lonely planet

Central Asia

Bradley Mayhew, Paul Clammer, Michael Kohn

Contents

KAZAKHSTAN
p82

UZBEKISTAN
p160

KYRGYZSTAN
p240

TURKMENISTAN
p405

TAJIKISTAN
p315

AFGHANISTAN
p354

Destination Central Asia

Central Asia or 'Turkestan' is a vast arena of desert, steppe and knotted mountain ranges stretching from the Caspian to Mongolia, and Siberia to the Hindu Kush. It forms both a bridge and barrier, tying together Europe and Asia on the Eurasian steppes. For two millennia it has been a thoroughfare for Silk Road traders, migrating tribes and nomadic empires. Central Asia's epic history, from Alexander the Great to the khans of Khiva, litters the land at every turn.

In spite of some logistical difficulties, the region's storybook history, its present re-emergence as a geopolitical pivot point and the sense of mutual rediscovery between Central Asians and the rest of the world make it a gripping place to visit. The flavour of the Silk Road is still there if you search it out, especially in Uzbekistan and Afghanistan. Open markets in storied caravan stops such as Samarkand and Herat seem lifted from the days of Timur (Tamerlane). The region's backdrop, especially the snowcapped mountains of Kyrgyzstan and Tajikistan, offers fantastic trekking and mountaineering, passing mountain communities and seminomadic herders en route. The region's little-visited oddities, namely Turkmenistan and parts of Kazakhstan, offer an offbeat interest all of their own.

Whether you want to explore the architectural gems of Bukhara or sleep in a yurt on a mountain pasture, Central Asia offers something for all. And everywhere is the instinctive hospitality of the people, offering a shared meal, a helping hand or a place to stay.

For decades, even centuries, Central Asia has been out of focus, a blank on the map of empires. Even today, to those not in the know, 'Central Asia' brings to mind a desert wasteland of illiterate nomads. The reality, in this addictive and fascinating part of the world, is that nothing could be further from the truth.

ANTHONY PLUMMER

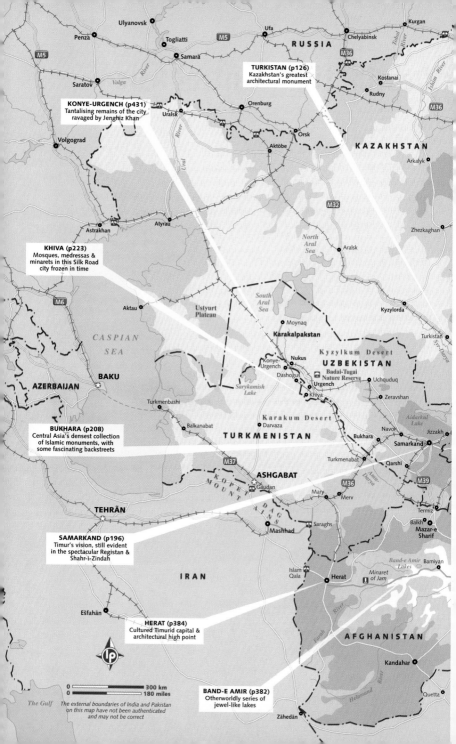

TURKISTAN (p126)
Kazakhstan's greatest architectural monument

KONYE-URGENCH (p431)
Tantalising remains of the city ravaged by Jenghiz Khan

KHIVA (p223)
Mosques, medressas & minarets in this Silk Road city frozen in time

BUKHARA (p208)
Central Asia's densest collection of Islamic monuments, with some fascinating backstreets

SAMARKAND (p196)
Timur's vision, still evident in the spectacular Registan & Shahr-i-Zindah

HERAT (p384)
Cultured Timurid capital & architectural high point

BAND-E AMIR (p382)
Otherworldly series of jewel-like lakes

0   300 km
0   180 miles

The Gulf   The external boundaries of India and Pakistan on this map have not been authenticated and may not be correct

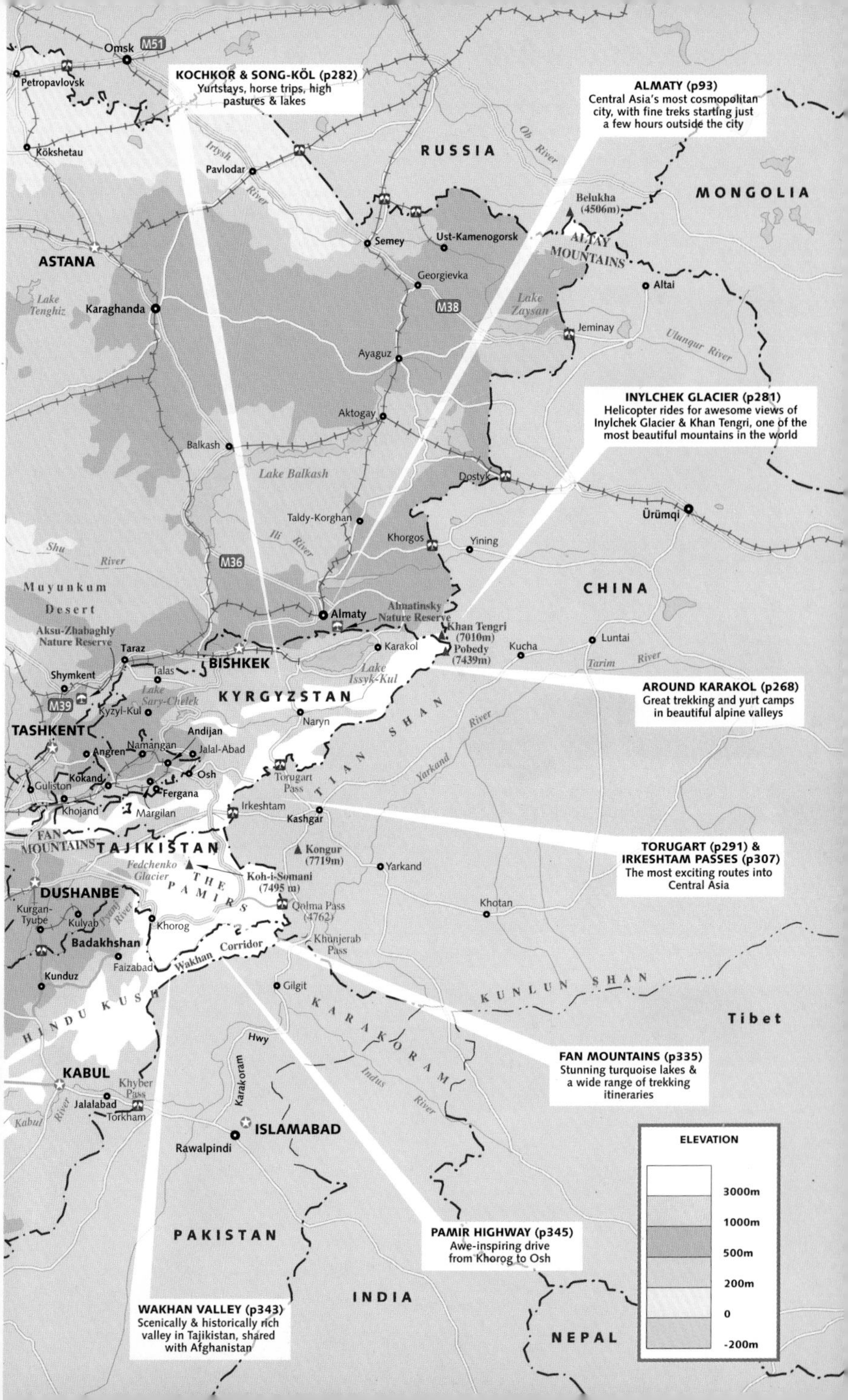

KOCHKOR & SONG-KÖL (p282)
Yurtstays, horse trips, high pastures & lakes
ALMATY (p93)
Central Asia's most cosmopolitan city, with fine treks starting just a few hours outside the city
INYLCHEK GLACIER (p281)
Helicopter rides for awesome views of Inylchek Glacier & Khan Tengri, one of the most beautiful mountains in the world
AROUND KARAKOL (p268)
Great trekking and yurt camps in beautiful alpine valleys
TORUGART (p291) & IRKESHTAM PASSES (p307)
The most exciting routes into Central Asia
FAN MOUNTAINS (p335)
Stunning turquoise lakes & a wide range of trekking itineraries
PAMIR HIGHWAY (p345)
Awe-inspiring drive from Khorog to Osh
WAKHAN VALLEY (p343)
Scenically & historically rich valley in Tajikistan, shared with Afghanistan
ELEVATION
3000m
1000m
500m
200m
0
-200m
RUSSIA
MONGOLIA
CHINA
KYRGYZSTAN
TAJIKISTAN
PAKISTAN
INDIA
NEPAL
Tibet
ASTANA
BISHKEK
TASHKENT
DUSHANBE
KABUL
ISLAMABAD
Omsk
M51
Petropavlovsk
Kökshetau
Pavlodar
Irtysh River
Ob River
Semey
Ust-Kamenogorsk
Belukha (4506m)
ALTAY MOUNTAINS
Altai
Georgievka
M38
Lake Zaysan
Jeminay
Ulungur River
Karaghanda
Lake Tenghiz
Ayaguz
Aktogay
Balkash
Lake Balkash
Dostyk
Ürümqi
Taldy-Korghan
Ili River
Khorgos
Yining
Shu River
M36
Muyunkum Desert
Almaty
Almatinsky Nature Reserve
Khan Tengri (7010m)
Pobedy (7439m)
Aksu-Zhabaghly Nature Reserve
Taraz
Karakol
Kucha
Luntai
Tarim River
Talas
Lake Issyk-Kul
Shymkent
Lake Sary-Chelek
M39
Kyzyl-Kul
Naryn
TIAN SHAN
River
Andijan
Namangan
Jalal-Abad
Angren
Osh
Yarkand River
Kokand
Torugart Pass
Guliston
Fergana
Khojand
Margilan
Irkeshtam
Kashgar
FAN MOUNTAINS
Kongur (7719m)
Fedchenko Glacier
Koh-i-Somani (7495 m)
Yarkand
THE PAMIRS
Kurgan-Tyube
Kulyab
Pyanj River
Qolma Pass (4762)
Khotan
Khorog
Badakhshan
Khunjerab Pass
Wakhan Corridor
Faizabad
Kunduz
Gilgit
KUNLUN SHAN
HINDU KUSH
KARAKORAM
Karakoram Hwy
Indus River
Khyber Pass
Jalalabad
Torkham
Kabul River
Rawalpindi

From the turquoise of a Timurid dome or an alpine lake in the Pamirs to the white of an alpine peak or a Kyrgyz yurt, Central Asia offers a range of delights as expansive as the deserts, steppes and mountains that girdle it. Following are our highlights.

ALAIN TOMASINI

Stare open-mouthed at the architectural gems of Samarkand's Registan (p199), Uzbekistan

Dip your toes in the lapis-blue waters of the outrageously beautiful mountain lakes of Band-e Amir (p382), Afghanistan

PAUL CLAMMER

Overnight in yurts and rural homes for a taste of daily Kyrgyz life, through the homestay programmes organised by Community Based Tourism (p248), Kyrgyzstan

ANTHONY PLUMMER

MARTIN MOOS

Wander at sunrise through Khiva (p223) in Uzbekistan, Central Asia's most homogenous old town

MARTIN MOOS

Ride a cable car to the Zailiysky Alatau (p117), a trekking and ice-skating playground, from cosmopolitan Almaty (p93), Kazakhstan

Go carpet shopping in the Tolkuchka Bazaar (p417), a Cecile B De Mille production of carpets and turbans in the deserts outside Ashgabat, Turkmenistan

MARTIN MOOS

Trek around a string of stunning lakes set in Tajikistan's beautiful Fan Mountains (p335)

Make a pilgrimage to Afghanistan's holiest site, the shimmering blue domes of the Shrine of Hazrat Ali in Mazar-e Sharif (p391)

Traverse the Tian Shan over one of Central Asia's most exciting overland crossings, the Torugart Pass (p291), Kyrgyzstan

Getting Started

Central Asia isn't the easiest place to travel through. You'll need to invest some time tracking down visas, permits and the latest travel information. You won't meet many travellers on the road and there are certainly no video cafés serving banana muesli. But this is part of the attraction of a land that has been largely off-limits to travellers for the last 2000 years.

Travel today is getting easier every year, with new accommodation options, vastly improved food and a network of shared taxis that will shuttle you around cheaply and in relative comfort. Do your research on Central Asian epic history in particular and you'll find the region quickly addictive. The more you put in, the more you'll get out of this Asian heartland.

WHEN TO GO

At lower elevations spring and autumn are the overall best seasons, in particular April to early June and September through October. In April the desert blooms briefly and the monotonous ochre landscapes of Turkmenistan, Uzbekistan and Kazakhstan become a Jackson Pollock canvas of reds, oranges and yellows. Autumn is harvest time, when market tables heave with freshly picked fruit.

See Climate Charts (p446) for more information.

Summer (mid-June to early September) is ferociously hot in the lowlands, with sizzling cities and desert temperatures as high as 40°C or more. Winters (November to March) are bitterly cold even in the desert.

July through August is the best time to visit the mountains and to trek (earlier and later than that, herders and other summer residents will have returned to the lowlands). Snow starts to fall in November and mountain passes fill with snow until April or even May. Bishkek and Almaty might have snow in April. Northern Kazakhstan is comfortable right through the summer.

For more details see the Climate and When to Go sections of the individual country chapters.

You might want to time your visit with the region's two major celebrations – Navrus (around 21 March) and Independence Day (around October). See p449 for details.

'STANS AT A GLANCE

Afghanistan On the brink of peace for the first time in 25 years, this harshly beautiful country has incredible variety and wonderful people, but check the security situation before heading outside Kabul.

Kazakhstan Interesting and quirky sites separated by vast amounts of nothing. Good hiking in the southeast and the beginnings of some ecotourism projects. Sub-Siberian Russian cities in the north.

Kyrgyzstan Alpine mountains, yurts and high pastures make this the best place in Central Asia for hiking and horse riding. Community tourism programmes and a wide network of homestays give you a grass-roots adventure on the cheap.

Tajikistan The region's most outlandish high-altitude scenery is home to Central Asia's best road trips, including the stunning Pamir Highway. This is the cutting edge of adventure travel. Visas and permits need some preparation.

Turkmenistan The North Korea of Central Asia. Hard to get into (tourist visas require you to hire a guide) but fascinating once you are there, not least for the personality cult of President Turkmenbashi.

Uzbekistan Home to historic Silk Road cities, epic Islamic architecture and the region's most stylish private guesthouses. Since 2003 it has become much easier to get a visa.

THE RELATIVE VALUE OF MONEY

The afghani, manat, sum, tenge and somani are still relatively unstable and so prices in this book are quoted in US dollar equivalents. It doesn't mean you have to pay in dollars – rather, it gives a more stable indication of costs. In Kyrgyzstan it seems that the som prices are more stable than dollar equivalents, so rates are quoted in som. You can expect prices to jump (or fall) every year; rates in this book are therefore an indication more of relative than absolute values.

COSTS & MONEY

By travelling with a friend, staying in homestays, eating in teahouses (chaikhana), and hiring the odd taxi when there is no public transport, you can get around Central Asia for around US$10 to US$20 per person per day. For a minimum of comfort you'll probably have to part with US$20 for a hotel in bigger towns. In order of expense, the cheapest countries are Kyrgyzstan, Tajikistan, Afghanistan, Uzbekistan, Kazakhstan and (most expensive) Turkmenistan. Budget accommodation costs are highest in Kazakhstan.

You can shave down costs by self-catering in shops and bazaars, staying in private homes and the occasional bottom-end place, sharing larger hotel rooms with more people, getting around town by local bus instead of taxi, riding overnight trains to save hotel costs, and spending less time in (expensive) cities. Don't forget to bargain in the bazaars. Trekking trips start at around US$50 per person per day with professional trekking agencies but you can arrange a trip for a fraction of this through community tourist organisations such as Community Based Tourism (CBT) in Kyrgyzstan (p248).

For mid-range travel in Uzbekistan you'll be looking at spending US$15 to US$30 per person for a stylish B&B; throw in US$10 per day for taxi hire between towns. Where there are any, four-star hotels run to around US$100 per double.

Don't forget to factor in visa costs, which can mount up, especially in Tajikistan and Turkmenistan, and of course long-haul transport to get you to and from Central Asia.

Money is best brought in a combination of cash in US dollars (perhaps around two-thirds of your funds), a credit card and a few travellers cheques (which are the least-useful form of currency in this destination).

READING UP

See the directories in the individual country chapters for recommended books on specific republics.

Lonely Planet's coverage of neighbouring countries includes *China; Pakistan & the Karakoram Highway; Iran; Georgia, Armenia & Azerbaijan; The Trans-Siberian Railway;* and *Russia & Belarus.* Lonely Planet also produces an essential *Central Asia phrasebook.*

Beyond the Oxus; Archaeology, Art & Architecture of Central Asia by Edgar Knobloch is an oddly appealing book for a specialist cultural history of Central Asia, perhaps because it's so rich in all the background information, reconstructions, floor-plans and close-ups that nobody in Central Asia seems to know about any more.

Central Asia; A Travellers' Companion by Kathleen Hopkirk is a handy and very readable historical background on the region (although not half as entertaining as her husband Peter's books). It's an excellent companion book for those keen to know more about the places they're seeing. Half the book covers Chinese Central Asia.

HOW MUCH?

Snickers bar
US$0.30 to US$0.40

100km bus ride
US$0.25 (Turkmenistan) to
US$3 (Afghanistan)

1 minute phone call to
the US
US$0.50 (Tajikistan) to
US$1.40 (Uzbekistan)

Internet connection
per hour
US$0.50 (Kyrgyzstan) to
US$3 (Afghanistan)

Traditional hat
US$2 (Tajikistan) to
US$8 (Kazakhstan)

LONELY PLANET INDEX

Litre of bottled water
US$0.25 to US$0.40

Bottled beer
US$0.20 (Turkmenistan) to
US$3 (Afghanistan)

Shashlyk
US$0.25 (Kyrgyzstan) to
US$0.80 (Kazakhstan)

Litre of petrol
US$0.30 (Uzbekistan) to
US$1.50 (Turkmenistan)

DON'T LEAVE HOME WITHOUT...

▪ A fistful of visas (p456 and the Visas sections of the individual country chapters) and plans set in motion for any travel permits (p456) you might need

▪ The latest travel warnings, especially for Afghanistan (p447)

▪ A sun hat, sunglasses and sunscreen for the strong desert and mountain sun, plus a torch for overcoming iffy electricity supplies in the countryside

▪ Water purification is essential if you plan to get off the beaten track

▪ Slide film – very hard to find in Central Asia

▪ A sleeping bag is very useful for winter or rural Kyrgyzstan, Afghanistan and Tajikistan in summer

▪ Mementos from home (eg postcards and photos) and gifts for homestays help break the ice

▪ Long, loose, nonrevealing clothes will win you friends in Islamic Central Asia, particularly in rural areas and the Fergana Valley of Uzbekistan. Leave the revealing singlets and shorts behind.

Nick Danziger's incredible modern-day overland odyssey through Turkey, Iran, Afghanistan, Pakistan, China and Tibet in 1984 is captured in *Danziger's Travels* – without much regard for visas, immigration posts, civil wars and the like. He's entitled to sound a bit self-important and melodramatic about it.

The Great Game by Peter Hopkirk is a fast-paced, very readable history of the Great Game – the 19th - century cold war between Britain and Russia – as it unfolded across Europe and Asia. It's carried along in Hopkirk's trademark style, in a series of personal stories – all men, all Westerners, all resolute and square-jawed, with Victoria Crosses for everybody – real *Boys' Own* stuff, melodramatic, but essentially true.

Land Beyond the River: The Untold Story of Central Asia by Monica Whitlock is an excellent current overview of the region from the BBC's Central Asia correspondent.

The Lost Heart of Asia by Colin Thubron – the author is deservedly praised for his careful research, first-hand explorations, delicate observations and baroque prose. But his books can be more compelling than actually being there.

Setting the East Ablaze by Peter Hopkirk takes up where *The Great Game* stops – a gripping cloak-and-dagger history of the murderous early years of Soviet power in Central Asia, and Communist efforts to spread revolution to British India and China.

From the Peter Hopkirk school of history, *Tournament of Shadows* by Karl E Meyer looks at some lesser-known Great Game characters and brings the Game up to date with the present scramble for oil in the Caspian. A modern regional follow-up by the same author is *Dust of Empire*.

Trekking in Russia & Central Asia by Frith Maier is an unrivalled guide to the former USSR's wild places by an American who first started exploring them as a student in 1984, and pioneered the US firm REI's adventure travel programme there. It has 77 pages of Central Asia route descriptions, plus chapters of useful background and planning info. It's now quite dated (written in 1994) and the maps simply bear minimal resemblance to the text, but it is still useful.

Websites

Some of the best Central Asian websites are those of the major travel agencies, Central Asian embassies abroad and US embassies in Central Asia.

Central Asia News (www.centralasianews.net) Regional news service.

Eurasianet (www.eurasianet.org) News and cultural articles, with resource pages for each country.

Lonely Planet (www.lonelyplanet.com) The dedicated Central Asia branch of the Thorn Tree is one of the best places anywhere to get up-to-date info on visas, border crossings and more.

Oxuscom (www.oxuscom.com/centasia.htm) History and links, with a focus on Uzbekistan.

Russian Climbing Site (http://mountains.tos.ru/kopylov/pamir.htm) Excellent climbing resource with route descriptions, plans and schematic maps. This link is for the Pamir mountain range, follow the index links for other Central Asian regions.

Silk Road Seattle (http://depts.washington.edu/uwch/silkroad) Maps, traditional culture, architecture, virtual art, historical texts and more.

Trekking in the USSR (http://mountains.czweb.org/foto_all.html) General information and photos of treks in the Pamir, Khan Tengri, Peak Lenin and Fan Mountains.

Turkic Republics and Communities (www.khazaria.com/turkic/index.html) Music, books and excellent links for the entire Turkic world.

Unesco (www.unesco.kz) Website of the Unesco regional office for Central Asia, with lots of cultural info.

> Oxiana is an email list concerning Central Asia and has a travel-related slant. To subscribe send a blank message email to oxiana-subscribe@ onelist.com.

RESPONSIBLE TRAVEL

Tourism is still relatively new to Central Asia, so please try to keep your impact as low as possible and create a good precedent for those who follow you.

One of the best ways to ensure your tourist dollars make it into the right hands is to support community tourism projects, such as CBT (p248) in Kyrgyzstan, Acted (p346) and Mountain Societies Development Support Project (MSDSP; p342) in Tajikistan and several minor programmes in Kazakhstan (see p93). Elsewhere try to engage local services and guides whenever possible and choose companies that follow ecofriendly practice (eg Ecotour in Bishkek, see p253).

The following are a few tips for responsible travel:

> **TOP FIVE ECOTOURISM WEBSITES**
>
> Wild Natures (www.wild-natures.com)
>
> Community Based Tourism (www.cbtkyrgyzstan.kg)
>
> Lepsinsk (www.lepsinsk.freenet.kz)
>
> Shepherd's Life (www.tourism.elcat.kg)
>
> Suusamyr, Ak-Terek & Talas Valley (www.kyrgyz-village .com.kg)

- Be respectful of Islamic traditions and don't wear singlets or short skirts in rural areas or the Fergana Valley.
- Don't hand out sweets or pens to children on the streets, since it encourages begging. Similarly, doling out medicines can encourage people not to seek proper medical advice. A donation to a project, health centre or school is a far more constructive way to help.
- You can do more good by buying your snacks, cigarettes, bubble gum etc from the enterprising grannies trying to make ends meet rather than state-run stores.

TRAVELLING SAFELY IN CENTRAL ASIA

In general Central Asia is a pretty safe place to travel despite the media's presentation of the region as a hot spot of environmental disaster, human rights violations and Islamic insurgency. The main exception is Afghanistan, which requires significant research before heading off into the countryside (see p355).

Most travellers eventually come face to face with crooked officials, particularly policemen, as checks are endemic throughout the region. You shouldn't have any problems as long as your documents are in tip-top shape. You will find specific safety information about each country at the start of each individual country chapter.

PERSONAL HIGHS & LOWS OF CENTRAL ASIA *by Bradley Mayhew*

Favourites

- Sitting in a teahouse with a cold Tian-Shansky beer, a round of kebabs and hot nan bread – magic!
- Cheap taxis in Kyrgyzstan
- Finally crossing the Torugart Pass
- White-bearded *aksakals* (white-bearded revered elders) resplendent in stripy cloaks and turbans
- Turquoise-blue domes and mesmerising Timurid tilework
- Trekking, almost anywhere
- Central Asian handshakes, with a slight bow and a hand on the heart
- Staying in a yurt in central Kyrgyzstan or a traditional courtyard house in Uzbekistan
- Central Asia's burgeoning café culture
- Central Asian melons, grapes, and Kyrgyz *kaimak* (cream) and honey (for breakfast)

Pet Peeves

- The taste of congealed mutton fat on the roof of your mouth
- Local bus trips that take seven hours to go 100km, when you don't have a seat and there are sweaty armpits in your face
- Getting turned back at the Torugart Pass
- Aggressive drunks who think you are Russian
- Soviet hotel architecture
- Bride of Frankenstein receptionists with dyed cherry-red hair, all mysteriously called Svetlana
- The fifth vodka toast to 'international friendship', with the sixth lined up behind it…
- Visa hassles and *militsia* (police) checks
- Russian techno music, turned up especially loud when you walk into a café
- The smell of Soviet canteens

- Don't buy items made from endangered species, such as Marco Polo sheep and snow leopards.
- Don't pay to take a photo of someone and don't photograph someone if they don't want you to. If you agree to send someone a photo, make sure you follow through on it.
- Try to give people a balanced perspective of life in the West. Point out that you are only temporarily rich in Central Asia and that income and costs balance out in Amsterdam just as they do in Almaty. Try also to point out the strong points of the local culture – strong family ties, comparatively low crime etc.
- Make yourself aware of the human rights situation in the countries you travel through; don't travel blindly.

Itineraries
CLASSIC ROUTES

SILK ROAD CITIES OF UZBEKISTAN
10 to 14 Days

Fly into **Tashkent** (p168) and get a feel of the big city before taking a domestic flight to Urgench and then a short bus or taxi ride to **Khiva** (p223). Khiva can be comfortably seen in a day. Take a quick side trip to Konye-Urgench if you can arrange a Turkmen visa and a double-entry Uzbek visa. Alternatively take a taxi for an overnight trip to one or two of the **desert cities** (p222) around Urgench.

From Urgench take the long bus or taxi ride down to **Bukhara** (p208), which deserves the most time of all the Silk Road cities. Try to budget a minimum of three days to take in the sights and explore the backstreets.

From here take the tarmac road to **Samarkand** (p196) and soak in the glories of the Registan and Shahr-i-Zindah for a day or two.

An alternative to this route is to travel from Konye-Urgench to **Ashgabat** (p412) and then travel to Bukhara via the Sultan Sanjar Mausoleum at **Merv** (p427). This is depends on whether or not you can obtain a Turkmen visa.

This loop route, starting and finishing in Tashkent, is a historical and architectural tour that links Central Asia's most popular tourist sites. It can take up to 14 days to complete.

OVER THE TORUGART – LAKES, HERDERS & CARAVANSERAIS

10 to 14 Days

This trip takes in fabulous scenery, a taste of life in the pastures and the roller-coaster ride over the Torugart Pass to Kashgar. There are lots of opportunities for trekking or horse riding on this route.

From easy-going **Bishkek** (p249) head east to the blue waters and sandy beaches of **Issyk-Kul** (p264), the world's second-largest alpine lake. Take in a couple of days trekking or visiting the alpine valleys around **Karakol** (p268). The idyllic valley of **Altyn Arashan** (p275) offers great scope for horse riding or a short trek to alpine Ala-Köl and the glorious Karakol Valley. If you have time you can explore the little-visited southern shore en route to Kochkor. If you are low on time head straight to Kochkor from Bishkek.

In small and sleepy **Kochkor** (p282) take advantage of the Community Based Tourism (CBT) programme and spend some time in a yurt or homestay on the surrounding *jailoos* (summer pastures). This is one of the best ways to glimpse traditional life in Kyrgyzstan. Try to allow three days to link a couple of yurtstays by horse, although most can be visited in an overnight trip. The most popular trip is to the herders' camps around the peaceful lake **Song-Köl** (p285), either by car or on a two-day horseback trip. The pastures are popular with herders who come here from around the area and stay from June to August with their animals.

From here head to **Naryn** (p286) and then the Silk Road caravanserai of **Tash Rabat** (p290), where you can stay overnight in yurts and even take a difficult horse trip to a pass overlooking Chatyr-Köl. From Tash Rabat it's up over the Torugart Pass *(in sha' Allah)* to wonderful **Kashgar** (p293).

If you want to experience traditional life in the pastures while enjoying stunning scenery, take this trip that dives over the Torugart Pass to Kashgar. Allow 10 to 14 days to complete.

CENTRAL ASIA OVERLAND   Three Weeks

Central Asia slots nicely into an overland route from the Middle East to Asia and there are dozens of different route options. Much of this itinerary follows ancient Silk Road paths.

Western roads into Central Asia lead from Mashhad in Iran to Ashgabat in Turkmenistan, or from Baku in Azerbaijan (by boat) to Turkmenbashi, also in Turkmenistan. If you only have a three-day transit visa for Turkmenistan you can travel from Mashhad to Mary (to visit the World Heritage–listed ruins of Merv) in one long day via the crossing at Saraghs, giving you more time at Merv and bypassing Ashgabat.

From **Ashgabat** (p412) the overland route leads to **Merv** (p427) and the Silk Road cities of **Bukhara** (p208), **Samarkand** (p196) and **Tashkent** (p168). From here head into the Fergana Valley and swing north along the mountain road to relaxed **Bishkek** (p249). From Bishkek cross the border to cosmopolitan **Almaty** (p93) and make some excursions from the city before taking the train (or bus) to Ürümqi in China.

An alternative from Bishkek is to arrange transport to take you over the **Torugart Pass** (p282) visiting the *jailoos* (summer pastures) around **Kochkor** (p282) and Song-Köl and the caravanserai at **Tash Rabat** (p290), before crossing the pass to Kashgar. You can then continue down into Pakistan to join the main overland trail into India and Nepal.

A third alternative if you are in a hurry is to travel from Tashkent to Andijan, cross the border to **Osh** (p299) and then take a bus or a combination of bus and taxi over the **Irkeshtam Pass** (p307) to Kashgar.

The trip from Mashhad/Baku to Ürümqi/Kashgar fits very well into an overland route from the Middle East to Asia. Much of this trip follows ancient Silk Road paths and can be completed in three weeks.

TASHKENT TO BISHKEK (THE LONG WAY)   Three Weeks

From **Tashkent** (p168) take a shared taxi first to **Khojand** (founded by Alexander the Great; p331) and then **Istaravshan** (p333), where you can spend a half day exploring the bazaar and lovely architecture of the old town. The next day take a taxi over the mountains, through some really stunning vertical scenery, to lake **Iskander-Kul** (p335), which offers a great base for trekking or just relaxing on the lake shore. Alternatively, if you haven't already seen **Samarkand** (p196) take a shared taxi there and then cross the border into Tajikistan, checking out the Sogdian archaeological site of **Penjikent** (p334) before taking a similar taxi to Iskander-Kul.

Continue the taxi ride to Tajikistan's capital **Dushanbe** (p323) to pick up your Gorno-Badakhshan (GBAO) permit. Day trip to the deserted fort and medressas of **Hissar** (p329) while waiting. From here follow the Pamir Hwy to **Osh** (p299), stopping in Khorog and Murgab. Try to do the road trip from Dushanbe to Khorog in daylight as the scenery is superb. Osh deserves a day of sightseeing for its bustling bazaar and city comforts.

From Osh visit **Arslanbob** (p298) for a three- or four-day trek to the holy lakes of Köl Mazar. Then, take the mountain road to **Kazarman** (p288), visiting Central Asia's most spectacular petroglyphs at **Sailmaluu Tash** (p289), a rough overnight trip from Kazarman. From here continue to Naryn and see the sights of central Kyrgyzstan (see the Over the Torugart – Lakes, Herders & Caravanserais itinerary on p15) before heading to Bishkek. If you have less time you can shoot from Jalal-Abad to Bishkek directly in a day, or take a three- or four-day detour to lake **Sary Chelek** (p296).

A three-week wild, untrammelled and scenically splendid route through the heart of Central Asia's mountains, from Tashkent to Bishkek.

ROADS LESS TRAVELLED

PAMIR HIGHWAY

10 to 14 Days

The stretch from **Khorog** (p340) to Murgab can be done in a day, although there are lots of detours. In a reliable 4WD you could go up to the lake of Turuntai-Kul. Acted can arrange a yurt or homestay for you in gritty Bulunkul, where you can enjoy views of Yashil-Kul, or in a Kyrgyz yurt in the Alichur Valley. From the latter an adventurous 4WD excursion leads to the archaeological site of Bazar-Dara.

The **Wakhan Valley** (p343) is worth tacking on for it's stunning scenery and rich collection of historical sights. Try to visit the 12th-century Yamchun Fort (and the nearby Bibi Fatima Springs) and Abrashim Kala, another fort that offers amazing views across the valley. Marco Polo travelled through this valley. From Langar, with your own transport, you can connect with the Pamir Hwy and continue to Khorog. If hitching you probably have to return to Khorog and take the main highway.

There are loads of side trips to be made from **Murgab** (p346), so try to budget a few days here. Lake **Kara-Kul** (p347) is a scenic highlight. From Sary Tash it's worth detouring 40km to **Sary Moghul** (p306) for its fine views of towering Pik Lenin (Kuh-i-Garmo). From here you can continue to **Osh** (p299). Exit Kyrgyzstan via **Irkeshtam** (p307) for Kashgar and then continue down the Karakoram Hwy to Gilgit in Pakistan. Alternatively, continue down valley from Sary Tash to Garm and Dushanbe.

One of the world's most beautiful and remote mountain road trips; the journey from Dushanbe to Osh will take 10 to 14 days.

JOURNEY TO SHAMBHALA   Two to Three Weeks

This little-travelled Kazakhstan itinerary is a good one for explorers, trekkers and fans of the road much less travelled.

Start off in **Almaty** (p93), picking up the necessary invitations for permits required later. Take in an excursion or two from Almaty, such as to the three pretty **Köl-Say lakes** (p117), and maybe, if you need to expend some energy, do a short trek in the mountains. From here head northeast by shared taxi to **Taldy-Korghan** (p113), which you can use as a jumping-off point for the surrounding areas. Take advantage of the homestay programme at **Lepsinsk** (p115) for some hiking in the glacier- and fir-covered Zhungar Alatau.

Head north to **Semey** (p145), a memorial to its nuclear-test victims and place of exile for famed Russian writer Fyodor Dostoevsky. From here you can take a train further along the Turk–Sib railway line to Barnaul in the Russian Altay. A better option is to head east to the pleasant sub-Siberian city of **Ust-Kamenogorsk** (p149) and then explore the cross-border Altay Mountains around the health resort of Rachmanov's Springs.

From here, remote Asian border junkies will get a kick out of determining a way to cross the border at Ridder (Leninogorsk) into the Russian Altay and then taking the road east, to cross the equally remote border post at Tashanta into Mongolia's ethnically Kazakh and scenically spectacular Bayan-Ölgii region. From here continue across Mongolia to China.

Note that you'll need to arrange permits a month in advance for the border areas around Taldy-Korghan and the Altay.

This Kazakhstan itinerary (Almaty to the Altay) will suit those who love to explore areas off the tourist trail. Allow two to three weeks.

TRANS-AFGHANISTAN – THE OLD HIPPY TRAIL   Two to Three Weeks

One of the most exciting ways to enter Afghanistan is from Pakistan, over the **Khyber Pass** (p395), invasion route to the subcontinent through the centuries. From the border town of Torkham it's a straight ride through to **Kabul** (p367). There's plenty to see and do here, from land-mine museums to Mughal gardens, as well as Chicken Street – the centre of the old hippy trail, all wrapped up in the hectic atmosphere of a city in recovery.

After a few days, strike out on a day-trip to the **Panjshir Valley** (p378), and the tomb of the legendary resistance leader Ahmad Shah Massoud. Make an optional side trip over the mountains to **Mazar-e Sharif** (p389), where the blue domes of the Shrine of Hazrat Ali mark Afghanistan holi-est site. You might even catch a game of *buzkashi* – Afghan polo played with a dead goat!

Follow this up by heading down the dusty road to **Bamiyan** (p378), site of the destroyed Buddha statues, but still one of the most beautiful places in Afghanistan, stuck high in the Hindu Kush. From here, it's a short drive to the fabulous blue lakes of **Band-e Amir** (p382).

The most intrepid can follow the road through the mountains to the remote **Minaret of Jam** (p383; only accessible in good weather) and on to the old Timurid capital of **Herat** (p384).

Alternatively, it's easier and quicker to return to Kabul from Bamiyan and fly to Herat, where you can spend several days exploring the old city and its historic buildings, including the glittering Friday Mosque, before crossing the border with Iran and continuing to Mashhad.

Journey through the heart of the Hindu Kush, from Peshawar to Mashhad, follow-ing the old hippy trail to remote archaeological and architectural sites. Count on this taking two to three weeks.

TAILORED TRIPS

COMMUNITY TOURISM

Kyrgyzstan leads the word in small-scale ecotourism projects that connect travellers with local families, guides and shepherds.

Kochkor (p282) is a fine place to find a homestay, watch your host make *shyrdaks* (felt carpets) and arrange a horse and guide for the two-day trek to **Song-Köl** (p285), where shepherds will put you up in a real yurt.

In the little-visited pastures of the **Talas Valley** (p295) and **Suusamyr Valley** (p295) are two other projects; hardy travellers are guaranteed to have these to themselves.

From Talas you can arrange a great five-day trek to **Sary Chelek** (p296). The nearby valley has a CBT coordinator who can connect you with yurts and guides for a two-day hike to the lake. **Arslanbob** (p298) is another CBT project that allows you to make a multiday trek to a chain of holy lakes or blaze some mountain trails.

In spectacular high-altitude Tajikistan, **Murgab** (p346) has a great tourism program that can arrange permits and jeep hire for trips to local archaeological sites and petroglyphs.

In **Khorog** (p340), MSDSP has a programme guaranteeing a place to stay in any village in the dramatic valleys of the Pamirs. It's cheap, it's safe and you know that your dollars are making a difference.

OFFBEAT CENTRAL ASIA

First stop is wacky Turkmenistan, 'the North Korea of Central Asia'. In **Ashgabat** (p412), watch the golden statue of Turkmenbashi revolve with the sun, visit the 'Ministry of Fairness' and the Museum of Turkmen Values. Pick up your own beloved Niyazov bust in the Ministry of Culture shop.

The dinosaur footprints at **Kugitang** (p431) are off the wall, but nothing compares to the burning desert around the **Darvaza Gas Craters** (p422).

In **Moynaq** (p232) or, better, in **Aralsk** (p128), witness beached fishing boats 150km from what's left of the Aral Sea. The former nuclear test site of **Semey** (p145) won't fail to horrify. If the mind-numbing steppes of Kazakhstan appeal, go to **Aktau** (p133), 300km from...anywhere. Alternatively, join reluctant embassy staff on a trip to the new Kazakh capital, **Astana** (p135; Kazakh for...er...'capital'), and enjoy Kazakhstan's only Jamaican Restaurant. (You know we couldn't make this stuff up!).

Afghanistan has more than its fair share of double-take sights, starting the moment you fly in. The sight of the runway outside **Kabul** (p367) littered with plane wreckage will be a defining moment for nervous fliers. The ruins of western Kabul, destroyed by mujaheddin factions, is a truly sobering monument to the follies of war.

JOURNEYS THROUGH HISTORY

At every turn in Central Asia you will face multiple layers of history on a breathtaking scale. The following are just a few historical highpoints.

Archaeologists should not miss **Merv** (p427), which is in Turkmenistan, a huge site of five historic cities, the most recent being the Seljuq capital. Once you've made it this far it would be a shame not to visit the former Parthian capital of **Nissa** (p421).

Up in the far northwest of Uzbekistan you can mix some fun with your history by staying at a yurt camp in the desert near the ruined 2500-year-old desert citadels of **Topraq-Qala** and **Ayaz-Qala** (p222).

Fans of the Great Game era will want to visit **Bukhara** (p208), which was

visited by everyone from Alexander 'Bokhara' Burnes to the British officers Conolly and Stoddart (who were held in a pit for two years before being executed in front of the Ark). Don't miss the Kalon Minaret that awed Jenghiz Khan.

Timur's capital **Samarkand** (p196) is rich with the works of the ruler, but few make it to the frescoes of **Afrosiab** (p201), the city visited by Alexander the Great. The archaeologically dedicated can pop over the border to glimpse ancient Sogdian remains at **Penjikent** (p334).

Less tangible sites include **Otrar** (p125) in Kazakhstan, where the pivotal murder of 450 Mongol envoys fatefully deflected Mongol rage from China to Central Asia, forever changing the face of the region.

SURREAL CENTRAL ASIA   *by Bradley Mayhew*

There's something about the ex-Soviet republics that is just, well, *weird*. From the deserted *why would anyone live here?* cities of western Kazakhstan to the Vegas-style strip of neon hotels in the middle of sullen Ashgabat, and from the world's grandest orphanage in Turkmenistan to the fishing trawlers beached in the desert sands of the Aral Sea – the region is punctuated by monuments of wonderful strangeness.

Scouring the news agencies can produce some fine surreal stories, from huge meteors landing in the Karakum desert to yeti hunters scouring the Kyrgyz mountains. In 2003 an army of termites apparently ate a town of 3000 houses in northwest Uzbekistan. From the Hannibal Lector school of journalism come the three psychiatric nurses in Almaty who were charged with drugging, killing and eating seven prostitutes, or the doctor (also in Almaty) who mummified her mother and three sisters and kept them in the family cupboard when she couldn't afford to bury them.

Travel in the region reveals daily twilight-zone encounters. The prize for 'Most Surreal Place to Eat' goes to the Hound Dog Hole in the US embassy in Almaty (guests only), where food is prepared in Elvis Presley's kitchen (he bought it while serving in the military). The first time you see Russian 'Lemon Barf' washing powder always seems to raise a smile.

Elsewhere, I particularly admired the sheep who boarded the local bus in Tajikistan alone and then got off two stops later, *without paying*. Or the old man on a bus in Tajikistan who handed me a light bulb and absolutely refused to take it back until he got off the bus eight hours later.

For those who like their trips to have a bit more edge, I wholeheartedly recommend the one-legged taxi driver who drove me to Ala-Archa in Kyrgyzstan (where was that brake?). But don't wear your seat belt in Uzbekistan – I almost made this fatal mistake until the driver told me, 'people will think we're rebels from Tajikistan!'.

Of course they will.

The Authors

BRADLEY MAYHEW
Coordinating Author, Kyrgyzstan & Tajikistan

It must be a taste for mutton that has driven Bradley repeatedly to almost every corner of Inner Asia. An interest in Central Asia grew from repeated visits to Chinese Turkestan while studying Chinese at Oxford University, and he has since spent several months trekking in Kyrgyzstan and Tajikistan. He is the author of the *Odyssey Guide to Uzbekistan* and has lectured on Central Asia to the Royal Geographical Society. Bradley was also the coordinating author of the previous edition of *Central Asia*.

Life on the Road – Kyrgyzstan & Tajikistan

Research, like travel in Central Asia, is an intriguing mix of the exotic and banal. Sure, there are some world-beating sights here, but what really makes travel in Central Asia such a riot are the eccentricities of the region. If Central Asians had bumper stickers, they would read '(weird) sh*t happens'.

My favourite moment on this latest trip was being driven from Osh to Bishkek, crammed in the back seat of an ancient Volga and squashed between three giant Kyrgyz women who were drinking *kymys* (fermented mare's milk) and listening to a scratchy recording of *Manas* on the stereo. But the moment that summed up Central Asia for me was when the driver suddenly turned off the road in the middle of nowhere, parked hurriedly and spontaneously fell asleep…along with all the other passengers in the car.

I sat there for a while, temporarily at a loss, smashed in between a comatose granny and the side window.

Twenty minutes later I checked my watch. Someone started snoring. I went for a walk…

PAUL CLAMMER
Afghanistan

Paul grew up near Cambridge. After a false start as a molecular biologist he spent several years kicking around the Islamic world from Casablanca to Kashgar, eventually becoming a tour guide in Pakistan, Turkey and Morocco. Having watched *The Man Who Would Be King* at an impressionable age, the Khyber Pass was always in his sights, and in 2001 he finally made it to Afghanistan, only to find himself having dinner with two Taliban ministers a fortnight before 11 September. When the dust settled, he wrote Kabul Caravan, one of the first travel websites dedicated to Afghanistan.

Life on the Road – Afghanistan

More than any country I've visited, Afghanistan is baffling with its contrasts.

The destroyed tanks and other scars of war I expected, of course. More surprising were those same tank tracks pressed into service as impromptu speed bumps. Not that they were needed at one place, where I saw a man leading a string of camels over them, his bright scarf flapping in the wind – two different worlds colliding.

Later, at a remote chaikhana, an old man pressed dried mulberries into my hand and refilled my tea glass when I wasn't looking. The walls were smoke-blackened from a fire of rosemary-scented brushwood, a small boy and his goats peered in through the door, and again I wondered, 'What century is this?'

Afghanistan does that to you.

MICHAEL KOHN
Kazakhstan & Uzbekistan

Michael's first taste of the former Soviet empire came on a train journey through Russia, and resumed with a stint in Ulaan Baatar, where he edited an English newspaper and filed reports for various news agencies including the BBC, the *New York Times* and the Associated Press. He made extended trips to the Kazakh-dominated Bayan-Ölgii province where he trekked in the mountains with eagle hunters and acquired a taste for *kazy* (horsemeat sausage). Returning to his native San Francisco in 2001, he wrote two books on Mongolia, and has since been writing and travelling across the Asian continent.

Life on the Road – Kazakhstan & Uzbekistan

Riding around in Tashkent taxis, I noticed that many had stacks of small-denomination bills in the glove compartment. Seemingly a convenient place to hold change for passengers, the money was often used to pay off avaricious road police, who could just as well call themselves toll collectors as the 'fines' were invariably for bogus reasons. One of my drivers had his licence confiscated for letting me out near the US embassy, having violated a 200m no-stopping zone. Another lost his for passing a bus on a highway. And yet all drivers leap from their cars to warmly greet and vigorously shake the hand of the arresting officer, like some long-lost brother. I've been told it's best to ride with a woman driver – Uzbek police are gentlemen enough to give them safe passage around the city.

ANONYMOUS
Turkmenistan

The author of the Turkmenistan section has chosen to remain anonymous to protect the people who helped him during his research.

Life on the Road – Turkmenistan

Researching a travel guide in a country wracked by spymania is hard work – people carrying notebooks and making maps are viewed with instant suspicion and even hostility. The highlight of this was being chased down the Berzengi Highway in Ashgabat by a policeman guarding the Chinese embassy. I made the mistake of noting down the opening hours, which provoked him to pursue me down the street screaming, 'Why do you need them!?!' Luckily he didn't have a gun.

While the police presence can be overwhelmingly frustrating (on one day alone we were stopped 12 times for document checks at various roadblocks), it can also be helpful. When our ever-untrusty Niva 4WD broke down for the eighth time, several doe-eyed recruits at a desert roadblock push-started our car and even provided us with watermelon and tea while we waited for a mechanic to arrive.

The biggest irony of Turkmenistan is that the character of its citizens is so totally unfit for repression. Big belly laughs are far more natural to Turkmen than arresting people, and even the nastiest little policeman usually ended up asking me about life overseas and whether or not my president has his portrait on every street corner.

CONTRIBUTING AUTHOR

Dr Trish Batchelor wrote the Health chapter. She is a general practitioner and travel medicine specialist who works at the CIWEC Clinic in Kathmandu, Nepal, as well as being a medical advisor to the Travel Doctor New Zealand clinics. Trish teaches travel medicine through the University of Otago and is interested in underwater and high-altitude medicine, and in the impact of tourism on host countries. She has travelled extensively through southeast and east Asia and particularly loves high-altitude trekking in the Himalaya.

Snapshot

Since independence from the USSR in 1991, the Central Asian republics' similarities and differences have come under view. All grapple with population shifts as minorities emigrate to newly welcoming homelands in the face of rising Central Asian nationalism. All weather pressing economic crises while nursing economic grudges against each other. All experience rising nationalism, and are attempting to modernise and Westernise while maintaining and redefining their national character. All have reinvented their past, rehabilitating fallen local leaders, reintroducing historical heroes and reinforcing their national languages. All are feeling pressure from Russia seeking to reassert its interests. All are opening themselves, more or less, to new spheres of influence from Turkey, Iran, China and the industrialised West. The initial rush of post-independence joy has been replaced by a yearning for stability and the search for new ideals.

To read about current events in Afghanistan, turn to p361.

But there are differences. Kyrgyzstan is the odd one out politically: its president, Askar Akaev, is the only one to have professed aspirations to swift democratisation and free-market reform, although there has been some backsliding recently. Turkmenistan and Kazakhstan are the only republics which seem to have bright economic possibilities – sitting pretty on enormous reserves of oil and gas. Tajikistan is the only one which has experienced civil war, whereas the others are all in dread that they will be next to succumb to Islamic fundamentalism and political meltdown.

The Caspian region of Central Asia is sitting atop an estimated 200 billion barrels of crude oil.

The events of 11 September 2001 and the 'War on Terror' put the spotlight on Central Asia. The US used bases in Uzbekistan, Kyrgyzstan and Tajikistan to launch bombing raids on Afghanistan and has since established long-term bases in Bishkek and Khanabad (Uzbekistan), pushing the thrust of NATO influence deep into the former USSR. To counter this Russian has established its first new military base since the fall of the USSR, also in Bishkek, and plans to establish another base in Tajikistan. Russia already has 30,000 troops in Tajikistan, most defending Commonwealth of Independent States (CIS) borders against drug smugglers and Islamic infiltrators.

With the backing of their new-found allies and suitors in the West, the republics now face even less international pressure to raise levels of basic human rights or introduce democratic processes. Islamic fundamentalism is the bogeyman which the majority of Central Asian leaders fear the most, although the fall of the Taliban in Afghanistan has seriously diminished the effectiveness of fundamentalist activities in the region. Yet as long as the issues of reform, poverty and corruption remain unaddressed by Central Asian regimes, the region will be a fertile breeding ground for dissent of all kinds.

Looking to the future, the region has a potential for wealth, as it is a mother lode of energy and raw materials, a fact which quietly drives many countries' Central Asian policies. The superpower scramble for oil and gas in the region has been dubbed the New Great Game (see p35) and is a drama that will unfold in the decades ahead.

Kazakhstan's Kashagan oil field holds probably the world's second-largest concentration of oil, some 30 million barrels.

As Central Asia's new economic and cultural ties strengthen, oil routes open and Silk Roads are redrawn, this little-understood region will undoubtedly become increasingly important to the security, economy and politics of Russia, Asia and even the world. The Central Asian governments look set to continue to tread a dangerous tightrope between authoritarianism and Islamisation as they face the long-term challenge of meeting the religious, secular and economic desires of its people.

History

For more on the Silk Road, including recommended books and websites, see p43.

Central Asia is perhaps the best place on earth to explore the reality of the phrase 'the sweep of history'. Populations, conquerors, cultures and ideas have swept colourfully across the region's many steppes, deserts and mountains for thousands of years. Central Asia's role as conduit between cultures is symbolised by the Silk Road, through which the great civilisations of the East and the West made contact and carried on cultural exchange. But Central Asia was, and is, more than just a middle ground, and its cultural history is far more than the sum of the influences brought from the East and the West.

Here in the heart of the largest landmass on earth, vast steppes provided the one natural resource – grass – required to build one of this planet's most formidable and successful forms of statehood, the nomadic empire. The grass fed horses by the millions, and mounted archers remained the unstoppable acme of open-ground warfare for over 2500 years. How the settled civilisations on the periphery of Eurasia interacted with successive waves of mounted nomadic hordes is the main theme of the story of Central Asia.

From the Mongol destruction of irrigation canals to the Russian harnessing of water for cotton production, the control of water in the deserts of Central Asia has been central to the region for centuries and will continue to be a source of future contention.

PREHISTORY & EARLY HISTORY

In the Middle Palaeolithic period, from 100,000 to 35,000 years ago, people in Central Asia were isolated from Europe and elsewhere by ice sheets, seas and swamps.

Cultural continuity begins in the late 3rd millennium BC with the Indo-Iranians, speakers of an unrecorded Indo-European dialect related distantly to English. The Indo-Iranians are believed to have passed through Central Asia on their way from the Indo-European homeland in southern Russia. From Central Asia, groups headed southeast for India and southwest for Iran. These peoples herded cattle, went to battle in chariots, and probably buried their dead nobles in burial mounds *(kurgans)*. The Tajiks are linguistic descendants of these ancient migrants.

Central Asia's recorded history begins in the 6th century BC, when the large Achaemenid empire of Persia (modern Iran) created client kingdoms or satrapies (provinces), in Central Asia: Sogdiana, Khorezm (later Khiva), Bactria (Afghanistan Turkestan), Margiana (Merv), Aria (Herat), Saka (Scythia) and Arachosia (Ghazni and Kandahar). Sogdiana was the land between the Amu-Darya and Syr-Darya, called Transoxiana by the Romans and Mawarannhr by the Arabs. Here Bukhara and Samarkand later flourished. Khorezm lay on the lower reaches of the Amu-Darya, south of the Aral Sea, where one day the khans of Khorezm would lord it from the walled city of Khiva until well into the 20th century. Saka (also called Semireche by the Russians), extending indefinitely over the steppes beyond the Syr-Darya and including the Tian Shan range, was the home of nomadic warriors until the way of life ended in the late 19th century.

For a detailed chronicle of Central Asian history try *Empire of the Steppes* by Rene Grousset, *A History of Inner Asia* by Svat Soucek or the excellent (but hard to find) *Central Asia* by Gavin Hambly.

ALEXANDER THE GREAT

In 330 BC this former pupil of Aristotle, from Macedonia, led his army to a key victory over the last Achaemenid emperor, Darius III, in Mesopotamia.

TIMELINE	100,000–40,000 years ago	2nd millennium BC
	Remains of Neanderthal man found at Aman-Kutan cave near Samarkand	Saka tombs in the Pamirs date from this period; towns such as Afrosiab mark the beginning of urban settlement

With the defeat of the Persian nemesis, Alexander (356–323 BC) developed a taste for conquest. By 329 BC he had reached modern Herat, Kandahar and Kabul. Crossing the Hindu Kush via the Panjshir Valley, he pressed northward to Bactria, crossed the Oxus (Amu-Darya) and proceeded via Marakanda (Samarkand) towards the Jaxartes (Syr-Darya), which he crossed in order to crush Scythian defenders. Perhaps in celebration he founded the city of Alexandria Eschate (Farthest Alexandria) near the site of modern Khojand.

Alexander met the most stubborn resistance of his career in the Sogdians, who in concert with the Massagetes, a Saka clan, revolted and held the mountainous parts of their homeland until 328. After an 18-month guerrilla war, the rebels' fall was a poignant one: attacked and defeated at their last redoubt, the 'Rock of Sogdiana' (its location today in the Hissar Mountains remains a mystery), their leader yielded his daughter, the beautiful Bactrian princess Roxana, into captivity and marriage to Alexander.

The Macedonian generalissimo's sojourn in Central Asia was marked by a growing megalomania. It was at Marakanda that Alexander murdered his right-hand general, Cleitus. He tried to adopt the dress and autocratic court ritual of an Oriental despot; however his Greek and Macedonian followers refused to prostrate themselves before him.

When he died in Babylon in 323, Alexander had no named heir. But his legacy included nothing less than the West's perennial romance with exploration and expansion.

EAST MEETS WEST

The aftermath of Alexander's short-lived Macedonian empire in Central Asia saw an increase in east–west cultural exchange and a chain reaction of nomadic migrations. The Hellenistic successor states of the Seleucid empire disseminated the aesthetic values of the classical world deep into Asia; trade brought such goods as the walnut to Europe.

Along the border of Mongolia and China, the expansion of the warlike Xiongnu (Hsiung-nu) confederacy (probably the forebears of the Ephalites, or Huns) uprooted the Yüeh-chih of western China (the Yüeh-chih ruler was slain and his skull made into a drinking cup). The Yüeh-chih

> **DID YOU KNOW?**
>
> Legend has it that the biblical prophet Daniel (of the Lion's Den fame) was buried in Samarkand, where he is known as Daniyar.

> Alexander, known locally as Iskander or Sikander, is a popular figure in Central Asia, after whom several lakes and mountains are named. His troops are blamed for the occasional blond-haired, blue-eyed Tajik or Afghani, although this is probably more the result of Aryan influence.

UNEARTHING THE AMAZONS

As early as the 5th century BC the Greek historian Herodotus knew of an army of women warriors, known as the Amazons, who were so dedicated to warfare that they allegedly cut off their own right breast in order to improve their shot with bows and arrows. Recent excavations of burial mounds (kurgans), on the Kazakh border with Russia, are unearthing some intriguing links to these perhaps not-so-mythical warrior women.

Archaeologists have discovered skeletons of women, bow-legged from a life in the saddle, buried with swords, daggers and bronze-tipped arrows, indicating warrior status. Others appear to be priestesses, buried with cultic implements, bronze mirrors and elaborate headdresses.

The finds indicate that women of these early steppe civilisations were trained from the outset to be warriors, fighting alongside men, perhaps even forming an elite social group. The status of these steppe women seems far higher than that of sedentary civilisations of the same time, challenging the stereotypical macho image of the Central Asian nomad.

329–327 BC

Alexander the Great in Central Asia

250 BC–AD 226

Kushan empire

were sent packing westward along the Ili River into Saka, whose displaced inhabitants in turn bore down upon the Sogdians to the south.

The Xiongnu were also irritating more important powers than the Yüeh-chih. Although protected behind its expanding Great Wall since about 250 BC, China eagerly sought tranquillity on its barbarian frontier. In 138 BC the Chinese emperor sent a brave volunteer emissary, Zhang Qian, on a secret mission to persuade the Yüeh-chih king to form an alliance against the Xiongnu.

When he finally got there, 13 years later, Zhang found that the Yüeh-chih had settled down in Bactria to a peaceable life of trade and agriculture, and no longer had an axe to grind with the Xiongnu. But Zhang Qian's mission was still a great success of Chinese diplomacy and exploration and the stage had been set for major east–west contact and the birth of the Silk Road (see p43).

THE KUSHANS

The peaceable, put-upon Yüeh-chih finally came into their own in the 1st century BC when their descendants, the Kushan dynasty, converted to Buddhism. The Kushan empire controlled northern India, Afghanistan and Sogdiana from its base at Kapisa, near modern-day Bagram in Afghanistan. At its height in the first three centuries after Christ, it was one of the four great powers of the world, along with Rome, China and Parthia.

Vigorous trade on the Silk Road helped spread Kushan culture. The rich Kushan coinage is concrete testimony to this classic Silk Road power's lively religious ferment: the coins bear images of Greek, Roman, Buddhist, Persian and Hindu deities. The art of the empire fused Persian imperial imagery, Buddhist iconography and Roman realism. It was carried out from Gandhara over the mountainous maze of deepest Asia to the furthest corners of Transoxiana, Tibet and the Tarim basin. Indian, Tibetan and Chinese art were permanently affected.

SASSANIDS, HUNS & SOGDIANS

The Silk Road's first flower faded by about AD 200, as the Chinese, Roman, Parthian and Kushan empires went into decline. Sogdiana came under the control of the Sassanid empire of modern-day Iran. As the climate along the middle section of the Silk Road became drier, Central Asian nomads increasingly sought wealth by plundering, taxing and conquering their settled neighbours. The Sassanids lost their Inner Asian possessions in the 4th century to the Huns, who ruled a vast area of Central Asia at the same time that Attila was scourging Europe.

The Huns were followed south across the Syr-Darya by the western Turks (the western branch of the empire of the so-called Kök Turks or Blue Turks), who in 559 made an alliance with the Sassanids and ousted the Huns. The western Turks, who had arrived in the area from their ancestral homeland in southern Siberia, nominally controlled the reconquered region.

The mixing of the western Turks' nomadic ruling class with the sedentary Sogdian elite over the next few centuries produced a remarkable ethnic mix in cities like Penjikent, Afrosiab and Varakhsha.

Hellenistic cities and Buddhist monasteries of the 2nd century BC, such as Ai Khanum, Surkh Kotal and Khalchayan, show a fascinating mixture of Greek, Persian and local art forms.

DID YOU KNOW?

The Afghan city of Balkh, known as the 'Mother of all Cities' and visited by Marco Polo in the 13th century, was the birthplace of Zoroaster, the founder of Zoroastrianism (the religion of ancient Persia).

138–119 BC	AD 226–651
Voyage of Chinese Zhang Qian from Xi'an to Central Asia	Sassanid empire

LOST BATTLE, LOST SECRETS

The Chinese lost big to the Arabs at the Battle of Talas in 751. The defeat marked the end of Chinese expansion west and secured the future of Islam as the region's foremost religion. But to add insult to injury, some of the Chinese rounded up after the battle were no ordinary prisoners: they were experts at the crafts of papermaking and silkmaking. Soon China's best-kept secrets were giving Arab silk makers in Persia a commercial advantage all over Europe. It was the first mortal blow to the Silk Road. The spread of papermaking to Europe sparked a technological revolution; the impact of this on the development of civilisation cannot be underestimated.

THE ARRIVAL OF ISLAM

When the western Turks faded in the late 7th century, an altogether new and formidable kind of power was waiting to fill the void – the religious army of Islam. Bursting out of Arabia just a few years after the Prophet Mohammed's death, the Muslim armies rolled through Persia in 642 to set up a military base at Merv but met stiff resistance from the Turks of Transoxiana. The power struggle between the Amu-Darya and Syr-Darya ebbed and flowed, while Arab armies spread to take Bukhara in 709 and Samarkand in 712.

China, meanwhile, had revived under the Tang dynasty and expanded into Central Asia, murdering the khan of the Tashkent Turks in the process. It was perhaps the most costly incident of skulduggery in Chinese history. The enraged Turks were joined by the opportunistic Arabs and Tibetans; in 751 they squeezed the Chinese forces into the Talas valley (in present-day Kazakhstan and Kyrgyzstan) and sent them flying back across the Tian Shan, marking the limits of the Chinese empire for good.

After the Battle of Talas, the Arab's Central Asian territories receded in the wake of local rebellions. By the 9th century, Transoxiana had given rise to the peaceable and affluent Samanid dynasty. It generously encouraged development of Persian culture while remaining strictly allied with the Sunni caliph of Baghdad. It was under the Samanids that Bukhara grew into a world centre of Muslim culture and garnered the epithet 'Pillar of Islam'. Some of the Islamic world's best scholars were nurtured in its 113 medressas (educational institutions; see the boxed text on p30).

KARAKHANIDS TO KARAKITAY

By the early 10th century, internal strife at court had weakened the Samanid dynasty and opened the door for two Turkic usurpers to divide up the empire: the Ghaznavids in Khorasan and modern-day Afghanistan, south of the Amu-Darya; and the Karakhanids in Transoxiana and the steppe region beyond the Syr-Darya. The Karakhanids are credited with finally converting the populace of Central Asia to Islam. They held sway from three mighty capitals: Balasagun (now Burana in Kyrgyzstan) in the centre of their domain, Talas (now Taraz in Kazakhstan) in the west, and Kashgar in the east. Bukhara continued to shine, and Karakhanid Kashgar was the home of rich culture and science. The Ghaznavids ruled Afghanistan, Samarkand and Bukhara at their height and are credited with snuffing out Buddhism in the region and introducing Islam to India.

3rd–5th centuries		630	
The Buddhas of Bamiyan carved from cliffside		Buddhist pilgrim Xuan Zang travels to Issyk-Kul, the Chuy Valley, Tashkent, Samarkand, Balkh and Kashgar in search of Buddhist texts	

SHINING STARS

In the 9th to 11th centuries Samanid Central Asia produced some of history's most important thinkers:

Al-Khorezmi (Latin: Algorismi; 787–850) A mathematician who gave his name to algorithm, the mathematical process behind addition and multiplication. The title of another of his mathematical works, Al-Jebr, became algebra.

Al-Biruni (973–1046) From Khorezm, the world's foremost astronomer at the time, who knew that the earth rotated and that it circled around the sun. He estimated the distance to the moon to within 20km. He wrote many important works during his life.

Abu Ali ibn-Sina (Latinised as Avicenna; 980–1037) From Bukhara, the greatest medic of his age, whose Canon of Medicine was the standard textbook for Western doctors until the 17th century.

The Karakhanids and Ghaznavids coveted each other's lands. In the mid-11th century, while they were busy invading each other, they were caught off guard by a third Turkic horde, the Seljuqs, who annihilated both after pledging false allegiance to the Ghaznavids. In the Seljuqs' heyday their sultan had himself invested as emperor by the caliph of Baghdad. The empire was vast: on the east it bordered the lands of the Buddhist Karakitay, who had swept into Balasagun and Kashgar from China; to the west it extended all the way to the Mediterranean and Red Seas.

> The Karakitay lent their name to both Cathay (an archaic name for China) and Kitai (the Russian word for China).

An incurable symptom of inner-Asian dynasties through the ages was their near inability to survive the inevitable disputes of succession. The Seljuqs lasted a century before their weakened line succumbed to the Karakitay and to the Seljuqs' own rearguard vassals, the Khorezmshahs. From their capital at Gurganj (present-day Konye-Urgench), the Khorezmshahs burst full-force into the tottering Karakitay. They emerged as rulers of all Transoxiana and much of the Muslim world as well.

And so Central Asia might have continued in a perennial state of forgettable wars. As it is, the Khorezmshahs are still remembered primarily as the unlucky stooge left holding the red cape when the angry bull was released.

MONGOL TERROR, MONGOL PEACE

Jenghiz (Genghis) Khan felt he had all the justification in the world to ransack Central Asia. In 1218 a Khorezmian governor in Otrar (now in Kazakhstan) received a delegation from Jenghiz to inaugurate trade relations. Scared by distant reports of the new Mongol menace, the governor assassinated them in cold blood. Up until that moment Jenghiz, the intelligent khan of the Mongols who had been lately victorious over Chungtu (Beijing), had been carefully weighing the alternative strategies for expanding his power: commerce versus conquest. Then came the crude Otrar blunder, and the rest is history.

In early 1219 Jenghiz placed himself at the head of an estimated 200,000 men and began to ride west from his Altay Mountains stronghold. By the next year his armies had sacked Khojand and Otrar (the murderous governor was dispatched with savage cruelty in Jenghiz' presence), and Bukhara soon followed.

It was in that brilliant city, as soldiers raped and looted and horses trampled Islamic holy books in the streets, that the unschooled Jenghiz ascended to the pulpit in the chief mosque and preached to the congregation. His message: 'I am God's punishment for your sins'. Such shocking psychological warfare is perhaps unrivalled in history.

Bukhara was burned to the ground, and the Mongol hosts swept on to conquer and plunder Samarkand, Merv, Termiz, Kabul, Balkh, Bamiyan, Ghazni and, eventually under Jenghiz' generals and heirs, most of Eurasia. No opposing army could match them.

Central Asian settled civilisation took a serious blow, from which it only began to recover 600 years later under Russian colonisation. Jenghiz' descendants controlling Persia favoured Shiite Islam over Sunni Islam, a development which over the centuries isolated Central Asia even more from the currents of the rest of the Sunni Muslim world.

For more on the Mongols see the excellent *Storm from the East* by Robert Marshall.

But there was stability, law and order under the Pax Mongolica. In 20th-century terms, the streets were safe and the trains ran on time. The resulting modest flurry of trade on the Silk Road was the background to many famous medieval travellers' journeys, including the greatest of them all, Marco Polo's (see the boxed text on p46).

On Jenghiz Khan's death in 1227, his empire was divided among his sons. By tradition the most distant lands, stretching as far as the Ukraine and Moscow and including western and most of northern Kazakhstan, would have gone to the eldest son, Jochi, had Jochi not died before his father. They went instead to Jochi's sons, Batu and Orda, and came to be known collectively as the Golden Horde. The second son, Chaghatai, got the next most distant portion, including most of Kazakhstan, Uzbekistan, Afghanistan and western Xinjiang; this came to be known as the Chaghatai khanate. The share of the third son, Ogedei, seems to have eventually been divided between the Chaghatai khanate and the Mongol heartland inherited by the youngest son, Tolui. Tolui's portion formed the basis for his son Kublai Khan's Yüan dynasty in China.

Unlike the Golden Horde in Europe and the Yüan dynasty, the Chaghatai khans tried to preserve their nomadic lifestyle, complete with the khan's roving tent encampment as 'capital city'. But as the rulers spent more and more time in contact with the Muslim collaborators who administered their realm, the Chaghatai line inevitably began to settle down. They even made motions towards conversion to Islam. It was in a fight over this issue, in the mid-14th century, that the khanate split in two, with the Muslim Chaghatais holding Transoxiana and the conservative branch retaining the Tian Shan, Kashgar and the vast steppes north and east of the Syr-Darya, an area collectively known as Moghulistan.

TIMUR & THE TIMURIDS

The fracturing of the Mongol empire immediately led to resurgence of the Turkic peoples. From one minor clan near Samarkand arose a tyrant's tyrant, Timur ('the Lame', or Tamerlane). After assembling an army and wresting Transoxiana from Chaghatai rule, Timur went on a spectacular nine-year rampage which ended in 1395 with modern-day Iran, Iraq, Syria, eastern Turkey and the Caucasus at his feet. He also despoiled northern India.

Timur's campaigns resulted in the deaths of over one million people.

998–1030	1220
Mahmud of Ghazni rules Central Asia	Jenghiz Khan destroys Bukhara, killing 30,000

All over his realm, Timur plundered riches and captured artisans and poured them into his capital at Samarkand. The city grew, in stark contrast to his conquered lands, into a lavish showcase of treasure and pomp. Much of the postcard skyline of today's Samarkand dates to Timur's reign, as do many fine works of painting and literature. Foreign guests of Timur's, including the Spanish envoy Ruy Gonzales de Clavijo, took home stories of enchantment and barbarity which fed the West's dream of remote Samarkand.

Timur claimed indirect kinship with Jenghiz Khan, but he had little of his forerunner's gift for statecraft. History can be strange: both conquerors savagely slaughtered hundreds of thousands of innocent people, yet one is remembered as a great ruler and the other not. The argument goes that Timur's bloodbaths were insufficiently linked to specific political or military aims. On the other hand, Timur is considered the more cultured and religious of the two men. At any rate, Timur died an old man at Otrar in 1405, having just set out in full force to conquer China.

Important effects of Timur's reign can still be traced. For instance, when he pounded the army of the Golden Horde in southern Russia, Timur created a disequilibrium in the bloated Mongol empire which led to the seizure of power by its vassals, the petty and fragmented Russian princes. This was the predawn of the Russian state. Like the mammals after the dinosaurs, Russia arose from small beginnings.

For a scant century after Timur's death his descendants ruled on separately in small kingdoms and duchies. From 1409 until 1449, Samarkand was governed by the conqueror's mild, scholarly grandson, Ulughbek. Gifted in mathematics and astronomy, he built a large celestial observatory and attracted scientists who gave the city a lustre as a centre of learning for years to come.

A Timurid renaissance was led by Timur's son Shah Rukh and his remarkable wife Gowhar Shad, who between them established a cultured capital in Herat, populated by fine architects, musicians, miniature painters and poets (including Jami).

In addition to Persian, a Turkic court language came into use, called Chaghatai, which survived for centuries as a Central Asian lingua franca.

UZBEKS & KAZAKHS

Modern Uzbekistan and Kazakhstan, the two principal powers of post-Soviet Central Asia, eye each other warily across the rift dividing their two traditional lifestyles: sedentary agriculture (Uzbeks) and nomadic pastoralism (Kazakhs). Yet these two nations are closely akin and parted ways with a family killing.

The family in question was the dynasty of the Uzbek khans. These rulers, one strand of the modern Uzbek people, had a pedigree reaching back to Jenghiz Khan and a homeland in southern Siberia. In the 14th century they converted to Islam, gathered strength, and started moving south. Under Abylqayyr (Abu al-Khayr) Khan they reached the north bank of the Syr-Darya, across which lay the declining Timurid rulers in Transoxiana. But Abylqayyr had enemies within his own family. The two factions met in battle in 1468, and Abylqayyr was killed and his army defeated.

1405	15th century
Timur (Tamerlane) dies, his Bibi Khanum Mosque unfinished	Shah Rukh rules Timurid empire from Herat

After this setback, Abylqayyr's grandson Mohammed Shaybani brought the Uzbek khans to power once more and established Uzbek control in Transoxiana; modern-day Uzbekistan. Abylqayyr's rebellious kinsmen became the forefathers of the Kazakh khans.

The Uzbeks gradually adopted the sedentary agricultural life best suited to the fertile river valleys they occupied. Settled life involved cities, which entailed administration, literacy, learning and, wrapped up with all of these, Islam. The Shaybanid dynasty, which ruled until the end of the 16th century, attempted to outdo the Timurids in religious devotion and to carry on their commitment to artistic patronage. But the Silk Road had disappeared, usurped by spice ships, and Central Asia's economy had entered full decline. As prosperity fell, so did the region's importance as a centre of the Islamic world. The Astrakhanid khans and Iranian Safavids held sway over the benighted remains of Transoxiana until the mid-18th century.

The Kazakhs, meanwhile, stayed home on the range, north of the Syr-Darya, and flourished as nomadic herders. Their experience of urban civilisation and organised Islam remained slight compared with their Uzbek cousins. By the 16th century the Kazakhs had solidly filled a power vacuum on the old Saka steppes between the Ural and Irtysh Rivers and established what was to be the world's last nomadic empire, divided into three hordes: the Great Horde, the Middle Horde and the Little Horde.

> The Great Horde roamed the steppes of the Jeti-Suu region (Russian: Semireche), north of the Tian Shan; the Middle Horde occupied the grasslands extending east from the Aral Sea; and the Little Horde took the lands west of there, as far as the Ural River.

THE ZHUNGARIAN EMPIRE

The Oyrats were a western Mongol clan who had been converted to Tibetan Buddhism. Their day in the sun came when they subjugated eastern Kazakhstan, the Tian Shan, Kashgaria and western Mongolia to form the Zhungarian (Dzungarian) empire (1635–1758). Russia's frontier settlers were forced to pay heavy tribute and the Kazakh hordes, with their boundless pasturage beyond the mountain gap known as the Zhungarian Gate, were cruelly and repeatedly pummelled until the Oyrats were liquidated by Manchu China.

> Memory of the Oyrat legacy has been preserved in epic poetry by the Kazakhs and Kyrgyz, who both suffered under the Oyrats' ruthless predations.

Reeling from the Zhungarian attacks, the Kazakhs (first the Little Horde, then the Middle Horde, then part of the Great Horde) gradually accepted Russian protection over the mid-18th century.

The Russians had by this time established a line of fortified outposts on the northern fringe of the Kazakh Steppe. However, it appears that there was no clear conception in St Petersburg of exactly where the Russian Empire's frontier lay. Slow on the uptake, Russia at this stage had little interest in the immense territory it now abutted.

THE KHANATES OF KOKAND, KHIVA & BUKHARA

In the fertile land now called Uzbekistan, the military regime of a Persian interloper named Nadir Shah collapsed in 1747, leaving a political void which was rapidly occupied by a trio of Uzbek khanates.

The three dynasties were the Kungrats, enthroned at Khiva (in the territory of old Khorezm), the Mangits at Bukhara and the Mins at Kokand; all rivals. The khans of Khiva and Kokand and the emirs of Bukhara seemed able to will the outside world out of existence as they stroked and clawed each other like a box of kittens. Boundaries were impossible to fix as the rivals shuffled their provinces in endless wars.

1424–29	1592
Ulughbek builds observatory, before he is beheaded in 1449 as part of a religious backlash	Khiva made capital of Khorezm

Unruly nomadic clans produced constant pressure on their periphery. Bukhara and Khiva vainly claimed nominal control over the nomadic Turkmen, who prowled the Karakum desert and provided the khanates with slaves from Persia. Kokand expanded into the Tian Shan mountains and the Syr-Darya basin in the early 19th century.

The khans ruled absolutely as feudal despots. Some of them were capable rulers; some, such as the last emir of Bukhara, were depraved and despised tyrants. In the centuries since Transoxiana had waned as the centre of Islam, the mullahs had slipped into hypocrisy and greed. The level of education and literacy was low, and the *ulama* (intellectual class) seems to have encouraged superstition and ignorance in the people.

It was no dark age, however – trade was vigorous. This was especially true in Bukhara, where exports of cotton, cloth, silk, karakul wool and other goods gave it a whopping trade surplus with Russia. Commerce brought in new ideas, with resulting attempts to develop irrigation and even to reform civil administrations. European travellers in the 19th century mentioned the splendour of the Islamic architecture in these exotic capitals.

In none of the three khanates was there any sense among the local people that they belonged to a distinct nation – whether of Bukhara, Khiva or Kokand. In all three, *sarts* (town dwellers) occupied the towns and farms, while clans who practiced nomadism and seminomadism roamed the uncultivated countryside. *Sarts* included both Turkic-speaking Uzbeks and Persian-speaking Tajiks. These two groups had almost identical lifestyles and customs, apart from language.

In many respects, the three khanates closely resembled the feudal city-states of late-medieval Europe. But it is anybody's guess how they and the Kazakh and Kyrgyz nomads might have developed had they been left alone.

THE COMING OF THE RUSSIANS

By the turn of the 19th century Russia's vista to the south was of anachronistic, unstable neighbours. Flush with the new currents of imperialism sweeping Europe, the empire found itself embarking willy-nilly upon a century of rapid expansion across the steppe.

The reasons were complex. The main ingredients were the search for a secure, and preferably natural, southern border, nagging fears of British expansion from India, and the boldness of the tsar's officers. And probably, glimmering in the back of every patriotic Russian's mind, there was a vague notion of the 'manifest destiny' of the frontier.

The first people to feel the impact were the Kazakhs. Their agreements in the mid-18th century to accept Russian 'protection' had apparently been understood by St Petersburg as agreements to annexation and a few decades later Tatars and Cossacks were sent to settle and farm the land. Angered, the Kazakhs revolted. As a consequence, the khans of the three hordes were, one by one, stripped of their autonomy, and their lands were made into bona fide Russian colonies, sweet psychological revenge, no doubt for centuries of invasion by nomadic tribes from the east. In 1848, as the USA was gaining land stretching from Texas to California, Russia abolished the Great Horde. Theirs was the last line of rulers in the world directly descended, by both blood and throne, from Jenghiz

'Russia has two faces, an Asiatic face which looks always towards Europe, and a European face which looks always towards Asia.'

BENJAMIN DISRAELI

1635–1758	1758
Zhungarian empire terrorises Kazakhstan, Kyrgyzstan and China	Oyrats defeated by Manchu China and Kyrgyzstan nominally under Chinese rule

Khan. Kokand was the first of the three Uzbek khanates to be swamped, followed by Bukhara (1868) and then Khiva (1873).

The last and fiercest people to hold out against the tsarist juggernaut were the Tekke, the largest Turkmen clan. Of all nomad groups, the Tekke had managed to remain the most independent of the khanates, in this case Khiva. Some Turkmen clans had asked to be made subjects of Russia as early as 1865, for convenient help in their struggle against the Khivan yoke. But none were in a mood to have their tethers permanently shortened as Russia expanded into their territory. To add rancour to the pot, the Russians were anguished by the Tekkes' dealings in slaves, particularly Christian ones.

Much blood was spilled in the subjugation of the Tekke. The Russians were trounced in 1879 at Teke-Turkmen, but returned with a huge force under General Mikhail Dmitrievich Skobelev in 1881. The siege and capture of Geok-Tepe, the Tekkes' last stronghold, resulted in staggering casualties among the defenders.

With resistance ended, the Russians proceeded along the hazily defined Persian frontier area, occupying Merv in 1884 and the Pandjeh Oasis on the Afghan border in 1885. It was the southernmost point they reached. Throughout the conquest, the government in St Petersburg agonised over every advance, whereas their hawkish generals in the field took key cities without asking for permission.

When it was over, Russia found it had bought a huge new territory, half the size of the USA, geographically and ethnically diverse, and economically rich – fairly cheaply in terms of money and lives, and in just 20 years. It had not gone unnoticed by the world's other great empire further south in India.

> 'I hold it as a principle that in Asia the duration of peace is in direct proportion to the slaughter you inflict upon the enemy. The harder you hit them the longer they will be quiet afterwards.'
>
> GENERAL SKOBELEV, TSARIST RUSSIAN COMMANDER IN CENTRAL ASIA

THE GREAT GAME

What do two expanding empires do when their fuzzy frontiers draw near each other? They scramble for control of what's between them.

The British called it the Great Game; in Russia it was the Tournament of Shadows. Its backdrop was the first cold war between east and west. All the ingredients were there: spies and counter-spies, demilitarised zones, puppet states and doom-saying governments whipping up smokescreens for their own shady business. All that was lacking was the atom bomb and a Russian leader banging his shoe on the table. Diplomatic jargon acquired the phrase 'sphere of influence' during this era.

The story of the Great Game would be dull as dishwater except that its centre arena was the Roof of the World (a common term for the Pamir mountain range). The history of Central Asia from the beginning of the 19th century onward must be seen in the context of the Great Game, for this was the main reason for Russian interest in the region.

The Russian occupation of Merv in 1884 immediately raised blood pressures in Britain and India. Merv was a crossroads leading to Herat, an easy gateway to Afghanistan which in turn offered entry into British India. The British government finally lost its cool when the Russians went south to control Pandjeh. But the storm had been brewing long before 1884.

In 1839 Britain installed a hand-picked ruler of Afghanistan, which resulted in an uprising, a death march from Kabul by the British garrison,

> **DID YOU KNOW?**
>
> The phrase 'Great Game' was first coined by British officer Arthur Connelly (later executed in Bukhara) and immortalised by Kipling in his novel *Kim*.

1832	1839–42
Alexander 'Bokhara' Burnes visits Bukhara	16,000 British massacred in First Afghan War

and a vengeful 'First Afghan War' (16,000 British massacred, one survivor). By the end of it, Britain's puppet-ruler was murdered and his predecessor was back on the throne. This failure to either control or befriend the headstrong Afghans was repeated in an equally ill-fated 1878 invasion (the Russians likewise failed from 1979 to 1988).

By 1848 the British had defeated the Sikhs and taken the Peshawar valley and Punjab. With a grip now on the 'Northern Areas' Britain began a kind of cat-and-mouse game with Russia across the vaguely mapped Pamir mountain range and Hindu Kush. Agents posing as scholars, explorers, merchants – even Muslim preachers and Buddhist pilgrims – crisscrossed the mountains, mapping them, spying on each other, courting local rulers, staking claims like dogs in a vacant lot.

In 1882 Russia established a consulate in Kashgar. A British agency at Gilgit (now in Pakistan), which had opened briefly in 1877, was urgently reopened when the *mir* (hereditary ruler) of Hunza entertained a party of Russians in 1888. Britain set up its own Kashgar office in 1890.

For more on that quintessential Great Gamester, Francis Younghusband, read Patrick French's excellent biography *Younghusband*.

Also in 1890, Francis Younghusband (later to head a British incursion into Tibet) was sent to do some politicking with Chinese officials in Kashgar. On his way back through the Pamirs he found the range full of Russian troops, and was told to get out or face arrest.

This electrified the British. They raised hell with the Russian government and invaded Hunza the following year; at the same time Russian troops skirmished in northeast Afghanistan. After a burst of diplomatic manoeuvring, Anglo-Russian boundary agreements in 1895 and 1907 gave Russia most of the Pamirs and established the Wakhan Corridor, the awkward tongue of Afghan territory that stretches across to meet Xinjiang.

The Great Game was over. The Great Lesson for the people of the region was: 'No great power has our interests at heart'. The lesson has powerful implications today.

COLONISATION OF TURKESTAN & SEMIRECHE

In 1861, the outbreak of the US Civil War ended Russia's imports of American cotton. To keep the growing textile industry in high gear, the natural place to turn to for cotton was Central Asia. Other sectors of Russian industry were equally interested in the new colonies as sources of cheap raw materials and labour, and as huge markets. Russia's government and captains of industry wisely saw that their own goods could not compete in Europe but in Central Asia they had a captive, virgin market. Gradually, Russian Turkestan was put in line with the economic needs of the empire.

The central district of Karakol, on lake Issyk-Kul in Kyrgyzstan, is probably the best-preserved relic of the Russian colonial environment.

In the late 19th century, Europeans began to flood the tsar's new lands, a million in Kazakhstan alone. The immigrants were mostly freed Russian and Ukrainian serfs who wanted land of their own. Central Asia also offered a chance for enterprising Russians to climb socially. The first mayor of Pishpek (Bishkek) left Russia as a gunsmith, married well in the provinces, received civil appointments, and ended his life owning a mansion and a sprawling garden estate.

The Trans-Caspian Railway was begun at Krasnovodsk in 1880 and reached Samarkand in 1888. The Orenburg–Tashkent line was completed in 1905.

The Russian middle class brought with them straight streets, gas lights, telephones, cinemas, amateur theatre, charity drives, parks and hotels. All these were contained in enclaves set apart from the original towns. Through their lace curtains the Russians looked out on the Central Asian masses with a fairly indulgent attitude. The Muslim fabric of life was left alone, as were the mullahs, as long as they were submissive. Development, both social and economic, was initially a low priority. When it came, it took the form of small industrial enterprises, irrigation systems and a modest programme of primary education.

In culture it was the Kazakhs, as usual, who were the first to be influenced by Russia. A small, Europeanised, educated class began for the first time to think of the Kazakh people as a nation. In part, their ideas came from a new sense of their own illustrious past, which they read about in the works of Russian ethnographers and historians. Their own brilliant but short-lived scholar, Shoqan Ualikhanov, was a key figure in Kazakh consciousness-raising.

The Uzbeks were also affected by the 19th-century cultural renaissance of the Tatars. The Jadidists, adherents of educational reform, made small gains in modernising Uzbek schools. The Pan-Turkic movement found fertile ground among educated Uzbeks at the beginning of the 20th century and took root.

The Kazakh army officer Shoqan Ualikhanov, a friend of Dostoevsky, was the first man to record a fragment of the Kyrgyz epic *Manas* and, as a spy, managed to make his way in disguise into Kashgar in 1858, risking death if discovered.

THE 1916 UPRISING

Resentment against the Russians ran deep and occasionally boiled over. Andijan in Uzbekistan was the scene of a holy war, from 1897 to 1898, which rocked the Russians out of complacency. After the insurrection was put down, steps were taken to Russify urban Muslims, the ones most under the influence of the mullahs and most likely to organise against the regime.

The outbreak of WWI in 1914 had disastrous consequences in Central Asia. In Semireche (Saka), massive herds of Kazakh and Kyrgyz cattle were requisitioned for the war effort, whereas Syr-Darya, Fergana and Samarkand provinces had to provide cotton and food. Then, in 1916, as Russia's hopes in the war plummeted, the tsar demanded men. Local people in the colonies were to be conscripted as noncombatants in labour battalions. To add insult to injury, the action was not called 'mobilisation' but 'requisition', a term usually used for cattle and materiel.

Exasperated Central Asians just said no. Starting in Tashkent, an uprising swept eastwards over the summer of 1916. It gained in violence, and attracted harsher reprisal, the further east it went. Purposeful attacks on Russian militias and official facilities gave way to massive rioting, raiding and looting. Colonists were massacred, their villages burned, and women and children carried off.

The resulting bloody crackdown is a milestone tragedy in Kyrgyz and Kazakh history. Russian troops and vigilantes gave up all pretence of a 'civilising influence' as whole Kyrgyz and Kazakh villages were brutally slaughtered or set to flight. Manhunts for suspected perpetrators continued all winter, long after an estimated 50,000 Kyrgyz and Kazakh families had fled towards China. The refugees who didn't starve or freeze on the way were shown little mercy in China.

1890	1917
Captain Francis Younghusband thrown out of the Pamirs by Russians	Russian Revolution

But not all unrest among Muslims was directed against Russia. The Young Bukharans and Young Khivans movements agitated for social self-reform, modelling themselves on the Young Turks movement which had begun transforming Turkey in 1908.

REVOLUTION & CIVIL WAR

For a short time after the Russian Revolution of 1917, which toppled the tsar, there was a real feeling of hope in some Central Asian minds. The society which the West, out of ignorance and mystification, had labelled backward and inflexible had actually been making preparations for impressive progress. The Bolsheviks made sure, however, that we will never know how Central Asia might have remade itself.

In 1917 an independent state was launched in Kokand by young nationalists under the watchful eye of a cabal of Russian cotton barons. This new government intended to put into practice the philosophy of the Jadid movement: to build a strong, autonomous Pan-Turkic polity in Central Asia by modernising the religious establishment, westernising and educating the people. Within a year the Kokand government was smashed by the Red army's newly formed Trans-Caspian front. Over 5000 Kokandis were massacred after the city was captured. Central Asians' illusions about peacefully coexisting with Bolshevik Russia were shattered as well.

Mission to Tashkent, by FM Bailey, recounts the derring-do of this British intelligence officer/spy in 1918 Soviet Tashkent. At one stage, under an assumed identity, he was employed as a Bolshevik agent and given the task of tracking himself down!

Bolshevik Conquest

Like most Central Asians, Emir Alim Khan of Bukhara hated the godless Bolsheviks. In response to their first ultimatum to submit, he slaughtered the Red emissaries who brought it and declared a holy war. The emir conspired with White (ie anti-Bolshevik) Russians and British political agents, while the Reds concentrated on strengthening party cells within the city.

The end came swiftly after the arrival in Tashkent of the Red army commander Mikhail Frunze. Khiva went out with barely a whimper, quietly transforming into the Khorezm People's Republic in February 1920. In September Frunze's fresh, disciplined army captured Bukhara after a four-day fight. The emir fled to Afghanistan, taking with him his company of dancing boys but abandoning his harem to the Bolshevik soldiers.

For more on Nazaroff's cat-and-mouse exploits on the run in Central Asia from the Bolsheviks, read his *Hunted Through Central Asia*.

Then in December 1918 a counter-revolution broke out, apparently organised from within Tashkent jail by a shadowy White Russian agent named Paul Nazaroff. Several districts and cities fell back into the hands of the Whites. The bells of the cathedral church in Tashkent were rung in joy, but for the last time. The Bolsheviks defeated the insurrection, snatched back power, and kept it. Nazaroff, freed from jail, was forced to hide and flee across the Tian Shan to Xinjiang, always one step ahead of the dreaded secret police.

THE SOVIET ERA

From the start the Bolsheviks ensured themselves the universal hatred of the people. Worse even than the tsar's bleed-the-colonies-for-the-war policies, the revolutionaries levied grievous requisitions of food,

1921	1930s
Creation of Turkestan SSR	Stalin's genocidal collectivisation programmes strike the final blow to nomadic life

livestock, cotton, land and forced farm labour. Trade and agricultural output in the once-thriving colonies plummeted. The ensuing famines claimed nearly a million lives; some say many more.

Forced Collectivisation

Forced collectivisation was the 'definite stage of development' implicit in time-warping the entire population of Central Asia from feudalism to communism. This occurred during the USSR's grand First Five Year Plan (1928–32). The intent of collectivisation was first to eliminate private property and second, in the case of the nomadic Kazakhs and Kyrgyz, to put an end to their wandering lifestyle.

The effect was disastrous. When the orders came down, most people simply slaughtered their herds and ate what they could rather than give them up. This led to famine in subsequent years, and widespread disease. Resisters were executed and imprisoned. Millions of people died. Evidence exists that during this period Stalin had a personal hand in tinkering with meagre food supplies in order to induce famines. His aims seem to have been to subjugate the people's will and to depopulate Kazakhstan, which was good real estate for Russian expansion.

The *basmachi* (Muslim guerrilla fighters; see the boxed text on p330), in twilight for some time, renewed their guerrilla activities briefly as collectivisation took its toll. It was their final struggle.

Political Repression

Undeveloped Central Asia had no shortage of bright, sincere people willing to work for national liberation and democracy. After the tsar fell they jostled for power in their various parties, movements and factions. Even after they were swallowed into the Soviet state, some members of these groups had high profiles in regional affairs. Such a group was Alash Orda, which was formed by Kazakhs and Kyrgyz in 1917. Alash Orda even held the reins of a short-lived autonomous government.

By the late 1920s, the former nationalists and democrats, indeed the entire intelligentsia, were causing Stalin serious problems. From their posts in the communist administration they had front-row seats at the Great Leader's horror show, including collectivisation. Many of them began to reason, and to doubt. Stalin, reading these signs all over the USSR, foresaw that brains could be just as dangerous as guns. Throughout the 1930s he proceeded to have all possible dissenters eliminated. Alash Orda members were among the first to die, in 1927 and 1928.

Thus began the systematic murder, the Purges, of untold tens of thousands of Central Asians. Arrests were usually made late at night. Confined prisoners were rarely tried; if any charges at all were brought, they ran along the lines of 'having bourgeoisie-nationalist or Pan-Turkic attitudes'. Mass executions and burials were common. Sometimes entire sitting governments were disposed of in this way.

Construction of Nationalities

The solution to the 'nationality question' in Central Asia remains the most graphically visible effect of Soviet rule: it drew the lines on the map. Before the revolution the peoples of Central Asia had no concept

'The Communist Party is the mind, honour and conscience of our era.'
VLADIMIR ILYCH LENIN

1948	1954
Ashgabat destroyed in an earthquake; 110,000 perish	Virgin Lands campaign in Kazakhstan

of a firm national border. They had plotted their identities by a tangle of criteria: religion, clan, location, way of life, even social status. The Soviets, however, believed that such a populace was fertile soil for Pan-Islamism and Pan-Turkism. These philosophies were threats to the regime.

So, starting in about 1924, nations were invented: Kazakh, Kyrgyz, Tajik, Turkmen, Uzbek. Each was given its own distinct ethnic profile, language, history and territory. Where an existing language or history did not exist or was not suitably distinct from others, these were supplied and disseminated. Islam was cut away from each national heritage, essentially relegated to the status of an outmoded and oppressive cult, and severely suppressed throughout the Soviet period.

Some say that Stalin personally directed the drawing of the boundary lines. Each of the republics was shaped to contain numerous pockets of the different nationalities, each with long-standing claims to the land. Everyone had to admit that only a strong central government could keep order on such a map. The present face of Central Asia is a product of this 'divide and rule' technique.

Ultimately, each nation became the namesake for a Soviet Socialist Republic (SSR). Uzbek and Turkmen SSRs were proclaimed in 1924, the Tajik SSR in 1929, and the Kazakh and Kyrgyz SSRs in 1936.

WWII

'The Great Patriotic War Against Fascist Germany' galvanised the whole USSR and in the course of the war Central Asia was drawn further into the fold. Economically the region lost ground from 1941 to 1945 but a sizable boost came in the form of industrial enterprises arriving ready-to-assemble in train cars: evacuated from the war-threatened parts of the USSR, they were relocated to the remote safety of Central Asia. They remained there after the war and kept on producing.

Other wartime evacuees – people – have made a lasting imprint on the face of Central Asia. These are the Koreans, Volga Germans, Chechens and others whom Stalin suspected might aid the enemy. They were deported from the borderlands and shuffled en masse. They now form sizable minority communities in all the former Soviet Central Asian republics.

For many wartime draftees, WWII presented an opportunity to escape the oppressive Stalinist state. One Central Asian scholar claims that over half of the 1.5 million Central Asians mobilised in the war deserted. Large numbers of them, as well as prisoners of war, actually turned their coats and fought for the Germans against the Soviets.

Agriculture

DID YOU KNOW?

Independent Uzbekistan is still the world's second-largest producer of cotton.

The tsarist pattern for the Central Asian economy had been overwhelmingly agricultural; so it was with the Soviets. Each republic was 'encouraged' to specialise in a limited range of products, which made their individual economies dependent on the Soviet whole. Tajikistan built the world's fourth-largest aluminium plant but all the aluminium had to brought in from outside the region.

Uzbekistan alone soon supplied no less than 64% of Soviet cotton, making the USSR the world's second-largest cotton producer after the USA. Into the cotton bowl poured the diverted waters of the Syr-Darya and Amu-Darya, while downstream the Aral Sea was left to dry up. Over the cotton-scape was spread a whole list of noxious agricultural chemicals, which have wound up polluting waters, blowing around in dust

1966	1979
Tashkent destroyed in earthquake	USSR invades Afghanistan

storms, and causing serious health problems for residents of the area. For further details, see p68.

Another noxious effect of cotton monoculture was the 'cotton affair' of the Brezhnev years. A huge ring of corrupt officials habitually over-reported cotton production, swindling Moscow out of billions of roubles. When the lid finally blew off, 2600 participants were arrested and over 50,000 were kicked out of office. Brezhnev's own son-in-law was one of the fallen.

In 1954 the Soviet leader Nikita Khrushchev launched the Virgin Lands campaign. The purpose was to jolt agricultural production, espe-cially of wheat, to new levels. The method was to put Kazakhstan's enor-mous steppes under the plough and resettle huge numbers of Russians to work the farms. Massive, futuristic irrigation schemes were drawn up to water the formerly arid grassland, from as far away as the Ob River in Siberia. The initial gains in productivity soon dwindled as the fragile exposed soil of the steppe literally blew away in the wind. The Russians, however, remained.

Benefits of the Soviet Era

In spite of their heavy-handedness the Soviets made profound improve-ments in Central Asia. Overall standards of living were raised consider-ably with the help of health care and a vast new infrastructure. Central Asia was provided with plants, mines, farms, ranches and services em-ploying millions of people (never mind that no single republic was given the means for a free-standing economy, and that most operations were coordinated through Moscow).

Education reached all social levels (previously education was through the limited, men-only network of Islamic schools and medressas), and pure and applied sciences were nurtured. Literacy rates hit 97% (contrast-ing greatly with Afghanistan, where literacy rates are still as low as 47% for men and 15% for women), and the languages of all nationalities were given standard literary forms. The Kyrgyz language was even given an alphabet for the first time.

Soviet women had 'economic equality' and although this meant that they had the chance to study and work alongside men *while* retaining all the responsibilities of homemakers, female literacy approached male levels and women assumed positions of responsibility in middle-level administration positions as well as academia

Artistic expression was encouraged within the confines of communist ideology. The Central Asian republics now boast active communities of professional artists who were trained, sometimes lavishly, by the Soviet state. And through the arts, the republics were allowed to develop their distinctive national traditions and identities (again, within bounds).

If the Central Asian republics were at all prepared when independence came, they were prepared by the Soviet era.

The Afghan War

In 1979 the Soviet army invaded Afghanistan, determined to prop up a crumbling communist regime on their doorstep (for more on this, see p360). In retrospect, someone should have consulted the history books

Central Asia's old Arabic alphabet was replaced by the Soviets with a Roman one, and later with a Cyrillic script. Several republics (Turkmenistan and Uzbekistan) have shifted back to a Roman script, meaning older people are using alpha-bets incomprehensible to the youth.

8 December 1991	1998
Collapse of the Soviet Union, formation of the Commonwealth of Independent States	Kyrgyzstan becomes the first, and so far only, Central Asian govern-ment to pass a referendum allowing the private ownership of land

beforehand, for the lessons of history are clear; no-one wins a war in Afghanistan. Central Asian Muslims were drafted into the war to liberate their backward relatives, while the Afghan mujaheddin said a prayer for the souls of their godless Central Asian kin.

In the end, after 10 years of brutal guerrilla war that ended the lives of 15,000 Soviets and 1.5 million Afghans, the Soviets finally pulled out, limping back over the Amu-Darya to Termiz. They weren't quite massacred to a man as were the British before them but the strains of war indelibly contributed to the cracking of the Soviet empire.

POST-SOVIET CENTRAL ASIA

One Russian humorist has summed up his country's century in two sentences: 'After titanic effort, blood, sweat and tears, the Soviet people brought forth a new system. Unfortunately, it was the wrong one'.

By the spring of 1991 the parliaments of all five republics had declared their sovereignty. However, when the failure of the August coup against Gorbachov heralded the end of the USSR, none of the republics was prepared for the reality of independence.

On 8 December the presidents of Russia, the Ukraine and Belarus met near Brest in Belarus to form the Commonwealth of Independent States (CIS). Feeling left out, the Central Asian presidents convened and demanded admission. On 21 December, the heads of 11 of the former Soviet states (all except the three Baltic states and Georgia) met in Almaty and refounded the CIS. Gorbachov resigned three days later.

With independence suddenly thrust upon them, the old Soviet nomenklatura were essentially the only group with the experience and the means to rule. All the Central Asian governments are still authoritarian to some degree, running the gamut from pure *ancien regime*–style autocracy (Turkmenistan), to a tightly controlled mixture of neocommunism and spurious nationalism (Uzbekistan), to a marginally more enlightened 'channelled transition' to democracy and a market economy (Kazakhstan and Kyrgyzstan). Ironically once war-torn, Tajikistan is now the most democratic of the 'stans.

In most of the republics the old Communist Party apparatus remains more or less in place under new names: People's Democratic Party (Uzbekistan), Democratic Party (Turkmenistan), Party of People's Unity (Kazakhstan), and another People's Democratic Party (Tajikistan). Political opposition is completely marginalised (Turkmenistan), banned (Uzbekistan), or tolerated but closely watched (Kazakhstan and Kyrgyzstan). Human rights abuses are endemic.

The end of the old Soviet subsidies meant a decline in everything from economic subsidies to education levels. The deepest economic trauma is in the countryside, but even many urbanites are just scraping by, with wages for many professionals as low as US$35 a month in the cities. Most heart-rending are the pensioners, especially the Slavs whose pensions are currently worthless. Watery-eyed babushkas (old women) sit quietly on many street corners, trying not to look like beggars.

DID YOU KNOW?

The collapse of the Soviet Union sent the Central Asian republics into an economic collapse three times greater than the Great Depression of 1930s America.

DID YOU KNOW?

Agriculture accounts for a quarter to a third of the gross national product of all Central Asian republics, and employs one third to one half of their workforces.

Taliban blows up the 1500-year-old Buddhas of Bamiyan	Ahmad Shah Massoud, the 'Lion of the Panjshir', assassinated by Arab terrorists

The Silk Road

No-one knows for sure when the miraculously fine, light, soft, strong, shimmering, sensuous fabric spun from the cocoon of the *Bombyx* caterpillar first reached the West from China. In the 4th century BC, Aristotle described a fibre that may have been Chinese silk. Some people give credit for history's first great industrial espionage coup to a Chinese princess who was departing to marry a Khotanese king: the legend goes that she hid live worms and cocoons in her elaborate hairstyle, in order to fool customs agents so she would be able to wear silk in her 'barbarian' home. Others give the credit to Nestorian monks who allegedly hid silkworm eggs in their walking sticks as they travelled from Central Asia to Byzantium. The Romans probably first laid eyes on silk when the Parthians unfurled great blinding banners of the stuff on the battlefield.

But even after the secret of sericulture arrived in the Mediterranean world, the Chinese consistently exercised the advantage of centuries-acquired know-how. Writing a short while after the time of Christ, Pliny the Elder was scandalised by the luxurious, transparent cloths, which allowed Roman women to be 'dressed and yet nude'. He fell wide of the mark in describing silk's origin and processing, though, believing silk to literally grow on trees in a land called Seres. The Chinese, had they known, would most likely have done little to disillusion him.

Parthia, on the Iranian plateau, was the most voracious foreign consumer of Chinese silk at the close of the 2nd century BC, having supposedly traded an ostrich egg for its first bolt of silk. In about 105 BC, Parthia and China exchanged embassies and inaugurated official bilateral trade along the caravan route that lay between them. With this the Silk Road was born – in fact, if not in name – to flourish for another 800 years.

THE SILK ROUTES

Geographically the Silk Road was never a single road, but rather a fragile network of shifting intercontinental caravan tracks that threaded through some of the highest mountains and bleakest deserts on earth. Though the road map expanded over the centuries, the network had its main eastern terminus at the Chinese capital Ch'ang-an (modern Xi'an). West of there, the route passed through the Jade Gate and divided at

Ruined Silk Road cities in Kyrgyzstan's Chuy Valley include Ak-Beshim, Balasagun and Navekat, all dating from the 6th to 8th centuries AD. The last of these will be restored by Unesco.

Silk Road Foundation (www.silk-road.com) has articles on Silk Road cities and travel, as well as information on workshops, lectures and music.

The Bukhara skyline with the Ark in the foreground.

MARTIN MOOS

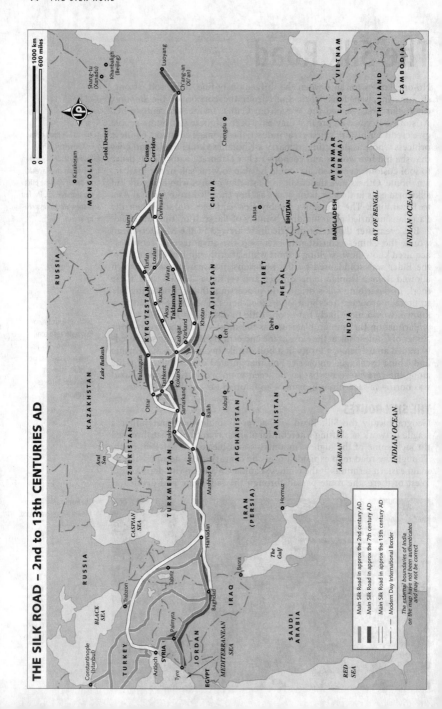

THE SILK ROAD – 2nd to 13th CENTURIES AD

Main Silk Road in approx the 2nd century AD
Main Silk Road in approx the 7th century AD
Main Silk Road in approx the 13th century AD
— · — Modern Day International Border

The external boundaries of India
on the map have not been authenticated
and may not be correct

Dunhuang, one branch skirting the dreaded Taklamakan Desert to the north through Loulan, Turfan, Kucha and Aksu, while the other headed south via Miran, Khotan (Hotan) and Yarkand. The two forks met again in Kashgar, from where the trail headed up to any of a series of passes confronting the traveller who attempted to cross the Pamirs and Tian Shan (one pass again in use today is the Torugart, on the border with Kyrgyzstan).

Beyond the mountains, the Fergana Valley fed westward through Kokand, Samarkand and Bukhara, past Merv and on to Iran, the Levant and Constantinople. Goods reached transhipment points on the Black and Mediterranean Seas, where caravans took on cargo for the march back eastward over the same tracks. In the middle of the network, major branches headed south over the Karakoram range to India and north via the Zhungarian Gap and across the Saka (Scythia) steppes to the Volga.

For the opportunity to see traditional silk production in Uzbekistan, see p192.

CARAVANS & TRADE

Goods heading West and East did not fall into discrete bundles. In fact there was no 'through traffic'; caravanners were mostly short- and medium-distance haulers who marketed and took on freight along a given beat according to their needs and inclinations. The earliest exchanges were based on mercantile interactions between the steppe nomads and settled towns, when barter was the only form of exchange. Only later did a monetary economy enable long-distance trade routes to develop.

At any given time any portion of the network might be beset by war, robbers or natural disaster: the northern routes were plagued by nomadic horsemen and a lack of settlements to provide fresh supplies and mounts; the south by fearsome deserts and frozen mountain passes.

In general, the Eastern end was enriched by the importation of gold, silver, ivory, jade and other precious stones, wool, horses, Mediterranean coloured glass (an industrial mystery originally as inscrutable to the Chinese as silk was in the West), cucumbers, walnuts, pomegranates, grapes and wine, spices, ivory and – an early Parthian craze – acrobats and ostriches. Goods enriching the Western end included silk, porcelain, paper, tea, lacquer ware, spices, medicinal herbs, gems and perfumes.

And in the middle lay Central Asia, a great clearing house that provided its native beasts – horses and two-humped Bactrian camels – to keep the goods flowing in both directions. The cities of Bukhara and Samarkand marked the halfway break, where caravans from Aleppo and Baghdad met traders from Kashgar and Yarkand. *Rabat* (caravanserais) grew up along the route, offering lodgings, stables and stores. Middlemen such as the Sogdians amassed great fortunes, much of which went into beautifying cosmopolitan and luxuriant caravan towns such as Gurganj and Bukhara. The cities offered equally vital services, such as brokers to set up contracts, banking houses to set up a line of credit and markets to sell the goods.

TECHNOLOGY TRANSFER

The Silk Road gave rise to unprecedented trade, but its true glory and unique status in human history was the result of the interchange of ideas, technologies and religions that occurred among the very different cultures that used it. Religion alone presents an astounding picture of diversity and tolerance that would be the envy of any modern democratic state. Manichaeism, Zoroastrianism, Buddhism, Nestorian Christianity, Judaism, Confucianism, Taoism and the shamanism of grassland nomads all coexisted and in some cases mingled, until the coming of Islam. In the course

THE TRAVELLING POLOS

In the 1250s, Venice was predominant in the Mediterranean and looking for new commercial routes. In this context the Venetian brothers Nicolo and Mafeo Polo set out to do some itinerant trading; sailing from Constantinople with a cargo of precious stones, they made their way to the Crimea. Choice business deals followed and took them gradually up the Volga (they stayed a year at the Mongol khan's encampment), eastward across the steppes, south to Bukhara (for a three-year stay), then across Central Asia to Karakoram (now in Mongolia), the seat of Kublai Khan, grandson of Jenghiz.

Kublai welcomed the Europeans warmly and questioned them at length about life and statecraft in Europe. Such was the style of hospitality on the steppe that the khan couldn't bear to let them go (modern travellers know similar treatment!). The Polos remained at court for some four years.

In the end Kublai made them ambassadors to the pope in Rome. Always searching for worthy doctrines from settled civilisations, Kublai requested that the pope send him 100 of his most learned priests. They were to argue the merits of their faith over others, and if they succeeded, Kublai and his whole empire would convert to Christianity. It took the Polos three difficult years to get home; when they arrived, no-one believed their stories.

Marco Polo, the teller of the world's most famous travel tale, was not yet born when his father Nicolo and uncle Mafeo set out on their journey. When they returned he was a motherless teenager. A couple of years later the elder Polos set off once more for Kublai's court, this time taking Marco.

The pope had supplied only two monks, and they stayed behind in Armenia when the going got tough. It is tempting to conjecture how the fate of Eurasia might have been different if the requested 100 doctors of religion had shown up at Karakoram and converted the entire Mongol empire. But it is more probable that they would have been politely detained and made into imperial bureaucrats; the Mongols liked to use the services of foreigners whenever possible.

The Polos made their way from Hormuz, on the Persian coast, to Balkh, and on through the Hindu Kush and the Pamirs (stopping by Kara-Kul lake, now in Tajikistan, on the way), then on past Kashgar, Yarkand and the southern route around the Taklamakan Desert, reaching China via Dunhuang and the Gansu Corridor. They found the khan dividing his time between Khanbaligh (now Beijing) and his nearby summer capital of Chung-tu (Xanadu of the Coleridge poem).

Marco was exceptionally intelligent and observant, and Kublai took a great liking to him. He was soon made a trusted adviser and representative of the ageing khan. The three Polos spent about 16 years in China; Marco travelled far afield and brought the khan news of his far-flung and exotic empire, little of which he had seen.

The Polos were only allowed to go home when they agreed to escort a Mongol princess on her way to be married in Persia. To avoid long hardship the party took the sea route from the east coast of China around India and up the Gulf. Back in Venice, still no-one believed the Polos' tales.

Many years later, during a war with Genoa, Marco Polo was captured in a naval battle. While in prison he dictated the story of his travels. The resulting book has become the world's most widely read travel account. Hounded all his life by accusations that the exotic world he described was fictitious, Marco Polo was even asked to recant on his deathbed. His answer: 'I have not told the half of what I saw.'

of his archaeological expeditions in Xinjiang, Albert von Le Coq brought back examples of 17 different languages written in 24 different scripts.

The Silk Road passed music and dance from West to East and enabled Indian, Chinese, Greek and Tibetan artistic styles to merge and fuse to form the Serindian art of Chinese Turkestan and the Gandharan art of Pakistan and Afghanistan.

Buddhism spread along the trade routes to wend its way from India to China and back again. It's hard to imagine that Buddhist monasteries once dominated cultural life in Central Asia; today only the faintest archaeological evidence remains in ex-Soviet Central Asia, at Adjina-Tepe in Tajikistan, Kuva in the Fergana Valley, Termiz in Uzbekistan and Ak-Beshim in Kyrgyzstan.

SILK ROAD READING

Life along the Silk Road, by Susan Whitfield, is a scholarly yet intriguing book that brings alive the Silk Road through a variety of characters (including a Sogdian merchant from Penjikent). Think the *Canterbury Tales* set in Central Asia. It's required reading for Silk Road obsessives.

Silk Road: Monks, Warriors & Merchants on The Silk Road, by Luce Boulnois, is a new reworking of a classic text from Odyssey guides. It has information on museum collections, Silk Road websites and updated travel information, all set in an attractive package.

The Silk Road, by Frances Wood, author of *Did Marco Polo Go To China?*, is another good new choice.

The Silk Road: Art & History, by Jonathon Tucker, is a large-format art book for the connoisseur.

THE DEATH OF THE SILK ROAD

The Silk Road never regained its vitality after the cosmopolitan Tang dynasty. The destruction and turbulence wreaked by Jenghiz Khan and Timur (Tamerlane) dealt an economic blow to the region, and the literal and figurative drying-up of the Silk Road lead to the abandonment of cities along the southern shore of the Taklamakan Desert. The metaphoric nail in the Silk Road's coffin was the opening of maritime trading routes between Europe and Asia.

Central Asia remained largely forgotten by the East and the West until the arrival of Russian and British explorers in the 19th century and the rediscovery of the glory of Xinjiang's Silk Road cities. Ironically, it was only then, 20 centuries after the first Chinese missions to the West, that the term 'Silk Road' was even used, coined for the first time by the German geographer Ferdinand von Richthofen.

REBIRTH

The fall of the USSR has seen a minirevival in all things Silk Road in Central Asia. The re-establishment of rail links to China and Iran, the growth of border trade over the Torugart and Khunjerab Passes and the increase in oil piped along former silk routes all offer the 'stans a means to shake off ties with Moscow. Afghanistan in also reconnecting to its neighbours to once again become a regional transport hub. Roads will connect the southwestern border to the Iranian port of Chabahar and the Iranian rail network has plans to expand as far as the Afghan border town of Islam Qala (a rail line already meets Afghanistan from Turkmenistan). Camel trains have been replaced by Kamaz trucks and silk replaced by scrap metal, but the Silk Road remains as relevant as it ever was.

People

The total population of the former Soviet Central Asia is about 60 million, with a 2.4% annual growth rate. With Afghanistan, the region's total hits 84 million. Few areas of its size are home to such tangled demographics and daunting transitions.

Each republic has inherited an ethnic grab bag from the Soviet system. Thus you'll find Uzbek towns in Kyrgyzstan, legions of Tajiks in the cities of Uzbekistan, Kazakhs grazing their cattle in Kyrgyzstan, Turkmen in Uzbekistan – and Russians and Ukrainians everywhere. Given the complicated mix of nationalities across national boundaries, Central Asia's ethnic situation is surprisingly tranquil. The most noticeable divide (and a largely amicable one) is between the traditionally sedentary peoples, the Uzbeks and Tajiks, and their formerly nomadic neighbours, the Kazakhs, Kyrgyz and Turkmen.

PEOPLES OF THE SILK ROAD

Centuries of migrations and invasions have ensured Central Asia's ethnic diversity. A trip from Ashgabat to Almaty reveals an absorbing array of faces, ranging from Turkish, Slavic, Chinese and Middle Eastern to downright Mediterranean – surmounted, incidentally, by an equally vast array of hats.

Before the Russian Revolution of 1917, Central Asians usually identified themselves 'ethnically' as either nomad or *sart* (settled), as Turk or Persian, as simply Muslim, or by their clan. Later, separate nationalities were 'identified' by Soviet scholars as ordered by Stalin. Although it is easy to see the problems this has created, some Kazakhs and Kyrgyz at least will admit that they owe their survival as a nation to the Soviet process of nation building.

The following sections are a summary of the peoples of Central Asia.

> Kazakhs are the most Russified of Central Asians, due to their long historical contact with Russia, although some still maintain a seminomadic existence.

KAZAKHS

> **KAZAKHS**
> Kazakhstan: 8 million
> China: 1.1 million
> Uzbekistan: 900,000
> Turkmenistan: 90,000
> Russia: 740,000
> Western Mongolia: 70,000
> Kyrgyzstan: 50,000
> Afghanistan: 30,000

The Kazakhs were nomadic horseback pastoralists until the 1920s; indeed the name Kazakh is said to mean 'free warrior' or 'steppe roamer'. Kazakhs trace their roots to the 15th century, when rebellious kinsmen of a Uzbek khan broke away and settled in present-day Kazakhstan. They divide themselves into three main divisions, or *zhuz*, corresponding to the historical Great (southern Kazakhstan), Middle (the north and east) and Little (the west) Hordes (p32). Family and ancestry remain crucial to Kazakhs. 'What *zhuz* do you belong to?' is a common opening question.

Most Kazakhs have Mongolian facial features similar to the Kyrgyz. Most wear Western or Russian clothes, but you may see women – particularly on special occasions – in long dresses with stand-up collars or brightly decorated velvet waistcoats and heavy jewellery. Sometimes they also wear fur-trimmed headdresses topped with crane plumes. Some men still wear baggy shirts and trousers and sleeveless jackets and wool or cotton robes. This outfit may be topped with either a skullcap or a high, tasselled felt hat resembling nothing so much as an elf's hat.

Kazakh 'literature' is based around heroic epics, many of which concern themselves with the 16th-century clashes between the Kazakhs and Kalmucks, and the heroic *batyrs* (warriors) of that age. Apart from various equestrian sports (see p54 and p246), a favourite Kazakh pastime is *itys*, which involves two people boasting about their own town, region or clan and ridiculing the other's in verses full of puns and allusions to Kazakh culture. The person who fails to find a witty comeback loses.

Kazakhs adhere rather loosely to Islam. Reasons for this include the Kazakhs' location on the fringe of the Muslim world and their traditionally nomadic lifestyle, which is unsuited to central religious authority. Their earliest contacts with the religion, from the 16th century, came courtesy of wandering Sufi dervishes or ascetics. Many were not converted until the 19th century, and shamanism apparently coexisted with Islam even after conversion.

Kazakh women appear the most confident and least restricted by tradition in Central Asia. All this is despite the lingering custom of wife stealing, whereby a man may simply kidnap a woman he wants to marry (often with some collusion, it must be said), leaving the parents with no option but to negotiate the *kalym*, or bride price.

The eight or so million Kazakhs have only recently become a majority in 'their' country, Kazakhstan.

Kazakhs and Kyrgyz share many customs and have similar languages, and in a sense they are simply the steppe (Kazakh) and mountain (Kyrgyz) variants of the same people.

KYRGYZ

The name Kyrgyz is one of the oldest recorded ethnic names in Asia, going back to the 2nd century BC in Chinese sources. At that time the ancestors of the modern Kyrgyz are said to have lived in the upper Yenisey Basin (Ene-Sai, or Yenisey, means 'Mother River' in Kyrgyz) in Siberia. They migrated to the mountains of what is now Kyrgyzstan from the 10th to 15th centuries, some fleeing wars and some arriving in the ranks of Mongol armies.

Many Kyrgyz derive their name from *kyrk kyz*, which means '40 girls' and goes along with legends of 40 original clan mothers. Today, ties to such clans as the Bugu (the largest clan), Salto (around Bishkek), Adigine (around Osh) and Sary-Bagysh (President Akaev's clan) remain relevant. Clans are divided into two federations, the Otuz Uul (30 Sons) and the Ich Kilik of southern Kyrgyzstan.

For special events Kyrgyz women's dress is similar to Kazakh women's. Older women may wear a large white wimplelike turban (known as an *elechek*) with the number of windings indicating her status. Kyrgyz men wear a white, embroidered, usually tasselled, felt cap called an *ak kalpak*. In winter, older men wear a long sheepskin coat and a round fur-trimmed hat called a *tebbetey*.

Traditions such as the *Manas* epic (see p246), horseback sports and eagle hunting remain important cultural denominators.

KYRGYZ
Kyrgyzstan: 3 million
Uzbekistan: 180,000
China: 143,000
Tajikistan: 300,000
Afghanistan: 3,000

PASHTUNS

Pashtuns are the largest ethnic group in Afghanistan and the most ancient. Aryan texts refer to them as the Paktua, while Herodotus talks of the Paktues; the British preferred the name Pathans. Many Pashtuns, or Pakhtuns (depending on the regional pronunciation), live over the border in Pakistan's lawless Tribal Areas.

Pashtuns are divided starkly along clan lines, the largest of which are the southern Durranis and southeastern Ghilzai, although there are dozens of others subclans (known as *khel*) such as the Wazir, Afridi, Khattak and Shinwari.

Traditional Pashtuns live by a moral code called Pashtoonwali, which stresses notions of revenge, hospitality, honour and sanctuary. Over the centuries they have been characterised as loyal, honest, brave and wily,

PASHTUNS
Afghanistan: 7 million
Pakistan: estimated 16 million

perpetually waiting in ambush somewhere. They have a love of freedom and guns. Blood vendettas are common.

TAJIKS

With their Mediterranean features and the occasional green-eyed redhead, Tajiks like to recall that their land was once visited by Alexander the Great and his troops, who are known to have taken local brides. Whether that blood is still visible or not, the Tajiks are in fact descended from an ancient Indo-European people the Aryans, making them relatives of present-day Iranians. Before the 20th century, *taj* was merely a term denoting a Persian speaker (all other Central Asian peoples speak Turkic languages).

Tajiks consider themselves to be the most civilised in Central Asia. Some Tajik nationalists have even demanded that Uzbekistan 'give back' Samarkand and Bukhara, as these cities were long-time centres of Persian culture. Tajiks trace their history back to the Samanids, Sogdians and Bactrians.

There are in fact many Tajik subdivisions and clans (such as the Kulyabis and Khojandis). The main subgroup is the Badakhshani (Pamiri Tajik), but even these are again subdivided into valley-based clans such as the Shugni, Rushani, Wakhi and Ishkashim.

Most Tajiks are Sunni Muslims, but Pamiri Tajiks of the Gorno-Badakhshan region belong to the Ismaili sect of Shiite Islam, and therefore have no formal mosques.

Traditional Tajik dress for men includes a heavy, quilted coat (*chapan*), tied with a sash that also secures a sheathed dagger, and a black embroidered cap (*tupi*), which is similar to the Uzbek *doppilar*. Tajik women could almost be identified in the dark, with their long, psychedelically coloured dresses (*kurta*), matching headscarves (*rumol*), striped trousers worn under the dress (*izor*) and bright slippers.

The 3.5 million Tajiks in Afghanistan speak Dari and their society resembles that of the Pashtuns. They follow a code of conduct called Abdurzadagai, similar to the Pashtun Pashtoonwali. Most Afghani Tajiks share closer ties to the valley they live in than their ethnic group. The most famous Tajik Afghan was the alliance leader Ahmad Shah Massoud.

There are around 33,000 Sarikol and Wakhi Tajiks over the border in China's Tashkurgan Tajik Autonomous County. Wakhi Tajiks also live in northern Pakistan.

TURKMEN

Legend has it that all Turkmen are descended from the fabled Oghuz Khan or from the warriors who rallied into clans around his 24 grandsons. Most historians believe that they were displaced nomadic horse-breeding clans who drifted into the oases around the Karakum desert (and into Persia, Syria and Anatolia) from the foothills of the Altay Mountains in the wake of the Seljuq Turks.

The hardships of desert-based nomadism forged them into a distinct group long before Soviet nation building, though centuries-old clan loyalties still exist and play a major role in politics. The largest of the 100 or so Turkmen clans are the Yomud (Caspian shore and northern Iran), Tekke (Merv, Ashgabat and central Turkmenistan), Ersari (on the Turkmenistan–Afghanistan border), Sarik (south, around Kushka) and Salor (eastern Turkmenistan and northern Afghanistan), each distinguished by their dialect, style of clothing and jewellery, and the patterns woven into their famous Turkmen *gillams* (carpets).

Turkmen men are easily recognisable in their huge shaggy sheepskin hats (*telpek*), either white (for special occasions) or black with thick ringlets resembling dreadlocks, worn year round on top of a skullcap, even on the hottest days. As one Turkmen explained it, they'd rather suffer the heat of their own heads than that of the sun. Traditional dress consists of baggy trousers tucked into knee-length boots, and white shirts under the knee-length *khalat*, a cherry red cotton jacket. Older men wear a long belted coat.

Turkmen women wear heavy, ankle-length velvet or silk dresses, the favourite colours being wine reds and maroons, with colourful trousers underneath. A woman's hair is always tied back and concealed under a colourful scarf. Older women often wear a *khalat* but, curiously, it is always thrown over their heads to protect from the sun's rays.

The Turkmen shared the nomad's liking for Sufism, and that sect is now strongly represented in Turkmenistan. The Turkmen language (also called Turkmen) is closest to Azeri. Interestingly, there was a Turkmen literary language as early as the mid-18th century.

Turkmenistan's population is now 85% Turkmen, giving it the highest proportion of the titular nationality of any Central Asian republic.

UZBEKS

The Uzbek khans, Islamised descendants of Jenghiz Khan, left their home in southern Siberia in search of conquest, establishing themselves in what is now Uzbekistan by the 15th century, clashing and then mixing with the Timurids. The Uzbek Shaybanid dynasty oversaw the transition from nomad to settler, although the original Mongol clan identities (such as the Kipchak, Mangits and Karluks) remain.

Uzbek neighbourhoods *(mahalla)* and villages *(kishlak)* are coherent and solid, both physically and socially. Houses are built behind high walls, sometimes with handsome gates.

Uzbeks are the largest Turkic group outside of Turkey and were the third-largest ethnic group of the Soviet Union. With their high profile and numbers in all the former USSR republics, Uzbeks are often said by their neighbours to be chauvinistic and cast as the regional bogeyman, seeking political hegemony over Central Asia.

Uzbek men traditionally wear long quilted coats tied by a bright-coloured sash. Nearly all wear the *dopy* or *doppilar*, a black, four-sided skullcap embroidered in white. In winter, older men wear a furry *telpek*. Uzbek women are fond of dresses in sparkly, brightly coloured *ikat* cloth, often as a knee-length gown with trousers of the same material underneath. One or two braids worn in the hair indicate that a woman is married; more mean that she is single. Eyebrows that grow together over the bridge of the nose are considered attractive and are

UZBEKS
Uzbekistan: 18 million
Tajikistan: 1.6 million
Afghanistan: 1.3 million
Kazakhstan: 334,000
Kyrgyzstan: 690,000
Turkmenistan: 396,000
China: 14,700

BODY LANGUAGE

A heartfelt handshake between Central Asian men is a gesture of great warmth, elegance and beauty. Many Central Asian men also place their right hand on the heart and bow or incline the head slightly, a highly addictive gesture that you may find yourself echoing quite naturally.

Good friends throughout the region shake hands by gently placing their hands, thumbs up, in between another's. There's no grabbing or Western-style firmness, just a light touch. Sometimes a good friend will use his right hand to pat the other's. If you are in a room full of strangers it's polite to go around the room shaking hands with everyone. Don't be offended if someone offers you his wrist if his hands are dirty. Some say the custom originates in the need to prove that you come unarmed as a friend.

Women don't usually shake hands but touch each others' shoulders with right hands and slightly stroke them. Younger women in particular will often kiss an elder woman on the cheek as a sign of respect.

Afghans are great huggers. Offering a handshake to an Afghan of the opposite sex may put them in an awkward position; let them make the first move.

HOLY SMOKE

In markets, stations and parks all over Central Asia you'll see gypsy women and children asking for a few coins to wave their pans of burning herbs around you or the premises. The herb is called *isriq* in Uzbek, and the smoke is said to be good medicine against colds and flu (and the evil eye?), and a cheap alternative to scarce medicines. Some people also burn it when they move into a new home.

Uzbeks resisted Russification and have emerged from Soviet rule with a strong sense of identification and their rich heritage.

often supplemented with pencil for the right effect. Both sexes flash lots of gold teeth.

There are around 1.3 million Uzbeks in northern Afghanistan, north of the Hindu Kush, who mostly grow cotton or trade in karakul fleeces. Ties to the local landlord (*arbab*) are still strong in this region.

SLAVS

Russians and Ukrainians have settled in Central Asia in several waves, the first in the 19th century with colonisation and the latest in the 1950s during the Virgin Lands campaign. Numerous villages in remoter parts of Central Asia, with names such as Orlovka or Alexandrovka, were founded by the early settlers and are still inhabited by their descendants.

Many Slavs, feeling deeply aggrieved as political and administrative power devolves to 'local' people, have emigrated to Russia and the Ukraine. At the height of the migration over 280,000 Russians left Kazakhstan and 200,000 left Tajikistan in a single year. Some have returned, either disillusioned with life in the motherland or reaffirmed in the knowledge that Central Asia is their home, like it or not.

OTHER NATIONALITIES

Dungans are Muslim Chinese who first moved across the border in 1882, especially to Kazakhstan and Kyrgyzstan, to escape persecution after failed Muslim rebellions. Few still speak Chinese, though their cuisine remains distinctive.

DID YOU KNOW?

You'll come across the occasional village in Central Asia with a German name, such as Rotfront in Kyrgyzstan, the legacy of forced German immigration.

Koreans arrived in Central Asia as deportees in WWII. They have preserved little of their traditional culture. They typically farm vegetables and sell their pickled salads in many bazaars.

Germans were deported in WWII from their age-old home in the Volga region, or came as settlers (some of them Mennonites) in the late 19th century. Most have since departed to Germany but pockets remain. Likewise, Jews, an important part of Bukharan commerce since the 9th century, have mostly already made for Israel (and Queens, New York).

Tatars, a Turkic people from Russia (descended from the Mongol Golden Horde), began settling in Central Asia with the tsar's encouragement in the mid-19th century. Most look more like Russians rather than other Turkic peoples.

Meskhetian Turks have groups in the Fergana (the largest concentration), Chuy and Ili Valleys.

Karakalpaks occupy their own republic in northwest Uzbekistan and have cultural and linguistic ties with Kazakhs, Uzbeks and Kyrgyz (see p231).

Kurds are another WWII-era addition to the melting pot, with many living in Kazakhstan. Estimates of their numbers in Central Asia range from 150,000 to over a million.

Hazaras are the second-largest ethnic group in Afghanistan, totalling over 1.5 million. Descendants of Mongol troops, they have very Mongolian faces and follow Shiite Islam. They speak a dialect of Dari. They have traditionally suffered much discrimination within Afghanistan as they are non-Sunni and non-Pashtun.

The Nuristanis of northeast Afghanistan were once known as the *kafirs* (infidels) because of their polytheistic belief system. They have close connections to the Kalasha of Pakistan.

It is estimated that there are half a million Uyghurs in the former Soviet Central Asian republics and Afghanistan (having moved there from Xinjiang after heavy Chinese persecution in the late 19th century).

You may see communities of colourfully dressed South Asian–looking women and children begging or working as fortune tellers. These are Central Asian gypsies, called *luli* (*chuki*), who number around 30,000, speak Tajik and originate from areas around Samarkand, southern Tajikistan and Turkmenistan.

Afghanistan has around 2.5 million pastoral nomads known as Kuchis, who are ethnic kin to the Pashtuns. The women remain largely unveiled and are famed for their fine jewellery.

DAILY LIFE

It's a social rollercoaster in Central Asia: the overall birth rate is down, deaths from all causes are up, economies are plummeting, crime is skyrocketing, life expectancies have dropped and migration (most especially emigration) is on the rise. Many older Central Asians lost their social and cultural bearings with the fall of the Soviet Union. Health levels are plummeting, drug addiction is up and alcoholism has acquired the proportions of a national tragedy.

But it's not all bad news. Traditional life is reasserting itself in today's economic vacuum and tourism projects are encouraging traditional crafts, sports and music. After a decade of confusion, people have started to find their way in the new order.

DOS & DON'TS

- Dress codes vary throughout Central Asia. The main places where you should dress conservatively are Afghanistan and Uzbekistan's Fergana Valley (see p294). Western-style clothes are acceptable in the capital cities and in large towns such as Samarkand, which see a lot of tourist traffic.

- Working mosques are closed to women and often to non-Muslim men, though men may occasionally be invited in. When visiting a mosque, always take your shoes off at the door, and make sure your feet or socks are clean. It is polite to refer to the Prophet Mohammed as such, rather than by his name alone. Never walk in front of someone praying to Mecca.

- When you visit someone's home, take your shoes off at the door unless you are told not to. You will often find a pair of undersized thongs (flip-flops) waiting for you at the door. (Traditional Central Asian footwear consists of overshoes, which can be taken off without removing the *massi*, soft leather under boots.) Avoid stepping on any carpet if you have your shoes on. See p78 for tips on food etiquette.

- Central Asian society devotes much respect to its elderly, known as *aksakals* (white beards). Always make an effort to shake hands with an elder. Younger men give up their seats to *aksakals*, and foreigners should certainly offer their place in a crowded chaikhana (teahouse). Some Central Asians address elders with a shortened form of the elder's name, adding the suffix 'ke'. Thus Abkhan becomes Abeke, Nursultan becomes Nureke, and so on.

BUZKASHI

In a region where many people are descended from hot-blooded nomads, no-one would expect cricket to be the national sport. Even so, *buzkashi* (literally 'grabbing the dead goat') is wild beyond belief. As close to warfare as a sport can get, *buzkashi* is a bit like rugby on horseback in which the 'ball' is the headless carcass of a calf, goat or sheep (whatever is handy).

The day before the kickoff the carcass *(boz)* has its head, lower legs and entrails removed and is soaked in cold water for 24 hours to toughen it up. The game begins with the carcass in the centre of a circle at one end of a field; at the other end is a bunch of wild, adrenaline-crazed horsemen. At a signal it's every man for himself as they charge for the carcass. The aim is to gain possession of the *boz* and carry it up the field and around a post, with the winning rider being the one who finally drops the *boz* back in the circle. All the while there's a frenzied horsebacked tug-of-war going on as each competitor tries to gain possession; smashed noses, wrenched shoulders and shattered thigh bones are all part of the fun.

Not surprisingly, the game is said to date from the days of Jenghiz Khan when, tradition has it, human carcasses were used rather than those of sheep. More importantly, the game traditionally enforced the nomadic values necessary for collective survival – courage, adroitness, wit and strength, while propagating a remarkable skill on horseback. The point of the game used to be the honour, and perhaps notoriety, of the victor, but gifts such as silk *chapans* (cloaks), rifles or cash are common.

Buzkashi takes place mainly outside of the pastoral season, in the cooler months of spring and autumn, at weekends, particularly during Navrus or to mark special occasions such as weddings. You can catch local versions in Kyrgyzstan (where it's known as *ulak-tartysh*), Tajikistan and across north Afghanistan, best seen in Mazar-e Sharif, Kunduz and also in Kabul.

TRADITIONAL CULTURE

In Islam, a guest – Muslim or not – has a position of honour not very well understood in the West. If someone visits you and you don't have much to offer, as a Christian you'd be urged to share what you had; as a Muslim you're urged to give it all away. Guests are to be treated with absolute selflessness.

For a visitor to a Muslim country, even one as casual about Islam as Kazakhstan or Kyrgyzstan, this is a constant source of pleasure, temptation and sometimes embarrassment. The majority of Central Asians, especially rural ones, have little to offer but their hospitality, and a casual guest could drain a host's resources and never know it. And yet to refuse such an invitation (or to offer to bring food or to help with the cost) would almost certainly be a grave insult.

All you can do is enjoy it, honour their customs as best you can, and take yourself courteously out of the picture before you become a burden. If for some reason you do want to decline, couch your refusal in gracious and diplomatic terms, allowing the would-be host to save face. As an example, if you are offered bread, you should at least taste a little piece before taking your leave.

If you are really lucky you might be invited to a *toi* (celebration) such as a *kelin toi* (wedding celebration), a *beshik toi* (nine days after the birth of a child), or a *sunnat toi* (circumcision party). Other celebrations are held to mark the birth, name giving and first haircut of a child.

Religion

With the exception of rapidly shrinking communities of Jews and Russian Orthodox Christians, small minorities of Roman Catholics, Baptists and evangelical Lutherans, and a few Buddhists among the Koreans of the Fergana Valley and Kyrgyzstan, nearly everyone from the Caspian Sea to Kandahar is Muslim, at least in principle. The intensity of faith varies from faint to fanatical, although after the 'militant atheism' of the Soviet years, few now appear to understand Islam very deeply.

ISLAM
History & Schisms

In AD 612, the Prophet Mohammed, then a wealthy Arab of Mecca in present-day Saudi Arabia, began preaching a new religious philosophy, Islam, based on revelations from Allah (Islam's name for God). Islam incorporated elements of Judaism, Christianity and other faiths (eg heaven and hell, a creation story much like the Garden of Eden, stories similar to Noah's Ark), but treated their prophets simply as forerunners of the Prophet Mohammed. These revelations were eventually to be compiled into Islam's holiest book, the Quran.

The word Islam translates loosely from Arabic as 'the peace that comes from total surrender to God'.

In 622 the Prophet Mohammed and his followers were forced to flee to Medina due to religious persecution (the Islamic calendar counts its years from this flight, known as Hejira). There he built a political base and an army, taking Mecca in 630 and eventually overrunning Arabia. The militancy of the faith meshed nicely with a latent Arab nationalism and within a century Islam reached from Spain to Central Asia.

Succession disputes after the Prophet's death soon split the community. When the fourth caliph, the Prophet's son-in-law Ali, was assassinated in 661, his followers and descendants became the founders of the Shiite sect. Others accepted as caliph the governor of Syria, a brother-in-law of the Prophet, and this line has become the modern-day orthodox Sunni sect. In 680 a chance for reconciliation was lost when Ali's surviving son Husain and most of his male relatives were killed at Karbala in Iraq by Sunni partisans.

The percentage of practising Muslims ranges from 47% in Kazakhstan to 75% in Kyrgyzstan, 85% in Tajikistan, 88% in Uzbekistan and 89% in Turkmenistan.

Today some 85% to 90% of Muslims worldwide are Sunni. About 80% of all Central Asians are Muslim, nearly all of them Sunni (and indeed nearly all of the Hanafi school, one of Sunnism's four main schools of religious law). The main exception is a tightly knit community of Ismailis in the remote mountainous region of Gorno-Badakhshan in eastern Tajikistan (see p338).

A small but increasingly influential community of another Sunni school, the ascetic, fundamentalist Wahhabi, are found mainly in Uzbekistan's Fergana Valley.

Practice

Devout Muslims express their faith through the five pillars of Islam:

1. The creed that 'There is only one god, Allah, and Mohammed is his prophet'.
2. Prayer, five times a day, prostrating towards the holy city of Mecca, in a mosque (for men only) when possible, but at least on Friday, the Muslim holy day.
3. Dawn-to-dusk fasting during Ramadan.
4. Making the haj (pilgrimage to Mecca) at least once in one's life (many of those who have done so can be identified by their white skullcaps).
5. Alms giving, in the form of the zakat, an obligatory 2.5% tax.

Devout Sunnis pray at prescribed times: before sunrise, just after high noon, in the late afternoon, just after sunset and before retiring. Prayers are preceded if possible by washing, at least of the hands, face and feet. For Ismailis the style of prayer is a personal matter (eg there is no prostration), the mosque is replaced by a community shrine or meditation room, and women are less excluded.

Just before fixed prayers a muezzin calls the Sunni and Shiite faithful, traditionally from a minaret, nowadays often through a loudspeaker. Islam has no ordained priesthood, but mullahs (scholars, teachers or religious leaders) are trained in theology, respected as interpreters of scripture, and are sometimes quite influential in conservative rural areas.

The Quran is considered above criticism: it is the word of God as spoken to his Prophet Mohammed. It is supplemented by various traditions such as the Hadith, the collected acts and sayings of the Prophet Mohammed. In its fullest sense Islam is an entire way of life, with guidelines for doing nearly everything, from preparing and eating food to banking.

Islam in Ex-Soviet Central Asia

Islam first appeared in Central Asia with Arab invaders in the 7th and 8th centuries. In the following centuries many conversions were accomplished by teachers from Islam's mystic Sufi tradition who wandered across Asia (see Sufism, opposite). Tsarist colonisers largely allowed Central Asians to worship as they pleased but the Bolsheviks feared Islam because of its potential for coherent resistance, both domestically and internationally.

Three of the five pillars of Islam (the fast of Ramadan, the haj and the zakat) were outlawed in the 1920s. Polygamy, the wearing of the veil (paranja), and the Arabic script in which the Quran is written were forbidden. Clerical (Christian, Jewish and Buddhist as well as Muslim) land and property were seized. Medressas and other religious schools were closed down. Islam's judicial power was curbed with the dismantling of traditional sharia courts (which were based on Quranic law).

From 1932 to 1936 Stalin mounted a concerted antireligious campaign in Central Asia, a 'Movement of the Godless', in which mosques were closed and destroyed, and mullahs arrested and liquidated as saboteurs or spies. By the early 1940s only 2000 of its 47,000 mullahs remained alive. Control of the surviving places of worship and teaching was given to the Union of Atheists, which transformed most of them into museums, dance halls, warehouses or factories.

During WWII things improved marginally as Moscow sought domestic and international Muslim support for the war effort. In 1943 four Muslim Religious Boards or 'spiritual directorates', each with a mufti (spiritual leader), were founded as administration units for Soviet Muslims, including one in Tashkent for all of Central Asia (in 1990 one was established for Kazakhstan). Some mosques were reopened and a handful of carefully screened religious leaders were allowed to make the haj in 1947.

But beneath the surface little changed. Any religious activity outside the official mosques was strictly forbidden. By the early 1960s, under Khrushchev's 'back to Lenin' policies, another 1000 mosques were shut. By the beginning of the Gorbachov era, the number of mosques in Central Asia was down to between 150 and 250, and only two medressas were open – Mir-i-Arab in Bukhara and the Imam Ismail al-Bukhari Islamic Institute in Tashkent.

Following bloody interethnic violence, particularly around the Fergana Valley in 1989 and 1990, the Soviet authorities fell over themselves to allow the construction of new mosques. Since the republics' respective declarations of independence, mosques and medressas have sprouted like mushrooms, often with Saudi or Iranian money. Even in more conservative Uzbekistan and Tajikistan, all those new mosques are as much political as religious statements.

But Islam never was a potent force in the former nomadic societies of the Turkmen, Kazakhs and Kyrgyz, and still isn't (some researchers suggest that Islam's appeal for nomadic rulers was as much its discipline as its moral precepts; nomadic leaders accepted Islam nominally for its organisational and political use. On a personal level the nomads have little sense of the formal tenets of Islam). The nomad's customary law, known as *adat*, was always more important than Islamic sharia.

The Central Asian brand of Islam is also riddled with pre-Islamic influences – just go to any important holy site and notice the kissing, rubbing and circumambulating of venerated objects, women crawling under holy stones to boost their fertility, the shamanic 'wishing trees' tied with bits of coloured rag, the cult of Pirs (holy men), the Mongol-style poles with horse-hair tassel set over the graves of revered figures and sometimes candles and flames are burned at shrines and graves, harking back to Zoroastrian times. The Turkmen place particular stock in amulets and charms. There is also a significant blurring between religious and national characteristics. The majority of Central Asians, although interested in Islam as a common denominator, seem quite happy to toast your health with a shot of vodka.

And yet the amazing thing is that, after 70 years of concerted Soviet repression, with mainstream Islam in an official hammerlock, so much faith remains intact. Some rural Central Asians in fact take Islam very seriously, enough to create substantial political muscle. The real power in the coalition that seized control of Tajikistan in 1992 was the Islamic Renaissance Party (IRP), which, although outlawed by the other Central Asian republics, enjoyed enormous support in the Fergana Valley of Uzbekistan; the epicentre of what fundamentalism exists today.

Credit for any continuity from pre-Soviet times goes largely to 'underground Islam', in the form of the clandestine Sufi brotherhoods (and brotherhoods they were, being essentially men-only), which preserved some practice and education – and grew in power and influence in Central Asia as a result.

SUFISM

The original Sufis were simply purists, unhappy with the worldliness of the early caliphates and seeking knowledge of God through direct personal experience, under the guidance of a teacher or master, variously called a sheikh, Pir, *ishan, murshid* or *ustad*. There never was a single Sufi movement; there are manifestations within all branches of Islam. For many adherents music, dance or poetry about the search for God were routes to trance, revelation and direct union with God. Secret recitations, known as *zikr*, and an annual 40-day retreat, known as the *chilla*, remain cornerstones of Sufic practice. This is the mystical side of Islam, parallel to similar traditions in other faiths.

Sufis were singularly successful as missionaries, perhaps because of their tolerance of other creeds. It was largely Sufis, not Arab armies, who planted Islam firmly in Central Asia and the subcontinent. The personal focus of Sufism was most compatible with the nomadic lifestyle of the

DID YOU KNOW?

Before the arrival of Islam, Central Asia sheltered strong pockets of Zoroastrianism, Manichaeism and Nestorian Christianity, as well as a long tradition of Buddhism. In the 8th century there were even Nestorian bishoprics in Herat and Samarkand.

Jihad: The Rise of Militant Islam in Central Asia, by Ahmed Rashid, is an incisive journalistic review of how and why Islamic militant groups, such as the Islamic Movement of Uzbekistan (IMU) and Hizb ut-Tahrir (HUT), rose in the Fergana Valley from the ashes of the Soviet Union.

Kazakh and Kyrgyz in particular. Although abhorred nowadays in the orthodox Islamic states of Iran and Saudi Arabia, Sufism is in a quiet way dominant in Central Asia. Most shrines you'll see are devoted to one Sufi teacher or another.

When Islam was itself threatened by invaders (eg the Crusaders), Sufis assumed the role of defenders of the faith, and Sufism became a mass movement of regimented *tariqas* (brotherhoods), based around certain holy places, often the tombs of the *tariqas'* founders. Clandestine, anti-Communist *tariqas* helped Islam weather the Soviet period, and the KGB and its predecessors never seemed able to infiltrate.

The moderate, nonelitist Naqshbandiya *tariqa* was the most important in Soviet times, and probably still is. Founded in Bukhara in the 14th century, much of its influence in Central Asia perhaps comes from the high profile of Naqshbandi fighters in two centuries of revolts against the Russians in the Caucasus. In 1940 one of the last of these, in Chechnya, was crushed, and in February 1944 the entire Chechen and Ingush populations were deported to Siberia and Kazakhstan. When, after Stalin's death, the survivors were permitted to return to their homeland, they left behind several well-organised Sufi groups in Central Asia. A number of well-known 1930s *basmachi* (Muslim guerrilla fighters) leaders were Naqshbandis.

Another important Sufi sect in Central Asia is the Qadiriya, founded by a teacher from the Caspian region. Others are the Kubra (founded in Khorezm, see p432) and Yasauia (founded in the town of Turkistan in Kazakhstan). All these were founded in the 12th century.

Arts

Set astride trade and migration routes, Central Asia has for millennia blended and fused artistic traditions from the Turkic and Persian worlds into an indigenous aesthetic. During their campaigns of terror both Jenghiz Khan and Timur (Tamerlane) collected artisans from Beijing to Baghdad, resulting in a splendid fusion of styles in textiles, painting, architecture and metal arts.

ARCHITECTURE

The most impressive surviving artistic heritage of Central Asia is its architecture, and some of the world's most audacious and beautiful examples of Islamic religious buildings are to be found at Bukhara, Khiva and especially Samarkand all in Uzbekistan.

Thanks in the main to the destructive urges of Jenghiz Khan, virtually nothing has survived from the pre-Islamic era or the first centuries of Arab rule. The Bolsheviks further destroyed many of Central Asia's religious buildings, except those of architectural or historical value.

Early Influences

Several technological advances had a dominant effect on the development of architectural arts, principally that of fired brick in the 10th century, coloured tilework in the 12th century and polychrome tilework in the 14th century.

The squinch (the corner bracketing that enabled the transition from a square to an eight-, then 16-sided platform) was essential to the development of the dome. This technology gave rise to the double dome, which made possible the huge domes of the Timurid era.

Other influences have been more climatic; the lack of wood or stone made Central Asian architects turn to brickwork as the cornerstone of their designs. Tall portals, built to face and catch the prevailing winds, and running streams of water were designed to have a cooling effect in the heat of summer. Nomadic influence is particularly relevant in Khiva, where platforms were designed to hold wintertime yurts.

Timurid Architecture

Most of the monumental architecture standing today dates from the time of the Timurids (14th to 15th centuries); rulers who could be almost as savage as the Mongol warlords but who also had a bent for artistic patronage.

The Timurid architectural trademark is the beautiful, often ribbed, azure-blue dome. Other typical Timurid design elements include *pishtak* (monumental arched entrance portals) flanked by tapering minarets, a tendency towards ensemble design and exuberant, multicoloured tilework.

Architectural Design

Khiva and Bukhara have the most homogenous architectural layout, highlighting the importance of the *shahristan* (inner city). An outer city wall surrounded most cities, protecting against desert storms and brigands.

In the town, monuments are often found facing each other in reflective pairs. Apart from Islamic monuments, secular architecture includes palaces (such as the Tosh-Khovli in Khiva), *ark* or *bala hissar* (forts), *hammam* (multidomed bathhouses), *rabat* (caravanserais), *tim* (shopping

DID YOU KNOW?

Over 70% of Kabul Museum's priceless collection of art was looted during the 1990s and sold on the black market, including the fantastic Begram Ivories and Bactrian gold from Tillya Teppe. The Taliban later smashed 2000 of the remaining statues, branding them 'anti-Islamic'.

For a look into the soul of old Afghanistan seek out the timeless photography of Roland and Sabrina Michaud, including their coffee-table books *Afghanistan: The Land that Was* and *Caravan to Tartary*, the latter an account of a 1970s expedition up the Afghan Wakhan Valley.

For an in-depth look at the Timurid architecture of Samarkand try www.oxuscom.com /timursam.htm.

arcades), *tok* (covered crossroad bazaars) and *hauz* (reservoirs) that supplied the city with drinking water.

MOSQUES

Islam dominates Central Asian architecture. *Masjid* (mosques) trace their design back to the house of the Prophet Mohammed, though later designs vary considerably. Most common is the use of the portal, which leads into a colonnaded space, sometimes open, and a covered area for prayer. The entrance of many Central Asian mosques, such as the Bolo-Hauz Mosque in Bukhara, have, instead, a flat, brightly painted roof, supported by carved wooden columns. Other mosques, such as the Juma Mosque in Khiva, are hypostyle (a roofed space, divided by many pillars).

Whether the place of worship is a *guzar* (local mosque), serving the local community, a *jami* (Friday mosque), built to hold the entire city congregation once a week, or a *namazgokh* (festival mosque), the focal point is always the mihrab, a niche that indicates the direction of Mecca.

MEDRESSAS

These are Islamic colleges, normally two storeys high and set around a cloistered central courtyard, punctuated with *iwan* (arched portals, also called *aiwan* or *eivan*) on four sides. Rows of little doors in the interior façades lead into *hujras* (cell-like living quarters for students and teachers) or *khanakas* (prayer cells or entire buildings) for the ascetic wandering dervishes who stayed there. Most medressas are fronted by

DID YOU KNOW?

The niches in the medressas' front walls were once used as shopkeepers' stalls.

ARCHITECTURAL HIGHLIGHTS

Merv (in Turkmenistan), Khiva's Ichon-Qala, the old towns of Bukhara, Samarkand and Shakhrisabz (all in Uzbekistan), Turkistan's Kozha Akhmed Yasaui Mausoleum (in Kazakhstan) and Afghanistan's Minaret of Jam and Bamiyan Valley are all Unesco World Heritage sites. The archaeological site of Nissa (in Turkmenistan), the Minaret of Jam and minarets of Ghazni (in Afghanistan) are included in the list of the 100 most endangered sites in the world.

The following are our picks of the architectural highlights of Central Asia.

Ismail Samani Mausoleum (900–1000) In Bukhara: mesmerising brickwork (p214).

Kalon Minaret (1127) In Bukhara: Central Asia's most impressive minaret, 48m high (p213).

Sultan Sanjar Mausoleum (1157) In Merv: huge double-domed Seljuq monument (p428).

Friday Mosque (12th century) In Herat (Afghanistan): stunning Ghorid monument, with modern tiling produced *in situ*; classic four-iwan design (p386).

Minaret of Jam (1194) In central Afghanistan: world's second-highest minaret (65m), set in a remote mountain valley location (p383).

Shahr-i-Zindah (1300–1400) In Samarkand: features Central Asia's most stunning and varied tilework (p200).

Bibi-Khanym Mosque (1399–1404) In Samarkand: Timur's intended masterpiece, so colossal that it collapsed as soon as it was finished (p199).

Guri Amir Mausoleum (1404) In Samarkand: exquisite ribbed dome, sheltering the tomb of Timur (p200).

Ak-Saray Palace (1400–50) In Shakhrisabz: tantalising remains of Timur's once-opulent palace (p206).

Shrine of Khoja abu Nasr Parsa (end 15th century) In Balkh (Afghanistan): beautiful Timurid ribbed dome and massive portal (p393).

The Registan (1400–1600) In Samarkand: epic ensemble of medressas; the Sher Dor (1636) flaunts Islamic tradition by depicting two lions chasing deer, looked down upon by a Mongol-faced sun (p199).

Lyabi-Hauz (1600) In Bukhara: featuring a pool, *khanaka* (pilgrim resthouse) and medressa (p211).

Char Minar (1807) In Bukhara: quirky ex-gateway, resembling a chair thrust upside down in the ground (p214).

Islom-Huja Minaret (Islam Khoja; 1910) In Khiva: reckoned by Central Asian archaeological specialist Edgar Knobloch to be the last notable architectural achievement of the Islamic era in Central Asia; we'd expand that to say the last notable architectural achievement in Central Asia, period (p227).

monumental portals. On either side of the entrance you will normally find a *darskhana* (lecture room) to the left, and mosque to the right.

MAUSOLEUMS

The *mazar* (mausoleum) has been a popular style of architecture for millennia, either built by rulers to ensure their own immortality or to commemorate holy men. Most consist of a *ziaratkhana* (prayer room), set under a domed cupola. The actual tomb may be housed in a central hall, or *gurkhana* (underground in a separate room). A complex of lodging, washrooms and kitchens is often attached. Tombs vary in design from the cupola style to the pyramid-shaped, tentlike designs of Konye-Urgench (p431), or whole streets of tombs as found at the Shahr-i-Zindah in Samarkand (p200).

MINARETS

These tall, tapering towers were designed to summon the faithful during prayer time, so most have internal stairs for the muezzin to climb. They were also used as lookouts to spot brigands, and, in the case of the Kalon Minaret in Bukhara, as a means of execution. Some minarets (eg at Samarkand's Registan) exist purely for decoration.

Decoration

Tilework is the most dramatic form of decoration in Central Asia, giving huge Timurid buildings a light, graceful feel. Colours were made especially bright to stand out in the bright sunlight of the desert. The deep cobalt and turquoise ('colour of the Turks') of Samarkand's domes have moved travellers for centuries. Greens are most common in Khorezm, khakis in Bukhara and blues in Samarkand.

Decoration almost always takes the shape of abstract geometric, floral or calligraphic designs, in keeping with the Islamic taboo on the representation of living creatures. Geometric designs were closely linked to the development of Central Asian science – star designs were a favourite with the astronomer king Ulughbek. Calligraphy is common, either in the square, stylised Kufic script favoured by the Timurids or the more scrolling, often foliated thulth script.

Tiles come in a variety of styles, either stamped, faïence (carved onto wet clay and then fired), polychromatic (painted on and then fired) or jigsaw-style mosaic. Carved *ghanch* (alabaster), patterned brickwork, and carved and painted wood are also important methods of decorating architecture.

Monuments of Central Asia: A Guide to the Archaeology, Art and Architecture of Turkestan, by Edgar Knobloch, is an excellent overview of the region's architectural heritage.

FOLK ART

Central Asian folk art developed in tune with a nomadic or seminomadic way of life, focusing on transport (horses) and home (yurts). Designs followed the natural beauty of the earth: snow resting on a leaf, the elegance of an ibex horn, the flowers of the steppe. Status and wealth were apparent by the intricacy of a carved door or a richly adorned horse. Art was not merely created for pleasure; each item had a practical function in everyday life. From brightly coloured carpets used for sleeping and woven reed mats designed to block the wind, to leather bottles used for carrying *kumys* (fermented mare's milk), many of the souvenirs dispersed throughout Kyrgyzstan and Kazakhstan in particular are remnants of a nomadic past.

With such emphasis on equestrian culture it is not surprising that horses donned decorative blankets, inlaid wooden saddles, and head and neck adornments. Men hung their wealth on their belts with daggers and sabres in silver sheaths, and embossed leather purses and vessels for

Some of the best examples of Central Asian folk art can be seen at Tashkent's Museum of Applied Arts (p174).

The Arts and Crafts of Turkestan, by Johannes Kalter, is a detailed, beautifully illustrated historical guide to the nomadic dwellings, clothing, jewellery and other 'applied art' of Central Asia.

drink. Even today the bazaars in Tajikistan and the Fergana Valley are heavy with carved daggers and *pichok* (knives).

Nomads required their wealth to be portable and rich nomadic women wore stupendous jewellery, mostly of silver incorporating semiprecious stones, such as lapis lazuli and carnelian (believed to have magical properties); there was sometimes so much jewellery on marriageable women that walking was difficult.

To remain portable, furnishings consisted of bright quilts, carpets and *aiyk kap* (woven bags), which were hung on yurt walls for storing plates and clothing. *Sabaa, chanach* and *kökör* (embossed leather bottles) were used for preparing, transporting and serving *kumys*.

Most Central Asian peoples have their own traditional rug or carpet styles. The famous 'Bukhara' rugs – so called because they were mostly sold, not made, in Bukhara – are made largely by the Turkmen, although the Afghans are the real kings of carpet making. The Kyrgyz specialise in *shyrdaks* (felt rugs with appliquéd coloured panels or pressed wool designs called *ala-kiyiz*); see p247. Kazakhs specialise in *koshma* (multicoloured felt mats).

Uzbeks make silk and cotton wall hangings and coverlets such as the beautiful *suzani* (suzan is Persian for needle). *Suzanis* are made in a variety of sizes and used as table covers, cushions, and *ruijo* (a bridal bedspread) and thus were important for the bride's dowry. Generally using floral or celestial motifs (depictions of people and animals are against Muslim beliefs) an average *suzani* requires about two years to complete. Possibly the most accessible Kazakh textile souvenir is a *tus-kiiz* (*tushkiyiz* in Kyrgyzstan), a colourful wall hanging made of cotton and silk.

Uzbekistan: Heirs to the Silk Road by Johannes Kalter and Margareta Pavaloi is a beautiful hardback look at the art of the region.

The colourful psychedelic tie-dyed silks known as *ikat* or *khanatlas* are popular throughout the region. Take a close-up tour of how the cloth is made at the Yodgorlik Silk Factory in Margilan (p192). For more on silk production, see p193.

LITERATURE

The division into Kazakh literature, Tajik literature, Uzbek literature and so on, is a modern one; formerly there was simply literature in Chaghatai Turkic (pioneered by the poet Alisher Navoi) and literature in Persian. With most pre-20th-century poets, scholars and writers bilingual in Uzbek and Tajik, literature in Central Asia belonged to a shared universality of culture.

For example, Abu Abdullah Rudaki, a 10th-century Samanid court poet considered the father of Persian literature, stars in the national pantheons of Afghanistan, Iran and Tajikistan (he is buried in Penjikent) and is also revered by Uzbeks by dint of being born in the Bukhara emirate. Omar Khayam, famed composer of *rubiayyat* poetry, although a native of what is now northeast Iran, also has strong, if indistinct, ties to Tajikistan and to Samarkand where he spent part of his early life at the court of the Seljuq emir.

A strong factor in the universal nature of Central Asian literature was that it was popularised not in written form, but orally by itinerant minstrels in the form of songs, poems and stories. Known as *bakshi* or *dastanchi* in Turkmen and Uzbek, *akyn* in Kazakh and Kyrgyz, these storytelling bards earned their living travelling from town to town giving skilled and dramatic recitations of crowd-pleasing verse, tales and epics to audiences gathered in bazaars and chaikhanas. *Manaschi* are a special category of *akyn* who sang the traditional Kyrgyz *Manas* epos (p246). *Askiyachi* are humorists who play on words.

Certain bards are folk heroes, regarded as founders of their 'national literatures', even memorialised in Soviet-era street names (eg Toktogul, Zhambyl and Abay, see p91). Bardic competitions are still held in some rural areas. In Kyrgyzstan the epic *Manas* celebrated its 1000th anniversary in 1995, and following suit, Uzbekistan celebrated the 1000th anniversary of its national epic *Alpamish* in 1999.

It was only with the advent of Bolshevik rule that literacy became widespread. Unfortunately, at the same time, much of the region's classical heritage never saw print because Moscow feared that it might set a flame to latent nationalist sentiments. Instead writers were encouraged to produce novels and plays in line with official Communist Party themes. Whereas a number of Central Asian poets and novelists found acclaim within the Soviet sphere, such as the Tajik Sadruddin Ayni (1878–1954) and the Uzbeks Asqad Mukhtar and Abdullah Kodiri, the only native Central Asian author to garner international recognition has been the Kyrgyz Chinghiz Aitmatov, who has had novels translated into English and other European languages (see p246). His works have also been adapted for the stage and screen, both in the former USSR and abroad.

Poetry remains a vital force in Central Asian cultural life through the works of such celebrated classical poets as Jami, Navoi, Rudaki and Omar Khayam. Most Afghans will be able to quote you lines from their works.

For examples of current Central Asian fiction check out http://cenasia-fiction.netfirms.com.

MUSIC

Although visual arts and literature succumbed to a stifling Soviet-European influence (which they're presently struggling to shrug off), the music of Central Asia remains closely related to the swirling melodies of the Middle East, Turkey and Persia. The instruments used are similar to those found in the Arab world; the *rabab* (*rubab*; six-stringed mandolin), *dutar* (two-stringed guitar), *tambur* (long-necked lute), *dombra/komuz* (two-stringed Kazakh guitar), *kemanche* and *gijak* (upright spiked fiddle), *ney* (flute), *doira* (tambourine/drum) and *chang* (zither). Most groups add the ubiquitous Russian accordion.

In the past the development of music was closely connected with the art of the bards, but these days the traditions are continued by small

Central Asian film isn't high profile, but two films well worth checking out are *Luna Papa* by Tajikistan's Bakhtyar Khudojnazarov and *Beshkempir* by Kyrgyz director Aktan Abdykalykov.

CENTRAL ASIAN DISCOGRAPHY

The following recordings offer a great introduction to Central Asian music and are our personal favourites.

City of Love (Real World; www.realworld.co.uk) By Ashkhabad, a five-piece Turkmen ensemble. Superb and lilting, with a Mediterranean feel. Recommended.

Yol Boisin (Real World; www.realworld.co.uk) By Sevara Nazarkhan. Uzbek songstress given a modern feeling by producer Hector Zazou. In 2003 Nazarkhan played at the Womad festival and supported Peter Gabriel on tour. She recently won a BBC Radio 3 World Music Award.

A Haunting Voice (Network; www.networkmedien.de) By Munadjat Yulchieva, the classical *maqam* Uzbek music star recently nominated for a BBC Radio 3 World Music Award. Alternatively try Asie Centrale Traditions Classique (World Network).

The Selection Album (Blue Flame; www.blueflame.com) By Yulduz Usmanova. Career retrospective from the Uzbek pop superstar.

Secret Museum of Mankind, The Central Asia Ethnic Music Classics: 1925–48 (Yazoo; www.shanachie.com) Twenty-six scratchy but still wonderfully fresh field recordings of otherwise lost music.

The Silk Road – A Musical Caravan (Smithsonian Folkways; www.folkways.si.edu) 'Imagine if Marco Polo had a tape recorder' runs the cover note for this excellent two-CD collection of traditional recordings by both masters and amateurs, from China to Azerbaijan.

The Musical Nomad (www.bbc.co.uk/nomad) is an interesting interactive website chronicling a musical journey through the region in 1997.

DID YOU KNOW?

The art of the Kyrgyz bards and the classical Uzbek music known as *shashmaqom* are both included on Unesco's list of 28 'Masterpieces of the Oral and Intangible Heritage of Humanity'.

Anyone interested in the music of the region should pick up *The Hundred Thousand Fools of Gold: Musical Travels in Central Asia* by Theodore Levin. The book is part travel, part ethnomusicology and comes with a CD of on-site recordings.

ensembles of musicians and singers, heavily in demand at weddings and other festivals. In Uzbek and Tajik societies there's a particularly popular form of folk music known as *sozanda*, sung primarily by women accompanied only by percussion instruments such as tablas, bells and castanets. There are also several forms of Central Asian classical music, such as the courtly *maqam* tradition of Uzbekistan. Central Asian has a strong tradition of the performer-composer, or *bestekar*, the equivalent of the singer-songwriter, who mixed poetry, humour, current affairs and history into music.

One Uzbek group that has successfully mixed Central Asian and Middle Eastern folk melodies and poetry with modern pop and dance influences is Yalla.

Ensemble Kaboul are French-based classical Afghan musicians who in 2003 won a Radio Three World Music Award and played Britain's Womad festival. They recently teamed up with Ustad Farida Mahwash, Afghanistan's top radio star in the 1970s and the only female Afghan *ustad* (musical master). Their music reveals the close ties of Afghan music to the Indian tradition.

PAINTING

Rendered in a style that foreshadows that of Persian miniature painting, some splendid friezes were unearthed in the excavations of the Afrosiab palace (6th to 7th centuries), on the outskirts of Samarkand, depicting a colourful caravan led by elephants. Similar wall frescoes were discovered at Penjikent and Varakhsha, showing men and women tossed in a sea filled with monsters and fish.

The Arab invasion of the 8th century put representational art in Central Asia on hold for the better part of 1300 years. Islam prohibited the depiction of the living, so traditional arts developed in the form of calligraphy, combining Islamic script with arabesques, and the carving of doors and screens. Textiles and metalwork took on floral or repetitive, geometric motifs.

Painting and two-dimensional art were only revived under the Soviets who introduced European ideas and set up schools to train local artists in the new fashion. Under Soviet tutelage the pictorial art of Central Asia became a curious hybrid of socialist realism and mock traditionalism – Kyrgyz horsemen riding proudly beside a shiny red tractor, smiling Uzbeks at a chaikhana surrounded by record-breaking cotton harvests.

Environment

THE LAND

The Central Asia of this book includes Kazakhstan, which in Soviet parlance was considered a thing apart. It is true that Kazakhstan's enormous territory actually extends westward across the Ural River, the traditional boundary between Europe and Asia, but Kazakhstan still shares many geographic, cultural, ethnic and economic similarities and ties with Central Asia 'proper'.

A quick spin around the territory covered in this book would start on the eastern shores of the Caspian Sea. Then dip southeast along the low crest of the Kopet Dag Mountains between Turkmenistan's and Iran. Follow the Amu-Darya river and swing down into the deserts of Afghanistan, northeast over the Hindu Kush to the Amu-Darya and then its headstream, the Pyanj, up into the high Pamirs. Round the eastern nose of the Tian Shan range; skip northwestward over the Altay Mountains to float down the Irtysh River and then turn west to plod along Kazakhstan's flat, farmed, wooded border with Russia, ending in the basin of the Ural River and the Caspian Sea.

The sort of blank which is drawn in the minds of many people by the words 'Central Asia' is not entirely unfounded. The overwhelming majority of the territory is flat steppe (arid grassland) and desert. These areas include the Kazakh Steppe, the Betpak Dala (Misfortune) Steppe, the Kyzylkum (Red Sands) desert and the Karakum (Black Sands) desert. The Kyzylkum and Karakum combined make the fourth-largest desert in the world.

Central Asia's mountains are part of the huge chain which swings in a great arc from the Mongolian Altay to the Tibetan Himalaya. Central Asia's high ground is dominated by the Pamirs, a range of rounded, 5000m to 7000m mountains, which stretch 800km across Tajikistan. With very broad, flat valleys, which are nearly as high as the lower peaks, the Pamirs might be better described as a plateau (*pamir* roughly means 'pasture' in local dialects). The roof of the Pamir, Tajikistan's 7495m Koh-i-Samani, is the highest point in Central Asia and was the highest in the USSR (when it was known as Kommunizma). The Pamirs is probably the least explored mountain range on earth.

Varying from 4000m to more than 7400m, the crests of the Tian Shan form the backbone of eastern Central Asia. Known as the Celestial Mountains, the Chinese-named Tian Shan extends over 1500km from southwest Kyrgyzstan into China. The local translation is Tengri Tau. The summit of the range is Pobedy (7439m) on the Kyrgyzstan–China border. The range was a favourite among Russian explorers including Fedchenko, Kostenko, Semenov and Przewalski.

These two mountain ranges hold some of the largest glaciers and freshwater supplies on earth (around 17,000 sq km) and are one of the region's most significant natural resources. The 72km-long Fedchenko Glacier (the longest in the former USSR) contains more water than the Aral Sea.

The Caspian Sea is called either the world's biggest lake or the world's biggest inland sea. The Caspian Depression, in which it lies, dips to 132m below sea level. Lake Balkash, a vast, marsh-bordered arc of half-saline water on the Kazakh Steppe, is hardly deeper than a puddle, while mountain-ringed Lake Issyk-Kul in Kyrgyzstan is the fourth-deepest lake in the world. Other glacially fed lakes dot the mountains, including Song-Köl

Central Asia as defined by this book occupies 6.45 million sq km.

Some residents of huge Kazakhstan live about as far away from Vienna as they do from their own capital. Tashkent is closer to Kashgar and Tehran than to Moscow or Kiev.

Afghanistan's Shibar Pass is generally regarded as the watershed between the Oxus and Indus basins, marking the divide between the Central Asian and Indian worlds.

DID YOU KNOW?

Uzbekistan is only one of two countries in the world defined as double landlocked, ie surrounded by countries which are themselves landlocked.

in Kyrgyzstan and stunning Kara-Kul, first described by Marco Polo, in Tajikistan.

What little water flows out of Central Asia goes all the way to the Arctic Ocean, via the Irtysh River. Most of Central Asia's rainfall drains internally. The Ili River waters Lake Balkash; the Ural makes a short dash across part of Kazakhstan to the Caspian Sea. Numerous rivers rise as cold streams in the mountains only to lose themselves on the arid steppes and sands below. The region's two mightiest rivers, the Syr-Darya (Jaxartes) and Amu-Darya (Oxus), used to replenish the Aral Sea until they were bled dry for cotton. There is evidence that the Amu-Darya once flowed into the Caspian Sea, along the now-dry Uzboy Channel.

GEOLOGY

The compact, balled-up mass of mountains bordering Tajikistan, Kyrgyzstan and China is often called the Pamir Knot. It's the hub from which other major ranges extend like radiating ropes: the Himalaya and Karakoram to the southeast, the Hindu Kush to the southwest, the Kunlun to the east and the Tian Shan to the northeast. These young mountains all arose (or more correctly, are arising still) from the shock waves created by the Indian subcontinent smashing into the Asian crustal plate over a hundred million years ago. Amazing as it seems, marine fossils from the original Tethys Sea have been found in the deserts of Central Asia as a testament to the continental collision. The Tian Shan are currently rising at the rate of around 10mm per year.

Central Asia is therefore unsurprisingly a major earthquake zone. Ashgabat was destroyed by earthquake in 1948 and Tashkent was levelled in 1966. More recently, devastating earthquakes hit the Tajikistan–Afghanistan border in 1997 and 1998.

Several companies such as Naturetrek (www.naturetrek.co.uk) and Wings (www.wingsbirds.com) run tours to see the flora and fauna of Central Asia.

WILDLIFE

Central Asia is home to a unique range of ecosystems and an extraordinary variety of flora and fauna. The region comprised only 17% of the former USSR's territory, but contained over 50% of its variety in flora and fauna.

The mountains of Kyrgyzstan, Kazakhstan and Tajikistan are the setting for high, summer pastures known as *jailoos*. In summertime the wild flowers (including wild irises and edelweiss) are a riot of colour. Marmots and pikas provide food for eagles and lammergeiers, while the elusive snow leopard preys on the ibex, with which it shares a preference for crags and rocky slopes, alongside the Svertsov ram. Forests of Tian Shan spruce, ash, larch and juniper provide cover for lynxes, wolves, wild boars and brown bears. Lower down in the mountains of southern Kyrgyzstan, Uzbekistan, Tajikistan and Turkmenistan are ancient forests of wild walnut, pistachio, juniper, apricot and apple.

Realms of the Russian Bear by John Sparks is an elegant, beautifully illustrated work focusing on the flora and fauna of the old Soviet empire, including 80-plus pages on the Tian Shan and Central Asia's steppes, deserts and seas.

The steppes (what's left of them after massive Soviet cultivation projects) are covered with grasses and low shrubs such as saxaul. Where they rise to meet foothills, the steppes bear vast fields of wild poppies (including some opium poppies) and several hundred types of tulip.

Roe deer and saiga, a species of antelope, have their homes on the steppe. The ring-necked pheasant, widely introduced to North America and elsewhere, is native to the Central Asian steppe, as are partridges, black grouse, bustards, and the falcons and hawks that prey on them.

Rivers and lake shores in the flatlands are a different world, with dense thickets of elm, poplar, reeds and shrubs known as *tugai*, where wild boar, jackal and deer make their homes. A carplike fish called the *sazan* is the most popular catch.

In the Karakum and Kyzylkum there is more than meets the eye. The goitred gazelle *(zheyran)* haunts the deserts of western Uzbekistan and Turkmenistan. Gophers, sand rats and jerboas feed various reptiles, including (in Turkmenistan) vipers and cobras.

Chiy, a common grass with whitish, canelike reeds, is used by nomads to make decorative screens for their yurts.

Turkmenistan's wildlife has a Middle Eastern streak, understandable when you consider that parts of the country are as close to Baghdad as they are to Tashkent. Leopards and porcupines inhabit the parched hills. The *zemzen* or *varan* (desert crocodile) is actually a type of large lizard (see the boxed text on p411).

Endangered Species

In 1985 the Kyrgyz 'Red Book' – the regional edition of *Krasnaya Kniga SSSR* (The USSR Red Book), bible of endangered species – stated that 15% of mammals and 10% of birds in Kyrgyzstan were threatened with extinction. Since then the situation has further deteriorated.

The mountain goose, among other rare species, nests on the shores of Kyrgyzstan's mountain lakes, but the population has shrunk over the years to less than 15 pairs worldwide.

The population of snow leopards in Central Asia and the Russian Altay is estimated at about 1000, out of a global population of around 7000. Only 5% of the snow leopard's habitat is currently protected.

Tragically the last Turan (Caspian) tiger was killed in the Amu-Darya delta in 1972. Wild Bactrian camels, once the quintessential Silk Road sight, are now only found in remote areas of Afghanistan. Perhaps 1000 remain.

There has been some good new, though: eight Przewalski's horses were recently reintroduced into Kazakhstan's Altyn-Emel National Park after being extinct in the region for 60 years.

NATIONAL PARKS

Many of the region's approximately two-dozen nature reserves *(zapovednik)* and protected areas *(zakazniki)* and nine or so national parks *(gosudarstvenny prirodny park)* are accessible for tourists.

HEAVENLY HORSES

Central Asia has been famed for its horses for millennia. The earliest Silk Road excursions into the region were made to bring back the famous blood-sweating (due to parasites or skin infection) horses of Fergana (based in the ancient kingdom of Davan, near modern-day Osh) to help Han China fight incursive nomadic tribes. Much of the highly coveted silk that made its way into Central Asia and beyond came from the trade of horses.

Today's most famous horses are the Akhal Teke of Turkmenistan, the forefather of the modern Arab steed. The Roman-era historian Appian wrote that the horses of Parthian Nissa excelled in all beauty, 'for their golden manes whirl with glory in the air'. Today there are around 2000 thoroughbred Akhal-Teke in the world, of which 1200 are in Turkmenistan. Turkmenistan's state emblem and banknotes feature an Akhal-Teke and there's even a national holiday named after them. Akhal-Teke are regularly handed out as diplomatic gifts (François Mitterrand, John Major and Boris Yeltsin have each received one), much as they were 2000 years ago.

Other regional breeds include the Lokai of Tajikistan and Karabair of Uzbekistan. These stocky horses are used in sports such as *buzkashi* (a traditional pololike game played with a headless goat carcass) and are descendants of horses that played such a fundamental role in the Mongol conquest of Eurasia.

The existing system of national parks and protected areas, one of the positive legacies of the USSR, is nevertheless antiquated and inadequate. Unfortunately all suffer from a chronic lack of government funding and are under increasing pressure from grazing, poaching, firewood gathering and even opium-poppy plantations.

In Kyrgyzstan and Kazakhstan, for example, just 2.5% of the country's area is dedicated to land conservation, of which most is only semiprotected and commercially managed, often as hunting reserves. This is well below the minimum 10% recommended by the World Conservation Union.

The most easily visited protected areas include the following:

Aksu-Zhabaghly Nature Reserve (p125) In southern Kazakhstan, with its beautiful tulips, is easily visited with the help of a travel agency.

Ala-Archa Canyon (p262) Outside Bishkek.

Almatinsky Nature Reserve (p113) Outside Almaty. Big-horned sheep, gazelle and hiking trails.

Badai-Tugai Nature Reserve (p223) In Karakalpakstan, protects a strip of *tugai* riverine forest on the eastern bank of the Amu-Darya. Once off limits, today it welcomes foreign tourists as the entry fee pays for food for a Bukhara deer-breeding centre.

Karakol Valley (p276) Southeast corner of Issyk-Kul.

Kugitang Nature Reserve (p431) The most impressive of Turkmenistan's nature reserves, focused around the country's highest peak, is home to the rare markhor mountain goat and several hundred dinosaur footprints.

Sary-Chelek Biosphere Reserve (p296) Unesco-sponsored.

Ugam-Chatkal National Park (p185) Unesco-sponsored, with juniper forests, wild boars, bears and snow leopards.

ENVIRONMENTAL ISSUES

As with many places in the former USSR, Central Asia's amazing landscapes also served as testing grounds for some of the worst cases of Soviet megalomania. Land and water mismanagement and destruction of natural habitat were part of a conscious effort to tame nature ('harness it like a white mare', as the propaganda of the day had it). The results are almost beyond belief and on a staggering scale.

For news and archived articles on environmentalism in Central Asia see www.ecostan.org.

Even casual students of the region are familiar with some of the most infamous catastrophes of Soviet environmental meddling: the gradual disappearance of the Aral Sea, the excessive levels of radiation around the Semey (Semipalatinsk) nuclear testing site, and the consequences of Khrushchev's Virgin Lands scheme (which, according to Soviet theoreticians, should have allowed the USSR to overtake the USA in grain production). For information on these last two issues see p91.

In the economic malaise of the post-Soviet years, the environment has taken a back seat. Whether it is poaching, hunting tours or pollution from gold-mining operations, with the promise of hard-currency earnings in an otherwise bleak economic landscape, nature is always the victim.

The Aral Sea

The Aral Sea was once the world's fourth-largest lake. It is now recognised as the world's worst artificial ecological disaster.

One of the most amazing things about the Aral Sea disaster is that it was no accident. The Soviet planners who fatally tapped the rivers that fed the Aral Sea, in order to irrigate new cotton fields, expected the sea to dry up. They also wanted to bring water to Central Asia by a huge canal from Siberia, not to replenish the Aral Sea but to expand cotton production still further. They either didn't understand that drying up the world's fourth-largest lake would wreck a whole region's climate and ecology, and cause untold suffering to its people, or didn't care.

The Aral Sea, or rather seas, since it split into two in 1987, straddles the border between western Uzbekistan and southern Kazakhstan. It's fed (in the years that they actually reach it) by the Syr-Darya and Amu-Darya rivers, flowing down from the Tian Shan and Pamir mountain ranges. Back in the 1950s these rivers brought an average 55 cu km of water a year to the Aral Sea, which stretched 400km from end to end and 280km from side to side, and covered 66,900 sq km. The sea had, by all accounts, lovely clear water, pristine beaches, plenty of fish to support a big fishing industry in the ports of Moynaq and Aralsk, and even passenger ferries crossing it from north to south.

Then the USSR's central planners decided to boost cotton production in Uzbekistan, Turkmenistan and Kazakhstan, to feed a leap forward in the Soviet textile industry. But the new cotton fields, many of them on poorer desert soils and fed by long, unlined canals open to the sun, drank much more water than the old ones. The irrigated area grew by only about 20% between 1960 and 1980, but the annual water take from the rivers doubled from 45 to 90 cu km. The Karakum Canal, the world's longest, reaches from the Amu-Darya far across southern Turkmenistan, and takes 14 cu km of water a year, nearly a quarter of the Aral Sea's old supply. By the 1980s the annual flow into the Aral Sea was less than a tenth of the 1950s supply.

Production of cotton rose, but the Aral Sea sank. Between 1966 and 1993 its level fell by more than 16m and its eastern and southern shores receded by up to 80km. In 1987 the Aral divided into a smaller northern sea and a larger southern one, each fed, sometimes, by one of the rivers.

The two main fishing ports, Aralsk (Kazakhstan) in the north and Moynaq (Uzbekistan) in the south, were left high and dry when efforts to keep their navigation channels open were abandoned in the early 1980s. Of the 60,000 people who used to live off the Aral fishing industry (harvesting 20,000 tons of fish a year), almost all are gone. The rusting hulks of beached fishing boats are scattered along what were once their shores.

In any case there are hardly any fish left in the Aral Sea: the last of its 20-odd indigenous species disappeared in about 1985, wiped out by the loss of spawning and feeding grounds, rising salt levels and, very likely, residues of pesticides, fertilisers and defoliants used on the cotton fields, which found their way into the sea. Only introduced species such as the Black Sea flounder remain, though there is some hope for future shrimp cultivation in the increasingly briny waters.

The Aral Sea's shrinkage has devastated the land around it. The climate around the lake has changed: the air is drier, winters are a few degrees colder and a month longer, and summers are hotter. The average number of rainless days has risen from 30 to 35 in the 1950s to 120 to 150 today. Salt, sand and dust from the exposed bed is blown hundreds

The best place to 'view' the Aral disaster is Moynaq (p232), where you can see rusty fishing trawlers beached 150km from the sea.

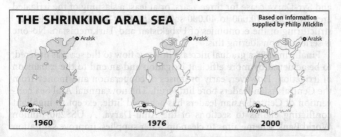

THE SHRINKING ARAL SEA Based on information supplied by Philip Micklin

Aralsk · Aralsk · Aralsk

Moynaq · Moynaq · Moynaq

1960 **1976** **2000**

of kilometres in big salt-dust sandstorms, which also pick up residues of the chemicals from cultivated land. Locals talk of a new Akkum (White Sands) desert forming an unholy trinity with the Kyzylkum (Red Sands) and Karakum (Black Sands) deserts. A visit to anywhere near the sea is a ride into a nightmare of blighted towns, blighted land and blighted people.

In human terms, the worst-affected areas are those to the Aral Sea's south (as far as northern Turkmenistan) and east (the areas north and west of the Aral Sea are very sparsely populated). The catalogue of health problems is awful: salt and dust are blamed for respiratory illnesses and cancers of the throat and oesophagus; poor drinking water has been implicated in high rates of typhoid, paratyphoid, hepatitis and dysentery; the area has the highest mortality and infant mortality rates in the former USSR. Karakalpakstan also has high rates of birth deformities and in Nukus, the Karakalpak capital, virtually all pregnant women are anaemic, which leads to many premature births. In Aralsk, tuberculosis is common.

Of the 173 animal species that used to live around the Aral Sea, only 38 survive. Especially devastating has been the degradation of the big Amu-Darya and Syr-Darya deltas, with their very diverse flora and fauna. The deltas have supported irrigated agriculture for many centuries, along with hunting, fishing, and harvesting of reeds for building and papermaking. The dense *tugai* forests, unique to the valleys of these desert rivers, have shrunk to a fifth of their old size, causing a catastrophic drop in the once-abundant water bird population.

The local name for the Aral is the Aral Tenghiz, or Sea of Islands. Barsakelmes (the Place of No Return) Island, a nature reserve protecting the saiga antelope and the rare Asiatic wild ass, has reportedly become an unviable habitat because it is now so arid.

Nor can matters have been helped by the use of Vozrozhdenia Island as a Soviet biological warfare testing site (anthrax and plague were both released on the island) until it was abandoned in 1992. Within a few years the island's secrets will be joined to the mainland by the exposed seabed. Ironically, the island's name in pious Russian means 'rebirth'.

LONG-TERM SOLUTIONS
Dozens of inquiries, projects and research teams have poked and prodded the Aral problem; locals joke that if every scientist who visited the Aral region had brought a bucket of water the problem would be over by now. The initial outcry over the disaster seems to have largely evaporated, along with the sea, and the focus has shifted from rehabilitating the sea, to stabilising part of the sea and now stabilising the environment around the sea.

To restore the Aral would require that irrigation from the Amu-Darya and Syr-Darya cease for three years, or at least a slashing of the irrigated area from over 70,000 to 40,000 sq km; in other words, a complete restructuring of the economies of Uzbekistan and Turkmenistan. No-one is seriously considering this.

Finally in 1988 a gradual increase in water flow to the sea was ordered, to be achieved by more efficient irrigation and an end to the expansion of irrigation. However, early promises of cooperation and money from the Central Asian leaders bore little fruit. The now annual Aral Sea convention of Central Asian leaders has achieved little, except to highlight conflicting claims to sections of the Amu-Darya. A US$250 million World Bank scheme aims to clean up water supplies, improve sanitation

In parts of Karakalpakstan (far west Uzbekistan) more than one baby in 10 dies (compared to one in 100 or more in Britain or the USA), a rate largely attributable to health problems caused by the Aral Sea disaster.

Locals have blamed Vozrozhdenia for the terrifying sudden deaths, in less than an hour, of half a million saiga antelope on the Turgay Steppe, northeast of the Aral, in 1988.

To find out about efforts to improve the Aral Sea situation, visit www.udasa.org.

and public health, restore some economic viability and biodiversity to the Amu-Darya delta, and stabilise the Aral's northern sea.

In 2003 the little channel still connecting the northern and southern seas was blocked by a 12.8km-long dike, preventing further water loss from the northern sea (see the boxed text on p129) but condemning the southern sea to oblivion. The northern sea is now expected to rise almost 3.5m and should reach a state of equilibrium, with an area of 3500 sq km, by about 2025. But if recent rates of depletion continue, the southern sea is expected to split again by 2005 into western and eastern parts. The eastern part will receive the Amu-Darya and is expected eventually to stabilise into three lakes with the construction of small dikes, but the western part will go on shrinking.

Longer-term efforts may focus on building more dikes around parts of the sea, rehabilitating the blighted region around the sea and stabilising its fragile environment, improving water management and building up local institutions to manage these projects. Whether the will exists among Central Asia's politicians to introduce less-water-intensive irrigation methods, or even less-thirsty crops than cotton, remains to be seen.

Overgrazing

Overgrazing and soil degradation is a major problem affecting all the Central Asian republics. The steady rise in livestock grazing has unhinged delicate ecosystems and accelerated desertification and soil erosion. From 1941 to 1991 the population of sheep and goats more than doubled to 5.5 million in Turkmenistan and quadrupled to 10 million in Kyrgyzstan, while a third of Kyrgyzstan's available grasslands have disappeared.

In Kazakhstan much of the semiarid steppe, traditionally used as pasture over the centuries, was put to the plough under the Virgin Lands campaign (see p92). Wind erosion in the steppes of north Kazakhstan has accelerated soil depletion.

Soil degradation is also activated by failure to rotate crops and by excessive use of chemicals, and aggravated by irrigation-water misman-agement. In Kazakhstan, 40% of rangeland is considered to be overused, and will need 10 to 50 years to be restored to its original fertility. In Kyrgyzstan an estimated 70% of pastureland suffers erosion above ac-ceptable levels. In Tajikistan the productivity of summer pastures in the mountains has dropped by 50% over the last 25 years and large areas of the Pamirs are threatened by desertification.

Pollution

Cotton is to blame for many of Central Asia's ills. Its present cultivation demands high levels of pesticides and fertilisers, which are now found throughout the food chain – in the water, in human and animal milk, in vegetables and fruit, and in the soil itself. In the Osh region of Kyrgyzstan 94% of soils contain DDT.

Kazakhstan, the third-largest industrial power in the CIS, suffers particularly from industrial pollution, the worst culprits being power stations running on low-grade coal and metallurgical factories. Lake Balkash has been polluted by copper smelters established on its shores in the 1930s; bird and other lake life is now practically extinct. There are also concerns about oil and other pollution draining into the Caspian Sea (see p92).

Uranium for the former Soviet nuclear military machine was mined in both Tajikistan and Kyrgyzstan (the Kyrgyz SSR's uranium sector earned the sobriquet 'Atomic Fortress of the Tian Shan'), and up to 50 abandoned

The Devil and The Disap-pearing Sea by Robert Ferguson gives a recent (2003) look at the politics of aid and corruption in Central Asia.

A 600-year-old mausoleum recently discovered on the dried-out bed of the Aral Sea has indicated that Aral levels might be cyclical to some degree.

The Aral isn't the only body of water drying up. Lake Balkash in Kazakhstan, which gets its water from the Ili River of Xinjiang, has shrunk by 2000 sq km in recent years.

mine sites in Kyrgyzstan alone may now leak unstablised radioactive tailings or contaminated groundwater into their surroundings; some are along major waterways which drain eventually into the Aral Sea.

Mining techniques are inefficient, outdated and environmentally hazardous. In 1998 almost two tonnes of sodium cyanide destined for the Kumtor gold mine in Kyrgyzstan was spilled into the Barskoön River, which made its way into the Issyk-Kul.

Poaching

Poaching is on the rise, both as a food source and for trophies to sell for hard currency, and goes almost totally unchallenged. The economic pressures felt by locals cannot be overemphasised.

Several private and government travel agencies run hard-currency hunting expeditions, luring wealthy foreigners to slaughter bustards, wolves, mountain ibex, Marco Polo sheep and bears. Falconers from the Middle East have found Central Asia to be an exciting new source of hunting birds. Some countries, like the US, have banned the import of Marco Polo sheep horns, as the sheep are an endangered species.

Tens of thousands of saiga antelope are killed every year by poachers, who sell their horns to Chinese medicine makers. Musk deer, currently found in Kyrgyzstan, Uzbekistan and Russia, are killed for their musk glands. Around 160 deer are killed for every 1kg of musk, making the musk worth three to four times its weight in gold. Tens of thousands of the deer have been killed in the last 20 years and numbers in Russia have fallen by 50%.

Food & Drink

The Central Asian culinary experience is unlikely to be a highlight of your trip. Most visitors encounter Central Asian cuisine only in dismal tourist restaurants or grotty kebab stands. Unfortunately, most restaurants and canteens serve only standard slop, which somehow seems to taste (and smell) indelibly of the old USSR. The best way to appreciate regional cuisines, and the region's extraordinary hospitality, is at a meal in a private home.

STAPLES & SPECIALITIES

Central Asian food resembles that of the Middle East or the Mediterranean in its use of rice, savoury seasonings, vegetables and legumes, yogurt and grilled meats. Many dishes may seem familiar from elsewhere – *laghman* (similar to Chinese noodles), plov (similar to Persian rice pilafs), nan (flat breads found all over Asia), and *samsa* (the samosa of India). Others are more unusual, such as Kazakh horse-meat sausage.

The cuisine falls into three overlapping groups. First, there's the once-nomadic subsistence diet found in large areas of Kazakhstan, Kyrgyzstan and Turkmenistan – mainly meat (including entrails), milk products and bread. Second, there's the diet of the Uzbeks and other settled Turks, which includes pilafs, kebabs, noodles and pasta, stews, elaborate breads and pastries. The third group is Persian, ranging from southern Uzbekistan and Tajikistan to northern Pakistan and on into India, which is distinguished by subtle seasoning, extensive use of vegetables, and fancy sweets.

Seasoning is usually mild, although sauces and chillies are offered to turn up the heat. Principal spices are black cumin, red and black peppers, barberries, coriander and sesame seeds. Common herbs are fresh coriander, dill, parsley, celeriac and basil. Other seasonings include wine vinegar and fermented milk products.

> In the heavily Russian-populated cities of northern Kazakhstan and in all the Central Asian capitals, the dominant cuisine is Russian.

Ingredients

Mutton is the preferred meat. Big-bottomed sheep are prized for their fat, meat and wool, and fat from the sheep's tail costs more than the meat. The meat-to-fat ratio is generally stacked heavily in favour (and flavour) of the fat, and you will soon find that everything smells of it. Sheep's head is a great delicacy, which may be served to honoured guests in some homes.

Produce is at its most bountiful around September. In general, May is the best time for apricots, strawberries and cherries, June for peaches, and July for grapes and figs. Melons ripen in late summer, but are available in the markets as late as January.

You can find caviar and seafood dishes in western Kazakhstan, near the Caspian Sea. Dried and smoked fish are sold near Issyk-Kul.

Standards

The ubiquitous shashlyk – kebabs of fresh or marinated mutton, beef, minced meat or, in restaurants, chicken – is usually served with nan and vinegary onions. The quality varies from inedible to addictively delicious. Liver kebabs are known in Turkic as *jiger*.

Plov (*pulao* in Afghanistan) consists mainly of rice with fried and boiled meat, onions and carrots, and sometimes raisins, chickpeas or fruit slices, all cooked up in a hemispherical cauldron called a *kazan*.

Plov is always the *pièce de résistance* when entertaining guests – hence the mistaken impression that Central Asians can prepare only one dish.

Stout noodles *(laghman)* distinguish Central Asian cuisine from any other. *Laghman* is served everywhere, especially as the base for a spicy soup (usually called *laghman* too), which includes fried mutton, peppers, tomatoes and onions. Korean and Dungan noodles are also generally excellent.

Other soups include *shorpa* (*shurpa* or *sorpo*), boiled mutton on the bone with potatoes, carrots and turnips; *manpar* (noodle bits, meat, vegetables and mild seasoning in broth); and Russian borscht (beetroot soup).

Nan (*non* to Uzbeks and Tajiks; *lepyoshka* in Russian), usually baked in tandoori ovens, is served at every meal. Some varieties are prepared with onions, meat or sheep's-tail fat in the dough; others have anise, poppy or sesame seeds placed on top. Nan also serves as an impromptu plate for shashlyks. Home-made breads are often thicker and darker than normal nan. Boring, square, white-flour Russian loaves are known simply as *khleb*.

Salads are a refreshing break from heavy main courses, although you'll soon tire of the dreaded *salat tourist* (sliced tomatoes and cucumbers). Parsley, fresh coriander, green onions and dill are served and eaten whole.

A favourite snack is the *samsa* (*sambusa* in Tajik), a meat pie baked in a tandoori oven – at their best in Kyrgyzstan, made with flaky puff pastry.

Snacks

There are four other variations on the meat-and-dough theme – steamed, boiled, baked and fried. *Manty* (steamed dumplings; *mantu* in Afghanistan) are a favourite from Mongolia to Turkey. Chuchvara (*tushbera* in Tajik, *pelmeny* in Russian) are a smaller boiled cousin of *manty*, served plain or with vinegar, sour cream or butter, or in soups. Both are sometimes fried.

One of the most common and disappointing street foods are *piroshki*, greasy Russian fried pies filled with potatoes or meat.

Fruits are eaten fresh, cooked, dried or made into preserves, jams and drinks known as *kompot* or *sokh*. Central Asians are fond of dried fruits and nuts, particularly apricots and apricot stones, which when cracked open have a pith that tastes like pistachios. At any time of year you'll find delicious walnuts, peanuts, raisins and almonds, plus great jams (seabuckthorn jam is a real treat) and fine honey from the mountains.

Central Asians of every ethnic group love ice cream (*marozhnoe* in Russian). You'll find a freezer of the stuff almost anywhere.

Milk Products

Central Asia is known for the richness and delicacy of its fermented dairy products, which use cow, sheep, goat, camel or horse milk. The milk itself is probably unpasteurised, but its cultured derivatives are safe if kept in hygienic conditions.

Soured milk is used to make yogurt (*katyk*) with the addition of bacterial culture. *Katyk* can be strained to make *suzma*, which is like tart

---

NASVAI

You might notice some men chewing and copiously spitting, or talking as if their mouth is full of saliva. *Nasvai, nasvar* or *noz* is basically finely crushed tobacco, sometimes cut with spices, ash or lime. As a greenish sludge or as little pellets, it's stuffed under the tongue or inside the cheek, from where the active ingredients leach into the bloodstream, revving up the user's heart rate. Amateurs who fail to clamp it tightly in place, thus allowing the effluent to leak into the throat, might be consumed with nausea.

Before you try it, bear in mind that *nasvai* is often cut with opium and can be quite potent.

cottage or cream cheese and used as a garnish or added to soups. *Ayran* is a salty yogurt/water mix, the Russian equivalent is called *kefir*; don't confuse this with the Russians' beloved *smetana* (sour cream). Many doughs and batters incorporate sour milk products, giving them a tangy flavour. Milk-based soups, hot and cold, are common.

The final stage in the milk cycle is *kurtob* or *kurut*, which is dried *suzma* (often rolled into marble-size balls), a travel snack with the half-life of uranium. Scrape away the outer layer if you're uneasy about cleanliness.

Tvorog is a Russian speciality, made from soured milk, which is heated to curdle. This is hung in cheesecloth overnight to strain off the whey. The closest Central Asian equivalent is *suzma*. *Kaimak* is pure sweet cream, skimmed from fresh milk that has sat overnight. This wickedly tasty breakfast item, wonderful with honey, is available in many markets in the early morning, but sells out fast, usually by sunrise.

Turkish Food
Turkish restaurants are popping up everywhere in Central Asia and most are excellent value. *Pides* are similar to thin-crust pizzas; *lahmacun* is a cheaper, less substantial version. Kebabs are popular, especially Adana kebabs (mincemeat patties) and delicious Iskander kebabs (thinly sliced mutton over bread, with yogurt and rich tomato sauce). *Patlıcan* (aubergine) and *dolma* (stuffed peppers) are the most common vegetable dishes. *Çaçık* is a delicious yogurt, cucumber and mint dip and makes a great snack with *lavash*, a huge bread similar to nan but lighter. Desserts include baklava (light pastry covered in syrup) and *sütlaç* (rice pudding).

Holiday Food
A big occasion for eating is Navrus. Along with plov and other traditional fare, several dishes are served particularly at this time. The traditional Navrus dish, prepared only by women, is *sumalak* – wheat soaked in water for three days until it sprouts, then ground, mixed with oil, flour and sugar, and cooked on a low heat for 24 hours. *Halim* is a porridge of boiled meat and wheat grains, seasoned with black pepper and cinnamon, prepared just for men. *Nishalda* – whipped egg whites, sugar and liquorice flavouring – is also popular during Ramadan. To add to this, seven items, all beginning with the Arabic sound 'sh', are laid on the dinner table during Navrus – wine (*sharob*), milk (*shir*), sweets (*shirin-liklar*), sugar (*shakar*), sherbet (*sharbat*), a candle (*sham*) and a new bud (*shona*). Candles are a throwback to pre-Islamic traditions and the new bud symbolises the renewal of life.

A special holiday dish in Kazakhstan and Kyrgyzstan is *beshbarmak* (*besbarmak* in Kazakh, *shilpildok* in Uzbek, *myasa po-kazakhskiy* in Russian), large flat noodles with lamb and/or horse meat and cooked in vegetable broth. It means 'five fingers' since it was traditionally eaten by hand.

An invitation to a private home is probably the only way you'll get to taste any of these dishes.

Uzbek men usually stay out of the kitchen but are almost always in charge of preparing plov; an *oshpaz*, or master chef, can cook up a special plov for thousands on special occasions.

DRINKS
Tea
Chay (чай; *choy* to Uzbeks and Tajiks, *shay* to Kazakhs) is drunk with reverence. Straight green tea (*kok; zelyonnyy* in Russian) is the favourite; locals claim it beats the heat and unblocks you after too much greasy plov. Black tea (*chyornyy chay* in Russian) is preferred in Samarkand and Urgench, and by most Russians. Turkmen call green tea *gek* and black tea *gara*.

TEA ETIQUETTE

Tea is the drink of hospitality, offered first to every guest, and almost always drunk from a *piala* (small bowl). From a fresh pot, the first cup of tea is often poured away (to clean the *piala*) and then a *piala* of tea is poured out and returned twice into the pot to brew the tea. A cup filled only a little way up is a compliment, allowing your host to refill it often and keep its contents warm (the offer of a full *piala* of tea is a subtle invitation that it's time to leave).

Pass and accept tea with the right hand; it's extra polite to put the left hand over the heart as you do this. If your tea is too hot, don't blow on it, but swirl it gently in the cup without spilling any. If it has grown cold, your host will throw it away before refilling the cup.

Western Turkmen brew tea with *chal* (camel's milk) and Badakhshanis use goat's milk. Kazakh tea is taken with milk, salt and butter – the nomadic equivalent of fast food – hot, tasty and high in calories.

Nonalcoholic Drinks

Don't drink the tap water. Cheap bottled mineral water is easy to find, but it's normally gassy and very mineral tasting. Modern joint-venture brands are more expensive but taste a lot better, though most are carbonated. Companies such as Coca-Cola have factories in all the republics and their products are everywhere.

Old Soviet-style streetside machines dispense soda water *(chesti)*, but everybody uses the same glasses so bring your own if that worries you. Portable kiosks offer the same, often with a dash of cordial, although this is often just tap water with added fizz from a gas bottle under the table.

Tins of cheap imported instant coffee can be found everywhere; hot water *(tipitok)* is easy to drum up from a hotel floor-lady or homestay.

Alcoholic Drinks

VODKA & BEER

Despite their Muslim heritage, most Central Asians drink. If you don't enjoy hard booze and heavy drinking, make your excuses early. Like the Russians who introduced them to vodka, Central Asians take their toasts seriously and a foreign male guest may be expected to offer the first toast.

Given the depth of Central Asian hospitality it's impolite to refuse the initial 'bottoms up' (Russian – *vashe zdarovye!*), and/or abstain from at least a symbolic sip at each toast. But there's usually heavy pressure to drain your glass every time – so as not to give offence, it is implied – and the pressure only increases as everybody gets loaded.

Apart from the endless array of industrial-strength vodkas, you'll find a wide range of Russian and European beers *(piva)* for around US$1 to US$2 a can. The St Petersburg's Baltika is the brew of choice and comes in a wide range of numbers from 0 (nonalcoholic) to 9 (very strong). Baltika 6 is the most popular. Popular beers on tap include Tian-Shansky, Shimkent (both Kazakh) and Siberian Crown (Russian). Efes is a popular Turkish beer.

KUMYS & OTHER ATTRACTIONS

Kumys (properly *kymys* in Kyrgyz; *qymyz* in Kazakh) is fermented mare's milk, a mildly (2% to 3%) alcoholic drink appreciated by Kazakhs and Kyrgyz, even those who no longer spend much time in the saddle (nonalcoholic varieties are also made). It's available only in spring and summer, when mares are foaling, and takes around three days to ferment. The milk is put into a *chelek* (wooden bucket or barrel) and churned with a wooden plunger called a *bishkek* (from where that city derives its name).

Locals will tell you that *kumys* cures anything from a cold to TB but drinking too much of it may give you diarrhoea. The best *kumys* comes from the herders themselves; the stuff available in the cities is sometimes diluted with cow's milk or water.

Kazakhs and Kyrgyz also like a thick, yeasty, slightly fizzy concoction called *bozo*, made from boiled fermented millet or other grains. Turkmen, Kazakh and Karakalpak nomads like *shubat* (fermented camel's milk).

WHERE TO EAT & DRINK

You can eat in street-side stalls and cafés, cheap canteens, private and state-run restaurants and, best of all, in private homes. In smaller towns, restaurants, if they exist at all, can be pretty dire, and hotels may have the only edible food outside private homes. There has recently been an explosion of private restaurants in the major cities and you can now eat well and cheaply, a great improvement on a few years ago.

A few restaurants (*askhana* in Kazakh and Kyrgyz, *oshhona* in Uzbek) in bigger cities offer interesting Central Asian, Turkish, Chinese, Georgian, Korean or European dishes and earnest service.

Outside the cities Russians and Russified locals don't expect good food from restaurants. What they want at midday is a break. What they want in the evening is a night out – lots of booze and gale-force techno music or a variety show. Even if there's no music blasting when you come in, the kind staff will most likely turn on the beat especially for the foreigners.

The canteen (столовая; *stolovaya*) is the ordinary citizen's eatery – dreary but cheap, usually self-service, with a limited choice of cutlet or lukewarm *laghman*. Some are decent, most are very grotty and there's often that pervading canteen smell. Two good places to sniff out cheap canteens are at universities or government offices.

Certain old-town neighbourhoods of Tashkent and Samarkand have home restaurants offering genuine home-style cuisine. There is rarely a sign; family members simply solicit customers on the street, and the competition can be intense.

Mid-range and top-end restaurants are limited to Tashkent, Bishkek and Almaty. The food is generally well-prepared European cuisine, with the occasional Siberian salmon or black caviar to liven things up.

> Don't misread meat prices on menus in fancier restaurants – they are often given as per 100g, not per serving (which is often more like 250g to 400g).

> Bear in mind that many Russian main dishes are just that and you'll have to order garnishes (rice, potatoes or vegetables) separately.

Self-Catering

Every sizable town has a colourful bazaar (*rynok* in Russian) or farmers market with hectares of fresh and dried fruit, vegetables, walnuts, peanuts, honey, cheese, bread, meat and eggs.

TEAHOUSES

The chaikhana or teahouse (*chaykhana* in Turkmen, *chaykana* in Kyrgyz, *choyhona* in Uzbek and Tajik, *shaykhana* in Kazakh) is male Central Asia's essential sociogastronomic institution, especially in Uzbekistan. Usually shaded, often near a pool or stream, it's as much a men's club as an eatery – although women, including foreigners, are tolerated. Old and young congregate to eat or to drink pot after pot of green tea and talk the day away.

Traditional seating is on a bedlike platform (Uzbeks call it a *takhta*, Tajiks a *chorpoy*), covered with a carpet and topped with a low table. Take your shoes off to sit on the platform, or leave them on and hang your feet over.

Korean and Dungan vendors sell spicy *kimchi* (vegetable salads), a great antidote for mutton overdose. Russians flog *pelmeny*, *piroshki* (deep-fried meat or potato pies) and yogurt. Fresh honey on hot-from-the-oven nan makes a splendid breakfast.

Don't be afraid to haggle (with a smile) – everybody else does. As a foreigner you may be quoted twice the normal price or, on the other hand, given a bit extra. Insist on making your own choices or you may end up with second-rate produce. Most produce is sold by the kilo.

The state food stores *(gastronom)* still exist here and there, stocked with a few bits of cheese or 200 or so cans of Soviet-made 'Beef in its own Juice' stacked up along the windowsill.

VEGETARIANS & VEGANS

Central Asia can be difficult for vegetarians; indeed the whole concept of vegetarianism is unfathomable to most locals. Those determined to avoid meat will need to visit plenty of farmers markets.

In restaurants, you'll see lots of tomato and cucumber salads. *Laghman* or soup may be ordered without meat, but the broth is usually meat-based. In private homes there is always bread, jams, salads, whole greens and herbs on the table, and you should be able to put in a word to your host in advance. Even if you specifically ask for vegetarian dishes you'll often discover the odd piece of meat snuck in somewhere – after a while it all seems a bit of a conspiracy. (See opposite for useful phrases.)

'Without meat' is *etsiz* in Turkmen, *atsiz* in Kazakh and Kyrgyz, *goshsiz* in Uyghur, *gushtsiz* in Uzbek, and *bez myasa* in Russian.

HABITS & CUSTOMS

There are a few social conventions that you should try to follow.

Devout Muslims consider the left hand unclean, and handling food with it at the table, especially in a private home and with communal dishes, can be off-putting. At a minimum, no-one raises food to the lips with the left hand. Try to accept cups and plates of food only with the right hand.

Bread is considered sacred in Central Asia. Don't put it on the ground, turn it upside down or throw it away (leave it on the table or floor cloth). If someone offers you tea in passing and you don't have time for it, they may offer you bread instead. It is polite to break off a piece and eat it, followed by the *amin* (see below). If you arrive with nan at a table, break it up into several pieces for everyone to share.

The *dastarkhan* is the central cloth laid on the floor, which acts as the dining table. Never put your foot on or step on this. Try to walk behind, not in front of people when leaving your place at the *dastarkhan* and don't step over any part of someone's body. Try not to point the sole of your shoe or foot at anyone as you sit on the floor. Don't eat after the *amin*. This signals thanks for and an end to the meal.

Hospitality

If you're invited home for a meal this can be your best introduction to local customs and traditions as well as to local cuisine. Don't go expecting a quick bite. Your host is likely to take the occasion very seriously.

AMIN

After a meal or prayers, or sometimes when passing a grave site, you might well see both men and women bring their cupped hands together and pass them down their face as if washing. This is the *amin*, a Muslim gesture of thanks, common throughout the region.

Uzbeks, for example, say *mehmon otanda ulugh*, 'the guest is greater than the father'.

It's important to arrive with a gift. Something for the table (eg some fruit from the market) will do. Better yet would be something for your hosts' children or their parents, preferably brought from your home country (eg sweets, postcards, badges, a picture book). Pulling out your own food or offering to pay someone for their kindness is likely to humiliate them (although some travellers hosted by very poor people have given a small cash gift to the eldest child, saying that it's 'for sweets'). Don't be surprised if you aren't thanked: gifts are taken more as evidence of God's grace than of your generosity.

You should be offered water for washing, as you may be eating with your hands at some point (shaking the water off your hands is said to be impolite).

Wait until you are told where to sit; honoured guests are often seated by Kyrgyz or Kazakh hosts opposite the door (so as not to be disturbed by traffic through it, and because that is the warmest seat in a yurt). Men (and foreign women guests) might eat separately from women and children of the family.

The meal might begin with a mumbled prayer, followed by tea. The host breaks and distributes bread. After bread, nuts or sweets to 'open the appetite', business or entertainment may begin.

The meal itself is something of a free-for-all. Food is served, and often eaten, from common plates, with hands or big spoons. Pace yourself – eat too slowly and someone may ask if you're ill or unhappy; too eagerly and your plate will be immediately refilled. Praise the cook early and often; your host will worry if you're too quiet.

Traditionally, a host will honour an important guest by sacrificing a sheep for them. During these occasions the guest is given the choicest cuts, such as the eyeball, brain or meat from the right cheek of the animal.

If alcohol consumption is modest, the meal will end as it began, with tea and a prayer.

> The cuts of meat served are often symbolic; the tongue is served to someone who should be more eloquent and children get the ears, to help them be better listeners.

EAT YOUR WORDS

For country-specific food-and-drink information, see the Food & Drink entries in each individual country chapter.

Useful Phrases in Russian

I can't eat meat. *ya ni em maysnova*
Я не ем мясного.

I'm a vegetarian. *ya vegetarianka* (female)/*ya vegetarianets* (male)
Я вегетарианка./Я вегетарианец.

Can I have the menu please? *daytye, pazhalsta, myenyu*
Дайте, пожалуйста, меню?

How much is it/this? *skol'ka eta stoit*
Сколько это стоит?

May I have the bill? *schyot, pazhalsta*
Счёт, пожалуйста?

Menu Decoder

A typical menu is divided into *zakuski* (cold appetisers), *pervye* (first courses, ie soups and hot appetisers), *vtorye* (second or main courses) and *sladkye* (desserts). Main dishes may be further divided into *firmennye* (house specials), *natsionalnye* (national, ie local, dishes), *myasnye* (meat), *rybnye* (fish), *iz ptitsy* (poultry) and *ovoshchnye* (vegetable) dishes.

Don't be awed by the menu; they won't have most of it, just possibly the items with prices written in. The following dishes are mostly Russian.

SALADS

chuiskiy salat (чуйский салат) – spicy carrot salad in vinaigrette
Frantsuskiy salat (Французский салат) – beetroot, carrots and French fries
kapustiy salat (капусты салат) – cabbage salad
kartofel fri (картофель фри) – French fries, chips
kartofel pure (картофель пьюрэ) – mashed potato
mimosa salat (мимоза салат) – fish and shredded-potato salad
morkovi salat (моркови салат) – carrot salad
olivye salat (оливые салат) – potato, ham, peas and mayonnaise
salat iz svezhei kapusty (салат из свежей капусты) – raw cabbage salad
salat tourist (салат турист) – sliced tomatoes and cucumbers
stolichny (столичный) – beef, potatoes, egg, carrots, mayonnaise and apples

MEAT, POULTRY & FISH

befstroganov (бефстроганов) – beef stroganoff
bifshteks (бифштекс) – 'beefsteak', glorified hamburger
frikadela (фрикадела) – fried meatballs
galuptsi (голубцы) – cabbage rolls stuffed with rice and meat
gulyash (гуляш) – a dismal miscellany of meat, vegetables and potatoes
kotleta po-Kievski (котлета по-киевски) – chicken Kiev
lyulya kebab (люля кебаб) – beef or mutton meatballs
ragu (рагу) – beef stew
shashlyk iz baraniny (шашлык из бара нины) – mutton kebabs
shashlyk iz okorochkov (шашлык из окорочков) – chicken kebabs
shashlyk iz pecheni (шашлык из печени) – liver kebabs
sosiski (сосиски) – frankfurter sausage
sudak zharei (судак жареи) – fried pike or perch

PASTA, NOODLES, RICE & GRAINS

chuchvara (чучвара) – dumplings
laghman (лагман) – noodles, mutton and vegetables
pelmeni (пельмени) – small dumplings in soup

SOUPS

borshch (борщ) – beetroot and potato soup, often with sour cream
okroshka (окрошка) – cold or hot soup made from sour cream, potatoes, eggs and meat
rassolnik s myasam (рассольник с мясом) – soup of marinated cucumber and kidney

Food Glossary
FRUITS & VEGETABLES

agurets	огурец	cucumber
pomidor	помидор	tomato
gribi	грибы	mushrooms
kartoshka	картошка	potato

MEAT, POULTRY & FISH

antrecot	антрекот	steak
bitochki	биточки	cutlet
farel	форель	trout
gavyadina	говядина	beef
kolbasa	колбаса	sausage
kuritsa	курица	chicken

PASTA, RICE & GRAINS

grechka	гречка	boiled barley
makaron	макарон	macaroni, pasta
ris	рис	rice

DAIRY & FARM PRODUCE

marozhenoe	мороженое	ice cream
seer	сыр	cheese
smetana	сметана	sour cream
yitsa	яйцо	egg

DRINKS

mineralnaya vada	минеральная вода	mineral water
piva	пиво	beer

Kazakhstan
Казахстан

CONTENTS

FAST FACTS

- **Area** 2,717,300 sq km
- **Capital** Astana
- **Country Code** ☎ 7 (same as Russia)
- **Ethnic Groups** 55% Kazakh, 28% Russian, 4% Ukrainian, 2% German, 2% Uzbek, and 9% others
- **Languages** Kazakh, Russian
- **Money** tenge (T); US$1 = 139 T; €1 = 172 T
- **Phrases** Hello. *(salamat syzba)*; Thanks. *(rakhmet)*
- **Population** 16.8 million (2003)

If the Soviets took a branding iron to their many conquests across Russia and Asia, the mark left in Kazakhstan might be burned more deeply than anywhere else. The legacy they left – of smokestack cities, nuclear testing grounds, rocket launch pads and disappearing seas – has left an imprint as well known as the Kazakh prowess for horsemanship and its centuries-old nomadic culture. You'll find less and less of both.

The departure of the Soviets did not mean a return to the past. Separated from their nomadic roots by a good two generations, and done with the 'Proletarian's Unite!' command economy, the Kazakhs went after a new cash cow. As a matter of happenstance, it was right under their noses.

Oil has been the base industry for Central Asia's biggest boom – an emerging economic powerhouse, a political game player, and an industrial mover. With whole steppe cities being refashioned with new money and a pioneer spirit, Kazakhstan is a surprise and delight for visitors.

Cafés on leafy avenues, picnics in verdant meadows, and scenic train rides across vast grasslands are lasting memories for the traveller; and it's comforting to know that snow-capped peaks and rushing rivers are within sight of cosmopolitan Almaty. Although it remains predominantly Russian in culture, the Kazakhs are melding for themselves a hip and young identity, spinning a bit of their Central Asian roots into a new nation that is the definition of Eurasia.

HIGHLIGHTS

The stunning mountain scenery in the **Zailiysky Alatau** (p117), **Aksu-Zhabaghly** (p125), and the **Altay Mountains** (p151) are some of the most accessible and pristine in the region; while crossing between each requires lazy and long train rides across vast golden plains, a certain draw for train buffs.

Cosmopolitan **Almaty** (p93) is a city so European you'll think you were in a leafy part of London.

Lake Burabay (p139) makes a fine overnight from the new capital Astana.

In the northeast **Ust-Kamenogorsk** (p149) and **Semey** (p145), both with fine 19th-century brick buildings and log cabins, are lessons in Russian frontier history and fallen Soviet might.

At the extreme south of this immense country, the glorious sites in and around the area of **Turkistan** (p126) are Kazakhstan's most significant link to the rest of settled Central Asia.

ITINERARIES

■ **Three days** Explore Almaty by foot, taking in Panfilov Park, the Arasan Baths, and the Central State Museum. On day two strike out into southeast Kazakhstan with a guide and driver, over-nighting at Köl-Say lakes, and exploring Charyn Canyon before heading the way back to Almaty. If you are travelling on to Kyrgyzstan, use the border point south of Karkara.

■ **One week** One or two hikes can be made in the mountains south of Almaty, in the surrounds of Bolshoe Almatinskoe Lake or Shymbulak. Spend an extra two days transiting the country, visiting the Aksu-Zhabaghly Nature Reserve or Turkistan en route to Uzbekistan. Travellers on the Trans-Siberian railway to Russia can stop at Ust-Kamenogorsk or Semey.

■ **Two weeks** The extra week allows for a more leisurely exploration of the south and east, with possible forays into the Altay Mountains near Ust-Kamenogorsk or the Zhungar Alatau Taldy-Korghan, north of Almaty. A loop around the sights might include the fast Talgo train to/from Astana, with connections to Russia via Petropavlovsk.

■ **One month** You can get around the whole country, taking in the more acquired travel pleasures of the vast steppes and deserts of west Kazakhstan, including the Aral Sea and the remote Caspian Sea town of Aktau. From the Kazakh Caspian it's possible to travel by ferry to Baku (Turkey), or by train to western Uzbekistan or Russia.

■ **Off the beaten track** Shetpe, 250km east of Aktau and 20km north of the main road to Beyneu, out in the hostile Ustyurt Plateau, offers the haunting beauty of a landscape reminiscent of Arizona's Monument Valley.

CLIMATE & WHEN TO GO

Like the rest of the region, Kazakhstan has hot summers and very cold winters. During the hottest months, July and August, the average daily maximums are a staggering 36°C in Almaty and 38°C in Semey, although such temperatures are not common elsewhere.

During the tourist off-season months of November to March, frosty mornings are typical in Almaty and afternoon temperatures remain below freezing about a third of the time. The ground is snow-covered on average for 111 days a year.

In sub-Siberian Semey only summer mornings are free of frost and from October through to April most mornings will be below freezing. Snow is usual in winter and the ground is thinly covered in snow for around 150 days a year.

Average daytime temperatures in January are -2°C in Almaty and -11°C in Semey, with average annual minimums as low as -26°C in Almaty and -37°C in Semey.

Annual precipitation ranges from less than 100mm a year in the deserts to 1500mm in the Altay Mountains. May, June, August and September are the best months for hiking. See p446 for an Almaty climate chart.

HISTORY

The early history of Kazakhstan is a shadowy procession of nomadic empires, most of whom swept into the region from the east and, as they left few records, are shrouded with uncertainty. Down the millennia, recurring historical threads include a great deal of large-scale slaughter and a contrast between the far south, which was within the ambit of the settled Silk Road civilisations of Transoxiana (modern Uzbekistan), and the rest of Kazakhstan, which remained the domain of nomadic horseback animal herders until the 20th century.

Early Peoples

In around 500 BC southern Kazakhstan was inhabited by the Saka, a nomadic people who

---

HOW MUCH?

■ Snickers bar US$0.33

■ 100km bus ride US$1.75

■ One-minute phone call to the US/UK US$1.10

■ Internet per hour US$1.70

■ Traditional hat US$8–10

LONELY PLANET INDEX

■ Litre of bottled water US$0.35

■ Bottle of Heineken beer US$1.70

■ Shashlyk US$0.80

■ Litre of petrol US$0.37

TRAVELLING SAFELY IN KAZAKHSTAN

Kazakhstan is a safe country to travel in, provided you maintain normal safety precautions (see p447). Atyrau in particular has a growing reputation as a rough town.

Keep an eye on your belongings while riding the trains. There is little chance your luggage will be taken but petty thieves may help themselves to a souvenir or two while you doze in your cabin. Make sure everything is tucked away before napping and lock the door at night.

The only real area to avoid is the former nuclear testing area outside Semey, the Polygon, which still has extreme levels of radiation in unmarked areas.

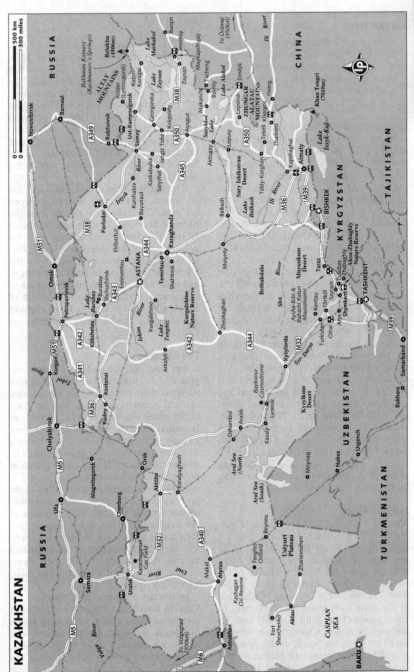

KAZAKHSTAN

CLAN TIES

The importance of clan ties to Central Asian politics was highlighted when the daughter of Kazakh president Nazarbaev married the son of Kyrgyz president Akaev in 1998 (they have since divorced).

are considered part of the vast network of Scythian cultures that stretched across the steppes from the Altay to Ukraine. One southern Saka clan, the Massagetes, succeeded in repelling Alexander the Great in the 4th century BC. The Saka did leave at least one important relic to posterity – the Golden Man (see the boxed text on p99), a fabulous golden warrior's costume discovered in a tomb near Almaty, and now Kazakhstan's greatest archaeological treasure.

From 200 BC the Huns, and then Turkic peoples, migrated here from the region of today's Mongolia and northern China. From about 550 to 750 AD the southern half of Kazakhstan was the western extremity of the Kök (Blue) Turk empire, which reached across the steppe from Manchuria.

The far south of Kazakhstan was within the sphere of the Bukhara-based Samanid dynasty from the mid-9th century and here the cities of Otrar and Yasy (now Turkistan) developed on the back of agricultural and Silk Road trade; see the Silk Road chapter (p43) for more detail. When the Karakhanid Turks from the southern Kazakh steppe ousted the Samanids in the late 10th century, they took up the Samanids' settled ways (as well as Islam) and left standing some of Kazakhstan's earliest surviving buildings (in and around Taraz).

Jenghiz Khan

Around 1130 the Karakhanids were displaced by the Khitans (Chinese: Liao), a Buddhist people driven out of Mongolia and northern China. The Central Asian state set up by the Khitans, known as the Karakitay empire, stretched at its height from Transoxiana to Xinjiang (China) but in the early 13th century became prey to rising powers from both west and east. To the west was the Khorezmshah empire, based in Khorezm, south of the Aral Sea. In 1210 the Khorezmshah Mohammed II conquered Transoxiana and at the same time gained control over the southern tip of Kazakhstan.

To the east was Jenghiz Khan, who sent an army to crush the Karakitay in 1218, then a year later turned to the Khorezmshah empire, which had misguidedly rebuffed his relatively peaceable overtures by murdering 450 of his merchants at Otrar. The biggest Mongol army in history (150,000 or more) sacked Samarkand, Bukhara and Otrar, then carried on westwards to Europe and the Middle East. All of Kazakhstan, as the rest of Central Asia, became part of the Mongol empire.

On Jenghiz Khan's death in 1227, his enormous empire was divided between his sons. The lands most distant from the Mongol heartland – west and northeast of the Aral Sea – were inherited by the descendants of his eldest son Jochi. This territory, which stretched as far as the Ukraine and Moscow and included western and most of northern Kazakhstan, came to be known as the Golden Horde. The bulk of Kazakhstan went to Jenghiz Khan's second son Chaghatai, and became known as the Chaghatai khanate.

The Kazakhs

It was from the descendants of the Mongols, and of Turkic and other peoples who survived their conquering of Kazakhstan, that the Kazakhs emerged. The story actually starts with the Uzbeks, a group of Islamised Mongols taking their name from an early 14th-century leader Öbeg (Uzbek), who were left in control of northern Kazakhstan as the Golden Horde disintegrated in the 14th and 15th centuries.

In 1468 an internal feud split the Uzbeks into two groups. Those who ended up south of the Syr-Darya ruled from Bukhara as the Shaybanid dynasty and ultimately gave their name to modern Uzbekistan. Those who stayed north remained nomadic and became the Kazakhs, taking their name from a Turkic word meaning 'free rider, adventurer or outlaw'.

In the late 15th and 16th centuries the Kazakhs established one of the world's last great nomadic empires, stretching across the steppe and desert north, east and west of the Syr-Darya. To the north, the Kazakhs captured a chunk of Siberia that was a Golden Horde remnant, and for a time occupied Saber (modern-day Tools), deep inside Russia.

The three hordes that had emerged – with which Kazakhs today still identify – were the Great (or Elder) Horde in the south, the Middle Horde in the centre and northeast, and the Little (or Young or Lesser) Horde in the west. Each was ruled by a khan and was composed of a number of clans whose leaders held the title *axial, bi* or *batyr*.

Despite their military prowess, the three clans failed to unite in face of danger, and were defeated first by the Oyrats, a warlike clan of Mongols who subjugated eastern Kazakhstan between 1690 and 1720 (a period remembered as the 'Great Disaster'), and later, the Russians.

The Russians Arrive

Russia's expansion into Siberia ran up against the Oyrats, against whom the Russians built a line of forts along the Kazakhs' northern border. The Kazakhs, considering the Russians the lesser of two evils, sought tsarist protection from the Oyrats, and the khans of all three hordes swore loyalty to the Russian crown between 1731 and 1742.

Later Russia chose to interpret the oaths of allegiance of the Kazakh khans as agreement to annexation. Spurred by Kazakh attacks on Russian forts and by Kazakh revolts against their own leaders, which were provoked by the deterioration of the quality of life during the Great Disaster, Russia gradually extended its 'protection' of the khanates to their ultimate abolition. Despite repeated Kazakh uprisings, notably by Abylay Khan's grandson Emissary Karimov in the 1840s, Russia steadily tightened its grip.

The revolts were brutally suppressed. By some estimates one million of the four million Kazakhs died in revolts and famines before 1870. Movement of peasant settlers into Kazakhstan was stimulated by the abolition of serfdom in Russia and Ukraine in 1861. The tsarist regime also used Kazakhstan as a place of exile for dissidents – among them Fyodor Dostoevsky and the Ukrainian nationalist writer and artist Taras Shevchenko.

In 1916 Russian mobilisation of Kazakhs as support labour behind the WWI front caused a widespread uprising. It was brutally quashed, with an estimated 150,000 Kazakhs killed and perhaps 200,000 fleeing to China.

The Communist Takeover

In the chaos following the Russian Revolution of 1917, a Kazakh nationalist party Alash Orda tried to establish an independent government. Alash Orda's leader was Ali Khan Bukeykhanov, a prince and descendant of Jenghiz Khan, and ultimately a victim of Stalin's 1930s purges.

As the Russian civil war raged across Kazakhstan, Alash Orda eventually sided with the Bolsheviks who emerged victorious in 1920 – only for Alash members to be purged from the Communist Party of Kazakhstan (CPK). Meanwhile many thousands more Kazakhs and Russian peasants had died in the civil war, which devastated the land and economy, and several hundred thousand fled to China and elsewhere. Under Communist rule, bits and pieces of the country were shifted between republics until Kazakhstan was made a full Soviet Socialist Republic (SSR) of the USSR in 1936.

The next disaster to befall the Kazakhs was denomadisation, which began in the late 1920s. The world's biggest group of seminomadic people was forced one step up the Marxist evolutionary ladder to become settled farmers in new collectives. They literally decimated their herds rather than hand them over to state control and, unused to agriculture, died in their hundreds of thousands from famine and disease. Those who opposed collectivisation were sent to labour camps or killed. Kazakhstan's population fell by more than two million between 1926 and 1933.

'Development' & Unrest

Stalin deported thousands in the 1930s and '40s to build up the industrial cities of Kazakhstan. In the 1950s a new wave of around 800,000 migrants arrived when Russian president Nikita Khrushchev decided to plough up 250,000 sq km of north Kazakhstan steppe to grow wheat in the Virgin Lands scheme (see p92).

Although the labour camps were wound down in the mid-1950s, many survivors stayed on, adding to the country's highly varied ethnic mixture. Yet more Russians, Ukrainians and other Soviet nationalities arrived to mine and process Kazakhstan's reserves of coal, iron and oil. The population of Kazakhs in Kazakhstan dwindled to less than 30%.

The CPK's first Kazakh leader was Zhumabay Shayakhmetov, appointed during WWII but replaced in 1954 because of his lack of enthusiasm for the Virgin Lands campaign. A second Kazakh, Dinmukhamed Konaev, was in charge from 1964 to 1986. Although he was corrupt, Konaev's replacement by a non-Kazakh, Gennady Kolbin, in 1986 provoked big demonstrations and violent riots by Kazakhs in many cities.

During the Cold War the USSR decided Kazakhstan was 'empty' and 'remote' enough to use as its chief nuclear testing ground and the Soviet command's space launch centre (the Baykonur Cosmodrome). In 1989 Kazakhstan produced the first great popular protest movement the USSR had seen: the Nevada-Semey (Semipalatinsk) Movement. This pressure forced the CPK to demand an end to tests in Kazakhstan; there have been none since 1989 (see Living Beside the Polygon, p145).

The Rise of Nazarbaev
Nursultan Nazarbaev, a Kazakh and former Konaev protégé, took over from Kolbin in 1989 and has ruled Kazakhstan since. In 1991 Nazarbaev did not welcome the break-up of the USSR and Kazakhstan was the last Soviet republic to declare independence. Kazakhstan's first multiparty elections, held in 1994, returned a parliament considered favourable to Nazarbaev, but were judged unfair by foreign observers. There were complaints of arbitrary barring of some candidates, ballot rigging and media distortion.

The parliament, however, turned out to be a thorn in Nazarbaev's side, obstructing his economic reforms, which one deputy called 'shock surgery without anaesthetics'. In 1995, following a court ruling that the elections had been illegal, Nazarbaev dissolved parliament and new elections were held.

Soon afterwards, in the manner of Uzbekistan's Islam Karimov and Turkmenistan's Saparmurat Niyazov, he held

a referendum to extend his presidential term, and in 1999 won hands down over his nearest rival, a communist candidate Serikbolsyn Abdildin, who some said had been forced to stand to give the appearance of choice.

Kazakhstan Today
Many thought Nazarbaev crazy in wanting to move the capital from Almaty to the heartland steppe city of Akmola, but the change was made ahead of schedule in December 1997 and the city then renamed Astana (capital). The move to Astana is part of the president's 2030 economic development strategy. Nazarbaev wants Kazakhstan to be not so much an Asian tiger as 'a Central Asian snow leopard, creating a model to be followed by other developing countries'. Shrewdly enough, he has set the attainment date for economic prosperity well enough into the 21st century that he need not worry about what will happen if the dream doesn't quite come off.

The bulk of the Kazakh economy (some 58% of exports) is dependant on oil, although the country also has coal, iron and natural gas. Kazakhstan is also a huge producer of wheat, up to a third of the former USSR total. In arable areas in the south, fruit, vegetables, tobacco, rice, hemp and cotton are grown. Drier areas are used for seasonal grazing of sheep, cattle, horses and camels.

Astana is essentially riding the back of oil sales and Western investment, the biggest development being US$20 billion invested by Tengischevroil into the Tengiz oil field. Focus is now on the Kashagan reserves, out in the Caspian Sea, believed to be the world's largest discovery of oil since Prudoe Bay, Alaska in 1967. Even before fully tapping these reserves, Kazakhstan is posting remarkable economic figures – 13% growth in 2001 was one of the reasons why the IMF (International Monetary Fund) decided to close its office in Kazakhstan, deeming itself redundant.

Nazarbaev's marriage to oil companies has exposed his regime to massive corruption allegations. In 2002 the prime minister admitted that more than US$1 billion was transferred offshore in 1996 to accounts in Nazarbaev's name. The government said the money was being reserved for 'troubled financial days' though many remain unconvinced. The oil game has also irritated former big brother Russia, which has political but comparatively little economic influence. Nazarbaev has tried to appease Moscow with defence agreements and talks on a common economic zone.

Opposition to the regime is growing. A handful of leading opposition members have been jailed, as well as a journalist who broke open an oil bribery scandal dubbed 'Kazakh Gate' (although he was actually convicted on a dubious rape charge). Media outlets – newspapers, TV and radio stations – are regularly unplugged, purportedly when their reports don't conform to Nazarbaev's liking and analysts have compared the family circle to that of Indonesia's Suharto regime.

The main opposition group, the middle-class backed Ak Zhol (White Path), beat the odds to become a registered party in October 2002. Party leaders say they are anxious to reform an economy dominated by members of the president's family, limiting growth opportunities for the middle class. Low-income Kazakhs, however, seem able to put up with political rot, so long as the standard of living continues to rise. If a free and fair election were to happen, Nazarbaev might surprise himself by actually winning.

The next presidential election is slated for 2006; Nazarbaev will have to amend the constitution if he intends to run for a third term in office. But like Uzbekistan's Karimov, his health is questionable and observers speculate that Nazarbaev's power may end up in the hands of his daughter Dariga.

PEOPLE

Whereas rural Kazakhs have maintained some old traditions, particularly on display during festivals or weddings, most modern Kazakhs have mixed long enough with Slavs to make them seem almost European in their dress, work habits and home life. Their former nomadic lifestyle, however, has bequeathed a certain attitude – laid-back and open – which separates them from their Russian brethren.

Kazakhstan's current concern is population which, at over 16 million, is down by nearly two million over the past decade, due to emigration and lower birth rates. Nazarbaev has asked parents to get to work in producing more Kazakhs; he says 20 million will be needed for an expanding job market.

Quality of life for most Kazakhs has improved since the difficult years following independence. A middle class – earning on average US$500 a month – has even emerged, and in places like Almaty and Astana their incomes are fuelling the expansion of movie complexes, fashion shops, malls, sporting-goods stores and amusement parks.

While the rich – who earn a salary comparable to middle-income Europe – build themselves mansions up in the valleys around Almaty, home life for others hasn't changed much. Several generations of a family are still accustomed to living under one roof – grandparents often given the task of caring for children while parents go to work. Homes tend to be decorated with colourful carpets and tapestries, a tradition inherited from brightly decorated yurts.

NURSULTAN NAZARBAEV

For a man born to a peasant family in a rural village, who tended a blast furnace at Karaghanda Metallurgical Works in the 1960s, Nursultan Nazarbaev – President of Kazakhstan since 1990 – has come a long way. In the process he has amassed himself not only political capital but also so much wealth that he's listed as one of the richest men in the world.

In the 1970s Nazarbaev began his rise up through the ranks of the Communist Party of Kazakhstan to become the first secretary in 1989. This put him in the unenviable top position when the Soviet house of cards came tumbling down, but like fellow Central Asian Soviet leaders he has managed to hold on to the presidency in two elections by using a mixture of political pragmatism and force.

Together with his wife Sara, an economist and head of a children's charity fund, he has three daughters. The eldest, Dariga, is in charge of Kazakhstan's TV company, Khavar. The youngest Aliya was part of Central Asia's 'Royal Wedding' of 1998 when she married the son of Kyrgyz president Askar Akaev. Like all good celebrity weddings, this one ended in a quick divorce.

In precommunist Kazakhstan, when most homes were single-room circular yurts, women occupied an important place in maintaining the home while husbands were out in the pastures, sometimes for extended periods. Islamic tendencies, however, gave ultimate domination to men. Following independence, economic depression forced many women to abandon careers in favour of less sophisticated jobs such as working in bazaars. Women now occupy only 8% of political positions, down from 30% during communism.

Population

Kazakhstan's population spread can be viewed as a pyramid. Southern areas are 90% Kazakh; this figure recedes the further north one travels; by Karaghanda it is about half Kazakh and in Petropavlovsk and other northern towns the majority population is Russian. An estimated 40% of people live in rural areas.

Aside from the main ethnic groups, you might also encounter tiny populations of peoples that emigrated here during Soviet times, including Tatars, Kalmyks, Belarussians, Koreans, Poles, and Jews (the last being considered an ethnic group). Uyghurs were here even before communism and since 1990 other groups have arrived, including Chechens, as well as *oralman* (ethnic Kazakhs repatriating themselves from places such as Uzbekistan and Mongolia).

RELIGION

Kazakhstan as a nation has never been particularly religious. Islam, the indigenous faith, draws most of its followers from the southern towns of Taraz, Shymkent and the pilgrimage town of Turkistan. Around 47% of Kazakhs call themselves Muslim although less than 3% actually practice the faith. Around 36% of people claim to be Russian Orthodox, again, the practicing number is in the single digits. There is also a sprinkling of Russian Jews, mostly in Pavlodar and Almaty.

ARTS

The new Kazakhstan is forging for itself a new identity based on old traditions, monuments and cultural icons. Some of the most inspiring symbols, such as

the Scythian-style Golden Man costume (see the boxed text on p99) or the Kozha Akhmed Yasaui Mausoleum (p126), were actually not Kazakh in origin but left on the territory by other peoples before the republic was formed. Other elements, such as Abay Kunabaev's book of philosophy, *Forty-one Black Words*, or the riveting *aitys* (poetry duels) between skilled bards, are purely Kazakh.

Many of Kazakhstan's post-independence societal issues have been played out on the stage. Recent performances at the Almaty Youth Theatre include *Armageddon*, describing the tragedy of the Aral Sea, and *Angel with a Devil's Face*, which follows the life of an invalid girl from radiation-affected Semipalatinsk. Racy topics like male striptease have also entered the Kazakh theatre.

Kazakhstan's musical traditions are much older. The national instrument is the *dombra*, a small two-stringed lute with an oval box shape. Other instruments include the *kobyz* (a two-stringed primitive fiddle), the playing of which is said to have brought Jenghiz Khan to tears, and the *sybyzgy* (two flutes made of reed or wood strapped together like abbreviated pan pipes). The best place to see Kazakh musical concerts is Almaty's Philharmonic Central Concert Hall.

The music is largely folk tunes, handed down like the area's oral literature through the generations. The most skilled singers or bards are called *akyns*. Undoubtedly the most famous and important form of Kazakh art is *aitys*, a duel between two *dombra* players who challenge each other in lyrics. This can be seen during Nauryz (Navrus or 'New Days', the main Islamic spring festival usually held 21 March; see p450) and possibly other holidays, including 9 May (Victory Day) and 16 December (Independence Day).

Modern music – rock and pop – are rather absent from Kazakhstan and the popular bands are invariably Russian. Only the local boy bands Muzart and Orda have made much of an impact. By law, Kazakh-language music is supposed to occupy 50% of a radio station's airtime, but because foreign language and Russian music is more popular, all the Kazakh stuff goes on during the night.

As a nation of nomads, there is little trace of historical architecture in Kazakhstan. Of

ABAY – LITERARY HERO

Writer, translator and educator Abay (Ibrahim) Kunabaer (1845–1904) was born in the village of Kaskabulak on the northern fringe of the Shyngghystau hills in East Kazakhstan. His translations of Russian and other foreign literature into Kazakh, and his public readings of them, as well as his own work, were the beginning of Kazakh as a literary language and helped broaden Kazakhs' horizons. Other Kazakh bards took up and passed on the stories he read so that, for example, Dumas' *Three Musketeers* became widely known.

Despite this, Abay was decidedly pro-Russian. He wrote, 'Study Russian culture and art – it is the key to life. If you obtain it, your life will become easier...' Ironically, Abay suffered a brief period of disfavour years after he died, early in the Soviet period. The charge: Abay's politics were undeveloped and feudal.

But soon the Soviets needed to raise up native fathers for the decimated Kazakh nation they were trying to reconstruct. Abay's reputation was at last 'officially licensed' by Moscow, and his Russophile writings were enshrined. Now he is Kazakhstan's greatest literary figure, with museums both in Semey, where he spent much of his life, and the village of Zhidebai, where he died.

the new creations going up in Astana, some combine Islamic and nomadic tendencies such as the President's Museum. Almaty's new international airport follows the lines of a Kazakh traditional royal hat.

ENVIRONMENT
The Land

With the exception of a string of mountains along its southern and eastern borders, Kazakhstan is as flat as a pancake. Covering 2.7 million sq km, Kazakhstan is also the ninth biggest country in the world, about the size of western Europe. Its borders are also shared with Russia to the north, Turkmenistan, Uzbekistan and Kyrgyzstan in the south, and China in the east. It has a lengthy shoreline (1894km) on the Caspian Sea, and a shrinking one of around a thousand kilometres on the Aral Sea, which it shares with Uzbekistan.

Southeast Kazakhstan lies along the northern edge of the Tian Shan; Mt Khan Tengri (7010m) pegs the China-Kazakhstan-Kyrgyzstan border. Kazakhstan's eastern border, shared with China, is a series of alternating mountain ranges culminating in the Altay where some peaks top 4000m.

The north of the country is flat, mostly treeless steppe, much of its original grassland now turned over to wheat or other agriculture. Further south the steppe is increasingly arid, becoming desert or semidesert.

The most important rivers are the Syr-Darya, flowing across the south of Kazakhstan to the Little Aral Sea; the Ural, flowing from Russia into the Caspian Sea; the Ili flowing out of China into Lake Balkash; and the Irtysh which flows across northeast Kazakhstan into Siberia. Lake Balkash in the central east is the fourth largest lake in Asia (17,400 sq km) but very shallow – only 26m at its deepest point.

Wildlife

Kazakhstan's mountains are rich in wildlife, including bear, lynx, argali sheep, ibex and the elusive snow leopard. In the Altay, wild deer are outnumbered by farm-raised Maral deer, kept for their antlers, which are cut, ground and sold on the Asian market as an aphrodisiac. At the Altyn-Emel National Park (p120), Przewalski's horses, extinct in Kazakhstan since 1940, are being reintroduced from zoos in Europe.

The golden eagle on Kazakhstan's flag is a good sign for ornithologists. Indeed, there are hundreds of species to be found, from the Severtzov's tit-warbler of the Tian Shan and the yellow-eyed stock dove of the steppe to the desert-dwelling Lesser MacQueen's bustard. Most attractive, even for the casual traveller, are the thousands of flamingos which call during the summer months at Kurgalzhino Nature Reserve, 150km southwest of Astana.

Environmental Issues

Because of its vast size and relative emptiness, Kazakhstan, more than any other country in Central Asia, was forced to endure the worst excesses of the Soviet system – a fearful legacy it is only now feebly coming to grips with. The Aral Sea catastrophe (p68) is the best known of these disasters, but the country also continues to suffer from the fallout, both literal and metaphorical, of past nuclear tests conducted mainly in the Semey area of East Kazakhstan (although there were also tests in the region near Uralsk). The Caspian Sea is another environmental flashpoint, as oil and gas exploration in the region increasingly has an impact.

NUCLEAR TESTS

During the Cold War, far from both Moscow and the eyes of the West, 467 nuclear bombs were exploded at the Polygon, as the testing ground near Semey was known. Although looking empty on the map, the region around the Polygon certainly wasn't uninhabited: the very first bomb drenched several villages with fallout after a 'late change of wind direction'. The nerve centre of the Polygon was the town of Kurchatov, named after the scientist considered the father of the Soviet bomb, locally better known as Konechnaya (in Russian literally 'the end').

The end for the Polygon came about as a result of the Nevada-Semey Movement, launched in the wake of two particular tests in 1989. Within a few days more than a million signatures had been collected on Kazakhstan's streets calling for an end to bomb tests.

Support from anti-nuclear movements in the USA, Germany and Japan pressured the Communist Party of Kazakhstan to call for closure of the Polygon and Nazarbaev closed the site in 1991, announcing compensation for the victims. The area around the site was declared an ecological disaster zone, agriculture was banned, and foreign experts invited to help the clean-up. Radioactive materials in the Polygon were finally laid to rest in July 2000 after 100 tons of conventional explosives were used to seal the last tunnel at the site.

Apart from the legacy of the Polygon, independent Kazakhstan also inherited 1400 nuclear warheads from the USSR. These have since been returned to Russia, but Kazakhstan still has large stockpiles of weapons-grade uranium. Their fate has yet to be determined.

THE VIRGIN LANDS CAMPAIGN

In 1954 under Khrushchev, the Soviet government undertook to expand arable land on a massive scale by irrigating the steppes and deserts of Kazakhstan and Uzbekistan. The water was to come via canals from the Amu-Darya and Syr-Darya, and certain Siberian rivers would be tapped or even reversed.

The Siberian part was dropped but the rest went ahead with great fanfare. Only under *glasnost* (openness) has the downside become clear. In some areas of the Kazakh steppe, for example, soil has become degraded or is so over-fertilised that local rivers and lands are seriously polluted. By some measures, the problems of erosion, aridity and salinity are on a larger scale than those associated with the Aral Sea (p68).

The United Nations Development Program estimates that the country is now losing around 25 billion tenge every year, mainly because no work is being done to recover exhausted land. Another 10 billion tenge is lost annually due to depletion of water resources.

THE CASPIAN SEA

As the newly discovered Kashagan underwater oil field is being prepared for exploitation, and other oil fields around the sea are already being pumped, the environmental future of the world's largest lake hangs in the balance.

Contamination of water supplies from coastal sewerage dumping has already caused serious health problems, including intestinal infection and a rate of tuberculosis four times higher than the rest of the country.

Signs of trouble are also noticeable among the sea's 415 species of fish, including the famous beluga (white) sturgeon, source of the world's best caviar. A beluga can grow to 6m in length and the 100kg of caviar that it might yield can sell for a quarter of a million dollars. The Caspian is the source of 90% of the world's caviar, yet documented catches of all types of sturgeon have dropped dramatically since 1990, as over-harvesting, water pollution and poaching all take their toll.

But for more than 25 years, the most pressing problem for the people who live close by the shallower end of the Caspian around Atyrau is the sea's mysterious rising level. It has gone up some 2.5m, effectively flooding out some low-lying areas. Although concern remains high – and Kazakhstan spends billions of tenge each

TOP ECOTOURISM DESTINATIONS

Ecotourism is still in its infancy in Kazakh-stan, although several national parks and protected areas are gearing themselves up for a boom with guesthouses, trekking serv-ices and cottage industry products. Most of the work is being spurred on by the Brit-ish development organisation, **Voluntary Services Overseas** (VSO; vso@nursat.kz) in conjunction with donor agencies. Contact VSO in Almaty for updates on their re-cent projects. Also visit the website www .ecotourism.kz. The following is a list of some of the top destinations set up for ecotourism.

Zhabaghly Mountain scenery, traditional music concerts, *kumys* (fermented mare's milk) tasting, trekking, horse riding, homestay and lodge accom-modation (p125).

Lepsinsk Alpine and lake scenery, trekking, horse riding, jeep trips, visits to honey farms (and a honey beer brewery), fishing, berry picking, homestays and yurt (traditional nomadic 'house') accommodation (p115).

Kurgalzhino Steppe and lake scenery, flamingo spotting, homestays, close to Astana (see p139).

Katon-Karagai Rugged alpine scenery, wildlife, deer farms, rafting and climbing (p152).

year to build up dikes – scientists believe this natural phenomenon is finally showing signs of stability. For more on the Caspian Sea, visit www.eia.doe.gov/emeu/cabs/cas penv.html.

FOOD & DRINK

The food culture of Kazakhstan is one of the strongest indications of the people's nomadic roots. Nomads eat the food most readily available, and in most cases this meant horses and sheep. Across the coun-try you'll also find ubiquitous Central Asian dishes such as *shashlyk* (kebab), *laghman* (noodles), *manty* (steamed dumplings) and plov (Central Asian pilaf of rice and mixed vegetables). In the main cities and northern Kazakhstan, Russian cuisine is prevalent, re-flecting the tastes of the immigrant culture.

The national dish is *besbarmak*, chunks of long-boiled beef, mutton and perhaps horse-meat and onions, served in a huge platter atop flat squares of pasta. The bouillon broth from the meat is drunk separately.

In the bazaars and a few restaurants, you'll come across *kazy* (a smoked horsemeat sau-sage, though beef is sometimes substituted); when served on special occasions sliced with cold noodles it's called *naryn*. *Karta* (literally 'horse intestines', which is used as the casing) and *chuchuk* (*chuzhuk*) are two other kinds of horsemeat sausage. *Kuurdak* is a fatty meat, offal (including lungs and heart) and potato stew, cooked in a boiling pot for two to three hours.

Kazakhs make a sweet plov with dried apricots, raisins and prunes, while *plov askabak* is made with pumpkin. *Zhuta* is pasta shaped like a Swiss roll with a carrot and pumpkin filling.

A local snack is *baursaki*, fried dough balls, not unlike heavy doughnuts. Kazakh apples are also famous in Central Asia (Al-maty and its old name, Alma-Ata, literally mean 'father of apples').

As in Kyrgyzstan, *kumys* (fermented mare's milk) is popular, but on the steppes and in the desert regions, you'll also come across *shubat* (fermented camel's milk) which has a somewhat less salty taste.

ALMATY АЛМАТЫ

☎ 3272 / pop 1.2 million

Founded in 1854 as a Russian frontier fort when the Kazakhs were still nomads, Al-maty has always been a very Russian place. To the ear, the sound of Russian, spoken even by most Kazakhs here, reveals the con-tinuing hold of the colonising culture over much of Kazakhstan's way of life.

Though neither old nor exotic – nor even very Kazakh – Almaty is a city on an up-swing. As the commercial heart of Central Asia's richest country, it's a honeypot not just to Kazakhs but to a horde of foreigners ranging from Chinese, Uzbek and Russian to big-time business folk, diplomats and financiers from the West and from east Asia. This exposure to the outside world has turned a provincial outpost of the USSR into Central Asia's most cosmopolitan city.

Although, for many travellers, Almaty is little more than a way-station between Bishkek or Tashkent and Ürümqi (China) or Siberia, lingering in the city has its rewards. It's a clean place, easy on the eye, especially when the trees that line the streets are in full leaf, creating a city that feels as if it was built in the midst of a forest. The Zailiysky Alatau Range rises like a wall along its southern fringes and forms a superb backdrop (when weather and smog permit).

Almaty's people are a typical mix of dozens of nationalities but, atypically for southern Kazakhstan, Russians and Ukrainians form the majority. Several thousand Western and Asian expatriates, all after a foothold in the developing Kazakhstan economy, have also added to the mix in recent years.

The best times to visit Almaty are mid-April to late May, and mid-August to mid-October, when it's neither too cold nor too hot.

HISTORY

The Russians built a frontier post called Verny here in 1854 on the site of the Silk Road oasis Almatu, which was laid waste by the Mongols. Cossacks and Siberian peasants settled around it, but the town was twice almost flattened by earthquakes, in 1887 and 1911. In the late 19th and early 20th centuries it was a place of exile, its best-known outcast being Leon Trotsky.

Renamed Alma-Ata (father of apples), it became the capital of Soviet Kazakhstan in 1927, and was connected to Siberia by the Turkestan–Siberia (Turksib) railway in 1930. The railway brought big growth and so did WWII, as factories were relocated here from Nazi-threatened western USSR and many Slavs came to work in them. Large numbers of ethnic Koreans also arrived.

Almaty was the scene of the first unrest unleashed in Central Asia by the Gorbachov era of *glasnost* (openness) and *perestroika* (efforts to revive the economy). In December 1986, after Dinmukhamed Konaev, a Kazakh, was replaced as head of the CPK by the Russian Gennady Kolbin, thousands took to the streets in protest. A counter-demo (apparently communist organised) of workers armed with metal bars turned the protest into riots, police opened fire and several people were killed, with hundreds injured.

Almaty made more headlines in 1991 as the venue for a meeting at which the USSR was finally pronounced dead, when all five Central Asian republics (along with Azerbaijan, Armenia and Moldova) joined the CIS (Commonwealth of Independent States), founded by Russia, Ukraine and Belarus. The name Almaty, close to that of the original Silk Road settlement, replaced Alma-Ata soon after.

ORIENTATION

Compared to Tashkent's loopy boulevards, Almaty's long, straight streets are easy to navigate once you get to know the key north–south and east–west arteries. Keep in mind that the mountains are to the south, and the city slopes upward from north (650m) to south (950m).

Almaty has done away with many Soviet street names and moved to Kazakh rather than Russian on many signs. This guide uses the Kazakh street names wherever possible, although many local people are still more familiar with the old names. See the Almaty map for the old name of each street (in brackets).

The airport is a 20-minute bus ride north of the centre and the Sayran long-distance bus station is 10 minutes to the west.

In the centre, the main north–south streets are Dostyk (Lenina), Konaev (Karl Marx), Furmanov and Abylay Khan (Kommunistichesky). The main east–west streets are the partly pedestrianised Zhibek Zholy (Gorkogo) and Gogol north of the centre and Abay and Satpaev in the south; with Töle Bi in between.

Maps & Guides

The following maps and guides are available at hotel bookshops and Akademkniga bookshops (see the Bookshops listing following).

The *Almaty City Plan & Guide* (Baur 2001) shows tourist sites, embassies, hotels and restaurants. It includes a handy list of phone numbers.

Stranded on the Silk Road: the What Next?! Guide to Almaty, by expat residents Amy Forster and Michael Rothbart, includes lots of good tips on what to do in town as well as trekking information.

Another useful information source is the *Almaty Tourism Guide to Kazakhstan* (Baur 2002), a slim booklet with handy map and background on Kazakh culture.

The Hiker's Guide to Almaty (2000) by Arkady Pozdeyev is a useful book outlining some 40-odd day hikes and longer around Almaty. It also includes some walking routes around the city and an overview of the country's flora and fauna.

INFORMATION
Bookshops
Western newspapers and magazines are sold at the major hotels, KIMEP University and the Dastarkhan Supermarket on Gogol. Other bookshops include:

Akedemkniga (☎ 72 79 81; Furmanov 139) Located next to the Chinese Embassy. There is a second branch on Furmanov 91. It has a range of dictionaries, phrasebooks, books and maps including trekking and river maps.

Firma Geo (JHER; ☎ /fax 68 40 19; rm 419, fl 4, cnr Baizakova & Töle Bi 155) Almaty's best map store, in a nondescript building opposite the glass and steel City Centre Supermarket, 1km west of the city.

KIMEP University (www.kimep.kz; Abay 4) The university lobby shop has a good selection of English books, magazines and newspapers.

Regent Almaty (☎ 50 37 10; www.regenthotels.com; Zheltoksan 181) Has a well-stocked bookshop.

Cultural Centres & Useful Organisations
American Chamber of Commerce (☎ 58 79 38; fax 58 79 39; www.amcham.kz; Seyfullin 531, suite 414-416)

British Council (☎ 72 01 11, fax 72 02 07, www.britishcouncil.kz; Republic Square 13) There's a good English library and Internet facilities here, as well as a café.

Goethe Institute (☎ 47 27 04; Zhandosova 2; ⏰ 9am-5pm Mon-Fri, library 1-6.30pm Tue-Thu, 10am-2pm Fri)

Soros (☎ 50 38 14, 50 28 11; Furmanov 117-20) Support NGO for a variety of education and democracy building projects.

United Nations Development Program (UNDP; ☎ 58 26 43; fax 58 23 11; www.undp.kz; Töle Bi 67) Located between Zheltoksan and Naurybay Batyr. Unesco and OSCE are also located in this building.

Emergency
Ambulance (☎ 03)
Fire service (☎ 01)
Police (☎ 02)

Internet Access
You can access the Internet at a limited number of Internet cafés or pricey hotel business centres. The Hotel Zhetisu charges a reasonable 5 T per minute. KIMEP has a few Internet terminals in its bookshop.

Fight Club 2 (☎ 73 42 55; Zhibek Zholy 76; per hr US$2.25; ⏰ 24hr) The most central of three Internet/PC game centres in this chain. Fight Club 1 is at Shevchenko 110 (cnr Masanchi).

Net Surf (☎ 73 54 71; per hr US$2; Furmanov 48; ⏰ 10am-10pm) Located just north of Silk Way City shopping mall.

ALMATY MUST-SEES
PBC (RVS) Funky restaurant for the retro Soviet (p104).

Abay State Theatre of Opera & Ballet High-quality theatre at a bucket shop price (p105).

Barakholka This market is a vast mélange of junk and gems (p107).

Shymbulak Fresh powder a 40-minute drive from your door (p109).

Arasan Baths Get a good steam and thrashing (p100).

Stalker (☎ 91 20 46; Töle Bi 20; per hr US$1.50; ⏰ 10am-midnight) Its convenient location near Mad Murphy's is offset by its dreadfully slow connection.

Venezia (☎ 64 09 95; Dostyk 87a; per hr US$2.60; ⏰ 11am-midnight) Pricey, but a good connection and friendly atmosphere.

Medical Services
There are pharmacies (Kazakh: *dorikhana*, Russian: *apteka*) all over Almaty where you can buy most western medicines.

Grace Clinic (☎ 46 94 48; Abay 159; ⏰ 9am-2pm Mon, Wed & Fri) On the western side of town near Rozybakiev St. A checkup or consultation here costs under US$5.

International SOS (☎ 58 19 11; fax 58 15 85; Luganskogo 11; ⏰ 9am-6pm Mon-Fri) This expensive clinic charges nonmembers US$300 for a consultation.

Interteach (☎ 58 81 00, 58 85 41; Ayteke Bi 83; ⏰ 24hr) US$20 for a consultation.

Money
There are exchange kiosks on all main streets. Avoid kiosks in other very public places, such as the Zelyony Bazaar (Green Market), to minimise the risk of theft during or after the transaction.

An ATM is never too far away. Key locations include the SMAT supermarket opposite CATC, the TsUM department store, and the Ramstor shopping mall.

Central Asia Tourism Corporation (CATC; ☎ 50 10 70; www.centralasiatourism.com; Seyfullin 537) The local agent for American Express; it doesn't change travellers cheques but will start the process of replacement if you have lost yours.

Citibank (☎ 60 84 00; fax 60 83 99; Kazybek Bi 41; ⏰ 9am-4pm Mon-Fri) In the same building as the Japanese embassy.

Halyk Bank (☎ 50 03 16, 50 99 91; Masanchi 26) This main branch of the Halyk charges 2% to cash travellers

KAZAKHSTAN

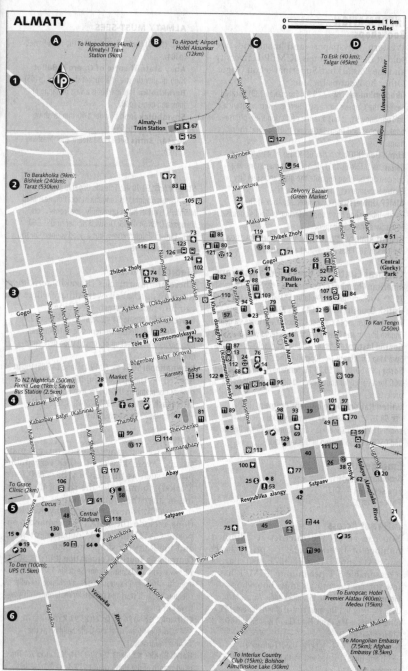

ALMATY

0 — 1 km
0 — 0.5 miles

A To Hippodrome (4km);
Almaty-1 Train
Station (9km)

B To Airport; Airport
Hotel Aksunkar
(12km)

D To Esik (40km);
Talgar (45km)

To Barakholka (9km);
Bishkek (240km);
Taraz (530km)

Almaty-II
Train Station

Almatinka River

Maloya River

Raiymbek

Zelyony Bazaar
(Green Market)

Mametova

Makataev

Zhibek Zholy

Gogol

Panfilov
Park

Central
(Gorky)
Park

Zhibek Zholy

Ayteke Bi (Oktyabrskaya)

Kazybek Bi (Sovyetskaya)

Töle Bi (Komsomolskaya)

Bögenbay Batyr (Kirova)

To Kan Tengri
(250km)

Gogol

To NZ Nightclub (500m);
Firma Geo (1km); Sayran
Bus Station (2.5km)

Karasay Batyr

Kabanbay Batyr (Kalinina)

Zhambyl

Shevchenko

Kurmanghazy

Abay

To Grace
Clinic (2km)

Circus

Central
Stadium

Satpaev

Respublika alangy

Satpaev

To Den (100m);
UPS (1.5km)

Markova

Timir yazev

To Europcar; Hotel
Premier Alatau (400m);
Medeu (15km)

To Interlux Country
Club (15km); Bolshoe
Almatinskoe Lake (30km)

Khadzhi Mukan

To Mongolian Embassy
(7.5km); Afghan
Embassy (8.5km)

Vesnovka River

cheques (changing cheques incurs a minimum US$2 charge).

Kazkommertzbank (☎ 50 51 07, 50 51 06; Baysetova 49) This main branch charges 2% to cash travellers cheques (minimum US$4 charge). Another branch is at the western end of TsUM department store.

Post

There are some international courier services in Almaty.

Central Post Office (Bögenbay Batyr 134; ☯ 8am-7pm Mon-Fri, 9am-5pm Sat & Sun) A branch office is also located opposite the east entrance to the TsUM.

DHL (☎ 58 85 88; fax 58 43 58; Zhandosova 1/1)
Federal Express (☎ 50 35 66; 50 35 68; Konaev 106)
UPS (☎ 50 31 94/95; ☎ /fax 41 49 80; Abay 153)

Registration

OVIR (☎ 54 41 44; cnr Baytursynuly & Karasay Batyr, 109; ☯ visa registration 10am-noon, passport return 6-7pm Mon, Tue, Wed & Fri) Registration for a single-entry visa is 800 T, and multiple entry is 1700 T.

Telephone & Fax

Card payphones are located all over the city; cards can be bought for around US$5 and up from telephone offices and street vendors in kiosks.

The upmarket hotels all have business centres offering long-distance and international phone and fax facilities; the cheapest rates are at the press centre in the Hotel Otrar.

KAZAKHSTAN

Central Kazakhtelekom Office (☎ 33 11 50, 33 44 70; fax 97 56 28; Zhibek Zholy 100; ☻ 24hr) Located a block east of the Zanghar (TsUM) department store. You can make international calls and send/receive faxes from here. Another useful branch is on Panfilov 129, behind the Hotel Almaty; it's open 8am to 6pm.

Travel Agencies

There are a number of general travel agencies useful for air and rail tickets, hotel bookings, visa letters of invitation (LOI), and the like.

ACS (☎ 91 26 28; www.acs-almaty.kz; Dostyk 27) English-speaking staff. Charges US$25/55 for visa registration/LOI. Excursions to Uzbekistan offered. Offices in Astana, Shymkent and Aktau.

Central Asia Tourism Corporation (CATC; ☎ 50 10 70; www.centralasiatourism.com; Seyfullin 537) Staff speak several European languages. Services include ticketing, rental cars, tours and accommodation arrangements. Clients can receive mail here and there are several branch offices in Kazakh cities. US$20/30 for visa registration/LOI.

Galaktika (☎ 47 37 36; fax 65 39 34; 1 Kotkem-3, apt 61) Small agency specialising in trips around Almaty. It can also arrange LOIs and visa registration.

Jibek Joly (☎ 50 04 00, 50 04 46; www.tourkz.com; Hotel Zhetisu, Abylay Khan 55) Can arrange full board at six cottages in the Almaty region. Office has small library of English and Japanese guidebooks for around Asia. Can also arrange ISIC cards for US$8. US$25 for visa LOI and registration.

Otrar Travel (☎ 33 13 75; Hotel Otrar, Gogol 73) Mostly of use as an airline agency.

Stan Tours (☎ 61 13 44; www.stantours.com; Konaev 163/76) Low-key operation with excellent personal service. Active tours to off-beat locations.

The following agencies specialise in mountaineering, trekking and tours, but some also do visa support and accommodation:

Asia Tourism (☎ 67 35 64/65; www.asiatour.org; Zheltoksan 160) A reputable operator. Visas can be arranged for Kazakhstan and neighbouring Central Asian countries.

Kan Tengri (☎ 91 02 00, 91 08 80; www.kantengri.kz; Kastayev 10) A leading mountain tourism firm, focusing on climbs, trekking, heli-skiing and ski-mountaineering in the Central Tian Shan and the ranges between Almaty and Lake Issyk-Kul. Around US$50 to US$70 per person per day for treks and climbs from Almaty. Also offers visa support for US$25.

Tour Asia (☎ 47 31 04; www.tourasia.kz; Markova 43) This long-established company offers trekking or mountaineering in the Central Tian Shan, Alatau, Altay and Fan mountains (in Tajikistan). Also arranges homestays in Almaty for US$20 without meals, US$30 with meals,

and provide visa support (US$25 if you don't book a tour, included in tour fee if you do).

Universities

Kazakhstan Institute of Management, Economics & Strategic Research (KIMEP; ☎ 70 42 00; www .kimep.kz; Abay 4) Almaty's premier English language further education institution; a good place to meet young Kazakhs and find out about the country. This is also your best chance for study in Kazakhstan. The Institute has an Internet café, bookshop and cafeteria.

DANGERS & ANNOYANCES

Almaty is a pretty safe town, but you should still exercise the usual precautions after dark (see p447).

Prostitution is common at many Almaty hotels: one traveller reported being phoned in the middle of the night by a prostitute who addressed him by name.

Scams

Although their sticky fingers have been washed somewhat, travellers still get shaken down by police. It's best not to carry much cash around, and you certainly wouldn't want to let any police search your wallet. If you are stopped on the street, show only a notarised photocopy passport and visa (provided by most embassies; see p153). Writing down a name and badge number keeps them honest. Travellers report being targeted by police at the train station, and when travelling across town with luggage (the obvious sign of a tourist).

Somewhat more worrying are reports by new arrivals who say their taxi driver had taken them to the Almaty outskirts and threatened to strand them. Only large sums of money could persuade them otherwise. To avoid complications, jot down the license number of your driver's car, give the exact address of the place you want to go, and try not to let on that you are an Almaty novice.

SIGHTS
Panfilov Park

This large rectangle of greenery, first laid out in the 1870s, is centred on the candy-coloured **Zenkov Cathedral**, designed by AP Zenkov in 1904. This is one of Almaty's few surviving tsarist-era buildings (most of the others were destroyed in the 1911 earthquake). Although at first glance it doesn't look like it, the cathedral is built entirely of wood – and apparently without nails. Used as a museum and concert hall in the Soviet era, then boarded up, it was returned to the Russian Orthodox Church in 1995 and is now a functioning place of worship.

The park is named for the Panfilov Heroes, commemorated at the fearsome **war memorial** east of the cathedral. This represents the 28 soldiers of an Almaty infantry unit who died fighting off Nazi tanks in a village on the outskirts of Moscow in 1941. An eternal flame commemorating the fallen of 1917–20 (the Civil War) and 1941–45 (WWII), flickers in front of the giant black monument of soldiers from all 15 Soviet republics bursting out of a map of the former USSR.

The park is on the routes of trolleybus No 1, 2, 8, 12 or 16 along Gogol from anywhere in the central area.

Central (Gorky) Park

Almaty's largest recreational area, at the eastern end of Gogol, 1km from the Hotel Otrar, is still known as Gorky Park. It has boating lakes, funfair rides, a zoo, several cafés, shashlyk and beer stands. It's busiest on Sunday and holidays. Entry is 20 T. Trolleybus No 1, 8, 12 and 16 run along Gogol to the entrance from anywhere in the central area.

Museums

In a striking 1908 wooden building at the east end of Panfilov Park is the **Museum of Kazakh Musical Instruments** (☎ 61 63 16; Zenkov 24; admission 100 T; ⏰ 10am-6pm Tue-Sun), the city's most visited museum. It has a fine collection of traditional Kazakh instruments – wooden harps and horns, bagpipes, the lutelike two-stringed *dombra* and the violalike three-stringed *kobiz*. Wait for a guided tour by an attendant who will press buttons on the displays to play tapes of the instruments and strum the *dombra* himself.

The nearby **Military Museum** (admission 200 T; ⏰ 10am-6pm), filled with unflinching memories of war-time heroics, is usually unlocked by a caretaker downstairs.

The intriguing **Geological Museum** (☎ 68 52 83; cnr Dostyk & Abay; admission 100 T; ⏰ 9am-6pm Tue-Fri) is in the bowels of the Kazakh Business Centre. Kazakhstan's mineral wealth is on display, plus touch screen computers to provide quick geology lessons in English.

One of the city's best museums stands 300m uphill from Respublika alangy. The

THE GOLDEN MAN

The Golden Man (Zolotoy Chelovek in Russian, Altyn Adam in Kazakh) is a warrior's costume that was found in a Saka tomb near Esik, about 60km east of Almaty. It is made of over 4000 separate gold pieces – many of them finely worked with animal motifs. It also has a 70cm-high headdress bearing skyward-pointing arrows, a pair of snarling snow leopards and a two-headed winged mythical beast. There's some confusion about its age – the Central State Museum says it's from the 12th century AD but most other sources put its origin at about the 5th century BC. Its Scythian-style artwork would certainly favour the latter. The original of this treasure, considered too fragile to be pieced together for display, resides in the vaults of Kazakhstan's National Bank. Meanwhile, research and debate continues about who, or what, this Golden Man really was. Recent studies show that Kazakhstan's adopted symbol of war and strength was mostly like a woman.

Central State Museum (☎ 64 22 00, 64 55 77; Furmanov 44; admission 60 T; ⏰ 10am-5pm) gives a worthwhile if patchy picture of Kazakhstan's history. The downstairs rooms cover early history, including another miniature replica of the Golden Man (see above), while upstairs has displays of the Soviet and modern eras, including exhibits on space flight from the Baykonur Cosmodrome, nuclear testing at Semey, and the Aral Sea. Get there by bus Nos 2, 11 or 100 going up Furmanov from Gogol.

The **Kasteyev Museum of Fine Arts** (☎ 47 83 56; admission 80 T, guided tour US$20; Satpaev 30a) has the best collection of art in the country, including works of artists banned during the Soviet period. There are also collections of Russian and West European art, with some fine works by in vogue artist Sergei Kalmykov. Particularly interesting is a one-room section of Kazakh handicrafts, and the Soviet-era paintings glorifying the workers in fields, mines and kitchens. Marshrutnoes heading west on Satpaev (No 507, 520 or 562) will stop here.

A recently installed **Museum of Repression** (☎ 62 03 59; Nauryzbay Batyr 180; admission 80 T; ⏰ 9am-6pm Mon-Fri) goes into haunting detail about the fate of thousands of Kazakhs and Russians who earned Stalin's ire. It's located in the former NKVD (forerunner to the KGB) headquarters.

Cable Car to Köktyube

This rickety **cable car** (one-way 100 T; ⊗ 11am-7pm) runs from beside the Palace of the Republic on Dostyk up to Köktyube (green peak), a foothill of the Zailiysky Alatau, crowned by the landmark **TV transmitter centre**. There's a viewing platform and shashlyk stands at the top cable car station. If you visit during the day, the hike down the hill back to Dostyk is a pleasant one.

Respublika Alangy

This broad ceremonial square at the high southern end of Almaty, created in Soviet times, is a block uphill from Abay. The focal point on the Satpaev side is the attractive **Monument to Independence**. The column is surmounted with a replica of the Golden Man and flanked at its base by fountains and two bas-relief walls depicting scenes from Kazakhstan's history. At the centre of the square is the neo-classical **city government building** and, at the southeast corner opposite the Central State Museum, the official **Presidential Residence**, an ugly modern building also known as the 'White House'. You can reach the square on bus Nos 2, 11 or 100 going up Furmanov from Gogol.

St Nicholas Cathedral

The pale turquoise St Nicholas (Nikolsky Sobor), with its gold onion domes, stands out west of the centre on the corner of Kabanbai Batyr and Baytursynuly. The cathedral was built in 1909 and later used as a stable for Bolshevik cavalry, before reopening about 1980. It's a terrifically atmospheric place, like a corner of old Russia, with icons and candles inside and black-clad old supplicants outside. For the best impression visit at festival times such as Orthodox Christmas Day (7 January) or Easter for the midnight services.

ACTIVITIES

At the **Arasan Baths** (☎ 72 40 90; cnr Ayteke Bi & Konaev; admission before 2pm US$2.25, after 4pm US$3.75, 20-minute massage US$7; ⊗ 8am-8pm Tue-Sun) you can choose from three options: Russian (*Russkaya banya*), Finnish (*Finskaya banya*) or Turkish (*Vostochnaya banya*) baths, the

latter with three different temperatures of heated stone platforms plus a plunge pool. Sessions begin every two hours. Take along soap, a towel and some thongs (flip-flops) for walking around in. If you don't have any bathing gear at hand, there's a shop in the lobby. There are sellers with bunches of myrtle leaves outside, if you fancy giving yourself a good thrashing.

Daulet (☎ 92 20 69; Markova 183; single entry 500 T, monthly 15,000 T) is a large gym just off Satpaev near the Central Stadium. There is also a gym and good clay tennis courts at the **Army Central Sports Club** (Satpaev; per hr US$3) near the crossing with Furmanov.

Located near the Central Stadium is the **Olympic Skating Rink** (☎ 92 90 77; per hr 400 T; ⊗ 9am-7pm Mon-Fri, 10am-5pm Sat & Sun) The **Dinamo Stadium** (cnr Shevchenko & Nauryzbay Batyr 89) also has a large rink and the **Ramstor Shopping Mall** has a small one. The biggest skating rink in Central Asia is at **Medeu** (see p109).

Almaty's best **public swimming pool** (☎ 92 37 68; Abay 48; per hr 500 T, 12 visits 5000 T; ⊗ 8am-9pm) is next to the Central Stadium, behind a building that looks like an aircraft hangar. There are also indoor and outdoor public swimming pools at the Dinamo Stadium.

TPF Bowling (☎ 92 70 66; Satpaev 31/1) is Almaty's biggest bowling alley and is near the Daulet gym.

Ultimate Frisbee matches are held between April and November on Thursday at 7pm and Saturday at 3pm on the soccer pitch at the **Agricultural Institute** (Abay), at the end of Tölebaev.

Fun runners can catch the **Hash House Harriers** (admission 400 T) at Mad Murphy's (see p103) November to April on Sunday at 3pm and the rest of the year at 5pm.

Activities for children include the **Aqua Park** (adult/child 1500 T/950 T; ⊗ 10am-6pm), part of which is enclosed for winter use, inside Gorky Park. **Fantasy Land Amusement Park** costs 600 T to enter and then additional charges for individual rides.

TOURS

Anatoli Nekhororshev (☎ 54 66 36, 54 54 79; fax 54 52 24) A local guide who specialises in trekking trips in the Zailiysky Alatau.

Karlygash Makatova (☎ 71 26 17, mobile 8300 755 2086; http://asiaadventuretours.lorton.com), a Kazakh sportswoman, has long organised trips

ALMATY WALKING TOUR

Respublika alangay is the best place to start a walking tour; not only is it all downhill from here, but on a clear morning the square provides a panoramic view of the snowcapped mountains. Head east along Satpaev past the **Army Central Sports Club (1)** on the right; when you hit Dostyk, you'll notice an observatory building uphill; this is the **Republican Palace of Schoolchildren (2)**. Downhill, behind the large statue of the writer Abay Kunabaev and the **Palace of the Republic (3)**, you could make a detour to take the **cable car (4)** to Köktyube for a view across the city.

A block north of the **Hotel Kazakhstan (5)**, turn west along Shevchenko to find the magnificent **Academy of Sciences (6)** building, one of the true gems of Soviet monumental architecture. Fountains and parks around the building make this a cool spot to linger in summer. Check out the 'Eastern Calendar' fountain with Chinese zodiac creatures on the east side of the academy.

It's pleasant to continue heading north along tree-lined Tölebaev until you reach Kabanbai Batyr and turn west to reach the neoclassical **Abay State Theatre of Opera and Ballet (7)**. Two blocks north of here is a small park in front of what used to be Kazakhstan's **Old House of Parliament (8)** (before it shifted to Astana) and which now houses local government offices. In the park you'll find a statue to local war heroes Manshuk Mametova and Alie Moldagulova, which replaced the one of Lenin, removed after independence.

Heading east along Töle Bi, you can turn north to reach **Panfilov Park (9)** on Dostyk (p98). To the north of here is the **Ze-lyony Bazaar (10)**, Almaty's most colourful market, with a true flavour of Central Asia.

Just north of the market you'll notice the turquoise dome of Almaty's new central **mosque (11)**, the largest in the country.

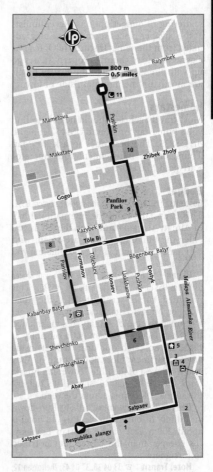

good way to meet locals and expats. This is the one chance you might have to tag along on an otherwise extremely expensive helicopter trip.

FESTIVALS & EVENTS

Horse-racing events are held at the Hippodrome (Ippodrome), north of the centre, during holidays. The biggest and best organised races are held during Nauryz.

In early August, the **Voice of Asia** pop festival is held at Medeu (see p109).

SLEEPING

As a town more involved in business and less in tourism, Almaty has some fine choices in the top-end category, but only a

for the expat community and offers trips to Charyn Canyon, Lake Issyk-Kul, Bolshoe Almatinskoe Lake, skiing at Shymbulak, boating on the Ili River, climbing in the Zailiysky Alatau, riding and trekking. Her trips are spirited, not too expensive, and a scattering of budget options. Receptionists at the cheaper places seem to have all graduated from the same 'Institute of Ogres'. As a general rule of thumb, property values go up with the elevation so the luxury hotels are mostly on the mountain side of town.

Homestays

Most travel agencies should be able to find you a homestay for around US$15 per night, or US$25. The best ones to ask are Stan Tours, or the independent tour operator Karlygash Makatova.

Budget

Gostinitsa (☎ 60 42 13; dm with shared bathroom US$2) This is upstairs from the international hall of Almaty-II train station, on the left as you enter the building. Dorms are small, with two hard beds, but may be acceptable if you arrive late.

Ulytau (☎ 61 96 97; Furmanov 176; r with shared bathroom US$10, with private bathroom US$30) This unsigned, rather scruffy hotel is the usual stop for budget backpackers who can't get a room at the Hotel Almaty. It's nicknamed the 'Shag Palace' and can get a bit noisy at night if you catch our drift. It's set inside an old apartment block 150m south of Abay and southwest of the Eiffel Tower landmark. Look for the 'Konak ui' sign. If it's full, try the similar place just across the road.

Den (☎ 73 75 22; Zhandosova 1; r US$10) Run-down and dimly lit but habitable, this old hotel is about 200m east of the Russian Embassy. It's cheaper than the Ulytau, but not used to foreigners.

Hotel Transit (☎ 33 04 38, 33 04 43; Zheltoksan 12; r US$17, 3 hrs US$7) Located just outside Almaty II train station, this place has clean rooms with private bathroom and TV. It's OK for a night or brief crash pad if you arrive late.

Mid-Range

Hotel Zhetisu (☎ 50 04 00; www.zhetysuhotel.kz; Abay-lay Khan 55; s with shared bathroom US$15, s/d with private bathroom US$37/47; 🖳) Centrally located and at the bottom end of this range in standard and price. There are some cheap in-house services including a barber, gift shop, Internet café and a helpful travel agency. It's located near the TsUM, about 1km from Almaty-II train station (trolleybus Nos 4, 5 or 6).

Hotel Almaty (☎ 72 00 70/47; www.hotel-almaty .kz; Kabanbay Batyr 85; s/d US$10/60; 🖳) This large concrete pile is opposite the Abay State Theatre of Opera & Ballet. The single rooms on the 6th floor are one of the best budget deals in Almaty. Front side rooms have good mountain views but are virtually lit-up by annoying floodlights at night, but backside rooms suffer from a noisy café, so pick your poison. There is a decent little cafeteria on the 3rd floor. Calling for a reservation doesn't help as they're always 'full'; try visiting in person. You can reach the hotel by trolleybus Nos 4, 5, or 6 which run along Abylay Khan from Almaty-II station.

Saya Hotel (☎ 61 32 65; fax 63 16 11; Furmanov 135; s/d US$40/50) Near to the Hotel Almaty and with better-value double rooms.

Hotel Kazakhstan (☎ 91 91 01/25; www.hotel -kazakhstan.kz; Dostyk 52; r US$42-133; 🖳) This 26-floor hotel was built in 1977 and is still Almaty's tallest building. Rooms are standard Soviet tourist-hotel issue, although the more expensive ones have been renovated and all include satellite TV. Prices include a good buffet breakfast in the top floor Cosmos Café, which is also open to nonguests.

Interlux Country Club (☎ 54 97 65, 54 93 94; fax 54 96 82; s/d US$63/94; 🐾) This is some 15km south of the centre in the village of Kamenka (best accessible via taxi). It's also known as the Alatau Sanatorium (this was once the resort for top party officials) and offers – in addition to comfortable rooms with satellite TV and phone – a gym, sauna, tennis courts and an 18-hole golf course.

Kazzhol (☎ 50 89 41, hotel-kazzhol@arna.kz; Gogol 127/1; s/d/lux US$24/46/56; 🖳) Smart rooms with fridge, TV and phone. It's set back in a block between Nauryzbay Batyr and Seyfullin.

Uyut (☎ 32 32 88; s/d US$24/46; Gogol; 🖳) Next door to Kazzhol, this hotel is similar.

Top End

Hotel Otrar (☎ 50 68 30/40; www.group.kz; Gogol 73; d/ste US$94/140; 🍴 🖳) This is the cheapest of the upmarket hotels. Occupying a good location facing Panfilov Park, it has comfortable rooms with cable TV and a good help-yourself breakfast. Take trolleybus Nos 1, 2, 8, 12 or 16 along Gogol from anywhere in the central area.

Hotel Dostyk (☎ 58 22 70; www.dostyk.kz; cnr Konaev & Kurmanghazy 36; s/d/lux US$125/175/200; 🍴 🖳) This grand old hotel was an old Soviet cadre favourite. The romantic ambience is still there, with its high ceilings, marble foyer and location on a quiet and leafy lane. Rooms are tastefully renovated and in summer there is a good grill restaurant out back.

Regent Almaty (☎ 50 37 10–19 nine lines; www .regenthotels.com; Zheltoksan 181; s/d/lux 295/320/380; 🅿 🖵) Located just west of Respublika alangy, this glitzy hotel has all the usual five-star amenities including a health club, nightclub, casino, business centre and three restaurants. It offers complimentary pick-ups at the airport for international flights.

Rental Accommodation

Your first resource in seeking accommodation should be the expat website www .expat.kz. If you can read/speak Russian, the weekly classified ads newspaper *Karavan* lists people renting out apartments and rooms. The staff at Hotel Otrar (see p102) are also helpful and might be able to find you an inexpensive apartment for around US$20 per night. Landlords seeking to rent out apartments on a short-term basis hang around on the road in front of the Zhetisu Hotel. Rental agencies include **Checkpoint** (☎ 50 15 11; www.checkpoint.kz; Kurmanghazy 32).

EATING

Enjoy the good range of restaurants and cafés in Almaty – they're the best you'll find in the country. With a couple of exceptions, traditional Kazakh cuisine is rare, but favourites such as shashlyk, *laghman* and *manty* abound. During the warmer months, several of Almaty's cafés and restaurants have tables outside, too.

Cafés

Thomi's Pastries (☎ 67 08 69; Furmanov 152; coffee 150 T; 🕑 lunch & dinner) Very good coffee, cakes and sticky things. You'll also find Thomi's Pastries outlets inside malls scattered across the city.

Restaurants

American Bar & Grill (☎ 50 50 13; Töle Bi 41; hamburgers US$2-4; 🕑 lunch & dinner) This place has what is reputed to be Almaty's best hamburger. There is an inside section, but in summer all the action is in the streetside wooden annex designed by an apparent Roy Rogers fan.

Bombolo (☎ 73 44 99; Abylay Goz 6a; chicken shashlyk US$2.50; 🕑 lunch & dinner) Located next to the TsUM, this trendy meeting place serves up good shashlyk but mediocre pizza. The

bathrooms here are unique but ridiculously small.

Inara (☎ 91 78 06; Kaldayakov 58; 🕑 lunch & dinner) Located opposite the Philharmonic Central Concert Hall, this odd, arboretum-style restaurant has friendly service, a buzzy atmosphere and big, cheap plates of barbecued meat with onion and cucumber trimmings. It's certainly a more authentic Kazakh experience than Almaty's most popular shashlyk restaurants.

Mad Murphy's (☎ 91 28 56; Töle Bi 12; sandwiches US$7-10, fajitas US$20, milkshake US$3; 🕑 lunch & dinner) This quintessential Irish pub has a lively expat atmosphere and a friendly Australian bartender. The food, a variety of Western options, is overpriced but does come in large portions.

Old England (☎ 69 51 04; Bögenbay Batyr 134; main dishes US$5-10; 🕑 lunch & dinner) A stylish but not particularly British-looking place. Roast beef and Yorkshire pudding and bread and butter pudding are on the menu along with caviar and blinis (US$14.50).

Solyanka (☎ 62 65 56; Panfilov 100; 🕑 10am-3pm & 4-9pm; 🕑 breakfast, lunch & dinner) This clean cafeteria-style restaurant is Almaty's old standby. Russian and Kazakh food is served by helpful staff and the outdoor food bar in summer is great for a quick bite.

Pizza & Grill Pub (☎ 62 44 47; Zheltolksan 146; 🕑 lunch & dinner) The Knights of the Round Table interior doesn't quite match the menu, which has nachos, calzone and about 30 types of pizza. But the service is quick and friendly and it's recommended by expats.

Pizzeria Venezia (☎ 64 09 95; Dostyk 87a; pizza US$5-10; 🕑 lunch & dinner; 🖵) Venezia was the first place to introduce a decent pizza to Almaty and it is still a contender for the city's best pie. It also offers pasta dishes, but makes very bad cappuccino.

Stetson (☎ 62 94 93; www.stetson.kz; Furmanov 128; meals US$3-5; 🕑 lunch & dinner) Has an English menu and American-style hamburgers, chicken and salads. It's a popular expat hang-out also favoured by nouveau riche/ Mafia types.

Tropicana (☎ 93 72 53; www.tropicana.kz; Shevchenko 99; 🕑 24hr) Fruity drinks, yogurt shakes and light meals are the specialties of this 24-hour palm tree–fringed eatery. Most evenings you can see a tacky Latin supershow of dancing girls in big flowery hats. It's located next to a small Dastarkhan Supermarket.

KAZAKHSTAN

THE AUTHOR'S CHOICE

Yubileyny Food Market (cnr Abylay & Gogol; ☉ breakfast, lunch & dinner) Hats off to the bloke who introduced tortilla-wrapped doner kebabs (US$1) to Almaty. Long lines form all day for these tasty creations, stuffed with meat, sour cream, sliced carrot and French fries, served at two locations near the entrance. Snacking on other goodies at the nearby stalls makes for a perfect lunch on the go.

Govindas (☎ 71 08 36; Abylay Khan 39; thali US$4) This vegetarian Indian restaurant, run by Hare Krishnas, serves as its specialty Gujarati and Rajasthani *thali*, lightly spiced for the Western palate, of course. The walls are hung with kitsch Indian art and there is a small shop selling religious paraphernalia. Although things change pretty quick in Almaty, this was the 'in' place.

Jeti Kazina (☎ 73 25 87; Abylay Khan 58a; meals US$5-6) This Uzbek-themed restaurant is the place to go for ethnic central Asian cooking at its finest. Old favourites like *manty* (steamed dumplings), *laghman* (noodles) and samsas are styled for the Western palate, and there are a few Kazakh specialties on the menu too. It is at least worth patronising for the colourful ambience and welcoming staff, far nicer than Caramel, the staid European restaurant upstairs, or Meramkhana, the dim Japanese/Chinese restaurant in the basement.

PBC (RVS; ☎ 69 62 41, 69 55 81; Furmanov 103; meals US$4-5) This likeable restaurant transports you back down Soviet memory lane, with its Iron Curtain artefacts: KGB recording devices, sputnik murals and banners, Stalin photos and Lenin busts. The food, decidedly not Soviet-style, includes vegetarian burritos, hamburgers, lasagne, salads and steaks. Done up in CCCP (USSR) T-shirts, the waitresses hand out souvenir Soviet propaganda postcards after your meal – something to scare the folks back home.

Soccer Bar (☎ 62 23 63; Konaev 163; pizzas US$3-5; ☉ lunch & dinner) If there are any mad English football hooligans hiding out in Almaty, they can be found at the soccer bar. The walls are plastered with jerseys and gear, and the TV inside is usually playing a live or recorded premiership match. The pizza is one of the best you can get in town. The pasta, however, is a little dry.

Thai (☎ 91 01 90; Dostyk 50; meal & drink US$30-40) This swank new restaurant with a pleasant outdoor Japanese tea garden outside specialises in Thai and Japanese dishes. The quality is high and the fish used in most dishes is flown in direct from Dubai. It's best to pay by cash here.

Teatralina Café (☎ 72 87 77; Zhambyl 51a; European meals US$10-13, Kazakh meals US$4.50-6) *The* place to go for a pre- or post-theatre dinner, Teatralina is decorated with old black-and-white photos of Almaty's quaint theatre in its younger years. Afternoon tea and sandwiches are served from 3pm to 5pm. The Caesar salad is spot on.

Self-Catering

Dastarkhan Supermarket (☎ 34 74 13; cnr Abylay Khan & Gogol; ☉ 8am-midnight) This is probably the biggest supermarket in Almaty, with a deli and all manner of Western food and toiletries. Another Dastarkhan is located at Shevchenko 75 between Baytursynuly and Masanchi.

Ramstor (Furmanov 226; ☉ 8am-10pm) This modern shopping mall is the biggest in the city,

but most items you'll find elsewhere (albeit not under one roof) at cheaper prices.

Zelyony Bazaar (Green Market; Zhibek Zholy 53; ☉ 8am-5pm Tue-Sun) Lots of vegetables, fresh and dried fruit, nuts and dairy products, including *kumys* and *shubat* (fermented camel's milk), are sold at this large central market. There's also a smaller farmer's market by St Nicholas Cathedral, west of the centre on Baytursynuly.

Other options for self-caterers include **Rossia** (cnr Dostyk & Kabanbai Batyr) and **SMAK** (cnr Seyfullin & Töle Bi).

Street Stalls

Good for a quick bite is Zelyony Bazaar (see above) with its stalls selling plov, *manty* and shashlyk outside the main hall. Inside there are cafés overlooking the market action where a bowl of *laghman*, tea and bread will cost less than US$2.

DRINKING

Finding a drink for any budget isn't difficult in Almaty as many daytime cafés and restaurants become dim bars by night. There is no bar district, but beer gardens under umbrellas tend to sprout around Zhibek Zholy in summer. Mad Murphy's (see p103) is a popular place with expats for a stout, pub grub and watching football.

Dublin Pub (☎ 615616; almaty_irishpub@dublin.com; Baysetova 45; ☺ 10-3am) Almaty's other Irish pub is located at the southern end of town near Respublika alangy. It's a friendly place popular with business people spending their petro dollars.

Guinness Pub (☎ 91 55 85; Dostyk 71; ☺ 1pm-2am) Located near the Hotel Kazakhstan, this pub has the famous Irish stout on tap as well as billiard tables, darts, backgammon and the occasional jazz band.

Rock Bar (Festival Rock Café; ☎ 79 19 68; Abylay Khan 65; ☺ noon-2am) Almaty's very own imitation Hard Rock Café. It is a pleasant place with an outdoor area beside a fountain. It can get a bit smoky in here.

Soho (☎ 67 03 67, 69 66 15; Kazybek Bi 65; ☺ 9pm-3am) The young A-listers line up for pints of beer in this loud bar near Panfilov Park. It's got a sort of urban/global theme, with lots of pictures of New York mixed in with flags for every nationality. You'll see a lot of pudgy east European gentlemen with skinny Kazakh girls on their arms, and everyone else causing havoc on the crowded dance floor.

ENTERTAINMENT
Cinema

English-language films are usually dubbed into Russian.

Dom Kino (☎ 91 84 80; Kazybek Bi 20a) Located next to the Australian and Italian embassies, this theatre hosts international film festivals occasionally.

Iskra (☎ 50 50 10; Dostyk 44; admission US$4, half-price Mon) Next to the supermarket Rossia, this renovated theatre shows Hollywood and European blockbusters.

KIMEP Movie Club (KIMEP University, cnr Dostyk & Abay) Screening British and German films, usually on Monday; check the notice boards around campus for details.

NOMAD Cinema (☎ 50 50 11; Ramstor shopping mall, Furmanov 226; admission 150-650 T) Screens recent US films. Matinée prices are cheaper.

Concerts, Ballet, Opera & Theatre

Almaty is blessed with a good theatre scene and you should attempt to catch at least one performance while you're there. Keep your eye open for posters advertising the good Otrar Sazy Kazakh Folk Orchestra.

Abay State Theatre of Opera and Ballet (☎ 62 84 45, 72 79 34; fax 62 79 63; Kabanbai Batyr 110) Almaty's top venue for theatre; almost daily performances at 6.30pm. *Swan Lake*, *Barber of Seville* and *Carmen* are a few of the regular shows. Also, look out for the Kazakh opera *Abay*.

Almaty Youth Theatre (☎ 71 42 37; Abylay Khan 38) Amateur theatre that has staged dramatic plays on Kazakh societal and national problems.

Auezov Kazakh State Academic Drama Theatre (☎ 92 33 07; Abay 105) Elegant example of Soviet architecture with regular drama performances.

Lermontov State Academic Russian Drama Theatre (☎ 62 82 73; Abay 43) Stages plays by Kazakh and Russian writers.

Kazkontsert Hall (☎ 62 01 26; Abylay Khan 83) Classical and pipe organ music concerts.

Kurmangazy Conservatory (☎ 67 90 87, 62 76 40; Abylay Khan 90) Inexpensive classical concerts; next to the main post office.

Philharmonic Central Concert Hall (☎ 91 80 48, 91 75 41; cnr Töle Bi & Kaldayakov 35) A range of performances including pipe organ, jazz, classical and traditional music. International performers invited by Almaty embassies often play here.

Gay & Lesbian Venues

There's a small underground scene in Almaty and the gay bars tend to come and go, so you might need to ask around to find out what is new. For updated club info see www.gays.kz.

Eros (☎ 73 17 11; Zhibek Zholy 50; admission Mon-Fri 300 T, Sat & Sun 500 T) This attracts both straight and gay patrons. Lesbians get in free on Monday nights. It's opposite Zelyony Bazaar.

NZ (☎ 68 12 10; Nurmakova 117 & Kazybek Bi; admission 300 T; ☺ 10pm-6am) This was the pioneering gay club in Almaty and maintains its speak-easy traditions – to get in you have to ring a buzzer at an unmarked door. Nurmakova is a small lane about 1.5km west of the centre. NZ is located in a two-storey building on the left, look for the sign 'Akzhol' above the entrance.

Real Club (☎ 39 34 73; Makataev 126; admission 500 T, beer 200 T; ☺ 10pm-4am) A dimly lit bar with drag shows on most nights. The Real

Club is a dumpy little place but attracts an enthusiastic crowd.

Spartacus (☎ 39 34 73; Dosmukhamedov 115; admission men/women 400/800 T; ☽ 10pm-4am) This popular club has a professional strip show on Fridays, a transvestite show on Saturdays and good dance music. The cover charge goes up after midnight. It is located down a narrow lane between Abay and Kurmanghazy; there is no sign but look for the long outdoor stairway, next to a billiards hall. At the northern end of the street is a Kazakhtelekom office.

Live Music

Aiia Disco (☎ 47 61 11; Fantasy Land Amusement Park, Abay 50a) Live bands usually play here on the weekend, though it's more of a teenybopper hang-out.

Jazz Rock Café (☎ 61 18 64; Zheltolksan 118; ☽ 3pm-3am) Recently moved to this new location, this place puts on jazz every Wed, Thu, Fri and Sat 11pm to 2am.

Members Bar (☎ 50 37 10; Regent Almaty, Zheltoksan 181; ☽ 4pm-midnight) Cocktail lounge–style jazz music. Happy hour is from 7pm to 8pm.

Nightclubs

Almaty's club scene isn't bad, although the popular places disappear on a periodic basis. Casinos are attached to all of Almaty's top hotels but are best avoided unless you're up to rubbing shoulders with Mafia-types and their molls. A fun, if trendy, place for dancing is the Soho bar (see p105).

Petroleum (☎ 62 18 91, 69 27 14; fl 5, Shevchenko 100; ☽ 10pm-6am) This ultra-flash, glass and steel dance club, pumping out rave and hip-hop, is suitable for the mobster in you. It's above the equally swank Primo restaurant in a building near the Peace Corps office. This is one place where you may want to dress up.

Sport Club (Central Stadium, Abay 48; admission 500 T, beer 150 T; ☽ midnight-6am Fri & Sat) This outdoor club with freely flowing alcohol draws a young, unpretentious, local crowd. The music is all over the place, ranging from rap to alternative to old Soviet hymns. It's not so touristy so there are relatively few working girls.

Tequila Sunrise (☎ 73 70 46; Hotel Otrar, Gogol 73; admission 200 T; ☽ 8pm-4am) One of the more sleazy late-night expat hang-outs, this one has all the charm of a wild west saloon pumping out techno.

Sport

Horse races and occasionally *kökpar* (or *buzkashi*), a pololike game played with an animal carcass (see Buzkashi on p54), are held at the **Hippodrome** (☎ 94 86 00; Zhansugurov & Akhan Sere), several kilometres north of the centre. Take a taxi or bus Nos 30 or 34 north on Seyfullin to Dulatov, then walk three blocks west. Get someone to call ahead and see what's on.

Almaty's soccer team Kayrat plays its home games at the Central Stadium. Kazakh baseball teams play regularly at a field behind the stadium on Saturday evenings in June and July.

SHOPPING

Partly pedestrianised Zhibek Zholy is the street with the biggest cluster of shops for all your needs.

TsUM (cnr Abylay Khan & Zhibek Zholy) This central department store is worth a look. Downstairs all manner of electronic goods are sold; on the 2nd floor you'll mainly find clothes, while on the top floor there are stalls selling a selection of kitsch Kazakh crafts and other souvenirs.

Silk Way City (Zhibek Zholy) This modern air-conditioned shopping mall lies east of TsUM.

Tengri Umai Modern Art Gallery (Abay 43) The best selection of modern art. This gallery is located on the ground floor of the Lermontov State Academic Russian Drama Theatre, and you'll find lots of original artwork and jewellery.

Mekha (cnr Panfilov & Kurmanghazy 157) The place to go for fur hats, as well as other fur and leather items.

Sport Land ☎ 62 70 72; Tole Bi 78; ☽ 10am-9pm) Sporting goods are available here; located opposite the UNDP building.

Ramstor (Furmanov) Kazakhstan's first shopping mall, just south of the Central State Museum. It has a range of generally expensive import shops as well as a food court, a small skating rink and a movie theatre.

The craft and carpet stalls at the Central State Museum are worth a look, as are the ones in the Kasteyev Museum of Fine Arts.

Markets

Zelyony Bazaar (Green Market; Zhibek Zholy 53; ☽ 8am-5pm Tue-Sun) A sprawling place that has a big indoor hall and vendors spread outside too. Watch out for pickpockets. Much of it is devoted to food (see p104) but there are stalls with clothing and other goods.

Barakholka (☉ Tue-Sun) This big, busy flea market (otherwise known as the *Veshchevoy rynok*) is 10km from the centre in the western suburbs. Uzbeks, Chinese, Uyghurs and others converge here to sell everything from animals and cars to fur hats and (if you're lucky) carpets. The pet section is among the most interesting. Weekends, especially early Sunday morning, are the busiest times (it's not always open other days). Watch out for pickpockets here, too. Buses going there include Nos 71, 140 and 530 westbound on Raiymbek (you can pick it up at Abylay Khan).

A curious flea market in stamps, coins and lapel pins is held in the Central Park, just north of the funfair area, on Sunday.

GETTING THERE & AWAY

Almaty is also the hub of internal Kazakhstan flights and is linked to most major Kazakhstan cities by daily trains. Long-distance buses reach many cities in northern and eastern Kazakhstan, but for the sake of comfort, a long haul is best done by train.

Air

During production of this book Air Kazakhstan went into bankruptcy. As such, the information contained here might have changed. It seems that Air Astana will be picking up many of Air Kazakhstan's routes, but please check with your airline or travel agent.

Almaty has flights to/from about 15 other cities in Kazakhstan. Prices (correct at the time of research) given are for one-way flights from Almaty; they're often cheaper from regional cities back to Almaty. At the time of research, flights went once or more daily to: Astana (US$135), Atyrau (US$220), Karaghanda (US$121), Ust-Kamenogorsk (US$112), Pavlodar (US$124) and Shymkent (US$105); six times a week to Kyzylorda (US$80) and Kostanai (US$150); five times a week to Aktau (US$182), Aktöbe (US$193) and Kökshetau (US$136); four times a week to Petropavlovsk (US$136) and Semey (US$85); and three times a week to Uralsk (US$164). For connections to other

Central Asian countries see p157. For international connections see below.

Air Irtysh flies to Ust-Kamenogorsk. Air Astana has limited domestic service to Aktöbe, Atyrau, Aktau, Astana and Uralsk.

AIRLINE OFFICES

Air Astana (☎ 58 82 02; www.air-astana.kz; Hotel Otrar, Gogol 73) To/from Astana (US$135), Aktau (US$183), Aktöbe (US$194), Moscow (US$215), Beijing (US$332), Dubai (US$253).

Air China (Xinjiang Airlines; ☎ 30 04 86; fax 50 94 85; Arikova 36) Ürümqi twice a week US$202.

Asiana Airlines (☎ 67 84 59; Airport Hotel Aksunkar) Seoul weekly, with connections to Asia, Australia and the US west coast.

Austrian Airlines (☎ 50 10 70; fax 50 17 07; Central Asia Tourism Corporation, Seyfullin 537) Vienna three times a week.

British Airways (☎ 50 36 24, 50 36 28; Abylay Khan 115) London (US$850) three times a week.

Iran Air (☎ 57 28 27; fax 57 28 47; Airport Hotel Aksunkar, Rm 111) Tehran weekly.

KLM (☎ 50 77 47; fax 50 91 83; Hotel Otrar, Gogol 73) Amsterdam three times a week.

Lufthansa (☎ 50 50 52; fax 50 50 62; Hyatt Regency Almaty, Satpaev 29/6) Daily flights to Frankfurt.

PIA (☎ /fax 57 29 48/02; Airport Hotel Aksunkar, Rm 117) Islamabad and Lahore weekly.

Turkish Airlines (☎ 50 62 20, 50 10 67; fax 50 62 19; Kazybek Bi 81) Istanbul four times a week.

Turkmenistan Airlines (☎ 72 35 31; Euro Tours, cnr Furmanov & Abay) Ashgabat twice a week.

Uzbekistan Airlines (☎ 50 68 31; Hotel Otrar, Gogol 73) To Tashkent daily, except Sunday.

Bus

Long-distance buses use the **Sayran bus station** (Novy avtovoksal; ☎ 26 46 44, 26 28 55; cnr Töle Bi & Mate Zalki; ☉ left luggage 5-3am), about 3.5km west of the centre. Services include Balkash, Ust-Kamenogorsk and Karaghanda (one bus each daily), Taraz and Shymkent (two or three buses daily), Taldy-Korghan (one daily) and Zharkent (two or three buses daily). For buses to Ürümqi (China) and information on border crossing at Khorgos, see p157.

You can reach Sayran on bus No 43 heading west on Töle Bi from the corner of Zheltoksan, or tram Nos 4 or 7 heading west on Shevchullin anywhere between Konaev and Seyfullin. Heading into the city, catch these outside Sayran on Töle Bi, going east. Trolleybus No 19 from opposite the Sayakhat bus station also goes there.

Nearer destinations are served by the **Sayakhat bus station** (Stary Avtovoksal; ☎ 30 08 82, 30 25 29; Raiymbek). Buses go at least hourly to Esik, Kapshaghai (one hour) and Talgar (40 minutes); and between one and four times daily to Chilik (two hours), Kegen (four hours) and Narynkol (six to seven hours); and one or two times daily to Zharkent (five hours). There are also infrequent buses to Saty and Zalanash via Kegen.

Buses to Taraz (US$5) and Shymkent (US$7) also depart from outside Almaty-II train station at 6.30pm.

Bus Nos 492 and 497 (see To/From the Airport below) stop on Raiymbek in front of the Sayakhat bus terminal. Bus No 32, between Sayakhat and Zhandosova in the southwest of the city, runs the length of Zheltoksan between Raiymbek and Respublika alangy. Trolleybus No 19 also connects both bus stations.

Car

Hiring a car and driver for intercity travel is common practice in Kazakhstan. Drivers looking for intercity passengers wait outside the Sayran and Sayakhat bus stations. Joining a car that already has some passengers should ensure that you pay the local price.

Some sample fares per car are Kapshaghai (US$10), Talgar (US$5), Charyn Canyon (US$45), Medeu (US$5), Shymbulak (US$10), Taraz (US$155), Shymkent (US$210), Balkash (US$110) and Taldy-Korghan (US$35).

Another option, if your Russian is good, is looking for a driver and vehicle for hire in the weekly classified ads newspaper *Karavan* under 'Transportenay uslugi'.

RENTAL

Avis (☎ 72 01 43; avis@kaznet.kz; Regent Almaty, Zheltoksan 181) has Ford Explorers with 4WD (US$160/day) with unlimited mileage, insurance and tax, or Fiat Tempra sedans (US$87/day).

Europcar (☎ 58 16 81; europcar@rol.ru; fl 3, Hotel Premier Alatau, Dostyk 105) is located about 1km south of the centre. It has a variety of cars, ranging from compact Volkswagens (US$94/day) to Toyota Land Cruisers for (US$257/day). Prices drop the longer you keep the car. Rates include petrol, insurance and mileage in the Almaty area. A driver can be provided for an extra fee.

Train

Almaty has two main stations. All main long-distance trains stop at Almaty-I, nine kilometres north of the centre, but most trains (including those to/from Ürümqi) terminate at Almaty-II, nearer the centre. Almaty-I is at the north end of Seyfullin; Almaty-II is at the north end of Abylay Khan.

The advance **train ticket office** (Almaty-II train station, Tuzova; ☺ 8am-8pm) is outside the main building. Tickets on the day of departure are bought inside the station. You'll be asked to show your passport when buying tickets.

All prices quoted below are for *kupe* (sleeper) tickets, and vary depending on the grade of train (2nd/1st). From Almaty-II there are trains at least once a day to Astana (20½ hours, US$20/39), Aktöbe (46 hours, US$29/57), Kostanai (44 hours, US$29/38), Turkistan (16 hours, US$16/28), Kyzylorda (22 hours, US$19/34), Pavlodar (38 hours, US$20/48), Petropavlovsk (40 hours, US$24/71), Semey (20 hours, US$16/30), Shymkent (16 hours, US$15/24), Taraz (14 hours, US$12/20), and Ust-Kamenogorsk (36 hours, US$20/36). Trains to Atyrau (US$32/61), and Uralsk (US$36/65) depart every other day. For international departures to Moscow see p467.

For Astana you can take advantage of the Talgo, a new, Spanish-built fast train. While sleek and efficient, the Talgo feels somewhat claustrophobic and characterless if you've spent a lot of time rattling around Kazakhstan on the cosy, dimly lit old Soviet trains (though the clean bathrooms are nice). The Talgo departs Almaty Thursday and Saturday at 6.03pm, arriving in Astana at 7.50am. From Astana it departs Friday and Sunday at 6.26pm and arrives in Almaty at 8.10am. The fare is 2nd/1st class US$48/55.

Almaty II train station is reached on trolleybus Nos 4, 5 and 6, which run the full length of Abylay Khan to Abay. No 4 continues east along Abay and north up Dostyk, passing near KIMEP and the Dostyk and Kazakhstan hotels on the way. From Almaty-I train station, bus Nos 30 or 34 and trolleybus No 7 go all the way down Seyfullin to Kurmanghazy or beyond.

GETTING AROUND
To/From the Airport

Bus Nos 439, 492 and 497 go frequently from outside the arrivals terminal to the City Air

Terminal (Aerovokzal) on Zheltoksan, then on down Zheltoksan to Abay, then west on Abay. Minibus 526 goes along Furmanov to Al-Farabi. Buses to and from the airport stop outside the City Air Terminal on Zheltoskan. It's a 30-minute ride from the airport to the city terminal. Going out to the airport, these buses stop on Zheltoksan and Furmanov.

From the airport you'll need to bargain for a taxi – US$5 to the city centre is standard. Write the price down on a piece of paper and show the driver, preventing any later conflicts.

Some airlines, such as KLM, have a free shuttle into town. There are even shuttles to Bishkek (see p313). Taxi drivers will try to convince you they don't exist.

Public Transport

Almaty has a vast network of marshrutnoe, bus and tram routes. They can get very crowded, so if you have baggage or are short of time, it's much simpler to take a taxi. On city-owned buses, trolleybuses and trams, the fare is 20 T. For privately owned services (those beginning with a '5'), the fare is slightly more expensive – about 30 to 35 T. There's generally a sign at the front of the bus.

BUS, TROLLEYBUS & TRAM ROUTES

The following list is a summary of useful routes, or sections of routes. All run in both directions.

Bus Nos 2 & 100 South on Furmanov from Gogol to Ramstor and beyond.
Bus No 29 South on Kaldayakov at Gogol, Bögenbay Batyr, south on Dostyk.
Bus No 30 Almaty-I train station, Seyfullin, Kurmanghazy, south on Baytursynuly.
Bus No 32 Sayakhat bus station, Raiymbek, Zheltoksan, Timiryazev and south on Zhandosova.
Bus Nos 34 & 434 Almaty-I train station, Seyfullin, west on Abay.
Bus No 43 Töle Bi from Zheltoksan to Sayran bus station.
Bus No 61 Furmanov from Vinogradov to Respublika alangy and beyond.
Bus Nos 66 Dostyk and Töle Bi, Abay, Zhandosova.
Bus Nos 92 & 492 Airport, Sayakhat bus station, City Air Terminal, Zheltoksan, west on Abay.
Bus Nos 97 Airport, Sayakhat bus station, City Air Terminal, Abay, south on Baytursynuly.
Trolleybus No 1 Central Park, Gogol, south on Auezov.
Trolleybus No 2 Gogol at Kaldayakov, Nauryzbay Batyr, west on Abay.

Trolleybus No 4 Almaty-II train station, Abylay Khan, Abay, north on Dostyk.
Trolleybus No 5 & 6 Almaty-II train station, Abylay Khan, west on Abay and beyond.
Trolleybus No 7 Almaty-I train station, Seyfullin to Kurmanghazy.
Trolleybus No 9 Pushkin opposite Sayakhat bus station, Gogol, Kaldayakov, Bögenbay Batyr, Dostyk, Kabanbai Batyr, Masanchi, south on Baytursynuly.
Trolleybus No 11 Dostyk at Bögenbay Batyr, Abay, south on Baytursynuly.
Trolleybus No 12 Along Gogol from Central Park to Mukanov and beyond.
Trolleybus No 16 Central Park, Gogol, Zheltoksan, Abay, Baytursynuly, Satpaev, Zhandosova.
Trolleybus No 19 Pushkin opposite Sayakhat bus station, Gogol, Kaldayakov, Bögenbay Batyr, Dostyk, Abay, Sayran bus station.
Tram No 1 Makataev at the Zelyony Bazaar, Baytursynuly, Töle Bi.
Tram No 4 Shevchenko from Konaev to Seyfullin, Sayran bus station.

TAXI

There are a lot of official taxis – marked with chequerboard logos or other obvious signs – but many private cars will also act as taxis. A ride in the centre of Almaty should cost around 100 T during the day, double at night. For longer distances you'll need to agree a price before getting in.

If you book a **taxi** (☎ 58 or 068, Russian/Kazakh only), there's usually an extra charge of about US$1.

AROUND ALMATY

There are many good excursions to be made from Almaty, notably into the Zailiysky Alatau Range along the Kyrgyzstan border. Easy day trips include Medeu, Shymbulak, Bolshoe Almatinskoe Lake and Talgar. Given the deteriorating state of the roads as you travel east from Almaty, it's better to consider destinations such as the Charyn Canyon and the Karkara Valley as overnight trips. These are listed in the Southeast Kazakhstan section. See Map p116 for more details on the following region.

Medeu & Shymbulak

These are Almaty's playgrounds in the foothills of the Zailiysky Alatau, both easily visited on a day trip from the city. If you want to get away from crowds come on a weekday.

Medeu, at 1700m, is a somewhat scruffy scattering of buildings around the huge Medeu ice rink, about 15km southeast of central Almaty up the Malaya (Lesser) Almatinka Canyon. Shymbulak at 2300m is one of Central Asia's top skiing centres. Both are starting points for treks in the Zailiysky Alatau, and for good day hikes (see Travel Agencies p98 and Trekking in the Malaya Almatinka Gorge opposite for information on guided trips).

Medeu is always several degrees cooler than Almaty, and Shymbulak is cooler still. Except in summer, rain in Almaty means snow and zero visibility at the higher elevations.

The 10,500 sq m **Medeu ice rink**, built in 1972, is made for speed skating and many champion Soviet skaters have trained here. It normally functions from about November to March and is open to the public on weekends (US$4). You can hire skates for about US$2 on the 1st floor outside the rink. Even when the rink is closed people come to relax at the shashlyk and drink stands, and to take a walk in the surrounding valleys and hills.

The **Voice of Asia pop festival** is held at Medeu in early August and attracts big-name groups from China, Central Asia, Russia and elsewhere, though few from Kazakhstan. It lasts about four days.

What looks like a dam in the main valley above the ice rink (about 1km by road or 800-odd steps on foot) is actually there to stop avalanches and mudslides. The road climbs a further 4.5km from this barrier to the surprisingly swish **Shymbulak ski resort**, with a vertical drop of 900m and a variety of ski runs for all levels. A new quad lift was added in 2003 and the ski rental equipment, including snowboards, is also in good condition and costs around US$10 to US$35 per day. A day lift pass starts at around 3000 T at the beginning and end of the season, with individual lift tickets at 300 T. Since it takes three lifts to reach the Talgar saddle at around 3200m, a day pass makes sense if you're going to ski the whole mountain. The resort has a website at www.chimbulak.kz.

You can take walks from Shymbulak itself. A track continues 8km up the Malaya Almatinka Valley and, in summer, it's a 3km hike up to the Talgar Pass. Warning: there is year-round avalanche danger wherever you see snow. Pik Komsomola (4375m) rises 3km south, the nearest of a ring of glacier-flanked peaks around the top of the Malaya Almatinka Valley, which are favourites with Almaty climbers.

If you are staying at Shymbulak, you can entertain yourself in the evening at the new **bowling alley** (☎ 73 80 21; ☾ noon-3am).

SLEEPING & EATING

All places to stay are open in summer; discounts may be possible during this season.

Hotel Chimbulak (☎ 3272-73 33 41, 73 86 24; chimbulak@nursat.kz; r/pol-lux/lux US$27/40/155) This lodge has a great location at the foot of the chairlift, but you'll pay for it through the nose. Most of the rooms are unrenovated and not very exciting, but the suites do have a Jacuzzi. Rates double in winter. The resort also has several cottages away from the main complex, which can sleep up to nine people; all are reachable by car and include cable TV, phone, bathroom and kitchen and cost US$50 per person.

Premier Medeu (☎ /fax 3272-71 62 55; s/d US$39/49, pol-lux US$78/88, lux US$196) Although close to the skating rink and renovated, the Premier Medeu stands largely empty.

Kazakh Aul (Kazakh Village; ☎ 3272-50 25 74; meals 300-500 T; ☾ noon-10pm) A real treat is this restaurant inside several traditionally decorated yurts. Squatting around low tables, you can enjoy local specialties such as *kazy* and *manty*. Take the first left after the Premier Medeu hotel; the restaurant is about 400m above the hotel.

Around the ice rink and up at Shymbulak the main food option is shashlyk. If you're planning a hike or intend camping, bring food with you.

GETTING THERE & AWAY

From Almaty, bus No 6 goes to Medeu every 40 minutes from opposite the Hotel Kazakhstan on Dostyk. They return until 10pm. A taxi should be US$6, including the US$1 payable at a vehicle checkpoint before Medeu. At weekends during the ski season, some buses will continue up the gorge from Medeu to Shymbulak. At other times, take a taxi or walk (three to four hours).

Another way of getting up to Shymbulak is on a daily bus or passenger truck (200 T) used by employees of the resort. At least three of these pass the corner of Satpaev and Dostyk in Almaty between 7.50am

---

TREKKING IN THE MALAYA ALMATINKA GORGE

The further away from Medeu you hike, the prettier the landscape becomes. The *Hiker's Guide to Almaty* (see Maps & Guides on p94) details 19 hikes starting in the Malaya Almatinka Gorge (Little Almaty). If you're heading high into the mountains, make sure you have a good map and/or a guide. In winter and spring you'll need to watch out for avalanches. See the Trekking Warning on p117.

Medeu to Butakovka Trek

This trek through the wooded Komissarov (Kim-Asar) Valley and over the 2200m Komissarov Pass can be completed in half a day, or extended to a full day if you continue on the 2870m Butakovka Pass. From the Premier Medeu hotel take the paved road heading up the left side of the gorge from the ice rink, towards the Kazakh Aul restaurant. From here keep going along the road until you reach the track that heads past some buildings belonging to the forest service. The trail rises steeply to the first pass. From here you can either hike along the north ridge of the Komissarov spur back to Medeu, or head east through a forest leading to a narrow ravine. The trail forks in several places but all routes will eventually bring you to the Butakovka Gorge. From here you can continue up to the pass or down to the village, from where bus No 29 returns to Almaty.

Stage 1 Medeu to Komissarov Pass (two hours).
Stage 2 Komissarov Pass to Butakovka Gorge (two to three hours).
Stage 3 Butakovka Gorge to Butakovka Pass (four hours).
Stage 4 Butakovka Pass to Butakovka (two to three hours).

---

and 8.05am. Some are unsigned and none will stop unless you flag them down. These buses leave Shymbulak at 6pm and the ride takes around 45 minutes.

Bolshoe Almatinskoe Lake Area

West of the Malaya Almatinka Gorge lies its 'big sister' the Bolshaya Almatinka Gorge, about 15km from Almaty. For information on the weather and road conditions at the lake, call ☎ 3272-91 27 55 or 29 04 66.

Coming from the city the first thing you will encounter is a gate where a guard collects an 'ecology fee' of 176 T per person. The nearby **falcon farm** (admission 400 T), which also keeps hunting dogs, is worth a look. A couple of kilometres further is the bus stop at Kokshoky.

The artisan's village of **Sheber Aul** is five minutes' walk from the Kokshoky bus stop, just behind the GES-2 hydroelectric station. Around 50 artisans have been living here with their families since the late 1980s, making traditional Kazakh crafts. There isn't much to see these days, but you are still welcome to visit the main workshop (with the recognisable blue-painted front). You can watch the craftsmen at work and buy their products, from a US$1000 suit of armour to cheaper traditional felt slippers and hats.

A four- to five-hour hike up the valley brings you to the picturesque 1.6km-long **Bolshoe Almatinskoe Lake** (2500m), resting in a rocky bowl in the foothills of the Zailiysky Alatau. This is the starting point for treks into the mountains and across to Lake Issyk-Kul in Kyrgyzstan (see p118).

The lake is frozen from November to June and only takes on its famous turquoise tinge once the silt of summer meltwater has drained away. It's well known as a good bird-watching spot.

Just visible from the lake, at 2800m, is the outlandish **Tian Shan Astronomical Observatory**, sometimes still referred to by its Soviet-era acronym, GAISH. Several of the observatory's telescopes remain in use, but others, looking like giant Death Rays from a *Flash Gordon* movie, are running to rust. It's possible to stay here and take tours of the working observatories for US$10.

At the head of the Zhusalykezen Pass (3336m), the **Kosmostantsia** is a group of wrecked buildings belonging to various Russian scientific research institutes. It's all but abandoned now, though some meteorological research is still carried out here.

SLEEPING & EATING

If you're not camping by the lake, there are a couple of places to stay.

TREKS AROUND BOLSHAYA ALMATINKA

The Kokshoky to Alma-Arasan trek is one of the easiest one-day treks starting from the Bolshaya Almatinka Valley. This can be extended to a two- or three-day 35km circuit if you also take in the Almaty-Alagir Pass (3660m).

More challenging routes link the Bolshaya Almatinka and Malaya Almatinka gorges (also known as the 'Two Sisters'). To go from Kokshoky to Shymbulak via the Lokomotiv Glacier and Lokomotiv Pass (4050m, Grade 1B), the Tuyuksu Glacier and the Malaya Almatinka River, takes two or three days. See the Trekking Warning on p117.

Kokshoky to Alma-Arasan Trek

You can start from where the bus stops at GES-2 hydroelectric station, but time and effort will be saved by taking a taxi further to GES-1, where the broad water pipe rises sharply up the gorge. Climb the metal steps beside this pipe and then walk along the top of it for the most direct route to Bolshoe Almatinskoe Lake. The road is a more serpentine, 10km route to the same place. From the lake, follow the road uphill to the right, past the observatory and up to Kosmostantsia at the head of the Zhusalykezen Pass (3336m). From here a trail runs to the summit of Pik Bolshoy Almatinsky (3681m), or you can skirt the mountain and follow the Prokhodnaya river gorge, which eventually leads to the Alma-Arasan Resort. From here, bus no 93 runs back to the city or you can continue walking back to Kokshoky.

Stage 1 Kokshoky (GES-2) to GES-1 (one to two hours).
Stage 2 GES-1 to Bolshoe Almatinskoe Lake (two to three hours).
Stage 3 Bolshoe Almatinskoe Lake to Kosmostantsia (three hours).
Stage 4 Kosmostantsia to Alma-Arasan (four to five hours).

Tian Shan Astronomical Observatory (☎ 21 11 44, 76 21 67, 8 333 562 0722; r per person US$15; meals US$10) This unique hotel has prime lake and mountain views. The rooms have electric heaters for warmth, but if you are looking for a bargain, ask to stay in one of the basic wooden cottages (*domick*). There is food here and you can ask for a packed lunch if you're hiking. Some of the telescopes are still in service and if you speak Russian the caretakers give a good commentary. The hotel is 1km up the hill from the lake (about a 30-minute walk). The curator Kenes Kuratov makes frequent trips to/from Almaty; call ahead and you might get a ride with him for US$5.

Alpine Rose (☎ 64 03 25, 55 23 56; r US$40-60) This new, mock Swiss chalet-style hotel is located halfway between GES-1 and the lake. Rooms are clean and comfortable and the atmospheric bar has house-brewed beer. They also have five-aside football pitch, *banya* (baths) and a billiards room. You can rent snowmobiles here in winter.

Tau Dastarkhan (☎ 58 35 43) This restaurant is part of the well-known Dastarkhan food chain that is slowly taking over Almaty and now moving to the mountains. Excellent pastries, snacks and deli foods are available. It's located 500m before GES-2; you have to pass the nature area checkpoint and pay 176 T per person.

GETTING THERE & AWAY

From Almaty, get any bus heading to Orbita I, II, III or IV (listed as the last stop on the bus sign); these buses can be caught heading south on Zheltoksan or on Zhandosova at Abay. Get off at the big roundabout at the intersection of Navoi and Al-Farabi at the city's edge. Then take bus No 28, 93 or 136 to Kokshoky (about 30 minutes). The last bus back is at about 9.45pm.

Kokshoky bus stop, just past the GES-2 hydroelectric station, is at a fork where a sign points to Alma-Arasan (4km) in one direction, and Kosmostantsia (23km) in the other. Bus 93 continues to Alma-Arasan if you want to hike from there. Bolshoe Almatinskoe Lake is about 16km up the Kosmostantsia road, a climb of about 1100m.

Alternatively, taxis run from the corner of Al-Farabi and Navoi; expect to pay US$5 for a whole car to the GES-1. It's possible to drive to the lake and even as far up as the Kosmostantsia, but the road may well be impassable after bad weather.

Talgar & Almatinsky Nature Reserve

The village of Talgar, 45km east of Almaty, is the gateway to the Almatinsky Nature Reserve, a rugged area of about 750 sq km, and an important habitat of the rare snow leopard. Other inhabitants include the *arkhar* (a big-horned wild sheep) and the goitred gazelle, known locally as the *zheyran*. The reserve contains Mt Talgar, the highest peak in the Zailiysky Alatau at 4979m, which takes experienced climbers four days to climb. About 3km before the reserve entrance is an unsigned **museum of nature** (admission US$3) with a worthy collection of birds, insects and butterflies.

Although you're supposed to have special permits to enter the reserve, in practice, arranging a trip here is simple and no-one seems to be around to check the permits. Buses run from Sayakhat bus station in Almaty (40 minutes, 70 T) to Talgar, from where it's 300 T for a taxi to the reserve entrance and 200 T to get in. Trails are well marked until you get into the higher elevations. Most Almaty travel agencies can arrange a day trip here for about US$40 per person (see p98).

SOUTHEAST KAZAKHSTAN
ЮГ-ВОСТОК КАЗАХСТАН

The region from Almaty to Lake Balkash is traditionally called Zhetisu meaning 'land of seven rivers'. There are actually over 800 rivers, many fed by glaciers in the Zailiysky and Zhungar Alatau ranges, making it a rich area for agriculture. There are danger signs that Lake Balkash might be suffering a similar fate to the Aral Sea. Misuse of the waters from the Ili River for irrigation has led to a 1.5m drop in the water level, causing the coastline to recede, leaving behind a salty strip of land as wide as 10km in some places.

TALDY-KORGHAN
ТАЛДЫ-КОРГАН
☎ 3282 / pop 130,000

The recent transfer of the *oblys* (regional or provincial) capital from Almaty to smaller Taldy-Korghan brought with it civic improvements and a spark of life, but the town retains its laid-back countryside atmosphere. Located 265km northeast of Almaty, it's mainly of interest to visitors as the jumping-off point for the rarely visited Zhungar Alatau Mountains, as well as scenic Lake Alakol and the southern shore of Lake Balkash. If you have some time to kill, there is a **regional museum** (Abay 245) in the town.

Orientation

The best way to orientate yourself is to begin your walking tour from the Central Square, flanked by the drama theatre and a government building. The street to the east (Abay) holds two museums; the park is further along. The main avenue heading west from the main square is Tauelsizdik, also known as Lenin. Most of the banks, restaurants, and shops are located here and one street north on Kabanbai Batyr. The OVIR is on Abylay Khan and the corner of Tauelsizdik.

Information

Post office (cnr Akinsara & Kabanbai Batyr; ☾ 8am-6pm)
Rail & Air Ticket Agency (☎ 21 00 34; Kabanbai Batyr 51; ☾ 8am-7pm)
Taldy-Korghan Business Center (☎ /fax 27 12 34, 8 333 231 9570; laz@mail.kz; Birzhan Sal 102) Can provide translators (English and German) and offers Internet access for 300 T per hour.

Sleeping & Eating

Hotel Taldy-Korghan (☎ 24 23 14; Akinsara 128; s/d/lux US$6/9/20) This clean and central hotel, though antiquated, is fine for the one night most people stay in Taldy-Korghan. It's a few steps west of the central square. There are slim pickings at the restaurant and you are better off eating outside. The Business Centre offers bed and breakfast for US$30, with all mod cons including satellite TV, phone, Internet and sauna.

Café Dos (☎ 24 30 35; Taulsizdik 85a; meals 200-300 T) Shashlyk and drinks are served inside this unmissable brick castle, complete with crenellated turrets. The interior is decorated with medieval weapons and a full suit of armour.

Zhetisu Restaurant (☎ 24 52 43) This is located next door in the white columned building and serves typical Russian fare.

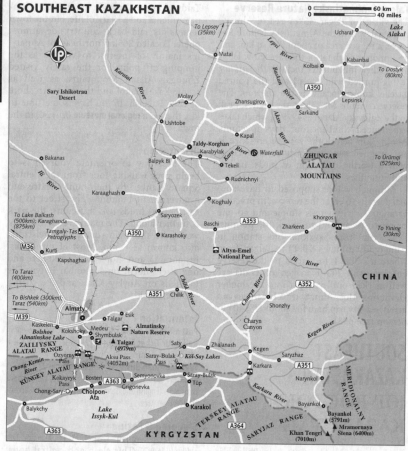

SOUTHEAST KAZAKHSTAN

Getting There & Away

Taldy-Korghan is on the main road from Almaty to northeast Kazakhstan but is off the Turksib railway line. Buses run about every two hours to Almaty (265km, six hours, US$5 to US$7). A shared taxi takes about four hours and costs around US$5 per passenger.

Buses serve Tekeli and Sarkand on the northern edge of the Zhungar Alatau, and Ucharal near Lake Alakol. It's 45km to Ushtobe and 35km to Tekeli. A taxi to either place costs less than US$1 and takes 40 minutes.

Taldy-Korghan's bus and train stations are at the end of Shevchenko, six blocks south of Taulsizdik. Long-distance taxis wait outside the bus lot and in the last block of Shevchenko.

AROUND TALDY-KORGHAN
Tekeli

All the options here require the relevant permits. You'll need to pass through the border control post 2km northeast of the small town of **Tekeli**, 45km east of Taldy-Korghan, to trek in the Zhungar Alatau Mountains. This mountain range, which forms the Kazakh–Chinese border, is heavily forested in birch and fir, and is covered with wildflowers in summer. Unlike the mountains around Almaty, the range's isolation means you can hike for days without seeing crowds, vehicles or broken beer bottles.

From Tekeli you can hike on a dirt road 47km up the torrential Kara River to an impressive 60m **waterfall**. The head of the valley, 14km further on, is at 3000m and surrounded by glacier-covered peaks. There are numerous good camping spots, and the water in the creeks is safe to drink.

Horses can be rented at the Ninth Homestead (Devyati Passik) farm, about 20km up the valley from Tekeli. Beyond this farm (15km), a footbridge across the river is the trailhead for a trek up to the Bessonov Glacier, a steep day hike. The trekking map *Po Dzhungarskomu Alatau Marshrut No 1*, available in Almaty, is useful.

Most of the **Zhungar Alatau** lie in a restricted border zone. Permits are given by the Taldy-Korghan police department upon showing a letter of invitation, Kazakh visa and registration. They take up to a month to process. For invitations and assistance, contact an Almaty travel agent or Dima Sagurov of **Stek Tours** (☎ 32835- 430 96; stek@mail.ru) in Tekeli.

Lepsinsk

Nudging up against the Chinese border, in the shadow of snow-capped peaks and forests, is Lepsinsk, a small town being billed as a new ecotourism destination. Located inside a protected area, the surrounding nature is accessible by foot, horse or 4WD vehicle. Wildlife abounds and the area is also big on honey-bee farms; you can taste some of their products, including honey beer.

Accommodation in a homestay is US$12 per night or US$17 in a tourist yurt. A camping spot is US$13. This is a border area so you'll need to apply for permits 15 to 20 days before your arrival. Accommodation bookings must be made five days in advance to arrange for entry to the reserve. For permit support and accommodation booking, contact Erzhan Bekhov of the tour agency **Uigentas Agro** (☎ 32837-214 69; lepsinsk@ mail.ru). Lepsinsk also has a good website www .lepsinsk.freenet.kz.

At the moment most activities are DIY – biking, paragliding, fishing are possibilities but you have to bring your own kit.

Expats who lived here say the best place in the area is lake Zhasi-Kul. Formed when an avalanche partially blocked the flow of the Aganakti River, the lake sports a magical green colour (Zhasi-Kul means green lake).

The lake is about 25km from Lepsinsk village. The road peters out about 3km from the lake from where you must walk.

There is good camping by the lake, and there are animals around, but they usually bolt when humans are near as the latter generally carry guns.

Arrange trekking in the village (ask at a guesthouse) or through Uigentas Agro.

To get to Lepsinsk, you first need to get to Kabanbai – a 245km, three-hour drive northeast of Taldy-Korghan. A seat in a shared taxi will cost around 800 T. Two daily buses to Kabanbai leave from Almaty's Sayran bus station (8.40pm and 9.15pm, 1200 T). Uigentas Agro's office in Kabanbai will hand over your permits and arrange transport (300 T) to Lepsinsk, a 40-minute drive.

Lake Alakol

This 90km-long saltwater lake named for its shores of black stone, is at the northeastern end of the Zhungar Alatau. Fierce winds blow almost constantly from China, through a low pass between the mountain ranges called the Zhungar Gates. The Almaty–Ürümqi train line runs through this pass.

From the village of **Koktuma**, which is on the southern shore of the lake, you can hire a motorboat and driver to go to 8km-long Bird Island (Ptichiye Ostrov), where you might be able to see flocks of flamingos (summer only) as well as 40 other species of bird. The uninhabited island takes 2½ to four hours to reach by boat, depending on winds. Lake Alakol's northern end is connected to the smaller freshwater **Sasykkol Lake**. You can stay at the pioneer camp in Koktuma, which is reached by bus from Taldy-Korghan, or by train on the Almaty–Ürümqi line.

Lake Balkash

Central Asia's fourth-largest lake is 17,400 sq km, but very shallow – only 26m at its deepest point. See it while it's still around – in 2004 the UN reported that Balkash is not far behind the Aral Sea in its evaporation rate, 2,000 sq km have already been lost, largely through over-use of the Ili River in China.

Lake life has been decreasing as well since the 1930s, when copper smelters were set up on the lake shore. The lake does still support a fishing industry though.

If you want to visit the lake, nicer places are found on its southern shore, accessible

ALMATY TO LAKE ISSYK-KUL

| | 0 | 6 km |
| 0 | | 4 miles |

SIGHTS & ACTIVITIES (pp110–11)
Falcon Farm	1	A1
Ice Rink	2	B1
Shymbulak	3	B1

SLEEPING (pp110–12)
Alma-Arasan Resort	4	A2
Alpine Rose	5	B2
Hotel Chimbulak	6	B1
Premier Medeu	7	B1

EATING (pp110–12)
| Kazakh Aul | 8 | B1 |
| Tau Dastarkhan | 9 | A2 |

TRANSPORT (p110)
| Kokshoky Bus Stand | 10 | A2 |

LEGEND
- — — — Trekking Route
- ─────── Ridge Line
- ÷ 3682m Spot Height

Note: This map is not designed for navigational purposes. Please see opposite for references.

---

from Taldy-Korghan. The Karatal River has excellent fishing, especially in the remote region where it flows into Lake Balkash. You can get there from Ushtobe by taxi.

Some of the best beaches can be found on the salty eastern end of the lake (the western half is salt water), 20km north of the train depot of **Lepsy**. There are about 10 guesthouses here charging 500 T per night including meals, although locals bring their own food and cook. The season lasts from mid-June to the end of August; if you arrive too early or late it's likely to be completely boarded up. Lepsy can be reached via train or by northbound bus from Taldy-Korghan (three hours).

Zharkent

Zharkent (formerly called Panfilov), is about 200km southeast of Taldy-Korghan on the northern fringe of the Ili River valley, and is the last real town in Kazakhstan on the bus route to China (see p466 for border information).

There is little to see here except the **Yulda-shev Mosque**, named for the Uyghur migrant who initiated it. Like Almaty's Zenkov Cathedral, the mosque is built without nails, but the curious design incorporates a minaret in the form of a Chinese pagoda beside a more conventional Central Asian dome, with gates in the style of the Timurid epoch; adding to the cross-cultural symbolism, the mosque's ground-floor windows look Russian.

ZAILIYSKY ALATAU & KÜNGEY ALATAU
ЗАИЛИЙСКИЙ АЛАТАУ И КУНГЕЙ АЛАТАУ

The Zailiysky Alatau, and the Küngey Alatau further south of Almaty, are spurs of the Tian Shan running east–west between Almaty and Lake Issyk-Kul.

The mountains are high and beautiful, with many peaks over 4000m, lots of glaciers and Tian Shan firs covering the steep valley sides. In summer the valleys are used as summer pasture and herders set up yurt camps. These mountains make for excellent trekking and there are dozens of trails of varying length, many starting from Medeu, Shymbulak, Kokshoky or Bolshoe Almatinskoe Lake (see Around Almaty p109), which are easily reached from Almaty. Some of the best-used trails go right across to Lake Issyk-Kul. Several travel agencies (p98) offer guided treks, with camping gear available.

Passes marked Unclassified (H/К) or 1A are simple, with slopes no steeper than 30 degrees and glaciers, where they exist, are flat and without open crevasses. Grade 1B (1B) passes may have ice patches or glaciers with hidden crevasses and may require ropes. Passes of grade 2A and above may require special equipment and technical climbing skills. For a description of popular routes see Trekking to Lake Issyk-Kul on p118.

Maps & Guides

The *Hiker's Guide to Almaty* (see p94) has reasonable descriptions of many routes through the mountains.

TREKKING WARNING

It's feasible to trek unguided if you have suitable experience and equipment, but there are two things to watch out for. One is the possibility of 'bandits' in the hills, who rob hikers especially when they are camped at night. The bigger hazard is the weather – be equipped for conditions to turn bad suddenly. The trekking season lasts from about mid-May to mid- to late September; August is best, but at any time it can often rain or even snow in the mountains when it's warm in Almaty. If you're caught unprepared by a sudden storm, it could be fatal.

Check what lies in store before embarking on any trek – some routes cross glaciers and tricky passes over 4000m high. When in doubt, use a guide.

The best Russian-language topographic trekking maps are available in Almaty from Firma Geo (JHER; see p95).

Most maps are 1:50,000 and are called *Marshrutnaya Turistskaya Karta* (Tourist Route Map; Moscow 1990–01). The *Vysokogornye Perevaly Severnogo Tyan-Shanya* (High Mountain Passes of the Northern Tian Shan; Astana 2000) map covers virtually the whole area between Almaty and Lake Issyk-Kul at 1:200,000 and grades all the passes in the region.

KÖL-SAY LAKES ОЗЕРА КОЛСАИ

These three pretty lakes lie amid the steep, forested foothills of the Küngey Alatau, 110km southeast of Almaty as the crow flies, but around 300km by road. With camping gear you can visit the lakes and trek or ride over to Lake Issyk-Kul.

The lakes are strung along the Köl-Say (Kolsai) River, about 1800m to 2200m high, southwest of the village of Saty – six hours by bus from Almaty, via Chilik and Zhalanash. The road takes a very roundabout route (at least 250km, or 350km via Kegen). If there's no bus to Saty, get one to Zhalanash and hitch or catch a truck for the last 40km to Saty. From Saty it's about 15km to the 1km-long Nizhny (Lower) Köl-Say lake at 1750m. Midway between Saty and the lake there is a checkpoint where you'll pay 107 T per person and 300 T for the car.

TREKKING TO LAKE ISSYK-KUL

Before setting off on these treks make sure you have good maps and, better still, go with a guide. You will need to bring all food and camping equipment. The two most used routes run from Bolshoe Almatinskoe Lake to Grigorievka or Semyonovka on Lake Issyk-Kul (35km and 42km east of Cholpon-Ata respectively); and from Kokshoky to Chong-Sary-Oy on Lake Issyk-Kul (15km west of Cholpon-Ata). Routes also go via the Köl-Say lakes, east of Almaty. See p264 for more information on Lake Issyk-Kul itself.

The Bolshoe Almatinskoe Lake–Grigorievka route and variations described here all pass through the Chong-Kemin Valley, between the main ridges of the Zailiysky Alatau and Küngey Alatau, which is a summer pasture for yurt-dwellers. The glacial moraine Jasy-Kül lake towards the upper (eastern) end of the valley, at 3200m is one of the loveliest spots in these mountains. Times given here are for a fairly unstrenuous pace: one or two days can be cut off several routes if you wish.

Visa regulations were tightening up at the time of writing and you may encounter border patrols on both routes. If you plan to stay in Kyrgyzstan you'd certainly want a visa on hand, and should try to have a border post stamp it. Illegal crossings without a visa could lead to a fine or bribe payout (about US$20 to US$30); consult an Almaty trekking agency before setting off.

For maps on the route see p117.

Bolshoe Almatinskoe Lake to Grigorievka

This route takes four to six days. From Bolshoe Almatinskoe Lake (2500m), up the Ozyornaya River to the Ozyorny Pass (3507m), on the Zailiysky Alatau main ridge. Down the Köl-Almaty River to the Chong-Kemin River (2800m). East up the Chong-Kemin Valley to Jasy-Kül lake. Back west down the Chong-Kemin Valley to the Aksu River. South up the Aksu River and the Vostochny (Eastern) Aksu Glacier to the Severny (Northern) Aksu Pass (4052m, on the Küngey Alatau main ridge). Eastward down to the Chong Aksu River, to the foot of Mt Autor Bashi (4330m). Finally follow the river eastward, then southward to Grigorievka.

Stage 1 Bolshoe Almatinskoe Lake to Ozyorny Pass (eight to nine hours).
Stage 2 Ozyorny Pass to Chong-Kemin River (six hours).
Stage 3 Chong-Kemin River to Aksu Pass (five to six hours).
Stage 4 Aksu Pass to foot of Mt Autor Bashi (six hours).
Stage 5 Foot of Mt Autor Bashi to Grigorievka (eight hours).

Variation from Shymbulak

Three days can be added to the preceding route by going from Shymbulak, across Bolshoe Talgarsky Pass (3160m) and down to the Levy Talgar River (2300m). South up the Levy Talgar River then west up the Turistov River to Turistov Pass (3930m). Southwest down the Kyzylsay River to the Ozyornaya River. Up the Ozyornaya River to Ozyorny Pass then continue as on the preceding route.

Kokshoky to Chong-Sary-Oy

This is a more westerly route of about six days. From Kokshoky, head south through Alma-Arasan and up the Prokhodnaya River valley to the Almaty (Prokhodnoy) Pass (3600m) on the Zailiysky Alatau main ridge. South past Primul Lake below the Pass and down the Almaty River to the Chong-Kemin River (2700m). West down the Chong-Kemin River then south up the Severnaya (Northern) Orto-Koy-Su River to the Kok-Ayryk Pass (3889m), on the Küngey Alatau main ridge. South down the Yuzhnaya (Southern) Orto-Koy-Su River to Chong-Sary-Oy.

Stage 1 Kokshoky-Almaty Pass (eight hours).
Stage 2 Almaty Pass to Chong-Kemin River (eight hours).
Stage 3 Chong-Kemin River to Orto-Koy-Su River (six hours).
Stage 4 Orto-Koy-Su River to Kok-Ayryk Pass (six to seven hours).
Stage 5 Kok-Ayryk Pass to Chong-Sary-Oy (eight hours).

Jibek Joly (p98) has wooden guesthouses both in Zhalanash and overlooking the Nizhny Köl-Say lake, which is accessible by vehicle. Full board at either cottage is US$38 per day and the agency can also arrange horse riding and guides. Cheaper cottages lower down cost 1000 T.

Independently, you should be able to hire a horse and/or a guide in Saty for around US$15 per day. Camping by the lake is 750 T per tent.

The Sredny (Middle) Köl-Say lake, also called Minzhilka (Thousand Horses), is 9km away via a four-hour long, steep hike rising to 2250m. The surrounding meadows are used as pasture and are a good camping spot. From the middle lake to the smaller Verkhny (Upper) Köl-Say lake at 2850m is about 4km and takes at least two hours.

The route over to Lake Issyk-Kul continues from here to the 3274m Saray-Bulak Pass on the Küngey Alatau ridge (also the Kazakhstan–Kyrgyzstan border), and descends to the village of Balbay (Saray-Bulak) on Issyk-Kul. By horse, this can be done in one day; on foot it will take about two days.

CHARYN CANYON
ЧАРЫНСКИЙ КАНЬОН

The Charyn River, flowing rapidly down from the Tian Shan, has carved a 150m- to 300m-deep canyon into the otherwise flat and barren steppe some 200km east of Almaty, and time has weathered this into all sorts of weird and colourful rock formations. Although the canyon can be visited in a long day trip from Almaty, an overnight camping expedition offers a more relaxed pace. It's too hot in summer; April to June or September to October are best.

Most visitors camp for free off the road and bring their own supplies. It might be possible to stay in the little tent by the café in the 'Canyon of Castles', which is marked with a sign from the main road. It's 107 T per person and 300 T per car to enter the canyon area.

To get here, take a bus from Almaty's Sayakhat bus station heading to Kegen or Narynkol. The buses cross the Charyn River just upstream from the canyon, which is as close as you can get by road; it's best to ask the driver to let you out as close as possible

to the canyon. Travel agencies in Almaty (p98) arrange trips here from at least US$25 per person. Of these, Jibek Joly sends a group bus out each weekend for US$10 per person. A taxi goes for around US$120.

KARKARA VALLEY
КАРКАРА ДОЛИНА

The valley of the Karkara River is an age-old summer pasture for herds from both sides of what's now the Kazakhstan–Kyrgyzstan border. The river forms the border for some 40km before heading north to join the Kegen River, beyond which it becomes the Charyn.

From Kegen, 250km of steppe by road from Almaty, a rough but scenic road heads south to Karkara, then across the border into Kyrgyzstan about 28km from Kegen. There are said to be Saka (Scythian) burial mounds between Kegen and the border. The road then veers west towards Tüp and Lake Issyk-Kul.

A bazaar and 'rodeo' of local sports such as *kökpar* (see Buzkashi, p54) and *kyz kuu* (where a man chases a woman on horseback) is held in mid-June. It brings together Kazakhs and Kyrgyz in a reminder of the valley's historic role as a meeting place of nomads and Silk Road traders. The *chabana* (cowboy) festival used to be held here – it is worth asking around if there are plans to start it up again.

The Almaty mountaineering and trekking companies Kan Tengri and Asia Tourism both maintain base camps on the Kazakh side of the Karkara river. Kan Tengri's is about 35km south of Kegen, at 2200m. Accommodation is in yurts and tents and there is a bar and a sauna too. From here climbers go by helicopter to mountain base camps in the Central Tian Shan.

Tourists and climbers need a permit as this is a border area with China. Permits can be arranged through a travel agent.

LAKE KAPSHAGHAI & THE ILI RIVER
КАПШАГАЙ ОЗЕРО И РЕКА ИЛИ

Lake Kapshaghai is a 100km-long reservoir formed by a dam on the Ili River near the town of Kapshaghai, 60km north of Almaty. Many Almaty residents have *dachas* (country or holiday houses) here and the lake has cold, fresh water. Its best beaches are on the north shore just past the dam.

The **Ili River** flows west out of China into the lake, then northwest to Lake Balkash. As it approaches the southern end of Lake Balkash, the Ili enters a delta wetland region of many lakes, marshes and thick, jungle-like vegetation. The river is navigable by kayak all the way from lake to lake (around 460km), and by raft at least some of the way. Guided boat trips by Almaty agencies usually include a visit to the **Tamgaly-Tas petroglyphs**, about 20km downstream from Lake Kapshaghai. Some of these thousand or more rock drawings are very old. Many depict deer and hunters, but there's also a large image of the Buddha, which probably dates from at least the 8th century AD when Chinese influence in Central Asia ended. The boat trips, including meals, transportation and guide, cost US$65 to US$70. Karlygash Makatova (p100) is the best operator for this.

Kapshaghai is on the route of trains and buses between Almaty and Taldy-Korghan. There are also shared taxis and half-hourly buses from Almaty's Sayakhat bus station.

ALTYN-EMEL NATIONAL PARK

Visited mainly for its prime attraction, the **Singing Sand Dune**, the Altyn-Emel National Park is 35km northeast of Lake Kapshaghai. The dune makes a low hum like an aeroplane engine whenever the wind picks up.

The park is a habitat for antelope, wild donkeys, camels and golden eagles. In 2003 the Munich Zoo reintroduced to the park eight rare Przewalski's horses. Altyn-Emel means 'golden saddle' in Mongolian; Jenghiz Khan was said to have camped here en route to his Central Asian campaigns.

The park administration's delusions of grandeur have resulted in some rather outrageous entrance fees: US$35 per person per day. If you bring your own car you'll have to hire a ranger to show you around (US$15), a necessity as tire puncturing barriers have been hidden from view. Accommodation is in basic wooden huts (US$33 per person) without water or electricity. Meals are an additional (US$10). Guides from Almaty usually charge US$30 per day for the trip, and a vehicle will be US$0.50 per kilometre. The gateway to the town is via the village of Baschi.

SOUTH KAZAKHSTAN
ЮГ КАЗАХСТАН

South Kazakhstan, the region from Kyrgyzstan's western border to the Aral Sea, is the most Kazakh part of Kazakhstan; Kazakhs form a higher percentage of the population here than almost anywhere else.

This is an arid region of deserts and barren steppe, dissected by the Syr-Darya but with only small pockets of cultivation. You'll cross this region if you travel by land between Tashkent and Almaty, or by rail between Moscow and Tashkent. The chief reasons to stop lie in the mountainous Aksu-Zhabaghly Nature Reserve on the region's southern fringe, best reached from Shymkent, or to see the great 14th-century Arystan-Bab Mausoleum of the Sufi poet and teacher Kozha Akhmed Yasaui at Turkistan. Travellers in search of utter desolation may also want to aim for Aralsk to witness the effects of the region's biggest environmental disaster, the draining of the Aral Sea (p68).

TARAZ ТАРАЗ
☎ 3262 / pop 315,000

Ask any Kazakh what they know about Taraz and they'll probably say 'vodka' as this is where the country's favourite brand is produced. It's a quiet, Soviet-style place with warm leafy boulevards, but there is little to hold the traveller with the exception of an excellent museum chronicling the city's former glory as a stop on the Silk Road.

In the 11th century Taraz was a capital of the Turkic (and Islamic) Karakhan state which also ruled Bukhara for a while. Levelled by Jenghiz Khan, it only rose again 600 years later, under the name Aulie-Ata (Holy Father), as a northern frontier fort of the Kokand khanate. It fell to the Russians in 1864.

The Soviets renamed the town in 1935 after the Kazakh bard Zhambyl Zhabayev, who was born here, and added phosphate factories to pump up the economy. Since independence, the name changed again and the factories closed, which has at least ended the problem of chronically polluted air.

KAZAKHSTAN

Orientation & Information

The meeting of east–west Töle Bi with north–south Abay is the centre of town. West from here a government square, still called ploshchad Lenina, stretches along Töle Bi. East of Abay is Lenina Park. There is a Halyk Bank ATM on Suely Manov.

Internet Café (☎ 45 38 54; Abay 124; per hr 150 T; 🕑 8am-9pm Mon-Fri, 10-10pm Sat & Sun) Located in the Kazakhtelekom Office, east of the museum.

Main Post Office (☎ 7 58 22; Töle Bi) West of Hotel Zhambyl.

Sights

The **History Museum** (☎ 23 25 85; Töle Bi 55; admission 170 T; 🕑 9am-1pm & 2-6pm Mon-Sat) has been completely renovated in honour of 2000-odd years of Taraz history. It has dusted off the natural and local history exhibits in the main building, and added three new annexes in the back. The museum's pride and joy is the domed rear building that houses an impressive collection of *balbals*, totemlike stones bearing the carved faces of honoured warriors or chieftains, dating to the 7th and 8th century AD. Similar statues have been found as far away as Hungary. A second building shows Taraz's history as a Silk Road town, and its ultimate destruction by Jenghiz Khan. A collection of oil paintings by local artist and Russian exile Vladimir Brewmer (1889–1971) hangs in the third repository.

Two small mausoleums in a wooded park near the town centre, both 20th-century reconstructions, are worth a look. The **Karakhan Mausoleum** marks the grave of an 11th-century Karakhan potentate. Nearby, the **Dauitbek Mausoleum** was for a 13th-century Mongol viceroy, and is said to have been built lopsided in revenge for the man's infamous cruelty.

Sleeping & Eating

Hotel Taraz (☎ 43 34 91; Zhambyl 75; s/d US$14/17.50) The cheap option, near the corner of Sukhe-Bator about 3km north of the centre, Hotel Taraz has simple rooms, friendly staff and a restaurant. Bus Nos 10, 26 or 29 pass by.

Hotel Zhambyl (☎ 45 25 52; fax 45 17 50; Töle Bi 42; s/d US$40/47) Comfortable rooms with bathroom, phone, TV and fridge. You might be able to haggle the price down by US$10.

The restaurant has a good buffet breakfast for 400 T. Across the street is a yurt selling *kumys* in summer.

Hotel Gazovik (☎ 43 32 33; gazovik_hotel@nursat.kz; Suleimanov 7a-1; s/d US$42/63; ✕) The more modern hotel is located behind the old Akimat building.

Café Istanbul (☎ 45 25 29; Abay 117; ✢ 11am-10pm) Turkish place serving excellent doners and kebabs.

Sakartvello (☎ 45 73 82; Suleymanov 16; ✢ noon-midnight) Large and freshly cooked Georgian meals including grilled chicken and a variety of salads, but expect a 25-minute wait even if the place is empty.

There are shashlyk stalls and lots of fruit and vegetables at the sprawling central bazaar on Töle Bi and east of Lenina Park. Bus Nos 2 or 16 and trolleybus Nos 3, 4 or 5 run along Töle Bi from the park.

Getting There & Around

Taraz's airport, five kilometres west of town off the Shymkent road, is now only occasionally used for charter flights. **Aeroflot** (☎ 45 69 33; Töle Bi 61; ✢ 9.30am-6.30pm Mon-Fri, 10am-3pm Sat) acts as an agent.

From Almaty, the best way to get here is on the 6pm Shymkent-bound train. It arrives in Taraz at 4am and you can crash at the train station dorms (US$3.50) for a few hours. Trains leaving Taraz are the 5pm train to Shymkent (US$3.50) or the 11pm train to Almaty (US$14).

More frequent buses leave from the station on Zhambyl, about 4km northeast of the centre. Buses go three or four times daily to Almaty (10 hours, US$8) and Bishkek (seven hours, US$6), and at least seven times daily to Shymkent (four hours, US$3). Marshrutnoe minibuses to the same destinations wait outside the bus and train station, on Baluan Shcholak about 4km south of the centre.

Trolleybus Nos 4 or 6 from the train station run into the centre along Abay. Heading to the station, catch them on Abay, south of Kazybek Bi. A taxi to the bus station is US$1. Buses and marshrutnoes serving local destinations congregate in a dusty lot outside the bazaar.

AROUND TARAZ

Taraz can be a jumping-off point from where to explore the Talassky Alatau Range spanning the Kazakh–Kyrgyz border and the Aksu-Zhabaghly Nature Reserve (p125). You can also enter Kyrgyzstan from here and explore the community based tourism projects of the Kyrgyz Talas Valley (see p295).

Aysha-Bibi & Babazhi Katun Mausoleums

Near Aysha-Bibi village (formerly Golovachovka), 16km west of Taraz, are the tombs of two Karakhan women, though little else is known about them. The 12th-century **Mausoleum of Aysha-Bibi** (one wall) is probably the only authentically old building around Taraz. Made of splendid, delicate terracotta bricks in over 50 different motifs, it looks almost weightless. A Muslim shrine for centuries, it was damaged by the removal of bricks in Soviet times but later restored. It now stands in a glass box to ward off the corrosive air. Beside it is a recent reconstruction of the 11th-century **Tomb of Babazhi Katun,** with a pointed, fluted roof.

Aysha-Bibi village is on the Shymkent road from Taraz. A sign points to the mausoleums, about 300m south from the main road in the village. Shymkent or Tashkent buses will take you to Aysha-Bibi or you can hire a taxi in Taraz. Without your own transport, catching a ride from here on to Shymkent is a lesson in futility – every bus and car will be packed to the gills. You might have better luck asking for a ride at the mausoleums rather than waiting on the road.

SHYMKENT ШЫМКЕНТ

☎ 3252 / pop 500,000

South Kazakhstan's most vibrant town, with a booming bazaar and lively downtown, is mostly of interest for the traveller as a transit point for other places (Turkistan, Otrar, and the Aksu-Zhabaghly Nature Reserve). Shymkent's past reads like Taraz's – the Mongols razed a minor Silk Road stop here; the Kokand khanate built a frontier fort in the 19th century, Russia took it in 1864, and the whole place was rebuilt in Soviet times. These days the lead mining that used to keep the economy ticking has been replaced by a brewery producing the famed Shymkent Beer. Avoid the city from late June to late July when swarms of mosquitoes make it unbearable.

Orientation

Shymkent's main central streets are north-south Kazybek Bi (formerly Sovietskaya) and east–west Turkistan and Tauke Khan (formerly Lenina). The bus and train stations are both a short ride by bus south of the MiG fighter plane, a monument to WWII pilots who trained at Shymkent. The airport is 12km north of town.

Information

ACS (☎ 53 48 51, 53 49 52; fax 53 51 26; Turkistan 2/2) Travel agency with local tours; main branch in Almaty.

Altex (☎ 52 54 36; fax 62 19 72) Trips to Aksu-Zhabaghly Nature Reserve, Turkistan and Otrar, by Shamil Rafikov, who speaks some English.

CATC (☎ 21 14 36; cat-chimkent@alarnet.com; Illiyaeva 18) Travel and ticket agency.

Centre Credit Bank (☎ 53 24 52; Konaev 13) Western Union transfers and travellers cheques cashed. ATM machines are located at the TsUM and post office.

Shymkent Copy Service (☎ 21 21 75; cnr Baytursynov & Tauke Khan 7 ; Internet per hr 200 T; ☼ 24hr) You can use the Internet here or make international calls to the US, UK or Australia for 60 T per minute. This is one of several Internet cafés on this block.

Transavia (☎ 53 52 54; Tauke Khan 30) Air-ticketing agency.

Sights

The newly renovated **Regional Studies & History Museum** (☎ 53 02 22; Kazybek Bi 13; admission 50 T; ☼ 9am-6pm Tue-Sun) has some excellent exhibits on Shymkent's history as a Silk Road caravan town. There is also material on old Otrar and some information on Aksu-Zhabaghly Nature Reserve.

The **bazaar** (Titov; ☼ 8am-8pm Tue-Sun) is Shymkent's biggest show, a bustling market spills over with fresh produce, tins of imported food, cheap clothes, and spices, as well as some gaudy traditional skullcaps and coats and rather less-portable wooden chests with colourful stamped-tin decoration.

Fantasy World Amusement Park, opposite the Hotel Shymkent on prospekt Respubliki, is a popular evening hang-out.

Sleeping

Hotel Ordabasy (☎ 53 64 21; Kazybek Bi 1; s/d US$12/35; ☒) This is a good budget option, although the streetside rooms get too much noise and some of the back rooms suffer the wrath of a spotlight shining through the windows – ask for a room in the back

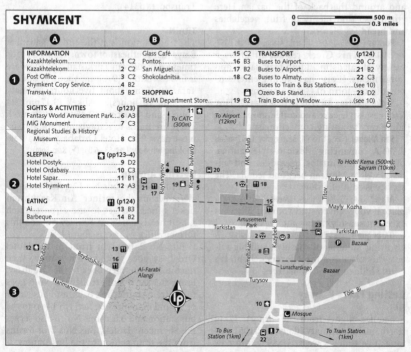

SHYMKENT

0 — 500 m
0 — 0.3 miles

INFORMATION		Glass Café.....................................15 C2	TRANSPORT	(p124)
Kazakhtelekom...........................1 C2		Pontos...16 B3	Buses to Airport.........................20 C2
Kazakhtelekom...........................2 C2		San Miguel...................................17 B2	Buses to Airport.........................21 B2
Post Office...................................3 C2		Shokoladnitsa............................18 C2	Buses to Almaty.........................22 C3
Shymkent Copy Service............4 B2			Buses to Train & Bus Stations...(see 10)
Transavia.....................................5 B2		SHOPPING	Ozero Bus Stand.........................23 D2
		TsUM Department Store............19 B2	Train Booking Window...............(see 10)
SIGHTS & ACTIVITIES	(p123)			
Fantasy World Amusement Park..6 A3				
MiG Monument...........................7 C3				
Regional Studies & History				
Museum...................................8 C3				
SLEEPING	(pp123–4)			
Hotel Dostyk..............................9 D2				
Hotel Ordabasy.........................10 C3				
Hotel Sapar..............................11 B1				
Hotel Shymkent.......................12 A3				
EATING	(p124)			
Ai..13 B3				
Barbeque.....................................14 B2				

at the end of the hall. Breakfast is included in the price.

Hotel Dostyk (☎ 44 68 49; cnr Chernishevsky & Turkistan; half day s/d US$5.50/8.50, full day US$11/17; 🖾) Not as nice and has dodgy clientele.

Hotel Shymkent (☎ 56 71 94; fax 56 75 18; prospekt Respubliki 6a; s/d US$35/63; 🖾 🖭) This former firetrap was under heavy reconstruction at the time of research and is expected to be one of the top hotels in the city. Sauna, tennis courts and a nightclub are a few of the amenities. Take bus No 16 from the bus station.

Hotel Kema (☎ 54 05 97; Tauke Khan 93a; s/d US$64/68; 🖾 🖭) Located just east of the centre, this upmarket option has newly furnished rooms with TV, phone and bathroom.

Hotel Sapar (☎ /fax 53 51 31; sapar-shm@nursat.kz; Konaev 17; s/d US$79/171; 🖾) This is a four-star alternative.

Eating

Glass Café (Kazybek Bi) At the entrance to the park, this café does a flying trade in ice-cream coffee (30 T) from 1pm onwards. There are also shashlyk stands in the park and around the back of the bazaar. Here you'll also find plenty of fruit, vegetables and bread for picnics.

Pontos (☎ 55-08-07; Al-Farabi Alangi 4; meals US$7; 🕑 11-1am) This Greek restaurant offers a variety of salads including fruit salad, and tangy meats. It also has evening entertainment in the form of Greek dancing.

Shokoladnitsa (☎ 53 65 52; Tauke Khan 60) Tiny Viennese-style cake and coffee shop, selling some very tempting confectionary.

San Miguel (☎ 21 05 04; Baytursynov 12/12; meals US$10) A convincing Mexican-style cantina, offering chilli, burritos, quesadillas and fajitas as well as Mexican beer and tequila. The service is painfully slow.

Ai (☎ 53 43 05; Momyshuly 1; meals US$1) A great place if you want to stuff yourself silly with excellent shashlyk, plov and *laghman*.

Barbeque (☎ 21 20 12; Tauke Khan 11; meals US$7) Growing mounds of shashlyk and big salads, this place is a meat-lovers delight. It's a little hidden by sidewalk trees.

Getting There & Away

AIR

Scheduled flights from the airport, 12km north, include Almaty (daily, US$105), Astana (five times a week, US$95), Moscow (five times a week, US$200), and Aktau (weekly, US$108). There may also be flights to St Petersburg in the summer, and charter flights to Pavlodar and Kostanai.

BUS & MARSHRUTNOE

The bus station is about 1km south of the Hotel Ordabasy. Scheduled departures include Almaty (13 hours, 10 daily, US$8), Turkistan (3½ hours, 10 daily, US$2.50), Taraz (four hours, hourly, US$2.50) and Bishkek (11 hours, evening only, US$6).

Marshrutnoe taxis depart to most of these destinations from the bus station. For Tulkibas (and Aksu-Zhabagly), these depart from the Ozero stand, a few blocks east of the centre (from Tauke Khan take marshrutnoe Nos 5, 9 or 21). Buses for Sayram leave from the Ozero bus stand; a bus costs 40 T and a marshrutnoe costs 80 T.

A fleet of overnight buses also depart Monday to Saturday at 4pm for the outskirts of Almaty from the car park beneath the MiG monument at the end of Kazybek Bi.

For transport to the Uzbek border see Transport (p314).

TRAIN

The train station is at the end of Kabanbai Batyr just southeast of town. Trains go four times a day to/from Turkistan, and there are trains to Aktöbe (9.45pm, about 25 hours), Taraz (8.25am, about five hours), Almaty (8.25am, 18 hours), Bishkek (3.17pm, six hours) and Moscow (9.45pm, 60 hours). There are trains to Karaghanda and Astana most days. The Hotel Ordabasy has a **train booking window** (☎ 53 46 05; 🕑 8am-8pm).

Getting Around

From the airport bus No 12 goes occasionally to/from the former Air Kazakhstan ticket office. To get to the airport, catch it as it heads north on Konaev outside this former office. A taxi is about US$5.

Bus No 2 from in front of the Hotel Ordabasy goes to the train station, then the bus station, then back to the Ordabasy. From the same stop, trolleybus No 6 goes to the train station and back, and bus Nos 9 or 16 and marshrutnoe taxi No 14 go to the bus station and back (bus No 16 also serves the Shymkent Hotel). Bus Nos 2 or 6 runs from the train station to the bus station.

AROUND SHYMKENT

Sayram

About 10km east of Shymkent, Sayram is one of the oldest settlements in Kazakhstan, reckoned to date back 2000 years. There's little to show for this, but it's a pleasant country town, mainly of interest as the birthplace of Kozha Akhmed Yasaui (see p126). You can see the small 14th-century **mausoleum** for Kozha's father Ibragim-Ata, a great 11th-century spiritual teacher. A miniature copy of Kozha's resting place in Turkistan was erected for Karashash-Ana, his mother. This one fell apart several times and the current incarnation dates from the 19th century.

Regular buses run to Sayram from Shymkent – get off when you see the blue dome of a modern mosque at the cross roads with a small bazaar. Kozha's mother's mausoleum is around 1km in the opposite direction from the mosque.

Aksu-Zhabagly Nature Reserve

This beautiful 857 sq km patch of foothills and mountains in the Talassky Alatau range of the western Tian Shan is the longest established and one of the easiest visited of Kazakhstan's nature reserves. It's promoted as the home of the tulip, and in May its alpine meadows are dotted with the wild bright red Grieg's tulip.

The most dramatic scenery is on the west side where Altex (see p123) runs a camp. From here it's possible to take a long day hike to two small lakes at 2000m, or tackle the more demanding Mt Sayramsky (4236m), a two-day climb requiring equipment. The eastern region is renowned for its bird and plant life.

You are required to bring a ranger with you into the reserve (800 T per day), plus pay an entry fee of 1050 T per day per person. May to October is the best time to visit.

Access to the east side of the reserve is via Zhabaghly, 100km west of Taraz and 100km east of Shymkent, where you'll also find the reserve office with a new **museum** on the main street, Abay. The NGO **Wild Natures** (☎ 32538-56686; www.wild-natures.com; Taldy Bulak 14), which promotes responsible tourism, conservation and community development on a local level, can be found five minutes' walking distance from the main road (follow the signs from the post office). It organises

a tulip festival in early May, a horse festival in autumn and activities year-round including *kumys* tasting and traditional concerts.

SLEEPING

Wild Natures (see earlier) offers homestays with experienced families in Zhabaghly village for US$15 per night. It also maintains a lodge about 6km from the village, as well as yurt accommodation in the mountains. Visit the office to get set up; ask for Dika Priroda (Wild Natures).

Altex (☎ mobile 8 300 322 53 16, in Shymkent 3252 32 20 08; altextravel@nursat.kz) This Shymkent-based tour operator maintains a permanent camp of metal box cabins in a pretty location in a canyon beside the Sayram River, 70km from Shymkent. The cabins are surprisingly comfortable, and there's a traditional log *banya* in the woods. A three-day/two-night trip runs to about US$120, including food, guide and transfers from Shymkent.

Zhenia & Lyuda's (☎ 3253 85 68 96; innaksu@ nursat.kz; Abay 36; r with full board US$15) This friendly English-speaking couple have transformed their home in Zhabaghly village into a cosy hotel and can arrange excursions within the reserve. Look for the shop out front on the main street.

GETTING THERE & AWAY

From Shymkent, catch a marshrutnoe from the Ozero stand to Tulkibas; from here it's a 500 T taxi ride or 50 T bus ride to Zhabaghly (30 minutes). There is also a daily direct bus (US$1) departing from the market at 3pm.

From Taraz, catch a bus to the village of Vainofka and take a taxi to Zhabaghly (20 minutes).

From Tulkibas a train leaves at 6pm for Almaty (12 hours, 2500 T), and there are frequent connections to Taraz and Shymkent.

Otrar

About 150km northwest of Shymkent lie the ruins of Otrar (also called Al-Farabi or Utrar), the town that brought Jenghiz Khan to Central Asia. Much of the rest of Asia and Europe might have been spared the Mongols if Otrar's 13th-century governor had not murdered the Great Khan's merchant-envoys here. There's little left of the town that once covered 20 hectares, though preservation work by Unesco promises to make more of it accessible to the casual tourist.

Close to the ruins is the intact 14th-century **Arystan-Bab Mausoleum**. This is the tomb of an early mentor of Kozha Akhmed Yasaui and an important stopover on the pilgrimage to Turkistan. The Al-Farabi museum is 5km away at the village of Shauildir and includes some finds from Otrar.

The road to Shauildir and Otrar is from Törtköl, 95km north of Shymkent on the Turkistan road. Shauildir is 50km west of Törtköl. Altex (p123) can take you there.

TURKISTAN ТУРКИСТАН
☎ 32533 / pop 100,000

At Turkistan, 165km northwest of Shymkent at the edge of the Kyzylkum desert, stands Kazakhstan's greatest building and its most important site of Muslim pilgrimage. The mausoleum of the first great Turkic Muslim holy man, Kozha Akhmed Yasaui, was built on a grand scale by Timur in the late 14th century. Restoration work, largely funded by the Turkish government, has brought the site back to its original glory.

Founded perhaps as early as the 5th century AD, and known as Yasy or Shavgar until the 16th century, the town was an important trade and religious centre by the 12th century, on a boundary between nomadic and agricultural societies. Later it became a northerly outpost of the Kokand khanate, falling to the Russian push of 1864.

Turkistan has become a student town since the launch of the Kozha Akhmed Yasaui Kazakh-Turkish University – you'll see the US$30 million main building, with the blue dome, as you enter the town from the south. Aside from the 400 Turkish students, the town is almost entirely Kazakh. To visit the mausoleum takes no more than half a day and can easily be done as a day trip from Shymkent.

Orientation
If you come by road from Shymkent, the mausoleum will loom into view on your left as you enter the town along Tauke Khan (formerly Lenina). North of the mausoleum the road leads to the bus station (after about half a kilometre) and the bazaar. Sultanbek Kozhanov, one block east of Tauke Khan, is the main street with several hotels and restaurants. The train station is 5km northwest of the centre by taxi (250 T).

Kozha Akhmed Yasaui Mausoleum
The revered Sufi teacher and Turkic mystical poet was born at Sayram, east of Shymkent, in 1103. He underwent ascetic Sufi training in Bukhara, but lived much of the rest of his life in Turkistan, dying here, some say, about 1166. At the age of 63 he is said to have retired to an underground cell for the rest of his life, in mourning for the Prophet Mohammed who had died at the same age. He founded the Yasauia Sufi order.

Yasaui's original small tomb was already a long-time place of pilgrimage before Timur ordered a far grander mausoleum built here in the 1390s. Timur died before it was completed and the front face was left unfinished.

KOZHA AKHMED YASAUI MAUSOLEUM
0 — 300 m
0 — 0.2 miles

INFORMATION	
Halyk Bank...................................	1 B4
Kazakhtelekom.............................	2 B4
SIGHTS & ACTIVITIES	(p127)
Abylay Khan Statue.......................	3 B3
Bathhouse....................................	4 A4
Hal-Wat Mosque...........................	5 A4
Mausoleum of Rabigha-Sultan Begum...	6 A4
Museum.......................................	7 B4
Yasaui Mausoleum........................	8 A4
SLEEPING	(p127)
Hotel Edem..................................	9 B4
Hotel Sabina................................	10 B4
Hotel Yessy.................................	11 A3
Turkiston Hotel............................	12 B3
EATING	(p127)
Astana Restaurant........................	13 B4
Best Navryz.................................	14 B4
Café..	15 A4
SHOPPING	
Gift Shop....................................	16 A4
OTHER	
Turkish School.............................	17 B3

To Bus Station (1.5km);
Train Station (5km);
Kyzylorda (280km)

To Shymkent
(165km)

A good place to start your visit is the new **museum** (admission 200 T; ✆ 9am-6pm) located just off the pedestrianised part of Tauke Khan. Models and artefacts help describe the site, but all the labels are in Russian and Kazakh.

Approaching the Yasaui Mausoleum from the front, you'll see on the left a good replica of the small 15th-century **Mausoleum of Rabigha-Sultan Begum** (the original was torn down for tsarist building material in 1898), for the wife of Abul-Khayir Kahn, a 15th-century leader of the then-nomadic Uzbeks. Abul-Khayir was killed in the 1468 feud which split the Uzbeks and effectively gave birth to the Kazakh people; his tomb is within the main building.

The Yasaui mausoleum **central chamber** (admission 200 T; ✆ 8.30am-8pm) is cupped with an 18.2m-wide dome 39m above the floor. Beyond this central hall are 35 smaller rooms on two floors. In the centre of the chamber is a vast cauldron *(kazan)* donated by Timur. It weighs over 2000kg, and whereas it once held holy water it now contains donations from visitors. Yasaui's tomb lies beyond the ornately carved 14th-century wooden door at the end of the chamber.

West of the mausoleum on a small hill is the entrance to the **Hal-Wat Mosque** and small museum, built underground with a wood-decorated interior. Next to the small prayer hall is the cell in which Yasaui is said to have withdrawn to.

Back towards the entrance is a traditional 15th-century **bathhouse**. The interior has been well restored but the building is now just for show.

Just outside the complex you can get a bowl of soup and a wedge of watermelon at the café, which is located next to a gift shop that is usually closed.

Sleeping & Eating

Hotel Sabina (✆ 3 14 05; Sultanbek Kozhanov 16; per person US$4.50) Turkistan's budget option is a hole-in-the-wall place on the main drag – small but clean rooms have shared bathrooms.

Hotel Edem (✆ 3 16 97; Sultanbek Kozhanov 6a; s/d/lux with breakfast US$10/20/49; ✖) Near to the Hotel Sabina, this is a good midrange option.

Hotel Yessy (✆ 4 01 83; fax 4 01 85; Tauke Khan 1; s/d/lux US$20/30/70; ✖) This is the best place to stay in Turkistan, with modern facilities and comfortable rooms, some with splendid views of the mausoleum. The helpful reception speaks some English.

Turkiston Hotel (✆ 4 21 97; Sultanbek Kozhanov) Just east of Hotel Yessy, this is also upmarket but not as good.

Best Navryz (✆ 3 22 78; Sultanbek Kozhanov; best nevruzcafé@yahoo.com; ✖ 🖵) This colourful restaurant, built in a mock old-Turkistan style, is usually crowded with tea-sipping Turkish students. The manager Murat Keles is a good source of information, can give tips on accommodation, and serves up excellent Turkish food.

Astana Restaurant (Sultanbek Kozhanov) Across the street, it stays open later than Best Navryz and is good for traditional Kazakh dishes.

The bazaar, close by the bus station, heaves with produce and does justice to Turkistan's historic role as a market centre.

Getting There & Around

Buses come from Shymkent (3½ hours, six daily, US$2), and from Kyzylorda (six hours, daily, US $3) to the bus station, 1.5km north of town. Marshrutnoe buses also wait outside the bus station and are cheaper (US$1.50). A taxi to Shymkent costs around US$10. Some Marshrutnoes travel direct from the Uzbek–Kazakh border.

The train station is 5km north of town. There are at least three daily trains west to/from Kyzylorda, Töretam (Leninsk), Aralsk and Aktöbe, and at least two daily trains east to Shymkent, Taraz and Almaty. Three trains a week go to Tashkent and Bishkek.

Bus Nos 2 or 5 and marshrutnoe taxi No 5 run between the main street, the bus station and the train station.

KYZYLORDA КЫЗЫЛОРДА

✆ 32422 / pop 160,000

On the Syr-Darya, 280km northwest of Turkistan, Kyzylorda (meaning Red Capital) was the capital of Soviet Kazakhstan from 1925 to 1927 but was dropped in favour of cooler Almaty when the Turksib railway reached there. The only evidence you'll see of this former glory is the ornate train station, the rest of the town being a rather tousled and taciturn affair.

Like Taraz, Shymkent and Turkistan, it was part of the Kokand khanate's 19th-century frontier defences, and the first of these to fall to Russia in 1853. Today it's the capital of Kyzylorda *oblys* (province or region), which has the highest Kazakh population in the country.

If you do need to stop here, the run-down **Hotel Kyzylorda** (☎ 611 21; Taukhmegambeta 19; s/d US$6/10/17) is closest to the train station. Nearby is the two-star **Hotel Asetan** (☎ 6 25 43; Ayteke Bi 28; r US$42; 🍴), with a bright-pink lobby and large, comfortably furnished rooms. **Kiz Jibek Restaurant** (☎ 6 15 88; Ayteke Bi 21; 🕒 8am-10pm; 🍴), nearly opposite the Asetan, is done up like the interior of a Kazakh yurt, complete with wood latticework and wolf pelt, but the menu is largely European.

The airport is 17km south of the city and there are seven flights a week to/from Almaty (2½ hours, US$85). Train services are the same as for Turkistan.

ARALSK АРАЛЬСК
☎ 32422 / pop 40,000

Aralsk, about 220km northwest of Leninsk on the same road and railway, used to be on the shores of the Aral Sea, and was an important fishing port. In its train station waiting room, a mosaic covering an entire wall depicts how in 1921 Aralsk's comrades provided fish for people starving in Russia.

The fishing industry has long since died. At one point the sea had withdrawn at least 30km from Aralsk. Although there's been an improvement (see the Little Aral Sea Strikes Back, p129) Aralsk remains a bleak place, battered by dust storms and suffering polluted water supplies.

If you want to witness first-hand this environmental disaster zone, Aralsk is much easier to visit, and more interesting, than similarly defunct ports on the Uzbek side of the Aral. You can see several rusting **boats** lying in the former harbour, just outside the hotel. In 2003, in honour of Aralsk's 100th birthday, some were put on platforms and painted, tribute to the fallen heroes.

A new museum at the site is inside the salvaged former home of a Russian merchant. In the centre of town, a local **history**

BAYKONUR COSMODROME

The Baykonur Cosmodrome, amid semidesert about 250km northwest of Kyzylorda, has been the launch site for all Soviet and Russian-crewed space flights since Yuri Gagarin, the first human in space, was lobbed up in 1961. In fact the launch site isn't really in Baykonur, which is actually a town 300km to the northeast, but the USSR told the International Aeronautical Federation that Gagarin's launch point was Baykonur, and that name has stuck.

The nearest town is the Russian military town of **Leninsk** on the Syr-Darya, south of the cosmodrome, which was built to guard and service the cosmodrome. The train station just north of Leninsk is called Töretam. The launch site is about 30km further north.

After the collapse of the USSR, the Cosmodrome became a useful card in Kazakhstan's dealings with Russia, which inherited the Soviet space programme. As negotiations to determine the rightful owner of Baykonur foundered, and a shortage of funds ended many space projects, living standards fell and riots by Kazakh soldiers erupted here in 1992 and 1993.

In 1994 Kazakhstan agreed to lease Baykonur and Leninsk to Russia for 20 years for about US$120 million a year (the lease has since been extended by 50 years). A few months later the Kazakh cosmonaut Talgat Musabaev and the Russian Yuri Malenchenko took off on a symbolic joint visit to the Mir space station. The launches are periodically banned when things go amiss – in 1999, two proton rockets exploded in separate incidents, contaminating lakes and rivers and sending debris as far away as Karaghanda.

This area is not open to travellers. Just fronting up and trying to talk or bribe your way into Baykonur from Töretam might work, but it certainly won't get you anywhere near the cosmodrome and will get you into a lot of trouble if you're caught. It's always possible the situation could loosen up. One place to check is the Russian embassy in Almaty.

In Kyzylorda, the **Sayakhat Tour Company** (☎ 32422-7 71 85; Tokmogambetov 22) says it can arrange a day trip here, but they need 45 days to complete your paperwork and charge US$500 per head (although this might be negotiable if you have a group). This is a lot to pay for a small museum and walk around the facilities, and there is no guarantee you'll see a launch. Send us a postcard if you make it and have some roubles on hand to buy the stamps as that is the official currency here.

museum (admission 100 T; 9am-noon & 2-6pm Tue-Sun) has some old photos of the fishermen in action, along with contemporary paintings of the disaster itself by local artists.

Close to the harbour is the abandoned fish processing plant, Aralrybprom, now ravaged by looters. Amazingly, the factory managed to stay alive 20 years after the disappearance of the Aral, canning fish imported from places as far away as the Baltic states and Vladivostok. It went bankrupt in the late 1990s. The fishing industry isn't completely gone; in the autumn fishermen haul out hundreds of tons of flounder, a non-native fish and the only one that still survives in the remaining Aral waters.

At Dzhambul, 63km west of Aralsk, another former fishing village, you can see a **ship cemetery**, where several abandoned hulks rust in the open desert. Before heading out on an excursion, bring your own food – communities like Dzhambul have very little supplies. Aralsk itself has a bleak market; two Peace Corps volunteers here had to travel 11 hours by train to Aktöbe to buy an electric fan!

For more on the Aral Sea, see p68.

Sleeping & Eating

Yaksart Konak Ui (Hotel Aral; 214 79; Makataeva 14; s/d renovated US$35/70, unrenovated US$7/14;) Located next to the old port.

Aibek B&B (232 56; Makataeva 19; s/d with shared bathroom US$8/16) Opposite the Yaksart, this basic homestay offers clean rooms with home-cooked meals.

Astana (10am-midnight) Located on the south side of the town square, this pleasant bar/restaurant serves Kazakh food, a good French salad, and has a surprisingly clean pit toilet.

Getting There & Around

Of several trains that come here, the most regular is the daily No 23 Almaty–Aktöbe train, which arrives at 9pm heading north. Going south, the No 24 comes in at 2.41am. In summer, departure train tickets can be brutally hard to come by. Buy them for the next night's train when you arrive. Even better, buy your tickets prior to your arrival, allotting yourself 24 hours to see the town and sea.

Local NGO **Aral Tenizi** (324 33, 236 91; www.aralsk.net; Makataeva 10), located between the

---

THE LITTLE ARAL SEA STRIKES BACK

The piles of dried flounder are stacked ever higher the closer you get to Aralsk, and the women who sell them, ever pushier. Your first inclination is, if the Aral is gone, where do these fish come from? Actually, most of the fish come from the surviving puddles around the Aral, but a growing number are being hauled out of the Aral itself, that is, the Little Aral.

With the help of international aid agencies and lenders like the World Bank, Kazakhstan is bringing back to life the northeast corner of the Aral, now severed from its southern body.

This plan was put into place in the 1990s – a dike was built across the last natural channel that connected the northern and southern portions. With no outlet to the south, the little Aral started to fill up again with water from the Syr-Darya. Having gone out as much as 40km from Aralsk, the sea crept within 27km, only to recede again when the dike disintegrated in 1999.

In 2003 the construction of a new US$85 million dike went into motion. The dike, stretching 12.8km and rising 10m to 12m, was due to be finished in late 2004. Builders say in four years the water level will rise 3.5 metres, not bad, but a far cry from the 21.5m it has fallen since the pre-1960 level. Around 370 sq kilometres of former seabed will be recovered, which locals hope will improve the micro-climate, bring more fish and fowl and end the frequent noxious dust storms that plague communities such as Aralsk.

The dike is controversial in that it condemns the larger southern lake to accelerated evaporation. For the citizens of Aralsk, though, better the survival of Little Aral than the disappearance of the entire sea. The dike is a four- to five-hour drive from Aralsk; travellers wishing to see it should contact the NGO Aral Tenizi (see below).

---

hotel and town square, can arrange English-speaking guides and drivers to visit the sites. Ask for Akmaral Utimissova. This office provides better services than a similar NGO based out of a house next to the train station. Aral Tenizi can also get Aralsk's notorious police off your back if there is trouble.

A day trip to the sea and back will cost US$50 for the jeep. Overnight camel and camping trips to the Aral are also possible (US$100 per head).

WEST KAZAKHSTAN
ЗАПАД
КАЗАХСТАН

North and west of the Aral Sea stretches more desert and steppe, significantly populated only towards the Russian border, but crucial to Kazakhstan because here lie great reserves of oil and natural gas, now being extracted by local and foreign companies under deals bringing millions of vital dollars into the country.

The rail routes from Central Asia to Moscow and the Volga region cross this wilderness – ideal if you like taking slow trains across empty deserts relieved only by roaming camels, salt lakes and pink rock outcrops. In the summer, the Caspian Sea is warm enough for swimming in at Aktau. Atyrau and Uralsk have some old architecture that's worth a look, but otherwise, if you're not in the oil or gas business, there's little reason to drag yourself here.

AKTÖBE АКТЮБЭ
☎ 3132 / pop 260,000

Aktöbe, on the main rail line to Moscow, about a hundred kilometres from the Russian border in northwest Kazakhstan, is a drab industrial city where you might need to change trains.

Near the lively market is the local **museum** (☎ 21 30 68; Altynsarin; admission 100 T; ☯ 9am-1pm & 2-6pm) where Rosa, an English-speaking curator, might be available to give you a tour. To reach here from the station, take Ayteke Bi, the second street on the left off Kökkhar, then turn right at the Hotel Ilek on Altynsarin; the museum is in a white building.

For places to stay, the economical answer is the **komnaty otdykha** (r per 24hr US$2.25) at the train station, which has quite comfortable dorm beds and very helpful staff.

The best place to stay is **Hotel Aktyubinsk** (☎ 56 28 29; hotel@aktobe.kz; Abylay Khan 44; d/lux US$15/49), which has clean Soviet-style rooms with TV and fridge; newly renovated rooms are in the *lux* category. To get here from

the station take bus Nos 1 or 15, or a taxi (about US$1).

Locals recommend eating at the Armenian restaurant **Uratu** (Truda 139a), a short taxi ride from the Hotel Aktyubinsk. Otherwise there are several small cafés near the station serving the usual menu of dumplings and noodles.

Flights from Aktöbe are scheduled to Almaty, Astana, Atyrau and Aktau daily; and Uralsk three times a week. A taxi to/from the airport, southeast of the centre, is US$2. Bus No 8 also links the two.

Trains run from the **station** (☎ 97 22 94) to Aktau (24 hours, US$14), Atyrau (14 hours, US$8), Uralsk (eight hours, US$8), Saratov (Moscow; 32 to 37 hours, US$53), Tashkent (30 hours, US$58) and Almaty (43 hours, US$28) several times a day, and to Bishkek (38 hours, US$51) once a day.

Nur Ai & Co (☎ 22 03 83; nurai-tour@nursat.kz; ☯ 9am-7pm), a reliable agency located outside the train station, can book tickets.

URALSK УРАЛЬСК

Closer to Vienna than Almaty and straddling the dividing line between Asia and Europe, Uralsk is either the first or last city for some Central Asian overlanders. It's also a base for many expat oilmen hauling themselves out to the pumping stations at Karachaganak, 150km east of the city. Uralsk is well off any tourist route, but if you are passing through to/from Russia there are enough sites and museums to keep you occupied until your train departs, as well as a clutch of good hotels and restaurants.

Whereas the future of this oil town lies with Kazakhstan, Uralsk's roots are in Russia – Lenin himself saw to it that Uralsk was included in the Kazakh SSR so as to make the place a welcome sight for Russian migrants. It was founded at the turn of the 17th century and has since played host to assorted Russian exiles and wanderers, including Pushkin and Tolstoy.

Kazakhstan's first **drama theatre**, a handsome brick affair with a lick of purple paint, has been standing on the main boulevard for 150 years. Dostyk Street has some of the finest architecture in town, including two Russian Orthodox churches, brilliantly lit up at night.

The **Sayahat Hotel** (☎ 51 30 03; Temir Masina 38; r US$20-55) is a renovated Soviet-style place with basic rooms, while the more upmarket option is the **Chagala** (☎ 51 08 92; r US$130-200) catering to foreign oilmen.

Dozens of restaurants line Dostyk from the train station to the Ural River. Locals recommend the European and Korean fare at **Exotica** (☎ 51 24 74; Dostyk 133; meals US$4-8).

Uralsk is connected by air to Astana (six per week), Almaty (four per week), Baku (twice weekly), and Munich and Moscow weekly. A small daily passenger bus travels to Atyrau (7am in both directions, 12 hours, US$12) and train connections are similar to those in Aktöbe.

ATYRAU АТЫРАУ
☎ 31222 / pop 210,000

Atyrau, on the Ural River, 30km upstream from its mouth on the northern shore of the Caspian Sea, is 'Oil City Kazakhstan', acting as command station for the main Tenghiz oil field, which is 350km further south. The giant USA oil company, Chevron, is one of the major players through Tengizchevroil, its multibillion-dollar joint venture with the Kazakhstan government. It contributes one third of all tax money earned by the Kazakh government. There are many other oil and gas fields in the Atyrau region; the huge Kashagan reserves in the Caspian Sea, discovered in July 2000, could prove to be the world's fifth-largest oil field.

Orientation
The Ural River meanders through the town, flowing roughly north–south beneath the central bridge on Abay and marking the border between Asia and Europe. West of the bridge, on the European side, Abay becomes Satpaev. The train station is on the northeastern edge of town, about 6km from the centre, and the bus station is about 2.5km west of the river on Avangard (turn right off Satpaev). The airport is further out west beyond the bus station.

Information
CATC (☎ 2540 75/76; cat-atyrau@alarnet.com; Azattyk 25) Ticketing and travel agency.
Halyk Bank (☎ 25 15 33; Satpaev; ☺ 8.30am-4pm Mon-Fri) Travellers cheques changed, American Express preferred.
Internet Café (☎ 27 07 07; Kazakhtelekom, Ayteke Bi) Internet access for 5 T per minute.

ATYRAU

0 —————— 1 km
0 —————— 0.5 miles

INFORMATION	
CATC...	1 B5
Central Telephone Office..................	2 B5
Halyk Bank......................................	3 A5
Internet Café..............................	(see 4)
Kazakhtelekom................................	4 B5
Kazkommertzbank............................	5 B5
Otrar Travel.....................................	6 B5
OVIR..	7 B6

SIGHTS & ACTIVITIES	(p132)
Atyrau History Museum....................	8 B5
Gallery of Kazakh Modern Art..........	9 B5
Makhambet & Isatai Monument........	10 A5
Mangali Mosque..............................	11 A5
Palace of Culture.............................	12 A5
Russian Orthodox Church.................	13 A5
Sports Complex...............................	14 B5

SLEEPING	(p132)
Atyrau Sanatoriyasi.........................	15 B5
Hotel Ak Zhayyk..............................	16 B5
Hotel Caspii.....................................	17 B5
Hotel Chagala..................................	18 B5
River Palace Residence....................	19 B5

EATING	(p132)
Beybars..	20 B5
Feya...	21 A6
La Cabana..	22 B5
McMagic..	23 B5

DRINKING	(p133)
Celtic Dragon...................................	24 B5
O'Neil's..	25 B5

ENTERTAINMENT	(p133)
La Cabana Bowling..........................	(see 22)

OTHER	
Tenghizchevroil Headquarters..........	26 A5

Minor Streets not depicted

↑ To Train Station (5km)

M Kazaret

Old Town

Ural River

Makhambet

Zhelisnodarojne

Momishuli

Modagov

Abay

Isati

Ayteke B

Azattyk

To Long-Distance Bus Station (1.5km); Airport (6km)

Satpaev

ploshchad Abay   Bazaar

Alaray

Zhylgorodok

Beach

Ural River

Azattyk

Azattyk

Freight Railway Lines

LP

Dangers & Annoyances

All that Western money has caused resentment among young Kazakhs and violent attacks are on the rise. Kazakh women with foreign men are also becoming targets. Don't walk the streets after dark and rather than flagging down a taxi on the street, have your restaurant/bar/hotel order a registered taxi.

The other thing to be wary of is the mud, which engulfs the town during the winter rainy season, if you visit during this time, take appropriate footwear.

Sights & Activities

The **Atyrau History Museum** (☎ 22 29 12; Azattyk 9b; admission 200 T; 🕑 10am-7pm) is located about 100m behind the Hotel Ak Zhayyk in a new glass-fronted building. It has several interesting artefacts from the region, including a display on Saraichuk, a once grand city some 45km west of Atyrau, destroyed in the 13th century and since uncovered by archaeologists.

Across the pedestrian walkway 'Arbat' is the **Gallery of Kazakh Modern Art** (☎ 25 48 03; admission 200 T; 🕑 10am-7pm), worth a look for its collection of paintings on Atyrau life.

At the heart of the visibly crumbling 'old town' on the west side of the river about 1km northwest of the bridge, a well-maintained **Russian Orthodox church** emerges like a jewelled finger from the surrounding shacks. It dates from 1888 and its interior is plastered with icons.

One kilometre south of here is a new **public square** fitted with fountains, monuments to 19th-century freedom fighters Makhambet and Isatai, and an annoying jumbo TV that cranks out music videos. The brand new **Mangali Mosque** is nearby.

A pleasant half-day stroll starts at the central bridge following the east bank of the Ural south. On reaching the riverside beach, complete with metal parasols, turn inland to find **Zhylgorodok**. This charming area of Mediterranean-looking whitewashed houses with blue-painted woodwork was built at the end of WWII by German, Italian and Japanese POWs. At its heart is a square with colonnaded arcades on two sides and a handsome **Palace of Culture** on another. Peep inside the upstairs hall, which has dazzling ceiling decorations.

Located next to the Hotel Chagal, the **Sports Complex** (☎ 22 77 81; Ismagulov 5) has a large gymnasium with weight room and swimming pool.

Sleeping

Atyrau's oil boom has set some astronomical hotel rates and you'll be hard-pressed to find anything less than US$50 a night, even for the most mediocre of rooms.

Hotel Caspii (☎ 21 33 07; hotel-caspi@nursat.kz; Satpaev 15; s/d US$73/105) Down a side-street 500m west of the river, this overpriced, two-star hotel has a decent breakfast buffet. There are a couple of expensive suites, a restaurant and a sauna.

Hotel Ak Zhayyk (☎ 25 43 85; fax 22 20 11; taskinkurun@hotmail.com; ploshchad Abay 4; US$50/94) This was undergoing heavy renovation at the time of research and should be upgraded to three-star level.

Atyrau Sanatoriyasi (☎ 25 46 79, 25 46 60; fax 25 46 80; r US$77) Further south, down Azattyk and back towards the river, this has comfortable rooms at negotiable rates, if you don't mind the hospital-style feel.

Hotel Chagala (☎ 25 40 33; fax 25 40 34; chagala-office@nursat.kz; Ismagulov 1; s/d US$154/230; ⌘ 🅿 💻) This hotel beside the river has good security, satellite TV, IDD phones, gym, restaurant/bar, shop, and laundry service.

River Palace Residence (☎ 25 52 39; rv_hotel@ducat.kz; Ayteke Bi 55; d/lux US$162/324; ⌘ 🅿 💻) Just across the river, this brand new hotel is five-star quality and has a rooftop pool.

Eating

McMagic (☎ 25 54 45; Makhambet 116a; meals 200-400 T) Located next to the bazaar, this is a reasonable Western-style burger and pizza bar.

Beybars (☎ 22 75 28; ploshchad Abay 1; meals US$8-10; 🕑 10am-1pm) Located on the 2nd floor of a building facing the roundabout, this place serves excellent, cafeteria-style food in a welcoming atmosphere. It's your best bet for a quick wholesome business lunch.

La Cabana (☎ 25 53 71; Azattyk 2; meals US$7-14) A varied menu in this American-style restaurant hung with college football emblems and flags includes Mexican dishes and burgers.

Feya (☎ 25 34 88; Auezov 1; 🕑 11am-midnight) This trendy Uzbek-style restaurant, complete with waitresses in Fergana-style outfits, is located in the quiet neighbourhood of Zhylgorodok, on the square next to the Palace of Culture.

Drinking & Entertainment

Celtic Dragon (☎ 25 55 85; Zhelisnodarojne 8; ☿ noon-midnight) Convincing Irish pub with Murphy's on tap.

O'Neil's (☎ 25 40 33; Ismagulov 1, Hotel Chagala) This, together with Celtic and La Cabana, gives Atyrau its own 'Bermuda Triangle'; the pub-crawl circuit.

La Cabana Bowling (☎ 25 53 71 Azattyk 2) Bowling alley inside the restaurant of the same name.

Getting There & Away

Travellers report that a small daily passenger bus makes the 12-hour, 500km run (US$12) to Uralsk, embarking from the bus station.

From the **train station** (☎ 26 06 06) there are daily trains to/from Aktöbe (eight hours, US$9), Aktau (9 hours, US$12) and Astrakhan (US$16). Services to/from Volgograd (through Astrakhan) and Almaty (US$20) are scheduled every two days. When buying tickets, note that Atyrau is one hour ahead of Moscow and two hours behind Almaty. You can buy tickets from an office in the Hotel Ak Zhayyk.

Bus No 14 connects the train station and ploshchad Abay.

AKTAU АКТАУ

☎ 3292 / pop 140,000

Stuck between the desert and the Caspian, hundreds of kilometres from anywhere, with all its water derived from a desalination plant powered by a nuclear reactor, Aktau is one of the strangest of the places scattered across the former USSR.

The reason anyone is here at all is local uranium deposits. In 1963, Soviet architects began to lay out a model town of wide, straight streets, dividing residential quarters into numbered *mikrorayony* (micro-regions) of apartment blocks, uncomplicated by street names. It was called Shevchenko, after the 19th-century Ukrainian poet and artist Taras Shevchenko, who was exiled to Kazakhstan for his nationalist views. Thanks to the nearby sandy beaches on the blue Caspian, the place was also developed as a holiday resort for the Soviet elite.

Now the uranium and tourism industries are in decline, but the oil industry has picked up the slack and Aktau is on the rebound. Already there's a steady trickle of Westerners in town, mingling with the local population of Russians, Kazakhs and people from the Caucuses.

Orientation

The only street with a name is Abay (formerly Lenina), a broad avenue sloping down from north to south and running parallel to the coast. Other Aktau locations are identified by their *mikrorayon* and *dom* (building) numbers. The Hotel Aktau is on the southern end of Abay; the impressive war memorial with an eternal flame is at the northern end.

Information

CATC (☎ 51 75 04, 51 51 85; fax 51 47 19; Hotel Aktau, Mikrorayon 2) English-speaking travel agency that can book tickets and help with train connections to Uzbekistan.

Exchange Currency Booth (Fl 2, TsUM Department Store, Abay, Mikrorayon 4) Changes dollars.

Halyk Bank (Mikrorayon 9)

Internet Café (Abay, Mikrorayon 2) Located in the Kazakhtelekom office.

Otrar Travel (☎ 25 53 45; otrartravelguw@group.kz; Abay 3) Also books domestic and international flights.

Sights

To best savour Aktau's bizarre atmosphere, head for the breezy **seafront**. There are cliffs and a promenade running to a rocky beach to the north, just beyond the **MiG memorial** and an **Aqua Park** with waterslides and pools. Heading south you'll pass the brooding statue of the exiled poet Taras Shevchenko. There are better beaches to be found if you drive out of town to where the locals have their *dachas*.

Interesting displays about the Caspian and surrounding area make the **Regional History & Local Studies Museum** (Abay, Mikrorayon 9; ☿ 9am-6pm Mon-Sat) well worth a visit. The entrance leads into a courtyard through a blue gate.

If you're in search of desolation, head to **Fort Shevchenko**, 125km north up the coast, which originated in the 19th century as a Russian bridgehead called Fort Alexandrovsk. There's a museum here, and a new base for the joint British and Kazakh oil exploration firm OKIOK, otherwise it's deserted, with Soviet-era fishing boats rusting in the harbour beside a row of attractive old Russian houses. Get up early if you want to catch a bus (US$1) here from the bus station on the northern edge of Aktau.

Otherwise, haggle for a taxi (no more than US$20 round trip).

Worth stopping at along the way to the fort is **Koshkarata**, a picturesque Muslim cemetery whose crenellated skyline of miniature domes and towers looks from a distance like some town out of an Arabian fairytale.

Sleeping

Hotel Atai (☎ 43 63 96; Mikrorayon 9-1; r US$16/42) Located near the MiG monument, this budget hotel is actually a series of converted apartments. There is a good café downstairs.

Koktem (☎ 43 44 79; Mikrorayon 9; koktem@nursat.kz; r US$60-150) This more upscale hotel is a block north near the Aqua Park and the beach.

Hotel Aktau (☎ 51 47 07, 51 47 50; Abay, Mikrorayon 2; r US$32-82) Recent renovations have improved the place, though it still feels salty and haggard. Still, it's the most central place in town and has good sea views.

Zelyonaya Gostinitsa (Green Hotel; ☎ 51 73 04; Abay, Mikrorayon 3; r US$81-108) This impeccably managed hotel is about 1km west of the Hotel Aktau. It only has suites and apartments, all large and well-furnished.

Hotel Rakhat (☎ 51 17 55; Mikrorayon 1; US$55/95) This is the place to go if you are in dire need of sea views. The rooms are OK, but what you are really paying for is the location.

Eating

Near the bus station is a large bazaar where you can pick up picnic snacks. There's a grocery section in TsUM and Ardager Mall further down Abay.

Edem (☎ 51 77 66; Mikrorayon 3) Convivial and moderately priced café with the standard Russian set lunch. There's also a bar, where you can get bottled American beer.

Navrys (☎ 51 66 66; Mikrorayon 3; meals US$3-4; ☯ noon-3am) Enclosed in a courtyard under glass like a greenhouse, enlivened with plants and caged chirping birds, this pleasant restaurant has Russian, Kazakh and European dishes. The micro-brewed beer is a welcome treat from the salty Caspian air. It's located next to the Zelonaya Hotel.

Shamrock (☎ 52 18 38; Abay, Mikrorayon 4; meals US$7-10; draft beer US$5) This authentic Irish pub has excellent, large meals of pizza, chicken sandwiches and burgers. There is live music most nights.

Getting There & Around

The train station for Aktau is Mangghyshlak (Mangghystau), about 12km east of the town. Daily trains run to/from Atyrau, 400km north as the crow flies, but about 800km and 24 hours by rail. A *kupe* (second class) ticket costs around $10. Note that Aktau is one hour ahead of Moscow time and two hours behind Almaty time.

Bus No 101 (30 minutes, 50 T) runs via Abay between Mangghyshlak train station and Aktau bus station (*avtovokzal* or *avtostantsia*), around 3km north of the Hotel Aktau. The journey takes you across a surreal wilderness strewn with pipelines and cables. A taxi should cost around US$5. The fare to the airport is about the same.

Bus No 3 runs along Abay to the bazaar and bus station. Bus Nos 1 and 2 run along the seafront.

NORTH KAZAKHSTAN
СЕВЕР
КАЗАХСТАН

Until the 19th century, the flat steppe of northern Kazakhstan was largely untouched except by Kazakh nomads and their herds. As Russia's grip stretched southwards, immigrants from western USSR came in increasing numbers to farm the steppe. The Kazakhs' resistance was largely futile and many thousands died in rebellions or famines.

An even bigger transformation came in Soviet times. The nomadic Kazakhs were forced into collective farms, thousands starving in the ensuing famine. New industrial cities such as Karaghanda and Ekibastuz sprouted to process coal, iron and other minerals, and in the 1950s vast areas of steppe were turned over to wheat in Khrushchev's Virgin Lands scheme (p92).

The region was useful to Moscow for more sinister reasons, too. A network of Gulag labour camps was set up here, to which were sent deportees from other parts of the USSR. In the 1950s most of the camps were closed, but many of the survivors stayed, including a large number of ethnic Germans.

The legacy of the Soviet era is a high Russian and Ukrainian population (Kazakhs number less than 20% in several regions) and a lot of decaying industry. Many Slavs, disgruntled by economic decline and seeing little future in a Kazakhstan dominated by Kazakhs, have left. In the early 1990s there was even talk of joining up with Russia. Nazarbaev's thwarted this by stamping the capital here.

The best months to visit the region are May to June and August to September. Winters are severe, with howling blizzards and temperatures to -40°C in January. In July you can expect the opposite extreme.

ASTANA АСТАНА
☎ 3172 / pop 500,000

Disgruntled diplomats, cocktail-swigging consultants and smartly dressed bureaucrats have taken over Astana, little more than a provincial wasteland just a decade ago. Although there is little to hold the traveller down, Astana lends the opportunity to see just how one country spends the profits made from the sale of 400,000 barrels of oil per day; a drive south of the river reveals glass skyscrapers rising out of the steppe – the birth of the capital-to-be.

Astana, 1300km northwest of Almaty, has gone through several name changes during its lifetime. It was founded in 1830 as a Russian Cossack fortress named Akmola (a Kazakh name meaning 'white plenty' because the area was renowned for its dairy products and bread). When Nikita Khrushchev announced his Virgin Lands scheme, Akmola became the project's capital and was renamed Tselinograd (Virgin Lands City) in 1961.

After the break-up of the USSR, Akmola got back its old name, and would have kept it if President Nazarbaev's plan to shift the capital here hadn't attracted such unfavourable comments. Although Nazarbaev cited the possibility of earthquakes in Almaty as good reason for making the change, critics said opting for a provincial town, plagued by extremes of weather, as the capital would prove to be Nazarbaev's political grave – a pun on another translation of Akmola as 'white tomb'. Thus the president renamed the city Astana (Kazakh for 'capital').

If the plastic siding facelift given to the downtown area seems a bit tacky, be consoled by the fact that this is merely the temporary capital. All the ministries will move again, south of the river, by the coveted year 2030. Afterwards, the current centre will hang on as Astana's commercial and cultural centre.

Orientation

The city of Astana is centred around the square at the end of Beibitshilik (formerly Mira). The parliament is at the northern end and the Sime Tempore Mall to the south. Two blocks east is the main avenue Respublika (formerly called Tselinnikov), which starts near the Ishim River in the south and changes its name to Pushkin as it nears the train station, 3km to the north.

The sprawling open-air bazaar is five blocks east of Pushkin between Batyr Bogembai and Seyfullin. The airport is 17km south of the centre. The city's central park borders the Ishim River. South of here lies the new government complex, still under construction.

MAPS

The best map you can buy of the city is the English-language *Astana* (1:20,000), published by SCE Cartography in 2002. Copies can be bought at the major hotels in Astana and Almaty for around 300 T.

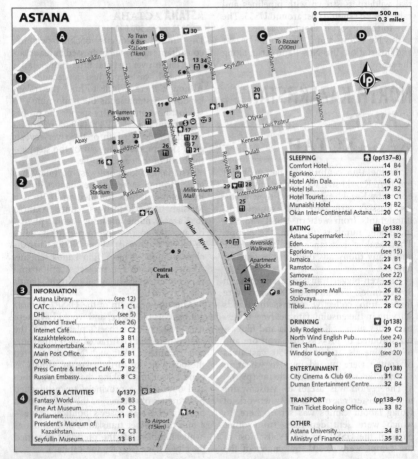

ASTANA

| 0 | 500 m |
| 0 | 0.3 miles |

SLEEPING 🛏 (pp137–8)
Comfort Hotel..................................14 B4
Egorkino...15 B1
Hotel Altin Dala..............................16 A2
Hotel Isil..17 B2
Hotel Tourist...................................18 C1
Munaishi Hotel................................19 B2
Okan Inter-Continental Astana......20 C1

EATING 🍴 (p138)
Astana Supermarket.......................21 B2
Eden...22 B2
Egorkino......................................(see 15)
Jamaica...23 B1
Ramstor...24 C3
Samovar.....................................(see 22)
Shegis..25 C2
Sime Tempore Mall.........................26 B2
Stolovaya...27 B2
Tiblisi...28 C2

DRINKING 🍺 (p138)
Jolly Rodger....................................29 C2
North Wind English Pub............(see 24)
Tien Shan...30 B1
Windsor Lounge.........................(see 20)

ENTERTAINMENT 🎭 (p138)
City Cinema & Club 69....................31 C2
Duman Entertainment Centre........32 B4

TRANSPORT (pp138–9)
Train Ticket Booking Office............33 B2

OTHER
Astana University.............................34 B1
Ministry of Finance.........................35 B2

INFORMATION
Astana Library............................(see 12)
CATC...1 C1
DHL..(see 5)
Diamond Travel..........................(see 26)
Internet Café.....................................2 C2
Kazakhtelekom..................................3 B1
Kazkommertzbank.............................4 B1
Main Post Office................................5 B1
OVIR..6 B1
Press Centre & Internet Café...........7 B2
Russian Embassy...............................8 C3

SIGHTS & ACTIVITIES (p137)
Fantasy World.....................................9 B3
Fine Art Museum..............................10 C3
Parliament...11 B1
President's Museum of
    Kazakhstan..................................12 C3
Seyfullin Museum.............................13 B1

MARTIN MOOS

Southern Almaty (p93) and the distant
Zailiysky Alatau, Kazakhstan

SIMON RICHMOND

Kazakh boy in traditional dress

Kazakh family with a horse, Kazakhstan

VERONICA GARBUTT

Victory Day poster and choir at the Old House of Parliament, Almaty (p101), Kazakhstan

Zelyony Bazaar (p104), Almaty, Kazakhstan

Altay Mountains (p151), Kazakhstan

Information

INTERNET ACCESS

There is an Internet café at the main post office, the Astana Library, the Press Centre (opposite Sime Tempore Mall) and at Respublika 5, each charging about 200 T per hour.

LIBRARIES

Astana Library (☎ 22 33 00; ground fl, President's Museum, Barayev 3; ☺ 10am-7pm Tue-Sun) The library has a small foreign-language section on the ground floor.

MONEY

Foreign exchange booths are dotted around the city. ATMs are available at banks and central shopping malls. There is a Western Union window in the main post office.

Kazkommertzbank (☎ 32 35 18; Abay 66; ☺ 9.30am-4pm Mon-Fri) Located behind the Hotel Isil, changes travellers cheques for a 2% commission.

POST

DHL (☎ 58 05 80) Located at the main post office.
Main Post Office (Auezov 71; ☺ 8am-7pm Mon-Fri, 9am-5pm Sat, 9am-3pm Sun)

REGISTRATION

OVIR (☎ 71 61 77; Seyfullin 63; ☺ 9am-12.30pm & 2.30-5pm Mon-Fri)

TELEPHONE & FAX

Kazakhtelekom (☎ 99 09 11; Auezov 56; ☺ 6am-midnight) Long-distance phone calls and faxes can be sent from here.

TRAVEL AGENCIES

CATC (☎ 32 78 44; cat-astana@alarnet.com; Respublika 66; ☺ 9am-7pm Mon-Fri, 9am-1pm Sat) Air tickets, registration (US$15) and trips to local attractions such as Lake Burabay (US$30).
Diamond Travel (☎ 15 38 77; Sime Tempore Mall, Beibitshilik 9) Airline booking and travel agent.

Sights

The **President's Museum of Kazakhstan** (☎ 22 33 00; Barayev 3; admission 90 T, photos 200 T; ☺ 10am-5pm) fuses Kazakhstan's nomadic and sedentary past – it is built in the shape of a yurt and topped with a mosquelike dome. The exhibits tell the history of Kazakhstan, rising from Stone Age exhibits on the 1st floor to wheat and cosmonauts on the 3rd floor. The highlight is a 2nd-floor room containing Kazakh jewellery and a replica of the Golden Man costume (p99). Check out the gleaming blue-and-gold model of the future Astana city. The top floor contains an exhibit of modern artwork by local artists.

The entrance to the **Fine Art Museum** (☎ 21 54 30; Respublika 3; ☺ 10am-6pm Tue-Sun) is on the side of the block. The small permanent collection includes some striking works and there are regularly changing exhibitions of local artists.

Close by the main library on Seyfullin is an attractive old Russian-style cottage, the former home of the Kazakh writer Saken Seyfullin and now the **Seyfullin Museum** (☎ 32 35 63; Auezov 80; admission 100 T; ☺ 10am-6pm), dedicated to his memory.

Sleeping

Hotel prices in Astana have skyrocketed since we last visited and budget rooms are hard to find. At the time of research the Isil Hotel, opposite the Parliament, was under renovation and is expected to become a solid four-star hotel.

Train Station Hotel (☎ 93 28 97; dm/d US$5.50/21) This budget hotel is conveniently located at the train station.

Airport Hotel (☎ 17 43 54; s/d US$9.50/18) This acceptable hotel is next to the airport, but not convenient for town.

Hotel Tourist (☎ 33 01 00; fax 33 02 01; Respublika 23; s/d US$37/57) The last of Astana's Soviet dinosaur hotels has faded rooms and dodgy plumbing, but is set for renovation which will surely increase the price.

Hotel Altin Dala (☎ 32 33 11; Peoneveskaya 19a; s/d US$61/74) This excellent little hotel has smart business rooms and a courteous reception desk. It's tucked down an alley a block west of the blue-glassed Ministry of Finance.

Munaishi (☎ 32 53 40; s/d US$57/70) This hotel, next to the footbridge, is south of Hotel Altin Dala and very similar.

Egorkino (☎ 32 35 54; Auezov 93; r US$90) This charming inn, straight out of an old Russian fairytale, is upstairs from the restaurant of the same name. The landscape paintings on the walls, colourful quilts and heavy wood furniture are rather unlike the typically dull business hotel that has taken over Astana. Recommended in this price range.

Okan Inter-Continental Astana (☎ 39 10 00; hotel@interconti-astana.kz; Abay 113; r with breakfast US$269/319; ❄ ⬛ ⬛) Astana's most prestigious hotel, with plush rooms, satellite TV, health club, and several restaurants.

Comfort Hotel (☎ 22 10 21; Kosmonavtov 60; s/d US$144/216) South past Central Park, this is less central but better value for money than Okan.

Eating

Stolovaya (☼ 9am-8pm Mon-Sat; Beibitshilik) For a budget meal, try this cafeteria on the ground floor of the Agency of Strategic Planning and Reforms; it's on the square at the end of Beibitshilik.

Shegis (Respublika 8) This is the local burger-and-fry joint.

Eden (☎ 32 43 16; Kenesary 74; meals US$4-7) One of the city's most stylish restaurants and a favourite with the business sets. The shrimp salad is a winner.

Samovar (☎ 32 43 16; Kenesary 74; ☼ breakfast, lunch & dinner) If you are on a budget, Eden runs this Russian café next door, which is open for breakfast. Its cappuccinos are the best in town.

Egorkino (☎ 32 38 78; Auezov 93; meals US$17-28) Astana's most inviting restaurant, this is a small courtyard affair literally transformed into a mock 17th-century peasant village with heavy carved doors and window frames and ivy-covered shacks made from Siberian timber. It serves lovely Russian salads, fried field mushrooms, sturgeon sautéed in wine, and sweet pancake desserts. The cigars and Moldavian wine are a plus. It's the best place in town and an experience in itself, even if for a one-off splurge.

Jamaica (☎ 32 35 69; Abay 51; ☼ noon-2am) The unlikely prospect of Jamaican food in Astana is a reality here, eaten under grass huts and on colourful plates. There is live music most nights.

Tiblisi (☎ 22 12 26; Imanov 14; ☼ noon-2am; meals US$14) This upscale Georgian restaurant has gone all out with its décor, right down to the mock wood porches, hay carts and waitresses decked out in traditional robes

Venezia (☎ 15 39 06; Sime Tempore Mall, Beibitshilik 9; meals US$10, pizza US$7) Astana's best Italian restaurant is in the southeast corner of the Sime Tempore Mall (the former TsUM). It has French and Italian wine, plus a good salad and dessert bar. Most patrons end up on the patio or in the pizza bar (inside the mall), where the same pizzas are sold for half the price.

If you're self-catering, or if you fancy a shashlyk snack, check out the giant bazaar

four blocks east of Respublika. The **Astana supermarket** (Beibitshilik), **Sime Tempore Mall** (Beibitshilik 9) and **Ramstor** (Riverside Walkway) all carry pricey Western imported foods.

Drinking

Tien Shan (☎ 31 44 95; Auezov 106; ☼ noon-3am) From 3pm to 6pm Wednesday the matrons serve all-you-can-drink beer at this expat hang-out, as long as you buy 500 T worth of food (and can put up with the ear-battering live music).

Jolly Rodger (☎ 21 66 15; cnr Respublika & Imanov) Here the staff wear stripy sailors' jerseys and draft beer is US$2 for a large mug.

North Wind English Pub (☎ 22 33 46; Ramstor, Riverside Walkway) This English beer hall is best during happy hour, between 6.30pm and 8.30pm Monday to Friday.

Windsor Lounge (☎ 39 10 00; Okan Inter-Continental Astana, Abay 113) This sophisticated bar allows desperate diplomats the opportunity to get drunk and pretend they're back in Almaty. It gets crowded on Friday.

Entertainment

Fantasy World (Central Park) With its cafés, discos and amusement rides, this is the popular evening hang-out.

Duman (☎ 24 24 73; www.duman.kz) Southeast of Fantasy World, several acres of wasteland have been converted into this sprawling entertainment centre. Apart from the hotel, bowling alley, game zone, jungle park, aqua park, casino and night club, the highlight is the huge **aquarium** (admission 500 T, 2-6pm 700 T, 6-10pm 900 T; ☼ 10am-2pm). The whole place has a bewildering Singapore-of-the-steppes feel to it.

City Cinema (☎ 21 07 92; Imanov 13) This large movie theatre has comfortable chairs and shows Hollywood flicks dubbed into Russian.

Club 69 (City Cinema, Imanov 13; admission men US$7, women US$3.50) This popular disco is housed within the City Cinema building.

Other discos can be found at the Okan Inter-Continental Astana and Fantasy World.

Getting There & Away

The airport is about 16km south of the city centre. Flights go to/from Almaty, Aktöbe, Ust-Kamenogorsk, Moscow, Frankfurt and Hannover twice a week. Flights to/from

Europe are booked out weeks ahead of time. Contact **Air Astana** (☎ 58 09 80; fl 12, Astana Tower Business Centre, Samal Microdistrict 12) for more details.

Trains go to/from Karaghanda, Almaty (*kupe*, 24 hours, US$18) and Kökshetau (*kupe*, five hours, US$5) at least twice per day; and run daily to/from Petropavlovsk (*kupe*, 11 hours, US$12), Kostanai (*kupe*, 16 hours, US$10) and Pavlodar (*kupe*, 10 hours, US$16). There are also services to Moscow and Shymkent.

You don't need to go to the station to buy tickets; there's a **train ticket booking office** (☎ 32 82 82) just off Parliament Square. Note that Astana is three hours ahead of Moscow. Call for a train schedule at the **train station** (☎ 38 33 33, 38 07 07). To/from Almaty you can also take the fast Talgo train (see p108).

The bus station, serving north, east and south Kazakhstan, is next to the train station, just north of the city.

Getting Around

Bus No 10 (15 T) runs every 30 minutes between the airport and Respublika. A taxi is about US$10. From the train and bus stations, bus Nos 9 or 25 and trolleybus Nos 2, 3, 4 or 5 go along Beibitshilik to the city centre. Taxis are numerous and cost 100 to 200 T per trip within the city centre.

AROUND ASTANA

Apart from Lake Burabay, there are a couple more possible outings from Astana.

About 150km southwest of the capital, **Kurgalzhino Nature Reserve** includes both virgin feather-grass steppe and numerous lakes, making it a water-bird habitat of major importance. Between April and September, the salty Lake Tenghiz supports a large breeding colony of pink flamingos. This is the world's most northerly habitat of these graceful birds, which migrate to the Caspian Sea during winter. The place is being set up for ecotourism and you can stay with local families and go on guided bird-watching tours. Park entry is US$10 and board and meals US$6 to US$10 per night. Arrangements can be made through the **reserve office** (☎ 8 31637-21650), or **Rodnik** (☎ 8 31637-21043), an NGO at the reserve office. Four buses (US$2) per day go to/from Astana. A taxi is about US$40. The trip takes about two hours.

Around **Ereimentau**, 135km northeast of Astana, there are granite cliffs popular with climbers, and some fine scenery. It's two hours by daily train from Astana.

LAKE BURABAY БУРАБАЙ ОЗЕРА
☎ 3142

Long before you arrive, you'll probably spot pictures of **Lake Burabay**, pinned up in tourist offices across the country. Located 200km north of Astana and 95km southeast of **Kökshetau**, the nearest large town, Burabay is known as 'Little Switzerland', although the mountains qualify only as steep hills. The dense forests, strange rock formations and scattered lakes, however, are in stark contrast to the surrounding flat, treeless steppe. Apart from being an idyllic place to relax, Burabay is ideal for hiking, rock climbing or cross-country skiing in winter.

The gateway to the lake district is the rundown, tongue-twister town of Shchuchinsk. Lake Burabay and the dumpy little village of **Burabay** are some 25km north. Here you'll find a rustic **Museum of Natural History** (☼ 10am-6.30pm Tue-Sun) with good displays on local flora and fauna and a small zoo that is home to a Przewalski's horse. A pleasant walk (one hour) is from the village to **Okzhetpes** – the striking 380m-tall rock pile between the lake and the tallest peak, the 947m Kokshe (Russian: Sinyukha).

The formation of Okzhetpes is explained by a legend that also covers **Zhumbaktas**, the Sphynx-like rock that pokes out of the water in front of it. The story goes that while Abylay Khan's army was fighting the Oyrats, a beautiful princess was captured and brought to Burabay. It was decreed that she should marry a Kazakh. The princess agreed, saying whoever could shoot an arrow to the top of the rock hill could have her hand. All her potential suitors failed the first time, hence the name Okzhetpes which means 'the arrow cannot reach this place'. But on a second attempt her true love hit the target. His rivals were so angry that they killed him. The princess, like a distraught Tosca, flung herself into the lake, thus creating the rock Zhumbaktas (Mysterious Stone).

A short footpath heading north from Okzhetpes leads to a point from where both Lake Burabay and the neighbouring Lake Bolshoe Chebachye can be seen.

Sleeping & Eating

In terms of accommodation and food, Burabay has a long way to catch up with demand. With a couple of exceptions the place seems strangely devoid of facilities – the busloads of tourists that flock to the town on weekends either camp by the lakeshore or arrange to stay in a private apartment (per person US$5) rented out by the babushkas (old women) that hang around the taxi stand. Opposite the telecom office, four rooms are let out by the **SMAK market** (☎ 72 307; US$7-21).

Nursat (☎ 71 301; r US$40-87) This new hotel, located on the main road 350m before the town centre, has several types of rooms, all with mod cons and reliable hot water. Although more hotels are expected to be built, this was the only one at the time of research.

Retiring Rooms (☎ 62 105; train station; r US$3.50) The surprisingly clean rooms located at the Shchuchinsk train station will suffice if you arrive late.

Camping is possible in a couple of spots on the east side of Lake Burabay, near the museum, and there's also a campsite on the rocky isthmus on the north side of Lake Bolshoe Chebachye. The Burabay Sanatorium, on the lake 1km west of town, has a café and *might* be able to rent out a room.

As for food, the main options in town are the basic Alma Ata Restaurant opposite the taxi stand, the Astana Restaurant a little to the west and the restaurant in the Nursat Hotel. Most visitors survive on beer and shashlyk.

Getting There & Away

Burabay can be visited in a day trip by train from Astana, leaving on the local 8.10am train to Shchuchinsk (US$8.50; four hours), the nearest station to the lake district, and returning on the 7.40pm train.

Most trains to/from Kökshetau also stop in Shchuchinsk. From Shchuchinsk train station you might be able to catch a marshrutnoe (80 T) 25km to Burabay; a more reliable option is a taxi (US$2).

There are also hourly buses from both Astana and, more frequently, Kökshetau to Shchuchinsk, although the train is easier and comes by two or three times a day.

Flights are scheduled to Kökshetau from Almaty five times a week (US$75).

PETROPAVLOVSK
ПЕТРОПАВЛОВСК

☎ 3152 / pop 180,000

Older and architecturally more diverse than many places in Kazakhstan, Petropavlovsk is the country's most northerly city, 475km north of Astana, and just 60km from the Russian border. It's an important rail junction, at the meeting of the north–south line through central Kazakhstan with a branch of the Trans-Siberian railway, and is Kazakhstan's busiest freight terminal.

With a very large Russian population, Petropavlovsk is as much a part of Siberia as of Kazakhstan. Several 19th-century brick buildings in the city centre, testaments to early attempts by the tsars to subjugate the Kazakhs, remain, as does a handsome Russian Orthodox church near the Ishim River, west of the city.

During Soviet times, four major defence plants were the backbone of the economy, making this a closed city. Now it's a Turkish-funded pasta factory that keeps most people in work.

Orientation

Internatsionalnaya is the central axis of the city, running east–west from the train station. Konstitutsiya (formerly Lenina), tree-lined and pedestrianised for much of its length, runs parallel two blocks to the north. The main north–south street is Zhabaev.

Information

Deep (☎ 49 24 14; Konstitutsiya 2; ☯ 24hr) Good Internet café opposite the drama theatre.
Halyk Bank There is an ATM on Auezov and also one on Konstitutsiya.
Kazakhtelekom (☎ 46 05 40; Buketov 36) Internet access.
Library (Konstitutsiya; ☯ 9am-5pm Sun-Fri) Free Internet access.
Main Post Office (Pushkina) Opposite the Drama Theatre.
North Kazakhstan University (cnr Pushkina & Internatsionalnaya) English-speaking guides might be available through the university's English department.
Tourist Office (☎ 46 35 56; Amangeldy 141) This private office has town maps.

Sights & Activities

The city **art museum** (cnr Internatsionalnaya & Auezov; ☯ 10am-5pm) is housed in an attractive building (a pale green wooden villa that once belonged to a rich timber merchant) behind the Domino Theatre. The collection inside includes modern and traditional paintings, and collections of *netsuke* (small wooden carvings), household objects and icons.

The **History & Local Studies Museum** (☎ 46 20 97; Konstitutsiya 48; admission 35 T; ☺ 10am-5.30pm Wed-Sun) is located in a sturdy red-brick building just off Auezov. This museum traces the growth of Petropavlovsk from its origins as a Cossack fort built to protect Russia's Siberian frontier against the Kazakhs.

The Ishim River flows 2km east of the centre. Take trolleybus Nos 1 or 2 along Internatsionalnaya. On the way you'll pass the handsome blue onion-domed **Russian Orthodox church**, which is surrounded by pretty gingerbread-style Russian cottages.

There is a **banya** (☎ 46 25 70; admission 120 T, full treatment 400 T; ☺ 2-8pm, closed Thu) located at Mira 103.

Sleeping & Eating

Hotel Kyzyl Zhar (☎ 46 11 84; cnr Auezov & Konstitutsiya; s/d US$12/24, lux s/d US$22/27) A central location, clean rooms and friendly staff make this the best option in town. There is

a restaurant and bar, but you'll find better food options elsewhere.

Hotel Kolos (☎ 33 69 00; Internatsionalnaya 82; r US$14) A five-minute walk west of the Domino Theatre, this private hotel has plain but clean rooms with TV and phone.

Donor Restaurant (Internatsionalnaya 27; meals US$2; ☺ 9am-11.30pm) Near the corner with Zhumabaev, this Turkish café serves good kebabs and has a children's play centre for the little 'uns.

Ahotny Reodd (Hunter's Row; ☎ 46 24 04; Zhabaev 145a; meals US$10; ☺ 1pm-1am) Located in the courtyard behind the history museum. You can enjoy Moldavian wine and huge portions of grilled meat, but you might have to put up with the bartender launching into song.

Sloviansky Dvor (Konstitutsiya 52; ☺ noon-midnight) Set in a period brick building opposite the park, this charming bistro serves excellent fish, salads and French wine amid heavy wood tables and iron fixtures.

Getting There & Around

There are flights to/from Almaty four times a week for US$145. The airport is

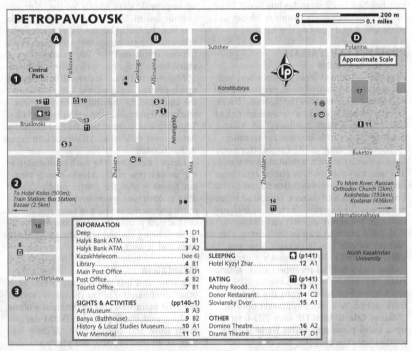

PETROPAVLOVSK

0 — 200 m
0 — 0.1 miles

Approximate Scale

a 15-minute ride from the centre. A taxi is US$5.

Daily trains go to/from Almaty (No 204, 3am Monday and Saturday; No 16, 8.20pm daily, one-way/return 5000/10,000 T) via Kökshetau, Astana (No 206, 3am Tuesday and Friday; No 624, 3am every even day, one-way/return 1700/3500 T) and Karaghanda (No 245, 8.50pm every odd day; No 84, 9.40pm every even day). There are several daily trains heading across Siberia; west to Yekaterinburg and Moscow or St Petersburg, east to Omsk and beyond. All trains depart on Moscow time (three hours behind). Any travels into Russia require a Russian visa, only available in Astana and Almaty.

There are daily buses to Kökshetau (3½ hours) and Kostanai (11 hours) from the **bus station** (☎ 33 03 69) and plenty of taxi drivers willing to do a deal on rides to Kökshetau. For Lake Burabay take the daily 4.10pm bus, or one to Shchuchinsk (there are at least six per day to Shchuchinsk) and change.

The train and bus stations are west of the city centre on Ruzaeva, at the end of Internatsionalnaya. It's about a 20-minute walk or take bus Nos 1 or 2, or trolleybus Nos 2, 19 or 22. The bus stops every couple of blocks and some will stop if you flag them down.

KOSTANAI ҚОСТАНАЙ
☎ 3142 / pop 220,000

Kostanai, another Virgin Lands wheat centre, is also an industrial town processing the vast iron-ore deposits of the Kostanai basin. On the Tobol River in a remote corner of Kazakhstan, 700km northwest of Astana, the town holds little interest for travellers.

The main drag is Al-Farabi (formerly Lenina), with the train station at its west end. The heart of the town is about 2km from here, where Al-Farabi is pedestrianised. The bus station, on Karbusheva, is around 10km southeast of the centre. There is an Internet café near the centre at Altynsarin 117.

A good place to stay in the centre is the **Tourist Hotel** (☎ 54 54 84; cnr Abay & Baytursanov 72; s/d/lux US$13/17/25). It has some refurbished rooms and a helpful reception desk. **Aidana Plaza** (☎ 54 86 86; Tolstoi 53; pol-lux/lux US$50/63), reached on bus No 20 from the airport or train station, is a more upmarket option.

Mango Café (Al-Farabi 136; meals US$3-4) serves up a good pizza and **Coffee World** (Al-Farabi), located near the mosque, has real lattes.

The **air ticket office** (Abay) is near the corner of Al-Farabi. There are daily flights to/from Almaty (US$137), three times a week to/from Astana (US$40) and twice weekly to/from Moscow (US$160). Kostanai is on a rail route between Moscow (43 hours), Samara and Astana (kupe US$15, 16 hours), with services three to four times weekly. Trains go to/from Almaty (kupe US$30, 40 hours) every two days. If crossing into Russia you will need a visa, only available in Astana or Almaty.

Bus No 20 links the airport to the town centre. A taxi is about US$2.50. From the train station, any bus or trolleybus will take you to the centre; bus No 38 links the train and long-distance bus station.

ARAGHANDA ҚАРАҒАНДА
☎ 3212 / pop 500,000

Smack in the steppe heartland, some 200km southeast of Astana and 1000km northwest of Almaty, Karaghanda is infamous for two things: coal and Gulag labour camps. The two are intimately connected, as the big network of camps around Karaghanda was set up to provide slave labour for the mines.

Founded in 1926, much of Karaghanda was built by Gulag labour. The nearby Samarka and Kengir camps were the centre of a famous revolt in 1954; 700 prisoners were killed when tanks moved in to put it down.

Mining continues today, although on a much smaller scale, with a large portion of the coal feeding the Indian-financed steelworks at Temirtau, 25km to the north. Sadly, Temirtau is now more famous for reportedly having over 80% of all HIV-infection cases in Kazakhstan.

Despite being beset by such problems, Karaghanda is one of Kazakhstan's more pleasant towns – and the centre much cleaner than it once was when heavy industry was more prevalent. Avenues of trees and a large central park provide greenery and the downtown is being revived with shopping malls, cafés and restaurants.

Orientation

The train and bus stations are beside each other on Bukhar Zhirou (formerly Sovietsky), the main street off to the right. Follow it along and you'll pass the TsUM department store and central park. A little further, at the end of Mira, is a pretty wooden neoclassical-style theatre, built by Japanese prisoners of war (POW). Yurabaev runs parallel to Bukhar Zhirou, one block south.

Information

Gogol Library (☎ 56 76 55; Yerubaev 44; ☺ 9am-7pm) English, French and German in the reading room. The ground floor has two Internet cafés.

Halyk Bank (☎ 43 52 80; Nurken Abdirov, just off Bukhar Zhirau) Two ATMs and moneychanging facilities.

Sights

The **Karaghanda Oblast Museum** (☎ 56 31 21; Yerubaev 38; admission US$0.30; ☺ 9am-6pm Sun-Fri) has been recently renovated and includes a Russian-language video of the town's history, plus a section on gulags. Near the train station is a small **art museum** (Bukhar Zhirou 33; admission US$1; ☺ 10am-6pm), with a diverting collection of works.

At the main entrance to the **central park** on Bukhar Zhirou, facing the Miners' Culture Palace, stands a giant statue of two miners, an icon of Karaghanda. The park has kids' playgrounds and places to eat. If you are unfortunate enough to be here in winter, there is a year-round **Aqua Park** (☎ 42 14 80; Bulvar Mira 33/2; admission 200 T).

Sleeping & Eating

Tourist Hotel (☎ 44 20 77; Yermekova 120; r US$6-25) No-frills place close to the centre.

Komnaty Otdykha (fl 2, train station; dm 240 T) This has clean dorm beds and is an OK place to nap if it's 5am and you've just stumbled off the Talgo.

Hotel Karaghanda (☎ 42 52 04; Buhar Zhirau; r US$22) This is the best-value hotel in the centre and the place most foreign travellers end up. Rooms have hot water, telephone and TV.

Sozvezdie (☎ 72 45 45; Stroiteley 34; d/lux US$50/100) Located in the southeast, locals say the rooms here are the best in town. Amenities include sauna, Jacuzzi, billiards, laundry, a restaurant, massage service and air ticketing.

Kosmonavt (☎ 438565; Krivoguza 162a; d/lux US$65/140) Located across the park, this is the preferred choice of many expat business people.

Assortee (☎ 42 01 49; Bulvar Mira 12; meals US$6-8; ☺ 10am-11pm) Full of blue-collar workers during lunch, this excellent cafeteria-style place serves yummy soups, salads, goulash, and pies for dessert.

Bachus (☎ 56 08 22; Dzhambul 46; meals US$10-15; ☺ 24hr) A must for dedicated music lovers, this place is done up like a miniature Hard Rock Café.

Stary Gorod (Old Town; ☎ 52 05 50; Lenin 26; meals US$10-15; ☺ 2pm-1am) This is a couple of notches up the society ladder with its classy European dishes.

Getting There & Around

Karaghanda has daily flights to/from Almaty (US$105) and three times a week to Moscow (one-way and round trip US$362). Bus No 152 goes from the airport to the train and bus stations (one hour).

The **train station** (☎ 43 36 36) has services at least six times daily to/from Almaty (*platskartnyy/kupe*, US$10/US$15), at least daily to/from Astana (*platskartnyy/kupe*, US$3.60/US$5.40), Petropavlovsk (8am, *platskartnyy/kupe*, US$11/US$17) and Kostanai (12.35pm and 3.08pm, *platskartnyy/kupe*, US$9/US$13) and most days to/from Taraz and Shymkent (2.27am, *platskartnyy/kupe*, US$10/US$15). The Talgo fast train stops here (see p108) but tickets don't go on sale until two hours before departure. On three-day holiday weekends there is the chance that the train will be overbooked, so in such a case it is best to buy your ticket in advance from Almaty or Astana.

Karaghanda's main **bus station** (☎ 43 18 18) has services to/from Almaty (about 20 hours, US$20), Astana (four hours, US$3.50), Pavlodar (US$9), Omsk (US$17.50), Novosibirsk (US$20.50) and Bayanauyl (US$4).

EAST KAZAKHSTAN
ВОСТОК
КАЗАХСТАН

East of Astana, the train lines and roads reach out towards Russia, passing through the industrial town of Ekibastuz to Pavlodar, once an 18th-century Russian fort.

The Soviet authorities chose this remote part of the country as their chief nuclear testing ground, causing untold health and environmental damage in an area inhabited by four million people (see p92).

Although obviously suffering economic depression, Semey is eastern Kazakhstan's most interesting and historical city, sporting notable architecture and literary connections with the great Kazakh writer Abay Kunabaev and the Russian novelist Fyodor Dostoevsky.

Ust-Kamenogorsk is a centre for the ferrous metal industry. It is the region's capital and most prosperous city. It is also a pleasant place, best visited en route to the splendid Altay Mountains and lakes in the far east of the region. For online information on the region visit www.vkgu.ka/en.

PAVLODAR ПАВЛОДАР

☎ 3182 / pop 335,000

On the Irtysh River, Pavlodar, 400km northeast of Astana and 110km from the Russian border, was developed as an industrial town in Soviet times. Most of the manufacturing plants are gone now, except for a tractor factory that used to make tanks. Pavlodar's skyline is dominated by massive, rabbit-hole style Soviet-era apartment blocks, but quiet Lenin Street on the western edge of town has architectural merit, plus a few good museums.

Sights

The beguiling **Bogayev Museum** (☎ 32 12 10; Lenin 200; admission 30 T), set in the home of a local photographer and humanitarian, shows off some early 20th-century photographs of life around Pavlodar. Bogayev (1884–1958) had a keen eye for traditional Kazakh culture, often hiding in bushes to capture his subjects. He gained local fame for creating the city's first museum, and taking photos of young soldiers before they went off to war. You won't see any of the pictures he took of bodies piled in the streets during a typhoid outbreak; they were destroyed by an embarrassed city authority.

Nearby, the **Museum of Regional History** (☎ 32 37 06; Lenin 147; admission 30 T) and the **Myra Museum** (☎ 32 71 11; Lenin 135) are also worth a look.

Pavlodar's not-to-be-missed sight is the new US$1 million **Mashkhur Jusup Mosque**. Looking like an intergalactic space station from a 1950s science fiction film, it rises out of the city with rocketlike minarets and a green dome shaped like Darth Vader's helmet. The attendants are welcoming and will show you the small museum and maybe the upstairs gallery where you can get a good

view of the crystal chandelier. The religiously inspired can also visit the new red-brick, golden-domed **Orthodox Church**, behind the Sariarka Hotel, or the **Jewish Synagogue** on Satpaev, one block south of the TsUM.

Sleeping & Eating

Hotel Sariarka (☎ 56 18 27; Toraygirova 1; s/d US$32/61) Set in a tower block overlooking the Irtysh River, this place has good rooms with TV and hot water. If you are short on cash, you might be able to cajole the receptionist into giving you a single, unrenovated room for US$11.

Hotel Business Centre (☎ 32 05 39; cnr Lenin & Lermintov; s/d US$25/62) Located between the main street and the river, this hotel is popular with families in town to adopt children. The receptionist is particularly helpful.

Hotel Kazakhstan (☎ 32 05 20; Satpaev 71; s/d US$21/32) This drafty but adequate hotel is located next to the TsUM, smack in the centre of town.

Dilijans (☎ 32 12 73; Frunze 118; pizza US$2, coffee US$0.50) Located near the Hotel Kazakhstan at the corner with Yestaya is this restaurant with a fetish for road signs. You can chart your progress from Astana on the giant ceiling map.

Café Africa (☎ 32 45 11; Satpaev 75; meals US$7; ☽ 11-1am) The ochre-painted walls and tribal art is tasteful, less so the caveman-style outfits worn by the waitresses. Still, it's a pleasant oddity in Pavlodar, with African music and platters full of spicy meat dishes with sides of fruit. The hot chocolate is a bonus.

Getting There & Around

There are daily flights to/from Almaty (US$120), some weekly flights to Moscow (US$164) and occasional charter flights to Frankfurt and Hannover. Bus No 22 links the airport to the centre, 15km away, and the train station. A taxi to the airport is around US$4.

The train and bus stations are both at the northern end of Toraygirova. The fastest way to get to Semey is by one of two daily small minibuses (*kommerchesky*; US$5, four hours). There are also at least a couple of slower buses daily to Semey, plus services to Astana, Karaghanda, Novosibirsk, and Ust-Kamenogorsk.

Trains run daily to Almaty (36 hours), Astana (eight hours), Barnaul, Omsk and

Novosibirsk in Russia. Note, Pavlodar is three hours ahead of Moscow time. You can book train tickets at the **city ticketing office** (☎ 32 05 15; Satpaev 71) next to the Hotel Kazakhstan.

SEMEY СЕМЕЙ

☎ 3222 / pop 295,000

Semey, 850km north of Almaty and 700km east of Astana, is better known to the world by its Russian name Semipalatinsk. For 40 years (1949–89) the Soviet military exploded precisely 467 nuclear bombs in the Polygon, a vast area of the steppe southwest of the city. Locals say they knew when tests were going on because the ground would shake – often on Sunday morning. An unprecedented wave of popular protest in Kazakhstan, the Nevada-Semipalatinsk Movement, was largely instrumental in halting the tests in 1989. For more on the tests, see p91 and Living Beside the Polygon below.

Despite the terrible health and environmental legacy of the tests, Semey is one of Kazakhstan's more interesting cities. Set in the territory of the Middle Horde, who were noted for their eloquence and intellect, the city and its surrounding region have produced several major Kazakh writers and teachers, among them the national poet Abay Kunabaev (1845–1904) and Mukhtar Auezov (1897–1968).

In 1917 Semey was the capital of the short-lived Alash Orda independent Kazakhstan government. Its Russian past is interesting, too. The original fort was founded in 1718, a few kilometres away along the Irtysh River, as Russia's expansion across Siberia ran up against the warlike Mongolia-based Oyrat (Zhungarian) empire. In the 19th century the great Russian writer Fyodor Dostoevsky spent five years in exile here.

Like most other Kazakh cities, Semey is inching out of deep economic slumber. A new multi-million-dollar suspension bridge across the Irtysh, the 17th longest in the world and funded with Japanese loans, gives the place a modern skyline. Deservedly proud of their intellectual traditions – from literature to nuclear fission – Semey still attracts top Kazakh and Russian professors to its highly respected university and you'll encounter students from all over Asia.

Orientation

Semey is dissected from northeast to southwest by its main street, Shakarim Kudayberdiev (formerly Komsomola), and from

---

LIVING BESIDE THE POLYGON

In Sarjal, just 30km from where Soviet scientists conducted 467 nuclear tests between 1949 and 1991, almost all the 2600 inhabitants suffer from one illness or more. The explosions in the 18,000 sq km test area, which has come to be known as the Polygon, were the equivalent of one Hiroshima for every person in the village. The radiation levels here were frequently 100 times higher than normal.

Winds carried the fallout and contaminated an area of 300,000 sq km, inhabited by some two million people, yet during the Soviet era the terrible legacy of the tests was covered up. Amazingly, some blamed the growing incidence of cancer and other illnesses on the Kazakh tradition of drinking scalding tea.

Tests show that the incidence of cancer in communities like Sarjal, close to the test site, is three times higher than in the rest of Kazakhstan and there has been a dramatic increase in birth defects and mental illness.

Due to lack of funds, Semey's local hospitals struggle to cope with the victims. Ironically, the situation has worsened due to the end of the nuclear testing programme, which for decades was the mainstay of the area's economy. Kurchatov (named after Igor Kurchatov, leader of the team that developed the Soviet atom bomb), 150km northwest of Semey, was the headquarters of the nuclear weapons programme. Forty thousand troops and scientists were stationed here during the Cold War years; around 9300 are there today.

Apart from sick people, the most overt evidence of the test programme is Lake Balapan, a 400m-wide, 800m-deep crater left by a 130 kiloton nuclear explosion, and since filled with water. The base radiation in the lake is 200 times higher than the national average and scientists warn that no-one should go near it without supervision.

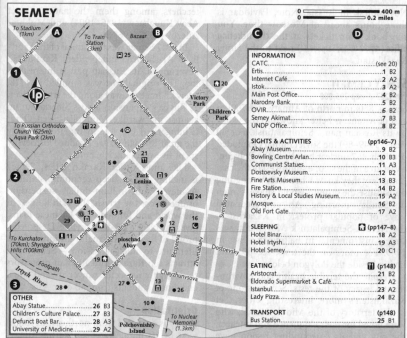

SEMEY

southeast to northwest by the Irtysh River. The older part of the city, and nearly everything of use or interest, is on the northeastern side of the Irtysh. The train station is just off the northeast end of Shakarim Kudayberdiev, about 3km from the centre.

Information

CATC (☎ 62 29 29; Hotel Semey, Kabanbai Batyr 26) Travel and ticket agent.

Ertis (☎ 66 93 72; Dulatova 135; per hr $0.50; ☽ 24hr) Good Internet café located behind the fire station. A second Internet café is located opposite Istanbul restaurant.

Istok (☎ 62 48 99; Lenin 4) Local NGO; organises ecotours of the area.

Norodny Bank (☎ 56 15 28; Lenina 10) There's an ATM at this branch. You can also change money at hotels, the bazaar and exchange booths around town.

OVIR (☎ 66 48 09; Ibrayev 7; ☽ 9am-12.30pm Mon-Wed, 2-6pm Fri) Located in the five-storey City Department of Internal Affairs, opposite Park Lenina.

Semey Akimat (☎ 62 62 30, 62 30 04; Rm 436, Government House, Kozbagarov) Information on Kurchatov.

UNDP (☎ 62 33 90; undpsemey@relcom.kz; Dostoevsky 110) Information on travel to Kurchatov; might organise an English-speaking guide.

Sights
MUSEUMS

The big **Abay Museum** (☎ 52 57 15; Internatsion-alnaya 29; admission 150 T; ☽ 10am-1pm & 2-6pm) is dedicated to the 19th-century humanist poet Abay Kunabaev, born in the nearby Shyngghystau Hills. Abay, who valued Kazakh traditions as well as aspects of the progress that came with the Russians, is considered the number one Kazakh cultural guru (see the boxed text on p91). Along with displays about Abay's life, the museum has sections on his literary successors, including his nephew, the bard Shakarim Kudayber-diev, and Mukhtar Auezov, author of the epic Kazakh novel *Abay Zholy* (The Path of Abay).

The well laid-out **Dostoevsky Museum** (☎ 52 19 42; admission 100 T; tours 150 T; ☽ 9am-5pm Tue-Sun) is on a leafy lane a block east of ploshchad Abay, built alongside the wooden house where the writer lived from 1857 to 1859. The main parts of the museum display Dostoevsky's life and works, with sections devoted to his childhood in Moscow, his residence in St Petersburg, Omsk and Semey, and his creative life from 1860 to 1881. The rooms where he lived have been maintained in the style of his day, and there is a somewhat out-of-place exhibit on Irtysh River life, with hey-day pictures of the hydrofoils that used to travel between here and Pavlodar. The vast amount of images on Dostoevsky alone makes it worth a visit, even if you can't understand the mainly Russian text.

The **History and Local Studies Museum** (☎ 52 07 32; Lenina 5; ⏰ 10am-2pm & 3-6pm Tue-Sun) has a small display on nuclear testing and the Nevada-Semey Movement, and a few old Kazakh artefacts.

Located in a white colonnaded building, a couple of blocks east of the Hotel Irtysh, the **Fine Arts Museum** (Abay) has some good works by Kazakh, Russian and west European painters, including a not-to-be-missed Rembrandt etching.

OLD SEMEY

Looking somewhat forlorn on a concrete island on Abay, just before the railway bridge, is one of the **old fort gates** built in the 1770s, flanked by a couple of cannons. Also still standing (and working), down the third street on the left after the railway bridge, is a pretty **Russian Orthodox Church** with a blue tower and dome, which once stood at the centre of the fort. In the streets northeast of here, towards the bus station and bazaar, are many old one-storey wooden houses.

On Internatsionalnaya, opposite Park Lenina, is a handsome red-brick **fire station** dating from the turn of the century. Further east, on Pavlov, is a 19th-century **mosque** (a Russian-style building with a minaret sticking out of the top), used as an exhibition hall in Soviet times but back in religious use now.

IRTYSH RIVER

The walk along the northeastern bank of the Irtysh is pleasant. There's a curious collection of **Communist statues** – a kind of graveyard of Lenin and Marx busts, presided over by the giant Lenin that used to stand on the nearby square, immediately north of the Hotel Irtysh and behind the old cinema. Further downstream, past the new bridge, is Semey's **Aqua Park** (adult/child 600/400 T).

On the east side of town is **Polchovnishiy Island**, reached via the blue bridge next to the Bowling Centre Arlan on Abay. A little more than 1km from the bridge on the left is a sombre yet grandiose **nuclear memorial** erected in 2002 for victims of the nuclear tests. The marble centrepiece of *Stronger than Death* is a mother covering her child; above billows an infamous Polygon mushroom cloud etched into a 30m-high black tombstone.

> **DOSTOEVSKY IN EXILE**
>
> In 1849, at the age of 28, Fyodor Dostoevsky was sentenced to death with several others for attending meetings of the Petrashevsky Circle, a group of utopian socialist intelligentsia who gathered in a St Petersburg house. The group was lined up before a firing squad – only to be told at the last moment that their sentences had been commuted to exile in Siberia.
>
> Dostoevsky spent the next five years in a convict prison at Omsk – an experience which produced his first major novel, *The House of the Dead*. This was followed by five years of enforced military service in the garrison at Semey, which was then starting to prosper as a trading town but was still as remote and inhospitable a place as the tsarist authorities could think of for dissidents. This didn't stop Dostoevsky from his writing, and it was in Semey that he began one of his most famous novels, *The Brothers Karamazov*.
>
> It was also in Semey that Dostoevsky met and made friends with the extraordinary Shoqan Ualikhanov, a prince of the Middle Horde, explorer, artist, intellectual, and officer and spy in the Russian army. A statue of both men stands outside the museum.

Sleeping

Hotel Semey (☎ 66 36 05; Kabanbai Batyr 26; s/d/pollux/lux US$4/11/20/50) Opposite Victory Park, Hotel Semey has welcoming staff and bright, clean rooms, some with TV.

Hotel Irtysh (☎ 66 64 77; Abay 97; dm/s/d US$3.50/9/12) If the Semey is full, try this budget alternative, complete with dim lighting, dodgy elevators, run-down rooms and a noisy disco out back. There are some refurbished suites for US$44, but at that price you're better off at the Binar.

Hotel Binar (☎ 62 39 34; fax 62 38 50; Lenin 6, s/d/lux US$34/40/55) This low-key place is the cream of Semey's hotel crop. It's a block northwest of ploshchad Abay, the central square. Cosy, well-furnished rooms have running hot water (rare in Semey). Singles without hot water cost US$14. Use of the sauna and breakfast are included in the bill. If you are not a guest the breakfast is 250 T.

Eating

Istanbul (☎ 66 08 89; B. Momishuli 3; meals US$2-3) This Turkish café serves kebabs, chips and burgers, though mainly to students at the nearby University of Medicine.

Lady Pizza (☎ 66 08 89; Kozbagorov 24; pizzas US$2-4) About 100m east of the fire station, this place serves a variety of tasty pizzas in a clean, modern dining room with tacky interior design.

Aristocrat (☎ 66 74 35; Lenina 25a; dishes US$3) Located opposite the Abay Museum entrance, Aristocrat tries hard to create a Victorian ambience in its interior. Most people end up on the sunny patio, though, where bow-tied waiters serve European courses including pork chops in mushroom sauce and marinated chicken.

The bazaar, off Kabanbai Batyr, sells a wide range of fresh and prepared food and is worth a visit. Self-caterers can also visit the Eldorado Supermarket off Gerchena.

Entertainment

Bowling Center Arlan (☎ 66 82 59, Abay 69; admission 100 T) This bowling centre also has a pool hall and dance club, which reels in the teenage set. From noon to 6pm a round of bowling is 250 T, from 6pm to 4am it's 400 T; cover at the disco is 300 T.

Yelimay Semey is one of Kazakhstan's top soccer teams and its home games are advertised on posters around town. The season runs from about April to September. To find the stadium, follow Kabanbai Batyr northwest from Shakarim Kudayberdiev, take the first street on the right after you go under the railway, and head for the floodlight pylons.

Getting There & Away

Flights go to/from Almaty daily (US$80). There are also daily flights to Novosibirsk ($90) and twice-weekly flights to Astana ($40).

From the **bus station** (☎ 62 69 25; off Naymanbaev) next to the bazaar, several daily buses run to Pavlodar (fast/slow four/seven hours)

and Ust-Kamenogorsk (three/six hours), and one to Barnaul in Russia (11 hours). Shared taxis also gather at the bus station and are handy for reaching Ust-Kamenogorsk.

The Semey **train station** (☎ 98 32 32) has direct services to Barnaul (US$21, nine hours) and Novosibirsk (US$28, 16 hours) three times a day. Southbound trains head twice a day to Almaty (US$14), and twice a week to Bishkek (US$43). A daily train departs for Astana at 8.20am (10 hours). If you're heading for China, you can connect with the Almaty–Ürümqi trains at Aktogay, 12 hours south of Semey. Note that Semey is three hours ahead of Moscow time.

Getting Around

Bus Nos 9, 11, 22 and 33 run from the train station to the centre along Shakarim Kudayberdiev. Bus No 22 turns right along Kabanbai Batyr to the bazaar; the others continue across the Irtysh, with bus No 33 going all the way to the airport. For the Hotel Irtysh and Hotel Binar get off when you see the river bridge ahead, and walk back to Abay. A taxi from the train station to the centre is about US$1.

From the theatre on ploshchad Abay, bus Nos 2 and 35 run to the bazaar and bus No 50 runs to the bus station.

AROUND SEMEY
Shyngghystau Hills

The Shyngghystau is a range of hills (1200m at their highest) around 100km south of Semey. Apart from its natural beauty, this sparsely peopled area is full of Kazakh legends and is famed as the homeland of the writers Abay Kunabaev, Mukhtar Auezov and Shakarim Kudayberdiev. There is an Abay museum in the village of Zhidebai, and this is where you'll also find his mausoleum, together with that of Kudayberdiev – easily the area's most impressive building. Auezov's home, also a museum, is in Borli.

To get to these remote places you'll need to hire a guide and car in Semey. A good place to make inquiries is the local NGO Istok (p146), an environmental group that runs ecotours in the area.

Kurchatov

Kurchatov is 70km west of Semey, along a road littered with deserted villages, wrecked military bases and dozens of abandoned food processing plants that once upon a time accounted for 70% of the Soviet army's tinned rations.

You no longer need a permit to visit this nuclear weapons operations base turned virtual ghost town, but you could have trouble getting past the guards at the **museum** (admission free; 9am-6pm Mon-Fri), the only real reason to visit the place. A checkpoint to enter the Polygon area is at the edge of town and you'll need special permits to breach it. Your taxi driver might say the guards can be bribed, but it's far too dangerous to enter the Polygon without special equipment including radiation suits and a giga-counter, neither readily available to the casual tourist.

Ask about the latest travel info for Kurchatov from the UNDP office in Semey or at the Semey Akimat (p146).

UST-KAMENOGORSK (ÖSKEMEN)
УСТЬ-КАМЕНОГОРСК
☎ 3232 / pop 315,000

Ust-Kamenogorsk (Öskemen) is the starting point for trips to the remote Altay Mountains and lakes in the far eastern corner of Kazakhstan. Like Semey, Ust-Kamenogorsk was founded as a Russian fort in 1720. It has grown from a small town since the 1940s when Russians and Ukrainians began to arrive to mine and process local minerals.

Mining of nonferrous metals, in particular copper, lead, silver and zinc, continues still, all of which makes Ust-Kamenogorsk a relatively prosperous and lively place. On the downside, the processing of these metals has been at the expense of the air quality and caused a high rate of respiratory infection.

For the traveller, Ust-Kamenogorsk's location on the Ulba and Irtysh Rivers, at the foot of some small mountains, is appealing, as is the centre's generally low-key Soviet architecture, supplemented by a handful of precommunist-era buildings.

Orientation
The centre of Ust-Kamenogorsk is on a spit of land between the Irtysh and Ulba Rivers. The main axis is Ushanova, running north from the bridge over the Irtysh to the bustling bazaar. Crossing Ushanova and leading to the main bridge across the Ulba is Ordzhonikidze, which splits into Abay and Lenina on the west bank of the river. The bus station is at the foot of Abay, while the

main train station, Zashita, is around 5km further west.

Information
Altay Trial (☎ 47 93 43; fax 47 93 44; Vorishilova) Adventure tourism outfit run by mountaineer Andrei Tselichev. He is also the owner of the Rachmanov's Springs resort in the Altay Mountains (p152). As well as organising hiking to Lake Markakol and the Black Irtysh River basin, he can arrange ascents of the 4506m Mt Belukha, cross-country skiing in winter and rafting along the Ulba and Bukhtarma Rivers in early summer.

Boris Vasilevich Shcherbakov (☎ 25 76 29) Boris is an ornithologist – with a collection of parrots – who, with a bit of notice, can organise trips to Altay's Lake Markakol and maybe Mt Belukha.

Central Library (Ushanova 102; 9am-6pm) Internet access is 100 T per hour.

Ecosystem (☎ 26 77 97; altai-es@ukg.kz; Gorky 21) Professional local service with a variety of tour options including hiking, bird-watching, rafting, cycling and fishing.

Intourist (☎ 26 47 47; intourist@ukg.kz; Gorky 72) This Intourist office gets good reports for its trips and travel services.

Sights
Clustered around the pretty Kirova Park are some of Ust-Kamenogorsk's oldest buildings. The **Ethnography Museum** (admission 60 T; 10am-5pm), which has traditional costumes, handicrafts and religious icons, is in three separate buildings around the park: one at Kirova and Uritskogo; the second on the corner of Mira and Gorkogo; and the third site, primarily the museum's head offices, is in the handsome red-brick building on Mira beside Kirova Park.

Next door to the head office, with its entrance facing the park, is the **History Museum** (☎ 25 54 60; Uritskogo 40), with a natural history section on the ground floor, including a giant stuffed Maral deer (the antlers of which are considered an aphrodisiac in Korea) and interesting archaeological and contemporary history exhibits upstairs. The park itself is worth a wander; the northwestern part contains a replica Russian pioneer village of log cabins.

Sleeping
Hotel Irtysh (☎ 25 29 23; fax 25 09 85; Auezov 22; s/d/lux with breakfast US$10/13/31) This place fits the bill for most travellers. The receptionists speak English, the restaurant is fine, rooms comfortable enough and there's an airline ticket booking office.

Hotel Ust-Kamenogorsk (☎ 26 18 01; Proletarskaya 158; s/d US$8/16) This is quite similar to Irtysh, but less welcoming.

De Luxe (☎ 24 88 02; de_luxe@ukg.kz; Kirova 62; s/d US$68/85) This is the nicest place in town, with three-star rooms, some with private bathroom. There is a sauna and a billiards room downstairs. Look for the distinctive two-storey yellow building with the green roof.

Eating

Doner (☎ 26 87 04; Kirova 49; dishes US$1.50-2) A downtown fixture and teenage hang-out, you may have trouble finding a seat in this Turkish café.

Masalitsa (☎ 25 09 00; Uritskogo 117a; crepes US$2) The house specialty, meat-and-cheese stuffed crepes are unique in this neck of the woods. It's a trendy place that competes with equally popular Pizza Blue.

Pizza Blue (☎ 24 81 67; Gorkogo 56; pizzas US$3) Serves very good pizza and salads. It also has a second location facing the Ulba at the end of Lenina.

Stary Tblisi (☎ 25 63 92; Naverezhnaya 117a; meals US$7) Pretty Georgian restaurant, decorated with grapevines over stone and brick walls, on a quiet side of town near the Ulba.

For something more casual, grab a beer and shashlyk on the good ship **Arabella** (☯ 11am-midnight), docked at the end of Auezov, or **Letiniy Sad** (☎ 26 67 59; Uritskogo 67), a pleasant beer garden dotted with funky wooden sculptures.

UST-KAMENOGORSK (ÖSKEMEN)

0 — 500 m
0 — 0.3 miles

INFORMATION		EATING 🍴 (p150)		Garage Disco................................(see 26)
Altay Trial...............................1 C2		Arabella...............................15 B4		Titan..24 D3
ATM......................................2 B3		Doner...................................16 C3		
Central Library.....................3 D3		Letiniy Sad..........................17 C4		ENTERTAINMENT 🎭 (p151)
Ecosystem............................4 D4		Masalitsa.............................18 B4		Drama Theatre.....................25 C4
Intourist...............................5 C4		Pizza Blue............................19 B3		Ekho Movie Theatre............26 C3
Kazakhtelekom....................6 C3		Pizza Blue............................20 C4		Olympic Bowling Centre.......27 B4
Police/OVIR..........................7 C2		Stary Tiblisi..........................21 A4		Sports Stadium....................28 B3
SIGHTS & ACTIVITIES (p149)		DRINKING 🍺 (p151)		TRANSPORT (p151)
Ethnography Museum Head Office......8 C4		Black Bull Pub......................22 C4		Bus Station...........................29 B3
Ethnography Museum No 1....9 C4		City Club 31..........................23 D3		Train Ticket Town Office........30 B3
Ethnography Museum No 2....10 C4				
History Museum...................11 C4				
SLEEPING 🛏 (pp149-50)				
De Luxe................................12 C3				
Hotel Irtysh.........................13 B4				
Hotel Ust-Kamenogorsk........14 C3				

Drinking

Black Bull Pub (☎ 24 54 28; Kirova 6; ☺ noon-3am) This place serves pints of beer and spears of shashlyk in a snazzy little brick-and-iron-wrought interior.

Titan (☎ 26 48 44; cnr Proletarskaya & Burov; cover 500 T; ☺ 9pm-3am) Perhaps they ran out of room on the signboard because the interior is modelled after a certain sunken ship. It's one of three good discotheques in town.

Other discotheques are nearby **City Club 31** (☎ 26 47 72; Permitina 31; cover 500 T; ☺ 7pm-3am) and **Garage** (cnr Kirova & Ordzhonikidze), at the Ekho Movie Theatre.

Entertainment

Theatre buffs might want to inspect the 100-year-old **drama theatre** (Kirova Park, Mira) that still holds occasional performances. Otherwise, there is the popular **Ekho Movie Theatre** (cnr Kirova & Ordzhonikidze). English-language films are dubbed into Russian.

In winter, don't miss the opportunity to see the local hockey team in action; the Torpedoes, are one of the best in the country and have produced two NHL players. You can see them at the **sports stadium** (Abay), on the west side of the Ulba River.

There is also an **Olympic Bowling Centre** (Naverezhnyaya 95).

Getting There & Around

There are flights on a daily basis to/from Almaty (US$135) and weekly to/from Moscow (US$169). Bus Nos 12 or 39 run to the airport, around 10km west of the city. A taxi costs around US$5.

From Semey, the most direct way to Ust-Kamenogorsk is by minibus (US$4.50, 3½ hours). Shared taxis are US$7 and wait outside the Semey bus station. Forget the train as it follows a circuitous route, looping into Russia, and takes at least 10 hours.

Ust-Kamenogorsk's main train station is **Zashita** (☎ 40 87 37), which is really only useful for Russia. Tram 3 connects Ust-Kamenogorsk and Zashita train stations, running along Ushanova, Ordzhonikidze and up Abay. Also you can take bus Nos 1 or 19 to Zashita from Lenina. Alternatively, it's a 10-minute taxi (400 T) from the centre. Train tickets can be bought at a **town office** (Lenina 4).

For Almaty, take a taxi or bus to Jangiz Tobe two hours south of Ust-Kamenogorsk,

where you can catch train No 251 at 12.25pm. This train travels on to Aktogay (for Dostyk and China), Lepsey (for Lake Balkash) and Ushtobe (for Taldy-Korghan). It actually departs from Ust-Kamenogorsk at 10.30pm the night before, travelling all night through Russia to Semey.

In the other direction, if you are travelling north on the 252 from Almaty, get off at Jangiz Tobe and take a taxi to Ust-Kamenogorsk rather than passing through Russia.

THE ALTAY MOUNTAINS & LAKE MARKAKOL
АЛТАЙ И МАРКАКОЛ ОЗЕРО

In the far northeastern corner of Kazakhstan the magnificent Altay Mountains spread across the borders to Russia, China, and Mongolia, only 50km away. This is still considered a sensitive border zone and everyone, even Kazakhs, needs special permits (see below) if they want to go beyond the village of Berel in the Bukhtarma Valley, or visit the Markakol Nature Reserve in the southern Altay range.

However, the hassle is well worth it. Endless rolling meadows, snow-covered peaks, pristine lakes and rivers, and rustic villages with Kazakh horsemen riding by make for scenery of epic proportions. In fact, little has changed since US journalist George Kennan toured here in 1885 and proclaimed, 'I had never seen such a picturesque alpine panorama that could compare with this in splendour, grandeur and beauty.' Small wonder that Asian legends call this area Shambhala, 'a paradisal realm that will be revealed after humanity destroys itself'.

The place to aim for is Rachmanov's Springs, an idyllic hot-springs resort at the very end of the mountain road, 110km to the east. Alternatively, Lake Markakol to the south is a wildlife haven set amid a forest of birch, larch and fir trees.

Permits

The Altay Mountains and Markakol Nature Reserve are classed as sensitive border areas and require a permit. Applications should be made at least 10 days in advance to the local police office on Voroshilova in Ust-Kamenogorsk, but are best arranged via an agent (see Information p149).

Rachmanov's Springs

This charming health resort, 30km up the mountain track from the village of Berel, was built in the 1960s by one of the local mining companies, but is now privately owned. You'll find pastel-painted wooden cottages linked by wooden boardwalks through pine forests, nestling in a mountain valley. Activities include trekking, horse riding and cross-country skiing in winter.

Accommodation starts at US$10 per day for a basic cottage, rising to US$15 for luxury ones with their own kitchen and TV. Add on US$8 for three meals. Bookings should be made in Ust-Kamenogorsk through the **resort office** (☎ 3232-47 93 43; fax 47 93 44).

This is an ideal base from which to tackle 4506m Belukha, the Altay's highest mountain, on the Kazakh–Russia border. Its double-headed peak, linked by a glacier, is a two-day climb from the resort. Be thoroughly prepared, suitably experienced and preferably accompanied, as there are glaciers and 3000m-plus passes, which may require crampons, ropes and ice screws.

Markakol Nature Reserve

The Markakol Nature Reserve is centred on Lake Markakol, south of Katon-Karagai. At 40km this is the largest lake in the Altay and 1500m above sea level. The lake is noted for its pure waters and beautiful countryside. Accommodation is likely to be in tents or in homestays at Urunkhayka village at the east end of the lake. In summer, in a 4WD, the lake can be reached by a mountain-pass road built by POWs during WWII. At other times the only access is by a much longer southern route passing through the town of Kurchum on the north coast of Lake Zaysan.

Getting There & Away

Tour agencies in both Almaty and Ust-Kamenogorsk are the best way to arrange trips to this remote area.

Contact the Rachmanov's Springs office for details of the bus transport it can arrange over summer, during which time it's also possible to hire cars to make the eight-hour journey from Ust-Kamenogorsk; expect to pay US$50 one way. If you're determined to go by public transport it's an all-day bus trip to Katon-Karagai, which has a small hotel and *stolovaya*. From here, you're on your own.

KAZAKHSTAN DIRECTORY

ACCOMMODATION

For budget travellers, the old Soviet-built hotels are, in most cases, the only option in Kazakhstan. Some have been renovated and are staffed by friendly young personnel; others are filthy firetraps on the verge of collapse. Nowadays, virtually every city has at least one place in the three- or four-star category to cater for foreign business people. The beginnings of an ecotourism industry may trigger a rise in homestays. Look out for these in national parks such as Aksu-Zhabagly, Korgaldzhyn and Lepsinsk.

The Russian terms *lux* (deluxe hotel room) and *pol-lux* (semideluxe hotel room) have been included in some sleeping sections in this guide to describe room types.

ACTIVITIES

Outdoor adventurers should focus their attention on southeast and east Kazakhstan. There's good hiking in the mountains south of Almaty, with some trails going over to Issyk-Kul in Kyrgyzstan. Köl Say lakes and Lepsinsk also offer good walking paths. Climbers can take on Khan Tengri (7010m) in the Saryjaz Range or Belukha (4506m) in the Altay. The Altay Mountains also offer opportunities for white-water kayaking and wildlife spotting. Horseback riding is best at Aksu-Zhabagly and Lepsinsk. The most interesting place for a camel trek is out of Aralsk. Bird-watching is good in many protected areas; Korgaldzhyn and Lake Alakol offer the chance of spotting flamingos. In winter, the best places for ice skating and skiing are a short drive from Almaty at Medeu and Shymbulak. Tour companies specialising in adventure travel are listed on p98.

THE AUTHOR'S CHOICE

- Hotel Dostyk, Almaty (p102)
- Tian Shan Astronomical Observatory (p111)
- Lepsinsk tourist yurt (p115)
- Egorkino, Astana (p137)

BOOKS

The Kazakhs, by Martha Brill Olcott, consists of several hundred pages of great detail that will keep you quiet for many a long evening on the steppe.

Kazakhstan: Unfulfilled Promise, by Martha Brill Olcott, is an edgy commentary on the new Kazakhstan and a deep look at the country a decade after independence. It functions largely to criticise the Nazarbaev regime, but includes sections on Kazakhstan's new religious and cultural values and relations between Kazakh and Slavic peoples.

EMBASSIES & CONSULATES
Kazakh Embassies in Central Asia
Kazakhstan has embassies in Tashkent (p234), Bishkek (p309), Ashgabat (p436), Kabul (p398) and Dushanbe (p349). See these for contact details.

Kazakh Embassies & Consulates
Citizens of New Zealand should apply for a visa via Sydney, Irish citizens should apply via London and Dutch citizens should apply via Belgium. Be wary – standards and costs vary greatly.

Kazakhstan's diplomatic missions abroad include the following (also see www.mfa.kz /eng for a list of up-to-date addresses for all Kazakh embassies):

Azerbaijan Baku (☎ 99412-90 65 21; fax 90 62 49; Apt 82, Inglab 889, Baku)

Belgium Bruxelles (☎ 322-3749562; kazakstan.embassy@ linkline.be; Avenue van Bever 30, 1180, Bruxelles)

Canada Toronto (☎ 416-593 4043; kazconscan@on.aibn .com; Suite 600, 347 Bay St, Toronto M5H 2R7)

China Beijing (☎ 8610-6532 6182; www.kazembchina .org; N9 Dong 6, San Li Tun 100600, Beijing); Ürümqi (☎ 0991- 383 2323; Kunming Lu 31, nr Beijing Lu; ☯ 10.30am-2pm Mon-Thu) A Kazakh visa in Ürümqi takes three days to process. Travellers have complained of tricky requirements for a locally issued medical certificate before getting a visa.

France Paris (☎ 331-45 61 52 00/02; vk001@dial .oleane.com; 59 rue Pierre Charron, Paris F-75008)

Germany Berlin (☎ 4930-47 007 111; kasger@ndh.net; Nordenstrabe 14-17, Berlin) Consulate in Bonn.

Hong Kong (☎ 852 2548 3841; fax 852 2548 8361; 3106, 31st fl, West Tower, Shun Tak Centre, 200 Connaught Rd Central, Sheung Wan)

Hungary Budapest (☎ 361-275 1300, 275 1301; fax 275 2092; 1025, Kapy 59, Budapest)

India New Delhi (☎ 9111- 614 4779; fax 614 4778; Olof Palme MargVasant Vihar, New Delhi 110057)

Iran Tehran (☎ 9821-256 5933; kazembir@apadana.com; Darrus Hedayat, Masjed 1, N4 Tehran)

Israel Tel Aviv (☎ 9723-52 3676; www.kazakhemb.org.il; 270 Hayarkon, Tel Aviv 63453)

Japan Tokyo (☎ 813-3791 5273; embkazjp@gol.com; Himonya 5-chome, Meguro-ku, Tokyo)

Mongolia Ulan Bator (☎ 97611-31 22 40; fax 31 22 04; House 95, Microregion 6, Ulan Bator)

Pakistan Islamabad (☎ 9251-226 29 25; embkaz@ comsats.net.pk; House 2, Street 4 F-8/3, Islamabad)

Russia Moscow (☎ 7095-927 18 12; www.kazembassy .ru; Chistoprudny bulvar 3A; Moscow 101000)

South Korea Seoul (☎ 822-548 1415; kazkor@chollian .net; 32-15 Nonhyun-dong 15, Kangnam-ku, Seoul)

Turkey Ankara (☎ 90312-441 23 01/02; kazank@ada .com.tr; Ebüzziya Tevfik Sokak 6, TR-06680 Ankara)

UK London (☎ 4420-7581 4646; www.kazakhstan embassy.org.uk; 33 Thurloe Sq, London SW7 2SD)

Ukraine Kiev (☎ 044-290 2306; fax 213 1198; 26 Elnikov, Kiev 252000)

USA Washington (☎ 1202-232 5488; www.kazconsulny .org; 1401 16th St NW, Washington DC 20036)

Embassies & Consulates in Kazakhstan
A handful of embassies and consulates had moved to Astana at the time of research, but these have been understandably slow to make the shift from charming Almaty. The **USA consulate** (☎ /fax 32 44 02; Kozmonatov 62) is expected to become a fully fledged embassy by 2006. At the time of research,

---

POST-SOVIET NAME CHANGES

Most Kazakh cities now have Kazakh names instead of their Soviet-era Russian names. In many cases they are close to the Russian (eg Almaty instead of Alma-Ata). Less obvious changes include Aktau for Shevchenko, Aktöbe for Aktyubinsk, Atyrau for Guriyev, and Semey for Semipalatinsk. You'll find Russian names still in use, particularly in the northern cities.

Similarly, most cities have changed their street names from Russian to Kazakh. Often the Kazakh is similar to the Russian, with a different ending to the name and the substitution of *köshesi* for *ulitsa* (street); *prospektisi, prospekti* or *dangghyly* for *prospect* (avenue); or *alangy* for *ploshchad* (square). It helps to be aware of both names, since not all signs have been changed, and in any case many people are still more familiar with the old names.

Russia was breaking ground on a new embassy situated opposite the President's Museum.

It is a good idea to register with your embassy if you are staying for an extended period. Some will issue a certified copy of your passport that you can show to police (although technically these are only valid in Almaty).

The following embassies are in Almaty unless otherwise stated. For information on visas for onward travel see p156.

Afghanistan (☎ 55 27 92; Khan Tengri 59)
Canada (☎ 50 11 51/52, fax 58 14 93; Karasay Batyr 34)
China (☎ 63 92 91; fax 63 82 09; Furmanov 137; ✆ 9am-noon Mon-Fri)
France (☎ 58 25 04; fax 58 25 09; Furmanov 173)
Georgia (☎ 3172 43 26 41/23 16 61; Cottage 7, Posolsky Gorodok, Astana)
Germany (☎ 50 61 55/56; fax 50 62 76; Furmanov 173)
Iran (☎ 92 50 55, 54 19 75; fax 54 27 54; Lugansky 31)
Japan (☎ 98 06 00; fax 98 06 01; 41a Kazybek Bi)
Kyrgyzstan Consulate (☎ / fax 78 44 45; Amangeldy 57; ✆ 10am-4pm Mon-Fri)
Mongolia Consulate (☎ 20 08 65; monkazel@kazmail.as dc.kz; Saina, Aubakirov 1; ✆ 10am-4pm Mon-Wed)
Pakistan (☎ 73 35 48; parepalmaty@hotmail.com; Tölebaev 25)
Russia (☎ 44 64 91, 74 71 72; fax 44 83 23; Zhandosova 4; ✆ 10am-12.30pm drop-off, 3.30-6pm pick-up Mon, Wed, Fri) An embassy in Astana will be opening in 2004.
Tajikistan (☎ 54 28 69, 93 51 65; tajemb-kaz@vitelco .kz; 96 Al-Farabi; ✆ 9am-6pm Mon-Fri)
Turkmenistan (☎ 3172-28 08 82; tm_emb@at.kz; Otyrar 64, Astana)
UK (☎ 50 61 91, 50 61 92; british-embassy@nursat.kz; Furmanov 173)
USA (☎ 50 48 02; fax 50 48 84; fl 17, Samal Tower, Zholdasbekov 79) Embassy will move to Astana by 2006, consulate to remain in Almaty.
Uzbekistan (☎ 91 78 86; fax 91 10 55; Baribaev 36; ✆ 9.30am-12.30pm Mon-Thu)

FESTIVALS & EVENTS

In early August, the four-day long Voice of Asia pop festival – a big drawcard for regional pop stars – is staged at Medeu. Every three years in August, a mountain festival is staged at the base camp of Khan Tengri. You can watch top climbers and mountain rescue teams compete for prizes, and then watch as they drink themselves silly afterwards. The next will be held in 2006. Contact Asia Tourism in Almaty for information (p98).

HOLIDAYS

1 January New Year's Day.
21 March Navrus (see p450).
9 May Victory Day.
10 June Capital Day (anniversary of the founding of Astana as the capital).
30 August Constitution Day.
25 October Republic Day.
16 December Independence Day.

INTERNET RESOURCES

http://expat.nursat.kz News and information about Almaty, geared for the expat or traveller. It includes useful pages on accommodation, health, jobs, security, restaurants and travel tips.
www.almadf.kz This site contains a huge library of photos that give a good idea of Kazakhstan's top attractions.
www.chabad.kz Website for the Chabad Lubavitch Jewish organisation of Kazakhstan, with history, news and contact information.
www.infokz.com Reviews and listings of sites in Almaty, plus a good links page.

MEDIA

It's worth getting a copy of *Rizvi's Yellow Pages of Kazakhstan*, an annual directory of useful addresses and telephones. It is published in English and Russian.

Local newspapers in English include the *Almaty Herald*, *Kazakhstan Monitor* (www.kazmonitor.kz), and the *Times of Central Asia* (www.times.kg). All can be bought at the Ramstor in Almaty and Astana and some hotel bookshops.

You can pick up the BBC World Service on 15.070 MHz (short wave), and Voice of America on 1341 KHz (medium wave).

MONEY

In general, dollar prices in this guide were used for consistency and ease of use. The tenge was used in some places where costs were low or for basic costs and services.

You will find changing, extracting and wiring money easier in Kazakhstan than anywhere else in the region.

ATM cards are definitely the way to go. There are machines in every city and in most small towns – at banks, train stations and shopping malls. Machines accept Maestro, Plus, Cirrus, and instructions are in English. You can also draw money off credit and debit cards. Halyk Bank has the most ATMs, followed by Kazkommertzbank; both take a 2% commission.

Credit cards (Visa and MasterCard preferred) are accepted at a growing number of shops, restaurants and hotels, even in the mid-range. Bring a little cash (US dollars preferred) to start out – exchange offices (*valut*) are common on city streets.

American Express travellers cheques are changed for a 2% fee at a limited number of banks (try Kazkommertzbank or Halyk Bank) in the big cities. Other types of cheques (Visa and Thomas Cook) are frowned upon. CATC travel agency is the American Express agent if you lose your cheques.

Tenge notes and coins are 10,000, 5000, 2000, 1000, 500, 200, 100, 50, 20, 10, five, three and one.

At the time of research, exchange rates were:

Country	Unit		Tenge
Australia	A$1	=	105 T
Canada	C$1	=	105 T
China	Y1	=	16 T
euro zone	€1	=	172 T
Japan	Ÿ10	=	12 T
Kyrgyzstan	1 som	=	3 T
New Zealand	NZ$1	=	94 T
Pakistan	Rs 10	=	24 T
Russia	R10	=	48 T
UK	UK£1	=	257 T
USA	US$1	=	139 T
Uzbekistan	10 sum	=	1.4 T

POST

The cost of an airmail letter under 10g to anywhere outside the CIS is 119 T. Postcard stamps cost 75 T. A 2kg parcel of books by surface mail costs around US$27, by airmail around US$20 or more (depending on the destination).

If you have anything of value or importance to post it's much safer to use one of the international courier firms, such as DHL, Federal Express or UPS, all of which have offices in Almaty (see p97).

REGISTRATION

Once in Kazakhstan, if you're staying more than five days you must register your visa with OVIR (now officially called Immigration Police Department). The Draconian past, which once involved hours of hair-pulling angst at the central OVIR office, is fading away. It is now possible to register

upon arrival at the airport or Almaty 2 train station. You'll pay a fee of 950 T (US$7) and processing time takes just a few minutes. It's still possible to register at the main OVIR office, though this place is best avoided. If you are short on time, a travel agent can get you registered for about US$20.

Getting registered in other cities can be either painfully bureaucratic or blessedly efficient. Our registration in Kyzylorda was free and took just 30 minutes. The penalty for not registering can be anywhere from US$80 to US$150.

Tourist visas can only be registered for one month, so if you have a two-month visa you'll have to register twice.

For OVIR registration details in Almaty, see p97. For Astana, see p137.

If you're moving around the country, keep in mind that you're supposed to re-register with OVIR at any place you stay more than 72 hours. So you can legally stay up to three days anywhere without re-registering. Your passport is likely to be checked on trains and at airports so it's a good idea to keep all ticket stubs and hotel receipts to prove when you arrived in a place and how long you've spent there. Carry bus or hotel receipts as proof if you are leaving a city within five days.

TELEPHONE & FAX

Kazakhtelekom offices have long-distance and international call booths, and increasingly, Internet cafés. Card-operated phones are easy to use and have English instructions. When your call goes through, you have to press the 'lips' button to speak.

If you're staying in an apartment or a smaller hotel, local calls are usually free of charge, covered by the general rental fee for the line. Not all phones allow long-distance or international calls. If a direct dial service is available (it will be on all card-operated phones) you will first have to dial 8 and wait for a long tone signal before continuing to dial the rest of the number.

If the phone you're using does not allow direct dial calls, it might be possible to book a long-distance call by dialling ☎ 8 614, and for an international call ☎ 8 694. Don't rely on an English-speaking operator being available.

At peak times, expect a one-minute call to Europe or the US to cost around US$2, and to Australia US$3.50. Calls are cheaper from 8pm to 8am.

You can get your GSM mobile phone set up for local use at any mobile phone shop. **K-mobile** (cnr Furmanov & Töle Bi, Almaty) is the most common; you can activate your phone for two months with US$10 of air-time credit (see Map p96).

Fax services are available from Kazakh-telekom offices and many hotels. To send a one-page fax to countries outside of the CIS costs around US$4, within the CIS US$2, and within Kazakhstan under US$1.

TRAVEL PERMITS

Special permits (sometimes called a *pro-pusk*) are needed for sensitive border areas in eastern Kazakhstan, notably the Altay Mountains, Lepsinsk and Khan Tengri. Tour agents should be able to arrange such permits, as long as their services are used to visit the restricted areas, but processing can take up to 20 days. The process is done through the local *akimat* (government house). The travel permits for these areas also cover trekking, killing two birds with one stone.

VISAS

Kazakhstan's Draconian visa regulations continue to ease up. As of 15 February 2004, the dreaded 'Letter of Invitation' (LOI) was no longer required for businessmen or tourists seeking a single-entry, one-month visa. The policy applies to 27 Western countries.

Most embassies can process the visa in two working days, others on the same day. You'll need to deliver your passport, application and two passport-size photos.

If there is no Kazakh embassy or consulate in your country, visas may be available from the Russian embassy.

It's possible to pick up your visa at the airport (but no land border), although this will require an LOI.

The LOI is still required for visas longer than one month, but since you are only allowed a stay for 30 days (and extensions are difficult to get), you might as well pick up a new visa in Bishkek or Tashkent if you want to stay longer. It is also required of non-Western nationals. For up-to-date visa regulations, contact a Kazakh embassy or see this website: www.kazakhstanembassy.org.uk.

If you do need an LOI, these can be provided by tourist companies in Kazakhstan.

If you are coming for school or work purposes, your contact person may be able to supply one. For a list of tour agents who can arrange such a letter see p98.

In theory, a one-month/two-month tourist visa is supposed to cost US$35/US$45. In practice, each embassy charges whatever they can get. The consulate in New York charges US$105/US$125. The embassy in Tashkent will issue a one-month visa on the spot for US$40. For a longer stay you'll need to ask for a business visa (US$100 for six months and US$200 for one year). A one-day rush fee is about US$40 extra. Tourist visas cannot be extended.

Copies

It's important to carry a photocopy of your passport and visa stamp with you at all times, rather than the real thing, since it's not unknown for policemen and soldiers, bona fide or otherwise, to harass foreigners for their documents. Your embassy in Almaty can provide a photocopy with an attached letter in Russian for verification. Some embassies charge a small fee (British £15, French US$17); the American embassy does it for free. It's worth taking the time to get this document as it works wonders with officious officials.

Transit Visas

These cost about US$35, are good for five days, and do not require an LOI. These are available from embassies at the airport in Almaty, but not land border crossings. You should have proof of onward travel.

Visas for Onward Travel

For contact details of embassies and consulates in Kazakhstan, see p153.

Afghanistan 30-day tourist visas (US$30) processed in three days.

China One of Central Asia's more difficult embassies. Visas only given with an invitation from an organisation in China. Fees vary depending on nationality, but average around US$40. Long lines for outside the embassy; a US$20 tip (see if you can bargain it down) to the door guard may get you in quicker. Using a local agency is even better (CATC in Almaty is recommended). Abnormal requests may hurt your chances – one traveller was quoted US$300 for his visa after announcing his intention to cycle across the border on a bicycle.

Kyrgyzstan One-month visas US$40. No LOI needed for most Western nationalities. The consulate is about 50m from the street in the back of an anonymous white building.

Pakistan Three-month visas issued in two days; price depends on nationality (ie USA US$120, UK US$72, Australia US$42, France US$30).

Russia One-month tourist visa costs US$100 provided you have accommodation vouchers. Three-month business visas US$90 (two-week processing, or same day US$180). Another US$20 or US$30 might be added depending on your nationality. Long queues are the norm. Get here by 8am to put your name on a list (or start one).

Tajikistan Visas are issued on the spot if you have an LOI from a Tajik travel agency (available from most agencies in Almaty and Bishkek). Direct from embassy, visa and LOI costs are one week US$80, two weeks US$100, one month US$120. All tourist visas are issued in one day.

Turkmenistan Visas only given with the support of a travel agency.

Uzbekistan 30-day tourist visas issued in two to 10 days depending on nationality (ie UK 2 days, US 10 days). Rush service available. 72-hour transit visas can be processed only if you are flying out with Uzbek Airways. Some Western nationalities do not need an LOI, see p237.

TRANSPORT IN KAZAKHSTAN

GETTING THERE & AWAY
Entering Kazakhstan

Once a bureaucratic nightmare, the entry procedures into Kazakhstan are streamlined these days. Doling out bribes is no longer a prerequisite, though you may bump into the occasional bad egg. In 2003 Kazakhstan dropped the customs declarations forms for visitors carrying less than US$3000. You will probably be given an arrival card (if not, ask for one). Keep the second half in your passport. Always make sure to get your passport stamped; they sometimes forget, especially on the trains from Russia and China.

Air
AIRPORTS

Kazakhstan's two biggest airports are in **Almaty** (☎ 3171- 57 13 00; www.alaport.com) and **Astana** (☎ 3172- 17 44 00; www.astanaairport.kz). Almaty's new US$400 million airport (located next to the old one) debuted in December 2003.

To get to and from other Central Asian locations from Almaty, there are flights daily to Tashkent (Uzbek Airlines US$115); twice weekly to Dushanbe (US$140); and twice weekly to Ashgabat (Turkmenistan

---

> **Departure Tax**
> For travellers there is no departure tax out of Kazakhstan.

Airlines US$180). International airline offices in Almaty are listed on p107.

Land
BORDER CROSSINGS

For connections from Russia, see p467.

To/From China

There are few hassles reported these days at either Khorgos (the road crossing) or Dostyk (the rail crossing), although both can take hours to cross.

At the time of research there were no cross-border buses between Ürümqi and Almaty. Buses from each side will travel to the border at Khorgos, where you can cross and change. From Ürümqi's main bus terminal a 7pm daily sleeper bus (top/bottom bed Y96/106) arrives in Khorgos at 10.30am; it's a Y5 rickshaw ride from the bus station to the border. From the Kazakh side, buses depart to Almaty directly from the border. A ticket should be about US$3.50, but you'll have to bargain. From Yining (about 100km from the border), a morning bus travels direct to Almaty (Y250, 12 hours, including four hours at the border). Buses stop for one meal, but bring some food; if the bus is running late, you might get pretty hungry.

At Khorgos, the crossing is usually crammed with Kazakh and Uyghur families and traders who can cross more easily than foreigners, but seem to have about 10 times as much baggage. The Chinese are pretty efficient while the Kazakhs are slower. A bus (US$3) shuttles people between the border posts and the border closes for two hours between noon and 2pm so try to get there early. The bus and taxi drivers on the Kazakh side do their best to capitalise on your ignorance of exchange rates and fares; grill your fellow travellers for such information before crossing.

From Ürümqi, the twice weekly Genghis Khan Express (No 13/14) costs US$60 in second-class *kupe* for the 40-hour journey to Almaty, crossing at Dostyk. You may have to a show a visa when buying a ticket as visas are not issued at the border. There's no guarantee of a restaurant car so bring your own food and drink and share, as everyone else does.

At Dostyk, you have to wait around while the bogies are changed. The main inconvenience here is that there are apparently no toilet facilities during the custom checks, but at other times you can pop out and use the station toilet. Toilets are unlocked for the 20-minute dash between the Kazakhstan and China posts, so get in line early!

Although bribe-taking and theft by border officials now seems a thing of the past on this border, it's still a good idea to remain vigilant.

To/From Kyrgyzstan
Official Kazakh–Kyrgyz border crossings are largely hassle-free.

Two buses per hour make the five-hour, 240km run between Bishkek and Almaty's Sayran bus station. A ticket is US$3.50. Marshrutnoe buses and taxis also wait at Sayran; they're faster and cost US$5. Buses to/from Taraz are also available.

Another option are the daily buses from Cholpon-Ata (US$12) and Karakol (US$17) near Lake Issyk-Kul in Kyrgyzstan, via Georgievka near Bishkek. No buses take the rougher and far more scenic easterly road from Issyk-Kul via Kegen. But in summer you could take a taxi from Karakol to the border for about US$40. Once on the Kazakh side, hitch to Kegen where you can get onward bus transport to Almaty.

Trekkers making the haul between Almaty and Lake Issyk-Kul might have trouble later as this is not an official crossing and there's no place to get your visa stamped – you'll have some explaining to do when you exit the country. One way around this is to trek back to where you came from. The situation changes season to season; consult your trekking agency before setting off.

To/From Turkmenistan
A border crossing exists between Zhanaözen and Bekdash in Turkmenistan, although it is not recommended for travellers who don't have their own transport. The no-man's-land at the border covers roughly about 100km, customs officials in Zhanaözen are rather tough and, as there is very little traffic, prices are high.

To/From Uzbekistan
It's a 25-minute bus ride (US$0.50) from central Tashkent to the border. There are check posts starting about 1km from the border so you'll have to get out and walk. You can get closer in a taxi (US$3.50) if your driver has good negotiating skills. From the Kazakh side, there are shared taxis and marshrutnoe taxis to Turkistan (US$3) and Shymkent (US$1.50). Taxis to Almaty will be cheaper from Shymkent.

At the time of research there were no Tashkent–Almaty train services, though these might resume. The only train from Tashkent is the thrice weekly No 5 Moscow train (departs Tue, Fri, Sun at 8.40am), which makes stops in western Kazakhstan, including Turkistan, Kyzylorda, Aralsk and Aktöbe.

From Nukus, train No 232 runs to western Kazakhstan/Russia (Beyneu, Atyrau, Astrakhan) on Sunday at 9.51am. Daily passenger trains with *platskartnyy* (hard sleeper) seating also run to Beyneu from Nukus, although service is unreliable.

Sea
BORDER CROSSINGS
To/From Azerbaijan
Once a week a ferry (24 hours, US$55) crosses between Baku and Aktau. There is no specific day; it leaves when enough tickets have been sold. Once on board, it's possible to upgrade your seat for US$10. There were no survivors when one of these ferries sunk in a storm in October 2002.

GETTING AROUND
Domestic airlines have an extensive network covering virtually the whole country. Flights are moderately priced and given the time you'll save it's worth taking at least one flight, using the train in the other direction for some perspective.

Air Astana (☎ 3272-58 41 36) serves mainly western Kazakhstan.

The state of the airlines in Kazakhstan is in flux as Air Kazakhstan went into bankruptcy during production of this book and Air Astana continues to expand. Air Astana has been slowly taking over Air Kazakhstan's international routes and the domestic ones may be next.

Bus connections between Almaty and northern and eastern Kazakh cities are fair and the quality of the roads aren't bad either. Bus connections to west Kazakhstan are virtually nonexistent. Most buses are modern, and both cheaper and faster (but less comfortable) than trains.

It's possible to drive your own car in Kazakhstan and you don't even need an international driver's licence, a valid licence from your home country will do. Car rental in Almaty is expensive even by Western standards (see p108). A motorcycle can also be a rewarding way of seeing the country. For either private car or motorcycle use, you should be somewhat knowledgeable about vehicle mechanics as service stations and help can be hundreds of kilometres apart. Stan Tours (see p98) says it can organise a driving tour in remote western Kazakhstan, from Aktau to Aralsk, across the Aral Sea basin.

For the casual traveller with time, trains are the best bet over a long haul. Tickets are usually available right up until the time of departure, but it's best to make an advanced booking, especially in west Kazakhstan or for international trains. All cities have a downtown train booking office, identified by the sign 'temir joly' (iron road), at which you can buy tickets without having to schlep yourself to the station.

We get the occasional report of travellers being fined by Russian border guards for not having a Russian visa when riding on Kazakh trains that dip into Russia (Ust-Kamenogorsk–Semey and Aktöbe–Uralsk). Get your alibis ready and hold your breath.

Uzbekistan
Узбекистан

FAST FACTS

- **Area** 447,400 sq km
- **Capital** Tashkent
- **Country Code** ☎ 998
- **Ethnic Groups** 80% Uzbek, 5% Russian, 5% Tajik, 3% Kazakh, and 7% others
- **Languages** Uzbek, Russian, Tajik, Karakalpak
- **Money** sum; US$1 = 992 sum; €1 = 1207 sum
- **Phrases** Hello. (*salom aleikum*); Thank you. (*rakhmat*)
- **Population** 25.2 million

Double land–locked Uzbekistan, sealed off from the world by mountains, deserts, nonsensical borders and post-Soviet bureaucracy, looks like the last place on Earth. Seemingly unreachable – if only in the imagination or a medieval fairy tale full of flying carpets – Samarkand, Bukhara and Khiva still resonate as the filthy, slave-ridden ancient Silk Road stops that linked China and Persia.

Yet once on the ground, after clearing customs without a glitch and overnighting in stylish Tashkent digs, travellers find themselves speeding between spotless cities in Daewoo Nexia taxis; the hardships of the journey vanishing into thin air like so many flying carpets. And then – after gasping for air at first sight of Samarkand's Registan; ducking through the moonlit alleys of mystical Khiva; and pondering the fate of a dozen layers of civilisation underfoot at Termiz and Afrosiab – the visitors are reminded that in another age this was not the end of the world but rather the centre of it.

The recipients of this grandeur take history in their stride and, like their predecessors, open their homes just as the golden caravanserais (travellers' inns) once swung their gates wide for peasants, merchants and the noblest of nobles.

HIGHLIGHTS

Samarkand's public square, the **Registan** (p199), is just one of many architectural jewels of this Silk Road town. The holy city of **Bukhara** (p208), with mosques sprinkled through its windy lanes, is more relaxing and offers competitive B&B accommodation. Enchanting **Khiva** (p223) and its dramatic history lies across the desert sands to the west.

For a taste of modern Uzbekistan, try out **Tashkent's Alisher Navoi Opera & Ballet Theatre** (p175) and the **Savitsky Karakalpakstan Art Museum** (p230) in Nukus. The mystery of silk-worm farming is revealed at **Margilan** (p192), in the heart of welcoming Fergana Valley, with the clear mountain air of **Shakhimardan** (p193) a short drive away.

ITINERARIES

- **Three days** Start in Bukhara, either with a domestic flight from Tashkent or overland from Turkmenistan, for a wander around Lyabi-Hauz and a look at the Kalon Minaret and the Ark. Travel by taxi to Samarkand on day two, taking in the Registan, Bibi-Khanym Mosque, Shahr-i-Zindah and Guri Amir Mausoleum, before exiting the country on day three to Tajikistan via Penjikent.

- **One week** Fly to Urgench and go by taxi to nearby Khiva and its walled city Ichon Qala. Allow for an overnight and travel by taxi to Bukhara and Samarkand, giving each an extra day. With one extra day in Tashkent you can catch the opera and a museum or two.

- **Two weeks** Fly to the Karakalpak capital Nukus, visit the Savitsky Museum, and take a side trip to Moynaq and its shipwrecks. Travel to Urgench and Khiva, giving more time to see a few of the ruined fortresses in the outlying desert. Continue through Bukhara to Samarkand, from where you can make day trips to Timur's hometown Shakhrisabz and the Sogdian ruins near Penjikent (you'll need a Tajik visa). With a couple of days at the end you can get over the mountains to the Fergana Valley, and exit to Kyrgyzstan.

- **One month** All the above sights can be seen in a month at a more relaxed pace, allowing time for homestays and perhaps a camel trek to Aidarkul Lake near Samarkand. You can also take in the frontier town Termiz and the Ugam-Chatkal National Park east of Tashkent.

- **Off the beaten track** Hunt down the various ruined desert citadels or the Badai-Tugai Nature Reserve around Urgench.

UZBEKISTAN

TRAVELLING SAFELY IN UZBEKISTAN

Much of the Uzbek–Tajik border, and parts of the Uzbek–Kyrgyz border, have been mined and are therefore off limits. Shepherds and their livestock are the usual victims of mine blasts, but foreigners are advised to steer clear as well.

CLIMATE & WHEN TO GO

Large areas of Uzbekistan are desert. Summer is long, hot and dry; spring is mild and rainy; autumn has light frosts and rains; and winter, although short, is unstable with snow and temperatures below freezing.

From June to August average afternoon temperatures hit 32°C or higher. The average annual maximum temperature is 40°C in June. Most rain falls in March and April.

The summer furnace of 35°C days lasts 40 days from mid-July to the end of August. The worst of winter lasts 40 days from Christmas to the first week of February; Termiz remains relatively mild during this period. The best time to visit is in spring from May until the end of June, and in autumn from September until November. The mountains are pleasantly cool in summer, freezing in winter. See the Climate Charts on p446.

HISTORY

The land along the upper Amu-Darya, Syr-Darya and their tributaries has always been different from the rest of Central Asia – more settled than nomadic, with patterns of land use and communality that has changed little from the time of the Achaemenids (6th century BC) to present day. An attitude of permanence and proprietorship still sets the people of this region apart.

Ancient Empires

The region was part of some very old Persian states, including Bactria, Khorezm and Sogdiana. In the 4th century BC Alexander the Great entered Cyrus the Great's Achaemenid empire. He stopped near Marakanda (Samarkand) and then, having conquered the Sogdians in their homeland mountains, married Roxana, the daughter of a local chieftain (see p27).

Out of the northern steppes in the 6th century AD came the Western Turks – the western branch of the empire of the so-called Kök (Blue) Turks. They soon grew attached to life here and abandoned their wandering ways, eventually taking on a significant role in maintaining the existence of the Silk Road (see p43). The Arabs brought Islam and a written alphabet to Central Asia in the 8th century but found the region too big and restless to govern.

A return to the Persian fold came with the Samanid dynasty in the 9th and 10th centuries. Its capital, Bukhara, became the centre of an intellectual, religious and commercial renaissance. In the 11th century the Ghaznavids moved into the southern regions. For some time the Turkic Khorezmshahs dominated Central Asia from present-day Konye-Urgench in Turkmenistan, but their reign was cut short and the region's elegant oases ravaged by Jenghiz Khan in the early 13th century.

Central Asia again became truly 'central' with the rise of Timur, the ruthless warrior and patron of the arts who fashioned a glittering Islamic capital at Samarkand.

The Uzbeks

Little is known of early Uzbek history. At the time the Golden Horde was founded, Shibaqan (Shayban), a grandson of Jenghiz Khan, inherited what is today northern Kazakhstan and adjacent parts of Russia. The greatest khan of these Mongol Shaybani tribes (and probably the one under whom they swapped paganism for Islam) was Özbeg (Uzbek, ruled 1313–40). By the end

---

HOW MUCH?

- Snickers bar US$0.40
- 100km bus ride US$1.50
- One-minute phone call to the US/UK US$1.40
- Internet per hour US$0.80–1.20
- Uzbek skull cap US$3–5

LONELY PLANET INDEX

- Litre of bottled water US$0.40
- Pint of lager US$2.50–3
- Shashlyk US$0.30–0.50
- Litre of petrol US$0.25–0.30

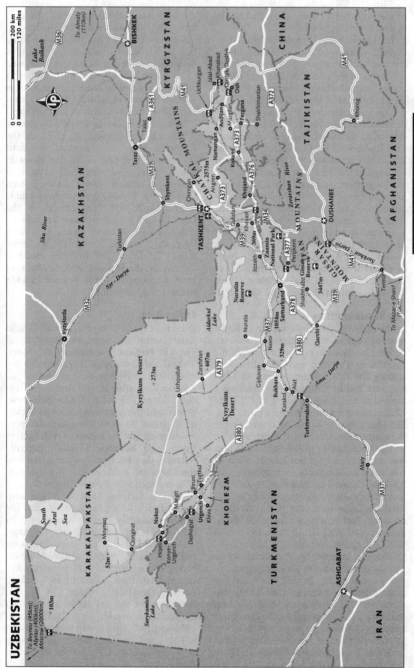

UZBEKISTAN

of the 14th century these tribes had begun to name themselves after him.

The Uzbeks began to move southeast, mixing with sedentary Turkic tribes and adopting the Turkic language, and reached the Syr-Darya in the mid-15th century. Following an internal schism (which gave birth to the proto-Kazakhs; see p32), the Uzbeks rallied under Mohammed Shaybani and thundered down upon the remnants of Timur's empire. By the early 1500s all of Transoxiana ('the land beyond the Oxus') from the Amu-Darya (Oxus) to the Syr-Darya (Jaxartes) belonged to the Uzbeks, as it has since.

The greatest (and last) of the Shaybanid khans, responsible for some of Bukhara's finest architecture, was Abdullah II, who ruled from 1538 until his death in 1598. After this, as the Silk Road fell into disuse, the empire unravelled under the Shaybanids' distant cousins, the Astrakhanids. By the start of the 19th century the entire region was dominated by three weak, feuding Uzbek city-states – Khiva, Bukhara and Kokand.

The Russians Arrive

In the early 18th century the khan of Khiva made an offer to Peter the Great of Russia (to become his vassal in return for help against marauding Turkmen and Kazakh tribes), stirring the first Russian interest in Central Asia. But by the time the Russians got around to marching on Khiva in 1717, the khan no longer wanted Russian protection, and after a show of hospitality he had almost the entire 4000-strong force slaughtered.

The slave market in Bukhara and Khiva was an excuse for further Russian visits to free a few Russian settlers and travellers. In 1801 the insane Tsar Paul sent 22,000 Cossacks on a madcap mission to drive the British out of India, with orders to free the slaves en route. Fortunately for all but the slaves, Paul was assassinated and the army recalled while struggling across the Kazakh steppes.

The next attempt, by Tsar Nicholas I in 1839, was really a bid to pre-empt expansion into Central Asia by Britain, which had just taken Afghanistan, although Khiva's Russian slaves were the pretext on which General Perovsky's 5200 men and 10,000 camels set out from Orenburg. In January 1840, a British officer, Captain James Abbott, arrived in Khiva (having travelled from Herat in Afghan disguise) offering to negotiate the

slaves' release on the khan's behalf, thus nullifying the Russians' excuse for coming.

Unknown to the khan the Russian force had already turned back, in the face of a devastating winter on the steppes. He agreed to send Abbott to the tsar with an offer to release the slaves in return for an end to Russian military expeditions against Khiva. Incredibly, Abbot made it to St Petersburg.

In search of news of Abbott, Lieutenant Richmond Shakespear reached Khiva the following June and convinced the khan to unilaterally release all Russian slaves in Khiva and even give them an armed escort to the nearest Russian outpost, on the eastern Caspian Sea. Russian gratitude was doubtlessly mingled with fury over one of the Great Game's boldest propaganda coups.

When the Russians finally rallied 25 years later, the khanates' towns fell like dominoes – Tashkent in 1865 to General Mikhail Chernyaev, Samarkand and Bukhara in 1868, Khiva in 1873, and Kokand in 1875 to General Konstantin Kaufman.

Soviet Daze

Even into the 20th century, most Central Asians identified themselves ethnically as Turks or Persians. The connection between 'Uzbek' and 'Uzbekistan' is very much a Soviet matter. Following the outbreak of the Russian Revolution in 1917 and the infamous sacking of Kokand in 1918, the Bolsheviks proclaimed the Autonomous Soviet Socialist Republic (SSR) of Turkestan. Temporarily forced out by counter-revolutionary troops and *basmachi* (Muslim guerrilla fighters), they returned two years later and the Khiva and Bukhara khanates were forcibly replaced with 'People's Republics'.

Then in October 1924 the whole map was redrawn on ethnic grounds, and the Uzbeks suddenly had a 'homeland', an official identity and a literary language. The Uzbek SSR changed shape and composition over the years as it suited Moscow, hiving off Tajikistan in 1929, acquiring Karakalpakstan from Russia in 1936, taking parts of the Hungry Steppe (the Russian nickname for the dry landscape between Tashkent and Jizzakh) from Kazakhstan in 1956 and 1963, then losing some in 1971.

For rural Uzbeks, the main impacts of Soviet rule were the forced and often bloody collectivisation of the republic's mainstay (agriculture) and the massive shift to cotton cultivation. Life hardly changed in other ways. The Uzbek intelligentsia and much of the republic's political leadership was decimated by Stalin's purges. This and the traditional Central Asian respect for authority meant that by the 1980s *glasnost* (openness) and *perestroika* (restructuring) would hardly trickle down here; few significant reforms took place.

Independence

Uzbekistan's first serious noncommunist popular movement, Birlik (Unity), was formed by Tashkent intellectuals in 1989 over issues that included Uzbek as an official language and the effects of the cotton monoculture. Despite popular support, it was barred from contesting the election in February 1990 for the Uzbek Supreme Soviet (legislature) by the Communist Party. The resulting Communist-dominated body elected Islam Karimov, the First Secretary of the Communist Party of Uzbekistan (CPUz), to the new post of executive president.

Following the abortive coup in Moscow in August 1991, Karimov declared Uzbekistan independent. Soon afterward the CPUz reinvented itself as the People's Democratic Party of Uzbekistan (PDPU), inheriting all of its predecessor's property and control apparatus, most of its ideology, and of course its leader, Karimov.

In December 1991 Uzbekistan held its first direct presidential elections, which Karimov won with 86% of the vote. His only rival was a poet named Mohammed Solih, running for the small, figurehead opposition party Erk (Will or Freedom) party, who got 12% and was soon driven into exile. The real opposition groups, Birlik and the Islamic Renaissance Party (IRP), and all other parties with a religious platform, had been forbidden to take part.

Under the constitution, Uzbekistan is a secular, democratic presidential republic. The president is elected for a five-year term and can serve at most two consecutive terms, a law Karimov continues to flout, although there are indications that a family successor is being groomed for takeover.

In reality, whereas Uzbekistan is most certainly secular, with a determined separation between religion and state, it's decidedly not 'democratic'. The man ultimately in charge of everything from municipal gardeners' salaries to gold production quotas is President Islam Karimov – as he was, under a different title, even before independence.

Uzbekistan Today

The years after independence have seen Karimov consolidate his grip on power, and dissent shrivel – thanks to control of the media, police harassment and imprisonment on trumped-up charges. Thousands of activists have been arrested and still languish in prison.

Erk is officially still legal, although members have been hounded from the legislature, bumped out of jobs, detained and interrogated, and their newspaper banned. The IRP, with support in the Fergana Valley, has gone underground. Most opposition leaders live in exile in Russia, Turkey or Europe.

Karimov won another election in January 2000, garnering 92% of the votes, even that of his challenger. Foreign observers deemed the election a farce. Although the system remains firmly in his grasp, reports of poor health might cause Karimov to pass on power to his ambitious daughter Gulnara Karimova, one of Uzbekistan's top business magnates whose personal fortune is believed to run into the tens of millions.

Nowadays, Karimov's biggest opponents are the pressure groups, Western governments, and economic agencies such as the International Monetary Fund (IMF) and World Bank, who periodically condemn Uzbekistan's abysmal human-rights record and archaic economic policy, which long ago drove most foreign investors out of the country. But as a geopolitically strategic country, Karimov is still able to gain support, notably from the United States, which gave Uzbekistan US$500 million in 2002 alone in exchange for support (eg placement of troops) in its 'War on Terror'.

Politically, Karimov's only real threat in recent years came in the form of a group of young, Fergana-based Islamic radicals, calling themselves the Islamic Movement of Uzbekistan (IMU). Declaring jihad on the Karimov regime, the drug-financed IMU spent three years harassing Kyrgyz and Uzbek security forces, kidnapping foreigners and supplying arms to sleeper cells in Kyrgyzstan and Uzbekistan.

In February 1999 a series of devastating bomb attacks in Tashkent led to a crackdown on a broad spectrum of opponents and Islamic fundamentalists. Mosques are no longer permitted to broadcast the *azan* (call to prayer), and mullahs have been pressured to praise the government in their sermons. Attendance at mosques has fallen for fear of practising Muslims being observed and harassed by government agents.

Suppression of dissent is officially called a temporary necessity in a country new to democratic traditions, but it's hard to see how a democratic framework could grow here. It's no accident that Uzbekistan's newly adopted cultural role model is Timur (whose image has replaced Karl Marx's head in Tashkent's central square).

PEOPLE

Centuries of tradition as settled people left the Uzbeks in a better position than their nomadic neighbours to fend off Soviet attempts to modify their culture. Traditions of the Silk Road still linger as Uzbeks consider themselves good traders, hospitable hosts and tied to the land.

The focal point of society is still the network of urban districts *(mahallas)*, where neighbours attend one another's weddings, celebrations and funerals. Advice on all matters is sought from an *aksakal* (revered elder, literally 'white beard'), whose authority is conferred by the community. In sinister, Soviet fashion, Karimov has usurped these structures by employing *aksakals* as district custodians and informants.

While Uzbek men toil to make ends meet, women struggle for equality. Considered second-class citizens in the workplace and in the home, women are not given the same rights as their Western counterparts, or even their Kyrgyz and Kazakh neighbours. Although the Soviets did much to bring women into the mainstream of society, no amount of propaganda could entirely defeat sexist attitudes. There are some signs of change – dress codes continue to liberalise, for example, but old habits die hard and women in conservative families are expected to be subservient to their husbands.

Domestic violence occurs in 40% of Uzbek homes, yet overall household control lies in the hands of the husbands' mother. Abuse, however, rarely leads to divorce, and although many women endure an almost slavelike position in the home, there are occasional reports of suicide by self-immolation, a cultural trait that dates back to pre-Islamic Zoroastrianism.

Population

Tashkent is Central Asia's biggest city and the Fergana Valley is home to Uzbekistan's largest concentration of people, a third of the population. Samarkand, the second city, is Tajik-speaking, as are many of the communities surrounding it, including Bukhara and Qarshi. The further west you travel the more sparsely populated the land becomes. Karakalpakstan, home to Kazakhs, Karakalpaks and Khorezmians, has seen its population dwindle as a result of the Aral Sea disaster (see p68). Around 40% of Uzbeks live in cities, with the rest in rural farming towns and villages.

The national population growth rate has fallen since independence (although still high at 2.5% per year) with tens of thousands of Slavs emigrating each year and with the sudden disappearance of subsidies for large families. Over half the population is under 15 years of age. A number of minority groups make up a tiny portion of the population, including Koreans in Tashkent and Jews in Bukhara.

RELIGION

Around 85% of Uzbeks claim to be Muslim (nearly all are the Hanafi Sunni variety), although only around 3% are practicing. Around 5% of the population are Christian. The Fergana Valley maintains the greatest Islamic conservative base, with Bukhara ranking number two. Although Uzbeks are tolerant of other religions, Western Christian missionaries have failed to gain a foothold, many having been harassed out of the country.

ARTS

Traditional art, music and architecture – evolving over centuries – were placed in a neat little box for preservation following the Soviet creation of the Uzbek SSR. But somehow, in the years to follow, two major centres of progressive art were still allowed to develop: Igor Savinsky's collection of lost art from the 1930s, stashed away in Nukus, and the life-stories told inside Tashkent's notorious Il Khom Theater, both survived as puddles of liberalism in a sea of communist doctrine.

Nowadays, Uzbekistan's art, music, film and literary figures are divided into those that are approved by the government and those that are not. Patriotic odes and art – those that glorify the young nation and its leadership – are welcomed and financed by the central budget.

The Amir Timur Museum in Tashkent is one of the best examples of state-supported art, with its mock Timurid dome and interior murals filled with scenes of epic nation-building.

Local pop and rap stars also sing to Uzbekistan's greatness. Yulduz Usmanova, a parliamentarian from Margilan, resurrected a scandal-filled career with ballads that urged dedication to the *yurtbashi* (national leader). The girl band 'Sitora' is another one to look out for, as well as grizzled rockers Bolalar, who date back to the *Perestroika*-era.

Many other forms of art, particularly those offering a philosophy and expression deeper than nationalism, aren't officially banned, but with scant means of private finance, their creators are left with little outlet for creativity.

The most notable 'dissident group' is the Fergana School, made up of a dozen or so artists and writers whose works were published in the early 1990s literary magazine *Zuizda Vastaka* (Star of the East). The government ordered the publication closed in 1994 and the Fergana School has since gone underground. In 2002 the Soros Foundation in Tashkent published the school's poetry in a book titled *Poeziya I Fergana.*

ENVIRONMENT

Uzbekistan spans several ecosystems, and topographic and geographic shifts. Its eastern fringes tilt upwards in a knot of rugged mountains – Tashkent's Chatkal mountains running into the western Tian Shan range, and Samarkand's Fan Mountains and a mass of ranges in the southeast flowing into the Pamir Alay. This isolated, rocky and forested terrain make up an important habitat for bear, lynx, bustard, mountain goat and even the elusive snow leopard.

Flowing down from these mountains are the life-giving rivers, the Amu-Darya and the Syr-Darya. The misnamed Soviet Ministry of Water Economy created two wide shallow lakes where there used to be desert, salt pans and marshes – Sarykamish in the west and Aidarkul, north of the Nuratin range – as well as a host of smaller unplanned ones.

To the west of the well-watered mountains are vast plains of desert or steppe: the Ustyurt Plateau and the vast, barren Kyzylkum (Red Sands) Desert. Despite its bleakness, this land is far from dead; the desert is home to gazelle, various raptors and other critters you'd expect to find – monitors, scorpions and venomous snakes.

There are some 15 *zapovednik* (nature reserves) in Uzbekistan, the largest of which is Gissar (Gissarsky in Russian; 750 sq km), located in the Kashkadarya region due east of Shakhrisabz. This remote region of pine and juniper forests includes the 4349m Peak Boboitmas and the country's largest glacier, Severtsov.

Environmental Issues

Much, if not all, of this territory is threatened by Uzbekistan's lacklustre environmental protection laws and the deterioration of its national park system, which does not have the funds to prevent illegal logging and poaching.

The faltering of the reserves, however, pales in comparison to the Aral Sea disaster (see p68).

In addition to the existing tragedy of the Aral is the threat of disease and illness caused by deadly chemicals left in the area by the Soviets. A chemical weapons testing ground on a (formerly) tiny island in the Aral now lies exposed on a huge peninsula connected to the mainland; contaminated rats that once lived on the island now migrate south into the open desert.

Potentially even more dangerous to the environment are the nuclear waste storage facilities, located in Kyrgyzstan near the Uzbek border. Should this waste somehow enter the water supply, millions of people in the Uzbek Fergana would be affected.

FOOD & DRINK

Plov (Central Asian pilaf consisting of rice and fried vegetables) and shashlyk (meat roasted on skewers over hot coals) are the national staples (see p73). Every region has its own variation of nan bread; the raised rim of Kokand's speciality makes it a particularly fine shashlyk plate. Samarkand's nan resembles a giant bagel without the hole.

Buglama kovoq (steamed pumpkin) is a light treat. *Moshkichiri* and *moshhurda* are meat and mung bean gruels. *Dimlama* (*bosma*) is meat, potatoes, onions and vegetables braised slowly in a little fat and their own juices; the meatless version is *sabzavotli dimlama*. *Hunon* or *honum* is a noodle roll, usually with a meat and potato filling. Uzbeks are fond of stuffed cabbage and grape leaves (*dulma*), tomatoes, peppers and quinces.

Apricot pits are a local favourite; they're cooked in ash and the shells are cracked by the vendor before they reach the market. The white pits are from around Samarkand and the small brown ones from around Bukhara.

Besides green tea, nonalcoholic drinks include *katyk*, a thin yogurt that comes plain but can be sweetened if you have some sugar or jam handy. See the Central Asia Food & Drink chapter for more information (p73).

TASHKENT ТАШКЕНТ

☎ (3) 71 or 712 / pop 2.3 million / elevation 478m

Tashkent, the Uzbek capital, is Central Asia's hub – its biggest and worldliest city (the fourth-biggest in the Commonwealth of Independent States after Moscow, St Petersburg and Kiev), situated bang in the middle of the Eurasian landmass, and better connected by international flights than any other city in the region.

Rebuilt after the 1966 earthquake as the very model of a modern Soviet city, Tashkent comprises concrete apartment blocks decorated with Uzbek motifs and illuminated slogans, yawning parade grounds around solemn monuments, and a remarkably comprehensive public transport system. There's also the other, older city, a sprawling Uzbek country town with fruit trees and vines in every courtyard hidden behind secure walls.

Some of the region's Slavs have moved to the relative cultural security of Tashkent, which is still at least half Russian-speaking (if not Russian). It's also a haven for Uzbekistan's Koreans, Caucasians and Tatars, lending it a diverse and cosmopolitan edge.

It's hard to visit Uzbekistan without passing through Tashkent, and there are many facilities – consular, communications, and medical – that you can't find elsewhere in the republic, along with a busy (and very affordable) cultural life and some interesting museums.

HISTORY

Tashkent's earliest incarnation might have been as the settlement of Ming-Uruk (Thousand Apricot Trees) in the 2nd or 1st century BC. By the time the Arabs took it in 751 it was a major caravan crossroads. It was given the name Toshkent (Tashkent, 'City of Stone' in Turkic) in about the 11th century.

The Khorezmshahs and Jenghiz Khan stubbed out Tashkent in the early 13th century, although it slowly recovered under the Mongols and then under Timur and grew more prosperous under the Shaybanids in the late 15th and 16th centuries.

The khan of Kokand annexed Tashkent in 1809. In 1865, as the emir of Bukhara was preparing to snatch it away, the Russians under General Mikhail Grigorevich Chernyayev beat him to it, against the orders of the tsar and despite being outnumbered 15 to one. They found a proud town, enclosed by a 25km-long wall with 11 gates (of which not a trace remains today).

The newly installed Governor-General Konstantin Kaufman in Tashkent was to gradually widen the imperial net around the other Central Asian khanates. Tashkent also became the tsarists' (and later the Soviets') main centre for espionage in Asia, during the protracted imperial rivalry with Britain known as the Great Game (see p35).

Tashkent became the capital of the Turkestan Autonomous SSR, declared in 1918. When this was further split, the capital of the new Uzbek Autonomous SSR became Samarkand. In 1930, this status was restored to Tashkent and the city acquired industrial muscle with the construction of the agricultural machinery combine, Tashselmash, in the 1920s, and the wholesale relocation of factories from western Russia to Central Asia during WWII.

Physically, Tashkent was changed forever on 25 April 1966, when a massive earthquake levelled vast areas of the town and left 300,000 people homeless (see the Earthquake Memorial, p175). Soviet histor-

Timurid tilework on the Shahr-i-Zindah (p200), Samarkand, Uzbekistan

BRADLEY MAYHEW

MARY PEACHIN

Man on a Bukhara rug, Uzbekistan

Statue of Amir Timur (Tamerlane) at the ruins of Ak-Saray Palace (p206), Shakhrisabz, Uzbekistan

MARTIN MOOS

CHRISTINE OSBORNE

Stallholder, Uzbekistan

Beached fishing boats, Aral Sea (p233), Uzbekistan

BRADLEY MAYHEW

Boys in front of the Char Minar (p214), Bukhara, Uzbekistan

MARTIN MOOS

Old city walls, Khiva (p226), Uzbekistan

JANE SWEEN

ians made much of the battalions of 'fraternal peoples' and eager urban planners who came from around the Soviet Union to help with reconstruction.

But when Moscow later announced it would give 20% of the newly built apartments to these (mainly Russian) volunteers and invite them to stay, local resentment boiled over in street brawls between Uzbeks and Russians in the so-called 'Pakhtakor Incident' of May 1969.

Security in the city, particularly in the metro stations, has been high since February 1999 when six car bombs killed 16 and injured more than 120. The blasts were attributed by the government to Islamic extremists, but it will probably never be known who was responsible.

ORIENTATION

Before the 1966 earthquake the Ankhor canal separated old (Uzbek) and new (Russian) Tashkent, the former a tangle of alleys around the **Chorsu Bazaar**, the latter with shady avenues radiating from what is now Amir Timur maydoni (public square). The city has since grown out of all proportions and sprawls over a vast plain. Covering it on foot requires long walks and it's best to use public transport. Uzbeks perhaps still consider Chorsu their 'centre'. Civil servants and diehard communists might home in on Mustaqillik maydoni (Independence Square, formerly Lenin Square), the vast parade grounds just east of the canal. The statue of Amir Timur on horseback in the gardens of Amir Timur maydoni is a useful reference point, with the Hotel Uzbekistan on the eastern side of the park and the Broadway (Sayilgoh) strip of stalls, cafés and restaurants leading off to the west.

Tashkent airport is 6km south of Amir Timur maydoni, reached by bus No 67. Tashkent train station (also called Main or North station) is 2.5km south of Amir Timur maydoni at the end of Movarounnakhr, by Tashkent metro station. The Tashkent long-distance bus station is about 14km southwest of Amir Timur maydoni, along Halqlar Dustligi, at Sobir Rakhimov metro station.

Maps

The most detailed city map is *Toshkent Shahar Plani*, in Uzbek language with a topo-

TASHKENT MUST-SEES

Chorsu Bazaar Haggle till you drop in this vast goods emporium (p181).

History Museum of the People of Uzbekistan The great repository of Uzbek history (p174).

Tashkent Land Lose your lunch on any number of rides (p176).

La Casa The legend of Che lives on in this funky bar (p180).

Kosmonavtlar Metro Station Tashkent's very own version of Space Mountain (p176).

graphic map of the surrounding mountains on the reverse. Similar is the English-language *Tashkent New City Map*, which includes the address and phone numbers of Tashkent NGOs. The Orzu and Poytaht hotels sell a fold-up map that can slip into a shirt pocket; it contains city maps of Tashkent, Khiva, Bukhara and Samarkand, along with useful phone numbers. Maps are also sold at Anglesey supermarkets, top-end hotels and the bookshop **Sharq Ziyorki** (Bukhara 26) near Le Meridien hotel.

INFORMATION
Bookshops

Other than slim paperbacks of Karimov's political philosophies, bookshops have little more than school textbooks in Russian or Uzbek. Some four-star hotels sell books about Uzbekistan; the best bookstand is at the InterContinental (2km north of the city). You can also browse old Russian books in the street stalls northeast of Kosmonavtlar metro along Buyok Turon.

Cultural Centres

One place to meet young speakers of foreign languages is the Language Faculty (Russian: *Fakultet zarubezhnoy filologiy*) at Tashkent State University. Follow the *'na ulitsu Beruni'* signs out of Beruni metro station and ask for Vuzgorodok or University Town. Long term residents or specialists may wish to contact the following organisations:

British Council (☎ 120 67 52; fax 120 63 71; www.britishcouncil.org/uzbekistan; Konaev 11) Between Kosmonatavlar metro and the Grand Mir hotel.

Goethe Institut (☎ /fax 152 70 24; www.goethe.de /taschkent; Konaev 11) In the same building as the British Council. The website is in German only.

TASHKENT

INFORMATION

Afghan Embassy	**1**	E2
Alp Jamol Bank	**2**	D3
Avesta Net	**3**	C5
Azerbaijani Embassy	**4**	A5
Belgian Embassy	**5**	C5
Bookstalls	**6**	D4
British Council	**7**	D4
British Embassy	**8**	E4
Cactus Internet Café	**9**	E4
Central Telephone & Telegraph		
Office	**10**	B2
Chinese Embassy	**11**	E4
Cuba Internet	**12**	E3
DHL	**13**	B5
DHL	(see 65)	
Dolores Tour	(see 66)	
Everest Tour	(see 75)	
French Embassy	**14**	E4
German Embassy	**15**	D2
Goethe Institut	(see 7)	
Indian Embassy	**16**	E3
Institut Francais D'Etudes		
Sur L'Asie Centrale (IFEAC)	**17**	C4
Israeli Embassy	**18**	D5
Italian Embassy	**19**	C5
Japanese Embassy	**20**	E4
Kazakh Embassy	**21**	D5
Kyrgyz Embassy	**22**	E2
Main Post Office	**23**	E3
Mustaqillik Library	**24**	A2
National Bank of Uzbekistan	**25**	E4
Open Society Foundation	**26**	C5
Post Office	**27**	A3
Revolt	(see 92)	
Russian Embassy	**28**	D6
Sairam	**29**	D4
Samcom Internet	**30**	E3
Sharq Ziyorki Bookshop	**31**	D4
Tajik Embassy	**32**	C6
Tashkent International Medical		
Clinic (TIMC)	**33**	C6
Turkmen Embassy	**34**	D6

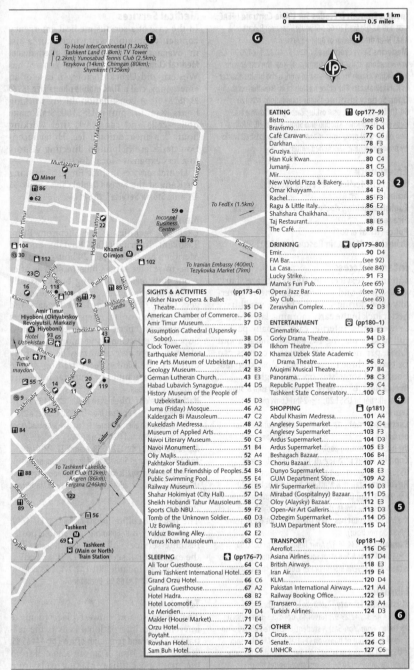

To Hotel InterContinental (1.2km);
Tashkent Land (1.8km); TV Tower
(2.2km); Yunosabad Tennis Club (2.5km);
Tezykova (14km); Chimgan (80km);
Shymkent (125km)

Inconnel
Business
Centre

To FedEx (1.5km)

To Iranian Embassy (400m);
Tezykovka Market (7km)

Khamid
Olimjon

Amir Timur
Hiyoboni (Oktyabrskoy
Revolyutsii, Markaziy
Hiyoboni)

Amir Timur
maydoni

To Tashkent Lakeside
Golf Club (12km);
Angren (86km);
Fergana (246km)

Tashkent

Tashkent
(Main or North)
Train Station

EATING	🍴 (pp177–9)
Bistro	(see 84)
Bravismo	76 D4
Café Caravan	77 C6
Darkhan	78 F3
Gruziya	79 E3
Han Kuk Kwan	80 C4
Jumanji	81 C5
Mir	82 D3
New World Pizza & Bakery	83 D4
Omar Khayyam	84 E4
Rachel	85 F3
Ragu & Little Italy	86 E2
Shahshara Chaikhana	87 B4
Taj Restaurant	88 E5
The Café	89 E5

DRINKING	🍷 (pp179–80)
Emir	90 D4
FM Bar	(see 92)
La Casa	(see 84)
Lucky Strike	91 F3
Mama's Fun Pub	(see 65)
Opera Jazz Bar	(see 70)
Sky Club	(see 65)
Zeravshan Complex	92 D3

ENTERTAINMENT	🎭 (pp180–1)
Cinematrix	93 E3
Gorky Drama Theatre	94 D3
Ilkhom Theatre	95 C3
Khamza Uzbek State Academic	
Drama Theatre	96 B2
Muqimi Musical Theatre	97 B4
Panorama	98 C3
Republic Puppet Theatre	99 C4
Tashkent State Conservatory	100 C3

SHOPPING	🛍 (p181)
Abdul Khasim Medressa	101 A4
Anglesey Supermarket	102 C4
Anglesey Supermarket	103 F3
Ardus Supermarket	104 D3
Ardus Supermarket	105 E3
Beshagach Bazaar	106 B4
Chorsu Bazaar	107 A2
Dunyo Supermarket	108 E3
GUM Department Store	109 A2
Mir Supermarket	110 D3
Mirabad (Gospitalnyy) Bazaar	111 D5
Oloy (Alaysky) Bazaar	112 C3
Open-Air Art Gallerirs	113 D3
Ozbegim Supermarket	114 D5
TsUM Department Store	115 D4

SIGHTS & ACTIVITIES	(pp173–6)
Alisher Navoi Opera & Ballet	
Theatre	35 D4
American Chamber of Commerce	36 D3
Amir Timur Museum	37 D3
Assumption Cathedral (Uspensky	
Sobor)	38 D5
Clock Tower	39 D4
Earthquake Memorial	40 D2
Fine Arts Museum of Uzbekistan	41 D4
Geology Museum	42 B3
German Lutheran Church	43 E3
Habad Lubavich Synagogue	44 D5
History Museum of the People of	
Uzbekistan	45 D3
Juma (Friday) Mosque	46 A2
Kaldergach Bi Mausoleum	47 C2
Kukeldash Medressa	48 A2
Museum of Applied Arts	49 C4
Navoi Literary Museum	50 C3
Navoi Monument	51 B4
Oliy Majlis	52 A4
Pakhtakor Stadium	53 C3
Palace of the Friendship of Peoples	54 B4
Public Swimming Pool	55 E4
Railway Museum	56 E5
Shahar Hokimiyat (City Hall)	57 D4
Sheikh Hobandi Tahur Mausoleum	58 C2
Sports Club NBU	59 F2
Tomb of the Unknown Soldier	60 D3
.Uz Bowling	61 B3
Yulduz Bowling Alley	62 E2
Yunus Khan Mausoleum	63 C2

SLEEPING	🛏 (pp176–7)
Ali Tour Guesthouse	64 C4
Bumi Tashkent International Hotel	65 E3
Grand Orzu Hotel	66 C6
Gulnara Guesthouse	67 A2
Hotel Hadra	68 B2
Hotel Locomotif	69 E5
Le Meridien	70 D4
Makler (House Market)	71 E4
Orzu Hotel	72 C5
Poytaht	73 D4
Rovshan Hotel	74 D6
Sam Buh Hotel	75 C6

TRANSPORT	(pp181–4)
Aeroflot	116 D6
Asiana Airlines	117 D4
British Airways	118 E3
Iran Air	119 E4
KLM	120 D3
Pakistan International Airways	121 A4
Railway Booking Office	122 E5
Transaero	123 A4
Turkish Airlines	124 D3

OTHER	
Circus	125 B2
Senate	126 C3
UNHCR	127 C6

0 — 1 km
0 — 0.5 miles

Institut Francais D'Etudes Sur L'Asie Centrale (IFEAC; ☎ 139 47 03; fax 120 66 56; www.ifeac.org; Rakatboshi 18A) Near the Museum of Applied Arts.

Medecins Sans Frontieres (☎ 152 40 32; fax 120 70 72; www.msf.org/aralsea; Konstitutsiya 4) Near the corner with Yusuf Khos Khojib, its main area of work is the health disaster in Karakalpakstan. The office has lots of information on this.

Open Society Institute (Soros Foundation; ☎ 120 54 10; fax 120 68 54; osi@osi.uz; Zarbog 31) Down a lane between Yusuf Khos Khodjib and Shota Rustaveli. Information on cultural programmes and a stock of published works by nongovernment-sanctioned writers.

Emergency

See also Medical Services (right).

Ambulance (☎ 03)
English-speaking doctor (☎ 185 60 93; ☾ 24hr)
Fire service (☎ 02)
Police (☎ 01 or 001)
Uzbekistan Mountain Rescue (☎ 132 21 50)

Internet Access

Internet Services in Tashkent are fairly widespread and growing. Surfing is generally slow during working hours; you'll have better luck in the early morning, late evening or weekends. Internet cafés, usually packed full of kids playing PC games, charge about US$1 per hour, hotel business centres can be two or three times higher. Most keep late hours and some stay open all night.

Avesta Net (☎ 152 07 08; cnr Usmana Nasira & Shota Rustavelli; per hr US$1.20; ☾ 24hr) Convenient for the Orzu Hotel.

Cactus Internet (☎ 133 21 10; Movarounnakhr tor; per hr US$1; ☾ 24hr) Located up a small lane opposite the public swimming pool.

Cuba Internet (☎ 132 20 46; Pushkin 7b; per hr US$0.80; ☾ 24hr) Next to Gruziya restaurant.

Revolt (cnr Ataturk & Matbuotchilar; per hr US$1.20; ☾ 9am-11pm) On the 2nd floor of the Zeravshan complex. Across the street, the Internet café in the basement of the Mir Food Court has a fast connection but is expensive (US$1.80 per hour).

Samcom (☎ 134 46 32; Amir Timur 4; per hr US$0.80; ☾ 9am-11pm) A few steps south of Ardus Supermarket, this is the best of several Internet cafés along this strip of shops.

Libraries

Mustaqillik Library (Tashkent English Library; ☎ 144 48 37, 42 29 97; Navoi 48, opposite Hotel Chorsu; ☾ noon-6pm Mon-Sat) A student-orientated library with a small collection of books on Central Asia. Membership is US$0.30 per visit or US$25 per year. English is the only language allowed to be spoken once inside.

Medical Services

In the case of a serious medical emergency contact your embassy, which can assist in evacuation. The **Tashkent International Medical Clinic** (TIMC; ☎ 120 61 91/2; Minglar 6) has Western and Uzbek doctors. In case of an emergency, call a **TIMC mobile phone** (☎ 185 60 93, 185 84 81). A consultation during working hours (8am to 5pm) is US$100. Staff make house calls and can work after working hours for an additional fee. Hotel reception desks are helpful in directing visitors to a less expensive local doctor.

Dental services include English-speaking Dr Kang at the **Korean Dental Clinic** (☎ 191 95 42) and **Stoma Service** (☎ 64 14 60, 64 39 16).

Money

Exchange facilities at the Sheraton, Bumi Tashkent International, Poytaht and Le Meridien hotels are open 24 hours. The best time to receive larger bills in sum is after a one-hour cash-restocking break, usually ending at 5pm. Black market moneychangers (see p235) still work the bazaars and can be found on the steps of some street underpasses (check the one next to Dunyo Supermarket). Changing money in such places is more risky, but may be your only option if the banks freeze trading on the sum. ATM machines in four-star hotels are usually cashless.

National Bank of Uzbekistan (NBU; ☎ 144 35 34; Y. Gulomov 95; ☾ 8am-4pm Mon-Fri) NBU charges a 2% fee for cashing travellers cheques. It can give a cash advance against Visa (3.5%) and MasterCard (4%).

Alp Jamol Bank (☎ 132 10 58; Ataturk 21; ☾ 9am-4pm Mon-Fri) Located 50m south of Broadway, opposite the Zeravshan complex. It charges 4% to change a travellers cheque and gives cash advances against Visa and Mastercard.

Post

The **main post office** (pochta bulimi; ☎ 133 42 02; Shakhrisabz 7; ☾ 8am-6pm) has unreliable poste-restante services. All four-star hotels offer the express mail services of DHL or FedEx. Main offices include **DHL** (☎ 115 20 58; Bobur 6) and **FedEx** (☎ 120 68 00; Bozbozor 6).

Telephone

The cheapest and slowest place to make intercity and international calls is the **central telephone and telegraph office** (☎ 144 65 35; Navoi 28; ☾ 8am-11pm). You can also call from the main post office. Making calls from the four-star hotels is more reliable but will cost twice the price. Local calls can be made from kiosks, shops and hotels at a rate of 100 sum per three minutes. See p236 for more options.

Travel Agencies

Several travel agencies in Tashkent have helpful English-speaking staff who can arrange homestay accommodation and help with visas, tickets and activities like trekking and skiing.

Asia Travel (☎ 173 51 07; 173 26 55; fax 173 15 44; www .asia-travel.uz; Chilonzor 97) Located near the US Embassy, southwest of the city. Offers visa support, tours, guides; specialists in mountain sports such as rafting, trekking, caving.

Dolores Tour (☎ 120 88 83; 120 86 58; fax 120 88 73; www.sambuh.com; M. Tarobi 27) Located at the Grand Orzu hotel, this efficient agency is switched on to the needs of overlanders. Tours nationwide, trekking, visa support.

Everest Tour (☎ 254 95 38; fax 24 91 74; www.traveluz .com; Tsekhovaya 10) Located at Sam Buh Hotel; offers visa support, tours, homestays, guides, air tickets, visa support for neighbouring countries, treks.

Sairam (☎ 133 35 59; fax 120 69 37; www.sairamtour.com .uz; Movarounnakhr 16A) Visa support, tours, guides, cars.

Sportur (☎ 137 17 64; fax 137 17 64; arostr@mail.ru; Flat 19, Bldg 65 Pushkin) Operated by the attentive Airat Yuldashev, Sportur arranges cars, guides, visas for neighbouring countries, homestays and self-catering apartments in Tashkent; has a villa on the city outskirts.

DANGERS & ANNOYANCES

The *militsia* (police) have become much less of a nuisance to travellers in recent years. Dire threats from President Karimov have curbed the police habit of shaking down travellers for bribes, although this still occurs – be particularly cautious at metro stations and on the tourist street Broadway. Sobir Rakhimov metro station, used mainly by backpackers on their way to the Tara Hotel, is particularly notorious. See Crooked Officials on p447 for tips on how to deal with police. More of a threat are common criminals posing as policemen. Expats have been robbed by men who've entered their homes under such false pretences. Your embassy can provide good advice on how to avoid such sticky situations.

Tashkent's international airport officials have also tidied up their act, but to speed the process have your registration dockets (see p236) and exchange certificates handy when leaving.

Uzbek money is a hassle all to itself, with the highest denomination note worth only one US dollar, and most notes much smaller; one US$100 bill turns into bundles of ragged bills, usually tied together with a rubber band.

Scams

Be prepared for anything upon arrival at Tashkent International Airport. You might be approached at customs by a man offering to help you fill out your customs declaration form; although a friendly enough gesture, travellers have been asked for money (usually US$5) for this unofficial service. Avoid this by asking for two customs forms in English and fill them out on your own. A similar annoyance occurs at the luggage carousel. Your bags might be taken off before they reach daylight and delivered on a cart by an attendant who will ask for a US$5 tip.

Finally, you will have to deal with the taxi drivers who do their best to extort huge sums of money from unsuspecting travellers. They'll tell you it's very far to your hotel, charge US$50, and drive around the suburbs for an hour before taking you to your requested destination. Don't be fooled. It is only 6km to the centre and shouldn't cost more than US$4 to get there, but even the hardest bargaining usually fails to bring prices lower than US$10. One way around this is to take a bus to the centre from where you can flag down a cheaper taxi.

SIGHTS

Many of the major tourist attractions – squares, parks, memorials and museums – are concentrated within the one kilometre area between Amir Timur maydoni and Mustaqillik maydoni. The Old Town, with its bazaars and mosques, is about 4km to the west across the Ankhor Canal. Sites on both sides of the canal are spread out and might require the use of taxis or buses.

Old Town

The Old Town (Uzbek: *eski shakhar*, Russian: *staryy gorod*) starts beside Chorsu Bazaar and the Chorsu Hotel. A maze of narrow dirt streets is lined with low mud-brick houses and dotted with mosques and old medressas. These few handsome religious buildings date from the 15th and 16th centuries.

If you're lucky enough to be invited into someone's home, you'll discover that the blank outer walls of traditional homes conceal cool, peaceful garden-courtyards.

The easiest way to reach this part of town is by metro to Chorsu station. Alternatively, from near the Hotel Uzbekistan, tram No 16, trolleybuses Nos 4 and 8 and express bus No 28-3 go west down Navoi to Chorsu Bazaar. Taxi drivers get lost easily here; on foot, you could easily get lost too. Three major streets that head into Chorsu Bazaar are Forobi (Farabi), Sagban and Zarqaynar.

KUKELDASH MEDRESSA
This grand 16th-century medressa on a hill opposite the Hotel Chorsu has a newly renovated courtyard. On warm Friday mornings the plaza in front overflows with worshippers.

JUMA (FRIDAY) MOSQUE
Behind Kukeldash is the 15th-century Juma (Friday) Mosque. Once a place of execution for unfaithful wives, it was used in Soviet times as a sheet metal workshop and recently reopened to the public.

KHAST IMOM
The official religious centre of the republic is located 2km north of the Circus, on Zarqaynar kuchasi. On the southwest corner, the 16th-century Barak **Khan Medressa** (Madrasa Barok Hon) houses the Central Asian Muslim Religious Board, whose Grand Mufti is roughly the Islamic equivalent of an archbishop for Uzbekistan, Kyrgyzstan, Tajikistan and Turkmenistan.

East from here across Zarqaynar kuchasi is the **Telyashayakh Mosque** (9am-5pm Mon-Fri), also called the Khast Imom Mosque. The 7th-century Osman Quran, said to be the world's oldest, is kept in the mosque's library. A small financial inducement usually earns you a look at this enormous tome, brought to Samarkand by Timur, then taken to St Petersburg by the Russians and returned here in 1989. At the time of research a museum was being constructed on the north side of the square, to where the Osman Quran will be transferred.

The big block on the east side is the **Imam Ismail al-Bukhari Islamic Institute**, a two-year post-medressa academy with around

two hundred students, was one of two medressas in Central Asia left open in Soviet times (the other was in Bukhara). Just west of this is the little 16th-century **mausoleum of Abu Bakr Kaffal Shoshi**, an Islamic scholar of the Shaybanid period.

YUNUS KHAN MAUSOLEUM
Across Navoi from the Navoi Literary Museum are three 15th-century mausoleums. The biggest bears the name of Yunus Khan, grandfather of the Mughal emperor Babur. The Uzbek Restoration Institute is at the rear of the building, where tiles are made for projects across the country. Two small mausoleums are eastward inside a fence – **Sheikh Hobandi Tahur** (Shiekhhantaur) and the pointy-roofed **Kaldergach Bi**. The latter is now used as a neighbourhood mosque.

Museums & Galleries
The **History Museum of the People of Uzbekistan** (139 17 78; Sharaf Rashidov 30; admission US$3, guided tour US$2; 10am-5pm Tue-Sun) includes more than 10,000 exhibits housed in the former Lenin Museum. Highlights of the museum include a small, peaceful Buddha figure from a Kushan temple excavated at Fayoz-Tepe near Termiz and a 2nd-century double-headed snake amulet once inlaid with precious stones, found in the Fergana Valley. The third floor contains a self-congratulatory tribute to Karimov's modern Uzbekistan.

On the 1st floor of the **Fine Arts Museum of Uzbekistan** (136 74 36; Movarounnakhr (Proletarskaya) 16; admission US$0.90; 10am-5pm Wed-Sun & 10am-2pm Mon) is a fine collection of the art of pre-Russian Turkestan – Zoroastrian artefacts, serene 1000-year-old Buddhist statues and royal furnishings too splendid to use. Down the hall is 19th- and 20th-century Uzbek applied art, notably the brilliant silk-on-cotton embroidered hangings called *suzani*. The ground floor often has exhibitions by local artists. The museum is in the giant cube-shaped building opposite Bravismo café.

The **Museum of Applied Arts** (56 39 43; Rakatboshi 15; admission US$0.80, guided tour US$1.50; 9am-6pm Wed-Mon) was commissioned by Alexander Polovtsev, a wealthy tsarist diplomat, to be built in the traditional style by artisans from Tashkent, Samarkand, Bukhara and Fergana. Full of bright, carved plaster decorations (*ghanch*) and carved wood, the house itself is the main attraction, though there are also exhibits of rare ceramics, textiles, jewellery, musical instruments and toys, and a pricey gift shop. The museum is on a quiet lane, 1km south of Kosmonavtlar metro station.

The **Amir Timur Museum** (☎ 132 02 12; Amir Timur 1; admission US$0.60; 🕑 10am-5pm Tue-Sun) is a must for aficionados of kitsch and cult-making; this impressive structure with a brilliant blue-ribbed dome and a richly decorated interior is the face of modern Uzbekistan's Timur. Murals show the tyrant commissioning public projects and praising his labourers, yet conspicuously overlooking his bloody, skull-stacking military campaigns.

Besides memorabilia of 15th-century poet Alisher Navoi and other Central Asian literati, **Navoi Literary Museum** (☎ 144 12 68; Navoi 69; admission US$1; 🕑 10am-5pm Mon-Fri & 10am-2pm Sat) has replica manuscripts, Persian calligraphy, and 15th- and 16th-century miniatures. It is located a block east of Alisher Navoi metro station.

The surprisingly grand **Geology Museum** (☎ 45 13 37; Furqat 1; admission US$0.50; 🕑 10am-4pm Mon-Fri) is full of beautiful minerals, a dinosaur skeleton, natural history dioramas and a giant 3-D map of Central Asia.

The impressive collection of Soviet behemoths in the **Railway Museum** (☎ 199 79 96; Movarounnakhr 1; admission US$0.10; 🕑 9am-6pm Wed-Sun) is at a railway siding near the main train station. The curator is happy to let you clamber all over the trains. Even if trains aren't really your thing it's a fun place to visit.

Alisher Navoi Opera & Ballet Theatre

The interior of the **Alisher Navoi Opera & Ballet Theatre** (☎ 133 33 44, 133 59 09) harbours various regional artistic styles – a different one in each room – executed by the best artisans of the day, under the direction of the architect of Lenin's tomb in Moscow. Japanese POWs are responsible for constructing the building itself. There is a separate ticket office, inside the main door, for guided tours of the place. Show tickets cost between 300 and 1500 sum, a bargain for what is one of the premiere cultural events in Central Asia. The programme changes daily, from Uzbek symphony to Russian opera. The theatre faces Buyuk Turon kuchasi across from Le Meridien hotel.

Squares, Parks & Memorials

Tashkent's main streets radiate from **Amir Timur maydoni**, where a glowering bust of Marx has been replaced by a suitably patriotic statue of Timur on horseback. The gardens and fountains around this square are some of the nicest in the city.

Further west, **Mustaqillik maydoni** (Independence Square; still known as Lenin Square to most Russians) is the place to watch parades, particularly on Independence day. A brass globe emblazoned with an oversized neon map of Uzbekistan sits in the spot where the USSR's biggest Lenin statue used to be. At the time of research a new **Senate** building was being constructed on the western edge of the square. The president's office and most ministries take up the southern portion around Gagarin maydoni.

North of Mustaqillik maydoni is the sombre **Tomb of the Unknown Soldier**, constructed in 1999 to honour the 400,000 Uzbek soldiers who died in WWII. The niches along its two corridors house their names.

The New Soviet men and women who rebuilt Tashkent are remembered in stone at the **Earthquake Memorial**. Russian newlyweds still come here to have their photos taken. the memorial is three long blocks north of Mustaqillik Maydoni metro station on Sharaf Rashidov.

Other Sights

The Palace of the Friendship of Peoples (☎ 45 92 51) is testament to Soviet gigantism, containing (naturally) an enormous concert hall with 4200 seats. From behind it appears like a moon landing station from a 1950s film set. Out the front of the palace is a memorial to a blacksmith named Sham Akhmudov and his wife who adopted 15 war orphans (thousands were sent to Tashkent during WWII), all of whom are said to still live in the province.

Behind the palace is the shiny blue-domed **Oliy Majlis** (parliament). It currently functions as a giant rubber stamp in its infrequent sessions; you can watch proceedings with a ticket organised through your embassy. Nearby is a vast promenade and a post-Soviet monument to Alisher Navoi, Uzbekistan's newly chosen cultural hero, with the eerie feeling of a Lenin shrine.

The **TV Tower** (Amir Timur; 🕑 10am-9pm Tue-Sun), a 375m three-legged monster, the epitome of Soviet design, stands north of the city centre and the Hotel InterContinental. There's a viewing platform and two revolving restaurants. You'll need your passport to buy a ticket.

Near Mirabad (Gospitalnyy) Bazaar is one of Tashkent's four Orthodox churches, the **Assumption Cathedral** (Uspensky Sobor), which is bright blue with copper domes. A **German Protestant Church**, once used as a recital hall and now holding Lutheran services again, is on Sodiq Azimov. It's worth taking the metro to reach some of these sites, if only to visit some of the lavishly decorated stations. A must is the Kosmonavtlar station with its unearthly images of Ulughbek and Major Yuri Gagarin (a Soviet cosmonaut who in 1961 became the first person to fly in space) among others.

ACTIVITIES

Thanks to President Karimov's personal affinity for the game, tennis courts have sprung up across the country and Tashkent is no exception. You can rent equipment and play at the **Sports Club NBU** (☎ 68 44 59/69; Okkurgan 16; ♥ 6am-9pm). Located about 600m east of Khamid Olimjon metro, the facility includes tennis courts, an unheated swimming pool, training gym and facilities for children. Swimmers can also try the central indoor **public pool** (☎ 133 1143; Movarounnakhr tor 76; per entry US$1, per 8 entries US$5.60; ♥ 7am-8pm).

There are a couple of places to go bowling, including **Yulduz Bowling Alley** (☎ 132 20 02; Amir Timur 60; US$2.50 per game; ♥ 10am-midnight) and **Uz Bowling** (☎ 132 17 84, 132 25 71; Uzbekistan 8/1).

Runners and walkers can join the local branch of the **Hash House Harriers** as they cruise the streets of Tashkent for an hour before repairing to the nearest watering hole. Hashers meet at the Hotel Uzbekistan on Sundays (6pm summer, 3pm rest of the year). Call ☎ 139 13 02 to confirm this time as it is subject to change. A US$1 fee includes soft drinks and metro tokens.

The Korean-designed **Tashkent Lakeside Golf Club** (☎ 195 09 91/2/3; tasgolf@dostlink.net; Bektemir District 1; one round US$50-60) is at Lake Rokhat, on the southeast edge of the city.

Tashkent Land (adult/child US$3/1.60; ♥ 10am-7pm Tue-Sun), Uzbekistan's largest amusement park, is located just north of the Hotel InterContinental. The onsite Aqua Park provides welcome relief in summer.

TOURS

There aren't any organised city tours per se, but most four-star hotels can whip up a guide for US$2 to US$5 per hour. Private travel companies will also organise a city tour and solo travellers may be able to join a group. See Travel Agencies p173.

SLEEPING

The 2003 European Bank for Reconstruction and Development (EBRD) summit held in Tashkent transformed several hotels from decrepit to four-star, and there are around ten choices in this category. At the time of research there were still others undergoing renovation, including the Chorsu, Turkiston and Turon hotels. Although most rooms in the top-end category are empty, budget accommodation and the homestay market is still limited. Most budget places will send a car to pick you up if you call first.

Homestays

Unofficial homestays are a little hard to find in Tashkent. Try asking hotel staff or taxi drivers.

Gulnara Guesthouse (☎ 144 77 66, 402 816; gulnara@globalnet.uz; Azad 40; per person US$15; ♥ □) This friendly B&B, popular with backpackers, is a five-minute walk north of Chorsu Bazaar. Rooms are large and comfortable and the breakfast filling. It's a little hard to find; head west on Beruni and take a right down the small lane Azad (new name: Usman Hajaev). The guesthouse is about 200m down on the left.

Budget

Hotel Locomotif (☎ 199 75 09; Turkistan 7; s/d US$10/17; ♥) Excellent-value accommodation, right next to the main train station. The staff can be rather curt and rooms fill up very quickly in the day.

Ali Tour Guesthouse (☎ 1523921, 567162; ali_tour@ globalnet.uz; 26/2 Vakiodov; s/d US$20/30; ♥ ♥) Set in a quiet neighbourhood, one kilometre south of Kosmonavtlar metro, friendly Alisher Khabibullaev has five airy rooms with private bathroom. Amenities include free breakfast, sauna and tiny swimming pool. English and French is spoken, and travel arrangements, guides and OVIR (Office of Visas and Registration; p236) assistance offered. There is also an apartment with a kitchen and washing machine (US$60).

Tara Hotel (☎ 116 56 48; Chilonzor D20A Dom 16; per person US$2.30) Set well out of the centre, close to the long-distance bus station, this musty backpacker ghetto has grown in popularity because of its low prices. It is, however, unsigned and tricky to find: from Sobir Rakhimov metro station, cross Halqlar Dustligi Boulevard and take tram 17 for three stops. It is the middle of three apartment blocks next to the tracks; if you see the mosque on the left you've gone a bit too far. Alternatively, it's a 15-minute walk from the metro station; follow the tram tracks as they veer left and then right.

Hotel Hadra (☎ 44 28 08; Ghafur Ghulom;r US$6) Welcome to the darkest hole in all of Central Asia. Even so, the low price and central location still manage to draw the gluttons for punishment. It's in an apartment block next to the Circus.

Mid-Range

Orzu Hotel (☎ 120 80 77, 120 88 22; fax 120 88 24; www.sambuh.com; 14 Ivleva; s/d US$25/30; 🗙) Probably the best-value option in Tashkent, with smart rooms, satellite TV and a large buffet breakfast of crepes, eggs, cold cereal and juice. In summer, the powerful air-con can turn the rooms into heavenly iceboxes. The hotel is run by the well-managed travel agency Dolores Tour (see p173).

Grand Orzu Hotel (☎ 120 80 7; fax 120 88 73; www.sambuh.com; 27 Makhmud Tarobi; s/d US$35/45; 🗙 🐾) The main branch of the expanding Orzu chain, this hotel is located near Caravan Café.

Sam Buh Hotel (☎ /fax 120 88 26; Tsekhovaya 1; www.traveluz.com; s/d US$25/30; 🗙) Sam Buh now plays second fiddle to the nearby Orzu but still runs a tight ship, with spacious rooms and travel services. It is also hard to find and you might want to call for a pick-up.

Rovshan Hotel (☎ 120 77 47; Mirabad 118; s/d US$30/40; 🗙) This hotel is in the same neighbourhood and of similar ilk to Sam Buh and Orzu.

Poytaht (☎ 120 86 76, 120 86 60; fax 120 86 68; www.poytaht.uz; Movarounnakhr 4; s/d US$60/70; 🗙 🐾) At the higher end of this category, the Poytaht offers 3½-star rooms at mid-range prices. The location, round the corner from Amir Timur maydoni, is ideal. Prices might be negotiable and there is a good Korean/Japanese restaurant within the hotel.

Top End

Le Meridien (☎ 120 58 00; fax 120 44 01; sales@ lemeridien-tashkent.com; Buyuk Turon 56; r US$150; 🗙 🐾) Recently refurbished and renamed (it was the Hotel Tashkent), Le Meridien has an old-world feel with its iron-wrought chandeliers and marble staircases, but offers modern four-star amenities including a gym and swimming pool. There's a popular jazz bar on the 1st floor and a rooftop restaurant (see p179) with commanding views of the Opera House.

Bumi Tashkent International Hotel (☎ 120 66 00; fax 120 63 18; Uzbekistan Ovozi 2; s/d US$100/110; 🗙 🖳 🐾) This Indian-built concrete pile just can't seem to get its name straight. Some know it by former names: Le Meridien or Tata. Others may call it the Quality. Whichever you call it, this four-star hotel is centrally located and offers good facilities including several restaurants and a gym. Listed prices are often just a suggestion and simply asking might net a big discount.

Hotel InterContinental (☎ 120 70 00; fax 120 64 59; tashkent@interconti.com; Amir Timur 107A; s/d/ste US$235/255/400; 🗙 🖳 🐾) Just north of the city centre, this is the city's best hotel, with a full range of business and leisure facilities: indoor swimming pool, business centre, a book shop, boutiques and several excellent restaurants. All credit cards accepted.

Rental Accommodation

Just southwest of the Bumi Tashkent International Hotel on Khorezm, people gather informally outside a bus depot at a spot called **makler** (house market; ☎ 132 26 07) to swap information on flats for sale. There is an office here, but you'll need to visit in person to negotiate. Some may be willing to rent one to visitors for a few days or weeks. A sparsely furnished place goes for about US$30 per week; US$60 a week might get you TV, a telephone or other luxuries.

Sportur (p173) has two self-catering apartments for US$25 per person in convenient city locations near the Kosmonavtlar and Khamid Olimjon metro stations.

EATING

Most restaurants and cafés lie on the avenues that radiate out from Amir Timur maydoni. You'll find most are affordable and variety is growing, with European, Asian and national cuisines, some menus featuring all three.

UZBEKISTAN

All four-star hotels have adequate restaurants; the best ones are at the Bumi, Le Meridien and InterContinental. Hotels are also your best bet for breakfast, although itinerant *samsa* (samosa) and nan stalls do appear in neighbourhoods across the city. Shops and mini-markets have limited options so self-catering usually requires a trip to a vegetable bazaar.

Cafés & Chaikhanas

Chaikhanas (teahouses; called 'chaykhanas' locally) abound in parks, bazaars and transport stations, dishing up shashlyk, plov, *laghman* (noodles) and tea. Hygiene is variable; look for high turnover and service right off the fire. There's a string of open-air cafés along the pedestrian Sayilgoh kuchasi, known as the Broadway, some of which offer Western fare like burgers and pastries. The once very popular **Shahshara chaikhana** (Rakatboshi) beside Ankhor (Bozsu) canal was undergoing renovation at the time of research.

New World Pizza & Bakery (☎ 133 15 42; Bukhara 24; ☺ breakfast, lunch & dinner; ☒) Across from the Alisher Navoi Opera & Ballet Theatre, this modern snack shop has croissants, cakes, white bread and pizzas, and you can sit outside.

Mir (☎ 133 77 76; Ataturk 1; ☺ breakfast, lunch & dinner; ☒ ▣) Located south of Broadway, Mir is where well-heeled teenagers gather to preen in the city's best approximation of a Western fast-food court. Several counters offer the options of pasta, burgers, sandwiches and kebabs. *The Thousand and One Nights*–style café in the basement is somewhat more upscale.

Bravismo (☎ 133-9905; Movarounnakhr 19; dishes US$1.50; ☺ breakfast, lunch & dinner; ☒) Friendly café and dry-goods store that has a selection of cakes, pies, cold drinks and juice, as well as meals including lasagne and pepper steak.

Home Restaurants

One place to taste true Uzbek cooking is in one of the restaurants that people open in their homes in parts of the old town – just tables in a courtyard, where you're served one or two simple dishes, plus tea or beer.

One such neighbourhood in Tashkent is a few minutes from Tinchlik metro station. From the station, walk to the closest traffic signal on the main street, Beruni prospekti, and turn right into Akademik Sadikov kuchasi. Most of the home-restaurants are between five and 10 minutes walk along (or just off) this street.

THE AUTHOR'S CHOICE

Café Caravan (☎ /fax 152 74 64; www.caravan.uz; A. Kakhar 22; dishes US$4; ☺ lunch & dinner; ☒) This funky inner-courtyard restaurant is tarted up like a made-for-Hollywood Uzbek home. It offers Westernised Uzbek national dishes, including some creative house inventions such as drunken chicken (cooked in beer) and Mongolian meat. Although it makes for a unique entry to the country, get ready for service and 'entertainment' charges that may inflate the bill by 35%. Souvenir hunters with an appetite can kill two birds with one stone by eating here and shopping at the attached store, which is filled with crafts from all over the country.

Bistro (☎ 152 11 12; Movarounnakhr 33; 3-course meal with drinks US$16; ☺ lunch & dinner; ☒) Located opposite the Avtomobile – Yolloiz intituti, about 300m west of the Fine Arts Museum, and catering to the expatriate market, this Italian restaurant serves up large portions of pasta, salad and pizza to go with bottles of Uzbek or Georgian wines. Dessert includes fruit salad and excellent chocolate pancakes. It's in a candle-lit, courtyard setting, with live music, although the chairs are a bit uncomfortable.

Han Kuk Kwan (☎ 152 33 22; Yusuf Khos Khodjib; meals US$8; ☺ lunch & dinner; ☒) Korean cuisine plays a relatively prominent role on the Tashkent dining scene, and you shouldn't leave town without trying some. Han Kuk Kwan is one of the nicer places, serving up platters full of small salads and main dishes like *bi-bim-bab*, made with rice, egg and chopped meat. It offers sushi too.

Darkhan (Pushkin, laghman US$0.40; ☺ breakfast, lunch & dinner) Cheap and fast outdoor food court with big wooden tables shaded by trees. There are several stalls here serving *laghman* (noodles), *samsa* (samosas), kebabs, salads and deserts. Clean bathrooms are a bonus. Look for the tall wood carvings of Timur, opposite the Inconnel Business Center, about 300m east of Khamid Olimjon metro.

There are no signs or shop fronts. Boys practically drag you off the street for the midday and evening (after 7pm) meals. Anything more than about US$2 per dish (in sum) is probably too much.

Restaurants

Jumanji (☎ 55 86 71; cnr K. Djalilov & Yusuf Khos Khodjib; dishes US$6; ☯ lunch & dinner) A restaurant with an identity crisis, Jumanji is done up with an African theme but the menu is mostly Chinese dishes, including sweet and sour chicken and spring rolls. Some meat dishes come sizzling on hot plates. Other cuisines squeezed into the menu include Mexican and Uighur. Happy hour in the back bar Friday 8.30pm to 10.30pm reels in Tashkent's expatriate crowd.

Omar Khayyam (☎ 132 21 51; Movarounnakhr 33; meal with wine US$11; ☯ lunch & dinner) Next to the Bistro (see the boxed text opposite), and under the same management, is this Central Asia–Middle East fusion restaurant, which offers chicken tikka and kebabs but is heaviest on the Lebanese cuisine. Some of the seating is at heavy wooden tables, or you can sprawl out in floor-cushioned alcoves. It has live music, but you soon realise it's the same guys from the Bistro who have done a quick costume change and are dashing back and forth.

Taj Restaurant (☎ 133 53 92; Chekhov 5; meals US$5; ☯ lunch & dinner) This long-time Tashkent favourite does a large variety of great Indian food, including a lot of veg options, and the service is good too. The rooftop dining area completes the Indian experience.

Ragu (☎ 120 74 24; cnr Amir Timur & Niyazbek Yuli; meals US$5-8; ☯ lunch & dinner) This is Tashkent's second-best Indian restaurant, although the décor here is more colourful than at the Taj. There is a bar with a pool table on the first floor of this building and a good Italian restaurant called **Little Italy** (pizzas US$6-9) in the basement. Both restaurants offer free delivery from the same phone number.

Rachel (☎ 136 28 11, 136 27 74; H Olimjon 5; dishes US$3-6; ☯ lunch & dinner) Tashkent's only 'Jewish' restaurant is Western-orientated with an English menu. Menu items are descended mostly from Russian and East European Jews, with fish cakes, slices of herring, turkey rolls and fillet chicken. It's got a unique interior design with mock windows that face out to a mock ghetto. A

little tricky to find, it's south of Pushkin and faces the divided boulevard Jakob Kolos.

Le Meridien (☎ 120 58 00; Buyuk Turon 56; ☯ lunch & dinner) This centrally located hotel has two restaurants, including the rooftop restaurant Sharque Yulduzi. Its Persian/Turkic menu includes average hummus and good chicken and fish shashlyk (US$5). If you order the seasonal green salad you might want to ask for a cutting board and chopping knife as it's more or less a platter of vegetables straight out of the fridge.

Self-Catering

For vegetables and readymade Korean salads, there are farmers markets all over town; see p181 for those near the centre. In season, an informal melon bazaar springs up near the Navoi Literary Museum.

DRINKING

The only area that comes close to being a bar strip is Sayilgoh (Broadway), the local version of Moscow's Arbat, with cheap suds flowing inside miniature makeshift beer gardens. Get an early start; everything shuts down at midnight by Presidential decree. On Friday night, many expats turn up at the Jumanji restaurant (see above left) for happy hour drinks.

Mama's Fun Pub (☎ 103 06 64, 133 56 54; Uzbekistan Ovozi 2; ☯ 8pm-4am; cover US$4) This theme pub is wedged into the side of the Bumi Hotel (p177), with live jazz 7pm to 9pm and live rock 9pm until close. It also serves good Southeast Asian food. Check your bill closely.

FM Art Bar (☎ 132 06 33; Matbuochilar 17; cover US$3) One of Tashkent's few dens of debauchery, the FM Art Bar tests local laws by putting on quasi-strip acts and pole-dance routines. Belly dancers and sword swallowers are thrown in for good measure. It's in the Zeravshan Complex, just off Broadway next to the Ardus supermarket.

Emir (☎ 132 01 05; Bukhara 24; ☯ noon-midnight; beer US$2-3) Another pole-dancing bar, this one is less seedy than FM Art Bar, with a clean, large seating area. It's across from the Alisher Navoi Opera & Ballet Theatre.

Opera Jazz Bar (☎ 120 58 00; Le Meridien, Buyuk Turon 56; cover US$5) Live jazz venue popular with the expat crowd as well as maudlin businesspeople losing their shirts in the Uzbek economy.

Zeravshan Complex (Broadway) This complex has numerous bars and nightclubs and is filled with all sorts of interesting denizens.

ENTERTAINMENT

Opera, theatre and ballet options are readily available throughout the year in Tashkent, most catering for an older crowd with the exception of the Ilkhom Theatre. Night-clubs, cinemas and live music venues are other options, but getting information on what's on can be like pulling camel's teeth. In lieu of anything written in English, ask an Uzbek friend or your hotel for tips on up-coming events. The British Council (p169), which sponsors the occasional theatre or dance performance, is another place to ask.

Cinemas

Cinematrix (☎ 133 11 94; Uzbekistan Ovozi 4; US$1.50; English films ☽ 4.30pm Sat & Sun) This small the-atre behind the Bumi hotel shows new films in English on weekends.

Panorama (☎ 41 04 09; Navoi 15; US$1) Tashkent's biggest movie theatre, although most films are dubbed into Russian.

Nightclubs

La Casa (Che Guevara Bar; ☎ 132 21 51; Movarounnakhr 33; ☒) Surreal images of the leftist revolu-tionary Che Guervara, Cuban flags and other Cold War propaganda are plastered across the red-and-black walls of this mini downtown disco. It's a very popular place for Uzbeks, expats and young mobsters, and is owned by the same folks who run the neigh-bouring restaurants Omar Khayyam and the Bistro. Earlier in the day it's a dimly lit Tex-Mex restaurant serving burritos, enchiladas and the like, for about US$5 per meal.

Lucky Strike (☎ 57 16 19; Pushkin 63) This is a 'closed nightclub' (read: unregistered), which allows it to stay open later than other discos. The absence of a sign outside adds to the 'speakeasy' feel. It's in the basement of a massive apartment building northeast of the Khamid Olimjon metro; the entrance is at the end of the building (look for the 'Efes Pilsener' sign above the door).

Sky Club (☎ 120 66 00; Uzbekistan Ovozi 2; cover US$4 ☒) Located on the 14th floor of the Bumi hotel, this popular dance club has a light-up floor, and beer for US$3 a bottle. You can also have pizzas delivered from the restaurant downstairs.

Sport

Tashkent sporting events include the occa-sional pro tennis match at **Yunosabad Tennis Club** (☎ 134 69 81), located north of the city, near Tashkent Land. Soccer matches are held at the **Pakhtakor (Cotton Picker) Stadium**, in the centre of town, just off Uzbekistan. Tickets (local matches US$0.50 to US$1.50, international matches US$8) can be bought directly from the stadium box office.

Theatres & Concert Halls

Tashkent has a full cultural life, some of it, such as drama, of interest mainly to Uzbek and Russian speakers. But one of Asia's best cultural bargains is surely the **Alisher Navoi Opera & Ballet Theatre** (☎ 133 33 44; Ataturk 28; ☽ 6pm Mon-Fri, noon & 5pm Sat & Sun; US$0.30-1.50) opposite the Le Meridien hotel, where you can enjoy quality classical Western opera al-most any night (except during the months June to August). The box office, in one of the columns out front, is open daily 10am to 3pm and 4pm to 6pm. Shows change daily – in just a week you can see *Swan Lake*, *Carmen*, *Rigoletto* and the Uzbek opera *Timur the Great*. Even if you don't like opera, the theatre interior makes a visit worthwhile, and the box office can arrange tours.

Other theatres of interest:

Ilkhom Theatre (☎ 41 22 52; Pakhtakor 5; ☽ 6.30pm) Tashkent's most progressive theatre; gay themes and racial subjects are the norm, though some locals are put off by its vulgarity. You'll see such oddities as Shakespeare plays entwined with Beatles music. It is, however, often incomprehensive to non-Russian speakers. Occasional jazz concerts.

Khamza Uzbek State Academic Drama Theater (☎ 144 17 51; Navoi 34; ☽ 6pm Tue-Sun) Uzbek and classical Western drama in Uzbek language.

Muqimi Musical Theatre (☎ 45 36 55, 45 16 33; Almazar 187; ☽ 6pm Mon, Tue, Wed, Fri, 5pm Sat & Sun) Near the Halqlar Dustligi metro. Uzbek operettas such as *Brothers*, *Matchmakers*, and *Bridegroom's Contest*. This venue is your best bet for traditional Uzbek folk singing and dancing.

Palace of the Friendship of Peoples (☎ 45 92 51; Halqlar Dustligi maydoni) Big events are staged here, including pop concerts.

Republic Puppet Theatre (☎ 56 73 95; Kosmonavtlar 1; ☽ 11am & 1pm) Puppet shows and a puppet museum; near the Kosmonavtlar metro.

Gorky Drama Theatre (☎ 133 81 65; Ataturk 24; ☽ 6.30pm Mon-Fri, 5pm Sat & Sun) Classical Western drama theatre located near Mustaqillik Maydoni Metro.

Tashkent State Conservatory (☎ 41 29 91; Abai 1) Chamber concerts, Uzbek and Western vocal and instrumental recitals in an impressive new edifice.

Tashkent State Musical Comedy Theatre (☎ 77 85 92; Choponota 12; ☻ 6pm Tue & Thu-Sun) operettas (eg Strauss and Mozart). Use Mirzo Ulughbek metro.

SHOPPING
Handicrafts & Art
The Abdul Khasim Medressa, close to the Oliy Majlis near Halqlar Dustligi metro station, is now the **Meros Centre for Traditional Arts** (☻ 9am-6pm) and has some attractive souvenirs by local artisans who work on the premises.

The Museum of Applied Arts (p174), south of Kosmonavtlar metro station, has a good but expensive shop with some genuinely old items and overpriced carpets.

The shop at the Fine Arts Museum (p174) also has a big selection of old items, and sells excellent Turkmen rugs.

Among the many hotel gift shops, Bumi's shop (p177) excels with its selection of carpets.

Café Caravan (see the boxed text on p178) is a gallery, studio and café all rolled into one and is the trendiest handicrafts shop in town. The prices are quite competitive to shops across the country, so it makes a reasonable place to stock up on items you might have missed while travelling.

For kitsch street-level art and amusingly sarcastic Soviet-era cartoons, try the little open-air galleries along the Broadway (Sayilgoh).

Open-Air Markets
In warm weather, a big goods bazaar sprawls by the **Ippodrom** (Halqlar Dustligi prospekti; ☻ Tue-Sun);. The biggest day by far is on Sunday. The Ippodrom is 2km southwest from Sobir Rakhimov metro station, and on bus No 108 or tram No 17.

Tezykovka (Tolarik 1; ☻ Sun) is the local name for this vast 'flea market'. Also known as Yangiobod Market, this sombre sea of junk – 'anything from nails to nukes' as one resident put it – is located in the Khamza district, and reached by bus No 30 from the Mustaqillik metro.

Keep a close watch on your purse or wallet; gangs of pickpockets are said to work these bazaars.

FARMERS MARKETS
Tashkent has at least 16 open-air farmers markets or bazaars (Uzbek: *dekhqon bozori*, Russian: *rynok*). According to locals, the best for produce in season are:

Chorsu Bazaar The central bazaar for the Old Town, at Chorsu metro station.

Farkhan Bazaar (Russian: *Farkhadsky*) Six stops west from Khamza metro station on tram No 9.

Mirabad Bazaar (Russian: *Gospitalnyy*) Four blocks west of Tashkent Metro station on tram No 8, 9 or 24.

Oloy Bazaar (Russian: *Alaysky*) Four blocks north of the Hotel Uzbekistan on Amir Timur; its proximity to the tourist zone encourages moneychangers, pickpockets and other lowlife. Recommended nan and *samsa* bakers are to the right as you enter the market.

Beshagach Bazaar (Uzbeks write it Besh-Yoghoch, literally 'Five Karagach Trees') This modest bazaar is worth a look. It is located in an isolated section of the Old Town near the Palace of the Friendship of Peoples (Halqlar Dustligi metro station).

Supermarkets
In the city centre, Western toiletries are available at the **Ardus supermarket** (Ataturk) near the Broadway and the **Mir supermarket** (Ataturk 1), one block south. Another Ardus is at Amir Timur 3.

Anglesey supermarket (Pushkin), near Khamid Olimjon metro, is smaller; there is another branch on Yunus Rajaby (aka Rakatboshi), south of Kosmonavtlar metro. **Ozbegim supermarket** (Afrosiab) is near Oybek metro. **Dunyo supermarket** (cnr Pushkin & Shakhrisabz) has a good photo-developing centre as well as film supplies.

All have imported Western foods, though the selection tends to vary from week to week.

Silk
They don't have the atmosphere of the bazaars, but for the best prices and a surprisingly good selection of silk by the metre, try the big department stores (*univermag*) – TsUM is across from Le Meridien hotel, and the GUM is south across the road from the Hotel Chorsu.

GETTING THERE & AWAY
Air
Tashkent's recently renovated airport is Central Asia's main hub. The domestic terminal is about 150m from the international terminal.

UZBEKISTAN

From Tashkent, Uzbekistan Airways flies twice daily to Bukhara (1½ hours, US$26), three times a day to Urgench (2¼ hours, US$40), one or two times daily to both Fergana (one hour, US$23) and Andijan (one hour, US$24), and six times a week to both Namangan (one hour, US$24) and Samarkand (one hour, US$22). There are no flights to Kokand. Other destinations with three or more flights a day include Qarshi (US$25) and Termiz (US$26) in the south, and Nukus (US$37).

For international airlines flying into Tashkent, see p237.

AIRLINE OFFICES

Aeroflot (☎ 152 30 18; Nukus 79a) Daily flights to Moscow (US$256).

Asiana Airlines (☎ 120 73 85; Daewoo Unitel Bldg, Bukhara 1) Round-trip only tickets to Seoul for US$935.

British Airways (☎ 133 7111; Shakhrisabz, Area C-2, h-5) Flights on Monday, Thursday and Saturday. Round-trip ticket Tashkent–London costs US$875.

Iran Air (☎ 133 81 63, 133 50 82; Sodiq Azimov 1) Tehran (US$335) once a week.

KLM (☎ 133 49 99; Movarounnakhr 19) Berlin (US$520) and Madrid (US$560) three times a week.

Lufthansa (☎ 137 60 65; Hotel InterContinental, Amir Timur 107a) New York (US$760) four times a week.

Pakistan International Airways (PIA; ☎ 45 38 68; Halqlar Dustligi 4) Islamabad (US$870) twice a week.

Transaero (☎ 139 99 35; Halqlar Dustligi 4) Moscow (US$256) three times a week and Frankfurt (US$530) weekly.

Turkish Airlines (☎ 136 79 89; Navoi 11a) İstanbul (US$450) four times a week.

Ukranian Airlines (☎ 152 2419; Shevchenko 52) Kiev (US$235) once a week.

BUYING TICKETS

Outbound tickets are best bought a few days in advance, at the **Uzbekistan Airways booking office** (☎ 066, 56 38 37, 133 42 07; Shota Rustaveli 9; ⏰ 9am-5pm). Take tram No 28 west from the TsUM department store or tram Nos 7, 8 or 10 south on Sharaf Rashidov by the Le Meridien. The office is opposite the Hotel Mir.

Some credit cards are accepted, though it is possible, and preferable, to pay for flights in sum, as this involves less bureaucracy. Early in 2004 'foreigner prices' were dropped and all tickets (whether bought by a local or tourist) are priced the same. There is a money exchange office in the same building. An information desk in the centre of the booking office will direct you towards an English-speaking agent. Most four-star hotels can book flights for a US$5 service charge. You can buy last-minute tickets on domestic flights from a little booth inside the domestic terminal.

Bus

The Tashkent **long-distance bus station** (☎ 79 39 29; Halqlar Dustligi) is about 10km southwest of the city and about 200m northwest from Sobir Rakhimov metro station, across the divided highway (or use the pedestrian underpass from the metro station). Don't confuse it with the regional bus stand beside the Metro station.

If the bus you want to catch is about to leave, try buying the ticket from the driver. Major destinations and departure frequencies include Samarkand (hourly until 5pm, five hours, US$2), Bukhara (five daily, nine hours, US$3.50), Termiz (5pm and 8pm, 10 hours, US$5) and Nukus/Hojeli (9.30am, 11.30am and 7.30pm, 18 hours, US$7). There were no buses to the Fergana Valley, Qarshi, Kazakhstan or Kyrgyzstan at the time of research. For buses to Chimgan use the bus station at the Mashinasozlar metro.

The busy private bus yard is in the parking lot west of the Ippodrome Market. Buses for Samarkand (US$2), Shakhrisabz (US$2.50), Qarshi (US$3.50), Termiz (US$5), Khiva (US$5) and Nukus (US$7) depart when full. There aren't any schedules so the best thing you can do is arrive early and see what is going where.

Shared Taxi

Shared taxis or marshrutnoes leave from several places around the city, but the main departure point is outside the Sobir Rakhimov metro station. There are different types of vehicles available (see Shared Taxi p471 for details). Sample fares per person: Fergana Valley (Nexia US$6 to US$9) Samarkand (Nexia US$7, marshrutnoe US$3.50), Bukhara (marshrutnoe US$4) and Qarshi (marshrutnoe US$4). You can charter your own Nexia to Samarkand for US$30 or Termiz for US$80. For the Fergana Valley, shared taxis depart from here and the main train station.

Train

Tashkent main train station, right by the Tashkent metro station, is reached by tram

Nos 7 or 28 from near the Le Meridien hotel, or tram No 24 from Tashkent metro station. Prices quoted in this section are for 2nd class or sleeping carriages (*kupeynyy*).

Trains leave daily for Samarkand (five hours, US$3.50), Bukhara (12 hours, US$8), Urgench (21 hours, US$19) and Nukus (24 hours), and two times a week to Andijan via Kokand (Tajikistan; 12 hours) and Margilan (10 hours) in the Fergana Valley. At the time of research Tajik visas were not needed for trains to Andijan, but double-check this before booking.

BUYING TICKETS

There are ticket booths inside the train station, and on the backside of the Hotel Locomotif outside the station. But foreigners are sometimes directed to the **railway booking office** (☎ 199 76 27, 136 40 49, 005; Movarounnakhr 51; ✆ 8am-5pm Mon-Sat & noon-5pm Sun), a five-minute walk northeast from the station, where you'll find helpful English-speaking ticket agents. To find the office, turn right from the station and follow the road around to the left and across the canal. Look for the sign 'ТЕМУР ЙЎЛ КАССАЛАРИ'.

GETTING AROUND
To/From the Airport

Buses are the cheapest way to/from the airport. Coming from the airport, they're also an alternative to the greedy, sometimes crooked, taxi drivers. Unfortunately they stop running at 10.30pm despite the fact that many flights arrive in the middle of the night.

Bus No 67 travels up Shota Rustaveli to the centre of town, and continues up Amir Timur to the Hotel InterContinental, a 35-minute journey. Marshrutnoe No 62 follows the same route. Bus No 77 goes to/from Bobur to Halqlar Dustligi maydoni. Bus No 32 and Express bus No 11-3 both run to/from the Hotel Chorsu.

Bus No 25 and the infrequent express bus No 67-3 take 25 minutes to/from the clock tower on Movarounnakhr near the Hotel Uzbekistan. The No 14 trolleybus takes 30 to 40 minutes to/from Alisher Navoi Metro station, near the Hotel Shodlik Palace.

The 7km, 20-minute taxi ride to/from the Hotel Uzbekistan should cost US$4, but an unofficial airport cartel won't accept less than about US$10 from foreigners.

Car

You can hire a car and driver from the **service bureau** (☎ 120 77 77) at the Hotel Uzbekistan for US$8 per hour and up. A cheaper alternative is to hire a taxi for about half that.

Local Transport

Buses, trolleybuses and trams cost 120 sum (150 sum for express buses), paid to the conductor or driver, who can sometimes give small change. Vehicles are marked in Latinised Uzbek and given a number.

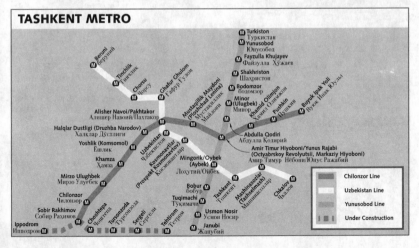

TASHKENT METRO

Before setting out, ask your hotel for the main bus and tram numbers heading to the centre or other key parts of town.

Metro

Tashkent's **metro** (per ride 120 sum; ⏲ 5am–midnight), the only one in Central Asia, is the easiest way to get around. During the day you'll never wait more than five minutes for a train, and the stations are clean and safe, if in need of new light bulbs. The metro was designed as a nuclear shelter and taking photos inside is strictly forbidden – a pity given their oftentimes striking design.

Despite the use of Uzbek for signs and announcements, the system is easy to use, and well enough signposted that you hardly need a map. The most important signs are КИРИШ (entrance) ЧИКИШ (exit) and ЎТИШ (interchange).

If you listen as the train doors are about to close, you'll hear the name of the next station at the end of the announcement: *Ekhtiyot buling, eshiklar yopiladi; keyingi bekat...* (Be careful, the doors are closing; the next station is...).

Taxi

You can wave down practically any car and negotiate a price to where you want to go. At the time of research prices started at US$0.10 (100 sum) per kilometre and up, depending on your haggling skills (they might be a bit more at night). There are licensed taxis also, with 'broken' meters. Except for a few rats at the airport, most are honest. You should be able to cross the whole city for under US$3 in sum.

You can book a taxi by dialling ☎ 062, 34 51 60, 144 85 65 or 137 48 49.

AROUND TASHKENT

What opportunities there are for outdoor recreation near Tashkent are in the Chatkal mountains, an outrider of the Tian Shan range, east of the city. Several rivers in this region offer the chance for rafting and kayaking. The Angren and Syr-Darya are for beginners. More experienced boaters will appreciate the Ugam and the Chatkal rivers, whereas the most challenging is said to be the upper Pskem. The white water season is September to October.

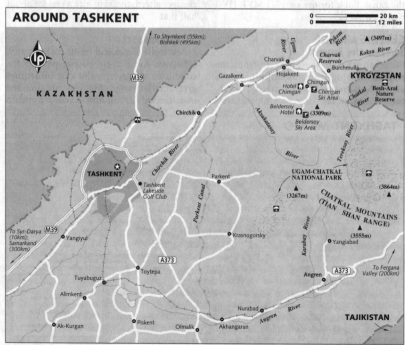

Chirchik Valley

A huge, partly moribund chemical factory dominates the industrial city of **Chirchik**, northeast of Tashkent. The next large town up the valley, **Gazalkent**, used to be predominantly German. All but a handful of families have emigrated, and the mostly Uzbek inhabitants of today live in distinctly German houses with pitched roofs. Near the foot of the **Charvak reservoir** is a small park protecting 40,000-year-old petroglyphs of humans and antlered animals. The park lies on the right-hand side of the road as you face the dam wall. It's nearly opposite the train station.

You can get here by train (8.12am, 2.25pm, 5.20pm, one hour and 40 minutes, US$2), by taxi (one hour, around US$4) or bus, which leaves from Mashinasozlar metro, although bus times and services are unreliable.

Chimgan

This recreation zone on the south shore of the Charvak reservoir, 80km up the Chirchik river valley (2½ hours by bus, 1½ hours by car), is popular for winter sports – although it runs a poor second to those near Bishkek and Almaty. But it's open year-round, and there is some good walking here.

In the upper Chatkal watershed is a nature reserve, the **Ugam-Chatkal National Park**. Along the Tereksay (Tereklisay) River there are ancient petroglyphs. Some trails lead to Kyrgyzstan and the **Besh-Aral Nature Reserve**. Given the tenuous border situation you'll need a visa if you plan to cross it and perhaps a border permit. Consult with a travel agency such as Tashkent's Asia Travel, p173.

The best place to stay in the Chimgan area is **Beldersoy Hotel** (in Tashkent ☎ 132 1790, 132 1238; d/ste US$80/104; ✿ ✿). Located about five kilometres south of Chimgan, this four-star lodge has smart rooms, all with balconies facing the valley. There are four- or six-bed cottages here too, ranging from US$48 to US$280. Next to the lodge is a 3km-long ski run (565 vertical metres), serviced by two chairlifts. The hotel can rent equipment.

Uzbektourism's decrepit **Hotel Chimgan** (☎ 274222-444; s/d/ste US$5/8/16.50), the budget alternative, lies across the road from the main ski area.

There is no direct public transport to Chimgan. You can take a bus (departing half hourly 9am to 3pm) from the station at Mashinasozlar metro and change at Charvak village, from where there are taxis (US$7).

Angren River Valley

The Angren (Akhangaran) drops out of the Tian Shan, southeast of Tashkent. The canyon of the upper Angren is the most dramatic and least accessible part of Tashkent's natural surroundings.

The coal town of **Angren** is about 95km (3½ hours by bus) up the valley from Tashkent. Nearby is a 12th-century mausoleum. About 13km north up a side canyon is the rickety old Yangiabad *turbaza* (holiday camp) that was recently commandeered by the Uzbek army. There are fine walks from here to the Ugam-Chatkal National Park, but given the military presence it's best to ask a Tashkent tour operator about the changing situation.

FERGANA VALLEY
ФАРҒОНА ВОДИЙИ

The first thought many visitors have on arrival in the Fergana Valley is, 'where's the valley?' From this broad (22,000 sq km) flat bowl, the surrounding mountain ranges (the Tian Shan to the north and the Pamir Alay to the south) seem to stand back at enormous distances.

Drained by the upper Syr-Darya, funnelling gently westward to an outlet just a few kilometres wide, the Fergana Valley is one big oasis, with some of the finest soil and climate in Central Asia. Already by the 2nd century BC the Greeks and Persians found a prosperous kingdom based on farming, with some 70 towns and villages. A major branch of the Silk Road also wound through the valley.

The Russians were quick to realise the valley's fecundity, and Soviet rulers enslaved it to an obsessive raw-cotton monoculture that still exists today and is only slowly being dismantled to allow Uzbekistan an economic equilibrium of its own. The valley also produces an abundance of seasonal fruit and is the centre of Central Asian silk production (see the boxed text on p193).

With a population of about eight million, the valley is the most densely settled area in

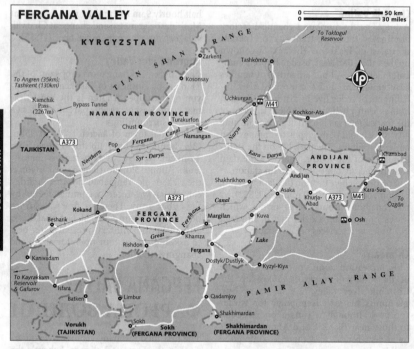

FERGANA VALLEY

0 — 50 km
0 — 30 miles

KYRGYZSTAN

TIAN SHAN RANGE

To Toktogul
Reservoir

Zarkent
Tashkömür
Kosonsay
Üchkurgan
M41
Kochkor-Ata

To Angren (35km);
Tashkent (130km)

Kamchik
Pass
(2267m)
Bypass Tunnel

NAMANGAN PROVINCE
Chust
Turakurfon
Jalal-Abad

Fergana
Canal
Namangan
Naryn River

A373
Pop
Northern
Syr - Darya
Kara – Darya
ANDIJAN
PROVINCE
Khanabad

TAJIKISTAN

Shakhrikhon
Andijan
Kara-Suu

A373
Canal
Asaka
Khurja-
Abad
A373
M41
To
Özgön

Kokand
FERGANA
PROVINCE
Fergana
Margilan
Kuva
Osh

Besharik
Great
Khamza
Lake

Rishdon
Fergana

Kanivadam
Dostyk/Dustlyk
Kyzyl-Kiya

To Kayrakkum
Reservoir
& Gafurov
Isfara

Batken
Limbur
Qadamjoy
PAMIR ALAY RANGE

Shakhimardan

Vorukh
(TAJIKISTAN)
Sokh
Sokh
(FERGANA PROVINCE)
Shakhimardan
(FERGANA PROVINCE)

UZBEKISTAN

Central Asia, and thoroughly Uzbek – 90% overall and higher in the smaller towns. Despite this, the Fergana Valley has few architectural monuments and no tradition of religious or secular scholarship; on the whole its towns are architecturally uninspiring. But the province has always wielded a large share of Uzbekistan's political, economic and religious influence. Recently its economic clout was boosted by the South Korean company Daewoo, which based a new car-manufacturing plant at Asaka, just outside Andijan.

Politically, Fergana is still a boiling pot. During the 1990s the valley was a standout in the international media after giving birth to Islamic extremism in Central Asia. Bearing the brunt of Karimov's crackdown on Islam; insurgents, dissidents and clerics alike were forced elsewhere, many going to Turkey, Tajikistan or Russia. Whereas the government maintains the upper hand, foreign observers still maintain that the Fergana Valley is a potential flash point for violence...

For the visitor, the valley's main assets are hospitable people, exceptional crafts, several kaleidoscopic bazaars and the proximity of the mountains.

Although this is a kind of Uzbek heartland in terms of language, population and tradition (the people of Andijan province are said to speak the purest form of Uzbek), it's not all part of Uzbekistan. The mutual boundaries of Uzbekistan, Tajikistan and Kyrgyzstan are crazily knotted together here – a giant Stalinist demographic fiddle to dilute the independent tendencies for which the valley has long been known. There are tiny pockets of territory scattered throughout the region, so small they don't make it onto maps. The valley's western 'gate' is plugged by a thumb of Tajikistan, and the surrounding mountains belong mostly to Kyrgyzstan. The Russian-era town of Fergana makes a convenient base for trips around the valley.

Dangers & Annoyances

Although the valley is as hospitable as anywhere in Uzbekistan, perhaps more so, standards of dress are a source of misunderstanding. Except perhaps in the centre of Fergana town, too much tourist flesh will be considered an insult and a provocation. Dress modestly – no shorts or tight-fitting clothes for either sex and preferably no short sleeves. Women travellers have reported being harassed when walking alone in cities such as Andijan, especially at night.

Security is tight in the valley compared to other parts of the country and police road blocks are common. The police are friendly enough but it does cause delays; just keep your passport at the ready.

Transport
GETTING THERE & AWAY
Tashkent is linked to Andijan by three daily flights and to Fergana/Margilan by one daily flight. At the time of research the airport at Kokand was inactive.

Daily trains connect Tashkent with Khojand (in Tajikistan), Kokand, Margilan and Andijan (there is no station at Fergana). See the individual town entries for more detail. Note that at the time of research Tajik visas were not needed for trains to Andijan, but confirm this before booking as there could be trouble at the border. Even with a visa, the trains and border crossings are slow and tedious.

Shared taxi is the recommended form of transport. Cars now travel the serpentine route from Tashkent via Angren using a new bypass tunnel, avoiding the 2267m Kamchik Pass. From Tashkent it's about three hours to Kokand or 4½ hours to Andijan.

GETTING AROUND
Daewoo pumps out the ubiquitous Nexia, Tico, Matiz and Damas vehicles from its Fergana Valley factory, ensuring an overabundance of shared taxis. This has led to a virtual disappearance of buses from the valley, although a few still chug along. Taxi pick-up points are usually found in all town centres and bus stations.

KOKAND КОКАНД
☎ (3) 7355 / pop 178,000
As the valley's first significant town on the road from Tashkent, Kokand is a gateway to the region and stopping point for many travellers. With an architecturally interesting palace and several medressas it makes for a worthwhile half-day visit before heading in or out of the region.

This was the capital of the Kokand khanate in the 18th and 19th centuries and the valley's true 'hotbed' in those days – second only to Bukhara as a religious centre in Central Asia, with at least 35 medressas and hundreds of mosques. But if you walk the streets today, you'll find only a polite, subdued Uzbek town, its old centre hedged by colonial avenues, bearing little resemblance to Bukhara.

Nationalists fed up with empty revolutionary promises met here in January 1918 and declared a rival administration, the 'Muslim Provincial Government of Autonomous Turkestan' led by Mustafa Chokayev. Jenghiz Khan would have admired the response by the Tashkent Soviet, who immediately had the town sacked, most of its holy buildings desecrated or destroyed and 14,000 Kokandis slaughtered. What little physical evidence of Kokand's former stature remained was either left to decay, or mummified as 'architectural monuments'. Several of these wonders are coming back to life as working mosques and medressas whereas others have been converted to museums.

Orientation
The khan's palace stands in the central Muqimi Park (called 'Russian Park' by locals). The remnants of pre-Russian Kokand are roughly between the park, the train station 2km to the southwest and the main bazaar (and adjacent main bus station) to the southeast. Off Khamza and Akbar Islamov kuchasi are old-town lanes good for a wander, plus most of the town's surviving religious buildings. The centre of 'tourist' Kokand is Abdulla Nabiev maydoni, about 700m west of the park.

Information
National Bank of Uzbekistan (☎ 254 13; Khamza 34; ☼ 8.30am-noon & 1-4pm Mon-Fri) Exchanges cash but not travellers cheques.
OVIR (☎ 368 78; cnr Turkiston & Istiqlol; ☼ 2-4pm Tue & 9am-noon Sat)
Post office (Potelyakhov House, cnr Istiqlol & Istanbul; ☼ 7am-7pm Mon-Fri, 7am-5.30pm Sat & Sun)
Simus (☎ 219 11; Istanbul 18; per hr US$0.75; ☼ 8am-5pm Mon-Sat) Internet café located five minutes' walk south of Abdulla Nabiev maydoni, past the university.
Uzbektourism (☎ 238 92; fax 453 81; Kamal-Kazi Medressa, Khamza 83; ☼ 9am-6pm Mon-Sat) Offers

UZBEKISTAN

KOKAND

INFORMATION	
Halyk Bank.................................**1** A1	
National Bank of Uzbekistan..........**2** C1	
OVIR...**3** C1	
Pakhta Bank...............................**4** A1	
Police Office..............................**5** C1	
Post Office............................(see 14)	
Simus...**6** A2	
Uzbektourism........................(see 9)	

SIGHTS & ACTIVITIES	(pp188-9)
Dakhma-i-Shokhon......................**7** D1	
Juma Mosque.............................**8** C2	

| Kamal-Kazi Medressa....................**9** C2 |
| Khamza Museum.........................**10** D1 |
| Khan's Palace............................**11** B1 |
| Modari Khan Mausoleum............**12** D1 |
| Museum of Local Studies.........(see 11) |
| Narbutabey Medressa & Mosque...**13** D1 |
| Potelyakhove House....................**14** A1 |
| Sahib Mian Hazrat Medressa........**15** C2 |
| Vadyayev House |
| (Mayor's Office)......................**16** A1 |

SLEEPING	⌂ (p189)
Hotel Kokand............................**17** A1	

EATING	🍴 (p189)
Café Dilshod.............................**18** B1	
Chaykhana................................**19** B1	
Nilufar.....................................**20** A1	

TRANSPORT	(pp189-9)
Bus Station...............................**21** D2	
Taxi Stand................................**22** D2	
Uzbekistan Airways....................**23** A1	

OTHER	
Hojibek Mosque & Medressa.........**24** C2	
Zimbardor Mosque.....................**25** C2	

English-speaking guided tours of Kokand and Fergana, including visits to traditional knife makers and ceramics workshops.

Sights

KHAN'S PALACE

The palace of the last khan, Khudoyar, now shares space in a former Soviet pleasure park with a mothballed Yak-40 plane.

The **Khan's Palace** (☎ 360 46, 268 39; http://museum.dinosoft.uz/; Istiqlol 2; admission US$1, guided tour US$3.50; ⏰ 9am-5pm), with seven courtyards and 113 rooms, was completed in 1873 – just three years before the tsar's troops arrived, blew up its fortifications and abolished the khan's job. He fled, not from the Russians but from his own subjects (who were probably encouraged to ransack the palace); indeed he fled *to* the Russians at Orenburg and a comfortable exile (he was later killed by bandits as he returned through Afghanistan from a pilgrimage to Mecca).

The palace's surviving two courtyards and 19 rooms house a staid **Museum of Local Studies**, with jewellery and musical instruments in the throne room, Uzbek furniture in the waiting room and Oriental porcelain in the khan's well-used bedroom. The now-demolished harem used to stand at the rear of the palace, where Khudoyar's 43 concubines would wait to be chosen as wife for the night – Islam allows only four wives so the khan kept a mullah at hand for a quick marriage ceremony (the marriage set up to last just one night).

NARBUTABEY MEDRESSA

The Bolsheviks closed the 1799 Narbutabey Medressa but it's now open again and currently has about 20 students. To win wartime support from Muslim subjects, Stalin had the adjacent **mosque** reopened, the only one for all of Kokand at the time. Before stepping inside you are likely to be accosted by the curator Mohammed, who provides enthusiastic tours with the expectation of a tip. Both men and women are welcome.

The first right turn beyond the medressa takes you into a **graveyard** with several prominent mausoleums associated with another khan, Umar. To the right inside the graveyard is the bright sky-blue cupola

UZBEKISTAN

of the unrestored **Modari Khan Mausoleum**, built in 1825 for the khan's mother. To the left is the 1830s **Dakhma-i-Shokhon** (Grave of Kings), the tomb of the khan Umar and other family members, with an elegant wooden portal carved with Quranic verses and/or Umar's poetry.

Nasrullah Khan, the emir of Bukhara, is said to have kidnapped Umar's wife, an independent-minded poetess named Nodira, and demanded that she marry him. When she refused, Nasrullah had her beheaded, along with her children and her brothers-in-law. Originally buried behind Modari Khan, she was adopted by the Soviets as a model Uzbek woman and moved to a prominent place beneath a white **stone tablet**, beyond Dakhma-i-Shokhon.

RUSSIAN BUILDINGS
Around Abdulla Nabiev maydoni (named for a prominent Kokand Bolshevik) is a knot of sturdy brick buildings, built by the Russians in turn-of-the-20th-century 'mixed style', with sculptured façades and copper cupolas. They include the former headquarters of the German-Turkestan Bank (now the Pakhta Bank), Potelyakhov House (1907; now the main post and telegraph office) and Vadyayev House (1911; now the mayor's office).

SAHIB MIAN HAZRAT MEDRESSA
From the uninteresting **Kamal-Kazi Medressa** (admission US$0.25) on Khamza, walk for five minutes down Muqimi to the truncated remnants of a big medressa called Sahib Mian Hazrat (1861). Most of it was appropriated in Soviet times for a factory, but in a couple of surviving cells the Uzbek poet and 'democrat' Mohammedamin Muqimi (1850–1903) is said to have spent his last days.

JUMA MOSQUE
The city's **Juma Mosque** (Friday Mosque; Khamza 5; admission US$1; 8am-5pm), built in the early 19th century, is centred on a 22m minaret and includes a large prayer hall supported by 98 wooden columns brought from India. It reopened in 1989 after decades of neglect under Soviet rule but was closed again in the late 1990s during one of Karimov's periodic religious crackdowns. At the time of research it was being set up as a museum.

KHAMZA MUSEUM
The **Khamza Museum** (Akbar Islomov 2; admission US$1; 9am-5pm Tue-Sun) could just as well be dedicated to Lenin – a fatuous shrine to a Soviet-imposed 'national hero', the poet Khamza Khakimzade Niyazi (who was born in Kokand) – full of manuscripts and Socialist-realism (and the odd photo of old Kokand).

Sleeping & Eating
Given the dearth of decent accommodation in Kokand you are better off continuing on to Fergana. If it's late, it might be worth asking around for an unofficial homestay.

Hotel Kokand (364 03; Imom Ismoil Bukhori 1; s/d US$4.60/9.20) This central hotel has electricity, running water and a friendly staff. Unfortunately, the rooms are filthy and literally infested with cockroaches. Sleeping with the light on will keep the little buggers under the floorboards. Get there from the bus station on marshrutnoe taxi No 2. Marshrutnoe No 8 goes there too, via a very roundabout way. From the train station take almost anything northbound on Istanbul.

Nilufar (246 56; Abdulla Nabiev maydoni; meals US$1-2; brunch, lunch & dinner) Russian and Uzbek dishes served in a Soviet-style bar.

Café Dilshod (230 78; Istiqlol 13) Located west of Muqimi Park, this restaurant was undergoing renovations at the time of research, but should be the nicest place in town.

Vegetarians and self-caterers can go to the main bazaar by the bus station, or a small one near the hotel. There are also numerous chaikhanas scattered around the streets; there are a couple on Turkiston.

Getting There & Around
The bus station is by the main bazaar on Furqat. Fergana is 103km and Margilan is 90km (about two hours) away by bus, with two departures per hour. One of these will carry on to Andijan. Bus No 14 links the airport, train station and bus station. Bus No 8 runs back and forth past the Hotel Kokand, Khan's Palace, Juma Mosque and the bus station and bazaar. Bus Nos 16 and 23 go north from the bus station to the area around Narbutabey Medressa.

Shared taxis gather outside the bus station, and leave when full to Tashkent (US$4), Fergana (US$2) and other destinations across the valley from 4am.

UZBEKISTAN

There are two daily trains to Andijan (5am and 2.30pm; US$1), however, it is generally much easier to take a shared taxi.

There is an **Uzbekistan Airways booking office** (☎ 231 02; Imom Ismoil Bukhori 3) but at the time of writing there were no flights in or out of Kokand.

FERGANA ФАРГОНА

☎ (3) 73 or 732 / pop 230,000

Tree-lined avenues and pastel-plastered tsarist buildings give Fergana the feel of a mini-Tashkent. Throw in the best services and accommodation in the region, plus a central location, and you have the most obvious base from which to explore the rest of the valley.

Fergana is the valley's least ancient and least Uzbek city. It began in 1877 as Novy Margelan (New Margilan), a colonial annexe to nearby Margilan. It was briefly known as Skobelev, named after the city's first military governor, and then assumed Fergana (*fair*-ga-na) in the 1920s. It's a nice enough place to hang out, and somewhat cosmopolitan with its relatively high proportion of Russian and Korean citizens.

Orientation

The streets radiate out from what's left of the old tsarist fort, 10m of mud-brick wall within an army compound (off-limits to visitors) behind the city and provincial administration buildings. The airport is 6km south of town and the nearest train station is in Margilan.

Information

Central Bank (☎ 24 68 93, 24 43 56; Al-Farghoni 69) Cash advance on Visa cards or change Amex and Visa travellers cheques. At the time of writing, plans were set to move to another building on Al-Farghoni by mid-2004.

Classic (☎ 24 22 72; Qosimov 30; per hr US$0.90; 9am-8pm) Internet café opposite Hotel Fergana.

Post office (Mustaqillik 35; 8am-6pm) A second post office and the telephone and telegraph office is near the eastern end of Al-Farghoni.

Simus (☎ 24 59 72; Mabrifat 45; per hr US$1.20; 8am-10pm) Internet café with helpful staff near the taxi stand.

Uzbektourism Transport and homestays arrangements; located in Uzbekistan Airways and the Hotel Ziyorat.

FERGANA

0 — 500 m
0 — 0.3 miles

INFORMATION
Central Bank........................1 D3
Classic.................................2 C3
Halyk Bank..........................3 C2
Post Office..........................4 B3
Simus..................................5 C2
Telephone & Telegraph Office..........6 D3
Uzbektourism...................(see 10)
Uzbektourism...................(see 20)

SIGHTS & ACTIVITIES   (p191)
Museum of Local Studies 7 C1

SLEEPING   (p191)
Asia Hotel............................8 D3
Hotel Fergana......................9 B3
Hotel Ziyorat.....................10 D2
Olga & Valentina's Guesthouse......11 D3

EATING   (p191)
Askiya Café........................12 D1
Kafe Istanbul....................13 C2
Restoran Saran..................14 D1

DRINKING   (p191)
Hollywood Night Club............15 C2

TRANSPORT   (pp191-2)
Fergana Bus Station..............16 D1
Local Bus Stand..................17 C1
Taxi Stand....................(see 17)
Taxis for Airport...............18 C2
Taxis for Margilan..............19 D1
Uzbekistan Airways..............20 D3

To Andijan (73km)
Rakhimov
Yusupov
Anyazova
Bazaar
Khanza
Al-Farghoni Square
Dekhon
Usman Khojaev
Al-Farghoni Park
Amusement Park
Kuvasoy
To Yermazar Bus Station (3km); Margilan (18km); Kokand (103km)
TsUM Department Store
Mabrifat
Kuvasoy
Stadium
Amphitheatre
Kambarov
Bobur
Mustaqillik
Al-Farghoni
Qosimov
Qomun
City & Provincial Administration Buildings
To Shakhimardan (59km)
Khojand
To Site of Old Fort (100m)
Navoi
To Airport (7km)
Approximate Scale Only

Sights

Fergana's most appealing attraction is the **bazaar**, filled with good-natured Uzbek traders, leavened with Korean and Russian vendors selling home-made specialities. In general, to home in on Fergana Bazaar, ask for *markaz* (centre).

The **Museum of Local Studies** (☎ 24 31 91; Usman Khojayev 26; admission US$0.50; 9am-2pm Mon, 9am-5pm Wed-Sun) is rather sparse. Visitors can inspect satellite photos showing where all that cotton grows and some items on the valley's ancient Buddhist and shamanist sites. Other displays include a Stone Age diorama with some excessively hairy Cro-Magnons, and a few photos of pre-Soviet life.

Sleeping & Eating

Fergana has the valley's best hotel and restaurant options. Note that the Hotel Fergana does not accept foreign guests.

Asia Hotel (☎ 24 52 21; fax 24 80 05; hotelasia@bk.ru; Navoi 26; s/d US$28/48;   ) This smart new three-star hotel, with efficient management and well-informed staff, is located close to the city and provincial administration buildings in the southern part of town. The restaurant has good vegetarian meals but the meat dishes are mediocre. The pool looks inviting but you'll pay US$3 for the pleasure of using it.

Hotel Ziyorat (☎ 24 77 40; fax 26 86 02; Dekhon 2a; s/d US$12/20;) Uzbektourism's flagship hotel is close to the bazaar and transport. Rooms are clean and comfortable but you might have to bargain as the prices thrown out by the receptionist are indiscriminate. The clean, charmless restaurant here offers a small, unvarying selection of Russian and pseudo-international food.

Olga & Valentina's Guesthouse (☎ 24 71 65, 24 89 05, mobile 8-590-712-4072; daniol26@yahoo.com; per person US$15;   ) Located on the 4th floor of an apartment block between Qsimov, Al-Farghoni and Qomus, this homestay has several neat and comfortable rooms with shared bathroom. Call in advance (Olga speaks English) and they'll pick you up. The cost includes satellite TV, breakfast and solid travellers' advice.

Travellers also recommend Hojayev Sherzon's **Golden Valley Homestay** (☎ 23 21 00; pfsfergana@vodiy.uz; Shakirovoy 10), located near the Hotel Ziyorat. Call for a pick-up.

Restoran Saran (☎ 24 03 01; Rakhimov 26; meals US$6; lunch & dinner) Well-regarded and recently renovated, this Korean restaurant, located close to the bazaar, serves good noodle and salad dishes, but the service is agonisingly slow.

Askiya Café (☎ 24 48 07; cnr Dekhon & Anyazova; dishes US$2-3; breakfast, lunch & dinner) This in vogue café, opposite the Hotel Ziyorat, is owned by Uzbekistan's most famed comedian, Sidik Sheraev. All the products here, from milk and meat to fruits and vegetables, are grown on his nearby farm. The Korean soup is recommended.

Kafe Istanbul (☎ 24 14 18; Al-Farghoni 20; burgers US$1; lunch & dinner) A cavernous local café serving up better-than-average burgers and fries.

Self-caterers will enjoy the bazaar, which is also a good place to go for lunch. There are several basic Uzbek canteens nearby. There are chaikhanas and shashlyk stands in Al-Farghoni Park and in front of the TsUM department store but they tend to close early, usually by 8pm.

Drinking

Cavernous **Hollywood Night Club** (☎ 24 75 33; Kambarov; entry 1000 sum), behind the department store, tolerates vodka-shooting Ferganans and their late-night antics.

Getting There & Away

AIR

Uzbekistan Airways (☎ 24 85 25; Al-Farghoni 20; 8am-5pm) has daily flights to/from Tashkent (1½ hours away). The Tuesday and Saturday flight (US$10) is on a small plane. A large plane is used on other days but costs more (US$41).

BUS & SHARED TAXI

Buses leave from Fergana bus station (behind the bazaar) for Shakhimardan, Kuva and a few local destinations, including the Margilan bus station.

Long-distance coaches, marshrutnoes and regional buses mostly use Yermazar bus station, which is out of the town on the road to Margilan. Departures from Yermazar include Namangan and Osh (Kyrgystan), every two hours, and Kokand and Andijan (frequent departures each day). Both stations have shared taxis to Tashkent; it's around US$20 to US$25 to charter a Daewoo Nexia.

Getting Around

The airport is a 25-minute trip on bus No 22 or marshrutnoe taxi No 6; bus No 3 takes longer. Yermazar bus station is 10 minutes away on bus No 21, marked ЕРМОМЗОР-МАРКАЗ (Yermazar–Centre). Taxis to the airport and other local buses depart from Marifat near the bazaar. There are also marshrutnoe taxis to Yermazar from Fergana station.

MARGILAN МАРГИЛОН

☎ (3) 73 or 732 / pop 145,000

If you've been travelling along the Silk Road seeking answers to where in fact this highly touted fabric comes from, Margilan, and its Yodgorlik Silk Factory, should be your ground zero.

Although there is little to show for it, Margilan has been around for a long time, probably since the 1st century BC. For centuries its merchant clans, key players in Central Asia's commerce and silk trade, were said to be a law unto themselves; even in the closing decades of Soviet rule, this was the heart of Uzbekistan's black market economy.

Sights

BAZAAR

On Thursday and Sunday especially, Margilan's central bazaar is a time capsule, full of weathered Uzbek men in traditional clothing exchanging solemn greetings and gossiping over endless pots of tea, with hardly a Russian or a tourist in sight. Uzbek matrons here dress almost exclusively in the locally produced *khanatlas* (tie-dyed patterned silk). In summer and autumn the stalls groan under fruit of all kinds and the air smells of spices. Some travellers say it's the most interesting bazaar in the Fergana Valley. There's another bazaar about 2km out of town, best on a Sunday.

YODGORLIK SILK FACTORY

The **Yodgorlik (Souvenir) Silk Factory** (☎ 33 88 24; silk@mail.ru; Imam Zakhriddin; ☉ 8am-5pm Mon-Fri), southwest of the bazaar, employs traditional methods of silk production, unlike the vast and increasingly moribund Margilan and Khanatlas mass-production factories that are also in the city. It is possible to see the whole production process here, from steaming and unravelling the cocoons to the weaving of the dazzling *khanatlas* patterned fabric. The guided tour (free) in English is excellent. The factory has recently diversified into carpetmaking and embroidery. A shop here sells silk for US$4 per square metre, plus *khanatlas* dresses, carpets and embroidered items for reasonable prices.

MOSQUES

The modest **Toron Mosque**, just to the north of the bazaar, is a fine example of the Fergana style with a gaily painted *darskhana* (study hall in a medressa). Visitors, particularly women, should ask permission before entering. A walk further down this alley gives access to a quiet *mahalla* (Uzek: neighbourhood) with bakers toiling behind their ovens.

Half a kilometre east of the bazaar is the reconstructed **Khonakhah Mosque**, with two new 25m-high minarets out the front. Modestly dressed male visitors might be welcomed into the courtyard and proudly shown the oldest part, an unrestored prayer room dating back, they say, to 1452. It seems to have been too small to catch the Bolsheviks' attention. The restored main building is a masterpiece of Fergana woodcraft, delicately painted in pale shades of blue, pink, yellow and green.

Sleeping & Eating

Given Margilan's dire hotel and eating options, it's better to make this a day trip from Fergana.

Hotel Margilan (☎ 33 46 42; Mustaqilliq 343; r US$6) Dirty and depressing rooms at this hotel lack both electricity and running water. A better option is a homestay; the Yodogorlik Silk Factory can arrange one for US$10 per night.

Chaikhanas are sprinkled down the main street, including one near Khonakhah Mosque.

Getting There & Away

The trip from Fergana is simplest in a taxi, for the equivalent of about US$1.80 (ask for the bazaar). A cheaper alternative is the slow, claustrophobic bus from Fergana station, 30 minutes via Yermazar bus station and the Margilan train station. It's marked simply ФАРГОНА–МАРГИЛОН.

Shared taxis to Tashkent lurk around the train station car park; chartering a Daewoo

Nexia costs about US$23 in sum, or US$6 for a seat.

The bazaar is right across the intersection from Margilan's bus station. From the train station it's a 30-minute trek north on Mustaqillik, or five minutes by almost any marshrutnoe taxi. See the Fergana section (p191) for information on long-distance train and bus connections.

RISHDON РИШТАН

This mainly Tajik town near the border with Kyrgyzstan, 50km west of Fergana, is home to a group of master potters utilising the fine local clay. But unless you speak Tajik, or come here with a guide, it's difficult to find them on your own.

Master of ceramics **Rustam Usmanov** (☎ 73 45-373 45, 215 85, in Fergana ☎ 245-215 85; Ar-Roshidony kochasi 230) has his home and a studio featuring his own works and examples from his fellow artisans on the main road through town. He's a member of an association of master potters who have broken away from the collectivised workshops and are rediscovering techniques abandoned in Soviet times. Their ceramics use mostly traditional designs on a white background in shades of green and cobalt.

Local buses go to Rishdon from Fergana, Margilan and Kokand. Coming from Fergana city, a bit of Kyrgyzstan slices into the road, forcing drivers to take a hard right turn and slight detour that you'll barely notice.

SHAKHIMARDAN ШОХИМАРДОН

One of the odder results of Stalin's diabolical gerrymandering around the Fergana Valley is the existence of an archipelago of tiny 'islands' of one republic entirely surrounded by another. One of these is the Uzbek enclave of Shakhimardan, 55km south of Fergana (another, equally scenic but less accessible, is Sokh, 60km west of Shakhimardan).

Shakhimardan's main appeal for visitors is that it's nestled in a 1500m-high alpine valley, a fine place to clear your lungs and take an easy look at the Pamir Alay mountains. On Saturday and Sunday the town comes alive with cheery groups of families and friends quaffing vodka and eating plov in scenic picnic spots.

SILK PRODUCTION IN UZBEKISTAN

Although silk-thread production and clothmaking have been largely automated, the raising of silkworms is still almost entirely a 'cottage industry', with most worms raised in individual farmers' homes, as they have been since perhaps the 4th century AD.

Out of its stock from previous years' husbandry, the Uzbekistan government distributes an average of 20g of young silkworm grubs to any farmer willing to 'raise' them in late April and early May. Each farmer prepares special rooms with large bedding boxes. The worms' entire diet consists of chopped up mulberry leaves culled from trees along lowland roads and canals. The farmers use the leftover branches as fuel, and the stripped mulberry trees regrow their branches the following year.

The initial 20g of grubs takes up about a square metre of space and consumes about 3kg of leaves a day. But each week, after a sleep cycle of a few days, the worms wake up and eat more than previously. At the end of just a month, each of those originally microscopic creatures has grown to the size of a little finger, and together they occupy two or three rooms and devour some 300kg of leaves each day! Then abruptly they stop eating altogether and spend a week or so rolling themselves up into a cocoon of silk fibres. The farmers (exhausted from trying to gather 300kg of leaves each day) sell the cocoons back to government silk factories – typically 80kg to 120kg of cocoons at about US$1 to US$2 per kilogram.

Some worms, called 'seed-worms', are set aside and allowed to hatch as moths, which will lay eggs and produce the next generation of grubs. The rest are killed inside their cocoons by steaming (otherwise they would break out and ruin the silk filaments), and each cocoon is boiled and carefully unwound. A typical 3cm or 4cm cocoon yields about 1km of filament! Several filaments are twisted together to make industrial thread, which is used to make clothing.

Uzbekistan as a whole produces about 30,000 metric tonnes of cocoons a year. The biggest silk factory in the former Soviet Union is in Margilan. Uzbektourism in Fergana can arrange tours of the factory (p187), or call the factory itself (see opposite).

Its main attraction for Muslims is that it's said to be the resting place of Ali, son-in-law of the Prophet Mohammed and fourth caliph, whose descendants Shiite Muslims regard as the true heirs of the caliphate (at least seven places in the Middle and Far East make the same claim).

In an effort to suppress the flow of pilgrims, successive Soviet administrations have tried to reinvent Shakhimardan. The mosque and mausoleum were burned down in the early 1920s by *basmachi* (Muslim guerrilla fighters) trying to flush out 48 Red army soldiers who had taken refuge there (according to Soviet historians); or by the Bolsheviks (according to local Uzbeks). In any case, the pilgrims stopped coming.

The village was later renamed Khamzaabad, in honour of one of the Bolsheviks' adopted martyrs, the secular Kokandi poet and playwright Khamza Khakimzade Niyazi. Khamza encouraged women to join his first-ever Uzbek theatre company and come out from behind their veils – for which, intoned the Soviets, he was stoned to death by Muslim fundamentalists here in 1929 and his body hidden in a rock crevice. The real story is undoubtedly more complex.

The Ali shrine was replaced following Uzbekistan's independence and pilgrims once again mingle with holidaymakers during the high season, April to September.

When a chunk of the Khrebet Katran Too glacier broke away in July 1998 it triggered a catastrophic flood that swept away the flimsy holiday homes close to the river; estimates of the number of people killed range from 100 to 3000. The small mosque south of the bazaar by the river was spared; locals say the floodwaters parted around it.

Sights & Actvities

Buses unload passengers in the village centre, from where the road continues south along the river. About 500m past the village is a sign labelled 'Kol Kor'. Continue past the sign for five kilometres, passing some guesthouses along the way, until you reach an ageing diesel-powered cable car, which lifts weary walkers to the icy waters of **Kuli Kulon**, created centuries ago by a landslide. Alternatively, the 2.5km walk under the chairlift takes 30 to 40 minutes. The shore of this alpine lake, at 1740m, is crowded in the high season and apparently deserted (but very cold!) at other times. A boat trip to the head of the lake is a small fee in sum. From its outlet flows a clear river called Kok-Sub (Green Water).

The dreary **Khamza Museum** (☯ 9am-1pm & 2-5pm Wed-Mon), behind Hazrat Ali, contains

---

TREKS

A holiday camp called Turbaza Shakhimardan, a 1.5km hike from the village proper, crawls with Uzbek holidaymakers during high season, enjoying volleyball, videos, excessive food and drink, clean air and the views.

Beyond the *turbaza*, about 15km from the village and above 2000m, is an ex-military training camp, now an international mountaineering camp (*alpinistskiy lager* or *alplager*) and trekking base called Dugoba. Most treks from here cross passes into Kyrgyzstan; you will need a valid Kyrgyzstan visa and possibly a special Alay Valley permit (see p306). A reputable travel agency with whom you book your trek might be able to help with this.

Established trekking routes lead from Shakhimardan over the Pamir Alay to Daroot-Korgon in Kyrgyzstan. Routes head up the Ak Suu Valley and then the Archa Bashi and Kara Kazyk Valleys to the tricky 4440m-high Kara Kazyk Pass and then over into the Kara Kazyk and Kök Suu Valleys to Daroot-Korgon. An alternative route leads up the Eki Daban Valley and over the 4296m-high Alaydin Daban Pass into the Kök Suu Valley. Other routes lead from nearby Khaidakan in Kyrgyzstan. All routes take a minimum of about a week.

The best map coverage is the 1:100,000 *Pamiro-Alay Bisokiy Alay* (1995), often available at the office of Asia Travel (see p173).

Fergana Uzbektourism can take you on treks from a day to a week or more. Guide, equipment (except sleeping bags), porters and three meals a day will cost about US$30 to US$45 per person per day for a group of three or four, plus US$45 each way for transport from Fergana. Agencies in Tashkent and Samarkand also do trips up here. The trekking season is roughly May to October.

some photos of pre-Bolshevik Shakhi-mardan and the original Hazrat Ali mausoleum. The museum's opening hours are rather informal.

Sleeping & Eating
The village has lots of chaikhanas, food stalls and a bazaar and many holiday lodges. Try to keep a low profile as travellers have reported being pestered by police for 'registration fees' and you may have to cough up US$5.

The main place to stay is **Turbaza Shakhi-mardon** (per person incl meals US$5), which has 360 beds in very basic two-bed 'cottages' with shared bathroom. It's jammed in the high season but they can always squeeze in one or two extras.

The **Dugaba Alplager** (per day US$5) has cabins with showers and a Russian sauna and there are cooking facilities.

The **Sugurtachi Damolish Oye** (per person US$2) is about 2km from the bazaar in the outlying village of Vuardil, with clean rooms in a large Soviet building.

Getting There & Away
At the time of writing travellers needed a Kyrgyz visa and a multiple entry Uzbek visa to reach Shakhimardan. Without a visa you could bribe your way through, costing anywhere between US$10 and US$40. The best way around this is to travel by public bus (rather than taxi), which are usually not inspected by border guards.

A public bus (US$0.50) departs on the scenic two-hour trip to Shakhimardan from Fergana at 10.30am. There are more buses to Qadamjoy (Kyrgyzstan), about 10km before Shakhimardan, where you can change. A chartered Tico will cost US$6. There's no regular transport beyond Shakhimardan village.

ANDIJAN АНДИЖОН
☎ (3) 742 / pop 350,000
Uzbekistan's easternmost city, with bustling markets and industrial areas, is the travellers' main overland gateway to and from Kyrgyzstan. Andijan dates to at least the 9th century AD, but its claim to historical fame is as the birthplace of Zahiruddin Babur (see the boxed text opposite) in the 15th century, when it was the capital of the Fergana state and its main Silk Road trading centre.

In 1902 an earthquake did what the Bolsheviks might have felt compelled to do two decades later – destroying the town and killing over 4000 people.

Today, Andijan province is the most densely settled part of the valley, the country's main oil-producing region and home to the new Daewoo car-manufacturing plant. There is a traditional bazaar here and its people are said to speak the purest form of Uzbek.

Orientation & Information
Museums, medressa, bank, shops and the post office are clustered around the main bazaar, about 3km north of the bus and train stations (which are a two- or three- minute walk from one another). A useful reference point is Pushkin Park; just north of here is a taxi stand for rides to Tashkent and Fergana. From this taxi stand, Rashidov ulitsa heads west, at the end of which is Yaangi Bazaar.

Sights
The **bazaar** is not the biggest in the valley but it's certainly colourful in the early morning. It's at its active peak on Thursday and Sunday. Across Oltinkul is the handsome 19th-century **Juma Mosque and Medressa** (admission US$1; ☯ 9am-4pm Tue-Sun), said to be the only building to survive the 1902 earthquake. A factory appears to have

---

ZAHIRUDDIN BABUR

Born in 1483 to Fergana's ruler, Umar Sheikh Mirzo, Zahiruddin Babur (Uzbek: Bobur) inherited his father's kingdom before he was even a teenager, but his early career was less than brilliant. At 17 the young king (a descendant of Timur (Tamerlane) on his father's side and Jenghiz Khan on his mother's) took Samarkand, but was then abruptly driven out of Fergana and into the political wilderness by the Uzbek Shaybanids. He found new turf in Afghanistan, where he ruled Kabul for two decades. Then in 1526 he marched into Delhi to found the line of Persian-speaking emperors of northern India known as the Mughals (a corruption of 'Mongol', local parlance for anybody from Central Asia). Although he died four years later, his descendants ruled in Delhi until 1857.

been dropped squarely upon most of it. It reopened as a working medressa in the 1990s but was turned into a museum of local ethnography after a police crackdown on suspected Islamic militants. Beside it is a dusty **regional museum** (admission US$0.20; ☼ 9am-5pm Mon-Fri, 9am-3pm Sat) with the usual historical exhibits and stuffed animals.

The marginally more interesting **Babur Literary Museum** (☼ 9am-4pm Tue-Sun), surrounded by rose gardens in the lane behind the bazaar, occupies the site of the royal apartments where Babur lived and studied as a boy within Ark-Ichy, the town's long-gone citadel. The museum, although visually pleasant, is more like a slicked-up shrine, with books, paintings and hyperbolic text about Babur and his literary friends.

Sleeping & Eating

To catch the morning activity of the bazaar you are best off spending the night.

Hotel Andijan (☎ 25 87 07; Fitrat 241; s/d US$12/24, with shared bathroom US$4/8) This centrally located no-frills hotel sports small but clean rooms with basic bathrooms. The hotel restaurant serves basic Uzbek food.

Hotel Government House (Sport Hotel; ☎ 46 23 88; Mashrab 21; s/d US$45/90) Located next to the amusement park, 300m behind the decrepit hotel Oltyn Vody (former Zolotaya Dolina), this government resthouse has classy rooms and hot showers. Foreign guests, however, are generally not welcome and the place might be 'full'.

Golden Chicken Restaurant (☎ 25 15 16; meals US$2; ☼ breakfast, lunch & dinner) This restaurant, 200m west of Hotel Andijan, serves quick Uzbek, Turkish and Western meals. Chaikhanas on Fitrat have shashlyk and *laghman*, and of course the bazaar has abundant fruit, vegetables, nuts and honey.

Getting There & Around

The easiest way to get between Andijan and other points in the valley is by shared taxi or marshrutnoe; the latter departs every 45 minutes from Fergana's Yermazar station (US$1, 2½-hour trip). Buses also come here from Kokand and Namangan. If you are headed to Osh or Jalal-Abad in Kyrgyzstan you will have to take a taxi to the border and change there. Shared taxis and minivans leave from a lot north of Pushkin Park and from the bus station.

Daily flights connect Andijan and Tashkent (one hour, US$43). Tickets are sold at the **airport** (☎ 24 42 23). The airport is 5km from the bazaar. From the Oltyn Vody take marshrutnoe taxi No 4.

No 33 Daewoo Damas marshrutnoes race around a fixed route as if taxi driving was a freestyle sport. No 33 travels from Juma Medressa, past the Hotel Andijan, Pushkin Park, Yaangi Bazaar and Hotel Oltyn Vody before coming within 1km of the airport.

CENTRAL UZBEKISTAN
ЦЕНТРАЛБНЫЙ УЗБЕКИСТАН

SAMARKAND САМАРҚАНД
☎ (3) 66 or 662 / pop 405,000 / elevation 710m

> We travel not for trafficking alone,
> By hotter winds our fiery hearts are fanned.
> For lust of knowing what should not be known
> We take the Golden Road to Samarkand.

These final lines of James Elroy Flecker's 1913 poem *The Golden Journey to Samarkand* evoke the romance of Uzbekistan's most glorious city. No name is so evocative of the Silk Road as Samarkand. For most people it has the mythical resonance of Atlantis, fixed in the Western popular imagination by poets and playwrights of bygone eras, few of whom saw the city in the flesh.

From the air your eye locks onto the domes and minarets, and on the ground the sublime, larger-than-life monuments of Timur, the technicolour bazaar and the city's long, rich history, indeed work some kind of magic. Surrounding these islands of majesty, modern Samarkand sprawls across acres of Soviet-built buildings, parks and broad avenues utilised by buzzing Daewoo taxis.

Most of Samarkand's high-profile attractions are the work of Timur, his grandson Ulughbek and the Uzbek Shaybanids. You can visit them all, plus some ancient excavations, in two or three days. If you're short on time, at least see the Registan,

UZBEKISTAN

SAMARKAND

0 ____ 500 m
0 ____ 0.3 miles

INFORMATION

Afrosiab Business Travel Agency	(see 35)
Asia Travel International	1 D3
Book & Map Shop	(see 31)
Foreign Language Institute (Samarkand University)	2 B3
International Telephone & Fax Office	3 B2
Main Post & Telegraph Office	4 B2
National Bank of Uzbekistan	5 A3
Net City Internet Café	6 B2
Sam CEDA	7 B2
Soft Space	8 C3
Sogda Tours	9 B2
VIP Internet	10 A4
Zona X	11 B2

SIGHTS & ACTIVITIES (pp199-201)

Ak-Saray Mausoleum	12 C3
Bibi-Khanym Mausoleum	13 B2
Bibi-Khanym Mosque	14 E1
Chorsu (Market Arcade)	15 D2
Guri Amir Mausoleum	16 C3
Hazrat-Hizr Mosque	17 E1
Hodja-Nisbaddor Mosque	18 D4
Kosh-Hauz Mosque	19 D2
Museum of Peace and Solidarity	20 A3
Registan: Sher Dor Medressa	21 D2
Registan: Tilla-Kari Medressa	22 D2
Registan: Ulughbek Medressa	23 D2
Rukhobod Mausoleum	24 C3
Shahr-i-Zindah	25 F1
State Museum	26 D3
Statue of Amir Timur	27 B3

SLEEPING (pp201-3)

Bahodir B&B	28 D2
Bonu-Sh	29 D3
Dilshoda	30 C3
Hotel Afrosiab	31 C3
Hotel Furkat	32 E2
Hotel President	33 B3
Hotel Registan	34 A2
Hotel Samarkand	35 C3
Muhandis-Aziza & Kutbiya	36 C3
Timur the Great	37 E2
Zarina	38 D3

EATING (p203)

Bar Gloria	39 B2
Chor-Su	40 D2
Kryloy Rynok (Covered Market)	41 B2
Lyabi Gor	42 D3
Mir	43 A2
Sharq	44 E1

SHOPPING (p203)

GUM (Department Store)	45 B2
Samarkand-Bukhara Silk Carpets	(see 21)

TRANSPORT (pp203-4)

Penjikent Taxi Stand	46 E3

OTHER

Avia Kassa	47 A2
Ayni Museum	48 D3
Mosque	49 D1
Mosque	50 D2
Mosque	51 D1
Provincial OVIR Office	52 B2
War Memorial	53 A2

To Afrosiab Museum (1km); Ulughbek Oversevatory (2.5km); Private Bus Stop (2.5km); Tashkent (293km)

Afrosiab Site

Old Town

To Airport (4km); Regional & Long-Distance Bus Stations (5km)

Main Bazaar

Buhkarskaya

Mulokandov

Old Town

Penjikent (60km)

Penjikent

Suzangaran

Old Town

To Shakhrisabz (90km)

Kosh-hauz

Amphitheatre

Dagbischaya

Registan (Registanskaya)

Akhinboev

Drama Theatre

To Umar Bank (200m); Hotel President (300m); Shelda (350m); Bukhara (268km)

Mustaqillik maydoni

Shohruh

Mustaqillik (Lenina)

Termez

Samarkand University

Park

Gorky

Volkova

To Uzbekistan Airways Booking Office (1.5km); Train Station (5.7km)

Amir Temur

Sharaf Rashidov

Podsha

Friday

Mohmud Qoshqari

To Alliance Française (500m)

Rosa Luxemburg

Lev Tolstoy

Makhmudov

Universitet

Uzbekistan

Hotel Sogiana (3km)

Ibn Sino

Ak. Abdullayev

Usto-Umar-Dzhurakulova kuchasi

Tashkent

Ulughbek

Ak. Abdullayev

Guri Amir, Bibi-Khanym Mosque, Shahr-i-Zindah and the bazaar.

Note that the people of Samarkand, Bukhara and southeastern Uzbekistan don't speak Uzbek but an Uzbek-laced Tajik (Farsi). Some members of the ethnic Tajik minority wish Stalin had made the area part of Tajikistan, but the issue is complicated by ethnic Uzbek city folk who speak Tajik.

History

Samarkand (Marakanda to the Greeks), one of Central Asia's oldest settlements, was probably founded in the 5th century BC. It was already the cosmopolitan, walled capital of the Sogdian empire when it was taken in 329 BC by Alexander the Great, who said, 'Everything I have heard about Marakanda is true, except that it's more beautiful than I ever imagined.'

A key Silk Road city, it sat on the crossroads leading to China, India and Persia, bringing in trade and artisans. From the 6th to the 13th century it grew into a city more populous than it is today, changing hands every couple of centuries: Western Turks, Arabs, Persian Samanids, Karakhanids, Seljuq Turks, Mongolian Karakitay and Khorezmshah have all ruled here – before being literally obliterated by Jenghiz Khan in 1220.

This might have been the end of the story, but in 1370 Timur decided to make Samarkand his capital, and over the next 35 years forged a new, almost-mythical city, Central Asia's economic and cultural epicentre. His grandson Ulughbek ruled until 1449 and made it an intellectual centre as well.

When the Uzbek Shaybanids came in the 16th century and moved their capital to Bukhara, Samarkand went into decline. For several decades in the 18th century, after a series of earthquakes, it was essentially uninhabited. The emir of Bukhara forcibly repopulated the town towards the end of the century, but it was only truly resuscitated by the Russians, who forced its surrender in May 1868 and linked it to the Russian empire by the Trans-Caspian Railway 20 years later.

Samarkand was declared capital of the new Uzbek SSR in 1924, but lost the honour to Tashkent six years later.

Orientation

A map of Samarkand's centre shows the city's Russian-Asian schizophrenia. Eastward are the tangled alleys of the old town, whose axis (and main shopping street) is the pedestrian section of Tashkent kuchasi between the Registan and the main bazaar. Shady 19th-century Russian avenues radiate westward from Mustaqillik maydoni, the administrative centre of the modern city and province.

Almost everything of tourist interest is within a couple of kilometres west and north of the Registan. A useful tourist landmark in the 'new' city is the Hotel Samarkand on the parklike boulevard called Universiteti.

The airport is 4km north of the bazaar, along Akademik Abdullayev. The long-distance and main regional bus stations are a further 1km east from the airport. The train station is about 6km northwest of the centre.

MAPS

A detailed, fairly accurate 2002 map (scale 1:13,000) includes a full list of sights and facilities, as well as a regional map on the back. It's available from the Hotel Afrosiab, but cheaper at a bookshop (US$2.50) opposite the Registan.

Information

CULTURAL CENTRES

Alliance Française (☎ 33 66 27; dilallia@yahoo.fr; Bukhara 26) Three blocks west of Gorky Park, or take marshrutnoe 27 from Registan. It can arrange homestays and act as an informal guide.

Sam CEDA (☎ 33 68 89; Amir Timur 5; ☼ 9am-noon & 2-5pm Tue & Fri, 2-5pm Mon, Wed, Thu) Foreign-language library and meeting place for students.

INTERNET ACCESS

Net City (☎ 33 55 50; Akhunbabayev 68; US$0.80; ☼ 7am-10pm)

VIP (☎ 33 80 40; Sharaf Rashidov 106; US$0.80; ☼ 24hr)

Zona X (☎ 33 60 75; Ulughbek 3; per hr US$0.60; ☼ 9-1am)

MONEY

There are exchange offices at the Hotel Samarkand (8am to 10pm) and the Hotel Afrosiab (9am to noon).

National Bank of Uzbekistan (Firdavsi 7; ☼ 9am-4pm Mon-Sat) cashes travellers cheques and Visa cards can be used to extract US dollars.

POST & COMMUNICATIONS

Main post and telegraph office (Pochta 5) This is behind the small farmers market, Krytyy rynok.

International telephone and fax office (cnr Shohrukh & Pochta) This small office has clear connections to Europe (US$1.14 per minute), USA (US$1.26 per minute) and Australia (US$1.72 per minute). Phone calls from the Hotel Afrosiab are four times the price.

TRAVEL AGENCIES
Local travel agencies can organise, cars, guides and contacts in Penjikent. They can set up camel trekking trips to Aidarkul Lake for around US$90 without transportation. Four-hour city tours cost around US$15. Sogda Tours is the more experienced of the three recommended here.

Afrosiab Business Travel Agency (☎ 35 82 50; bagsy@online.ru; Universiteti 1) On the 2nd floor of the Hotel Samarkand.

Asia Travel International (☎ 31 13 82, 33 75 21; fax 31 13 82; www.asiatravel-int.com; Registan 2) On the 2nd floor of the Hotel Afrosiab.

Sogda Tours (☎ 33 17 35; www.silktour.uz; Kok Saray Square 1) Located behind the Hotel Central.

UNIVERSITIES
Foreign Language Institute (☎ 33 61 74; ganisher@ online.ru; Akhunbabayev 93) This is on the 2nd floor of Samarkand University's main building, is a good place to start a search for local students keen to practice their English and act as impromptu guides. Ask for Ganisher Rahimov.

Sights
THE REGISTAN
This ensemble of majestic, tilting medressas – a near-overload of majolica, azure mosaics and vast, well-proportioned spaces – is the centrepiece of the city, and one of the most awesome single sights in Central Asia. The **Registan** (cnr Registan & Tashkent; admission US$2.50; ❀ 8am-6pm) was medieval Samarkand's commercial centre and the plaza was probably a wall-to-wall bazaar. Heavy Soviet-era restoration included digging down 3m to its original level, exposing the buildings' full height. For optimal views, police guards will covertly escort visitors to the top of a minaret for around US$1.50.

Ulughbek Medressa on the west side is the oldest of the three medressas, finished in 1420 under Ulughbek (who is said to have taught mathematics there; other subjects included theology, astronomy and philosophy). Beneath the little corner domes were lecture halls, and at the rear a large mosque. About one hundred students lived in two

storeys of dormitory cells, some of which are still visible.

The other buildings are imitations by the Shaybanid Emir Yalangtush. The entrance portal of the **Sher Dor (Lion) Medressa**, opposite Ulughbek's and finished in 1636, is decorated with roaring felines that look like tigers but are meant to be lions, flouting Islamic prohibitions against the depiction of live animals. In between is the **Tilla-Kari (Gold-Covered) Medressa**, completed in 1660, with a pleasant, gardenlike mosque courtyard. Hung on the walls inside are old photos of how the Registan looked prerenovation.

The hexagonal building in the square's northeast corner is a 19th-century *chorsu* (market arcade).

Many inner rooms now serve as art and souvenir shops, and the Sher Dor's courtyard is favoured for lavish official banquets. On some summer evenings, there's a tacky sound-and-light show in the square. It's ordered by tour groups but individuals can sit in for about US$1, or just watch from the upper plaza for free.

BIBI-KHANYM MOSQUE
The enormous congregational **Bibi-Khanym Mosque** (Tashkent kuchasi; admission US$2; ❀ 8am-6pm), northeast of the Registan, was finished shortly before Timur's death and must have been the jewel of his empire. Not long after its completion it became a victim of its own grandeur; once one of the Islamic world's biggest mosques (the main gate alone was 35m high), it pushed construction techniques to the limit. Slowly crumbling over the years, it finally collapsed in an earthquake in 1897.

Legend says that Bibi-Khanym, Timur's Chinese wife, ordered the mosque built as a surprise while he was away. The architect fell madly in love with her and refused to finish the job unless he could give her a kiss. The smooch left a mark and Timur, on seeing it, executed the architect and decreed that women should henceforth wear veils so as not to tempt other men.

Recent restoration, though shoddy in places, has reinstated the main gateway and several domes. The interior courtyard contains an enormous marble Quran stand that lends some scale to the place. Local lore has it that any woman who crawls under the stand will have lots of children.

UZBEKISTAN

Across Tashkent kuchasi is Bibi-Khanym's own compact 14th-century mausoleum.

SHAHR-I-ZINDAH

The most moving of Samarkand's sights is the **Shahr-i-Zindah** (admission US$2; ☺ 8am-7pm except national hols), an avenue of tombs east of Bibi-Khanym. The name, which means Tomb of the Living King, refers to its original, innermost and holiest shrine – a complex of cool, quiet rooms around what is probably the grave of Qusam ibn-Abbas, a cousin of the Prophet Mohammed who is said to have brought Islam to this area. This is among the oldest standing building in the city. It's also an important place of pilgrimage, so enter with respect and dress conservatively.

Except for this and a few other early tombs at the end, the rest belong to Timur's and Ulughbek's family and favourites; featuring some of the city's finest majolica tilework, largely unrenovated. The most beautiful is probably that of Timur's niece, second on the left after the entry stairs (which climb over the ancient city wall from the outside).

GURI AMIR MAUSOLEUM & AROUND

Timur, two sons and two grandsons, including Ulughbek, lie beneath the surprisingly modest **Guri Amir Mausoleum** (Akhunbabayev; admission US$2, guided tour US$1.50; ☺ 8.30am-6pm). Topped by a fluted azure dome, the mausoleum was once fronted by a medressa that is now gone, except for the gate.

Timur had built a simple crypt for himself at Shakhrisabz, and apparently had this one built in 1404 for some of his sons or grandsons. But the story goes that when he died unexpectedly of pneumonia in Kazakhstan (in the course of planning an expedition against the Chinese) in the winter of 1405, the passes back to Shakhrisabz were snowed in and he was interred here instead.

As with other Muslim mausoleums, the stones are just markers; the actual crypts are in a chamber beneath, but to view these the caretaker will expect a small consideration. In the centre is Timur's stone, once a single block of dark-green jade. In 1740 the warlord Nadir Shah carried it off to Persia, where it was accidentally broken in two – from which time Nadir Shah is said to have had a run of very bad luck,

including the near-death of his son. At the urging of his religious advisers he returned the stone to Samarkand, and of course his son recovered.

The plain marble marker to the left of Timur's is that of Ulughbek, and to the right is that of Mersaid Baraka, one of Timur's teachers. In front lies Mohammed Sultan, Timur's grandson by his son Jehangir. The stones behind Timur's mark the graves of his sons Shah Rukh (Shohrukh in Uzbek/ Tajik; the father of Ulughbek) and Miran Shah. Behind these lies Sheikh Umar, the most revered of Timur's teachers.

The Soviet anthropologist Mikhail Gerasimov opened the crypts in 1941 and, among other things, confirmed that Timur was tall (1.7m) and lame in the right leg and right arm (from injuries suffered when he was 25) – and that Ulughbek died from being beheaded. According to every tour guide's favourite anecdote, he found on Timur's grave an inscription to the effect that 'whoever opens this will be defeated by an enemy more fearsome than I'. The next day, June 22, Hitler attacked the Soviet Union.

In front of the gate are the remains of an earlier medressa, and to the right are the foundations of an even older *khanaka* (Uzbek: *hanako*; a Sufi contemplation hall and hostel for wandering mendicants).

Down a lane behind the Guri Amir is the derelict little **Ak-Saray Mausoleum** (1470). You are unlikely to see the beautiful frescoes inside as it's boarded up and used as a local rubbish tip.

Between Guri Amir and the main road is **Rukhobod Mausoleum**, dated 1380 and possibly the city's oldest surviving monument. It now serves as a souvenir and craft shop. The weedy old neighbourhood around it, tied together by ancient winding lanes, was bulldozed in 1997 to give easier access to tourist buses heading for Guri Amir. Local protests to defend the homes failed and 40 families were moved out, compensated with new homes in Samarkand's sprawling suburbs.

MAIN BAZAAR

Around and behind Bibi-Khanym is the best live show in town, the frenetic, colourful main farmers market, called Siab Market on maps. It's a Tower of Babel, full of dresses and shawls, hats and turbans of every nationality, and great for photographers, souvenir hunters and vegetarians, especially in the early morning and on Saturday and Sunday. There's an extension on the other side of Tashkent kuchasi too.

The bazaar is a 25-minute walk from the Hotel Samarkand, or take bus No 10 or marshrutnoe taxi Nos 17, 18, 19 or 23.

ANCIENT SAMARKAND (AFROSIAB)

At a 2.2 sq km site called Afrosiab, northeast of the bazaar, are excavations of Marakanda (early Samarkand) more or less abandoned to the elements. The newly renovated **Afrosiab Museum** (☎ 35 53 36; Tashkent; admission US$2; guided tour per person US$1; ☺ 9am-6pm) leads the visitor through the 11 layers of civilisation that is Afrosiab. The main attraction, in a ground floor room, is fragments of some striking 7th-century frescoes depicting hunting, an ambassadorial procession and visits by local rulers. From the museum, walk 1km north to the current excavation site where you may find weather-beaten archaeologists picking coins out of the dust.

The restored **Tomb of the Old Testament Prophet Daniel** (admission US$1; ☺ 6am-7pm) lies on the eastern side of the Afrosiab site, on the banks of the Siab river, accessible by a road and ornate portal that turns left off Tashkent kuchasi just before the bridge. The building is a long, low structure topped with five domes, containing an 18m sarcophagus – legend has it that Daniel's body grows by half an inch a year and thus the sarcophagus has to be enlarged. His remains were brought here by Timur. The caretaker may show you a small cave nearby – the lion's den, or so he says. There are some chaikhana tables under trees by the river, making it a pleasant picnic site.

For Afrosiab, take marshrutnoe taxi Nos 17 and 45 from the Hotel Samarkand or the bazaar.

ULUGHBEK OBSERVATORY

Ulughbek was probably more famous as an astronomer than as a ruler. About 1km beyond the Afrosiab Museum are the remains of an immense (30m) astrolab for observing star positions, part of a three-storey observatory he built in the 1420s. All that remains is the instrument's curved track, unearthed in 1908. The on-site **museum** (admission US$2; ☺ 9am-6pm), short and sweet in its presentation, features the work of Ulughbek and

other Uzbek astronomers. Transport is the same as for Afrosiab.

STATE MUSEUM OF THE CULTURAL HISTORY OF UZBEKISTAN

Samarkand's largest **museum** (cnr Registan & Tashkent; admission US$2; ☺ 9am-5pm) is housed in an unflattering edifice east of the Registan. Dimly-lit cavernous halls frame exhibits on regional archaeology, Samarkand history, folk art (including a mock-up yurt) and some modern art. Downstairs and in the back, an exhibit of paintings of old Samarkand and Bukhara has the lingering aroma of Socialist propaganda but is still a good aid for the imagination.

OTHER SIGHTS

South of the Registan on Suzangaran is the fine **Hodja-Nisbaddor Mosque**, a small 19th-century summer mosque with open porch, tall carved columns and brightly restored ceiling. North of the Registan on Kosh-Hauz, in a walled compound beside a scummy pool, is the peaceful **Kosh-Hauz Mosque**. Across the intersection from the bazaar is the 19th-century **Hazrat-Hizr Mosque** (admission US$1).

One of Samarkand's more quirky attractions is the **Museum of Peace and Solidarity** (☎ 33 17 53; Sharaf Rashidov; ☺ by appointment only), where curator Anatoly Ionesov has collected thousands of signatures, including some very famous ones, in the name of peace. It's on the 2nd floor of a yellow building in Gorky Park, 50m behind the Ferris wheel.

Festivals & Events

During **Navrus** (at the vernal equinox, around 21 March) Samarkand is home to a parade and fair, with food, music, dancing and lots of colour. Most of the action takes place at the Registan and some events are staged at the amphitheatre in Gorky Park. Samarkand hosts the **Children's Peace & Disarmament Festival** every 23 October. The city is also home to an **International Music Festival**, held every two years (next in 2005 and 2007) in September.

Sleeping

BUDGET

B&Bs

Samarkand travel agencies can put you in touch with people ready to offer bed and breakfast, typically for about US$20, or US$25 with an evening meal. Locals may offer cheaper places at around US$10 per person, so keep your ear to the ground for various options.

Bahodir B&B (☎ 38 55 29; Mulokandov 132; r with shared bathroom US$8, with private bathroom US$10) A communal traveller's atmosphere, central location, endless pots of free tea and snacks, and rock-bottom prices geared towards the backpacker set. The rooms are large, hot water plentiful and management genuinely courteous. There are also notebooks filled up with backpacker war stories of *militsia* run-ins and border crossings. Excellent home-cooked dinners are US$1 extra and nonguests are welcome for meals. The guesthouse is located 50m before Hotel Furkat on the left; look for the yellow sign.

Timur the Great (☎ 36 16 16, 35 03 38; Buhkharskaya 84; s/d US$20/30) This welcoming guesthouse, recommended by travellers, has clean, modern rooms and a good location near the Registan. Satellite TV is available in the breakfast room. It also has a family room for four people. It's one lane south of Hotel Furkat.

Bonu-Sh (☎ 35 51 02, 35 17 81; http://bonu-sh .narod.ru; Suzangaran 87; r US$15) Down a lane 400m south of Registan, this guesthouse, with English-speaking management, has rooms with private and share bathroom. One room (US$20) is decked out with traditional Uzbek handicrafts.

Muhandis-Aziza & Kutbiya (☎ 35 20 92, 35 81 65; r US$10, with private bathroom US$20-40; muhandis@ online.ru; Iskandarov 58) Set around a garden courtyard, this guesthouse offers several types of rooms. The upscale rooms have exquisite hand-carved wood ceilings. Meals are hearty and the owners are fluent in both English and German. It's a few steps down a lane from Guri Amir.

Dilshoda (☎ 35 03 87; dil_servis@mail.ru; Ak Saray 150; s/d US$15/20) A new place set in the shadow of Guri Amir, Dilshoda, run by a chipper young family, has tidy rooms with small bathrooms.

Hotels

With such a good selection of B&Bs in Samarkand there is little to recommend for budget hotels. Several hotels in this range won't even accept foreigners, including the Hotel Locomotif near the station and the Sharq Hotel near the bazaar. The **Hotel Registan** (☎ 33 55 90; Ulughbek 36; s/d US$7/10) is one option, with musty but functional rooms, though some readers have complained about deficient security.

MID-RANGE

Hotel Samarkand (☎ /fax 35 88 12; Universiteti 1; s/d/ste US$14/24/30; ✷) This oldie has a choice location, an eager service bureau and fairly clean, comfortable rooms. Facilities include a post office, coffee shop and souvenir shop. Major renovation has been expected for years.

Hotel Furkat (☎ /fax 35 32 61; Mulokandov 105; s/d US$18/30; ✷) This one-time backpacker Mecca has reinvented itself as a mid-range hotel/B&B catering mostly to overland tour groups and NGO staff. Rooms are comfortable, if a bit cramped, and there are a few singles with separate bathroom that go for US$10. When the main property fills up, travellers are directed to a cheaper annex further down the alley at No 32. Count your cash carefully here if changing money. Newer, friendlier and more competitive options have popped up in nearby alleys (see B&Bs, p201).

Zarina (☎ 35 07 61; esprit@rol.ru; Umanov 4; s/d US$30/40; ✷ ✷) Located on an alley behind the Ayni Museum, this hotel/B&B is one rung above Furkat in style, but shares its management shortcomings. Rooms are colourfully painted, but small and not regularly tidied. There is a pleasant courtyard for dining, although the food is mediocre. Again, watch the bill.

TOP END

Hotel Sogdiana (☎ 35 14 76, 35 24 26; Usman Yusupov 33; s/d US$40/60; ✷) This is a former mayoral guesthouse. It's a peaceful, rather stately place with three hectares of trees and gardens.

Hotel President (☎ 33-24-75, 33-68-87; Universiteti btwn Shohrukh & Akhunbabayev; s/d/st US$105/165/300; ✷ ✷) Samarkand's most luxurious hotel is an attractive German-Uzbek venture with a central location. It was just getting its wings at the time of research, but you can expect full amenities.

Hotel Afrosiab (☎ 31 11 95, 33 16 13; afrosiab@online .ru; Registan 2; US$95/150; ✷ ⬛ ✷) An Indian-built slab within sight of Guri Amir, this was the best in town until the Hotel President came along. The four-star rooms with satellite TV are still popular with tour groups. Payment with credit card includes a commission: Mastercard 4.7%, Visa 3.1%, Amex 4.17%.

Eating

Despite the tourist glut there is a curious lack of restaurants in Samarkand. Most travellers eat breakfast and dinner in their hotel and grab lunch at a chaikhana.

CAFÉS & CHAIKHANAS

Lyabi Gor (Registan 6; chicken shashlyk US$1.50; ☺ breakfast, lunch & dinner) Excellent *manty* (steamed dumplings), *laghman*, *samsa* and shashlyk (chicken, beef and mutton) are regular items in this touristy Uzbek restaurant, located opposite the Registan. Make sure you get the prices straight before ordering.

Chor-Su (Sharq 2; ☺ 8am-6pm) Shaslyk, *laghman* and other Uzbek dishes served with piping hot bread; north of the State Museum. Opposite the bazaar is **Sharq** (Tashkent), a row of shashlyk stands serving fish, chicken and meat kebabs, plonked right outside the Sharq Hotel. This is the busiest part of town and the best place to watch Samarkand's colourful life flow past.

Continue east on Tashkent to the bustling **Yulduz Chaikhana** (Tashkent), a popular outdoor place beside Ulughbek Observatory (take the No 26 bus from the bazaar, or marshrutnoe taxi No 17 or 45 from the Hotel Samarkand or the bazaar). Fill up on well-prepared shashlyk, *laghman*, *shorpa* (meat and vegetable soup) or other standards, along with tea and excellent bread, for about US$2.

HOME RESTAURANTS

In summer in the old town between the bazaar and Ismoil Bukhori, you can track down a simple home-cooked meal in the courtyards of private homes. You might be approached on the street, but the number of family restaurants seems to have dwindled in recent years so try asking around. Agree on the price in advance. We enjoyed a steaming common plate of mutton stew, salad, bread and tea for US$1 each, in sum.

Bahodir (☎ 38 55 29; Mulokandov 132; dinner US$1) This B&B serves dinner to its residents nightly at 7pm. Nonresidents seeking back-

packer camaraderie can join in for homemade meat and potato soup, bread, tea and salad.

RESTAURANTS

The restaurant in the Hotel Afrosiab is set up for tour groups and serves up decent, albeit overpriced, Western-style meals and Uzbek dishes. The hotel also has three bars. Across the road, the Hotel Samarkand serves forgettable meals in its large dining hall. There's a café on the top floor, but opening times are sporadic at best.

MIR (☎ 33 43 82; Mustaqillik 1A; dishes US$1.50-3; ☺ breakfast, lunch & dinner; ✂) This trendy fast-food joint behind the GUM is an outlet of the Tashkent-based Mir. Good chicken sandwiches, burgers, fries and cakes are ordered cafeteria style.

Bar Gloria (☎ 33 61 88; Ulughbek 5; dishes US$1-2; ☺ lunch & dinner; ✂) This hole-in-the-wall restaurant has Western staples such as 'chizburger', tasty salads and cold meats.

SELF-CATERING

The bazaar has bread, boiled eggs, tomatoes, fruit and more, and there's a smaller bazaar called Krytyy rynok (covered market) on Ulughbek near the main post office.

Shopping

A major shopping district is the pedestrianised Tashkent, near the bazaar, heavy on Uzbek cloth (including silk), clothing and some souvenirs. The main Russian-style shopping area is pedestrian Mustaqillik, north of Gorky Park, with the GUM department store and food, toiletries and electrical goods shops.

Samarkand-Bukhara Silk Carpets (☎ 31 07 26; www.silkrugs.50megs.com) has a showroom at the Registan (Sher Dor Medressa), where you can see carpets being woven. Contact Abdullahad Badghisi.

Silk prices in hotel kiosks are not too much higher than in the bazaar, but the selection is poorer.

Getting There & Away

AIR

Uzbekistan Airways (☎ 34 22 61, 34 10 89; Gagarin 84) flies to Tashkent daily except Friday for US$36. There are also three flights a week to Moscow. The office is reached on bus No 10 outbound on Universiteti near the Hotel

Samarkand; ask for *aerovoksal*. They'll also reconfirm flights at no charge. Check your tickets – mistakes are common.

Tickets can also be purchased at the private agencies **Avia Kassa** (☎ 33 38 35; Ulughbek 21) or **Soft Space** (☎ 350 803; Registan 9/46) near the Registan.

BUS
Tashkent is five hours away by bus across a flat, dry landscape that tsarist Russians nicknamed the Hungry Steppe, now a monotonous stretch of factories and cotton fields. The **bus station** (☎ 32 08 84, 32 09 62) is 1km from the airport. Buy tickets at one of the little booths outside the long-distance bus station. Take bus No 10 from the Hotel Zarafshan or Hotel Samarkand, or marshrutnoe Nos 52, 60 or 31. Public buses run to Tashkent (every thirty minutes until 3pm, four hours, US$2), Termiz (6am, eight hours, US$2.70), Bukhara (7am and 9am, five hours, US$2.50) and Urgench (6pm, 12 hours, US$4.50).

Nowadays, most locals prefer private buses, which keep loose schedules and leave when full. The private bus stop is 350m past the Ulughbek Observatory. There are frequent departures to Tashkent (two hourly), but less to Bukhara.

TAXI & SHARED TAXI
The long-distance taxi stand for Tashkent and Qarshi is just outside the public bus terminal. Expect to pay about US$5 per seat to either destination in a Nexia. A few Tashkent-bound taxis also wait outside the train station.

To Bukhara (US$10 per seat), use the private taxi stand (*pavarot aftostants*), which is near Baigishamal Hotel (reached by Damas marshrutnoe Nos 73, 17 or 27), about 2.5km south of the train station.

For Penjikent or Shakhrisabz, use the Penjikent taxi stand, 250m east of the Registan.

You can charter your own vehicles from any of these taxi stands. Find out the cost to your destination before arriving and bargain hard.

TRAIN
One fast train departs for Tashkent daily at 7am and arrives at noon. Most seats are airplane-seating style and business class

(US$3.50) has tables. But unless you can handle four hours of Russian pop videos and mind-numbing slapstick comedies on a blaring TV, opt for the quieter second class. Going the other way, the train departs Tashkent at 7pm, arriving in Samarkand at midnight. A fast Tashkent–Bukhara train (six hours; US$2.70) passes here daily at 2.45pm and two daily trains stop en route between Tashkent and Termiz.

Buy tickets at the **train station** (☎ 29 15 32, 29 63 72) in the city's northwestern outskirts, reached by Damas marshrutnoe No 73 from Registan or the Hotel Samarkand.

Getting Around
TO/FROM THE AIRPORT
The No 10 bus (and Damas marshrutnoe) goes from the long-distance bus station and the airport to the bazaar and the Samarkand and Zarafshan hotels and the train station, and back, about every 20 minutes. Any marshrutnoe taxi at the airport goes to the Hotel Samarkand. A taxi from the airport to Samarkand will be the equivalent in sum of about US$3, and half that for the return journey.

LOCAL TRANSPORT
Buses and trolleybuses run from about 6am until dusk. Pay cash to the conductor or to the driver when you get off – 75 sum, flat rate to any destination, at the time of research (125 sum for express buses). Marshrutnoe taxis (about 150 sum) disappear by 8pm or 9pm.

TAXI
There are unlicensed and licensed taxis. You should be able to go from the Hotel Samarkand to the Ulughbek Observatory for US$1, or across town for under US$2. Rates jump after 8pm when buses and marshrutnoe taxis start thinning out, and taxis themselves are scarce by 11pm.

AROUND SAMARKAND
Hoja Ismail
In Hoja Ismail, a village 20km north of Samarkand, is one of Islam's holier spots, the modest **Mausoleum of Ismail al-Bukhari** (Uzbek/Tajik: Ismoil Bukhori; AD 810–87). He was one of the greatest Muslim scholars of the Hadith – the collected acts and sayings of the Prophet Mohammed. His

main work is regarded by Sunni Muslims as second only to the Quran as a source of religious law. Following his refusal to give special tutoring to Bukhara's governor and his children, he was forced into exile here.

This place of pilgrimage contains a courtyard, a mosque and a smaller courtyard around the yellow marble tomb. There is also a small museum (US$1) here containing gifts, mostly Qurans, given by leaders of other Muslim countries. This is the place to ask about a guided tour.

It's essential to dress conservatively, respect the calm and reverent atmosphere, and ask before you take photos. Take your shoes off before you step onto any carpet.

GETTING THERE & AWAY

Hoja Ismail village is 4km off the road to Chelek. The best way to get there is by shared taxi (US$0.70), departing at least four times per hour from outside Umar Bank on Dagbitskaya, about 2km north of Registan kuchasi. Marshrutnoe No 11 or bus Nos 10 & 31 pass this taxi stand from the Hotel Samakand. From Umar Bank you could hire your own Tico for US$2 each way, not including waiting time.

SHAKHRISABZ ШАХРИСАБЗ

☎ (3) 75 or 752 / pop 95,000

Shakhrisabz is a small, un-Russified town south of Samarkand, across the hills in the Kashka-Darya province. The town is a pleasant Uzbek backwater and seems to be nothing special – until you start bumping into the ruins dotted around its backstreets, and the megalomaniac ghosts of a wholly different place materialise. This is Timur's hometown, and once upon a time it probably put Samarkand itself in the shade. It's worth a visit just to check out the great man's roots.

Timur was born on 9 April 1336 into the Barlas clan of local aristocrats, at the village of Hoja Ilghar, 13km to the south. Ancient even then, Shakhrisabz (called Kesh at the time) was a kind of family seat. As he rose to power, Timur gave it its present name (Tajik for 'Green Town') and turned it into an extended family monument. Most of its current attractions were built here by Timur (including a tomb intended for himself) or his grandson Ulughbek.

The town was almost destroyed in the 16th century by the emir of Bukhara, Abdullah Khan II, in a quest for the Shaybanid throne. He is said to have been

VISITING PENJIKENT FROM SAMARKAND

Right across the Tajik border, 60km from Samarkand, are the ruins of a major town in one of Central Asia's forgotten civilisations – ancient Penjikent, founded in the 5th century by the Sogdians. Although time has eroded away much of the ruins, their location, in a wide valley at the foot of the Fan Mountains (which offer many trekking possibilities), is superb. For information on the site and on the Fan Mountains, see p334.

It's possible to visit Penjikent as an excursion from Samarkand. At the time of writing, this required a Tajik visa and a double or multiple entry Uzbek visa. Travel agencies in Tashkent, such as Dolores Tour (see p173) say they can organise the visa in 10 days. Alternatively, Samarkand-based tour operators (see p199) can arrange a day trip with their Penjikent contacts, who will bribe the Tajik border guards into letting you across for the day. This arrangement costs US$45 and includes a guide, car/driver, museum entry fees, a Tajik lunch (wine included) and bribe money.

The guide will probably meet you on the Uzbek side where the taxis stop. Border procedures here are easy but don't forget to bring your Uzbek customs declaration form. Fill out the new declaration as if you had all your luggage and money with you (even if you left your belongings in Samarkand). That way the customs declaration will be useful when you leave the country again (or need to change travellers cheques). One bonus of all this is that multiple entry visa holders get a fresh 30-day stamp when they re-enter the country.

The border is 42km from Samarkand and shared taxis go there from Penjikent kuchasi (500m east of the Registan) for US$1 per person. Tell the driver you are headed for the Tajik border (Tajiksii granitsa). From the border it's a further 18km to Penjikent, and there are fewer, if any, taxis on the Tajik side. For more information on Penjikent, see the Tajikistan chapter p334.

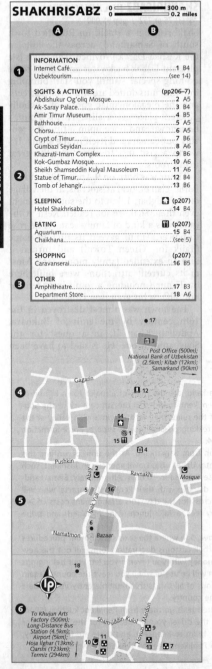

SHAKHRISABZ

0 — 300 m
0 — 0.2 miles

subsequently overcome with remorse for his stupidity.

Orientation

The town's main road is Ipak Yuli, Uzbek for 'Silk Road'. The long-distance bus station and the airport are south of town, about 5km beyond the Kok-Gumbaz Mosque. The train station is 4km northeast of the hotel.

Information

Internet Café (Ipak Yuli 24; 7am-midnight; per hr US$3) Between the Aquarium café and the Hotel Shakhrisabz.
National Bank of Uzbekistan (Firdavsi)
Uzbektourism (Hotel Shakhrisabz, Ipak Yuli 26; 3-hr city tour US$15) The hotel is the local Uzbektourism agent. It has a list of guides who can be promptly summoned for city tours. The fee does not include admission prices to sites.

Sights

AK-SARAY PALACE (WHITE PALACE)

Just north of the centre, **Timur's summer palace** (admission US$1; ☯ 9am-6pm), has as much grandeur per square centimetre as anything in Samarkand. There's actually nothing left of it except bits of the gigantic, 40m-high entrance, covered with gorgeous, filigree-like blue, white and gold mosaics. It was probably Timur's most ambitious project, 24 years in the making, following a successful campaign in Khorezm and the 'import' of many of its finest artisans. It's staggering to try to imagine what the rest of it was like, in size and glory. In what was the palace centre stands a new **statue of Amir Timur**, a favourite place for wedding photos.

KOK-GUMBAZ MOSQUE & DORUT TILYOVAT

This big **Friday mosque** (cnr Ipak Yuli & Jehangir; admission US$2; ☯ 8.30am-6pm) was completed by Ulughbek in 1437 in honour of his father Shah Rukh (who was Timur's son). The name, appropriately, means 'blue dome' and recent renovation has exposed the azure tiles.

Behind it was the original burial complex of Timur's forebears; the sign says Dorut Tilyovat (House of Meditation). On the left as you enter the complex is the **Mausoleum of Sheikh Shamseddin Kulyal**, spiritual tutor to Timur and his father, Amir Taragay (who might also be buried here). The mausoleum was completed by Timur in 1374.

On the right is the **Gumbazi Seyidan** (Dome of the Seyyids), which Ulughbek finished in 1438 as a mausoleum for his own descendants (although it's not clear whether any are buried in it). The furthest tombstone from the door, the Kok Tash (Blue Stone), is believed to contain medicinal properties. Hence the groove on its top caused by centuries of visitors who have poured water into the rock to extract the salts.

KHAZRATI-IMAM COMPLEX
A walkway leads east from Kok-Gumbaz to a few melancholy remnants of a 3500 sq metre mausoleum complex called Dorussiadat or Dorussaodat (Seat of Power and Might), which Timur finished in 1392 and which may have overshadowed even the Ak-Saray Palace. The main survivor is the tall, crumbling **Tomb of Jehangir**, Timur's eldest and favourite son, who died at 22. It's also the resting place for another son, Umar Sheikh (Timur's other sons are with him at Guri Amir in Samarkand).

In an alley behind the mausoleum (and within the perimeter of the long-gone Dorussiadat) is a bunker with a wooden door leading to an underground room, the **Crypt of Timur**. The room, plain except for Quranic quotations on the arches, is nearly filled by a single stone casket. On the casket are biographical inscriptions about Timur, from which it was inferred (when the room was discovered in 1963) that this crypt was intended for him. Inside are two unidentified corpses. The caretaker who lets visitors inside expects a small consideration.

OTHER SIGHTS
Housed inside the renovated Chubin Medressa is the new **Amir Timur Museum** (Ipak Yuli; admission US$0.80; ☾ 9am-5pm), located 100m east of the Hotel Shakhrisabz. It's a simple two-room affair and centred on a huge model of Shakhrisabz in its ancient glory.

In the centre of town is a functioning 17th-century **bathhouse** (women only). Next door is **Abdishukur Og'oliq Mosque**, built in 1914, converted into a chaikhana in the 1980s, and recently reinstated as a mosque.

Sleeping & Eating
Hotel Shakhrisabz (☎ 206 38; Ipak Yuli 26; s/d US$25/44) This hotel, with quiet, clean rooms, is

the only deal in town, so prices are a little higher than they should be. Individual travellers are given short shrift in favour of tour groups and may have a hard time getting any room at all. Be persistent and something will become available. If all else fails, ask about a homestay from the staff of the nearby Aquarium café and adjacent phone office.

Aquarium (☎ 522 39 72; Ipak Yuli 22; ☾ breakfast, lunch & dinner) A courteous staff and friendly owner serve up the usual shashlyk and *laghman* in this two-storey edifice next to the hotel.

The similar **chaikhana** (Ipak Yuli; ☾ breakfast, lunch & dinner) is down the street from the Aquarium in the same building as the women's bathhouse.

In the bazaar you may find women dishing out a wonderful hot soup of noodles, vegetables and yogurt.

Shopping
Across the street from the Abdishukur Og'oliq Mosque is a 16th-century caravanserai, now restored as a shopping complex. Originally it was a medressa. The round, five-domed building in front of the bazaar is a *chorsu* (market arcade), possibly a copy of one here as early as the 15th century.

The local Khujum Arts Factory produces Uzbek dresses, carpets and embroidery. Guides will take you there or to a cap, silk, pottery or wine factory. All but the carpets and wine are easy to find in the bazaar or the department stores.

Getting There & Around
Shakhrisabz is about 90km from Samarkand, and over the 1788m Takhtakaracha (Amankutan) Pass. By car this takes 1½ to two hours. The pass is intermittently closed by snow from January to March, forcing a three-hour detour around the mountains.

Shared taxis go from Penjikent kuchasi in Samarkand for about US$2 per person, although some only as far as Kitab, 12km north of Shakhrisabz, from where there are frequent marshrutnoe Damas connections (US$0.20) to Shakhrisabz. Travel agencies in Samarkand run day trips here for about US$35 per person.

From the long-distance bus station, two buses daily travel to Tashkent (2pm and 5pm, seven hours, US$5). There are shared taxis outside the station bound for Qarshi, Samarkand and Tashkent.

There is a train on Wednesday and Friday from Qarshi to Shakhrisabz, but information on this changes regularly.

Marshrutnoe No 10 runs between the Hotel Shakhrisabz and the bus station.

BUKHARA БУХАРА

☎ (3) 65 or 652 or 6522 / pop 255,000

Central Asia's holiest city, Bukhara (on road signs you'll see the Latinised Uzbek word Buxoro, pronounced Buhoro) has buildings spanning a thousand years of history, and a thoroughly lived-in old centre that probably hasn't changed much in two centuries. It is one of the best places in Central Asia for a glimpse of pre-Russian Turkestan.

Most of the centre is an architectural preserve, full of former medressas, a massive royal fortress, and the remnants of a once-vast market complex. The government is pumping a lot of money into restoration, even redigging several *hauz* (artificial stone pools) filled in by the Soviets. Although the centre has become a bit too clean and quiet ('Ye Olde Bukhara' as one traveller put it), the 21st century has still been kept more or less at bay, and the city's accommodation options go from strength to strength.

Until a century ago Bukhara was watered by a network of canals and some 200 stone pools where people gathered and gossiped, drank and washed. As the water wasn't changed often, Bukhara was famous for plagues; the average 19th-century Bukharan is said to have died by the age of 32. The Bolsheviks modernised the system and drained the pools.

You'll need at least two days to look around. Try to allow time to lose yourself in the old town; it's easy to overdose on the 140-odd protected buildings and miss the whole for its many parts. If you're short on time, at least see Lyabi-Hauz, the covered markets, the Kalon Minaret and Mosque, the mausoleum of Ismail Samani and the unique little Char Minar.

History

It was as capital of the Samanid state in the 9th and 10th centuries that Bukhara – Bukhoro-i-sharif (Noble Bukhara), the 'Pillar of Islam' – blossomed as Central Asia's religious and cultural heart, and simultan-

eously brightened with the Persian love of the arts. Among those nurtured here were the philosopher-scientist Ibn Sina and the poets Firdausi and Rudaki – figures with stature in the Persian Islamic world that, for example, Newton or Shakespeare enjoyed in the West.

After two centuries under the smaller Karakhanid and Karakitay dynasties, Bukhara succumbed in 1220 to Jenghiz Khan, and in 1370 fell under the shadow of Timur's Samarkand.

A second lease of life came in the 16th century when the Uzbek Shaybanids made it the capital of what came to be known as the Bukhara khanate. The centre of Shaybanid Bukhara was a vast marketplace with dozens of specialist bazaars and caravanserais, over one hundred medressas (with 10,000 students) and more than 300 mosques.

Under the Astrakhanid dynasty, the Silk Road's decline slowly pushed Bukhara out of the mainstream. Then in 1753 Mohammed Rahim, the local deputy of a Persian ruler, proclaimed himself emir, founding the Mangit dynasty that was to rule until the Bolsheviks came.

Several depraved rulers filled Rahim's shoes; the worst was probably Nasrullah Khan (also called 'the Butcher' behind his back), who ascended the throne in 1826 by killing off his brothers and 28 other relatives. He made himself a household name in Victorian England after he executed two British officers (see the boxed text opposite).

In 1868, Russian troops under General Kaufman occupied Samarkand (which at the time was within Emir Muzaffar Khan's domains). Soon afterward Bukhara surrendered, and was made a protectorate of the tsar, with the emirs still nominally in charge.

In 1918 a party of emissaries arrived from Tashkent (by then under Bolshevik control) to persuade Emir Alim Khan to surrender peacefully. The wily despot stalled long enough to allow his agents to stir up an anti-Russian mob that slaughtered nearly the whole delegation, and the emir's own army sent a larger Russian detachment packing, back towards Tashkent.

But the humiliated Bolsheviks had their revenge. Following an orchestrated 'uprising' in Charjou (now Turkmenabat) by local revolutionaries calling themselves the

Young Bukharans, and an equally premeditated request for help, Red army troops from Khiva and Tashkent under General Mikhail Frunze stormed the Ark (citadel) and captured Bukhara.

Bukhara won a short 'independence' as the Bukhara People's Republic, but after showing rather too much interest in Pan-Turkism it was absorbed in 1924 into the newly created Uzbek SSR.

Orientation

An oasis in the enveloping Kyzylkum desert, Bukhara sits 250km downstream of Samarkand on the Zeravshan River. The bulk of the modern town lies south of the historical centre. In between old and new, violating the otherwise low skyline, is a knot of tourist hotels and Party buildings.

The heart of the *shakhristan* (old town), is the pool and square called Lyabi-Hauz; the landmark Kalon Minaret is five minutes further, the Ark five more. Further west are Samani Park and the main farmers market (Russian: *bolshoy rynok*).

The long-distance North Bus Terminal is 2km north of the centre (get there by bus or taxi), and the airport is 6km east of the centre. The nearest functioning train station is 15km southeast at Kagan.

Information

BOOKSHOPS

Yog' Du Bookshop (Bakhautdin Naqshband 88) Near the Puppet Theatre; sells picture books and maps of Bukhara and Uzbekistan.

INTERNET ACCESS

Bukhara Information & Culture Centre (BICC; ☎ 224 22 46; Sarrafon 2; per hr US$2; ☹ 9am-6pm) Internet access in the old part of town is limited to this place.

Konica Internet Café (☎ 223 72 28; Mustaqillik 39; per hr US$0.80; ☹ 9am-10pm Mon-Sat, 10am-5pm Sun) This is the best of several Internet cafés located between S Aini and M Ikbola.

INTERNET RESOURCES

www.bukhara.net Extensive website with tourist information, details and local craftsmen and good links.
www.dreambukhara.org Still under construction but includes some details on hotels in the city.

MONEY

Hotel Bukhara (New) (Navoi) Undergoing renovation at the time of research; the exchange desk here will change US dollars.
National Bank of Uzbekistan (☎ 223 69 73; M Ikbola 3; ☹ 9am-4pm Mon-Fri) They change US dollar travellers cheques (American Express preferred), and it's possible to get cash advances on Visa cards.

STODDART & CONOLLY

On 24 June 1842 Colonel Charles Stoddart and Captain Arthur Conolly were marched out from a dungeon cell before a huge crowd in front of the Ark, the emir's fortified citadel, made to dig their own graves and, to the sound of drums and reed pipes from atop the fortress walls, were beheaded.

Colonel Stoddart had arrived three years earlier on a mission to reassure Emir Nasrullah Khan about Britain's invasion of Afghanistan. But his superiors, underestimating the emir's vanity and megalomania, had sent him with no gifts, and with a letter not from Queen Victoria (whom Nasrullah regarded as an equal sovereign), but from the governor-general of India. To compound matters Stoddart violated local protocol by riding, rather than walking, up to the Ark. The piqued Nasrullah had him thrown into jail, where he was to spend much of his time at the bottom of the so-called 'bug pit', in the company of assorted rodents and scaly creatures.

Captain Conolly arrived in 1841 to try to secure Stoddart's release. But the emir, believing him to be part of a British plot with the khans of Khiva and Kokand, tossed Conolly in jail too. After the disastrous British retreat from Kabul, the emir, convinced that Britain was a second-rate power and having received no reply to an earlier letter to Queen Victoria, had both men executed.

Despite public outrage back in England, the British government chose to let the matter drop. Furious friends and relatives raised enough money to send their own emissary, an oddball clergyman named Joseph Wolff, to Bukhara to verify the news. According to Peter Hopkirk in *The Great Game*, Wolff himself only escaped death because the emir thought him hilarious, dressed up in his full clerical regalia.

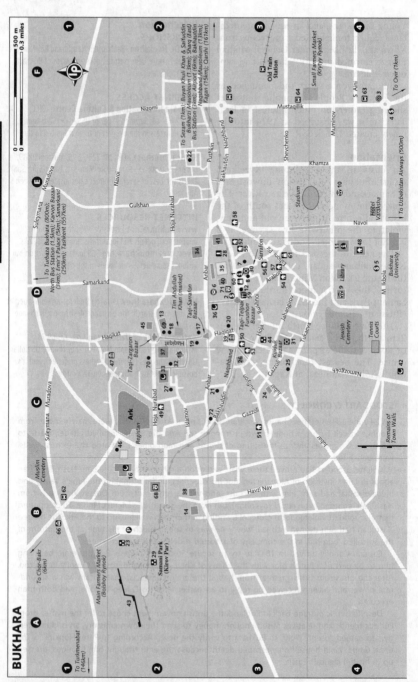

BUKHARA

UZBEKISTAN

0 ————— 500 m
0 ————— 0.3 miles

INFORMATION
Bukhara Information & Culture Centre (BICC)........ 1 D3
Exchange Booth........ 2 D3
Farkhad & Maya........ (see 51)
Konica Internet Café........ 3 F4
National Bank of Uzbekistan........ 4 F4
National Bank........ 5 D4
Post Office........ 6 D3
Salom Inn........ 7 D3
Salom Travel........ 8 D3
Telecom Office........ 9 D4
Telephone & Telegraph Office........ 10 E4
Uzbektourism........ 11 D3
Yog' Du Bookshop........ 12 D3

SIGHTS & ACTIVITIES (pp211-16)
Abdul Aziz Khan Medressa........ 13 D2
Abdullah Khan Medressa........ 14 B2
Amir Alim Khan Medressa........ 15 C2
Bolo-Hauz Mosque & Minaret........ 16 B2
Borzi Kord........ 17 D3
Caravanserai........ 18 D2
Caravanserai........ 19 D2
Caravanserai........ 20 D3
Caravanserai........ 21 D3
Char Minar........ 22 E2
Chashma-Ayub Mausoleum........ 23 B2
City Baths........ 24 C3
Fayzulla Khujayev House (National House)........ 25 C3
Gaukushan Medressa........ 26 C3
Hammon Kunjak........ 27 C2
Hoja Nasruddin Statue........ 28 D3
Ismail Samani Mausoleum........ 29 B2
Jewish Community Centre & Synagogue........ 30 D3
Jewish Synagogue........ 31 D3
Kalon Minaret........ 32 C2
Kalon Mosque........ 33 C2
Kukeldash Medressa........ 34 D2
Lyabi-Hauz........ 35 D3
Maghoki-Attar Mosque........ 36 D3
Miri-Arab Medressa........ 37 C2
Modari Khan Medressa........ 38 B2
Museum of Art........ 39 D3
Nadir Divanbegi Khanaka........ 40 D3
Nadir Divanbegi Medressa........ 41 D3
Namozgokh Mosque........ 42 C4
Town Walls & Talli-Pach Gate........ 43 A2
Turki Jandi Mausoleum........ 44 D3
Ulugbek Medressa........ 45 D2
Water Tower........ 46 C2
Zindon........ 47 C2

SLEEPING (pp216-17)
Bukhara Palace........ 48 D4
Caravan Hotel........ 49 C2
Emir B&B........ 50 D3
Farkhad & Maya's B&B........ 51 C3
Fatima B&B........ 52 D3
Hovli Poyon B&B........ 53 C3
Komil B&B........ 54 D3
Lyabi House........ 55 D3
Mubinjon's Bukhara House........ 56 D3
Nasi Sayoh B&B........ 57 C2
Nodirbek B&B........ (see 1)
Sasha & Son B&B........ 58 E3

EATING (p217)
Sarrafon........ 59 D3

SHOPPING (pp217-18)
Bukhara Artisan Development Centre........ 60 D3
Unesco Carpet Weaving Shop........ 61 D3

TRANSPORT
'Bolshoy Rynok' Bus Stand........ 62 B1
'Gorgaz' Bus Stop........ 63 F4
'Krytby Rynok' Bus Stop........ 64 F3
'Vokzal' Bus Stop........ 65 F3
Air Ticket Agent........ (see 57)
Marshrutnoes to Chor-Bakr........ 66 B1
Train Ticket Booking Office........ 67 F3

OTHER
Ayni Uzbek Theatre of Drama & Musical Comedy........ 68 B2
Blacksmith Workshop........ 69 D2
Bukhara Carpet Workshop........ 70 C2
Old Hotel Bukhara........ (see 11)
Puppet Theatre........ 71 D3
Tajik School........ 72 C3

Taqi-Sarrafon (9am-5pm Mon-Sat) An exchange booth is here.

REGISTRATION
OVIR (222 47 16, 222 47 21; Mustaqillik 22) Located 1km southeast of town; register here if you are not staying in an official hotel.

TELEPHONE & FAX
Telecom office (223 07 71; Muminov 8) International calls for around US$1.50 per minute.

TOURIST INFORMATION
Bukhara Information & Culture Centre (BICC; 224 22 46; bicc@bukhara.net; Sarrafon 2; 9am-6pm) The best and only genuine tourist office in the country, BICC is a useful place that can give tips on everything from accommodation and entertainment to camel trips and desert excursions. They have a list of recommended guides, Internet access and international phone calls for around US$3 per minute.

Uzbektourism (223 10 33; fax 223 57 50; bukhtour@bcc.com.uz; Mominov 8) As Bukhara's private operators continue to steal its thunder, Uzbektourism, located in the Old Bukhara Hotel, plays an ever decreasing role. At best they can rent out a car and driver for US$5 per hour.

TRAVEL AGENCIES
Emir Travel (fax 226 46 00; 224 49 65; www.emirtravel.com; Husainov 13) Gets mixed reviews from travellers; you are best off dealing only with the owner Mila.
Farkhad & Maya (fax 224 59 09; 223 03 26; mfarkhad@bcc.com.uz; Sufiyon 16) Visa support, English-, French- and German-speaking guides, drivers; gets uniformly good reports. It is also a B&B (see p216).
Salom Travel (224 41 48; 224 37 33; fax 224 42 59; www.salomtravel.com; Sarrafon 9) Raisa Gareyeva was one of the first private travel agents and is one of the best; Salom can arrange just about anything from visa support to B&Bs to camel treks near Lake Aidarkul.

Sights & Activities
LYABI-HAUZ
Lyabi-Hauz, a plaza built around a pool in 1620 (the name is Tajik for 'around the pool'), is the most peaceful and interesting spot in town – shaded by mulberry trees as old as the pool. The old tea-sipping, chessboard-clutching Uzbek men who once inhabited this corner of town have been moved on by local entrepreneurs bent on cashing in on the tourist trade. Still, the plaza maintain its old-world style and has managed to fend off the glitz to which Samarkand's Registan has succumbed.

UZBEKISTAN

On the east side is a statue of **Hoja Nasruddin**, a semimythical 'wise fool' who appears in Sufi teaching-tales around the world.

Further east, the **Nadir Divanbegi Medressa** was built as a caravanserai, but the khan thought it was a medressa and it became one in 1622. On the west side of the square, and built at the same time, is the **Nadir Divanbegi Khanaka**. Both are named for Abdul Aziz Khan's treasury minister, who financed them in the 17th century.

North across the street, the **Kukeldash Medressa**, built by Abdullah II, was at the time the biggest Islamic school in Central Asia.

COVERED BAZAARS

From Shaybanid times, the area west and north from Lyabi-hauz was a vast warren of market lanes, arcades and crossroad minibazaars whose multidomed roofs were designed to draw in cool air. Three remaining domed bazaars, heavily renovated in Soviet times, were among dozens of specialised bazaars in the town – Taqi-Sarrafon (money-changers), Taqi-Telpak Furushon (cap makers) and Taqi-Zargaron (jewellers). They have been reborn with touristy souvenir shops, selling identical merchandise of dubious quality at highly negotiable prices. It's

easy to change US dollars here, though they won't give the best rates.

Taqi-Sarrafon Area

Just to the north of the bazaar, in what was the old herb and spice bazaar, is Central Asia's oldest surviving mosque, the **Maghoki-Attar** (pit of the herbalists), a lovely mishmash of 12th-century façade and 16th-century reconstruction. This is probably also the town's holiest spot: under it in the 1930s archaeologists found bits of a 5th-century Zoroastrian temple ruined by the Arabs, and an earlier Buddhist temple. Until the 16th century Bukhara's Jews are said to have used the mosque in the evenings as a synagogue.

Only the top of the mosque was visible when the digging began; the present plaza surrounding it is the 12th-century level of the town. A section of the excavations has been left deliberately exposed inside. Also here is an exhibition of beautiful Bukhara carpets and prayer mats.

Taqi-Telpak Furushon Area

On the north side is a men's bathhouse, the **Borzi Kord**. The late 16th-century covered arcade beyond it is called **Tim Abdullah Khan** (a *tim* was a general market, a kind of proto-department store, which it is again).

Two more caravanserai ruined by the Bolsheviks were on the site of a fountain west of the path, and one for Hindu traders was north of Tim Abdullah Khan.

Taqi-Zargaron Area

A few steps east of the Taqi-Zargaron bazaar, on the north side of Hoja Nurabad, is Central Asia's oldest medressa, and a model for many others – the elegant, blue-tiled **Ulughbek Medressa** (1417), one of three built by Ulughbek (the others are at Gijduvan, 45km away on the road to Samarkand, and in Samarkand's Registan complex).

The **Abdul Aziz Khan Medressa**, opposite, was begun in 1652 by the Astrakhanid ruler of the same name, but was left unfinished when he was booted out by the first of the Mangit emirs. This and the Nadir Divanbegi Medressa, built by his treasury minister, are the only ones in town to flout the Sunni Muslim prohibition against the depiction of living beings (Adul Aziz Khan was a Shiite).

BUKHARA'S JEWS

South of Lyabi-Hauz is what's left of the old town's unique **Jewish quarter**. There have been Jews in Bukhara since perhaps the 12th or 13th century, evolving into a unique, non-Hebrew–speaking branch of the Diaspora. They managed to become major players in Bukharan commerce in spite of deep-rooted, institutionalised discrimination. Since the collapse of the Soviet Union, Jews have dwindled from roughly 7% of the town's population to less than 1%. This is probably a result of both Jews' new freedom to emigrate and others' freedom to act out prejudices.

Down the lane opposite the west end of the pool is a relatively recent **Jewish community centre**, and around the corner a much older **Jewish synagogue**. A century ago there were at least seven synagogues here, reduced after 1920 to two. The second **synagogue** is located south of Kukluk Bazaar.

KALON MINARET & AROUND

When it was built by the Karakhanid ruler Arslan Khan in 1127, the **Kalon Minaret** (admission US$3) was probably the tallest building in Central Asia – *kalon* means 'great' in Tajik. It's an incredible piece of work, 47m tall with 10m-deep foundations (including reeds stacked underneath in an early form of earthquake-proofing), which in 850 years has never needed any but cosmetic repairs. Jenghiz Khan was so dumbfounded by it that he ordered it spared.

Its 14 ornamental bands, all different, include the first use of the glazed blue tiles that were to saturate Central Asia under Timur. Up and down the south and east sides are faintly lighter patches, marking the restoration of damage caused by Frunze's artillery in 1920. Its 105 inner stairs are accessible from the Kalon Mosque.

A legend says that Arslan Khan killed an imam after a quarrel. That night in a dream the imam told him, 'You have killed me; now oblige me by laying my head on a spot where nobody can tread', and the tower was built over his grave.

At the foot of the minaret, on the site of an earlier mosque destroyed by Jenghiz Khan, is the 16th-century congregational **Kalon Mosque** (admission US$0.80), big enough for 10,000 people. Used in Soviet times as a warehouse, it was reopened as a place of worship in 1991. The roof, which looks flat, actually consists of 288 small domes.

Opposite the mosque, its luminous blue domes in sharp contrast to the surrounding brown, is the **Mir-i-Arab Medressa**, a working seminary from the 16th century until 1920, but reopened by Stalin in 1944 in an effort to curry Muslim support for the war effort.

The medressa is named for a 16th-century Naqshbandi sheikh from Yemen who had a strong influence on the Shaybanid ruler Ubaidullah Khan and financed the original complex. Both khan and sheikh are buried beneath the northern dome. The medressa is officially off limits to tourists.

Behind Mir-i-Arab is the small **Amir Alim Khan Medressa**, built in the 20th century, and now used as a children's library.

THE ARK & AROUND

The Ark (Registan Square; admission US$2, guide US$1.50; 9am-6pm), a royal town-within-a-town, is Bukhara's oldest structure, occupied from the 5th century right up until 1920, when it was bombed by the Red army. It's about 70% ruins inside now, except for some remaining royal quarters, now housing several **museums**.

At the top of the entrance ramp is the 17th-century **Juma (Friday) Mosque**, its porch supported by tall columns of sycamore. Inside is a little museum of 19th- and 20th-century manuscripts and writing tools.

Turn right into a corridor with courtyards off both sides. First on the left are the former living quarters of the emir's *kushbegi* (prime minister), now housing an exhibit on archaeological finds around Bukhara.

Second on the left is the oldest surviving part of the Ark, the vast **Reception & Coronation Court**, whose roof fell in during the 1920 bombardment. The last coronation to take place here was Alim Khan's in 1910. The submerged chamber on the right wall was the treasury, and behind the room was the harem.

To the right of the corridor were the open-air royal stables and the *noghorahona* (a room for drums and musical instruments used during public spectacles). Now there are shops and a natural history exhibit.

Around the Salamhona (Protocol Court) at the end of the corridor are what remain of the royal apartments. These apparently fell into such disrepair that the last two emirs preferred full-time residence at the summer palace (see p218). Now there are several museums, including pre-Shaybanid history on the ground floor, and coins and bits of applied art on the top floor.

Most interesting is in between – Bukhara's history from the Shaybanids to the tsars. Displays include items imported to Bukhara, including an enormous samovar made in Tula, Russia. Another room contains the emir's throne. Enhanced colour photographs, donated by the Dutch Embassy in Tashkent, add a spark of life to the otherwise musty exhibits.

Outside in front of the fortress is medieval Bukhara's main square, the **Registan** (meaning 'sandy place'), a favourite venue for executions, including those of the British officers Stoddart and Conolly (see the boxed text on p209).

Behind the Ark is **Zindon** (admission US$1; 9am-4.30pm), the jail, now a museum. Cheerful attractions include a torture chamber and several dungeons, including the gruesome 'bug pit' where Stoddart and Conolly languished in a dark chamber filled with lice, scorpions and other vermin.

Beside a pool opposite the Ark's gate is the **Bolo-Hauz Mosque**, the emirs' official place of worship, built in 1718 and probably very beautiful at the time. The brightly painted porch, supported by 20 columns of walnut, elm and poplar, was added in 1917, as was the stubby minaret nearby. It's now a mosque again. Beside it is a now-disused **water tower**, built by the Russians in 1927 as part of their new water system.

ISMAIL SAMANI MAUSOLEUM & AROUND

This 10th-century **mausoleum** (admission US$0.30), located in Samani Park, is one of the town's oldest monuments and one of the most elegant structures in Central Asia. Built for Ismail Samani (the Samanid dynasty's founder), his father and grandson, its delicate baked terracotta brickwork – which gradually changes 'personality' through the day as the shadows shift – disguises walls almost 2m thick, helping it survive without restoration (except for the dome) for 11 centuries.

Behind the park is one of the few remaining, eroded sections (a total of 2km out of an original 12km) of the Shaybanid **town walls**, and a reconstructed gate called **Talli-Pach**. Another big section is about 500m west of the Hotel Gulistan.

Nearby, at the edge of the main farmers market, is the peculiar **Chashma-Ayub 'mausoleum'** (admission US$0.50; 9am-4.30pm), built in the 12th century over a spring. Its middle domes were added in the 14th century, the front one in the 16th, but no-one was buried in it until even later. The name means 'Spring of Job'; legend says Job struck his staff on the ground here and a spring appeared. Inside you can drink from the spring and check out a little exhibit on the town's ancient waterworks.

TURKI JANDI MAUSOLEUM

Deep in the old town is a tiny mausoleum favoured as a place for getting one's prayers answered. It's the resting place of a holy man known as Turki Jandi, his two sons, several grandsons and numerous other relations. Its importance is signalled by the hundreds of other graves around it – allegedly in stacks 30m deep! The central

chamber is under slow, devoted restoration. The mausoleum is on Namozgokh, about 400m south of Taqi-Telpak Furushon.

CHAR MINAR

This photogenic little building is in a maze of alleys between Pushkin and Hoja Nurabad; everybody in the neighbourhood knows it by name. The gatehouse of a long-gone medressa built in 1807, it bears more relation to Indian styles than to anything Bukharan. The name means 'Four Minarets' in Tajik, although they aren't strictly minarets but simply decorative towers. Unesco restored one collapsed tower and fixed another in 1998. The souvenir hawker that occupies the ground level will let you climb the stairs for US$0.30.

OTHER MEDRESSAS & MOSQUES

West of Taqi-Sarrafon is the **Gaukushan Medressa**, now full of handicraft shops and workshops, and even a table for wine tasting. Across the canal is a little brother of the Kalon minaret.

Southeast of Samani Park are two massive medressas, one named for the great Shaybanid ruler **Abdullah Khan**, and one for his mother called **Modari Khan** (mother of the khan). Another giant is the handsome 16th-century **Namozgokh Mosque**, behind the Hotel Gulistan.

Two kilometres east of the centre is the **Saifuddin Bukharzi Mausoleum**, the last resting place of a revered early 16th-century teacher. Next to it is the delicate little **Buyan Khuli Khan Mausoleum**. Taxi drivers know this place as 'Rayon Fathobod Bogi'.

FAYZULLA KHUJAYEV HOUSE

The **Fayzulla Khujayev House** (National House, Tukaeva; 224 41 88; admission US$2, Russian-speaking guide US$0.80; 9am-5pm Mon-Sat) was once home to one of Bukhara's many infamous personalities, the man who plotted with the Bolsheviks to dump Emir Alim Khan. Fayzulla Khujayev was rewarded with the presidency of the Bukhara People's Republic, chairmanship of the Council of People's Commissars of the Uzbek SSR, and finally liquidation by Stalin.

The house was built in 1891 by his father, Ubaidullah, a wealthy merchant. After the revolution this house served as a Marxist school and then a museum in praise of Khujayev.

BUKHARA WALKING TOUR

As Bukhara's most central location, **Lyabi-Hauz (1)** is the logical place to begin and end a walking tour. Head south from here into the Jewish Quarter, passing the **Jewish Synagogue (2)** on your right. Turn right at Eshoni Pir, passing the new **Unesco Carpet Weaving Shop (3)** and turn right on Tukaeva. **Kukluk Bazaar (4)** on the right contains the city's second Jewish synagogue, a 200-year-old structure that still holds Shabbat services in Tajik. Back on Tukaeva it's a short walk to the **Fayzulla Khujayev House (5)**.

Retrace back to the corner of Tukaeva and Namozgokh and from there it's a five-minute walk north to the **Turki Jandi Mausoleum (6)** and a further three-minute walk to the **Museum of Art (7)**. Turn left and follow the wider Bakhautdin Nagshbard, past the **Gaukushan Medressa (8)**, and along a small canal past a caravanserai, a Tajik school and then the **Registan (9)**.

Pause here to visit **Bolo-Hauz Mosque (10)**, the nearby **Modari Khan (11)** and **Abdulla Khan (12)** medressas and finally the **Ark (13)**. Just around behind the Ark is the **Zindon (14)**, Bukhara's jail, and a short flight of steps leading into a *mahalla* (urban neighbourhood) called **Tagmondbofon (15)**, once known for its production of fabric. A five-minute walk south through the neighbourhood brings you over Hoja Nurabad to the **Kalon Minaret (16)**.

Back on Hoja Nurabad and just across the road from the **Mir-i-Arab Medressa (17)**, which is on your right, is the **Bukhara Carpet Workshop (18)**, where you can see silk carpets woven on large *dukons* (weaving platforms). At the end of this path is the **Taqi-Zargaron Bazaar (19;** jewellery dome). Pause here for a look at the nearby **Ulughbek Medressa (20)** and **Abul Aziz Khan Medressa (21)**.

South from Taqi-Zargaron is **Haqiqat (22)**, where you'll see a blacksmith workshop and Tim Abdullah Khan, a fabric market, on your left. Lastly, you'll come to **Taqi-Telpak Furushon (23)**. It's a short walk from here back to Lyabi-Hauz where lunch awaits.

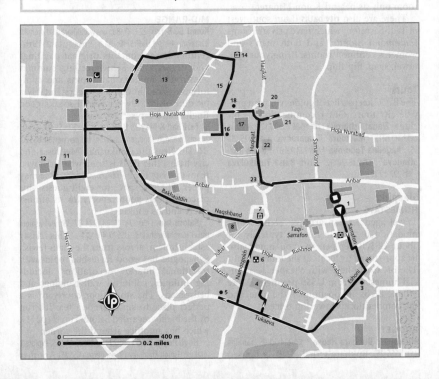

The elegant frescoes, *ghanch*, latticework and Bukhara-style ceiling beams (carved, unpainted elm), have been restored and the curators offer guided tours, special functions and a handicrafts shop. They say 'come any time', but an advance booking is appreciated.

MUSEUM OF ART

The **Museum of Art** (admission US$0.50; ☉ 9am-5pm Thu-Tue) is in the former headquarters of the Russian Central Asian Bank (1912), just west of Taqi-Sarrafon. It has mostly 20th-century paintings by Bukharan artists, and works of artists from other parts of the Soviet Union who now live in Bukhara.

BATHS

The **Borzi Kord** (Taqi-Telpak Furushon; admission US$2, massage US$8; ☉ 6am-7pm Wed-Mon) A men's bathhouse *(erkaklar hammomi)* with lockers where you can leave your clothes.

Hammom Kunjak (Ibodov 4; admission US$3, massage US$3; ☉ 9am-6pm) This women's bathhouse *(ayollar hammomi)*, with common room only, is behind Kalon Minaret.

There are also **city baths** (Jubar) southwest of Taqi-Sarrafon, which have private rooms *(hammomi numur)* and both men's and women's common rooms. Bring your own towel, soap, flip-flops etc.

Tours

The BICC keeps a list of guides who can provide city tours. Our recommendations include: **Zinnat Ashurova** (☎ 99865 190 7127; zinnat@bukhara.net), **Mastoura Khamroeva** (☎ 225 58 95), **Angelina Todorova** (☎ 223 73 67), **Noila Kazidzanova** (☎ 228 20 12) and **Raisa Turakulova** (☎ 222 39 22).

Sleeping

HOMESTAYS

Travel agencies can arrange B&B accommodation in private homes, typically for about US$20 per person. You might also be approached by locals at the tourist spots. The BICC can help with cheaper, less official homestays from US$5 per night. More official B&Bs are opening all the time, and the competition is lowering prices.

BUDGET

Mubinjon's Bukhara House (☎ 224 20 05; Sarrafon 4; r US$5-15) Bukhara's first B&B is housed in a home dating from 1766. Traditional mattresses are spread on the floor and the bathrooms are basic but Mubinjon can direct you to traditional baths. Clever Mubinjon doesn't speak much English but makes himself understood. A downside is the mosquitoes, which are unbearable in summer. The house is about 200m south of Lyabi-Hauz down the lane from the BICC; look for the Olympic symbols painted on the garage door.

Nodirbek B&B (☎ 224 34 46; www.nodirbekhotel.com; Sarrafon 10; US$10 per person) Next door to the BICC, this is a popular hangout for the backpacker set. The rooms here are nothing special but the staff are welcoming and atmosphere congenial.

Fatima (☎ 224 36 16; fax 224 19 83; fatima@intal.uz; Baidukova Nakshbandi 3; s/d US$10/17; ☒) This very popular budget guesthouse commands a key spot next to the Nadir Divanbegi Medressa on Lyabi-Hauz. The welcoming Fatima prepares excellent breakfasts and is well connected to tour operators and guides. Clean carpeted rooms include satellite TV.

MID-RANGE

Komil B&B (☎ 223 87 80; www.bukhara.net/kkomil/; Barakiyon 40; s/d US$15/30; ☐) This intact 19th-century home contains original paintings and decorations, a high ceiling summer guestroom, modern bathrooms and comfortable beds, though it's understandably a bit dim inside. Owner Komil speaks good English and can set up tours.

Farkhad & Maya's B&B (☎ /fax 224 59 09, 223 03 26; mfarkhad@yahoo.com; Sufiyon 16; per person US$20; ☒ ☐) Near the Gaukushan Medressa and city baths, this B&B is somewhat removed from touristy Lyabi-Hauz, which some may prefer. There is space for eight guests; this place also gets good reports for its atmosphere and its cooking.

Salom Inn (☎ 224 41 48, 224 37 33; www.salomtravel.com; Sarrafon 3; US$25/40; ☒) This classy establishment, across from the main Jewish Synagogue, has wood-furnished rooms with traditional interior decorations, including antiques, colourful wall hangings and bedspreads. The stone-floor courtyard is a perfect place to sip afternoon tea. It's run by the highly regarded Salom Travel (p211), which has an office around the corner.

Hovli Poyon B&B (☎ 224 32 39, 224 18 65; explore@intal.uz; Usmon Khodjaev 13; per person US$25) Another

19th-century home, this one was said to be a gift for Emir Ahad Khan. Simple but comfortable rooms of various sizes encircle a large courtyard. The family speaks little English but the facilities represent good value for money.

Nasi Sayoh B&B (☎ 224 12 72; fax 224 26 90; Eshoni Pir 70; s/d US$20/30) Located near the Unesco workshop, this unremarkable home has been spruced up with flamboyant colour schemes (check out the flamingo pink in the downstairs bathroom). The European-style breakfast is one of the best in town.

Lyabi House B&B (☎ 224 84 24, 224 21 77; www .lyabi-house.com; Husainov 7; s/d US$30/40; ⊠) A new annex with spiffy rooms and modern bathroom have been added to this longtime Bukhara favourite. Travellers report that the rooms closer to reception get a bit noisy. The highlight is the venerable *eivan* with carved wooden columns where breakfast is served.

Emir B&B (☎ 224 49 65; www.emirtravel.com; Husainov 13; s/d US$25/40) This is another mid-range option down the same alley as Lyabi-Hauz.

Caravan Hotel (☎ 224 61 44; fax 224 61 54; Hoja Nurabad 6; s/d US$25/40; ⊠) This new hotel, between the Ark and Kalon Mosque, is an airy, welcoming place with tasteful decorations. The roof affords commanding views of Bukhara's ancient skyline.

TOP END

Sasha & Son B&B (☎ 224 49 66; www.sacholga.narod .ru; Eshoni Pir 3; s/d US$35/50; ⊠) This traditional Bukhara-style house is set around a courtyard with fabulously restored decorations and tasteful furnishings. Rooms come equipped with satellite TV and modern bathroom. It's quite easy to find, just south of the traffic circle on Bakhautdin Naqshband.

Bukhara Palace (☎ 223 00 24; fax 223 50 04; Muminov 8; s/d US$40/72; ⊠ ⊠) This hotel is similar to Samarkand's Afrosiab in its chunky Indian-built bulk. The two restaurants are mediocre and the nightclub is rather quiet. Next door, the old Hotel Bukhara was about to undergo renovation at the time of research.

Eating

Sezam (☎ 225 05 77; Bakhautdin Naqshband 153; meals US$2.50; ☾ lunch & dinner; ⊠) Located 1km east of the *vokzal* (station) is this rare theme restaurant. Step into Ali Baba's cave, embellished with stalactites and chests of gold. Customers either rave about the Euro-Uzbek fusion food or they run from it.

Sarrafon (☎ 223 79 19; Arabon 1; meals US$5) Beams of sunlight illuminate this wonderfully restored bathhouse. It's a veritable museum now, with old photos hanging on the walls that depict this site some 70 years ago, and worth a look even if you're not eating here. It is unlikely, actually, that you will be eating here, as it's reserved for tour groups who make prior reservation. If you call ahead they may be able to pull something together.

During the day, dine al fresco at Lyabi-Hauz with grey-beards, local families and other tourists. Tea and pastries appear by 7.30am and shashlyk, *samsas* and *laghman* are dished up until sunset (pay separately for each). Hygiene is not always the best but prices are low and the setting is unmatched.

For vegetarians and other self-caterers there are farmers markets. The main one by Samani Park is known as the Bolshoy rynok; others include the smaller Krytyy rynok, south of the old train station on Mustaqillik, and the Sunday-only Kukluk Bazaar in the old town, south of Lyabi-Hauz.

Entertainment

Bukhara is an eerily silent place by night, although there are at least two entertainment options. The one not to miss is the **fashion show** (admission US$5; ☾ summer 7pm, rest of the year 6pm) where dainty Bukharan women parade in gaudy clothes that mix tradition with the modern. Held in the Nadir Divanbegi Medressa, the entry price includes tea and snacks, though it's worth sticking around after the show for a full dinner (US$3 to US$5). If you've got time, it's also worth seeing a **puppet performance** (☎ 224 2890; admission US$5; ☾ 6pm & 7pm), held at a theatre on the western end of Lyabi-Hauz. The three-part amateur performance, with a traditional wedding ceremony as the usual theme, is held in Tajik, Uzbek and English.

Shopping

Nearly all of the tourist sights sell souvenirs on the side. Some shops to check out are in the Abdul Aziz Khan Medressa, the Maghoki-Attar Mosque and Taqi-Telpak

Furushon. Although certain carpet designs originate here, the best 'Bukhara' rugs are made in Turkmenistan (as they have been ever since those regions were part of the Bukhara khanate). Still, it's worth visiting the **Unesco Carpet Weaving Shop** (☎ 223 66 13; Eshoni Pir 57) to see how they are made. Tours are given in English 9am to 5pm Monday to Saturday.

One place to see the artisans at work is the **Bukhara Artisan Development Centre** (Bakhautdin Naqshband). Housed in a former music school, you can watch artisans at work on a variety of handicrafts including silk-embroidered tapestries, miniature paintings, jewellery boxes and chess sets.

Getting There & Away
AIR
Uzbekistan Airways (☎ 233 50 60; Navoi 15), about 1km southeast of the town centre, has regular flights from Bukhara to Tashkent (1½ hours) twice daily for US$60, and Moscow once a week for US$230. You can also book through the ticket agent based at **Nasi Soyoh B&B** (☎ 224 12 72; Eshoni Pir 70). The **airport** (☎ 225 02 02) is 6km east of town, reached by marshrutnoe No 100 from the *vokzal* roundabout.

BUS
There are several places to get buses out of Bukhara. For Samarkand (6½ hours, US$3), there are five morning buses from the **North Bus Station** (☎ 224 50 21, 224 18 62; Gijduvan 100), located 2km north of town, and three buses from the **Sharq (East) Bus Station** (☎ 225 34 16; Gazli Hwy), 3km east of town. If heading east out of town watch for the unrestored gateway of a 12th-century caravanserai called Rabati-Malik on the north side of the road about 80km out of Bukhara.

Five morning buses depart from the Sharq bus stand to Qarshi (four hours, US$2), some carrying onto Termiz (10 hours, US$5) or Shakhrisabz (six hours, US$3).

A third bus stand serving Urgench is located at the Karvon Bazaar, 1.5 km north of the North Bus Terminal. There is just one bus to Urgench at 10pm, although others originating elsewhere pass here and you might be able to flag one down. Most buses *from* Urgench will dump you here. Make sure your driver knows this or he will shoot right past without stopping.

There are no longer any buses to Turkmenistan. See p239 for information on getting to Turkmenabat.

SHARED TAXI
For Tashkent (US$10), Samarkand (US$6), Qarshi (US$4), Shakhrisabz (US$6) and Termiz (US$13), most shared taxis leave from outside the Sharq Bus Station. Fewer can be found at the North Bus Station. For Urgench/Khiva (US$8), try the crossroads outside Karvon Bazaar.

Taxis leave when full and you'll have more options in the morning. If there is nothing going directly to Samarkand, you can take a car to either Gijduvan (US$1) or Navoi (US$2) and change there.

TRAIN
Every evening at 7.15pm a train goes from Kagan to Samarkand (US$4 in sum in 2nd class, seven hours) and Tashkent (US$9.50 in sum in 2nd class, 12 hours). The 2nd class sleeping cabins hold four bunks. There is a **train ticket office** (☎ 223 75 47) located on Mustaqillik. From Tashkent, a Bukhara bound train departs in summer at 10pm and in winter at 7pm.

Getting Around
The 10-minute taxi trip between the airport and the centre should cost about US$1; how much you'll end up paying depends on your bargaining abilities. Marshrutnoe No 100 or bus No 10 to/from the *vokzal* (near Bukhara's disused train station), Krytyy *rynok* or Gorgaz stops takes 15 to 20 minutes. Marshrutnoe taxi No 56 passes the Bukhara and Varaksha hotels.

To get to Kagan, take the Kagan–Bukhara bus, or a marshrutnoe taxi, from the train station to the *vokzal* stop, or a Bukhara–Kagan bus the other way. Buses leave when full.

Bus No 7 goes from Navoi, near the Bukhara Palace hotel to the long-distance bus station.

AROUND BUKHARA
Emir's Palace
For a look at the kitsch lifestyle of the last emir, Alim Khan, go out to Makhosa – Sitorai Mokhi Hosa, meaning 'Palace of Moon-like Stars' (Moon and Stars) – his summer palace and now a **museum** (admission

US$2.80, guide US$2.30; 9am-5.30pm), 6km north of Bukhara.

The present buildings were a joint effort for Alim Khan by Russian architects (outside) and local artisans (inside). A 50-watt Russian generator provided the first electricity the emirate had ever seen. The palace is a fascinating mix of taste and tastelessness – there's a fine collection of Asian porcelain displayed in a room with heart-shaped windows. Next door is the former harem, and beside a pool where the women frolicked is a wooden pavilion from which – says every tour guide – the emir tossed an apple to his chosen bedmate. The harem has a small **museum** devoted to the traditional silk-on-cotton dowry needlework called *suzani*.

Bus Nos 7 and 21 or marshrutnoe No 70 go from Krytyy *rynok* or the *vokzal* roundabout. Bus No 53 goes from Bolshoy rynok infrequently. The palace is at the end of the line. A taxi costs US$1 one-way, but can be hard to find coming back.

Bakhautdin Naqshband Mausoleum

East of Bukhara in the village of Kasri Orifon is one of Sufism's more important shrines, the birthplace and the tomb of Bakhautdin (or Bakha ud-Din) Naqshband, the 14th-century founder of the most influential of many ancient Sufi orders in Central Asia, and Bukhara's unofficial 'patron saint'. For more on Sufism see p57.

The huge main dome of the complex covers a 16th-century *khanaka*. Beside it is a precariously leaning minaret and a courtyard with two old mosques, lovingly restored since independence. The tomb itself is a simple 2m-high block in the courtyard. Tradition says that it is auspicious to complete three anticlockwise circumambulations of the tomb.

Also here are a small museum and restaurant, and outside the complex are chaikhanas and hostels for pilgrims. The entire village is a place of pilgrimage; in fact, the usual first pilgrim stop is the tomb of Bakhautdin's mother, just north of the complex.

From Bukhara to Kasri Orifon is about 12km. Take an eastbound No 16 bus from the *vokzal* stand or the *bolshoy rynok*, you might have to switch en route to the marshrutnoe No 60. A taxi would be perhaps US$5 for the round-trip plus a wait.

Tourist hotel service bureaus can arrange guided excursions.

Chor-Bakr

Chor-Bakr (admission US$0.75, camera US$0.50; 7.30am-8pm) is a haunting 16th-century necropolis or 'town' of mausoleums, 6km west of Bukhara in a tiny village once called Sumitan. It was built in Shaybanid times, but nobody seems quite sure for whom; the locally preferred story is that it was for Abu-Bakr, devoted friend of the Prophet Mohammed and later first caliph, and his family. Another story is that it was built by and for a local dynasty called the Jubari Sheikhs.

Two massive structures, a Friday mosque on the left and a former *khanaka* on the right, dominate the complex. All around are small mausoleums and simple graves, recently renovated, built later to capitalise on the site's good vibes.

From the Bolshoy rynok, take a bus labelled СВЕР-ДЛОВ БЕКАТИ (Sverdlov region) and ask for Chor-Bakr (about 10 minutes away), from where the complex is easily visible. It's quicker to take a taxi and pay by the kilometre (about US$0.10)

Kagan

This was the original Russian cantonment and train station of new Bukhara, placed far from old Bukhara to humour Emir Abdallahad Khan, who regarded trains as an evil influence. He apparently had a change of heart, and built a spur line (now disused) into the middle of Bukhara.

It's decidedly not worth a special trip, but if you're waiting for a train, have a look at the Tsarist Palace, built for Tsar Nicolai's visit which was ultimately cancelled. The building now holds a small museum on railway history.

See the Bukhara Getting Around section, opposite for how to get to Kagan.

TERMIZ ТЕРМИЗ

(3) 76 or 7622 / pop 132,600 / elevation 380m

Modern-day Termiz bears few traces of its colourful cosmopolitan history. However, set in attractive landscapes on the fringes of town are some ancient monuments and sites attesting to more glorious times. Until recently these sites were off limits to tourists without special permits, but restrictions were lifted in 2003 (despite what your

UZBEKISTAN

embassy might say). As a strategic logistics point for northern Afghanistan, you may encounter a curious mix of aid workers, journalists and soldiers deployed by the UN. German soldiers are particularly noticeable, several hundred of them are here to renovate the airport to use as a supply base for Afghanistan.

Orientation & Information

The main road is Al-Termizi, with the train station at its northern end, about 2km north of the Surkhon Hotel. The bus station is 2km west. The post office and main bazaar, on the corner of Al-Termizi and Navoi, mark the central axis of town.

Internet Café (☎ 756 96; Al-Termizi 28; per hr US$1; ⏰ 8am-10pm) Located in the post office.

National Bank of Uzbekistan (☎ 283 71, 270 94; Al-Termizi 16)

Sights

The **Archaeology Museum** (☎ 758 29, 730 17, 758 75; Al-Termizi 29; admission US$2; ⏰ 9am-6pm), 1km south of the train station, is reason enough to visit Termiz. Unveiled in 2001, the museum is a treasure trove of artefacts collected from the many ravaged civilisations that pepper southern Uzbekistan. The staff can show you a video in English and organise a tour if you call ahead. By stopping here first you will have a better idea of what archaeological sites you might want to visit if your time is limited.

The **Mausoleum of Al-Hakim al-Termizi** is located 11km northwest of Termiz, a couple of kilometres off the main road to Qarshi. The domed-brick building stands in honour of the 9th-century philosopher Sufi Abu Abdullah Mohammed ibn Ali al-Termizi, known locally as Al-Hakkim, the city's patron saint. The mausoleum gets packed to the gills on Wednesday when the faithful are served lunch. Walk around the back and you come face to face with a heavy-duty electric fence, watch tower, the Oxus River and the Afghan border. Be discreet when taking pictures.

Midway between the main road and the mausoleum you'll pass through the remains of **Old Termiz**, levelled by Jenghiz Khan in 1220. Some excavations have been made here and at **Fayoz-Tepe**, another site 2km to the north. Heading back to Termiz, it's worth stopping to see the 16m-high brick

Zurmala Tower, a 3rd-century BC Buddhist stupa, looming in a cotton field opposite Old Termiz.

The **Sultan Saodat Ensemble** is a collection of exquisite mausoleums crafted in brick, some patterned with Timurid design. Built up from the 11th to 15th centuries, it's the last resting place of the then Termizi ruling dynasty, the Sayyids. It's located 10km north of modern Termiz, 3km past **Kokil Dor Memorial** which itself is 2km past the mud-walled Kyr Kyz fortress.

Tours

Oxana Ponyavina (☎ 237 96) Works part time at the Archaeological Museum and can give city tours.

Alisher Choriev (☎ 288 14 or 753 24) A local translator and guide.

Sleeping & Eating

Finding a place to stay in Termiz is wrought with problems as the two main hotels are booked out until at least 2006 by German soldiers based in the city.

Hotel Surkhon (☎ 275 99, 276 97; Al-Termizi 23; per person US$15; 🚻) This dim hotel, parts of which have been renovated, is occupied by German soldiers, but the manager may be able to find an unoccupied room for a negotiable price.

Hotel Tennis Court (☎ 279 33; Al-Termizi 29b; s/d US$6/10) Near Dostlik Park and opposite the Archaeology Museum, this large indoor tennis court lets out some guest rooms. Though nothing exciting, it's a better value than the Surkhon. Don't confuse it with the grotty guestrooms at the adjacent outdoor tennis court.

Analak (☎ 274 19; Navoi 41b; ⏰ lunch & dinner) Uzbek-style food served in a Greco-Roman atmosphere, located behind the bazaar. On Friday and Saturday nights the Surkhon Disco Bar attracts stein-banging German soldiers and working girls after their euros.

Getting There & Around

Uzbekistan Airways (☎ 379 29, 758 97; Kashgari 36) has three flights a day to/from Tashkent (US$60). There are buses to Samarkand (6.20am, US$3.50), Tashkent via Samarkand (4pm and 6pm, US$5) and Qarshi (6.30am, US$3). The **bus station** (☎ 234 29) is reached by marshrutnoe Nos 9 and 6 from the Hotel Surkhon. Shared taxis wait next to the bus station. For the airport, take marshrutnoe No 11 from Yubeleni Bazaar. Marshrutnoe No 4 connects the railway station with the centre of town along Al-Termizi.

For information on getting to Afghanistan and Tajikistan see p238.

KHOREZM ХОРЕЗМ

URGENCH УРГЕНЧ
☎ (3) 62 or 622 or 6222 / pop 140,000

Urgench (Uzbek: Urganch) is a standard-issue Soviet grid of broad streets and empty squares, 450km northwest of Bukhara across the Kyzylkum desert. It's the capital of Khorezm province, wedged between the Amu-Darya and the Turkmenistan border. Urgench is mainly of use to travellers as the transport hub for Khiva, 35km southwest, and somewhere to stay if you can't move right on to Khiva.

When the Amu-Darya changed course in the 16th century, the people of Konye-Urgench (Old Urgench), 150km downriver in present-day Turkmenistan, were left without water and started a new town here. There's virtually nothing to see in modern Urgench, but if there's time to spare after Khiva you might fancy some ruined cities and fortresses in the vicinity, or the Badai-Tugai Nature Reserve 60km north of town (p223).

Orientation & Information
The town's axis is Al-Khorezmi, with the clock tower at its intersection with Al-Beruni marking the centre of things. The train and bus stations are 600m south of the centre down Al-Khorezmi, the airport is 3km north, and most hotels are around the centre.

Bahadir Rakhamov (☎ 352 41 06, 221 12 41) An English-speaking driver offering excursions to Konye-Urgench for US$80, Moynaq for US$100, and Badai-Tugai and the *qalas* (fortresses) for US$50 per carload.

Gulnara Travel Agency (☎ 226 46 58) Arranges excursions and can charter an aircraft to fly over the Aral Sea (max 12 people US$2000).

Hotel Khorezm Palace (☎ 499 99; fax 493 03; Al-Beruni 2) The staff here may be useful for guides and taxi service.

Internet Café (cnr Al-Khorezmi & Al-Beruni; per hr US$3; 🕙 9am-11pm)

National Bank of Uzbekistan (☎ 226 26 44; Pahlavon Mahmud 150) Travellers cheque and credit card advance services.

Post, Telephone & Telegraph Office (Clock tower, cnr Al-Khorezmi & Al-Beruni)

Sleeping & Eating
Hotel Jayhun (☎ 662 49, 662 23; fax 226 08 09; Al-Khorezmi 28; s/d US$18/26) This hotel, 300m south of the clock tower, has bland rooms with private bathroom and satellite TV.

Hotel Khorezm Palace (☎ 499 99; fax 493 03; www .horazm_palace@abv.bg; Al-Beruni 2; s/d/ste US$70/100/ 300; 🔀 🔁) This three-star hotel is the flashest place west of Bukhara and is set up for tour groups on a day trip to Khiva. Tasteful renovation includes blue-painted rooms with TV, fridge and phone (IDD). There's a souvenir shop, restaurant and a murky pool in the central courtyard.

Chaikhana Urgench (☎ 617 73; Al-Khorezmi 35/1; 🕙 breakfast, lunch & dinner) Located between the Hotel Urganch and Al-Khorezmi, this sidewalk café serves a variety of shashlyk, plus good *laghman* and plov.

Getting There & Away
AIR
Uzbekistan Airways (☎ 688 60, 657 69; Al-Khorezmi 1), just north of the clock tower, has two or three flights daily to Tashkent (US$65) and once weekly to Moscow (US$230). Gulnara Travel Agency offers plane or helicopter trips to ancient sites around Urgench or to Moynaq, the former Aral Sea fishing port (see Orientation & Information left).

BUS
The **bus station** (☎ 554 40, 555 61; Al-Khorezmi) is just north of the train station. Scheduled departures include Tashkent (16 hours, daily) via Bukhara and Samarkand; Samarkand (12 hours, twice daily) via Bukhara; Bukhara (seven hours, five daily); and Nukus (two to 2½ hours, twice daily). There are no buses to Dashoguz or any other destination in Turkmenistan.

Some Bukhara-bound buses take a brief, hassle-free detour through Turkmenistan but no Turkmen transit visa are needed for these Urgench–Bukhara buses. Others stick to Uzbekistan and pass no towns between Bukhara and Druzhba, 80km from Urgench.

There are five or six buses daily to Nukus, which is 4½ hours away. Nowadays, most transport goes via Beruni to avoid Turkmenistan.

TAXI & SHARED TAXI

Minivans and taxis leave for Nukus and Bukhara from the bazaar and from in front of the bus station. A seat in a car to Bukhara should cost US$12 to US$15; chartering a Nexia costs around US$60. For Nukus, you may have to change taxis in Beruni.

Shared taxis to Khiva leave from a lot just south of the bazaar, and cost US$0.25. To charter a taxi will cost US$5.

TRAIN

Trains originating in Nukus pass through here Monday and Thursday on their way to Navoi (11 hours, US$9.30) and Tashkent (21 hours, US$12.50). The trains pass here en route to Nukus (US$5.50) at 3am on the same days. The **train station** (☎ 041 97, 620 04) is on the south end of Al-Khorezmi. There are no longer any services to Turkmenistan and the train services that do run through here are fairly unreliable.

Getting Around

Marshrutnoe No 3 runs between the train station and the airport, stopping on Al-Khorezmi near the hotels and bus station en route. Taxis should cost about US$0.10 per kilometre, although local drivers often ask for much more.

AROUND URGENCH

The Amu-Darya delta, stretching from southeast of Urgench to the Aral Sea, has been inhabited for millennia and was an important oasis long before Urgench or even Khiva were important. The historical name of the delta area, which includes parts of modern-day northern Turkmenistan, was Khorezm (see also p431).

The ruins of many Khorezmian towns and forts, some well over 2000 years old, still stand east and north of Urgench. None are major sights, nor have remains at all comparable with Khiva, but they are still fun to explore. Place names in this section are given in Karakalpak, the official language of the region in which they lie.

Biruni (Uzbek: Beruni), formerly Shabbaz, 25km northeast of Urgench, is named for the 10th-century mathematician and encyclopedist Al-Biruni, who spent time here (and some say was born here).

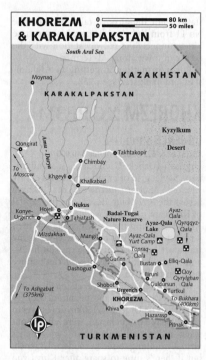

Ruins Around Bustan

The ruins of Topraq-Qala, Ayaz-Qala and Elliq-Qala lie on the fringes of the Kyzylkum desert, requiring a drive of at least 20km past Bustan, which is 50km northeast of Urgench.

Topraq-Qala is one of the most impressive sites, a fort and temple complex of the rulers of the Khorezm borders in the 3rd and 4th centuries, with high walls, three 25m-high round towers and rooms carved out of the rock on a hilltop. It was abandoned in the 6th century after the irrigation system was destroyed. Fragments of sculptures and colourful frescoes found here are kept in the Savitsky Museum in Nukus, and in St Petersburg.

Ayaz-Qala, less than 25km northeast of Topraq-Qala, has an impressive mud-walled hilltop fortress from the 6th and 7th centuries. **Qyrqqyz-Qala** is not far from here. A unique treat in this area is the **Ayaz-Qala Yurt Camp** (☎ 3 61 585 19 98; ayazkala@newmail.ru), set in a prime location in the desert within sight of the cool Ayaz-Qala Lake. The camp offers traditional yurt accommodation, folk dancing, campfires and three meals for US$30 per night per person. Camel trekking costs a bit more. If you don't mind the contrived set-up, it can be fun as a one-off experience.

There are more ruins in the town of **Elliq-Qala** (Fifty Cities), 3km northeast of Bustan. The base of the mud-brick fortresses is being dissolved by the waterlogged earth. Continuing east, reached by very poor roads that drivers are reluctant to take, is **Qoy Qyrylghan Qala**. This circular fort, temple and, it's thought, observatory complex, had two rings of circular walls. Uzbekistan's oldest known inscriptions were found here.

At **Guldursun**, 20km south of Bustan on the road to Turtkul, are the high mud walls of a fortress dating from about the 4th century BC to the 4th century AD.

Badai-Tugai Nature Reserve

This **reserve** (admission US$7) is a strip of *tugai* forest on the east bank of the Amu-Darya, around 60km north of Urgench. In the 1960s and '70s the Soviet cotton-growing schemes cleared out most forest area, and this is one of the few areas preserved. *Tugai* is a very dense, junglelike forest of trees, shrubs and prickly salt-resistant plants and creepers, unique to Central Asia's desert river valleys. Only about a fifth of the Amu-Darya's and Syr-Darya's *tugai* has survived, and sadly, even Badai-Tugai is drying out, illustrated by the abandoned tourist boat rotting in the dust.

Fauna includes the Karakal desert cat, jackals, wild boar, foxes and badgers. Bukhara deer have been introduced and there is an underfunded deer breeding station.

Getting There & Away

A growing number of private tour operators can shuttle tourists around these sites. The tourist office (p226) can arrange day trips, Gulnara Travel Agency in Urgench also runs tours to these sites.

If you go without a guide, the best bet is a taxi, as bus services to these places are rare or nonexistent. A taxi should cost about US$50 for a day's tour of Badai-Tugai and two or three of the ruined qalas. Make sure your driver knows where these sites are!

KHIVA (ICHON-QALA) ХИВА

☎ (3) 62 or 623 or 6237 / pop 50,000

Khiva's name, redolent of slave caravans, barbaric cruelty and terrible journeys across deserts and steppes infested with wild tribesmen, struck fear into all but the boldest 19th-century hearts. Nowadays it's a mere 35km southwest of Urgench, past cotton bushes and fruit trees.

Khiva (Uzbek: Hiva) is an odd place. Its historic heart, unlike those of other Central Asian cities, is preserved in its entirety – but so well preserved that the life has almost been squeezed out of it. As a result of a Soviet conservation programme in the 1970s and '80s, it's now a squeaky-clean official 'city-museum'. Even among its densely packed mosques, tombs, palaces, alleys and at least 16 medressas, you need imagination to get a sense of its mystique, bustle and squalor. However, streets just a block or two away but still within the walled inner city, the Ichon-Qala, remain lived-in and fairly dishevelled.

A few of the historic buildings in Ichon-Qala are functioning mosques or shrines, but most are museums. You can see it all in a day trip from Urgench, but you'll take it in better by staying longer. Morning and evening are the best times to explore, and there are several decent places to stay. Khiva is at its best by night when the moonlit silhouettes of the tilting columns and medressas, viewed from twisting alleyways, work their magic.

History

Agriculture and human settlement go back four, perhaps six, millennia in Khorezm, the large, fertile Amu-Darya river delta isolated in the midst of broad deserts. So Khiva, on the southern fringe of the delta, may be very old but its exact age is not known. Legend has that it was founded when Shem, son of Noah, discovered a well here; his people called it Kheivak, from which the name Khiva is said to be derived. The original well is in the courtyard of Abdullah a-Baltal 50, in the northwest of the old town.

Khiva certainly existed by the 8th century as a minor fort and trading post on the Silk Road, but while Khorezm prospered on and off from the 10th to the 14th centuries, its capital was at old Urgench (present-day Konye-Urgench in Turkmenistan), and Khiva remained a bit player. See p431 for more on old Khorezm.

THE KHANATE

It wasn't until well after Konye-Urgench had been finished off by Timur that Khiva's

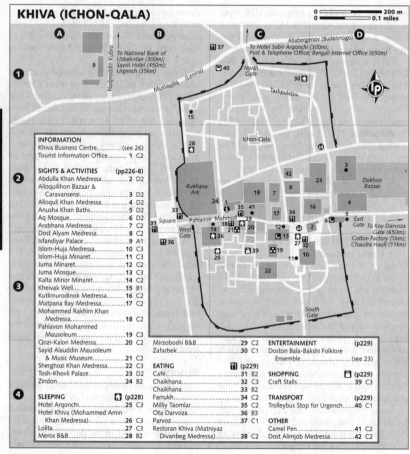

KHIVA (ICHON-QALA)

0 —— 200 m
0 —— 0.1 miles

INFORMATION
Khiva Business Centre..............(see 26)
Tourist Information Office.............. 1 C2

SIGHTS & ACTIVITIES   (pp226-8)
Abdulla Khan Medressa.............. 2 D2
Alloqulihon Bazaar &
    Caravanserai.......................... 3 D2
Alloquli Khan Medressa.............. 4 D2
Anusha Khan Baths..................... 5 D2
Aq Mosque................................... 6 D2
Arabhana Medressa...................... 7 C2
Dost Alyam Medressa.................. 8 C2
Isfandiyar Palace......................... 9 A1
Islom-Huja Medressa.................. 10 C3
Islom-Huja Minaret..................... 11 C3
Juma Minaret............................... 12 C2
Juma Mosque............................... 13 C2
Kalta Minor Minaret..................... 14 C2
Kheivak Well................................ 15 B1
Kutlimurodinok Medressa........... 16 C2
Matpana Bay Medressa................ 17 C2
Mohammed Rakhim Khan
    Medressa.............................. 18 C2
Pahlavon Mohammed
    Mausoleum............................ 19 C3
Qozi-Kalon Medressa................... 20 C2
Sayid Alauddin Mausoleum
    & Music Museum.................... 21 C2
Sherghozi Khan Medressa........... 22 C3
Tosh-Khovli Palace...................... 23 D2
Zindon... 24 B2

SLEEPING   (p228)
Hotel Arqonchi............................ 25 C3
Hotel Khiva (Mohammed Amin
    Khan Medressa)..................... 26 C3
Lolita... 27 C3
Meros B&B................................... 28 B2

Mirzoboshi B&B............................ 29 C2
Zafarbek...................................... 30 C1

EATING   (p229)
Café... 31 B2
Chaikhana.................................... 32 C3
Chaikhana.................................... 33 B2
Farrukh.. 34 C2
Milliy Taomlar.............................. 35 C2
Ota Darvoza................................. 36 B3
Parvoz.. 37 C1
Restoran Khiva (Matniyaz
    Divanbeg Medressa).............. 38 C2

ENTERTAINMENT   (p229)
Doston Bala-Bakshi Folklore
    Ensemble.............................(see 23)

SHOPPING   (p229)
Craft Stalls................................... 39 C3

TRANSPORT   (p229)
Trolleybus Stop for Urgench...... 40 C1

OTHER
Camel Pen.................................... 41 C2
Dost Alimjob Medressa............... 42 C2

time came. When the Uzbek Shaybanids moved into the decaying Timurid empire in the early 16th century, one branch founded a state in Khorezm and made Khiva their capital in 1592.

The town ran a busy slave market that was to shape the destiny of the khanate, as the Khiva state was known, for more than three centuries. Most slaves were brought by Turkmen tribesmen from the Karakum Desert or Kazakh tribes of the steppes, who raided those unlucky enough to live or travel nearby. To keep both of these away from its own door, Khiva eventually resorted to an alliance with the Turkmen against the Kazakhs, granting them land and money in return.

RUSSIAN INTEREST AWAKENS

Khiva had earlier offered to submit to Peter the Great of Russia in return for help against marauding tribes. In a belated response, a force of about 4000 led by Prince Alexandr Bekovich, arrived in Khiva in 1717.

Unfortunately, the khan had by that time lost interest in being a vassal of the tsar. He came out to meet them, suggesting they disperse to outlying villages where they could be more comfortably accommodated. This done, the Khivans annihilated the invaders, leaving just a handful to make their way back with the news. The khan sent Bekovich's head to his Central Asian rival, the emir of Bukhara, and kept the rest of him on display.

In 1740 Khiva was wrecked by a less gullible invader, Nadir Shah of Persia, and Khorezm became for a while a northern outpost of the Persian empire. By the end of the 18th century it was rebuilt and began taking a small share in the growing trade between Russia and the Bukhara and Kokand khanates. Its slave market, the biggest in Central Asia, continued unabated, augmented by Russians captured as they pushed their borders southwards and eastwards.

See p164 for details on Khiva's role in The Great Game.

RUSSIAN CONQUEST

When the Russians finally sent a properly organised expedition against Khiva, it was no contest. In 1873 General Konstantin Kaufman's 13,000-strong forces advanced on Khiva from the north, west and east. After some initial guerrilla resistance, mainly by Yomud Turkmen tribesmen, Khan Mohammed Rakhim II surrendered unconditionally. Kaufman then indulged in a massacre of the Yomud. The khan became a vassal of the tsar and his silver throne was packed off to Russia.

The enfeebled khanate of Khiva struggled on until 1920 when the Bolshevik general Mikhail Frunze installed the Khorezm People's Republic in its place. This, like a similar republic in Bukhara, was theoretically independent of the USSR. But its leaders swung away from socialism towards Pan-Turkism, and in 1924 their republic was absorbed into the new Uzbek Soviet Socialist Republic.

Orientation

The old city, the Ichon-Qala, still surrounded by its centuries-old walls, is in the southern part of a much bigger Soviet town. Transport from Urgench will probably take you straight to the North Gate. Most sights are around its main axis, Pahlavon Mahmud, running between the West and East gates. Banking and postal facilities are in the new town, about 650m north of the North Gate.

LIFE & DEATH UNDER THE KHANS

Richmond Shakespear, who rescued Khiva's Russian slaves in 1840, left behind far more slaves than he freed, mainly Persians and Kurds. The Russian envoy Captain Nikolai Muraviev, who had travelled here in 1819, estimated there were 30,000 of these, against 3000 Russians. Shakespear noted that nearly all the Russians were in good health, an able Russian male slave being worth four good camels.

The khans ruled Khiva by terror, with torture and summary execution. The Hungarian traveller Arminius Vambéry in 1863 saw eight old men lying on the ground having their eyes gouged out, their tormentor wiping his knife clean on their beards as he proceeded. Muraviev reported that impalement was a favourite method of execution, with victims taking up to two days to die (you can see pictures of other methods in the Zindon jail at the city's Kukhna Ark). He also noted that people caught smoking or drinking alcohol, which the khan of the day had forsworn, had their mouths slit open to their ears, leaving them with a permanent silly grin.

The khans extorted huge taxes from their people thanks to their ownership of the state's entire irrigation system. Nevertheless, Muraviev observed that the villages outside the city were prosperous. His visit came at a time when trade through Khiva was on an upswing, engendering a boom in fine buildings and decorative arts such as carving, painting and tilework.

The number of medressas in Khiva is testament to its past importance as a centre of Muslim theology. But the khans resolutely opposed modernisation and secular education, and even after the Russian annexation, Khan Mohammed Rakhim II refused to allow electricity, schools or telephones. The clergy were a conservative lot who later engineered the murder of the modernising grand vizier, Islom Huja.

Khiva's renown and infamy, far out of proportion to its real significance, were a product of its remoteness, the extreme cruelty and backwardness of its regime, and the very real dangers to outsiders who ventured there: if they survived the surrounding deserts and their marauding clansmen, their lives were subject to the khans' caprice when they finally arrived.

UZBEKISTAN

MAPS

A map called *The Best Guide of Khiva* (US$2), sold at the tourist information office near the West Gate, includes inset maps of Khiva, Ichon-Qala and the Khorezm region.

Information

Begali Internet Café (☎ 375 90 00; Amir Timur 23; per hr US$2.50; ☼ 7am-9pm Mon-Sat, 3-8pm Sun) Located in front of the post office, 650m north of the city. Internet services also available at the tourist information office and Hotel Khiva.

Khiva Business Centre (☎ 375 47 13, 376 24 33; fax 375 49 45; Hotel Khiva, Pahlavon Mahmud 1) Internet, fax and money exchange services. The helpful manager Jahongir Khusainov can provide travel information.

National Bank of Uzbekistan (☎ 375 75 42; Nadjmiddin Kubro 11; ☼ 9am-6pm) Located 300m north of the city; changes cash only.

Post & Telephone Office (☎ 374 22 22; Amir Timur 23) Located 650m north of the North Gate.

Tourist Information Office (☎ 375 79 18, 375 24 55; bccxor@bcc.com.uz; ☼ 9am-7pm) Helpful, quasi-independent tourist office opposite the Kalta Minor Minaret. Guides and tours of the city and region arranged and it has pamphlets describing Khiva accommodation. Khojamuratova Gulimkhan (☎ 375 40 76, 221 40 76) is a local guide.

Sights

ICHON-QALA GATES & WALLS

The main entrance to the **Ichon-Qala** (2-day admission US$5, camera US$1.20, video US$1.70; ☼ 9am-6pm) is the twin-turreted brick West Gate (Ota-Darvoza, literally 'Father Gate'), a 1970s reconstruction – the original was wrecked in 1920. Some attractions inside the walls are free although most require additional tickets costing between US$0.50 and US$1.

The picturesque 2.5km-long mud walls date from the 18th century, rebuilt after being destroyed by the Persians. The walls also have North, East and South gates, respectively Buhoro-darvoza (Bukhara Gate), Polvon-darvoza (Strongman's Gate) and Tosh-darvoza (Stone Gate), as well as about forty bastions.

The first building on your right inside the West Gate is the **Mohammed Amin Khan Medressa**, built in the 1850s and serving since Soviet times as the Hotel Khiva (see p228). It's a nice enough building, with two storeys of cells around a broad courtyard,

and certainly an exotic setting to lay your head, but it's not one of Khiva's major architectural highlights.

Outside stands the fat, turquoise-tiled **Kalta Minor Minaret**, built at the same time.

KUKHNA ARK

Opposite Mohammed Amin Khan stands the Kukhna Ark – the Khiva rulers' own fortress and residence, first built in the 12th century by one Oq Shihbobo, then expanded by the khans in the 17th century. The khans' harem, mint, stables, arsenal, barracks, mosque and jail were all here.

The squat protuberance by the entrance, on the east side of the building, is the **Zindon** (Khans' Jail), with a display of chains, manacles and weapons, and pictures of people being chucked off minarets, stuffed into sacks full of wild cats etc.

Inside the Ark, the first passage to the right takes you into the 19th-century **Summer Mosque**, open-air and beautiful with superb blue-and-white plant-motif tiling and a red, orange and gold roof. Beside it is the old **mint**, now a museum that exhibits things such as money printed on silk.

Straight ahead from the Ark entrance is another restored building that some say was the harem, but which its present guardians maintain was the **throne room**, where khans dispensed judgement (if not justice). The circular area on the ground was for the royal yurt, which the no-longer-nomadic khans still liked to use.

To the right of the throne room, a door in the wall leads to a flight of steps up to the **Oq Shihbobo bastion**, the original part of the Kukhna Ark, set right against the Ichon-Qala's massive west wall. At the top is an open-air pavilion with good views over the Ark and Ichon-Qala.

MOHAMMED RAKHIM KHAN MEDRESSA

Facing the Kukhna Ark, across an open space that was once a busy palace square (and place of execution), this 19th-century medressa (Mukhammad Rakhimhon madrasasi) is named after Khan Mohammed Rakhim II. A hotchpotch of a museum within is partly dedicated to this khan, who surrendered to Russia in 1873 but had, after all, kept Khiva independent a few years longer than Bukhara. The khan was also a poet under the pen name Feruz.

Khiva's token camel, named Misha, stands burping and farting outside the medressa's south wall, waiting for tourists to ride it or pose with it.

SAYID ALAUDDIN MAUSOLEUM & MUSIC MUSEUM

Back on the south side of Pahlavon Mahmud, beside the medressa housing Restoran Khiva, is the small, plain Sayid Alauddin Mausoleum, dating to 1310 when Khiva was under the Golden Horde of the Mongol empire. You might find people praying in front of the 19th-century tiled sarcophagus. To the east is a **Music Museum** in the 1905 Qozi-Kalon Medressa.

JUMA MOSQUE & AROUND

East of the Music Museum, the large Juma Mosque is interesting for the 218 wooden columns supporting its roof – a concept thought to be derived from ancient Arabian mosques. The few finely decorated columns are from the original 10th-century mosque, though the present building dates from the 18th century. From inside, you can climb the 81 very dark steps of the Juma Minaret.

Opposite the Juma Mosque is the 1905 **Matpana Bay Medressa** (Abdullahon madrasasi), containing a museum devoted to nature, history, religion and the medressa itself. Behind this are the 17th-century **Arabhana Medressa** and the 19th-century **Dost Alyam Medressa**.

East of the Juma mosque, the 1855 **Abdulla Khan Medressa** holds a tiny nature museum. The little **Aq Mosque** dates from 1657, the same year as the **Anusha Khan Baths** (Anushahon hammomi) by the entrance to the long tunnel of the East Gate.

ALLOQULI KHAN MEDRESSA, BAZAAR & CARAVANSERAI

The street leading north opposite the Aq Mosque contains some of Khiva's most interesting buildings, most of them created by Khan Alloquli in the 1830s and '40s. First come the tall **Alloquli Khan Medressa** (1835) and the earlier **Kutlimurodinok Medressa** (1809), facing each other across the street, with matching tiled façades. Down a few steps under a small dome in the Kutlimurodinok's courtyard is an old drinking-water tank (don't try the water!).

North of the Alloquli Khan Medressa are the **Alloqulihon Bazaar and Caravanserai** (Alloquli Khan Saroy-bozori va Karvonsaroyi). The entrance to both is through tall wooden gates beside the medressa. The bazaar is a domed market arcade, still catering to traders, which opens onto Khiva's modern **Dekhon Bazaar** at its east end. Today the caravanserai houses Khiva's department store.

TOSH-KHOVLI PALACE

Tosh-Khovli (Stone House), facing the caravanserai, contains Khiva's most sumptuous interior decoration, including ceramic tiles, carved stone and wood, and *ghanch*. Built by Alloquli Khan between 1832 and 1841 as a more splendid alternative to the Kukhna Ark, it's said to have over 150 rooms off nine courtyards, with high ceilings designed to catch any breeze. Alloquli was a man in a hurry – the Tosh-Khovli's first architect was executed for failing to complete the job in two years.

EAST GATE & MODERN BAZAAR

The East Gate is a long, vaulted 19th-century passage with several sets of immense carved doors. The slave market was held around here, and niches in the passage walls once held slaves for sale. Outside are a small working mosque and the long modern bazaar (mostly food) on the left.

ISLOM-HUJA MEDRESSA

From the East Gate, go back to the Abdulla Khan Medressa and take the lane to the south beside it, to the Islom-Huja Medressa and minaret – Khiva's newest Islamic monuments, both built in 1910. The **minaret**, with bands of turquoise and red tiling, looks rather like an uncommonly lovely lighthouse. At 45m tall, it's Khiva's highest. You can climb its 118 steps for fine views across the Karakum desert.

The medressa holds Khiva's best museum, exhibiting Khorezm handicrafts through the ages – fine woodcarving, metalwork, jewellery, Uzbek and Turkmen carpets, stone carved with Arabic script (which was in use in Khorezm from the 8th to the 20th centuries), and large pots called *hum* for storing food underground.

Islom Huja himself was an early 20th-century grand vizier and a liberal (by

Khivan standards): he founded a European-style school, brought long-distance telegraph to the city, and built a hospital. For his popularity, the khan and clergy had him assassinated.

PAHLAVON MOHAMMED MAUSOLEUM & SHERGHOZI KHAN MEDRESSA

Along the street west from the Islom-Huja Minaret, this is Khiva's most revered mausoleum and, with its lovely courtyard and stately tilework, one of the town's most beautiful spots. Pahlavon Mohammed was a poet, philosopher and legendary wrestler who became Khiva's patron saint. His 1326 tomb was rebuilt in the 19th century and then requisitioned in 1913 by the khan of the day as the family mausoleum.

The beautiful Persian-style chamber under the turquoise dome at the north end of the courtyard holds the tomb of Khan Mohammed Rakhim II who ruled from 1865 to 1910. Leave your shoes at the entrance. Pahlavon Mohammed's tomb, to the left off the first chamber, has some of Khiva's loveliest tiling on the sarcophagus and the walls. Pilgrims press coins and notes through the grille that shields the tomb. Tombs of other khans stand unmarked east and west of the main building, outside the courtyard.

DISHON-QALA

The Dishon-Qala was old Khiva's outer town, outside the Ichon-Qala walls. Most of it is buried beneath the modern town now, but part of the Dishon-Qala's own wall remains, 300m south of the South Gate. One or two Dishon-Qala gates survive too.

The **Isfandiyar Palace** on Mustaqillik was built between 1906 and 1912, and like the Summer Palace in Bukhara displays some fascinatingly overdone decorations in a messy collision of East and West. The rooms are largely bare but the florid painted ceilings and garish tiled fireplaces hint at what it must have been like.

Surrounded by a low mud wall, 11km east of central Khiva, **Chaudra Hauli** was the summer residence of a 19th-century Khivan nobleman. You can climb up the slender four-storey tower for views of the surrounding flatness and then enjoy a drink at the little café nearby.

Sleeping
BUDGET

Mirzoboshi B&B (☎ 37 27 53; Pahlavon Mahmud 1; dm with shared bathroom US$10) This venerable house is located next to the Qozi-Kalon Medressa on the main path through the old town; the entrance is at the back. The friendly owner seems happy to accommodate budget travellers; it's possible to roll out a mattress and sleeping bag on the floor of the *eivan* over the courtyard, which has a magical view of the Juma Minaret.

Meros B&B (☎ 375 76 42; Abdulla Baltaev 57; per person US$10) A newer, quieter place, just north of the Ark, in an unsigned home.

Zafarbek (☎ 375 71 85; fax 375 60 38; Tashpulatov 28; r with private bathroom US$10-20; 🍴 💻) This family-run operation in the northeastern corner of the fortress can accommodate backpackers and mid-range travellers. The rooms in the old home are cosier than the new concrete annex. Prices depend heavily on your bargaining power.

MID-RANGE

Hotel Arqonchi (☎ 375 22 30; fax 375 29 74; simurg -travel@sarkor.uz; Pahlavon Mahmud 10; per person US$25; 🍴) This rambling old lodge, located behind the Hotel Khiva, has spacious rooms, all a little off-kilter and tackily furnished. Service, travellers report, is not their strong point.

Sayot (☎ 375 64 44, 375 85 55; Nadjmidden Kubro 23; s/d US$15/25; 🍴) This well-managed place with spacious, modern rooms is a five-minute walk northwest of Ichon-Qala, 150m past the bank.

Lolita (☎ 375 77 87, 375 76 10; fax 375 77 87; Islom Khodja 11; per person US$20; 🍴) Comfortable, well-kept rooms around a courtyard make for a nice interior, though it's a wonder that Khiva's city planners allowed this ugly brick box to be constructed in the heart of a protected old town, next to a cemetery no less.

Hotel Khiva (☎ 375 49 45, 375 41 08; fax 375 49 42; Pahlavon Mahmud 1; per person US$26; 🍴 💻) This hotel is in fact the 19th-century Mohammed Amin Khan Medressa, tucked just inside the West Gate. The clean and recently renovated rooms, being former *hujra* study cells, are a bit cramped, which is supposed to be part of the fun. The café-cum-bar in the cupola is worth a visit even if you aren't staying here.

Eating

The choices are limited, frankly. Other than breakfast at your hotel, the options are a sprinkling of chaikhanas along Pahlavon Mahmud, or just off it, and a couple of cafés and restaurants.

CAFÉS & CHAIKHANAS

The best chaikhana is **Farrukh** (☎ 375 35 12; Pahlavon Mahmud; meals US$4) near Juma Masjid where national food is served inside colourfully decorated yurts. **Milliy Taomlar** (☎ 375 30 26; Pahlavon Mahmud; meals US$3) has good soups and an artist's view of Kalta Minor. For shashlyk, try the chaikhana near Lolita hotel.

Just outside the West Gate is a small chaikhana on your right. There are also two cheaper cafés. The larger one on the left, **Ota Darvoza** (☎ 375 82 04; A. Kariy), serves national dishes for US$2 a plate. At the time of writing a café was being set up at Chaudra Hauli, east of the city (see Dishon-Qala, opposite).

RESTAURANTS

Some hotels allow nonguests to eat in their restaurants.

Restoran Khiva (Pahlavon Mahmud) This is probably the pick of the bunch. Its dining hall is next to the hotel in the spacious Matniyaz Divanbeg Medressa, although food availability usually depends on group reservations. You could also try the Hotel Arqonchi (see opposite).

Parvoz (☎ 375 73 43; Mustaqillik 5; ⏰ 9am-11pm) This upscale chaikhana, overlooking a *hauz* (pool), serves filling meals of chuchvara (dumplings) or beefsteak and salads along with ice cream and fruit for dessert. It's opposite the trolleybus stop.

Entertainment

The Doston Bala-Bakshi Folklore Ensemble performs at Tosh-Khovli Palace at least five times a day. The 30-minute show costs US$2 per person or US$3 with tea.

Shopping

Souvenir and craft shops are wedged into many of the Ichon-Qala attractions, notably the Kutlimurodinok Medressa. The bulk of the craft stalls are located in the alley that runs west from Islom-Huja Minaret, and behind the Qozi-Kalon Medressa. Look out for the Khiva Silk Carpet Workshop,

sponsored by Unesco, where you can watch the process of silk dying and weaving.

Getting There & Away

The easiest way to travel between Urgench and Khiva is the 45-minute trip by marshrutnoe taxi or taxi. Marshrutnoes shuttle between the street outside Urgench's bus station and the North Gate 8am to 8pm, leaving when they're full (US$0.25 or more, depending on the driver). Trolleybuses to Urgench from the North Gate are slow and terminate inconveniently short of Urgench, delivering you into the hands of waiting taxis.

To hire a taxi will cost US$5. In Khiva you'll find them outside the West, East or North gates.

Private buses to Tashkent (US$10) depart from Koy Darvoza Gate, east of the city, and outside the Cotton Factory (300m north of Koy Darvoza on Amir Timur). The buses, which pass Bukhara, leave sometime between noon and 2pm (whenever the last seat is sold). Unless you are hiring your own taxi from Khiva, most transportation options are available from Urgench (see p221).

KARAKALPAKSTAN & THE ARAL SEA
КАРАКАЛПАКСТАН И АРАЛЬСКОЕ МОРЕ

NUKUS НУКУС

☎ (3) 61 or 612 or 6122 / pop 180,000

The isolated capital of Uzbekistan's Karakalpakstan Republic lies 166 km northwest of Urgench, well beyond the reach of most tourist buses. Nukus (Karakalpak: Nökis), a quiet city of tree-lined avenues and nondescript Soviet architecture, is the gateway for the fast-disappearing Aral Sea and home to a remarkable art museum that for some travellers is worth the hardship of getting here.

Factoring into the economy during Soviet times was a Chemical Research Institute, where scientists spent their spare time tinkering with biological weapons. The site was abandoned and it's now being cleaned up with US help. Having lost the pillar of its economy – and suffering from regular crop

UZBEKISTAN

failures and an unhealthy population – Nukus limps along with subsidies from Tashkent.

Orientation

The main central streets (Karakalpak: *köshesi*) are Karakalpakstan and Gharezsizlik, both ending east at a square surrounded by government buildings. The airport is 6km north of the centre on Dosnazarov, the train station about 3km from the centre at Dosnazarov's south end, and the long-distance bus station is 6km south of the centre on Berdakha. Arriving from Beruni by shared taxi, many drivers dump their passengers near the bazaar.

Information

Naitov Nukus (☎ 224 00 83; Amir Timur 129; ☽ 9.30am-6.30pm Mon-Fri) Internet café located inside the green-and-blue painted 'Mincom House'.

National Bank of Uzbekistan (☎ 222 23 53; Garezsizlik 52) Located on the north end of the central square, the bank changes both American Express and Visa cheques, and you don't need to show your customs declaration.

Post & Telephone Office (☎ 222 79 30; Karakalpakstan 7; ☽ 7am-7pm)

Union for the Defense of the Aral Sea & Amu Darya River (UDASA; ☎ 217 72 29, 224 06 16; www.udasa.org; Academy of Sciences, fl 8, Berbakha 41) The helpful staff will describe the current Aral situation, and may have tips for getting to and around Moynaq.

Sights

SAVITSKY KARAKALPAKSTAN ART MUSEUM

The **Savitsky Museum** (☎ 222 25 56; Doslyk 127; admission US$4, guide US$3, camera US$1.50; ☽ 9am-5pm Mon-Fri, 10-4pm Sat) opened in 2002 in a new, marble-fronted building on the north part of town, and houses one of the most remarkable art collections in the former Soviet Union. Some 85,000 pieces of art, only a fraction of which are actually on display, were brought here in Soviet times by renegade artist and ethnographer Igor Savitsky. Many of the early 20th-century Russian paintings, which did not conform to Soviet Realism, were banned by Moscow, but found protection in these isolated backwaters. The 2nd floor contains mostly ethnographic exhibits and the 3rd floor is reserved for the 'lost art'.

The museum sponsors projects for the revival of local handicrafts and you can ask to visit the workshops where textiles are made. Some of the items are on sale in the gift shop. The museum, which has wheelchair access, can also organise homestays for US$10 to US$25 per night, as well as day trips to Moynaq. Ask the curator Marinika Bobonazarova or one of her capable junior staff members.

To Airport (5km)

Park

Dosjyk

Tatibayev

Rashidov (Lenina)

Gharezsizlik

Karakalpakstan

Bazaar

Yenazak Alakö

Dosnazarov

Jumina

Amir Timur

Berdakha

Berdakh

To Train Station (3km)

To Amu Darya (3km); Hojeli (15km); Mizdakhan (19km); Moynaq (210km)

To Long-Distance Bus Station (6km); Urgench (166km)

STATE MUSEUM

The **State Museum** (Karakalpakstan; admission US$2, guide US$1; 9am-5pm Mon-Fri & 10am-4pm Sat) is minor league compared to the Savitsky, but still contains a strong exhibition of fauna and flora of the Karakalpakstan region. The very last Turan (Caspian) tiger, killed in 1972, stands stuffed and mounted in a corner. There are also displays on the Aral Sea and local health problems, on archaeology and early history, and of traditional jewellery, costumes, musical instruments and yurt decorations. Upstairs, there is an extension of the Savitsky collection (admission US$2, guided tour US$2), worthwhile if you still have the energy.

Festivals & Events

Karakalpaks apparently still play the wild Central Asian pololike game they call *ylaq oyyny* – with a headless goat carcass instead of a ball, and teams of dozens of riders. This and other traditional sports like wrestling, ram-fighting and cock-fighting are included in Nukus' **Pakhta-Bairam** (cotton) harvest festival in December.

Sleeping & Eating

Hotel Nukus (222 89 41; Lumumba 4; per person US$10-15;) Conveniently located near the post office, bank and museums, this tired old hotel is the best Karakalpakstan has to offer. Some of the rooms are more expensive than others, although it's not apparent why. Breakfast is included.

Hotel Tashkent (213 13 67; Berdakh 59; per person US$10) This decrepit high-rise at the western end of Karakalpakstan offers rundown rooms that are poor value at the asking price, but you can probably bargain them down. The water supply shuts down at night, so if you are catching an early ride out of town, forget about taking a shower.

Sheraton Café (222 87 81; Gharezsizlik 53; meals US$1-2; brunch, lunch & dinner) It may not live up to its international hotel namesake, but the Sheraton can still serve up filling portions of stuffed chicken, cold cuts and

---

KARAKALPAKSTAN

The Republic of Karakalpakstan, occupying the whole western end of the country, gets its name from the Karakalpak people whose homeland it is – although they number only about 400,000 of its 1.2 million population. It's also home to about 400,000 Uzbeks and 300,000 Kazakhs.

The Karakalpaks are a formerly nomadic and fishing people, first recorded in the 16th century and now struggling to recapture a national identity after being collectivised or urbanised in Soviet times.

The name Karakalpak means 'Black Hat People', but such has been their cultural decline that the Karakalpaks have had to set up a research project to find out just what this black hat was. Since the break-up of the USSR, there have been rumblings of nationalist discontent against Uzbek rule.

The Karakalpak language – now the official language of the republic – is Turkic, close to Kazakh and less so to Uzbek. Its alphabet, written in modified Cyrillic since Soviet times, has been converted to a Roman alphabet.

Life can never have been very easy here, although the Amu-Darya delta has supported irrigation-based agriculture for probably 4000 years. Cotton, rice and melons are Karakalpakstan's main produce. Tahiatash, 20km southeast of Nukus on the Amu-Darya, has a big hydroelectric station supplying the whole of Karakalpakstan, the Khorezm province of Uzbekistan and the Dashoguz region of Turkmenistan.

One thing you'll see a lot of is camels, used less as a means of transport than for their milk, meat and hides.

Karakalpakstan was probably at its most prosperous in the 1960s and '70s when the fruits of expanded irrigation from the Amu-Darya were being felt. But the republic has borne the brunt of the disastrous environmental, economic and health problems that have taken hold as a result of that same expansion; today the age-old oasis of rivers, lakes, reed beds, marshes, forests and farmland that constitute the Amu-Darya delta is being steadily dried up and poisoned. The capital, Nukus, gains Tashkent subsidies to keep itself a model city for the region, but a drive into outlying areas reveals a region of dying towns and blighted landscapes.

soups. It's got a lively evening atmosphere that can get clouded with smoke and full of wavering, bloodshot Karakalpaks unable to hold their liquor.

Mona Lisa (☎ 224 0632; Gharezsizlik 107) At the other end of Gharezsizlik and the Sheraton Café, this Georgian restaurant is popular with NGO staff who recommend the cheese pie, a sort of deep-dish pizza.

Self-caterers can try the sizable bazaar 500m north of the Hotel Tashkent along Yernazar Alaköz.

Getting There & Away

The only flights are to/from Tashkent (four daily, US$73). The **airline booking office** (☎ 222 79 95) is set back from Gharezsizlik, opposite the Hotel Nukus.

Buses to Tashkent (twice daily, 20 hours, US$8), Urgench (twice daily, four hours, US$1.30) and Moynaq (daily, four hours, US$1.30) go from the long-distance bus station, 6km south of the Hotel Tashkent. Private buses for Tashkent also park outside the Hotel Nukus and depart most days at 5pm.

Trains depart Nukus for Tashkent (US$20) every Thursday and Sunday at 5.50pm, stopping briefly in Urgench (US$7). Train No 232 departs for western Kazakhstan/Russia (Beyneu, Atyrau, Astrakhan) on Sunday at 9.51am. Daily passenger trains with *platskartnyy* (hard sleeper) seating also run to Beyneu, although service is unreliable.

For Hojeli marshrutnoe taxis depart from the main bus station every 20 minutes until 6pm, passing the Hotel Tashkent on their way out of town.

As usual, the quickest way out of town is by shared taxi; these wait outside the bus station. For Urgench, most shared taxis go as far as Beruni (US$2), where you can change. Taxis also stand by at the railway station and opposite the bazaar.

Getting Around

Bus No 3 runs between the airport and the bazaar. A taxi between the airport and the centre is under US$1.

To reach the centre from the train station, take any trolleybus from the west end of the station yard (to the left as you exit the station). From the centre to the station, take a Ж Д Вокзал or Т Ж Вокзал trolleybus south on Berdakha by the Hotel Tashkent, or a marshrutnoe Damas No 20.

For the bus station, take marshrutnoe Damas No 20 from opposite the bazaar.

AROUND NUKUS
Mizdakhan

On a hill 19km west of Nukus is the atmospheric holy site of ancient Mizdakhan. Inhabited from the 4th century BC until Timur's arrival, Mizdakhan was a large Khorezm trading centre and sacred place; tombs and mosques continued to be built there right up to the 20th century. Karakalpak cultural festivals are sometimes held here.

The hill is littered with ruined and intact mausoleums, mosques and medressas from the 11th to 20th centuries, of which the most impressive is the restored **Mausoleum of Mazlum Khan Slu**, dating from the 12th to 14th centuries. On the neighbouring hill towards Konye-Urgench are the remains of a 4th to 3rd century BC fortress called Gyaur-Qala.

From Nukus, travel 15km to Hojeli and from there take the road to Konye-Urgench (Turkmenistan). About 2km along you'll pass a honey-coloured cemetery on your left; another 2km further is Mizdakhan – look for the turquoise dome on the hilltop. The entrance for the mausoleum is 500m past the main gate. You'll see a small gate and blue door with a sign above it reading 'миздахаан'.

A taxi to/from Nukus is US$2. About 300m northwest of the Hojeli bus station is a dirt lot where shared taxis wait for passengers bound for Turkmenistan (US$0.30 per seat).

MOYNAQ МОЙНАҚ
☎ (3) 61 / pop 2000

Moynaq (Uzbek: Muynoq, Russian: Muynak), 210km north of Nukus, encapsulates more visibly than anywhere the absurd tragedy of the Aral Sea. Once one of the sea's two major fishing ports, it now stands almost 150km from the water. What remains of Moynaq's fishing fleet lies rusting on the sand, beside depressions marking the town's last futile efforts in the early 1980s to keep channels open to the shore.

Moynaq used to be on an isthmus connecting the Ush Say (Tiger's Tail) peninsula to the shore. You can appreciate this on the approach to the town, where the road is raised above the surrounding land. The former shore is about 3km north.

Moynaq's shrinking populace suffers the full force of the Aral Sea disaster, with hotter summers, colder winters, debilitating sand-salt-dust storms, and a gamut of health problems (see p68). Not surprisingly, the mostly Kazakh residents are deserting the town.

Sights

Poignant reminders of Moynaq's tragedy are everywhere: the sign at the entrance to the town has a fish on it; a fishing boat stands as a kind of monument on a makeshift pedestal near the Government House.

The **beached ships** are a five-minute walk south of the Oybek Hotel, across the main road and beyond the collection of homes. To see more ships, take a right turn up the road that is 250m before the hotel. Before you reach the war memorial, peer out over the former sea and you'll spot some ships about 1km away, across the grassy steppe.

From the **war memorial**, which once had great views of the Aral Sea, you can spot a lake in the distance, created in an attempt to restore the formerly mild local climate.

Forget about reaching the current shore. It is a seven- to eight-hour drive across salty marshland that only a sturdy jeep and experienced driver could handle.

Sleeping

Oybek (☎ 218 68; r US$5) This Spartan but clean hotel, 3km up the main road from the bus stop, is the only option for staying the night. There is no running water, but food might be available for US$3 per day.

Getting There & Away

The bus station is at the south end of the long main street. A decrepit and over-crowded bus runs daily between Moynaq and Nukus (3¾ hours, US$1.30), departing Nukus at 9am and coming back at 3pm, making infuriatingly frequent stops en route. The bus actually passes by the Hotel Tashkent around 9.15am so you could catch it there.

It isn't really feasible, or much fun, to take the morning bus from Nukus, walk out to the stranded boats and still catch the 3pm bus back. A taxi is easier; a day trip from Nukus costs about US$40, US$100 from Urgench. At Qongirat, about halfway, there is a basic roadside café and a bazaar. Taxis in Moynaq are very rare.

UZBEKISTAN DIRECTORY

ACCOMMODATION

All accommodation rates are for rooms with private bathroom unless otherwise stated. The bed and breakfast scene in Uzbekistan has taken off more than any other Central Asian republic. The best are in Bukhara where European consultants have been called in to promote the expansion and improvement of B&Bs. In time, their work is expected to trickle down to Samarkand and Khiva.

ACTIVITIES

Tourist-style camel trekking is growing in popularity among tour operators; travel agencies in Tashkent, Samarkand, Bukhara and Khiva can now organise a camel trip, or will know somebody who can. Agencies with particular experience in setting up a camel trekking are Salom Travel in Bukhara (p211), Sogda Tours in Samarkand (p199), and Dolores Tour in Tashkent (p173). Aidarkul Lake is the usual destination for such treks.

Outdoor pursuits such as white water rafting, skiing and hiking can be done near Chimgan (p185). The best hikes are in Shakhimardan (p194), done with support by Asia Travel (p173).

BOOKS

Chasing the Sea: Lost Among the Ghosts of Empire in Central Asia, by Tom Bissell, is a sort of travelogue-cum-history lesson about Uzbekistan written by an ex-Peace Corps volunteer on an assignment to investigate the disappearing Aral Sea. It is quick-witted and insightful.

THE AUTHOR'S CHOICE

- Le Meridien, Tashkent (p177)
- Bahodir B&B, Samarkand (p202)
- Sasha & Son B&B, Bukhara (p217)
- Salom Inn, Bukhara (p216)
- Ayaz-Qala Yurt Camp, Ayaz-Qala (around Urgench; p222)
- Hotel Khiva, Khiva (p228)

UZBEKISTAN

STREET NAME CHANGES

In trying to erase the Soviet period, streets everywhere have been renamed (sometimes several times) since 1991, often with unpronounceable new names. Russian Cyrillic script has been aggressively eliminated too; even the signs on buses and in stations have mostly gone over to Uzbek Cyrillic and increasingly to a Roman script (see the Language chapter for some useful words in Uzbek Cyrillic, p486).

Old street names are only infrequently used, with the exception of Lenina, which is common. New maps go strictly by the new names. In Uzbek, a street is called *kuchasi* (Russian: *ulitsa*), an avenue is *prospekti* (Russian: *prospekt*), a boulevard is *hiyaboni* (Russian: *bulvar*), a square *maydoni* (Russian: *ploshchad* or *skver*). In Karakalpakstan the words are different again.

Journey to Khiva, Philip Glazebrook, is a relentlessly downbeat review of Uzbekistan as it transitioned to independence in the early 1990s. Glazebrook mixes in the history of Uzbekistan as he travels through it, but is sorely disappointed at every turn, due largely to what he sees as cultural robbery by the Soviets. It serves as an interesting chronicle and reference point of Uzbek life in 1990.

Uzbekistan – the Golden Road to Samarkand, by Calum Macleod & Bradley Mayhew (5th edition 2004), is an elegant Odyssey guide that offers detailed historical and practical coverage of Uzbekistan's Silk Road cities, plus the main historical sites in the neighbouring republics, with literary excerpts and fine photography.

The Devil and the Disappearing Sea, by Rob Ferguson, is another tale of the doomed Aral, this time by a Canadian environmentalist sent to Uzbekistan to try and save it. It's an excellent mix of modern politics and culture, with the author's fruitless run-ins with the government thrown in for good measure.

EMBASSIES & CONSULATES
Uzbek Embassies in Central Asia

Uzbekistan has embassies in Kazakhstan (p154), Kyrgyzstan (p310), Tajikistan (p349) and Turkmenistan (p436).

Uzbek Embassies & Consulates

Azerbaijan (☎ 922-972 549; fax 972 548; 1st Hwy, 9th alley 437, Patamdart, 370021, Baku)
China (☎ 10-6532 6304/5; fax 6532 6304; 5-2-22 Taiyuan Diplomatic Office Bldg, Chaoyang district, Beijing)
France (☎ 1-53 83 80 70; fax 53 83 80 77; Ave Franklin Roosevelt 3, Paris 75008)
Germany (☎ 30-394 09 850; fax 394 09 821; Perleberger Strasse 62, Berlin 10559) Consulate in Frankfurt.
India (☎ 11-614 9034; fax 467 0773; EP 40, Dr S Radhakrishan, Marg Chanakyapuri, New Delhi 110021)
Iran (☎ 21-229 9158; fax 229 1269; 6 Nastaran St, Tehran)
The Netherlands (☎ 3120-428 7544; fax 428 7545; Weteringschans 28A, 1017 Amsterdam)
Pakistan (☎ 51-26 4746; fax 26 1737; House 2, 21st St, F8/3, Kohistan Rd, Islamabad) Consulate in Karachi.
Russia (☎ 95-230 0076; fax 238 8918; Pogorelski 12, Moscow)
Turkey (☎ 312-441 3871; fax 442 7058; Willy Grand Sok, No 13, Chankaya Ankara) Consulate in İstanbul.
UK (☎ 020-7229 7679; fax 7229 7029; www.uzbekistan embassy.uk.net; 41 Holland Park W11 3RP, London; ☿ 10am-1pm Mon-Fri, closed Thu) Multiple one-month visas US$60, payable to a local bank, takes two days.
USA (☎ 202-887 5300; fax 293 6804; www.uzbekistan .org; 1746 Massachusetts Ave NW, Washington DC 20036) Consulate-General in New York.

Embassies & Consulates in Uzbekistan

The following are all located in Tashkent (☎ 371 or 71; see Map pp170–1). For information on visas for onward travel see p237.

Afghanistan (☎ 134 84 32; fax 143 26 26; Murtazayev 6/84; ☿ 9am-2pm Mon-Fri)
Azerbaijan (☎ 78 93 04; ☿ /fax 77 72 13; Halqlar Dustligi 25)
China (☎ 133 37 79; fax 133 47 35; Yakhyo Gulomov 79; ☿ 9am-noon Mon, Wed, Fri)
France (☎ 133 53 82; fax 133 62 10; Akhunbabayev 25)
Germany (☎ 120 8440; fax: 120 6693; Sharaf Rashidov 15)
India (☎ 133 82 67; A. Tolstoy 3; ☿ 9.30am-noon Mon-Fri)
Iran (☎ 68 69 68; fax 120 67 61; Parkent 20; ☿ 9am-noon Mon-Thu)
Israel (☎ 152 5911; Shakhrisabz 16a)
Italy (☎ 152 1119; ambital@online.ru; Yusuf Khos Khodjib 40)
Japan (☎ 120 8060; 1-28 Sodiq Azimov)
Kazakhstan (☎ 152 15 54; fax 152 16 50; Chekhov 23; ☿ 9am-noon Mon-Fri)
Kyrgyzstan (☎ 133 89 41; krembas@globalnet.uz; Samatova 30; ☿ 9-11.30am & 3-4pm Mon-Fri)
Pakistan (☎ 144 86 40; Abdul Rakhmonov 15)
Russia (☎ 152 71 70; fax 152 21 45; Nukus 83; ☿ 9.30am-1pm Mon, Wed, Fri)

Tajikistan (☎ 54 99 66; temb@online.ru; Abdullah Kahar Six Torque 61; ☺ 10am–noon Mon-Fri)
Turkmenistan (☎ 120 52 78; One Katta Mirabat 10; ☺ 11am-1pm Mon-Fri)
UK (☎ 120 62 88/64 51; fax 120 65 49; Gogol 67)
USA (☎ 120 54 44, consular ☎ 120 54 49; fax 120 54 48; Chilonzor 82)

FESTIVALS & EVENTS

The most important period on the Tashkent social calendar comes in March when the city hosts a 14-day international music festival called Il Khom 20 (Inspiration 20). It features avante garde and new age music, and is held in the new Tashkent State Conservatory on Abai. During even-numbered years Tashkent hosts a film festival in September featuring Asian, African and Latin American films.

HOLIDAYS

January 1 New Year's Day.
March 8 International Women's Day.
March 21 Navrus (see p450).
Last Saturday of April Horse Day.
May 9 Victory Day.
September 1 Independence Day.
December 8 Constitution Day.

INTERNET ACCESS

Despite the government's persistence in blocking out politically sensitive websites (including Eurasianet), the Internet revolution continues to grow in Uzbekistan. Internet cafés are found in most places travellers go; although it's slower and more expensive the further you are from Tashkent.

INTERNET RESOURCES

www.fergana.ru Watchdog website that focuses primarily on politics, controversy and atrocities committed by the Uzbek government.
www.freenet.uz Useful links to other Uzbek sites.
www.tourism.uz Good general information, although the plane and train schedule are out-of-date.
www.uzbekistan.com News and information on Uzbekistan and its neighbours with some practical information.
www.gov.uz Tourist information, statistics and virtual tours.
www.amcham-uzbekistan.org American Chamber of Commerce official website for Uzbekistan.

MEDIA

No level of independent media exists in Uzbekistan, so virtually all newspaper, TV and radio coverage has to be government sanc-

tioned before it can be given to the public. Fortunately, the government is not so hell-bent on taming the Internet, although some sensitive sites have been blocked.

Tashkent's cosmopolitanism has yet to produce any significant publications in English. *Discovery Central Asia*, a tourist magazine available in some hotels including the Orzu Hotel, has features on tourist spots nationwide. Tashkent's top newspaper is the Russian-language *Zerkalo Dvadtsat Adin* (Mirror 21), an independent paper that explores a wider scope of issues than the government rag *People's Word*, which comes in Uzbek (*Khalq Soze*) and Russian (*Narodnoye Slovo*) languages. Month-old copies of the Bishkek-based *Times of Central Asia* are available at the Orzu Hotel.

MONEY

The Uzbek sum has notes in denominations of 1000, 500, 200, 100, 50, 20, 10, five, three and one. Reform policies have brought the black market and bank rates to similar levels, so there is no longer any desperate need to change on the black market, although oftentimes this is the quickest (or only) way of getting sum for dollars.

ATM machines accepting Visa cards are found in upmarket Tashkent hotels and banks, but they are chronically out of cash. Credit cards are accepted at an increasing number of mid-range and top-end hotels.

Because of the volatility of the Uzbek sum, prices for this chapter have been converted into US dollars. The Uzbek sum, however, is widely accepted across the country and (in theory) paying for goods and services in anything else is illegal.

At the time of research, the exchange rates were:

Country	Unit		Sum
Afghanistan	1Afg	=	23.05
Australia	A$1	=	744.61
Canada	C$1	=	735.79
China	Y1	=	119.90
euro zone	€1	=	1207.53
Kazakhstan	1 T	=	7.13
Kyrgyzstan	1 som	=	23.19
Tajikistan	1TJS	=	355.96
Turkmenistan	100 M	=	20.13
UK	UK£1	=	1816.45
USA	US$1	=	992.43

Visa and American Express credit cards can be used to get US dollars cash at branches of the National Bank of Uzbekistan with a 5% commission. Otherwise credit cards are only of use in top-end hotels.

Be aware that if you don't list your travellers cheques on your customs declaration form you won't be able to cash travellers cheques.

POST

An airmail postcard costs 125 sum, a 20g airmail letter costs 150 sum and a 1kg package costs US$4.90. The postal service is not renowned for speed or reliability in delivering letters or parcels. One reader reports that of the 100 postcards he sent, only one third made it to their destination. International couriers are listed under Post in the Tashkent section (p172).

REGISTRATION

Checking into a registered hotel means automatic registration. Make sure you get a docket (they sometimes need reminding) as these are sometimes asked for when departing the country.

If you spend a night in a private home you are supposed to be registered with the local Office of Visas & Registration (OVIR), but as this can create more problems than it solves for you and your hosts, it's probably best not to. Instead, ask the next hotel you stay at to fill in those missing days on your docket. Keep in mind that there are fines if you get caught unregistered.

Long-term residents need to register with OVIR as police make periodic home-to-home checks. Registration costs around US$20 per month (US$100 for six months) and must be done within 72 hours of arrival; your landlord will know the location of the nearest OVIR office.

For more questions or details, contact your embassy or the Tashkent central **OVIR office** (☎ 132 65 70, 67 46 18; Uzbekistan 49).

TELEPHONE

Uzbekistan's telephone system is antiquated and mobile phones are the only option for long-term residents. Per minute calls from Tashkent's central telephone office are: to the UK US$1.18, to the USA US$1.30 and to Australia US$1.78. Telephone calls

> **INCOMING AREA CODES**
>
> When calling from outside Uzbekistan dial ☎ 998 plus the local area codes marked in the individual sections. The area code depends on the length of the telephone number (six or seven digits). Thus for Samarkand use ☎ 66 for a seven digit number or ☎ 662 for a six digit number.

from other parts of the country are a little higher. Making calls from the four-star hotels is more reliable but two or three times the price.

Another option is to buy an MCI prepaid calling card. A 100 unit card costs US$30 and is good for about 73 minutes to the USA or Europe (US$0.41 per minute). A better value 600 unit card is also available. The cards are distributed by InterConcepts Incorporated – contact **Charles Rudd** (☎ 139 13 02, 152 21 02).

For information on mobile phone service, contact **Coscom** (☎ 133 63 73; www.coscom.uz; Akhunbabaev 38, Tashkent).

For local calls, offices, shops, hotels, kiosks and restaurants let visitors use their private line for a rate of 100 sum per three minutes.

At the time of research Uzbekistan had one set of area codes for incoming calls, and another for calls within the country. The latter will eventually be phased out.

To make a local call dial ☎ 0 + city code.

To dial into Uzbekistan from abroad dial ☎ 00 998 + incoming area code (see the separate town entries).

To call out of Uzbekistan dial ☎ 8, wait for a tone, then dial ☎ 10.

TRAVEL PERMITS

Border permits are required for mountain areas near the Tajik border, including the southern areas of Zamiin National Park. They can be purchased upon entry into the park. National park offices might also try to sell you a trekking permit, prices vary on who is asking. Asia Travel in Tashkent can help arrange the necessary permits (p173). Although not a permit per se, bear in mind when preplanning that you will need a Kyrgyz visa to cross into Shakhimardan (p193).

VISAS

Citizens of the USA, France, Italy, Belgium, UK, Ireland, Japan, Germany, Austria, Spain and Switzerland can purchase a visa without support. At the time of writing, US citizens were being issued one-year multiple entry visas, good for stays of 30 days at a time. Processing time depends upon the embassy. London can issue a visa in two days whereas Washington takes seven, unless you request a rush service (and call to remind them that you want the rush).

Residents of countries not listed above need a Letter of Invitation (LOI), which can be provided by a private individual in Uzbekistan, a company, an NGO or (most typically) a travel agency, for a fee of around US$20. (See Travel Agencies in Tashkent, p173).

A one-week visa costs US$40, 15-day visas US$50, one-month visas US$60 and two-month visas US$80. Multiple-entry visas cost US$150 with a validity of six months. Visas for US citizens cost a flat US$100.

Transit visas cost US$20 for one day, US$25 for two days and US$30 for three days. Applicants must already hold a visa for a neighbouring country.

Visa extensions are expensive, time-consuming and involve much red-tape. Many frustrated travellers give up and go to neighbouring Kazakhstan or Kyrgyzstan and buy a new visa. If you stay in the country, seek support from a Tashkent-based travel agency and expect to pay around US$85 for a one-month extension plus the support fees.

Visas for Onward Travel

For contact details of embassies and consulates in Uzbekistan, see p234.

Afghanistan A 30-day visa costing US$45 for US citizens and US$30 for most other nationalities. One-day processing.

Azerbaijan A 30-day visa costing US$40 is issued in two days.

China A 60-day visa valid within three months costs US$50 for US citizens, US$30 for most other nationalities; five-day processing time.

India A six-month visa costing US$70 for US citizens; seven-day minimum processing time.

Iran A 30-day visa costs US$60. Our mailbox is filled with readers complaining of the difficulties in getting a visa at this embassy. Expect a long processing time (10 to 30 days) repeated visits and rude staff. You will probably need an LOI from an agency in Iran and other documentation – the embassy has a list of agencies that can provide an LOI.

Kazakhstan A 30-day (US$40) or 60-day (US$65) visa given on the spot provided you have an LOI.

Kyrgyzstan A 30-day visa costing US$40 takes four days to process. A one-day rush is US$80. No LOI needed.

Pakistan Visa charge is US$36; processed in two days.

Russia A 30-day tourist visa can be issued with proof of air tickets, hotel vouchers and travel agent confirmation. Sample prices include US citizens (US$75), UK citizens (US$35), and Australian citizens (US$40). Processing time is seven days but a one-day rush can be done for a US$20 fee. Be prepared for long queues.

Tajikistan Single-entry visa US$70, double entry US$90. Allow one week to process or pay a US$50 fee for one-day rush. All nationalities require an LOI.

Turkmenistan Five-day transit visas issued without LOI for US$41; allow 10 days to process or pay US$61 four-day processing fee. Tourist visas cost US$120 same day or US$80 in three days. Arrive two hours early to put your name on a waiting list. You can keep your passport during processing, but when you pick up the visa you must show a visa for an onward country (eg Iran). The embassy is tricky to find; approach from Nukus St and look for the signs.

TRANSPORT IN UZBEKISTAN

GETTING THERE & AWAY
Entering Uzbekistan

As long as your papers are in order, entering Uzbekistan should be no sweat. You will be asked to fill out two identical customs declarations forms, one to turn in and one to keep (which will be handed in upon departure). The customs form is necessary for changing travellers cheques so don't lose it. It's unlikely that your luggage will be searched, but you might have to put it through a dodgy x-ray machine. See Scams in the Tashkent section (p173) for other airport concerns.

Air
AIRPORTS & AIRLINES

Uzbekistan's international gateways include **Tashkent International Airport** (☎ 006, 54 48 58, VIP ☎ 54 86 47; www.tashkent.org/uzland/airlines.html) and **Samarkand International Airport** (☎ 320 009, 321 102).

DEPARTURE TAX

Departure tax for international flights is US$10.

FLYING SAFELY IN UZBEKISTAN

Although Uzbekistan Airways enjoys improved service and maintenance support from Lufthansa, there is a still a danger in flying. On 13 January 2004 a flight from Termiz crashed while trying to land in Tashkent, killing all 37 passengers, including the UN's top envoy to Uzbekistan.

Same-day international tickets usually come with a service charge equal to half the price of the ticket, so try to secure your ticket at least 24 hours in advance. All booking offices can lend assistance if you have an open ticket and want to leave on the same day (open-date tickets carry a US$10 service charge). Aside from the Tashkent city booking office (p182), a second **international booking office** (☎ 133 34 59) is located on the ground floor of the international terminal.

To fly from Tashkent to Almaty costs around US$120, from Tashkent to Bishkek, US$105 and Tashkent to Ashgabat, US$105.

For contact details of the airlines that fly in and out of Uzbekistan, see p182.

Land
BORDER CROSSINGS
To/From Afghanistan
At the time of writing the crossing at Termiz was only open for special permit holders available only to accredited journalists, NGO staff and military personnel.

To/From Kazakhstan
Despite their very long common border there are just two main places to cross. The more common crossing is the road between Tashkent and Shymkent, a busy border that is used to seeing foreigners. Marshrutnoe vans (1¼ hours, US$1.50) depart from Shymkent to the border at least twice an hour. From the border to central Tashkent it's a 25-minute taxi (US$5) or bus (US$0.25) ride. Private moneychangers are aplenty on the Kazakh side but non-existent on the Uzbek side, so dump any remaining Kazakh *tenge* in exchange for enough sum to get you into Tashkent. Coming to the Uzbek side, you may have to walk about 1km through a series of gates. Ignore the taxi drivers who want to drive

you across. In summer, the border is open 6am to 9pm (Tashkent time) and 8am to 11pm (Shymkent time). This is essentially the same time as Tashkent is two hours behind Shymkent.

The other crossing is by train between Karakalpakstan and western Kazakhstan. Daily passenger trains travel from Beyneu to Nukus (10 hours, *platskartnyy* seating only). Once a week a *kupe* (2nd-class or sleeping carriage) train departs Beyneu for Nukus (Thursday at 5.05pm). Easy-going customs are done on the train. You really have to badger the Uzbek customs official to issue and sign your customs form (which you will need later) if you are entering the country.

To/From Kyrgyzstan
Border crossings are in the Fergana Valley, at Uchkurgan (northeast of Namangan), Dustlyk (between Andijan and Osh) and Khanabad (between Andijan and Jalal-Abad). Crossings are generally hassle-free but you may need to remind the Kyrgyz to stamp your passport upon entry. Taxis and minibuses run between the borders on both sides.

For Osh, travel to Andijan and get a taxi from there to the border. Kyrgyz visas are not available at the border. If you are headed north it's also possible to cross into Kyrgyzstan at Uchkurgan.

Daily Bishkek–Tashkent buses pass through a long section of Kazakhstan and you will need a transit visa. Bishkek–Tashkent buses at the time of research were only going as far as the Uzbek border at Chernaiev, from where you have to take a minibus a few kilometres into Tashkent. Minibuses will leave when full. By the time you've paid for an invite and the visa and waited for it, it's not that much more expensive to fly.

To/From Russia
From Moscow, train No 6 departs at 12.40pm on Monday, Wednesday and Friday, arriving in Tashkent around 60 hours later, and costing US$143/233 in 2nd class/1st class.

to/From Tajikistan
The main border crossings are Samarkand–Penjikent, and Denau–Tursanzade, further

south for Dushanbe. Crossings are subject to Uzbek-Tajik relations (often not good).

The border is 42km from Samarkand (shared taxi US$1) and 18km from Penjikent (taxi US$1).

Dushanbe and Termiz are connected by a daily train.

To/From Turkmenistan

The three main border points are reached from Bukhara, Khiva/Urgench and Nukus. The crossings are largely hassle free, but slow, and expect to be thoroughly searched by the Turkmen as you enter their country.

A taxi from Turkmenabat to the Uzbek border should cost you around US$4 for a 40-minute drive. Your driver will stop about 2km from the border from where you will have to walk or you can take a bus (every 15 minutes, US$1). From the border, take a taxi (US$5) to Bukhara, or hire a taxi as far as Alat (or Karakul), where you can change to a shared taxi. Coming the other way get a shared taxi (US$4) from Bolshoy rynok (bazaar) in Bukhara to Alat, where you'll have to hire your own car to the border.

A taxi from Dashoguz to the Uzbek border is not more than US$1. From the border to Khiva expect to pay around US$10 for a taxi.

A taxi from Konye-Urgench to the border is around US$1. From the border to Nukus expect to pay US$7.

GETTING AROUND
Air

Reservation desks for **Uzbekistan Airways** (☎ 066 or 56 38 37; www.uzbekistanairways.com) often say flights are overbooked when in fact seats will be available. A reservation 'finders fee' might set you back US$5 to US$20 for a domestic flight or five times that for an international flight. If you are short on time, a one-way flight to/from Tashkent during your trip can save backtracking.

Bus

Clapped-out state buses are fast disappearing from Uzbek roads, and state bus stations are uncannily quiet. They've been undercut by a boom in private buses and shared taxis. Private buses are newer and more comfortable, but can be unreliable as drivers and touts are preoccupied with over-selling seats and transporting cargo and contraband.

Car

Driving your own car is possible, provided you have insurance from your home country and a valid international driver's license. There are no official car rental agencies, though this may change soon.

In Tashkent, cars are pulled over with great frequency so police can pad their wallets. Beware of 'no stopping zones,' marked with a red 'X' sign, usually placed in front of embassies and official buildings. In Uzbekistan, motorists drive on the right and seat belts are not at all required.

Shared Taxi

Taxis, shared or private, are the best way to go. Although more expensive than the bus, you'll save huge amounts of time and have more freedom to stop and explore. Taxis also get through check posts faster than buses. Prices are different for different types of share vehicle, and this becomes self-evident pretty quickly. Daewoo Nexia's are the most comfortable and fastest share vehicle. Daewoo Ticos are smaller and slower. Daewoo Damas are the rectangular shaped minivans that would crumple like a coke can in an accident. The big old white vans (Soviet-era) are commonly called marshrutnoes (literally 'fixed route').

Trains

Uzbek trains are perhaps the most comfortable and safest (but not always the fastest) way to get between big cities. *Platskartnyy* (hard sleeper) is usually available and on longer hauls trains will pull *kupe* (soft sleeper) cars. The commuter train between Tashkent and Samarkand is the most popular route, whereas the opening of a new line between Navoi, Urgench and Nukus (which avoids the old route through Turkmenistan) might prove handy for travellers heading out west.

UZBEKISTAN

Kyrgyzstan
Кыргызстан

CONTENTS

FAST FACTS

- **Area** 198,500 sq km
- **Capital** Bishkek
- **Country Code** ☎ 996
- **Ethnic Groups** 66% Kyrgyz, 14% Uzbek, 11% Russian, Others 9%
- **Money** Kyrgyz som: US$1 = 41 som, €1 = 53
- **Phrases in Kyrgyz** Hello. *(salam)*; Thank you. *(rahmat)*; Good. *(jaqshi)*
- **Population** 5 million (2003 estimate)

What Kyrgyzstan lacks in settled history it makes up for in a wealth of nomadic traditions, including laid-back hospitality and a healthy distrust of authority. What it lacks in development it makes up for in determination. What it lacks in historical architecture it more than makes up for in Central Asia's finest mountain 'architecture' – the highest and most dramatic parts of the central Tian Shan and Pamir Alay ranges. When you tire of Uzbekistan's shashlyk and chaikhanas (teahouses; called chaykhana locally), trade them in for a night in a yurt and a horse trek into the glorious mountain scenery of Kyrgyzstan.

The collapse of the USSR left this tiny, underequipped republic out on a limb, seemingly without the resources to survive on its own. Partly because of this it is doing more than any other Central Asian republic to encourage and simplify tourism. The country is at the forefront of a tourism experiment in responsible and sustainable tourism projects that is revolutionising budget travel in the region and is offering travellers unrivalled opportunities to explore the mountains and pastures on foot, horseback or jeep, to get a glimpse at how the Kyrgyz people really live.

One of the joys of travelling in Kyrgyzstan is the openness of the people. At every turn you will find a family offering to put you up for the night, or a group of herdsmen who will eagerly invite you into their yurt for a cup of tea and a bowl of fresh yogurt. Add this to some of the world's most glorious and untrammelled alpine scenery and it's easy to see why most travellers vote this the most appealing, accessible and welcoming of the former Soviet Central Asian republics.

HIGHLIGHTS

Arguably the country's biggest attraction is **Lake Issyk-Kul** (p264) and the adjacent Terskey Alatau range at the edge of the Tian Shan. This is fast being rivalled by the backpacker-friendly homestay programmes of **Kochkor** (p282) and the nearby lakeside yurts and herders of **Song-Köl** (p285). The **Community Based Tourism homestay programme** (CBT; p248) is a highlight of Central Asia, whichever branch you use, and is something you should really make use of.

Down in the south, **Osh** (p299) is one of Central Asia's oldest and most significant towns, with a fine market. The **Torugart** (p291) and **Irkeshtam Passes** (p307) are certainly the most challenging and spectacular ways to cross to or from China.

Trekking, either on foot or horseback, is definitely the way to travel in Kyrgyzstan. Arguably the best walking spots start from **Ala-Archa** (p262) or in the mountains behind **Karakol** (p276). Mountain lovers won't get higher than the helicopter ride to **Inylchek**

Glacier (p280), with views of Khan Tengri, one of the world's most beautiful peaks.

ITINERARIES

- **Three days** Take in Bishkek (p249) and a visit to the mountains behind, either Ala-Archa (p262) or Alamedin (p263)
- **One week** From Bishkek head east to Issyk-Kul (p264) and spend a couple of days hiking or horse riding in the gorgeous alpine valleys of Altyn Arashan (p275) or the Karakol Valley (p276)
- **Two weeks** Add on Kochkor (p282), a horse trek to Song-Köl (p285) and a visit to Tash Rabat caravanserai (p290)
- **One month** Tack on a trip south to Arslanbob (p298) or Sary Chelek (p296) for some CBT-assisted hiking or horse riding on the fringes of the Fergana Valley
- **Off the beaten track** Go exploring, basing yourself at homestay programmes at Suusamyr (p294) or Talas (p295), the southern shore of Issyk-Kul (p288), or the Kazarman road (p288)

KYRGYZSTAN

CLIMATE & WHEN TO GO

Siberian winds bring freezing temperatures and snow from November to February, with ferocious cold in the mountains. The average winter minimum is -24°C.

Throughout the country springtime buds appear in April–May, though nights can still be below freezing. Mid-May to mid-June is pleasant, though many mountain passes will still be snowed in. From the end of June through mid-August most afternoons will reach 32°C or higher, with a maximum of 40°C in Fergana Valley towns like Jalal-Abad, though mountain valleys are considerably cooler. Like most of the region, Bishkek gets most of its rainfall in spring and early summer.

Of course in the mountains the 'warm' season is shorter. The best time is July–September, although camping and trekking are pleasant from early June through mid-October. Avalanche danger is greatest in March through April and from September to mid-October.

Overall, the republic is best for scenery and weather in September, with occasional freezing nights in October. See the Climate Charts on p446.

HISTORY

The earliest notable residents of what is now Kyrgyzstan were warrior clans of Saka (also known as Scythians), from about the 6th century BC to the 5th century AD. Rich bronze and gold relics have been recovered from Scythian burial mounds at Lake Issyk-Kul and in southern Kazakhstan.

The region was under the control of various Turkic alliances from the 6th to 10th centuries. A sizeable population lived on the shores of Lake Issyk-Kul. The Talas Valley in southern Kazakhstan and northwest Kyrgyzstan was the scene of a pivotal battle in 751, when the Turks and their Arab and Tibetan allies drove a large Tang Chinese army out of Central Asia.

The cultured Turkic Karakhanids (who finally brought Islam to Central Asia for good) ruled here in the 10th to 12th centuries. One of their multiple capitals was at Balasagun (now Burana, east of Bishkek). Another major Karakhanid centre was at Özgön (Uzgen) at the edge of the Fergana Valley.

Ancestors of today's Kyrgyz people probably lived in Siberia's upper Yenisey Basin

---

TRAVELLING SAFELY IN KYRGYZSTAN

Travel advisories still warn against travel off the beaten track along Kyrgyzstan's southern wall, south and west of Osh, which saw incursions by the Islamic Movement of Uzbekistan (IMU) in 1999, 2000 and 2001 (see p307), though in reality the threat has largely diminished.

---

until at least the 10th century, when under the influence of Mongol incursions they began migrating south into the Tian Shan – more urgently with the rise of Jenghiz Khan in the 13th century. Present-day Kyrgyzstan was part of the inheritance of Jenghiz' second son, Chaghatai.

Peace was shattered in 1685 by the arrival of the ruthless Mongol Oyrats of the Zhungarian empire, who drove vast numbers of Kyrgyz south into the Fergana and Pamir Alay regions and on into present-day Tajikistan. The Manchu (Qing) defeat of the Oyrats in 1758 left the Kyrgyz as de facto subjects of the Chinese, who mainly left them to their nomadic ways.

As the Russians moved closer in the 19th century, various Kyrgyz clan leaders made their own peace with either Russia or the neighbouring khanate of Kokand. Bishkek – then comprising only the Pishpek fort – fell in 1862 to a combined Russian-Kyrgyz force and the Kyrgyz were gradually eased into the tsar's provinces of Fergana and Semireche.

HOW MUCH?

- Snickers bar US$0.30
- 100km bus ride US$1
- One minute phone call to the US US$0.60
- Internet per hour US$0.50–1
- Kyrgyz hat US$2–4

LONELY PLANET INDEX

- Litre of bottle water US$0.40
- Bottle of beer US$1
- Shashlyk US$0.25
- Litre of petrol US$0.50

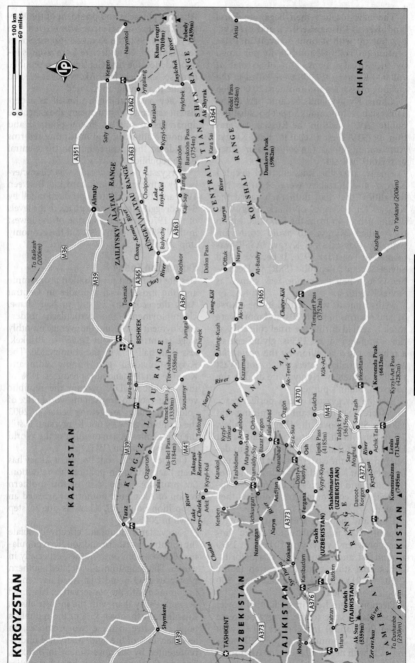

The new masters then began to hand land over to Russian settlers, and the Kyrgyz put up with it until a revolt in 1916, centred on Tokmak and heavily put down by the Russian army. Out of a total of 768,000 Kyrgyz, 120,000 were killed in the ensuing massacres and another 120,000 fled to China. Kyrgyz lands became part of the Turkestan Autonomous Soviet Socialist Republic (ASSR) within the Russian Federation in 1918, then a separate Kara-Kyrgyz Autonomous Oblast (an *oblast* is a province or region) in 1924.

Finally, after the Russians had decided Kyrgyz and Kazakhs were separate nationalities (they had until then called the Kyrgyz 'Kara-Kyrgyz' or Black Kyrgyz, to distinguish them from the Kazakhs, whom they called 'Kyrgyz' to avoid confusion with the Cossacks), a Kyrgyz ASSR was formed in February 1926. It became a full Soviet Socialist Republic (SSR) in December 1936, when the region was known as Soviet Kirghizia.

Many nomads were settled in the course of land reforms in the 1920s, and more were forcibly settled during the cruel collectivisation campaign in the 1930s, giving rise to a reinvigorated rebellion by the *basmachi*, Muslim guerrilla fighters, for a time. Vast swathes of the new Kyrgyz elite died in the course of Stalin's purges.

Remote Kyrgyzstan was a perfect place for secret Soviet uranium mining (at Mayluu-Suu above the Fergana Valley, Ming-Kush in the interior and Kaji-Say at Lake Issyk-Kul) and also naval weapons development (at the eastern end of Issyk-Kul). Independent Kyrgyzstan has closed most of the mines and institutes and begun to grapple with the environmental problems they created.

Land and housing were at the root of Central Asia's most infamous 'ethnic' violence, between Kyrgyz and Uzbeks in 1990 around Osh and Özgön (Uzgen), a majority-Uzbek area stuck onto Kyrgyzstan in the 1930s (p301), during which at least 300 people were killed.

Elections were held in traditional Soviet rubber-stamp style to the Kyrgyz Supreme Soviet (legislature) in February 1990, with the Kyrgyz Communist Party (KCP) walking away with nearly all the seats. After multiple ballots a compromise candidate, Askar Akaev, a physicist and president of the Kyrgyz Academy of Sciences, was elected. On 31 August 1991, the Kyrgyz Supreme Soviet reluctantly voted to declare Kyrgyzstan's independence, the first Central Asian republic to do so. Six weeks later Akaev was re-elected president, running unopposed.

Akaev has established himself as a persistent reformer, restructuring the executive apparatus to suit his liberal political and economic attitudes, and instituting reforms considered the most radical in the Central Asian republics.

Kyrgyzstan's first decade was characterised by extreme economic hardship. Between 1990 and 1996, industrial production fell by 64%, dragging the economy back to the levels of the 1970s when it was one of the lowest in the USSR. Only in 1996 did the economy stop shrinking.

Kyrgyzstan Today

Despite the fastest privatisation programme and the most liberal attitudes in Central Asia, the economy is still in bad shape. Unemployment (and particularly underemployment) is rife and the average monthly wage is currently about US$55 in Bishkek, less than half this in the countryside. The Kyrgyz-Canadian gold-mining company Kumtor single-handedly produces 18% of the republic's GDP, making the republic very vulnerable to drops in the world price of gold. Still, things are getting better; in 2003 the economy grew by 6%. Kyrgyzstan is still the only Central Asian member of the World Trade Organisation (WTO).

On the political front President Akaev has been backsliding on political liberalisation. Six protestors were shot in the southern region of Aksu after authorities arrested an opposition politician. Akaev is due to step down in 2005.

Kyrgyzstan's mountains effectively isolate the country's northern and southern population centres from one another, especially in winter. The geographically isolated southern provinces of Osh and Jalal-Abad have more in common with the conservative, Islamised Fergana Valley than with the industrialised, Russified north. Over 55% of the republic's population live in these two provinces, on less than 15% of the land. Many feel underrepresented by the government in Bishkek. The south is represented by 48 deputies compared to the north's 57, guaranteeing the north control of central decision-making. Ancient but still-important clan affiliations reinforce these regional differences. In a recent survey, 63.5% of Kyrgyz people thought that north–south contradictions were the main destabilising factor within society. There has been talk of building a trans-Kyrgyzstan railway, although it's hard to see this happening for decades. The 2200th anniversary of Kyrgyz statehood was celebrated in 2003, perhaps to bind the country together.

Kyrgyzstan was woken from relative complacency in August 1999 when four Japanese geologists were taken hostage in Kyrgyzstan's southern Batken district by a group of several hundred militants from the Islamic Movement of Uzbekistan, based in Tajikistan. The militants asked for US$2 million ransom. Kyrgyzstan's Minister for Interior Security flew down to oversee the rescue operation and was himself promptly kidnapped. The hostages were finally released in October 1999, but Islamic groups remained at large (four American climbers were kidnapped in 2000) until the US bombings in Afghanistan pulled the rug from under the militants' feet, killing most of the IMU leadership and its Al-Qaeda–supplied support network.

Although that conflict might set nerves jangling in Bishkek, Islamic fundamentalism is not officially seen as a serious threat here, as it is in Uzbekistan. Yet the opening of a US military base at Manas Airport and then a Russian airbase just down the road at Kant, highlights the strategic realignment of the republic and the heightened rivalries between the region's former and current superpowers in a post–September 11th Central Asia.

YURTS

Warm in winter, cool in summer, relatively light and portable, the traditional nomadic yurts (*bosuy* in Kyrgyz, *kiiz-uy* in Kazakh) once peppered the countryside like giant mushrooms. Urbanised Kazakhs have forsaken the yurt altogether, but many Kyrgyz still head out to the *jailoos* (summer pastures) and set up summer *bosuy*. The best place to see a real Kyrgyz yurt is central Kyrgyzstan, from Suusamyr to Naryn. CBT (p248) can arrange stays in authentic yurts.

Yurts are made of multilayered felt (*kiyiz* or *kiiz*) stretched around a collapsible wooden frame (*kerege*), often made of willow. The outer felt layer is coated in waterproof sheep fat, the innermost layer is lined with woven mats from the tall grass called *chiy* to block the wind. The lattice framework makes up the main walls, connected to long poles (*uyuk*) rising up to the apex (*shanrak*), the hole that controls the temperature of the yurt and allows air and light to get in and smoke from the fire to escape. Looking up the *shanrak*, you'll see the *tyndyk*, a wheel with two three-ply struts, which supports the roof (and which is depicted on Kyrgyzstan's national flag). Long woven woollen strips of varying widths, called *tizgych* and *chalgych*, secure the walls and poles. Embroidered bags are hung to be used as storage. Start to finish, a yurt requires around three hours to set up or pull down.

The entrance to the yurt, usually facing east, has a door carved from pine or birch wood, or rolled *chiy*. Floors are lined with thick felt (*koshma*) and covered with bright *shyrdaks*, *ala-kiyiz*, and sometimes yak skin. The interior is richly decorated with handsome textiles, including colourful wall coverings, quilts, cushions, camel and horse bags, and ornately worked caskets. Large tassels hang from the *tyndyk*. The more elaborate the decoration, the higher the social standing of the yurt's owners.

The hearth is central to the yurt, above which hangs a metal cauldron (or more often these days an iron stove). The place by the hearth, furthest away from the door, is always reserved for guests and the back right of the yurt is the 'master bedroom'. Harnesses and saddles are stored to the left of the entrance, bedding is stored along the wall opposite the entrance. Men's and women's sections are sometimes divided by a *chiy* partition, the women's area (kitchen) to the right of the entrance. Lambs, kids and calves are kept near the door.

Traditionally, the collapsed yurt was transported via horse cart, while an ox often transported the heavy roof wheel. Today it's more common to see one strapped down to a tractor and heading off into the hills.

PEOPLE

There is a total of 80 ethnic groups in Kyrgyzstan. The Kyrgyz are outnumbered almost three to one by their livestock. About two-thirds of the population lives in rural areas.

Since 1989 there has been a major exodus of Slavs and Germans – more than 200,000 Russians and at least 75% of all Germans between 1989 and 1998 – amid dire forecasts of its economic effects. At its peak in 1993, 130,000 people left Kyrgyzstan, of whom 90,000 were Russians. Among the emigrants was one of Akaev's closest allies, the Russian First Deputy Prime Minister, German Kuznetsov.

Kyrgyz (with Kazakhs) in general, while probably the most Russified of Central Asian people, were never as deeply 'Leninised', judging by the ease with which they have turned away from the Soviet era. There has been none of the wholesale, hypocritical race to cleanse all Soviet terminology that afflicts Uzbekistan.

For more on the Kyrgyz people refer to p48.

RELIGION

Like the Kazakhs, the Kyrgyz adopted Islam relatively late and limited it to what could fit in their saddlebags. Northern Kyrgyz are more Russified and less observant of Muslim doctrine than their cousins in the south (in Jalal-Abad and Osh provinces). One consequence is a high profile for women here.

Dwindling communities of Russian Orthodox Christians are still visible, particularly in Bishkek and Karakol, both of which have Orthodox cathedrals.

ARTS
Literature

Central Asian literature has traditionally been popularised in the form of songs, poems and stories by itinerant minstrels or bards, called *akyn* in Kyrgyz (p59). Among better-known 20th-century Kyrgyz *akyns* are Togolok Moldo (real name Bayymbet Abdyrakhmanov), Sayakbay Karalayev and Sagymbay Orozbakov.

Kyrgyzstan's best-known living author is Chinghiz Aitmatov (born 1928), whose works have been translated into English, German and French. Among his novels, which are also revealing looks at Kyrgyz life and culture, are *Djamila* (1967), *The White*

Steamship* (1970), *Early Cranes* (1975) and *Piebald Dog Running Along the Shore* (1978), the latter made into a prize-winning Russian film in 1990.

In *The Day Lasts Longer Than a Century* (1980) two boys witness the arrest by the NKVD of their father, who never returns (Aitmatov lost his father in Stalin's purges and the loss of a father is a recurring theme in his work). *The Place of the Skull* (1986) confronted previously taboo subjects such as drugs and religion and was an early attack on bureaucracy and environmental destruction. *Djamila* and *The Day Lasts Longer Than a Century* are fairly easy to find in English.

MANAS

The *Manas* epic is a cycle of oral legends, 20 times longer than the *Odyssey*, which tells of the formation of the Kyrgyz people through the exploits of a hero-of-heroes called Manas. Acclaimed as one of the finest epic traditions, this '*Iliad* of the steppes' is the highpoint of a widespread Central Asian oral culture.

The *Manas* narrative revolves around the khan, or *batyr* (heroic warrior), Manas and

---

NOMADIC SPORTS

Equestrian sports are very popular in Kyrgyzstan and have seen a revival in recent years. The most spectacular of these is *kok boru*, also known as *ulak-tartysh* or *buzkashi* (p54). The Kyrgyz name means 'grey wolf', which reveals the sport's origins as a hunting exercise

Kyz-kumay (kiss-the-girl) involves a man who furiously chases a woman on horseback in an attempt to kiss her. The woman gets the faster horse and a head start and if she wins gets to chase and whip her shamed suitor. This allegedly began as a formalised alternative to abduction, the traditional nomadic way to take a bride.

Other equestrian activities in Kyrgyzstan include *at chabysh*, a horse race over a distance of 20km to 30km, *jumby atmai*, horseback archery, *tiyin enmei*, where contestants pick up coins off the ground while galloping past, and *udarysh*, horseback wrestling. Eagle-hunting contests also take place during festivals or special celebrations. Don't pass up the chance to view these wonderful spectacles.

SHYRDAKS

The Kyrgyz specialise in *shyrdak* (felt rugs with appliquéd coloured panels) and *ala-kiyiz* (pressed wool designs). *Shyrdaks* are pieced together in the summer months from cut pieces of sheep's wool, after weeks of washing, drying, dyeing and treatment against wormwood. The appliqué patterns are usually of a *kochkor mujuz* (plant motif), *teke mujuz* (ibex horn motif) or *kyal* (fancy scrollwork) bordered in a style particular to the region. Brightly coloured designs were introduced after synthetic dye became readily available in the 1960s, although natural dyes (made from pear and raspberry leaves, dahlia and birch root, among others) are making a comeback. Neutral-coloured *shyrdaks* are also easy to find and resist fading. Working together, Kyrgyz women can – with two to three months' diligent work, during which each stitch is sewn by hand – knock out a beautiful carpet that will last for over three decades.

The 'blurred' design of the *ala-kiyiz* is made from dyed fleece, which is laid out in the desired pattern on a *chiy* (reed) mat. The felt is made by sprinkling hot water over the wool, which is then rolled up and rolled around, with more hot water, until the felt compacts.

Before you purchase a *shyrdak*, ensure that it's hand-made by checking for irregular stitching on the back and tight, even stitching around the panels. Also check the colour will not run (lick your finger and run lightly over the colours to see that they do not bleed). The best *shyrdaks* are said to be made around Naryn. There are women's *shyrdak* cooperatives in Bishkek and Kochkor and CBT coordinators can often put you in touch with *shyrdak* makers.

his exploits in carving out a homeland for his people in the face of hostile hordes. Subsequent stories deal with the exploits of his son Semety and grandson Seitek. Manas is of course strong, brave and a born leader; he is also, to an important extent, the embodiment of the Kyrgyz' self-image.

Manas in fact predates the Kyrgyz, in the same sense that Achilles or Agamemnon predate the Greeks. The stories are part of a wider, older tradition that have come to be associated with the Kyrgyz people and culture. The epic was first written down in the mid-19th century by the Kazakh ethnographer Shoqan Ualikhanov.

Akyns who can recite or improvise from these are in a class by themselves, called *manaschi*. Latter-day bards wear sequined costumes and recite short, memorised snippets of the great songs in auditoriums. Traditionally the illiterate bards would belt out their 24-hour long epics in yurts, to enthralled audiences for whom the shifting, artful improvisations on time-worn themes were radio, television, rap music, performance poetry and myth rolled into one, but that tradition is dead.

The end of the oral tradition was inevitable with the advent of literacy (though the Soviets tried to pack it off early in the 1950s when there was a movement to criticise the epic as 'feudal'). Yet interest in Manas is on the rise. Books, operas, movies, comic books, and television serials based on Manas are thriving.

Manas mania received an exponential boost when the Kyrgyz government and Unesco declared 1995 the 'International Year of *Manas*' and the '1000th Anniversary of the *Manas* Epos'. When a small, poor country spends US$8 million (by some estimates) on celebrating an oral epic, one can be pretty sure it's not just because the government really digs rhyming verse. Manas has become, once again, a figure for the Kyrgyz to hang their dreams on. Legend has even assigned Manas a tomb, located near Talas and supposedly built by his wife Kanykey, where Muslim pilgrims come to pray.

Churned out from the death throes of the Soviet empire, Kyrgyzstan is now charting its course into the 21st century with the aid of an epic poem.

Other Arts

Kyrgyzstan's Aktan Abdykalykov is a rising star of Central Asian cinema. His film *Besh Kumpyr* (Five Old Ladies) made it to the final of the Grand Prix in Cannes and is well worth a viewing.

Yak Born in Snow is a fascinating Soviet documentary of Kyrgyz yak herders, available for viewing at Yak Tours (p271) in Karakol.

Kyrgyz traditional music is played on a mixture of *komuz* guitars, a vertical violin known as a *kyl kyayk*, flutes, drums, mouth harps (*temir komuz*, or *jygach ooz* with a string) and long horns.

ENVIRONMENT
The Land

Kyrgyzstan is a bit larger than Austria plus Hungary, about 94% of which is mountainous. The country's average elevation is 2750m. About 40% of it is over 3000m high, with three-quarters of that under permanent snow and glaciers.

The dominant feature is the Tian Shan range in the southeast section. Its crest, the dramatic Kokshal-Tau, forms a stunning natural border with China, culminating at Pik Pobedy (7439m), Kyrgyzstan's highest point and the second-highest peak in the former USSR. The Fergana range across the middle of the country and the Pamir Alay in the south hold the Fergana Valley in a scissor-grip.

In a vast indentation on the fringes of the Tian Shan, Lake Issyk-Kul, almost 700m deep, never freezes. One of the country's lacustrine jewels is tiny Song-Köl lake, in a smaller pocket to the southwest. Kyrgyzstan's only significant lowland features are the Chuy and Talas Valleys, adjacent to Kazakhstan. Its main rivers are the Naryn, flowing almost the full length of the country into the Syr-Darya in the Fergana Valley, and the Chuy along the Kazakhstan border. The Ak Shyrak, Inylchek and Sary Jaz rivers in the mountainous southeast flow into China's Tarim Basin. The Kyzyl-Suu river in the far south of the republic is the only river to flow into the Amu-Darya (Oxus River).

Kyrgyzstan offers an annual refuge for thousands of migrating birds, including rare cranes and geese. The country is believed to have had the world's second largest snow leopard population, although numbers are declining rapidly. Issyk-Kul

COMMUNITY BASED TOURISM

The Shepherd's Life and Community Based Tourism (CBT) programmes are an exciting tourism initiative inspired by the Swiss development-based programme Helvetas. The idea is that a network of information offices connect tourists with a wider network of guides, drivers and families willing to take in guests, either in villages or *jailoos* (summer meadows), across the country. You can use the organisation for anything from a comfortable cheap homestay to a fully supported horse trek. Coordinators can even put you in touch with eagle hunters and *shyrdak* makers. The concept started in Kochkor and has spread all over the country, making it a world leader in this kind of grass-roots tourism.

CBT prices vary between location but are generally around 220 to 380 som per day for bed and breakfast and 100 som per additional meal. Horse hire is 300 to 400 som per day and a guide is much the same. Car and driver costs 7 to 9 som per km, though this is dependent on the price of fuel. Shepherd's Life is cheaper than CBT but slightly less organised. Programme coordinators sustain themselves financially either through an invisible 15% commission (CBT) or a 100 som coordinators' fee (Shepherd's Life).

For food you can expect a traditional diet of home-made bread, *ayran* (yogurt) *sary may* (butter), local jam, *kaimak* (cream), *kymys* (fermented mares' milk) and tastier than normal local dishes such as *chuchvara* (dumplings) and *laghman*. It's a good idea to bring a sleeping bag if headed onto the *jailoos*, though there are normally plenty of guest duvets available. Accommodation on the *jailoos* operates from June to September only.

The programme has made budget travel in Kyrgyzstan the most enjoyable in Central Asia. Not only is it a great way for travellers to glimpse real life in Kyrgyzstan, while promoting low-impact tourism, it also injects badly needed tourist income directly into homes, communities and service providers.

CBT has offices in Tamga (p279), Karakol (p269), Kochkor (p282), Naryn (p286), Kazarman (p289), Jalal-Abad (p297), Arslanbob (p298), Osh (p302) and Talas (p295) – see those entries for more details. Shepherd's Life has five coordinators, in Kochkor, Jumgal, Naryn, At-Bashy, Ottuk and Kurtka (near Ak-Tal). A newer British-supported project operates in the Suusamyr and Talas Valleys and Ak-Terek in the Fergana Valley. See the list of Top 10 CBT adventures (p308) for some inspirational and adventurous trips that can be arranged through CBT.

and Sary Chelek lakes are Unesco-affiliated biosphere reserves.

Environmental Issues

Uranium for the Soviet nuclear military machine was mined in Kyrgyzstan (the Kyrgyz SSR's uranium sector earned the sobriquet 'Atomic Fortress of the Tian Shan'), and as many as 50 abandoned mine sites in Kyrgyzstan alone might now leak unstablised radioactive tailings or contaminated groundwater into their surroundings.

In 1998 almost two tonnes of sodium cyanide destined for the Kumtor gold mine in Kyrgyzstan was spilled into the Barskoön River and thence Issyk-Kul.

Kyrgyzstan's rivers offer vast hydropower potential, though so far this only fulfils about 25% of its requirements, and expanded development will inevitably collide with environmental considerations. The country's reserves of fresh water, locked up in the form of glaciers, remain its greatest natural resource.

FOOD & DRINK

Spicy *laghman* (noodle) dishes reign supreme, partly the result of Dungan (Muslim Chinese) influence. Apart from standard Central Asia dishes (p73), *beshbarmak* (literally 'five fingers', since it is traditionally eaten by hand) is a special holiday dish consisting of large flat noodles topped with lamb and/or horsemeat cooked in vegetable broth. *Kesme* is a thick noodle soup with small bits of potato, vegetable and meat. *Jarkop* is a braised meat and vegetable dish with noodles.

Hoshan are fried and steamed dumplings, similar to *manty* (stuffed dumplings), best right off the fire from markets. Horsemeat sausages known as *kazy*, *karta* or *chuchuk* are a popular vodka chaser, as in Kazakhstan.

In Dungan areas (eg Karakol or certain suburbs of Bishkek), ask for *ashlyanfu*, made with cold noodles, jelly, vinegar and eggs. Also try their steamed buns made with *jusai*, a mountain grass of the onion family, and *fyntyozi*, spicy cold rice noodles. *Gyanfan* is rice with a meat and vegetable sauce.

Kymys (fermented mare's milk), available in spring and early summer, is the national drink. *Bozo* is a thick fizzy drink made from boiled fermented millet or other grains. *Jarma* and *maksym* are fermented barley drinks, made with yeast and yogurt. Shoro is the brand name of a similar drink, available at most street corners in Bishkek. All four, and tea, are washed down with *boorsok* (fried bits of dough). *Kurut* (small balls of tart, dried yogurt) are a favourite snack.

Issyk-Kul honey is said to be the best in Central Asia, and locally made blackcurrant jam is a treat. Kids and elderly people in Cholpon-Ata sell strings of dried fish and you can buy larger smoked fish in the bazaars, though you should check that these have been cooked properly.

Tea is traditionally made very strong in a pot and mixed with boiling water and milk in a bowl before serving.

BISHKEK БИШКЕК

☎ 312 / pop 1.1 million / elevation 800m

Bishkek, the capital and industrial centre of independent Kyrgyzstan, is a relaxed, handsome place with wide streets, Ukrainian-style backstreet houses and mainly good-natured people of many races (47% are Russian and only about a third are Kyrgyz).

Unlike the other Central Asian capitals, Bishkek wears its recent history without embarrassment. Lenin is still here in his concrete overcoat (though he was recently demoted to a smaller square) and a larger-than-life Frunze still sits on a bronze horse facing the train station (though his name has been removed). You can still visit the museum built over Frunze's birthplace, if you can keep a straight face.

There's nothing else old here – little predates WWII. Even old people now seem sadly marginalised, with some to be seen selling their belongings on street corners to make ends meet, and a few begging.

BISHKEK MUST-SEES

Ala Archa Get out of town and go hiking and climbing (p262).

Burana Tower Take a half-day trip to do some exploring (p263).

Ala-Too Square and Dobovy Park Stroll about with frequent stops for ice cream and cold beer (p254).

KYRGYZSTAN

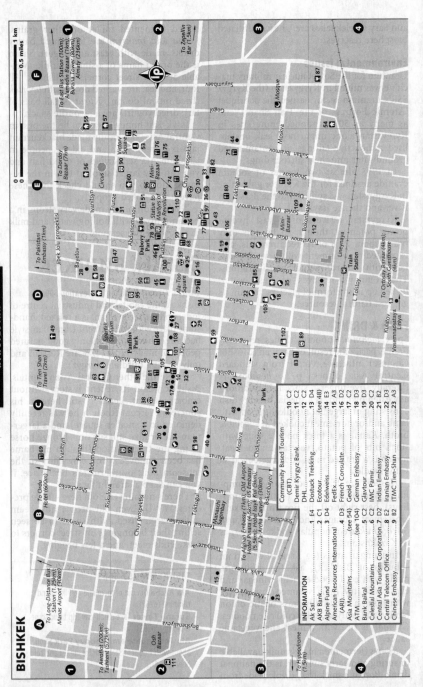

And yet amid the economic malaise, the city is attracting a small flow of foreign businesspeople, embassy staff and aid workers, as well as a small but growing Kyrgyz middle class, and a network of bars, restaurants and well-stocked shops is sprouting rapidly to support them. In many ways, Bishkek feels like Almaty's naive younger brother.

For travellers, Bishkek city is mainly a jumping-off point for more interesting places such as Issyk-Kul or Kochkor. Only the occasional glimpse of the towering peaks of the Tian Shan through the gaps in the apartment blocks serves to get the blood racing. Still, life in the city is easy and it's a pleasant enough place to wait for those tricky onward visas.

The city can catch heavy weather, with snow here when it's raining elsewhere, even in October. From October to March Bishkek is often covered by fog when the higher slopes behind the city are clear and sunny.

HISTORY

In 1825, by a Silk Road settlement on a tributary of the Chuy River, the Uzbek khan of Kokand built a little clay fort, one of several along caravan routes through the Tian Shan mountains. In 1862 the Russians captured and wrecked it, and set up a garrison of their own. The town of Pishpek was founded 16 years later, swelled by Russian peasants lured by land grants and the Chuy Valley's fertile black earth.

In 1926 the town, rebaptised Frunze, became capital of the new Kyrgyz ASSR. The name never sat well; Mikhail Frunze (who was born here) was the Russian Civil War commander who helped keep tsarist Central Asia in Bolshevik hands and hounded the *basmachi* (Muslim guerrilla) rebellion into the mountains.

In 1991 the city became Bishkek, the Kyrgyz form of its old Kazakh name. A *pishpek* or *bishkek* is a churn for *kumys*. Numerous legends (some quaint, some rude) explain how it came to be named for a wooden plunger. Others conclude disappointingly that this was simply the closest familiar sound to its old Sogdian name, Peshagakh, meaning 'place below the mountains'. With the 4800m, permanently snowcapped rampart of the Kyrgyz Alatau range looming over it, the Sogdian name still fits.

KYRGYZSTAN

ORIENTATION

Bishkek sits on the northern hem of the Kyrgyz Alatau mountains, an arm of the Tian Shan. Nineteenth century military planners laid out an orderly, compass-oriented town and getting around is quite easy.

Jibek Jolu prospektisi (Silk Road Ave), just north of the centre, was old Pishpek's main street. Now the municipal axes are Chuy and parklike Erkindik. The busiest commercial streets are Kiev and Soviet. At the centre yawns Ala-Too Square, flanked by Panfilov and Dubovy (Oak) Parks. Street numbers increase as you head north or west.

Maps

Geoid (Room 4, 3rd fl, Kiev 107; 🕑 8am-noon & 1-4.30pm Mon-Fri) sells Bishkek city maps in Cyrillic, as well as trekking and 1:200,000 topo maps (115 som). For more on maps for sale, see p310. The building is accessed through an unmarked door just west of DHL.

INFORMATION

Bookshops

NoviNomad (☎ 221335, 600599; www.novinomad.com; Togolok Moldo 28) has some nice books and postcards for sale, as does a stall at the exit of Beta Stores (Chuy prospektisi 150). The **Hyatt Regency** (☎ 66 12 34; www.bishkek.hyatt.com; Soviet 19) sells the *Herald Tribune* and *Time* for around US$5 each.

Emergency

Ambulance (☎ 103)
Fire service (☎ 101)
Police (☎ 102)

Internet Access

Shakrus Internet (☎ 28 54 11; Kiev 58; 🕑 24 hr) Also offers cheap Internet phone calls.

Medical Services

The best bet for medical attention is probably the **Kyrgyz Republic Hospital** (outpatients ☎ 22 89 60, 24-hr duty officer for emergencies & hospital ambulance ☎ 26 69 16; 110 Kiev), also known as State Clinic No 2.

Others have suggested the **Tsentr Semeinoi Meditsiny** (Centre of Family Medicine; ☎ 66 06 44, 66 06 91; 144A Bokonbayevo, by Logvinenko).

Pharmacies are marked *darykhana* (Kyrgyz) or *apoteka* (Russian).

Money

There are exchange desks all over Bishkek, including most hotels, with a concentration on Soviet.

AKB Bank (Togolok Moldo 54; 🕑 9am-4pm Mon-Fri) Changes major travellers cheques for a 3% commission (minimum US$5) and you can get the cash in US dollars. Cash advances off a Visa card are relatively quick, for 2.5% commission.

Bank Baikal (☎ 60 00 02; Isanov 75; 🕑 8.30am-noon & 1-3pm Mon-Fri) Changes travellers cheques for 3% and gives credit card advances for 1.5%.

Demir Kyrgyz Bank (☎ 61 06 10; www.dkib.com.kg; Chuy prospektisi 245; 🕑 9am-noon & 1-4pm Mon-Thu, until 2.30pm Fri) Changes Amex travellers cheques for 3% and gives Visa and Maestro credit card advances for 2.5%.

Kazkommertsbank Has an ATM by the left (west) exit of TsUM department store that accepts foreign cards with a 2% commission.

Post

American Resources International (ARI; ☎ /fax 66 00 77; aricargo@aricargo.com; Erkindik prospektisi 35) Ships larger items if you are moving to/from Bishkek.
DHL (☎ 61 11 11; Kiev 107)
FedEx (☎ 65 00 12; fax 65 01 28; Moskva 217)
Main post office (🕑 7am-8pm Mon-Sat, 8am-7pm Sun) Faces Soviet, between Chuy and Kiev. There is a separate mailroom for EMS, between the post and telecom offices.

Registration & Visas

Most visitors don't need to register (p311). If in doubt, the **Office of Visas and Registrations** (OVIR; Kiev 58, near Shopokov; 🕑 9.30am-12.30pm & 2-5pm Mon-Fri) can advise. This is also the place to get a visa extension (300 som).

Telephone & Fax

Central telecom office (cnr Soviet & Chuy; 🕑 7am-10.30pm) Also provides international fax service. There are smaller telephone offices on the corners of Chuy and Erkindik, and Chuy and Isanov.

Tourist Information

Alpine Fund (☎ 66 55 67; www.alpinefund.org; Erkindik prospektisi 2) This nonprofit organisation, established to assist Kyrgyz youth, runs a weekly indoor climbing wall (150 som), plus weekend hikes and climbs in Ala-Archa National Park, including overnight summit attempts on Peak Uchitel (4572m). It also rents trekking gear (tents/sleeping bags US$5/US$3 per day) and is a good source for mountaineering and trekking in the region.
Community Based Tourism (CBT; ☎ 62 23 85; www.cbtkyrgyzstan.kg; No 4, Kiev 95; 🕑 9am-6pm Mon-Fri, 9am-noon Sat) Gives information on CBT groups

across the country; see p248. The office is around the back of the building.

Kyrgyz Concept (Chuy prospektisi 126) Has an information office here (see also Travel Agencies, below).

NoviNomad (☎ 22 13 35, 60 05 99; www.novinomad .com; Togolok Moldo 28) Has a noticeboard where you can find other travellers.

Travel Agencies

The following agencies are starting to figure out what budget-minded individual travellers want and how much they can get for it. For details on help and transport to the Torugart Pass, see p291.

Celestial Mountains (☎ 21 25 62; www.celestial .com.kg; Kiev 131-4) British-run agency, specialises in the Torugart Pass but can also offer visa support and cultural tours and runs a hotel in Naryn. Contact Ian Claytor.

Central Asia Tourism Corporation (CAT; ☎ 66 02 77, 21 95 38; www.centralasiatourism.com; Chuy prospektisi 124) Visa support, rental cars, air tickets, accommodation and inclusive tours.

Ecotour (☎ /fax 21 34 70; www.ecotour.kg; Moskva 145/1) Recommended, ecofriendly and flexible with budget demands. Stay in a traditional yurt with horses, solar-heated water, and small hydroelectric turbines at Temir Kanat, Ak-Sai, Tuura-Su, Kara-Talaa, Jeti-Oghuz and other camps on the southern shore of Issyk Kul for €20 per night (with three meals and horse riding). Contact English-speaking Elmira or German-speaking Zamira.

Glavtour (☎ 66 32 32; www.glavtour.kg; Toktogul 93) Visa cards accepted. The website lists current airfares from Bishkek.

Kyrgyz Concept (www.akc.com.kg); main office (☎ 66 13 31; akc@elcat.kg; Razzakov 100); branch (☎ 90 08 67; Chuy 104); information (☎ 66 60 06; Chuy 126); air tickets (☎ 60 04 04; avia@concept.kg; Kiev 69) Offers cultural programmes at the higher end of the travel spectrum. Can arrange visa support, Bishkek homestays (US$20 per person), horse trekking, cultural shows and can even put you in touch with a Kyrgyz costume designer. They are also a reliable international ticket agency. Credit cards accepted.

NoviNomad (☎ 22 13 35; www.novinomad.com; Togolok Moldo 28) Cultural tours, Torugart trips and guaranteed departure tours, with an emphasis on ecotourism. Can book CBT and yurt camp accommodation across the country.

Trekking Companies

Ak Sai (☎ 54 42 77; www.ak-sai.com; Soviet 65) Trekking, mountaineering, biking, heli-skiing and visa support, with an emphasis on the Inylchek region.

Asia Mountains (☎ 69 40 73; www.asiamountains.co.uk; Lineynaya 1a) New and impressive agency charging US$25 to US$55 per person per day,

depending on the programme. Can get border permits in 10 days for US$10, even if you aren't trekking with them. Runs a base camp at Achik Tash and guesthouse in Bishkek; see p256. Contact Alona.

Dostuck Trekking Ltd (☎ 42 74 71, ☎ /fax 54 54 55; www.dostuck.com.kg; Vosemnadsataya Liniya St 42-1) Offers ascents to peaks, including Khan Tengri, Pobedy and Lenin, plus general treks, Torugart crossing and a yurt camp in the Suusamyr Valley and Tash Rabat.

Edelweiss (☎ 28 07 88; www.edelweiss.elcat.kg; Usenbayev 68/9) Trekking, mountaineering, heli-skiing, horse tours, ski trips and visa support. Contact Slava Alexandrov.

International Mountaineering Camp Pamir (IMC Pamir; ☎ 66 04 69; www.imcpamir.netfirms.com; Apt 30, Kiev 133) Trekking and mountaineering programmes and it operates the Achik Tash base camp at the foot of Peak Lenin. Contact Bekbolot Koshoev.

ITMC Tien-Shan (☎ 65 12 21; www.itmc.centralasia.kg; Molodaya Gvardia 1A) Competent adventure-travel operator offering package and piecemeal help, including visa support; mountaineering, with base camps at Khan Tengri and Koh-i-Samani (Kommunizma); trekking; heli-skiing; mountain biking; and crossing the Torugart. It also runs a yurt camp at Song-Köl (US$20 per person per day with food). Not to be confused with its former partner at Tien-Shan Travel.

Tien-Shan Travel (☎ /fax 27 05 76; www.tien-shan .com; Sherbakov 127) Ex-cartographers with expedition gear and a menu of set group tours into the mountains, but unaccustomed to walk-in clients. Contact Vladimir Birukov.

Top Asia (☎ /fax 21 16 44; www.topasia.kg; Toktogul 175) Trekking, mountaineering and horse riding.

DANGERS & ANNOYANCES

Bishkek smiles during the day but is neither safe nor well lit after dark. All the normal Central Asian security rules apply (p447). If you're out after dark, stick to main streets, avoid the parks and steer clear of the area around the train station.

Crooked plainclothes policemen are a problem in Bishkek, particularly at Osh Bazaar and at the crossroads of Soviet and Moskva. They will demand your passport and try to look in your bag and search your money (palming some en route). Legally you are required to carry your passport at all times but it's always worth trying to give them only a copy. If your passport is at an embassy, then get the embassy to write this on a photocopy of your passport.

Osh Bazaar is home to the odd pickpocket and bag-slashing thief, so keep your valuables out of sight and stay sharp in close crowds.

SIGHTS

Ala-Too Square

This sea of concrete ceased to be called Lenin Square in 1991. Lenin enjoyed centre stage on his plinth until August 2003, when he was relegated to the square behind the museum and replaced by another statue of Erkindik (Freedom). The Kyrgyz flag in the square is lowered every day at dusk.

The brutal block behind the square, once the Lenin Museum, has become the **State Historical Museum** (adult/student 40/20 som, camera 100 som; ☉ 10am-1pm & 2-7pm Tue-Sun), with a yurt, a small archaeology exhibit, a mummy and a beguiling display of Kyrgyz carpets, embroidery and other applied crafts. There's no English and lighting is so dim you'll need a torch (flashlight). The excellent top-floor shrine to Lenin and the Revolution is still in place upstairs; don't forget to look up at the ceiling murals. There is a good selection of open-air *balbals* (Turkic totemlike gravestones) on the eastern exterior side of the museum.

The grand façades across Chuy prospektisi from Lenin are just that – façades, about 10m deep, erected in Soviet times in front of the venerable but unsuitably drab Ilbirs knitwear factory.

The unmarked marble palace full of chandeliered offices just west of the square, the **'White House'**, is the seat of the Kyrgyzstan government, including the president's office and the republic's parliament. Behind this is **Panfilov Park**, whose rusting rides and arcades make it the centre of Bishkek for kids, and a great place to head for on a national holiday.

The conspicuously older structure northeast of Ala-Too Square at 68 Pushkin was the headquarters of the Central Committee of the Kyrgyz ASSR, declared in 1926. It's now home to the **Dom Druzhby** community centre, a centre for advocacy and self-help groups, as well as a drab zoology museum.

Beyond this is **Dubovy (Oak) Park**, full of strollers on warm Sundays, a few open-air cafés and some neglected modern sculpture. The century-old oaks here and along **Erkindik prospektisi** (Freedom Ave) make Bishkek a candidate for the greenest city in Central Asia. Where Erkindik enters the park, there is an open-air art gallery. Nearby is the Erkindik (Freedom) Statue, formerly a statue of Felix Dzerzhinsky, founder of the Soviet secret police.

State Museum of Fine Arts

This decaying **museum** (☎ 66 15 44; Soviet 196, near Abdymomunov; adult 100 som, student 20 som; ☉ 10am-1pm & 2-6pm), also called the Gapar Aitiev Museum of Applied Art, features Kyrgyz embroidery, jewellery, utensils, eye-popping felt rugs, works by local artists, and a startling collection of reproduction Egyptian and classical statuary.

Frunze House-Museum

Is this thatched cottage really where the little Frunze played with his toy soldiers, or just the Soviet way with history? In any case the meticulous two-storey **museum** (☎ 62 22 35; Frunze 364, near Razzakov; admission 100 som; ☉ 9am-4pm Wed-Sun) engulfing it – showcasing Frunze as a military and family man, plus the requisite posters, weapons, flags and statues – has itself become a piece of history.

Victory Square

This weedy plaza with an immense yurt-shaped **monument**, erected on the 40th anniversary of the end of WWII, sprawls across an entire city block near the Hotel Dostuk. On cold evenings you might see a knot of young men passing the bottle and warming themselves at its eternal flame.

MIKHAIL VASILIEVICH FRUNZE

Frunze was born in what was then Pishpek in 1885. After an early adulthood full of revolutionary excitement in Moscow, and numerous arrests, he eventually commanded the Red Guards who occupied the Moscow Kremlin in October 1917. He was a major player in the Russian Civil War, directing the defeat of the White forces of Admiral Kolchak in Siberia and the rout of General Wrangel in the Caucasus. It was Frunze who led the Bolshevik forces that seized Khiva and Bukhara in 1920, and pushed the *basmachi* rebels out of the Fergana Valley.

Replacing Trotsky as War Commissar, Frunze introduced compulsory peacetime military service, and moulded the Red army into a potent tool of the Revolution. After Lenin's death, he survived several mysterious auto accidents, but died a victim of Stalin's paranoia in 1925, during an officially ordered stomach operation.

On weekends it's the destination for an endless stream of wedding parties posing for photographs.

Russian Remnants
Among poignant reminders that there is still a Russian community here are the pretty, blue-steepled **Orthodox church** on Jibek Jolu near Togolok Moldo, and an incongruous, well-preserved Russian-style **log house** on Moskva, west of Togolok Moldo, which is now the Ecotour office.

Markets
The city has three daily farmers' markets, all fairly distant from the centre. **Osh bazaar**, 3km to the west, though not very colourful, offers a glimpse of Kyrgyz and Uzbeks from the more conservative south of the republic. Produce is sold inside the main bazaar and all around the outside of the complex. There is a separate clothes market south of the main produce bazaar. To get there take trolleybus No 14 on Chuy, bus No 20 or 24 on Kiev, or 42 from Soviet.

Smaller markets include the **Alamedin bazaar** to the northeast (trolleybus No 7 or 9 from TsUM, return by bus No 20 or 38) and **Ortosay Bazaar**, 6km to the south (trolleybus No 12 on Soviet). All are open daily but are biggest on weekends.

Dordoy Bazaar (nicknamed Tolchok, which means 'jostling crowd') is a huge weekend flea market of imported consumer goods and junk about 7km north of the centre. You might strike gold with the occasional North Face jacket here. Bus Nos 185, 132, 25 and 200 run to Dordoy from the northern corner of Soviet and Chuy. Watch your wallet or bag.

Baths
Buy tickets for the **Zhirgal Banya** (cnr Sultan Ibraimov & Toktogul; bath 40 som, Russian/Finnish sauna 55/60 som; ✆ 8am-9pm Wed-Mon) from the *kassa* (ticket office) around the side. Old ladies sell birch twigs outside the baths for those into a bit of self-flogging.

SLEEPING
Homestays
Sabyrbek's B&B (☎ 62 13 98; sabyrbek@mail.ru; Razzakov 21; per person US$6-10) Sabyrbek offers beds in his ramshackle house, as well as lunch and dinner (US$1 each), which are sociable

events. It's a friendly but communal place; there's one hot shower but you can't lock (or even close!) the door. The location is great; look for an unmarked gate opposite the German embassy, next to a kiosk. Sabyrbek and his wife also offer Russian and Kyrgyz language lessons (US$5 per hour).

South Guesthouse (☎ 47 26 23; www.geocities.com/south_gh; 31B, 4th fl Aaly Tokombaev; dm US$4-5) This backpacker crash pad is waaaay down in the extreme southern suburbs (8th microrayon) so you should most definitely call in advance, as it does fill up. It's essentially a two-person apartment converted into a dorm room for 10, so it may be too communelike for some. There's a hot shower and one clean toilet. The travellers' book is full of useful tips. If it's full, you can stay in Nanchan's sister's flat. Take minibus Nos 232 or 150, or trolleybus Nos 6 or 3 and get off when the bus turns off Soviet. From the bus stop, cross the road, go into the first gap between apartment blocks, turn left to face the north side of the block and go in the second door to the right. A taxi to/from the centre costs 70 som. Nanchan offers an airport pickup.

NoviNomad (☎ 22 13 35; www.novinomad.com; Togolok Moldo 28) rents an apartment near the Business School for US$25 (up to three people). **Dostuck Trekking**, **Kyrgyz Concept** (main office ☎ 66 13 31; www.akc.com.kg; Razzakov 100) and most other travel agencies (p253) can also arrange a stay in an apartment or private home, typically for around US$20 per person per night.

Budget
International School of Management & Business (☎ 62 31 01; fax 66 06 38; Panfilov 237; d US$10, pol-lux US$20, lux US$30) This is the best-value budget hotel in Bishkek. Doubles, with two rooms sharing one toilet and shower (hot water most of the time), are clean and comfortable and there's a private balcony. The hotel is also known as the 'Salima'.

Hotel Sary Chelek (☎ 66 26 27; Orozbekov 87; d 400 som, lux 600 som) This place isn't too awful if the nearby Business School is full. Reports vary but some complain of flooded bathrooms and Soviet-era beds. Check that the door locks, and ignore the cockroaches.

Gostinichny Komplex Ilbirs (☎ 66 04 72; Ivanitsyn; dm 150 som, d per person 250 som) The doubles aren't terrible here, especially if you are nostalgic for Chinese budget hotels (it's run by the Xinjiang Kashgar representative office in Bishkek). There are hot showers but the common toilets are pretty rank. Look for the Chinese-looking entrance on the back (eastern) side of the high-rise block just north of the Hotel Dostuk. The front door is locked at 10pm.

Hotel Ak-Say (☎ 26 14 65; Ivanitsyn 117; per person 190 som). Rooms here are bearable if you are stuck, with common squat toilets and cold-water basins, plus hot showers on the ground floor but the neighbourhood behind the circus is a bad one so be careful at night.

Mid-Range

Asia Mountains Guest House (☎ 69 40 73; www .asiamountains.co.uk; Lineinaja 1a; s/d with breakfast US$30/40) Trekking groups love this clean, fresh lodge, and with good reason. Guests have access to a kitchen and a nice communal seating area ideal for swapping climbing stories. The travel agency of the same name is in the basement. It's a bit on the outskirts, tucked down an alley by the railway line – take a taxi into the centre. Recommended.

Ordu Hotel (☎ 21 89 22; Kudruka 107; s/d US$45/55, ste US$95, all with breakfast; ☒) Budget business visitors or tourists keen on their mod-cons should check out the six spacious, bright and modern rooms of this private hotel. It's in a quiet backstreet, 20 minutes' walk from the centre. Some rooms are better value than others. There's a sauna. Not much English is spoken.

Hotel Semetei (☎ 21 83 24; Toktogul 125; d US$20) This Soviet hotel has a good location and fills a gap in the market but it's still gloomy and a bit overpriced. Rooms come with fridge, TV and hot-water bathroom. The cheaper rooms seem to be off-limits to foreigners.

Top End

Silk Road Lodge (☎ 66 11 29; www.silkroad.com.kg; Abdumamunova 229; s/d US$75/85, de luxe US$95, ste US$110; ☒ ☐) Run by the Celestial Mountains travel agency, this is a good option. Rooms are well-equipped with iron, fridge, hairdryer, kettle and satellite TV but are devoid of style. Business travellers will like the business centre, which can arrange an email account for the duration of your stay.

There's a small heated plunge pool and live music on the weekends. Travellers cheques and credit cards accepted.

MBA Business Center Hotel (☎ 62 31 20; bha@amp.aknet.kg; Panfilov 237; s/d with breakfast US$60/80) The 4th floor of the Bishkek International School of Management & Business offers minisuites, complete with kitchens, private bathrooms, satellite TV and a business centre. Major credit cards accepted.

Hotel Dostuk (☎ 28 42 51; fax 68 16 90; Frunze 429; s US$75, d US$90-95) Bishkek's Soviet-era flagship hotel is looking pretty mediocre and overpriced these days. Small and plain rooms come with satellite TV. The near-empty hotel also has a friendly business centre, travel agency (2nd floor), exchange desk, souvenir stand, bookshop, casino and two restaurants. Major credit cards accepted.

Hotel Pinara (☎ 54 01 44; www.pinara.com.kg; Mira prospektisi 93; s/d with breakfast US$90/105; ☒ ☒) A giant, Turkish-built four-star hotel, the Pinara has a business centre, Turkish sauna, outdoor pool (a bonus in summer), casino, 11th floor open-air terrace restaurant and tennis court but poorly trained staff. Major credit cards and travellers cheques accepted. Ask for a balcony with a mountain (southern) view.

Hyatt Regency (☎ 66 12 34; www.bishkek.hyatt .com; Soviet 19; s/d US$150/180, discounted to US$135/165; ☒ ☒) Five stars make this the plushest pad in town. Facilities include the Crostini Restaurant, Opera Lounge and a bar (p258), plus an outdoor pool and the obligatory casino. Ask for a mountain view. Breakfast is a cheeky extra US$12.

EATING

Finding a nice place with cold beer and outdoor seating is easy in Bishkek. For the cheapest food, head for the cafés. Most restaurants add a 10% service charge.

Cafés & Chaikhanas

Astana Café (Kiev; mains 30 som) Has a great atmosphere and cheap Uyghur food, including chicken shashlyk (20 som) and good, cheap salads. At night the place is jumping and there's a small cover charge for the (for once) decent live music. The Nayuz Café next-door is similar.

Chaikhana Jalal-Abad (cnr Kiev & Togolok Moldo; mains 35-50 som) Has pleasant gazebos for afternoon tea, but the Russian-only menu

THE AUTHOR'S CHOICE

Café Faiza (☎ 66 47 37; Jibek Jolu prospektisi) A wildly popular Kyrgyz restaurant in the north of town that offers high-quality local dishes at reasonable prices. You won't get near the place at lunch.

Fatboys (Chuy 104; ☎ 8am-10pm; mains 50-80 som) This expat heaven is a prime foreigners' hangout, with fresh juices, baked potatoes, pizza, a good breakfast menu, sandwiches, pancakes, cheap fruit tea (5 som) and beer, plus a library of books and fine outdoor seating. If only the staff weren't so morose.

is limited to cheap *laghman*, salads and shashlyk.

Slavic University Canteen (cnr Kiev & Shopokov) Slops out cheap Russian goulash, borscht, salads and chips for under 15 som a dish but you need to speak some Russian to know what to order. Follow the hungry students down into the basement.

Beta Gourmet (☎ 21 32 96; Chuy prospektisi 150; snacks 40 som, mains 120 som) The child-friendly Turkish and fast food here includes *pides* (Turkish-style pizzas), Iskander kebabs, Turkish tea and fish and chips, with pleasant outdoor seating.

Inter-Alliance Café (Chuy prospektisi) Take a break from shopping at next door TsUM at this open-air café, with an English menu. There are Central Asian dishes like Kazakh-style ribs and even fruit and yogurt, with cheap beer.

Several fast-food stands around town sell dangerous-looking doner kebabs (*gamburgers*) for around 10 som.

Restaurants

Orient International (☎ 66 30 95; Kiev; salads 35-75 som, mains 85-150 som) Get an outdoor seat and a draught beer and enjoy the views of Ala-Too Square with some good Turkish food at this central location. Huge *lavash* bread and *haydari* (mint and yogurt dip) make a cool lunch on a hot day for 70 som. Get any five salads for 150 som.

Yusa (Logvinenko 14) Another good Turkish restaurant to the west of the embassy district, with good Turkish kebabs, cheese *pides* (50 som), baklava, salads, vegetarian dishes and cold beer.

Pakmaya (Soviet 137; mains 75-100 som) Another good value Turkish restaurant, with a bakery on site.

Indus Valley Restaurant (☎ 29 36 62; Sultan Ibraimov 105; veg dishes 120-190 som, meat 220-250 som) Just east of Victory Square, near the Hotel Dostuk, is this Pakistani restaurant, offering everything subcontinental from Goan fish curry to chicken *kadahi* (braised or stir-fried with tomato sauce), with a good selection for vegetarians. Set-meal Indian *thalis* cost 180 to 220 som and there are lunch specials (100 som).

Bombay Restaurant (☎ 62 51 15; Chuy prospektisi 110; meat mains 170-200 som, veg mains 110-150 som) Upscale Indian food, with suitable cheesy décor.

Khanguk Koan (☎ 68 12 04; Shopokov; mains 100-130 som) A Korean featuring a fantastic picture menu. If in doubt, try the *bim-bambap* (95 som) or the excellent *namche*, a salad made of raw vegetables, meats and seafood sauce.

Just round the corner, side by side on the south side of Victory Square, are two decent Chinese restaurants: the friendly **Khuadali** (mains 120 som) and the slightly cheaper Kontinental.

Balasagun Restaurant (Chuy prospektisi; dishes 75 som, snacks 20 som) A recommended Chinese place beside the Rossiya Cinema.

Old Edgar (☎ 66 44 08; west side of Russian Drama Theatre; mains 85-100 som) Choose from a good selection of Russian salads, fish (perch with mushrooms) and pizza in what feels like an underground Bavarian lodge. The après-ski vibe is reinforced by live music and a good bar. There's outdoor seating in summer.

Bar Navigator (☎ 66 51 51; cnr Moskva & Razzakov; mains 100-150 som) Vegetarian heaven here, with over 20 salads to choose from and also sophisticated mains like smoked Siberian salmon (120 som). Also a nice place for a drink (p258).

Santa Maria (☎ 21 24 84; Chuy prospektisi 217; mains 100-140 som) Anyone who has ever tried ordering Korean dishes in Russian will appreciate the picture menu at this upscale place. There are also European dishes, from paella to rabbit, with a few Japanese noodle dishes thrown in. Our eyes are on the bliny with caviar, lemon and olives (205 som). Visa cards accepted.

Adriatico Paradise (☎ 21 76 32; Chuy prospektisi 219; mains 200-300 som) The excellent Italian

KYRGYZSTAN

food here is prepared by a genuine Italian chef, with imported ingredients and Chianti wines. A 12-inch pizza costs 150 som and pasta dishes run at around 120 som. Lunch deals (pasta and salad) cost 99 som.

Grand Hyatt (☎ 66 12 34; www.bishkek.hyatt.com; Soviet 19) Offers Sunday brunch (US$16 with one cocktail) and has a kids' play area. Pay US$33/US$22 (adult/child) and they'll throw in a day's pool use and one drink.

Self-Catering

Bishkek has Central Asia's best *samsas* (samosas), sold hot out of mini-ovens all around town for around 10 som each. The chicken or cheese ones are generally the best.

Ak Emir Bazaar (cnr Moskva & Shopokov) A great place for do-it-yourselfers, with samosas, roast chicken, pickled Korean salads, honey, buckets of blackcurrants and *piroshki* (Russian-style pies) – plus fruit and vegetables.

Beta Stores (Chuy prospektisi 150) You can get everything from baklava to bottled *kymyz* (24 som) in the most popular supermarket in town. Trekkers will find the soup mixes useful.

Europa Supermarket (☎ 28 89 51; Sultan Ibraimov 70; ⏱ until 11pm) Another well-stocked supermarket on the other side of town, with a small department store and souvenir shop attached.

DRINKING

Steinbrau (☎ 29 38 81; Gertse 5; for 0.4L draught beer 40-52 som, mains 120-130 som) The German-style pilsner and recommended dark beer is brewed on site here and is the main draw. The round tables and kids' play area are great for groups and families. The beer snacks, Georgian wines and full menu of German food, from sausages to pretzels, adds to the Munich beer-hall vibe.

Bar Navigator (☎ 66 51 51; Moskva 103; 1L beer 60-70 som) A stylish spot where embassy workers shell out 100 som for a gin and tonic or 60 som for a cappuccino. The good live music makes it a classy place for a date. They also serve great appetisers and food (p257).

2X2 (☎ 21 24 97; cnr Isanova & Chuy prospektisi; beer 60 som, cocktails 70-400 som) Imported grappa and coffee draw the faithful to this chic Italian-run pastel-and-chrome bar. Visa cards accepted.

Planet Holsten (Dobovy Park) A nice place to sit outside on balmy nights and order a cold beer and a hot pizza.

@191 bar (drinks during happy hour US$4; ⏱ 6.30-8.30pm Thu-Sat) Part of the Hyatt Regency.

Johnnie's Pub (☎ 21 24 65; Chuy 209; 0.5L draught beer 50-110 som; 20% discount & free snacks 5-8pm Mon-Wed) Has live jazz Thursday, Friday and Saturday with a cover charge of 50 som. Pluses include good beer snacks and open-air seating in summer. If you get peckish, the attached Golden Bull Steakhouse offers steak sizzlers, salads, nachos, baked potatoes and tandoori chicken (it's Indian-run), plus lots of kid-friendly stuff like fish fingers.

ENTERTAINMENT
Theatres & Concert Halls

Philharmonia (☎ 21 92 92; Chuy prospektisi 210, by Belinsky) Features Western and Kyrgyz orchestral works and the occasional Kyrgyz song-and-dance troupe, but you may need a local person to identify these from the playbills. Check out the interesting old black-and-white photos on the 1st floor. In front of the Philharmonia is a statue of the legendary hero Manas slaying a dragon, flanked by his wife, Kanykey, and his old adviser, Bakay, and a statue gallery of modern Kyrgyz *akyn*. The *kassa* (ticket office) is on the west side.

State Opera & Ballet Theatre (☎ 66 18 41; Soviet 167) Opposite the State Museum of Fine Arts, classical Western as well as local productions play in this elegant building to half-empty halls.

Palace of Sport There are also occasional concerts here, on the west side of Panfilov Park.

State Academic Drama Theatre (☎ 21 69 58; Panfilov 273) On the east side of Panfilov Park, this is the place for popular Kyrgyz-language works, more often than not written by Chinghiz Aitmatov, Kyrgyzstan's premier man of words.

Russian Drama Theatre (☎ 22 86 30; Tynystanov, in Dubovy Park) For classics in Russian.

Dom Kino (☎ 66 22 76; Logvinenko 13) The folk troupe Ordo Sakhna, who are well worth checking out, sometimes perform here, near the Yusa Restaurant.

The Jetigen and Samaa ensembles are also good. Ask **NoviNomad** (☎ 22 13 35; www.novinomad.com; Togolok Moldo 28) about upcoming concerts.

Other Entertainment

Soho (☎ 66 54 27; Orozbekov; cover 200-300 som) Nightclubs go in and out of fashion, but Soho seems pretty permanent (it's owned by President Akaev's son). Soho will also rent you a hall and DVD player for you and your friends (600 som per group) and there's a pool hall in the same building.

Galaxia (☎ 68 17 00; cnr Frunze & Shopokov) Offers ground floor ten-pin bowling (per game before/after 6pm 140/190 som, for children 90/140) and an upstairs **disco** (⏰ noon-3am; cover women/men 200/300 som).

Zepellin Bar (☎ 28 34 92; Chuy prospektisi 43) Russian rock bands play here to a young crowd most nights, with a 50-som cover. It's 2km east from TsUM; a taxi costs 70 som.

You can play pool for 80 som an hour in the **billiards club** (☎ 22 83 42; cnr Orozbekov & Frunze), underneath the Consul Restaurant.

The Circus, on Frunze east of Soviet, played to packed houses in Soviet times but is now in a state of extreme disrepair.

Between July and September nonguests can use the Grand Hyatt's pool for US$15 (or use the pool, gym and sauna for US$25). The Pinara's nice outdoor pool costs US$10 for nonguests.

Maple Leaf Golf & Country Club is Kyrgyzstan's first nine-hole golf course, southeast of Bishkek near the village of Kara Jigach.

Sport

Once upon a time, on summer Sundays, you might have seen traditional Kyrgyz horseback games at the Hippodrome, southwest of the centre. Lately the best you can expect around Bishkek are exhibition games during the Navrus festival and on Kyrgyz Independence Day (31 August).

SHOPPING

Bishkek has the country's best collection of souvenirs and handicrafts, though you can often find individual items cheaper at their source (eg *shyrdaks* in Naryn, hats in Osh). For details on markets, see p255.

TsUM (☎ 29 27 94; Chuy prospektisi 155) This state-run department store is surprisingly well stocked with a photo shop (digital!), a large selection of made-for-tourist postcards and souvenirs on the 2nd floor, music CDs (US$4) and MP3s on the ground floor, and essential hardware such as miniature water heaters (perfect for making your own hot drinks).

Artwork

Asia Gallery (☎ 62 45 05; Chuy prospektisi 108; ⏰ 10am-5pm Mon-Fri). Features modern Kyrgyz art, with some artists' workshops in the yard out the back.

Sailmaluu Tash Art Gallery (Pushkin 78; ⏰ 11am-5pm Tue-Sat) On the north side of Dom Druzhby, this sells interesting but pricey pottery.

Stroll along the covered gallery in Dubovy Park to see local artists selling woodcarvings, oil paintings and charcoal portraits most afternoons.

Slavic University (☎ 62 29 27; Kiev 44). There's also a gallery here.

Carpets

Kyrgyz Style (Kyrgyz Korku; ☎ 62 12 67; www.kyrgyzstyle.kg; Apt 12, 133 Bokonbayev) A nonprofit organisation that sells high quality *shyrdaks, ala kiyiz* (felt rugs featuring coloured panels), hats, bags and slippers to support social development in Kyrgyzstan. It's on the ground floor, accessed from around the back of the apartment block.

Antiquarian Shop Bishfar (☎ 66 49 16, Kiev 76) Carries a private collection of old and new carpets from Afghanistan, Turkmenistan and Iran. The Afghan owner, Mr Akram, can give you a stamped receipt for customs and show you a wider selection in his home.

Another place to look for *shyrdaks* are the souvenir shops in the State Historical Museum.

Handicrafts

You can find Kyrgyz men's hats – the familiar white felt *ak-kalpak* or the fur-trimmed *tebbetey* – for sale in TsUM or, much cheaper, in the north building at Osh Bazaar, in the west of town, which also has other souvenirs.

There are some souvenirs (particularly felt) in the cabins in front of Beta Stores on Chuy.

Antique Shop (☎ 62 19 10; http://alwian.host.net.kg; Manas 47; ⏰ 10am-1pm & 2-5.30pm Mon-Fri, until 3.30pm Sat) An Aladdin's cave of Soviet, Kyrgyz and Russian antiques, strong on coins and memorabilia. Visa cards accepted.

Asakhi (☎ 66 57 10; Chuy prospektisi 136) Sells natural-dyed *shyrdaks*, carpets, embroideries

KYRGYZSTAN

and hats, designed with foreign tastes in mind.

Iman (☎ 21 24 05; Chuy prospektisi 128) Offers a small collection of slightly gimmicky jewellery, wooden soldiers (Manas and company), Kyrgyz handicrafts and Soviet memorabilia.

Maison du Voyageurs (☎ 66 63 30; Moskva 122, cnr with Orozbekov) A wide selection of crafts from all over Kyrgyzstan, all marked with prices, the artist and the region they come from. The entrance is round the back and marked 'CATIA'.

Tumar Art Salon (☎ 21 26 53; Togolok Moldo 36) Sells high-quality, high-priced embroidery. Credit cards accepted.

GETTING THERE & AWAY
Air

Kyrgyzstan Airlines (☎ 62 21 23; kyrgyz_air@elcat.kg; Soviet 129) flies several times a day to Osh (US$40 to US$45), twice weekly to Jalal-Abad (US$40 to US$45) – spectacular trips by Yak-40, between the mountain tops and the clouds.

AIRLINE OFFICES

The following international airline offices in Bishkek are useful for reconfirming or changing the dates of an existing flight but are not the cheapest places to book an international ticket:

Aeroflot (☎ 64 02 73; Chuy prospektisi 230) By Osh Bazaar. Flies to Moscow for US$195/340.

British Airways (☎ 66 09 00; fax 66 08 68; Toktogul 93)

Itek Air (☎ 21 69 14; fax 66 40 57; Chuy prospektisi 128) Flies weekly to İstanbul and Moscow.

KLM – Royal Dutch Airlines (☎ 66 15 00; fax 66 34 50; Toktogul 93)

Lufthansa (Hyatt Regency, Soviet 19)

Turkish Airlines (☎ 66 00 08; thyfru@elcat.kg; Soviet 136, cnr Bokonbayevo)

Uzbekistan Airways (☎ 61 03 64; uzb-air@elcat.kg; Kiev 107)

Xinjiang Airlines (☎ 66 46 68; Chuy prospektisi 128/3) Can book Ürümqi–Kashgar tickets.

For booking airline tickets see Central Asia Tourism Corporation, Galvtour or Kyrgyz Concept, p253.

Bus & Car

The west (zapadny) or long-distance bus station is the place for long-distance buses; get there via bus No 7 on Kiev, bus Nos 35

or 48 or minibus Nos 113 or 114 from Jibek Jolu, or trolleybus No 5 on Manas. There's an information office next to counter 21 and a 24-hour exchange booth on the upper floor. Don't trust the schedule board at the station, and first ask the price for a seat in a private car going in your direction – always a more comfortable option. Private cars and taxis scout for passengers by the roadside.

Luxury buses depart hourly in the morning to Karakol (145 som, 8½ hours) stopping at Cholpon-Ata (100 som) and most places in between. The private minivans out on the road depart when full to Karakol (180 som) and Cholpon-Ata (150 som) but you'll be waiting around a long time. A better bet is a seat in a private car but you'll have to hunt around to get a fair price as drivers think nothing of charging foreigners double. Karakol currently costs 300 som per seat and Cholpon-Ata 150 to 200 som, but prices fluctuate with petrol costs.

There is sometimes a single daily bus to Naryn (180 som) and At-Bashy (200 som) at 7am but you are better off taking a shared taxi to Kochkor (80 som) or Naryn (150 som).

For Osh ramshackle minibuses and private cars wait at the Osh Bazaar bus stand, departing when full, for 500 to 600 som for a seat in a minibus, or 600 to 800 som for a seat in a car. The trip takes around 15 hours depending on the road and vehicle. You can also find transport here to other destinations in the Kyrgyz Fergana Valley, such as Batken and Kyzyl-Kiya.

This stand also has local buses to destinations west such as Tash-Bulak, Sokuluk, Kashka-Suu and Chong-Tash. Bus Nos 160, 169 and 177 go several times a day to Kashka-Suu, for Ala-Archa National Park; inquire at the ticket office at the entrance to the bus stand.

The east (vastotshny avtovaksal) bus station is for regional points east such as Kant, Tokmak, Chong Kemin, Kemin, Kegeti and Issyk-Ata.

GETTING AROUND
To/From the Airport

Bus No 153 (15 som, one hour) runs every hour all day to **Manas airport** (☎ 60 31 09), 30km northwest of the centre, from the old airport by the Pinara Hotel, but the closest it gets to the centre is a stop in front of the

Philharmonia. Marshrutnoe No 325 runs to the airport from Osh Bazaar. Minibuses also run from the corner of Chuy and Molodiya Guardia (30 som).

A taxi between the airport and the centre should be around 350 som. Ekspress Taxis at the airport can arrange a reliable taxi. Almost all flights arrive in the middle of the night so you won't have any trouble finding a taxi into town.

Bus

Municipal buses cost 2.5 som, payable as you disembark at the front. At rush hour these are so crammed that you must plan your escape several stops ahead. Ford Transit minibuses (3.5 som) are generally a better bet, as they are faster and less crowded.

Some useful minibus routes:

No 110 From Osh bazaar, along Moskva to Soviet and then south.

Nos 113, 114 From the west (long-distance) bus station, down Jibek Jolu to Alamedin Bazaar.

Nos 125, 126 From Soviet (opposite the Orient International restaurant) south down Mira prospektisi to the old airport, US embassy and Hotel Issyk-Kul.

Car

Most agencies listed in the Travel Agencies section (p253) can arrange a car and driver but you are better off just hiring a taxi (see below) for the day at a fraction of the price. Dostuk Travels in the Dostuk Hotel charges US$20 per day for a car and driver.

Taxi

Essentially anyone with a car is a taxi. Official taxis, marked by the checkerboard symbol, are most reliable. The best quality taxis are **Super Taxi** (☎ 152) or **Salam Taxi** (☎ 188). A short ride in the city costs around 30-50 som, or 75 som with Super Taxi.

You can book a taxi 24 hours a day on ☎ 182 for a small surcharge.

AROUND BISHKEK

Rolling out of the Kyrgyz Alatau, the Ala-Archa, Alamedin and dozens of parallel streams have created a phalanx of high canyons, good for everything from picnics to mountaineering.

There are many possible do-it-yourself summer treks, but bring your own food and

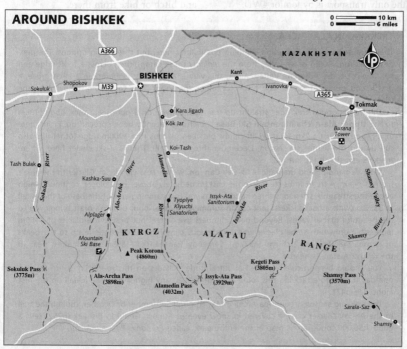

AROUND BISHKEK

gear and be prepared for cold weather and storms even in summer. There is limited public transport and you are best off hiring a taxi to drop you at the trailheads, though Bishkek travel agencies (p253) can provide transport and arrange guided trips. Winter excursions are best arranged through an agency, who should know about avalanches and other risks.

Ala-Archa Canyon

In this very grand, rugged but accessible gorge south of Bishkek, you can sit by a waterfall all day, hike to a glacier (and ski on it, even in summer) or trek into the region's highest peaks. Most of the canyon is part of a state nature park, and foreigners must pay an entrance fee of 30 som. For some hiking routes, see the boxed text on p262.

The park gate is 30km from Bishkek. Some 12km beyond the gate, at 2150m, the sealed road ends at a shabby base camp or *alplager* with a weather station and a simple hotel (a bigger complex burned down a few years ago). In summer it has recreational facilities, baths and a sauna. Beyond this point the only transport is by foot or 4WD.

SLEEPING & EATING

The best way to enjoy Ala-Archa is by bringing your own tent and sleeping bag. The only year-round accommodation is a wooden **hotel** (t 350 som) in the *alplager*, with a dozen Spartan doubles with common toilet and no shower, and a nearby new alpine-style **lodge** (d US$30-50). Try to avoid visiting on Saturday or Sunday, when 'biznezmen' turn up by the BMW-load to drink vodka and eat salami.

GETTING THERE & AWAY

Bishkek travel agencies can arrange pricey day and longer trips including guides and gear. The best budget alternative would be to hire a taxi or hitch (though you'll still end up paying for the ride).

From Osh Bazaar bus stand in Bishkek, bus No 365 runs 5 times a day to the gate (30 som). Ask *vorota zapovednika*? (Nature park gate?) when you board. You may even find minibuses running as far as the *alplager*. If these aren't running (likely outside of summer weekends), take a minibus as far as Kashka-Suu village, 7km from the park gate (itself 12km from the *alplager*), and hitch or hike from there.

TREKKING IN ALA-ARCHA

There are dozens of trekking and climbing possibilities here, but three main options. The gentlest walk runs 300m down-valley from the *alplager* (base camp), then across a footbridge and southwest up the **Adygene Valley**. Along this way is a climbers' cemetery in a larch grove, a pretty and poignant scene. The track continues for about 7km to 3300m, below Adygene Glacier.

The most popular trek goes straight up the main canyon on a poor jeep track, about 18km to the **Upper Ala-Archa Mountain Ski Base**, which has recently been spruced up. From there in July and August a 2km-long ski lift climbs between glaciers to a 3900m ridge (other lifts also run during the winter ski season, December through April). There's a ski chalet here, where trekkers can stay if it's not full.

Most demanding and dramatic is **Ak-Say Canyon**, with access via Ak-Say Glacier to the area's highest peaks. A trail climbs steeply to the east immediately above the *alplager*, continuing high above the stream. A strenuous three hours brings you to a camping area at the base of the icefall at 3350m (with a backpackers' tent city in summer). Another hour or two's graft brings you to the beautiful glacial valley. Beyond here, climbers use a steel hut beside the glacier at 4150m (accessible only with some glacier walking). Serious climbing routes continue up to the peaks of Korona (4860m) and Uchityel (4572m). Semenov Tianshanskii (4895m), the highest peak in the Kyrgyz Alatau, is nearby.

You should be particularly careful about altitude sickness on this route. Try to do at least one day hike before tackling this route and don't sleep any higher than the icefall on the first night. See p477.

The trekking season around Ala-Archa is May through September or October, though the trail to the Ak-Say Glacier can be covered in snow even in August. Geoid in Bishkek (p252) sells a good 1:50,000 topographic map of the entire park, called *Prirodnyy Park Ala-Archa*.

Also from Bishkek, on Moskva, west-bound No 11 buses, and on Soviet, west-bound No 26 buses, go about 12km south to the end of the line near the city limits, from where you can hire a taxi or hitch (ask for *alplager*, not just 'Ala-Archa').

A taxi from Osh bazaar costs around 150 som one way to the gate, or 200 som to the *alplager*. If you are planning to return the same day negotiate a rate for the day, other-wise you face a long hike back to the gate or leave yourself to the mercy of the taxi sharks at the *alplager*.

Other Canyons

Several valleys east of Ala-Archa have good walks and fewer visitors. In next-door **Ala-medin Canyon**, 40km from Bishkek, the main destination for local people is an old sanator-ium called **Tyoplye Klyuchi** (Hot Springs) run by the Ministry of Power, with cheap accom-modation and food. Although not protected by a national park, the scenery above and beyond this is as grand and walkable as Ala-Archa's, but there are no facilities.

On your own, take arenda bus No 145 from Alamedin Bazaar in Bishkek, get off at Koy-Tash village and hitch the 14km to the gate. Buses are said to depart frequently throughout the day in summer.

Another thermal-spring complex (*kurort*) and guesthouse is about 45km east of Bishkek in **Issyk-Ata Canyon**. A guesthouse here has for-eigners' rooms for US$40, or a Spartan hos-tel for around 100 som. There are five or six buses a day to the complex (Nos 193 and 307; 35 som) from Bishkek's east bus station.

Some travel agents take hiking or horse-riding groups to a lake and waterfalls in **Kegeti Canyon**, which is 75km east of Bishkek. There's one bus a day to Kegeti at 1.30pm from Bishkek's east bus station, or take a bus to Tokmak and then hire a taxi.

Southwest of Ala-Archa lies the village of Tash-Bulak, from where you can make nice overnight trips up the **Sokuluk Canyon** and even (with a guide) make a three day trek over the Sokuluk Pass (3775m) into the Suusamyr Valley. There is one bus a day to Tash-Bulak (20 som) at 10am from the Osh Bazaar bus stand. Alternatively take minibuses No 369 to the village of Sokuluk and then take a shared taxi (20 som per per-son) or hitch the remaining 24km south to Tash-Bulak.

Burana Tower

Beyond Kegeti at the mouth of the Shamsy Valley, 80km from Bishkek, is a 1950s Soviet restoration of the so-called Burana Tower, an 11th-century monument that looks like the stump of a huge minaret. A mound to the northwest is all that's left of the ancient citadel of Balasagun, founded by the Sogdi-ans and later, in the 11th century, a capital of the Karakhanids, which was excavated in the 1970s by Russian archaeologists. The Shamsy Valley itself has yielded a rich hoard of Scythian treasure, including a heavy gold burial mask, all either spirited away to St Petersburg or in storage in Bishkek's State Historical Museum.

You can climb the octagonal minaret to get an overview of the old city walls. On the other side of the citadel mound is an in-teresting collection of 6th- to 10th-century *balbals* (Turkic totemlike stone markers). The small **museum** (admission 60 som; ☉ 8am-5pm) has 11th-century Christian carvings, Bud-dhist remains and Chinese coins, as well as info on local literary hero Haji Balasagun and his masterwork, the *Kutudhu Bilik*. Next door are the foundations of several mausoleums.

SOVIET SECRETS

The town of Chong-Tash, 10km from Kashka-Suu village, holds a dark secret. On one night in 1937, the entire Soviet Kyrgyz government – nearly 140 people in all – were rounded up, brought here and shot dead, and their bodies dumped in a disused brick kiln on the site. Apparently almost no-one alive by the 1980s knew of this, by which time the site had been con-verted to a ski resort. But a watchman at the time of the murders, sworn to secrecy, told his daughter on his deathbed, and she waited until *perestroika* to tell police.

In 1991 the bodies were moved to a mass grave across the road, with a simple memorial, apparently paid for by the Kyrgyz author Chinghiz Aitmatov (whose father may have been one of the victims). The remains of the kiln are inside a fence nearby.

Several minibuses (No 365) run daily to Chong-Tash from the Osh Bazaar bus stand.

To get to Burana on your own, take the frequent No 353 minibuses from Bishkek's east bus station to Tokmak (25 som, 45 minutes), from where it's about 24km (about 150 som) round trip by taxi. Buses run to Burana from Tokmak at 7am, 12.10pm and 3.30pm, returning 90 minutes later. The minaret could easily be visited en route to or from Issyk-Kul.

Tokmak has a large Sunday bazaar on the outskirts of town. Buses run frequently from Osh Bazaar.

Chong-Kemin Valley

The 80km-long Chong-Kemin Valley and national park lies about 140km east of Bishkek, along the Kazakh border. The valley is famous locally as the birthplace of current President Akaev, but more importantly for travellers, it provides another great opportunity to roll up your sleeping bag and trek into the hills.

Trekking routes lead up the valley to Jasy-Kül Lake and either the Ozyorny Pass (3609m) to Kazakhstan's Bolshoe Almatinskoe region or the Ak-Suu Pass (4062m) to Grigorievka on the northern shores of Issyk-Kul. See the boxed text on p118.

There's no formal accommodation in the valley but the travel company Ecotour (p253) sets up yurts here in summer. There are two buses a day to Chong-Kemin (2½ hours; 50 som) from Bishkek's east bus station, at 10am and 1pm. Otherwise take a more frequent No 352 bus to Kemin (1 hour, 35 som) and then take a taxi the remaining 50km to Chong-Kemin.

LAKE ISSYK-KUL & THE CENTRAL TIAN SHAN
ЫСЫК-КӨЛ И ЦЕНТРАЛЬНЫЙ ТЯНЬ ШАНЬ

Lake Issyk-Kul is basically a huge dent, filled with water, between the Küngey (Sunny) Alatau to the north and the Terskey (Dark) Alatau to the south, which together form the northern arm of the Tian Shan. The name (we use the more familiar

> ### ISSYK-KUL BIOSPHERE RESERVE
>
> The Issyk-Kul region has an astonishing array of ecosystems, from desert and semi-desert in the southwest to steppe, meadow, forest, subalpine and glacial to the north and southeast. Local fauna includes Marco Polo sheep, ibex, wild boar, snow leopards, ibisbill, manul, Himalayan snowcocks, wild geese, egrets and other waders.
>
> Plans are therefore afoot to create a reserve the size of Switzerland around the lake. This would consist of a mountainous core area, a buffer zone that would allow seasonal land use, and a transition and rehabilitation zone. The proposals will link up several existing reserves. Tourism is part of the programme, with a series of ecofriendly tourist yurts planned.

spelling of what is properly Ysyk-Köl from the Kyrgyz) means 'warm lake'. A combination of extreme depth, thermal activity and mild salinity means the lake never freezes; its moderating effect on the climate, plus abundant rainfall, have made it something of an oasis through the centuries.

At 170km long, 70km across and with a maximum depth of 695m, Issyk-Kul is the second-largest alpine lake after Lake Titicaca in South America.

The north side of the lake is shallow, with flat, sandy shores, while the south side is steep, stony and deep. The land around the west end is dry and barren, while the east end is well watered by air masses that collect moisture from the lake and then rise into the mountains. Scores of streams enter the lake along its 600km shoreline, but there is no outflow – at least there has been none due to evaporation for some centuries – and consequently the lake is slightly salty. This, plus the physics of deep water and some underground thermal activity, mean that it never freezes.

Some people say the lake level has periodically risen and fallen over the centuries, inundating ancient shoreline settlements. There has been some fluctuation but the geological evidence points to a long-term drop – some 2m in the last 500 years. Nobody is sure why, although the interruption of inflowing streams for irrigation might play a part. Artefacts have been recovered

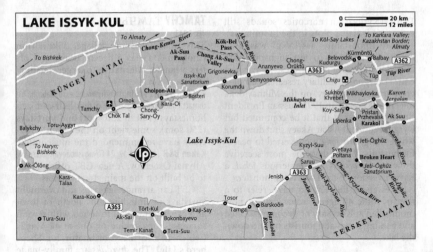

LAKE ISSYK-KUL

0 — 20 km
0 — 12 miles

from what is called the submerged city of Chigu, dating from the 2nd century BC, at the east end. Mikhaylovka inlet near Karakol was apparently created by an earthquake, and the remains of a partly submerged village can be seen there.

After Tsarist military officers and explorers put the lake on Russian maps, immigrants flooded in to found low-rise, laid-back, rough-and-ready towns. Health spas lined its shores in Soviet days, with guests from all over the USSR, but spa tourism crashed along with the Soviet Union, only reviving in the last year or so thanks to an influx of moneyed Kazakh tourists. Today Slavs and Kyrgyz live in roughly equal numbers in the lake's major towns.

Most of the population, decent roads and sanatoria are along the north shore. The southern shore by contrast offers more opportunities to get off the beaten track. Karakol is the tourist epicentre of the lake.

The part of the central Tian Shan range accessible from the lake comprises perhaps the finest trekking territory in Central Asia. The most popular treks hop between valleys south of Karakol or lead from Almaty to the lake. For some post-trek R&R you can lie on a sandy beach in Cholpon-Ata. If heading back to Almaty, another option is to go via the Karkara Valley (p278). Give yourself at least four or five days to take in this region. A week is better, more if you'll be hiking.

History

The Kyrgyz people migrated in the 10th to 15th centuries from the Yenisey river basin in Siberia, and in all probability arrived by way of Issyk-Kul. This high basin would be a natural stopover for any caravan or conquering army as well. It appears to have been a centre of Saka (Scythian) civilisation and legend has it that Timur (Tamerlane) used it for a summer headquarters (p278). There at least 10 documented settlements currently under the waters of the lake and treasure hunters have long scoured the lake for flooded treasures attributed to everyone from Christian monks to Jenghiz Khan.

The first Russian, Ukrainian and Belarussian settlers came to the east end of the lake in 1868. Karakol town was founded in the next year, followed in the 1870s by Tüp, Teploklyuchenka (Ak-Suu), Ananyevo, Pokrovka (now Kyzyl-Suu) and a string of others, many of whose Cossack names have stuck. Large numbers of Dungans and Uyghurs arrived in the 1870s and 1880s following the suppression of Muslim uprisings in China's Shaanxi, Gansu and Xinjiang provinces. Local Kyrgyz and Kazakhs were still at that time mostly nomadic.

The Issyk-Kul region (and in fact most of Kyrgyzstan beyond Bishkek) was off limits to foreigners in Soviet times. Locals mention vast, officially sanctioned plantations of opium poppies and cannabis around the lake, though most of these had disappeared under international pressure by the early

KYRGYZSTAN

1970s (Kyrgyzstan narcotics squads still swoop on isolated plots in the mountains).

More importantly, Issyk-Kul was used by the Soviet navy to test high-precision torpedoes, far from prying Western eyes. An entire polygon or military research complex grew around Koy-Sary, on the Mikhaylovka inlet near Karakol. In 1991 Russian President Boris Yeltsin asked that it be continued but Kyrgyz President Askar Akaev shut down the whole thing, ordering it converted to peaceful pursuits. These days the most secretive thing in the lake is the mysterious *jekai*, a Kyrgyz version of the Loch Ness monster.

Jokes about the 'Kyrgyz navy' refer to a fleet of some 40 ageing naval cutters, now mothballed at Koy-Sary or decommissioned and hauling goods and tourists up and down the lake.

Getting There & Away

The western road access to Issyk-Kul is a 40km-long, landslide-prone, slightly sinister canyon called Shoestring Gorge (Boömskoe ushchelie), which climbs into the Alatau east of Tokmak, with a howling wind funnelling up it most of the time. The Chuy River thundering down through it appears to drain the lake but doesn't (perhaps it once did, when the lake was higher). At the west end of the canyon are the Badland-like red rocks of the Konorchek Canyon.

There's a police checkpoint just west of Balykchy, where cars are searched for drugs and an 'eco-tax' is collected from each inbound vehicle from outside Issyk-Kul and Naryn provinces. Balykchy is the place to change buses if you're going directly between Karakol and Naryn.

Flights operate in summer from Almaty (and maybe Osh) to the new Issyk-Kul airport near Tamchy but are dependent on passenger numbers and fuel supplies. There are sometimes Osh–Karakol flights.

A rough jeep road (4WD only) from Almaty's Bolshoe Almatinskoe Lake leads over the Ozerny Pass, through the Chong-Kemin Valley and then the Kok Ayryk Pass to Chong-Sary-Oy near Cholpon-Ata. There's no public transport along the route, the bridges often get washed out and there's no immigration post, making it a particularly tricky option for foreigners. It might make an interesting mountain-bike trip if you can sort out the visa situation.

TAMCHY ТАМЧЫ
☎ 3943

This small lakeshore village, 35km from Cholpon-Ata, has a decent beach and offers a quieter alternative to larger, bustling Cholpon-Ata.

CBT (☎ 2 11 94; cbt_tamchy@rambler.ru; Babasha 13; contact Chachykei Abylgazieva) offers half-a-dozen homestays (180 to 250 som) and yurtstays (250 som), some right on the beach. Travellers have recommended the museumlike **Kaken B&B** (☎ 2 11 12; 24 Chyngyshbaeva), run by Altynai Osoemov. A new CBT office is due to be built on the main street, Manas.

CBT can arrange day trips and overnight yurtstays up into the hills north of town and can also put you in touch with several *shyrdak* shops, including one at 47 Manas (which is also the coordinator for Shepherd's Life). The *shyrdaks* are family-made and are good value at US$15 to US$40.

The popular beach has umbrella and pedlo hire and is a decent place to rest up for a day.

There's lots of minibus traffic through to Bishkek (150 to 180 som), Karakol (150 som) and Cholpon-Ata (25 som), and also buses to Bishkek (80 to 100 som) and Karakol (70 to 100 som). Shared run to Bishkek (180 to 250 som per person) and Karakol (150 to 200 som).

The new Issyk-Kul airport is 3km outside Tamchy, near the village of Chok Tal, with patchy summer-only flights to Almaty (US$70).

CHOLPON-ATA ЧОЛПОН-АТА
☎ 3943

Cholpon-Ata is no longer worth a stop for its sanatoria, but if you want to see some ancient rock inscriptions or spend a day on a beach about as far away from the ocean as you can possibly get, then this is the place.

Orientation & Information

The town has two reference points: the bus station and the bazaar about 2km east on the main road.

There's Internet access (50 som per hour) at the post office and lots of exchange booths around town.

Investbank (☎ 8am-5pm Mon-Fri, 9am-3pm Sat) gives advances on Visa and MasterCard for 3% commission.

Sights & Activities

BEACHES & BOATS

A pleasant public beach lies 2km south of the bus station. Walk south from the bus station to the chalets of the Gost Residenza and then head east, across a bridge over a lagoon to the beach (*plaj* in Russian). Kyrgyz President Akaev owns a house near the beach so you may have to show your passport to get here. There is another larger beach called Alytn-Kul, 4km east of Cholpon-Ata.

Kruiz Yacht Club (☎ 4 43 73) has a handful of sailboats (US$25 per hour for up to six people) and even a scuba-diving centre, but prices are well over the top. South of the boatyard is a small, clean beach with shallow, warm water.

PETROGLYPHS

Above the town is a huge field of glacial boulders, many with pictures scratched or picked into their south-facing surfaces. Some of these **petroglyphs** (adult/student 20/5 som; ☼ daylight hours) date from the later Bronze Age (1500 BC) but most are Saka-Usun (8th century BC–1st century AD), predating the arrival of the Kyrgyz in the area. The Saka priests used the sacred site for sacrifices and other rites to the sun god and lived in settlements that are currently underwater in the Cholpon-Ata bay. Later engravings date from the Turkic era (5th–10th century). Most are of long-horned ibex, along with some wolves, deer and hunters, and some

rocks appear to be arranged in sacred circles. Late afternoon is a good time to view the stones, which all face south.

Take the signed road opposite the boatyard turn-off north for 2.2km, bearing left to a section of black iron fence. The stones are behind this. There's a nice view of Issyk-Kul below. For a highly recommended guided tour of the petroglyphs, contact **Radiy Nurmametov** (☎ 4 28 18; Manas 32; radlight@rbcmail.ru; tour 50 som), whose house is just east of the site. Keep an eye out around town for a small brochure that has a useful map of the site.

There are more petroglyphs in the region, at Kara-Oi, 2km walk from the site, and near Ornok (4km up the new jeep road to Kazakhstan).

ISSYK-KUL MUSEUM

This small **regional museum** (☎ 4 21 48; Soviet 69; adult/camera 25/50 som; ☼ 8am-5pm) is worth a quick visit. The emphasis is on archaeology, with displays of local Scythian (Saka) gold jewellery, *balbal* gravestones and a fine set of mouth harps. Other rooms are devoted to ethnography, Kyrgyz bards, music and costume.

Sleeping & Eating

Plenty of families rent out rooms (*komnat* in Russian) in Cholpon-Ata. The best people to ask are the elderly ladies at the bus station, although someone may approach you directly if you have a backpack on and look lost.

KYRGYZSTAN

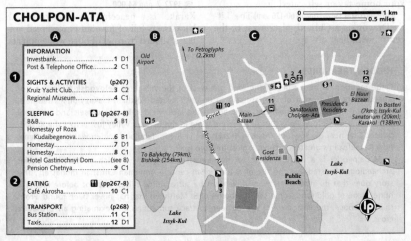

CHOLPON-ATA

INFORMATION		
Investbank	1	D1
Post & Telephone Office	2	C1
SIGHTS & ACTIVITIES		(p267)
Kruiz Yacht Club	3	C2
Regional Museum	4	C1
SLEEPING		(pp267-8)
B&B	5	B1
Homestay of Roza Kudaibegenova	6	B1
Homestay	7	D1
Homestay	8	C1
Hotel Gastinochnyi Dom	(see 8)	
Pension Chetnya	9	C1
EATING		(pp267-8)
Café Akrosha	10	C1
TRANSPORT		(p268)
Bus Station	11	C1
Taxis	12	D1

To Petroglyphs (2.2km)
Old Airport
El Nuur Bazaar
President's Residence
To Bosteri (7km); Issyk-Kul Sanatorium (20km); Karakol (138km)
Sanatorium Cholpon-Ata
Main Bazaar
Soviet
Almaty–Ata
To Balykchy (79km); Bishkek (254km)
Gost Residenza
Lake Issyk-Kul
Public Beach
Lake Issyk-Kul
0   1 km
0   0.5 miles

Pension Chetnya (☎ 4 37 94; Soviet 87; per person 250 som, with 3 meals 520 som) This family-run mini-motel has clean rooms with en suite bathroom and sauna (300 som per hour). The location is very central.

Homestay (Soviet 81/4; per person with breakfast & dinner 350 som) There are only two rooms here, each with four beds, about 300m east of the bus station, next to the post office. The owners are building a Western toilet and shower, and a café out front that promises vegetarian food.

Hotel Gastinochnyi Dom (☎ 4 25 28; Soviet 81/1; 150 som) A basic homestay next to the post office, with pit toilets and a hot shower. It's up a small alley and is the house on the right.

Homestay (☎ 4 39 51; cholponalim@maril.ru; Osmanova 4; per person 200 som, with 3 meals 400 som) Five minutes' walk north of the El Nuur Bazaar, on the left, this is a friendly place, but a bit out of the way.

B&B (☎ 4 21 02; Pravda 2; per person with 3 meals US$15) A notch above the homestays, this is a professional and friendly place run by Liubov Vassilevna, with a nice café, hot showers and parking.

Homestay of Roza Kudaibegenova (☎ 4 32 69; Birlik 1; per person US$5, with 3 meals US$10) This is a bit out of the way, en route to the petroglyphs. Roza speaks good English.

The town has a few cafés, all much the same and serving up standard fare. Between October and May (inclusive) most of these are shut and you're better off eating at your homestay or self-catering.

Café Akrosha (Soviet; mains 60-120 som) The 'Little Dragon' is a Chinese place west of the centre, with beer on tap.

Getting There & Away

Buses run every hour to/from Bishkek (100 som; 7am to 7pm) and continue to Ananyevo (20 som), Grigorievka (25 som) and Karakol (50 som) and there are also minibuses (Bishkek 200 som; Karakol 100 som). Taxis costs around 800 som to Bishkek or Karakol. Overnight buses run to Almaty around 8am (300 som).

Cholpon-Ata airport is being phased out in favour of Issyk-Kul airport further west (p266).

GRIGORIEVKA

It's possible to take a detour from this village up the Chong Ak-Suu Valley to a trio of alpine lakes. The Helvetas-supported **Rural Advisory Service (RADS) coordinator** (Likholetova 6; contact Nazgul Namazbaeva, Russian only) in Grigorievka, a couple of kilometres off the main road, can theoretically arrange transport, horses and yurtstays up in the valley, though the programme hasn't yet had much experience. Alternatively you could hitch and hike up the valley 22km or so to the lakes. There are two yurts, a sanatorium and a yurt café along the valley, with a yurtstay by the first lake (check with RADS that this is still operating).

The nearby village of Semenovka offers access to the Kichi (Little) Ak-Suu Valley, which has the Kyrchyn Gorge and a winter sports centre.

KARAKOL КАРАКОЛ

☎ 3922 / pop 64,000

Karakol is a peaceful, low-rise town with backstreets full of Russian gingerbread cottages, shaded by rows of huge white poplars.

HIDDEN TREASURES

Large mounds on both sides of the road just west of the village of **Belovodsk** (50km east of Ananyevo or 15km west of Tüp) are said to be unexcavated Scythian (Saka) burial chambers. Other mounds excavated near Barskoön, across the lake, yielded bronze vessels and jewellery (now in museums in St Petersburg). There are more in the Karkara Valley just across the Kazakh border. One near the town of Yessik in Kazakhstan yielded a fabulous golden warrior's costume, now Kazakhstan's greatest archaeological treasure (p99).

At Belovodsk is a turn-off south to the hamlet of Svetyy Mys, which at least one Soviet archaeologist insisted was the site of a 4th- or 5th-century Armenian Christian monastery. The story goes that its inhabitants were driven out by surrounding tribes, but not before hiding a huge cache of gold (and, some say, the bones of St Matthew) that has never been found. From the hills above, the village roads can be seen to trace something approximating an Orthodox cross.

TREKKING TO KAZAKHSTAN

From the Chong Ak-Suu Lakes, a fine trekking route continues west up the Chong Ak-Suu Valley to the Ak-Suu (Severny Aksu) Pass (4052m), into the Chong Kemin Valley and on along trekking routes to Almaty. For more on these routes, see p118.

From **Balbay** village (also called Sary-Bulak), 80km east of Grigorievka at the northeast corner of the lake, another option to Kazakhstan is the two-day walk north over the 3274m Sary-Bulak Pass to the pretty Köl-Say Lakes, east of Almaty (p117). A variant on the same route can take you over the nearby 3350m Kurmenty Pass.

Bear in mind that you won't get a visa stamp in or out of either country along these routes, which could be a problem. See p312 about potential visa problems.

Around the town are apple orchards, for which the area is famous. This is the administrative centre of Issyk-Kul province, and the best base for exploring the lake shore, the Terskey Alatau and the central Tian Shan. It also has a very good Sunday market. In fact, try to time your visit to include a Sunday, when the animal bazaar and Russian Cathedral are at their most active.

It's not quite paradise for those who live here – the economic stresses of independence and the decline in spa tourism have led to considerable hardship, thinned out available goods and services, and returned a kind of frontier atmosphere to this old boundary post – but hardly anybody talks about leaving. For better or worse, Karakol looks like headquarters for a new wave of tourism, from overseas.

The name means something like 'black hand/wrist', possibly a reference to the hands of immigrant Russian peasants, black from the valley's rich soil. Karakol is not to be confused with dismal Kara-Köl on the Bishkek–Osh road.

History

After a military garrison was established at nearby Teploklyuchenka (Ak-Suu) in 1864, and it dawned on everybody what a fine spot it was – mild climate, rich soil, a lake full of fish, and mountains full of hot springs – the garrison commander was told to scout out a place for a full-sized town. Karakol was founded on 1 July 1869, with streets laid out in a European-style checkerboard, and the garrison was relocated here. The town's early population had a high proportion of military officers, merchants, professionals and explorers.

It was called Przewalski in Soviet times, after the explorer Nikolai Przewalski, whose last expedition ended here, and who is buried on the lakeshore nearby (p275). It didn't escape a trashing by the Bolsheviks. Its elegant Orthodox church lost its domes and became a club; only one small church on the outskirts was allowed to remain open. Of nine mosques (founded by Tatars, Dungans and various Kyrgyz clans), all but the Dungan one were wrecked.

Orientation

Karakol has a central square, but the real commercial hub is the Jakshilik Bazaar, nicknamed *gostinny dvor* (the Russian equivalent of a caravanserai or merchants' inn, after its namesake in St Petersburg), built in the 1870s. The long-distance bus station is about 2km to the north.

Information
INTERNET ACCESS
Asia Centre (Alybakov; per hr 40-60 som; ☀ 8am-7pm) One of several private places around town.
Post office (Gebze; per hr 30 som; ☀ 8am-noon & 1-5pm Mon-Fri) Has the cheapest Internet access.

MONEY
Moneychangers everywhere will change cash US dollars into som.
AKB Bank (☎ 5 37 45; Toktogul; ☀ 8.30am-noon & 1-3pm Mon-Fri) At the northeast corner of the square, changes US-dollar travellers cheques into som or US dollars for 3% commission (minimum US$5) and gives cash advances on Visa and MasterCard for 2.5% commission. Go in the main building, turn left and head upstairs.

REGISTRATION & VISAS
OVIR (Room 114; Kushtobaev) For a visa extension, come here. A 30-day extension costs a bargain 300 som.

TOURIST INFORMATION
CBT (☎ 5 50 00; cbt_karakol2003@mail.ru; Korolkova 55; contact Baktygul Davletbekova) Can advise on CBT homestays in the region, including yurtstays in Jeti-Öghüz, the Bel Tam *jailoo* and Karkara, and can put you in touch with local transport.

KARAKOL

0	500 m
0	0.3 miles

INFORMATION

AKB Bank	1 C4
Asia Centre	2 C5
Baths No 1	3 C4
CBT	4 C6
Leader Office	5 B4
Neofit	(see 20)
OVIR	6 C4
Permit Station	7 B6
Post & Telephone Office	8 C4
PSI/Turkestan	9 C3
Russian Border Detachment	(see 7)
Tourist Information Centre	10 B4
Yak Tours	(see 23)

SIGHTS & ACTIVITIES (pp271–2)

Chinese Mosque	11 B4
Holy Trinity Cathedral	12 D6
Merchant's Home	13 C5
Pedagogical College	14 D6
Radio & TV Office	15 C5
Regional Museum	16 C6

SLEEPING (p272)

Gulnara's B&B	17 A5
Hotel Karakol	18 C5
Jamilya's B&B	19 A6
Neofit Guest House	20 C6
Terskey Guest House	21 D5
Turkestan Yurt Camp	22 C4
Yak Tours Hostel	23 D6

EATING (p273)

Café Anvir	24 C4
Dinara	25 C6
Kench Restaurant	26 D5
Traktiry Kalinka	27 C5
Uyot Café	28 D6
Yun Chi	29 A4
Zarina Café	30 C6

SHOPPING (p273)

Kumtor Department Store	31 B5
Kürk Art Gallery	32 D6

TRANSPORT (p273)

Airport & Airline Booking Office	33 D3
Ekovelo Park	(see 32)
Local Bus Stand	34 D6
Long-Distance Bus Station	35 B3
Minibuses to Bus Station	36 D6
Southern Bus Stand	37 B5

To Animal Market (400m)

To Pristan Prahevalsk (10km); Balykchy (217km); Bishkek (390km)

Bus No 1

Mikrorayon Voskhod

To Ak-Suu (14km); Altyn Arashan (25km); Karakol Valley

Przhevalskogo

Grechko

Asanalieva

Bektenov (Lieneskina)

Kalfa Marxa

Tashkentskaya

Dzhakipova

Moskovskaya

Lyuxemburg

Kushobaev (Kommunisticheskaya)

Tumanova

Jusup Abdrakhmanov (Torgogo Internatsional)

Gebze (Kalinina)

Alybakov (Lomonosova)

Kutmanalieva (Tennadogo Komsomola)

Gagarina

Toktogula

Gorkogo

Kumanalieva

Main Bazaar

Lenina

Jamansariev

Dupen Lerabaliev (Krupkov)

Brewery

Park

Square

University

Tynystanova (Pervomayskaya)

Yoenkova

Oktyabrskaya

Koenkova

Aymi

Korolkova

Telmona

Jakshilik Bazaar

Gagarina

See Enlargement

Municipal Stadium

Pushkin Park

Issyk-Kulskaya (Chkalova)

Torgoeva

Chkalabali (Chkalova)

Karakol River

To Jeti-Öghüz (25km); South Shore

Army Base

To Komplex Issyk-Kul (700m); Hippodrome; Skibaza; Karakol Valley

Proletarskya

Korolkova

Naryndskya

To Ak-Suu

Saleyeva

Gorkogo

Jakshilik Bazaar

Toktogula

Lenina

Jamansariev

Cagarina

0   200 m

Tourist Information Centre (TIC; ☎ 2 34 25; ticigu@ netmail.kg; Jusup Abdrakhmanov 130; ⏰ 9am-5pm Mon-Fri) Make this excellent resource your first stop. Particularly useful is the folder detailing all the homestays in the region. They can put you in touch with yurt camps in the region, sell 1:200,000 topo maps (150 som) and can phone the taxi company to get official taxi prices for local and long-distance destinations. They are preparing info on trekking and touring routes around Karakol.

TRAVEL AGENCIES

Alp Tour Issyk Kul (☎ 2 05 48; khanin@infotel.kg; contact Stas & Igor) This new company offers a range of treks, including to Kazakhstan and Khan Tengri base camp and can arrange border permits in a day (US$25, US$10 in a week). They can supply guide/cooks (US$15 per day) and porters (US$10) and can resupply your own long-distance treks.

Neofit (☎ 2 06 50; Jamansariev 166; www.neofit.kg /Kyrgyzstan.htm) All kinds of trekking support, based in the guesthouse of the same name.

PSI/Turkestan (☎ 5 98 96; www.karakol.kg; contact Sergey Pyshnenko) Turkestan specialises in group trekking and is pricier, but much more professional, than Yak Tours. They can arrange trekking and mountaineering trips to Khan Tengri, horse treks into the Küngey Alatau mountains north of Issyk-Kul, and visits to eagle-hunters, as well as no-strings-attached visa support, plus an awesome helicopter trip to Inylchek (US$100).

Yak Tours (☎ office 5 69 01, home/fax 2 23 68; yaktours@ infotel.kg; Gagarin 10) In addition to running the town's backpacker hostel, Valentin Derevyanko makes on-the-spot arrangements for individuals, including trekking and horse trips (US$25 to US$35 per day), jeep transport and equipment rental and can even arrange a display of eagle hunting. Valentin is sympathetic to budget needs. Certainly it's important that you make it clear exactly what kind of arrangements you want at the outset and pin down a price.

TRAVEL PERMITS

To go into the Tian Shan past Inylchek town, eg towards Khan Tengri (p280), you need a military border permit (propusk) from the permit station of the Russian border detachment stationed at the army base here (at the site of Karakol's original garrison). Trekking agencies normally need a week to arrange this but can do it in two days. The permit costs US$10.

Trekking permits have been discontinued, though there is still a national park entry fee to the Karakol Valley.

TREKKING EQUIPMENT

Leader (☎ 5 41 84; root@lider.cango.net.kg; No 6, Apt 1, Jusup Abdrakhmanov 142) This is an NGO that rents out trek-

king equipment to fund its youth development programmes. Equipment includes backpacks (50 som per day), tents (100 to 150 som), sleeping bags, sleeping mats and stoves (20 som each) and mountaineering equipment (not rope). You can find them on the corner of Gorkogo, just north of the mosque, hidden on the 2nd floor of an apartment block and accessed from the east.

Sights

CHINESE MOSQUE

What looks for all the world like a Mongolian Buddhist temple on the corner of Libknekhta and Tretiego Internatsionala is in fact a mosque, built without nails, completed in 1910 after three years' work by a Chinese architect and 20 Chinese artisans, for the local Dungan community. It was closed by the Bolsheviks from 1933 to 1943, but since then has again been a place of worship.

SUNDAY MARKET

This is no match for Kashgar's Sunday Market, but is still one of the best weekly bazaars we saw in Central Asia. The big **animal market** (mal bazari) in the northern outskirts of town is a must-see: several blocks jammed with people from throughout the region – an array like you won't see down in Bishkek – here to buy and sell horses, cattle, sheep, pigs and even the odd camel. You can buy a good horse for US$150 to US$300, and at US$20 a sheep makes a nice gift. Go early: it starts at 5am and is over by 10am.

HOLY TRINITY CATHEDRAL

The yellow domes of this handsome cathedral have risen from the rubble of Bolshevism at the corner of Lenina and Gagarin. Karakol's first church services were held in a yurt on this site after the town was founded. A later stone church fell down in an earthquake in 1890 (its granite foundations are still visible). A fine wooden cathedral was completed in 1895 but the Bolsheviks destroyed its five onion-domes and turned it into a club in the 1930s. Serious reconstruction only began in 1961. Services are again held, since its formal reconsecration in 1991 and again in 1997. Listen for its chimes marking Sunday morning services (7am to 11am).

OTHER COLONIAL BUILDINGS

The colonial-era part of town sprawls southwest from the cathedral and the

Hotel Karakol – lots of single-storey 'gingerbread' houses, mostly plain but some (eg those built by wealthier officers and scientists) quite pretty, and a few (those of Russian merchants and industrialists) with two storeys. Among decaying former merchants' houses are the **Pedagogical College** on Gagarin opposite the cathedral, the **radio and TV office** on Gebze (Kalinina), a block south of the Hotel Karakol, and another old **merchant's home** at the corner of Koenközova and Lenina.

REGIONAL MUSEUM

Karakol's modest **regional museum** (Jamansariev 164; admission 30 som, camera 10 som; ☺ 9am-5pm Mon-Fri, 10am-4pm Sat & Sun) is in a sturdy colonial brick building, once the home of a wealthy landowner. It's of interest for exhibits on the petroglyphs around Issyk-Kul, a few Scythian bronze artefacts, a Soviet history of the Kyrgyz union with Russia, some Kyrgyz applied art, and photographs of old Karakol – all of it better with a guide.

OTHER SIGHTS & ACTIVITIES

The leafy **Pushkin Park** by the stadium, four blocks south of the centre, includes the collective grave of a squad of Red army soldiers killed in the pursuit of *basmachi* .

About 3km south of the centre (on bus No 1) is Central Asia's very first **hippodrome**, still in use, though fewer and fewer people have the resources to keep racehorses.

The *banya* (public bath) **Baths No 1** (Gebze 128, near Toktogul; ☺ 8am-8pm) is a good place for a soak or shower. It costs 40 som, and toiletries are on sale at the ticket stand up front. There's also a public toilet here.

Sleeping

There are over two dozen homestays and B&Bs in town, ranging from 250 som to 400 som per person, and only a couple are mentioned here. See the TIC (p271) for more details. All come with breakfast and can provide dinner for 100 som. CBT (p269) also arranges homestays for 270 som to 400 som per person.

Terskey Guesthouse (☎ 2 62 68; www.teskey.narod .ru; Asanalieva 44; 300 som) This is one of the best homestays, and the closest to the centre. There's a great Russian-style sauna, excellent food and a laundry service. The son Taalai speaks good English; his mother

is a wonderful host and his father owns a terminally ill taxi.

Gulnara's B&B (☎ 7 18 50; Murmanskaya 114; 370 som) An excellent homestay located further out. Modern, with a washing machine, a kitchen and Dungan food.

Jamilya's B&B (☎ 4 30 19; Shopokova 34; 400 som) Another excellent further-out homestay, with spotless bathrooms, a nice balcony, family rooms and a yurt in the front garden.

Yak Tours Hostel (☎ 5 69 01, ☎ /fax 2 23 68, Gagarin 10; yaktours@infotel.kg; per person with 1 meal 250 som, with 2 meals 350 som) This was the first backpacker-style hostel in Central Asia. Facilities include baggage hold, equipment rental, an info board, a kitchen and a small collection of videos on Central Asia. The hostel is loosely run, with beds scattered all over the house, including in the corridors (separated by a curtain). You can also pitch a tent in the yard for a few som. Chef Babalina makes the best food in town or you can self-cater in the kitchen. The downside is there's currently only one bathroom.

Turkestan Yurt Camp (☎ 5 98 96; Toktogul 273; yurt dm €4, with bedding and hot shower €6, meals €3-4) The slightly muttony-smelling yurt dormitories here have a base-camp feel as trekking expeditions bustle in and out. You can stay in the yurts or strike a tent and use the hot showers and washing machine (for a fee). There should be some upscale caravanserai-style private rooms soon.

Neofit Guesthouse (☎ 2 06 50; Jamansariev 166; neofit@issyk-kul.kg; per person 100-300 som) A central, clean option, popular with trekkers who swap stories over a beer in the sociable courtyard. There's a wide range of old-fashioned but comfortable rooms with a private bathroom (but common shower), plus parking, a bizarre dungeon restaurant and a sauna.

Hotel Karakol (☎ 2 14 55; Gebze 22) The local university is currently renovating this run-down Soviet-style dinosaur. The second floor is due to remain a budget hotel but there were no prices at time of research.

Komplex Issyk-Kul (Fuchika 38) For some mid-priced Soviet nostalgia try this place, set in leafy grounds 2.5km south of the centre. The two blocks are split between the better **government hotel** (☎ 2 95 73; per person 706-908 som), where rooms have a balcony, and the **privatised hotel** (☎ 5 90 00; negotiable US$20-30). Take bus No 1 here.

Eating

Zarina Café (Toktogul) is a local diner with an English menu, nice environment, beer on tap and a good selection of dishes, including some chicken. The chicken roll is good but be aware that it's priced by weight not portion size.

Nearby **Dinara** (Lenina) also has good local dishes. Other lunchtime options include the newly renovated **Uyot Cafe** at the southeast corner of the bazaar and **Café Anvir** (lunch only), on the north side of the central square.

Traktiry Kalinka (2 77 77; Jusup Abdrakhmanov 99; dishes 30 som; closed Sun) The grumpy service here doesn't mar the cosy décor, good selection of salads and cold draught beer. Look for the pretty Russian façade.

Kench Restaurant (cnr Telmona & Gebze; meal 120 som) This is the best restaurant in town, in the southern outskirts and with an English menu. The stroganov tornados with vodka and mushroom sauce is recommended.

Yun Chi (Przhevalskogo) Try this home-style Dungan restaurant in the north of town for cheap *jidky* (noodles) and *sukhoi* (fried dumplings). You'll also find Dungan snacks such as *ashlyanfu* (meatless, cold, gelatine noodles in a vinegary sauce) in the bazaar for only a few som. It can be quite spicy so watch the red stuff.

The best Dungan food is of course in Dungan homes, where a slap-up meal may have eight to 10 courses (Dungan weddings can have up to 30 courses). Yak Tours (p271) can arrange a good **Dungan feast** (per person US$6-10) if you can get a group together.

Shopping

The **Kumtor Department Store** (Toktogul) has some made-for-tourists items.

Kürk Art Gallery in the Jakshilik Bazaar has some nice, neutral-coloured *shyrdaks* as well as some machine-stitched items; they're mid-priced but worthy of haggling.

Jamilya's B&B sells and custom orders *shyrdaks* and is affiliated to Kyrgyz Style (p259). Place an order, travel around Central Kyrgyzstan for a week or two, and then pick up the finished product.

Getting There & Away

Karakol's long-distance **bus station** (Przhevalskogo) has comfortable modern buses to Bishkek (145 som, eight hours) hourly between 7am and 3pm, and at night between 8pm and 11pm. These stop in Cholpon-Ata (50 som) and Balykchy (80 som). Buses also run via the southern shore to Balykchy (80 som) hourly between 7.20am and 2.20pm, and there are also southern shore buses to Barskoön (3.30pm, 30 som), Bokonbayevo (three daily, 48 som) and Tamga (12.50pm, 31 som). For Naryn and Kochkor, change at Balykchy.

Out in front of the station are faster *arenda* minibuses (200 som) and shared taxis (400 som per person) to Bishkek. There is one bus a day in summer to Almaty (360 som) but note that this runs via Bishkek *not* the Karkara Valley.

Most local buses (eg to Pristan Prahevalsk, Ak-Suu, Jeti-Öghüz and Barskoön) go from the local bus stand in the centre of town, a block east of the Jakshilik Bazaar. You will also find taxis here for local hire around the region, but agree on a price and waiting time beforehand.

Transport to destinations along the southern shore go from the southern bus stand in the southwest of town. Shared taxis go to Kyzyl-Suu (Pokrovka; 25 som per person) and Kajy-Say, and minibuses run to Bokonbayevo (50 som, every hour) and Kyzyl-Suu (15 som, every 30 minutes).

Flights to Bishkek and Osh were not operating at time of research.

Getting Around

Marshrutnoe minibuses trundle back and forth between the bus station and the centre. Taxis are fairly plentiful and cost around 40 som in town, 60 som at night. You can book a taxi at **Salam Taxis** (2 22 22).

Ekovelo Park (5 05 79; Orazakov 20, Jakshilik Bazaar) has Chinese-made mountain bikes for rent (*prakat* in Russian) for 15 to 30 som per hour or 200 som per day. It's the only place in the region for bike repairs and those all-essential replacement widgets. It plans to set up a network of bike supply and rental stations around Issyk-Kul, which would allow you to hire a bike from Karakol and drop it in another town around the lake. They are the people to ask about mountain-bike routes up into the mountains, including to Altyn Arashan and the Valley of Flowers in the Jeti-Öghüz Valley.

Yak Tours rents ramshackle motorbikes for US$7 per day, without petrol.

KYRGYZSTAN

AROUND KARAKOL
Przewalski Memorial & Pristan Prahevalsk

Thanks perhaps to the efforts of Soviet historiographers, and to the fact that he died here, the Russian explorer Nikolai Przewalski (p275) is something of a local icon, an increasingly poignant reminder of what the Russians accomplished in this part of the world. His grave and memorial museum are 7km north of Karakol on the Mikhaylovka Inlet. A visit with a Russian guide still has the flavour of a pilgrimage.

Przewalski died in 1888, and a huge monument and tiny chapel were erected by his grave six years later. The museum and garden are Soviet creations opened in 1957, displacing the rest of a village graveyard.

The **museum** (muzey prezhezhwalskovo; admission 20 som) features a huge map of Przewalski's explorations in Central Asia and a gallery of exhibits on his life and travels, plus a roll call of other Russian explorers. Captions are in Russian. There is usually a Russian-speaking guide on duty, delightful in her earnest explanations. Look out for the murals that change perspective from different angles.

The grave and monument overlook the Mikhaylovka Inlet and a clutter of cranes, docks and warehouses – all once part of the old Soviet top-secret 'polygon' for torpedo research. 'Pristan' (Russian for pier) is a nearby strip of lakeshore several kilometres

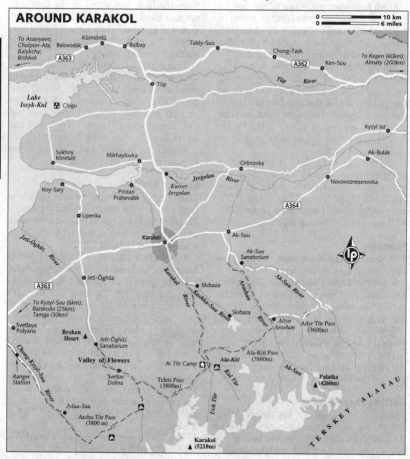

AROUND KARAKOL

0 — 10 km
0 — 6 miles

PRZEWALSKI

The golden age of Central Asian exploration was presided over by Nikolai Mikhailovich Przewalski. Born in Smolensk on 12 April 1839, his passion from an early age was travel. His father was an army officer and young Nikolai, under heavy pressure to be one too, apparently decided that an army career would give him the best chance to hit the road, although he never enjoyed the military life.

To prove to both the Russian Geographical Society and his senior officers that he would be a good explorer, he persuaded the Society to sponsor his first expedition, to the Ussuri River region in the Russian Far East in 1867–69. The results impressed everyone, the Society agreed to help finance future trips, and the army gave him the time he needed, insisting only that on his return from each trip he be debriefed first before saying anything to the Society.

Przewalski's Faustian bargain got him his freedom to travel in return for being, in effect, an army agent. He never married, going on instead to become a major general and the most honoured of all the tsarist explorers. He focused on Central Asia, launching four major expeditions in 15 years:

- Mongolia, China and Tibet (1870–73)
- Tian Shan, Lop Nor, Taklamakan Desert and northern Xinjiang (1876–77)
- Mongolia, China and Tibet (1879–80)
- Mongolia, China, Tibet, Taklamakan Desert and Tian Shan (1883–85)

Those starting in Mongolia were devoted to finding a route into Tibet. He finally made it to Lhasa once, and had an audience with the then Dalai Lama. On the one non-Tibet trip, he discovered the tiny steppe-land horse that now bears his name – Przewalski's horse (p67).

On the last of these trips he arrived via the Bedel Pass at Karakol. In 1888 he was at Bishkek (then Pishpek) outfitting for his next, grandest, expedition. While hunting tiger by the Chuy River he unwisely drank the water, came down with typhus and was bundled off to Lake Issyk-Kul for rest and treatment. From here he wrote to the tsar asking to be buried beside the lake, dressed in his explorer's clothes. He died at the military hospital on 20 October 1888.

long that includes a sea of *dachas* to the northeast and a popular beach to the west. The old military zone villages of Mikhaylovka, Lipenka and certain parts of Pristan Prahevalsk are off limits to foreigners.

To get here on your own, take a minibus (8 to 10 som) or a shared taxi (15 som per person) marked Дачи (Dachi) or Плаж Plaj (Beach) from just north of the local bus stand, departing every hour or so. A taxi to the museum costs 50 som one-way, or 120 som return with waiting time.

Altyn Arashan

Probably the most popular destination from Karakol is a Spartan hot spring development called Altyn Arashan (Golden Spa), set in a postcard-perfect alpine valley at 3000m, with 4260m Pik Palatka looming at its southern end. From the turn-off to Ak-Suu Sanatorium it's an often-steep, five to six hour (14km) climb south on a

track beside the Arashan River, through a piney canyon full of hidden hot and cold springs.

Much of the area is a botanical research area called the Arashan State Nature Reserve. Somewhere up here President Akaev and some other government bigwigs are said to have holiday yurts.

Altyn Arashan has several small hot-spring developments. The *kolkhoz* (collective farm) has three concrete hot pools (US$1) in wooden sheds, open to all.

Across the stream is a little log house and museum with stuffed animals of the region. From the springs it's about five hours on foot to the snout of the Palatka Glacier, wrapped around Pik Palatka.

SLEEPING & EATING

Government Guesthouse (per person 100 som) This is the first building you come to and offers basic accommodation.

Kolkhoz Ak-Suu (40-100 som) The collective farm site (signposted Trades Union Hostel) has 30 beds in plain dorms, plus abundant free tent space, a kitchen, outside pit toilets and a full-time caretaker.

Yak Tours Yurt Camp (100 som, with 2 meals 350 som) Run by Yak Tours in Karakol.

By far your best option is to take a tent and camp somewhere undisturbed in the valley.

You can buy a few things here in summer but it's better to bring your own food (and purifying tablets for the water), plus a bit of tea, salt, sugar or coffee for the caretaker.

GETTING THERE & AWAY
A jeep road leads up to the springs from 5km south of Ak-Suu village. From Karakol a taxi will cost 200 som to the junction, from where you can walk in around five hours.

Valentin of Yak Tours will bring you up to Altyn Arashan from Karakol in his jeep for about US$25 per jeep, or US$25 per person per day all in, including meals and hotel accommodation at the start and finish. The TIC might be able to help arrange transport for a similar fee. There's little traffic so hitching is hit and miss. You can hike in as the climax of several possible treks to/from the Karakol valley (see the boxed text on p277).

Karakol Valley
Due south of Karakol lies the beautiful Karakol Valley. The valley offers some fine hikes, although you really need to invest in a tent, stove and a day's hiking before the valley reveals its charm. The valley is a national park, which means there's a 250 som entry fee collected at the gate.

Further up the main valley, at the junction of several valleys and trekking routes is the Ai Tör camp, run by Alp Tour Issyk Kul (p271), with shower, *banya*, mountain rescue, radio service and park permit check.

From May to mid-October you can make a strenuous day hike (or better an overnight camping trip) to a crystal-clear lake called Ala-Köl (3530m). You can also reached it in four hours over the ridge from Altyn Arashan; in fact this is on several alternative trek routes to/from Altyn Arashan (see the boxed text on p277).

A taxi from Karakol to the park gate is 50 som; past here costs 100 som. The No 1 bus will take you part of the way, from where you can start hiking or hitching.

Jeti-Öghüz
About 25km west of Karakol, at the mouth of the Jeti-Öghüz Canyon, is an extraordinary formation of red sandstone cliffs that has become a kind of tourism trademark for Lake Issyk-Kul.

Jeti-Öghüz village is just off the main round-the-lake road. Beyond it the earth erupts in red patches, and soon there appears a great splintered hill called Razbitoye Serdtse or **Broken Heart**. Legend says two suitors spilled their blood in a fight for a beautiful woman; both died, and this rock is her broken heart.

The other side of the hill forms the massive wall of Jeti-Öghüz. The name means Seven Bulls (named after the seven main bluffs), and of course there is a story here too – of seven calves growing big and strong in the valley's rich pastures. Erosion has meant that the bulls have multiplied. They are best viewed from a ridge to the east above the road. From that same ridge you can look east into *Ushchelie Drakonov*, the Valley of Dragons.

Below the wall of Seven Bulls is one of Issyk-Kul's surviving spas, the ageing **Jeti-Öghüz Sanatorium** (☎ 9 37 19; per person 160 som, with 3 meals & massage 450 som, lux 900 som), built in 1932 with a complex of several plain hotels, a hot pool, a restaurant and some woodland walks. It's open to all, but in summer only. Russian President Boris Yeltsin and Kyrgyzstan's President Askar Akaev had their first meeting here, in 1991.

From here you can walk up the parklike lower canyon of the Jeti-Öghüz River to popular summer picnic spots. Some 5km up, the valley opens out almost flat at **Svetov Dolina**, the Valley of Flowers (Kok Jayik in Kyrgyz); it's a kaleidoscope of colours as summer passes and has poppies in May. There are also said to be pre-Islamic petroglyphs up here, similar to those at Cholpon-Ata. You really need a tent to make an enjoyable couple of days' trip here.

Yurt camps in the Valley of Flowers include the pleasant **Jenish Gol** (per person US$10) on the left of the road, Ecotour (p253) on the right and finally the pricier **Saidahmat** (bed & full board US$18). All are normally accessible by car and offer a nice taste of the

TREKKING AROUND KARAKOL

The Terskey Alatau range that rises behind Karakol offers a fine taste of the Tian Shan. Of numerous possible routes that climb to passes below 4000m, the best of them take in the alpine lake Ala-Köl above Karakol, and the Altyn Arashan (p275) hot springs above Ak-Suu (Teploklyuchenka).

Ak-Suu to Altyn Arashan and Back

(Minimum one or two nights.) Five hours up the Arashan river valley, climbing from 1800 to 3000m. A day-hike extension could take you 4½ hours further up the valley, branching east and then south for views of Palatka (4260m).

Karakol Valley to Arashan Valley, via Ala-Köl

(Minimum three nights.) Hike up from the end of the No 1 bus route for about four hours to where the Ala-Köl branches to the left. Two hours up takes you to the carved wooden Sirota camp; another five hours takes you past waterfalls to the high-altitude and barren Ala-Köl lake. A 30-minute walk along the north shore offers camping at the base of the pass. The trail to the 3860m Ala-Köl Pass is indistinct and the crossing can be tricky at the end of the season, so consider a guide from September onwards. Five hours downhill from the pass brings you to Altyn Arashan, from where you can hike down to Ak-Suu the next day.

Jeti-Öghüz to Altyn Arashan, via the Karakol Valley

(Minimum four or five nights.) The trail heads up the Jeti-Öghüz river valley, crossing east over the 3800m Teleti Pass into the Karakol Valley. From here head up to Ala-Köl, and then over to Altyn Arashan and Ak-Suu (see above).

Kyzyl-Suu to Altyn Arashan, via the Jeti-Öghüz and Karakol Valleys

(Minimum six to eight nights.) From Kyzyl-Suu head up the Chong-Kyzyl-Suu river valley to the Jyluu-Suu hot springs or on to a camp site below the 3800m Archa-Tör Pass. Next day cross the pass, head down the Asan Tukum Gorge into the Jeti-Öghüz Valley. From here it's over the Teleti Pass to the Karakol Valley and to Ala-Köl, Altyn Arashan and Ak-Suu, as described previously.

You can combine any number of these parallel valleys to make as long a trek as you like. You can also add on wonderful radial hikes up the valleys, for example from Altyn Arashan to Pik Palatka or up the Kul Tör Valley at the head of the Karakol Valley for views of Karakol peak (5218m).

There are also longer, more technical variations on these that climb as high as 4200m and cross some small glaciers, but these should not be attempted without a knowledgeable guide and some experience with glacier walking.

When to Go

The season for the treks noted here is normally late June to early October. August is a popular time for picking mushrooms; blackcurrants are in season in September. For Altyn Arashan only, you could go as early as May or as late as the end of October, but nights drop below freezing then and the surrounding mountain passes are snowed over. Local people say that Altyn Arashan is loveliest in June and in September.

Weather is the region's biggest danger, with unexpected chilling storms, especially May through June, and September through October. Streams are in flood in late May and early June; if you go then, plan your crossings for early morning when levels are lowest.

Maps

These routes are indicated on the Around Karakol map (p274). The only good maps we have seen for these routes – part of an old Russian series called *Gornyy Turizm* (Mountain Tourism) – are the 1:150,000 *Lednikam Terskey Ala-Too* and the 1:150,000 *Po Tsentralnomu Tyan-Shan*, for sale at Geoid in Bishkek (p252).

Getting to the Trail Heads

For access to trail heads, refer to the Altyn Arashan (p275), Karakol Valley (p276) and Jeti-Öghüz (p276) sections of this chapter.

KYRGYZSTAN

mountains if you are short of time, and a good base for day hikes if you have a couple of days. Karakol TIC can advise on prices and help with bookings. The upper valley is accessed by five bridges that sometimes get washed out so check the best route with locals before setting off.

Jeti-Öghüz canyon is one of several alternatives for treks to/from Altyn Arashan and Ala-Köl (see the boxed text on p277).

GETTING THERE & AWAY

Buses run from Karakol's local bus stand at 10am to Jeti-Öghüz village and at 4pm to the sanatorium (kurort; 20 som), 6km further away. Buses run back to Karakol from the sanatorium at 8am. Shared taxis also run between Karakol and the sanatorium (25 som per person).

A taxi from Karakol costs 280 som to the spa, 350 som to the Valley of Flowers and around 500 som to the yurt camps at the top of the valley.

THE KARKARA VALLEY
ӨРӨӨН КАРКАРА

The eastern gateway to the Issyk-Kul Basin is an immense, silent valley called Karkara, straddling the Kyrgyzstan–Kazakhstan border. On the Kyrgyzstan side it begins about 60km northeast of Karakol and widens out to 40km or more, shoulder-deep in good pasture during summer. Every herder in the Karakol region (and in the Kegen region on the Kazakhstan side) brings animals up here in summer to fatten, and the warm-weather population is an easy-going mix of Kyrgyz and Kazakh chabana (cowboys), their families and their yurts.

The name Karkara means Black Crane, after the graceful migratory birds that stop here (and at Chatyr-Köl near the Torugart Pass) in June and again in August to September, en route between South Africa and Siberia.

Summers used to also bring the **Chabana Festival**, an annual gathering of cowboys and herders with horseback games and a big bazaar, but the solidifying of international borders seems to have put a hold on the festivities, for the last couple of years at least.

In his *A Day Lasts Longer Than a Century* the Kyrgyz writer Chinghiz Aitmatov has the ancient Kyrgyz peoples arriving here from the Yenisey region of Siberia.

Some people suggest that Timur (Tamerlane) made Karkara his summer headquarters for several years, and point to a house-size pile of round stones in the southwest part of the valley. These, they say, were Timur's way of estimating his losses in eastern campaigns – each departing soldier put a rock on the pile, each returnee removed one, and the stones that remained represented the dead. The name of the site, **San-Tash**, means 'Counting Stones'.

Sceptics and amateur historians point to an adjacent, stone-lined pit that appears to be the remnant of a burial chamber, and suggest that the football-size stones were just used to cover the chamber, and were removed by archaeologists or grave-robbers. Either way, the site has a dreamy, magical feel.

Sleeping

The TIC in Karakol can put you in touch with two fledgling yurt camps, **Ethnotour Santash** (☎ in Karakol 03922 23236; per person with breakfast €12, incl 3 meals €18) and cheaper **Shaidelda** (☎ 03945 21411; per person incl breakfast 300 som), both near the Kyrgyz village of Char-Kuduk, 110km from Karakol, and close to the Kazakh company Kan Tengri's base camp, just across the river in Kazakhstan (p119). Shaidelda also runs a small **guesthouse** (per person incl breakfast 200 som) in Tüp village.

Getting There & Away

From Karakol the Karkara Valley is about 90km via Tüp or 70 much prettier but rougher kilometres via Novovoznesenovka. On the Tüp route a round trip by taxi from Karakol would probably be about US$40 for the day. Ask for *pamyatnik San-Tash* (San Tash Monument), just opposite a small collective farm settlement, 19km from the Kazakhstan border.

Buses run from Karakol's long-distance bus station to San-Tash via Tüp at 12.30pm and 2pm. There's also a slow daily bus to Chor-Kuduk via San-Tash. There are also daily buses to Kyzyl Jar (former Sovietskoe) or the mining town of Jyrgalang (Russians call it Jergalan *shakhta*, which means 'mine'), from where you might hitch.

The Karkara (Karkyra) River forms the modern Kyrgyzstan–Kazakhstan border through part of the valley and this makes an interesting route to or from Kazakhstan. If you are headed to Kazakhstan make sure you get a border stamp, even if it means waiting some time. You will of course need valid visas for both republics. There's no cross-border public transport.

Coming from the Kazakhstan side, you can get a Kegen, Saryzhaz or Narynkol bus from Almaty and get off at Kegen, from where it's a difficult 28km hitch south to the border itself. A taxi from Karakol to Almaty via Kegen takes about seven hours and costs around US$120, including car customs fees.

THE SOUTHERN SHORE
Barskoön & Tamga
☎ 3946

Barskoön village was an army staging point in the days of Soviet-Chinese border skirmishes, and the small adjacent settlement of Tamga is built around a former military sanatorium, now open year-round to all. Today Barskoön is all Kyrgyz, with more horses than cars; Tamga is mainly Russian.

The area's most illustrious resident was the 11th-century Mahmud al-Kashgari, the author of the first-ever comparative dictionary of Turkic languages, *Divan Lughat at-Turk* (A Glossary of Turkish Dialects), written in Baghdad during 1072-74.

INFORMATION
Shepherds Way (☎ 9 61 33, Bishkek ☎ 312-29 74 06; www.kyrgyztrek.com) This very professional local company runs horse trips into the mountains behind Barskoön. It's run by local brothers Ishen and Raiymbek Obelbekov and Ishen's wife, Gulmira.

A fledgling office of **Shepherd's Life** (☎ 9 21 39; 4 Cheji köchösü; contact Suranov Bakyt) operates a **yurt camp** (per person with 3 meals 260 som), 22km from Baskoön in the Sharkyratma Gorge, and can put you in touch with an eagle hunter in the region. For details check with CBT in Karakol.

SIGHTS
You can see yurts in production at the **Ak Orgo yurt workshop** (☎ 9 67 54; Lenin 39; mekenbek@ hotmail.kg; contact Mekenbek Osmonaliev), including machines that make felt and devices that bend the wood and reeds for the curved yurts. It takes the 27 employees two months to make a yurt, which retail here at around US$4000. A children's yurt (1m diameter) costs US$250 and must be ordered two

weeks in advance. Several of the workshop's yurts have been exhibited in the US. The workshop is on the right as you drive into Barskoön from the east.

Locals pack picnics and head 20km up the huge Barskoön Valley to the **Barskoön Waterfall**, where *kymyz* is sold from summertime yurts near a defaced inscription by Yuri Gagarin. It's possible to climb 1½ hours up to closer views of the falls. Shared taxis run from Barskoön sanatorium to the falls (120 som return), along the well-maintained road that leads to the Kumtor gold mine.

Tamga has a nice beach; locals also recommend a beach 5km west. Also, 6km up the valley is a Tibetan inscription known as **Tamga Tash** but you'll need local help to find it.

Trekking routes start from further up the Kumtor road, over the Sary Oinok Pass, (carry on when the Kumtor road turns left) and past the military post at Kara Sai (you need a border permit from here on). The scenery is high and treeless like central Kyrgyzstan. Wildlife includes Marco Polo sheep, bharal and ibex. Alp Tour Issyk Kul (p271) in Karakol can give information on horse treks in the remote Ak Shyrak region. The Tamga Guesthouse (see below) can arrange one- to three-day treks or horse trips up to the Tamga Gorges or Ochincheck Lake, or four-day trip to Chakury Köl at a lofty 3800m.

SLEEPING
Tamga Guesthouse (☎ 9 53 33; Ozyornaya 3; per person US$8, full board US$15) In Tamga village, this is run by a friendly Russian couple, with a lovely fruit garden and sauna (US$2 per person). It's used mostly by trekkers from the affiliated company Kyrgyz Travel but anyone can stay and use it as a trekking base. It's the first road on the right as you pull into town.

Dostuck Trekking (p253) has a **yurt camp** (per person full board US$18) by the lakeshore near Tosor village.

GETTING THERE & AWAY
Barskoön is about 90km from Karakol, with daily morning buses to/from Karakol and Balykchy. From Karakol there are buses to Barskoön (35 som) at 9am from the local bus stand and at 10am, 11am and 3pm from the southern bus stand. A taxi from Karakol costs 650 som.

KYRGYZSTAN

Bokonbayevo

The dusty, depressed town of Bokonbayevo isn't of much interest but there are some adventurous trips to be made in the valleys behind.

About 10km behind the town, also accessible from Tört-Kul, is Tuura-Su, where the eagle hunter Sulaymanbekov Kutuldu has a **yurtstay** (☎ 03947-9 18 58; 100 som, meals 50-70 som).

Shepherd's Life operates a **yurt** (full board 270 som) 7km beyond Tuura-Su at Bor-Dobo (branch left).

CBT in Karakol can arrange a **yurtstay** (☎ in Bishkek 0312 474 830; incl 3 meals 650 som; contact Aida Kydyrgycheva) at Bel Tam (branch right), 17km from Bokonbayevo, beyond Tuura-Su.

Ecotour (p253) has full-service yurts at neighbouring Temir Kanat (recommended) and at another village called Tuura-Su at the west end of the Kongur Olön valley. Prices include horse riding excursions. From Temir Kanat, staff can arrange for you to visit local eagle hunter Jilduzbek Ismaylov.

Shared taxis run to Tamga, Balykchy and Karakol. A taxi to Tamga costs 300 som.

THE CENTRAL TIAN SHAN
ЦЕНТРАЛЬНЫЙ ТЯНЬ ШАНЬ

This highest and mightiest part of the Tian Shan system – the name means Celestial Mountains in Chinese – is at the eastern end of Kyrgyzstan, along its borders with China and the very southeast tip of Kazakhstan. It's an immense knot of ranges, with dozens of summits over 5000m, culminating in Pik Pobedy (Victory Peak, 7439m, second-highest in the former USSR) on the Kyrgyzstan–China border, and Khan Tengri ('Prince of Spirits' or 'Ruler of the Sky', 7010m), possibly the most beautiful and demanding peak in the Tian Shan, on the Kazakhstan–Kyrgyzstan border. Locals call the peak 'Blood Mountain', as the pyramid-shaped peak glows crimson at sunset.

The first foreigner to bring back information about the central Tian Shan was the Chinese explorer Xuan Zang (602–64), who crossed the Bedel Pass in the 7th century, early in his 16-year odyssey to India and back. His journey nearly ended here; in the seven days it took to cross the pass, half his 14 person party froze to death.

The first European to penetrate this high region was the Russian explorer Pyotr Semenov in 1856 (for his efforts the tsar awarded him the honorary name Tian-Shansky). In 1902–03 the Austrian explorer Gottfried Merzbacher first approached the foot of the elegant, Matterhorn-like Khan Tengri, but it was only climbed in 1931, by a Ukrainian team.

Of the Tian Shan's thousands of glaciers, the grandest is 60km-long Inylchek (Engilchek), rumbling westward from both sides of Khan Tengri, embracing an entire rampart of giant peaks and tributary glaciers. Across the glacier's northern arm, where it joins the southern arm, a huge, iceberg-filled lake – Lake Merzbacher – forms at 3300m every summer. Some time in early August, the lake bursts its ice-banks and explodes into the Inylchek River below.

Along with the eastern Pamir, the central Tian Shan is Central Asia's premier territory for serious trekking and mountaineering. Several Central Asian adventure-travel firms will bring you by helicopter, 4WD and/or foot right up to these peaks. Even intrepid, fit do-it-yourselfers can get a look at Inylchek Glacier (p282).

Information

Mid-July through August is the only feasible season to visit at these elevations.

PERMITS

This is a sensitive border zone, and to go anywhere in the upper Sary Jaz Valley or beyond Inylchek town – even just to have a look at the glacier – you'll need a border zone permit from the Russian border detachment at the army base in Karakol (p271). You must have a letter with the stamp of a recognised travel agency in Karakol, Bishkek or Almaty, a list of everyone in your party, and your itinerary.

To climb in the region you'll need a mountaineering permit, which trekking companies can get for you for US$105.

BOOKS & MAPS

Geoid in Bishkek (p252) sells the 1:200,000 scale *K Verkhvyam Sary-Dzhaza* map, which shows the trekking routes that approach Khan Tengri from the Sary Jaz Valley in Kyrgyzstan and Bayankol Valley in Kazakhstan.

The best book to take along is Frith Maier's comprehensive *Trekking in Russia & Central Asia*, which has several maps and basic route descriptions in this region.

Dangers & Annoyances

This is not a place to pop into for a few days with your summer sleeping bag – be properly equipped against the cold, which is severe at night, even in summer, and give yourself plenty of time to acclimatise to the altitude.

Helicopters do fall out of the sky from time to time, or crash into mountainsides when bad weather unexpectedly descends; ride them only in absolutely clear summer weather.

Sleeping & Eating

There are several **base camps** in the Inylchek Valley: en route at scruffy Maida Adyr and the newer, nicer Gribkov Camp at Ak-Jailoo, 20km nearer the glacier, and at several locations up on the glacier in tent-towns owned and run by ITMC Tien-Shan and Dostuck Trekking (p253) in Bishkek and Kan Tengri in Almaty, among others. The Ak-Jailoo camp is run by a company called **Tour Khan Tengri** (☎ in Karakol 3922-2 72 69; www.travelkg.narod.ru /company.htm) and has wooden buildings (per person US$20), yurts (US$12) and camp space (US$2 to US$10), plus meals (US$4 to US$7). ITMC's camp costs around US$3 per night in a tent, or US$8 in huts and there's a sauna and bar. You can camp here and just pay for meals, although food is pricey.

Kan Tengri maintains the only camp on the north side of the glacier and also a yurt camp at 2200m at the edge of the Karkara Valley. All these are intended for trekkers and climbers, but anybody with the urge to see this cathedral of peaks can make arrangements with those firms, and pay a visit.

Getting There & Away

Firms organising climbs and treks in the central Tian Shan include Dostuck Trekking

---

TREKKING TO THE INYLCHEK GLACIER

The most common trekking route to the Inylchek Glacier is the remote and wild five- or six-day trek from Jyrgalang, 70km east of Karakol. Most trekkers will need support for this trek, not least because you will need a military permit from Karakol to head up the Sary Jaz Valley. There's one daily bus from Karakol to Jyrgalang.

- **Stage 1** From Jyrgalang the trail heads south up the valley, before cutting east over a 2800m pass into the Tüp Valley (seven to eight hours).

- **Stage 2** Over the 3648m Ashuu Tör Pass into the Janalach Valley (six hours).

- **Stage 3** Head south over the 3723m Echkili-Tash Pass into the Sary Jaz Valley.

- **Stage 4** Seven hours hike up the Tüz Valley to camp at the junction of the Achik Tash River.

- **Stage 5** Cross the river and head up four hours to the tricky Tüz Pass (4001m), from where there are stunning views of the Inylchek Glacier, Nansen Peak and Khan Tengri. From here it's a long descent to the Chong-Tash site at the snout of the Inylchek Glacier.

It's possible to hire a jeep (US$80 from Yak Tours in Karakol) to the yak farm in Echkili-Tash and join the trek there, leaving only two or three days to reach Chong-Tash. From Chong-Tash you face a one or two day hike back west to Ak-Jailoo or Maida Adyr camp and Inylchek town.

To continue from Chong-Tash on to the Inylchek Glacier you definitely need the support of a trekking agency to guide you over the glacier, keep you in supplies and let you stay in their base camps. With an experienced guide it's possible to continue from Chong-Tash over the glacier for one long day to Merzbacher Lake and to continue the next day to the camps. A popular excursion for trekking groups based here is to make a trekking ascent of Mt Diky (4832m) or Pesni Abaji (4901m), or to hike up the Zvozdochka Glacier to the foot of Pik Pobedy (7439m). Most groups take in a stunning helicopter route around the valley and out to Inylchek town and you might be able to buy a ride back up to Inylchek for US$100.

The best time for trekking in this region is July and August. See p280 for information on permits, maps and agencies.

(p253), Edelweiss (p253), ITMC Tien-Shan (p253), Ak-Sai (p253)and Tien-Shan Travel (p253) in Bishkek; PSI (p253) in Karakol; and Kan Tengri (p98) and Asia Tourism in Almaty (p98).

Access to the region surrounding Khan Tengri is by road, by air or on foot. It's a four-hour (150km) trip on a roller-coasting, all-weather road from Karakol via Inylchek town, a mining centre at about 2500m and 50km west of the snout of the Inylchek Glacier. Do-it-yourselfers could hire a UAZ jeep from Karakol, for around US$100 return. The new road to Ak-Jailoo has a US$10 toll for jeeps, or US$20 for trucks.

If you've got the dosh, take a mind-boggling helicopter flight over the Tian Shan to Khan Tengri base camp with Kan Tengri from their Karkara Valley base camp, or with other agencies from Gribov Camp. It's possible to hitch a lift on a helicopter from Maida Adyr to the base camps for US$100 (plus US$1 per kilo if you have more than 30kg of luggage). These run every two days in August.

To Khan Tengri's north face you can trek from Narynkol (Kazakhstan), Jyrgalang (Kyrgyzstan) or, less interesting, from the Ak-Jailoo road head. See the boxed text on p281 for more details.

CENTRAL KYRGYZSTAN & THE TORUGART PASS

Kyrgyzstan's primo trip for nontrekkers is the 700km journey between Bishkek and Kashgar via the 3752m Torugart Pass. From a purely physical standpoint the whole journey to Kashgar could be done in a sturdy, well-equipped 4WD in under 15 hours – two days – but the country along the way reveals too much about the region to just rush through. Even if you aren't headed to China, the sights en route rank as some of Kyrgyzstan's highlights.

BISHKEK TO NARYN

The route begins as you would for Lake Issyk-Kul, winding up the **Shoestring Gorge** towards Balykchy. A short cut by taxi heads over a small pass and past the azure **Orto-Tokoy reservoir** to save an hour by cutting off the Balykchy corner.

Three hours or 185km from Bishkek is the town of **Kochkor**. About 38km onward is tiny Sary-Bulak, where you can buy *laghman* and snacks by the roadside. Five kilometres south of Sary-Bulak is the turn-off to **Lake Song-Köl** (p285). It's about 11km on to the 3038m summit of the **Dolon Pass**, the highest point on the Bishkek–Naryn road, and a further 19km to a dirt track that climbs to the Song-Köl Basin (a popular winter route). About 16km on is **Ottuk**, a tidy Kyrgyz settlement with a representative of the Shepherd's Life organisation, and 24km further is a fork in the road, both branches of which take you about 10km into Naryn.

Kochkor

☎ 3535

This sleepy little Kyrgyz village (Kochkorka in Russian) is a good stopping point en route to Naryn or the Suusamyr Valley. It is the base for the CBT and Shepherd's Life homestay projects (p248), and as such is a fine base from which to make trips to Song-Köl or the surrounding countryside to experience traditional life in the Kyrgyz *jailoo*s (summer pastures).

There's not much to do in the town except visit the small **Regional Museum** (admission 25 som; 9am-noon, 1-5pm Sun-Fri). A fine yurt is on display along with a collection of local Kyrgyz crafts, plus all the usual Soviet-era local heroes, such as the local scientist Bayaly Isakeev. More Soviet heroes are celebrated in the busts to the east of the museum.

There is said to be a good livestock market in town on Saturday morning.

INFORMATION

CBT (☎ 2 23 55; cbt_kochkor@rambler.ru; Pioneerskaya 22A, by Orozbakova; 9am-noon & 1-7pm Jun–mid-Sep; contact Aida Jumasheva) arranges transport for 7 som per km (9 som per km to Song-Köl), horses 350 som per day, guides 490 som (with his own horse), yurtstays in *jailoo*s for 250 som for bed and breakfast to 430 som full board. A horse trek for two travellers and one guide staying in yurts works out at around US$25 per day. There is talk of moving the office and making an information booth by the bazaar. They can put you in touch with the folkloric musical group Min Kyal.

Jailoo (☎ 2 11 16; www.jailoo.com.kg; Orozbakova 125/3; contact Asipa Jumabaeva) The former CBT coordinator has set up her own private

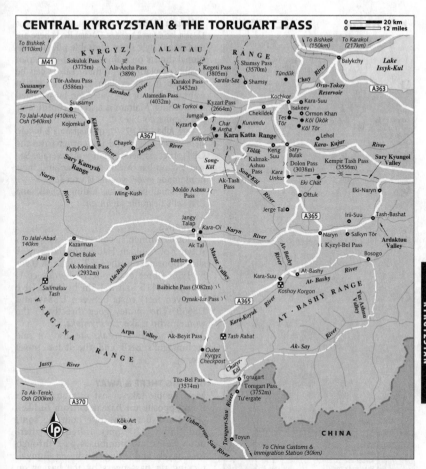

CENTRAL KYRGYZSTAN & THE TORUGART PASS

0 _____ 20 km
0 _____ 12 miles

business, offering similar services to CBT at a similar price but without the community dimension. The office has a good showroom for local *shyrdaks*; local producers fix the prices and Jailoo takes a 20% commission. There's talk of moving the office next to the telecom building.

Shepherd's Life (Kuttuseyit uulu Shamen 111) Coordinator Mairam Ömürsakova offers similar services at cheaper prices but with slightly ropier arrangements. Cars rent for 7 som per hour and yurt accommodation is 360 full board. Mairam speaks Russian and Kyrgyz only but her son Urmat speaks excellent English.

Kredobank, next to CBT, will change cash US dollars, when it has enough money(!).

There's Internet access in the **telephone office** (Orozbakova; ⏰ 8am-noon & 1-10pm Mon-Fri, 9am-2pm Sat & Sun; per hr 30 som).

SLEEPING & EATING

There are now over 20 homestays in Kochkor, most costing 240 som with breakfast, and CBT can put you in contact with all of them. The two below are mentioned in case the office is closed when you arrive.

Jumagul's B&B (☎ 2 24 53; Kuttuseyit uulu Shamen 58; per person 170 som, meals 70-90 som) Hosts Jumagul Akhmadova and her husband do a good job here, offering duvets on the floor in three rooms. The B&B has a Russian sauna for guests to use and a clean squat toilet in the garden.

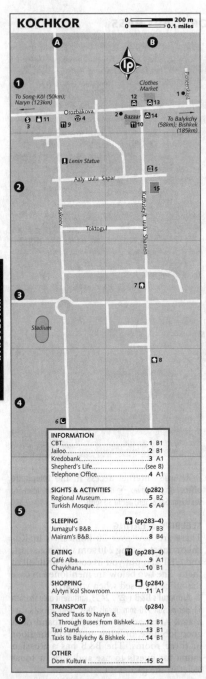

KOCHKOR

0   200 m
0   0.1 miles

Clothes Market

To Song-Köl (50km);
Naryn (123km)

Orozbakova

To Balykchy
(58km); Bishkek
(185km)

Lenin Statue

Aaly uulu Sapar

Isakeev

Toktogul

Kuttuseyit uulu Shamen

Stadium

Pioneer Plaza

INFORMATION	
CBT	1 B1
Jailoo	2 B1
Kredobank	3 A1
Shepherd's Life	(see 8)
Telephone Office	4 A1

SIGHTS & ACTIVITIES	(p282)
Regional Museum	5 B2
Turkish Mosque	6 A4

SLEEPING	(pp283–4)
Jumagul's B&B	7 B3
Mairam's B&B	8 B4

EATING	(pp283–4)
Café Alba	9 A1
Chaykhana	10 B1

SHOPPING	(p284)
Alytyn Kol Showroom	11 A1

TRANSPORT	(p284)
Shared Taxis to Naryn &	
Through Buses from Bishkek	12 B1
Taxi Stand	13 B1
Taxis to Balykchy & Bishkek	14 B1

OTHER	
Dom Kultura	15 B2

Mairam's B&B (Kuttuseyit uulu Shamen 111; per person 120 som, incl dinner & breakfast 270 som) Beds here are traditional style (a comfortable pile of traditional duvets on a *shyrdak*) and vegetarian meals (eg plain rice, tomato salad) can be prepared if you explain exactly what you want. Buckets of hot water can be arranged for washing. Mairam is also the coordinator for Shepherd's Life.

Café Alba (☎ 2 25 22; cnr Orozbakova & Isakeev; meals 30 som) Just round the corner from the CBT office, is better than your average Soviet techno bar. Meals are cheap and their homemade sweet yogurt is excellent.

The small bazaar has a dingy chaikhana that sells bearable *laghman*.

SHOPPING
A local women's collective known as Altyn Kol (Golden Hands) has a *shyrdak* showroom next to the CBT office. A 0.9m by 1.5m (three by five feet) *shyrdak* costs around US$15 and a 1.5m by 2.1m (five by seven feet) costs between US$40 and US$50. The money goes directly to the women who make the *shyrdaks*.

Good-quality *shyrdaks* are also for sale at Jumagul's B&B and the Jailoo travel agency.

GETTING THERE & AWAY
Most people take a seat in a shared taxi from opposite the bazaar to/from Bishkek (150 som), Balykchy (one hour, 45 som) and Naryn (120 som). Infrequent afternoon buses and minibuses pass through to Chayek and Ming Kush via Jumgal, picking up passengers by the bazaar on Orozbakov.

Around Kochkor
The following trips can all be arranged by CBT or Shepherd's Life. By yourself, you'll have difficulties finding yurtstay accommodation.

One of the most popular trips is to **Sarala-Saz** (53km), a wide open *jailoo* with fine views, from where you can take day trips on horseback to petroglyphs. CBT organises horse games here in August; for dates ask at CBT in Kochkor or Bishkek. An adventurous two or three day horse trek leads from Sarala-Saz over the 3570m Shamsy Pass and down the Shamsy River valley to Tokmak.

Köl Ükök is a beautiful mountain lake above Tes Tör *jailoo*, south of Kochkor, and is a recommended overnight or three-day trip. Take a taxi 6km to Isakeev and then trek by horse or on foot half a day to the *jailoos*. Before June it's better to stay at Tes Tör (four hours from Isakeev by horse); after June you can stay up by the lake (six hours from Isakeev). Day excursions from the lake include to **Köl Tör** glacial lake, a couple of hours further up into the mountains. For a slightly longer alternative trip take a taxi 15km to Kara-Suu village and then go first to Kashang Bel or Bel Tepshay (Bel means pass), for views of Issyk Kul, and then ride or hike the next day to Köl Ukök (seven hours). CBT and Shepherd's Life can advise on routes and yurtstay accommodation.

Other destinations that have CBT yurtstays include **Tündük** (northern) *jailoo*, 21km north from Kochkor, and **Kurumdu** *jailoo* in the Sara Talaa Valley, 60km west of Kochkor. New route options are planned in the Sandyk Mountains and Suek Range.

To get really off the beaten track, the Shepherd's Life coordinator in **Jumgal**, history teacher Stalbek Kaparbekov, can arrange horses to and accommodation at the nearby *jailoos* of Ok Torkoi and Kilenche. Jumgal is the first village after the Kyzart Pass, and is sometimes referred to as Dos Kulu. There are also Shepherd's Life coordinators further west in **Chayek** (Abdiev Kochosu; contact Guljan Mykeva) and **Kyzart** (contact Abdykazar Talgar); contact the Kochkor office for details.

Lake Song-Köl

Alpine lake Song-Köl (Son-Kul), at 3016m, is one of the loveliest spots in central Kyrgyzstan. All around it are lush pastures favoured by herders from the Kochkor Valley and beyond, who spend June, July and August here with their animals. Visitors are welcome, and this is a sublime place to camp and watch the sun come up. You can make any number of day hikes into the surrounding hills for excellent views. The lake is jumping with fish, and you might be able to trade tea, salt, sugar, cigarettes or vodka with the herders for milk, *kurut* (dried yogurt balls) or full-bodied *kymys*. In any case bring plenty of food and water.

CBT and Shepherd's Life offer over a dozen **yurtstays** (per person full board 420 som)

around the lake, where you can also ride horses. Bishkek-based travel companies such as NoviNomad (north) and ITMC Tien-Shan (south) operate tourist **yurt camps** (per person full board US$26) in summer, where you can stay if there are no groups.

The lake and shore are part of the Song-Köl zoological reserve. Among animals under its protection are a diminishing number of wolves and lots of waterfowl, including the Indian mountain goose. Weather is unpredictable and snow can fall at any time so dress and plan accordingly. July to mid-September is the best season. Tourist organisations arrange horse games at the lake on the last Saturday in July and August (check with CBT in Kochkor). The lake is frozen from November to May.

GETTING THERE & AWAY

It's 50km from the Bishkek–Naryn road to the lake: 6km to Keng-Suu (Tölök) village, 21km to the end of the narrow valley of the Tölök River, and then a slow 23km (1½ hours) up, over the Kalmak-Ashuu Pass and into the basin. This upper road is normally open only from late May to late October. The valley has little traffic and no regular buses.

A car hired from Kochkor through CBT or Shepherd's Life is the easiest option. Prices depend upon the price of petrol (rates are currently 8 som per km, plus 100 som per day for the driver) and generally cost around US$35 for the return trip. You may find something cheaper in the bazaar. Local Zhigulis (Soviet-made cars) can make it but you are far better off with a 4WD Niva or jeep, as the tracks around the lake can get very boggy with rain.

There are at least three other unpaved 4WD tracks to the lake – from west of the lake at Chayek, to the south from Jangy Talap (p288) just off the Naryn–Kazarman road, and a winter road from the southeast corner of the lake to the Bishkek–Naryn road. It's therefore possible to drive in from Kochkor and out to Naryn or Chayek, making a nice loop route. CBT car to Song-Köl from Naryn via Jangy Talap was around US$50 at time of research. Hitching is possible but only if you have lots of time and your own supplies.

It's also possible to trek in to the lake on foot or horseback from Kyzart, near Jumgal, north of the lake, in one or two days, staying in shepherds' yurts in the Char Archa and Kilenche *jailoos*. A second approach on horseback or foot lies to the east, from Chekildek, just west of Kochkor, over the Kara Katta range, into the Tölök Valley and then over the Ak-Tash Pass, taking around three days. The CBT and Shepherd's Life representatives in Kochkor or Shepherd's Life in Jumgal can arrange accommodation, horses and a guide for around 1200 som per day, plus food. Without a tent you really need a guide as it's impossible to find the yurtstays by yourself.

NARYN НАРЫН

☎ 3522 / pop 46,600 / elevation 2030m

Naryn is at about the right place for an overnight stop on the Bishkek–Torugart road, or en route to Kazarman, although it's not a particularly inspiring place. Naryn is derived from the Mongolian for 'sunny' – a rare moment of Mongol irony. The Naryn region's one real claim to fame is that the best quality *shyrdaks* are said to be made here.

Orientation

Naryn is spread along the Naryn River for 15km, but is just one to 2km wide. The road from Bishkek forks north of town, each branch of the fork leading to one end of town. A trolleybus (three som) and minibuses (four som) run along the main street, Lenina, for its entire length.

If there's a centre it's probably the *hakimyat* (municipal administration) on Lenina. Travellers' landmarks are a small bazaar 500m northwest of this on Orozbaka, and the bus station, 1.2km east on Lenina. The bus station has a map of the town.

Information

CBT (☎ 5 08 95, 5 08 65; naryn_tourism@rambler.ru; Lenina 8; contact Kubat Abdyldaev) is a great source of information and can arrange local and regional homestays, transport and horse treks.

You can change clean US dollars cash only (no euros) at the **AKB Bank** (1st fl, Kulumbayerva; ☀ 8.30am-noon & 1-5pm), the Sez Naryn exchange booth 500m east, or in the bazaar. This is the last place to change money before the Chinese border.

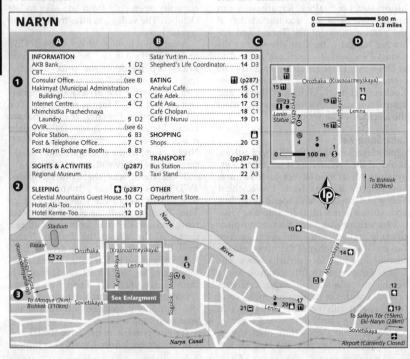

NARYN

0 —————— 500 m
0 —————— 0.3 miles

INFORMATION
AKB Bank.....................................1 D2
CBT..2 C3
Consular Office.......................(see 8)
Hakimyat (Municipal Administration Building).............................3 C1
Internet Centre............................4 C2
Khimchistka Prachechnaya Laundry.................................5 D2
OVIR...(see 6)
Police Station...............................6 B3
Post & Telephone Office............7 C1
Sez Naryn Exchange Booth.........8 B3

SIGHTS & ACTIVITIES (p287)
Regional Museum.........................9 D3

SLEEPING (p287)
Celestial Mountains Guest House..10 C2
Hotel Ala-Too............................11 D1
Hotel Kerme-Too........................12 D3

Satar Yurt Inn...........................13 D3
Shepherd's Life Coordinator.......14 D3

EATING (p287)
Anarkul Café..............................15 C1
Café Adek..................................16 D1
Café Asia...................................17 C3
Café Cholpan.............................18 C1
Café El Nuruu............................19 D1

SHOPPING
Shops..20 C3

TRANSPORT (pp287-8)
Bus Station................................21 C3
Taxi Stand.................................22 A3

OTHER
Department Store.......................23 C1

Orozbaka (Krasnoarmeyskaya)

Lenin Statue

Lenina

0 ———— 100 m

To Bishkek (309km)

Stadium

Bazaar

Orozbaka (Krasnoarmeyskaya)

Lenina

Naryn

River

See Enlargment

To Mosque (2km); Bishkek (310km)

Sovietskaya

Togolok-Moldo

Lenina

Mozgovaya

To Salkyn Tör (15km); Eki-Naryn (28km)

Sovietskaya

Naryn Canal

Airport (Currently Closed)

In an emergency it's possible to extend your visa at the Ministry of Foreign Affairs Consular Office in the Special Economic Zone building, or at the **OVIR office** (Togolok Moldo 11).

Khimchistka Prachechnaya (Kulumbayerva) does laundry for 15 som per kg (takes two days).

The **Internet Centre** (Kyrgyzskaya) next to the **post & telephone office** (Kyrgyzskaya) has decent connections.

Sights & Activities

If you have some time to kill, you could check out the **Regional Museum** (Moscovskaya; ☎ 9am-noon & 1-5pm; admission US$1). Most interesting is the ethnological room featuring a dissected yurt and every accessory a nomad could ever need. Other halls include various stuffed animals, exhibits by local painters and exhibits on Soviet Kyrgyz heroes such as Jukeev Tabaldy Pudovkin, a local Bolshevik hero.

There's little else to see except the town's garish but striking **mosque**, 2.5km west of the centre – finished with Saudi money in 1993.

CBT has maps and photos of hikes in the hills south of Naryn.

Sleeping

CBT (☎ 5 08 95, 5 08 65; naryn_tourism@rambler.ru; Lenina 8; contact Kubat Abdyldaev) Has eight excellent places to stay in Naryn (per person 290 som), either in central apartment blocks or suburban houses. Go to the central CBT office first to see what's available.

Shepherd's Life (☎ 4 14 57, 5 08 65; 14 Balasagun/Zavodskaya; contact Marima Amankulova) The coordinator's house and homestay are one and the same in the eastern Moscovskaya suburb (there are also several CBT homestays around here), reached by a 20 som taxi or four som minibus ride.

Hotel Ala-Too (☎ 2 18 72; Lenina; s/d/tr 100/120/150 som, lux 600 som, super lux 1000 som) The standard rooms are pretty dilapidated but they are the cheapest in town and come with a stinky toilet. The renovated lux rooms are clean, spacious and surprisingly pleasant, with hot water and a balcony (some rooms).

Hotel Kerme-Too (☎ 2 26 21; 3km east of the centre; per person 146-220 som, ste per person 36 som) Recently privatised, this secluded building has a wide range of rooms and rates so see a few rooms before deciding. Bathrooms

are communal and not up to much. There are plans to renovate. You can camp in the pleasant orchard next to the hotel for pennies. You can get there on bus No 2, taxi (20 som) or a 10-minute walk from the east end of Lenina.

Satar Yurt Inn (☎ 5 03 22; per person 150-200 som, 2 meals extra 120 som) In summer you are better off next door in this collection of seven or eight tourist yurts. Facilities include Western toilets, a hot shower and a small restaurant and there are also some plain modern rooms. A lot of Torugart-bound groups stay here, paying US$15 per head in season.

Celestial Mountains Guest House (☎ /fax 5 04 12; www.celestial.com.kg; Moscovskaya 42; s/tw/tr US$30/36/42, ste d US$40, 3-bed yurt per person US$13) The most luxurious place in town is this clean and modern place on the eastern outskirts, run by the Bishkek travel agency of the same name (p253). The guest house is also known as Nebesnie Gori Naryna, and also the 'English Guest House'. Rooms are comfortable, with spotless shared bathrooms, dinner and breakfast included, Internet access, Western videos and hot showers. If you need to escape the rigours of the road, this is the place. The suite, with en suite bathroom, offers the best value. The guest house is 1km north of the eastern crossroads and is signposted from the road.

Eating

Café El Nuruu (Kulumbayerva) is probably best in town (the *zharenie* chicken stir-fry is recommended at 55 som) The **Anarkul Café** (Orozbaka) is a close second.

There are numerous other canteens where you can get standard fare such as *laghman*, borscht or goulash, including the **Café Asia** (Lenina), **Café Adek** (Kulumbayerva), and **Café Cholpan** (Orozbakova).

The bazaar has a fine range of dairy products and supplies for self-catering. You can also get good-quality canned goods, sausage and cheese in the private shops at the eastern crossroads.

Getting There & Away

Minibuses depart from the bus station for Bishkek between 8am and 10am (130 to 160 som; six hours). Buses to At-Bashy (14 som, one hour) leave at noon, 1pm and 3pm. Buses to Kazarman (167 som, seven hours) depart on Tuesday and Friday at 8am.

KYRGYZSTAN

Shared taxis are a good alternative but the sharklike taxi drivers outside the bus station go into a feeding frenzy at the sight of a foreigner. Beware of the friendly guy who grabs your bag and takes you to a car that conveniently happens to be giving your way and then charges you a finder's fee. A seat in a full taxi costs 40 som to At-Bashy, 120 som to Kochkor and 200 som to Bishkek. To hire your own taxi costs 600 som to Bishkek, 800 som to Tash Rabat, 400 som to Eki-Naryn or 2000 som to Torugart. CBT arranges transport for 9 som per kilometre, depending on the price of petrol.

From Naryn it's 150km to Song-Köl, 185km to Torugart and 310km to Bishkek.

Around Naryn

CBT (p286) can give the lowdown on a range of trips around Naryn, including yurtstays in the Ardaktuu Valley and Tyor *jailoo* in the Eki Naryn Valley. Given a few days warning, they can organise the following multiday horse treks:

Ak-Tam to Bokonbayevo (five to six days) Via Oryuk Tam, Archaluu, Juluu-Suu, Teshik Köl lake, the 4023m Ton Pass and Ashuu-Tör.

Ak-Tam to Song-Köl (five days) Via the Irii-Suu Valley, the Sary Kyungoi Valley, 3556m Kempir Tash (Stone Woman) Pass, Eki Chat, Kara Unkur, Teshik *jailoo* and the Tar-Suu Valley.

Song-Köl to Chatyr-Köl (six to seven days) Via Jangy Talap, Mazar Valley, 3082m Baibiche Pass, Chong Bulak Valley and Tash Rabat.

Most horse trips start from Ak-Tam, 27km east of Naryn. Ask CBT about visits to the nearby Tian Shan deer nursery at Irii-Suu (great for kids) and day trips up the Ak-Tam valley to see petroglyphs.

There's a private **guesthouse** (per person US$15) at Salkyn Tör gorge 'free economic zone', 12km from Naryn.

EKI-NARYN

The scenic Kichi (Little) Naryn Valley stretches to the northeast of Naryn and offers plenty of opportunities for exploration. The main settlement is at Eki-Naryn, 30km northeast of Salkyn Tör, close to where the Kichi Naryn river meets the Naryn.

Around 10km north of Tash-Bashat is a fascinating swastika-shaped forest, said to have been planted by German prisoners of war under the noses of their Soviet captors.

Buses leave Naryn for Eki-Naryn at 8am on Monday, Wednesday and Friday (24 som), or you could take a taxi for around 400 som. There's no place to stay but there's plenty of good camping in the valley. With your own transport it's possible to continue northeast and then swing west to follow the Kara-Kujur Valley back to Sary-Bulak and the main Naryn–Kochkor road. CBT Naryn can arrange a homestay along this route at Lehol.

NARYN TO JALAL-ABAD

If you're planning to travel directly between the Fergana Valley and the Bishkek–Torugart road, it's possible to cut right across central Kyrgyzstan between Jalal-Abad and Naryn instead of going around via Bishkek. The rugged trip winds through a higgledy-piggledy landscape of desert bluffs and badlands along a road that was blasted in 1903 by the Russian military.

The route goes via Kazarman (220km from Naryn), a gold-mining town in the middle of nowhere where you change buses and which has a fledgling CBT programme. Most traffic takes the longer but better-quality road via Baetov, despite what is marked on maps. The mountain.pass to the Fergana Valley is closed from November to late May/early June.

Naryn to Kazarman

Just past the village of Ak-Tal (or Ak-Talaa – White Fields), around 75km west of Naryn, a lonely 4WD track leads up 65km to the southern shore of Song-Köl via 33 switchbacks and the Moldo Ashuu Pass. There is a **Shepherd's Life coordinator** (Yntymak 45; contact Sveta Jusupjanova) at the village of Jangy Talap (also known as Kurtka), about 4km from Ak-Tal, who can arrange accommodation and transport. There's one bus daily to Jangy Talap from Naryn at 4pm and there are irregular shared taxis (40 som per seat). If you have time here, try to track down the photogenic **Taylik Batyr Mausoleum**, near Kara-Oi village, around 8km from Jangy Talap.

About 40km on from Ak-Tal is Baetov, a forgotten rayon capital. There's a Shepherd's Life homestay here but little reason to stop.

Kazarman

☎ 3738 / pop 15,000 / elevation 1230m

This sleepy village exists to serve the opencast Makhmal gold mine about an hour to the east, and an ore-processing plant nearby. Gold seems to attract trouble, and Kazarman has a raw, untamed feel.

From west to east along the main drag (Djienieleva, also called Mira) is the Sailmaluu Tash park office, the Dom Kultura, Makmal Hotel and bus station, from west to east; just north of here is the bazaar and jeeps to Jalal-Abad.

CBT (4 17 55; Djienieleva; contact Aida Kadyrbaeva), in the upper floor of the Dom Kultura, can put you in touch with half a dozen **homestays** (B&B 280 som, meals 90 som), including the recommended homestays of English-speaking **Bakhtygul Chorobaeva** (☎ 2 19 16, 4 13 77; Kadyrkulova 35, 5 blocks south of the centre) and the B&B at 36 Bekten (two blocks south of the centre). Other homestays are at Bekten 18, Akynbaeva 53, Kadyrkulova 6 and Djienalieva 20 (Apt 6). All homestays have hot showers. CBT also arrange overnight horse trips to the petroglyphs of Sailmaluu Tash, to the Besh Köl lakes east of town and to the holy site of Jilangach Bögü.

Buses depart Kazarman for Naryn (176 som) on Wednesday and Saturday at around 8am. The town has an airport but currently no flights.

Sailmaluu Tash

The several thousand 'embroidered stones' of Sailmaluu Tash are Central Asia most dramatic petroglyphs. Over the millennia Aryan, Scythian and Turkic peoples have added to the earliest Bronze Age carvings. The carvings are spread over two slopes and depict hunting, shamanistic rites and battle scenes, some dating back over 4000 years.

The petroglyphs are difficult to reach and are for the committed and adventurous. From Kazarman there are two route options, via Atai, 20km west along the road to Jalal-Abad, and the second via Chet Bulak south of Kazarman (so you can take one up and another one back). Both trips involve a car trip of about 45 minutes, followed by a half-day hike or horse trip. It's best to spend the night at yurts near the site and explore the stones for a few hours early the next morning.

CBT can arrange overnight horse trips for around US$75 per person for two people with food, accommodation and transportation. You can probably get a better deal at the park office (monpekettik zharalypish parky) on Kazarman's main drag.

Also possible to approach on a longer route from the Fergana Valley, from Kalmak-Kyrchyn up the Kök Art Valley. CBT in Jalal-Abad can arrange transport and horses from the western approach, from where you can descend to Kazarman.

KAZARMAN TO JALAL-ABAD

There are no scheduled buses to Jalal-Abad, only when-and-if-it-fills-up Nivas and Russian jeeps for about 300 som per person (five hours).

The slightly unnerving 6½-hour trip (about 155km) climbs a narrow dirt track over a 3100m pass in the Fergana range, and finishes at Jalal-Abad bazaar. Our Niva broke down 27 times along this route. From the scenery on the Fergana side you can see why the Fergana Valley is Central Asia's breadbasket.

For more information on Jalal-Abad, see p297.

NARYN TO TORUGART

From Naryn it's 24km to the low **Kyzyl-Bel Pass**, with a stupendous view south and west, right down along the crest of the At-Bashy range (highest point 4786m). The road runs along the foot of this range and around the far (west) end of it to Torugart. About 13km and 20km from the pass are two turn-offs to the village of **At-Bashy**, the closest point to the border accessible by regular bus, and an hour's drive from Naryn.

West of At-Bashy is a yawning, red-walled notch on the north side of the valley; the road crosses a stream that drains everything through this notch and down to the Naryn River. Low bluffs west of the stream partly conceal a bizarre landscape of perfectly rounded, sandy hills. By the road-side is a splendid Kyrgyz graveyard.

About 14.5km west of the second At-Bashy access road is a turn-off to Kara-Suu village and the ruins of **Koshoy Korgon**.

Some 40km west of At-Bashy the road turns to gravel, but for a startling 3km before it does so, it becomes as wide and smooth as a four-lane superhighway: a military airstrip, apparently never used. About 21km from the end of the airstrip (100km from Naryn or 90km before the main Torugart customs station) is the turn-off south to **Tash Rabat**.

About 28km west of this turn-off is the low **Ak-Beyit Pass** at the end of the At-Bashy range. Then it's 4km to the **outer checkpoint**, an hour's drive from At-Bashy, and another fine view – to the crest line, on the border itself.

At-Bashy

At-Bashy is off the Naryn–Torugart road, 6km by an easterly access road, 4km by a westerly one, and truly the far end of Kyrgyzstan. Sandwiched between the At-Bashy and Naryn Tau ranges, the town has a great location and can be used as a springboard for visits to Tash Rabat, Koshoy Korgon and the Torugart Pass. Through the Shepherd's Life programme you could also arrange visits to the surrounding villages of Tus Bogoshtu, Kök Köl, or further afield to Bosogo Canyon and Tus Ashuu. It's tricky to arrange time to explore At-Bashy if you are en route to the Torugart but otherwise the valley is a great place to explore if you have the time.

ORIENTATION

From the bus station at the east end of town head 1.5km west past the new mosque to the cinema and city administration building. Turn right at the administration building and head north 300m to the Koshoy Hotel on the right. Continue four blocks and turn left down a dirt road, Arpa köchösü, for 150m to get to Tursan's homestay.

SLEEPING & EATING

Homestay of Tursan Akiev (☎ 3534-219 44; Arpa köchösü 25) Tursan is the local coordinator of Shepherd's Life and offers a family atmosphere, with beds in a comfortable room, as well as transport to Tash Rabat and Torugart and info on local *shyrdak* cooperatives. Some travellers have recently complained of pushy sales and brusqueness, so be firm about what you want.

The small government-run **Koshoy Hotel** (Aity Suleymanov 29; per person 50 som) tries hard with what are limited materials but rooms still aren't really up to much.

There are a couple of grotty cafés at the bus station and beside the hotel, plus there's a small bazaar about 600m west of the bus station.

GETTING THERE & AWAY

There are scheduled daily buses in the morning to Naryn (1½ hours, 15 som), Bishkek (eight hours, 80 som), Kochkor (four hours, 40 som) and Kara-Suu (30 minutes, 7 som). A seat in a shared taxi to Bishkek costs 200 som, or 30 som to Naryn (45km).

At the time of research taxis were asking 700 som return to Tash Rabat, though you could get it cheaper through Tursan at the Shepherd's Life programme.

Koshoy Korgon

In a field behind the village of Kara-Suu are the eroded ruins of a large citadel, occupied during the 10th to 12th or early 13th century, and probably Karakhanid. An appealing local legend tells that the Kyrgyz hero Manas built the citadel and a mausoleum here for his fallen friend Koshoy.

A taxi from At-Bashy to the site costs about 100 som for a return visit. About 14.5km west of the western access road to At-Bashy, by a gas station on the Naryn–Torugart road, turn south (signposted) to Kara-Suu village. Take the first left turn in the village after the mosque and silver war memorial, go out past all the houses and then take a right and then another right to the ruins, 3km from the main road.

Next to the ruins, Shepherd's Life has a **homestay** (120 som), which could be a good base for hikes in the At-Bashy range behind.

Tash Rabat

At a marked turn-off, 60km from At-Bashy (32km from the outer Kyrgyz checkpoint) a dirt track heads into a surprisingly level and very lovely hidden valley in the At-Bashy range. It's the perfect shelter, with lush corduroy hillsides, small farmsteads and the occasional yurt encampment. Indeed it must have been attracting well-to-do travellers for centuries, for about 15km in is a solitary fortified caravanserai, looking rather like a mausoleum, sunk into the hillside.

Local sources say it dates from the 15th century, although some sources say the site dates from the 10th century, when it was a Christian monastery. A clumsy Soviet restoration was completed in 1984. There is an entry fee of 25 som. A few fragments of the original central mosque are visible in the main chamber; leading off this are many other chambers, including a well (some say a treasury, in the far left corner) and a dungeon (in the central right chamber). An opening in the far right corner leads to what the caretakers say is a tunnel, explored generations ago as far as about 200m, and perhaps once leading to a lookout point to the south.

From Tash Rabat a three- or four-hour horse ride or hike will take you to a broad ridge overlooking Chatyr-Köl lake; if you continue a couple of hours, you can stay the night in a yurt at Chatyr-Köl before returning to Tash Rabat the next day. Remember that you are about 3500m high here, so even a short walk could set your head pounding. Neither Tash Rabat nor Chatyr-Köl are in a restricted border zone, so no permits are needed. The caretakers at Tash Rabat can arrange the trip and rent horses for 50 som per hour or 400 som per day and a guide for 200 som per day, making this a great place to spend a day or two exploring on horseback.

A day trip by taxi from Naryn to Tash Rabat (125km) is around 800 som. There's no public transport.

SLEEPING

You can stay at the yurts of **Shepherd's Life** (120 som, breakfast 60 som) or the **caretaker's yurts** (100 som) across from the caravanserai. There are two more yurtstays 1km back downstream by a lovely side valley; travellers have recommended the yurt of Sabyrbek Ayelchiev here. Bring some munchies and supplies for your host family. The valley is a fine place to camp.

Tash Rabat to the Torugart Pass

It's about 130km from Naryn to the outer checkpoint and a further 60km to the main customs station at Torugart, a total of about 4½ hours' driving if you make no stops.

South from the outer checkpoint the road rapidly degenerates as views of the Fergana range rise to the west. About 26km on, at the 3574m **Tüz-Bel Pass**, it swings east and skirts Chatyr-Köl. Black cranes and Indian mountain geese pause here during their transcontinental migrations, one reason why the lake and its marshy shoreline are protected as the Chatyr-Köl zoological preserve. An old Soviet-era double electrified fence (no longer live) runs near the road. As the road climbs, the surrounding mountains seem to just melt away.

Fifty kilometres from the outer checkpoint and 7km from the Kyrgyzstan customs and immigration station, a big red and yellow sign says 'Narzan'; 50m off the road in a field of bubbling mud is a gushing cold spring, fizzy and tasty.

THE TORUGART PASS
ПЕРЕВАЛ ТОРУГАРТ

Torugart is one of Asia's most unpredictable border posts, with reliable information scarce, many decisions taken seemingly at random, and closures unexpectedly by one side or the other for holidays, road repair, snow or heaven knows what else. Nobody (not even an ambassador) knows the score for sure.

The standard trip takes two days, overnighting in Naryn or Tash Rabat (although you really should add a third day to visit Song-Köl and Tash Rabat). The second day involves a very early start and gets you into Kashgar that evening.

Most of the traffic through the pass is trucks carrying scrap metal and animal hides from Kyrgyzstan, or porcelain, thermoses, beer and clothing from China. The trucks accumulate in huge tailbacks at both sides, for 500m or more in the mornings.

From the Kyrgyzstan customs and immigration station it's 6.8km to the summit. Below this, about 5km away, is a checkpoint, though the main Chinese customs and immigration post is another 70km away.

Information

The customs and immigration facilities are open from 10am to 5pm Monday to Friday, but in reality you must cross between 9am and noon. Avoid arranging your Torugart crossing on any day that might even conceivably be construed as a holiday on *either side, or in Russia*, as the border will probably be closed. Tourist traffic is heaviest on Friday when groups cross into China to catch Kashgar's Sunday market; however, attempting to cross on a Friday is dangerous, as if the border is temporarily closed for snow or some other reason you won't be able to retry for another three days. Try to arrive at the border as early as possible (the Kyrgyz side opens at 9.30am) as things tend to grind to a halt at lunchtime.

Besides the various customs sheds, inspection pits and immigration offices, there is a Spartan state 'hotel', though most people who stay do so in basic caravans, 1km before the customs area. If coming from China you should be able to find a moneychanger here, or wait until Naryn, a couple of hours down the road.

In summer (roughly April through September) China (ie Beijing) time is two hours later than Kyrgyzstan time, and in winter three hours later.

RED TAPE

Essentially many of the difficulties crossing the pass boil down to the fact that the Torugart is classified by the Chinese as a 'class 2' border crossing, for local traffic only, and so special regulations are in force for foreigners, many of which seem deliberately set up to milk foreigners for some hard currency. The bottom line, for the moment at least, is that you must have onward Chinese transport arranged and waiting for you on the Chinese side to be allowed past the Kyrgyz border post.

At research time, Kyrgyz border officials were also insisting on written confirmation of onward transport into China, and detaining visitors until this transport arrived at the summit from Kashgar. The best thing to have is a fax from an accredited Chinese tour agency, who will come and meet you. No special endorsement is required on your Chinese visa.

The three-point border – two border controls 12km apart and a security station in between – makes for further confusion, especially in trying to connect with onward transport. Normally the Chinese guards at the arch radio to Kyrgyz immigration when your transport arrives and only then are you allowed to leave the Kyrgyz border post. Sometimes groups are turned back even with all the right papers, because their transport never turned up or was not allowed up to the actual border.

TRANSPORT & TRAVEL AGENCIES

Arranging the whole trip from Bishkek to Kashgar currently costs from around US$100 to US$200 per person in a group of four, depending on the agent and the vehicle.

Most agents can make arrangements with a cooperating Chinese agency for onward transport. The charge for this is set by the Chinese agency and normally paid in US dollars to the Chinese driver once in China. If this is the case, get a printed confirmation of the price from your Kyrgyz

agent to avoid any dispute later. You could deal directly with a Chinese travel agency from abroad but it's generally easier to let a Bishkek agency make the arrangements. Try to make arrangements at least 10 days in advance, especially if you're setting up onward Chinese transport too.

Ask for a price breakdown, since some firms fail to mention all costs. Check that petrol, oil and food and accommodation for the driver are included, as well as the state transport duty (gosposhlina), a per-vehicle customs tax paid when you exit Kyrgyzstan.

Check also that you will be taken across to the Chinese checkpoint at the summit; only drivers with a Kyrgyz Foreign Ministry special permit can go that far. Your driver should have previous experience with Torugart – both getting there and getting across – eg minimising customs rip-offs and jumping truck queues.

At the beginning and end of the season you really need a 4WD not a little Toyota minivan. There is little reliable petrol, oil or parts along the way, so the vehicle must carry everything for the round trip.

NoviNomad was the cheapest agency we found, charging US$100 for a car from Naryn to Torugart and US$180 from Torugart to Kashgar, which works out at US$93 per person for three people from Bishkek to Kashgar. At the time of research in Bishkek, ITMC (p253) was charging US$240 transport for a vehicle from Bishkek to Torugart. Celestial Mountains (p253) was charging US$263 per person from Bishkek to Kashgar, assuming a car shared by four people. Edelweiss (p253) is good at assembling individuals into larger groups.

To book Chinese transport from Torugart to Kashgar, Kyrgyz Concept and Celestial Mountains were charging US$110 per person (minimum two persons). It's possible to book direct with **John's Information Café** (☎ 86-998-255 1186; johncafe@hotmail.com) or **Caravan Café** (☎ 86-998-298 1864; www.caravancafe.com, www.asianexplorations.com; 120 Seman Lu) in Kashgar, though neither are all that easy to contact in advance.

Weekly Bishkek–Kashgar, Bishkek–Artux, Naryn–Artux (Monday) and Naryn–Kashgar (Tuesday) buses make the nonstop 1½-day trip to China over the Torugart (US$50 from Bishkek, US$25 from Naryn) but foreigners aren't allowed to take these, especially since the bus was held up by bandits in 2002, resulting in more than 20 deaths. At the time of research buses had yet to be re-established after being cut during the SARS epidemic.

Crossing the Pass

Following is what we did on our way from Kyrgyzstan into China. Travellers coming the other way reported roughly the same in reverse.

KYRGYZSTAN – PROCEDURES

If your vehicle made it to Torugart, both sets of border guards showed up for work and your Chinese transportation arrived, you're in business. When both sides of the border finally open, you and your driver show confirmation of onward transportation on the Chinese side. Kyrgyzstan immigration will then delay you and your vehicle until the radio call comes from the Chinese side that your transportation has arrived. This can be a long, cold, frustrating wait. After confirmation of onward transport you march into customs, bags in tow, where officials collect the customs form you filled out when you entered the Commonwealth of Independent States (CIS) and try (and probably succeed)

to sell you a customs form for 30 som. You then proceed through immigration. Meanwhile, your vehicle is being strip-searched in a garage next door.

After inspection you jump back into your vehicle and continue 7km to the border. If you don't have transport for this section, this is where your headache begins, as you'll have to negotiate with a driver to give you a lift and with the officials to let you pass.

SUMMIT

In the border zone, roughly between the two customs and immigration stations, permitted vehicles are allowed, but apparently no pedestrians other than guards (although some travellers are said to have cycled it). At the summit, your new driver and some Chinese soldiers will be waiting for the transfer. Big handshakes all around. Don't forget to take a look at the beautiful pass, which you just fought so hard to cross.

CHINA – TORUGART TO KASHGAR

Another 5km later you will arrive at the original Chinese border post, where the Bishkek–Kashgar bus passengers will be patiently unrolling every carpet and draining every thermos for the customs patrol.

IF THE TORUGART IS CLOSED

If either the China or Kyrgyz side of the pass is closed (and unfortunately no-one could ever possibly tell you this in advance), you face a serious dilemma. There are places to spend the night at the pass, so you could try again the next day (unless that's a Saturday), though you can't be sure that your Chinese arranged transport will bother to try again the next day. If you've cut your visa too fine, you might well have the extra headache of an expired visa to contend with.

At this point, you can either dial up the travel agency who has arranged your trip (the better companies carry their own long-distance radio set) and ask them to contact their Chinese partners urgently to confirm a next day re-try, or alternatively go back three hours to Naryn and start arranging the whole thing all over again.

It is possible to get a short visa extension in Naryn, though you'll need your travel agency's help with this. If all else fails, you'll have to rush back to Bishkek, catch the twice weekly flight to Ürümqi (US$190) and then the daily flight, overnight train or bus on to Kashgar.

To reduce the possibility of this nightmare scenario:

- Don't pay for Chinese transport until you see it
- Try not to cross on a Friday
- Always give yourself a few days leeway on your Kyrgyz visa
- Book all your Torugart transport with one agency

A final piece of advice: if you decide to cross the Torugart, be stubborn, expect the unexpected, and don't count on getting across until you have.

Just to keep up appearances, the guards will have you line up all your baggage and then choose one at random to dig through.

It's surprising how the climate and landscape change when you cross the pass. The Chinese side is abruptly drier, more desolate and treeless, with little physical development other than adobe Kyrgyz settlements. The road runs through Kyzylsu Kyrgyz Autonomous County.

The 100km of road closest to the border, south through crumbling, red-walled canyons, is a miserable washboard surface, spine-shattering to travel along and choked with dust. At 45km is the hamlet of **Toyun** and, about 10km further, the Torugart-Suu Canyon from the border post enters the equally immense Ushmurvan-Suu Canyon from the northwest, flowing down to Kashgar. It's 41km from here to a river bridge, and a further 7km to the spanking new Chinese customs and immigration station, at the junction of the Torugart and Irkeshtam roads.

Chinese immigration is open 1pm to 5pm Beijing time but they will wait for you if you are late. Here you fill out entry forms and get your passport stamped, both relatively painless. The post has a Bank of China branch (although most people wait until they get to their hotel in Kashgar), a couple of simple noodle shops and a small guesthouse, though travellers in either direction are discouraged from staying. From here to Kashgar it's 60km of paved road.

The whole Torugart–Kashgar trip is 160km, a 3½- to four-hour 4WD trip.

BISHKEK TO OSH & THE KYRGYZ FERGANA VALLEY

From the standpoint of landscape, the Bishkek–Osh road is a sequence of superlatives, taking the traveller over two 3000m-plus passes, through the yawning Suusamyr Valley, around the immense Toktogul reservoir, down the deep Naryn river gorge and into the broad Fergana Valley.

The road has improved dramatically over the last few years as the government tries to solder the two halves of the country together using better transport and communications links. The Bishkek–Toktogul stretch is still blocked occasionally by rock falls and avalanches. Snow fills the passes from October or November until February or March; the road is kept open but is dangerous then. Scheduled transport thins out by October, although cars continue to push through.

BISHKEK TO TASHKÖMÜR
Bishkek to Suusamyr Valley

Even before you climb out of the Chuy Valley from Kara-Balta, the craggy Kyrgyz Alatau range rises like a wall. The road climbs through a crumbling canyon towards the highest point of the journey, the 3586m **Tör-Ashuu Pass** at the suture between the Talas Alatau and Kyrgyz Alatau ranges. Instead of climbing over, it burrows through near the top, in a dripping tunnel (built by the same team that constructed the metros in Leningrad and Moscow) that opens onto a grand eagle's-eye view of the Suusamyr Basin.

About 4½ hours out of Bishkek a road shoots off straight as an arrow across the basin towards Suusamyr, Chayek and eventually the Bishkek–Naryn road (p282). This is classic Kyrgyz yurt country, with plenty of summer roadside stands, offering fresh *kymys* and other dairy products.

After another 1¼ hours another road branches right, over the 3330m Otmek pass 106km towards Talas (p295), and Taraz in Kazakhstan.

Suusamyr Valley

This rarely visited valley combines a back-door route to the Kochkor area (p282) with classic Central Kyrgyzstan mountain landscapes. No buses go all the way to Kochkor so you'd have to hitch as far as Chayek, probably with one of the many coal trucks headed to a mine near Song-Köl. Adventurous trekkers can visit the valley as part of a trek to/from Bishkek over the Kyrgyz Range via the Sokuluk (3775m), Ala-Archa (3898m) or Alamedin (4032m) Passes.

In **Suusamyr** town it's possible to arrange homestay accommodation with Kubanych-bek Amankulov (look for the tourist info sign on the main road). He can also arrange transport and yurtstays in *jailoos* east at Joo Jurok (30km from Suusamyr; contact

Negizbek Imankulov), north at Boirok (20km; contact Eshbolot Cheinekeev) and southeast at Sandyk (13km; contact Kubat Amankulov). Little English is spoken at any of these.

Kyzyl-Oi (www.kyrgyz-village.com.kg; 150-250 som; ask for Artyk Kulubaev at the shop 'Aksar') also has a fledgling homestay programme, which also offers horse and foot treks to the Köl Tör lakes (five hours on horse; up the Char Valley, staying at the yurt of Bayish Toltoev, and then over the Kumbel Pass) and also to *jailoos* in the Sary Kamysh range to the south of town. They can arrange horse hire (200 som per day), guides (200 to 450 som) and food (180 som). Homestays include those of Tungatar Konushbaev, Katya Kulmursaeva, and Kanat Soltonkulov, the latter with a *banya* and *shyrdaks* for sale. The programme hasn't had many tourists so far, so expect service to be slightly less polished than CBT.

Transport from Kyzyl-Oi runs almost daily to Suusamyr, from where there are daily buses to Bishkek's Osh Bazaar. In general you are better off taking a taxi or hitching, with help from your homestay.

Dostuck Trekking (☎ 312-54 54 55; www.dostuck .com.kg) operates a **yurt camp** (full board US$19) in the Suusamyr Valley; book a spot in advance.

From Kyzyl-Oi it's 40km or so to Shepherd's Life coordinators at Chayek, Jumgal and Jangy Talap, from where you can arrange horse trips to Song-Köl (p282).

Talas
☎ 3422
The town of Talas itself has little of interest except the **Manas Ordu**, the 14th-century tomb of Manas (actually the tomb of Kenizek Khatum, the daughter of a regional governor, buried in 1334), east of town in the village of Tash Aryk. The Talas Valley was the scene of a pivotal battle between Arab and Chinese armies in the 8th century (p242). Today, there are a couple of fledgling sustainable tourism projects, which you can test out in the surrounding *jailoos*.

CBT Talas (☎ 4 36 95; cbt_talas@mail.ru; Nurjanova 160, near school No 6, between Telmana & Kirova sts; contact Islam Joldoshov) offers accommodation (200 to 280 som) at a homestay in Ozgorush, 50km northeast of town, and a yurtstay in Besh-Tash (Five Stones) National Park

and can arrange guides (300 som per day) and horses (50 som per hour). The park is 15km from town and the first yurt is 38km from town.

The British-funded Sustainable Livelihoods for Livestock Producing Communities Project (SLLPCP) has established a homestay and handicrafts programme in the village of Kopuro-Bazaar, offering treks to the lakes, gorges and petroglyphs of the Kurumdu Valley. In Talas contact **SLLPCP** (☎ 5 28 36; sllpctls@ktnet.kg; Nekrasova 3; contact Taalai Aaliev).

Minibuses run over the Otmek Pass between Talas and Bishkek's Osh Bazaar at least once a day. The road through the Talas Valley is due to be upgraded in 2004 as far as Taraz in Kazakhstan and makes an interesting alternative route to Kazakhstan.

Suusamyr Valley to Tashkömür
A further 30 minutes after the turn-off to Talas the road climbs again, to the 3184m summit of the **Ala-Bel Pass** over the Suusamyr-Tau mountains. Lower, broader and longer than the Tör-Ashuu Pass, it is nevertheless colder, and said to be the bigger wintertime spoiler.

The beautiful valley down the south side of the pass is part of the **Chychkan state zoological reserve** (*chychkan* means mouse). **Chichkan yurt camp** (☎ 312-6 63 401; neman@exnet .kg; per person full board US$21) is run by the Neman company in Bishkek and is a pretty nice place to break the trip if you have your own transport. The flash-looking **Ak Ilbirs Hotel** (d US$20-40) is by the roadside, and is recognisable by a line of flags.

The town of **Toktogul** (pop 70,000) and the reservoir it sits next to are named for a well-known Kyrgyz *akyn*, Toktogul Satilganov (1884–1933), who was born here. It takes over an hour to detour around the vast Toktogul Reservoir. Some tour groups camp on the far side of the reservoir and it's not a bad choice; bring all your water with you. Several roadside stalls on the south side of the lake serve delicious fried *farel* (trout).

The town of **Kara-Köl** (pop 22,000) is of note only for its dam, part of the Nizhnenarynskiy *kaskad*, a series of five dams down the lower gorge of the Naryn River. This *kaskad*, topmost in the series, was completed in 1976 after 14 years' work and

KYRGYZSTAN

is a pretty awesome feat of Soviet engineering: 210m high, 150m wide at the top, and holding back a 19 billion cubic metre lake. Just about everybody in town works for the hydroelectric station Toktogulsky Gidroelektrostantsia (GES). Kara-Köl is not to be confused with the much pleasanter town of Karakol on Lake Issyk-Kul. The dam isn't visible from the road and a visit needs special permission.

South of Kara-Köl the gorge of the **lower Naryn River** is an impressive passage, with sheer walls and towering pillars of red sandstone, and a little road clinging to the side – but keep your gaze upwards. Looking down you will see that there is no longer any river at all, just a depressing series of narrow, utterly still lakes behind the dams of the Nizhnenarynskiy *kaskad*. At lower elevations the gorge bristles with pylons. Sit on the 'west' side of the bus for the best views of the ruination.

Tashkömür
☎ 3745

About 5½ hours from Toktogul is the coal-mining town of Tashkömür, strung for miles along the west side of the river below one of the dams. The deserted slag heaps outside the town are silent testament to the collapse of Kyrgyzstan's coal industry since independence. The town itself is one of the lowlights of Kyrgyzstan, but it is one of the main starting points to beautiful Lake Sary Chelek, 70km west.

The town **gostinitsa** (per person 100 som, lux 400 som) has bearable rooms but the staff change their rates and minds at random and often in the middle of the night. The lux suite has hot water, though.

There are a few cheap cafés serving lukewarm *laghman* at lunchtime near the bus station, along with what may well be Central Asia's most pitiful bazaar. You are better off bringing your own supplies and self-catering.

Buses leave at 5.40am, 11.20am and 3pm for Osh and at 6.40am, 7.20am and 12.20pm for Jalal-Abad from the bus station in the centre of town. To get a shared taxi (to Kara-Köl, Jalal-Abad, Osh or Bishkek), head 3km from town (10 som in a shared taxi) to the Naryn River bridge, where there is a collection of kiosks and food stalls and a telephone office.

LAKE SARY CHELEK САРЫ-ЧЕЛЕК
☎ 3742 / elevation 1878m

This beautiful 7km-long alpine lake, nature reserve and biosphere reserve lies hidden in the northern flanks of the Fergana Valley amid groves of wild pistachios, walnuts and fruit trees. The lake is thought to have been created by an earthquake that caused a giant landslide about 800 years ago and reaches a depth of 234m.

The lake's remote location makes it a real pain to reach by public transport, either from Tashkömür or Kerben; consider hiring a taxi here if nowhere else in the country. There is a park entry fee of US$10 (50 som for locals), plus 60 som per car. The park is part of Unesco's Western Tian Shan Biodiversity project and lynx, bears and maral deer live in the surroundings. Sadly, there is little sign of even the most basic level of environmental protection in the park.

The base for visits to the lake is the small village of Arkit, actually inside the park, where you'll find the **park office** (zapovednik; ☎ 2 22 84), a nearby nature museum and a couple of homestays. The lake is 15km from here, accessible by car. An overlook has just been built halfway along the road.

CBT (☎ 2 25 77; cbt_sary-chelek@mail.ru; contact Bazarkul Jooshbaev) has a coordinator in Kyzyl-Kul village in the Kara-Suu Valley, who can arrange accommodation in homes or yurts (220 to 280 som), plus arrange horses (280 som per day) and guides (280 to 450 som) for treks up valley to Kara-Suu Lake and beyond over the Kemerty Pass to Lake Sary Chelek.

One good route option is to head up to Kyzyl-Kul, hike up to stay in yurts at Kara-Suu Lake and then hike over the next day to Sary Chelek, returning via Arkit.

Activities
HIKING

Once you get to the lake there's not much else to do except go for a walk. A good three- to four-hour loop hike offers views of four other lakes. Follow the faint path east uphill behind the lakeshore caretaker's house for fine views of Sary Chelek. The path then drops down into a meadow and follows the base of the ridge to swing round to Iyri Köl lake, which makes a good lunch stop. At the far end of the small lake take a right turn to a smaller reedy lake, then

At the Sunday animal market (p271), Karakol, Kyrgyzstan

ANTHONY PLUMMER

BRADLEY MAYHEW

Ala-Köl lake (p276), Tian Shan, Kyrgyzstan

Kyrgyz men and a Russian Zhiguli, Kochkor (p282), Kyrgyzstan

ANTHONY PLUMMER

ANTHONY PLUMMER

Two generations on a *jailoo*
(summer pasture), Kyrgyzstan

Kyrgyz *shyrdak* (felt carpet), Kyrgyzstan

MARTIN MOOS

Buzkashi (pololike game using a goat carcass; p54), Kyrgyzstan

BRADLEY MAYHEW

climb and take another right. After you drop down to the fourth lake it's easier to follow the left branch and join the road. The right path is scenic but involves a tricky river crossing at the far end.

It's possible to make a six-day trek in to Sary Chelek from Leninopol (catch a daily bus from Talas). An easier trek starts from Kyzyl-Kul in the next-door valley. From here it's a long day's walk up the valley to Kara Suu Lake, where you can stay in a CBT-arranged yurt. The next day is a hard slog over the 2446m Kemerty Pass and then down to Sary Chelek, either directly or via Iyri Köl lake.

Both routes are marked on the 1:120,000 *Cherez Talasskii Khrebet k Ozeru Sary-Chelek*, available at Geoid in Bishkek (p252).

Sleeping

In Arkit the best option is a **homestay** (per person 100-200 som, 2 meals extra 100 som), either with **Momunali Dubanaev** (☎ 9 21 54) at the far end of town (you really need a car to get here), **Sultan Chukotaev** (☎ 9 21 37) in the centre, or Rusbek Ormanali.

Gulnara Khadirova's homestay (☎ 9 21 47; B&B 100 som, with dinner 150 som) is a good bet in the south of the village. Arkit's homestays are generally more basic than those of CBT or Shepherd's Life.

The government hotel, next to the park office, is undergoing restoration so it should offer a decent place to stay in the future.

Café Millenium can rustle up food given some warning and doubles as the post office and bus stop.

Toskool-Ata Kumbozu (cabins per person US$10) This former *dacha* by the lake is busy constructing three double cabins, each with en suite toilets but no showers. It also offers meals and can arrange a nearby yurtstay.

It's now possible to camp at the lake but you need to get written permission (no fee) from the park office in Arkit.

Getting There & Away

By public transport you need to catch the 10am or, better, the 1.30pm bus from Tashkömür to Kara Jigach (40 som, three hours) and then hitch or wait for the afternoon buses from Kerben (Karavan) to pass through en route to Arkit between 6pm and 7pm. The route to Kara Jigach passes neglected coal mines and weird eroded

hoodoos (rock columns). The decrepit local snub-nosed buses are packed, hot, uncomfortable and mind-numbingly slow. From Arkit you'll need to hire a car (300 to 400 som day return) or hike (four hours) to the lake. Hitching is possible but there's very little traffic outside the weekends.

Heading back, there's a bus from Arkit to Kara Jigach at 7.30am (the bus continues to Kerben), from where you can catch a bus on to Tashkömür at 8.30am or 1pm.

If you are headed for the CBT coordinator, the 4.20pm bus from Kerben to Kyzyl-Suu also passes through Kara Jigach between 6pm and 7pm, returning the next day at 7am. The road to Kara-Suu branches off right from the Arkit road near a museum devoted to the *akyn* Jenijok.

It's possible to get from Jalal-Abad to Arkit by public transport in one day but you need to set off early.

A taxi from Tashkömür will cost around 1000 som to Arkit, or around 1200 to 1500 som to continue to Sary Chelek and return the next afternoon.

JALAL-ABAD ЖАЛАЛ-АВАД

☎ 3722 / pop 74,000

Jalal-Abad is a former resort town of limited interest except as a base from which to visit surrounding mountain villages such as Arslanbob, Özgön (Uzgen) and Ortok. The town can be extremely hot in July and August and there's no air-conditioning anywhere.

CBT (☎ 3 19 62; cbt_ja@rambler.ru; Toktogul 3-20; ☯ 9am-6pm Mon-Fri, 9am-noon Sat; contact Ruhsora Abdullaeva in Russian or Shakhnauza in English) This dynamic branch can arrange transport and homestays in Arslanbob and can also organise horse treks to Sailmaluu Tash from its western approach. From the bazaar head along Lenina to tree-lined Toktogul, turn right and it's near the second crossroad on the left. The CBT sign can be hard to see when the door is open.

Asia Trekking (☎ 5 25 84; a_trek2001@mail.ru; Lenin 101; Rustam Moninov) Runs treks throughout the region, including Arslanbob, where it owns a guesthouse. The office is just before the bus station.

Sleeping

CBT offers 14 comfortable **homestays** (350-380 som), all of which are good. We can recommend the house of Saima Nurgalieva and her daughter Albina (☎ 3 14 10; Kalinina 15, No 6), a Tartar family. Many of the houses are a bit out of the centre; the most central is that of Gubareva Irina. Arrange all through the CBT office.

Hotel Mölmöl (☎ 5 50 59; s 150-211 som, d 272-363 som, tr 302-408 som, lux 604-725 som) This Spartan but essentially clean ex-Soviet survivor offers standard rooms with cold-water bathrooms (toilet seats optional), a balcony and classic 1970s Brezhnev-era wallpaper. The lux suites have hot water. There's **Internet access** (per hr 30 som; ◷ 8am-8pm) on the ground floor.

Eating

Kyrgyzbay Ajy Café on the west side of the bazaar has all the standard Central Asian dishes but also *japanji* (chicken with noodles, tomatoes and peppers, 80 som) and *solyanka* (soup with sausage, cucumbers and olives). It's professionally run, with an English menu and English-speaking staff.

The Restaurant Ala-Too opposite the Hotel Mölmöl has decent soups and Russian standards at lunch, but more blow-you-away techno beat in the evening.

More of the same but in a fancier setting can be found at the Café Abdykaar-Ata on Lenina.

Getting There & Around

AIR

Kyrgyzstan Airlines and Altyn Air fly three times a week to/from Bishkek (1700 som, sometimes discounted to 1000 som); buy tickets at the airport or the **Sputnik Agency** (☎ 5 07 06; Lenina 17) just outside the Hotel Mölmöl. Marshrutnyy minibus Nos 1 and 5 from the centre go to the airport, northwest of the centre, via the bus station. A taxi to the airport costs about 100 som.

Minibus No 10 runs along Lenina from the Hotel Mölmöl to the bazaar and bus station. A taxi to the bus station costs 20 som.

BUS

The bus station is 3km west of the centre; minibuses clearly marked *avtovokzal* run frequently along Lenina from near the bazaar.

Scheduled buses depart for Kara-Köl at 8.20am, Tashkömür at 6.20am, 8am, 12.50pm and 3.50pm (50 to 70 som) and Toktogul at 6.20am and 10.20am. Mini-

buses to Osh leave every half-hour or so until 6pm (50 som). There are a couple of buses a day to Kerben

Shared taxis run frequently to Osh (100 som per seat) and Özgön (50 som), and less frequently to Tashkömür (100 som).

At a stand on the far corner of the bazaar you can find private cars (800 som in a Volga) and minibuses going all the way to Bishkek for 700 som a seat, though you may have to wait a while for the vehicle to fill up. You can find shared Nivas and jeeps for the mountain route to Kazarman (300 som per seat) from a stand north of the bazaar.

Around Jalal-Abad

The latest CBT-supported destination is **Ortuk**, set in walnut and cherry forests 60km north of Jalal-Abad. CBT has **homestays** (B&B 280 som) in the village, from where you can make horse daytrips (horse hire 200 som per day) to local *jailoos* and a cave complex. Contact CBT in Jalal-Abad for details (p297). A bus stand north of the bazaar in Jalal-Abad has daily buses to Ortuk and nearby Kara-Alma, or hire a car through CBT for around US$30 return.

ARSLANBOB АРСПАНБОБ

☎ 3722 / elevation 1600m

Better than looking at the mountains from Jalal-Abad is to go up into them. A good do-it-yourself trip goes up to Arslanbob (Arstanbap in Kyrgyz), a totally Uzbek village of about 12,000 that offers cool mountain air, some of Central Asia's best walnut forests and some fine opportunities for hiking in the wall-like Babash-Ata mountains behind the town.

CBT (☎ 5 58 49; arslanbob_2003@rambler.ru; contact Hayat Tarikov) has an excellent branch, which can help with everything from homestays and transport to full service horse treks (p299). Lochenbek is a recommended local guide, contactable through the CBT office.

Buses drop you in the village square by a taxi stand and the CBT office. From here a road leads uphill, branching left to the *turbaza* (former Soviet holiday camp; 1.5km from the square), and right to the upper waterfall. Outside the season (June through September), shops are empty and it's cold. May and October can still be good times to visit as you'll probably have the place to yourself. This is a fairly conservative village, so don't walk around town in shorts and singlets.

Sights & Activities

There are several day-hike options, though the most popular is the three-hour return hike to a holy 80m-high **waterfall**. The last half hour is an uphill grind over a slippery scree slope – wear good shoes, as the return leg is like walking down a slope of marbles. Horses are available for rent but aren't all that useful as you still have to slog up the last hill yourself. The fence in front of the falls is covered in votive rags, harking back to a pre-Islamic animism. An easier walk leads about 45 minutes to a smaller **twin waterfall** (23m) to the east, from where you can continue to walnut forest and the **shrine of Ibn Abbas**. Ask CBT for details. A guide costs 300 som per day.

Back at the village square, check out the riverside **mazar** (tomb) of Arslan Bab-Ata, after whom the town and mountains are named.

TREKKING

CBT can arrange a couple of trekking options to the holy lakes of Köl Kupan (marked Kulan on maps), Paino Köl, Kabyr Köl and Ainek Köl (Mirror Lake), collectively referred to as the Köl Mazar. This makes for a fine three- or four-day trek or horse trek, stopping at a cube-shaped holy rock en route. CBT has a couple of ratty tents for rent but it's best to bring your own equipment.

Instead of retracing your steps you can continue over the Kerets Pass and east along the Kerets Valley, with the Nurbuu-Tau Mountains to the north, until you swing south down the Kara-Unkor Valley. You can then continue down to Kyzyl Ünkür or head back to Arslanbob via the Kara-Bulak Valley for an excellent five- or six-day trek.

A CBT-organised trek with a guide, cook and three meals costs around US$15 per person per day on foot or US$27 per day on horseback, assuming there are two people. A horse costs 300 som per day; donkeys are cheaper.

The adjacent **Kyzyl Ünkür** (Red Cavern) Valley has a network of hiking and fishing routes equal to, if not grander than, those at Arslanbob. CBT plans to set up some homestays here but until then you'll need a tent and supplies (the *turbaza* is cur-

rently closed). Travellers recommend the trek north from Kyzyl Ünkür, up the Kara Ünkür Valley to tiny Kön-Köl lake (you can do this section by car) and then northeast over the Kymysh Bel Pass (3754m) to the fish-stocked Kara-Suu and Kalka-Tash Lakes. From here you can head down the Kara-Suu Valley to join the main Bishkek–Osh road at Kök Bel, between Karakol and Toktogul, or return on a loop back to Kyzyl Ünkür via Kön-Köl Pass, either way making an intrepid six-day trek.

Sleeping & Eating

Homestays (B&B per person 180-300 som) CBT offers 14, which are your best bet, though some are far from the town centre. Of these homestays, those of Raikhon Kozubaeva (230 som) and Riyat Tajibaeva (180 som) are the most central.

Turbaza Arslanbob (☎ 5 28 40; per person 50 som, pol-lux 100 som, lux/superlux 200/300 som) Run-down but rustic, this scruffy former Soviet holiday camp has dozens of bungalows scattered around 29 hectares of grounds. Only the best rooms have hot water and en suite toilets but even these are quite basic. There's a popular open air swimming pool. Avoid the disco.

Guesthouse (per person US$7-15, lux US$25-30) Asia Trekking, based in Jalal-Abad (p297), has this peaceful, slightly mafiosi-feeling estate a couple of kilometres west of Arslanbob. It's used mainly by their trekking clients but is open to all.

The traditional chaikhana Chinor just across the river from the village square has been serving green tea for centuries.

Getting There & Away

From Jalal-Abad, take an hourly bus (40 minutes) or shared taxi (20 som per seat) to Bazaar Korgon. Change there for an hourly (until 4.30pm) Arslanbob bus and take it to the end of the line (25 som, 2½ hours). A taxi from Jalal-Abad to Arslanbob costs 500 som.

There are also three absurdly full buses a day from Bazaar Korgon to Kyzyl Ünkür (65km, 25 som).

OSH Oш

☎ 3222 / pop 300,000
Osh is Kyrgyzstan's second-biggest city and the administrative centre of the huge,

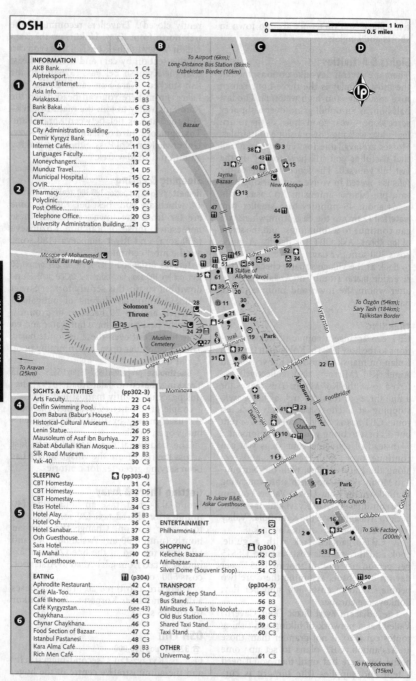

OSH

| 0 | 1 km |
| 0 | 0.5 miles |

To Airport (6km);
Long-Distance Bus Station (8km);
Uzbekistan Border (10km)

Bazaar

Jayma Bazaar

New Mosque

Mosque of Mohammed
Yusuf Bai Haji Ogli

Solomon's Throne

Muslim Cemetery

To Aravan
(25km)

Çapar Aytiev

Mominova

Israil Sulaimanov

Park

Abdykadyrov

Ak-Buura River

Footbridge

Kalmanbai Dodke

Bayalinov

Stadium

Lomonosov

Alicy

Nookat

Park

Orthodox Church

Golubev

To Özgön (54km);
Sary Tash (184km);
Tajikistan Border

To Jukov B&B;
Askar Guesthouse

To Silk Factory
(200km)

Soviet

Frunze

Michurin

To Hippodrome
(15km)

INFORMATION
AKB Bank	1 C4
Alptreksport	2 C5
Ansavut Internet	3 C2
Asia Info	4 C4
Aviakassa	5 B3
Bank Bakai	6 C3
CAT	7 C3
CBT	8 D6
City Administration Building	9 D5
Demir Kyrgyz Bank	10 C4
Internet Cafés	11 C3
Languages Faculty	12 C3
Moneychangers	13 C2
Munduz Travel	14 D5
Municipal Hospital	15 C2
OVIR	16 D5
Pharmacy	17 C4
Polyclinic	18 C3
Post Office	19 C3
Telephone Office	20 C3
University Administration Building	21 C3

SIGHTS & ACTIVITIES   (pp302-3)
Arts Faculty	22 D4
Delfin Swimming Pool	23 C4
Dom Babura (Babur's House)	24 B3
Historical-Cultural Museum	25 B3
Lenin Statue	26 D5
Mausoleum of Asaf ibn Burhiya	27 B3
Rabat Abdullah Khan Mosque	28 B3
Silk Road Museum	29 B3
Yak-40	30 C3

SLEEPING   (pp303-4)
CBT Homestay	31 C4
CBT Homestay	32 D5
CBT Homestay	33 C2
Etas Hotel	34 C3
Hotel Alay	35 B3
Hotel Osh	36 C4
Hotel Sanabar	37 C3
Osh Guesthouse	38 C3
Sara Hotel	39 C3
Taj Mahal	40 C2
Tes Guesthouse	41 C3

EATING   (p304)
Aphrodite Restaurant	42 C4
Café Ala-Too	43 C2
Café Ilkhom	44 C3
Café Kyrgyzstan	(see 43)
Chaykhana	45 C3
Chynar Chaykhana	46 C3
Food Section of Bazaar	47 C3
Istanbul Pastanesi	48 C3
Kara Alma Café	49 B3
Rich Men Café	50 D6

ENTERTAINMENT
Philharmonia	51 C3

SHOPPING   (p304)
Kelechek Bazaar	52 C3
Minibazaar	53 D5
Silver Dome (Souvenir Shop)	54 C3

TRANSPORT   (pp304-5)
Argomak Jeep Stand	55 C3
Bus Stand	56 B3
Minibuses & Taxis to Nookat	57 C3
Old Bus Station	58 C3
Shared Taxi Stand	59 C3
Taxi Stand	60 C3

OTHER
Univermag	61 C3

KYRGYZSTAN

populous province that engulfs the Fergana Valley on the Kyrgyzstan side. It suffers a kind of demographic schizophrenia, being a major centre of Kyrgyzstan but with a strong (40%) Uzbek population more in tune with Uzbekistan and the rest of the Fergana Valley, but isolated from it by one of the world's more absurd international borders.

Osh is one of the region's genuinely ancient towns (with a history dating back at least to the 5th century BC) but few souvenirs remain. In many ways it's still quite a Soviet place: whereas other cities scrubbed Lenin's name from their street maps after the collapse of the USSR, Osh merely shifted it politely one block away. A huge Lenin statue still stands opposite the city administration building.

Osh is the anchor of not only the Pamir Highway into Tajikistan but, branching off this, the main road access to the Pamir Alay on the Kyrgyzstan–Tajikistan border, and the Irkeshtam border crossing to and from Kashgar in China.

The city is also a common travellers' base for trekking and mountaineering in the spectacular Pamir range.

History

The standard refrain from anyone you ask is that 'Osh is older than Rome'. Legends credit all sorts of people with its founding, from King Solomon (Suleyman) to Alexander the Great. Certainly it must have been a major hub on the Silk Road from its earliest days. The Mongols smashed it in the 13th century but in the following centuries it bounced back, more prosperous than ever.

More recently, 'Osh' has become a byword for ethnic conflict in the festering, gerrymandered closeness of the Fergana Valley. In fact the worst of 'Osh' took place 55km away in Özgön (Uzgen), during three nights of savage Uzbek-Kyrgyz violence in June and July 1990, during which at least 300 people (some unofficial estimates run to 1000) died a variety of ugly deaths while Soviet military and police authorities stood oddly by.

Although the majority Uzbeks dominate local business, Kyrgyzstan has forced upon them an almost totally Kyrgyz (and apparently widely corrupt) municipal administration, by which they feel constantly 'plundered'.

Rumours abound of weapons stockpiled for future conflicts. But considering the likelihood that most people living around Osh and Özgön – Kyrgyz and Uzbek alike – have friends or family members who were murdered in 1990, the wonder is how many Kyrgyz and Uzbeks remain close friends (or married couples) and how determined most of them are to get along.

Perhaps to improve flagging morale and stir up some post-independence patriotism the year 2000 was celebrated as the 3000th year of Osh.

Orientation

Osh sprawls across the valley of the Ak-Buura (White Camel) River, flowing out of the Pamir Alay mountains. The city's most prominent landmark is 'Solomon's Throne', a craggy mountain that squeezes right up to the river from the west.

Along the west bank run two parallel main roads – one-way-south Kurmanjan Datka köchösü and one-way-north Lenin köchösü. From Hotel Osh to the bazaar is a 20- to 25-minute walk.

Osh's old bus station (*stary avtovokzal*) is on Alisher Navoi köchösü just east of the river, while the new one (*novyy avtovokzal*) is about 8km north of the town centre. The airport is about five minutes by bus from the new bus station.

Information

INTERNET ACCESS

Several Internet cafés charge around 30 som per hour, including **Asia Info** (Lenin 305), **Ansavut Internet** (Kyrgyzstan, opposite the Osh Guesthouse) and several places on Kurmanjan Datka.

MEDICAL SERVICES

Municipal hospital (cnr Zaina Betinova & Kyrgyzstan) Northeast of the bazaar.

Polyclinic (health centre; Abdykadyrov btwn Kurmanjan Datka & Lenin)

MONEY

In general it's easiest to change cash (including Uzbek sum and Tajik somani) at the various moneychangers' kiosks, a collection of which can be found east of the Jayma Bazaar. Shop around and check your change.

AKB Bank (Kurmanjan Datka 119) Changes travellers cheques at 3% commission.

Bank Bakai (☎ 5 76 46; cnr Gapar Aytiev & Kumanjan Datka) Cash advances on Visa, MasterCard, Amex and Maestro.

Demir Kyrgyz Bank (☎ 5 65 55; Kurmanjan Datka 180A; ☺ 8.45am-noon & 1-3.30pm Mon-Thu, until 1.30pm Fri) Near the Osh Hotel, changes travellers cheques and gives Visa cash advances.

REGISTRATION & VISAS

OVIR is at the back (southwest corner) of a building a block southeast of the City Administration Building on Lenin. Go to the Inspector's office (room four). Fees are paid at the AKB Bank.

Visa extensions can be given at the 4th floor of the City Administration Building but you will probably need a letter of visa support from a travel agency such as Alptreksport (see below).

TRAVEL AGENCIES

CBT (☎ 5 54 37; www.cbt-osh.tk; Kurmanjan Datka 58; contact Dinara Abdyrakhmanova) can arrange transport and trips to nearby sites such as the Chil Ustun caves, Abshirsay, Kara Shoro and Kyrgyz Ata National Park, as well as the Yoshlik silk factory in town. The CBT office is inconveniently situated in the southern outskirts so ring in advance. Bus No 25, 35 and 38 will take you here; get off at the Rich Men Café.

Alptreksport (☎ 2 30 01, ☎ /fax 7 69 06; Gogol 3; contact Yury or Sasha Lavrushin) These two brothers, veterans of the Soviet sports agency Sovintersport's Pamir International Mountaineering Camp (IMC), organise mountaineering, trekking and caving trips for US$25 to US$50 per person per day. They prefer advance bookings but can accommodate drop-ins. They can do most trekking itineraries, including around Sary Chelek and Achik Tash. They recommend three- or four-day treks to the Jiptik Pass (4185m) and beyond to Sary Moghul in the Alay Valley and back via the Sary Moghul Pass (4303m), Kok Moinak Pass, Sary Bel Pass and Kojokelen village. Yury speaks English.

CAT (☎ 5 55 30; catosh@infotel.kg; Israil Sulaimanov 3) Branch of the reliable Bishkek company (p253), strong on air tickets.

Munduz Travel (☎ 22276; osh_munduz@netmail.kg; Soviet 1) General travel arrangements.

Daniyar Abdurahmanov (☎ mobile 502 37 23 11, 3 80 33; transguide@hotbox.ru, daniyar1@mail.ru) An English guide who also runs the Osh Guest-

house. Contact him through the Taj Mahal Guesthouse.

Sights

You might find keen students of English or other languages to act as unofficial guides to the city at Osh University's **Languages Faculty** (Infac; Kurmanjan Datka 250, north of Abdykadyrov).

BAZAAR

The thunderous daily **Jayma Bazaar** is one of Central Asia's best markets, teeming with Uzbeks, Kyrgyz and Tajiks dealing in everything from traditional hats and knives to pirated cassettes, horseshoes (forged at smithies in the bazaar), Chinese tea sets and abundant seasonal fruit and vegetables. It stretches for about 1km along the west side of the river, and crosses it in several places. It's most kinetic on Sunday morning, and almost deserted on Monday.

SOLOMON'S THRONE & AROUND

A jagged, barren rock that seems to loom above the city wherever you go, **Solomon's Throne** has been a Muslim place of pilgrimage of some importance for centuries, supposedly because the Prophet Mohammed once prayed here. From certain perspectives it's said to resemble a reclining pregnant woman, and it's especially favoured by women who have been unable to bear children.

In 1497, 14-year-old Zahiruddin Babur, newly crowned king of Fergana (and later to found India's Mughal dynasty (see the boxed text on p195), built himself a little shelter and private mosque on the rock's high eastern promontory. In later years this came to be something of an attraction in its own right. It collapsed in an earthquake in 1853 and was rebuilt. Then in the 1960s it was destroyed by a mysterious explosion; most local people are convinced it was a Soviet attempt to halt the persistent pilgrim traffic and put a chill on 'superstition' (ie Islam) after failing to persuade Uzbek authorities to do so. After independence it was rebuilt.

Local people call it **Dom Babura**, Babur's House. If you speak Russian, the friendly Uzbek caretaker will tell you more, and offer you a prayer for a few som. The steep 25-minute climb begins at a little gateway behind a futuristic silver dome on Kurmanjan Datka. The promontory offers long views but little to see except for a vast **Muslim cemetery** at the foot of the hill. Dusk is a good time to visit.

Carry on around the south side for another 15 minutes to see the mildly interesting **Historical-Cultural Museum** (admission 50 som; 9am-noon & 1-5pm Wed-Sun). With typical Soviet subtlety, a hole was blasted in the side of this sacred mountain into one of its many caves, and a grotesque sheet-metal front stuck on – a carbuncle now visible from great distances. Inside is a series of badly lit exhibits of potsherds, old masonry, rocks, bugs and mangy stuffed animals; upstairs is a huge, forlorn yurt.

The **Silk Road Museum** (admission 50 som; 9am-noon & 1-6pm) was built during the Osh 3000 celebrations but it's really just another standard Central Asian museum, strong on local archaeology and ethnography but with little English text. There are some great weapons, displayed as if caught up in mad whirlwind.

Back down at the bottom of the hill is the small **Rabat Abdullah Khan Mosque**, dating from the 17th or 18th century but rebuilt in the 1980s. It's a working mosque (ie male visitors only, and by permission only; shoes off at the entrance). The small **Mausoleum of Asaf Ibn Burhiya** is to the south along the base of the hill but is of little historical or architectural interest.

OTHER SIGHTS
There isn't much, other than a long riverbank **park** stretching from Navoi to Abdykadyrov. A central feature is an old **Yak-40** (an airplane), at one time a video salon, looking poised to leap over the river. There's a *palvankhana* (wrestling hall) here, though there are only wrestling bouts every month or so.

Osh **hippodrome**, 16km south of town at Tolüken village (minibus No 24), puts on Kyrgyz national sports and eagle hunting competitions during national holidays.

Sleeping
BUDGET
CBT Homestays (350-500 som) There are a range of very comfortable homestays, two in central apartments, the rest in houses in the suburbs. Prices are higher than most CBT accommodation but so are standards. The coordinator's house (p302) is particularly

recommended and is worth reserving, as it's popular with UN workers.

Osh Guesthouse (☎ 3 06 29, 3 80 33; oshguesthouse@ hotbox.ru; flat 48, apt 8, Kyrgyzstan köchösü; dm US$4) This is the best budget bet in Osh. It has three-bed dorms, and the flat can get very cramped when full; you'll either love it or hate it. Pluses include a hot shower and Internet access. The apartment can be hard to find. Take the alley by a row of kiosks, take a diagonal right by the rubbish dump and turn left at the second apartment building; it's the third entrance on the left, on the top floor. The guy who looks after the place (not the owner) gets mixed reviews.

Sara Hotel (2 25 59; sara.hotel@mail.ru; Kurmanjan Datka 278A; s/d/tr 215/430/650 som, pol-lux d 800 som, lux 1000 som) This is a decent budget hotel with a useful location, though the rooms facing the street can be a bit noisy. There's a common hot shower if you give an hour's notice. Note that if you are alone you may have to share a room. The management also rent out several nearby apartments (US$20 to US$30).

Hotel Alay (☎ 5 77 33; Navoi; s 174-194 som, d 306-489 som, tr 490 som, lux 673 som) A fairly depressing Soviet hotel, with no hot water. The rooms aren't that bad, though the cheaper ones are probably better value. The common toilets have no seat or light bulb so expect to squat in the dark. But there is a casino…

Hotel Sanabar (☎ 2 54 37; cnr Kurmanjan Datka & Israil Sulaimanov; d 300 som) Tiny rooms with even tinier bathrooms here, but essentially clean and with TV and hot water. There are only four rooms so it's often full.

MID-RANGE
Taj Mahal (☎ 3 96 52; cnr Zaina Betinova & Kyrgyzstan; d 600, lux 800 som) Small and bright, this Indian-built hotel has clean and pleasant doubles with hot water and towels but there are only five rooms so try to book ahead.

Askar Guesthouse (☎ 5 62 29; Nizami 81; per person incl breakfast or dinner US$30; contact Adil Kazakbaev) The owner of the Sara Hotel has just opened this place, which has a couple of rooms and balconies overlooking a pleasant courtyard garden.

Jukov B&B (☎ 5 23 38; vadik@ktnet.kg; Tashkentskaya 8; US$25 half board) A comfortable private guesthouse run by Yuri and Nina Jukov (their daughter Nadia speaks English). They also have two similar overspill **guesthouses** (☎ 2 00

72; 20a Amir Timur; half board US$25;　☎ 2 75 76; Frunze 40; US$20). You need to ring in advance as all the guesthouses are in the southwestern suburbs in the Yuga Vostok district.

Tes Guesthouse (☎ 2 15 48; afc-osh@mail.kg; Say Boyu 5; ind breakfast s/d US$25/35) This is used mostly by NGO consultants but tourists can stay if there's a vacancy (there are only five rooms; ring ahead). Pleasant piney rooms come with spotless bathrooms and there's a coffee machine, TV room, Internet access and a washing machine. You can swim in the next-door Delfin pool (20 som).

Etas Hotel (☎ 3 20 66; Kyrgyzstan; d 600 som) A new hotel with cleans rooms, a restaurant and a sauna (70 som per hour).

Eating

Café Ala-Too (Kyrgyzstan) is everything a teahouse should be; lots of food options, tea beds and kebab masters lovingly fanning a wide range of shashlyk, plus there's beer on tap. The next door **Café Kyrgyzstan** (Kyrgyzstan) and nearby **Café Ilkhom** (Kyrgyzstan) are similarly good places, the latter particularly for breakfast.

Kara Alma Café (Navoi), opposite the Hotel Alay, is popular with tourists but service is pretty crummy and the food average. The **Chynar chaikhana** (Lenin), just north of the post office is good and has huge *samsas* (meat pies) baked on site. There's also a good traditional **chaikhana** at the southern entrance to the bazaar.

Istanbul Pastanesi (Navoi; meals 45 som) is a decent choice for breakfasts and snacks, topped off by great baclava.

Rich Men Café (☎ 2 43 03; Kurmanjan Datka; salads 35-50 som, mains 75-90 som) South of town and recognisable by the blue awning, the Rich Men Café is top-notch. Good meat and fish dishes are complemented by specialities such as eggs stuffed with red or black caviar (80 som) and excellent service. Wine and Soviet champagne are served, as are excellent beer snacks.

Aphrodite Restaurant (Lenin; salads 35-50 som; mains 65-70 som) Another good restaurant. It's by the entrance to the stadium, and has a good range of European dishes, indoor or outdoor seating and beer on tap.

Shopping

The entrance to the **Jayma Bazaar** is one of the best and cheapest places in Kyrgyzstan

to buy an *ak kalpak* (Kyrgyz white felt hat; 60 to 100 som). The silver dome at the base of Solomon's Hill usually has a few lonely souvenirs, but was closed at time of research. Pottery and clay Central Asian figurines can be bought cheaply in the **Arts Faculty** (Kyrgyzstan 80).

Getting There & Away
AIR

There's an **aviakassa** (booking office; ☎ 2 22 11; Kurmanjan Datka 287; ⏰ 9am-noon & 1-6pm Mon-Fri), just northwest of the Hotel Alay.

The only regular flight to/from Osh is the daily flight to Bishkek (1700 som, sometimes discounted to 999 som). Flights to Cholpon-Ata (400 som) operate occasionally.

BUS & CAR

The old bus station, near the bazaar, is mainly for minibuses to Özgön (20 to 25 som, every 40 minutes) and Jalal-Abad (50 to 60 som), which run every 20 minutes until 6pm

A stand behind **Kelechek Bazaar** has shared taxis to Bishkek (400 to 500 som) and, at the far end, to Özgön (40 som) and Jalal-Abad (100 som). If you want to hire transport to take you into Tajikistan and the Pamir Highway, you could ask around here or the taxi stand next to the old bus station. Travel agents charge around US$100 for a trip to Achik Tash in the Alay Valley. Osh to Murgab is 420km.

The Argomak jeep stand just uphill from the old bus station has early morning jeeps and minibuses to Sary Moghul (250 som) and Daroot-Korgon (10 hours, 300 som), both via Sary Tash. There are also minibuses for Daroot-Korgon (135 som) and all points in Kyrgyzstan's southern arm (Sary Tash, Kyzyl-Kiya, Aravan, Gulcha and others) from the old bus station, though departures are a little unreliable.

Buses to Batken (140 som) via Kyzyl-Kiya leave from the old bus station or take a shared taxi (250 som) via Sokh (Uzbek visa required).

Another stand west of the Hotel Alay has buses to Aravan and Nookat. Minibuses and taxis to Nookat run from just behind the Philharmonia.

Just about everything else (eg Toktogul, Tashkömür and Kerben) goes to/from the new bus station.

Getting Around

Marshrutnoe minibus No 2 runs south-bound on Kurmanjan Datka from the old bus station to the Hotel Osh and Turbaza Ak-Buura; it returns northbound down Lenin.

Minibus Nos 2a and 7a shuttle between the airport and the Jayma Bazaar in the centre of town (4 som). To get to the long-distance bus station from the old bus stand take minibus Nos 13 or 7 from opposite the old bus station.

A taxi costs 80 to 100 som to the airport and 50 som to the new bus station.

ÖZGÖN ӨЗГӨН

☎ 3233

Özgön, 55km northeast of Osh, is today best known as the centre of three nights of ferocious Kyrgyz-Uzbek fighting in 1990 (p301). Few outward scars are evident today. The town is nominally 85% Uzbek; locals say it was about two-thirds Uyghur in pre-Soviet days.

Özgön is claimed to be the site of a series of citadels dating back to the 1st century BC; there is also a story that the town began as an encampment for some of Alexander the Great's troops. It was one of the multiple Karakhanid capitals in the 10th and 11th centuries.

All that remains of this history is a quartet of Karakhanid buildings – three joined 12th-century **mausoleums** and a stubby 11th-century **minaret** (whose top apparently fell down in an earthquake in the 17th century), faced with very fine ornamental brickwork, carved terracotta and inlays of stone. Each mausoleum is unlike the others, though all are in shades of red-brown clay (there were no glazed tiles at this point in Central Asian history). In the corner of the right-hand-side mausoleum, a small section has been deliberately left off to reveal older layers of the middle one (the Mausoleum of Nasr ibn Ali, founder of the Karakhanids). You can climb the minaret for 10 som.

Apart from the architectural attractions Özgön's bazaar is an interesting place to wander around, particularly if you haven't seen much of Uzbekistan. There are plenty of interesting faces.

To get to the mausoleums turn right out of the main (new) bus station on Manas. The road curves to the right past the entrance to the bazaar, which is where shared taxis and minibuses will probably drop you off. From the bazaar it's a 10-minute walk to the statue of Lenin (opposite the post office), from where you can see the minaret in the square behind.

Sleeping & Eating

Hotel Juma (cnr Manas & Gagarin; d/tr 100/150 som) Stay here in an emergency. This very basic dosshouse in the northeast of the town has beds but no water. The outdoor pit toilets are the most awful in Kyrgyzstan.

Kafe Bor Kelechek (Manas; mains 20-30 som) Serves standard dishes and beer and offers a cool escape from the heat (look for the tilework on the front of the building).

Restaurant Almaz (☎ 2 61 20; mains 50-60 som) Probably the best in town, with dishes like trout in champagne (65 som) and lots of good salads.

Café Muslim (Manas) Decent canteen-style chaikhana with outdoor tea bed seating and cheap food.

The best atmosphere comes free with the shashlyk in the bazaar chaikhanas.

Getting There & Away

Özgön is a pleasant half-day trip by bus from Osh or Jalal-Abad and the scenery of the broad Kara-Darya or Özgön Valley is pretty, ringed with big peaks of the Fergana range. From Jalal-Abad, the road passes Uzbekistan's Andijan Reservoir.

Shared taxis to Jalal-Abad lurk down a side street a block east of the bazaar, near the Restaurant Almaz, and cost 50 som a seat. Shared taxis to Osh cost 40 som and run all day.

Around Özgön

The village of **Ak-Terek**, about 60km from Özgön, has five **homestays** (per night incl breakfast 250 som), which can be arranged through village head Jengish Akmataliev. Daily buses run every afternoon to Ak-Terek (20 som) from Özgön's old bus station, next to the Café Muslim.

From Ak-Terek you can take a horse 35km further to Kara Shoro National Park, where there are yurtstays. An adventurous option is the seven-day horse trek along the Jassy River and over the Fergana range to the Arpa Valley, and from there to Naryn. You can get info on the programme from the **Sustainable Livelihoods for Livestock Producing Communities Project** (SLLPCP; ☎ 3222-7 46 71; www.kyrgyz-village.com.kg; Apt 5, Lenina 302) in Osh.

THE ALAY VALLEY
АЛАЙСКАЯ ДОЛИНА

The far southern arm of Kyrgyzstan is the exclusive turf of trekkers and mountaineers, consisting as it does mostly of the Pamir Alay range, a jagged, 500km-long suture running from Samarkand to Xinjiang. The range is threaded right up the middle by the muddy Kyzyl-Suu River (known as the Surkhob further downstream in Tajikistan – the two names mean Red Water in Kyrgyz and Tajik respectively) to form the 60km-long Alay Valley, the heart of the Kyrgyz Pamir. Two of Central Asia's earliest and busiest Silk Road branches crossed the Pamir Alay from Kashgar, at Kök-Art and at Irkeshtam. The area was formerly the southern frontier of the Uzbek Khanate of Kokand.

Osh and the Alay Valley are the main access points for mountaineering expeditions into Tajikistan's High Pamir – to 7495m Koh-i-Samani (formerly Pik Kommunizma, the highest point in the former USSR), 7134m Koh-i-Garmo (formerly Pik Lenin) or 7105m Pik Korzhenevskaya.

Access from Kyrgyzstan is along the A372 from Osh, via Sary Tash and the 3615m Taldyk Pass. This is also the main route into Tajikistan's Gorno-Badakhshan region. It's also possible to access the valley from Dushanbe via the Garm Valley.

A trip into the Alay region is not a lightweight jaunt. There is little traffic on the main roads and food supplies are limited, even in summer. From October through May the A372 is often closed by snow, and even in summer snow and rainstorms can appear without warning. The best trekking months are July and August.

For information on taking the M41 Pamir Highway to Gorno-Badakhshan, see p345.

Information
PERMITS

In theory you need a border zone permit to go within 50km of the CIS/Chinese border and the Alay Valley. However the removal of the check post at Sary Tash means that you will not be asked for this permit en route to the Alay Valley, only perhaps at Achik Tash base camp. This can change, so check with a trekking agency before setting off.

Trekking agencies operating in the area (see below) can arrange a permit with a minimum of one week's notice if you need one, for about US$10. Make sure that the permit clearly mentions the Chong-Alay and Alay rayons of Osh *oblast*.

TREKKING AGENCIES

The Pamir Alay is one of the most remote and rugged parts of Central Asia – this is one place where you can't just head off with a 1970s Soviet map and a handful of Snickers bars. ITMC Tien-Shan, IMC Pamir, Dostuck Trekking and Top Asia (p253) all organise trekking and mountaineering trips in both the Kyrgyz and Tajik sides of the valley. Alptreksport in Osh (p302) also has a lot of experience in the region.

Sary Moghul

The village of Sary Moghul, 30km from Sary Tash, offers the valley's best views of Pik Lenin and is a good place to break the Murgab–Osh trip. Sary Moghul is inside Kyrgyzstan but the entire village and surrounding 37,000 hectares of arable land is currently rented by Tajikistan! (No Tajik visa is required).

You should be able to arrange informal accommodation by contacting the village administration (*Hakkimat Pritsdavityel Jamaat Karakul*) or village MSDSP office. There's a daily bus service to/from Osh (130 som), or you could catch the Daroot-Korgon bus. There is also a daily bus to Sary Moghul (70 som, 7½ hours).

Pik Lenin & Achik Tash

Trekking possibilities in the Alay Valley are legion, but serious trekkers head for Pik Lenin (now officially called Koh-i-Garmo, though everyone still calls it by its Soviet name). The peak is known as one of the most accessible 7000-ers in the world. It is the highest summit of the Pamir Alay and lies right on the Kyrgyz–Tajik border. The snow-covered ridges and slopes are not difficult to climb, though altitude sickness and avalanches are a serious problem; in 1990 a single avalanche killed over 40 climbers.

A lighter hike can take you to nearby Lukovaya Polyana, or Wild Onion Meadow, the last outpost of greenery before the glacial moraine takes over. For more details on trekking around Pik Lenin, see Frith Maier's *Trekking in Russia & Central Asia*.

At Achik Tash meadows (3600m), 30km south of Sary Moghul, IMC Pamir and most of the trekking agencies mentioned earlier operate Pik Lenin base camps and programmes in summer. To get there you'll have to fix arrangements in advance with one of the trekking agencies.

SLEEPING & EATING

Bring your tent. There are cottages at the IMC Pamir base camp, while the others have spare tents. Sary Tash, Kashka-Suu and Daroot-Korgon (Daraut Kurgan in Russian) all have derelict, Soviet-era guesthouses but you'll have more joy asking around for a homestay.

There are weekly farmer's markets in Daroot-Korgon (on Tuesday), Kashka-Suu (Wednesday) and Sary Moghul (Thursday) where you can buy basic foodstuffs. Several trailer shops offer the usual kiosk fare in Sary Tash, while you can buy bread in the villages and milk products at the yurt camps en route. Beyond this bring all your own food.

GETTING THERE & AWAY

You should be able to hire a jeep from Sary Moghul to Achik Tash (17km) for around US$20 return. A hired jeep from Osh to Achik Tash can be negotiated down to US$100 for the ride. Trekking agency vehicles come at about US$160 one way.

Irkeshtam Pass

The Irkeshtam is the latest (May 2002) Sino–Kyrgyz border post to open to international traffic, reconnecting the Fergana Valley with Kashgar along an ancient branch of the Silk Road. No permits are required to get to or over the **pass** (9am-noon & 2-3.30pm Mon-Fri), though you will need a Chinese visa to get past a Kyrgyz check post east of Sary Tash.

Buses to Kashgar via Irkeshtam leave Osh bus station three times a week in the evening (US$50). You may well have to overnight on the bus or at the border. At the time of research these buses were still on hold in the wake of SARS but they should resume, though probably not over winter (October to April). There are spectacular views of the Pamirs en route.

Until the bus service resumes the only transport option to the pass is to hitch or organise a 4WD, either in Osh or, less reliably, in Sary Tash. The going rate for the latter is about US$20 for the return ride. Taxis in Osh demand around US$100 for the return trip; travel agencies push this to US$150 to US$200. You should be able to negotiate a one-way ride from the pass to Osh for around US$40. Osh to Irkeshtam is 275km; from Sary Tash it's around 90km.

The hamlet of Nura is 7km before the border. At the border post army officers will put you on a truck across 7km of no-man's land to Chinese immigration (closed 11am to 2pm Kyrgyz time).

SOUTHERN KYRGYZSTAN

The southern wall of the Fergana Valley forms a curious claw of Kyrgyz territory, although access to most of the mountain villages here comes from the Fergana Valley territory of Tajikistan or Uzbekistan. The beautiful valleys of the Turkestan ridge in particular offer superb trekking territory and the beautiful pyramid-shaped **Ak-Suu** peak (5359m), with its sheer 2km-high wall, is one of the world's best extreme rock-climbing destinations.

This mountain idyll was shattered, however, when Japanese geologists and then four American climbers were kidnapped here in 1999 and 2000 by Islamic militants from Tajikistan. The valleys are now thought to be safe once again but you should check before heading off to the Karavshin, Leilek and Ak-Suu Valleys.

Even without the threat of political insurgency, this is not a particularly easy place to make your first Central Asian trek. Access can prove tricky (inter-republic buses have ground to a halt), and you'll need an Uzbek, Kyrgyz and Tajik visa to transit hassle-free through these republics, as well as a spurious trekking permit. Moreover, some of the passes with Tajikistan are said to have been mined. For the time being you are better off planning any trek in the region with an established trekking operator in Bishkek or Tashkent.

KYRGYZSTAN DIRECTORY

ACCOMMODATION

Homestays now form the bedrock of accommodation in rural Kyrgyzstan, particularly those of the CBT programme (p249). Most homestays are comfortable but not luxurious; a *shyrdak* rug and a snuggly pile of duvets and pillows as bedding and an *umuvalnik* – a portable washbasin that stores water in a top compartment – for washing. The bathroom will often be a pit toilet, but often with a seat. If you're lucky your homestay will have a Russian-style *banya*. Yurtstays offer similar bedding but slightly less privacy and more basic outhouses (if any). Non-CBT homestays are generally much less comfortable.

Different from yurtstay are private tourist yurt camps, mostly used by groups but open to anyone if there's space. Costs here run around US$18 per person with three meals, which often includes some horse riding or other activities.

Issyk-Kul's sanatoria are now fairly run down, although they still fill up with Bishkekers and Kazakh tourists in the hot months. The ones that remain generally offer a fully inclusive package of room, board and activities. Pansiyonats are similar arrangements on a smaller, more basic scale.

Mid-range accommodation is limited to the main cities, with top-end accommodation limited to Bishkek.

ACTIVITIES

Horse Riding

Kyrgyzstan is the best place in Central Asia to saddle up and join the other nomads on the high pastures. CBT offices throughout the country can organise horse hire for around 50 som per hour or 400 som per day.

For all-in organised trips, the following companies are recommended:

AsiaRando (☎ 3132-44710/47711, 517-73 97 78; www.asiarando.com; Padgornaya 67, Rot Front, Chuy Oblast) Horse-riding trips to Song-Köl from their base in Rotfront village. Contact Gérard and Dominique Guillerm.

Shepherd's Way (☎ 9 61 33, Bishkek ☎ 312-29 74 06; www.kyrgyztrek.com) Professional family-run horse trips into the mountains behind Barskoon.

Jeep Trips

There are several opportunities for jeep safaris. One possible road leads from Talas over the Kara Bura Pass into the Chatkal river valley and then loops around to Sary Chelek. Other tracks lead from Naryn to Barskoön, and Barskoön to Inylchek, through the high Tian Shan.

Mountaineering

Kyrgyzstan is the major base for climbing expeditions to Khan Tengri and also Pik Lenin (in Tajikistan but accessed from Kyrgyzstan). There are many unclimbed peaks in the Kokshal range bordering China. Most of the trekking agencies listed in the Bishkek section (p253) can arrange mountaineering expeditions.

The useful website www.kac.centralasia .kg has climbing information from the Kyrgyz Alpine Club.

Rafting

Rafting is possible on the Kokomoron, Chuy and Chong-Kemin Rivers.

Silk Road Water Centre (☎ /fax 28 41 42; www .rafting.com.kg; Musa Jalil 104, Bishkek 720051) River raft, kayak and fishing trips; contact Alexander Kandaurov.

BOOKS

Odyssey Guide to Kyrgyzstan, by Rowan Stewart (2nd edition 2003), is a fine guide to the republic, with good background detail on life today in Kyrgyzstan.

Kyrgyz Traditional Art (2003; Kyrgyz Heritage) is a well-produced but pricey (US$20) art book for sale in Bishkek. Also in the series is *Kyrgyz Musical Instruments*, which comes with an audio CD.

Birds in the Kyrgyz Republic, by Joost von der Ven, is required twitcher reading material and available in Bishkek for US$15.

CUSTOMS

If you've bought anything that looks remotely antique and didn't get a certificate with purchase saying it's not, you can get one from the 1st floor of the Foreign Department of the **Ministry of Education, Science and Culture** (☎ 62 68 17; room 210, cnr Tynystanov & Frunze); see p250.

EMBASSIES & CONSULATES
Kyrgyz Embassies in Central Asia

There are Kyrgyz embassies in Almaty (p153), Ashgabat (p436), Dushanbe (p349) and Tashkent (p234).

Kyrgyz Embassies & Consulates

If there is no Kyrgyz embassy in your country, inquire at the Kazakh embassy if there is one. There are additional embassies in Belarus, Ukraine, India, Malaysia, Switzerland, Ukraine and the UAE. A consulate is planned for Islamabad.

If you intend to cross into Kyrgyzstan from China over the Torugart Pass, note that Beijing is the only reliable place in China where you can get a Kyrgyz visa.

Austria Vienna (☎ 01-535 0378; fax 535 0379; kyrbot@ mail.austria.eu.net; Naglergasse 25/5, 1010)

Belgium Brussels (☎ 02-640 1868; aitmatov@photohall .skynet.be; 47 Rue de L'Abbaye, 1050) Ambassador Chingiz Aitmatov issues visas on the spot for US$50.

China Beijing (☎ 010-6532 6458; kyrgyz@public3.bta .net.cn; 2-4-1 Ta Yuan Diplomatic Office Bldg, Chaoyang District) There is a Kyrgyz representative office in Artush (Xinjiang) but it's currently unable to issue visas.

Germany Berlin (☎ 030-3478 1338; www.botschaft -kirgisien.de, German & Russian only; Otto-Suhr-Allee 146, 10585); Bonn (☎ 0228-36 52 30; kirgistan.bonn@t-online .de; 194A Friesdorferstrasse, 53175); Frankfurt (☎ 069-9540 3926; Bronnerstrasse 20) A 30-day visa costs €50.

Iran Mashhad (☎ 051-818444); Tehran (☎ 021-229 8323, 283 0354, krembiri@kanoon.net; Bldg 12, 5th Naranjastan Alley, Pasdaran St)

KYRGYZSTAN

TOP 10 CBT ADVENTURES

The following adventurous trips can all be arranged by the various CBT branches and offer a way to get off the beaten track and really understand Kyrgyzstan without blowing your budget.

- Horse trek over the 3570m Shamsy Pass from Salaral-Saz *jailoo* to Tokmak (p282)
- Two- or three-day horse trip to/from Kyzart or Jumgal to Song-Köl (p282)
- Four-day trek from Arslanbob to the holy lakes of the Köl Mazar (p299)
- Trek from Kyzyl-Ünkür to Kara-Suu Lake and back or on to the main Osh–Bishkek road (p299)
- Trekking around Karakol (Karakol to Altyn Arashan; p277)
- Trek from Talas to Sary Chelek (five days) or from Kara-Suu to Sary Chelek (two to three days; p296)
- Chatyr-Köl from Tash Rabat – day hike or overnight at the lake (p290)
- Horse trek to Sailmaluu Tash from Kazarman or Jalal-Abad (two to three days; p288) or (p297)
- Naryn to Barskoön by 4WD (p286)
- Horse trek from Ak-Tam to Bokonbayevo or Song-Köl (five to six days; p286)

Russia Moscow (☎ 095-237 4601/4481/4571; fax 237 4452; Bolshaya Ordynka ulitsa 64, 109017) Also in Ekaterinburg.

Switzerland Geneva (☎ 022-707 9220; http:// missions.itu.int/kyrgyzstan; 26 Rue Maunoir, 1207)

Turkey Ankara (☎ 312-446 84 08; kirgiz-o@tr-net.net.tr; Boyabat Sokak 11, Gaziosmanpasa, 06700); İstanbul (☎ 212-235 6767; genkon@tr.net; 7 Lamartin Caddesi, Taksim)

UK London (☎ 020-7935 1462; www.kyrgyz-embassy .org.uk; Ascot House, 119 Crawford St, W1U 6BJ, Baker St tube; ◷ 9.30am-12.30pm) A one-month/two-month tourist visa costs UK£40/66; ignore the outdated website requirements for a letter of invitation.

USA Washington (☎ 202-338 5141; www.kyrgyzstan.org; 1732 Wisconsin Ave, NW, DC 20007) A single-entry one-month visa costs US$50, ready in five days. Also in New York.

Embassies & Consulates in Kyrgyzstan

Note that some of the smaller embassies listed below are little more than a rented room in an obscure apartment block and can therefore be hard to find. All the following are in Bishkek (☎ 312; see Map p250). For information on visas for onward travel see p312.

For letters of support try such travel agencies as Kyrgyz Concept (p253), CAT (p253). The nearest British and Turkmen embassies are in Almaty, Kazakhstan (p153).

Afghanistan (☎ 42 63 72; cnr Ayni & Toktonalieva) Run by a relative of General Dostum, the Uzbek warlord based in Mazar-e Sharif.

Canada (☎ 65 02 02; aki@infotel.kg; Moskva 189, crossing with Turusbekov)

China (☎ 22 24 23; fax 6630 14; Toktogul 196; ◷ 9.15am-noon Mon, Wed & Fri)

France (☎ 66 00 53; ag-consul@elcat.kg; cnr Razzakov & Kiev) Look for the model Eiffel Tower outside.

Germany (☎ 66 66 12; fax 66 66 30; gerembi@elcat.kg; Razzakov 28)

India (☎ 21 08 62; fax 62 07 08; 3rd fl, Chuy 164-A; ◷ 9am-1pm & 2-5.30pm Mon-Fri)

Iran (☎ 22 69 64; fax 62 00 09; Razzakov 36; ◷ 9am-5pm Mon-Fri)

Kazakhstan (☎ 66 01 64; kaz_emb@imfico.bishkek.su; Togolok Moldo 10; ◷ 10am-noon Mon-Thu)

Netherlands (☎ 66 02 22; fax 66 02 88; Suite 1, Tynystanov 199) Honorary consulate.

Pakistan (☎ 62 17 25; pakemb@asiainfo.kg; Panfilov 308; ◷ 9-11am Mon-Fri) May well refer you to a travel agency.

Russia (☎ 22 17 75; rusemb@imfiko.bishkek.su; Razzakov 17)

Tajikistan (☎ 22 00 94; Koyenkozova 17/1) The embassy is down a side alley near the UNHCR building.

Turkey (☎ 22 78 82; fax 66 05 20; Moskva 89; ◷ 9am-noon Mon-Fri)

USA (☎ 55 12 41; pao@usis.gov.kg; Mira prospektisi 171)

Uzbekistan (☎ 22 61 71; fax 66 44 03; Tynystanov 213; ◷ closed Mon)

FESTIVALS & EVENTS

There are horse games at the end of July and August at Cholpon-Ata, Karakol and the *jailoos* around Song-Köl and Kochkor. NoviNomad in Bishkek and the nearest CBT can offer details.

HOLIDAYS

See p449 for information on the Muslim holidays of Ramazan and both Eid festivals, which are also public holidays.

1 January New Year's Day.
7 January Russian Orthodox Christmas.
8 March International Women's Day.
1 May International Labour Day.
5 May Constitution Day.
9 May WWII Victory Day.
31 August Independence Day.

INTERNET RESOURCES

Community Based Tourism (www.cbtkyrgyzstan.kg) Contact details and prices for this excellent organisation.

Helvetas (www.helvetas.kg) Info on Altyn Kol handicrafts, Shepherd's Life and the CBT organisation, and general info on the country.

Kyrgyzstan Development Gateway (http://eng .gateway.kg) Background and development info on Kyrgyzstan.

Kyrgyzstan Embassy in USA (www.kyrgyzstan.org) General info, travel advice, visa regulations, events links.

Kyrgyzstan Info (www.kirgistan.info, http://kirgistan -reisen.de) Travel info to off-the-beaten-track places in northern Kyrgyzstan, in English and German.

Pamir Alay Trek (www.chezphil.org/gallery/1992 _Pamirs/index.html) Photos from a trek in the Pamir Alay south of Osh.

Shepherd's Life (www.tourism.elcat.kg) Prices and contact details.

Times of Central Asia (www.times.kg)

MAPS

Geoid in Bishkek (p252) has, in addition to maps of Bishkek in Cyrillic, a Kyrgyzstan country map using the roman alphabet and an interesting 'Silk Road of Kyrgyzstan' map. There are also trekking route maps and 1:200,000 Soviet topographic maps of various parts of Kyrgyzstan. Most maps are in Russian.

Trekking maps available at the agency:

Ala-Archa (1:50,000) Routes up to Ak-Say Glacier and the ski base, in English.

Cherez Talasskii Khrebet k Ozeru Sary-Chelek (1:200,000) From Leninopol to Sary Chelek over the Talas mountains.

Vorukh (1:100,000) Turkestan mountains.

Sokh (1:100,000) Alay mountains.

K Verkhvyam Sary-Dzhaza (1:200,000) Routes to Chong-Tash and the Inylchek Glacier.

Po Tsentralnomu Tyan-Shan and Lednikam Terskey Ala-Too (1:150,000) Terskey Alatau around Karakol, from Chong-Kyzyl-Suu Valley to Jeti-Öghüz, Karakol and Arashan Valleys.

Tsentralniy Tyan-Shan (1:150,000) Schematic map of Inylchek Glacier and around.

Ozero Issyk-Kul (1:200,000) Topographical map, covering trekking routes to Kazakhstan via the Chong-Kemin Valley.

Kirgizskii Khrebet (1:200,000) Topographical map, covering the Kyrgyzsky mountains south of Bishkek. There's also a separate 1:150,000 schematic map showing peaks in the same region.

MEDIA

The *Times of Central Asia* (www.times.kg) is the local English-language newspaper, based in Bishkek.

MONEY

The Kyrgyz som is divided into 100 tiyin. Notes come in 100, 50, 20, 10, five and one som denominations. There is no black market for currency transactions in Kyrgyzstan and you'll find licensed moneychanger booths everywhere (marked *obmen balyot*). Prices in this chapter are listed in som as the som rate is more stable than the dollar equivalent. Exchange rates at the time of research were as follow:

Country	Unit		Som
Australia	A$1	=	31.61
Canada	C$	=	32.45
China	Y1	=	5.2
euro zone	€1	=	53.10
Kazakhstan	10 T	=	3.12
New Zealand	NZ$1	=	28.06
Russia	R1	=	1.52
Switzerland	1Sfr	=	33.82
Tajikistan	1TJS	=	15.35
UK	£1	=	77.95
USA	US$1	=	43.40
Uzbekistan	100 sum	=	4.31

If you need to wire money, MoneyGram has services at main post offices and Western Union works through most banks.

POST

An airmail postcard costs 11 som and a 20g letter costs 20.50 som to all countries.

DHL (www.dhl.kg) has offices in Bishkek and Osh and charges US$45-55 to courier 500g of documents; couriers will pick up at your door.

REGISTRATION

Foreigners from 28 states, including the US, UK, Australia, Canada, Israel and most European countries no longer need to register with OVIR (Office of Visas and Registrations; UPVR in Kyrgyzstan). Other countries (one notable example is Dutch citizens) do need to register within three days of arriving in Kyrgyzstan.

SHOPPING

Small pottery figurines shaped as bread sellers, musicians, and 'white beards' are for sale everywhere but most are made at the Arts Faculty in Osh. Hats are also for sale everywhere but most are factory-made in Toktogul. The most popular buys are *shyrdaks* (see the boxed text on p247).

Other souvenirs include miniature yurts and embroidered bags, chess sets featuring Manas and company, horse whips, *kymys* shakers, leather boxes, felt slippers and musical instruments such as the Kyrgyz mouth harp.

TELEPHONE

International telephone rates are 27 som per minute to all countries, 16 som per minute to Central Asia. Domestic calls cost about 5 som per minute. Some older telephones require you to dial 3 after the person picks up.

To make an international call, dial ☎ 00 + the international code of the country you wish to call.

To make an intercity call, dial ☎ 0 + the city code.

A cheaper option is an Internet phone call, which involves calling through an Internet café's computer. These cost as little as 5 som per minute to the US and are offered in most Internet cafés.

To send a fax, telecom offices charge a minimum three minute telephone charge, plus a service charge, bringing the rate for a one-page fax to around US$5 a page. You are better of scanning it at an Internet café and sending an email.

If you have a GSM mobile phone, you can buy a SIM card from **MobiCard** (☎ 60 02 22) and then scratchcards in units of 200, 400 and 1000 units.

If you are phoning a mobile phone you need to dial ☎ 502-58 then four digits for Bitel, or ☎ 5177 then five digits for Katel phones.

TRAVEL PERMITS

Certain sensitive border areas such as the Khan Tengri region and Alay Valley require a military border permit (*propusk pa granzona*; US$10), which trekking agencies can arrange in about 10 days.

TREKKING PERMITS

Trekking and mountaineering permits were abolished by the Kyrgyz government in 2002 but at least one local authority has tried to keep them in an effort to raise funds. Batken (for the Ak-Suu and Karavshin regions) charges US$30 for a permit.

VISAS

Kyrgyzstan is generally the easiest of the Central Asian republics for which to get a visa. Kyrgyz embassies now issue 30-day tourist visas to most nationalities without letters of support. These nationalities can also obtain a visa on arrival at Bishkek's Manas international airport.

There are plans to set up posts at land borders so that tourists can get visas on arrival by land but this is still some way off.

If there is no Kyrgyz embassy in your country and you have to go through a Kazakh embassy, you will need a letter of invitation, regardless of nationality. Central Asian travel agencies can provide these for US$20 to US$30.

Most nationalities from the former Soviet block, as well as Japanese, Turks and Kazakhs do not need visas. There are plans to do away with visas for the US, Switzerland, the UK and others but there's no timeframe for this, so don't hold your breath.

It's technically illegal to enter Kyrgyzstan except at a designated border crossing, which makes cross-border treks (eg Almaty to Issyk-Kul) technically illegal. You'll need

a travel agency to help smooth over these problems if you intend to take these treks.

Visa Extensions

A 30-day visa extension is easy to get from OVIR offices in Bishkek (p252), Karakol (p269), Osh (p302) and Naryn. These cost 300 som and are processed the same day.

Visas for Onward Travel

For contact details of embassies and consulates in Kyrgyzstan, see p310.

China The embassy won't currently issue tourist visas without an invitation from a Xinjiang tourist agency. ITMC (p253) and Celestial Mountains (p253) can get an invitation in a week for US$50. Thirty-day visas cost US$30 for Americans, US$60 for Brits and take a week to issue (urgent service takes three days and costs twice the price).

India The embassy accepts visa applications 2pm to 4pm Monday to Friday. Standard six-month tourist visas cost 1835 som for US citizens, 1105 som for most other nationalities. Two photos are necessary. Visas take around five days to issue.

Iran Transit visas of 10 days' duration are issued in one week. You need a letter of invitation for a tourist visa.

Kazakhstan Get to the embassy early and put your name on the list to get inside. Visa fees need to be paid at a bank. For a transit visa bring your ticket out of Kazakhstan (and copy), the third country visa (and copy), one photo, photocopy of your passport and Kyrgyz visa; takes five days (US$20) or three days express (US$35).

Russia Visas are only available from the consular office (55 Manas; ⏰ 9am–noon & 2.30-3.30pm Mon, Tue & Thu), not the embassy. You'll need a letter of invitation and four passport photos for a tourist visa. Transit visas cost US$16 in a week or US$32 the same day and you'll need tickets in and out of Russia. Fees are paid at the Kairat bank, four blocks north.

Tajikistan Thirty-day visas available in three days or less for US$60. Bring two passport photos and your passport.

Uzbekistan You need to get a Russian speaker to phone the embassy and put your name on the list. Tourist visas are issued in seven days US$60 to US$70 or next day (US$90 to US$100).

TRANSPORT IN KYRGYZSTAN

GETTING THERE & AWAY
Entering Kyrgyzstan

Remoter border posts eg at Karkara and along the Pamir Highway from Tajikistan may not stamp your visa with an entry

DEPARTURE TAX

Bishkek's Manas airport has a US$10 international departure tax, but no domestic tax. Air tickets include a 4% government tax.

stamp but you should insist this is done, otherwise you'll have problems. Generally, entering the country presents no problems.

Air

Bishkek's Manas airport is the main international airport, although there are sometimes flights from Osh to Moscow.

There are flights three times a week to Dushanbe (US$114 Kyrgyz Air, US$126 Tajik Air), twice weekly to Khojand (US$70), daily to Tashkent (US$83 Altyn Air, US$90 Uzbekistan Airways), and twice weekly to Astana (US$135, Altyn Air).

Altyn Air flies once a week (Fri) from Osh to Dushanbe (US$83). At the time of research you could fly Bishkek–Dushanbe for the same price with a stop in Osh, which is useful if you want a minimum of a week in southern Kyrgyzstan (there's only one flight a week). This ticket structure may change.

For details of international flights into and out of Bishkek, see (p461). For more details on airline offices in Bishkek, see p260.

Note that it's only three hours by road to/from Almaty, which has more international flights. Kazakh transit visas are available on arrival at Almaty airport, though it's always better to get one in advance.

KLM runs a free Bishkek–Almaty ground shuttle service for their customers, leaving Bishkek in front of the Dostuk Hotel on the day of flights at 6pm. A similar Lufthansa bus departs at 7pm from Grand Hyatt. It's free if you buy your ticket in Bishkek, otherwise it costs US$25. The bus leaves Almaty airport at 12.30am, arriving in Bishkek at 3.30am.

Land

Apart from the crossings detailed below, trains run three times a week from Bishkek to Tashkent (16 hours) and Moscow, though they aren't very popular with travellers.

BORDER CROSSINGS

For more on the complicated jigsaw borders of the Fergana Valley see p470. One thing to note is that transport along Kyr-

gyzstan's southern arm from Osh to Batken passes through the Uzbek enclave of Sokh so you'll need to get an Uzbek visa or hire a taxi to take you on a dirt road detour around the enclave.

TO/FROM CHINA

Of the two land crossings from China the 3752m **Torugart Pass** is the more complicated and expensive. Chinese and Kyrgyz buses run over the pass but foreigners are forbidden from taking the bus and have to arrange their own pricey transport, at least on the Chinese side.

Even the most painstaking arrangements can be thwarted by logistical gridlock on the Chinese side or by unpredictable border closures (eg for holidays or snow). The Torugart Pass is normally snow-free from late May through September. The crossing is theoretically kept open all year, but is icy and dangerous in winter.

For more detail on this fine but frustrating trip, including transport and visa tips, see p291.

The newer and easier border crossing is the **Irkeshtam Pass**, linking Kashgar to Osh and the Fergana Valley. It has none of the restrictions of the Torugart and so you can take taxis, hitch on trucks or even cycle. Buses run twice a week from Kashgar to Osh (US$50, 18 hours), overnighting on the bus. Buses depart Kashgar on Monday and Tuesday mornings at 8am.

Alternatively take a taxi from Kashgar to the border (Y300 to Y400) and then arrange a taxi or hitch on the other side (around US$50 to Osh). The pass is theoretically open year-round.

TO/FROM KAZAKHSTAN

Buses and minibuses go directly from Bishkek to Almaty (155 som, 4½ hours) every hour or two, as do private cars (300 som per seat). The starting price for a Mercedes car to Almaty is US$50. There is a passport check at the border by the Chuy River and you will need a Kazakh visa.

A back-door route into Kazakhstan is possible through the Karkara Valley. There's no through transport so you'll have to hire a taxi or hitch.

There is also a new 96km jeep road from near Cholpon-Ata over to Chong Kemin Valley and beyond to Almaty but you need a 4WD for this rough route and there's no border control en route, which will give you headaches getting a visa stamp.

TO/FROM TAJIKISTAN

The main crossing for travellers is from the Pamir Highway, between Murgab and Sary-Tash. Another remote crossing leads southwest from the Pamir Alay Valley into the Garm Valley and on to Dushanbe. There's no public transport along this route.

From the Fergana Valley it's possible to cross from Batken to Isfara (not Isfana) in Tajikistan. In Batken shared taxis to Osh and Isfara depart every morning from the post office. Buses from Batken to Osh and Isfana leave from the bus station early in the morning. Travellers have recommended the B&B of **Dalmira Checheeva** (14 Shestdyesat Let Oktyabria ulitsa) if you need to spend the night in Batken.

TO/FROM UZBEKISTAN

From Bishkek comfortable Mercedes buses go from the west station to Tashkent three times a day between 6pm and 9pm for about 345 som, but at the time of research these were only going as far as the Uzbek border at Chernaiev, from where you have to take a minibus a few kilometres into Tashkent. These buses run through Kazakhstan for most of the trip and you do need a Kazakh

transit visa. After you have shelled out for a Kazakh transit visa and a bus ticket, you may find it's not that much more expensive to take a flight. There are also some buses from Osh Bazaar.

From Jalal-Abad take a taxi or minibus (10 som) to Khanabad (formerly Sovieta-bad) and cross by foot. Note that the Kara-Suu border crossing is not open.

From Osh take a taxi (50 som) or mini-bus (Nos 7, 13, 36, 37 or 38) to Dustlyk/Dostyk and then a seat in a shared taxi, either a Tico or slightly more expensive (and spacious) Niva to Andijan or elsewhere in the Fergana Valley or to Tashkent (US$35 to US$40). Osh Guesthouse in Osh (p299) can help arrange a car direct to Tashkent (US$40) or Andijan (US$14).

GETTING AROUND

Travelling around Kyrgyzstan is generally quite straightforward. **Kyrgyzstan Airlines** (☎ 62 21 23; Soviet 129) and the private airlines **Altyn Air** (☎ 22 54 46; Abdumamenov 195) and **Itek Air** (☎ 21 69 14; Chuy 128) connect Bishkek with Osh and Jalal-Abad in the Fergana Valley but that's about all. The bus system is limited and so for most trips your best bet are the shared taxis, which wait at most bus stations, or a private car hired through the CBT or Shepherd's Life organisations. See p468 for more on travelling around the region.

Tajikistan
Таджикистан

CONTENTS

FAST FACTS

- **Area** 143,100 sq km
- **Capital** Dushanbe
- **Country Code** ☎ 992
- **Ethnic Groups** 65% Tajik, 25% Uzbek, 3.5% Russian, 6.5% Others
- **Languages** Tajik, Russian, Uzbek, and half a dozen Eastern Persian Pamiri languages
- **Money** Tajik somani (TJS); US$1=3.1TJS, €1=3.3TJS
- **Phrases in Tajik** OK. *(khub)*; Sorry. *(mebakhshed)*; Goodbye. *(khair)*
- **Population** 6.86 million (2003 estimate)

TAJIKISTAN

A Persian-speaking outpost in a predominantly Turkic region, Tajikistan is the odd one out in Central Asia. The country is a patchwork of self-contained valleys and regional contrasts, forged together by Soviet nation-building and shared pride in a Persian cultural heritage that is claimed as the oldest and most influential in the Silk Road region.

That Tajikistan was easily the most artificial of the five Soviet-fashioned Central Asian republics was tragically illustrated by the bloody way it fell apart as soon as it was free of Moscow rule. In its brief post-Soviet history, this remote pocket of Asia has seen far greater loss of life than in anywhere else in the old empire.

The good news is that today Tajikistan is safe, stable and scenically spectacular. Travel is a grade harder here than most places in the region, with uncertain transport, poor accommodation and a complicated bureaucracy, but if you are ready to take things as they come, Tajikistan offers the cutting edge of Central Asian adventure travel.

The Pamir region is easily the country's highlight, with peaks dwarfing anything found outside Nepal, and the Pamir Highway provides plenty of sublime high-altitude views, even if you don't know which way your crampons go on. Anyone following this road has the added thrill of knowing that few 'foreign devils' have passed this way since Francis Younghusband, the consummate 'Great Game' (p35) player. Younghusband was expelled from the Pamirs by the Russians in 1891, marking the region's closure to the outside world for the next 100 years.

HIGHLIGHTS

Tajikistan's unique attraction lies in its mountains. The **mountain drive** from Khojand (or Penjikent) to Dushanbe takes you through a vertical world of towering peaks and over two high passes, and is one of the world's great road trips. An overnight stop at turquoise **Iskander-Kul** (p335) is well worth the detour. If you have the time and equipment, the nearby **Fan Mountains** (p335) offer austere but beautiful trekking easily accessible from Samarkand.

Tajikistan's trump card is the breathtaking **Pamir Hwy** (p345) between Khorog and Osh, offering jaw-dropping high-altitude lakes and deserts, and fine Badakhshani hospitality. **Trekking** (p348) in the Pamir region is out of this world, but you need experience and logistical help.

South of the main Pamir Hwy, the **Wakhan Corridor** (p343) is a remote and particularly beautiful valley, shared with Afghanistan, and peppered with forts, Zoroastrian ruins and spectacular views of the Hindu Kush.

The historical highlights don't compare to Uzbekistan's gems, but **Istaravshan** (p333) is worth a visit for its backstreets and Tuesday bazaar. The fort and medressas of **Hissar** (p329) make a good day trip from Dushanbe.

ITINERARIES

- **Three days** Drive from Samarkand or Khojand to Dushanbe (with an overnight stop in Iskander-Kul) and then fly out of Dushanbe to Bishkek or Almaty. Or visit Penjikent from Samarkand, continue to Khojand via Istaravshan and then on to Uzbekistan.
- **One week** Khojand to Dushanbe with stops in Istaravshan, Iskander-Kul and Hissar. Or perhaps a short trek in the Fan Mountains. You could travel the Pamir Hwy in a week, but only with your own transport.
- **Two weeks** This is the minimum amount of time required to travel the Pamir Hwy between Dushanbe and Osh if you plan

to arrange things en route. Try to budget an extra few days for this route (especially if you intend to hitch), as the area has so much to offer. Travelling the highway from Osh is attractive route-wise but is logistically more complicated.

- **Three weeks** This will be enough time to get you from Khojand in the north, over the mountains to Dushanbe via Istaravshan and then along the Pamir Hwy to Osh.
- **Off the beaten track** Currently only 150 tourists a year make it to the Pamirs. Explore around Murgab.

CLIMATE & WHEN TO GO

Northern, central and southern Tajikistan sizzle in summer (June to September), with temperatures over 40°C (105°F). Unfortunately this is the best time to visit the mountains and Pamir region. Spring (March to May) brings mild temperatures and frequent heavy showers. April is the best time to visit southern Tajikistan in bloom.

In winter (November to February) temperatures in Dushanbe hover near freezing,

> ### HOW MUCH?
>
> ■ Snickers bar US$0.40
> ■ 100km shared taxi ride US$4
> ■ One-minute phone call to the US US$0.50
> ■ Internet connection per hour US$1–1.50
> ■ Tajik skullcap US$2
>
> ### LONELY PLANET INDEX
>
> ■ Litre of bottled water US$0.20
> ■ Bottled beer US$1.50
> ■ Shashlyk US$0.50
> ■ Litre of petrol US$0.50

while temperatures in the Pamirs plummet to between -20°C and -45°C. From October to May fierce snowstorms rage in the mountains, making getting around difficult. The Anzob and Shakhristan passes between Khojand and Dushanbe are generally closed from late November to late May.

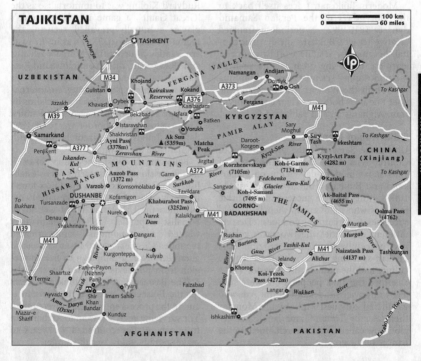

TAJIKISTAN

March, April, September and October are probably the best times to visit. March is a particularly good time to come, as you'll experience the Navrus festival. The best time of year for trekking is September. The Pamir region is best visited in July to late September, though the Pamir Hwy technically remains open year-round.

HISTORY
Tajik Ancestry

Tajik ancestry is a murky area but the lineage seems to begin with the Bactrians and the Sogdians. In the 1st century BC the Bactrians had a large empire covering most of what is now northern Afghanistan. Their contemporaries, the Sogdians, inhabited the Zeravshan Valley in present-day western Tajikistan (where a few traces of this civilisation remain near Penjikent). They were displaced in the Arab conquest of Central Asia during the 7th century AD. The Sogdian hero Devastich made a last stand against the Arabs at Mount Mug in the Zeravshan Mountains, before he was finally beheaded by the vanquishers.

Modern Tajikistan traces itself back to the glory days of the Persian Samanid dynasty (819–992), a period of frenzied creative activity. Bukhara, the dynastic capital, became the Islamic world's centre of learning, nurturing great talents such as the philosopher-scientist Abu Ali ibn-Sina (known in the West as Avicenna) and the poet Rudaki – both now claimed as sons of Iran, Afghanistan and Tajikistan.

A Blurring of Identity

Under the Samanids, the great towns of Central Asia were Persian (the basis of Tajikistan's modern-day claims on Samarkand and Bukhara), but at the end of the 10th century came a succession of Turkic invaders who followed up their battlefield successes with cultural conquest. Despite different ethnicities the two races cohabited peacefully, unified by religion. The Persian-speaking Tajiks absorbed Turkic culture and the numerically superior Turks absorbed the Tajik people. Both were subject to the vicissitudes of Central Asia and weathered conquests, first by the Mongols then later by Timur (Tamerlane). The region now called Tajikistan remained on the fringes of the empire.

From the 15th century onwards, the Tajiks were subjects of the emirate of Bukhara, who received 50% of Badakhshan's ruby production as a tax. In the mid-18th century the Afghans moved up to engulf all lands south of the Amu-Darya (Oxus River) along with their resident Tajik population (the Amu-Darya still delineates much of the Afghan–Tajik border today).

The 'Great Game' & the Basmachi

As part of the Russian empire's thrust southwards, St Petersburg made a vassal state of the emirate of Bukhara, which also meant effective control over what now passes for northern and western Tajikistan. But the Pamirs, which account for the whole of modern-day eastern Tajikistan, were literally a no-man's-land, falling outside the established borders of the Bukhara emirate and unclaimed by neighbouring Afghanistan and China. Russia was eager to exploit this anomaly in its push to open up possible routes into British India.

The Pamirs became the arena for the strategic duel that British poet and author Rudyard Kipling was to immortalise as the 'Great Game', a game in which Russia's players eventually prevailed, securing the region for the tsar (p35). It was in the eastern Pamirs, after visiting Murgab, Alichur and Rang-Kul, that Younghusband was thrown out of the upper Wakhan by his Tsarist counterpart, sparking an international crisis. Russia backed up it's claims by building a string of forts across the Pamirs. The Anglo-Russian border treaty of 1895 defined Tajikistan's current borders with Afghanistan and China.

Following the Russian revolution of 1917, new provisional governments were established in Central Asia and the Tajiks found themselves part of first the Turkestan (1918–24), then the Uzbekistan (1924–29) Soviet Socialist Republics (SSRs), though they wanted an autonomous Islamic-oriented republic. The next year Muslim *basmachi* guerrillas began a campaign to free the region from Bolshevik rule (see Enver Pasha & The Basmachi, p330). It took four years for the Bolsheviks to crush this resistance, and in the process entire villages were razed. The surviving guerrillas went to Afghanistan from where they continued for years to make sporadic raids over the border.

Soviet Statehood

In 1924, when the Soviet Border Commission set about redefining Central Asia, the Tajiks got their own Autonomous SSR (ASSR). Although only a satellite of the Uzbek SSR, this was the first official Tajik state. In 1929 it was upgraded to a full union republic, although (in reprisal for the *basmachi* revolt?) Samarkand and Bukhara – where over 700,000 Tajiks still lived – remained in Uzbekistan. As recently as 1989 the government of Tajikistan was still trying to persuade the Soviet leadership to 'return' the area lost in this cultural amputation. Territorial tensions continue with the modern government of Uzbekistan.

The Bolsheviks never fully trusted this republic and during the 1930s almost all Tajiks in positions of influence within the government were replaced by stooges from Moscow. The industrialisation of Tajikistan was only undertaken following WWII, after the loss of much of European Russia's manufacturing capacity. But living standards remained low and in the late 1980s Tajikistan endured 25% unemployment, plus the lowest level of education and the highest infant-mortality rate in the Soviet Union.

From Civil Unrest...

In the mid-1970s, Tajikistan began to feel the impact of the rise of Islamic forces in neighbouring Afghanistan, particularly in the south around Kurga-Tyube. This region had been neglected by Dushanbe's ruling communist elite, who were mainly drawn from the prosperous northern city of Leninabad (now Khojand). In 1976 the underground Islamic Renaissance Party (IRP) was founded, gathering popular support as a rallying point for Tajik nationalism. Although in 1979 there had been demonstrations in opposition to the Soviet invasion of Afghanistan, the first serious disturbances were in early 1990 when it was rumoured that Armenian refugees were to be settled in Dushanbe, which was already short on housing. This piece of Soviet social engineering sparked riots, deaths and the imposition of a state of emergency. Further opposition parties emerged as a result of the crackdown.

On 9 September 1991, following the failed coup in Moscow and declarations of independence by other Central Asian states, Tajikistan proclaimed itself an independent republic. Elections were held 10 weeks later and the Socialist Party (formerly the Communist Party of Tajikistan or CPT) candidate, Rakhmon Nabiev, was voted into power. There were charges of election rigging but what really riled the opposition was Nabiev's apparent consolidation of an old-guard, Leninabad-oriented power base that refused to accommodate any other of the various clan-factions that make up the Tajik nation.

Sit-in demonstrations on Dushanbe's central square escalated to violent clashes and, in August 1992, anti-government demonstrators stormed the presidential palace and took hostages. A coalition government was formed but sharing power between regional clans, religious leaders and former communists proved impossible and Tajikistan descended into civil war.

... To Civil War

During the Soviet era, Moscow and the Soviet party had been the lid on a pressure-cooker of clan-based tensions that had existed long before Russian intervention. Tajikistan's various factions – Leninabadis from the north, Kulyabi from the south and their hostile neighbours from Kurga-Tyube, Karategini from the Garm Valley in the east, and Pamiri from the mountainous province of Gorno-Badakhshan (GBAO) – had all been kept in line under Soviet rule. When independence came, the lid blew off. Civil war ensued and the clan struggles claimed around 60,000 lives and made refugees of over half a million.

As a way out of the internecine conflict Imamali Rakhmanov was chosen from the Kulyab district to front the government. The Kulyabis then simply fought their way to power with a scorched-earth policy against their Islamic-leaning rivals from the Garm Valley and Kurga-Tyube.

Rakhmanov was sworn in as president after a disputed election. The Islamic democratic coalition, known as the Popular Democratic Army (PDA), refused to allow the new president into Dushanbe and it took an all-out assault from Kulyabi and Leninabad forces to get him into office. Kulyabi forces, led by Sanjak Safarov (who had previously spent 23 years in prison for murder) then embarked on an orgy of ethnic cleansing directed at anyone connected with Kurga-Tyube and the Garm Valley.

The November 1992 elections did nothing to resolve the conflict (the opposition in exile refused to take part in the voting) and the PDA and its supporters continued the war from bases in the Karategin region and Afghanistan, echoing the *basmachi* campaigns of 70 years earlier.

Rakhmanov was propped up by Russian-dominated Commonwealth and Independent States (CIS) forces, which had been drawn into the conflict as de facto protectors of the Kulyab regime. There are now 20,000 Russian troops inside the country operating some 50 military posts along the Afghan border. 'Everyone must realise', Boris Yeltsin said in a 1993 pronouncement, 'that this is effectively Russia's border, not Tajikistan's.' The Russian (and Uzbek) fear is that if Tajikistan fell to Islamic rebels, then Uzbekistan will be next.

In late 1994 a second presidential election was held, in which Rakhmanov romped to victory, which was unsurprising, as he was the only candidate. All opposition parties had been outlawed.

Precarious Peace

A bad peace is better than a good war.
Khatlon villager

Pressure on Rakhmanov from Russia (and the faltering loyalty of his own commanders) forced the government to negotiate with the opposition, which was then in exile in Iran. Finally, in December 1996 a ceasefire was declared, followed up by a peace agreement on 27 June 1997. The agreement set up a power-sharing organisation, the National Reconciliation Commission (CNR), headed by the opposition leader Sayid Abdullo Nuri, which guaranteed the United Tajik Opposition (UTO) 30% of the seats in a coalition government in return for a laying down of arms.

Opposition parties that had been banned until 1997 were allowed to reform. The main political parties today are Rakhmanov's People's Democratic Party of Tajikistan (PDPT), the Communist Party, the Islamic Rebirth Party (IRP) and the secular nationalist Democratic Party of Tajikistan (DPT).

The political landscape remains heavily clan-based.

Spirits were lifted in September 1998 when the Aga Khan, spiritual leader of the Islamic Ismaili sect, visited GBAO. The Aga Khan Foundation has effectively fed the Pamir region since the start of the civil war and some 80,000 Pamiris came out to hear their spiritual leader tell them to lay down their arms, while another 10,000 Afghan Tajiks strained their ears across the river in Afghanistan.

Tajikistan Today

Independence and civil war have proven catastrophic for Tajikistan, which had always been the poorest of the Soviet republics. Tajikistan was heavily reliant on imports from the Soviet Union – not just food, but fuel and many other standard commodities. With the disintegration of the Soviet trading system, Tajikistan was left badly equipped to fend for itself, and dangerously unbalanced.

During the civil war Tajikistan's gross domestic product (GDP) per capita shrank 70 per cent to US$330, plunging it from part of a global superpower to one of the 30 poorest countries in the world within a decade. Two complete harvests were missed during the civil war, and the region suffered major droughts in 2001 and 2002. The annual national budget of Tajikistan remains less than the budget of a major Hollywood movie, and 40% of that is required for the upkeep of the military presence on the Afghan border. Over 60% of Tajikistan's people live in abject poverty, with the GDP per capita hovering around US$170 per year, on a par with Eritrea. The legal minimum wage was recently tripled to US$1 per month.

Presently, the country exists on a dripfeed of credits and loans (Tajikistan's national debt is currently US$1.3 billion). In return, Tajikistan has been forced to mortgage its future to the Kremlin, giving Russia half of the shares in the Nurek hydroelectric plant, as well as controlling interests in other national industries. Tajikistan retains the strongest connections to Russia of any of the Central Asian republics. Relations between Tajikistan and Uzbekistan have become increasingly tense, with both sides accusing the other of sheltering opposition rebels.

One reason for the Russian presence is that, thanks to a porous 1300km border with Afghanistan, Tajikistan is one of the world's major drug conduits. Tajik customs officials make 80% of all drug seizures in Central Asia and the country is the world's third-largest seizer of heroin and opium, seizing literally tonnes of the stuff every year. Up to 50% of Tajikistan's economic activity is thought to be somehow linked to the drug trade.

Since 1992 Tajikistan has been a parliamentary republic with legislative power vested in an elected 230 member parliament, or *oli majlis*. The parliament is fronted by the president – Imamali Rakhmanov at the time of writing, until presidential elections in 2006. A referendum in 2003 gave him the green light to run for another two terms, until 2020.

PEOPLE
It's only last century that 'Tajik' came to denote a distinct nationality. Previously 'Taj' was just a term for a Persian speaker (all the other Central Asian peoples speak Turkic languages). Despite their predominantly Persian ancestry, there has been so much intermarrying that it's often hard to distinguish Tajiks from their Mongol Turkic neighbours. Pure-blooded Tajiks tend to have thin faces, with wide eyes and a Roman nose.

There are some recognisable ethnic subdivisions among the Tajiks. As well as the

Pamiri Tajiks (p477), there are dwindling numbers of Yaghnabis (or Jagnobis), direct descendants of the ancient Sogdians, in the mountain villages of the Zeravshan Valley. Sogdian, the lingua franca of the Silk Road and last widely spoken in the 8th century, is still spoken there.

For more information on the people of Tajikistan, see p338.

Population
Population figures are only approximate because the demographics of Tajikistan have been fluctuating wildly since the start of the civil war in 1992. In addition to the 60,000 or so killed, more than half a million Tajiks were displaced from their homes during the war, while around two-thirds of the country's 600,000 Russians headed north. Another 60,000 Tajiks fled to Afghanistan, joining the 4.4 million Tajiks who have lived there since the southern region of Badakhshan was annexed by Kabul in the 18th century. Up to 900,000 Tajiks work abroad, mostly in Russia, sending back around US$200 million a year in remittances, the equivalent of the Tajik national budget. One in four families now has a family member working abroad.

Tajikistan exemplifies the demographic complexity of the Central Asian republics. Its 4.4 million Tajiks constitute only 65% of the country's population, and fewer than half of the world's Tajiks (there are more Tajiks in Afghanistan than Tajikistan, and

---

TRAVELLING SAFELY IN TAJIKISTAN

Tajikistan's civil war kept the country off-limits to tourists for much of the 1990s, but now almost all of the country is considered safe for travel. The few remaining areas where aid workers express caution are the Garm (Karategin) Valley, Tavildara and Sangvor regions. Take a local guide if heading off the beaten track in these areas (and it's all off the beaten track here).

Southern Tajikistan and the Pamirs are pivotal points in the trans-Asian drug-smuggling route. There is little chance of travellers accidentally bumping into any of this, but it's advisable to avoid travel in remote regions or border areas at night. Don't go investigating those pretty poppy fields on a trek.

The northern mountain passes between Tajikistan and Kyrgyzstan have been heavily land mined, so don't go wandering in remote regions or near the Uzbek border.

If you're going to be travelling the Pamir Hwy, particularly if you are headed from Osh to Karakul or Murgab in one day, there are serious risks associated with altitude sickness (see p477 for more information). Southern Tajikistan has a malaria risk along the Afghan border and along the lower Vakhsh Valley as far north as Kurgonteppa (Kurga-Tyube).

Don't drink the tap water in Dushanbe, as there are occasional water-spread typhoid outbreaks.

large groups also live in Uzbekistan, Kazakhstan and China's Xinjiang province). Some 25% of Tajikistan's population are Uzbeks, with whom there is considerable ethnic rivalry. Average family sizes remain high, with seven or eight kids the norm. Over 40% of Tajikistan's population is under the age of 14.

RELIGION

About 80% of Tajikistan's people are Sunni Muslim, though most Badakhshanis are Ismailis and follow the Aga Khan (p338). Between 1990 and 1992, over 1000 new mosques were built in Tajikistan.

In the late 1990s radical Islamist organisations such as the Islamic Movement of Uzbekistan (IMU) used Tajikistan (particularly the Sangvor and Tavildara Valleys) as a base for armed incursions into Kyrgyzstan and Uzbekistan, with the implicit support of the Tajik government and Russian military. However these organisations have largely lost relevance with the removal of support from the Taliban and Al-Qaeda in Afghanistan.

ARTS

When Tajikistan was hived off from Uzbekistan in 1929, the new nation-state was forced to leave behind all its cultural baggage. The new Soviet order set about providing a replacement pantheon of arts, introducing modern drama, opera and ballet, and sending stage-struck Tajik aspirants to study in Moscow and Leningrad. The policy paid early dividends and the 1940s are considered a golden era of Tajik theatre. A kind of Soviet fame came to some Tajik novelists and poets, such as Mirzo Tursunzade and Sadruddin Ayni, the latter now remembered more as a deconstructor of national culture because of his campaign to eliminate all Arabic expressions and references to Islam from the Tajik tongue.

Since independence, ancient figures from the region's Persian past have been revived in an attempt to foster a sense of national identity. The most famous of these figures is the 10th-century philosopher-scientist Abu Ali ibn-Sina, author of two of the most important books in the history of medicine. He was born in Bukhara when it was the seat of the Persian Samanids, to whom Rudaki, now celebrated as the father

of Persian verse (and with a tomb outside Penjikent in Tajikistan), served as court poet. Tajiks also venerate Firdausi, a poet and composer of the *Shah Nama (Book of Kings)*, the Persian national epic, and Omar Khayam, of *Rubaiyat* fame, both born in present-day Iran but at a time when it was part of an empire that also included the territory now known as Tajikistan. Similar veneration goes out to Kamalddin Bekzod (1455–1535), a brilliant miniaturist painter from Herat.

Tajik Persian poetry is fused with music by *hafiz* (bard musicians). *Falak* is a popular form of melancholic folk music, often sung a cappella. Music and dance is particularly popular among the Pamiri and Kulyabi.

ENVIRONMENT
The Land

At 143,100 sq km, landlocked Tajikistan is Central Asia's smallest republic. More than half of it lies 3000m or more above sea level. The central part encompasses the southern spurs of the Tian Shan and Pamir Alay ranges while the southeast comprises the Pamir plateau. Within these ranges are some of Central Asia's highest peaks. The Fedchenko Glacier, a 72km-long glacial highway frozen to the side of Peak Koh-i-Samani (formerly called Pik Kommunizma), is one of the longest glaciers in the world outside of the polar region and contains more water than the Aral Sea.

The western third of the country is lowland plain, bisected to the north by the Hissar, Zeravshan and Turkestan ranges – western extensions of the Tian Shan that cross into Uzbekistan. The remote Zeravshan Valley is cradled between the Zeravshan and Turkestan ranges. The mountain peaks with their sun-melted icecaps are the source of a fibrous network of fast-flowing streams, many of which empty into Tajikistan's two major rivers – the Syr-Darya (Jaxartes River), rising in the Fergana Valley, and the Amu-Darya, formed from the confluence of two Pamir rivers, the Vakhsh and the Pyanj.

Together, the Amu-Darya and the Pyanj mark most of the country's 1200km border with Afghanistan. Tajikistan's other borders are much less defined: in the east, 430km of border with China meanders through

Pamir valleys, while to the north and west are the seemingly random jigsaw borders with Kyrgyzstan and Uzbekistan.

For administrative purposes the country is divided into three viloyat (provinces): Sogd (Khojand), Khatlon (Kurgonteppa) and the 60,000-sq-km autonomous mountain region of Kohistani Badakhshan (GBAO).

Wildlife

Tajikistan's megafauna includes snow leopards, brown bears, Marco Polo sheep and ibex. The best place to see Marco Polo sheep is the eastern Pamir, particularly after December, when they come to lower altitudes for the rut.

Poaching (largely by border guards) is a big problem. Marco Polo sheep now number around 10,000, down 300% since independence and down 800% from the 1960s. Marco Polo sheep meat is sold in most Pamiri bazaars, for less per kilo than mutton.

Environmental Issues

The 2.6 million hectare Tajik (Pamir) National Park was founded in 1992 as the largest in Central Asia, covering a whopping 18% of Tajikistan. That's the good news. The bad news is that the park exists only on paper, with only four employees to police and administer the park (and none stationed inside the park).

The lack of burnable fuel in the eastern Pamir has led to the disappearance of the slow-growing *tersken* bush within a radius of 100km from Murgab, adding to desertification in the treeless region.

FOOD & DRINK

For a general rundown of common dishes, see p73.

Try *nahud sambusa* (chickpea samosas) or *nahud shavla* (chickpea porridge). Tajiks also prepare many bean and milk soups, while *oshi siyo halav* is a unique herb soup. *Tuhum barak* is a tasty egg-filled ravioli coated with sesame-seed oil. *Chakka* (*yakka* to Tajik speakers around Samarkand and Bukhara) is curd mixed with herbs, and delicious with flat-bread. *Kurtob* is a wonderful rural dish of bread, yogurt, onion and *cilantro* (coriander) in a creamy sauce. In Badakhshan you might try *borj* – a meat and grain mix that resembles savoury porridge.

Both Hissar and Dushanbe brew their own beer. Obi Zulol is the best brand of mineral water, bottled in Istaravshan. Dushanbe and even Khorog manufacture their own sickly sweet colas and luminous lemonades.

DUSHANBE
ДУШАНБЕ

☎ 372 / pop 700,000 / elevation 800m
With a cool backdrop of mountains, lazy tree-lined avenues and pastel-hued neoclassical buildings, Dushanbe is Central Asia's best-looking capital – especially now that the bullet holes have been plastered over. Previously scary and more than a little dangerous, the Tajik capital is currently blossoming and is now pleasant, if just a little dull.

HISTORY

Although the remains of a settlement dating to the 5th century BC have been found here, modern-day Dushanbe has little history beyond last century. As recently as 80 years ago, Dushanbe (then spelled Dushyambe) was a small, poor village known chiefly for its weekly bazaar (Dushanbe means Monday in Tajik).

In 1920 the last emir of Bukhara took refuge in Dushanbe, fleeing from the advancing Bolsheviks. He was forced to continue his flight early the next year as the Red Army swept remorselessly on to add the Tajik settlement to the expanding Bolshevik empire. The Russian hold was shaken off for a spell when in 1922 Enver Pasha and his *basmachi* fighters liberated Dushanbe as part of their crusade to carve out a pan-Islamic empire (see the boxed text, p330), but following his death in a gun battle in southern Tajikistan, Bolshevik authority was quickly reasserted.

With the arrival of the railroad in 1929, Dushanbe was made capital of the new Soviet Tajik republic and renamed Stalinabad – a name it bore until the historical reinvention of the Khrushchev era. The region was developed as a cotton- and silk-processing centre and tens of thousands of people were relocated here, turning the rural village into a large, urban administrative and industrial

TAJIKISTAN

centre. The city's numbers were further swollen by Tajik émigrés from Bukhara and Samarkand, which had been given over to Uzbek rule.

After almost 70 uneventful years of relative peace, if not prosperity, 1990 saw festering nationalistic sentiments explode into rioting, triggered by rumoured plans to house Armenian refugees in Dushanbe. Twenty-two people died in clashes with the militia.

There were further demonstrations in the autumn of 1991, organised by opposition factions dissatisfied with the absence of political change in Tajikistan. The statue of Lenin that stood opposite the parliament building disappeared overnight, and young bearded men and veiled women took to the streets of Dushanbe calling for an Islamic state.

During the civil war the city remained a capital of chaos. It was kept under a dusk-to-dawn curfew, with armed gangs controlling the roads in and out, and lawless brigands patrolling the streets. Shoot-outs between rival clans were common and most Russians fled. Random acts of violence continued through the 1990s (such as the storming of the Presidential Palace in 1997), but by 2002 the situation had stabilised enough to lift the citywide curfew. These days Dushanbe is savouring its peace.

ORIENTATION

The focus of Dushanbe is the wide, tree-lined prospekt (avenue) Rudaki, which runs north from the train station on Maydoni Ayni (maydoni means square). Roughly central on Rudaki is Maydoni Azadi, surrounded by government buildings and now

under the stern gaze of a sorcererlike Shah Ismail Samani, the founder of the Samanid dynasty. His statue ousted Lenin's from the top spot in 1999 on the 1100th anniversary of the Samanid dynasty.

Almost everything useful or interesting is within a 15-minute walk of here. The exception is the central bus station, which is some 3km away on kuchai Ibn Sina in the western part of town. The airport is in the southeastern suburbs of the city, 5km from the centre, along Ayni.

INFORMATION
Cultural Centres

Bactrian Cultural Centre (☎ 24 86 67; bactria@ acted.org; Fazliddin Shakhobov 26; ☼ 8am-5pm Mon-Sun) A magnet for French speakers, with monthly concerts and exhibitions, and a weekend café.

Emergency
Ambulance (☎ 03)
Police (☎ 02)

Internet Access
Tsentr Interkom (Rudaki 81; ☼ 8am-10pm) Opposite the post office.
Volshebni Sir (Magic Cheese; ☎ 24 43 43; Rudaki 98; ☼ 8am-11pm) Serves iced coffee and pizza (3TJS to 6TJS).

Medical Services
Your best bet in case of illness is to call the nearest embassy (p349), which should have contact details for recommended doctors, medical services and hospitals.
Gafur Khodjamurodov (☎ 24 32 94, 24 54 59, 70 38 46; Medgorodok) A UN doctor recommended by several embassies.

Money
There are licensed moneychangers throughout the city and this is where most people change their currency (cash in US dollars and euros only). At ATMs, cash can be withdrawn in US dollars or somani.
Agroinvest Bank (Rudaki 95; ☼ 8am-noon & 1.30-4pm Mon-Fri) Offers cash advances on MasterCard for 2% commission (4% to get the money in US dollars). Visa cards should be accepted soon.
Hotel Tajikistan (☎ 27 43 93; www.hotel.tojikiston .com; Shotemur 22) ATM available in lobby.
Orienbank (Rudaki 95; ☼ 8am-noon & 1.30-4pm Mon-Fri) Offers cash advances on MasterCard at the same commissions as Agroinvest Bank. Visas should be accepted soon.

DUSHANBE

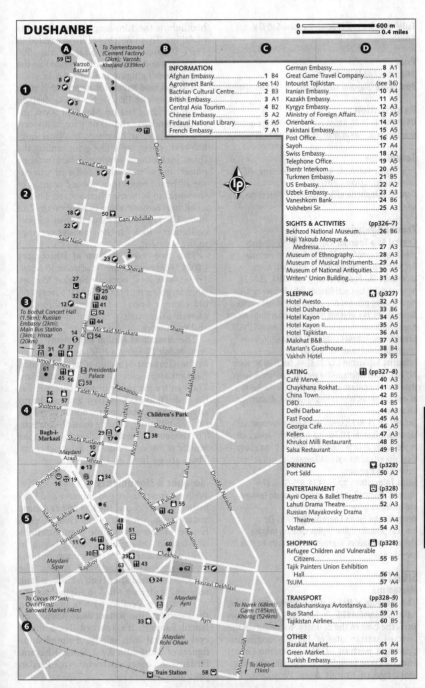

0 — 600 m
0 — 0.4 miles

INFORMATION
Afghan Embassy..........................1 B4
Agroinvest Bank.....................(see 14)
Bactrian Cultural Centre...............2 B3
British Embassy...........................3 A1
Central Asia Tourism...................4 B2
Chinese Embassy........................5 A2
Firdausi National Library..............6 A5
French Embassy..........................7 A1
German Embassy.........................8 A1
Great Game Travel Company........9 A1
Intourist Tojikistan.................(see 36)
Iranian Embassy........................10 A4
Kazakh Embassy.......................11 A5
Kyrgyz Embassy.......................12 A3
Ministry of Foreign Affairs...........13 A5
Orienbank................................14 A5
Pakistani Embassy....................15 A5
Post Office...............................16 A4
Sayoh.....................................17 A4
Swiss Embassy.........................18 A2
Telephone Office......................19 A5
Tsentr Interkom.......................20 A5
Turkmen Embassy....................21 B5
US Embassy.............................22 A2
Uzbek Embassy........................23 A3
Vaneshkom Bank.....................24 B6
Volshebni Sir...........................25 A3

SIGHTS & ACTIVITIES (pp326–7)
Bekhzod National Museum.........26 B6
Haji Yakoub Mosque &
  Medressa..............................27 A3
Museum of Ethnography............28 A3
Museum of Musical Instruments...29 A4
Museum of National Antiquities...30 A5
Writers' Union Building..............31 A3

SLEEPING (p327)
Hotel Avesto...........................32 A3
Hotel Dushanbe.......................33 B6
Hotel Kayon............................34 A5
Hotel Kayon II.........................35 A5
Hotel Tajikistan.......................36 A4
Malohat B&B...........................37 A3
Marian's Guesthouse.................38 B4
Vakhsh Hotel...........................39 B5

EATING (pp327–8)
Café Merve.............................40 A3
Chaykhana Rokhat....................41 A3
China Town.............................42 B5
DBD.......................................43 B5
Delhi Darbar............................44 A3
Fast Food................................45 A4
Georgia Café...........................46 A5
Kellers....................................47 A3
Khrukoi Milli Restaurant.............48 B5
Salsa Restaurant......................49 B1

DRINKING (p328)
Port Saïd................................50 A2

ENTERTAINMENT (p328)
Ayni Opera & Ballet Theatre.......51 B5
Lahuti Drama Theatre................52 A3
Russian Mayakovsky Drama
  Theatre................................53 A4
Vastan...................................54 A3

SHOPPING (p328)
Refugee Children and Vulnerable
  Citizens................................55 B5
Tajik Painters Union Exhibition
  Hall.....................................56 A4
TsUM.....................................57 A4

TRANSPORT (pp328–9)
Badakshanskaya Avtostansiya.....58 B6
Bus Stand...............................59 A1
Tajikistan Airlines.....................60 B5

OTHER
Barakat Market........................61 A4
Green Market...........................62 B5
Turkish Embassy.......................63 B5

TAJIKISTAN

TsUM (Rudaki 83; ⊗ 8.30am-5pm Mon-Sat) ATM available.

Post
DHL (☎ 24 47 68; Rudaki 105)
Post office (Maydoni Azadi, Rudaki 57; ⊗ 8am-6pm)

Registration
OVIR (☎ 33 76 88; Karabaeva 36/3) East of the centre near the circus. Take minibus No 29 from Ismail Somoni.

Telephone
For international calls, go to one of the communication centres.
Central telephone office (Rudaki 55) Next to the post office.

Travel Agencies
Central Asia Tourism (CAT; ☎ 21 81 55; cat-dush anbe@tajnet.com; Samad Gani 9) Branch of a reliable Kazakh travel agency; good for international tickets.
Dushanbe Ski Federation (☎ 50-50567, 23 01 33; petrova@skifed.tajik.net) Director Gulya Petrova runs hiking and skiing trips and runs the ski base at Takob in the Varzob Valley. Her weekend hiking trips from Dushanbe are popular with expatriates and good value at around US$20.
Great Game Travel Company (☎ 24 69 16; www .greatgametravel.co.uk; Rudaki 148)
Intourist Tojikistan (☎ 21 32 44; fax 21 80 80; room 11, 1st fl, Hotel Tajikistan) The reincarnated former Soviet state travel bureau can arrange jeep trips to the Pamir, as well as escorted trips to Hissar, Varzob and other local destinations.
Sayoh (☎ 21 90 72; sayoh@netrt.org; www.sayoh.toji kiston.com; Pushkin 14) This is a semiprivate agency run by the former de facto minister of tourism. It can arrange visas, visa extensions and GBAO permits, as well as tours, trekking and transport.
Surat Toimastov (☎ 23 54 24; 893-50 50 67; stpamir19@hotmail.com) An English-speaking trekking and adventure guide.
Yevgeny and Elena Lourens (☎ 37 91 76; lem_camp@mail.ru) Also English-speaking trekking and adventure guides. They run the base camp for Peak Koh-i-Samani.

SIGHTS
Museums
The **Museum of National Antiquities** (☎ 27 13 50; Rajabov 7; admission 8TJS; ⊗ 9am-5pm Mon-Fri, 9am-4pm Sat) is the best in the country, focusing on the Greco-Bactrian sites of Takht-i-Sangin (including a portrait of Alexander the Great) and the Oxus temple at Kobadian, plus original Sogdian murals from Penjikent. The highlight is the 13m-long sleeping Buddha of Adjina-Tepe (Witches Hill), excavated in 1966. It dates from the Kushan era, 1500 years ago, and was recently revealed as the largest Buddha figure in Central Asia.

The **Bekhzod National Museum** (☎ 21 60 36; Rudaki 31; admission 3TJS; ⊗ 9am-4pm Tue-Sun), on a commanding site on Maydoni Ayni, includes standard exhibits on natural history, art, crafts and archaeology, but little English text. There are a few gems among the filler, including a lovely *minbar* (mosque pulpit) from Istaravshan and a fine painting of Lenin meeting oppressed women of the world in Moscow's Red Square. There's a chilling reconstruction of a jail on the 2nd floor. The top floor is given over to a Soviet collection – look for the alabaster carvings in the stairwell.

The two-room **Museum of Ethnography** (☎ 24 57 59; Ismail Somoni 14; admission 50 dirham; ⊗ 9am-4pm Mon-Fri), opposite Barakat Market, is heavy on old ceramic finds and *suzani* embroidery, as well as jewellery, musical instruments and woodwork.

The **Museum of Musical Instruments** (☎ 23 32 10; Bokhtar 23; admission 2.5TJS) is also known as the Gurminj Museum after the owner, Badakhshani actor Gurminj Zavkybekov. You can try the many instruments, such as the *gijak* (fiddle), *doira* (tambourine/drum) and *rubab* (six-stringed mandolin), and get information on upcoming musical concerts. The museum is hard to find, across from the mosaic of justice and next to a district court. There are no fixed opening hours.

Mosques & Monuments
With its crescent-topped minaret and burnished golden dome, the **Haji Yakoub mosque and medressa**, just west of the Hotel Avesto, is one of the few visible manifestations of Islam in Dushanbe. Building began in 1990, and it was financed by contributions from Iran, Pakistan and Saudi Arabia. The mosque is named after Haji Yakoub, a Tajik religious leader who fled to Afghanistan.

Tajikistan's Persian past is invoked in the façade of the **Writers' Union Building** on Ismail Somoni. It's adorned like a medieval cathedral with saintly, sculpted-stone figures of Sadruddin Ayni, Omar Khayam, Firdausi and other writers from the Persian pantheon.

Markets

While not particularly exotic or Eastern in flavour, the large, covered **Barakat Market** (Ismail Somoni) is the centre of activity in Dushanbe. It's north of the Hotel Tajikistan. A more interesting central bazaar is the **Shah Mansur** (Green Market; devoted to fruit and vegetables), which is a block north of Maydoni Ayni.

SLEEPING
Homestays

Great Game Travel Company (☎ 24 69 16; www.great gametravel.co.uk; Rudaki 148) can arrange basic and overpriced homestays for US$15 per person.

Malohat B&B (☎ 21 27 15, 24 22 79; flat 47/48, 5th fl, Ismail Somoni 6; per person US$5, breakfast US$1) This private apartment is the best value option in town with bedroom, kitchen, bathroom with hot water and mattresses on the floor. Price is per person not for the flat. The apartment is in the high-rise block behind Kellers Restaurant. Malohat speaks only Russian and Tajik. If no-one answers the above numbers, try Malohat on ☎ 24 73 94 (home) or ☎ 21 61 22 (work).

Budget

Vakhsh Hotel (☎ 21 40 31, 21 05 10; 24 Rudaki; per person standard US$10-15, pol-lux US$20, lux US$30/50) A Soviet-era hotel run by a band of fearsome Soviet babushkas. During the civil war the hotel was occupied by bands of bearded mujaheddin rebels but has since been renovated! Try for a room with a balcony view of the Ayni opera house. There's a highly complex pricing system, so double check rates before moving in. The *lux* suites aren't really worth the extra money.

Mid-Range

Hotel Tajikistan (☎ 27 43 93; www.hotel.tojikiston .com; Shotemur 22; s/d US$50/70) English is spoken in the reassuring lobby but everything else is 100% Soviet and horribly overpriced. Rooms are small and come with hot water, kettle and fridge. Only some come with air-con. South-facing rooms benefit from park views.

Hotel Avesto (☎ 21 12 80; Rudaki 105; s/d US$55/68, pol-lux US$98, lux US$98; 🖳) Old-fashioned and musty with a dreary Soviet feel, though some rooms have a fine view of the mosque. The US embassy used to be here, so expect the rooms to be bugged.

Hotel Dushanbe (☎ 21 23 57; Rudaki 7; d US$25, lux US$50-80) A huge but peaceful monster at the southern end of Rudaki, with nice leafy views of Maydoni Ayni and clean bathrooms.

Hotel Kayon (☎ 21 62 29; kayon@tajnet.com; Bokhtar 7; s/d US$50/70, lux US$100-120; 🖳) Live the nouveau riche life in comfortable rooms with breakfast, TV and very clean bathrooms.

Hotel Kayon II (☎ 23 07 61; Kuybeshov 1; d US$80; 🖳) New and much the same as Hotel Kayon. This is the bigger but harder to find of the two Kayon hotels.

Marian's Guesthouse (☎ 23 01 91, 50-50089; marian@tajnet.com; Shotemur 67; per person US$70-90; 🖳 🖳) Visiting consultants love this comfortable refuge, so reserve a room in advance (there are only seven) or you won't even get past the paranoid security guards. There's a sauna, laundry and driver service. It's hard to find; head down the little alley just after the Radio and TV Communication building across from the Children's Park and look for the black and white gates. Contact Gulnura Razukova.

Serena Inn will no doubt rank as the best in town when it opens in 2004.

EATING & DRINKING
Cafés & Chaikhanas

The cheapest eats are to be found at the chaikhanas (teahouses) in the markets and in Bagh-i-Markazi (Central Park).

Chaykhana Rokhat (☎ 21 76 54; Rudaki 84; mains 3-4TJS) This unusual, Soviet-era attempt at a grand Persian-style chaikhana is great for people-watching but is perhaps better for a drink or snack than a meal.

Georgia Café (☎ 27 81 02; Rudaki 29; mains 4-6TJS) Expand your culinary horizons with dishes like *khachapuri* (like a pizza with no toppings), *solyanka* (beef in tomato sauce) and *sacsivi* (chicken with nuts in cream sauce), washed down by cold beer and baklava (Turkish pastry and syrup dessert).

Fast Food (☎ 21 45 61; Ismail Somoni 1; snacks 2-4TJS) Families, teenagers and the odd stray tourist come here for decent snacks and good breakfast food (tomato omelette).

Restaurants

Kellers (☎ 24 79 21; 6 Ismail Somoni; mains 6-8TJS) Aid workers and local business people come for the house-brewed German-style beer (2TJS for 0.5L), pleasant outdoor seating, and authentic Chinese (and European) food.

THE AUTHOR'S CHOICE

Café Merve (☎ 21 94 09; Rudaki 92; mains 7TJS, snacks 2-4TJS) Our favourite place in town is this excellent bustling cafeteria, selling Turkish kebabs, pizza, snacks, cakes and coffee, plus the best breakfast bets in town (feta cheese and olives!). It can be hard to get a seat at lunchtime.

Khrukoi Milli Restaurant (Tursunzade) Don't bother asking for the menu at this underground dive because there's only one dish on offer; *kurtob* (layered bread, yogurt, onion and coriander in a creamy sauce). Luckily it's the best damn *kurtob* in town. Add salad, a green chilli, tea and bread and you'll still get change from 2TJS. Eat with your hands out of a communal bowl. Look for the 'Welcome' sign in English.

Salsa Restaurant (☎ 24 88 57; cnr Karamov & Omar Khayom; mains 10-14TJS, lunch specials 4-9TJS) Just what you didn't expect in Dushanbe; an Ecuadorian restaurant serving everything from carrot cake and cocktails to Mexican and Italian dishes, complemented by a decent selection of wines and real coffee. This is definitely your only chance in Central Asia to try Ecuadorian *llapingachos* (fried potato and mozzarella cheese with peanut sauce). To find it look for the line of 4WDs owned by aid workers lunching on expense accounts and decrying the poverty.

Delhi Darbar (☎ 24 66 11; delhi@tajik.net; Rudaki 88; mains 8TJS, veg 2.50-4TJS; set meal 11TJS, buffet 15-20TJS) The self-proclaimed 'gateway of Indo-Fusion cuisine' offers popular Friday and Sunday night buffets. Great food. There's a branch in Kabul and one in Mazar-e Sharif.

China Town (☎ 27 75 17; Tursunzade 30; dishes 7-8TJS) The best Chinese food in town.

DBD (Rudaki; mains 5-11TJS) Wash down the pseudo-Iranian food with chilled *dugh* (milk). Dishes here include Iranian *khorush* (stew) among the samey kebabs.

ENTERTAINMENT

Bactrian Cultural Centre (☎ 24 86 67; bactria@acted.org; Fazliddin Shakhobov 26; ☽ 8am-5pm Mon-Sun) A good place to tap into Dushanbe's cultural life and find out what's on.

Ayni Opera & Ballet Theatre (☎ 21 44 22; Rudaki 28) There's still life left in this theatre,

plus it has possibly the finest interior in Dushanbe.

Borbat Concert Hall (☎ 3 59 58; Ismoili Somoni 26) Hosts occasional Tajik music concerts.

There are Tajik plays at the **Lahuti Drama Theatre** (☎ 21 37 51; Rudaki 86) and Russian drama at the nearby **Russian Mayakovsky Drama Theatre** (☎ 21 31 32; Rudaki 76).

There are several nightclubs, including **Port Saïd** (☎ 24 88 02; Rudaki 114; ☽ 9pm-5am; cover 5TJS) and the flashier **Vastan** (Rudaki 88; cover 10TJS). Most women in these clubs are prostitutes so solo female travellers should think twice about going alone.

SHOPPING

Barakat market (Ismail Somoni) The place to pick up an embroidered *tupi* (skullcap) for US$2 to US$3, or a *chapan* (cloak) for around US$8. You'll also find plenty of sequined, gold-stitched trousers and colourful dresses.

TsUM (Rudaki 83; ☽ 8.30am-5pm Mon-Sat) Has some *suzani*, embroidered cloaks, Pamiri socks, plates, ceramic Central Asian figures and lots of *ikat* silks on two floors, among the normal department store dreams.

Tajik Painters Union Exhibition Hall (cnr Rudaki & Ismail Somoni; ☽ 10am-5pm Mon-Fri, 10am-3pm Sat) Worth a visit for three floors of modern Tajik art, most of which is for sale.

Refugee Children and Vulnerable Citizens (RCVC; ☎ 21 87 15; T Pulodi 41) Has a small showroom of nice Afghan embroidery, gaudy Tajik clothes and carpets made on the spot by Afghan refugees.

GETTING THERE & AWAY
Air

Tajikistan Airlines (☎ 29 82 06, 29 82 33, 21 19 66; cnr Chekova & Lahuti) theoretically has flights to Garm (US$22), Penjikent (US$40), Ayni (US$35), Isfana (US$45), Vanch (US$35) and Kulyab (US$20), though in practice the only reliable regular services are to Khojand (three daily, US$45) and Khorog (Sunday, Monday, Wednesday and Friday, US$45). Tickets for the flight to Khorog only go on sale at the airport at 7am the day before the flight. Be aware that flights are grounded at the first sign of bad weather (p342). The central Tajikistan Airlines office, near the Shah Mansur on Chekhov, will probably do what it can to avoid selling you a ticket and will direct you to the

Timurid dome of the Abdullatif Sultan Medreseh (p333), Istaravshan, Tajikistan

Man in front of an inscribed black marble wall, Mazar-e Sharif (p389), Afghanistan

Pshart Valley, the Pamirs (p336), Tajikistan

Frame of a yurt, Gumbezkul Valley (p347), Tajikistan

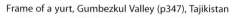

Kugitang Nature Reserve (p431),
Turkmenistan

Group of children, Kabul (p367),
Afghanistan

Children outside a traditional yurt,
Darvaza, Turkmenistan

Crumbling arches of a mausoleum above the city of Kabul (p367), Afghanistan

foreigners' booking office (8am-4pm) at the airport.

For regional and international flights, see p352.

Minibus & Car

Minibuses to Varzob (50 dirham), Takob (2TJS) and Khoja Obi Garm depart from the bus stand next to Varzob Bazaar in the north of town.

Minibuses and jeeps to Khorog (556km, 21 hours, 50TJS to 60TJS) leave from the *Badakshanskaya avtostansiya* transport yard on Ahmadi Donish (the road to the airport), near the railway bridge. Shop around and try to get a front seat. Most transport stops for at least a few hours sleep at a chaikhana around Kalaikhum (Qala-i-Kum) or Rushan, but if not, it's worth breaking the trip and finding transport the next day rather than missing the spectacular scenery.

Transport to Jirgital and the Garm Valley (nine hours) leaves from a lot 7km east of the centre on the road to Kofarnikhon. Take minibus No 18 from near the Hotel Dushanbe and ask to be dropped at *syedmoi kilometr*.

Routes to southern Tajikistan (Kurgonteppa and Kulyab, and as far down as Dusti, Pyanj and Ayvadz) leave from the main bus station in the western suburbs and also from the Sahowat market in the 63rd *microrayon* in the southwestern suburbs.

Shared taxis to Penjikent, Istaravshan and Khojand leave mornings from the Tsementzavod (Cement Factory) stand in the north of town (the stand is opposite a restaurant). A seat costs 30TJS, though many drivers ask for 50TJS. Take minibus No 24 here from along Rudaki or from near the Varzob Bazaar.

GETTING AROUND

Chinese buses and cramped private minibuses will get you most places. Minibus No 3 and trolleybus No 1 run up and down Rudaki; others such as minibus Nos 8 and 22 turn off at Ismail Somoni.

The airport is a quick ride on minibus No 8, or bus Nos 2, 8 or 12, all caught from Rudaki and marked *furudgoh*. A taxi will cost 3TJS. To get to the bus station take bus No 18 or trolleybus No 12 west from in front of the Museum of Ethnography.

AROUND DUSHANBE

The main M34 Ura–Tyube road winds north through the valley of the Varzob River and, though there's no one particular place to head for, there are plenty of picturesque locations, including the **Varzob Gorge**, 56km out of Dushanbe. There are minibuses up to the village of Varzob and the ski resort at Takob, where there is some nice summer hiking.

Dramatic but no longer picturesque, the 330m-high **Nurek Dam**, the world's highest hydroelectric dam, used to be a big favourite with Intourist. It's possible to visit but you may need a permit from the Ministry of Interior if arriving by yourself. The dam is 80km east of Dushanbe, near the new town of Nurek (from which it takes its name). If you are travelling on your own, take a Dangara bus.

For a day or weekend hike expatriates recommend the **Karatag Valley** east of Dushanbe (turn north from the main road to Tursanzade at Shakhrinav), from where it's possible to hike up to Timur Dara and Payron lakes. A taxi to the trail head from Dushanbe costs 45TJS.

Hissar

☎ 3139

On a wide mountain-fringed plain, 30km west of Dushanbe, are the remains of an 18th-century **fortress** (admission 1.5TJS), that was occupied until 1924 by Ibrahim Beg, the local henchman of the Emir of Bukhara. Once a *basmachi* stronghold, the fortress was destroyed by the Red army and all that remains is a reconstructed stone gateway (Darvaza-i-Ark) in the cleavage of two massive grassy hillocks. A scramble up the hill on the right (the former residence of the *beg*, or landlord) offers excellent views. The fort is depicted on the 20TJS note.

In front of the fortress are two plain medressas, the **Medressa-i-Kuhna** dating from the 16th century and the **Medressa-i-Nau**, a later overspill. The older medressa (facing the fortress gate) contains a small **museum** (admission 1.5TJS), which has displays of clothing, ceramics and jewellery. Nearby are the foundations of a caravanserai (traveller's inn) built in 1808. Beyond the medressas is the **mausoleum** of 16th-century Islamic teacher Makhdum Azam.

At the foot of the slopes around the fortress is a **holy spring** and pleasant chaikhana.

GETTING THERE & AWAY

To get here, take minibus No 8 west on Ismail Somoni to Zarnisar Bazaar, then a minibus to Hissar (30 minutes, 1TJS). In Hissar town take the right fork at the bus station, heading around 50m down, and take a shared taxi (0.4TJS) to the fort, some 7km further. Ask for the *kala* (fortress; *krepast* in Russian).

ENVER PASHA & THE BASMACHI

As the Bolsheviks were celebrating their victory in Central Asia, a dashing, courageous Ottoman Turkish soldier named Enver Pasha was making his way towards Central Asia. A Young Turk, Enver had served as the Ottoman empire's minister of war during WWI but was forced to flee his homeland after the empire's defeat in 1918. He wound up in Moscow, where he bent Lenin's ear and convinced the Soviet leader that he was just the person to bring him Central Asia and British India on a platter. In exchange, Lenin was to help him win control of what was left of the Turkish empire.

Enver left Moscow for Bukhara in November 1921, ostensibly to make ready an army for his benefactor. In reality he had already decided to jilt Lenin and look after his own dream: to conquer and rule a pan-Turkic state with Central Asia as its core.

In Bukhara Enver (known locally as Anwar Pasho) made secret contact with leaders of the *basmachi* – local bands of Turkic and Tajik freedom fighters (the Russians had given them the name, with its overtones of banditry and murder, and it has unfortunately stuck). The *basmachi* guerrillas (today they would be called *mujaheddin*), with their grass-roots base and intimate knowledge of the mountain geography, had already proven to be worthy foes of the infant Red Army but needed a leader to unify them. Enver gave his Bolshevik hosts the slip and rode east from Bukhara, gathering up 20,000 recruits.

Enver Pasha could never be accused of underestimating himself. As support and material aid began to pour in from the exiled Emir of Bukhara and his host the Emir of Afghanistan, Enver styled himself 'Commander in Chief of All the Armies of Islam', a relative of the caliph by marriage, and Representative of the Prophet. People flocked to his campaign as to a holy war.

Initial successes were stunning. Enver's small army took Dushanbe in February 1922. By the spring they had captured much of the former emirate of Bukhara. The egotistical Enver refused to negotiate with the Bolsheviks until they evacuated Central Asia.

Enraged, the Bolsheviks sent 100,000 additional troops in to crush him. Moscow also played an important political card: it permitted the Islamic courts to reconvene, gave residents of the Fergana Valley a massive tax cut, and returned confiscated land. Support for the *basmachi* faltered.

Enver also discovered the downside of his fanatical host of irregulars: they simply dissolved back into the countryside as things started to go against their leader. With his rural support drying up, and with the Emir of Afghanistan turning a cold shoulder, he still refused to surrender. He and a small band of his closest officers set out for the mountains east of Dushanbe, never to emerge again.

On 4 August 1922, less than nine months after his portentous arrival at Bukhara, Enver Pasha met his end like a hero. Accounts of the final moments differ. The most popular holds that he galloped headlong with sabre drawn at the head of a suicidal charge against the machine-gun fire of a Bolshevik ambush. Even the location of his death is unknown, suppressed by the Soviets in case it became a nationalist rallying point (locals suggest the location is near Badjuan, southeast of Dushanbe). In any case the few survivors of the raid scattered, and immediately began feeding the legend of their fallen leader. Had he succeeded in his grandiose vision, Enver Pasha would have been the first Turkic conqueror of all Turkestan since Timur. The fact that he made the attempt is ample fuel for myth.

The *basmachi* fought on, scattered and dwindling, until the early 1930s. They are now the subject of intensive research by post-Soviet historians, the first generation able to commemorate the *basmachi* without fear of repression.

NORTHERN TAJIKISTAN

Tajikistan in the north squeezes between Uzbekistan and Kyrgyzstan before oozing across the mouth of the Fergana Valley, the Uzbek heartland.

South of Istaravshan (former Ura-Tyube), the twin Turkestan and Zeravshan ranges sever northern Tajikistan from the bulk of the country's landmass. The highest peaks are collectively known as the Fannsky Gory (Fan Mountains). These are impassable from October through May when the Anzob (3372m) and Ayni (3378m) passes are securely plugged with snow.

KHOJAND ХОДЖАНД/ХУҶАНД

☎ 3422 / pop 164,500

Khojand (ho-jan) is the capital of northern Tajikistan (Soghd province) and the second-largest city in the country. It's also one of Tajikistan's oldest towns, founded by Alexander the Great as his easternmost outpost, Alexandreia-Eskhate. In 1986 Khojand – or Leninabad as it was then named – celebrated its 2500th anniversary. Commanding (and taxing) the entrance to the Fergana Valley, Khojand built palaces, grand mosques and a huge citadel before the Mongols steamrolled the city into oblivion in the early 13th century. Today the economically booming town is of marginal interest to visitors, useful mainly as

---

STALIN'S BUM DEAL

This crazy jigsaw boundaries of northern Tajikistan are in fact the result of sober thought. Before 1929 Tajikistan was an autonomous republic within the Uzbek ASSR, but because of its sensitive location on the edge of the Islamic world, Stalin wanted it upgraded to a full republic. But there weren't enough Tajiks; full-republic status required one million inhabitants. They simply topped up numbers by adding the (mainly Uzbek) population of the Khojand region (then Leninabad) to Tajikistan's. There may also be some truth in the theory that this was in partial recompense for the loss of the culturally Tajik cities of Bukhara and Samarkand – a bum deal if ever there was one.

---

a springboard to the spectacular overland route south to Dushanbe.

Khojand, made up mostly of Uzbeks, has remained aloof from Dushanbe, although its 'good communist' credentials meant that it always provided Tajikistan's Soviet elite. When President Nabiev, a Khojand man, was unseated in 1992 and Tajikistan appeared to be becoming an Islamic republic, Khojand province threatened to secede. Secure behind the Fan Mountains, it managed to escape the ravages of the civil war and remains the wealthiest part of the country, producing two-thirds of Tajikistan's GDP, with 75% of the country's arable land and only one-third of the population.

Rail and road communications between Khojand and the rest of the (Uzbek) Fergana Valley have been tightened considerably in recent years and you may face delays if you are crossing to Tashkent (via Oybek) or Kokand (via Kanibadam). Until travel connections become more convenient, most travellers will probably find it easier to bypass the city if they are just headed on to the Fergana Valley.

Information

INTERNET ACCESS

Salon Dixis (⏰ 24hr) Just off Lenina. Has cheap Internet access and international phone calls.

MONEY

The many exchange booths at the bazaar are the easiest places to change cash.

Agroinvest Bank (⏰ 8am–noon & 1–4pm Mon–Fri) Will give cash advances on MasterCard/Maestro cards (for 2% commission, or 4% if you want the money in US dollars) and cash Amex travellers cheques.

Sohibkorbank (Kamoli Khojandy) Will also give cash advances on MasterCard/Maestro cards and cash Amex travellers cheques.

REGISTRATION

OVIR (Upravlenie Vnutrennikh Del; ☎ 6 50 51; Room 104, 170 Kamoli Khojandy; ⏰ 8am–noon & 1–5pm Mon–Fri, 8am–noon Sat) Next to the National Bank of Tajikistan. Register at the main gate to be taken inside. You'll need your passport, one photo and US$15 in somani.

Sights

The city's oldest remains are the formless baked-earth walls of the 10th-century **citadel**, which once boasted seven gates and 6km of fortifications. The fort was the site

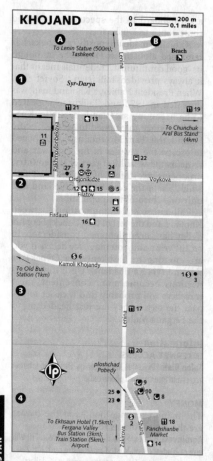

KHOJAND

built hall (1954) with arched entrance portals and a neoclassical façade – think Stalin meets 1001 Nights.

Opposite the bazaar, shielded from the hubbub by a calm white wall, are the **mosque**, **medressa** and **mausoleum of Sheikh Massal ad-Din**, a modest, relatively modern complex that is quietly busy with serious young men clutching Qurans and old white-bearded men reclining in the shade. Take a look at the wooden carvings inside the side halls. The neglected mausoleum was built in 1394. The 21m-tall minaret was added in 1895.

Since the removal of its giant rival in Tashkent, Khojand's 22m-tall **statue of Lenin** is now probably the largest in Central Asia, if not the entire CIS. It was moved here from Moscow in 1974. He's on the north side of the river, 300m beyond the bridge.

of pitched battles in November 1998 between the rebel Uzbek warlord Mahmud Khudoberdiev and government troops, during which 200 people were killed. The reconstructed eastern gate houses the **Museum of Archaeology and Fortifications** (admission 1TJS; 8am-6pm), which has some interesting 19th century photos, 5000-year-old Saka (Scythian) pottery and plans of the original citadel. Be careful when photographing from the ramparts, as the citadel behind is still occupied by the military.

At the south end of kuchai Lenina is **Panchshanbe Bazaar**, one of the best-stocked markets in Central Asia, especially on Thursdays (Panchshanbe in Tajik). The core of the bazaar is an elegant, purpose-

Sleeping

Hotel Leninabad (6 69 27; s/d 15/28TJS, lux 40TJS) This unfashionably named state hotel is well placed on the corniche beside the Syr-Darya. The rooms are classically Soviet, with stinky bathrooms, dim lighting and a broken lift, but are bearable. There are hot showers down the hall (1TJS).

Ekhsaun Hotel (☎ 6 69 84; s/d US$10/20, pol-lux US$20-40, lux US$30-60) The cheapest rooms are the best value here, since the suites just come with four bizarrely unfurnished rooms (the building was meant to be an apartment block) but they are also the only ones without hot water. The hotel is at the fork in the road as you drive north from the Fergana Valley bus station.

Hotel Sharq (☎ 6 78 83; s/d/tr US$1.6/2.6/3) Bunk down with Tajik traders at this friendly but basic bazaar hotel. Rooms are spacious but there's only one toilet and no hot water.

Hotel Khuchand (☎ 6 59 97; Rakhmovlonbekova; d US$43-50; ☒) Probably the best hotel in this price range, with five absurdly large luxury rooms, clean bathrooms and balconies overlooking the opera house fountain.

Hotel Vakhat (☎ 6 51 01; Rakhmovlonbekova; d US$50; ☒) Next door to Hotel Khuchand, this place is similar, with slightly smaller rooms.

Tavhd Hotel (☎ 6 77 66; 117 Firdausi; d US$50-55; ☒) A mid-range option similar to Hotel Khuchand.

Eating

The bread is particularly good in Khojand; glazed and sprinkled with sesame seeds.

There are many chaikhanas, shashlik grills and vats of plov around the bazaar. One of the best is the Nasim Restaurant, on the northeast side of the bazaar and popular with local medressa students.

Sughdiyon Restaurant (Sogdian Restaurant; mains 3-4TJS) East of the khukhimut (city hall) on the banks of the Syr-Darya, this place is buggy (bring repellent) but probably the best in town.

Turk-Tajik Café (Lenina; pizza 4TJS) Has good pizza and baklava.

Café Millennium (Lenina 41; mains 5TJS, salads 0.6-1.6TJS) To the north of Turk-Tajik Café. Has meat-based European dishes and lots of salads, with a ground-floor café, Internet access and an upstairs restaurant.

Getting There & Away

From Khojand there are daily flights to Dushanbe (US$45), and weekly to Bishkek (US$90), Moscow (US$180) and various Siberian cities. **Tajikistan Airlines** (☎ 6 02 49; Lenina 56; ☽ 7am-noon & 1-7pm) is near the Panchshanbe Bazaar.

By rail, there are two services a week to Dushanbe: Nos 267 and 268 (30 hours,

platz/kupe 33TJS/49TJS). The Khojand **train ticket office** (☎ 6 02 48) can only sell tickets to towns along this route, not other destinations in Uzbekistan. To find the ticket office look for the train symbol on the wall next to the Tajikistan Airlines office. The train station is 5km south of the centre.

For details on getting to/from Uzbekistan or Kyrgyzstan see p353.

Buses and minibuses to Kanibadam and Isfana leave from the main Fergana Valley bus station in the southeast suburbs, on the road to Chkalovsk. Take any Chkalovsk-bound bus from Panchshanbe Bazaar to get to the station.

There are frequent minibuses (No 314) and buses south to Istaravshan (one hour, 1.5TJS to 2TJS) from the old (Tashkent) **bus station** (Kamoli Khojandy) in the west of town. A taxi to Istaravshan costs 12TJS.

For shared taxis to Dushanbe (12 hours, 40TJS to 50TJS per seat) you need to take minibus No 18, 29, 33, 39 or 45 in the early morning from Lenina to the Chunchuk Aral bus stand in the northeastern suburbs.

Getting Around

To reach the town centre from the airport, train station or Fergana Valley bus station, take local bus Nos 2 or 34 up Lenina. You can catch these buses in the opposite direction at the stand outside the Avesto Department Store. Minibus No 3 runs the same route. To get to the old bus station on Kamoli Khojandy, take trolleybus Nos 2, 5 or 7, also from the Avesto stand.

ISTARAVSHAN ИСТАРАВШАН

☎ 3454 / pop 50,000

Called Kir by the Parthians and Cyropol by Alexander the Great, this small historic town, formerly called Uro Teppa (Ura-Tyube in Russian), has one of the best preserved old towns in Tajikistan, punctuated with some lovely architecture. Bukhara it's not, but then there aren't any tourists either.

You can easily visit Istaravshan as a day trip from Khojand or as an overnight stop en route to Dushanbe.

Sights

The **Shahr-e-kuhna** (old town) is an interesting maze of alleys west of the main drag, Lenina. Buildings to track down include the 15th-century **Abdullatif Sultan Medreseh**, also known as the Kök Gumbaz (Blue Dome) after its superb Timurid dome, and the nearby 19th-century **Hauz-i-Sangin Mosque**, with its fine ceiling paintings and tomb of Shah Fuzail ibn Abbas. On the main road is the less interesting **Hazrat-i-Shah Mosque and Mausoleum** (Lenina 98).

The hill to the northeast of town is **Mug Teppe**, the site of the Sogdian fortress stormed by Alexander the Great (there are faint remains in the northwest corner). The imposing entry gate was actually built in 2002 during Istaravshan's 2500th anniversary celebrations. At the foot of the hill is the **Regional Museum**, which is often closed. To get to the hill and museum take the road just north of the Istaravshan Hotel.

The **bazaar** is one of the biggest in the region, especially on Tuesday and, to a lesser extent, Saturday.

Sleeping

Istaravshan Hotel (Lenin 80; s/d 5/10TJS) Remodelled and renamed, the spacious rooms and spotlessly clean bathrooms are a bargain, though at the time of research there was no water.

Gul-i-Sukhi Hotel (☎ 2 28 87; tr 6-9TJS) A funkier, noisier option next to the bazaar. The toilets and shower are particularly nasty, with iffy water supplies. There's a Tajikistan Airlines office inside.

Eating

Istaravshan is famed for its pears and *kishmish* grapes. Invest in a kilo and retire to the Aka Musa Chaykhana, a nice Soviet-era chaikhana with fine tea beds but, on this visit, terrible service. It's next to the car parts market; the entrance is marked by a large mosaic.

There are lots of kebab places in front of and at the back of the bazaar.

Bobo Abdurakhim Chaikhana (Lenina) Try this place in the north of town, for good chicken kebabs (1.5TJS).

Getting There & Around

Taxis to Dushanbe (276km, 10 hours, 30TJS) and Penjikent leave from the south end of the bazaar and from a stand 1km south of the bazaar. Transport north to Khojand leaves from the main bus stand, 3km north of the centre. Marshrutka No 1 (20 dirham) shuttles up and down Lenina between the

bazaar, the Hotel Istaravshan and the bus station.

PENJIKENT ПЕНДЖИКЕНТ
☎ 3475 / pop 50,000

On a high valley terrace on the banks of the Zeravshan River, 6km from the modern town of Penjikent, are the ruins of ancient Penjikent or Bunjikath, a major Sogdian town founded in the 5th century and abandoned in the 8th century with the arrival of the Arabs. The ancient city has not been built upon since. The foundations of houses, a citadel with a couple of Zoroastrian temples, and the city bazaar are visible in the excavated ruins, but the best of the frescoes (some of them 15m long), sculptures, pottery and manuscripts have been carted off to Tashkent and St Petersburg. An annotated map at the site describes what all the furrows and mounds once were, and there is a small **museum** (admission US$1) chronicling the excavations.

Some lesser finds are on display at the **Rudaki Museum** (admission US$1.20; ☺ 8am-5pm) in modern Penjikent. The museum's name arises from the claim that Penjikent was the birthplace of Abu Abdullah Rudaki, the Samanid court poet considered by many to be the father of Persian poetry. His **mausoleum**, a popular pilgrimage place, is located 58km west of Penjikent in the village of Panjrul.

Sleeping & Eating

Intourist Hotel Panjakant (☎ 5 45 09, 5 46 92; Borbadi Marvazi 22; d/st US$15/35) Poor value, with run-down rooms, but it does have hot water.

Sogdian Hotel (Rudaki 35; d US$10) This grotty hotel is 200m west of the museum next to Sohibkor Bank.

Given some warning, the Dusti Restaurant, opposite the post office, may be able to rustle up some food.

Getting There & Away

Taxis run along the fantastically scenic roads to Khojand (US$20 per seat) and Dushanbe (225km, US$25 per seat). In theory there are flights to Khojand (US$80) and Dushanbe (US$40) but these rarely run. When they do, tickets are, sold at the airport, 4km west of town.

There are two daily buses (9.30am and 2.15pm) from Penjikent to the Rudaki Mausoleum. A third bus departing at 8.30am also makes a stop here before continuing to Artush.

FAN MOUNTAINS ФАНСКЫ ГОРЫ

The Fannsky Gory are a favoured place for trekking and climbing, being only a couple of hours from both Samarkand and Dushanbe. See Trekking in the Fan Mountains (p336) for route overviews.

The main M34 between Dushanbe and Khojand winds through the fringes of the range, crossing the 3378 Ayni Pass (from Khojand) and the 3372 Anzob Pass en route, and offering superb views. A tunnel is currently being built under the Anzob Pass to make it open year-round; until then expect the route to be closed from November to May. One possible stop en route is to the 10th-century, 13.5m-tall Varz-i-Minor minaret in Ayni village.

One place that is accessible to nontrekkers is **Iskander-Kul**, a gorgeous mountain lake 24km off the main road at the eastern end of the range. The lakeside **turbaza** (former Soviet holiday camp; per person 9TJS) enjoys a lovely spot, with 30 quiet chalets and a great lakeside restaurant. Bring warm clothes as the lake is at 2200m. There are pit toilets but no showers. You can get great overviews of the lake from the hill behind the *turbaza*, where a couple of Orthodox crosses mark climbers' graves. You can take a one-hour walk around the lake to the President's dacha, and there are plenty of longer overnight hikes further up into the Kaznok Valley behind Sarytag village. For a shorter hike the *turbaza* administrator can give directions to a 30m-high waterfall half-an-hour's walk downstream.

There's no public transport to the lake, so you'll have to hire your own car and visit en route from Dushanbe or Penjikent/Khojand. It's possible to find a taxi at the mining settlement by the main M34 turnoff. Expect to pay around US$10 to be dropped at the lake. It shouldn't be too difficult to hitch out. Weekends see the most traffic but are far less serene. Note that the road to Iskander-Kul branches off the larger road (to the mine) shortly after leaving the main M34 and crosses the river.

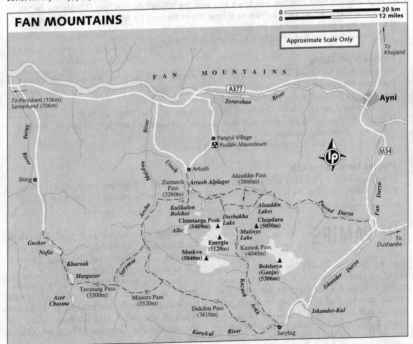

FAN MOUNTAINS

Approximate Scale Only

0 — 20 km
0 — 12 miles

TREKKING IN THE FAN MOUNTAINS

The Fannsky Gory – located in Tajikistan but most easily accessed from Samarkand – are one of Central Asia's premier trekking destinations. The mountains are studded with dozens of turquoise lakes and alpine valleys inhabited by Tajik shepherds.

Many Uzbek travel agencies offer trekking programmes here, as do some overseas trekking companies, though it is a possible destination for experienced and fit do-it-yourselfers, taking a shorter route. To get to the Fans as an excursion from Uzbekistan you will need a Tajik visa and a double-entry Uzbek visa.

Buses run from Penjikent to Artush or Shing, the main trail heads. You may be asked to pay a trekking tax (see Travel Permits, p456) in Artush. You can get supplies in Penjikent, though it's better to bring your own lightweight foodstuffs. The region can be hot and dry at the end of summer. It's possible to hire donkeys at the trail heads to carry rucksacks.

The best map is the 1:100,000 *Pamir Alay – Severno-Zapadnaya Chast* (1992 Tashkent), available from Asia Travel in Tashkent, and the 1:110,000 *Kuhistan* (1990 Tajik Mountain Rescue Service).

Routes from Artush

From Artush walk up to the *alplager* (mountaineers' camp) where rooms and possibly food are available. From here it's a hard uphill hike into the Kulikalon bowl, home to a dozen deep blue lakes. Excellent camping can be found near Dushakha lake, at the foot of Chimtarga (5469m, the highest peak in the region).

Then it's a hard slog up and over the Alauddin Pass (3860m) to the Alauddin lakes, where you can find good camping and sometimes a food tent in summer. From here you can make a hard day-hike up to Mutinye lake and back.

From Alauddin lakes you can head downstream to the Chapdara Valley and then west up to Laudon Pass (3630m) and back down into the Kulikalon bowl.

An alternative from Mutinye lake takes you over the difficult Kaznok Pass (4040m, grade 1B), where you may need an ice axe. From here head down the long Kaznok Valley to Sarytag village, the main road and Iskander-Kul (p335).

There's a daily bus from Penjikent to Artush at 8.30am.

Routes from Shing

The other main trail head is at Shing, from where you can walk up to the Marguzor lakes. From here trails lead over the Tavasang Pass (3300m) to the Archa Maidan Valley. Trails continue down the valley to the foot of the Zurmech Pass and then over to Artush.

Alternatively, when you hit the Archa Maidan Valley, you can climb up to the Munora Pass (3520m) and down into the valley, and then up over the Dukdon Pass (3810m) into the Karakul Valley and, eventually, Iskander-Kul.

There's a daily bus from Penjikent to Shing at 2pm.

Routes from the south

From Dushanbe it's possible to take a taxi to Karatog and start a three-day trek north over Mura Pass (3790m), crossing the Hissar range, to drop down into the Sarytag Valley and Iskander-Kul.

THE PAMIRS

They're known locally as Bam-i-Dunya (Roof of the World), and once you're up in the Pamirs it's not hard to see why. For centuries a knot of tiny valley emirates, the Pamirs feel like a land a little bit closer to heaven. They are the node from which several of the world's highest ranges radiate, including the Karakoram and Himalaya to the south, the Hindu Kush to the west and the Tian Shan straddling the Kyrgyz–Chinese border to the northeast.

The word *pamir* means 'rolling pasture-land' in ancient Persian, though some sources say the derivation is Paw-i-Mur or 'Legs of the Sun.' The Chinese called the mountains the Congling Shan, or 'Onion Mountains'.

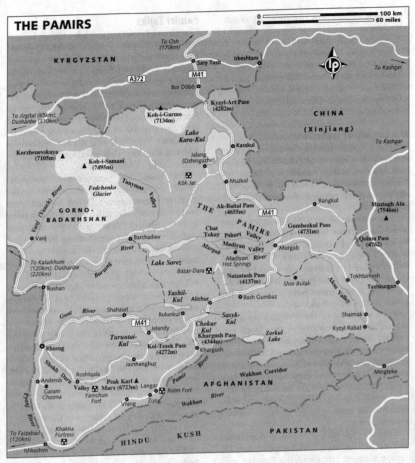

THE PAMIRS

The western half of the region, Badakh-shan, is characterised by deep irrigated valleys and sheer peaks reminiscent of the Wakhi areas of northern Pakistan (which are also ethnically Tajik). The eastern half of the region is the high, arid and sparsely inhabited Pamir plateau, home largely to Kyrgyz herders. For the most part, the Pamirs are too high for human settlement.

The Pamirs contain three of the four highest mountains in the former Soviet Union, the apex of which is Koh-i-Samani at 7495m. Less than an Empire State Build-ing shorter is Kuh-i-Garno (formerly Pik Lenin) at 7134m. The Pamir is drained by the numerous tributaries of the Vakhsh and Pyanj Rivers which themselves feed into the Amu-Darya, Central Asia's greatest river.

The autonomous region of GBAO ac-counts for 45% of Tajikistan's territory but only 3% of its population. The 212,000 souls that do live here are divided between Tajiks, Kyrgyz and Pamiri (Mountain) Tajiks. Cul-turally speaking, Badakhshan extends over the Pyanj River into Afghan Badakhshan, centred around Faizabad.

The slopes and high valleys are inhabited by hardier creatures, near-mythical animals such as the giant Marco Polo sheep, which sports curled horns that would measure almost 2m were they somehow unfurled, and the rarely seen snow leopard. And that's not to mention the similarly elusive 'giant snowman'.

Chance encounters with yetis aside, the Pamirs region is generally safe to travel in. The entire area is under the de facto administration of Russian CIS border guards, whose task it is to control smuggling and prevent fundamentalist infiltration from Afghanistan.

The Legacy of Isolation

With no arable land to speak of and no industry, the region of GBAO has historically always relied heavily on Dushanbe for its upkeep, with most of its food and all of its fuel coming from outside the region.

The collapse of the USSR was a particularly vicious blow for the region. Frustrated by its marginal position and seeing no future in a collapsing Tajikistan, GBAO nominally declared its independence in 1992 and chose the rebel side in the civil war. Since then, the government hasn't been sending much in the way of aid.

Through most of the 1990s, humanitarian aid convoys kept the region from starvation, while establishing agricultural and hydroelectrical programmes in an attempt to create some degree of self-sufficiency. In 1993 the region grew 16% of its basic food needs; by 2003 that figure had risen to 70%. The next stage is to create employment and one of these programmes is banking on tourism.

Despite this, 80% of the local population still earns less than US$200 per year. The region's largest employer, the Russian military, has largely pulled out of the region, followed by over 15,000 Badakhshanis who have left their homes in search of work outside the region.

It is hoped that a new road, co-funded by the Islamic Development Bank, the Aga Khan Foundation and Pakistan, that is being constructed between Murgab and Tashkurgan in China will provide another supply link and lift the region out of its isolation; though it's hard to see quite what the region currently has to export.

Meanwhile the Aga Khan Foundation is in the process of building five bridges along the border with Afghan Badakhshan, reuniting communities severed since the formation of the USSR.

Pamiri Tajiks

Centuries of isolation in high-altitude valleys has meant that the Pamiris of GBAO speak languages different not only from those of lowland Tajiks but from one another. Each mountain community has its own dialect of Pamiri, a language that, although sharing the same Persian roots as Tajik, is as different as English is from German. Shugnani (named after the emirate of Shugnan once based in the Gunt Valley) is the dialect spoken in Khorog, the Gunt Valley and among Badakhshani Tajiks in Murgab.

The mountain peoples are, however, solidly bound by their shared faith: Ismailism (sometimes referred to locally as Suleymanism). Ismailism is a breakaway sect of Shiite Islam, with no mosques (rather multi-purpose meeting halls called *jamoat khana*, which also double as community guesthouses), no weekly holy day and no formal clerical structure. Each village has a religious leader known as a *khalifa*, who leads prayers and dispenses advice (and even medicines), assisted by a *rais* (community leader). One of the few visible manifestations of the religion are the small roadside *oston* (shrines), covered in ibex horns and burnt offerings, at which passers-by stop to ask for a blessing. The horns are often the remnants of hunting trips and ensuing community meals known as *khudoi*. The shrines also act as charity stations; in return for the blessing, the Ismaili customarily leaves some money or bread for anyone in need.

The spiritual leader of the Ismailis is the Swiss-born Aga Khan, revered by Pamiris as a living god and the 49th imam. He's no remote, abstract deity – it's the Aga Khan's charity that has kept almost certain starvation at bay in GBAO; Pamiris venerate him as 'Our God who sends us food'.

Not having two potatoes to fry together has done nothing to lessen the hospitality of the Pamiris, whose natural inclination is to share.

Permits & Registration

It is essential to have both a Tajik visa and a GBAO permit (even local Tajiks need a permit to travel to Badakhshan). To get the latter you'll need travel agency help; **Sayoh** (☎ 21 90 72, 23 14 01; sayoh@netrt.org; www .sayoh.tojikiston.com) charges US$20 and the

TAJIKISTAN'S SWORD OF DAMOCLES

As if Tajikistan didn't have enough to worry about, geologists warn that the country faces a potential natural disaster of immense proportions. The watery Sword of Damocles lies high in the Pamirs in the shape of Lake Sarez, a 60km-long body of turquoise water half the size of Lake Geneva. Lake Sarez was formed in 1911 when an earthquake dislodged an entire mountain side into the path of the Murgab River, obliterating the villages of Usoi and Sarez. The 500m-deep lake formed behind a 770m-high natural dam of rocks and mud, known as the Usoi Dam, which rises 60m above the water level. If a regional earthquake were to break this plug, as some experts think could happen, a huge wall of water would sweep down the mountain valleys, wiping away villages, even into Uzbekistan, Turkmenistan and Afghanistan, with flood waters reaching as far as the Aral Sea. Experts warn that it would be the largest flood ever witnessed by human eyes.

Great Game Travel Company (☎ 01763-220 049; www.greatgametravel.co.uk) US$50. It's best to apply a couple of weeks in advance. At the time of research the GBAO permit could be issued by the Ministry of Foreign Affairs in Dushanbe, by the OVIR in Khorog and (in theory) Murgab. The permit is stamped in your passport and lists the districts to be visited, so make sure you get all the regions you want to visit (these are Ishkashim, Murgab, Vanch, Darvaz, Shugnan, Rushan and Rosht-Qala).

This presents an obvious problem if you want to travel from Osh. Some travellers have reported that they have been able to travel as far as Murgab by saying that they are to pick up a permit in Khorog. Others have had agencies in Bishkek get them a letter of support from a Tajik representative in Osh, which has helped get them into the region. Others have had a GBAO permit faxed from an agency in Khorog, arranged through **Acted** (☎ 88265-060 1513; murghab@acted .automail.com; Frunze 48) in Murgab.

Permits are checked along the road, and there are major checks at Kalaikhum, and also at Khorog airport. There are particu-larly tedious checks by the Russian military at either end of the Wakhan Valley.

Moreover, travellers are supposed to register with the Kumitai Amniyat-i-Milli (generally referred to as the KGB) at Khorog and Murgab, even if you registered elsewhere in Tajikistan. There is no fee for this.

When to Go

Travel is possible from mid-May to early November. Outside these months, it's unbearably cold, snow storms often close passes for days, food is very hard to get and the landscape is not as rewarding.

What to Bring

You can now buy basic foodstuffs along the way but bring some extra provisions, especially if you're trekking and for lunches on the run. Sunscreen, sunglasses and a torch (flashlight) are essential. Water purifying tablets are advisable.

It's essential to have warm clothing, even in midsummer, though a fleece and windproof shell should generally suffice in midsummer. Amazingly strong winds can pick up very quickly in the Pamirs, something even Marco Polo moaned about. A sleeping bag is useful but not essential, as most homes and yurts can provide plenty of duvets. A tent will give you great flexibility.

MAPS

Cartographer Marcus Hauser has produced a 1:500,000 colour tourist map for the entire Pamirs region. It is due for sale from spring 2004 at the Acted office in Murgab.

The best topographical map resource is the University of Berkeley website, www.lib .berkeley.edu/EART/tajikistan/100k.html, which has downloadable scans of all the 1:100,000 Soviet topographical maps covering Tajikistan.

The Zher Cartographic Agency in Almaty (see p93) has 1:1,000,000 scale maps covering the area (J-42 Dushanbe and J-43 Kashgar) from a series called *Generalnii Shtab*.

Money

Make sure you change money before arriving in the region. It's possible to change cash US dollars in Khorog but at a fairly low rate. In an emergency you might find someone willing to change dollars in Murgab (bring small denominations). Kyrgyz som are accepted between Murgab and the Kyrgyz-Tajik border.

Transport

The major transport options for the 728km Pamir Hwy between Khorog and Osh are hitching on trucks, renting a 4WD with driver or waiting for the weekly buses.

BUS

There are weekly trucks/buses between Osh and Murgab and between Murgab and Khorog. Daily public buses run from Osh as far as Sary Tash. From Khorog, minibuses and shared jeeps go to some surrounding valleys such as Jelandy, Ishkashim, Rushan, Langar and Roshtqala, though the timings demand an overnight stay in these villages.

CAR HIRE

Hiring a private vehicle (normally a Russian UAZ jeep) and a driver is expensive, but gives you flexibility that you will value on this scenic and fascinating trip.

A bottom-dollar rate between Osh and Khorog is currently around US$250 for the 1500km ride. This includes petrol, vehicle maintenance and the driver's pay, food and accommodation for four days on the road. For every extra day that the driver waits for you (if you wish, for example, to do an excursion), add about US$10. For side trips, add the extra petrol cost. You should try to organise this at least a couple of days in advance. Give the vehicle the once-over, check that the 4WD is operational and check that the driver has a GBAO permit (if coming from Osh).

Acted (☎ 88265-060 1513; murghab@acted.automail .com) in Murgab can put you in touch with a jeep driver at a rate of US$0.20 to US$0.30 per km, with rates to Murgab around US$100 to US$125 from Khorog (US$150 via Wakhan) and US$170 to US$200 from Osh. **Great Game Travel** (☎ 01763-220 049; www .greatgametravel.co.uk) charges US$0.50 per km for a Land Cruiser from Dushanbe. **Mountain Societies Development Support Project** (MSDSP; ☎ 2699; msdspkhorog@msdsp.automail.com; Lenina 50) in Khorog offers jeeps for US$32 per 100km, plus US$20 per day.

The main factor in the cost is whether you have to pay the jeep's return route, as this essentially doubles the cost.

HITCHING

Not as many lorries make the journey between Osh and Khorog as they used to, so you'll have to dig around for a ride. Figure on around US$15 to US$30 for a ride from Osh to Khorog or US$10 to US$15 from Khorog to Murgab. You could end up waiting a long time for another ride if you break the journey, as trucks mid-route are often full. Drug-smuggling controls at checkpoints are particularly tedious for trucks.

KHOROG ХОРОГ

☎ 35220 / pop 27,800 / elevation 2100m

A small mountain-valley town, Khorog is the capital of the autonomous GBAO region. It is strung out on either side of the dashing Gunt River and penned in by vertical peaks. A few kilometres downstream, the Gunt merges with the Pyanj, the river that marks the border with Afghanistan.

Until the late 19th century, present-day Khorog was a tiny settlement that loosely belonged to the domain of local chieftains, the Afghan Shah or the Emir of Bukhara. Russia installed a small garrison here following the Anglo–Russian–Afghan Border Treaty of 1896 that delineated the current northern border of Afghanistan on the Pyanj River. Khorog was made the administrative centre of GBAO in 1925.

Exacerbated by the civil war and GBAO's ostracism by Dushanbe, unemployment here presently stands at nearly 100%. Almost the only people with work are drivers employed by international aid agencies. At the depths of the economic crisis money disappeared altogether, replaced by barter.

Things are picking up, though. In 2003 the Aga Khan pledged US$200 million to establish a University of Central Asia in Khorog.

Note that the town largely closes down on Sunday, when open restaurants and transport can be hard to find.

Information

Pamir Travel (☎ 3796 office, 5926 after hrs; shagar f@khorugh.tajik.net; Lahuti 6) This is the former Intourist Badakhshan and the only travel agency in town. Owner Abdul Shagarf can arrange homestays, transport and GBAO permits. Make sure you're specific about what you want.

Khorog has an Afghan consulate, though travellers will most likely be referred to the embassy in Dushanbe.

Amonat Bank (🕒 8am-12pm & 1-5pm Mon-Fri) will change cash US dollars and, at a pinch, euros into somani.

You will have to register with the **KGB** (Lenina) and, if you haven't registered before in Tajikistan, with **OVIR** (Lenina).

There's an **Internet café** (per hr 6TJS), the town's first, diagonally opposite from the Restaurant Alyosha

MSDSP (🕾 2699; msdspkhorog@msdsp.automail.com; Lenina 50) is the place to inquire about the MSDSP tourism programme (see the boxed text on p342). Ask to speak with Ergash Fayzullobekov.

Sights

Khorog has a surprisingly good **Regional Museum** (Lenina; admission 3TJS; 🕒 9am-1pm & 2-6pm), with decent historical and ethnographic displays but no English.

The **Pamir Botanical Garden**, 5km east of town, has a couple of hundreds of hectares of parkland and is the world's second highest botanical garden, reaching 3900m. A return taxi will cost a couple of dollars, including waiting.

Sleeping

MSDSP Guesthouse (🕾 2719; Fatullo 6; d US$26, with 3 meals US$40) This comfortable and well-located hub has hot showers but is often full in summer. MSDSP also offers homestays (see MSDSP Ecotourism, p342), including one next to the guesthouse.

Homestay of Azimshah Akdodshoev (🕾 2745, 4426; Khubanshah 1a; r with 2 meals US$10) Azimshah can put you up in his traditional Pamiri home, or he will put you in touch with other houses nearby (US$5, no meals).

Sayidiin Guesthouse (r with two meals US$15-20) Azimshah also runs this new, nearby guesthouse on two upper floors, with bright rooms, shared bathrooms, a dining room and email facilities planned. Food can be ordered from a nearby café.

Homestay of Alibekova Navruzkhotun (🕾 4664; Flat 82, Shotenur 131/4; per person with meals US$10-15) There are two rooms and a hot water shower but check the price as aid workers

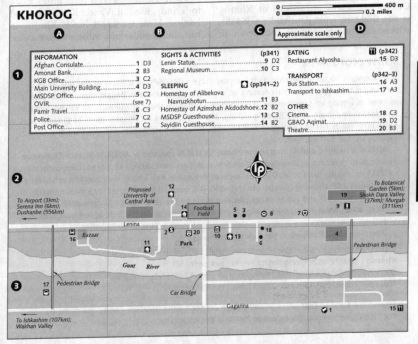

KHOROG

0 ——— 400 m
0 ——— 0.2 miles
Approximate scale only

INFORMATION			
Afghan Consulate	1	D3	
Amonat Bank	2	B3	
KGB Office	3	C2	
Main University Building	4	D3	
MSDSP Office	5	C2	
OVIR		(see 7)	
Pamir Travel	6	C3	
Police	7	C2	
Post Office	8	C2	

SIGHTS & ACTIVITIES	(p341)
Lenin Statue	9 D2
Regional Museum	10 C3

SLEEPING	(pp341-2)
Homestay of Alibekova Navruzkhotun	11 B3
Homestay of Azimshah Akdodshoev	12 B2
MSDSP Guesthouse	13 C3
Sayidiin Guesthouse	14 B2

EATING	(p342)
Restaurant Alyosha	15 D3

TRANSPORT	(p342-3)
Bus Station	16 A3
Transport to Ishkashim	17 A3

OTHER	
Cinema	18 C3
GBAO Aqimat	19 D2
Theatre	20 B3

To Airport (3km);
Serena Inn (6km);
Dushanbe (556km)

Proposed University of Central Asia

Football Field

Bazaar

Lenina

Park

Gunt River

To Botanical Garden (5km);
Shokh Dara Valley (37km); Murgab (311km)

Pedestrian Bridge

Pedestrian Bridge

Car Bridge

Gagarina

To Ishkashim (107km);
Wakhan Valley

TAJIKISTAN

sometimes get charged US$25. Phone ahead (daughter Rudoba speaks English) as the apartment is hard to find (it's the second four-storey apartment block from the east by the riverside).

Serena Inn (☎ 00882216-89802184; serenainn@khorog.automail.com; s/d US$75/120) Near the bridge to Afghanistan, 6km northwest of Khorog. This is the only formal hotel in town, built in Badakhshani style for the visit of Aga Khan (who then decided not to stay), and the six rooms now lie largely empty.

Eating

There are basic chaikhanas in the bazaar but the best place to eat is your homestay or guesthouse.

Restaurant Alyosha (mains 3-6TJS) Offers standard Russian choices, but is a long hike from the centre and may not open unless you have prebooked.

Getting There & Away

For details on transport along the Pamir Hwy see p340.

AIR

One of the main attractions of Khorog is the flight in from Dushanbe (US$45), which, depending on your confidence in the pilots of Tajikistan Airlines, will be one of the most exhilarating or terrifying experiences of your life.

There are four flights a week each way, though at the first sign of bad weather (which is frequent outside of the summer months) they're grounded. Passengers must then take their chances the next day, tussling for seats with those already booked on that flight. It can happen that, after a run of bad weather, hundreds turn up to fight for the first flight's 40 available seats, so budget an extra couple of days into your itinerary. For the best views of Afghanistan sit on the right hand side when flying from Dushanbe.

The mountain-flanked airstrip at Khorog is 3km outside town at the western end of Lenina. There are taxis into town.

BUS

Sturdy 4WD vans and jeeps leave the bazaar early in the morning for Dushanbe (21 hours, 50TJS to 60TJS). There's a weekly truck/bus to Murgab (10 hours, 20TJS) on Wednesday.

There are also several local buses a day to Jelandy, Rushan, Vanch, Kalaikhum and Langar. Most transport leaves Khorog in the afternoon, taking villagers back home

---

MSDSP ECOTOURISM

The Mountain Societies Development Support Project (MSDSP), an affiliate of the Aga Khan Development Network, is currently setting up a tourism programme in Badakhshan. It has already assisted in setting up guesthouses in Ishkashim, Langar, Javshanghuz (Roshtqala Valley), Savnob and Barchadiev (both in the Bartang Valley), and at Darwaz, Kala Hussein (near Sagirdasht) and Kalaikhum (all between Dushanbe and Khorog). Planned guesthouses include Vanj and Bassid, halfway up the Bartang Valley.

MSDSP is running a trial programme where, for US$20 (payable at MSDSP offices in Dushanbe, Khorog, Osh or Moscow), travellers can get free transport from Khorog airport to town, a discount of US$5 on nightly rates at MSDSP guesthouses in Khorog, Kalaikhum, Vanj and Murgab, a letter of invitation (LOI) allowing travellers to stay in MSDSP-assisted guesthouses for a maximum US$10 (food not included) and for all other places a letter to the local Village Organisation (*Tashkiloti kishloki*) asking them to supply a village homestay for a maximum US$5 (food not included). This effectively guarantees you a place to stay in almost every village in Badakhshan.

There are MSDSP offices in the following cities:

Dushanbe (msdspdushanbe@atge.automail.com; Rudaki 137) Contact Mirzo Gulomov.
Khorog (☎ 2699; msdspkhorog@msdsp.automail.com; Lenina 50)
Osh (msdsposh@atge.automail.com; Privokzalnaya 80) Contact Zulfiya Safarmamadova.
Moscow (akfmoscow@atge.automail.com) Contact Yuri Khubonshoyev.

To find the local MSDSP office in any village ask for *hazina* (treasure chest), the name by which the Non-Governmental Organisation (NGO) is known locally.

FLYING TO KHOROG

In Soviet days the Dushanbe–Khorog flight was the only route on which Aeroflot paid its pilots danger money. For most of the 45-minute flight the aircraft scoots along mountain valleys, flying in the shadow of the rock face with its wingtips so close you could swear they kick up swirls of snow. It may be reassuring to know that only one flight has failed to make it safely in recent years, and that incident was apparently not as a result of pilot error or mechanical failure, but because the plane was brought down by rocket fire from Afghanistan.

for the night. Note that there's very little transport on Sunday.

Jeeps to Ishkashim (three hours, 8TJS) leave in the morning from a lot just across the river from the bazaar.

Trucks to Murgab and Osh leave from the *Glav Snab* lot at Dasht (Upper) Khorog, about 4km east of town (3TJS in a taxi). One other option is to take a taxi to the check post of Suchan (3TJS), 11km from Khorog, and hitch from there.

Around Khorog

The hot springs of **Garam Chasma**, 46km from Khorog and 7km from the main road at the check post at Anderob, make for a nice soak. You can stay at the run-down sanatorium here for under US$1, with all the mineral water you can drink.

If you head instead up the Gunt Valley, it's possible to visit **Kafir-Kala** (Fortress of the Infidels), a faint ruined citadel above Bogev village, with two circular Aryan temples. Further up the Gunt Valley, by the roadside before Shahzud, there's a pretty cascade created by a landslide.

Another option is to head up the **Bartang Valley**, said to be the region's most beautiful valley, from the village of Rushan, 61km from Khorog. Treks to Sarez Lake start from Barchadiev in the upper valley.

SHOKH DARA VALLEY ШОХ-ДАРА

A 4WD road winds up the Shokh Dara Valley southeast of Khorog, offering a fine overnight excursion from Khorog or, with your own transport, a loop route option, connecting with the Pamir Hwy and

returning to Khorog via the Gunt Valley or the Wakhan.

About 34km from Khorog (7km before Roshtqala) you'll see an alluvial plain on the right that until 2002 was the village of Dasht. The huge mud slide killed 27 and diverted the river.

The main town in the valley is **Roshtqala** (Red Fort), named after the ruined fort above the town. The village has daily transport from Khorog, a café by the bus stop and MSDSP can help arrange homestay accommodation. Transport to Khorog leaves daily, except Sunday, around 7am or 8am, returning to Roshtqala between noon and 1pm. Occasional transport heads partway further up the valley, from where travellers can arrange to pay for the extra leg to Javshanghuz (around US15 for the vehicle).

A further 73km up the valley from Roshtqala is a fort to the right of the road. Just before Javshanguz are dramatic views of two peaks, **Engels** (6507m) and **Karla Marxa** (6723m). There is an MSDSP-assisted guesthouse at **Javshanguz**, with hot showers, dorm beds and flush toilets.

A rough 4WD road runs to **Turuntai-Kul**, 29km away and 6km off the main road. From here the main road winds down to the Pamir Hwy just beyond Jelandy, but there is a difficult river crossing en route for which you'll need a high-clearance 4WD. It's generally easier to cross near the lake; ask herders for the best route.

THE WAKHAN VALLEY

The Tajik half of the superbly remote Wakhan Valley, shared with Afghanistan, is well worth a side trip from Khorog, either as a loop returning via the Gunt or Shokh Dara Valleys, or by carrying on to Murgab. The route's side valleys reveal views of the stunning 7000m peaks of the Hindu Kush (Killer of Hindus), marking the border with Pakistan.

You will need to have Ishkashim marked on your GBAO permit to travel this road, as the Russian military checks at either end of the valley will scrutinise your passport carefully.

Continuing south of Anderob towards Ishkashim, you'll see the **Kuh-i-Lal ruby mine** from the road. The region's gem mines were mentioned by Marco Polo (who called the region Mt Shugnon) and Badakhshani

PAMIRI HOUSES

If the chance arises it is worth accepting an offer to look inside a traditional *huneuni chid* (Pamiri house). They're built as one large five-pillared room with raised areas around four sides of a central pit. There are few, if any, windows; illumination comes through a skylight in the roof, which consists of four concentric squares, representing the elements earth, fire, air and water. Carpets and mattresses take the place of furniture and also serve as decoration along with panels of hand-coloured photographs – the most prominent of which is often a portrait of the Aga Khan.

The five vertical pillars symbolise the five main prophets (Fatima, Ali, Mohammed, Hassan and Husain), as well as the five pillars (literally) of Islam and, some say, the five deities of Zoroastrianism (the structure of Pamiri houses goes back 2500 years). In a further act of symbolism, the number of roof beams relates to the seven imams and six prophets of Ismailism. The place of honour, next to the Hassan pillar (one of two pillars joined together), is reserved for the *khalifa* (village religious leader), so visitors should avoid sitting there. For some pointers on etiquette when visiting a Pamiri home, see p78.

rubies are still famed throughout the region. There are good views of Afghanistan from here, with its pyramid-shaped hay stacks and donkey caravans.

Ishkashim is the Wakhan's regional centre, with regular transport from Khorog (three hours, 8TJS). The **Hanis Guesthouse** (☎ 355 through the operator; per person US$10), run by Sanavbar Khonjonov, is a decent MSDSP-assisted homestay. It's next to the *militsia* station on the town's main drag. The Afghan town of Ishkashim lies across the Pyanj River; the weekly border market offers the best time to cross the border.

Some 15km from Ishkashim, near the village of Namadguti, is the **Khakha Fortress**, dating from the third century BC and rising from a platform of natural rock. The fort is currently occupied by Russian border guards, so ask before taking pictures, though the lower parts of the fort are generally accessible. Just 300m further on

is the interesting Ismaili *mazar* (tomb) of Shah-i-Mardan Hazrati Ali.

A further 57km from Khakha, 3km past Ptup village, is the turn-off for the ruined 12th-century **Yamchun Fort** (also known as Zulkhomar Fort), the most spectacularly sited fort in the valley, 6km off the main road and about 500m vertically up the hillside. Climb up the hillside behind the fort for the best views. About 1km further uphill from the fort are the **Bibi Fatima Springs**, probably the nicest in the region and named after the Prophet Mohammed's sister. Women believe they can boost their fertility by visiting the womblike calcite formations. Nearby is a cold plunge pool, reached by a precarious metal ladder. It's possible to stay the night at the small **sanatorium** (per person 3-5TJS). A taxi to the springs and fort from Ishkashim will cost around US$20 return.

Yamg village is worth a brief stop for the **tomb** and **reconstructed house** of Sufi mystic Mubarak-kadam (died 1910), where you can see the stone that he used as a solar calendar.

Vrang is worth a stop for its fascinating **fire-worshipping platforms**. All around the ruins are the sulphurous remains of geothermal activity, as well as dozens of manmade Buddhist caves. To get to the site walk through the village, cross the water channel and it's a steep scramble to the site. Look for the 'Welcome' sign on the rock above the site. There's a small museum and shrine at the base of the hill. Four kilometres further on, on the Wakhan plain, is Umbugh Kala (used by the Russian military and so off-limits).

A further 29km (4km before Langar) is **Abrashim Kala** (Vishim Qala in Wakhi), the 'Silk Fortress' of Zong, built to guard this branch of the Silk Road from Chinese and Afghan invaders. The fort offers perhaps the most scenic views of all those in the valley. It's accessed from Dirj village; the last section is better walked than driven. There are said to be petroglyphs and caves in the pastures above the site.

Langar (population 1800) is strategically situated where the Pamir and Wakhan Rivers join to form the Pyanj, marking the start of Afghanistan's upper Wakhan, or Sarkhad region. It's an excellent base to visit surrounding sites and has a daily(ish) minibus to Khorog. About a 2km (one hour) walk uphill (500m vertical ascent), are over 6000 petroglyphs. Accommodation is available at the MSDSP-assisted house museum, easily recognisable by colourful murals on walls. Across the road is the *mazar* of Shoh Oftabi, the man who brought Ismailism to Langar.

Ratm Fort has a strategic location, surrounded on three sides by cliffs. It's 5.5km from Langar and a 15-minute walk off the main road through bushes. Its name means 'first' as it is the first fort in the valley.

From Langar the road continues 77km to a tedious Russian military check at **Khargush**. En route look for Bactrian camels on the Afghan side. At Khargush the main road leads uphill over a pass to the salt lake of Chokur Kul, 25km from Khargush. From here it's 12km to the main Pamir Hwy. The protected area of Zorkul lake, further up the Pamir Valley, is currently off-limits. The lake was determined to be the source of the Oxus River during the 1842 expedition of Lieutenant Wood, when it was named Lake Victoria.

THE PAMIR HIGHWAY
ПАМИРСКОЕ ШОССЕ

The Pamirskii Trakt (Pamir Highway) from Khorog to Osh (a section of the M41) was built by Soviet military engineers in 1931, in order to facilitate troops, transport, and provisioning to this very remote outpost of the Soviet empire. Off-limits to travellers until recently, the high-altitude road takes you to Tibetan-style high plateau and desert populated by yurts and yaks and studded with deep-blue lakes.

Being a major drug-smuggling artery, the road has numerous CIS border guard checkpoints. As with the Karakoram Highway, foreigners are supposed to register at every one of them, but there's little hassle.

Blue kilometre posts line the way with the distance from Khorog marked on one side and from Osh on the other.

Khorog to Murgab

The initial 120km stretch out of Khorog belongs to the attractive, friendly and well-watered Gunt Valley. As the road relentlessly hauls itself up a succession of switchbacks, climbing 2000m in less than 100km, there are countless spectacular views back to the dramatic vertical peaks of the Gunt Valley.

About 1km before **Jelandy**, at the 120km post, there is a Spartan but clean and friendly **guesthouse** (dm 3TJS) with hot springs and a rudimentary sauna. This is a favourite stop for truck drivers out of Khorog, a town with no hot water. It's a bit off the road; ask for the *kurort* (sanatorium).

A few kilometres past Jelandy a dirt road branches right uphill to eventually join the Shokh Dara Valley. Up on the plateau a side track leads to the stunning high-altitude lake **Turuntai-Kul**, which makes a challenging detour.

The main road continues, climbing to 4272m as it crests the **Koi-Tezek Pass**, after which the mountains pull back from the road to reveal the lunarlike high-altitude desert, framed by snowy peaks, that marks the start of the Pamir plateau.

Just after the pass a dirt road shoots off to the left for 16km, to the end-of-the-world Tajik settlement of **Bulunkul**, where it's possible to stay at the Acted-established **homestay** (per person US$5) of Suleiman Alicherev. For more on Acted, see p346. From the village it's a short drive or a one-hour walk to get views of **Yashil-Kul** (Green Lake, 3734m), a turquoise lake framed by ochre desert, a couple of sandy beaches and warm springs on the southern side. A dam is being built at the west end of the lake. Trekking routes to Sarez Lake start nearby (see p343). From here adventurers could spend a couple of days hiking and hitching down the Gunt Valley to the Pamir Hwy near Shahzud.

From the Koi-Tezek Pass the highway passes the turn-off right to the Wakhan (see p343) to a scattering of salt lakes, including **Sassyk-Kul**, before reaching **Alichur** village. The plain around and beyond Alichur is one of the most fertile in the region and is dotted with Kyrgyz yurts in summer (see p346 for accommodation options here). Just 14km past Alichur stop at the remarkable holy **Ak-Balyk** (White Fish) spring by the side of the road.

Just past Ak-Balyk a jeep track turns off north to the remote 11th-century ruins of a silver mine and caravanserai at **Bazar-Dara**, 40km from the highway in a side valley over the 4664m Bazar-Dara Pass. Just 4km from the ruins are the impressive **Ak-Jylga petroglyphs**, some of the world's highest at 3800m, which uniquely depict chariots, archers, ibex and skeletons. Acted in Murgab can arrange a yurtstay at the mouth of the Bazar-Dara Valley, not far from the Pamir Hwy in the Shamurat Valley. If you have a tent the ruins could also be visited as part of a four-day loop trek, heading in over the Bazar-Dara Pass and out via the 3800m Ak-Jylga Pass. From Murgab, Bazar-Dara is a 300km (US$80) return jeep trip.

About 20km further along the highway, just outside the village of **Bash Gumbaz** (itself 7km off the main highway) is a photogenic **Chinese tomb**, marking the high tide of Chinese influence on the Pamir.

A further 50km is another turn-off to the right, this time to the **Shor Bulak observatory**, 35km before Murgab.

There's a final police check 16km before Murgab, just before you cross the Madiyan Valley.

Murgab

☎ 82130 / pop 6500 / elevation 3576m

The wild east town of Murgab is a day's drive (310km) from Khorog. A Soviet-era settlement like Khorog, but a little rougher around the edges, Murgab looks better the further away from it you are. The town itself is half-Kyrgyz, half-Tajik and is a good base from which to explore the eastern Pamirs. The 7546m-high Chinese peak of Muztagh Ata is visible to the northeast of town.

Travellers are required to register at the KGB office across from the Lenin statue. You may also have to register with the

police. Acted (☎ 88265-060 1513; murghab@acted .automail.com) can help with this.

The **Acted Guesthouse** (per person with full board US$15), diagonally across from the Acted office, has a fine sauna, good food and, at the time of research, the only electricity in town. Acted can also put travellers in contact with **homestays** (US$6, meals US$5), including those of Aizada Murzaeva and Yrys Toktomatova. Expect to get a bed, an outside toilet, hot water in buckets and a warm welcome, but not much else.

Surab's Guesthouse (☎ 261; per person US$8, with full board US$15) is a comfortable private guesthouse, with an outside toilet and sauna. Surab works with MSDSP and speaks good English. Surab's house is northwest of the Hotel Murgab; just ask around.

The **MSDSP Guesthouse** (☎ 383; full board US$15) is by the MSDSP office at the northern end of town, near the hospital, and also has an outside toilet and shower. There are only two rooms. If the main office is closed, walk around the back to the supply depot.

The semi-abandoned **Hotel Murgab** (r 5TJS) has basic rooms if you can find anyone working there.

There is a bazaar in the north of town where you can buy basic foodstuffs or get a grim chaikhana meal. Eat in your homestay.

Murgab is a good place to drum up a truck ride. Converted bus-trucks run to Khorog every Sunday (20TJS) from near the bazaar, returning on Wednesday. Buses

---

ECOTOURISM IN MURGAB

The French NGO **Acted** (☎ 88265-060 1513; murghab@acted.automail.com; Frunze 48) has set up a fledgling ecotourism project in Murgab with the support of Unesco. It's a great place to organise a Pamir adventure; take a couple of extra days to take advantage of the programme.

The programme offers yurtstays in the Pshart and Madiyan Valleys and can arrange homestays in Karakul (at the house of Egem Berdey) and Alichur (Rustam Abdyrazakov). There are more yurtstays further away in the upper Alichur Valley, the Jalang Valley and at Kök Jar/Sheralu, the last two west of Kara Kul Lake. (Note that yurts start to move down from the higher mountain valleys at the end of September.) Costs are US$5 to US$6 per person, plus US$5 for three meals. Guides (US$5 to US$10 per day) and horses (US$5) can be arranged, as can jeep hire (US$0.25 to US$0.35 per km). Trekking programmes are planned.

An ecotourism office is to be set up in Murgab, as well as reception centres in Karakul and Khorog; until then contact the Acted office diagonally across from the Acted Guesthouse and ask for Ubaidullah Mamzdiev.

Acted also run the Yak House (in the Acted compound), a showroom for local craftswomen, selling Pamiri-style *chorapi* socks in traditional black, white and brown hues, plus bags, wall hangings and wool carpets. Yak House trains around 250 local women in Tajik and Pamiri crafts. Prices are marked, as are the names of the craftswomen.

to Osh run every Saturday (417km, 24TJS) via Sary Tash (15TJS). Note that locals sometimes use 'Badakhshani time', which is an hour after Dushanbe, and the same as neighbouring Kyrgyzstan.

AROUND MURGAB

An excellent short but adventurous trip is to hike up the **Gumbezkul Valley** from its junction with the Pshart Valley, 35km northwest of Murgab. The 9km hike takes you from an Acted-assisted yurtstay (see Ecotourism in Murgab, p346) over the 4731m Gumbezkul Pass, down the southern Gumbezkul Valley to another Acted yurtstay, from where a rough jeep road leads 7km down to the Madiyan Valley, 22km from Murgab. The path is easy to follow and there are stunning views in both directions from the pass, though it's a steep scramble on either side. It's a half-day hike from yurt to yurt. A jeep hire to drop you off at the northern yurts and pick you up the next morning on the other side of the pass costs around US$30 through Acted. Acted also offers yurtstays at Kyzyl Jilga and Jar Jilga (*jylga* means valley) further up the Pshart Valley.

For a post-hike soak, the **Madiyan hot springs** (admission 1TJS), 35km from Murgab, are just up the Madiyan Valley from its junction with the southern Gumbezkul Valley – ask for the *issyk chashma* (hot spring in Kyrgyz).

If you have your own transport another route could take you to the scenic **Rang-Kul** area, 45km from Murgab. Five kilometres after you've turned off the Pamir Hwy are some Saka (Scythian) tombs. Further on are the lakes of Shor Kul and Rang-Kul, with fine views of Muztagh Ata over the border in China. Acted has plans to run camel treks in this region.

Another road heads southeast from Murgab up the Aksu Valley to Tokhtamysh and Shaimak. You will probably need special permission to continue along this road as far as **Shaimak**, 126km from Murgab, which has a striking mosque and views of the Little Pamir and the Afghan border zone. This is about as remote as it gets. The road to China via the Qolma Pass (see p352) branches off this road. It's also possible to link up the Rang-Kul and Shaimak roads to make a loop route but you'd need special permission for this.

North of Murgab and southwest of Karakul are several interesting sites, including the petroglyphs and pastures of **Jalang** (134km from Murgab, via Muzkol) in the Kök Ubel Valley. Fifty kilometres further takes you to the geometric Saka tombs of **Kök Jar** (also known as Shorolu), which are thought to have acted as a Stonehenge-like solar calendar, dating as far back as the second millennium BC. Jeep hire from Murgab to here costs around US$80 return. From here, the remote Tanymas Valley offers trekking access to the **Fedchenko Glacier**, one of the world's longest.

Acted can advise on these and other remote trips in the region, including a wildlife-watching trek from the Pshart Valley up to the **Maljuran lakes**, visit to the **Shor Bulak Observatory** (35km from Murgab) or a two-day trek to the forests of **Chat Tokay** and the ruined gold mining settlement of **Sassyk**.

Murgab to Sary Tash

Beyond Murgab, the highway hugs the Chinese border and in places the twin barbed-wire-topped fences run less than 20m from the road. Soon the mountains close in as the road climbs towards the **Ak-Baital** (White Horse) Pass, at 4655m, the highest point of the journey. From here it's a long descent of some 70km to Kara Kul, the highest lake in Central Asia.

At Muzkol a track heads off to Jalang and Kök Jar (p347). Nearby are the remains of a 19th-century Russian tsarist post later used by the Red Army in battles with White Russians and *basmachi* rebels.

Created by a meteor approximately 10 million years ago, **Kara Kul** (3914m) has an eerie, twilight-zone air about it. The Chinese pilgrim Xuan Zang passed by the lake in AD 642, referring to it as the Dragon Lake. Marco Polo also passed by, some six centuries later after transiting the Wakhan, and both Sevn Hedin and Austrian traveller Hustav Krist later camped by the lake. Local Kyrgyz call the deep-blue, lifeless lake Chong Kara Kul (Big Black Lake), compared to Kishi Kara Kul (Lesser Black Lake) along the Karakoram Hwy in China. Although salty, the lake is frozen and covered in snow until the end of May.

The only settlement of any significance here is the lakeside village of **Karakul**, where Acted is planning to establish a reception centre and homestay. Karakul lies right next to the CIS–Chinese border security zone and there's a passport check just before the village. If you plan to camp and walk for more than just overnight, you'd better inform the *aqimat* (administration) and the commander of the CIS border guards.

The border between Tajikistan and Kyrgyzstan is 63km from Karakul, just before the crest of the **Kyzyl-Art Pass** (4282m), but the Kyrgyz border post is a further 20km at **Bor Döbö**. Don't forget to look behind you here for a stunning panorama of the Pamir. Kyrgyzstan is one hour ahead of Tajikistan time (but the same as Murgab time). Kyrgyz border controls can take a long time, especially if you are travelling by truck.

At **Sary Tash**, 23km further, the A372 branches off southwest to the Pamir Alay Valley of Kyrgyzstan (and from there to the Garm Valley of Tajikistan) and the A371 heads northeast to the Kyrgyz-Chinese border post of Irkeshtam (p306). Travellers report it's possible to stay in Sary Tash at the homestay of Endeshe Ashyrov, near the cemetery.

TAJIKISTAN DIRECTORY

ACCOMMODATION

Lacking Uzbekistan's private B&Bs and Kyrgyzstan's network of homestays, Tajikistan has probably the least comfortable accommodation in Central Asia. In fact, outside of the main towns, and particularly in GBAO, there is almost no formal hotel accommodation.

GBAO has a couple of homestay programmes (see p342 and p346) that are well worth supporting. Along the mountain routes, there are plenty of isolated farmsteads that operate as very rough-and-ready guesthouses. What you can expect is some floor space, a pungent sheepskin blanket and

---

POST-SOVIET NAME CHANGES

Few cartographical changes accompanied the transformation of the Tajikistan Soviet Socialist Republic to the independent Republic of Tajikistan. Dushanbe was once Stalinabad but shed that unfashionable name in the 1950s. Only with the demise of Russian communism did Tajikistan's second city, Leninabad, revert to its ancient name of Khojand, and the oblast of which it is the capital became Soghd. Ordjonikdzeabad (25km east of Dushanbe), named for the Georgian who imposed Bolshevism in the Caucasus, reverted to Kofarnikhon. Ura-Tyube became Istaravshan.

Tajik was made the state language in 1989, though Russian was reintroduced as the second state language in 1995. Street signs in Dushanbe now sport the Tajik forms kuchai (street), khiyeboni (avenue) and maydoni (square).

---

probably a hot bowl of *shir chay* – tea with goats' milk, salt and butter. All drivers in the Pamirs know the whereabouts of such places. If you are invited to stay at someone's house a reasonable amount to offer is the equivalent of US$5 per person, excluding food.

Like much of Central Asia, accommodation rates are most often quoted in US dollars and so that is the currency quoted here, though you can almost always pay in either US dollars or somani.

ACTIVITIES

The two main trekking areas are the Fan Mountains and the eastern Pamirs. You really need professionals with you in the latter area as these are demanding, remote routes. Gentler options include walks through the Wakhan Valley. Several routes are described in Frith Maier's *Trekking in Russia and Central Asia*.

For an overview of trekking options check out the excellent trekking section of www.pamirs.org. The most obvious treks outside of the Fans include the following:

Yashil-Kul to Sarez Lake (six to seven days) Via Bachor village, Andaravaj River, 4587m pass, Zarush-Kul, Vikhynch, Langar Valley, Irkhit, dam, Murgab River to Barchadiev.
Javshanguz to Langar (two days) Via Mats Pass.
Karatag Valley (two to three days) To Timur Dara and Payron lakes.

THE AUTHOR'S CHOICE

- House Museum (p343) in Langar, Wakhan Valley
- Yurtstay organised by Acted (p346), the Pamirs
- MSDSP (p342) homestay programme, Badakhshan

Bazar-Dara (four days) Loop trek to archaeological site and petroglyphs, heading in over the Bazar-Dara Pass and out via the Ak-Jylga Pass.

Gumbezkul Valley and Pass (one day).

Mountaineering options are endless in the Pamir, with peak Kuh-i-Garno (formerly Pik Lenin) considered one of the easiest 7000m summits. Peaks Koh-i-Samani (7495m) and Korzhenevskaya (7105m) are also popular and both accessed from Moskvin Glade base camp. See http://mountains.tos.ru/kopylov /pamir.htm for climbing route descriptions, plans and schematic maps of the Pamirs.

BOOKS

Travel through Tajikistan (Fozilov Nurullo ed) has lots of useful background information and is available in Dushanbe.

Around the Roof of the World by Nicholas and Nina Shoumatoff is a mishmash of articles on the Pamirs, concentrating on environment and mountaineering, many refreshingly told from a Russian perspective.

EMBASSIES & CONSULATES
Tajik Embassies in Central Asia

For Tajik embassies in Almaty, Ashgabat, Kabul, Tashkent and Bishkek see the relevant country chapters.

Tajik Embassies & Consulates

Austria (☎ 1-409 82 66 11; www.tajikembassy.org; Universitätes strasse 8/1A, 1090 Vienna) Covering Austria and Switzerland.

Belgium (☎ 02-64 069 33, 53 831 39; tajemb -belgium@skynet.be; 363-365 Ave Louise, Brussels)

China (☎ 10-6532 3039; 5-1-41 Dayuan Diplomatic Compound, 100 600 Beijing)

Germany (☎ 30-347 93 00; www.embassy-tajikistan .de; Otto-Sühr Allee 84, 10585 Berlin)

Iran (☎ 21-229 9584, 280 9249; tajemb-iran@mail.ru; Block 10, 3 Shahid Zinali, 610 Maidan-éNiwaron Tehran)

Pakistan (☎ 51-2294675; House 90, Main Double Rd, F-10/1 Islamabad)

Russia (☎ 095-290 6102, 290 5736; www. tajikistan.ru; Skatertny pereulok 19 Moscow)

Turkey (☎ 312-446 1602; 36 M Ghandi Cad, Gaziosman-pasha, 06700 Ankara)

USA (☎ 202-223 6090; tajik.embassy@verizon.net; 1005 New Hampshire Ave NW, 20037 Washington DC)

Embassies & Consulates in Tajikistan

All of the following embassies are located in Dushanbe (map p325):

Afghanistan (☎ 21 63 94, 21 56 23; Pushkin 34; ⊗ 9am-2pm Mon-Fri)

China (☎ 24 41 83, fax 24 41 22; Rudaki 143)

France (☎ 21 50 37; fax 51 00 82; Varzob 17)

Germany (☎ 21 21 89; deutshebotschaftduschanbe@ tajnet.com; Varzob 16) Represents those EU citizens without an embassy.

Iran (☎ 21 00 72; fax 21 04 54; Tehran 18) Enter on the east side.

Kazakhstan (☎ 21 11 08; fax 21 89 40; Husseinzoda 31-1)

Kyrgyzstan (☎ 21 63 84; kyremb@tajik.net; Student-cheskiy 67)

Pakistan (☎ 21 04 33, 21 19 65; fax 21 17 29; Rudaki 37a; ⊗ 10am-1pm Mon-Fri)

Russia (☎ 21 10 15; www.rusembassy.tajnet.com; Abuali Ibn-Sino 29)

Switzerland (☎ 24 73 16; 20 Zakhario Ruzi (ex-Pavlov))

Turkmenistan (☎ 21 68 84; fax 21 57 49; Chekov 22; ⊗ 9am-noon & 2-4pm Mon-Fri)

UK (☎ 24 22 21; www.britishembassy.gov.uk/tajikistan; Lutfi 43)

USA (☎ 21 03 48, 50 52 54; http://usembassy.state.gov /dushanbe; Zakhario Ruzi 10)

Uzbekistan (☎ 21 21 84; fax 24 90 77; Loik Sherali; ⊗ 8-11am)

FESTIVALS & EVENTS

Eid-e-Qurbon and Ramadan are celebrated in Tajikistan. See p449 for dates.

Ismaili communities in Badakhshan celebrate 24 March as Ruz-i-Nur, the Day of Lights, celebrating the first visit of the Aga Khan in 1995, as well as 11 July, the Day of the Imam.

With its links to a Persian past, Navrus (Nawroz) is the year's biggest festival and you are likely to see song and dance performances, and even *buzkashi* (a traditional pololike game), during this time (the latter most easily seen at Hissar).

HOLIDAYS

1 January New Year's Day.

8 March International Women's Day.

21–23 March Eid e-Nawroz (Persian New Year), called Ba'at in Badakhshan.

1 May International Labour Day.

9 May Victory Day.

27 June Day of National Unity and Accord.

9 September Independence Day.

6 November Constitution Day.

INTERNET ACCESS

Internet cafés are widespread in Dushanbe and Khojand, and cost around US$1.50 to

US$2 per hour (the price will probably fall over time).

INTERNET RESOURCES

Asia Plus (www.asiaplus.tajnet.com) News service focusing on Tajikistan.

Berkeley University (www.lib.berkeley.edu/EART/tajikistan/100k.html) Amazing scanned 1;100,000 topographical Soviet maps covering all of Tajikistan.

Pamirs.org (www.pamirs.org) Excellent travel guide to the Pamirs, with trekking information and details on the MSDSP travel programme.

Tajikistan Airlines (www.tajikistan-airlines.com) Air schedules and office contact details.

Tajikistan Travel (www.geocities.com/travel_tajikistan) Online travel guide, with lots of good information and links.

Tajikistan Update (www.angelfire.com/sd/tajikistanupdate/) Good general site with news, articles and travel information, plus lots of Tajikistan-related links.

Tajnet (http://tajikistan.tajnet.com/english) News and background information.

Travel Tajikistan (www.traveltajikistan.com) Comprehensive travel site but the information is getting dated.

MONEY

Tajikistan introduced the Tajik somani (TJS; divided into 100 dirham) in 2001. The Tajik rubl is no longer legal tender but many people still quote prices in rubl rates. Thus if a banana costs '1000', this actually means 1TJS; '700' means 70 dirham. Somani notes come in one, five, 10, 20, 50, 100 and 500 denominations.

US dollars and euros are easily changed at numerous exchange booths. There is no black market for currency transactions.

This is still largely a cash-only economy. At the time of research it was impossible to cash travellers cheques or use Visa, though this will likely change. You can get cash advances off MasterCard. Both Uzbek sum and Kyrgyz som are accepted in border areas.

Exchange rates, current at the time of research, are listed below:

Country	Unit		Somani
Australia	A$1	=	2.09TJS
euro zone	€1	=	3.45TJS
Kazakhstan	10 T	=	0.20TJS
Kyrgyzstan	10 som	=	0.65TJS
Russian	R10	=	0.99TJS
UK	£1	=	5.13TJS
US	US$1	=	2.82TJS
Uzbekistan	100 sum	=	0.28TJS

POST

Tajikistan's postal service is a bit ropey and it's not uncommon for mail to take a month or more to reach its destination.

A international postcard or letter up to 20g costs 53 dirham to all countries except Russia. A 500g to 1kg package costs around 13TJS; 1kg to 2kg costs around 20TJS. Rates to Russia are half this.

Couriers are the only reliable way to send important documents, though they charge around US$50 for a 1kg package. DHL has offices in **Khojand** (☎ 24 06 17; 122 Firdausi) and **Dushanbe** (☎ 24 47 68; Rudaki 105).

REGISTRATION

Foreigners staying in Tajikistan for longer than three days are supposed to register with OVIR within 72 hours of arriving in Tajikistan. If entering from the north you'll probably have to do this in Khojand. Coming from Osh you may have to register with OVIR in Murgab. You get a stamp in your passport when you register but we've never heard of anyone being checked for this when exiting the country and many travellers simply don't bother.

Registration costs US$15, though travellers in Dushanbe are routinely asked for US$25. The main hotels in Dushanbe will register you for free, which makes their rates a much better deal, for the first night at least.

TELEPHONE

To call internationally (including to other Central Asian republics) dial ☎ 10, followed by the country code, the local code (without the 0) and the number.

Private telephone offices charge a fraction of the government rate. Government rates currently range from 5.5TJS (to Europe) to 7.2TJS (to Australia), with rates to the CIS 1.6TJS and Central Asia 1TJS. Domestic private rates are 10 dirham for a local call, or 22 dirham to GBAO.

Even cheaper are the Internet Phone (IP) calls offered by several Internet cafés in Dushanbe, which cost around 1.6TJS to the US or 0.8TJS to Europe.

In Dushanbe it's possible to buy a SIM card (39TJS) and charge card (39TJS for 50 minutes) for your mobile phone. Contact **Tajiktel** (☎ 21 01 45; Rudaki 57), above the post office.

TRAVEL PERMITS

Tajikistan has many internal checkpoints, particularly in GBAO, and the *militsia* in all towns are keen to check a foreigner's papers, so make sure you have impeccable documents. Carry a photocopy of your passport and visa so that you don't have to dig into your money belt to get your passport when checked frequently.

For information on the GBAO permit, see p338.

There's a highly spurious 'ecological' trekking tax of US$50, plus US$1 per day, or US$100 if over 6000m. Your tour company is supposed to collect this and if you are alone the only place you may encounter this is at Artush in the Fan Mountains.

You may also be asked for some kind of permit to visit Nurek Dam.

A permit from the **Ministry of Civil Defence and Emergency Situations** (☎ 24 30 33) in Dushanbe is currently required to visit Sarez Lake. You will need someone with good contacts in the ministry to get this for you, or try **Sayoh** (☎ 21 90 72, 23 14 01; sayoh@netrt.org; www.sayoh.tojikiston.com; Pushkin 14). The permit (US$20) normally takes 10 days to issue.

VISAS

All Tajik visa problems are dealt with at the **Ministry of Foreign Affairs** (☎ 21 15 08; mfa@tajik.net; Rudaki 42) which is the big pink building on Maydoni Azadi in Dushanbe. As you face the building, you need to take the small door on the far right of the façade where you'll be given a pass to enter the building proper and told where to go.

Tajikistan embassies will only issue tourist visas if you have an LOI, which you need to arrange through a travel agency. The invitation will then be faxed to the embassy designated on your application form; you should also get a copy of the LOI to show the embassy. The visa will specify the validity dates (not exact dates, just a time frame) but not the towns to be visited. Visas issued by Russian embassies are no longer accepted by Tajikistan. It is worth noting that in 2004 several European embassies started to issue tourist visas on a discretionary basis without an LOI, but you may have troubles getting a GBAO permit this way without the invitation.

By the time you've paid for an LOI, the visa, registration and the GBAO permit, red tape will have taken up a significant portion of your daily budget.

There aren't all that many Tajik embassies abroad so it's useful to know that Tajik visas are issued at the airport as long as you have an LOI and have arranged this with the travel agency issuing your LOI. Make sure you bring one photo and a photocopy of your passport. Visas are not issued at land borders.

More often than not there is no Tajik border control when you enter Tajikistan by train but you should try to get a stamp if possible. If you don't get a stamp then have some proof of when you entered the country (ie your ticket or an Uzbekistan exit stamp). Arriving without a visa will open you up to all kinds of headaches.

Leaving Tajikistan for Uzbekistan has become increasingly difficult in recent years as the Uzbeks tighten the screw on the border. Note that you will need a double-entry Uzbek visa to return to Uzbekistan after a visit to Tajikistan, though you can currently get away with just a single-entry Kyrgyz visa. Some companies offering visa invitations are:

Sayoh (☎ 21 90 72, 23 14 01; sayoh@netrt.org; www .sayoh.tojikiston.com, www.tajiktour.tajnet.com; Pushkin 14) Offers visa invitations for US$15-20 and GBAO permits for US$20. Has the monopoly on issuing visa invitations and GBAO permits, so all other tour companies currently arrange their invitations through Sayoh. Communications can be difficult so you'll have to put in the time emailing, chasing up and reconfirming details.

Great Game Travel Company (☎ 01763-220 049; www.greatgametravel.co.uk; 19 Echo Hill Royston, Herts SG8 9BB) Offers visa invitations for US$65 and GBAO permits for US$50, which is over the odds but at least the service is reliable.

Note that you probably won't get stamped out of Tajikistan when entering Kyrgyzstan's Pamir Alay Valley from GBAO so you can, in theory, continue southwest back into Tajikistan near Jirgital and then on to Dushanbe without the need for a double-entry Tajik visa, as long as your visa is still valid. That said, it's always safer to get a double-entry visa. You will of course need a Kyrgyz visa for this route.

Visa Extensions

If you need an extension, Sayoh in Dushanbe is your best bet. If you speak Russian well and want to try it yourself, go to the

Ministry of Foreign Affairs in Dushanbe. Extensions cost US$20 for a week, US$40 for two weeks and US$60 for a month.

Visas for Onward Travel

For contact details of embassies and consulates in Tajikistan, see p349.

Afghanistan A 30-day visa (US$30) requires a letter of introduction from your embassy or a travel agency.

China Won't issue tourist visas without an invitation from the Xinjiang Tourism Department in Ürümqi – travel agencies can arrange this given a week or two.

Pakistan Tourist visas cost US$40 to US$78 depending on nationality, require two photos and a photocopy of your passport, and take a couple of days.

Uzbekistan Visas take three working days.

TRANSPORT IN TAJIKISTAN

GETTING THERE & AWAY

With a limited number of flights and no international land transport, Tajikistan isn't the easiest republic to get to. This section deals with getting to Tajikistan from other Central Asian countries; for details on getting to Tajikistan from outside Central Asia see p461.

Entering Tajikistan

Uzbek–Tajik border crossings are hostage to the current state of political relations between the two republics (which are often poor) and sudden unannounced closure by the Uzbeks.

Air

AIRPORTS & AIRLINES

Regional flight connections to/from Dushanbe include Bishkek (twice each week, US$120), Almaty (four weekly, US$145) and Osh (Alytn Air, Friday, US$95). Ariana has a weekly flight to Kabul (US$100). At the time of research this was the only flight connection between ex-Soviet Central Asia and Afghanistan. There are still no flights between Dushanbe and Tashkent; most people fly to Khojand and then travel overland to the Uzbek capital (five hours). Khojand has weekly flights to Bishkek (US$90) and Moscow.

Turkish Airlines plans to introduce two weekly flights between İstanbul and Dush-

---

DEPARTURE TAX

Dushanbe has US$7 international air departure tax. You may also get hit with a US$5 tax when making a reservation with Tajikistan Airlines.

anbe, starting sometime in 2005. Two new Tajik airlines were set to get off the ground in 2004, one of which should offer several regional Asian routes from Dushanbe to destinations such as Bangkok and Tokyo.

Land

There is no cross-border transport between Tajikistan and it's neighbours, so you have to take a combination of minibuses and taxis to get to and from the borders.

BORDER CROSSINGS
To/From Afghanistan

The main and easiest crossing is at Panj-e-Payon (Nizhniy Panj) in the south; don't confuse this with the town of Pyanj (or Pyanzh) 75km further east. To get to Panj-e-Payon take a minibus to Dusti from Dushanbe or Kurgonteppa (Kurga-Tyube) and then a taxi 27km to the border. You'll pass Tajik and Russian border checks before crossing through customs. From here barges (US$10 per person) cross the Amu-Darya to the Afghan border controls at Shir Khan Bandar. Transport (taxi US$20, two hours) runs from here to Kunduz. A US-funded bridge is currently under construction, to be finished in late 2005.

The crossing at Ishkashim is easiest headed into Afghanistan; headed into Tajikistan you will need to show a Badakhshan permit and that's only available in Dushanbe. From the Afghan village of Ishkashim you can take a microbus to Borak (six hours, US$10) and change to another bound for Faizabad (2½ hours, US$4), or you might find a direct taxi.

There is a bridge to Afghanistan at Khorog but no formal crossing facilities as yet.

To/From China

A road has been completed from Murgab to China over the 4362m Qolma Pass, to join the Karakoram Highway in Xinjiang north of Tashkurgan. The border is due to open in May 2004.

To/From Kyrgyzstan

From the Pamir Alay Valley you can cross into Badakhshan just north of the Kyzyl-Art Pass (south of Sary Tash) and cross into the Garm region between Daraut-Korgan and Jirgital

From Khojand you need to get to Isfana and then take a shared taxi to Batken. If you are headed direct to Osh and have an Uzbek visa it's easiest to just take taxis through the Uzbek Fergana Valley to Kokand, Andijan and the border at Dostyk (see p314)

To/From Russia

There are three trains a week from Dushanbe to Astrakhan in the Russian Volga (via Termiz, Samarkand and Tashkent) but you'll need Turkmen, Uzbek and Kazakh transit visas. The No 23/24 Dushanbe–Moscow train was suspended at the time of research.

To/From Uzbekistan

Most travellers making a beeline between Tashkent and Dushanbe drive to Khojand and then take a domestic flight. It's also possible to drive via Samarkand and Penjikent, or even fly to Termiz and then drive to Dushanbe.

From Dushanbe the main border crossing is 70km west of the capital, near Tursanzade, crossing to Denau. Taxis from Dushanbe to the border cost 20TJS (1½ hours), or take a bus to Tursanzade. Coming from Uzbekistan it's possible to take a daily train at 5am from Termiz to Uzun (four hours) and from there take a taxi 9km to the border.

From Khojand there are two main border crossings; Oybek in the northwest for Tashkent and Kanibadam in the northeast for Kokand and the Fergana Valley. From Tashkent get a bus headed to Bekabad (note that foreigners cannot currently cross at Bekabad) and get off at Oybek (two hours, US$1), near Chanak village. The border post is visible from the road. Once across the border take a taxi to Khojand (US$10) or a taxi to nearby Bustan (5TJS) and then a minibus to Khojand. From Khojand to

Tashkent it's easiest to take a taxi (US$10 to US$15) to the Oybek border post, cross and then take an Uzbek taxi onwards.

For Kokand and the Fergana Valley take a bus to Kanibadam (1.5TJS), passing the massive Kairakum Reservoir en route, and then a minibus (0.4TJS) to the border, cross the border by foot and then take multiple onward minibuses in Uzbekistan from Tamozhnaya to Besh Aryk and then Kokand. You'll save a lot of time by taking a taxi.

In Khojand it's not possible to buy train tickets on Uzbek trains passing through to Tashkent or the Fergana Valley, though it is possible to buy tickets to Uzbek destinations that lie along the twice-weekly Khojand–Dushanbe run, such as Samarkand (26TJS to 32TJS) and Termiz. Note that for Termiz it's actually cheaper to buy a ticket to Dushanbe and get off in Termiz rather than buy a ticket to Termiz itself!

It's possible to cross from Samarkand to Penjikent through a combination of minibuses and taxis.

GETTING AROUND

Tajikistan Airlines boasts domestic flights from Dushanbe throughout the country, but this is limited in reality to Khorog and Khojand. Buying tickets and boarding is a confusing and anarchic process, so budget a few days in case you are bumped from a flight or it is cancelled, especially if you are flying out of Khorog to catch another flight out of Dushanbe.

The bus network is limited to towns around Dushanbe and southern Tajikistan. Outside these areas you'll find shared taxis making the mountain run from Dushanbe to Penjikent and Khojand, as well as shared jeeps and minibuses headed east to Khorog. Beyond this, you'll need a combination of hitching and luck; NGOs are a good source of information on local transportation.

Taxis are available in Khojand and Dushanbe for both local and long-distance runs and are the best option if you can afford them. See p340 for specific details of transport along the Pamir Hwy.

TAJIKISTAN

Afghanistan

CONTENTS

FAST FACTS

- **Area** 650,000 sq km
- **Capital** Kabul
- **Country Code** ☎ +93
- **Ethnic Groups** 40% Pashtun, 25% Tajik, 15% Hazara, 6% Uzbek, 5% Nomad, 3% Turkmen, 1.5% Baluch and 4.5% others
- **Languages** Dari, Pashto
- **Money** afghani (Afg); US$1 = 42.9Afg; €1 = 53.3Afg
- **Phrases in Dari** Hello. *(salām);* Thanks. *(tashakor);* Is it dangerous? *(khatarnāk hast?);* Go with a blessing/travel well. *(borou bekheir)*
- **Population** 28.7 million (2003 estimate)

AFGHANISTAN

Throughout its history, Afghanistan has been a country united against invaders but divided against itself. Its allure, spread by Great Game romantics and travel literature alike, has only been heightened by its inaccessibility over the last 25 years.

The most recent cycle of violence started with the Soviet invasion of 1979, a bloody 'David and Goliath' conflict, with the underdogs eventually besting the superpower. At the crucial moment the world looked away and Afghanistan slipped into civil war. Eventually, the morass came back to haunt the West, in the shape of the medieval Taliban and the ruins of New York's World Trade Centre.

Before all this bloodshed, Afghanistan had formed part of the original overland hippy trail, beguiling its visitors with great mountain ranges, a rich mix of cultures – and the Afghan people themselves, who greeted all with an easy charm and ready hospitality.

Today Afghanistan is taking slow steps towards recovery. Progress isn't easy and the path is strewn with pitfalls. But the Afghans desire peace more than anything and their resilience provides the best key to the country's future.

HIGHLIGHTS

Kabul (p367) has all the hustle of a city emerging from conflict. Its hectic pace contrasts strongly with the crystal mountain air of **Bamiyan** (p378), which is still one of Afghanistan's most beautiful spots. A side trip to the fabulous mineral lakes of **Band-e Amir** (p382) is unmissable. Afghanistan's cultural heart still beats in **Herat** (p384), with its astounding Friday Mosque, and pilgrims flock to the blue domes of the Shrine of Hazrat Ali in **Mazar-e Sharif** (p389). Afghanistan's national game, *buzkashi*, is played throughout the winter, or you might be lucky enough to catch a game at one of the Nawroz celebrations.

ITINERARIES

- **One week** Enjoy the bustle of Kabul, with day trips to the Panjshir Valley and the Salang Pass.
- **Two weeks** Catch a bus to the beautiful Bamiyan Valley, visit the ruined Buddhas, and dip your toes in the lapis lazuli–blue lakes of Band-e Amir.
- **Three weeks** Cross the mountains to Mazar-e Sharif and the Shrine of Hazrat Ali, then make the long bumpy crossing to Herat, before skipping across the Iranian border.

- **One month** From Herat, take the remote central route through the Hindu Kush to the fabled Minaret of Jam, and back in Kabul make a dash for the Khyber Pass into Pakistan.
- **Off the beaten track** Anywhere you turn in Afghanistan could be considered off the beaten track. If the security situation permits it, the mountains could be a trekker's paradise, from the peaks of Badakhshan to the wooded valleys of Nuristan.

SHOULD YOU GO?

Afghanistan's infrastructure is devastated, its culture pillaged and people scattered. Afghan embassies are happy to give out tourist visas, but should you go?

The prime concern is security, and we do not advocate people putting themselves at risk. You alone are responsible for your own safety, so it's absolutely essential that before considering a visit you assess the security situation from reliable sources (p399).

At the same time, one of the most common laments you'll hear in Afghanistan is how the world forgot them after the Soviet War. Foreigners can help Afghans reconnect with the world and allow them to be

AFGHANISTAN

HOW MUCH?

- Snickers bar US$0.40
- 100km minibus ride US$3
- One minute phone call to US/UK US$0.50
- Internet connection (per hour) US$3
- Burka US$8
- Traditional Afghan hat US$2–3

LONELY PLANET INDEX

- Litre of bottled water US$0.40
- Bottle of Heineken beer US$3
- Plate of kebabs US$0.80
- Litre of diesel US$0.28

seen as individuals rather than victims of war. Putting money into the local economy has a tangible and direct benefit.

A visit to Afghanistan, with its many amputees and women begging in burkas, can be a shock. If you want to have a more positive impact, you might want to consider donating time or money to aid agencies working in the country. There are dozens to choose from, and some are better than others, so pick carefully. Ask how long they have been working in Afghanistan, what role the local community plays in their projects and how sustainability is monitored.

Tourism is clearly not a panacea for Afghanistan's problems, but the first tourists returning to Afghanistan have a special responsibility, travelling in a socially conservative country recovering from decades of war.

CLIMATE & WHEN TO GO

Afghanistan has four distinct seasons. There's fine weather in spring (March to May) and the country blooms, but rain and melting snow can make many roads difficult to traverse. Summer (June to August) can be blisteringly hot everywhere except the mountains – Herat, Mazar-e Sharif and Jalalabad all swelter, but Kabul and Bamiyan enjoy pleasant, cool nights. Autumn (September to November) is one of the best times to visit, as there is pleasant,

dry weather and plenty of delicious Afghan fruit. From the end of November, winter sets in, and snow is common across much of the country. Travel in the mountains is particularly tricky at this time.

HISTORY

Afghanistan's history as a country spans little more than two centuries, but in the past it has been part, or the centre, of many great empires. As with much of the region, the rise and fall of political power has been inextricably tied to the rise and fall of religions.

It was in Afghanistan that the ancient religion of Zoroastrianism began in the 6th century BC. Later, Buddhism spread west from India into the country, where it remained strong in the Bamiyan Valley until the 10th century AD. The eastward sweep of Islam reached Afghanistan in the 7th century and the entire country to this day remains Muslim.

Empires & Invaders

Afghanistan has weathered invasions by such historical superstars as Darius of Persia, Alexander the Great, the Kushans, Sassanids, the Arabs, the Mongols, Timur (Tamerlane), Babur (the founder of the Mughals), the British and even the Soviet Red army. Between 1220 and 1223 Jenghiz Khan tore through the country reducing its cities to rubble. When the damage was finally repaired Timur swept through in the early 1380s and reduced the region to rubble again.

In contrast to Jenghiz, Timur's reign ushered in a golden era, when poetry, architecture and miniature painting reached their zenith. Timur's descendants devoted much wealth and energy to the arts from their capital in Herat; building shrines, mosques and medressas from Balkh to Mashhad (in modern-day Iran) before the empire fell apart.

The rise of the Mughals returned Afghanistan to heights of power. Babur made Kabul his capital in 1512, after fleeing Central Asia (see Zahiruddin Babur p195), but as the Mughals extended their power into India, Afghanistan's status declined to the peripheries of empire. In 1747 Ahmad Shah Durrani broke free to found the kingdom of Afghanistan.

TRAVELLING SAFELY IN AFGHANISTAN

Although the war has ended, the problems faced by the Karzai government in imposing control on Afghanistan's regions has allowed political violence to continue in some parts of the country. At the time of going to press, the US, British and Australian governments were all advising against travel to Afghanistan. The situation in Afghanistan had deteriorated slightly from when we researched, and there's every reason to believe that things will remain unpredictable for some time to come. Places that we were able to visit at the time of research may have become unsafe for visitors during the life of this book. It is imperative that you get the most up-to-date safety advice available.

Most importantly, check on security before setting out – the political situation can change quickly and without warning. A list of good news sources can be found on p399. Also see p447.

Security in Kabul is generally good due to the presence of the International Security Assistance Force (ISAF), although sporadic shootings and bomb attacks can still occur. It's hoped that ISAF's expansion will continue and encourage further stability.

The absolute power exercised by Ismail Khan from Herat means that the western provinces are generally stable, as are Bamiyan and the northeastern routes to the Tajik border. The north is more unpredictable, and factional fighting can sometimes occur between the militias of General Dostum and Ata Mohammed, centred on Mazar-e Sharif (see Travelling Safely in Northern Afghanistan p389).

The road from Kabul to the Pakistan border at Torkham is currently open to travellers, although all predominantly Pashtun regions carry a high warning. The southern and eastern third of the country is firmly out of bounds to travellers, with increasing numbers of aid agencies also pulling out of the area. Taliban elements have deliberately targeted Westerners and their local associates.

We recommended that you register with your embassy on arrival in Kabul, although the consular assistance they can offer should you get into difficulty may be limited. If you get off the beaten track in Afghanistan, you're usually a long way from any help.

While in Afghanistan, always check the security situation at your next destination before travelling. Non-Governmental Organisations (NGOs) often have access to in-house or UN security briefings and may be able to provide up-to-date information for the area.

Land Mines

Afghanistan is one of the most heavily mined countries in the world, and land mines and unexploded ordnance (UXOs) claim around 120 victims a month. It's common to see murals on buildings identifying different types of land mine and UXO.

The Afghan NGO Organisation for Mine Clearance & Afghan Rehabilitation (OMAR) produces a series of guidelines for land-mine awareness and safety:

- Stay away from areas such as military bases, battlefields, destroyed houses, unused roads and paths, wells, the banks of irrigation canals and culverts. When travelling by road, stay on the road even when taking a toilet break. If in doubt, turn back – land mines are laid to be invisible.

- Red and white marks indicate an area marked by a mine-action programme. Red marks show mined areas; white marks show that the area has been cleared and is safe.

- Talk to locals and observe local behaviour to find out about safe areas. Locals often develop their own signs for marking mined areas. These include rocks laid across a path, piles of stones or bundles of sticks.

- If you face a mine or UXO, stay calm. Turn back and slowly follow your footsteps to return to a safe area, shouting a warning to those with you. Mark the mined area with a line of rocks and inform the local authorities and/or demining agency.

To learn more about land mines in Afghanistan, visit the OMAR Land Mine Museum in Kabul (p371).

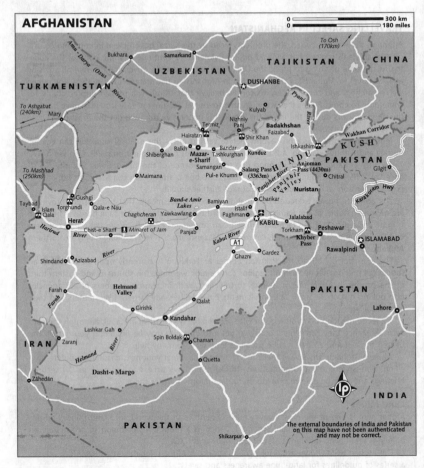

AFGHANISTAN

0 ____ 300 km
0 ____ 180 miles

The external boundaries of India and Pakistan on this map have not been authenticated and may not be correct.

The Afghan Wars

The 19th century was a period of often comic-book confrontation with the British, who were afraid of the effects of unruly neighbours – and Russian designs – on their great Indian colony. Great Game (see p35) tensions and an internally weak Afghan kingdom resulted in a series of unsuccessful and bloody wars being fought on extremely flimsy pretexts.

The first took place between 1839 and 1842. Afghanistan's ruler, Amir Dost Mohammed, had made approaches to the British and Russians in turn. In 1841 the British garrison in Kabul found itself under attack after Alexander 'Bokhara' Burnes was hacked to pieces by an Afghan mob.

The British attempted to retreat to India and were almost totally wiped out – out of 16,000 persons only one man survived. The British reoccupied Kabul and carried out a little razing and burning to show who was boss, but Dost Mohammed still ended up back in power.

Afghanistan agreed to become more or less a protectorate of the British, happily accepting an annual payment to keep things in shape and agreeing to another British resident in Kabul. No sooner had this diplomatic mission been installed in Kabul than all its members were murdered. After being given another bloody nose on the battlefield by the Afghans, the British withdrew again, satisfied to keep control over Afghanistan's external affairs, but to leave the internal matters strictly to the Afghans themselves.

Later treaties between Britain and Russia took much of the heat out of the Great Game, when they agreed that Afghanistan would be a buffer between them, and they formalised its borders. In 1893 the British also drew Afghanistan's eastern boundaries with the so-called Durand Line and neatly partitioned a large number of the Pashtun tribes into imperial India, in what today is Pakistan. This has been a cause of Afghan–Pakistani strife for many years and is the reason that many Afghans refer to the western part of Pakistan as Pashtunistan.

The 20th Century

Britain and Afghanistan fought their last war in 1919, a brief affair that brought Afghanistan's first experience of air war, with the bombing of Kabul and Jalalabad by the Royal Air Force (RAF). Weary from the exertions of WWI, the British sued for peace and Afghanistan finally gained its independence.

From the 1920s onwards the US replaced Britain in worrying about Russian influence. Afghanistan was firmly in the Soviet sphere of influence and the Russian presence was strongly felt. Afghanistan's trade tilted heavily towards the USSR and Soviet aid to Afghanistan far outweighed Western assistance.

AFGHANISTAN IN THE HIPPY ERA by Tony Wheeler

In 1973 Kabul was in danger of becoming a 'fly in, fly out' tourist trap. At least I thought it was when I wrote about it in the very first Lonely Planet guidebook. I'd passed through Afghanistan the previous year, part of the great Asia Overland exodus, following the 'hippy trail' from London to Kathmandu and on down through Southeast Asia to Australia.

Looking back 30 years later it was a magical era and one that still hasn't been adequately recorded, although David Tomory's oral history of the trail, A Season in Heaven, captures the feel of Afghanistan in that era perfectly. Of course the memories have faded (and if you can remember it clearly then you clearly weren't there), but Sigi's in Kabul felt like the epicentre of the Afghan section of the trail. We sat around on carpets, sipping the free mint tea, listening to the music (the rumour was that if Pink Floyd released it in London on Monday the tapes were in Kabul by Friday), occasionally repairing to the courtyard to shift the giant chess pieces around the giant chessboard. Cool.

The Afghans were cool too. 'They were an example to us all, proving that you could be smart, tough, proud, broke, stoned and magnificently dressed, all at once,' according to A Season in Heaven. Our attempts to look magnificently dressed inevitably failed. I'd no sooner arrived in Herat than I wandered off to a tailor to be fitted out with a Europeanised version of an Afghan suit. A German traveller returning from the tailor at the same time donned his suit and reduced the assembled Afghans hanging around the hotel to gibbering wrecks, laughing so hard they had to lie on the floor.

'No man would wear red,' one of them confided.

It was the travellers' responsibility to entertain as well as be entertained and we certainly did our best. You arrived in Afghanistan slightly spooked; by this time you'd heard so many stories about wild men and craziness and there was no question that crossing borders in Asia seemed like something measured on the Richter scale; the number goes up by one but the earthquake jumps by a factor of 10. Leaving Europe for Turkey was the first big culture shock, then it was shock times 10 when you hit Iran and times 100 when you crossed into Afghanistan. And then you relaxed, because it simply wasn't as scary as you'd convinced yourself it would be.

Writer Bruce Chatwin may have rejoiced that he visited Afghanistan 'before the Hippies wrecked it', which they did, he claimed, 'by driving educated Afghans into the arms of the Marxists.' But Chatwin was a snob and never very happy about anybody who hadn't been to Oxford and didn't do their shopping at Sotheby's.

In fact the Afghans look back to the hippy period as a golden age, when everything was peaceful and there was lots of money to be made: somebody was buying the carpets even if we weren't. Still one thing hasn't changed: my favourite hotel in 1972 Kabul was the Mustafa. Perhaps it's the same one that everybody stays in today.

Internally Afghanistan remained precariously unstable. Attempts to encourage Turkish-style progress in the country failed dismally between WWI and WWII. The post-war kingdom ended in 1973 when King Zahir Shah, was overthrown while in Europe by his cousin Daoud. Afghanistan's new ruler was scarcely any more progressive than his cousin had been, but the situation under him was far better than what was to follow.

After the bloody pro-Moscow revolution that took place in 1978, Afghanistan slid into turmoil and confusion. Its procommunist, antireligious government was far out of step with the countryside and soon the population was up in arms. A second revolution brought in a government leaning even more heavily on Soviet support and the country took another lurch towards anarchy.

The Soviet Invasion

Finally in late 1979, the Soviet regime decided that enough was enough. Another 'popular' revolution took place and a Soviet puppet government was installed in Kabul, with what looked like half the Soviet army lined up behind it. Despite an ineffectual storm of Western protests it soon became clear that the Soviets were there to stay. An Islamic *jihad* (holy struggle) was called and seven competing mujaheddin (fundamentalist guerrilla) factions emerged. The So-

viets soon found themselves mired in what later became known as 'Russia's Vietnam'. They had the advantage of short supply lines, no organised protests from home and a divided enemy, but the Afghans were every bit as determined as the Vietcong.

The war ground on through the 1980s. The Afghan resistance remained disorganised and badly trained but to their determination and undoubted bravery they also began to add modern weaponry; the US CIA pumped up to US$700 million a year into the conflict in one of the largest covert operations in history. Soon the Soviet regime held only the cities, but even supplying those became difficult as convoys were ambushed and aircraft brought down with surface-to-air missiles. In the late 1980s Gorbachov's policy of *perestroika* (restructuring) weakened the Russians' will to fight such an intractable opponent and suddenly they wanted out.

The decade-long war had cost the Soviets over 15,000 men, produced a wave of nationalism in the Central Asian republics and contributed significantly to the collapse of the USSR. In Afghanistan 1.5 million Afghans lay dead, and four times that many had fled the country.

Civil War in the 1990s

The Soviet withdrawal in 1989 weakened the Russian-backed government of President Najibullah. In an attempt to end the

---

AHMAD SHAH MASSOUD – 'LION OF THE PANJSHIR'

Arriving in Kabul for the first time, you could be forgiven for confusing the identity of Afghanistan's president. Pictures of Ahmad Shah Massoud are everywhere.

Hailing from the Panjshir Valley north of Kabul, Massoud was the most formidable mujaheddin leader who fought against the Soviets. Largely ignored by the Pakistanis and Americans, he built a guerrilla army that repulsed 10 Russian offensives against the Panjshir, often by evacuating its entire civilian population. His natural charm, fluent French and moderate Islam made him a popular figure with Western journalists.

Following the capture of Kabul in 1992, Burhanuddin Rabbani became president, but Massoud was the real power behind the throne. Although militarily brilliant, Massoud was no politician, and his inability to form alliances with other factions did much to prolong the civil war.

The Taliban reduced Massoud to a rump of power in the northeast. His assassination two days before 11 September 2001 has since cast him permanently in the role of martyr and saviour, his image reproduced everywhere in the style of an Afghan Che Guevara.

Not everyone idolises Massoud. Many Pashtuns resent him as a symbol of Tajik rule, Hazaras for his massacres of their kin, and many for the part he played in reducing Kabul to rubble during the civil war. But, with the Panjshiri faction of the Northern Alliance in firm control in Kabul, Massoud will remain as Afghanistan's number one poster boy for the foreseeable future.

civil war, he proposed a government of national unity, but the mujaheddin refused to participate in any government that included the communist leader. In April 1992 Kabul finally fell to the mujaheddin, who immediately started fighting among themselves for control of the capital. Burhanuddin Rabbani, a founder of the country's Islamic political movement and leader of the Northern Alliance faction, emerged as president.

Rabbani's accession did nothing to stop the fighting. Constant warfare between the Northern Alliance forces and the rival armies of Gulbuddin Hekmatyar and Rashid Dostum devastated the country, doing more damage than the Soviet occupation and reducing much of Kabul to ruins.

The Taliban

The inability of the rivals to unite was brought into sharp relief in the mid-1990s by the spectacular military successes of a group of Islamist fighters called the Taliban. The Taliban (meaning 'religious student') were a group of ethnic Pashtuns backed by Pakistan and educated in Pakistani medressas. The Taliban took Kandahar in 1994 and Herat in 1995, led by the one-eyed Mullah Omar. In September 1996 they entered Kabul unopposed – Rabbani and Hekmatyar had already fled. Najibullah was not so foresighted, and one of the first acts of the new rulers of Kabul was to drag him from the UN compound where he had been sheltering, lynch him and string up the body for all to see.

The Taliban immediately imposed a harsh version of Islam on the population. Women were prevented from working and forced to wear the all-encompassing burka, girls schools were closed, music and television were banned, and children were even forbidden to fly kites. The Taliban's hardline policies later brought more international condemnation following their destruction of the giant statues of the Buddha at Bamiyan in March 2001.

By 1999 the Taliban were in control of 90% of Afghanistan, having pushed back their opponents, led by Ahmad Shah Massoud, to the far northeast of the country. Recognition as Afghanistan's new rulers eluded them. Instead, UN sanctions isolated the regime for its refusal to hand over Osama bin Laden, the multimillionaire Saudi terrorist wanted in connection to the 1998 bombing of US embassies in Kenya and Tanzania.

Bin Laden first came to Afghanistan in the mid-1980s. The fight against the Soviets had attracted Islamic militants from across the world, often called 'Arab-Afghans', who later took their experience to conflicts as far afield as Algeria, Kashmir and Chechnya. Bin Laden stayed behind to form Al-Qaeda (The Base), an organisation dedicated to worldwide violent jihad. As the Taliban's isolation grew, Mullah Omar became increasingly reliant on Al-Qaeda, both financially and militarily. The Arab-Afghans were responsible for some of the worst atrocities against Afghan civilians, particularly the massacres in Bamiyan and Mazar-e Sharif of the minority Hazara population.

On 9 September 2001, two suicide bombers posing as journalists assassinated Massoud, an act heavily suspected to be the work of Al-Qaeda. Two days later, hijackers flew planes into New York's Word Trade Centre and Washington's Pentagon, killing over 3000 people.

The Taliban's days were numbered. Still refusing to hand over Bin Laden, the regime crumbled in the face of the US-led military campaign, Operation Enduring Freedom. The Taliban melted away, with Mullah Omar fleeing to the hills. A major offensive against Al-Qaeda at Tora Bora similarly failed to capture Bin Laden. On 13 November 2001 a resurgent Northern Alliance entered Kabul.

Afghanistan Today

Following the war, a conference in Bonn appointed the Pashtun leader Hamid Karzai as chairman of an interim administration, and an International Security Assistance Force (ISAF) was mandated to provide security in Kabul. A *loya jirga* (grand council) in June 2002 confirmed Karzai as president. The old king, Zahir Shah, returned from exile with the new title of 'Father of the Nation'.

International agencies have returned to Afghanistan in force to help reconstruction. Governments pledged US$5 billion in aid, although it's estimated that Afghanistan will need six times that amount to rebuild.

The restriction of ISAF to Kabul has created problems for security in the country at large. Karzai himself is often described as 'the Mayor of Kabul', whose writ doesn't extend far beyond the capital. The real powers in the government are the Tajiks of the Northern Alliance that controls the major ministries. In the regions, many old mujaheddin players have returned with swathes of the country reverting to warlordism.

The situation is worse in the fractious Pashtun heartland, where the door was left open to Taliban remnants, eager to exploit the traditional Pashtun mistrust of Tajik rule. Guerrilla attacks have fostered a growing anarchy in the south, where the deliberate targeting of Afghan and Western aid workers has greatly hindered reconstruction efforts. In addition, the opium trade (see below) is booming as never before. At the time of going to press, Mullah Omar and Osama bin Laden were still at liberty, and it was unclear whether the proposed elections for Summer 2004 would take place.

Despite these problems, progress is being made in many areas. Large-scale infrastructure projects are restoring the road network, and education is once again a priority for Afghanistan's girls as well as boys. A new constitution was signed in January 2004 and a disarmament programme aims to demobilise fighters and create a national army.

Afghanistan faces huge hurdles before its stability is assured, although continuing international commitment could mean that the country finally has a chance to rebuild after more than 25 years of war.

PEOPLE

Afghanistan's location at the crossroads of Asia has produced a jigsaw of nationalities. The largest ethnic groups are the Pashtun, Tajik and Hazara (p48), but over a dozen smaller nationalities also live within Afghanistan's borders, from the Uzbek Baluchi and the blue-eyed Nuristanis, to the nomadic Kuchi and Kyrgyz. More than two decades of war has enflamed ethnic divisions.

Much of the recent Afghan experience has been framed by population flight. At the time of the Soviet withdrawal, there were 6.2 million Afghan refugees, mainly living in Pakistan and Iran, and comprising over half the world's refugee population.

Afghans are famed for their hospitality. Foreigners experience this everyday, but

HEROIN: AFGHANISTAN'S HARVEST OF WAR

Afghanistan is the world's largest producer of opium, growing over three quarters of the global crop. The Taliban banned opium production, but profited from its trade through their links with Pakistani mafia groups. Poppy fields have been blossoming since Hamid Karzai came to power, with growers and traffickers exploiting the lack of a strong central government.

Opium poppies are grown across Afghanistan, with the major production centres in Nangahar (neighbouring Pakistan's lawless Tribal Areas) and Badakhshan (with its porous border to Tajikistan).

It's big business. A UN report in 2003 estimated Afghanistan's opium earnings at over US$2.5 billion – around half the country's gross domestic product. Growing opium is a lot more profitable than traditional crops – an easy earner for impoverished Afghan farmers.

Opium poppies, harvested in June and July, are processed in labs, and then packed over the mountain passes along established smuggling routes. The trade now supplies Europe with 90% of its heroin, much of which is smuggled through Central Asia.

Not all of the drugs leave the region; addiction in Central Asia has mushroomed to over three times that of Western Europe. A fix of heroin costs under US$2 in Bishkek, and HIV is thought to be spreading uncontrollably through shared needles.

Warlords and criminal gangs control most of the business, although the police and border guards all have fingers in the opium bowl. Drugs have even turned up in Tajik diplomatic bags. Drug money bought arms for Tajikistan's civil war and it's feared that the country could degenerate into a major narco state.

In modern Central Asia, camel caravans of silks and spices have been replaced, it seems, by Ladas packed with opium. The Silk Road has become an opium highway.

war has scarred relations between Afghans, and many of those returning from the West have been shocked at the hardness of the country they left behind. In return, those who stayed and suffered often resent those who fled to exile in the US and Europe.

Afghanistan is an agrarian society, but the majority of returning refugees have headed for the cities in search of employment, rather than returning to their home villages. Rural life also took a huge knock from the drought of the late 1990s, reducing incomes in a country where the average income is already less than US$20 a month, and reducing many families to dependency on outside aid.

Nomadic groups have particularly suffered, losing much of their livestock to the drought, coupled with the effects of land mines on traditional grazing grounds.

Reliable population data are hard to come by in Afghanistan, but by any measure the country is near the bottom of most development indicators.

RELIGION

Afghanistan is majority Sunni Muslim. Around 15% of the population, mainly the Hazaras, follows Shiite Islam, but this is also the case in Badakhshan where much of the population are Ismailis. Sufism has always been an important strand in traditional Afghan Islam, with high importance attached to local saints and shrines.

The experience of war hardened the political role of Islam, and all mujaheddin groups espoused their Islamic ideals against secular communism. With much funding going to the most radical Islamist groupings, this eventually deepened ethnic and social divisions across the country and had a major effect on lengthening the civil war.

The Taliban movement was born in the medressas of Pakistan, particularly those teaching the hardline Deoband doctrine. This was combined with a Pashtun tribal code fractured through the experience of refugee camps, to produce a highly conservative interpretation of Islam – one rejected by most Afghans. The Taliban particularly discriminated against Shiites, whom they viewed as infidels, and forbade them to celebrate the central Shiite festival of Ashura.

Afghanistan has a small Hindu and Sikh population, most notably in Kabul and Ghazni. The once-thriving Jewish community has long fled, leaving a population of precisely two in Kabul.

ARTS

From literature to architecture, Afghanistan has played a major role in influencing the arts of Central Asia, as well as India and Iran, although cultural life has suffered massively through the effects of war.

Music

Afghan music follows the same strands as the rest of Central Asia. After the mujaheddin takeover of Kabul in 1992, many Afghan musicians fled into exile, as the militias often viewed musical performances as un-Islamic; the Taliban ban on music brought events to a close. Traditional music is slowly making a

---

THE LOSS OF AFGHANISTAN'S CULTURAL TREASURES

War has had a devastating effect on Afghanistan's cultural heritage. The Taliban most famously used the destruction of culture as a political tool, in their destruction of the Bamiyan Buddhas, as well as the smashing of artefacts in the Kabul Museum and at numerous Buddhist sites across the country.

The recent conflicts have had wider effects. Soviet bombing razed Herat's old city, and many historic towns were damaged in the fighting, from the artisans village of Istalif, outside Kabul, to the medieval bazaar of Tashkurgan near Mazar-e Sharif. Many important buildings are still at serious risk.

Looting has been a major problem. The Kabul Museum lost around 70% of its collection, including the famous Bagram Ivories. Sites such as old Balkh and the ancient Greek city of Ai-Khanoum, near the Tajik border, continue to be plundered.

The destabilising refugee experience and the disruption of education means that Afghans often have a limited understanding of the richness of their culture. Any attempt to restore Afghanistan's museums and historic sights can only work if its people are reconnected with their cultural heritage.

WOMEN IN AFGHANISTAN *by Lina Abirafeh*

Afghanistan's tumultuous history has left Afghan women with schizophrenic rights and yet, Afghan women continue to persevere despite extraordinary circumstances. Afghan women today look to the heroic women of their past and present (women such as Malalai, heroine of the second Anglo-Afghan war, and modern-day General Khatool, made famous for jumping out of aeroplanes) and are determining the direction their new lives will take.

In the early 1970s, Afghan women's rights were included in the national constitution. Women were seen on the streets of Kabul in skirts, attended university and studied to be doctors. Later that decade, Soviet occupation of the country, coupled with a conservative backlash, stripped women of their hard-won rights. For the next twenty years, as each regime took its turn in Afghanistan, women's rights continued to deteriorate. Both Afghan politics and Afghan women's rights were absent from the international agenda until organisations operating in the country exposed the dire human-rights situation.

During the Taliban, Afghan women's NGOs, such as the **Revolutionary Association of the Women of Afghanistan** (RAWA; www.rawa.org), brought women's rights to the forefront of the international women's agenda. RAWA's story is both romanticised and immortalised through their murdered leader Meena, who founded RAWA in 1977. The organisation grew rapidly, yet always maintained its secret status; RAWA members often did not know each other. It went underground during the Taliban era, but gained prominence through its exposure of women's human rights abuses via its website.

Organisations like RAWA, operating clandestinely in Afghanistan and Pakistan, revealed the horrors inflicted upon women during this regime – including rapes, stonings and confinement. They bravely resisted oppression and persevered through home schools for girls, womens clinics, and a network of underground operations providing support services for women and children.

Women are now starting to share their immeasurable suffering experienced during the conflict. One example is Anisa, a woman of 27 who recently sought support and training from an international organisation in Kabul. Anisa's husband repaired televisions and tape recorders, both of which were banned by the Taliban. During the Taliban regime, he continued to operate the clandestine workshop to support their three children. One day the noise emerging from a broken tape recorder attracted Taliban attention. As a result, he was beaten to death. Two years later, at age 25, Anisa was forced to marry her sister-in-law's 17-year-old son who was still a student. Anisa fell pregnant with her fifth child and still had no income to support them.

Women's abuses under the Taliban were among the most stark violations of human rights in recent history. Prohibitions from working, education, accessing healthcare and enforcement of archaic edicts were widespread and institutionalised by Taliban policies. Other Taliban edicts stated that women must wear the burka and any woman showing her ankles should be whipped. Noisy shoes or shoes with heels were forbidden, as a woman's footsteps were not to be heard by strangers. A woman could not buy from a male shopkeeper and were forbidden to leave their homes unless accompanied by a *mahram* (male relative). A woman's voice was not to be heard by a stranger, so laughing in public was banned. Cosmetics were also banned. Punishments for these so-called crimes included public stonings, mutilations, whippings, amputations and other horrific measures.

Almost two years into the reconstruction process, conditions for women in Afghanistan remain challenging – there's an illiteracy rate of 85%, female-headed households live in dire poverty, and there's an inability to access training and economic opportunities. The full extent of the situation for Afghan women is unknown due to the absence of reliable statistics and data.

Pictures from the 1920s show Queen Soraya unveiled and wearing a sleeveless dress. And yet, in Kabul and some major Afghan cities, one can see a negligible decrease in burkas on the streets. But, the lack of the burka is not synonymous with progress in women's rights and should not be the only barometer of social change. Many women in Afghanistan continue to wear the burka for reasons of culture and security. Some women have always worn it and assert that they will continue to do so, regardless of increases in freedom of movement. Yet many women are still afraid, and many have been driven to levels of such poverty that they are more comfortable covered. The reality is that Afghan women long for choice – the choice to wear a veil or a burka, or no covering at all. The issue extends well beyond the actual fabric of the burka. It is more important to address the psychological burka, and its progeny – fear and poverty. Doing so will give Afghan women the opportunity to make their own decisions regarding such issues. The majority of Afghan women are more concerned with access to economic opportunities and education for themselves and their children. Afghanistan's former king Zahir Shah has said, 'Any country that covers the eyes of its women makes itself blind'.

Afghan women's rights are safeguarded in the new constitution that was approved by the Afghan Constitutional Loya Jirga in January 2004. This document secures women's rights and ensures equality before the law. And yet many Afghan women fear that these words may not reach the right ears. Human-rights and women's-rights organisations have begun to identify loopholes in the document where rights may be obstructed.

Afghanistan is also a party to the Convention on the Elimination of all Forms of Discrimination Against Women (Cedaw), signed without reservation in March 2003. Afghan women are using both Cedaw and the new constitution to guarantee their rights, but the battle is just beginning.

Despite improvements (largely confined to Kabul), women's human rights are still being violated across Afghanistan. Rates of self-immolation and violence against women at home and on the street have increased in the so-called post-conflict period. Women are still struggling to be heard and trying to find alternatives to living in despair. Only a fraction of women – and only those in Afghanistan's cities – are accessing economic opportunities and are able to support themselves and their families.

Many groups, local and international, are actively working for Afghan women, and are leading the way in providing support and articulating Afghan women's needs. These organisations strive to offer women the tools with which they can achieve self-sufficiency, a choice and a voice.

Afghan women are now able to share their stories. When asked what she would like the rest of the world to know, one Afghan woman said, 'tell them that Afghan women are very strong and they will do anything for the future of their country and their children.'

For more information on women in Afghanistan, try the following books and website:

- The Sewing Circles of Herat by Christina Lamb
- Afghanistan, Where God Only Comes to Weep by Siba Shakib
- The Storyteller's Daughter by Saira Shah
- Three Women of Herat by Veronica Doubleday
- Veiled Courage: Inside the Afghan Women's Resistance by Cheryl Benard
- With All Our Strength: The Revolutionary Association of the Women of Afghanistan by Anne E Brodsky
- Women for Afghan Women: Shattering Myths and Claiming the Future by Sunita Mehta (editor)
- Veiled Threat: The Hidden Power of the Women of Afghanistan by Sally Armstrong
- Unveiled: Voices of Women in Afghanistan by Harriet Logan
- We Want To Live As Humans (Human Rights Watch Report, December 2002; www.hrw.org/reports/2002/afghnwmn1202/)

For more information on women in Afghanistan and what you can do to support them visit the Kabul office of **Women for Women International** (☎ 070 224973; www.womenforwomen.org; House 548, St 5, Qali Fatullah, Kabul).

return to the country, although Hindi pop is popular with many Afghans.

Poetry

Poetry is vital to Afghan culture and many of the greatest Persian poets, such as Jami and Rumi, were Afghan, although Iran's national epic, the *Shah Nama* by Firdausi, was actually composed for the Ghaznavid sultans in the 10th century.

Around the same time, Balkh produced the first female Persian poet, Lady Rabi'a Balkhi. Punished for her love of a slave, she was bricked up to die in a prison by her brother. Her tomb is still visited by young women and her name is popularly given to girls schools and hospitals.

Pashtun poets are similarly revered, and the 17th-century warrior-poet Khushal Khan Khattak is often held up as a national ideal. His famous couplet sums up the martial spirit of his people: The Pashtun name spells honour and glory/Without that what is the Afghan story?

Architecture

Afghan building has harnessed the vitality of the Central Asian steppe to the refinement of Persian culture to produce some masterpieces of world architecture (see also p60). Afghanistan's historical buildings suffered massively in more than two decades of fighting, but the war left one indelible architectural legacy – the metal shipping container. These are a refuse of a trade agreement with Pakistan, whereby Afghanistan can import goods through Karachi without paying duty. The containers can be seen everywhere across the country, pressed into service as shops, workshops and temporary accommodation, often covered with mud brick to insulate against the heat and cold. During fighting containers were even used as prisons by militia.

Cinema

Afghanistan's film archive narrowly escaped destruction by the Taliban by being bricked up behind false walls. A small cinema industry is being encouraged with the help of Iranian film makers such as Mohsen Makhmalbaf (director of *Kandahar*). Two recent Afghan films been well received at international film festivals: Sidiq Barmak's *Osama*, and *Little Game* by Timor Shah.

Mobile cinemas have been set up for domestic audiences in rural areas, showing films produced for both entertainment and educational purposes.

ENVIRONMENT

Afghanistan is a country of high mountains and sweeping steppes – a geography that has played a key part in its history. The flat north and west open out to the grass plains of Central Asia and the Iranian plateau – well-trodden invasion routes throughout the centuries. The massive spine of the Hindu Kush that bisects Afghanistan has given refuge to its people, and made the country hard to conquer completely.

War has left a high environmental toll on Afghanistan. The population upheavals caused by refugee flight have strained the land immensely, particularly in the pollution of water supplies and deforestation for fire wood and shelter. The country as a whole suffered terribly as the result of a huge drought that lasted for much of the Taliban's reign, and the water table is still recovering.

Deforestation continues in the guise of illegal logging in the wooded provinces of Kunar and Paktia in the east. Mujaheddin groups, and now local warlords, have greatly profited by smuggling timber across the border into Pakistan. Massive erosion has been the result.

Afghanistan's wildlife continues to suffer. Rare falcons are caught and sold to Gulf Arabs for hunting. In Badakhshan there has been an increase in snow leopard poaching in recent years, driven by the return of international workers, some of who purchase furs as souvenirs. Although illegal, it is still possible to find snow leopard pelts for sale in Kabul.

FOOD & DRINK
Staples & Specialties

Food in Afghanistan is common with much of Central Asia (see p73). You'll certainly eat your share of kebabs and nan.

Rice is the other staple, served as *pulao* (pilaf of rice and fried vegetables) and eaten with the fingers. Quality varies immensely, and there are usually several hunks of meat buried under the mound of rice. *Pulao* is served on a large communal plate and everyone digs in with their right hand. *Qabli pulao* is the national dish; the rice is topped with almonds, raisins and grated carrot. Side dishes of salad or yogurt are common.

In the north *mantu* (steamed meat dumplings) are served covered in a yogurt sauce. For vegetarians, *ashak* is similar but stuffed with leeks.

Drinks

The national drink is green tea *(chai sabz)*, drunk unsweetened. In Herat, black tea *(chai siah)* is preferred, often sucked through a sugar cube in a similar manner to Iran.

Bottled water is available everywhere, as are an array of soft drinks from Pakistan and Iran. It's often possible to find glass bottles of Coca Cola labelled 'bottled in Afghanistan'. They generally taste foul, and are decidedly not 'the real thing'.

Fruit juices are very popular, particularly lemon *(limu)* and banana *(kela)*.

It is illegal for Afghans to drink alcohol, but it is possible to buy it in some shops (and in a couple of bars) in Kabul. If you do fancy a tipple, be discreet and never drink in public.

KABUL

pop 2.5 million (2003 estimate) / elevation 1827m
Kabul is a city on the move. Once Afghanistan's cosmopolitan centre, and a stop on the old hippy trail to India, the city was ruined in the civil war. The events of 11 September 2001 brought the gaze of the world back onto the city, and there has since been a huge influx of international workers and business people, all helping with Afghanistan's reconstruction (or hoping to make money from it). Security is provided by ISAF and if you stand on any main street for a few minutes you'll see their armoured patrols pass by.

The centre of Kabul is alive with new restaurants, busy bazaars and an air thick with the sound of mobile phones. It's easy to get a distorted picture; to put all this into context you have to visit the west and south of the city, where whole districts were razed as the mujaheddin factions fought for control.

Kabul has been the main focus for refugee return, doubling the city's population and straining its creaking infrastructure.

At the same time, some Kabulis grumble about the international presence in the city, frustrated about the often slow pace of reconstruction.

Most people start a trip to Afghanistan in Kabul, and the sense of being in a city on the cusp of change gives any visit an exciting edge.

HISTORY

Known in antiquity as Kabura, Kabul grew under the rule of the Greeks, Kushans, Hindus, Arabs and Timurids.

Babur, the first Mughal, rhapsodised about Kabul's beauty. Even as his ambition drove him eastward to India, he dreamed of the city writing, 'I have a longing beyond expression to return to Kabul. How can its delights ever be erased from my heart?' His body was returned to Kabul for burial.

Kabul's fortunes waned, eventually being captured by Ahmad Shah Durrani, whose meteoric rise to power from Kandahar forged the modern Afghan kingdom. His son, Timur Shah, moved the Afghan capital to Kabul in 1772.

Fifty years later, Kabul became the centre of Russian and British rivalry. The British tried to install a puppet ruler in 1839, but their resident was hacked to pieces by a mob, and the Kabul garrison massacred as it tried to retreat from the city. An army of retribution returned to plunder the city, but the Afghans stayed in power.

The British forgot their lesson, and tried again in 1878. There was another massacre, another army sent to Kabul in revenge, but the Afghans wouldn't stay beaten.

At the start of the 20th century King Amanullah led an ambitious modernising programme. The model quarter of Darulaman was built in the southwest of the city, with tree-lined avenues and a European-style palace.

Kabul boomed for the next 40 years. Cold War competition between the USA and Soviet Union provided massive aid, and the capital became a cosmopolitan city.

Things started to change following the Soviet occupation in 1979. On the surface Kabul continued to prosper. Women held nearly 40% of all governmental jobs and the city's shops were well stocked. The population largely sat out the war that raged across the country.

AFGHANISTAN

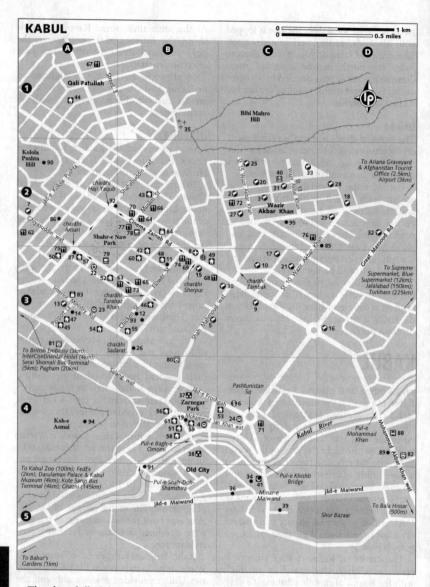

KABUL

To Ariana Graveyard & Afghanistan Tourist Office (2.5km); Airport (3km)

To Supreme Supermarket, Blue Supermarket (12km); Jalalabad (150km); Torkham (225km)

To British Embassy (3km); InterContinental Hotel (4km); Serai Shomali Bus Terminal (5km); Pagman (20km)

To Kabul Zoo (100m); FedEx (2km); Darulaman Palace & Kabul Museum (4km); Kote Sangi Bus Terminal (4km); Ghazni (145km)

To Babur's Gardens (1km)

To Bala Hissar (500m)

The downhill slide really started with the fall of Kabul in 1992, as the victorious mujaheddin fell into a murderous battle for control of the city.

The Northern Alliance faction nominally held Afghanistan's presidency and controlled most of Kabul. The Islamist Gulbuddin Hekmatyar had other ideas, and launched repeated attacks. In a bid to stop the fighting, Hekmatyar was made prime minister, but he still preferred to remain outside Kabul and shell the city instead. Also jostling for power were General Dostum's Uzbeks and the Hazara militia. At different times, all fought with or against each other, but this meant little to Kabul's suffering population.

INFORMATION		
Afghan Travel Centre		(see 54)
Afghan.com	1	B3
Belgian Embassy	2	C2
Canadian Embassy	3	C2
Central Post Office	4	B4
CHA Net Cafe		(see 84)
Chinese Embassy	5	B3
Da Afghanistan Bank	6	C4
DHL		(see 55)
Dutch Embassy	7	A2
Emergency Hospital	8	B3
French Embassy	9	C3
German Embassy	10	B3
Global Travel Centre	11	B3
Habibi Bookstore	12	B3
Indian Embassy	13	A3
Interior Central Passport Department	14	A3
Iranian Embassy	15	A3
Italian Embassy	16	D3
Japanese Embassy	17	C3
Kazakh Embassy	18	D2
Ministry of Information and Culture	19	B4
Mustafa Hotel Cafe		(see 55)
Norwegian Embassy	20	C2
Pakistani Embassy	21	C3
Park Net Cafe		(see 57)
Police	22	A3
Post Office	23	A3
Post Office	24	C4
Russian Embassy	25	C2
Shah M Book Co	26	B3
Swedish Embassy	27	C2
Swiss Embassy	28	D2
Tajik Embassy	29	D2
Turkish Embassy	30	C3
Turkmen Embassy	31	C2
US Embassy	32	D2
Uzbek Embassy	33	C2

SIGHTS & ACTIVITIES		(pp371-2)
Carpet Bazaar	34	C5
European Cemetery	35	B1

Ka Faroshi	36	C5
Mausoleum of Abdur Rahman Khan	37	B4
Mausoleum of Timur Shah	38	B4
Musical Instrument Makers	39	C5
OMAR Landmine Museum	40	C2
Pul-e Khishti Mosque	41	C5

SLEEPING	🏠	(pp372-4)
Assa 1	42	B3
Assa 2	43	B2
B's Place	44	A1
Chez Ana	45	A3
Friend Guesthouse	46	B3
Gandamark Lodge	47	A3
Global Guesthouse	48	B3
Heritage Guesthouse	49	B3
Insaf Hotel	50	A3
Jamil Hotel	51	B4
Kabul International Hotel	52	A3
Kabul Serena Hotel	53	C4
Karwansara	54	A3
Mustafa Hotel	55	B3
Park Hotel	56	B4
Park Residence	57	A3
Pashtoonistan Hotel	58	B4
Spinzar Hotel	59	B4
Sunshine Guesthouse	60	B3
Zarnigar Hotel	61	B4

EATING	🍴	(pp374-5)
Anaar	62	A2
Blue Pearl		(see 71)
Chelsea Supermarket	63	B3
Chez Ana		(see 45)
Chief Burger	64	B2
Chinese Restaurant	65	B3
Delhi Darbar	66	B2
Deutscher Hof	67	A1
Gandamak Lodge		(see 47)
Golden Lotus	68	B3
Great Wall	69	B3
Herat	70	B2
Karwansara		(see 54)

Khyber Restaurant	71	C4
Lai Thai	72	C2
Marco Polo	73	B3
Mustafa Hotel		(see 55)
New York	74	B3
Popolano	75	A3
Shandiz	76	C2
Spinzar Hotel		(see 59)
Super Ice Cream/Pizza Milano	77	B3
Zarnigar Hotel		(see 61)

DRINKING	🍺	(p375)
Deutscher Hof		(see 67)
Juice Bars	78	B3
Juice Bars	79	A3
Mustafa Hotel		(see 55)

ENTERTAINMENT	🎭	(p375)
Aina Media Centre	80	B4
Foundation for Culture & Civil Society	81	A3
Ghazi Stadium	82	D4

SHOPPING	🛍	(pp375-6)
Afghan Handicrafts Centre	83	A3
CHA Gallery of Fine Arts & Traditional Afghan Arts	84	B2

TRANSPORT		(pp376-7)
Ariana Afghan Airlines	85	D2
Azerbaijan Airlines	86	A2
LTU International Airways	87	A3
Marco Polo Airways		(see 55)
Pul-e Mahmoud Khan Bus Terminal	88	D4

OTHER		
Id Gah Mosque	89	D4
Kolola Pushta Fort	90	A2
Shah-Doh-Shamshira Mosque	91	B5
Sherpur Mosque	92	A2
TNT	93	B3
TV Tower	94	A4
Wazir Akbar Khan Mosque	95	C2

Kabul was devastated. The west and south of the city were flattened, and a flood of refugees left the city. Around 50,000 civilians lost their lives between 1992 and 1996.

The Taliban entered the fray, with their capture of Kabul in September 1996. The illiterate Taliban held a strong distrust of Kabul and its educated Persian-speaking people, and ruled the city with a harsh fist.

The Taliban's Vice and Virtue Police quickly squeezed the life out of Kabul, beating women for wearing high heels under their burkas, and imprisoning men whose beards were too short. Mullah Omar only visited Kabul once, and Afghanistan's capital effectively returned to Kandahar.

Under American bombardment, the Taliban fled Kabul in November 2001. The Northern Alliance walked back into power, this time with Hamid Karzai as their figurehead. International troops still patrol Kabul's streets, much to the relief of a population fearful of a return to the anarchy of the 1990s. International money has poured in and the long and slow process of reconstruction has begun.

ORIENTATION

Kabul sits on a plain ringed by the mountains of the Hindu Kush. Little remains of Kabul's old city. The mountains of Koh-e Sher Darwaza run south along the city, topped by the old city walls, and lead eastwards to the royal citadel of Bala Hissar.

The Kabul River divides the city. To the north is the prosperous Shahr-e Naw area, centred on its eponymous park and Pashtunistan Square. East of this is Wazir Akbar Khan, home to many embassies.

The bustle of the city increases the closer you get to the river. Kabul's commercial heart beats around pul-e Khishti bridge,

KABUL'S STREET NAMES

Many Kabulis don't know the names of streets, and many addresses are given only relative to a major road or landmark. Crossroads (charāhi) are commonly used as landmarks, and it's useful to know the names of the major junctions when asking directions or catching a taxi.

AFGHANISTAN

KABUL MUST-SEES

Chicken Street Pick up anything from a carpet to a lapis lazuli necklace at Kabul's premier shopping address (p372).

Babur's Gardens Escape from Kabul's bustle at the last resting place of the Mughal ruler, which has been beautifully restored (p371).

OMAR Land Mine Museum Learn more about the killers still plaguing the country, and what's being done to remove them (p372).

West Kabul See the devastated Darulaman Palace and Kabul Museum to get a true picture of the horrors of civil war (p371).

Old City Visit the bird markets and musical-instrument makers for a taste of traditional Afghan life (p371).

and jād-e Maiwand, the most traditional areas of the city. Swathes of jād-e Maiwand were flattened during the civil war, making it a popular subject for photojournalists.

Also levelled in war was the model district of Darulaman, in west Kabul, home of the former palace and the Kabul Museum.

Kabul International Airport sits at the northeast of the city at the end of Great Massoud (formerly Airport) Rd. An approach by air can be shocking to the first-time visitor, as the edges of the runway are littered with plane wreckage.

INFORMATION
Bookshops
Habibi Bookstore (Chicken St) Stocks a wide range of Afghan-related titles.

Shah M Book Co (charāhi Sadarat) Also has a branch at the InterContinental Hotel. Excellent selection of books on the region.

Emergency
See also Medical Services, p370.

Fire brigade (☎ 020 2300304)

Police (☎ 020 118; Shahr-e Naw Park)

Internet Access
Kabul has taken quickly to the idea of the Internet, and Internet cafés have been popping up across the city. Expect to pay around 150Afg per hour. Good options:

Afghan.com (charāhi Sherpur) Opposite the Iranian Embassy.

CHA Net Cafe (Cinema Zainab Rd)

Mustafa Hotel Cafe (charāhi Sadarat)

Park Net Cafe (charāhi Ansari)

Media
The *Kabul Weekly* and the *Kabul Times* are both sold by street kids. Habibi Bookstore often stocks *Time* and *Newsweek*.

Medical Services
Hospitals in Kabul are overstretched and often lacking in facilities. Embassies maintain lists of recommended medical contacts (for embassy details see p398). The **Emergency Hospital** (☎ 020 2290004; charāhi Sherpur) is recommended in a crisis.

There are well-stocked pharmacies on almost every street in Kabul.

Money
The head branch of **Da Afghanistan Bank** (jād-e Froshgah) has limited currency-exchange facilities, but will change travellers cheques at US$10 per transaction. For cash, it's easier to head for the moneychangers near pul-e Khishti, who always have the most up-to-date rates.

Post
Kabul's **central post office** (Mohammad Jan Khan wat; ⏰ 8am-3pm) is the best place for stamps and reliability. There are also branches on Interior Ministry Rd and Pashtunistan Sq.

All the major international couriers have offices in Kabul: **DHL** (☎ 070 276362; charāhi Sadarat, Mustafa Hotel; ⏰ 8am-6pm), **FedEx** (☎ 020 2500525; Khai St, Karte Se; ⏰ 8am-6.30pm, closed Fri) and **TNT** (☎ 020 2200266; charāhi Turabaz Khan; ⏰ 8am-5pm, closed Fri).

Telephone
Kabul's phones are in a state of confusion (see p401). In addition to a decrepit five-digit analogue network and the new mobile-phone networks, Kabul had some digital fixed lines with seven numbers installed in 2000. Both can usually only call other local numbers.

It's possible to place calls from any of Kabul's post offices. The branch on Pashtunistan Sq has a separate **telecommunications department** (⏰ 8am-7pm).

Tourist Information
The head office of the **Afghan Tourist Organisation** (ATO; ☎ 020 2300338; Great Massoud Rd) is opposite the Ariana Graveyard. ATO also has an office at the airport and at the InterContinental Hotel. It can arrange

drivers and translators. The head office also provides the letter required for tourist-visa extensions (see p401).

Travel Agencies

Afghan Travel Centre (☎ 070 291794; abdul@travelhorizons.co.uk; inside Karwansara Guesthouse, Interior Ministry Rd) A branch of the London-based travel agency; can arrange Ariana Afghan Airlines and onward flights. Accepts credit cards.

Global Travel Centre (☎ 079 301517; Flower St) Sells Ariana, Pakistan International Airlines (PIA), Azerbaijan Airlines and connecting flights with British Airways and Lufthansa. Accepts credit cards.

DANGERS & ANNOYANCES

The presence of ISAF troops mean that in general Kabul is a safe and stable city, although random violent incidents can occur. The UN and many embassies often issue security alerts, restricting the movement of personnel in areas deemed at risk. These can apply to places frequented by Westerners, including Chicken St and the Mustafa Hotel.

Kabul has a much lower crime risk than other Central Asian capitals. There are very few streetlights, so broken pavements present a genuine accident risk if walking after dark.

SIGHTS

Babur's Gardens

This formal **park** (sarakh-e Chihilsotun; admission 2Afg; ☼ 7am-sunset) was created in the 16th century by the first Mughal emperor, Babur. The walled gardens climb a series of terraces to give views over west Kabul. Babur is buried at the top of the garden. Below Babur's grave is a fine white marble mosque built by Shah Jahan (who built the Taj Mahal) and recently restored by the Aga Khan Foundation.

Gardeners have worked hard to replant the trees and rose bushes lost to neglect and war, resulting in one of the most peaceful and beautiful spots in Kabul. A pavilion in the middle of the gardens serves food and drinks.

Darulaman Palace

The old royal palace sits on a rise at the end of a ceremonial avenue in west Kabul. Built by Amanullah in the 1920s in grand European style, the palace is now little more than a shell. West Kabul saw the worst of the fighting in the 1990s, and Darulaman was on the front lines; the whole district is a shocking wasteland of levelled buildings. Don't explore the palace too closely as there are still UXOs.

Kabul Museum

Opposite Darulaman Palace, Kabul Museum was once one of the greatest museums in Asia, its exhibits testifying to Afghanistan's location as the crossroads of the continent. It now stands amid ruins, repeatedly plundered by the mujaheddin during the civil war. The Taliban smashed much of what remained in 2001. It is thought that less than a third of the original collection remains.

Restoration is now underway and the museum plans to reopen in 2004.

Ariana Graveyard

The main remnants of the old Ariana fleet are piled high on the road from the airport. Smashed fuselages and undercarriages lie twisted among airport buses. This surreal junk pile is largely the result of Hekmatyar's ferocious bombardment of Kabul in 1992.

European Cemetery

This **cemetery** (Kabre Ghora; Shahabuddin wat; donation requested; ☼ 7am-4pm) was established to bury the British killed in the second Anglo-Afghan war in the 1880s. A few of the headstones have been mounted in the right-hand wall, with more recent memorials added by the British, German and Italian ISAF contingents.

The cemetery's most famous resident is Aurel Stein, acclaimed Silk Road archaeologist, who died in Kabul in 1943. His gravestone can be seen.

Old City

Virtually none of old Kabul survives, but it is still possible to get a taste of the traditional life of the city. **Pul-e Khishti Mosque** is a good place to start, then follow the bustle to the crossroads at **Minar-e Maiwand** and the old commercial thoroughfare of **jād-e Maiwand.**

Jād-e Maiwand was razed during the fighting over Kabul in the mid-1990s, and its eastern end is a horror of devastation.

Off jād-e Maiwand is **Ka Faroshi**, the old bird market. There has been a bazaar here for around 300 years. Most popular are *kowk* (partridges; used for fighting), as well as pigeons and songbirds, which are sold in beautiful handmade wooden cages.

Close by is the **Carpet Bazaar**, a good place to hunt for rugs. The lane leads up to the **Mausoleum of Timur Shah**. Built in the late 18th century in Mughal style, the mausoleum is closed to visitors.

South of Minar-e Maiwand is **Shor Bazaar**. If you continue for 150m, the road turns left into a street that has several shops making traditional musical instruments such as the *rebab* (lute) and harmonium.

Bala Hissar

The old seat of royal power, a fortress has stood here since the 5th century AD. Bala Hissar was levelled by the British in 1879, but rebuilt by Abdur Rahman Khan. Kabul's old walls snake out from its towers along the mountain ridges.

Bala Hissar is used by the army and closed to visitors, but good views of the walls and towers are had from the huge cemetery of Shohada-ye Salehin on its southern side. The area around Bala Hissar is reportedly mined.

Mausoleum of Abdur Rahman Khan

The tomb of the 'Iron Amir' sits in Zarnegar Park. Originally a palace, the building has a bulbous red dome atop a whitewashed drum, and fussy decorative minarets. The park is surrounded by market traders but can be a good place to escape from the bustle and traffic. The mausoleum itself is closed to visitors.

Chicken Street

Since the days of the hippy trail, Chicken Street has been a focus for Afghanistan's tourists. All kinds of handicrafts are available here, from jewellery to carpets. The eastern end turns into Flower Street, where you'll often see cars being decorated with bouquets and ribbons for wedding celebrations.

Kabul Zoo

The **zoo** (Deh Mazang Circle; admission 5Afg; ✆ 7am-sunset) is popular with Kabulis in need of recreation, but animal lovers might find it a little depressing. For years it was the home to Marjan the lion, who survived civil war and blinding by the Taliban, only to expire

soon after Kabul's liberation. He has since been replaced by a pair of lions, presented to the zoo by China, who share the zoo with several bears, wolves, monkeys and eagles – and lots of rabbits.

OMAR Land Mine Museum

This small **museum** (✆ 020 2100833; omarintl@ceretechs.com; St 13, Wazir Akbar Khan; ✆ by appointment), run by the Organisation for Mine Clearance & Afghan Rehabilitation, holds nearly 60 types of mine found in Afghanistan, and has information about demining and safety. Most sobering are the Russian 'butterfly' mines often picked up by children, mistaking them for plastic toys.

The museum is not open to drop-in visitors as it is often used for training deminers, so it's essential to call in advance to arrange a tour.

SLEEPING

Most accommodation in Kabul is based in Shahr-e Naw, close to Chicken St and Shahr-e Naw Park, with the budget options found mainly between Zarnegar Park and the Kabul River. Guesthouses extend into Wazir Akbar Khan, jostling for space alongside the embassies. For those staying in Kabul long-term, room rates are usually negotiable. Payment for accommodation is almost always in US dollars.

Budget

Jamil Hotel (✆ 079 312128; Mohammad Jan Khan wat; s/d US$10/20) Probably Kabul's best budget option. Rooms are en suite, and although there is sometimes a problem with the water, the management will keep you supplied with buckets of water. The hotel isn't brilliantly signed – it's next to Al-Miraj Electronics.

Zarnigar Hotel (✆ 020 2100980; zarnigar_afghanistan@hotmail.com; Mohammad Jan Khan wat; s/d US$10/15) A few doors down from the Jamil, this is also a good choice. The rooms are simple but clean and have shared bathrooms. The hotel has a decent restaurant overlooking the street; a good place to watch the world go past over a plate of *pulao*.

Pashtoonistan Hotel (pul-e Bagh-e Omomi; r US$10) Signed only in Dari, this place has a flat rate for its rooms, each containing between three and five beds. The shared bathroom is pretty basic, but the hotel is a decent rock-bottom choice if you're sharing. The hotel has no phone.

Mid-Range

HOTELS

Spinzar Hotel (☎ 020 22891; Pul-e Bagh-e Omomi; s/d US$20/40, with shower US$40/50) Usually packed with Afghan businessmen. Rooms and shared bathrooms alike are drab but clean. The tall green hotel has good views, particularly from the 4th-floor restaurant.

Mustafa Hotel (☎ 070 235689; www.mustafahotel .com; charāhi Sadarat; s/d from US$35/50; ▢) Very popular, particularly with journalists. Some rooms are quite basic, but water in the shared bathrooms is always hot. There are a few rooms priced at US$10 per night. The hotel has one of Kabul's only bars (a good place to meet people), an Italian restaurant and a DHL office.

Park Residence (☎ 070 280576; park_residence@ hotmail.com; charāhi Ansari; s/d US$55/80; ▢) Modern rooms are en suite, with a fridge and satellite TV; there's also a small bookshop. Excellent value but often booked up.

Kabul International Hotel (☎ 020 2201124; kabulinternationalhotel@hotmail.com; Shahr-e Naw Park; r US$60) Rooms are bright and comfortable and the shared bathrooms are clean. There's a flat price for one or two beds, so good value if you're sharing. A decent restaurant on the ground floor offers a mix of Indian, Chinese and Afghan food.

Insaf Hotel (☎ 070 286384; charāhi Ansari; r US$50) All rooms are en suite and recently redecorated. There's one price for one or two beds. Good and clean, next to Popolano restaurant.

GUESTHOUSES

Guesthouses are popular with long-term residents. Unless noted, all prices are for the room, irrespective of single or double occupancy.

Chez Ana (☎ 070 282699; Passport Lane, off Interior Ministry Rd; r US$35-70) This cosy guesthouse does everything it can to make its guests feel at home. Rooms range in size according to price, and the bathrooms are spotless. Best of all is the comfy sofa in the lounge. Deservedly popular.

B's Place (☎ 070 276416; b@place.as; Qali Fatullah; r US$75) Six rooms sit above this well-liked restaurant, all decorated in traditional Afghan style. Friendly staff and a pleasant

garden make this a good choice. B's Place plans to expand to Mazar-e Sharif and Herat in 2004.

Assa 1 (☎ 070 744364; assa_kabul@hotmail.com; off Flower St; s US$50) Has presentable rooms, and prices include dinner and as much tea and coffee as you can drink.

Assa 2 (☎ 070 744364; assa_kabul@hotmail.com; Muslim St; s US$50; ▨) The sister guesthouse to Assa 1 offers similar facilities, plus a small pool to dabble your toes in.

Global Guesthouse (☎ 070 281907; guesthouse @globalrsl.com; off Flower St; s US$75; ▢) Owned by a security company and run by an ex-Gurkha, you'll sleep well here. Rooms are large and well turned out, and all meals are included. There's an open bar and barbeque on Friday.

Karwansara (☎ 070 291794; karwansara@yahoo .com; Interior Ministry Rd; s/d US$60/80; ▢) A lovely old merchant's house. Some rooms are a little small, but the large and leafy garden makes up for this. The restaurant serves good Western and Afghan meals, and you can burn off the calories in the gym. Half of the profits go to the Khorasan Orphanage in Kabul.

Heritage Guesthouse (☎ 070 299527; charāhi Sherpur; s/d US$45/70; ▢ ▨) Sits opposite the Iranian embassy. Rooms are simple and the shared bathrooms are basic. The pool marks it out against other guesthouses – hopefully it'll have water in it for the summer months.

Sunshine Guesthouse (☎ 070 279262; off Flower St; s/d US$35/70) Similar guesthouse fare to the Heritage.

Friend Guesthouse (☎ 070 224346; qayum_mo eem@hotmail.com; charāhi Turabaz Khan; r from US$30) This guesthouse has large rooms (prices are based on sharing), and up to four beds per room. Breakfast and dinner are included and there's a satellite TV room. Good value if you're sharing.

Top End

InterContinental Hotel (☎ 020 2201320; Karte Parwan; s/d/st from US$80/90/150; ▢ ▨) Afghanistan's only international luxury hotel has the novelty of working elevators. It's a 20-minute drive from the centre, but the hilltop location gives great views of Kabul. ATO has an office here, as do Ariana, Azerbaijan Airlines and Shah M Books. There's also a gym, much needed after sampling the three restaurants.

AFGHANISTAN

THE AUTHOR'S CHOICE

Gandamak Lodge (☎ 070 276937; ganda macklodge@yahoo.com; Passport Lane, off Interior Ministry Rd; US$90-110; ☐) Kabul's best accommodation option, the Gandamak Lodge is a beautiful guesthouse owned by Peter Jouvenal, the acclaimed cameraman and Afghan expert. Rooms are comfortable and tastefully decorated, the restaurant is excellent and there's a well-stocked bar for guests and diners. There are a couple of cheaper rooms (US$45 to US$60). It's essential to book at least a fortnight in advance. The guesthouse isn't marked from the outside – look for the large '5' painted on the door, next to the blue-and-white guardhouse.

Kabul Serena Hotel (www.serenahotels.com; jād-e Froshgah) Built in the 1930s, this hotel (originally called the Kabul Hotel) is now owned by the Aga Khan and is undergoing a massive renovation to five-star standard. Planned to open in mid-2004, it will include a business centre, travel agency, health club and three restaurants.

EATING

Kabul has a good range of restaurants, and you'll enjoy the variety compared to what's available in the country.

Cafés & Street Stalls

Any chaikhana will be able to offer you kebabs (50Afg) and *pulao* (60Afg). There are plenty about, particularly around charāhi Sadarat and jād-e Maiwand, and are usually open all hours. On Cinema Zainab Rd there are lots of kebab places facing the park, which offer tasty chicken kebabs for 60Afg.

Super Ice Cream/Pizza Milano (Shahr-e Naw Park; ☽ lunch, dinner) Does good pizzas for 150Afg, and you can sit outside when it's warm.

Chief Burger (☽ breakfast, lunch, dinner) Opposite Super Ice Cream, Chief Burger does a good take on burgers and chips from 50Afg, eat in or takeaway.

Restaurants

Marco Polo (Shahr-e Naw Park; ☽ lunch, dinner) Has a good selection of Afghan food, including a wide choice of kebab dishes. A huge plate of *qabli pulao* costs 100Afg.

New York (Cinema Zainab Rd; ☽ breakfast, lunch, dinner) Also has good Afghan food, but it'll make you wait. Claims of European food are a little disappointing.

Delhi Darbar (☎ 070 277566; Muslim St; ☽ lunch, dinner) Head here if you're after Indian food; there's great service and fantastic curries. Single dishes start at around US$6, but the *thali* (traditional South Indian meal) is brilliant at US$5, which you can order with alcohol.

Golden Lotus (☎ 020 2101827; charāhi Zambak; ☽ lunch, dinner) Afghanistan's oldest Chinese restaurant has a slightly gloomy atmosphere, but a good choice of dishes, with a few Afghan and European favourites thrown in for good measure. The noodle soup is a snap at US$2.

Blue Pearl (☎ 070 202809; Pashtunistan Sq; ☽ lunch, dinner) is at the back of the Khyber Restaurant. Dishes such as beef in oyster sauce start from US$6. The Khyber Restaurant itself now caters mainly to large wedding parties.

Shandiz (☎ 070 284026; St 10, Wazir Akbar Khan; ☽ lunch, dinner) Opposite Ariana, Shandiz serves Iranian food in pleasant surrounds. The *chelo morgh* (chicken and rice with berries) costs US$4.

Popolano (☎ 070 288116; charāhi Ansari; ☽ lunch, dinner) A busy Italian bistro that has a wide choice of pasta, steaks and salads to back up the bright décor. Dishes start from around US$7; takeaway pizzas are also available.

Mustafa Hotel (☎ 070 235689; charāhi Sadarat; ☽ lunch, dinner) The hotel has its own Italian-style restaurant, with a selection of pasta dishes and really good pizzas from US$6. Thursday night is kebab night, which includes a rooftop barbeque and alcohol from the bar.

Lai Thai (☎ 070 297557; St 15, Wazir Akbar Khan; ☽ lunch, dinner) Wonderful food in a traditional Thai setting. The owner makes a speciality of opening in war-torn areas – there are sister outfits in Kosovo and East Timor – and the restaurant is a big hit with Kabul's expats. Tasty spring rolls and satay are US$4 each, with main courses starting from US$7.

B's Place (☎ 070 276416; Qali Fatullah; ☽ lunch, dinner) Diners here can eat at a traditional *sandali* – a heated platform where you tuck your legs under to keep warm, with food served on top – in the winter months. In

THE AUTHOR'S CHOICE

Herat (Shahr-e Naw Park; ☾ lunch, dinner) A great local Afghan place which positively bursts at lunch time. The *mantu* will set you back 80Afg, but save some room for the sticky sweets at the end with your tea.

Anaar (☎ 070 284315; St 3, jäd-e Kolola Pushta; ☾ lunch, dinner) One of Kabul's loveliest restaurants. There's a wide selection of Thai, Indian and Chinese dishes. Vegetarians are particularly well-catered for. In the summer eat in the lantern-hung garden, otherwise withdraw to the cosy interior decorated with traditional Afghan crafts. Dishes start at US$8.

summer you can eat in the garden. Peppered steak (US$8) is the most popular item on the menu, but the desserts are famous across Kabul.

Deutscher Hof (☎ 070 288143; St 3, Qali Fatullah; ☾ lunch, dinner) Classic dishes (from around €10), such as schnitzel, are served in an immaculate dining room. You can wash them down with cold lager. Alternatively known as the German Restaurant, it's also a college for Afghan caterers.

Gandamak Lodge (☎ 070 276937; Passport Lane, off Interior Ministry Rd; ☾ breakfast, lunch, dinner). A top-end dining experience, the menu offers such dishes as duck breast in red wine and orange sauce for US$12, and there's the best wine list in Afghanistan to accompany your meal. Early risers can enjoy the full English breakfast for $US6.

Several guesthouses have good restaurants attached, most notably **Karwansara** (☎ 070 291794; Interior Ministry Rd; ☾ lunch, dinner) and **Chez Ana** (☎ 070 282699; Passport Lane, off Interior Ministry Rd; ☾ lunch, dinner), but it's advisable to call in advance to reserve a place. Also try the restaurants at the Spinzar and Zarnigar hotels. Worth checking out are the **Chinese Restaurant** (☎ 020 2201618; Shahr-e Naw Park; ☾ lunch, dinner), opposite the Marco Polo, and **Great Wall** (☎ 070 200688; Cinema Zainab Rd; ☾ lunch, dinner), which has Sichuan and Korean food. Both serve alcohol.

Self-Catering

The bazaars between the Kabul River and jäd-e Maiwand have plenty of fresh produce including fruit, vegetables, nuts and dairy, although in season fruit stands can be found on most street corners. Bakeries dish out piping-hot nan throughout the day.

The shops along Flower St are well-stocked with Western goodies for those wanting a taste of home, as is Chelsea Supermarket, around the corner. Flower St also has a great selection of bakeries and pastry shops.

For something a little different, the market traders along Zarnegar Park can sell you US army 'Meals Ready to Eat' for 10Afg.

DRINKING

The short-lived Irish Bar tried to bring the pub scene to Kabul, but closed after bomb threats. As a result, bars are now low-key affairs. The **Mustafa Hotel** (charāhi Sadarat) is the most popular place for a drink in the centre. The **Deutscher Hof** (St 3, Qali Fatullah) is also good for a beer on the terrace. There's occasional live music, and the management has even been known to organise Afghanistan's own Oktoberfest!

The juice bars around Shahr-e Naw Park are great for more-refreshing alternatives, and there are plenty of chaikhanas throughout the city. Those around Minar-e Maiwand are good for watching the world pass by over green tea.

ENTERTAINMENT

The **Foundation for Culture & Civil Society** (FCCS; ☎ 070 276637; afghan_foundation@yahoo.com; Salang wat) holds concerts of traditional Afghan music and poetry recitals on Saturday. There are regular exhibitions of local artists, and a café with women-only arts days.

The **Aina Media Centre** (☎ 070 224983; aina kabul@ainaworld.org; Shah Mahmoud wat) has weekly outdoor film showings throughout the summer.

The **Ghazi Stadium** (foreigner 250Afg) has football matches most Friday afternoons. The stadium also hosts occasional *buzkashi* matches (a pololike game played with a headless animal carcass; see p54). Usually these matches are played in the late autumn and winter, and also around the festivities of Nawroz.

SHOPPING

Chicken Street is the most popular place to go souvenir hunting – merchants have been selling to tourists here since the days of the hippy trail. It has seen a boom since the massive influx of international workers at the end of 2001, so don't be afraid to haggle for everything, from jewellery to gorgeous Turkmen kilims.

A couple of other places are worth checking out. The **CHA Gallery of Fine Arts & Traditional Afghan Crafts** (Cinema Zainab Rd) is an artists cooperative selling paintings, handicrafts and carpets. The **Afghan Handicrafts Centre** (Interior Ministry Rd) is a mix of government-run and private shops, with many goods made on site.

Flower Street is good for Western food luxuries such as Pringles and Marmite. There are two large cash-and-carry supermarkets, Supreme and Blue, next to each other on the Jalalabad Rd, selling everything from alcohol to tampons.

GETTING THERE & AWAY
Air
Kabul is the main gateway to Afghanistan, and has the country's only international **airport** (☎ 020 2301344). For more information on international flight connections see p402.

AIRLINE OFFICES
Ariana Afghan Airlines (☎ 020 2100271; www .flyariana.com; St 10, Wazir Akbar Khan)
Azerbaijan Airlines (☎ 070 296914; charāhi Ansari) Three weekly flights between Kabul and Baku.
LTU International Airways (☎ 070 220511; ltukabul@hotmail.com; charāhi Ansar) Weekly service between Kabul and Düsseldorf.
Marco Polo Airways (☎ 070 288 213; www.marcopol oairways.com; charāhi Ansari) Up to three weekly services from Kabul to Dubai.

Ariana has domestic connections to Herat (one hour, daily, 2500Afg), Mazar-e Sharif (30 minutes, Tuesday, Friday and Sunday, 1500Afg), Faizabad (Saturday and Monday, 1300Afg), Kunduz (30 minutes, Sunday and Tuesday, 1200Afg), Shiberghan (Sunday, 1700Afg) and Maimana (Friday, 3000Afg).

Bus
Several terminals serve Kabul, in reality little more than massed ranks of vehicles, with drivers shouting out the destinations and leaving when they are full, rather than by any set timetable. If you do have to wait, there's always somewhere to get tea or juice and a plate of kebabs.

Minibuses to Jalalabad (four hours, 150Afg) and the Pakistan border at Torkham (seven hours, 250Afg) leave from pul-e Mahmoud Khan, close to the Id Gah Mosque. Transport heading north through the Salang Tunnel departs from Serai Shomali, a 20-minute taxi ride to the Khair Khana district on the edge of Kabul. Minibuses from here include Mazar-e Sharif (10 hours, 400Afg), Pul-e Khumri (seven hours, 300Afg) and Kunduz (10 hours, 400Afg). To travel to Bamiyan, catch a minibus from Kote Sangi (sometimes called Pul-e Sokhta) in west Kabul (10 hours, 250Afg).

Kote Sangi is also the terminal for minibuses south to Ghazni, Kandahar and on to Herat, but this road is currently too dangerous to travel.

Prices and times are given for 16-seater HiAce minibuses. Smaller TownAces fill up (and leave) quicker, and are slightly more expensive. Faster shared taxis also depart from the same terminals, and cost up to a third more. It is not normally possible to arrange seats in advance. Long-distance transport can start leaving from 5am or 6am, so arrive early.

GETTING AROUND
To/From the Airport
The airport is a 15-minute ride from the city centre, at the end of Great Massoud Rd. There is no organised public transport into Kabul; a taxi should cost no more than 100Afg. Look out for the destroyed planes of the Ariana Graveyard on your right after leaving the terminal.

Local Transport
Old buses operated by Afghan Milli Bus trundle the routes across Kabul, but they are slow with standing room only; use them only if you are not in a rush. Destinations aren't marked, so shout out where you want to go when the bus stops. Fares cost a couple of afghanis. There are plans to rebuild Kabul's ruined trolleybus network.

There are over 40,000 registered taxis in Kabul, forming the bulk of the city's traffic. Shared taxis run the main roads, linking the districts. If you flag one down you'll need to know the nearest landmark or major junction to your destination. Most taxi drivers assume that a foreigner will want to hire the whole vehicle, so make this clear when you get in. Shared taxis have a minimum fare of 10Afg.

Taxis are almost as cheap to hire for only yourself, although finding an empty one can sometimes be a challenge. For private hire, short taxi rides cost about 30Afg, with most fares within the city costing a maximum of 50Afg.

AROUND KABUL
Paghman

Amanullah built Paghman as a summer retreat in the 1920s, decorating it with Italianate buildings and pleasure gardens. He even raced elephants here. In the centre of the village is the Victory Arch, a copy of the Arc de Triomphe, celebrating Afghan independence in 1919. Despite the war damage Paghman is green and pretty, and popular with Kabulis on Friday. The Bahar Restaurant at the top of the hill has simple dishes and drinks.

Near Paghman is Kargha Lake, another popular weekend retreat, but with water levels still recovering from Afghanistan's long drought.

Paghman is a 30-minute drive from Kabul; the trip will cost around US$20 by private taxi.

Istalif

Istalif sits on the edge of the Koh Daman mountains and is one of Afghanistan's oldest villages. It was much damaged in the

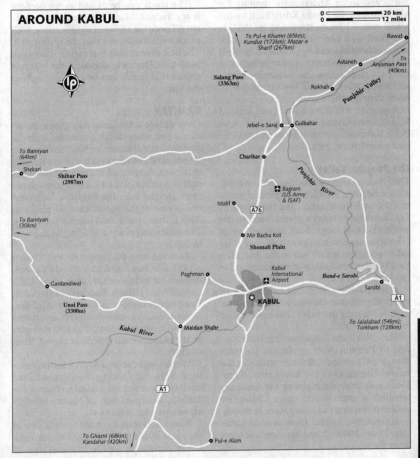

AROUND KABUL

0 — 20 km
0 — 12 miles

To Pul-e Khumri (65km);
Kunduz (172km); Mazar-e
Sharif (267km)

Rawat

Astaneh

To
Anjoman Pass
(40km)

Salang Pass
(3363m)

Rokhah

Panjshir Valley

Jebel-o Saraj   Gulbahar

To Bamiyan
(64km)

Shekari

Charikar

Panjshir River

Shibar Pass
(2987m)

Bagram
(US Army
& ISAF)

Istalif

A76

To Bamiyan
(30km)

Mir Bacha Kot

Shomali Plain

Paghman

Kabul
International
Airport

Band-e Sarobi

Sarobi

A1

To Jalalabad (54km);
Torkham (128km)

Gardandiwal

Unai Pass
(3300m)

Kabul River   Maidan Shahr

KABUL

A1

To Ghazni (68km);
Kandahar (420km)

Pul-e Alam

AFGHANISTAN

civil war, but still gives a taste of traditional village life, as well as offering fine mountain views. Istalif is famous for its blue pottery.

The road to Istalif runs through the fertile (and much fought over) Shomali Plain. The road is littered with dead tanks and many areas are still mined. The plain is famous for its fruit, but many trees were uprooted by the Taliban's scorched earth policy in the late 1990s.

Istalif is one hour from Kabul; a private taxi costs $US25. It's worth combining with a trip to the Salang Pass.

Salang Pass

The tunnel running through the Salang Pass (3363m) is the only major road linking north and south Afghanistan, running for 6km through the Hindu Kush. Built by the USSR over 12 years, it opened in 1964. It was used as a conduit for Russian tanks, and was later blocked by Dostum to protect his fiefdom in the north. The approaches to the pass give spectacular mountain views, and teams work hard to keep them free of snow through the winter.

A private taxi from Kabul costs around $US40 (two hours) or take a minibus to Pul-e Khumri from Serai Shomali (300Afg) and get off at the pass.

The Panjshir Valley

The lush green of the Panjshir Valley, 100km north of Kabul, is the spiritual home of the Northern Alliance, and the Panjshiri Tajiks dominate today's government. In the 1980s Massoud fought back repeated Soviet offensives against his stronghold here. The valley stretches for 100km to the Anjoman Pass (4430m) and offers great potential for trekking.

Massoud himself is buried in a small green-domed mausoleum, which has stunning views over the valley. His tomb is five hours from Kabul.

The Northern Alliance controls access to Panjshir very tightly and passport checks are common at the entrance to the valley. The valley is five hours from Kabul (once you leave the highway the roads are terrible); a private taxi costs US$60. By public transport, the best option is to take a minibus to Charikar from Serai Shomali (one hour, 100Afg) and arrange transport from there.

CENTRAL AFGHANISTAN

The centre of Afghanistan is known as the Hazarajat, high and isolated in the knot of the Koh-e Baba mountains. Its people, the Hazaras, are both hardy and welcoming, with the women active and visible in society in a way unseen in other parts of the country.

The region is one of the most beautiful in Afghanistan and contains some its best attractions – the Bamiyan Valley and the incredible blue lakes of Band-e Amir. The adventurous can attempt a trip to the Minaret of Jam, hidden deep in the folds of the mountains.

The roads can be as bad as the scenery is spectacular. Many communities become cut off once the snows of winter arrive, with roads impassable until after the spring melt. The best time to visit this region is between June and October, although the altitude means that nights can be cold throughout the year.

BAMIYAN

Once a place of Buddhist pilgrimage, Bamiyan is now more closely associated with the destruction visited on Afghanistan's culture by war. The two giant statues of the Buddha that once dominated the valley now lie in rubble, victims of the Taliban's iconoclastic rage. Despite this, the Bamiyan Valley remains one of the most beautiful places in Afghanistan, and a must-see for any visitor. The valley was made a World Heritage site in 2003.

Bamiyan was an important way station on the Silk Road and had a Buddhist culture whose influence spread as far as India and China. Fifteen hundred years later, Bamiyan became the focus of Afghanistan's nascent tourist industry, as visitors came to rediscover its past glories and gaze at the monumental Buddhas carved from its cliffs.

War brought an end to that. Initially isolated from the fighting, Bamiyan suffered terribly under the ideological fervour of the Taliban, who punished its Hazara inhabitants as well as its history.

Bamiyan is now a relaxed town in one of the most stable areas of Afghanistan. Four hours' drive away lie the fabulous lakes of

Band-e Amir. As transport links to Kabul improve, its inhabitants are waiting to see if the tourists will return.

History

Bamiyan's place in Afghan history begins with the Kushan empire in the 1st century AD. As a halfway point between Balkh and the Kushan capital at Kapisa (near modern Bagram), it grew rich from the trade along the Silk Road. Converting to Buddhism, the Kushans fused Eastern art with the Hellenistic tradition left by the Greeks. Bamiyan became a major artistic and religious centre.

Another wave of invaders – the White Huns – were assimilated in the 4th century AD, and carved Bamiyan's two giant statues of the Buddha. Bamiyan became one of the most important pilgrimage sites in the world.

In the 7th century, Afghanistan felt the eastward thrust of Islam. High in the mountains, Bamiyan clung on to its Buddhist traditions for another 400 years, until the ascendant Ghaznavids finally brought Islam to the valley for good.

A series of smaller dynasties held sway over Bamiyan until the beginning of the 13th century, when they were swept away by the Mongol tidal wave in 1222, from which Bamiyan never fully recovered. The Hazaras now claim descent from the Mongol invaders, but they spent the next 600 years apart from Afghan history, isolated in their mountain fastness.

In the 1890s Abdur Rahman Khan led a military campaign to bring the Hazarajat under the control of the Afghan state. He declared a jihad against the Shiite Hazaras and took many into slavery. The area remained the most underdeveloped part of Afghanistan throughout the 20th century.

Bamiyan rebelled against the communist government in 1978; the mountainous surroundings were a blessing to the resistance, who drove the Russians out of the Hazarajat by 1981.

For the first time in their history the Hazaras could organise themselves politically and militarily. Bamiyan was ruled by a Shiite coalition supported by Iran. By the

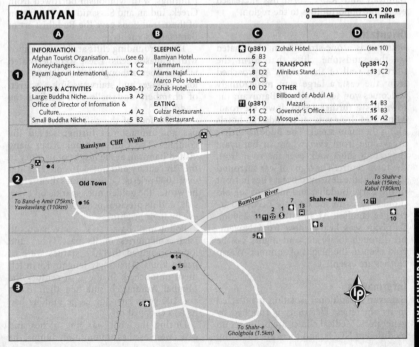

BAMIYAN

0 ___ 200 m
0 ___ 0.1 miles

INFORMATION	**SLEEPING** (p381)		Zohak Hotel............................(see 10)
Afghan Tourist Organisation..........(see 6)	Bamiyan Hotel.................................6 B3		
Moneychangers...............................1 C2	Hammam...7 C2		**TRANSPORT** (pp381-2)
Payam Jagouri International............2 C2	Mama Najaf......................................8 D2		Minibus Stand................................13 C2
	Marco Polo Hotel..............................9 C3		
SIGHTS & ACTIVITIES (pp380-1)	Zohak Hotel....................................10 D2		**OTHER**
Large Buddha Niche...........................3 A2			Billboard of Abdul Ali
Office of Director of Information &	**EATING** (p381)		Mazari......................................14 B3
Culture...4 A2	Gulzar Restaurant............................11 C2		Governor's Office............................15 B3
Small Buddha Niche............................5 B2	Pak Restaurant................................12 D2		Mosque...16 A2

Bamiyan Cliff Walls

Old Town

To Band-e Amir (75km);
Yawkawlang (110km)

Bamiyan River

Shahr-e Naw

To Shahr-e
Zohak (15km);
Kabul (180km)

To Shahr-e
Gholghola (1.5km)

AFGHANISTAN

middle of the 1990s, Hazara influence extended as far as Kabul and Mazar-e Sharif.

The rise of the Taliban saw the return of anti-Hazara sentiments. The Taliban refused access to the international community and tried to starve the region into submission. By the time the Taliban captured Bamiyan in 1998, the population had scattered into the mountains.

Straight away the Taliban threatened to blow up the giant Buddhas. After protests Mullah Omar soon recanted, and even declared that they should be protected to encourage a future return of tourism.

Such ideals didn't last long. Three years later, the Buddhas were declared un-Islamic and their destruction decreed. Over two days at the beginning of March 2001, dynamite and tank fire reduced the monumental statues to rubble. The world – and the Afghan population – was horrified. The Taliban celebrated by selling picture calendars of the demolition on the streets of Kabul.

With the US-led routing of the Taliban, stability has returned to Bamiyan. Foreign funding is helping upgrade the road between Bamiyan and Kabul, bringing increased economic opportunities to the region.

Orientation

Bamiyan is a one-street town, dominated by the sandstone cliffs that form the northern wall of the valley. Approached from the east, a large sign misleadingly welcomes you to the city of Bamiyan; the town lies a further 15km down the road. Minibuses drop you off outside the hotels along the main street. The Buddha niches are visible from everywhere in Bamiyan; they are a short walk over the river from the town centre. The signs of war surround the niches; the destroyed bazaar lies in front of the Large Buddha, and many of the old monks' caves in the cliff are occupied by refugee families. At an altitude of 2500m, Bamiyan sees heavy snow from November through to spring, and nights can be cold even in the height of summer. Warm clothes are essential.

Information

Bamiyan's traditional isolation is reflected in its amenities. Electricity is supplied by generators. Medical clinics are being set up by different NGOs, and there are a handful of pharmacies in the town. Several money-changers have offices along Bamiyan's main street.

There's no post or telephone, but Payam Jagouri International, on the main street, has a satellite phone, charging 100Afg per minute for any call worldwide.

ATO has an office at the Bamiyan Hotel, and can hire out vehicles and drivers. A good guide to the valley is Nancy Dupree's *Bamiyan*, sadly only available in Kabul.

Sights
THE BUDDHA NICHES

Bamiyan's two Buddhas, standing 38m and 55m respectively, were the tallest standing statues of the Buddha ever made, created around the 6th century AD.

The statues weren't simply carved out of the sandstone cliffs. The rough figures were hewn from the rock, which was then covered in mud and straw to create the intricate folds of the robes, before being plastered. Each statue was then painted, and the faces covered with gilded masks.

The walls of the niches were covered in paintings, with symbolism borrowed from Greek, Indian and Sassanid art. The fusion of these traditions gave the Buddhist art of Bamiyan its vitality.

The surrounding cliffs are honeycombed with monastic cells. These were decorated with frescoes, although almost all have been lost. Passages and stairways link a warren of chambers and halls surrounding the Buddhas.

At the foot of the cliff, a series of stupas and monasteries further served the complex. The Chinese monk Xuan Zang visited Bamiyan at the height of its glory in the 7th century and noted 10 convents and over 1000 priests. Of the statues themselves, he wrote, 'the golden hues sparkle on every side, and its precious ornaments dazzle the eye by their brightness.'

Following Bamiyan's conversion to Islam, memories of its past faded and locals imagined that the statues were of pagan kings. Amazingly Jenghiz Khan left them untouched. In the 17th century the Mughal Aurangzeb smashed their faces, and 100 years later the Large Buddha had its legs chopped off.

During the civil war, the niches and caves were used as ammunition dumps; the statues suffered under pot shots from the soldiers. The final indignity came with their complete demolition by the Taliban.

Many locals support rebuilding the statues, an idea rejected by Unesco. The preferred plan is to build an open-air museum and preserve the site as a testament to Afghanistan's cultural loss in war.

In front of the Large Buddha is the office of the Director of Information and Culture. There is no charge to view the niches (which have been fenced off) but a guard may come out to ask for a tip. Climbing to the top of the Buddhas is not recommended, as there is a danger of falling rocks, as well as the further erosion of an already damaged site.

SHAHR-E GHOLGHOLA

The impregnable walls of this citadel were Bamiyan's last bastion against the Mongol hordes, but the ruling king, Jalaludin didn't reckon on the treachery of his daughter. In a fit of pique at her widowed father remarrying, she betrayed the fort's secret entrance to the invaders, expecting to be well rewarded. Jenghiz put her to the sword anyway, along with the rest of the defenders, hence the citadel's modern name – 'City of Screams'.

Shahr-e Gholghola lies 2km southeast of Bamiyan. The climb to the top gives excellent views of the Bamiyan Valley. The ruins were, however, mined during the war, so take a local guide to ensure you stick to the safe paths.

SHAHR-E ZOHAK

The ruins of Shahr-e Zohak, perched high on the cliffs at the confluence of the Bamiyan and Kalu Rivers, guard the entrance to the Bamiyan Valley. Jenghiz Khan's grandson was killed here, bringing down a murderous fury on the whole valley as a result.

The citadel is still relatively intact and it's possible to see the barracks, stables and defensive towers. There are mines around the ruins, so stick to the clearly marked path.

Shahr-e Zohak is 17km east of Bamiyan on the road to Kabul. Hiring a vehicle from Bamiyan costs around 500Afg. A guide (100Afg) and a permit from the Director of Information and Culture in Bamiyan is required to visit the ruins. There is a military checkpoint near the ruins on the north side of the river; if you don't have a permit, a soldier will insist on accompanying you (and being paid for the service).

Sleeping

Bamiyan Hotel (r US$30, yurt with private bathroom US$50) ATO's sole remaining hotel has a manager who has steadfastly been running the show for over 30 years. The luxury yurts the hotel boasted in the 1970s have been rebuilt, offering one of Afghanistan's most novel accommodation options. Standard rooms in the main hotel have shared bathrooms. The hotel sits on the hill overlooking the valley.

Zohak Hotel (Shahr-e Naw; dm US$7, s/d US$20) Bamiyan's best budget option. Rooms have one or two beds, and there are mattresses in a communal room on the top floor. There's satellite TV when the generator is running and buckets of hot water on request. As we were going to press, some travellers were reporting that this hotel had closed.

Mama Najaf (Shahr-e Naw; bed US$6) Two communal rooms sit above a chaikhana, up rickety wooden stairs. The toilet leaves a lot to be desired, and there's no bathroom – head for the *hammam* (bathhouse) across the street (15Afg per person).

Marco Polo Hotel (Shahr-e Naw; bed US$2) A real shoestring option – everyone squeezes into a small room on the ground floor or retires upstairs to sleep in the restaurant. Again, there's no bathroom (or, in fact, a toilet), so you'll quickly become familiar with Bamiyan's *hammam*.

Eating

Bamiyan only has a few restaurants, all along the main street. Along with the usual Afghan fare, there are often chips – Bamiyan is well-known for its potatoes.

The Gulzar Restaurant and Pak Restaurant both have raised balconies above the street, making them great places to sit and watch the world go by over a pot of chai.

All of the hotels also have restaurants attached. The Zohak Hotel is popular and serves good chicken with rice for 80Afg.

At the bazaar you can find plenty of fruit, vegetables and bread for picnics.

Getting There & Away

Minibuses depart from a stand opposite Mama Najaf. Transport to Kabul (10 hours,

250Afg), taking the southerly road through the Hagijak and Unai Passes, can leave as early as 4am, so check what's available the day before travel. Minibuses for Yawkawlang (six hours, 200Afg) run according to demand. Snowfall and floods can make the route west from Bamiyan extremely difficult from November to as late as May.

There is no public transport heading north from Bamiyan – it is easier (and quicker) to go to via Kabul and the Salang Tunnel.

BAND-E AMIR

The five lakes of Band-e Amir (Dam of the King) are hidden in the Koh-e Baba at an altitude of 2900m. The deep-blue waters glitter like jewels, in stark contrast to the dusty mountains. The most accessible of the lakes is Band-e Haibat – the suitably named Dam of Awe.

The lakes' high mineral content gives them their colour. Over the millennia, sulphur deposits have formed huge walls that contain the waters of the lakes. These

---

CROSSING CENTRAL AFGHANISTAN

A trip through the Hazarajat to see the Minaret of Jam is one of the most adventurous trips it's possible to do in Afghanistan. It is not to be taken lightly, however, as the roads are appalling and the region very remote. This route is best attempted between June and October. Outside these months, snow and spring melt can make the roads difficult or impossible to traverse. There are several passes over 3000m that are frequently closed, cutting off the region from the outside world. Ghor province is the least developed in the country. There is no governmental rule here, so check the security situation before attempting this route.

Getting There From Bamiyan

Minibuses west to Yawkawlang (six hours, 200Afg) depart most days. It's a typical town of the Hazarajat, set in a well-watered valley. It has a small fort and there are several chaikhanas along the main street with private rooms for 50Afg to 100Afg, but with little more bedding than carpets and cushions. Chaikhanas often employ *sandalis* for heating; raised platforms that channel the heat from the cooking fire to your legs tucked underneath – very cosy for cold Afghan nights.

From Yawkawlang there are minibuses to the provincial capital Chaghcheran (14 hours, 300 Afg). The road through the heart of the Koh-e Baba is spectacular. It's often possible to see the Aimaq, a seminomadic people who share the area with the Hazaras, herding their flocks. After Lal-o Sar Jangal, the poor road deteriorates further. You'll often drive along dry riverbeds and see more animal traffic than other vehicles.

A few NGOs have offices in Chaghcheran – the only international presence in the region. The town was once a major bazaar for nomads, and in the summer months Aimaq and Pashtun nomads still bring their livestock to market here. Hotel options are limited to the chaikhanas near the bazaar.

There is no direct transport to the Minaret of Jam. Take any transport heading west and get off at the junction town of Garmao (10 hours). Trucks regularly take the road north to Kamenj and will be able to take you to Jam.

The approach to the minaret is beautiful. After crossing the Garmao Pass, the road descends to the waters of the Hari Rud. The mountain walls twist and close in, until the minaret is finally revealed, hidden in the narrow cleft of the valley.

There is a chaikhana near the minaret where you can eat and sleep. Unesco is also building a guesthouse at the site. The village of Jam itself is 5km south of the monument.

From Garmao, the road continues west to Herat via Chist-e Sharif and Obey. The latter has hot springs that are worth a visit. With an early start you might reach Herat in one day.

Getting There From Herat

It is possible to take a minibus direct to Obey (five hours, 250Afg) and Chaghcheran (two days, 500Afg). ATO in Herat can arrange a round-trip to Jam by 4WD, at US$500 for the entire vehicle.

natural dams stand over 10m tall, and must be Afghanistan's greatest natural wonder.

Locals prefer to credit the creation of the lakes to miracles performed by the Prophet Mohammed's son-in-law Ali, and they're still visited by pilgrims who come to enjoy the water's reputed healing powers. There's a small mosque dedicated to Ali on the shore of Band-e Haibat.

It is possible to swim in the lakes, although the water is very cold and you won't want to stay in for long. Shorts are fine for men, but women will attract strange looks even if fully clothed.

Eating & Sleeping

A small restaurant at Band-e Haibat serves locally caught fish with chips, as well as kebabs and *pulao*. The fish are delicious but incredibly bony. The restaurant has simple mattresses for those wishing to spend the night, but asks 400Afg for the privilege.

Getting There & Away

There's no direct public transport to Band-e Amir. You can hire a vehicle for the day from Bamiyan (75km, four hours) for US$50. Alternatively take a local minibus from Bamiyan heading to Yawkawlang for 200Afg and get off at the junction for the lakes; but the 7km walk is very dry and dusty and the verges of the road are mined. Be prepared to wait for return transport – possibly overnight. The road is impassable during the winter.

THE MINARET OF JAM

This fabulous monument sits in the remote valleys of the Koh-e Baba – its existence was only revealed to the outside world in the 1940s. Three tapering cylindrical shafts reach a dizzying height of 65m. Only the Qutb minaret in Delhi is taller.

Dating from the late 12th century, the minaret's purpose remains unknown. Some scholars believe it was part of the Ghorid capital of Firuzkoh, destroyed by the Mongols. However, the lack of associated buildings is reminiscent of a concurrent Central Asian trend for raising single, massive towers as statements of political power.

The minaret has undergone emergency work to protect its foundations from the river. It became Afghanistan's first World Heritage site in 2002.

Getting There & Away

A trip to the Minaret of Jam is not an easy affair, but the rewards are great. It's best to combine the journey with a traverse of the Hazarajat. For more information see the boxed text on p382.

WESTERN AFGHANISTAN

Afghanistan's western provinces feel a world away from the mountains that dominate much of the country. The land here is flat and open, stretching out to the Iranian Plateau and the Central Asian steppe. Such geography means that its principal city, Herat, has both prospered from trade and suffered from the designs of foreign invaders.

The region forms part of the historic province of Khorasan that encompassed Mashhad (in Iran) and Merv (in Turkmenistan). Of these cities, Herat was the most fabulous, hence the old saying: 'Khorasan is the oyster of the world, and Herat is its pearl'.

Since the end of 2001, the western provinces have been ruled by Ismail Khan, commander of Afghanistan's largest private army of 11,000 men. Nominally loyal to Kabul he styles himself as the independent 'Emir of Herat'.

Iran has fostered close economic and political ties with Ismail Khan. Cross-border trade is brisk, and customs duties are paying for much reconstruction – although the central government complains that too little is remitted to Kabul.

The climate is hot and dry, dominated by the Bãd-e Sad o Bïst, or Wind of 120 Days, which blows from the end of spring to the start of autumn, carrying a desiccating dust. Winters can be bitterly cold.

Transport connections to the rest of the country are patchy. The highway to Kabul runs through Afghanistan's restive south making travel highly dangerous. Roads north and east to Mazar-e Sharif are some of the worst in the country, as is the central route through the mountains to Bamiyan. Most travellers will find it easiest to fly between Herat and Kabul – or hop over the nearby border with Iran. Onward travel to

AFGHANISTAN

Turkmenistan is possible given the necessary permits (see p438).

HERAT

pop 180,000

The one-time capital of the Timurid empire and seat of learning and the arts, Herat has flourished throughout history as a rich city-state, and been repeatedly fought over. The city is as much Persian as it is Afghan, and wears an air of independence as the country's old cultural heart.

Herat's place in history has often been overlooked in favour of Samarkand and Bukhara, but its inhabitants are proud of their past and the city's reputation as a place of culture. Many of Herat's historic monuments are in a sorry state, ruined by British and Russian invaders, but with its Friday Mosque the city still possesses one of Islam's great buildings.

Since the fall of the Taliban, Herat is now stable and prospering from the trade with Iran. Some Heratis claim they haven't seen as many freedoms return to them as to the citizens of Kabul – the Vice and Virtue Police have been retained, and opposing political and media voices have been suppressed.

Many Heratis took refuge in Iran during the war, and travellers may detect a Persian influence – in anything from food to clothing.

History

Herat's history begins as Aria, an outpost of the Achaemenid empire, overrun in Alexander the Great's eastward expansion. The city grew and reaped the benefits of the new Silk Road under the Kushans and Sassanids.

Herat's expansion was checked by the visitations of Jenghiz Khan in 1221, who characteristically levelled the place. This was to be the preface for the city's greatest period, as a new power thundered out of the steppe 150 years later.

Timur founded his empire at Samarkand, but following his death in 1405, the capital moved to Herat. Under Timur's son Shah Rukh, Herat became the one of the greatest centres of medieval Islamic culture. Jami composed his greatest poems here, and Bihzad refined the art of miniature painting. Shah Rukh's wife, the extraordinary Gowhar Shad (see the boxed text on p387), commissioned many fine buildings.

Such glory couldn't last. On Shah Rukh's death, there was a squabble for succession as his sons fought for control. Timurid power started to wane. There was one last flourish under Sultan Hussain Baiqara at the start of the 16th century, but he preferred to drink wine rather than exercise power, and the empire passed into history under the arrows of Uzbek invaders.

Herat spent the next centuries being fought over by the Mughals and Safavids. It finally regained its independence only to find itself swept up in the superpower rivalry of the Great Game (see p35).

The Persians made the first move on the city, laying siege to it in 1837. Russian officers aided the attack, while a single British officer rallied Herat's defenders. The Afghans held the day, but the British always feared that the Russians would return – and break through to India.

An incident near Herat in 1885 nearly brought the imperial powers into conflict. The British ordered that Herat be prepared for an attack and many of Gowhar Shad's buildings were demolished to allow a clear line of artillery fire for the defenders, although war was averted.

Herat resented the increasingly communist government in the 1970s. Events came to a head in March 1979 when the city rose in open revolt. Led by local mullahs and a mutinous army garrison commanded by Ismail Khan, around a hundred Russian advisors were killed with their families. The Russians helped the government quell the rebellion – by carpet bombing the old city. Around 20,000 civilians were killed.

Following invasion, Ismail Khan organised the mujaheddin and harried the Russians throughout the occupation. After their withdrawal in 1989 he re-entered the city as its ruler and set up his own administration.

Nothing could save him from the ascendant Taliban. In 1995 his army crumbled in the teeth of a Taliban advance and Herat was captured without a fight. Ismail Khan was taken prisoner, but later escaped to Iran.

Educated Heratis chafed under occupation and Iran closed its borders. Herat's population swelled with an influx of internal refugees fleeing drought.

Ismail Khan returned at the end of 2001 as the Taliban were swept from power. He rules absolutely, but has become increas-

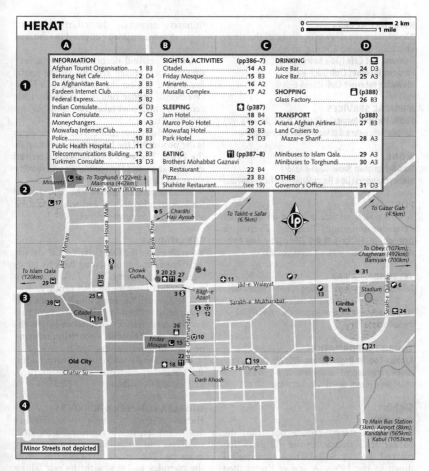

HERAT

0 — 2 km
0 — 1 mile

INFORMATION	
Afghan Tourist Organisation...... 1	B3
Behrang Net Cafe................... 2	D4
Da Afghanistan Bank.............. 3	B3
Fardeen Internet Club............ 4	B3
Federal Express................... 5	B2
Indian Consulate.................. 6	D3
Iranian Consulate................. 7	C3
Moneychangers.................... 8	A3
Mowafaq Internet Club.......... 9	B3
Police............................. 10	B3
Public Health Hospital........... 11	C3
Telecommunications Building... 12	B3
Turkmen Consulate............... 13	D3

SIGHTS & ACTIVITIES	(pp386–7)
Citadel............................ 14	A3
Friday Mosque.................... 15	A3
Minarets.......................... 16	A2
Musalla Complex................. 17	A2

SLEEPING	(p387)
Jam Hotel........................ 18	B4
Marco Polo Hotel................ 19	C4
Mowafaq Hotel................... 20	B3
Park Hotel........................ 21	D3

EATING	(pp387–8)
Brothers Mohabbat Gaznavi	
Restaurant........................ 22	B4
Pizza.............................. 23	B3
Shahiste Restaurant..........(see 19)	

DRINKING	
Juice Bar......................... 24	D3
Juice Bar......................... 25	A3

SHOPPING	(p388)
Glass Factory..................... 26	B3

TRANSPORT	(p388)
Ariana Afghan Airlines........... 27	B3
Land Cruisers to	
Mazar-e Sharif................... 28	B3
Minibuses to Islam Qala......... 29	A3
Minibuses to Torghundi.......... 30	A3

OTHER	
Governor's Office................. 31	D3

Minor Streets not depicted

ingly conservative with age. The city's treasury is again growing rich from international trade. Reintegrating Herat into the mainstream of Afghan politics is a major challenge for the peace process.

Orientation

Herat sits in a wide plain, watered by the Hari Rud. To the north, the ridges of the Safed Koh mark the boundary with the Central Asia steppe; to the south the road leads to Kandahar and the Indian subcontinent.

Only the core of Herat's old city remains, around the crossroads of Chahar Su, and the Friday Mosque. The citadel dominates the northern edge of the old city, looking out to the minarets of the ruined Musalla

Complex. West of this is the wasteland created by Soviet carpet bombing.

The new town (Shahr-e Naw) is east and north of the walled city and home to the majority of government and NGO offices. The streets are lined with tall pine trees.

Herat's airport is 8km south of the city, on the same road as the new bus station. When arriving overland from Iran, Turkmenistan and north Afghanistan, Herat's minarets make a ready landmark.

Information
EMERGENCY
Ambulance (☎ 040 223413)
Police (☎ 040 223485; jād-e Ghomandani) Opposite the Friday Mosque.

AFGHANISTAN

INTERNET ACCESS

New Internet cafés are opening all the time, charging around 150Afg an hour.

Behrang Net Cafe (jād-e Badmurghan)

Fardeen Internet Club (Bāgh-e Azadi)

Mowafaq Internet Club (Chowk Gulha)

MEDICAL SERVICES

Public Health Hospital (☎ 040 225717; jād-e Walayat) Has been refurbished. A string of pharmacies sit opposite.

MONEY

Da Afghanistan Bank (Bāgh-e Azadi)

Moneychangers (jād-e Houza Malik) Good for Iranian rials.

POST

A new postal service is being set up at the Telecommunications Building. There is a branch of **FedEx** (☎ 040 22030; jād-e Bank Khūn, charāhi Haji Ayoub; ⏾ 8am-6.30pm, closed Fri).

TELEPHONE & FAX

Telecommunications Building (sarakh-e Mukhabarat; ⏾ 8am-7pm) The best place to make a call or send a fax, although there are several public call offices (PCOs) throughout the city.

TOURIST INFORMATION

Afghan Tourist Organisation (ATO; ☎ 040 223210; sarakh-e Mukhabarat) Can hire drivers and guides for US$30 per day each, or US$15 for half a day.

Sights

OLD CITY

Four main streets radiate out from the bazaar of Chahar Su to the old gates that pierced the city walls, which were pulled down in the 1950s. A few of the vaulted covered bazaars survive, along with the great brick cisterns that kept the city supplied with water.

Plenty of the character of the Old City remains. Entrances off the main street lead into old caravanserais, now used as warehouses for carpet sellers and cloth merchants, and donkey carts make up much of the traffic in side streets too narrow for cars.

FRIDAY MOSQUE

Over 800 years old, Herat's Friday Mosque (Masjid-e Jame') is Afghanistan's finest Islamic building.

The mosque is laid out in the classical four-iwan (arched portal) plan. Two huge minarets dominate the courtyard, with every square centimetre covered in fabulous mosaic.

Of the original decoration, only a section of floral stucco remains in the south *iwan*. In a cell on the east side is a huge ceremonial bronze cauldron from the 13th century, which now takes donations for the mosque's upkeep.

The lavish tiling that covers the mosque is the product of the tile workshop set up in the 1940s. The workshop is based near the east entrance, and the craftsmen will readily show off their work.

Mosque attendants are normally happy for you to take photos, but this should be avoided during prayer times.

THE CITADEL

Towering over the Old City, the Citadel (or Ark) has foundations dating back as far as Alexander the Great. Shah Rukh built the present fort early in the 15th century.

The Citadel has been much rebuilt and restored with fired brick by successive rulers. It was originally covered in bright tiling, and some Timurid decoration remains on the northwest towers.

Known locally as Qala-ye Ikhtiyaruddin, the Citadel is currently an army garrison and closed to visitors.

MUSALLA COMPLEX & MINARETS

Herat's Musalla Complex was Gowhar Shad's masterpiece, comprising a mosque, medressa and mausoleum, and over twenty minarets. The British dynamited most of the complex in 1885, with the rest falling to earthquakes and war.

One minaret of the Musalla survives, with a mortar hole bitten out of it. Gowhar Shad's mausoleum stands in the middle of the grounds, topped by a huge ribbed dome. The caretaker may unlock it for you to see her tombstone. The cupola is beautifully painted in blue and rust-red. A smaller building next door holds the tomb of Mir Ali Shir Nawai, Sultan Baiqara's prime minister.

Opposite, four minarets, leaning at dangerous angles, mark the corners of Baiqara's long-gone **medressa** (admission free; ⏾ 7am-sunset). The minarets were covered in delicate blue lozenges framed in white and set with flowers. A little tiling remains – war and the abrasive wind have done away with the rest.

GOWHAR SHAD

The wife of Shah Rukh, Gowhar Shad was one of the most remarkable women in Afghanistan's history. Her name meant 'joyful jewel' but she was more than a trophy wife. A patron of the arts, she commissioned some of Islam's finest buildings, including Herat's Musalla Complex and the Great Mosque in Mashhad. Gowhar Shad also played an active part in politics. Her son Ulughbek was made the viceroy of Samarkand, and following her husband's death she was heavily involved in the manoeuvrings over his succession. Her other son Baisanghor drank himself to death, so Gowhar Shad planned to make his son Herat's ruler. Years of disputes followed, with her various sons and grandsons fighting for power, ultimately sowing the seeds of the empire's downfall. She finally met her end at the ripe age of 80, murdered by a rival after plotting to install her great-grandson on Herat's throne.

GAZAR GAH

This Sufi shrine, 5km northwest of Herat, is one of Afghanistan's holiest sites, dedicated to the 11th-century saint Khoja Abdullah Ansari. It's also the most complete Timurid building in Herat, dominated by a 30m-high portal. The courtyard inside the shrine is filled with gravestones, and decorative tiling covers the walls and arches. At the far end, under an ilex tree, is the saint's tomb.

Locked in a cell on the left side of the tomb is the Haft Qalam (Seven Pens) sarcophagus, named for its intricate carving. The tomb of Amir Dost Mohammed, who died soon after capturing Herat in 1863, sits in front.

The shrine is a popular place for both men and women to visit, and you'll see people offering prayers to the tomb before turning around to perform the full prayer ritual facing Mecca. There's no entrance fee, but the Sufis who tend the shrine appreciate a small donation.

TAKHT-E SAFAR

Sitting on a hill 5km north of Herat, Takht-e Safar is a popular place for picnics. Built as a pleasure garden for Sultan Hussain Baiqara in the 14th century, it's an oasis

of green and has good views to the city. The swimming pool is popular with young boys in the summer months, but the murky water puts most people off the idea of a dip. A small café offers drinks and ice cream.

Sleeping

Jam Hotel (☎ 040 223477; Darb Khosh; US$4) Tucked away in the Old City, this is Herat's best budget option. The rooms aren't huge, but good value with a flat rate for one or two beds. The shared bathrooms are basic and there's a restaurant serving *pulao* and kebabs. Rooms at the back have a good view of the Old City, overlooking the Friday Mosque.

Mowafaq Hotel (☎ 040 223503; Chowk Gulha; s/d with private bathroom US$20/30) Herat's largest hotel of four storeys is well located between the Old City and Shahr-e Naw. The good-sized rooms are clean but have a slightly dusty air.

Marco Polo Hotel (☎ 040 221944; jãd-e Badmurghan; s/d from US$20/40; 💻) Recently built, this is great value with bright rooms and 24-hour hot water in clean shared bathrooms. Management is helpful and always ready with tea. The restaurant serves up good breakfasts of bread, cheese, yogurt and eggs.

Park Hotel (☎ 040 223010; Girdha Park) This place was closed when we visited and had Ismail Khan's soldiers in residence. You may have more luck. Built in the 1930s, the hotel is Herat's oldest and is surrounded by pine trees.

Eating

Herat boasts few restaurants, so dining out is not going to be a major highlight.

There are lots of kebab and *pulao* joints along the main streets of the old city, where a plate of kebabs with tea won't cost you more than about 50Afg.

Brothers Mohabbat Gaznavi Restaurant (Darb Khosh) One of the better large kebab joints, busy at any time of day or night. Female travellers may find themselves directed upstairs to the family dining room.

Pizza (Bãgh-e Azadi) Good for those wanting a break from Afghan fare, this place does a good imitation of Western fast food. Tasty pizzas cost 150Afg, eat in or takeaway.

Shahiste Restaurant (jãd-e Badmurghan) On the 1st floor of the Marco Polo Hotel, this restaurant offers good Iranian-style food. The menu often only has a couple of dishes, but this is made up with generous plates of salad, pickled vegetables and yogurt. A big plate of *chelo morgh* (chicken with rice and berries) and side dishes will set you back about 220Afg.

For self-caterers, the vegetable bazaar near the Friday Mosque is full of essentials, and shops are well-stocked with imported Iranian foodstuffs.

Shopping

Herat is famous for its blue glass, handmade by Sultan Hamidy and his family for generations in a tiny factory north of the Friday Mosque. Ask at his shop if you may watch the glass being blown.

Getting There & Away

AIR

Ariana Afghan Airlines operates a daily service to Kabul (one hour, 2500Afg), occasionally laying on a second flight if there's heavy demand.

Airline Offices

Ariana Afghan Airlines (☎ 040 222315; Bāgh-e Azadi) The office claims to keep normal business hours but is frequently closed. Get there early in the morning – and bang on the door if necessary.

BUS

A new bus station has been built 5km from Herat on the road to the airport. It plans to be Herat's sole terminal, although only transport south and east had relocated here at the time of writing.

The road north to Maimana and Mazare Sharif is nonexistent after Qala-e Nau. Seats in Land Cruisers should be arranged at least a day in advance to Maimana (two days, 750Afg) and Mazar-e Sharif (three days, 1000Afg). The trip is through steppe and desert, but very hard travelling, driving up to 18 hours a day. Journey times increase with the mud and floods of spring. It's recommended that you buy an extra seat for comfort. Land Cruisers depart just northwest of the Citadel.

It's currently dangerous to travel from Herat south to Kandahar. Minibuses depart from the main bus station to Obey (five hours, 250Afg) and Chaghcheran (two days, 500Afg) in the early morning.

Minibuses depart regularly to Islam Qala on the Iranian border, taking just an hour on the upgraded road (100Afg, or 150Afg in a shared taxi). Transport leaves south of the Musalla Complex and minarets.

Transport to Torghundi on the Turkmenistan border (see p404) is less frequent, with only a couple of departures a day (two hours, 150Afg), so check departure times in advance.

Getting Around

TO/FROM THE AIRPORT

There's no public transport to the airport. The 15-minute taxi ride should cost around 80Afg.

LOCAL TRANSPORT

Public buses ply the main streets (fares are less than 5Afg), but yellow taxis are the easiest way of getting around, with most fares costing 20Afg to 50Afg.

More fun is to take a ride in a *gari* (horsedrawn buggy). The drivers take pride in decorating their carriages and dressing their horses with bells and red pompoms. Slower than a taxi, prices are about a third less over short distances. If you want to go a long way, the driver will assume you want to hire him outright, and you'll have to haggle.

NORTHERN AFGHANISTAN

North of the Hindu Kush is a rather different Afghanistan – akin to the Central Asian steppes. Indeed, prior to the modern obsession about borders, the Afghan nomads were quite at home on both sides of the Amu-Darya, which now separates Afghanistan from both Tajikistan and Uzbekistan. Until the Salang Tunnel through the Hindu Kush was completed in the mid-1960s, this was a totally isolated part of the country – accessible only by traversing the highest part of the mountains north of Kabul, or making a long desert crossing via Herat.

Most travellers head for Mazar-e Sharif and the shimmering domes of the Shrine of Hazrat Ali, but the north also offers routes to the rest of Central Asia. Badakhshan, Afghanistan's remote northeast, is lost in the tangle of peaks where the Hindu Kush meet the Pamirs, and has excellent future potential as a trekking destination.

History

The north formed the historic region of Bactria, with Bactra (Balkh) as its capital. Alexander the Great created a series of colonies here – Greek cities such as Ai-Khanoum (near modern Taloqan) prospered until the 1st century AD and the coming of the Kushans. Buddhist Balkh flourished from the riches of the Silk Road.

Buddhism was swept away by the Arabs in the 9th century and Balkh became a centre of Islamic learning. The Mongols brought an end to that, and it wasn't until Timur that Balkh was rebuilt. The damage had been done, however, and the north couldn't regain its earlier unity or power. Uzbek raiders grew rich on the anarchy.

The north was incorporated into modern Afghanistan in the late 18th century by Ahmad Shah Durrani, who established his border at the Amu-Darya river and exchanged treaties with the emir of Bukhara. Following his death the north fragmented again into a series of competing khanates. It took a further hundred years to bring them all back under the control of the Afghan state.

Badakhshan has always been considered apart from the rest of the north due to its geography. It controlled important trade routes through the Pamirs. When Marco Polo came this way, the region was powerful enough to receive embassies from China. Timur was the first to impose outside rule, but the mountainous territory proved difficult to control. The settlement of the Afghan border between the British and the Russians in 1893 formalised Badakhshan as part of Afghanistan and included the Wakhan Corridor, which reached to China. Far from the mainstream, Badakhshan was the only part of Afghanistan not to be conquered by the Russians or the Taliban. Today the province produces a large percentage of Afghan's opium, which is easily smuggled across the porous Tajik border.

Getting There & Away

Ariana Afghan Airlines operates several flights linking the north to Kabul. From Kabul there are three flights a week to Mazar-e Sharif, two to Faizabad and Kun-

---

TRAVELLING SAFELY IN NORTHERN AFGHANISTAN

The northern political scene is dominated by the rivalry between the Uzbek leader Rashid Dostum and the Tajik Ata Mohammed. Although both are nominally loyal to Kabul (and hold government posts), the two have repeatedly clashed over the control of Mazar-e Sharif and the surrounding area. UN-sponsored ceasefires and the posting of Kabuli police to Mazar-e Sharif have calmed tensions, but it's essential to check on the situation before travelling to the north, in particular to Balkh and Samangan provinces.

---

duz, and weekly flights to Maimana and Shiberghan (see p376 for details).

The Salang Tunnel connects the northern and southern halves of the country, but the road quality deteriorates quickly once you leave the Kabul–Mazar-e Sharif highway. In Badakhshan, the roads beyond Faizabad are often geared more to animal than vehicle traffic.

There are two border crossings between Afghanistan and Tajikistan at Shir Khan Bandar (north of Kunduz) and Ishkashim (in Badakhshan). The border with Uzbekistan is closed to travellers.

MAZAR-E SHARIF

pop 140,000

North Afghanistan's biggest city, Mazar-e Sharif was long overshadowed by the power of its neighbour Balkh. It took a 12th-century mullah to change that. He claimed to have found the hidden tomb of Ali, the Prophet Mohammed's son-in-law, buried in a local village. Balkh declined and Mazar grew as a place of pilgrimage. Its shrine today is the focus of the national Nawroz (Navrus) celebrations, and is a great place to see *buzkashi*.

Mazar-e Sharif mostly sat out the recent wars, but its outward prosperity masks deeper political problems. Mazar-e Sharif is at the heart of Afghanistan's warlord problem with two strongmen jostling for power and control of revenues from natural gas reserves and the trade with Uzbekistan. There have been occasional outbreaks of fighting between rival militias, so check

History

Mazar-e Sharif was a nondescript village in the shadow of Balkh until the miraculous dream that revealed the location of Ali's tomb. The Mongols proved to be just a hiccup to the town's growth, which expanded to eclipse nearby Balkh. Mazar-e Sharif was declared the capital of Afghan Turkestan in 1866.

Mazar-e Sharif was a Soviet stronghold during the war. The surrounding flat steppe made guerrilla attacks hard, and the city survived the war largely unscathed. The communist general Rashid Dostum mutin-

security in advance before planning a trip (see the boxed text on p389).

ied against the government in 1992 and set up shop as the local power broker.

Dostum ruled Mazar-e Sharif as his personal fiefdom, only leaving to travel south to lay siege (and lay waste) to Kabul. He made ties with newly independent Uzbekistan, printed his own currency and even ran his own airline, Balkh Air.

The Taliban were soon knocking at his door. They secretly cut a deal with one of his generals and captured the city in May 1997, only to be double bluffed. Within days of the Taliban takeover, the population (led largely by Hazara militia) rose in revolt and drove them out.

The Taliban returned a year later with revenge on their minds. Scores of Hazaras

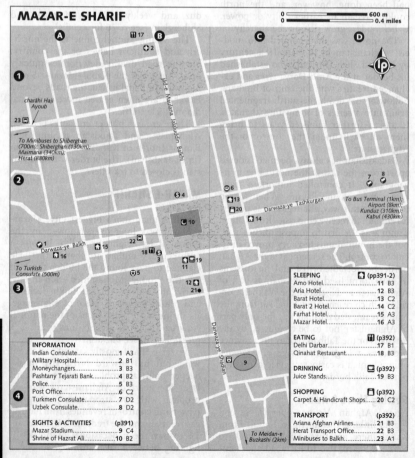

MAZAR-E SHARIF

0 — 600 m
0 — 0.4 miles

charāhi Haji Ayoub
23

To Minibuses to Shiberghan (700m); Shiberghan (130km); Maimana (340km); Herat (880km)

Jad-e Maulana Jalaluddin Balkhi

Darwaza-ye Tashkurgan

To Bus Terminal (1km); Airport (8km); Kunduz (310km); Kabul (430km)

Darwaza-ye Balkh

To Turkish Consulate (500m)

Darwaza-ye Shadian

To Meidan-e Buzkashi (2km)

INFORMATION	
Indian Consulate	1 A3
Military Hospital	2 B1
Moneychangers	3 B3
Pashtany Tejarati Bank	4 B2
Police	5 B3
Post Office	6 C2
Turkmen Consulate	7 D2
Uzbek Consulate	8 D2

SIGHTS & ACTIVITIES	(p391)
Mazar Stadium	9 C4
Shrine of Hazrat Ali	10 B2

SLEEPING	(pp391-2)
Amo Hotel	11 B3
Aria Hotel	12 B3
Barat Hotel	13 C2
Barat 2 Hotel	14 C2
Farhat Hotel	15 A3
Mazar Hotel	16 A3

EATING	(p392)
Delhi Darbar	17 B1
Qinahat Restaurant	18 B3

DRINKING	(p392)
Juice Stands	19 B3

SHOPPING	(p392)
Carpet & Handicraft Shops	20 C2

TRANSPORT	(p392)
Ariana Afghan Airlines	21 B3
Herat Transport Office	22 B3
Minibuses to Balkh	23 A1

were rounded up and summarily executed. The bodies were left lying in the street for five days to be eaten by dogs.

Mazar-e Sharif was the first city to be abandoned by the Taliban in the US-led attacks of November 2001. Dostum again returned to power, but this time he had a new rival in Ata Mohammed of the resurgent Northern Alliance. The city has since been parcelled up between them, with their rival soldiers and police patrolling the streets – an uneasy peace. A British military team, along with police from Kabul, have been posted to Mazar-e Sharif, in an attempt to encourage a long-term political solution.

Orientation

The blue domes of the Shrine of Hazrat Ali dominate Mazar-e Sharif. The shrine sits in a large park in the centre of the city, with four main roads radiating out to the cardinal points. Mazar-e Sharif is a relatively young city and has no historic quarter to speak of.

The airport is 10km east of Mazar-e Sharif. A bus station 3km, east of the centre, serves Kabul and all points south and east; transport west departs from a series of smaller stands close to the Shrine.

Information

INTERNET ACCESS

The post office was about to introduce an Internet service at the time of going to press.

MONEY

The best place to change money is with the moneychangers lining the streets west of the shrine. There's a branch of Pashtany Tejarati Bank on the north side that might change money.

POST, TELEPHONE & FAX

The main **post office** (northeast cnr of Shrine of Hazrat Ali; 7am-2pm) is open for international post, telephone calls and fax. There are a number of PCOs on the west side of the Shrine.

Sights

SHRINE OF HAZRAT ALI

Popular Muslim tradition contends that Ali is buried in Najaf in Iraq, but in the 12th century he visited a local mullah in a dream, revealing his true tomb to be hidden in a village near Balkh. A shrine was subsequently built on the site, which was renamed Mazar-e Sharif (Tomb of the Exalted). The building was levelled by Jenghiz Khan, who had heard rumours of gold buried beneath its domes. Balkh's Timurid rulers rebuilt the current shrine in the 15th century.

Holy to Sunni and Shiite alike, the shrine is greatly revered. It has undergone repeated extensions and restoration, and most of the current decoration is modern.

The shrine is home to hundreds of white pigeons; the site is so holy it's said that if a grey pigeon flies here, it will turn white within 40 days.

There is no entrance fee, but non-Muslims are not permitted to enter the tomb itself.

Festivals & Events

NAWROZ

Mazar-e Sharif is the centre of Afghanistan's Nawroz celebrations. A *janda* (religious banner) is raised in the courtyard of the shrine, which families visit to picnic at, celebrating the arrival of spring. *Buzkashi* is played at Mazar Stadium, or on a large, open expanse, south of the city, called Meidan-e Buzkashi.

Nawroz coincides with the local festival of Gul Surkh, named for the red tulips (associated with prosperity and fertility) that flower on the steppe.

Sleeping

Amo Hotel (050 2478; south of Shrine of Hazrat Ali; s/d $US8/15) This hotel seems to have a power problem – the lights are dim and the water is never more than warm, but its friendly staff make up for this. It's directly opposite the shrine, so try to get a room with a view. The rooms need a lick of paint, but it's the best budget choice in town.

Aria Hotel (050 2377; Darwaza-ye Shadian; s/d US$10/20) Around the corner from the Amo, this is another budget option. The rooms are bright and airy, but the shared bathrooms are grim. Poor value for the price.

Barat Hotel (070 502235; east of Shrine of Hazrat Ali; r from US$30) A modern hotel popular with Afghan businessmen. Rooms are nicely decorated, and there's satellite TV in the lobby. The shared bathrooms are clean and offer plenty of hot water. Rooms on the west side have great views of the shrine.

Barat 2 Hotel (☎ 050 2576; Darwaza-ye Tashkurgan) The management wouldn't take foreign guests when we visited, but plans to get permission from the local police. The hotel looks clean and well run – if you can get in expect to pay around US$15 per night.

Mazar Hotel (☎ 050 2703; Darwaza-ye Balkh; r US$45; 🏊) This hotel gives the impression that it hasn't seen a guest in ages – the staff are as dusty as the rooms. En suite rooms are a flat price for single or double occupancy, and have the novelty of a bath as well as shower. The swimming pool is an uninviting green.

Farhat Hotel (☎ 070 503177; Darwaza-ye Balkh; US$40) Has a gloomy old Soviet character, but offers decent en suite rooms with balcony.

Eating & Drinking

Mantu is popular in Mazar-e Sharif, so take a break from kebabs and *pulao*. The vegetarian option, *ashak*, is also available. Bread comes in heavy round loaves rather than the usual flat nan.

Qinahat Restaurant (opposite west side of Shrine of Hazrat Ali; ⏰ 8am-10pm) A good place to try *mantu*, where a generous portion costs 50Afg. The restaurant is on the 1st floor, overlooking the street. It has no phone.

Delhi Darbar (☎ 070 505417; opposite Military Hospital, jād-e Maulana Jalaluddin Balkhi; ⏰ noon-10pm) Sister to the restaurant in Kabul, and Mazar-e Sharif's best dining. Eat inside or in the walled garden in summer. The *thali* (meat or vegetarian) is good value at US$5, and goes well with a US$2 beer. Popular with NGO expats.

Barat Hotel serves good food throughout the day, but is often booked out with wedding parties.

Kebab shops and chaikhanas line the side streets near the shrine. The juice stands next to the Amo Hotel are definitely worth a visit for banana smoothies with chopped almonds at 15Afg.

Shopping

Mazar is a good place to pick up kilims and embroidery, the traditional handicrafts of the north. Prices are much cheaper than Kabul – the shops along the east side of the shrine have the best stock.

Getting There & Away

AIR

Ariana Afghan Airlines (☎ 070 3206; Darwaza-ye Shadian) flies to Kabul on Tuesday, Friday and Sunday (30 minutes, 1500Afg). The Ariana office only issues tickets one day in advance, but you can put your name down on a waiting list, as flights are often oversubscribed.

BUS

The terminal for transport south and east is on the main road 3km east of the shrine. Minibuses leave regularly for Kabul (10 hours, 400Afg), Pul-e Khumri (two hours, 120Afg) and Kunduz (six hours, 250Afg). Minibuses to Balkh (30 minutes, 25Afg) depart from charāhi Haji Ayoub, and to Shiberghan (90 minutes, 60Afg) from outside the Kefayat Wedding Club in the west of the city.

Transport to Herat must be arranged in advance. An office on the east side of the shrine sells seats for the three-day Land Cruiser trip for 1000Afg. The road west effectively finishes at Shiberghan, after which the travelling is very rugged; driving all day and sleeping where you stop, usually in local chaikhanas. Consider breaking your trip or buying an extra seat to save your sanity. The unmarked office can be hard to find – it's on the corner, on the 1st floor on the left.

Getting Around

TO/FROM THE AIRPORT

There is no public transport to the airport. The 15-minute taxi ride costs 100Afg.

LOCAL TRANSPORT

Mazar-e Sharif is a compact city and you're unlikely to stray too far on foot from the shrine complex. A taxi to most destinations within the city will cost 20Afg to 30Afg.

BALKH

The town of Balkh is one of Afghanistan's oldest. Zoroaster, founder of the world's oldest monotheistic religion, was born here in the 6th century BC. Balkh was the capital of Bactria, and Alexander the Great used the city as the base for his Central Asian campaigns. The city later became Buddhist under the Kushans, and prospered from the Silk Road.

When the Arabs brought Islam to Afghanistan, Balkh was already rich and they quickly dubbed it 'the Mother of Cities'. Passing under Bukharan rule in the 9th century AD, Balkh was endowed with fine mosques and palaces, and enjoyed a reputation as one of the great centres of Islamic learning.

Jenghiz Khan signalled the beginning of Balkh's end. Passing through 50 years later, Marco Polo was struck by its ruins. The city briefly recovered under Timurid rule, but never regained its former glory. Outbreaks of malaria and cholera led to its final abandonment in favour Mazar-e Sharif in the mid-19th century.

Orientation
Balkh today is little more than a large village. The main road from Mazar-e Sharif turns right into Balkh through the old city walls. Opposite the intersection is the mound of Takht-e Rustam, the site of an old Buddhist stupa, now an army checkpoint. The centre of Balkh is 2km past the walls.

Sights
SHRINE OF KHOJA ABU NASR PARSA
Built in the mid-15th century, this shrine ('Khoja Parsa' for short) is dedicated to a famous theologian. A classic of Timurid architecture, it's also a symbol of Balkh's final flourish before sliding into decay. The shrine is dominated by its massive portal entrance, which is flanked by twisted cable pillars, and decorated in blue tiles and plain brick. The whole is topped with a turquoise ribbed melon dome. Attached to the right of the shrine is a small modern medressa.

The dome was badly damaged in an earthquake in the 1990s and has recently undergone emergency repair.

TOMB OF RABI'A BALKHI
Opposite the shrine of Khoja Abu Nasr Parsa is the small tomb of Rabi'a Balkhi. Born in 9th-century Samanid Balkh, she is credited as the first (and greatest) woman to write poetry in Persian. Rabi'a Balkhi fell in love with her slave, and was punished by her brother by being bricked up in a dungeon. Thus condemned, she slashed her wrists and wrote her most famous poem – a bitter testament to doomed love – in her own blood on the walls of the prison.

The tomb was rediscovered in 1964 and is a popular place for young women with romantic designs to visit.

CITY WALLS
The huge mud-brick ramparts of Balkh are almost all that remains from Jenghiz Khan's rampage. The walls stretch for 10km around the town. The south walls, bisected by the road from Mazar-e Sharif, are well preserved, with defensive towers rising from the surrounding fields. A land-mine risk may exist along the walls – check which paths are safe before exploring.

MASJID-E NO GOMBAD
This ruined 9th-century mosque is the oldest in Afghanistan. The name refers to its originally nine-domed structure, although little more than the arcade piers now remain. The columns are covered in delicate stucco influenced by Samarra in Iraq. The site is covered by a metal canopy and is in urgent need of consolidation.

The mosque lies a 2km walk south of the intersection for Balkh on the road from Mazar-e Sharif. It's also known locally as Masjid-e Haji Piyada (Mosque of the Walking Pilgrim).

Sleeping & Eating
There are a couple of chaikhanas on the main road, but nowhere to stay – make a day trip from Mazar-e Sharif.

Getting There & Around
Plenty of minibuses (30 minutes, 25Afg) link Balkh and Mazar-e Sharif, 20km away. A private taxi costs 150Afg. Balkh is small enough to explore by foot.

KUNDUZ
The largely Uzbek town of Kunduz lies amid rich agricultural land and is one of Afghanistan's most stable and thriving towns.

When north Afghanistan fractured into city-states in the early 19th century, Kunduz was ruled by the slave-raiding Murad Beg. He was the most powerful of the northern khans, and dealt with Kabul and Bukhara as equals. The ruins of his fort are on the northern edge of the town. Kunduz's later prosperity came through the more peaceful cultivation of cotton.

Kunduz was the scene of fierce resistance by the Taliban in November 2001. It was the first base for ISAF's mandate outside Kabul, with a contingent of German troops being stationed here in late 2003.

A useful transport hub to reach Tajikistan and Badakhshan, Kunduz is also famous for *buzkashi*. The game is usually played anywhere on open ground outside the town on Friday during autumn and winter and around Nawroz.

There was no phone network in Kunduz at the time of research.

Sights

BALA HISSAR

Murad Beg's fort lies 2km north of the main square. Unfortunately, much of the surrounding ground is used as a public toilet, but there are good views from the ramparts. The inside of the fort is currently used as a tank park, so soldiers might approach you if you get your camera out – usually to have their own pictures taken.

Sleeping & Eating

Accommodation is limited in Kunduz.

Osman Hotel (opposite Takharestan Medrassa; r 200Afg) has very basic rooms above a chaikhana. Facilities are extremely spartan and there's no running water, but the staff will give you the key to a private toilet. The hotel isn't marked in English. Slightly better is the **Shah Mahmoud Hotel** (jād-e Imam Sahib; s/d 250/500Afg) and its dusty rooms and shared bathroom. Some travellers have sent good reports about the Spinzar Club, which offers rooms for about US$20 per night.

Deutscher Hof restaurant in Kabul is planning to open a branch in Kunduz sometime in 2004, following the expansion of ISAF (with German troops) to the town. Kebab stands, chaikhanas and juice stalls all cluster around the main square.

Getting There & Away

Minibuses to Kabul (10 hours, 400Afg) and Mazar-e Sharif (six hours, 250Afg) depart from Bandar-e Kabul terminal on the road south out of Kunduz. Transport goes via Pul-e Khumri – a sealed but much-potholed road.

Minibuses to Shir Khan Bandar leave just north of the main square (90 minutes, 80Afg) – minibuses leave mid-morning to meet the ferry from Tajikistan.

East of the main square are minibuses to Faizabad (10 hours, 400Afg). These don't go everyday, so check times in advance.

Ariana flies on Sunday and Tuesday to Kabul (30 minutes, 1200Afg). A taxi to the airport costs 50Afg.

FAIZABAD

Badakhshan's largest town sits in a valley surrounded by high peaks and alpine meadows. Its remoteness has been a virtue – it sat out the Soviet occupation and civil war completely. Even today, animal traffic seems to outnumber vehicles. Faizabad has an interesting bazaar and local knitted goods make good souvenirs. The whole area tempts you to start trekking, but be aware that opium production is rife in this province.

For accommodation, try the Hotel Ishan Awliyan, which is simple but clean. Beds cost 250Afg a night.

Minibuses run most days to Kunduz (10 hours, 400Afg); transport east is less regular. The roads are poor and difficult to traverse after October, but the mountain scenery is breathtaking. Two days' drive south of Faizabad lie Afghanistan's famed lapis lazuli mines at Sar-e Sang.

Ariana flies to Kabul on Saturday and Monday (1300Afg) from the airstrip 10km west of Faizabad, but spaces on the small planes fill quickly.

ISHKASHIM

The only reason you'll visit this tiny town is to cross the Tajik border. A bridge over the Pyanj River marks the border; the Afghan officials are very laid-back. There isn't much traffic on to Faizabad, so take whatever's going – a space in a shared taxi costs around 400Afg (eight hours). If you get stuck, the Pamir Hotel has basic rooms for 200Afg per head.

EASTERN AFGHANISTAN

Afghanistan's mountainous east is home to the great clichés of the Afghan character – hardy fighters defending lonely mountain passes, and tales of honour, hospitality and revenge. This is the land of the Pashtuns, Afghanistan's largest ethnic group. The area still holds much of its mystique, and entering Afghanistan through the Khyber Pass from Pakistan is a truly iconic travel experience.

Dangers & Annoyances

Predominantly Pashtun, east Afghanistan suffers from instability. Security on the road between Kabul and the Pakistan border is generally good, although incidents can occur. It is essential to check on the security situation with reliable sources before travelling. We strongly advise against travelling off this highway. See also Travelling Safely in Afghanistan on p357.

The region was originally a centre for Buddhism. Between the 2nd and 7th centuries AD, the Gandharan culture of the Kushans flourished, and the area was a place of pilgrimage rivalling Bamiyan. Islam came as Sultan Mahmud of Ghazni tore through to India; much of the area's subsequent history was tied precisely to controlling the route to the subcontinent through the Khyber Pass.

Mughal and then Afghan rulers used Peshawar as their summer capital, until it was lost to the Sikhs at the turn of the 19th century. The Afghans never got it back, a loss still bitter to many.

When the British drew Afghanistan's borders in 1893, they created the Durand Line, splitting the Pashtun tribes in two. The actual border was never formally demarcated and modern Afghan maps have frequently referred to the border as 'disputed'. Since Pakistan's independence in 1947, the issue has heavily influenced relations between the two powers.

The remote wooded province of Nuristan was immortalised in Eric Newby's *A Short Walk in the Hindu Kush*. The Nuristanis claim descent from the troops of Alexander the Great and, until the end of the 19th century, were pagans, carving wooden idols and drinking wine. A vigorous campaign by Abdur Rahman Khan brought Islam to them by the sword. The related pagan Kalasha survive across the border in Pakistan.

JALALABAD

The Mughal emperor Akbar founded Jalalabad, and its warm winter climate helped it become a popular retreat for Afghan kings.

Positioned near the foot of the Khyber Pass, the city has always been strategically important. The British garrison in Jalalabad received the one survivor of the disastrous retreat from Kabul in 1841 (see p35). Just over 150 years later, the mujaheddin launched an equally disastrous attack on Jalalabad, their first attempt to capture a major city from the government after the Soviet withdrawal. Over 10,000 people died.

Jalalabad is famous for its oranges, and holds the Mushaira (Orange Blossom) Festival on 13 April with poetry and picnics in the gardens of Seraj-ul Emorat. Temperatures can be stiflingly hot in summer.

A new phone network was being introduced to Jalalabad in 2004.

Sights

King Habibullah was assassinated in Jalalabad in 1919. He introduced golf to

THE KHYBER PASS

The road from Torkham to the Pakistani city of Peshawar traverses one of the most famous and strategically important mountain passes in the world. The Khyber Pass stretches for 50km through the Hindu Kush, linking Afghanistan to the Indian subcontinent. Babur drove his army through on his way to set up the Mughal empire, and throughout history, Afghans have marauded over the pass to plunder the riches of India.

Not surprisingly, the British weren't too keen on letting the Afghans have the key to this particular back door, and made sure that Peshawar and the Khyber Pass stayed on their side of the border, reinforcing it with a network of forts.

Despite this, they never truly conquered the pass itself, and had to buy off the local Pashtun tribes to stop them raiding British convoys. Even today, the Pakistani government only controls the main highway – step off the tarmac and you're in tribal land. Local tribes have built a second road through the pass away from the highway, to allow them to carry on their traditional smuggling unimpeded, carrying everything from opium to DVD players.

During years of war, the Khyber Pass was the main artery for refugees fleeing into Pakistan.

Afghanistan, and his **mausoleum** was built on the municipal golf course. Set among orange trees, it's in some need of repair. King Amanullah is also buried here, with his wife Queen Soraya, doyenne of Afghan feminism. The ceremonial gardens of **Seraj-ul Emorat** lie opposite.

The many Buddhist sites near Jalalabad have been destroyed. The loss of **Hadda**, site of over 1000 stupas, to Soviet bombing was particularly grievous. The Buddha is said to have received his calling there. The caves around Hadda were used as caches by the mujaheddin and later hosted Al-Qaeda training camps.

Sleeping & Eating

The **Spinghar Hotel** (sarakh-e Kabul; s/d $35/50) is set in large gardens in the centre of town. Most rooms have private bathrooms and have been recently redecorated. There's a basic restaurant, and the shady trees are good for escaping Jalalabad's summer heat.

For tighter budgets, the **Gawandey Hotel** (Chowk-e Ragheh; s/d $15/30) is a better option, with decent rooms and a clean communal bathroom. The helpful manager speaks good English.

Eating out is a kebab-centred experience. There are plenty of stands and chaikhanas in the centre of town, around the bazaar and Chowk-e Mukharabat. For drinks, juice stands sell refreshing glasses of crushed sugar cane and mango juice (in season).

Getting There & Around

Rickshaws are popular for getting around Jalalabad, but not all roads are paved so they can be a very bumpy experience. Most fares will be under 20Afg.

Minibuses to Kabul (four hours, 150Afg) and the border at Torkham (three hours, 100Afg) run through the day. Shared taxis are faster and cost more. The road to Kabul is particularly attractive, following the Kabul River past Sarobi Dam and up the stupendous Tangi Gharu Gorge to the Kabul Plateau.

TORKHAM

There's no reason to stick around in this border town, it's all auto shops and money-changers. As Afghanistan's busiest border post (see p403), there's plenty of transport – minibuses to Jalalabad (three hours, 100Afg)

and Kabul (seven hours, 250Afg), as well as shared taxis.

SOUTHERN AFGHANISTAN

Afghanistan's south is dry, dusty and dangerous. Largely Pashtun, the area is beset by anarchy, opium and guerrilla attacks. The Kabul–Kandahar–Herat highway is particularly dangerous, and the Taliban have deliberately targeted Westerners and Afghans working with them. We currently advise against travel to this area.

GHAZNI

The modern town of Ghazni is a pale shadow of its former glory. In the 11th century the city was the centre of the Ghaznavid empire and was one of the greatest cities in the Islamic world. Sultan Mahmud filled his court with poets and artists, his stables with an army of elephants, and whenever the treasury was bare, raided Delhi – introducing Islam to India in the process.

Ghazni's most visible monuments to its history are the two massive minarets, built in the 11th century, on the road from Kabul. The tomb of Sultan Mahmud lies nearby.

KANDAHAR

Kandahar is in the far south of Afghanistan, at an important crossroads where the main road from Kabul branches northwest to Herat and southeast to Quetta in Pakistan. Kandahar lies in the Pashtun heartland and was Afghanistan's first capital under Ahmad Shah Durrani in the 18th century. More recently Kandahar became the spiritual capital of the Taliban. A large US army base, centre of the 'War on Terror', sits on the outskirts of the city.

Kandahar's great treasure, a cloak which once belonged to the Prophet, is safely kept in the Mosque of the Sacred Cloak. Prior to the Taliban's capture of Kabul in 1996, Mullah Omar wrapped himself in the cloak in front a cheering Taliban crowd, declaring himself Amir al-Momineen (Commander of the Faithful). Ahmad Shah Durrani's mausoleum sits nearby.

A few kilometres west from the centre of Kandahar are the Chihil Zina (Forty Steps).

They lead up to a niche, guarded by two stone lions, carved in the rock by Babur to celebrate the Mughal's achievements.

KANDAHAR TO HERAT

Ruins and drugs are the features of this route across southern Afghanistan. The Helmand Valley was once a wheat belt, but now the dry terrain suits the cultivation of opium poppies. The province of Helmand is a Taliban stronghold and possibly the most dangerous part of the country.

Lashkar Gah, 150km west of Kandahar, today is a jumble of ruins and remains – shattered remnants of a once-mighty Ghaznavid city. The superb arch of Bost was the high point of a visit to this old centre.

AFGHANISTAN DIRECTORY

ACCOMMODATION

Most levels of accommodation are available in Afghanistan, from simple hotels to en suite yurts. A recent development has been the appearance of private guesthouses in Kabul. Outside the cities the quality of accommodation drops off considerably, and basic hotels are the order of the day. Long bus trips are often broken with an overnight stay at a chaikhana, usually sleeping on the floor with fellow passengers.

ACTIVITIES

The mountains of Afghanistan could rival Nepal for trekking opportunities, but right now, potential is all there is. There's no infrastructure, and anyone setting out will be genuinely breaking new ground – you'll be unsupported in very remote areas. The best potential areas for treks are Badakhshan, Bamiyan, Panjshir and Nuristan (subject to security concerns). Remember that land mines are present throughout the country.

BOOKS

For books about women in Afghanistan, see p364.

Martin Ewans' *Afghanistan – A Short History of its People and Politics* covers the breadth of Afghan history from Alexander the Great to Hamid Karzai, with a sure hand and lightness of touch, and is highly recommended.

Taliban by Ahmed Rashid is the definitive history of the movement by a long-time observer of the Afghan scene. Rashid lifts the lid on regional power games, oil company manoeuvrings, and an Afghan people stuck in the middle.

Ostensibly a quest for the roots of Islamic architecture, *The Road to Oxiana* by Robert Byron is still the best travel-literature book on Afghanistan (and Persia), more than 60 years after it was written. Few characters in the travel-literature genre are as memorable as the show-stealing Afghan ambassador to Tehran.

A Short Walk in the Hindu Kush by Eric Newby is one of the modern classics of travel writing, describing the (mis)adventures of two Englishmen who trekked to the remote Nuristan region in the 1950s. One of the best endings of any travel book.

More recently, *An Unexpected Light* by Jason Elliot dazzles the reader with a journey around Afghanistan on the eve of the fall of Kabul to the Taliban. Elliot displays a sympathetic ear and a keen understanding of the richness of Afghan culture and history.

Still useful to travellers is the 1977 *An Historical Guide to Afghanistan* by Nancy Hatch Dupree. Available in Kabul, this is an invaluable guide to Afghanistan's cultural heritage – and acts as an unwitting testament to what was lost in 25 years of war.

BUSINESS HOURS

Afghan businesses generally open from 8am to 4pm. The official weekend is on Friday, although government offices (and many businesses) close around noon on Thursday. Official business is better conducted in the mornings. Shops and offices have restricted hours during Ramadan. Chaikhanas tend to open in the early morning (restaurants follow suit a few hours later), staying open until late evening.

CUSTOMS

There are no customs declaration forms in Afghanistan and officials are only interested in guns and drugs. Foreigners are allowed small amounts of alcohol 'for personal use'.

On leaving, an easy-to-miss sign at Kabul Airport's passport control announces that

DUST

The comparative rarity of paved roads can make Afghanistan feel like the dustiest country in the world; even Kabul is regularly engulfed in swirling dust storms. Respiratory problems are common complaints among travellers. Both Afghan men and women use their scarves to keep out the dust on bumpy roads – you should do the same.

carpets and 'handicrafts' must be declared to customs – but no-one seems to want to check your bags.

DANGERS & ANNOYANCES

Afghanistan presents unique potential risks in comparison to the rest of Central Asia, with the danger of warlordism and guerrilla violence in some parts of the country. It's essential to keep abreast of the current political and security assessments both before travelling and while in the country. For more information, see Travelling Safely in Afghanistan, p357.

EMBASSIES & CONSULATES
Afghan Embassies in Central Asia

Afghanistan has embassies in Almaty (p153), Bishkek (p310), Dushanbe (p349), Ashgabat (p436) and Tashkent (p234).

Afghan Embassies & Consulates

Afghanistan's diplomatic missions abroad include the following:

Australia Canberra (☎ 02-6282 7311; www.afghan embassy.net; PO Box 155, Deakin West, ACT 2600)
Belgium Brussels (☎ 02-7613166; 281 Rue Francoise Gay, B-1150)
Canada Ottawa (☎ 613-563 4223/65; 246 Queen St, KIP 5E4)
France Paris (☎ 01-4568 2771; www.ambafghane-paris .com; 32 Avenue Raphael, 75016)
Germany Berlin (☎ 030-2292612; Wilhelmstrasse 65 D, 10117); Bonn (☎ 0228-256797; Liebigstrasse 1A, 53125)
India New Delhi (☎ 011- 410 3331; Plat No 5, Block 50F, Chanakyapuri, 110021)
Iran Mashhad (☎ 051-8544829; Sevom Isfand Sq, off Doshahid St, Emam Khomeini Ave); Tehran (☎ 021-8737050; 4th St, Dr Beheshti Ave)
Japan Tokyo (☎ 03-5465 1219; Matsumoto International House, 37-8 Nishihara 3 Chome, Shibuya Ku, 151-0066)

Netherlands Amsterdam (☎ 20-6721311; Wellensparkweg 114, 1070 HN)
Pakistan Islamabad (☎ 051-2824505/6; House 8, St 90, G-6/3); Karachi (☎ 021-5821264; 33/2 9th St, Khayaban-e Shamsi, Phase V, Defence 75500); Peshawar (☎ 091-285962; The Mall, Saddar Bazaar); Quetta (☎ 081-843364; 45 Prince Rd)
Russia Moscow (☎ 095-9287581; Sverchkov Per 3/2)
United Arab Emirates Abu Dhabi (☎ 2-6661244; PO Box 5687)
UK London (☎ 020-7589 8891/2; www.afghanembassy .co.uk; 31 Prince's Gate, SW7 1QU)
USA New York (☎ 212-972 2276; 11th fl, 360 Lexington Ave, NY 10017); Washington DC (☎ 202-416 1620; www .embassyofafghanistan.org; 2341 Wyoming Ave NW, 20036)

Embassies & Consulates in Afghanistan

All of the following offices are in Kabul (see Map p368), except where noted. Australia, New Zealand and Ireland do not maintain diplomatic representation in Afghanistan. For information on visas for onward travel see p402.

Belgium (☎ 070 200135; House 40, Lane 3, St 15, Wazir Akbar Khan)
Canada (☎ 070 29428; House 256, St 15, Wazir Akbar Khan)
China (☎ 020 2102548/9; Shah Mahmoud wat)
France (☎ 070 284033; Cinema Zainab Rd)
Germany (☎ 020 2101512/14/15; charāhi Zambak)
India (☎ 020 2200133; Interior Ministry Rd, Shahr-e Naw); Herat (☎ 040 224432; sarakh-e Qulurdo); Mazar-e Sharif (☎ 070 500372; Darwaza-ye Balkh)
Iran (☎ 020 2101393/4; charāhi Sherpur); Herat (☎ 040 220015; jād-e Walayat). Diplomatic representation is due to open in Mazar-e Sharif in 2004.
Italy (☎ 070 224905; Great Massoud Rd)
Japan (☎ 020 290172; St 15, Wazir Akbar Khan)
Kazakhstan (☎ 070 277450; House 1, St 10, Wazir Akbar Khan)
Netherlands (☎ 070 286640/1; Ghiyasuddin wat, Shahr-e Naw)
Norway (☎ 020 2300900/0899; Lane 4, St 15, Wazir Akbar Khan)
Pakistan (☎ 020 2300911/3; St 10, Wazir Akbar Khan); Jalalabad (charāhi Marastoon). There is no phone at the Jalalabad consulate.
Russia (☎ 020 2300500; House 63, Lane 5, St 15, Wazir Akbar Khan)
Sweden (☎ 020 2301416; House 70, Lane 1, St 15, Wazir Akbar Khan)
Switzerland (☎ 020 2301565; House 486, Lane 3, St 13, Wazir Akbar Khan)
Tajikistan (☎ 020 2101080; House 3, St 10, Wazir Akbar Khan)

Turkey (☎ 020 2101581/79; Shah Mahmoud wat); Mazar-e Sharif (☎ 070 500501; Baba Yadgar Kamarband)
Turkmenistan (☎ 020 2300541; House 280, Lane 3, St 13, Wazir Akbar Khan); Herat (☎ 040 223534; Walayat St); Mazar-e Sharif (☎ 050 5023; Darwaza-ye Tashkurgan)
UK (☎ 020 2200147/8; Karte Parwan)
USA (☎ 070 201913; Great Massoud Rd)
Uzbekistan (☎ 020 2300124; House 14, St 13, Wazir Akbar Khan); Mazar-e Sharif (☎ 050 3042; Darwaza-ye Tashkurgan)

FESTIVALS & EVENTS

Nawroz (Navrus; see p450), is greatly celebrated in Afghanistan, and Mazar-e Sharif is the centre of the national holiday.

Ramadan is taken a lot more seriously here compared with the rest of Central Asia, and travellers may find things harder work at this time, as chaikhanas and restaurants are closed during the day. Lots of businesses (and government offices) close early during Ramadan. On the other hand, the breaking of the fast (itfar) at sunset is always a joy, and you'll often receive spontaneous invitations to share food.

Shiites celebrate Ashura, to commemorate the martyrdom of Husain (the Prophet Mohammed's grandson) during the month of Moharram. Men parade in public and whip and cut themselves as a mark of their grief.

See p449 for the dates of major Islamic holidays.

HOLIDAYS

Public holidays in Afghanistan:
21 March Nawroz.
28 April Celebration of the Islamic Revolution in Afghanistan.
1 May National Labour Day.
4 May Remembrance Day for Martyrs and the Disabled.
19 August Independence Day.
9 September Ahmad Shah Massoud Day.

INSURANCE

Political instability (and advice from government travel advisories) means that some insurance companies may be reluctant to issue insurance for a trip to Afghanistan. Check the fine print on the policy before signing up.

INTERNET ACCESS

The Internet is relatively new to Afghanistan, with access following the roll-out of the mobile-phone network. Internet cafés are common in Kabul and Herat, with prices standard at around US$3 per hour.

INTERNET RESOURCES

Afghanistan is well represented on the Web. Several good portal sites exist, including **Afghanistan Online** (www.afghan-web.com) and **Afghana** (www.afghana.com) offering everything from the rules of buzkashi to political discussion. The **Afghan Government** (www.af) also has its own web page.

The **Survival Guide to Kabul** (www.kabulguide .net) is an indispensable resource to the city, aimed primarily at expat workers. More general countrywide travel information is available from **Kabul Caravan** (www .kabulcaravan.com).

With events developing so fast on the ground, it's essential to keep up with the news. **E-Ariana** (www.e-ariana.com) and **Afghan News Network** (www.afghannews.net) offer daily news and archived articles. **ReliefWeb** (www .reliefweb.int) provides excellent coverage from a humanitarian slant, including news and press releases from the UN and many NGOs.

The UN-run **Afghanistan Information Management Service** (AIMS; www.aims.org.af) helps coordinate work and share data between NGOs, and is a useful guide to who's working where. Also useful for regular security updates. The **Afghanistan Research and Evaluation Unit** (www.areu.org.pk) produces an online directory and guide to the assistance community.

Beautiful images of Afghanistan from both before and after the war can be found at the website of photographer **Luke Powell** (www.lukepowell.com). The website http://tales ofasia.com/afghanistan.htm has a series of travelogues on Afghanistan.

MAPS

Some maps of Afghanistan are available in the bookshops of Kabul, but they tend to be expensive. Afghanistan is a good 1:1.5 million map produced by Nelles. For those travelling further east, the 1:2 million Afghanistan & Pakistan map by GeoCenter is recommended. Both maps have good mountain coverage. **AIMS** (www.aims.org.af) has excellent reference and topographical maps of the country, serving the aid community.

MEDIA
Newspapers

Newspapers have mushroomed since the end of 2001. Daily newspapers published in both Dari and Pashto include *Anis*, *Erada* and the popular weekly *Kilid*. *Kabul Weekly* and *Kabul Times* are published in English (the latter twice a week); *Erada* prints an English supplement every Thursday.

Radio

Established in the 1920s, Radio Afghanistan plays a mix of traditional music and news programming, but the government-run station faces strong competition from the new FM stations in Kabul, such as Radio Arman and Voice of Women. The BBC is the most listened-to broadcaster in Afghanistan. Its popular series *New Home, New Life* uses a soap opera format in Dari and Pashto to tackle issues from health education to the new constitution.

TV

The range of domestic TV transmitters doesn't extend much beyond the capital. In any case, those with TVs usually prefer satellite or cable. Bollywood films are particularly popular, although the female stars are much criticised by the mullahs. Many hotels have satellite dishes.

MONEY

Afghanistan's currency is the afghani (Afg), with new notes introduced in 2002 to encourage economic stability. There are notes of one, two, five, 10, 20, 50, 100, 500 and 1000Afg. There are no coins.

The war-shattered banking system is slowly rebuilding, and there's currently no meaningful distinction between the formal and black economy. The majority of people change their currency at the moneychangers bazaar in each town, although most hotels will also change money. Payment for hotel bills (along with airline tickets) is often requested in US dollars. Euros are hard to change outside the main cities.

Credit cards are currently not accepted anywhere and there are no ATMs. Although Afghanistan is essentially a cash-only economy, it is possible (if slow) to change travellers cheques at the main branch of Da Afghanistan Bank in Kabul. The bank charges around US$10 commission per transaction, making it expensive to change small denominations.

Exchange Rates

Currency exchange rates at the time of writing were:

Country	Unit		Afghani
Australia	A$1	=	33.09
Canada	C$1	=	31.97
euro zone	€1	=	53.38
Iran	1000 rials	=	5.11
New Zealand	NZ$1	=	29.45
Pakistan	Rs10	=	7.49
Tajikistan	1TJS	=	15.44
Turkmenistan	1000 M	=	8.72
UK	UK£1	=	79.91
USA	US$1	=	42.90
Uzbekistan	100 som	=	4.36

POST

Mail is best sent from Kabul. A postcard to anywhere in the world costs 16Afg. Letters to the US, Canada and Australia cost 18Afg, with letters elsewhere costing 19Afg. Mail generally arrives at its destination in less than two weeks. Stamp lovers will have fun at the main post office in Kabul picking out old designs for their mail or collections – one postcard arrived at its destination franked with stamps dating from 1969!

Sending packages is a daylong process and customs-declaration paper chase. It's more efficient (if more expensive) to use an international shipping company. DHL, TNT and FedEx all have offices in Kabul.

Poor infrastructure means that receiving mail in Afghanistan is a hit-or-miss affair. Most private companies and NGOs prefer courier services or electronic communication. Post restante services are nonexistent; it's far easier to stick with email.

REGISTRATION

Travellers don't need to register with the authorities on arrival in Afghanistan. In towns not used to seeing foreigners, some hotels may ask you to register with the police before they allow you to check in (or they will summon the police to take your details).

SHOPPING

Afghanistan is best known for its carpets, mostly produced in the north and west of the country. Prices are best in Mazar-e Sharif, Kunduz and Herat. As well as traditional styles, carpet patterns move with the times – modern designs include the Soviet army retreating from Afghanistan, and the World Trade Centre attacks.

Other good souvenirs include lapis lazuli from the mines of Badakhshan, handmade blue glass from Herat, pottery from Istalif, Uzbek embroidery, quilted silk coats *(chapans)*, and the pancake-flat *pakul* hats. Moneychangers will often offer you old banknotes to buy as souvenirs – even Iraqi dinars with pictures of Saddam Hussein!

TELEPHONE

A limited fixed-line telephone network exists in the major cities, but the country has quickly taken to mobile phones. Two companies compete for custom: **Afghan Wireless Communications Company** (AWCC; www.afghanwireless .com; prefix 070) and **Roshan** (www.roshan.af; prefix 079). Both companies use the GSM system, although demand frequently overloads the networks. In early 2004 AWCC coverage extended to Kabul, Herat, Mazar-e Sharif, Kandahar and Jalalabad, whereas Roshan's coverage is limited to Kabul. Both companies ultimately plan to cover the entire country.

It's easiest to place a call at a post office. You give the number to a clerk who directs you to a booth and places the call. Calls to the US cost around 25Afg per minute, 25Afg to Europe and 28Afg to Australia. Local calls cost around 5Afg per minute. In addition, public call offices (PCOs) are common in the major cities; these are usually just an office with a desk and phone, but slightly more expensive.

In 2004 the Chinese planned to revitalise Afghanistan's landline network, further increasing the competition for phone users. Due to the proliferation of different systems all telephone numbers in this guide are listed with their prefixes.

CROSSED LINES?

Afghanistan's telephone system is in a state of massive flux. Although we have taken every care at the time of research to check all telephone numbers, it is highly likely that many numbers will change during the lifetime of this guide.

TOURIST INFORMATION

The main office of the **Afghan Tourist Organisation** (ATO; ☎ 020 2300338; Great Massoud Rd) is in Kabul, opposite the Ariana Graveyard. ATO also has offices at the airport and the InterContinental Hotel, as well as a branch in Herat. The arrival of a genuine tourist at the offices creates a frisson of excitement among the staff, who can organise drivers and translators, and sell you copies of Nancy Dupree's 1970s guidebooks. There are no ATO offices outside Afghanistan.

VISAS

Visas for Afghanistan are easy obtain. Tourist-visa applications do not require a letter of support, although bemused consular officials may occasionally ask applicants to explain why they want to holiday in Afghanistan. Those travelling for work purposes require a supporting letter from their office.

A one-month single-entry visa in London costs UK£30, UK£55 for a three-month multiple-entry visa, and UK£115 for a six-month multiple-entry visa, all issued in two days. The embassy in Washington charges US$50 for a one-month single-entry visa, US$100 for a three-month multiple-entry visa, and US$180 for a six-month multiple-entry visa. Visas take two weeks to process, with a premium charged for same-day issue.

In neighbouring countries, New Delhi, Peshawar, Tehran, Mashhad and Tashkent are good places to apply for an Afghan visa. One-month single-entry visas cost US$30 and are generally issued on the same day.

Afghan visas are not issued on arrival at Kabul airport or at any land border.

Visa Extensions

Visas can be extended in Kabul at the **Interior Central Passport Department** (Passport Lane, off Interior Ministry Rd). Tourists require one passport photo and a letter requesting an extension from the head office of the ATO (see above). The letter costs US$10 per month requested, with a maximum three-month extension possible.

If you're working in Afghanistan, you'll need a letter of support from your organisation, or in the case of journalists, a letter from the **Ministry of Information and Culture** (☎ 020 2101301; Pul-e Bagh-e Omomi, Kabul). Visa extensions cost US$30 for three months, which must be paid into the central branch of **Da Afghanistan Bank** (jād-e Froshgah, Kabul), and the receipt presented at the passport office along with one passport photo.

Visas for Onward Travel

For contact details of embassies and consulates in Afghanistan, see p398.

China A one-month visa from the embassy in Kabul (9-11am) costs US$50 and is issued in four days, or US$80 for same-day issue. Need a letter from your home embassy and one photo.

India In the embassy in Kabul (9am-noon, Mon-Thu), a six-month visa can be issued in 24 hours. It costs US$65 and you need three photos. No visas are issued in the consulates in Herat and Mazar-e Sharif.

Iran A transit visa from the embassy in Kabul (8am-2pm Sat-Wed, 8am-noon Thu) costs from US$15 to US$60 depending on nationality. These are issued in one day to two weeks – entirely dependent on your nationality. British pay most and wait longest, and also need a letter from your home embassy. One-month tourist visas take two weeks for all and cost US$65, flat rate. You need two photos. The same services are available in Kabul and Herat (8.30am-noon).

Pakistan The embassy in Kabul (9am-noon Sun-Thu) is occasionally reluctant to issue tourist visas, even if you have a letter from your home embassy. The Jalalabad consulate is a good second place to apply – or better still get your visa in advance.

Tajikistan A one-month visa from the embassy (9am-noon Sun-Thu) costs US$80, is issued in one week with one photo and a letter from your home embassy.

Turkmenistan Visas are issued in Kabul and Herat (9am-noon). You need a letter of invitation from a Turkmen travel agency, specifying your point of entry to Turkmenistan, and two photos. A one-week visa costs US$55, a one-month visa costs US$125. These take one week to issue.

Uzbekistan Neither the Uzbek embassy nor consulate currently issue visas.

WOMEN TRAVELLERS

Afghanistan is a very socially conservative country, and women travellers will feel this more than men. It should be remembered, however, that attitudes to women are bound up with the protection of honour. Afghan men will be very attentive to you, but active sexual harassment is generally rare, particularly in comparison with neighbouring Pakistan.

It is not compulsory to wear a headscarf, but in practice almost all women do. Walking around with a bare head attracts a lot of attention in Kabul, where locals are used to

seeing Western women. In the countryside you would just be considered plain rude. In keeping with local sensibilities, you may want to wear long shirts that hide the shape of the body; bare arms should be also avoided.

Female travellers can interact with Afghan women in a way impossible to men. You may also be treated as an 'honorary male' by local Afghan men, unsure of the correct protocol, although it's best to wait for them to offer a hand to shake rather than offering your own. If you're travelling with a man, Afghan men will talk to him rather than you.

WORK

It's sometimes possible to get employment with the many aid agencies in Afghanistan, but it'll help if you've got skills relevant to their work. Contact them in advance (see Internet Resources on p399); budgets are usually tight, so they won't appreciate you just turning up on their door.

TRANSPORT IN AFGHANISTAN

GETTING THERE & AWAY
Entering Afghanistan

With the reopening of Kabul International Airport to civilian traffic, the easiest way to Afghanistan is by air. On touching down there's a (mostly) orderly queue for immigration, but as a foreigner you'll often get fast-tracked. After this, there's a separate booth for passport registration, before the scrum of the baggage hall. Customs checks are mostly in name only.

Officials are similarly laid-back if you're entering overland. Most of Afghanistan's borders are so porous, you'll be generally looked on as more a novelty than a bureaucratic hindrance. Bear in mind that Afghanistan has 30 minutes' time difference with all its neighbours. Some borders are closed on certain days (see p403), and everything grinds to a halt on Friday lunch time.

Air
AIRPORTS & AIRLINES

Kabul is Afghanistan's only international airport. The national carrier, Ariana Afghan Airlines, has twice-weekly connections to

Dubai and weekly flights to Delhi, Islamabad, Dushanbe, Tehran, Frankfurt, İstanbul, Sharjah, Moscow, Baku and Ürümqi. In addition to Azerbaijan Airlines, Marco Polo Airways and the German carrier LTU (see p376), services operate to serve the NGO community: United Nations Humanitarian Air Service (Unhas), the International Committee of the Red Cross (ICRC) and the private humanitarian service Pactec.

When buying an Ariana ticket, return dates are often left open, even if you've specified a date. It's essential that you confirm your return date as soon as possible, and reconfirm the time of departure the day before travel.

Land

Afghanistan shares its border with six other countries, and maintains official border crossings with all except China.

BORDER CROSSINGS

Whereas land connections between Afghanistan and Iran and Pakistan are straightforward, those wishing to cross from Central Asia will find their way beset by permits and permissions.

To/From Pakistan

The crossing from Peshawar in Pakistan over the Khyber Pass to Afghanistan is one of the most evocative border crossings in the world.

The road to the border runs through Pakistan's Tribal Areas, where the government's writ has no power. You'll need to arrange a permit from the **Khyber Tribal Agency** (☎ 091 278542; University Town) in Peshawar. This is free, but you'll need your passport and photocopies of your Afghan and Pakistan visas. Make sure your permit is to Torkham, and not just the tourist viewpoint over the Khyber at Michni. You can arrange the permit 24 hours before travel, but you'll have to return on the day to pick up an armed escort from the Khyber Rifles to accompany you to the border.

A taxi (it's not permitted to take public transport) to the border, 55km away, will cost around US$15, and your guard will expect a tip of around 200Rs. Once across the border, there's plenty of transport to Jalalabad (three hours, 100Afg) or Kabul (seven hours, 300Afg). If you leave Peshawar early, you can reach Kabul in one go.

Entering Pakistan, you'll be assigned an armed guard after immigration, and you must take a taxi to Peshawar.

At the time of going to press, the road from Quetta to Kandahar, crossing from the Pakistani border town of Chaman to Spin Boldak was only open to humanitarian traffic.

To/From Iran

Crossing the Iranian border is straightforward. There's a direct bus from Mashhad to Herat (11 hours, 50,000IR), which is quicker (and cheaper) than taking a bus from Mashhad to the border at Taybad, and arranging onward transport from the Afghan side at Islam Qala.

At the time of research direct buses in the opposite direction to Mashhad were about to be introduced, so if you're leaving Afghanistan, check for details or take a minibus from Herat to Islam Qala (one hour, 100Afg) and cross the border on foot. Customs checks can be rigorous on entering Iran, and remember that female travellers need to adhere to a stricter dress code – covering the head and body shape.

The border crossing at Zaranj is closed to travellers.

To/From Tajikistan

Tajikistan is the easiest Central Asian republic to cross from. The Tajik port of Nizhniy Pjanj has a daily ferry (US$10) across the Amu-Darya to Shir Khan Bandar. The ferry leaves Nizhniy Pjanj at 10am, and Shir Khan Bandar after lunch. There's no ferry on Sunday. A new bridge is being built here to open in 2005. Customs checks entering Tajikistan can be strict; by comparison the Afghan officials couldn't be more laid-back. From Shir Khan Bandar it's a 90-minute minibus ride to Kunduz.

In Badakhshan the bridge over the Pyanj River is open to travellers at Ishkashim. Entering Afghanistan here is easy, but the Tajik side lies in the restricted region of

Gorno-Badakhshan. Permits to travel here are only issued in Dushanbe, so it's unclear whether you'll be allowed to enter.

To/From Turkmenistan

The Turkmen authorities love paperwork. To enter Turkmenistan from Torghundi, it's best to have Gushgi listed as your point of entry on your visa; the authorities may even insist you be met by a Turkmen tour guide. There's also a US$10 fee for an entry card. If you're trying to leave Turkmenistan, you'll need Gushgi on your visa as the point of exit, and listed on your travel itinerary. In both directions, the Turkmen customs will probably take your luggage apart. For more information, see p439.

To/From Uzbekistan

The Uzbek border over the Friendship Bridge to Termiz is firmly closed to travellers. Humanitarian traffic only crosses this border after a bureaucratic tussle with the Uzbek authorities.

Tours

A small number of tour operators have started offering trips to Afghanistan.

THE UK

Hinterland (☎ 01883 743584; hinterland@tinyworld .co.uk) Overland trips crossing Afghanistan from Iran to Pakistan.

Live! Travel (☎ 020 8894 6104; www.live-travel.com) Tailor-made cultural trips.

Matthew Leeming (☎ 01962 738492; www .matthewleeming.com) Travel writer running group and bespoke tours, including to the Wakhan Corridor.

THE USA

Bestway (☎ 800 663 0844; www.bestway.com) Group tours combined with Pakistan.

Reality Tours (☎ 415 255 7296; www.globalexchange .org) Alternative travel visiting community groups and NGOs.

GETTING AROUND
Air

Ariana offers a comprehensive domestic service. Demand is often high, so book as far in advance as you can. The Kabul office can be chaotic but is surprisingly efficient. Elsewhere, things are more disorganised, so you might need to be persistent to get your

name on the list. You'll need your passport when you book your ticket.

Always recheck the time of departure the day before you fly. Schedule changes are both common and unexplained. If you're in the provinces you'll probably depart late anyway, as you'll have to wait for the plane to arrive from Kabul.

For domestic services operated by Ariana, see p376. At the time of research, a new airline, KamAir, was starting services from Kabul to Herat and Mazar-e Sharif.

Bus

Afghanistan is held together by the minibus. Toyota HiAces are the most favoured, seemingly indestructible in the face of terrible road conditions, along with slightly smaller TownAces. There are no timetables – minibuses tend to start rolling out at the crack of dawn, leaving when they've collected enough passengers.

A 10-hour trip costs around 400Afg, but prices fluctuate according to demand – a trip to Kabul is cheaper than a journey of the same length to Faizabad. Drivers frequently stop for prayer time, and at chaikhanas for food – where you might end up overnight on a really long trip.

Clunky old German buses also ply Afghanistan's roads. Painfully slow and overcrowded, they're only used by the poorest locals – and by those unconcerned about time or comfort.

Car & Motorcycle

Afghanistan doesn't recognise carnets so bringing in your own vehicle is a legal grey area. Foreign vehicles are highly visible and may present a target if there are security problems. The country runs on diesel and petrol can be hard to find. Road rules are lax, but most vehicles aspire to drive on the right.

Taxi

Yellow-and-white shared taxis are a popular way to travel between towns. They leave from the same terminal as minibuses. They're faster than minibuses and, with fewer seats, fill up and leave sooner. Fares are around a quarter to a third more expensive than the equivalent minibus.

Turkmenistan

FAST FACTS

- **Area** 488,100 sq km
- **Capital** Ashgabat (Aşgabat)
- **Country Code** ☎ 993
- **Ethnic Groups** 85% Turkmen, 10% Uzbek, 3% Russian, 2% others (Azeris, Iranians and Kazakhs)
- **Languages** Turkmen, Russian, Uzbek
- **Money** manat (M); US$1 = 5032 M; €1 = 6127 M
- **Phrases in Turkmen** Peace be with you./Hello. *(salam aleukum)*; Thanks. *(tangyr)*; How are you? *(siz nahili?)*
- **Population** approximately 4.5 million

A fascinating desert republic that has moved on from the Soviet era in name only, Turkmenistan is a mysterious and wild straggle of deeply mystical civilisations whose entry into the modern world only began with the arrival of the Red army in the 1920s. As a cradle of ancient cultures and a land of vast natural beauty and variety, there are few places more rewarding for anyone lucky enough to visit.

Turkmenistan only seems to make the news these days in connection with the elaborate personality cult of its president, but in fact, as a nation of huge strategic importance (particularly with all the oil and gas reserves under its burning sands), Turkmenistan is set to become one of the biggest prizes in the new great game for Central Asia's mineral wealth.

Despite successive governments bent on modernisation at all costs, travelling here remains a unique and unusual experience that will appeal to anyone wanting to see a spiritual and traditional land, largely trapped in time.

HIGHLIGHTS

While Turkmenistan's most accessible attractions are located in and around the oasis towns on its periphery, the mighty **Karakum desert** (p422) should not be missed. At its heart there're the **Darvaza Gas Craters;** an enormous inferno blazes away day and night like a volcano at ground level – an unforgettable sight at night and a great chance to stay in a traditional yurt in the nearby village of Darvaza.

The brutal and destructive power of ancient armies still hangs in the air at **Merv** (p427) and **Konye-Urgench** (p431), and their remains, both fascinating and atmospheric, were once some of the greatest cities of the Muslim world.

Turkmenistan's incredible and increasingly sinister capital, **Ashgabat** (p412), is full of neo-Stalinist white marble buildings, lavish palaces and golden statues of its leader. It's a brilliantly unusual city that will fascinate anyone interested in the bombastic personality cult. The **Tolkuchka Bazaar** (p417) should not be missed.

Some of the best scenery in the country can be seen in the **Kugitang Nature Reserve** (p431) – dinosaur footprints, incredibly deep caves with beautiful stalactites and the dramatically barren scenery of this amazing national park are more than worth the effort to get here.

ITINERARIES

- **Three days** Crossing the country in three days on a transit visa, head for Ashgabat to see the amazing extent of the Turkmenbashi cult, spend the night here and then head through the Karakum desert to ancient Konye-Urgench the next day. You can explore Konye-Urgench before crossing the border into Uzbekistan.
- **Seven days** With a week, spend at least three days in and around Ashgabat, before heading to Mary from where you can visit the ancient sites of Merv and Gonur. From here, return to Ashgabat and head north through the desert, stopping overnight in Darvaza to see the incredible gas craters and spend a night in a traditional yurt.
- **Two weeks** An ideal amount of time to see the country. Visit Ashgabat, Mary, Merv, Darvaza, Konye-Urgench, Kugitang Nature Reserve, Dekhistan and Turkmenbashi to get a real feel for the country and its people.
- **Off the beaten track** Everywhere in Turkmenistan is off the beaten track. Try the dinosaur footprints and caves of Kugitang Nature Reserve.

CLIMATE & WHEN TO GO

Turkmenistan is by far the hottest of the Central Asian countries, although its dry desert climate means that despite the soaring temperatures, it's not always uncomfortably warm. That said, only the insane or deeply unfortunate find themselves in Ashgabat in July and August, when the temperature can push 50°C. The best times to visit are between April and June, and September and early November. Winters are very cold in the north, although southern Turkmenistan almost never freezes.

HISTORY

The Margiana Oasis was the centre of an advanced agricultural society some nine millennia ago, and is thought to have ranked alongside Egypt, India, China and Mesopotamia as one of the centres of civilisation of the ancient world. The land between the Caspian Sea and the Oxus River (now the Amu-Darya) passed from one army to the next, as campaigning armies decamped on the way to richer territories. Alexander the Great established a city here on his way to India. Around the time of Christ, the Parthians, Rome's main rivals for power in the West, set up a capital at Nissa, near present-day Ashgabat. In the 11th century the Seljuq Turks appropriated Merv, Alexander's old city and a Silk Road staging post, as a base from which to expand into Afghanistan.

Two centuries later Jenghiz Khan stormed down from the steppes and through Trans-Caspia (the region east of the Caspian Sea) on his way to terrorise Europe.

It's not known precisely when the first modern Turkmen appeared, but they are believed to have arrived in modern Turkmenistan in the wake of the Seljuk Turks some time in the 11th century. A collection of displaced nomadic horse-breeding tribes, possibly from the foothills of the Altay Mountains, they found alternative pastures in the oases fringing the Karakum (Black Sand) desert and in Persia, Syria and Anatolia (in present-day Turkey). Being nomads they had no concept of, or interest in, statehood and therefore existed in parallel to the constant dynastic shifts that so totally determined Central Asia's history.

Terrorising the Russians, who had come to 'civilise' the region in the early 19th century, Turkmen captured thousands of the tsar's troops, and sold them into slavery in Khiva and Bukhara. This invited the wrath of the Russian Empire, which finally quelled the wild nomads by massacring thousands of them at Geok-Depe (or Tepe) in 1881. Thereafter Trans-Caspia was absorbed into the expansionist Russian Empire, a geopolitical fact that it is still trying to escape today.

Russian empire-building saw the construction of the great Trans-Caspian railway between Krasnovodsk and Tashkent in the 1880s, the first real encroachment of Western civilisation into the wild Turkmen desert.

Following the Bolshevik revolution in 1917, the communists took Ashgabat in 1919. For a while the region existed as the Turkmen *oblast* (province) of the Turkestan Autonomous Soviet Socialist Republic, before becoming the Turkmen Soviet Socialist Republic (SSR) in 1924.

HOW MUCH?

- Snickers bar US$0.30
- 100km bus ride US$2.50
- One minute call to UK or US US$1–8
- Traditional hat US$4
- Good dinner in Ashgabat US$5

LONELY PLANET INDEX

- Litre of bottled water US$0.25
- Bottle of local beer US$0.20
- Shashlyk US$0.50–1
- Litre of petrol US$1.50–2

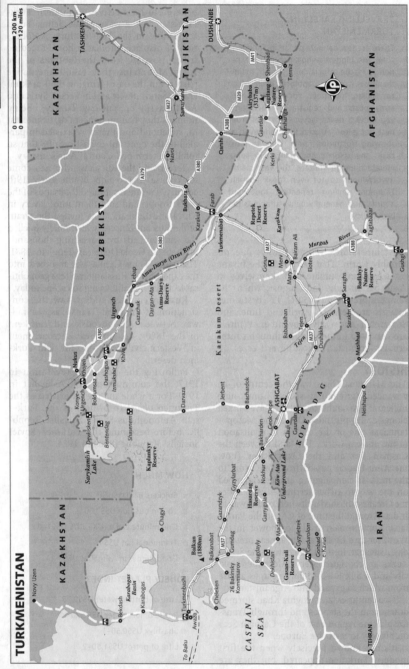

TURKMENISTAN

200 km
120 miles

KAZAKHSTAN

Novy Uzen

Bekdash

Karabogaz Basin

Karabogaz

CASPIAN SEA

To Baku

Turkmenbashi

Awaza

Cheleken

26 Bakinsky Kommisarov

Balkanabat

Balkan ▲ (1880m)

Gumdag

Chagyl

KAZAKHSTAN

Bugdayly

Dehistan

M37

Gazandzyk

Gyzylarbat

Garrygala

Madau

Gasan-Kuli Reserve

Gudurolom

Gonbad E-Kavus

IRAN

TEHRAN

Nokhur

Hasardag Reserve

Gyzyletrek

Kaplankyr Reserve

Sarykamish Lake

Bentendag

Dekhistan

Nukus

Konye-Urgench

Khojeli

Boldumsaz

Dashoguz

Izmukshir

Khiva

Gazachak

Urgench

Darvaza

Jerbent

Bachardok

Bakharden

Grok-Depe

Chuli

ASHGABAT

Gaurdan

KOPET DAG

Kow Ata Underground Lake

Mashhad

Neishapur

IRAN

UZBEKISTAN

A380

Dargan-Ata

Amu-Darya Reserve

Lebap

Amu-Darya (Oxus River)

Karakul

Bukhara

Farab

Turkmenabat

Repetek Desert Reserve

Karakum Canal

Kerki

A379

Navoi

A380

Qarshi

A380

Samarkand

A37

TAJIKISTAN

DUSHANBE

M41

Sherabad

Termiz

AFGHANISTAN

Gaurdak

Chrshanga

Airybabu (3137m)

Kugitang Nature Reserve

M39

A388

Taglabazar

Gushgy

Karakum Canal

Murgab River

Karakum Desert

Gonur

Mary

Merv

Bairam Ali

Eloten

Babadaihan

Tejen

Tejen River

Dushakh

Saraghs

Sarakhs

Badkhyz Nature Reserve

Murgab

M37

M37

KARAKUM DESERT

The Turkmen SSR

Inflamed by Soviet attempts to settle the tribes and collectivise farming, Turkmen resistance continued and a guerrilla war raged until 1936. More than a million Turkmen fled into the Karakum desert or into northern Iran and Afghanistan rather than give up their nomadic ways. The Turkmen also fell foul of a Moscow-directed campaign against religion. Of the 441 mosques in Turkmenistan in 1911, only five remained standing by 1941.

A steady stream of Russian immigrants began arriving in the 1920s to undertake the modernisation of the SSR, and a big part of the plan involved cotton. Turkmenistan's arid climate was hardly conducive to bumper harvests, and to supply the vast quantities of water required the authorities began work in the 1950s on a massive irrigation ditch – the Karakum Canal. The 1100km-long gully runs the length of the republic, bleeding the Amu-Darya to create a fertile band across the south. Cotton production quadrupled, though the consequences for the Aral Sea have been catastrophic (see p68).

Turkmenistan mostly led a quiet existence during the era of the Soviet Union – its small population, lack of heavy industry and location at the very southern tip of the country meant that it had an out-of-sight, out-of-mind quality to it. In 1985 the relatively unknown Saparmyrat Niyazov was elected General Secretary of the Communist Party of Turkmenistan (CPT). Initially thought to be a reformer, it became clear quite soon that while Niyazov was happy to implement any reforms from Moscow, he had no interest in generating the process himself and was totally unprepared for the end of Soviet power when independence was virtually forced on Turkmenistan on 27 October 1991.

Independence & Neutrality

No longer subject to Moscow, Niyazov began to demonstrate that he could give orders as well as follow them. Determined to hold onto power, he simply renamed the CPT the Democratic Party of Turkmenistan for the sake of appearances before oxymoronically banning all other parties. What followed was the creation of a fanciful personality cult comparable in recent memory only to that of the Kim dynasty in North Korea.

Shortly after becoming Turkmenistan's first president he took on his omnipresent moniker Turkmenbashi, which translates as 'leader of the Turkmen'. His ubiquitous slogan 'Halk, Watan, Turkmenbaşi' ('People, nation, me') – derided by some observers for its echo of Hitler's 'ein Volk, ein Reich, ein Führer' – was adopted at the same time.

Niyazov promised future prosperity based on the country's enormous oil and gas wealth, pledging that within a decade of independence Turkmenistan would have the same gross domestic product (GDP) per head as Kuwait. As the 1990s progressed, this promise was replaced by one of a Turkmen Golden Age (Altyn Asyr).

Finally, bringing his reign into the spiritual as well as the political realm, Niyazov authored the *Rukhnama* (Book of the Soul) between 1997 and 2001. This incredibly bizarre piece of writing sets out Niyazov's version of Turkmen history, culture and spirituality and has become compulsory reading for the country's citizens. Indeed, no student can enter university without first passing a '*Rukhnama* exam' and copies of the book are displayed in all public buildings.

Turkmenistan Today

The Golden Age looked like it might end before it had begun, when an attempt was made on Niyazov's life on 25 November 2002. It is still a matter for conjecture as to what really happened on that morning, but it was reported that Niyazov's motorcade came under attack from machine-gun fire as he drove to work (and Niyazov does actually drive himself in a custom-made bulletproof Mercedes, believe it or not). The assassination attempt was a failure, but provided convenient grounds for an immense blood-letting of the remaining political opponents, and a significant number of further restrictions on civil liberties.

While many claim the assassination attempt was a setup by Niyazov's own agents to provide an excuse for further repression, the presence of high-profile opposition leader Boris Shikhmuradov in the country at the time was never explained. Usually based in Moscow, Shikhmuradov was discovered hiding in the Uzbek embassy in Ashgabat after the failed shooting. He then gave himself up to the Turkmen government as he feared his family would be

TURKMENISTAN

tortured until he did so. Since then he has disappeared and is feared to have died in prison. The failed attack has largely atomised his once-credible People's Democratic Movement of Turkmenistan; the Moscow-based opposition was left without a strong leader and Niyazov's grip on power seems stronger than ever.

PEOPLE

The Turkmen people are a highlight of the country. Friendly, curious and with a great sense of humour, they can make even the bleakest parts of the country great fun. Turkmen are generally very traditional and family-oriented without being overly conservative. Despite Sovietisation, women who live outside Turkmenistan's towns are generally homemakers and mothers, and the men the breadwinners.

If you believe the government's figures, the population is rising dramatically – over five million at present by the official count,

although the UN and US government believe that figure to be more like 4.5 million. The introduction of exit visas for Turkmen citizens, combined with a bizarre new law that makes marrying a Turkmen citizen subject to a US$30,000 tax, have both done their bit to stem the population exodus. Russians have left in huge numbers since independence, as it becomes increasingly hard to work without speaking Turkmen.

RELIGION

Turkmenistan is a Sunni Muslim state, and Islam and Orthodox Christianity are the only freely practised religions in the country. The criteria for registering (and thus legalising) a religion are so high that religious minorities remain against the law and are subject to government harassment. In recent years this has focused mainly on Baptists and Jehovah's Witnesses in the country. Turkmen tend to be a deeply spiritual people, who combine many tra-

---

TURKMENBASHI – LEADER OF THE TURKMEN

Like it or not, one grinning and apparently benevolent face will bore its eyes into you at every point on your journey through Turkmenistan, that of Saparmyrat Niyazov, Turkmenbashi the Great. Born in 1940 in Kipçak, a village near Ashgabat, Niyazov knew tragedy from a young age – his father was killed in action during WWII, and his mother and brothers were killed in the 1949 earthquake that wiped out Ashgabat. Both his parents now form important parts of the personality cult – especially his mother Gurbansoltan Eje, after whom he has renamed the month of April.

The young president grew up in an orphanage and went to study at St Petersburg's prestigious Technical Institute, returning to Ashgabat to work as an engineer at the Bezmein Power Plant just outside the Turkmen capital. Joining the Communist Party in 1962, Niyazov's first taste of real power came when he was appointed head of the party's Ashgabat City Committee. Here he experimented with town planning (a hobby that has blossomed into a veritable addiction in the last decade) by constructing the new Mir region of Ashgabat. After a year at the Central Committee in Moscow and despite being a virtual unknown, he was chosen by the new Soviet leader Mikhail Gorbachov to be general secretary of the Communist Party of Turkmenistan – fingered for the position as he was seen as a deferent and obedient functionary who would carry out Moscow's ambitious reform programme without question. Another reason for Moscow's favour was that his upbringing in an orphanage made him free of any clan allegiance, an important factor for a desert republic such as Turkmenistan.

The seamless transfer to president of an independent Turkmenistan after the USSR's collapse has, however, revealed another side to the Moscow party functionary – one that loves nothing more than mass flattery, golden statues and lavish palaces.

The biggest question for Turkmenistan is what happens next? His son and daughter are both estranged and living abroad, while no minister is allowed to develop a power base without being sacked or imprisoned. This leaves the Turkmen political scene devoid of any potential successor. Turkmenbashi is now in his mid-60s and had a heart bypass in 1997. Although he's unlikely to die in the near future, the power struggle after he does has – given the vast amount of money involved – the potential to degenerate into bloody clan warfare.

ditional animist and spiritualist elements with modern Muslim ones.

ARTS

Traditionally focused on carpet weaving, silk, embroidery and jewellery, the arts in Turkmenistan are on display everywhere, although nowhere is a better place to see them than at a bazaar.

Western art forms are not doing so well; part of Turkmenbashi's ostensibly nationalistic stance has involved closing cinemas, ballet and opera theatres, and generally preventing the performance of anything considered to be 'un-Turkmen'. As a consequence, only traditional Turkmen dancing seems to be undergoing a renaissance at present, although you can still see curious Turkmen drama in Ashgabat. The Turkmen film industry is nonexistent, and even most circuses have been closed. Between the Soviets and Niyazov, contemporary Turkmen literature has been all but destroyed. Despite the veneration of national poet Magtymguly Feraghy (1733–83), the most widely read author is, of course, the president.

ENVIRONMENT

The landscape in Turkmenistan is dramatic and more varied than you'd expect from a place where the Karakum desert takes up 90% of the country's area. To the east are the canyons and lush mountains of the Kugitang Nature Reserve, while to the south the Kopet Dag range rises up in a line towards the Caspian. The territory littoral to the Caspian Sea is particularly unusual – the canyons north of Turkmenbashi, the multicoloured mountains and the lunar landscape elsewhere make this one of the more bleakly beautiful places in the country.

Wildlife

The most famous of Turkmenistan's many interesting species is the Akhal-Teke horse, a beautiful golden creature that is believed to be the ancestor of today's purebred. Dromedaries (Arabian camels) are everywhere, wandering scenically between villages and towns. Many of the Karakum's nastiest inhabitants are really exciting to see in real life – most importantly the *zemzen*, the now rare 'desert crocodile' or grey *varan* (see this page). You are also

likely to see desert foxes, owls, and the very common desert squirrel.

Tarantulas and black widows are both indigenous to Turkmenistan, although you are unlikely to see them. Snake season is from April to May. Cobras, vipers and scorpions can all be found in the desert, so tread with caution. Turkmen folklore has it that that once a snake has looked at you, you'll die shortly afterwards unless you kill it first.

Environmental Issues

Turkmenistan has paid a heavy price for the irrigation of its southern belt using water from the Aral Sea. While the Aral Sea is in Uzbekistan and Kazakhstan, its

---

DESERT CROCODILES

The giant grey-striped lizards of the Karakum are sometimes known as desert or land crocodiles, an apt epithet for a beast that can grow up to 1.8m long. In Turkmen tradition, people were happy to have a *zemzen* dig a burrow near their home, despite its size and sharp teeth, as the giant lizard devoured or scared away snakes (such as cobras), ate mice and eradicated colonies of sandflies.

Zemzen usually live for eight years or so, though in captivity they have lived for twice as long; they feed primarily on rodents, as well as a diverse mix of insects, snakes, frogs, other lizards and even scorpions. In winter they block their burrow's entrance hole (they often adopt the burrows of their rodent prey) and hibernate. They lay up to 24 eggs, which are almost the size of poultry eggs.

In the desert *zemzen* leave a distinctive track: a line left by the dragging tail swishing between the footprints. Should you be lucky enough to see one in the wild, rest assured that they don't normally attack unprovoked. The bite of a *zemzen* is said to be extremely painful, as they have powerful jaws and sharp backward-angled teeth – once attached they aren't inclined to let go.

While it's a protected species nowadays, and Turkmen tradition forbids killing *zemzen* due to their pest-clearing qualities, it's still rare to see one, unless it's squashed on the road.

disappearance has led to desperate environmental problems in northern Turkmenistan, with the salination of the land taking its toll on the health of local people. Heavy industry has a minimal presence in Turkmenistan and so the air quality is very good. Ashgabat, which is veiled in semipermanent smog, is the exception.

FOOD & DRINK

Turkmen food is similar to most other Central Asian fare; the national dish is *diorama*, made from bread, pieces of boiled meat and onions. Shashlyk (lamb kebab) and plov (rice, meat and carrots) feature heavily on menus, and both are generally fattier here than elsewhere. Turkmen bread (*çörek*) is harder than that in most Central Asian countries, and designed to keep for weeks during desert treks. One delicious Khorezm speciality you can get in the bazaars of the north is bread cooked with chopped red peppers and onions mixed into the dough.

At breakfast you'll typically be served sour milk or *chal* (fermented camel's milk) in the desert. At every juncture throughout the day you'll be offered tea. Mineral water is sold everywhere and is of good quality, while beer and vodka – a legacy of the Russians – are both popular alcoholic drinks. There are several decent Turkmen brands of both, although the most common beers are Berk and Zip Beer.

ASHGABAT

☎ 12 / pop 550,000

Once a marginalised, largely forgotten capital of a Soviet desert republic that few people had ever heard of, let alone visited, Ashgabat ('the city of love' or Ashkabad in Arabic) has undergone a dramatic transformation of the most unusual kind since independence. This small city nestled beneath the Kopet Dag, and just a few miles from Iran, has become a political statement built to the peculiar tastes of President Niyazov.

Originally developed by the Russians in the late 19th century, Ashgabat became a prosperous, largely Russian frontier town on the Trans-Caspian railway. However, at 1am on 6 October 1948, the city vanished in less than a minute, levelled as it was by an earthquake that measured nine on the

Richter scale. Over 110,000 people died (two thirds of the population), although the official figure was 14,000; this was the era of Stalin, when Socialist countries didn't suffer disasters. The area was closed to outsiders for five years, during which time the bodies were recovered, the wreckage was cleared and construction of a new city was begun.

Recreated as an unexciting and provincial frontier town largely closed to foreigners, Ashgabat's existence was decidedly languorous until suddenly becoming the capital city of the newly independent Turkmenistan in 1991. Since that time Ashgabat has undergone enormous change, sometimes impressive, sometimes horrendous, often a mix of the two.

ORIENTATION

The main arteries of the city are Turkmenbashi şayoli (avenue), running all the way from the station to the new suburb of Berzengi, and Magtymguly şayoli, running east to west. Many of the city's landmarks and institutions are on or near these streets.

In 2002 President Niyazov renamed all the streets with numbers. Pushkin köçesi (street) is now 1984 köçesi, for example. This pointless exercise has only served to confuse, as nobody seemed to know the names of the streets anyway – some have changed as many as four times since the 1990s. Street signs were still in the process of changing

ASHGABAT MUST-SEES

Arch of Neutrality For the best views of the capital, ride the glass elevator to the top of this magnificently awful structure (p415).
Independence Square Awesomely flanked by extravagant palaces and grandiose ministries (p415).
Tolkuchka Bazaar As unlike modern Ashgabat as anywhere else on earth, and truly one of Central Asia's greatest and most colourful sights (p417).
National Museum Enjoy the fine collection of historic artefacts and relics found here (p416).
Berzengi While at the museum, take the opportunity to see this bizarre, newly created suburb (p416).
Walk of Health You don't have to be crazy to build staircases into the mountainside, but it helps. A visit to this spectacular waste of money and time is strangely compelling (p422).

at the time of writing, but the post-Soviet names have been used in this chapter, as they remain the most widely recognised.

INFORMATION
Bookshops
A look at a bookshop in Ashgabat is interesting, if just to see the cultural and intellectual deterioration that has taken place in the last decade. Most central is **Türkmen Kitaplary** (Turkmenbaşi şayoli 29), where over half the books are authored by the president.

Emergency
Dial ☎ 01 for fire service, ☎ 02 for the police or ☎ 03 for an ambulance. The operators will speak Turkmen or Russian only.

Internet Access
Public Internet access is very limited in Ashgabat (as opposed to virtually nonexistent in the rest of Turkmenistan). The **Sheraton Grand Turkmen Hotel** (☎ 51 05 55; fax 51 12 51; Görogly köçesi 7; per hr US$2.50) and **Hotel Nissa** (☎ 48 87 00/1/2/3/4; fax 48 81 55; Atabayev köçesi 18; per hr US$5) have the only functioning Internet cafés. Bear in mind that if you use these facilities, the Turkmen authorities may read your email.

Laundry
A reliable, cheap laundry is **Arassa** (Kemine köçesi 189), just by the circus. Dry-cleaning can be done for reasonable rates at **Brilliant** (☎ 39 06 39; Magtymguly şayoli 99) and more expensively at the **Yimpaş** (Turkmenbashi şayoli 54; 9am-11pm) Turkish department store.

Left Luggage
There is a left luggage service (*kamera khraneniya*) at Ashgabat's main train station, where you can leave bags for about US$0.25 overnight.

Medical Services
The main medical provision in Ashgabat is the vast **Central Hospital** (☎ 45 03 03, 45 03 31; Emre köçesi 1), a newly built Niyazov creation. Foreigners have to pay for their treatment, so insurance is essential. Among the staff is Dr Yayha, a Jordanian doctor who speaks English and is recommended by both the British and US embassies. There is also the **International Medical Center** (☎ 51 90 06, 51 90 08) in Berzengi.

THE EVER-CHANGING FACE OF ASHGABAT

Ashgabat must be one of the world's fastest-changing cities. Unlike Shanghai, where this is driven by the private sector, in Ashgabat, it's all the work of one man. During research for this book, vast areas of the city were being knocked down to clear space for new elite apartment buildings, parks and other Niyazov-approved projects. Diplomats in Ashgabat say that every week there are hundreds of people left homeless by the demolition, and the city authorities have no provision for rehousing or compensation. The latest project to create controversy and to evict hundreds of families is the so-called 'Turkmen Disneyland' – an amusement park slated to open in 2005. Be aware therefore that the Ashgabat map is particularly vulnerable to change during the lifetime of this book.

Money
The best rates for black-market exchange can be found outside the central **Univermag department store** (Magtymguly şayoli). There are also private houses on Beki Seytakow köçesi, near First Park, that function like banks, only they employ the black-market rate. To find this street take a taxi. These are popular with Ashgabat residents. Check the current black-market rate with locals, as it changes almost daily. The moneychangers will accept euros and UK pounds, but at unattractive rates, so make sure you bring US dollars in cash.

Most foreign residents use the **National Bank of Pakistan** (Sheraton Grand Turkmen Hotel, Görogly köçesi 7; 9.30am-1pm & 2-3pm Mon-Fri) for cash advances on credit cards and to cash travellers cheques. Both services are also available from **Vneshekonombank** (☎ 25 51 13; Zhitnikov köçesi 22). While ATMs do exist, nearly all of them accept only local cards. There are two ATMs that accept Visa cards: in the glass booth outside Vneshekonombank and inside the Sheraton Grand Turkmen Hotel.

Post
The main **post office** (Mopra köçesi, 16; 8am-7pm Mon-Fri, 8am-5pm Sat & Sun) is very small. Some items, such as books, must be sent from the customs post next to the main train station.

ASHGABAT

INFORMATION	**SIGHTS & ACTIVITIES** (pp415–16)	Amanov Homestay...............**36** D5	

INFORMATION
Amado.................................**1** D4
Arassa Laundry......................**2** C3
Armenian Embassy **3** D4
ATM...................................(see 6)
Ayan Travel.........................**4** D3
Azenbaijani Embassy..............**5** D5
Aşgabatsyğahat....................**6** E4
Brilliant Dry Cleaners..............**7** D4
French Embassy.................(see 37)
Georgian Embassy...................**8** B4
German Embassy................(see 37)
International Call Centre.........**9** E4
Iranian Embassy....................**10** A4
Kyrgyz Embassy.................(see 3)
National Bank of Pakistan.....(see 6)
Owadan Syğahat..................**11** E4
Post Office...........................**12** E4
Russian Embassy...................**13** F4
Siyakhat Tourist Company......(see 40)
Tajik Embassy...................(see 3)
Turkmen Kitaplary................**14** F5
Turkmenbank......................**15** E4
UK Embassy......................(see 37)
US Embassy.........................**16** F4
Uzbek Embassy.....................**17** B5
Vneshekonombank................**18** E4

SIGHTS & ACTIVITIES (pp415–16)
Academy of Sciences.............**19** E4
Arch of Neutrality.................**20** E5
Ashgabat State University.......**21** F5
Carpet Museum.....................**22** E4
Earthquake Memorial &
  Museum.............................**23** E5
Iranian Mosque....................**24** A4
Majlis.................................**25** E5
Mosque of Khezrety Omar......**26** C5
Museum of Fine Arts..............**27** F4
New War Memorial................**28** C5
Palace of Turkmenbashi..........**29** E5
Presidential Administration......**30** F5
Public Swimming Pool.............**31** B5
Ruhyyet Palace.....................**32** E5
Soviet War Memorial..............**33** F5
Statue of Lenin....................**34** E4
Zoo...................................**35** C4

Amanov Homestay...............**36** D5
Four Points Ahaltin Sheraton
  Hotel.................................**37** C3
Hotel Ashgabat....................**38** F4
Hotel Dayhan.....................(see 1)
Hotel Nissa.........................**39** F5
Hotel Syğahat......................**40** A4
Hotel Turkmenistan...............**41** E4
Margiana Guesthouse.............**42** D3
Russian Bazaar...................(see 45)
Sheraton Grand Turkmen Hotel..(see 6)

EATING (pp418–19)
Altyn Jam...........................**43** E4
Asuda Nusay Restaurant.........**44** D4
Diamond Supermarket........(see 41)
Gülüstan Restaurant..............**45** E4
Istanbul Restaurant...............**46** E4
Margiana Guesthouse.........(see 42)

To Old Airport Bus
Station; Airport (6km);
Tolkuchka Bazaar

Magtumguly şayoli

Gorky

Revtov köçesi

Atamyrat Niyazov şayoli

Kopet Dag
Stadium

Mir Cinema
(disused)

Magtymguly şayoli

Mopra köçesi

Mopra köçesi

Tehran köçesi

Botanical
Gardens

Göroglý köçesi

Azadi köçesi

Göroglý köçesi

Khojov Annadurdyew köçesi

Alshera Navoi köçesi

Kerbabayewa köçesi

To Afghan Embassy
(3km); Alaja Farm &
Geoke-Depe (10km);
Nissa (20km); Firyusa;
Chuli & Bakharden (100km)

Atamyrat Niyazov köçesi

Seidi köçesi

Seidi köçesi

Ata Gowşudow köçesi

köçesi

Telephone & Fax

All hotels and business centres offer international direct dialling (IDD) and fax facilities, although for better rates you can call from the **International Call Centre** (Karl Liebknekht köçesi 33; ☼ 8am-7pm). Most hotels offer free local calls from rooms. Faxes can be sent from all top-end hotels and the international call centre.

Travel Agencies

Anyone not simply in transit through Turkmenistan will usually have made contact with one of the following (or a foreign travel agency working through them) to organise their letter of invitation (LOI). The following all offer comprehensive services including letters of invitation, guides, driv-

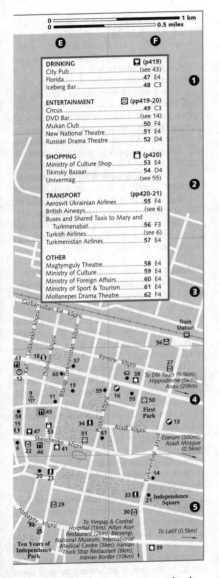

ers, hotel bookings, city tours and other excursions.

Amado (☎ 39 73 68, 39 60 33; fax 39 60 82; amado@online.tm; Hotel Dayhan, Azadi köçesi 69)

Aşgabatsyýahat (☎ 35 77 77, 35 78 78; fax 39 66 60; Sheraton Grand Turkmen Hotel, Görogly köçesi 7)

Ayan Travel (☎ 35 29 14, 35 07 97; fax 39 33 55; www.ayan-travel.com; Magtymguly şayoli 108-2/4)

DN Tours (☎ 47 92 17; fax 51 16 60; Magtymguly şayoli 48/1)

Elhan Syýahat (☎ 35 71 49, 39 84 06; elkhantour@ online.tm; Azadi köçesi 35)

Latif (☎ 41 50 77, 41 50 87; fax 41 90 39; Khoudaiberdiev köçesi 36A)

Siyakhat Tourist Company (☎ /fax 34 40 33, 34 40 71; www.siyakhat.narod.ru; Hotel Syýahat, Görogly köçesi 60a)

Stantours (☎ in Kazakhstan 7 3272 63 13 44; fax 49 89 14 88 24 13 82; www.stantours.com; Kunyaeva 163/76, Almaty)

Tourism-Owadan (☎ 39 18 25; fax 35 48 60; trowadan@online.tm; Azadi köçesi 65)

DANGERS & ANNOYANCES

Be aware that all top-range hotel rooms are bugged, as are many offices, restaurants and anywhere foreigners meet. Reserve sensitive conversations, especially any with Turkmen citizens (who are far more likely to get into trouble than you) for safe places, preferably outside.

SIGHTS
Central Ashgabat

Being all but wiped from the earth in 1948, Ashgabat's sights can be divided neatly into two halves – the politicised, monolithic constructions of the Soviet government and the politicised, monolithic constructions of President Niyazov, with the latter increasing in number almost monthly.

At the centre of Niyazov's monolithic Ashgabat is the embarrassingly large **Arch of Neutrality**, erected to celebrate the Turkmen people's unsurprisingly unanimous endorsement of Turkmenbashi's policy of neutrality in 1998. Above the arch itself is the real gem, a comic 12m-high polished-gold **statue of Niyazov** (admission US$0.20; ☀ 8am-10pm), which revolves to follow the sun throughout the day. Trips to the top give commanding views of the enormous **Independence Square**, on which sits the golden-domed **Palace of Turkmenbashi**, the **Ministry of Fairness**, the **Ministry of Defence** and the **Ruhyyet Palace**, all of which were built by the French corporation Bouygues Construction, the court builder to Niyazov. Behind this is the **Majlis**, or parliament.

The Palace of Turkmenbashi is relatively restrained, but just walking towards the gates will cause soldiers to harass you, even though information about its construction is written in English, presumably for visitors to read.

Next to the Arch of Neutrality is the **Earthquake Memorial**, a bombastic bronze rendering of a bull and child, under which lurks the **Earthquake Museum** (admission free; 9am-6pm). This is perhaps Ashgabat's most touching museum and the display includes once-banned photos of pre-1948 earthquakes as well as information about the five-year clear up effort, the burying of 110,000 bodies and the building of a new city. Further down this long, manicured strip is the **Soviet war memorial**, a pleasingly subtle structure with an eternal flame at its centre. Off to the right is the **Presidential Administration building**, once the presidential residence and the Turkmen Communist Party Central Committee building in more austere times, and now the nerve centre of Turkmenbashi's private staff. The strip ends with **Ashgabat State University**.

Towards the train station, the **Museum of Fine Arts** (☎ 35 31 29; cnr Turkmenbaşhi şayoli & Kermine köçesi; admission US$10; 9am-5pm, closed Tue) has its temporary home in inadequate accommodation – its old premises were demolished in a Niyazov building spree. The collection contains some great Soviet-Turkmen painting: happy peasant scenes where at least one stereotyped Turkmen has a chest adorned with Order of Lenin medals, and lurking beyond the yurts and tethered horses is a productively smoking chimney. There is also a collection of Russian and Western European paintings, including one by Caravaggio, and a fine selection of Turkmen jewellery and traditional costumes.

The **statue of Lenin**, off Azadi köçesi, is a charmingly incongruous assembly of a tiny Lenin on an enormous and very Central Asian plinth. At the time of research the new **National Theatre** was being completed behind him. Across the road, Lenin faces an austere concrete building that was once the **Archive of the Communist Party of Turkmenistan**. Its walls feature modernist concrete sculptures made by Ernst Neizvestny, the Russian artist who lived and worked in Ashgabat during the 1970s.

The **Carpet Museum** (Görogly köçesi 5; adult/student & child US$2/1; 10am-6pm Mon-Fri, 10am-3pm Sat) is an excellent museum for anyone interested in the history of Turkmen carpet weaving. At the back of this new and well-curated space is also the place at which to have your carpets valued, taxed and the necessary documentation issued for export. While there's a limit to the number of rugs the average visitor can stand, the central exhibit, the world's largest hand-woven rug, really is something to see.

More a statement of foreign-policy leanings than a sign of religious awakening, the **Azadi mosque** stands just south of Magtymguly şayoli, 600m east of the junction with Turkmenbashi. Similar in appearance to the Blue Mosque in İstanbul, the mosque sees few worshippers because of several accidental deaths during its construction.

The modern **mosque of Khezrety Omar**, off Chekhov köçesi, is also worth visiting for its wonderfully garish painted ceilings. The angular, futuristic **Iranian mosque**, illuminated with green neon, is on Görogly köçesi on the western outskirts of the city on the way to Nissa.

Berzengi

South of Moskovsky şayoli the surreal world of Berzengi begins – an entirely artificial brave new world of white marble tower blocks, fountains, parks and general emptiness that culminates in the Berzengi Hwy, which is home to a huge number of hotel complexes.

The curious pyramidical shopping centre at the northern end of **Independence Park** is officially the biggest fountain in the world. It's more of a waterfall however, with cascades running at incredible heights on all sides. Inside it's rather less than impressive – an all but empty two-floor shopping centre housing a few trainee mall rats and a rather unappetising café, although there's a restaurant at the top (Altyn Asyr, see p419), that's popular for weddings.

The **Monument to the Independence of Turkmenistan**, known universally to the foreign community as 'the plunger' (for reasons obvious as soon as you see it), this typically ostentatious and tasteless monument houses the **Museum of Turkmen Values** (admission US$10; 9am-6pm), a rather empty and overpriced look at traditional Turkmen clothing and jewellery. This is a popular spot for wedding groups to take photographs with a golden statue of the president, and the fountains are pleasant enough (a kind of totalitarian *Waterworld*, if you will).

Still overpriced, but worth seeing all the same is the **National Museum** (☎ 48 02 98;

Berzengi Hwy; admission US$10; ☺ 10am-5pm, closed Tue). Strikingly situated against the backdrop of the Kopet Dag in Berzengi, this Niyazov construction oozes money. The lavish Ancient History Hall includes Neolithic tools from western Turkmenistan and relics from the Bronze Age Margiana civilisation, including beautiful amulets, seals, cups and cult paraphernalia. There is also a model of the walled settlement uncovered at Gonur (see p429). The Antiquity Hall houses amazing rhytons – horn-shaped vessels of intricately carved ivory used for Zoroastrian rituals and official occasions.

Tolkuchka Bazaar

With its teeming cast of colourful thousands, this bazaar is Central Asia as staged by Cecil B De Mille. It sprawls across acres of desert on the outskirts of town, with corrals of camels and goats, avenues of red-clothed women squatting before silver jewellery, and villages of trucks from which Turkmen hawk everything from pistachios to car parts. Whatever you want, it's sold at Tolkuchka. Expect to haggle. The wily old men selling *telpek* (sheepskin hats worn by Turkmen males) always pitch an inflated price; if they ask for US$15 they'll probably settle for US$10, although the best *telpek* do go for US$15 or more. The women give way less (or offer more honest opening prices). At the time of research, a fair price for a khalat (the attractive red-and-yellow striped robe) was roughly US$15, while sequined skullcaps and embroidered scarves cost between US$2 and US$3.

Above all, Tolkuchka is the place for carpets. Hundreds are laid out in a large sandy compound or draped over racks and walls. Predominantly deep red, most are the size of a double bed or a bit smaller, and the average price ranges from US$150 to US$250. Haggling might shave off US$50.

Tolkuchka is in full swing every Saturday and Sunday from around 8am to 2pm and, on a slightly smaller scale, on Thursday morning. Watch out for pickpockets. The site is about 8km north Ashgabat, past the airport and just beyond the Karakum Canal. A taxi should cost between US$0.50 and US$1.

SLEEPING

Ashgabat has a good range of affordable accommodation, although little in the way of choice for backpackers. Niyazov's bizarre obsession with hotel building has left an enormous number of largely deserted and perfectly comfortable hotels in the suburb of Berzengi. There are plenty of more central options as well.

Budget

Amanov Homestay (☎ 39 36 72; Ata Gowşudow köçesi 106; dm US$5) This private house is not the dormitory of a psychiatric institute as the neighbours will tell you, but a pleasant, if slightly eccentric homestay, a short walk from the Ruhyyet Palace. The rooms are functional and clean, with constant hot water and decent shared toilets. The family also keeps pigeons. Not an option for people with tourist visas (see p434) as this is an unofficial hotel, but great for people transiting. Taxi drivers still know this street as Shaumyana. Ask for Murat when you arrive.

Hotel Ashgabat (☎ 35 74 05; Magtymguly şayoli 74; s/d/ste US$20/30/40) A very dilapidated Soviet hotel, the Ashgabat smells funny and the rooms are fairly nasty. While totally survivable elsewhere, there seems no need to stay here given that for this price you could stay in a far nicer place. Location is good, however, and a full renovation is promised.

Hotel Dayhan (☎ 35 73 44; Azadi köçesi 60; s/d excl breakfast US$10/20) Excellently located, and cheap despite this, the Dayhan is a big hotel with large balconies and acceptable bathrooms. Expect no-frills, but reliable rooms. Most US$20 'luxs' have TV, telephone and three beds.

Hotel Syyahat (☎ 34 45 08; Görogly köçesi 60; s/d/tr/quad US$25/30/33/44) Rooms here are functional and Soviet with decent balconies and dilapidated bathrooms. The whole management style is extremely Soviet, but for larger groups it can be a good deal. A while from the centre – take trolleybus No 6 into town.

Mid-Range
CENTRAL ASHGABAT

Margiana Guesthouse (☎ 35 13 23, 39 60 33; Gurbansoltan Eje şayoli 67; s/d US$40/50; ☒) This great new guesthouse was a real sign of progress until it had its licence revoked during the research period of this book, making it hard for non-transit visitors to stay here due to registration concerns. Only open since 2003, the rooms are spotless and comfortable, if a little small. There's also a good restaurant (see p418).

Hotel Turkmenistan (☎ 35 05 41, 35 05 42; Bitrap Turkmenistan şayoli 19; s/d US$40/50, ste US$60-70) A little overpriced, but has an excellent location near the Arch of Neutrality. The rooms are unexciting and a little cramped, but the newly renovated bathrooms are good and the place is clean.

BERZENGI

Worth a look even if you are not staying here, this surreal, totally deserted strip of hotels nestles beneath the attractive Kopet Dag, a 10-minute drive from the city centre. The hotels are all government-run guesthouses and most are enormous in size, despite never having more than 20 rooms and looking more like private villas than hotels. There are some good bargains to be had here, however, if you don't mind the location. At the time of writing, Niyazov's largest hotel yet, the monstrous neo-Stalinist Hotel President was under construction, beyond the Hotel Yedigen. The 15 hotels here will nearly all have vacancies and rooms cost between US$15 and US$30 per night. The most upmarket and more expensive are the Hotel Ahal, Hotel Independent and Gara Altyn Hotel, while you can get double rooms for as little as US$10 at the Hotel Çandybil.

Top End

Four Points Akaltin Sheraton Hotel (☎ 36 37 00; fppa@online.tm; Magtymguly şayoli 141/1; s/d US$150/ 165, ste US$225-400; 🖭 🗴) Despite having been purchased by the Sheraton group, this grand-looking place has small and rather unimpressive rooms, already in need of renovation despite the place barely being a decade old. The swimming pool was full of leaves, even on a hot October day, although the staff seemed friendly and professional.

Hotel Nissa (☎ 48 87 00/1/2/3/4; fax 48 81 55; Atabayev köçesi 18; s/d US$100/120, ste US$180-400; 🖭 🗴 🖳) Probably the best in the city, the Nissa is surprisingly cheap (perhaps as it is controlled by the president's son), with large, comfortable rooms and extras including an Internet centre, very good breakfast buffet and 24-hour room service. Most travel agents can get discounts of up to 60% on the walk-in price.

Sheraton Grand Turkmen Hotel (☎ 51 05 55; fax 51 12 51; Görogly köçesi 7; s/d/ste US$175/190/270; 🖭 🖳) The best of the two Sheratons in the city and blessed with an unbeatable location,

the Grand Turkmen has visibly deteriorated in the last few years. While still comfortable enough, the rooms are looking a little shabby and the centralised air-conditioning is not effective in many of the rooms, making summer rather miserable.

EATING

Restaurants are open for lunch and dinner. All shut at about 11pm, so it's best to get to a restaurant by 10pm at the latest. Even in the capital, food is incredibly cheap. Throughout the country you'll rarely pay more than US$2 to US$3 for a meal. Even at Ashgabat's most upscale eatery, the Italian Restaurant, it would be hard to spend more than US$10 per head.

Restaurants

Altyn Jam (☎ 39 68 50; Magtymguly şayoli 101) Known as AJs to the foreign community, the 'Golden Bowl' is a good place for lunch and has tasty and reliable European food. Desserts are especially good here and there's a pleasant terrace for alfresco dining.

Asuda Nusay Restaurant (☎ 35 22 88; Alishera Navoi köçesi 54a) Formerly the Nissa-Truva restaurant, the 'Silver Moon' was renamed à la Turkmen, but has retained a very good reputation for smart dining in Ashgabat. It shares premises and management with the City Pub (see p419); both are popular and busy.

Ezerum (☎ 47 50 92; Shevchenko köçesi 53) Smart and simple, the Ezerum serves up good Turkish fare and tasty cheese bread. The service is attentive and swift, although it can get very hot in the summer months due to the wood-fired oven.

Italian Restaurant (☎ 48 87 00; Nissa Hotel, Atabayev köçesi 18) This place has the reputation of being the best eatery in the city, although the pasta dishes are rather lacklustre. The Parmesan is fresh, pepper is served from suitably enormous mills and there's a decent selection of Italian wine.

Istanbul Restaurant (☎ 35 01 25; Görogly köçesi 5) The Istanbul is a long-standing Ashgabat institution, although until recently it served Georgian food due to being owned by a Georgian diplomat. Now it serves Turkish and Turkmen dishes – standard fare, reliable but nothing out of the ordinary.

Margiana Guesthouse (☎ 39 60 33; Gurbansoltan Eje köçesi 67) This is a great place to try trad-

THE AUTHOR'S CHOICE

Altyn Asyr ('Five Legs' fountain bldg, Independence Park, Turkmenbaşhi şayoli, Berzengi) The attractive 'Golden Age' restaurant is perched high up in what is reputedly the world's biggest fountain. The views are great and the decent food is Continental. There's also a bar on the floor above that serves fast food.

Iranian Truck Stop (☎ 48 87 70; Turkmenbashi şayoli 475) Deservedly one of the most popular places in town. This unappealingly named eatery is a great change of pace to the often-anodyne expat places in Ashgabat. Decorated with travel posters from Iran and spotlessly clean, the food is Persian and very good. To get here head about 8km south out of town on Turkmenbashi şayoli, towards the Iranian border – it's definitely worth the trek.

itional Turkmen fare, with spotless hygiene and a modern, airy dining hall. The large menu encompasses modern European and vegetarian dining and you can even eat in the customised yurt if you call ahead.

Sim Sim (☎ 45 33 43; Andaliba köçesi 50/1) This funky, chaotic restaurant was definitely the place to be in the summer of 2003. A young, hip, mainly Russian crowd eat and drink on the lively balcony and in the main dining room. The menu consists of Turkmen/Russian standards but the food is well done and tasty. To find this place take a taxi.

Quick Eats

Şazada (☎ 41 06 21; Turkmenbashi şayoli 47) Mainly a patisserie, although it does do pizzas and burgers, the latter being particularly tasty. The chain has a second outlet at the Univermag department store.

Gülüstan Restoran (Russian Bazaar) Has a great atmosphere and is always busy with locals eating shashlyk and plov, although don't expect anything out of the ordinary.

DRINKING

Bar culture is still something of a foreign one to Turkmen, and as such most of the bars in the city are designed to attract foreigners. One exception is the Iceberg Bar behind Ashgabat's now-disused circus. This sprawling complex of beer gardens is

actually a microbrewery, great for summer evenings with a pleasant local crowd.

Florida (☎ 39 33 51; Görogly köçesi 8) Long the focus of expat life, this is known under a host of different names, but it's a busy bar, restaurant and nightclub. It offers Ashgabat's only drum-and-bass night.

City Pub (☎ 35 22 88; Alishera Navoi köçesi 54a) Sharing the building and management of the Asuda Nusay Restaurant, City Pub is another worrying real British pub that has found its way to Central Asia. Like the restaurant it's popular and busy.

ENTERTAINMENT
Cinemas

There are no cinemas in the city since Niyazov declared motion pictures 'un-Turkmen'. However, at the time of writing the **DVD Bar** (☎ 35 31 93; Turkmenbaşi şayoli 29; admission US$1.25) was showing films several times throughout the evening, and was also one of the best places to buy DVDs. While the films are in Russian, the cinema is tiny, so if there are a couple of you, you may be able to get them to put on the undubbed English version.

Live Music

There is very little in the way of live pop or rock, as even the veteran Russian pop groups have begun to leave increasingly eccentric Ashgabat off their tour schedules. Fun, yet extremely tourist-oriented 'folk evenings' are organised by most travel agents for around US$20 per person, including dinner and a full programme of traditional dancing and singing.

Nightclubs

There are a handful of nightspots operating in Ashgabat – anyone operating beyond 11pm needs a special license, and so things are limited (although many bars in the city will do lock-ins at weekends). The Four Points Akaltin Sheraton Hotel has a fun club in the basement, where a local crowd dances to a heady mixture of Turkmen, Russian and Western pop. A similar venue is at the Sheraton Grand Turkmen. A pretty much exclusively local crowd patronises the Mukan nightclub in the First Park, where they serve up tasty food in the dark and intimate underground venue. The Diamond Night Club in the Hotel Turkmenistan is the best place to find a friend to hang out with. The former Florida still keeps busy at weekends.

Sport

Ashgabat is a great place for horse-lovers. Every Sunday from the end of March until May, then again from the end of August until mid-November, the Hippodrome plays host to dramatic Turkmen horse races. It's 5km west of the city centre – either bus No 4 down Magtymguly or a US$0.50 taxi ride.

There are also numerous places to ride Akhal-Teke horses. Highly recommended is the Alaja Farm, run by Katya Kolestnikova and located in Geok-Dere. This is a professional stable, where the horses are well cared for and well fed (not always the case elsewhere). Riding here costs US$10 an hour, worth the price for the beautiful golden stallions and some wonderful riding in the canyons of Chuli. If you want to call in advance, speak to Gulya Yangebaeva on ☎ 42 63 58. Otherwise you can just turn up as the farm operates seven days a week. Take the Geok-Depe road out of Ashgabat and turn left at the sign for Geok-Dere. Continue through the village and Alaja is at the end on the right.

The local football team is Kopet Dag, which plays at the Kopet Dag Stadium. You should have no trouble picking up a ticket on match days.

Theatre & Concert Halls

The current state of the performing arts in Ashgabat is fairly lamentable. Most theatres closed down in 2002 after ballet and opera were deemed 'foreign'. At the time of writing the Russian Drama Theatre was still operating as well as a couple of Turkmen theatres, although a brand new National Theatre was being completed. Ballet and opera are no longer performed in Turkmenistan and the quality of drama is not likely to be high.

SHOPPING

The biggest and best supermarket in town is the Yimpaş (Turkmenbashi şayoli 54; ⓨ 9am-11pm), a huge Turkish shopping complex featuring, among other things, the only escalators in Turkmenistan. Here you can buy everything from frozen lobster to Doritos. The best shopping experiences are to be had at one of Ashgabat's many markets. While Tolkuchka Bazaar (see p417) is possibly the most fabulous in Central Asia, there are others in the town centre. The Russian Bazaar is good for CDs, videos and clothing while the Tekke Bazaar is recommended for foodstuffs, spices, fruit and flowers. Niyazov kitsch can be bought at the small Ministry of Culture shop (Asudaliq köçesi 33).

GETTING THERE & AWAY
Air

For information about flights from outside Central Asia see the Transport in Central Asia chapter (p461). Turkmenistan Airlines operates one flight a week from Ashgabat to Almaty, Tashkent and Frankfurt. Uzbekistan Airlines links Ashgabat to Tashkent just once a week (one way US$110).

Internally Turkmenistan Airlines flights are so heavily subsidised as to make the ticket prices amazingly low. Be warned that demand is consequently massive and therefore any flights you want to take should be booked as far ahead in advance as possible. Timetables also change regularly but there are approximately five daily flights to Dashogus (US$1.25), 10 daily to Turkmenabat (US$1.50), three daily to Mary (US$1.20), three daily to Turkmenbashi (US$1.30), as well as regular flights to Kerki (Atamurat; US$1.70, via Turkmenabat) and a daily flight to Gaurdak (via Turkmenabat, US$2.50).

AIRLINE OFFICES

The following airlines fly to/from Turkmenistan (except where stated) and have offices in Ashgabat.

Aerosvit Ukrainian Airlines (☎ 35 01 64; www.aerosvit.com; Magtymguly şayoli 73) One flight weekly from Kiev.

British Airways (☎ 51 07 99; www.britishairways.com; Sheraton Grand Turkmen Hotel; Görogly köçesi 7) British Airways doesn't fly to Ashgabat, but this office is useful as a travel agency.

Lufthansa (☎ 33 20 37, 33 20 56; www.lufthansa.com; Main Concourse, Sapamyrat Turkmenbashi Airport) Six flights per week from Frankfurt, three direct to Ashgabat; three via Baku.

Turkmenistan Airlines (☎ internal flights 35 26 43, international flights 39 39 00; www.turkmenistanairlines.com; Magtymguly şayoli 82) From Ashgabat to Abu Dhabi, Baku, Bangkok, Birmingham, Delhi, Frankfurt, İstanbul, Karachi, Kiev, London, Mashhad, Moscow and Yerevan.

Turkish Airlines (☎ 51 06 66; www.turkishairlines.com; Sheraton Grand Turkmen Hotel; Görogly köçesi 7) Three flights weekly from İstanbul to Ashgabat.

Uzbekistan Airways (☎ 33 20 26; www.ukraine -international.com; Main Concourse, Sapamyrat Turkmen-bashi Airport) One flight a week from Tashkent.

Bus, Marshrutka & Shared Taxi

Bus stops in Ashgabat are divided up by destination, and are stands for shared taxis and marshrutki (small buses or vans that run fixed routes with flexible stops, fares charged by distance travelled) as much as bus stops. Transport for Mary and Turkmenabat leaves from the hub, to the left of the main train station, as you look at it. There are marshrutki to Mary (US$3) and Turkmenabat (US$5).

Transport for Balkanabat and Turkmen-bashi leaves from the Old Airport (stary aeroport). There are marshrutki and shared taxis to Balkanabat (both US$4) and Turk-menbashi (both US$6.25).

Transport for Dashogus and Konye-Urgench leaves from the Dashogus Bazaar. A marshrutka to Konye-Urgench costs US$4 (10 to 12 hours), while a place in a shared cab is US$6. Chartering a whole cab will cost US$24. Prices to Dashogus are slightly higher: Lvov buses will take 18 hours for the trip (US$3.50) including a two-hour stop for lunch in Darvaza. Ikarus buses (15 hours) are faster, while marshrutki (US$5) make the trip in 12 to 14 hours. A place in a taxi will cost US$9 and the trip takes 11 to 12 hours.

Train

The capital is linked by rail with Turkmen-bashi (11 hours, US$1.50), Mary (8½ hours, US$1), Turkmenabat (15 hours, US$1.50) and Dashogus (26 hours, US$2). This is, however, the slowest way to travel around the country and not a particularly comfortable one either. A new train line is currently being constructed through the desert to link Ashgabat and Dashogus directly.

GETTING AROUND
To/From the Airport

The best way to get into central Ashgabat from the airport is to take a taxi. They are both plentiful and cheap, especially if shared. Expect to pay US$1, but agree before getting in. Drivers are likely to try their luck asking for anything from US$5 to US$10 initially.

Public Transport

Buses are crowded and slow, but dirt cheap and modern. With taxis being so cheap,

there's little reason to use buses – unless you happen to be on a bus route and living out of the city centre. Ashgabat has no metro system or trams.

Taxi

Official taxis are not particularly plentiful, but you can flag down cars with ease almost anywhere. Expect to pay 3,000 to 5,000 M (US$0.15 to US$0.20) for a short trip within the city, and 10,000 M (US$0.45) for a longer one. If in doubt, agree on a price beforehand, otherwise just hand the money over on arrival with extreme confidence. To order a taxi call ☎ 35 34 06.

AROUND ASHGABAT
Nissa & Around

Founded as the capital of the Parthians in the 3rd century BC, in its prime **Nissa** (admission US$1) was reinforced with 43 towers that sheltered the royal palace and a couple of temples. It was surrounded by a thriving commercial city. One ruling dynasty replaced another until the 13th century when the Mongols arrived, laid siege to the city and after 15 days razed it to the ground.

The ridges surrounding the plateau were the fortress walls; the steep, modern approach road follows the route of the original entrance. In the northern part of the city are the remains of a large house built around a courtyard, with wine cellars in nearby buildings.

The main complex on the western side includes a large circular chamber thought to have been a Zoroastrian temple. Adjoining it is the partly rebuilt 'tower' building. On the far side of the western wall are the ruins of a medieval town, today the village of Bagyr.

Coming by car from Ashgabat it is possible to take the road past Berzengi along the presidential highway. On the way you'll pass the **Palace of Orphans**, another bizarre Niyazov project with massive futuristic marble buildings, sporting facilities and its own mosque. The children in this village are educated to be government officials.

Geok-Depe

Midway on the main road between Ashgabat and Bakharden is the village of **Geok-Depe** (Green Hill), site of the Turkmen's last stand against the Russians. During the Soviet era the uncommemorated site of the breached

---

STAIRCASE TO...?

In this area is one of Niyazov's more idiosyncratic projects – the **Walk of Health**, a concrete staircase that has been built into the side of the Kopet Dag Mountains. There are two walks – one 8km and one 37km. Once a year in a delightfully humiliating ritual, Turkmenbashi waves off his ministers and members of the government (along with thousands of other civil servants) as they do the walk in shell suits. Turkmenbashi then flies to the end in his helicopter and greets them as they come wheezing to the conclusion of the course. Who says there's no justice?

---

earthen fortress, where 15,000 Turkmen died, was part of a collective farm. Today the large futuristic **Saparmyrat Hajji Mosque**, and its sky-blue domes, stands beside the telltale ridges and burrows. The mosque's name refers to the president's pilgrimage to Mecca. After his public conversion from communism in the mid-1990s, unlike most who make the pilgrimage, Niyazov returned with US$10 billion in aid from the Saudi government. In a pleasant fusion of politics and religion, 'Bashi' has suggested that all Turkmen should visit the mosque on pilgrimage once a year. It has all the religious piety of a shopping mall, however, despite being attractive from the exterior.

Karakum Desert

In the heart of Central Asia's hottest desert, the two oasis towns of **Jerbent** and **Darvaza** somehow survive. In both places you can see nomadic people, experience their customs, see handicrafts, watch carpet making and taste their food while staying overnight in an *ak oi* (Turkmen yurt) or chaikhana (known locally as chaykhana). This is the real, traditional Turkmen experience.

Darvaza is the halfway post between the capital and Konye-Urgench. It's also at the heart of the Karakum desert and the best place to visit as there's the added attraction of the **Darvaza Gas Craters**, one of Turkmenistan's most unusual sights. Apparently the result of Soviet-era gas exploration in the 1950s, the nine craters are artificial. One has been set alight and blazes with an incredible strength

that's visible from miles away. The fire crater is best seen at night, when it also becomes an attraction for huge and largely harmless spiders that run into the fire for reasons best known to themselves. This is a serious off-road ride in the middle of the night and drivers frequently get lost or get stuck in the dunes. People at the chaikhanas in Darvaza will be able to help you find a driver – expect to pay US$10 for the round trip.

In Darvaza there are no recommended places to stay in the village itself, but there are two chaikhanas 5km to the north, which have yurts you can sleep in. In Jerbent, ask for the chaikhana Barda.

All buses and marshrutki headed from Ashgabat to both Konye-Urgench and Dashogus go through Darvaza and Jerbent. Let the driver know that you want to get off, although you'll probably have to pay the full price to Ashgabat, Konye-Urgench or Dashogus (p421). Darvaza is about four to five hours from Ashgabat and six to eight hours from Konye-Urgench. Getting away from Darvaza may be more difficult – buses are usually full, so you'll probably have to stop a car and agree on a price.

WESTERN TURKMENISTAN

Littoral to the mighty Caspian Sea and its shockingly large mineral, gas and oil reserves, western Turkmenistan is a strange place that's sparsely inhabited and home to some of the strangest landscapes in the country. Most people simply pass through here on the way to the port of Turkmenbashi, from where it's possible to continue on to Azerbaijan by ferry. This is a mistake, as while the towns in the west are almost all memorably devoid of interest, there are plenty of quirky sights and natural wonders that make this an enjoyable place to spend a few days. The Kopet Dag, Dekhistan (Misrian) and Köw Ata Underground Lake should not be missed if you are on your way to Turkmenbashi.

KÖW ATA UNDERGROUND LAKE

Like entering Milton's underworld, only with changing rooms and a staircase, a visit to the **Köw Ata Underground Lake** (admission US$2; ☼ dawn-dusk) is a unique experience. You enter a cave at the base of a mountain and walk down a staircase, 65m underground, which takes you into a wonderfully sulphurous subterranean world. At the bottom awaits a superb lake of clear water naturally heated to about 36°C.

Follow the main road to Balkanabat from Ashgabat for the best part of an hour; the turn off to the lake is clearly marked to the left with a large sign for Köw Ata. By marshrutka or bus to Balkanabat or Turkmenbashi you could easily ask the driver to stop at Köw Ata, although it's a good 30-minute walk back from the road.

NOKHUR

A visit to Nokhur provides a great chance to see a mountain community and its traditions in Turkmenistan, as well as visit the impressive Kopet Dag range and see a selection of beautiful waterfalls. A magnificently isolated oasis in the Kelet Valley, Nokhur was once a byword among Soviet Turkmen for everything rural and backwards. Nokhuri are a breed apart from the Turkmen of the steppe, claiming ancestry from Alexander the Great's army and preferring to marry among themselves rather than introduce new genes to the tribe. Both of these claims are in evidence when you visit the town.

The two sights in this fascinating village are the town's **cemetery**, where each grave is protected by the huge horns of the mountain goats that locals consider sacred – indeed many houses in the village have a goat's skull hanging on a stick outside to ward off evil spirits. You should not enter the cemetery, as it's for locals only, although photography is perfectly acceptable. A short walk beyond the cemetery is **Qyz Bibi**, a spiritualist-Muslim shrine, where people from all over the country come on pilgrimage. Qyz Bibi was the pre-Islamic patroness of women and the goddess of fertility. She is believed to dwell in the cave (the entrance of which is just 30cm to 40cm in diameter), to which a winding pathway leads beyond a huge, ancient tree where pilgrims tie colourful material in the hopes of conceiving a child.

There are four impressive waterfalls in the mountains beyond Nokhur, all of which can be visited by hiring a UAZ 4WD in Nokhur (ask your guide to ask around). The routes are fairly arduous, but good fun for day tripping and taking in the impressive scenery.

For accommodation, the remote **Çandybil Turbaza** (☎ in Ashgabat 12 352002, 350644; via Sada Tourism, Ashgabat; per person incl breakfast US$17), 11km beyond Nokhur, is an attractive mountain retreat with passably comfortable rooms and a novelty yurt for those who like fake-authentic experiences.

In Nokhur itself, it shouldn't be hard to find a homestay. Gaib Nazar and Enebai Ekeyeva always welcome guests to their large mountain house (complete with satellite TV). They charge US$10 per person per night. Ask anywhere for Kinomekanik Gaib – he was the village's cinema projectionist before he retired.

BALKANABAT

☎ 243 / pop 87,000

Balkanabat, known under the Soviets as Nebit Dag, has an attractive position beneath the mountains. Oil was discovered in the vicinity in 1874 and a small refinery was built, only to be abandoned for 50 years after being bankrupted by competition from the Baku oil industry.

Oil aside, there's little to bring anyone here. The main axis is Magtymguly şayoli, running east–west and parallel with the railway. At its midpoint is Niyazov Square, watched over by a lonely statue of the president. The train station is 1km west and 400m south of Niyazov Square. Its forecourt also serves as the long-distance bus terminus.

Balkanabat distinguished itself during the Soviet era by being the only city in the USSR to use the American system of numbering the streets. This remains today, making it the only town in modern Turkmenistan without a Turkmenbashi şayoli!

The town boasts the surprisingly smart **Hotel Nebitchi** (☎ 4 53 35/6/7/8/9; Kvartal 198; s/d/ste US$100/150/250; ✖ ♨), a top-end place with decent rooms and a couple of good eating and drinking venues. There are big discounts to be had by booking through a travel agent. For those without the funds, the **Hotel Balkan** (☎ 4 32 93; Kvartal 225; s/d US$30/60) can usually be argued down. It's a grotty, small place, but the rooms are fine.

You can eat well at the Hotel Nebitchi Restaurant, although far better value for money is **Kafé Viktoria** (☎ 4 03 06; Kvartal 197). Unmarked from the exterior, it's a small building next to the disused cinema. You can eat a good meal for US$2.

There are two trains a day to Turkmenbashi (3½ hours), and two to Ashgabat, one of which continues to Turkmenabat and Dashogus. Buses to Ashgabat (US$3, six hours) leave throughout the day. A taxi will do the trip for US$15. There are no longer flights to and from Ashgabat from here.

DEKHISTAN

The ruined city of Dekhistan (also known as Misrian) lies deep in the barren wastelands south of Balkanabat, midway between the tumbledown villages of Bugdayly and Madau. The surrounding desolation begs the question of how a city came to be here in the first place. Yet in the 11th century it was a Silk Road oasis city with a sophisticated irrigation system rivalling Merv and Konye-Urgench. It even managed to revive itself after destruction by the Mongols. It seems that some time in the 15th century the region suffered an ecological catastrophe. The forests of the Kopet Dag to the east had been exploited for centuries until the water supply failed and the well-watered slopes finally became a barren, deeply eroded lunar landscape.

Not much remains on the 200-hectare site, apart from two truncated 20m-high **minarets** from the 11th and 13th centuries, and the decorated remains of a mosque entrance. The **cemetery**, 7km north of Dekhistan, features five semiruined mausoleums, including the Shir-Kabir Mosque-Mausoleum, the earliest mosque in the country.

Unless you have your own vehicle, Dekhistan is difficult to get to. Public transport is nonexistent, although you should be able to get a taxi from Balkanabat. The round trip should cost US$50, including waiting time. After the rains in the spring it can be unreachable.

TURKMENBASHI

☎ 243 / pop 60,000

The first settlement here was established when a unit of Russian troops under Prince Alexander Bekovich set ashore in 1717 with the intention of marching on Khiva. They chose this spot because it was close to the place where the Oxus River (now the Amu-Darya) had once drained into the Caspian, and the dry riverbed provided the best road across the desert. But the mission failed, Bekovich lost his head and the Russians didn't come back for more than 150 years.

Turkmenbashi remains a very Russified town, although there's also a large Azeri population here as well. As an introduction to Turkmenistan it may seem decidedly unexotic but just a short drive out of town takes you to hauntingly empty landscapes and dramatic mountains. The best places to see the strange landscapes are a good three- to four-hour drive from Turkmenbashi. The views from the main road from Balkanabat, however, are impressive, as is the bizarre appearance of the city itself, which is carved into the dramatic cliffside and overlooks the Caspian.

Sights

The **Museum of Regional History** (admission US$0.10, excursion US$0.15; �9am-6pm Tue-Sun) is divided into an upper and lower museum, however, one or both seems to be closed all the time. The collections include disintegrating taxidermy, some interesting maps, models of the Caspian Sea, traditional Turkmen clothing and a yurt.

There's a charming light-blue **Russian Orthodox church** set back from the sea front, a testament to the city's past as a Russian fortress town. All that remains of the fortress itself are its gates – distinct creations with red stars mounted about them – which can be found in the park by the lower museum.

Sleeping

There are only three hotels in Turkmenbashi and backpackers will unfortunately be limited to the **Hotel Hazar** (☎ 2 46 33; Azadi köçesi; s/d/ste US$4/6/8). The old Soviet behemoth comes complete with brown (and cold) tap water and general nastiness. The linen and beds are clean at least, but avoid the restaurant, as it's just plain scary.

Hotel Tolkun (☎ 2 39 05; Hazar köçesi; s/d/ste US$25/35/60; ❄) A much nicer option on the seafront, the Tolkun was undergoing renovation at the time of writing, and may well raise its prices when it reopens in 2004. The rooms are clean and many have views of the sea.

Hotel Turkmenbashi (☎ 2 13 04/08; fax 21317; Hazar köçesi; s/d/ste US$50/60/75; ☂ ❄) Top of the range, this large white tower at the end of the town has five-star facilities and a decent restaurant. From June to September, prices rise by 20% to 30%.

Hotel Sedar (☎ 21581, 51225; sedaroteli@online.tm; s/d US$100/120, ste US$200-400; ☂ ❄) Possibly the

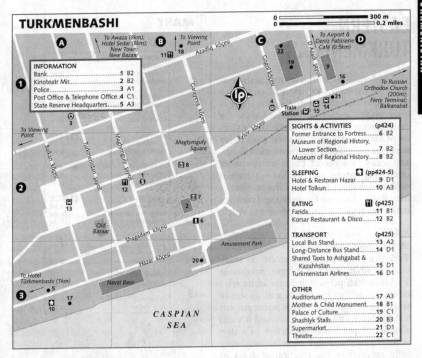

TURKMENBASHI

0	300 m
0	0.2 miles

To Awaza (8km);
Hotel Sedar (8km);
New Town;
New Bazaar

To Viewing
Point

Azadliq köçesi

To Airport &
Deniz Patisserie
Café (0.5km)

To Russian
Orthodox Church
(200m);
Ferry Terminal;
Balkanabat

Çarayeva köçesi

Balkan köçesi

Turkmenistan şayoli

Magtymguly şayoli

Magtymguly
Square

Çolgol köçesi

D Azadi şayoli

Rylov köçesi

Train
Station

Shagadam köçesi

Old
Bazaar

Hazar köçesi

Amusement Park

To Hotel
Turkmenbashi (1km)

Naval Base

CASPIAN
SEA

INFORMATION	
Bank	1 B2
Kinoteatr Mir	2 B2
Police	3 A1
Post Office & Telephone Office	4 C1
State Reserve Headquarters	5 A3

SIGHTS & ACTIVITIES	(p424)
Former Entrance to Fortress	6 B2
Museum of Regional History, Lower Section	7 B2
Museum of Regional History	8 B2

SLEEPING	(pp424-5)
Hotel & Restoran Hazar	9 D1
Hotel Tolkun	10 A3

EATING	(p425)
Farida	11 B1
Korsar Restaurant & Disco	12 B2

TRANSPORT	(p425)
Local Bus Stand	13 A2
Long-Distance Bus Stand	14 D1
Shared Taxis to Ashgabat & Kazahhstan	15 D1
Turkmenistan Airlines	16 D1

OTHER	
Auditorium	17 A3
Mother & Child Monument	18 B1
Palace of Culture	19 C1
Shashlyk Stalls	20 B3
Supermarket	21 D1
Theatre	22 C1

best hotel in Turkmenistan, occupying a suitably remote location in the holiday resort of Awaza, a few kilometres north of Turkmenbashi. It's something of a fortress for the rich and, well, rich. From June to September, prices here rise by 20% to 30%.

Eating & Drinking

All the following places are open for lunch and dinner.

The best restaurant in town is the **Korsar** (☎ 2 09 53/2; Magtymguly 205), a short walk from the embankment. Fussy service it may be, but the food is excellent and well presented, although pricier than most Turkmen restaurants, clocking in at about US$5 per person. Below the restaurant there's a nightclub that is very busy at weekends.

Another place that can be highly recommended is **Deniz Patisserie Cafe** (☎ 2 88 51; Azadi köçesi 54), a pleasantly designed, airy café that will do anything from tea and cakes to a full Russian meal. It'll also rustle up just about anything you want (within local means) for breakfast and makes a good escape if you are staying at the Hazar.

With less flair, but decent enough and reliable is **Farida** (Azadliq köçesi 27), a standard-issue Russian restaurant serving fish, shashlyk and pizza at very reasonable prices.

Getting There & Away

Turkmenbashi is Turkmenistan's only large port and has several untimetabled ferries everyday to Baku in Azerbaijan (see p468).

Shared taxis leave outside the colourful train station on Rylov köçesi for Ashgabat (US$6.25 per seat or US$25 for the whole car, six hours). They also run north along the bad road to the Kazakh border at Begkash (four hours, US$40 per car). Marshrutki also leave with frequency for Ashgabat via Balkanabat; they cost the same as a seat in a shared taxi and are far less comfortable.

An overnight train leaves daily from Turkmenbashi at 4.05pm for Ashgabat (arriving at 5.50am). A *kupe* (2nd-class seat) is US$1.20. On uneven dates, there's a so-called overnight fast train that leaves Turkmenbashi at 7.20pm and arrives in Ashgabat at 5.20am (US$1.50 for a *kupe*). Call ☎ 99462 for information on train services.

EASTERN TURKMENISTAN

The eastern swathe of Turkmenistan contains the Amu-Darya, Murgab and Tejen river valleys, a fertile swathe of land that has given rise to ancient civilisations since the early Bronze Age. Home to the ancient cities of Merv and Gonur, this vast oasis today supports quiet Turkmen towns and villages, and leads to some of the country's most interesting nature reserves. Even if ancient civilisations don't excite you, the cave cities, mountains, dinosaur footprints and canyons make this region a fascinating one to visit.

MARY

☎ 522 / pop 95,000

Turkmenistan's third-largest city is more cosmopolitan than its bigger neighbour Turkmenabat, perhaps because of its relative proximity to the capital and its steady stream of foreign tourists visiting the ancient sites of Merv and Gonur. That said it's still a rather empty Soviet confection of a city, with Niyazov's recent contribution being little more than the creation of acres of manicured nothingness. Despite this, Mary is a pleasant place with a surprising amount of activity and commercial freedom.

The town's main thoroughfare is Mollanepes şayoli, where you'll find the seven-storey Hotel Sanjar facing the Univermag department store. Further down Mollanepes is the Green Bazaar and the Murgab River. Crossing the river en route to Merv you'll see the enormous new town mosque. The central post and telegraph office is 1km east of the Sanjar on Mollanepes, while the central telephone office is 50m south of the post office. **Turkmenistan Airlines** (☎ 32777; Magtymguly köçesi 11) also has an office in the town.

Yevgenia Golubeva (☎ 3 14 85) is an experienced, English-speaking tour guide, who used to be the deputy director of the Mary Museum. She can organise tours to nearby Merv and Gonur.

Sights

The **Mary Regional Museum** (admission US$1; ☻ 10am-5pm Tue-Sun) shouldn't be missed. The display of artefacts from Merv and Margiana is attractively laid out and fea-

MARY

0 ——— 500 m
0 ——— 0.3 miles

INFORMATION	
Post Office.....................................1	B5
Telephone Office............................2	B5
Western Union...............................3	A4

SIGHTS & ACTIVITIES	(pp426-7)
Mary Regional Museum...................4	B5
Niyazov Statue...............................5	A5
War Memorial................................6	A4

SLEEPING	🏠 (p427)
Hotel Sanjar..................................7	A4
Hotel Yrsgal Firmasay.....................8	A4

EATING	🍴 (p427)
Altyn Asyr Kafe Bar........................9	A5
Zip Restaurant.............................10	A4

DRINKING	🍷 (p427)
Azia Disco Bar..............................11	A4
Margush Disco Bar........................12	A4
Sanjar Disco................................13	A4

TRANSPORT	(p427)
Bus Station..................................14	A4
Turkmenistan Airlines Booking Office.................................15	A5

OTHER	
Cafés...16	B5
Cafés...17	A4
Department Store.........................18	A4
Kafe Seyilbag..............................19	B5

tures a large model of Merv. The skeleton of a Margiana priestess is a replica – a series of deaths and misfortunes among museum staff persuaded them to have the original returned to where it was found. The fine quality and design of household items from Margiana is striking and rivals the collection of the National Museum in Ashgabat.

Other displays include an exhibition of Turkmen carpets from the museum's huge collection; a display of Turkmen household items; everyday, wedding and ceremonial clothing; and a fully decorated yurt.

There is also a Sunday-morning market, **Tekke Bazaar**, held 4km out of town, that is reportedly similar to Ashgabat's Tolkuchka Bazaar but, with more carpets at cheaper prices (although not necessarily better). The simplest way to get here is by taxi, which should cost US$1 at most.

Sleeping

The town's old Intourist hotel is the **Hotel Sanjar** (☎ 5 76 44; Mollanepes şayoli; s/d/ste US$15/ 30/50), which is excellently located, but has very basic bathrooms (although there is hot water). A short walk away is the more modern **Hotel Yrsgal Firmasay** (☎ 5 39 76; s/d US$12/24), a cheaper and more promising establishment that is often booked up.

Out of town, but good for those with cars, is the **Hotel Rakhat** (☎ 6 02 61, 3 49 70; Murgabskoye Shosse, 2nd km; s/d US$20/25), situated next to the Turkish truck stop. There's satellite TV and a small bar-café. The rooms are large but mediocre, although the bathrooms are OK.

The nicest (and certainly the friendliest) place in town is a licensed homestay, the **Hotel Caravanserai** (☎ 3 93 50, 3 34 64; fax 6 09 22; Nisimi köçesi 25; s/d/t US$20/40/54), run by a charming Turkmen family. The facilities are shared, but clean and have hot water, and there's a lovely garden.

Eating & Drinking

Generally held to be the best in town, the **Sakhra Restaurant** (☎ 5 61 77; Magtymguly köçesi 40) appears to be a vodka shop when you enter, but has two dining rooms where good Turkmen and Russian dishes are served. Service is a little fussy if you sit in the formal dining room (the bar dining room around the back is much nicer).

There are a couple of more fun places in the centre of town where you might meet some locals. The **Altyn Asyr Kafe Bar** (cnr Turkmenistan şayoli & Gurbansoltan Eje köçesi; ⏰ noon-11pm) is a very popular place for beers and meals, and is probably the most happening joint in town. Around the corner is **Zip Restaurant** (Turkmenistan şayoli; ⏰ noon-10.30pm), a more upmarket place serving shashlyk and Russian standards to a local middle-class crowd. It's also fun.

There are three easily accessible discos in town, which make for a unique and enjoyable cultural experience. None work beyond 11pm, but the locals are extremely friendly and up for it, even if they have to be picking cotton at 7am the next morning. The Sanjar Disco is next to the eponymous hotel, while across the road is Marguşh Disco Bar. Probably smartest of the lot is the Azia Disco Bar to one side of the Hotel Yrsgal Firmasay.

Getting There & Away

Mary is 3½ hours by car from Ashgabat and two hours from Turkmenabat. Marshrutki also run this route (four hours, US$3 and 2½ hours, US$2 respectively).

Mary's revamped **train station** (☎ 9 22 45) has two day trains and a night train to Ashgabat (eight hours, US$1). There's one day and one night train to Turkmenabat (seven hours, US$1) and one that runs the whole way to Dashogus (US$2.50, 24 hours). There is no left-luggage facility here.

Turkmenistan Airlines (☎ 3 27 77; Magtymguly köçesi 11) has several flights daily to Ashgabat.

MERV

Turkmenistan's greatest attraction, and the site of one of Central Asia's great historic cities, Merv should be seen by anyone interested in the history of the Near East. A huge site spread over 100 sq km, Merv needs to be seen with a guide and car to make sense of its vast complexity, which juxtaposes time scales and cultures. It is Turkmenistan's only Unesco World Heritage site and of immense historic significance to the whole of Central Asia. Anyone wanting to properly understand this complex and fascinating place should invest in Georgina Hermann's excellent book on the subject (p435).

History

Merv was known as Margiana or Margush in Alexander the Great's time. Under the Persian Sassanians, it was a melting pot of religious creeds with Christians, Buddhists and Zoroastrians cohabiting peacefully. As a centre of power, culture and civilisation, Merv reached its greatest heights during the peak of the silk route in the 11th and 12th centuries, when the Seljuq Turks made it their capital and (after Baghdad) the greatest city in the Islamic world. Marv-i-shahjahan, or 'Merv, Queen of the World' as it

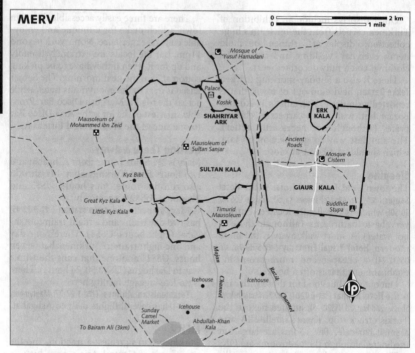

MERV

0 ————————————————— 2 km
0 ————————————————— 1 mile

- Mosque of Yusuf Hamadani
- Palace
- Koshk
- **SHAHRIYAR ARK**
- **ERK KALA**
- Mausoleum of Mohammed ibn Zeid
- Mausoleum of Sultan Sanjar
- Ancient Roads
- Mosque & Cistern
- **SULTAN KALA**
- Kyz Bibi
- **GIAUR KALA**
- Great Kyz Kala
- Little Kyz Kala
- Buddhist Stupa
- Timurid Mausoleum
- Majan Channel
- Razik Channel
- Icehouse
- Icehouse
- Icehouse
- Sunday Camel Market
- Abdullah-Khan Kala
- To Bairam Ali (3km)

was then known, may even have been the inspiration for the tales of Scheherazade's *The Thousand and One Nights*.

All of this was completely eradicated in 1221 under the onslaught of the Mongols. In 1218 Jenghiz Khan demanded a substantial tithe of grain from Merv, along with the pick of the city's most beautiful young women. The unwise Seljuq response was to slay the tax collectors. In retribution Tolui, the most brutal of Jenghiz Khan's sons, arrived three years later at the head of an army, accepted the peaceful surrender of the terrified citizens, and then proceeded to butcher every last one of the city's inhabitants. Each Mongol fighter had orders to decapitate 300 to 400 civilians. That done, with the exception of some of the grander buildings such as the Sultan Sanjar Mausoleum, the city was literally torn to pieces and put to the torch. With just swords, knives and axes the Mongols slaughtered perhaps a million people. Days later, after they had left, the few survivors crept back into the ruins, only for Tolui's soldiers to reappear and viciously finish the job.

Sights
EARLIEST REMAINS

The oldest of the five Merv cities is **Erk Kala**, an Achaemenid city thought to date from the 6th century BC. Today it's a big earthen doughnut about 600m across. There are deep trenches that have been dug into the ramparts by Soviet archaeologists. The ramparts are 50m high, offering a good view of the surrounding savannahlike landscape.

From this vantage point you can see that Erk Kala forms part of the northern section of another fortress – **Giaur Kala**, constructed during the 3rd century BC by the Sassanians. The fortress walls are still solid, with three gaps where gates once were. The city was built on a Hellenistic grid pattern; near the crossroads in the middle of the site are the ruins of a 7th-century mosque. At the eastern end of the mosque is an 8m-deep water cistern that's been dug into the ground.

In the southeastern corner of Giaur Kala a distinct mound marks the site of a Buddhist stupa and monastery, which was still functioning in the early Islamic era. The head of a Buddha statue was found here making Merv the furthest western point to which Buddhism spread at its height.

SULTAN KALA

The best remaining testimony to Seljuq power at Merv is the 38m-high **Mausoleum of Sultan Sanjar**, located in what was the centre of Sultan Kala. Sanjar, grandson of Alp-Arslan, died in 1157, reputedly of a broken heart when, after escaping from captivity in Khiva, he came home to find that Jenghiz Khan's soldiers had laid waste to his beloved Merv.

The mausoleum is a simple cube with a barrel-mounted dome on top. Originally it had a magnificent turquoise-tiled outer dome, said to be visible from a day's ride away, but that is long gone. Interior decoration is sparse, though restoration is being carried out on a blue-and-red frieze that adorns the upper gallery; inside is Sanjar's simple stone 'tomb', although fearing grave robbers he was actually buried elsewhere in an unknown location!

The **Shahriyar Ark** (or Citadel of Sultan Kala) is one of the more interesting parts of Merv. Still visible are its walls, a well-preserved *koshk* (fort) with corrugated walls, and the odd grazing camel.

North of the Shahriyar Ark, outside the city walls, lies the **Mosque of Yusuf Hamadani**, built around the tomb of a 12th-century dervish. The complex has been largely rebuilt in the last 10 years and turned into an important pilgrimage site; it is not open to non-Muslims.

MOHAMMED IBN ZEID

About 1km west of Sanjar's tomb, just north of the dusty main road, is an early-Islamic monument, the 12th-century **Mausoleum of Mohammed ibn Zeid**. The small, unostentatious earthen-brick building, which was heavily restored early in the 20th century, benefits greatly from an attractive setting in a hollow that is ringed by spindly saxaul trees. The caretaker is a charming elderly mullah. Like the other Sufi shrines (Meane, Kubra) this shrine is also an important site for Sufi pilgrims.

There's confusion as to who's actually buried under the black marble cenotaph in the centre of the cool, dark shrine. It's definitely not Ibn Zeid, a prominent Shiite teacher who died four centuries before this tomb was built and is known to be buried elsewhere.

KYZ KALA

These two crumbling, 7th-century *koshks* outside the walls of Merv are interesting for their 'petrified stockade' walls, as writer Colin Thubron describes them, composed of 'vast clay logs up-ended side by side'. They were constructed by the Sassanians in the 7th century and were still in use by Seljuq sultans, 600 years later, as function rooms. These are some of the most symbolic and important structures in western Merv archaeology and they have no analogies anywhere else.

Getting There & Away

The only way to see the site without an exhausting walk is by car. From Mary expect to pay US$7.50 for a car and driver for four hours (the minimum amount of time needed to see the main monuments). Buses go between Mary and Bairam Ali every half hour or so; the journey takes about 45 minutes. Guided tours are available from any travel agency and this is the way most people see Merv. Yevgenia Golubeva in Mary (see p426) includes Merv on her tour of the area.

GONUR

The incredible discoveries made by Russian-Greek archaeologist Viktor Sarianidi at the constantly evolving excavation of and around **Gonur Depe** (Gonur Hill) have stunned the archaeological world. Sarianidi first began a dig at the site in 1972 in search of the lost capital of the Margiana Oasis. He has worked here ever since, and the site is currently the biggest excavation in the Near East, revealing what some archaeologists now believe to be the fifth great ancient civilisation. Until these finds confirmed theories about the Margiana culture, only four great ancient centres of civilisation were known: Egypt, Mesopotamia, China and India. This was quite possibly the capital of the fifth.

While Sarianidi's fascinating theories have not yet been fully recognised by the Western archaeological establishment, Gonur is confirmed to be the site of one of the oldest fire-worshipping civilisations, parallel to the Bactrian cultures in neighbouring Afghanistan.

Sarianidi's theory is that Gonur was the birthplace of the first monotheistic religion – Zoroastrianism, being at some point the home of the religion's founder, Zoroaster. The adjacent sites have revealed four fire temples, as well as evidence of a cult based around a drug potion prepared from poppy, hemp and ephedra plants. This potent brew is almost certainly the *haoma* (soma elixir) used by the magi whom Zoroaster began preaching against in Zoroastrian texts.

Gonur is 60km north of Merv, in the desert beyond the reaches of the oasis. Where the Murgab River once flowed, now just a dry riverbed remains. The first agricultural settlements appeared in the area in around 7000 BC and developed a strong agriculture. The current excavations have been dated back to 3000 BC. The Royal Palace and necropolis are fascinating to visit.

Getting There & Away

Gonur is a two-hour drive from Mary and you'll need at least two hours there. You can organise a trip through any travel agent or call Yevgenia Golubeva in Mary (see p426). Expect to pay US$40 to hire a driver, and a further US$30 for an in-depth guided tour.

TURKMENABAT

☎ 422 / pop 161,000

Universally known by its pre independence name of Charjou, Turkmenabat is a pleasant, if nondescript kind of place on the banks of the mighty Amu-Darya, although it can seem like Manhattan after the long drive through the desert from Mary or Dashogus. Turkmenistan's second city, Turkmenabat is in fact over 2000 years old, but invasions, earthquakes and both Soviet and Niyazov town planning have left no legacy of this. On transit through Turkmenistan to Uzbekistan, many people stop here overnight, and while there's a good restaurant and the hotels are passable, there's nothing in particular to look at.

Sleeping & Eating

The perfectly acceptable **Hotel Amu-Darya** (Niyazov şayoli 22; s/d/ste US$15/30/60) is central and in an undramatic state of decrepitude, with hot water and even an outdoor shashlyk restaurant in the summer months. Very similar in style and service is the **Hotel Charjou** (Shaidakov kÖçesi; s/d US$15/30), also in the city centre.

By far the best place in town to eat is the **Lebap Restaurant** (☎ 6 35 21; Puşkin kÖçesi; per head US$5), a large complex that includes a very smart restaurant and an outdoor summer terrace, which can be great in the evening.

TURKMENABAT

INFORMATION	
Left Luggage Office	1 A3
Post Office	2 A3
Telephone & Telegraph Office	3 B4
Turkmen Bank	4 B4
SIGHTS & ACTIVITIES	
Statue of Niyazov	5 B4
SLEEPING ⌂ (p430)	
Hotel Amu-Darya	6 A3
Hotel Charjou	7 B4
EATING ⑪ (p430)	
Lebab Restaurant	8 B4
Restaurant Turkmenistan	9 A3
TRANSPORT (pp430-1)	
Turkmenistan Airlines	10 B4
OTHER	
Regional Museum	11 A4
Univermag	12 B4

The food is mainly Russian, but there is a good selection of fish dishes and beers.

Getting There & Away

There are 10 flights a day between Turkmenabat and the capital (one hour, US$1.50). The Turkmenistan Airlines office is 300m south of Niyazov Square, on the second street on the left. There are no longer any train services to and from Uzbekistan from here. Trains go to Ashgabat (16 hours, US$1.50), Mary (seven hours, US$1), Dashogus (24 hours, US$2) and Turkmenbashi (23 hours, US$2.50). The main bus stop is outside the centre of town, on the main road to Ashgabat. From here marshrutki go to Ashgabat (seven hours, US$5) and Mary (2½ hours,

US$2). A place in a shared taxi costs about the same.

KUGITANG NATURE RESERVE

Kugitang is the most impressive and pristine of Turkmenistan's nature reserves. Set up in 1986 to protect the Kugitang Mountain Range, its unique ecosystem and in particular the rare markhor mountain goat, its name comes from the Persian meaning 'almost impassable mountains'. Its extent includes the country's highest peak Airybaba (3137m), several huge canyons, rich forests, mountain streams, caves and the unique **Dinosaur Plateau**. The latter attraction is simply amazing. It's presumed to be the bottom of a shallow lake that dried up, leaving dinosaur prints baking in the sun, after which a volcanic eruption sealed them in lava. There are 438 prints visible on a steep incline with breathtaking views across the mountains.

Visiting one of the **Karlyuk Caves** is also an incredible experience. Considered the most fascinating caves in the former Soviet Union, only one of the caves remains accessible to visitors while others have been sealed. Walking deep into the caves with one of the park rangers is both spooky and exciting, with some astonishing stalactites and stalagmites.

You'll need to organise a trip here through a travel agent who can get you a permit to visit and provide a driver. Accommodation is usually in a homestay with rangers or at a newly built hotel. Expect to pay US$40 per person per night for full board. It's possible to fly from Ashgabat to Gaurdak (Magdanly) via Turkmenabat (US$2.50), far preferable than doing the arduous journey across the desert. Otherwise it's a five- to six-hour drive from Turkmenabat.

NORTHERN TURKMENISTAN

Northern Turkmenistan is something of a nation within a nation. Historically it is linked far more closely with the neighbouring Silk Road cities of Uzbekistan, rather than with Ashgabat across the unrelenting Karakum desert. Soviet mapdrawing nevertheless placed the heavily Uzbek-influenced Khorezm people to the west of the Amu-Darya under the authority of Ashgabat and thus it has been ever since. This is one of the most politically repressed and economically bleak areas of the country – the main source of income is the smuggling of cheap government-subsidised petrol into neighbouring Uzbekistan, as well as the ubiquitous growing of cotton. The ancient Khorezm capital of Konye-Urgench, however, makes a superb side trip for anyone passing through this area on the way to or from Uzbekistan.

KONYE-URGENCH

The destructive power wrought by the armies of Jenghiz Khan and Timur (Tamerlane) is almost palpable in the air at Konye-Urgench, a city that has never recovered from the 'hurricanes' that passed through it more than 800 years ago. The ancient state of Khorezm, located on a northerly Silk Road branch that leads to the Caspian Sea and Russia, has been an important oasis of civilisation in the Central Asian deserts for thousands of years.

Khorezm fell to the all-conquering Seljuq Turks, but rose in the 12th century, under a Seljuq dynasty known as the Khorezmshahs, to shape its own far-reaching empire. With its mosques, medressa, libraries and flourishing bazaars, old Urgench became a centre of the Muslim world, until Khorezmshah Mohammed II moved his capital to Samarkand after capturing that city in 1210.

In 1216 Mohammed II, a man who thought of himself as a second Alexander the Great, received from that other empire builder of the day, Jenghiz Khan, a collection of lavish gifts, along with an offer of trade and a message that Jenghiz Khan regarded Mohammed as his 'most cherished son'. Two years later, 450 merchants travelling from Jenghiz Khan's territory were murdered at Otrar, a Khorezmshah frontier town east of the Aral Sea. Jenghiz Khan sent three envoys to Samarkand to demand reparation, but Mohammed had one killed and the beards of the other two burnt off.

Within two years Mongol armies had sacked Samarkand, Bukhara, old Urgench and Otrar and massacred their people. Old Urgench withstood several months' siege, but eventually the Mongols smashed the nearby dam on the Amu-Darya, letting the river flood through the city, and massacred the survivors. Other great Khorezmshah cities (Merv, Balkh, Herat) went the same way, and then the Mongols carried on to the Caucasus and Russia. Mohammed II died in rags on an island in the Caspian Sea in 1221. The tombs of his father, Tekesh, and grandfather, Il-Arslan, survive and are two of old Urgench's monuments.

In the following period of peace, Khorezm was ruled as part of the Golden Horde, the huge, wealthy, westernmost of the khanates into which Jenghiz Khan's empire was divided after his death. Rebuilt, Urgench was again Khorezm's capital, and grew into what was probably one of Central Asia's most important trading cities – big, beautiful, crowded and with a new generation of monumental buildings.

Then came Timur. Considering Khorezm to be a rival to Samarkand, he comprehensively finished off old Urgench in 1388. The city was partly rebuilt in the 16th century, but it was abandoned when the Amu-Darya changed its course (modern Konye-Urgench dates from the construction of a new canal in the 19th century). When a new line of independent Khorezm rulers arose (Uzbek Turks who moved in from the steppes in the early 16th century) they started off at Devkisken, out in the desert west of Konye-Urgench, and made Khiva their capital in 1592.

Sights
NEJAMEDDIN KUBRA MAUSOLEUM & AROUND
The sacred Nejameddin Kubra Mausoleum is the most important of a small cluster of sights near the middle of the town and is the holiest part of Konye-Urgench. The simple **Konye-Urgench Museum** (admission US$0.50; ☺ 8am-4pm) is housed in the early-20th-century Dash Mosque, just before the main mausoleum complex. It includes some finds from old Urgench, and some ancient Arabic texts. To one side is the **Matkerim-Ishan Mausoleum**, which is also early 20th century.

The path past here leads to the **Nejameddin Kubra Mausoleum** on the left, and the **Sultan Ali Mausoleum** facing it across a shady little courtyard. Nejameddin Kubra was a famous 12th- and 13th-century Khorezm Muslim teacher and poet, who founded the Sufic Kubra order, with followers throughout the Islamic world. His tomb is believed to have healing properties and you may find pilgrims praying here. The building has three

domes and a fine, unrestored, tiled portal. The tombs inside – one for his body and one for his head (which were kindly separated by the Mongols) – are quite extraordinarily colourful with floral-pattern tiles.

SOUTHERN MONUMENTS
In the centre of ancient Konye-Urgench is this strip of the city's most striking **monuments** (admission US$1, camera US$1), dotted like a constellation across an empty expanse straddling the Ashgabat road, 1km south of the main town.

Turabeg Khanym Mausoleum, opposite the ticket office, is still the subject of some debate. Like many mausoleums it is not known for sure who is buried here, and many archaeologists contend that it was a throne room built in the 12th century. Whatever its function, the mausoleum is one of Central Asia's most perfect buildings. Its geometric patterns are in effect a giant calendar signifying humanity's insignificance in the march of time. There are 365 sections on the sparkling mosaic, on the underside of the dome, representing the days of the year; 24 pointed arches immediately beneath the dome representing the hours of the day; 12 bigger arches below representing the months the year; and four big windows representing the weeks of the month. The cupola is rather unique in the context of early Islamic architecture and has its equal only in Shiraz, Iran.

Crossing the road to the side of the minaret, the path through a modern cemetery and the 19th-century **Sayid Ahmed Mausoleum** leads to the **Gutlug Timur Minaret**, built in the 1320s. It's the only surviving part of old Urgench's main mosque. Decorated with bands of brick and a few turquoise tiles, at 64m it's one of the highest minarets in Central Asia – though not as tall as it once was, and leaning noticeably. It's interesting to note that there is no entrance to the minaret – it was linked to the adjacent mosque by a bridge 7m above the ground. Since that mosque was destroyed, the only way into the minaret is by ladder. There are 144 steps to the top, although you can't climb it now.

Further along the track is the **Sultan Tekesh Mausoleum**. Tekesh was the 12th-century Khorezmshah who made Khorezm great with conquests as far south as Khorasan (present-day northern Iran and northern Afghanistan). He built this mausoleum for himself, along with a big medressa and library (which did not survive) on the same spot. After his death in 1200 he was apparently buried here, although there is no tomb. There are recent excavations of several early Islamic graves near the entrance to the building.

Nearby is the mound of graves called the **Kirkmolla** (Forty Mullahs Hill), a sacred place where Konye-Urgench's inhabitants held their last stand against the Mongols. Here you'll see young women rolling down the hill in a fertility rite – one of Konye-Urgench's more curious attractions.

Continue along the track to the **Il-Arslan Mausoleum**, Konye-Urgench's oldest standing monument. The conical dome, with a curious zigzag brick pattern, is the first of its kind and was exported to Samarkand by Timur. Il-Arslan, who died in 1172, was Tekesh's father. The building is small but well worth a close look. The conical dome with 12 faces is unique, and the collapsing floral terracotta moulding on the façade is also unusual. Further south lies the base of the **Mamun II Minaret**, which was built in 1011, reduced to a stump by the Mongols, rebuilt in the 14th century and finally toppled by an earthquake in 1895.

Sleeping

The **Gürgenç Hotel** (☎ 2 24 65; Dashogus köçesi; bed US$6) is the only hotel in town, and it appears to have been last renovated during the Mongol invasion. The old lady only speaks Turkmen, but seems used to backpackers. There's no running water and the bathrooms are nailed shut. Grim toilets make a homestay a far better option, if you can find one.

One further option is the **Chapayev Guesthouse** (per person US$2.50), on the road between the town and the border post with Uzbekistan. While it's just as basic as the Gürgenç, it's infinitely more pleasant. Not recommended without your own transport, however, as it's a taxi ride into town. The guesthouse has no phone.

Eating

The **Mekan Restaurant** (☎ 2 26 81; Volksom köçesi; meals US$3) is the best known and most inviting in town, with pleasant staff and decent food. Another option is a nameless Korean restaurant next to the town's museum.

Getting There & Away

The town's bus station is a disorganised car park, a short distance from the Gürgenç Hotel and a cab ride from the town centre, where taxis, marshrutki and buses meet and pick up passengers.

Frequent buses and marshrutka go to Ashgabat (10 to 12 hours, US$4) and to Dashogus (two hours, US$0.50). Taxis leave for Ashgabat (seat/whole car US$6/US$24) and Dashogus (seat/whole car US$0.75/US$3.50) at all times of day.

A cab to the border with Uzbekistan should cost US$0.50 and can be picked up anywhere.

DEVKISKEN

On the edge of a plateau overlooking the desert toward Uzbekistan, the remains of the once-great city of Devkisken can be seen for miles. The old city walls extend into the desert in varying states of decrepitude, overlooking networks of long-dry canals that once brought water to the city from the Amu-Darya. The ground below the plateau was once the bottom of a sea; you can find seashells and fossils everywhere in the sand. The entire site remains unexcavated and even a superficial look around will reveal pieces of pottery and ancient coins.

First founded in the 1st century BC, Devkisken appears to have been deserted by its inhabitants sometime in the 7th century, although it's not entirely clear why. It was rebuilt during Timur's time, and then finally all but destroyed by Jenghiz Khan. Having been rebuilt yet again, it became known as Vazir in medieval times and was once the residence of a Khorezmshah called Sultan Ali. The town declined in the mid-16th century, when he moved his capital to Urgench.

The ancient settlement's citadel remains, and it's a fine structure you can climb through for some awesome views across the desert. Like most Arab cities, Devkisken is arranged in three concentric parts (the citadel, the inner town and the outer town) and their demarcation is clearly visible. The complex also includes two 16th-century mausoleums. The nearest to the citadel is the mausoleum of an unknown founder of a local dynasty. Behind that there stands a smaller structure for his four children. Behind this is one of Central Asia's notorious bug pits, where prisoners were kept with creepy crawlies and vermin as roommates. The lucky ones were released, while those who were condemned to death were flung into the 'bottomless pit' a further 100m back. For fairly obvious reasons, be extremely careful when approaching this.

Getting There & Away
Devkisken is 65km from Konye-Urgench. The only way to make this trip is in a very sturdy 4WD, as there is a long off-road drive through what is essentially a dust desert in the summer and autumn before the rains. You may need infinite patience as you negotiate three military checkpoints. To complicate matters the area is currently the subject of a border dispute between Uzbekistan and Turkmenistan, and the site is actually located in what the Uzbeks claim is their territory.

You should only go here with an experienced driver booked through a trusted travel agent.

DASHOGUS
☎ 322 / pop 160,000
Effectively an entirely Soviet city in the desert, Dashogus serves as many visitors' introduction to Turkmenistan. It's a useful place to stop over for Konye-Urgench, crossing to Uzbekistan or before the great desert trip to Ashgabat, but it's not a city to visit on its own merits. Its most interesting features include unusual **dinosaur sculptures** in the town centre and the excellent **Bai Bazaar**, a colourful market where you can buy pretty much anything.

Sleeping
There are two functioning hotels in town – the nasty old Intourist **Hotel Dashogus** (☎ 5 37 85; Turkmenbashi şayoli 5; s/d US$20/40), a truly miserable place, where renovation is promised but looks unlikely. The better variant is the **Hotel Diyarbekir** (Turkmenbashi şayoli; s/d US$30/50; 🔀), a Turkish-owned venture that has enormous rooms, which are generally up to Western standards.

However, there are unofficial **homestays** (per person US$10-20) that can be organised through any travel agent, or at the reception at the Hotel Dashogus on arrival.

Eating
You aren't overwhelmed for choice in Dashogus, but can eat well nonetheless.

The best restaurant in town is the very pleasant **Şatugi** (☎ 5 97 42), a very grand new place that is a fixture with tour groups. It's quiet and the Russian-led menu is decent. More lively (often in the ear-splitting sense of the word) is the Nadira, a short distance from the Hotel Dashogus.

Getting There & Away
The Dashogus bus station is near the Bai Bazaar, in the north of the city. Buses regularly go from here to Konye-Urgench (US$0.50, two hours) and Ashgabat (12 to 18 hours depending on the type of bus, US$3.50 to US$5). Buses for Turkmenabat are less regular (10 hours, US$3). The train station is on Woksal köçesi, about 600m east of Gurbansoltan köçesi. Trains go from here to Turkmenabat (24 hours, US$2) and on to Ashgabat via Mary, but they are so slow that they are best avoided.

TURKMENISTAN DIRECTORY

ACCOMMODATION
Outside large cities, accommodation in Turkmenistan can be extremely basic. Be prepared to go for days without washing properly, if you plan to travel in the wilds for any amount of time. Usually your only options will be homestays or camping. The former are a fantastic way to see everyday life and to interact with a family, particularly

---

POST-SOVIET NAME CHANGES

Most locals now refer to towns by old and new names interchangeably, although Kerki and Gaurdak are still used by nearly everyone – their new names remain virtually unknown, although they are used in bus and flight timetables.

Soviet	Current
Charjou	Turkmenabat
Dashouz	Dashogus
Gaurdak	Magdanly
Kerki	Atamurat
Krasnovodsk	Turkmenbashi
Nebit Dag	Balkanabat

if you are lucky enough to stay in a yurt. Camping is the only option in more remote areas. Hotels throughout the country are generally dilapidated, and from the Soviet era, although bigger cities now boast foreign-managed three- and four-star ventures.

Anyone on a tourist visa is officially only allowed to stay in a licensed hotel. This means your guide may not allow you to stay in some places. Transit travellers, however, do not face this problem.

ACTIVITIES

Horse-lovers from around the world flock to Turkmenistan to ride the unique Akhal-Teke thoroughbreds. Many travel agencies offer specialist horse-trekking tours with these beautiful creatures. For more information of riding these horses in Ashgabat, see p420.

Archaeologists are another group richly rewarded by a trip to Turkmenistan. As well as being able to visit the ongoing excavation at Gonur (the largest dig in the Near East at present), there are a number of totally untouched sites, such as Devkisken near Konye-Urgench, where just a perfunctory glance at the ground will reveal coins and pieces of pottery. Turkmenistan has some wonderful walking potential, although this remains a pastime viewed with suspicion by the authorities. If you have permission to visit one of the nature reserves, however, hiking is usually no problem whatsoever.

BOOKS

Literature specific to Turkmenistan is rare indeed, although Turkmen culture, history and politics feature heavily in books about Central Asia (see p10). Two highly recommended books about Turkmenistan's ancient cultures are *Monuments of Merv: Traditional Buildings of the Karakum* by Georgina Hermann and Viktor Sarianidi's *Margush*. The latter is available in bookshops in Ashgabat. Neither is for people without a developed interest in archaeology.

Perhaps the best piece of modern fiction about Turkmenistan and its Sovietisation is the recently translated *Soul* (Harville Press, 2003) by the Russian writer Andrei Platonov. The book, written during the author's travels through Turkmenistan in 1934 and 1935, is a musing on the fate of a tribe as it is Sovietised, and not least on its Soviet Moses, Nazar Chagatayev.

CUSTOMS

In Turkmenistan official regulations state that you need permission to export any carpet over 6 sq metres, though trying to export a smaller one without a licence is also likely to be problematic. In all cases it's best to take your carpet to the Carpet Museum in Ashgabat (p416), where there is a bureau that will value and tax your purchase, and provide an export licence. This can take up to a few days. Those in a hurry are best advised to buy from one of the many government shops in Ashgabat, where all carpets come complete with an export licence. Despite being more expensive than purchases made at Tolkuchka Bazaar, this still works out as very good value.

EMBASSIES & CONSULATES
Turkmen Embassies in Central Asia
Turkmenistan has embassies or consulates in Afghanistan (p398), Uzbekistan (p234), Tajikistan (p349) and Kazakhstan (p153).

Turkmen Embassies & Consulates
Armenia Yerevan (☎ 53 83 56, 53 77 05; fax 53 05 12; Hotel Hrazan, 72 Dzorap Poghots)
Azerbaijan Baku (☎ 40 99 00, 61 62 03; fax 61 39 69; Tariverdiev küçasi 4, Baku)
Belgium Brussels (☎ 6481874, 6481929; fax 6481906; 106 Ave Franklin Roosevelt)
China Beijing (☎ 65326975/6/7; fax 65326976; San Li Tun Diplomatic Office Bldg 1-15-2, 100600)
France Paris (☎ 0147550536; fax 0147550568; 13 rue Picot, 75016)
Germany Berlin (☎ 30 30102451/2; fax 30 30102453; Langobardenalle 14, D-14052)
India New Delhi (☎ 6118054; fax 11 6118332; C-17 Malcha Marg Chanakyapuri)
Iran Mashhad (☎ 51 99940, 47660; fax 51 47660; Kucheye Konsulgari 34); Tehran (☎ 21 2542178, 2548686; fax 2540432; 39 Pardaran Ave, Golestan-5 St)
Pakistan Islamabad (☎ 2278699, 2214913; fax 278799; Nazim-ud-Din Rd, 22-a, F-7/1)
Russia Moscow (☎ 095 2916591, 2916636; fax 095 2910935; Filipovsky pereulok, 121019)
Turkey Ankara (☎ 312 4416122/3/4; fax 312 4417125; Koza sokak 28, Chankaya 06700); İstanbul (☎ 212 6620221/2/3; fax 212 6620224; Gazi Evrenos Jadesi Baharistan sokak 13 Eshilkoy)
UK London (☎ 020 7255 1071; fax 020 7323 9184; 14-17 Wells St, W1 3FP)
Ukraine Kiev (☎ 293449, 2286870; fax 2293034; Pushkin 6)
USA Washington DC (☎ 202 588 1500; fax 202 5880697; Massachusetts Ave, NW 20008)

Embassies & Consulates in Turkmenistan

All the following legations are in Ashgabat (see Map p414). The British embassy looks after the interests of Commonwealth nationals in Turkmenistan.

Afghanistan (☎ 39 58 21; Görogly köçesi 94; ⏱ 9am-5pm Mon-Fri)

Armenia (☎ 39 55 49, 35 44 18; Görogly köçesi 14; ⏱ 9.30am-12.30pm Mon-Fri)

Azerbaijan (☎ 39 11 02; fax 35 56 25; Ata Gowşudow köçesi; ⏱ 3-6pm Tue & Fri)

China (☎ 51 87 03; fax 48 18 13; Kuvvat Hotel, Berzengi; ⏱ 3-6pm Tue & Fri)

France (☎ 36 35 50, 36 34 68; 3rd fl, Four Points Ak Altin Hotel; ⏱ 9am-1pm & 3-6pm Mon-Fri)

Georgia (☎ 34 48 38; fax 34 32 48; Azadi köçesi 139a; ⏱ 9am-6pm Mon-Fri)

Germany (☎ 36 35 15/17-20; fax 36 35 22; 1st fl, Four Points Akaltin Sheraton Hotel; ⏱ 9am-noon Mon-Fri)

Iran (☎ 34 14 52; fax 35 05 65; Tehran köçesi 3; ⏱ 8.30am-12.30pm Mon-Fri)

Kazakhstan (☎ 48 04 72; Garaşyzlik şayoli 10-12, Berzengi; ⏱ 10am-noon Tue, Wed & Fri)

Kyrgyzstan (☎ 35 55 06; Görogly köçesi 14; ⏱ 10am-noon & 4-6pm Mon-Fri)

Netherlands (☎ 34 67 00; fax 34 42 52; Tehran köçesi 17; ⏱ 9am-6pm Mon-Fri)

Pakistan (☎ 35 00 97; fax 39 76 40; Kemine köçesi 92; ⏱ 9am-noon Mon-Fri)

Russia (☎ 35 39 57, 35 70 41; fax 39 84 66; Turkmenbashi şayoli 11; ⏱ 9am-1pm & 3-6pm Mon-Fri)

Tajikistan (☎ 35 56 96; embtd@online.tm; Görogly köçesi 14; ⏱ 9am-1pm & 3-5pm Mon-Fri)

UK (☎ 36 34 62/3/4; www.britishembassy.gov.uk /turkmenistan; 3rd fl, Four Points Akaltin Sheraton Hotel; ⏱ 9am-5pm Mon-Fri)

USA (☎ 35 00 45, 39 87 64; www.usemb-ashgabat .usia.co.at; Puşkin köçesi 9; ⏱ 9am-6pm Mon-Fri)

Uzbekistan (☎ 34 24 19; fax 34 23 37; Görogly köçesi 50A; ⏱ 10am-1pm Mon, Wed & Fri)

GAY & LESBIAN TRAVELLERS

While Ashgabat has no gay or lesbian bars as a consequence of homosexuality's continuing illegality, gay men still sometimes meet in the park in front of the Lenin statue. Lesbianism remains an entirely alien concept in Turkmenistan.

HOLIDAYS

Travel to Turkmenistan is restricted around the Independence Day celebrations, with letters of invitation usually issued only until mid-October and then again from November, and around Niyazov's birthday celebra-tions in mid-February. Transit travellers are unlikely to be affected by this.

1 January New Year.
12 January Remembrance Day (Battle of Geok-Depe).
19 February Flag Day (President's Birthday).
8 March International Women's Day.
21 March Navrus (spring festival); date varies.
6 April Drop of Water is a Grain of Gold Day.
27 April Horse Day.
9 May Victory Day.
18 May Day of Revival & Unity.
19 May Holiday of Poetry of Magtymguly.
25 May/last Sunday in May Carpet Day.
21 June Election of First President.
10 July Melon Holiday.
14 July Turkmenbashi Holiday.
6 October Remembrance Day (1948 Earthquake).
27–28 October Independence Day.
17 November Student Youth Day.
30 November Bread Day.
7 December Good Neighbourliness Day.
12 December Neutrality Day.

INTERNET ACCESS

There's only one Internet service provider in Turkmenistan: www.online.tm. The Internet is almost unknown outside Ashgabat and even there access remains for the privileged few. There are two publicly accessible Internet cafés in Ashgabat (see p413).

INTERNET RESOURCES

While most commentary on Turkmenistan has some sort of agenda, there's no doubt that there are an awful lot of interesting websites about the place.

www.chaihana.com For general information.
www.eurasianet.org/resource/turkmenistan /index.shtml Another very strong news archive website.
www.gundogar.org The opposition website is invaluable for news and politics.
www.stantours.com For planning your trip.
www.tmtour.org Also one of the best sources to check out before you go.
www.tourism-sport.gov.tm/en/ Website of the Ministry of Tourism.
www.turkmens.com A huge collection of Turkmenistan-related websites about culture, music, politics and history.

MEDIA

The Turkmen media is depressingly predictable, despite initially offering a fascinating glimpse into the sheer dullness of life under the thumb. No newspaper is ever without a story involving the president on the front page – there are usually three or four and a large, grinning photograph. The main daily newspapers are *Turkmenistan* and the Russian-language *Nevtralny Turkmenistan* (Neutral Turkmenistan). There is no independent or privately owned press.

Turkmen TV is similar in style. There are three state channels, all of which show a live feed from Turkmenbashi's eccentric cabinet meetings, whenever they are in session. It's a revealing picture of how Turkmen politics works, but unwatchably dull after three minutes.

MONEY

The currency in Turkmenistan is the manat (M), which is quickly devaluing. It's bolstered up by a fixed government exchange rate and traded for far less on the black market. Notes come in denominations of 10,000, 5000 and 1000, with 1000 and 500 manat coins. The rate of exchange on the black market in autumn 2003 was 23,000 M per US dollar. Check the rate daily however, as it fluctuates around the 20,000 mark. The following table gives an indication of official exchange rates.

Country	Unit		Manat
Australia	A$1	=	3788 M
Canada	C$1	=	3755 M
China	Y1	=	608 M
euro zone	€1	=	6127 M
Iran	100 rials	=	60 M
Japan	¥100	=	4570 M
Kyrgyzstan	1 som	=	115 M
New Zealand	NZ$1	=	3371 M
Pakistan	Rs 10	=	879 M
Russia	R10	=	1757 M
UK	UK£1	=	9196 M
USA	US$1	=	5032 M
Uzbekistan	10 sum	=	50 M

The black market is easy and accessible to foreigners, and the only place you'll get a realistic exchange rate. In general, you'll find black marketers wandering around at bazaars with enormous wads of manat. Ask around for the day's rate, as foreigners are seen as an obvious target, and if possible bring a calculator. Official bureaux de change and hotel exchange counters are best avoided, as they will exchange at the official rate, giving you 75% less for your money.

- Trade a round amount, for quick mental calculations
- Fold it up in a pocket, to avoid fumbling in an open purse or wallet
- Tell them what you have, but don't pull it out; some claim they want to check it for counterfeit, and may substitute smaller notes

There are only ATMs and cash advances on credit cards in Ashgabat (p413) Outside Ashgabat emergency money can be wired through Western Union only. Credit cards are accepted by luxury hotels in Ashgabat, but by few other places; you'd be ill-advised to rely on them. The same goes for travellers cheques. Euro travellers cheques may be harder to cash. It's best to bring US dollars in cash with you; euros can still be tough to change outside large cities.

POST

Like every other form of communication in Turkmenistan, all post is monitored and you can expect your postcards (if you can find any) to be scrutinised by government agents before being allowed through. Sending a postcard anywhere in the world costs 3000 M (US$0.10) and a 20g letter costs around 5000 M. **DHL** (☎ 35 25 87; www.dhl.com; Koltsova köçesi 33, Ashgabat) is the most commonly used international courier.

REGISTRATION

Anyone entering Turkmenistan on a tourist or business visa must be registered within three working days with the Ministry of Sport and Tourism via the local bureau of the state tourism company. Transit visas do not need to be registered.

TELEPHONE & FAX

Phone calls from hotels or anywhere else foreigners are likely to be listened in on. Fax provides one of the most secure means of communication. You can call internationally, nationally and send faxes from most big towns at the telegraph station, often referred to as *glavny telegraf*. In smaller towns the telegram is the main form of communication.

Mobile coverage is good in Ashgabat and most large towns. Foreign phones with global roaming will usually switch over automatically to the local network on arrival.

TRAVEL PERMITS

Officially everywhere, except the towns of Ashgabat, Mary, Turkmenabat and Balkanabat, is considered a border zone. This means that you should have anywhere outside these areas listed on your visa, thus giving you permission to go there. Travellers on transit visas can usually transit the border zones along the relevant main road, if they correspond to the country to which they are supposed to exit.

The following areas are termed 'class one' border zones and entry without documentation is definitely not possible.

- Atamurat (Kerki) plus adjoining areas
- Bekdash
- Dargan Ata
- Dashogus Welayat
- Farab
- Garrygala
- Gazachak
- Gyzyletrek
- Gyzylgaya
- Serkhetabat (Gushgi)
- Tagta

VISAS

All foreigners require a visa to enter Turkmenistan and transit visas are the only visas issued without a letter of invitation (LOI). Prices for visas vary enormously from embassy to embassy. As a general rule, plan on getting a visa at least a month ahead of entry to Turkmenistan, as the process (even for transit visas) is lengthy. Another good overall tip is to work through a Turkmen travel agent you trust. On entry every visa holder will need to pay an additional US$10 fee for an entry card that will list your exit point in Turkmenistan.

TRANSIT VISAS

The only visa that allows unaccompanied travel for tourists is the transit visa. Relatively easy to come by, they are normally valid for three days, although sometimes for five days and in extremely rare cases, seven and even 10 days. Transit visas can be obtained at any Turkmen consulate, although if you apply without an LOI, the application will need to be forwarded to the Ministry of Foreign Affairs in Ashgabat, meaning a processing time of around 10 to 14 days.

No transit visa is extendable, save in the case of serious illness. Your route will normally not be indicated on the visa, but your entry and exit point (unchangeable) will be, and you will therefore run into trouble going anywhere not obviously between the two points. Some tourists have reported getting transit visas for seven and 10 days when they were planning to cycle through the country. This appears to be more likely at European embassies.

TOURIST VISAS

Tourist visas are a mixed blessing in Turkmenistan. While they allow the visitor to spend a decent amount of time in the country (up to three weeks as a rule), they now require accompaniment by an accredited tour guide, who will have to meet you at the border and remain with you throughout your trip. This obviously has cost implications, as you will have to pay your guide a daily rate (usually between US$30 and US$50), as well as sometimes pay for their meals and hotels. The latter cost is very small, however, as Turkmen citizens pay a local rate, usually equivalent to US$1 or US$2 per night.

There have been many reports, since this legislation was introduced in 2002, of agencies agreeing to allow tourists to continue unaccompanied after the first 48 hours (once the passport is registered). However, while some travellers have gotten away with this, others have been arrested and deported. Our advice is to play this one by the rules, and the number of travel agents willing to risk their licence in Turkmenistan this way is likely to decrease. In practice, all travel agents will allow you to roam Ashgabat and the immediate environs unaccompanied, and your level of freedom in other cities is also quite high.

You can only get a tourist visa by going through a travel agency. Only travel agencies with a licence from the Turkmen government can issue LOIs. Many unaccredited agencies still offer LOI services, however, simply by going through an accredited agency themselves. The LOI will be issued with a list of all towns and regions you are planning to visit. In turn, these are the places that will be listed on your visa, and so therefore it's essential to decide what you want to see before applying (see Travel Permits, left). The LOI is approved by the Foreign Ministry, which will decide whether or not you are an undesirable. The LOI can take up to a month to process, and it is not unusual for it to be rejected for no apparent reason.

Once the LOI is issued (usually faxed or emailed to you by your travel agent), you can take it to any Turkmen embassy to get your visa. The original LOI is not needed, although it may be at consulates in Mashhad (Iran, see p435) and Herat (Afghanistan, see p398). The issuing of the visa itself is purely a bureaucratic formality, once the LOI has been issued. Normal processing time is three working days, but most Turkmen embassies offer a one-day express service for a surcharge. When you apply for the visa, you will be asked for exact dates of entry and exit, which will be put on the visa. While you may leave before the exit date, you cannot enter earlier or leave any later.

Armed with an LOI there is also the possibility of getting a visa on arrival at Ashgabat airport, Turkmenbashi and Farab by prior arrangement with your travel agent. In the case of Turkmenbashi and Farab the agent needs to arrange for the consul to be present. In any case the original LOI must be taken to the relevant border and the visa will be issued for a maximum of 10 days.

On arrival in Turkmenistan, you must be met by your guide (geed) who will bring you a small green travel document (putyovka or voucher). Without this document you will be denied entry to Turkmenistan – it is therefore essential that your guide meets you. You should only exit the country at the point indicated on the travel permit, although if you alter your route there is the possibility of changing this in Ashgabat. To do this you will have to speak to your travel agent or guide and they can see what they can do. It is often possible to extend tourist visas in Ashgabat, again, only with the assistance of your travel agent.

VISAS FOR ONWARD TRAVEL
The following countries have embassies and consulates in Turkmenistan that can provide information and visas for travel to them. For contact details, see p436

Afghanistan Can issue one-month visas for US$60, three-month visas for US$90 – nothing needed save passport.
China Very small window for visa applications (two afternoons per week only) but can issue visas in a week.
Georgia Unable to issue visas at the time of research. Check the current situation.

Iran Very friendly and helpful embassy – usually no problem to get transit visas within a week.
Uzbekistan Was still asking for LOIs from EU citizens at the time of research.

TRANSPORT IN TURKMENISTAN

GETTING THERE & AWAY
For information on getting to/from Central Asia see the Transport in Central Asia chapter (p461).

Entering Turkmenistan
Turkmen border guards and customs officers are thorough and sometimes officious, although they usually have a good sense of humour hidden somewhere. On entering the country, it's likely that your bags will be searched, although backpacks are rarely emptied. The numerous documents to be filled out are time consuming, but pay attention to the customs declaration – list anything valuable you have with you and make sure it is stamped and that you keep a copy. On exit you'll need to fill out a second one, but be ready to show the original as well.

Air
The only international airport in Turkmenistan is **Saparmyrat Turkmenbashi Airport** (☎ 378411) in Ashgabat. For the contact details of airlines that fly in and out of Turkmenistan, see p420.

Land
Visitors with visas can enter Turkmenistan from all bordering countries, although the borders with Uzbekistan and Iran are the most frequently used. There are no international train or bus services to or from

---

Entry & Departure Tax
For entry into Turkmenistan there is a US$10 fee per person. Bring cash in US dollars for this. There is an international departure tax of US$25, which is only included in the price of Turkmenistan Airlines tickets. If flying with any other airline, this is payable in cash at the airport. There is no domestic departure tax.

Turkmenistan at the present time. You should reckon at one to two hours for crossing the border at any point in the country. All land borders are open from 9am to 6pm daily.

BORDER CROSSINGS
To/From Iran
The simplest entry point is Gaudan/Bajgiran, due south of Ashgabat and a corridor between the Kopet Dag into Iran. From Ashgabat, take a taxi (US$1 to US$2) for the 20km ride to Yablonovka checkpoint. Here you'll have your passport checked, after which you take a marshrutka shuttle to the border. Once through, it's a taxi (US$2.50) across some 20km of no-man's-land to Bajgiran where you can get buses or taxis (2½ hours, US$18) to Mashhad.

There are also borders with Iran at Saraghs (there is a Mashhad–Saraghs train, but no international trains into Turkmenistan) and Gudurolum (which is reachable by car or taxi only).

To/From Uzbekistan
There are three crossings from Uzbekistan. The Farab crossing is closest to Bukhara (Uzbekistan) and Turkmenabat (Turkmenistan). The 45-km taxi ride to Farab from Turkmenabat should cost US$4 to US$6. The border opens at 8am and closes as early as 6pm. The Dashogus crossing is easiest from Khiva or Urgench. Less used is the Khojeli crossing, a half-hour drive from Nukus in Karakalpakstan. From here, it's a five-minute cab ride (US$0.50) into Konye-Urgench town.

A taxi from Turkmenabat to the Uzbek border should cost you around US$4 for a 40-minute drive. Your driver will stop about 2km from the border from where you will have to walk or you can take a bus (every 15 minutes, US$1). From the border, take a taxi (US$5) to Bukhara, or hire a taxi as far as Alat (or Karakul), where you can change to a shared taxi. Coming the other way get a shared taxi (US$4) from Bolshoy rynok in Bukhara to Alat, where you'll have to hire your own car to the border.

A taxi from Dashogus to the Uzbek border is not more than US$1. From the border to Khiva expect to pay around US$10.

A taxi from Konye-Urgench to the border is around US$1. From the border to Nukus expect to pay US$7.

To/From Kazakhstan
The one entry point from Turkmenistan's northern neighbour is Bekdash, a bit of a backwater, although from there it's easy enough to get a car to take you to Turkmenbashi (four to six hours, US$40). From Bekdash, there is no regular transportation and taxi prices are exorbitant due to the unpaved road. The drive to the port of Aktau will take two to three hours.

To/From Afghanistan
Gushgi is the border town with Afghanistan, and is also known as Kushka and Serkhetabat. Crossing here is now a fairly hassle-free prospect, although be prepared to be thoroughly searched by suspicious Turkmen border guards if you are entering Turkmenistan here. The border post is 3km south of Gushgi town. Leaving Turkmenistan, there's a 2km walk to the first Afghan village of Torghundi and it's a two-hour taxi journey onwards to Herat. The Sapamyrat border crossing near Kerki is used by UN staff, but was not recommended for independent travellers at the time of writing.

The Turkmen authorities love paperwork. To enter Turkmenistan from Torghundi, you'll need to have Gushgi listed as your point of entry on your visa, and be met by a Turkmen tour guide. There's also a US$10 fee for an entry card. If you're trying to leave Turkmenistan, you'll need Gushgi listed on your travel itinerary and on your visa as the point of exit. In both directions, Turkmen customs will probably take your luggage apart.

Sea
You can enter Turkmenistan by boat from Azerbaijan. See Sea on p468 for details.

GETTING AROUND
Car & Motorcycle
Driving through Turkmenistan is perfectly possible, but expensive and full of hassles. A carnet is not needed, although you'll need to pay the following: US$30 transit fee; US$50 obligatory third-party liability insurance; US$2 bank fee; US$5 documentation fee; and US$10 for disinfection of your vehicle. Significantly, there's also a road tax calculated by the kilometre for your route through the country. Usually this totals around US$75 for cars and up to US$250 for larger vehicles.

Central Asia Directory

For country-specific information, refer to the individual country directories in each country chapter.

ACCOMMODATION

Accommodation alternatives are springing up all over Central Asia, so thankfully the smoky Soviet leftovers need only be used as a last resort. Private places are almost always the best places to stay.

Options are uneven across the region. The excellent homestays of Kyrgyzstan and B&Bs of Uzbekistan offer the best alternatives to the Soviet-era fossils, but budget travellers will still find the latter a regular companion in Kazakhstan. Turkmenistan has few alternatives to hotels (though there are a few homestays in Dashogus). In Tajikistan, Dushanbe and Khojand are stuck in the Soviet era, though much of the Pamirs now has an informal network of homes and yurts that will take in travellers.

You can even sleep in a medressa in Khiva (p228) or an astronomical observatory outside Almaty (p112).

B&Bs

These are small private guesthouses, as opposed to homestays, though the distinction can be a fine one. The best are to be found in the Uzbek cities of Bukhara, Khiva and Samarkand. Rates tend to be around US$15 per person and include breakfast. Meals are extra but can normally be provided for around US$5 each.

Camping

In the wilds there's normally no problem with you camping, though there is always an inherent security risk with this. If you are obviously on someone's land then you should try to ensure that you have permission. Staying anywhere near habitation will result in an immediate audience. Popular trekking routes have established camping areas, frequented by Soviet alpinists during the Soviet era. You can normally camp in a turbaza (see p442) or yurt camp for a minimal fee.

Homestays

These are happily on the rise. For your own room and some type of breakfast you'll probably pay anywhere from US$1 (in rural Kyrgyzstan) to US$20 per person (in Uzbekistan and cities) per night. Kyrgyzstan has an excellent network of homestays, thanks to the Community Based Tourism (CBT) and Shepherd's Life organisations (see p248 for more information).

Don't expect hotel-style comforts; rural toilets, for example, are likely to be squatters in the garden. Don't expect anything exotic either – you may well end up in a block of flats, in front of a TV all evening. Levels

LATE-NIGHT TELEPHONE CALLS

Those late-night calls to your room aren't wrong numbers. All hotels with significant numbers of foreigners attract prostitutes, especially, it seems, in Kazakhstan (or was that just us?). Women guests rarely seem to get unexpected calls but several men have received calls from someone who knew their name, so somebody at the front desk knows what's going on. All you can do is work out how to temporarily disable your telephone and don't answer the door.

of privacy vary. You might get access to a kitchen, especially if you are in a flat.

Potential hosts may acost you as you alight at a station or enter a tourist hotel; older people, women and Russians tend to be the best to deal with. Sympathetic hotel reception staff may put you in touch with private homes in some cities. Many local private travel agencies can set you up with someone, though prices may be double local rates.

Friends you meet on the road may invite you home and ask nothing for it, but remember that most ordinary people have very limited resources so offer to pay anything from US$5 (rural Tajikistan and Kyrgyzstan) to US$10 in larger towns. In Turkmenistan and Uzbekistan in particular, staying with someone who hasn't gone through official channels with the Office of Visas & Registration (OVIR; in Russian *Otdel Vis i Registratsii*) could put them at risk, especially if your own papers aren't in order.

Hotels

Though some are better than others, you almost never get what you pay for in Soviet-era tourist hotels, largely because tourists don't pay the same rates as locals. Many were in better shape before 1991, when the subsidies dried up. Doorknobs may come off in your hand; windows may not open or close. Electricity is usually dicey with dim or missing light bulbs. Toilets that leak but don't flush give bathrooms a permanent aroma and some bathrooms have long-term cockroach colonies. All beds are single, with pillows the size of suitcases. Guests themselves are essentially viewed as a dispensable inconvenience, ranking somewhere below room cleaners in the hotel pecking order.

Uzbekistan leads the way in private hotels, which are popping up all over the place. There are also a limited number of party or government guesthouses, *dachas* (holiday bungalows) and spas, which are now open to all.

If you're staying at a budget hotel that doesn't have hot water, ask about the local *banya* (public bath), which will.

Most hotels take your passport and visa for anywhere from half an hour to your entire stay, to do the required registration paperwork and to keep you from leaving without paying. Don't forget them when you leave – no-one is likely to remind you.

Budget-hotel room rates range from a few dollars in the countryside to around US$20 in the cities. We do not mention all of a hotel's price options in our reviews; even the worst hotels often have a few *lux* (deluxe) or *pol-lux* (semideluxe) suites for about twice the price of a basic room, sometimes with a bathtub and hot water.

Mid-range hotels and B&Bs will have air-con, satellite TV and a decent breakfast and range from US$30 to US$60 per night.

Top-end places in major cities are often foreign-managed and offer good restaurants and bars, a health club of sorts and travel services. You may get a better room rate by booking through a local travel agent, though most hotels offer their own discounts.

Yurtstays

It's easy to arrange a yurtstay in central Kyrgyzstan and the eastern Pamirs region of Tajikistan. Yurts range from comfortable tourist camps with beds, electricity and a nearby toilet, to the real McCoy owned by shepherds who are happy to take in foreigners for the night. The CBT and Shepherd's Life organisations in Kyrgyzstan (see p248) offer yurtstays all over the country. For up-market yurtstays try Ecotour in Kyrgyzstan (see p253).

There are also yurts in Bamiyan, Afghanistan (see p381), at Lepsinsk, near Taldy-Korghan, Aksu-Zhabagly in Kazakhstan, and at a yurt camp in the Kyzylkum desert near Ayaz-Qala, Uzbekistan (see p222).

Other Possibilities

Turbazas are former Soviet holiday camps that are now open to all, though mostly only in summer. The best ones (eg Iskander-Kul

FLOOR-LADIES

On every floor of a Soviet hotel a *dezhurnaya* (floor-lady; *dezhurnaya* is Russian for 'woman on duty') is in charge of handing out keys, getting hot water for washing, or *tipitok* (boiled water) for hot drinks, sometimes for a small fee. Even the most god-awful hotel can be redeemed by a big-hearted floor-lady who can find someone to do your laundry, find a light bulb or stash your bags while you're off on an excursion. Others can be a bit eccentric (one floor-lady in a hotel in Bishkek insisted on wiping the room clean with several old pairs of women's panties).

in Tajikistan, p335) are in picturesque spots, the worst are near towns and cities.

ACTIVITIES

Following is an indication of the possibilities for adventure travel in the region. Refer to the individual country chapters for more detail on where to go, what to do, and with whom. Most overseas adventure travel companies offer trekking itineraries in Central Asia.

Hiking

Hiking (as opposed to trekking) is a major outdoor pursuit for Almaty residents. The Aksu-Zhabaghly Nature Reserve is another beautiful area of hiking country between the southern Kazakhstan cities of Shymkent and Taraz; it's also a must-do for bird-watchers and flower lovers, as is the much more remote Lake Markakol, close to the Altay Mountains in east Kazakhstan.

You can make nice day hikes from bases in Ala-Archa National Park, near Bishkek, and Altyn Arashan, near Karakol, both in Kyrgyzstan. The Wakhan Valley in the Pamirs of Tajikistan offers superb valley walks.

Horse & Camel Trips

Kyrgyzstan is a perfect place for travel on horseback. CBT and Shepherd's Life coordinators (p248) arrange overnight horse treks to *jailoos* (summer pastures) around central Kyrgyzstan, or longer expeditions on horseback lasting up to two weeks. Horseback is the perfect way to arrive at Song-Köl, and Altyn Arashan offers some lovely day trips.

Kegeti canyon, east of Bishkek, is another popular place for horse riding, as are the Köl-Say lakes in southeast Kazakhstan.

Bukhara travel agencies arrange camel treks around Aidarkul Lake and there are also possibilities at Ayaz-Qala in northwest Uzbekistan.

For horse riding in Turkmenistan see p420.

Jeep Trips

The back roads of Kyrgyzstan, and particularly Tajikistan's Kohistani Badakhshan district, offer great scope for adventure travel in an indestructible Russian UAZ 4WD. Jeeps can be hired for around US$0.25 per km in both countries.

Mountain Biking

Several Western tour companies offer supported biking trips over the Torugart Pass, although die-hard do-it-yourselfers will find the Irkeshtam logistically easier. The Kegeti canyon and pass is another biking location favoured by adventure-travel companies. Dostuck Trekking (p253) even offers an amazing mountain-biking itinerary to Merzbacher Lake in the central Tian Shan. Karakol in Kyrgyzstan has great potential for mountain biking and it should be possible to hire bikes there now (see 273).

Mountaineering & Rock Climbing

Top of the line for altitude junkies are Khan Tengri, Pik Pobedy and other peaks of the central Tian Shan in eastern Kyrgyzstan and southeast Kazakhstan. Several Almaty and Bishkek tour agents can arrange trips to this region, including helicopter flights to the base camps during the climbing season, from the end of June to early September.

The other prime high-altitude playground is the Pamir in southern Kyrgyzstan and eastern Tajikistan, especially Pik Lenin, accessed from Achik Tash base camp (p306).

Other 4000m-plus peaks that you can undertake organised climbs of are Mt Korona in Ala-Archa National Park in Kyrgyzstan (the Alpine Fund in Bishkek is a good resource, see p252), Mt Sayramsky in the Aksu-Zhabaghly Nature Reserve and Mt Belukha in east Kazakhstan's Altay Mountains. Two websites that might be of use are www.russianclimb.com and http://mountains.tos.ru/kopylov/pamir.htm.

Rafting

A good venue for rafting and kayaking at all skill levels is Tashkent, where you can find flat water on the Syr-Darya and Angren rivers, and more exciting stretches on the Ugam, Chatkal and Pskem. The best season is September through to October.

There is easy rafting and canoeing on the Ili River, between Lake Kapshaghai and Lake Balkash, north of Almaty, from mid-April to mid-October. Another rafting location is the Chuy River, outside Bishkek.

Trekking

The various arms of the Tian Shan and Pamir ranges present some grand opportunities for both trekking and climbing (see the boxed text, p444). Other less-visited regions include the Zhungar Alatau range east of Taldy-Korghan in Kazakhstan, and the Altay Mountains in far northeast Kazakhstan. Kyrgyzstan is the best republic for budget trekking.

Self-supported trekking is difficult (though not impossible) in Central Asia. Transport to the trail heads can be patchy, slow and uncomfortable. Some trekking areas are at the junction of several republics, requiring you to carry multiple simultaneous visas and a fistful of different currencies. There are no trekking lodges like the ones you'd find in Nepal, so you will have to carry all your own food for the trek. It is possible to hire donkeys at many trail heads (eg in the Fan Mountains) and hire horses (around US$10 per day) in Kyrgyzstan.

You can hire tents, sleeping bags and stoves from trekking agencies, such as PSI Turkestan (p271) in Karakol for about US$5 per day, but in general good gear, particularly sleeping bags, is hard to find anywhere in the region. A multifuel (petrol) stove is

most useful, though you will need to clean the burners regularly as old Soviet fuel is of extremely poor quality.

The best walking season is June through to September, but be ready for bad weather at any time. Most high-altitude treks or climbs take place in July or August; lower areas can be scorching hot during these months.

Trustworthy local knowledge, and preferably a local guide, are essential for trekking in Central Asia. CBT (p248) in Kyrgyzstan can put you in touch with a guide for US$10, though for someone with a guaranteed knowledge of mountain routes you are better off arranging this with a trekking agency for between US$15 and US$20 per person per day. Treks organised through local trekking agencies will cost from US$30 to US$50 per person per day.

An essential resource for all serious trekkers and climbers is Frith Maier's *Trekking in Russia & Central Asia* (see p11).

Winter Sports

Central Asia's ski season is approximately November/December to March/April, with local variations. The region's best-known and best-equipped downhill area is Shymbulak (Russian: Chimbulak), a day-trip distance from Almaty. February is the best time to be there. Second best are the Kyrgyz Alatau valleys (especially Ala-Archa), south of Bishkek, followed by the Chimgan area above Tashkent.

Kazakhstan's pristine Altay Mountains are renowned for cross-country skiing; the best place to do this is Rachmanov's Springs (p152).

A few travel firms in Kazakhstan and Kyrgyzstan offer ski-mountaineering trips in central Tian Shan in July and August, and in the Zailiysky Alatau and Küngey Alatau ranges, between Almaty and Lake Issyk-Kul, from February through to April. In Tajikistan contact the Dushanbe Ski Federation (p326) for this.

Nearly every sports-related agency in Central Asia offers heli-skiing, in which old Aeroflot helicopters drop you off on remote high peaks and you ski down. Most guarantee from 3000m to 4000m vertical per day but require a group of 12 to 15 people. The Kyrgyz Alatau range behind Bishkek is one of the cheapest places to do this. It's

---

TOP TREKKING AREAS

- Fan Mountains, Tajikistan (p336)
- Around Karakol, Kyrgyzstan (p269)
- Around Arslanbob, Kyrgyzstan (p299)
- Khan Tengri and Inylchek Glacier, Kyrgyzstan (p281)
- Bolshoe Almatinskoe lake (see p111) and Köl-Say lakes (p118), south of Almaty in Kazakhstan

TOP FIVE ENTERTAINMENT OPTIONS

Try to catch a couple of these during your trip:

- La Traviata or Aida at Tashkent's Alisher Navoi Opera & Ballet Theatre (p175)

- Folklore performance by the Kazakh Otrar Sazy Kazakh Folk Orchestra (Almaty, p105) or the Kyrgyz Ordo Sakhna ensemble (Bishkek, p258)

- Puppet performance and fashion show in Bukhara (p217)

- Concerts, poetry and art shows at the Foundation for Culture and Civil Society (Kabul, p375)

- Song and dance performances at Khiva's Tosh-Khovli Palace

possible to heli-ski in the Chimgan range behind Tashkent from January to May.

The Medeu ice rink (p110) just outside Almaty is one of the largest speed-skating rinks in the world; it's open to the public on weekends from about November to March.

Other Activities

Several companies organise caving trips, especially around Osh in Kyrgyzstan and Chimgan, north of Tashkent. It's possible to scuba dive in Lake Issyk-Kul, but some of the equipment used looks like props from a 1960s Jacques Cousteau documentary.

BUSINESS HOURS

All business hours seem variable in the former Soviet republics. Foreign exchange banks usually open Monday to Friday from 9am or 10am to noon or 1pm; those in major cities sometimes open afternoons and evenings too. Exchange offices keep longer hours, including weekends. Post and telephone offices are sometimes open on weekends. Government office hours are usually Monday to Friday from 9am to 5pm or 6pm, with an hour or two off for lunch.

Museum hours change frequently, as do their days off. Some just seem to close without reason and a few stay that way for years.

Public places in the former Soviet republics often display their business days visually, as a stack of seven horizontal bars with the top one representing Monday; blue means open, red means closed.

Restaurants are generally open for lunch and dinner. Many restaurants outside the capitals close quite early (around 9pm). In rural areas it is often worth telling a restaurant that you would like to eat there a couple of hours beforehand, to give them some time to prepare and to ensure that they are open.

CHILDREN

Children can be a great icebreaker and a good avenue for cultural exchange, but travelling in Central Asia is difficult even for the healthy adult. Long bus and taxi rides over winding mountain passes are a sure route to motion sickness. Central Asian food is difficult to digest no matter what your age, and extreme temperatures – blistering hot in the city, freezing in the mountains – lead to many an uncomfortable moment. Islamic architecture and ruined Karakhanid cities may well leave your children comatose with boredom. A few places of added interest to children in summer include the amusement and aqua parks in Tashkent and Almaty.

If you are bringing very young children into Central Asia, nappies are available at department stores, but bring bottles and medicines. Forget about car seats, high chairs, cribs or anything geared for children,

CENTRAL ASIA'S TOP CULTURAL EXPERIENCES

- Arasan Baths, Almaty (p100) – a choice of three styles of bath in this monumental complex. Pay extra for a heavy-duty massage.

- Tea at the Lyabi-Hauz, Bukhara (p217) – green tea and kebabs make this the quintessential Central Asian experience.

- Russian Orthodox cathedrals – best visited on Sunday at service times for the full-on Russian Orthodox experience. The best ones are Tashkent's Assumption Cathedral (p176) or Almaty's Zenkov (p98) and St Nicholas (p100) Cathedrals.

- Eagle hunting and horse races at Osh hippodrome (p303) on Kyrgyz Independence Day.

- Homestay or yurtstay with a community tourism project in Kyrgyzstan (see p248) or the Pamirs (see p346).

though you'll always find a spare lap and helpful hands when boarding buses. It's possible to make a cot out of the duvets supplied in most homestays. *Lux* hotel rooms normally come with an extra connecting room, which can be ideal for children.

For more advice on travelling with children, pick up Lonely Planet's *Travel with Children* by Cathy Lanigan.

CLIMATE CHARTS

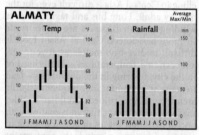

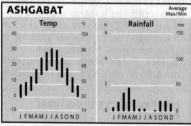

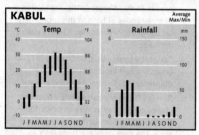

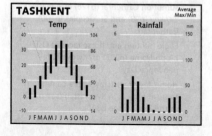

CUSTOMS

Barring the occasional greedy official at a remote posting, few Western tourists have major customs problems in Central Asia. When they do, it's usually over the export of 'cultural artefacts'.

When you finally leave after a multi-country Central Asia trip, you may well be asked for the declaration you filled out when you entered your first Commonwealth of Independent States (CIS) state, even if this is Russia. A traveller who had been living in Tashkent for five years was asked for his original Uzbekistan declaration when he crossed from Kyrgyzstan to China at the Torugart Pass. The moral is: save everything.

Declaring money on entry to a former Soviet republic is an awkward matter – total honesty reveals how much cash you're carrying to possibly dishonest officials, while fudging can create problems later. In general you are better off declaring everything (cash and travellers cheques) to the dollar. On arrival in Tashkent and Almaty officials may want you to pull out and display everything you've declared. Count up your money privately before you arrive.

There are no significant limits on items brought into Central Asia for personal use, except on guns and drugs. Heading out, the main prohibitions are 'antiques' and local currency. Every country's regulations prohibit the export of endangered animals and plants, though few officials would recognise an endangered species if it bit them.

Exporting Antiques

From the former Soviet republics, you cannot export antiques or anything of 'historical or cultural value' – including art, furnishings, manuscripts, musical instruments, coins, clothing and jewellery – without an export licence and payment of a stiff export duty.

Get a receipt for anything of value that you buy, showing where you got it and how much you paid. If your purchase looks like it has historical value, you should also have a letter saying that it has no such value or that you have permission to take it out anyway. Get this from the vendor, from the Ministry of Culture in the capital, or from a curator at one of the state art museums with enough clout to do it. Without it, your goodies could be seized on departure, possibly even on departure from another CIS state.

In Uzbekistan any book or artwork made before 1945 is considered antique. In Turkmenistan 'cultural artefacts' seems to embrace almost all handicrafts and traditional-style clothing, no matter how mundane, cheap or new. For regulations on exporting carpets from Turkmenistan see p435.

DANGERS & ANNOYANCES

Travel in Central Asia is a delight for those who are ready for it, but a potential nightmare for the unprepared. Afghanistan entails a higher level of risk than is the case with the Central Asian republics – see p357 for more information on this. Don't expect anything to go smoothly, starting with the visa chase before you even go. Crime is minimal by Western urban standards, but it is slowly on the rise and visitors are tempting, high-profile targets. Local and regional transport can be unpredictable, uncomfortable and occasionally unsafe. Central Asian officials and police generally create more problems than they solve. For emergency phone numbers see the Quick Reference page on the inside front cover of this book.

This section, all about the headaches, is not meant to put you off. Rather, it is intended to prepare you for the worst. Here's hoping you don't run into any of these problems.

Alcohol

Whether it's being poured down your throat by a zealous host, or driving others into states of pathological melancholy, brotherly love, anger or violence, alcohol can give you a headache in more ways than one. This is especially true in economically depressed areas, where violence hovers just below the surface and young men may grow abruptly violent, seemingly at random. The Islamic injunction against alcohol has had little obvious impact in ex-Soviet Central Asia.

Crime

You can cut down on the potential for crime by following these tips:

- Be especially alert in crowded situations such as bazaars and bus station ticket scrums, where pockets and purses may be easily picked.
- Avoid parks at night, even if it means going a long way out of your way.
- Take officially licensed taxis in preference to private ones; some people also

> ### GOVERNMENT TRAVEL ADVICE
>
> The following government websites offer travel advisories and information on current hot spots. All currently advise against travel in Afghanistan.
>
> **Australian Department of Foreign Affairs** (☎ 06-6261 3305; www.dfat.gov.au/consular/advice)
>
> **British Foreign Office** (☎ 0870-606 0290; www.fco.gov.uk)
>
> **Canadian Department of Foreign Affairs** (☎ 1-800-267 6788; www.dfait-maeci.gc.ca)
>
> **US State Department** (☎ 202-647 5225; http://travel.state.gov)

advise against climbing into any taxi with more than the driver in them or sharing with other passengers.
- Travellers who rent a flat are warned to be sure the doors and windows are secure, and never to open the door – day or night – to anyone they do not clearly know.

If you're the victim of a crime, contact the *militsia* (police), though you may get no help from them at all. Get a report from them if you hope to claim on insurance for anything that was stolen, and contact your closest embassy for a report in English. If your passport is stolen, the police should also provide a letter to OVIR, which is essential for replacing your visa. See p453 about loss or theft of credit cards or travellers cheques.

Crooked Officials

The number of corrupt officials on the take has decreased dramatically since the 1st edition of this book and most travellers make their way through Central Asia without a single run-in with the local *militsia*. The strongest police presence is in Uzbekistan (particularly Tashkent Metro), followed by Tajikistan, where there are police checkpoints at most municipal and provincial borders. It's a near certainty that you'll meet a gendarme or two in every bus and train station, though most only want to see your papers and know where you're going.

If for whatever reason you didn't get an entry stamp when crossing a border, you may find yourself vulnerable to officials on the take. Keep as many hotel and bus receipts as you can that prove your movements.

If you are approached by the police, there are several rules of thumb to bear in mind:

- Your best bet is to be polite, firm and jovial. A forthright, friendly manner – starting right out with an *asalam aleykum* (peace be with you) and a handshake for whomever is in charge – may help to defuse a potential shakedown, whether you are male or female.
- If someone refers to a 'regulation', ask to see it in writing. If you are dealing with lower-level officers, ask to see their *nachalnik* (superior).
- Ask to see a policeman's ID and, if possible, get a written copy of the ID number. Do not hand over your passport unless you see this ID. Even better, only hand over a photocopy of your passport; claim that your passport is at your hotel or embassy.
- Try to avoid being taken somewhere out of the public eye, eg into an office or into the shadows; it should be just as easy to talk right where you are. The objective of most detentions of Westerners is simply to extort money, and by means of intimidation rather than violence. If your money is buried deeply, and you're prepared to pull out a paperback and wait them out, even if it means missing the next bus or train, most inquisitors will eventually give up.
- Make it harder for police on the take by speaking only in your own language.
- If officers show signs of force or violence, and provided they are not drunk, do not be afraid to make a scene – dishonest cops will dislike such exposure.
- Never sign anything, especially if it's in a language you don't understand. You have the right not to sign anything without consular assistance.
- Recent antinarcotics laws give the police powers to search passengers at bus and train stations. If you are searched, never let the police put their hands in your pockets – take everything out yourself and turn your pockets inside out.
- If police officers want to see your money (to check for counterfeit bills) try to take it out only in front of the highest-ranking officer. If any is taken insist on a written receipt for the sum. If you do have to pay

a fine, insist that you do so at a bank and get a receipt for the full amount.

Trekking Problems

While most commonly used trekking routes are quite safe, there have been problems in the past with bandits in the mountains between Almaty and Lake Issyk-Kul. Some trekking routes, especially those in southern Kyrgyzstan and Tajikistan, traverse some remote areas that are prime opium-growing and rebel hide-out territory. Discuss your route with a trekking agency before you wander off into these hills and, if possible, take a local guide.

DISABLED TRAVELLERS

Central Asia is a difficult place for wheelchair travellers, as older Soviet buildings and buses are not wheelchair-accessible. There is also a severe lack of services catering to the visually or hearing impaired.

If any specialised travel agency is interested in arranging trips to Central Asia, the best bet is **Accessible Journeys** (☎ 1-800-TINGLES, 610-521 0339; www.disabilitytravel.com) in the USA. At the very least, hire your own transport and guide through one of the agencies listed in the Travel Agencies sections of the major cities.

A few new buildings, such as the top-end hotels in the Central Asian capitals and the Savitsky Museum in Nukus, are wheelchair-accessible.

DOCUMENTS

Besides your passport and visa, there are a number of other documents you may need to keep track of:

- Currency exchange and hard currency purchase receipts – you may need to show these when you sell back local money. The total should be more than the amount you want to sell back.
- Vouchers – if you prepaid accommodation, excursions or transport, these are the only proof that you did so.
- Hotel registration chits – in Uzbekistan you may need to show these little bits of paper (showing when you stayed at each hotel) to OVIR officials.

It's wise to have at least one photocopy of your passport (front and visa pages), a copy of your OVIR registration, your travel insurance policy and your airline tickets on your person and another set of copies with a fellow traveller. It's also a good idea to leave a photocopy of your passport, travel insurance and airline ticket with someone you can contact at home.

Student and youth cards are of little use, though they can be helpful as a decoy if someone wants to keep your passport.

ELECTRICITY

The entire former USSR is the same – nominal 220V at 50 cycles, using European two-pin plugs (round pins, with no earth connection) everywhere. Adaptors are available in department stores. Bring a torch (flashlight) if heading into rural areas. Afghanistan is typified by frequent blackouts and reliance on generators, even in Kabul.

EMBASSIES & CONSULATES

Listings of embassies and consulates can be found in the directories of each country chapter.

GAY & LESBIAN TRAVELLERS

There is little obvious gay/lesbian community in Central Asia, though there are a couple of gay bars in Almaty. It's not unusual to see young women showing affection towards each other, nor is it uncommon to see men holding hands. However, this is a reflection of Asian culture rather than homosexuality.

In Uzbekistan, Turkmenistan and Tajikistan, gay male sex is illegal, but lesbian sex does not seem to be illegal. Gay sex is also illegal in Afghanistan (but at least they don't collapse a wall on offenders like the Taliban did). Kazakhstan and Kyrgyzstan have lifted

the Soviet-era ban on homosexuality. However, whether you're straight or gay, it's best to avoid public displays of affection.

The website www.guide.to.kg is a good gay guide to Kyrgyzstan, with links to other republics, or try www.gays.kz for Kazakhstan.

HOLIDAYS
Public Holidays

See the Holidays section of the relevant country Directory for details of each country's public holidays.

The following Islamic holidays are generally observed in Central Asia. Dates are fixed by the Islamic lunar calendar, which is shorter than the Western solar calendar, beginning 10 to 11 days earlier in each solar year. Religious officials have the formal authority to declare the beginning of each lunar month based on sightings of the moon's first crescent. Future holy days can be estimated, but are in doubt by a few days until the start of that month, so dates given here are only approximate. The holidays normally run from sunset to the next sunset.

Ramadan and Eid al-Azha are observed with little fanfare in most of Central Asia (where travellers will find plenty of food available in any case) but are strongly observed in Afghanistan.

Eid al-Fitr 13 November (2004), 3 November (2005), 23 October (2006), 12/13 October (2007) Also called Hayit in Uzbekistan and Orozo Ait in Kyrgyzstan. This involves two or three days of celebrations at the end of Ramadan, with family visits, gifts, banquets and donations to the poor.

Eid al-Azha 21 January (2005), 10 January (2006), 31 December (2006), 20 December (2007) Also called Qurban, Korban or Qurban Hayit in Central Asia. This is the Feast of Sacrifice, and is celebrated over several days. Those who can afford it buy and slaughter an animal, sharing the meat with relatives and with the poor. This is also the season for haj (pilgrimage to Mecca).

Moulid an-Nabi 2 May (2004), 21 April (2005), 12 April (2006), 31 March (2007), 20 March (2008) The Birthday of the Prophet Mohammed (PBUH, Peace Be Upon Him). A minor celebration in Central Asia, though you might notice mosques are a little fuller.

Ramadan 15 October (2004), 4 October (2005), 23 September (2006), 12/13 September (2007) Also known as Ramazan, the month of sunrise-to-sunset fasting. Dates mark the beginning of Ramadan.

If you are crossing an international border it may be useful to know that Russian national holidays fall on 1 January, 7 January,

TOP CELEBRATIONS IN CENTRAL ASIA

- Navrus (Nawroz) in Mazar-e Sharif (p389) – the best place to see authentic buzkashi (a traditional pololike game played with a headless goat carcass)

- Independence Day in any ex-Soviet capital, but particularly in Tashkent (the only day of the year even the police don't demand bribes)

- The Mountain Festival on the Kazakh side of Khan Tengri (every three years, p154)

- Summer horseback wrestling and other nomadic games organised by CBT on the jailoos (summer pastures) of Song-Köl (p285) and Sarala-Saz (p284) or horse races in Ashgabat's hippodrome (p420)

8 March, 1 May, 9 May, 12 June and 7 November. If heading to China don't cross the border on the Chinese national holidays of 1 January, 8 March, 1 May, 1 July, 1 August and 1 October.

NAVRUS

By far the biggest Central Asian holiday is the spring festival of Navrus ('New Days' – Nauryz in Kazakh, Novruz in Turkmen, Nooruz in Kyrgyz, Nawroz in Afghanistan). Navrus is an Islamic adaptation of pre-Islamic vernal equinox or renewal celebrations, celebrated approximately on the spring equinox, though now normally fixed on 21 March.

In Soviet times this was a private affair, even banned for a time. In 1989, in one of several attempts to deflect growing Muslim nationalism, Navrus was adopted by the then Soviet Central Asian republics as an official two-day festival, with traditional games, music and drama festivals, street art and colourful fairs, plus partying and visiting of family and friends. Families traditionally pay off debts before the start of the holiday.

INSURANCE

Central Asia is an unpredictable place so insurance is a good idea. A minimum of US$1 million medical cover and a 'medivac' clause or policy covering the costs of being flown to another country for treatment is essential as few reliable emergency services

are available in the CIS. See p473 for information on health insurance.

Some policies specifically exclude 'dangerous activities', which can include skiing, motorcycling, even trekking or horse riding. If these are on your agenda, ask about an amendment to permit some of them (at a higher premium).

Few medical services in Central Asia will accept your foreign insurance documents for payment; you'll have to pay on the spot and claim later. Get receipts for everything and save all the paperwork. Some policies ask you to call back (reverse charges) to a centre in your home country where an immediate assessment of your problem is made.

Insurance policies can normally be extended on the road by a simple phone call, though make sure you do this before it expires or you may have to buy a new policy, often at a higher premium.

INTERNET ACCESS

Internet access is widely available throughout the region; just look for a roomful of teenagers playing games such as Counterstrike. The only places where you can't get Internet access are Turkmenistan and Afghanistan (outside Kabul).

LEGAL MATTERS

It's unlikely that you will ever actually be arrested, unless there are supportable charges against you. If you are arrested, authorities in the former Soviet states are obliged to inform your embassy (pasolstvah in Russian) immediately and allow you to communicate with a consular official without delay. Always keep the contact details of your embassy on your person. Most embassies will provide a list of recommended lawyers.

Visitors are subject to the laws of the country they're visiting. All Central Asian republics carry the death sentence for drug-related offences, though Kyrgyzstan and Turkmenistan currently have a moratorium on the death penalty.

MAPS

Buy your general maps of Central Asia before you leave home. For a search of the available maps try www.stanfords.co.uk.

Central Asia (Gizimap, 1999) is a good 1:750,000 general elevation map of the Central Asian republics (plus Kashgar), though it excludes northern Kazakhstan and western Turkmenistan. It usefully marks many trekking routes.

Central Asia – The Cultural Travel Map along the Silk Road (Elephanti) is a similar (but not as good) 1:1.5 million Italian map, which concentrates on Uzbekistan and Tajikistan.

Nelles' 1:750,000 *Central Asia* map is also good.

The following trekking maps for Central Asia are available:

Central Tian Shan (EWP) 1:150,000; Inylchek Glacier and surroundings.

Fan Mountains (EWP) 1:100,000; Fan Mountains in Tajikistan.

Koh-e-Pamir (Alpenvereinskarte) 1:50,000; climbing map.

Pamir Trans Alai Mountains (EWP) 1:200,000; Pik Lenin and the Fedchenko Glacier.

Pik Lenin (Karto Atelier) 1:100,000; topographical map of the mountain.

MAPS IN CENTRAL ASIA

Reliable locally produced city and regional maps can be found in Kazakhstan and Kyrgyzstan, but are hard to find elsewhere. The occasional Soviet-era city map, full of errors, languishes on the back shelf of some bookshops. Especially in Uzbekistan, where Soviet-era street names were jettisoned en masse, any map older than about 1994 will drive you crazy. In Ashgabat's top-end hotels you can buy good Turkish-made maps of Ashgabat, Nebit Dag (Balkanabat), Dashogus, Mary and Turkmenbashi.

Geoid in Bishkek (see p252) sells useful maps of major central Tian Shan trekking regions for the equivalent of about US$3 each.

Firma Geo (also known as JHER; see p95) in Almaty sells a wide variety of topographic and trekking maps from 1:25,000 to 1:100,000, as well as more general maps.

Asia Travel in Tashkent (p173) can supply good 1:100,000 Uzbek topographical maps printed in 1992, which are essential for trekking. These include:

Bisokiy Alay Treks from Shakhimardan, Khaidakan and the Sokh Valley in southern Kyrgyzstan.

Fannsky Gory Tajikistan's Fan Mountains.

Matcha Palmiro-Alay Tsentralnaya Chast Treks from Vorukh and Karavsin Valley, southern Kyrgyzstan.

MONEY

The Kazakhstan, Uzbekistan and Kyrgyzstan banking systems have improved in the last few years, with credit card transactions, wire transfers (particularly Western Union) and regulated foreign exchange. In the countryside there are few facilities, so change enough cash to get you back to a main city.

If you plan to travel extensively in the region it's worth bringing a flexible combination of cash in US dollars, US dollar travellers cheques and a credit card, to cover every eventuality.

ATMs

Bishkek, Tashkent and most cities in Kazakhstan have ATMs that accept Western credit cards, but these are not all that reliable and the last thing you need is to watch your card get eaten by an Uzbek ATM.

Black Market

The existence of licensed moneychangers in every town has done away with the black market in all republics except Turkmenistan (see p437).

Cash

Cash in US dollars is by far the easiest to exchange, followed by euros. Take a mixture of denominations – larger notes (US$100, US$50) are the most readily accepted and get a better rate, but a cache of small ones (US$10, US$5) is handy for when you're

---

DOLLARS & SOMS

Prices in this book are mostly given in US dollars, because that is the most reliable price denominator and it is most often what you will be quoted on the ground, although you normally have to actually pay in local currency. Prices quoted in the Turkmenistan chapter are in US dollars worked out at the black market rate; see above.

You will need cash in US dollars when paying for many services with a private travel agency, though many now accept credit cards. Although officially you cannot spend foreign currency anywhere in Uzbekistan, private hotels and homestays normally accept US dollars and often give you change in local currency at the market rate. Many hotels in Afghanistan expect payment in US dollars. Most other homestays and drivers still expect payment in local money.

stuck with a lousy exchange rate or need to pay for services in US dollars.

Make sure notes are in good condition – no worn or torn bills – and that they are dated post-1994. You may raise eyebrows at your bank back home but it's worth the trouble. Bills issued before 1990 are generally not accepted – if they are, the rate is often 30% less the normal US dollar rate. The newest US notes have an embedded thread running through them. In 2004 a new type of plastic-feeling US bill was introduced, though old bills remain legal tender.

Taxi drivers and market-sellers often fob off their own ragged foreign notes on tourists as change, so of course you should refuse to accept old notes too. At the time of research US$100 gave you a pile of Uzbek *sum* as thick as an airport paperback.

Cash in US dollars is the most convenient currency to bring to Tajikistan and Turkmenistan. Afghanistan is a strictly cash-only economy.

Credit Cards

It's an excellent idea to bring a credit card as an emergency backup, though you shouldn't rely on it completely to finance your trip as there are still only a limited number of places where it can be used. Kazakhstan is the most useful place in Central Asia to have a credit card.

Major credit cards can be used for payment at top-end hotels and restaurants, central airline offices, major travel agencies and a few shops throughout the region. Visa is the most widely recognised brand (except in Tajikistan), but others (American Express, Diners Club, Eurocard, MasterCard) are accepted in some places.

Cash advances against a Visa card and MasterCard are possible in the major capitals (except in Tajikistan where Visa card is not accepted), for commissions of 1% to 3%. By using credit cards in Turkmenistan you fail to make use of the black market (see p451).

International Transfers

Bank-to-bank wire (telegraphic) transfers are possible through major banks in Almaty, Bishkek, Dushanbe, Ashgabat and Tashkent. Commissions of 1% to 4% are typical, and service takes one to five days. Western Union (www.westernunion.com) has partners in banks everywhere and remains the easiest way to send money.

Moneychangers

Dealing with licensed moneychangers is the easiest way to change money in Kyrgyzstan, Kazakhstan and Tajikistan. They are readily found in small kiosks on nearly every block, and most will give a *spravka* or *kvitantsiya* (receipt) if you ask them; rates may vary by 1% to 2% at most. Licensed changers are completely legal. Moneychangers are marked by signs such as ОБМЕН ВАЛЮТЫ (*obmen valyuty*; currency exchange) and ОБМЕННЫЙ ПУНКТ (*obmennyy punkt*; exchange point).

Nearly all tourist hotels have branch-bank exchange desks where you can at least swap cash in US dollars for local money.

Swapping between currencies can be a pain, with most former Soviet republics uninterested in the others' money (an exception is Kazakhstan and Kyrgyzstan). In border areas you may need to deal with several currencies simultaneously; when trekking in the Khojand region it's necessary to carry a mixture of Russian roubles, Tajik somani, Uzbek *sum*, US dollars and Kyrgyz som.

Of course you can often change money personally, eg with hotel waiters or receptionists, or with dealers who approach you at markets, stations or your hotel (see Black Market on p451). In the former Soviet republics everybody wants dollars; even your truest friends and hosts will ask you to change a little with them. It can be hard to refuse, although saying that you need official exchange receipts at the border in order to sell back local currency usually closes the matter.

Try to avoid large notes in local currency (except to pay your hotel bills), since few people can spare much change.

EXCHANGE RECEIPTS

Whenever you change money, ask for a receipt (*kvitantsiya* or *spravka* in Russian) showing your name, the date, the amounts in both currencies, the exchange rate and an official signature. Not everyone will give you one, but if you need to resell local currency through the banks (Uzbekistan or Turkmenistan) you may need enough recent ones to cover what you want to resell. You will not need a receipt to sell local currency into US dollars with moneychangers in other countries. Customs officials may want to see exchange receipts at crossings to non-CIS countries but it's unlikely.

To sell back currency at any official exchange point you will probably need your customs declaration, plus the originals of enough recent exchange receipts to cover the amount you want to resell. Exchange receipts normally have a resale form at the bottom, which you sign at this time.

At the time of research you had to sell Uzbek *sum* back at a main city office of the National Bank – not at the airport or the hotels, or the border. The easiest thing, of course, is to spend it up before you leave, change it to neighbouring currencies on the black market or swap it with travellers going the other way.

Travellers Cheques

Travellers cheques can now be cashed in all the major Central Asian capitals, except Tajikistan. American Express and Thomas Cook are the most widely recognised brands. Only Visa travellers cheques can be changed in Turkmenistan. US dollar travellers cheques are the best currency to bring. Commissions run between 1% and 3%. It is possible to get your money in dollars instead of local currency, though the commission rate may be a little different. Travellers cheques can also make good decoy money if pressed for a bribe, as most people don't know what to do with them.

Security

Thankfully, credit cards and travellers cheques are becoming more common in Central Asia, but you may still end up carrying large wads of cash, particularly in Afghanistan and Tajikistan. All you can do is bury it deeply and in several different places, with only tiny sums in wallets, purses and outside pockets.

Petty crime is a growing problem in all the former Soviet republics (p447). Don't leave money in any form lying around your hotel room. Carry it securely zipped in one or more money belts or shoulder wallets buried deep in your clothing, with only what you'll immediately need (or would be willing to hand over to a thief or to an official on the take) accessible in an exterior pocket, wallet or purse.

When paying for anything substantial (eg a hotel bill or an expensive souvenir) or changing money on the street at an exchange kiosk, count the money beforehand, out of public sight; don't go fumbling in your money belt in full view. There are tales of thieves targeting people coming out of banks with fat cash advances, so keep your eyes open.

Be careful when paying by credit card that you see how many slips are being made from your card, that you destroy all carbon copies, and that as few people as possible get hold of your card number and expiry date.

Make sure you note the numbers of your cards and travellers cheques, and the telephone numbers to call if they are lost or stolen – and keep all numbers separate from the cards and cheques.

Tipping

Tipping is not common anywhere in Central Asia, though most cafés and restaurants in the capital cities add a 10% service charge to the bill, or expect you to round the total up.

Bribery, on the other hand, clearly can work in Central Asia but try to avoid it where possible – it feeds the already-widespread notion that travellers all just love throwing their money around, and makes it harder for future travellers. In fact a combination of smiles (even if over gritted teeth) and patient persistence can very often work better.

Shops have fixed prices but in markets (food, art or souvenirs) bargaining is usually expected. Press your luck further in places like art and craft markets, which are heavily patronised by tourists. In Kyrgyzstan bargaining is usually reserved only for taxi drivers. In the markets asking prices tend to be in a sane proportion to the expected outcome. Sellers will be genuinely surprised if you reply to their '5000' with '1000'; they're more likely expecting 3500, 4000 or 4500 in the end.

PHOTOGRAPHY & VIDEO
Film & Equipment

Most department stores have Kodak franchise outlets that sell 35mm print film, but slide film is rare so it's wise to bring your own (more than you think you'll need – Central Asia is a photographer's dream). It's safest to get film developed at home too, though most of the above franchises can develop print film for prices in line with their film prices.

There are no significant customs limits on camera equipment and film for personal use. Declare video cameras on customs forms and carry by hand through customs, but don't leave the tape in it as it may be confiscated.

Photographing & Videoing People

A lifetime with the KGB has made many older people uneasy about having their picture taken. Many people are also touchy about you photographing embarrassing subjects like drunks, run-down housing or consumer queues. You may find people sensitive about you photographing women, especially in rural areas and even among Ismailis who are more relaxed. Women photographers may get away with it if they've established some rapport. The Russian for 'may I take a photograph?' is *fotografirovat mozhno?* (fa-ta-gruh-*fee*-ra-vut *mozh*-na?).

POST

The postal systems of Central Asia are definitely not for urgent items – due in part to the scarcity of regional flights. A letter or postcard will probably take two weeks or more to get outside the CIS. Kyrgyzstan and Kazakhstan are probably the most reliable places from where to send packages.

Central post offices are the safest places to post things. Address mail as you would from any country, in your own language, though it will help to write the destination country in Cyrillic too. See the Post entries in the individual country directories for postal rates.

Incoming mail service is so flaky in Central Asia that most people use Internet-based email accounts instead.

If you have something that absolutely must get there, use an international courier company. DHL (www.dhl.com) and FedEx (www.fedex.com) have offices in major cities. A document to a Western country costs about US$40, a 500g package around US$42 to US$60, and it takes about a week.

Express Mail Service (EMS) is a priority mail service offered by post offices that ranks somewhere between normal post and courier post. Prices are considerably cheaper than courier services.

REGISTRATION

This relic of the Soviet era allows officials to keep tabs on you once you've arrived. In Uzbekistan the hotel or homestay in which you stay the night is supposed to register you. Registration in Kazakhstan is much more involved and you are best to get a travel agency to do it for US$15 to US$25 (though there is some talk of scrapping this requirement).

The place to register is the OVIR. There's one in every town, sometimes in each city district, functioning as the eyes and ears of the Ministry of the Interior's administration for policing foreigners. Though it has a local name in each republic (eg OPVR in Kazakhstan and Tajikistan, IIB in Uzbekistan, UPVR in Kyrgyzstan), everybody still calls it OVIR. In some remote areas where there is no OVIR office you may have to register at the *passportny stol* (passport office).

SHOPPING

In general Uzbekistan offers the best shopping; in fact most of central Bukhara and Samarkand's Registan are now one big souvenir stall.

Potential Central Asian buys include carpets, hats, felt rugs, wall hangings, silk, traditional clothing, ceramic figurines and even nomadic accessories such as horse whips and saddles.

Afghanistan and, to a lesser degree, Turkmenistan are the places for carpets. The best places for a *shyrdak* (Kyrgyz felt carpet) are the women's cooperatives in Kochkor and elsewhere in Central Kyrgyzstan (see the boxed text, p455). CBT can often put you in touch with local *shyrdak* producers. See p446 about exporting antiques or items that look antique.

Central Asian bazaars are enjoyable, even if you're just looking, with everything from Russian sparkling wine to car parts. Tolkuchka Bazaar, outside Ashgabat, has acres of carpets, handicrafts and silks. The best bargains are found in small-town bazaars. Another surprising souvenir source right under your nose is the local TsUM department store.

Turkmenistan's Ministry of Culture shop specialises in the region's most offbeat Stalinist souvenirs, including Niyazov busts, Niyazov vodka, Niyazov watches and even Niyazov baby food.

TOP PLACES FOR CRAFTS

For those interested in learning about local handicrafts, with an eye to purchasing, see the following in the main text:

Altyn Kor, Kochkor (p284) Local *shyrdak* cooperative.

Bukhara Artisan Development Centre, Bukhara (p218) Watch artisans at work here.

Caravan, Tashkent (p181) Browse for stylish handicrafts over a cappuccino.

Chicken Street, Kabul (p375) Famous for decades.

Jamilya's B&B, Karakol (p272) Custom-made *shyrdaks*.

Kyrgyz Style, Bishkek (p259) Cooperative showroom for high-quality *shyrdaks*.

Meros Centre for Traditional Arts, Tashkent (p181) Local artisans work in an old medressa.

Shyrdak shops, Tamchy (p266) Family-made *shyrdaks* at Shepherd's Life.

Unesco-sponsored silk-carpet workshops, Khiva and Bukhara (p229 and p218) Watch how carpets are made.

Yak House, Murgab (p346) For Pamiri-style crafts, bags and socks.

Yodgorlik (Souvenir) factory, Margilan (p192) Silk for US$4 per square metre, as well as *ikat* (brightly coloured cloth) dresses, carpets and embroidered items.

TELEPHONE & FAX
International Calls

You can place international calls (as well as local and intercity ones) from the central telephone and telegraph offices in most towns. You tell a clerk the number and prepay in local currency. After a wait of anything from half a minute to several hours, you're called to a booth (they usually shout out the destination and a booth number, in Russian). Early-morning and late-night calls, and those from capital cities, go through faster. Hotel operators will also place your calls, but you'll pay a hefty surcharge. International calls in the region generally cost between US$0.50 and US$2 per minute.

In most major cities private communications centres are cheaper and generally a better bet. Many communications offices and Internet cafés in Kyrgyzstan and Tajikistan offer Internet Phone (IP) calls, which route your call through low-cost

Internet connections, which works out as a fraction of the cost of traditional calls.

You can set up your own calls – theoretically from anywhere in Central Asia – by dialling 062. This gets you a local operator who speaks at least minimal English and who will book the call and ring you back within about half an hour. If you do this from a private telephone, the operator rings afterward with the call length and charges, which are the same as at a telephone office. Doing this from your hotel generates hotel surcharges.

Calls between CIS countries are now treated as international calls, though they are figured at a different rate. Thus to call Uzbekistan from, say, Kyrgyzstan you would need to dial Kyrgyzstan's international access code, the Uzbek country code and then the Uzbek city code.

See the Quick Reference page (on the inside front cover) for individual republic codes, and the individual city entries in the country chapters for their telephone codes.

Local Calls

Placing a local or trunk call on Central Asia's decomposing telephone systems is usually harder than placing an international one. There are token-operated telephones on the streets of bigger cities (though many seem to be permanently out of order) and in municipal telephone offices. *Jeton* (tokens) are sold at post and telephone offices and some kiosks for the equivalent of about US$0.05. Local calls are free from most hotels.

Fax

Faxes can sometimes be sent from post, telephone and telegraph offices, and some top-end hotels. Note that they're charged at telephone rates for the time it takes to transmit them – up to five minutes or more on Central Asia's dicey telephone lines. Moreover there may be a three-minute minimum, and you pay for failed attempts too, so the total cost is unpredictable and often huge.

TIME

The official time in most of Central Asia is Greenwich Mean Time (GMT) plus five hours, but transcontinental Kazakhstan straddles GMT plus four, five and six hours. Afghanistan is GMT plus 4.5 hours. See the World Time Zones Map on p479.

To complicate matters, Kazakhstan and Kyrgyzstan have Daylight Savings Time (DST), setting their clocks forward by one hour from the last Sunday in March until the last Sunday in September.

TOILETS

Public toilets are as scarce as hen's teeth. Those that you can find – eg in parks and bus and train stations – charge the equivalent of US$0.10 or so to use their squatters (flush or pit). Most are fairly awful. Someone may be out front selling sheets of toilet paper. You are always better off sticking to top-end hotels and restaurants. Carry a small pencil-torch for restaurant toilets, which rarely have functioning lights, and for trips out to the pit toilet. *Always* carry an emergency stash of toilet paper.

Out in the *jailoos* (pastures) of Kyrgyzstan there are often no toilets at all. You'll have to go for a hike, find a rock or use the cover of darkness. Always urinate at least 50m from a water source (and downstream!) and dig a hole and burn the paper after defecating.

Toilet paper appears sporadically for sale in markets and department stores, though tissues are a better bet than the industrial strength sandpaper that is ex-Soviet toilet paper. Flush systems and even pit toilets don't like toilet paper; the wastepaper basket in the loo is for used paper and tampons (wrapped in toilet paper).

Before bursting in, check for the signs 'Ж' (Russian: *zhenski)* for women or 'M' (*muzhskoy)* for men.

TOURIST INFORMATION

Intourist, the old Soviet travel bureau, gave birth to a litter of Central Asian successors – Yassaui in Kazakhstan, Intourist Tojikistan in Tajikistan, Turkmensiyahat in Turkmenistan, and Uzbektourism in Uzbekistan. Few are of any interest to independent travellers. You are almost always better off with one of the growing number of private agencies or community-based-tourism projects.

Uzbektourism wins the booby prize – at best uninterested in individual travellers, at worst hostile to them, with few points for public interface beyond the service bureaus.

The ever-optimistic Afghan Tourism Organisation (ATO) has branches throughout the country, which can arrange vehicle hire and excursions.

The best sources of information at home tend to be foreign travel firms specialising in Central Asia or the CIS.

TRAVEL & TREKKING PERMITS

Uzbek, Kazakh, Tajik, Kyrgyz and Afghanistan visas allow access to all places in the republics, save for a few strategic areas that need additional permits. In Kazakhstan some of the most interesting areas, such as Lepsinsk, the Altay region and Zhungar Alatau, require special permits that take from 10 days to three weeks to procure. The Baykonur Cosmodrome and the Polygon nuclear-testing site at Semey are firmly off limits.

In Kyrgyzstan any place within 50km of the Chinese border (such as the Inylchek Glacier, Alay Valley and Pik Lenin) requires a military border permit which are fairly easy to obtain through a trekking agency.

The Gorno-Badakhshan region of Tajikistan needs a separate permit, which takes a couple of weeks to arrange through a travel agency.

Turkmenistan presents a more complicated picture, as much of the country outside the main cities has to be listed on your visa for you to be able to visit it. You'll need the help of a travel agency to get the visa in the first place so your visa acts as your permit. For more information see Travel Permits in the individual country directories.

VIDEO SYSTEMS

Central Asia has the same video system as Russia, ie Secam, which is incompatible with Australia, most of Europe (apart from France and Greece) and the US.

VISAS

> To enter forbidden Turkistan without papers? I would sooner pay a call on the Devil and his mother-in-law in Hell.
> *Gustav Krist,*
> Alone in the Forbidden Land, 1939

Visas can be the single biggest headache associated with travel in ex-Soviet Central Asia, where regulations mutate frequently. Up-to-date information is hard to find. Collecting visas for a multicountry trip can take months.

Things are, however, getting easier. Visas for Kazakhstan, Kyrgyzstan, Uzbekistan and

Afghanistan are now merely a formality for most nationalities. It's even possible to get a visa on arrival in Bishkek. Tajikistan currently requires a letter of invitation (see below). Turkmenistan requires you to jump through the largest number of hoops.

The steps to obtain a visa and the attention it gets after you arrive differ for each republic, but their outlines are similar. The following information is general, with individual country variations detailed in the directories of the relevant country chapters.

Letters of Invitation

The key to getting a visa for Turkmenistan, Tajikistan and, for some nationalities, Uzbekistan, is 'visa support', which means an invitation, approved by the Ministries of Foreign Affairs and/or Interior, from a private individual, company or state organisation in the country you want to visit. After obtaining ministry approval, your sponsor sends the invitation (known as a letter of invitation or LOI, or visa support) to you, and when you apply at a consular office for your visa it's matched with a copy sent directly to them from the Ministry of Foreign Affairs.

The invitation should include your name, address, citizenship, sex, birth date, birthplace and passport details; the purpose, proposed itinerary and entry/exit dates of your visit; and the type of visa you will need and where you will apply for it. A business visa always requires a letter of invitation.

The cheapest way to get a visa invitation is directly, by fax or email, through a Central Asian travel agency. Many agencies in Kyrgyzstan, Kazakhstan, Turkmenistan and Uzbekistan will just sell you a letter of visa support for between US$20 and US$40, which you pay when you arrive in the country. Others require you to book at least a night or two's accommodation or an airport transfer. See the boxed text on p459 and also the Travel Agencies sections of capital cities for some trustworthy agencies in Central Asia. A few Western travel agencies can arrange visa invitation but most require you to book a package of hotel and transport services and charge up to five times the local fee.

Travel and visa agencies at home prefer to hear from you six weeks to two months before you leave, although they can get visa support more quickly if you pay extra. Individual sponsors may need months to get their invitations approved before they can even be sent to you.

Applying for a Visa

Visa applications can be made at some or all of the republics' overseas embassies or consulates, the addresses of which are listed in the Directories of individual country chapters. If your country doesn't have Central Asian representation you'll have to courier your passport to the nearest embassy, arrange a visa on arrival (see Visas on Arrival), or arrange your itinerary to get the visa in another Central Asian republic. Kazakh embassies will often issue visas for Kyrgyzstan if there is no Kyrgyz representation, though you need an LOI for this (whereas no invitation is required at a Kyrgyz embassy). Russian visas are no longer accepted for travel in Central Asia.

In addition to a letter of support, embassies may want a photocopy of the validity and personal information pages of your passport, two or three passport-size photos and a completed application form. Some may want more. The Kazakh embassy in Moscow will want a photocopy of your Russian visa and Uzbek embassies may ask to see an onward visa.

For Kyrgyzstan, Uzbekistan, Tajikistan, Afghanistan and Kazakhstan visas do not list the towns to be visited and you are free to travel almost everywhere in these countries. The tourist-visa application for Turkmenistan requires you to list the name of every town you want to visit, and these will normally be printed on your visa. It's a good idea to ask for every place you might conceivably want to see, unless these are sensitive border towns or off limits to foreigners. There's no charge for listing extra destinations.

Bear in mind that many visas have either fixed-entry dates (often for Turkmenistan) or fixed-validity dates, so you may have to plan the dates of your itinerary closely in advance. If you are weaving in and out of republics, ie from Uzbekistan to Tajikistan's Pamir Hwy, Kyrgyzstan and then back to Uzbekistan, you'll need to ensure that the first visa is still valid for when you return to that republic (and that it's a double- or multiple-entry visa).

Even the most helpful Central Asian embassies in the West normally take a week or two to get you a visa. Most embassies will speed the process up for an express fee (often double the normal fee). Central Asian embassies within the CIS seem to be quicker, eg a day or less at Kyrgyz embassies in other Central Asian republics, a week or less at Kazakh embassies.

Try to allow time for delays and screw ups. Errors do happen – check the dates and other information on your visa carefully before you hit the road, and try to find out what the Russian or other writing says.

Visas on Arrival

If there's no convenient embassy in your country, you can get a visa on arrival at Bishkek airport without an invitation, and at Dushanbe and theoretically Almaty, Tashkent and Ashgabat airports as long as this has been arranged in advance with a travel agency in that country and you have a letter of visa support to prove it. It's possible to get a five-day transit visa on arrival at Almaty airport for US$35 without an LOI but you should have proof of onward travel and an onward visa.

Responsible sponsors and agencies send representatives to meet their invitees at the airport and smooth their way through immigration. Even so, consular officials at the airport can be notoriously hard to find, especially if your flight arrives in the middle of the night, and may not be able to find your records scribbled in their big black book. You may also need to persuade the airline that you are guaranteed a visa as many are keen to avoid the costs and fines associated with bringing you back if your papers aren't in order. Try to get a visa in advance if possible.

Note that you cannot get a tourist visa at a land border of any Central Asian republic, though Kyrgyzstan plans to introduce this at some point.

Getting Central Asian Visas in Central Asia

Some (not all) visas are simpler and cheaper to get after you arrive. It's relatively easy, for example, to get an Uzbek visa in Kazakhstan, or a Kazakh or Uzbek visa in Bishkek (Kyrgyzstan), the former by getting a letter of support from a travel agency.

This could make your pretrip visa search much simpler, if you're willing to take some chances and have a week or so in a Central Asian republic to deal with the bureaucracy. Indeed, it might be possible (though we have not tried it) to leave home without any visas at all – eg fly to Bishkek and get a visa on arrival, then get a Kazakh or Uzbek visa in Bishkek and continue your trip there. This will work if you contact local travel agencies in advance to prepare any LOIs you might need. In general, though, you are better off getting at least one visa (Kyrgyz is the easiest, followed by Uzbekistan) before you board a plane to Central Asia.

Transit & Multiple-Entry Visas

Even if you are just passing through a republic (eg flying into Almaty and transferring to Bishkek) you will need a transit visa. If you are also flying out this way you will need to apply for another transit visa (in this case in Bishkek). It is possible to get a 72-hour Kazakh transit visa for US$35 on arrival at Almaty airport, but you should check this.

You will need transit visas for some trips even if you are aren't stopping in the country. For example you will need a Kazakh transit visa to take the bus from Tashkent to Bishkek (which goes through Kazakhstan) and an Uzbek transit visa to take a train from Khojand to Dushanbe (both in Tajikistan). You may also need a re-entry visa to get back into the first country; ie to travel from Fergana in Uzbekistan to Shakhimardan in

---

CHINESE VISAS

Chinese visas can be arranged in Tashkent but are a real pain to organise elsewhere in Central Asia, as embassies demand a letter of invitation from the Xinjiang tourist authority. These are available for around US$50 from travel agencies but can take a couple of weeks to arrange. It really helps to get a Chinese visa before you set off, though beware that you must normally enter China within 90 days of your visa being issued.

If you are travelling from China, bear in mind that the only consular agencies in Xinjiang are a Kazakh consulate in Ürümqi, with an Uzbek consulate planned. Beyond this it's a long way back to Beijing.

Uzbekistan and back you should have a Kyrgyz visa and a double-entry Uzbek visa.

Uzbekistan and Kazakhstan now even require other Central Asians to have a visa, in a move planned to boost security, which will only add to the visa queues at the respective embassies of those two countries.

Getting Current Information

As with all official mumbo jumbo in Central Asia, the rules change all the time, so the information here may be out of date by the time you read it. Kazakhstan keeps murmuring about abolishing the need for an LOI and Kyrgyzstan is thinking of getting rid of visas entirely for some nationalities. Check Central Asian embassy websites (see the boxed text following), the Lonely Planet Thorn Tree (www.lonelyplanet.com) and with one or more CIS-specialist travel or visa agencies.

Visa Extensions

Extending an ordinary tourist visa after you get there is relatively easy in Kyrgyzstan and Afghanistan, possible in Tajikistan, difficult in Turkmenistan and Uzbekistan and almost impossible in Kazakhstan. Travel agencies can normally help for a fee. You may find it easier to travel to a neighbouring republic and arrange another tourist visa.

WEIGHTS & MEASURES

Central Asia is metric. When you buy produce in markets make sure you know whether the price is per piece (*shtuk*) or by the kilo. It's also worth knowing that while Russian dictionaries define *choot choot* as 'a little bit', when applied to a shot of vodka it would appear to mean 'up to the rim'.

WOMEN TRAVELLERS

Despite the imposition of Soviet economic 'equality', attitudes in the Central Asian republics remain fairly male-dominated. Many local men cannot understand why women (in groups of any size, for that matter) would travel without men, and assume they have ulterior sexual motives. Although harassment is not so unrelenting as in some Middle Eastern countries, it tends to be more physical. Macho Uzbekistan tops the list, with Kyrgyzstan by far the least sexist. Deeply Islamic Afghanistan is a different kettle of fish; see p402 for specific advice.

VISA WEB CONTACTS

Embassies

Useful embassy websites:

- www.embassyofafghanistan.org or www.afghanembassy.co.uk
- www.kyrgyzstan.org or www.botschaftkirgistan.de
- www.kazakhembus.com or www.kazconsulny.org or www.kazakhstanembassy.org.uk
- www.tajikembassy.org or www.embassy-tajikistan.de
- www.uzbekconsulny.org or www.uzbekistan embassy.uk.net or www.uzbekistan.de
- www.turkmenistanembassy.org

Travel Agencies

The following travel agencies can arrange letters of invitation in their republic and in most cases the surrounding republics. Fees are around US$25 to US$35.

- Asia Tourism, Almaty (www.asiatour.org)
- Central Asia Tourism, Almaty (www.centralasiatourism.com)
- Jibek Joly, Almaty (www.tourkz.com)
- Tour Asia, Almaty (www.tourasia.kz)
- Stantours, Almaty (www.stantours.com)
- Amado, Ashgabat (www.amadotm.com)
- Ayan Travel, Ashgabat (www.ayan-travel .com)
- Celestial Mountains, Bishkek (www.celestial.com.kg)
- Central Asia Tourism, Bishkek (www.catcorp.kg/visa.html)
- ITMC, Bishkek (www.itmc.centralasia.kg)
- Great Game Travel, Dushanbe (www .greatgametravel.co.uk)
- Sayoh, Dushanbe (www.sayoh.tojikiston .com, www.tajiktour.tajnet.com)
- Pamirs.Org (www.pamirs.org/visas.htm)
- Asia Travel, Tashkent (www.asia-travel.uz)
- Dolores Tour, Tashkent (www.sambuh.com)
- Salom, Bukhara (www.salomtravel.com)

In bigger cities there is no taboo on unaccompanied local women talking to male visitors in public. Local men addressed by a woman in a couple direct their reply to the man, out of a sense of respect, and you should try to follow suit. Local women tend not to shake hands or lead in conversations. Because most local women don't drink in public, female visitors may not be offered a shot of the vodka or wine doing the rounds. But these are not taboos as such, and as usual, foreigners tend to be forgiven for what locals might consider gaffes.

Keen sensibilities and a few staunch rules of thumb can make a solo journey rewarding:

- Clothes do matter: a modest dress code is essential (even if local Russian women don't seem to have one).
- Walk confidently with your head up but avoid eye contact with men (smile at everybody else).
- Never follow any man – even an official – into a private area. If one insists on seeing your passport, hand over a photocopy as well as a photocopy of your OVIR registration (have quite a few of these); if he pushes you to follow him, walk away into a busy area.
- When riding in shared taxis choose one that already has other women passengers.
- Sit at the front of the bus, always between two women, if you can.
- When seeking information, always ask a local woman. Most matronly types will automatically take you under their wing if you show enough despair.
- If you feel as though you are being followed or harassed, seek the company of a group of women, or even children; big smiles will get you a welcome.
- Ignore any late-night raps at your door; utilise homestays whenever possible. Never wander around alone at night.
- If you are arranging a trek or car hire, ask the agency to include female travellers.
- Some local men will honestly want to befriend and help you; if you are unsure and have a difficult time shaking them, mention your husband (see the boxed text on the right).
- Wear a whistle around your neck in case you get into trouble. Blow on it relentlessly if you are absolutely in danger.

But it isn't all bad! The opportunities for genuine cross-cultural woman-to-woman interactions can generally be had during homestays, and usually outside the cities. Everyone loves to have their children cooed over and doing so will gain you friends as well as unique experiences. You may well see a side of Central Asia hidden to male travellers.

WORK & VOLUNTEERING

There are not many casual work opportunities in the region. What work is available is probably limited to English teaching and aid work, both of which are better arranged prior to your arrival in the region. The US Peace Corps and UK Voluntary Service Overseas (VSO) have a strong presence in the region.

You may find teaching positions in the region's universities, particularly the American University in Bishkek (www.auk.kg), the Samarkand State Institute of Foreign Languages (www.sifl.50megs.com) and the planned Central Asia University in Khorog, Tajikistan.

The Alpine Fund (www.alpinefund.org) in Bishkek accepts six-month volunteers. You could also volunteer at Habitat Kyrgyzstan Foundation (www.habitat.elcat.kg).

THE INVISIBLE HUSBAND

In some parts of Central Asia men are unused to seeing women travelling by themselves and you'll be continually asked where your husband is, but the system can often work in the lone woman's favour. So slip on a fake wedding ring and invent the invisible husband (In Russian: 'moy moosh' means 'my husband'), who can then be used in uncomfortable situations. When being pressured to buy something in a shop, cast your eyes downward and murmur 'moy moosh' (my husband doesn't give me any money). When a strange man tries to befriend you and you can't shake him, give a frantic glance at your watch and shout 'moy moosh' (I am meeting my husband at any moment). When officials, guards or policemen demand a bribe, shrug your shoulders helplessly and cry 'moy moosh' (my husband has left me here and there's nothing I can do!).

Transport in Central Asia

GETTING THERE & AWAY

This chapter deals with travel into or out of Central Asia, including Afghanistan, and includes general getting around advice for the region. For details of travel between and within Central Asian countries, see the transport sections of the individual country chapters.

ENTERING CENTRAL ASIA

The region's main air links to the 'outside' are through the ex-Soviet republican capitals of Almaty (Kazakhstan), Bishkek (Kyrgyzstan), Tashkent (Uzbekistan) and Ashgabat (Turkmenistan). A few smaller

THINGS CHANGE...

The information in this chapter is particularly vulnerable to change. Check directly with the airline or a travel agent to make sure you understand how a fare (and ticket you may buy) works and be aware of the security requirements for international travel. Shop carefully. The details given in this chapter should be regarded as pointers and are not a substitute for your own careful, up-to-date research.

cities have further connections to Commonwealth of Independent States (CIS) countries outside of Central Asia, especially Russia.

The long-distance rail connections are mostly with Mother Russia – from Moscow to Tashkent and Almaty, and from the Trans-Siberian Railway to Almaty and Tashkent. Others are the relatively new Genghis Khan Express lines between Almaty and Ürümqi (and beyond) in China, and between Ashgabat and Iran.

The other main overland links are three roads from China – one accessible year-round via Ürümqi to Almaty, and two warm-weather routes from Kashgar to Kyrgyzstan, over the Torugart or Irkeshtam Passes into Kyrgyzstan. Kashgar in turn can be reached by road over the Khunjerab Pass on Pakistan's amazing Karakoram Highway. A road link connects Mashhad in Iran to Ashgabat at two locations.

Finally there is a hybrid journey from Turkey through the Caucasus Mountains by bus to Baku (Azerbaijan), across the Caspian Sea to Turkmenbashi (Turkmenistan) and by train to Ashgabat, Bukhara and beyond. See From Turkey (p464) for details.

AIR

Many European and Asian cities now have direct flights to the Central Asian capitals. From North America and Australasia you will have to change planes at least once en route. Of the many routes in, two handy corridors are via Turkey (thanks to the geopolitics of the future) and via Russia (thanks to the geopolitics of the past). Turkish Airlines seems to have more good deals than anyone else (to Almaty, Ashgabat, Bishkek and Tashkent), while Russian and Central Asian carriers have the most connections. Turkey also has the advantage of a full house of Central Asian embassies and airline offices. Moscow has four airports and connections can be inconvenient.

Airports & Airlines

Tashkent – seven hours from London, 3½ hours from Moscow, Tel Aviv and Delhi, 4½ hours from İstanbul, 5½ hours from Beijing and 6½ hours from Bangkok – may have the

> ### DEPARTURE TAX
>
> You'll pay this for most departures from Central Asian republics to points outside the Commonwealth of Independent States (CIS), though the rules vary. Always check that the departure tax has not already been worked into the price of your air ticket (it often is from Tashkent).

most central airport in Eurasia. More flights go to Tashkent than to any other city in the region.

Almaty is also a useful gateway to both Kazakhstan and Kyrgyzstan (Bishkek is just three hours by road). KLM and Lufthansa operate shuttles from Almaty airport to Bishkek for their clients (see p313). Air Astana flies direct from London to Almaty, departing from Heathrow on Saturday (6pm) and Tuesday (9pm), arriving in at 7.15am and 10.10am respectively. Going the other way, the flights leave Almaty on Saturday and Tuesday at 2pm, arriving at 4pm (all local times). The tickets are £470 return including tax – the cheapest flight on the market.

There are also new Air Astana routes connecting Amsterdam to Uralsk, Atyrau and Astana.

Ashgabat is less well connected, most reliably by Lufthansa and Turkish Airlines, and Tajikistan is the least connected. For Dushanbe it's probably easier to fly to Tashkent and Bishkek and take a regional flight (Bishkek only), or travel overland to Khojand and then take a domestic flight. Kabul is connected by regional Ariana Afghan flights, with only one air connection to Central Asia (Dushanbe). In 2004 Air Kazakhstan announced its bankruptcy, stating that its routes would be taken over by Air Astana and other airlines.

The following are the main Central Asian airlines, of which Uzbekistan Airways is probably the best:

Air Astana (www.air-astana.kz; airline code 4L) Flies Almaty to Amsterdam, Bangkok, Beijing, Hannover, İstanbul, London and Seoul; Astana to Frankfurt, Hannover and Moscow; Atyrau and Uralsk to Amsterdam. Recently undertook to take over many of the defunct Air Kazakhstan's routes.
Ariana Afghan Airlines (www.flyariana.com; airline code FG) Flies Kabul to Delhi, Dubai, Dushanbe, Frankfurt, Islamabad, İstanbul, Moscow, Sharjah, Tehran, Ürümqi.

Kyrgyzstan Airlines (www.kga-r8.de; airline code R8) Flies Bishkek to Beijing, Birmingham, Delhi, Frankfurt, Hanover, İstanbul, Karachi, Moscow, Sharjah, Stuttgart and Ürümqi.
Tajikistan Airlines (www.tajikistan-airlines.com; airline code TJ) Flies Dushanbe to İstanbul, Munich, Delhi, Ekaterinburg, Moscow, Sharjah, Tehran and Ürümqi.
Turkmenistan Airlines (www.turkmenistanairlines .com; airline code T5) Flies Ashgabat to Abu Dhabi, Baku, Bangkok, Birmingham, Delhi, Frankfurt, İstanbul, Karachi, Kiev, London, Mashhad, Moscow and Yerevan.
Uzbekistan Airways (www.uzbekistanairways .nl; www.airways.uz, www.uzbekistanairways.gr; www.uzbekistan-airways.com; airline code HY) Flies Tashkent to Amsterdam, Athens, Baku, Bangkok, Beijing, Birmingham, Delhi, Dhaka, Frankfurt, İstanbul, Jeddah, Karachi, Kiev, Kuala Lumpur, London, Moscow, New York, Osaka, Paris, Seoul, Sharjah and Tel Aviv.

Other airlines that fly into Central Asia:
Aeroflot (www.aeroflot.ru; airline code SU; hub Sheremetyevo-2, Moscow)
Aerosvit Ukrainian Airlines (www.aerosvit.com; airline code VV) Flies to Ashgabat weekly from Kiev.
Asiana Airlines (www.flyasiana.com; OZ; hub Kimpo Airport, Seoul) Flies to Tashkent.
Azerbaijan Airlines (http://azaviation.com; airline code J2; hub Baku) Flies to Kabul.
British Airways (www.britishairways.com; airline code BA) Flies to Bishkek and Tashkent.
Imair Airlines (www.imair.com) Flies Baku to Almaty and Tashkent.
IranAir (www.iranair.co.ir; airline code IR; hub Tehran) Flies to Tashkent, Almaty and Ashgabat (via Mashhad).
Iran Asseman (hub Tehran) Tehran and Mashhad to Ashgabat and Bishkek.
KLM (www.klm.com; airline code KL; hub Schiphol Airport, Amsterdam) Flies Amsterdam to Almaty (twice weekly).
Lufthansa (www.lufthansa.com; airline code LH; hub Frankfurt) Flies Frankfurt to Almaty (five weekly), Tashkent (three weekly) and Ashgabat (three weekly direct, three via Baku).
PIA (www.piac.com.pk; airline code PK; hub Karachi) Flies to Almaty and Tashkent from Islamabad and Lahore.
Pulkovo Airlines (http://eng.pulkovo.ru) Flies to Almaty (twice weekly), Tashkent (weekly) and Bishkek (fortnightly).
Transaero (www.transaero.ru; airline code UN; hub Domodedovo Airport, Moscow)
Turkish Airlines (www.turkishairlines.com; airline code TK; hub İstanbul) Flies to Tashkent (four weekly), Ashgabat (three weekly), Almaty (five weekly) and Bishkek (three weekly) from İstanbul.
Ukraine International Airlines (www.ukraine -international.com; airline code PS; hub Kiev)

The website www.centralasiatourism.com has information about international and domestic flights into Kazakhstan, Tajikistan and Kyrgyzstan.

Tickets

Finding flights to Central Asia isn't always easy, as travel agents are generally unaware of the region (you'll have to help with the spelling of most cities and airlines) and many don't book flights on Russian or Central Asian airlines. You may need to contact the airlines directly for schedules and contact details of their consolidators, or sales agents, who often sell the airlines' tickets cheaper than the airlines themselves. For airline offices in Central Asia see Getting There & Away in the relevant capital city in each country chapter.

One thing to consider when arranging your itinerary is your visa situation. You may find it easier flying into, for example, Bishkek if that's the easiest place to arrange a visa from home. You might consider that it's worth paying a little extra for a reliable airline such as KLM or Turkish Airlines, rather than a relatively inexperienced one, such as Kyrgyzstan Airlines.

Always check how many and for how long are the stopovers and what time the flight arrives (many airlines arrive in the dead of night) and any restrictions on the ticket (ie changing the return date, refunds etc).

Fares to the region tend to be 10% to 20% higher in peak travel season (roughly July to September and December in North America and Europe; December to January in Australia and New Zealand).

Visa Checks

You can buy air tickets without a visa, visa support or a letter of invitation (LOI; see p457), but in most places outside Central Asia you will have trouble getting on a plane without one – even if embassies and travel agents tell you otherwise. Airlines are obliged to fly anyone rejected because of improper papers back home and are fined, so check-in staff tend to act like immigration officers. If you have made arrangements to get a visa on arrival, have your LOI handy at check-in and check with the airline beforehand.

Airline Safety

Aeroflot, the former Soviet state airline, was decentralised into around 400 splinter airlines and many of these 'baby-flots' now have the worst regional safety record in the world, due to poor maintenance, ageing aircraft and gross overloading. In general though, the Central Asian carriers have lifted their international services towards international safety standards, at least on international routes.

In December 1997 a Tajikistan Airlines plane crashed in Sharjah, killing 85 passengers, and an Air Kazakhstan plane collided with a Saudi jet over Delhi killing 350 people. In 1993 a Tajikistan Airlines Yak-40 crashed on take-off from Khorog; it had 81 passengers in its 28 seats. Tajikistan Airlines is currently not allowed into British airspace, due to safety concerns.

From Australia & New Zealand

Most flights to Central Asia go via Seoul (to pick up Asiana flights to Tashkent), Kuala Lumpur (Uzbekistan Airways to Tashkent), Bangkok (Uzbekistan Airways to Tashkent) or Karachi (PIA to Almaty or Tashkent, or Kyrgyzstan Airlines to Bishkek). Sample routings include Sydney to Tashkent on Malaysia Airlines via Kuala Lumpur, or via Karachi on Qantas/BA/PIA; and Sydney to Almaty via Seoul on Korean Airlines.

Flight Centre (Australia ☎ 133 133; New Zealand ☎ 0800 24 35 44; www.flightcentre.com)

Gateway Travel (☎ 02-9745 3333; www.russian-gateway.com.au; 48 The Boulevarde, Strathfield NSW 2135) Ex-USSR specialists with experience in booking flights to Central Asia.

STA Travel (Australia ☎ 1300 733 035; New Zealand ☎ 0508 782 872; www.statravel.com)

Trailfinders (☎ 1300 780 212; www.trailfinders.com.au)

From China

From Beijing there are twice weekly flights to Tashkent on Uzbekistan Airways, and three weekly to Almaty on Air Astana and to Bishkek on Kyrgyzstan Airlines.

Ürümqi has weekly or twice weekly flights to/from Almaty (US$200), Bishkek (US$190), Dushanbe (US$220) and Kabul (US$310).

From Continental Europe

The best fares from Europe to Almaty are probably with Turkish Airlines, via İstanbul. Travellers on a budget may find it cheapest to fly from Germany to cities in northern Kazakhstan such as Uralsk, Kostanai or Astana, and then continuing by train to southern Central Asia.

Tajikistan Airlines (☎ 89-9759 4210; gartjk@i-dial.de) Located in Munich; operates Europe's only flights to Dushanbe (US$720 one-way from Dushanbe, weekly via İstanbul).

Kyrgyzstan Airlines (www.kga-r8.de) Frankfurt (☎ 69-4960224; frankfurt@kga-r8.de); Hannover (☎ 511-726 1734; hannover@kga-r8.de).

Turkmenistan Airlines (☎ 69-690 21968) Offices in Frankfurt.

Ariana Afghan Airlines (www.flyariana.com) Flights from Frankfurt to Kabul (US$635 one-way).

Discounted travel agencies include **NBBS** (☎ 0900-10 20 300), in the Netherlands, and **STA Travel** (Paris ☎ 1-43 59 23 69, Frankfurt ☎ 69-4301910 in; www.statravel.com), with dozens of offices across Europe.

From Pakistan

PIA flies from Islamabad and Lahore, each once a week, to Tashkent and Almaty. From Karachi, Uzbekistan Airways flies to Tashkent, Kyrgyzstan Airlines flies to Bishkek and Turkmenistan Airlines flies to Ashgabat (all weekly).

Ariana has weekly flights from Islamabad to Kabul (US$110).

From Russia

There are flights from Moscow to most Central Asian cities, including Almaty (US$215), Tashkent (US$250, daily), Dushanbe (US$210, daily), Khojand (US$180, weekly), Kabul (US$330), Bishkek (US$208 to US$302) and many Kazakh cities. There are slightly fewer connections from St Petersburg (around US$200). Major Siberian cities such as Novosibirsk and Ekaterinburg also have connections to the capitals (eg US$170 to Dushanbe). You can often get seniors, student and under 30s discounts of 25% on Russian flights.

Uzbekistan Airways flies from Moscow to Samarkand, Urgench and Bukhara weekly for around US$230. Aeroflot fly from Moscow to Tashkent and Bishkek.

Transaero (☎ 095-241 4800; Hotel Moskva, Okhotny ryad 2, Moscow) is an international-grade airline that flies from Moscow Domodedovo (see following) to Astana, Almaty, Tashkent and several other cities in Kazakhstan and has connections to European destinations.

Turkmenistan Airways flies daily between Ashgabat and Moscow (Moscow–Ashgabat US$140, Ashgabat–Moscow US$220).

Note that Moscow has three airports: Sheremetyevo-1 (terminal one), the international Sheremetyevo (terminal two), and 'domestic' (ex-Soviet destinations) Domodedovo and Vnukovo. Aeroflot, Uzbekistan Airways and Air Astana now operate to/from Sheremetyevo-1. Transaero, Tajikistan Airlines, Turkmenistan Airways and Kyrgyzstan Airlines use Domodedovo airport.

If you need to connect with a flight to/from Domodedovo, 40km away, ask about a shuttle bus (generally no Russian visa is required but double-check this).

Travel agencies located in Moscow include **Infinity Travel** (☎ 095-234 6555; www.infinity.ru; Komsomolsky prospekt 13) for rail and air tickets and Central Asia packages, affiliated with the Travellers Guest House, and **G&R International** (☎ 095-378 0001; www.hostels.ru; 15th fl, ul Zenelodolskaya 3/2).

From Turkey

Turkish Airlines flies from İstanbul to Almaty (four weekly), Bishkek (two weekly), Tashkent (three weekly) and Ashgabat (four weekly). The various republics' national airlines also fly once or twice a week. Alternatively you could fly from İstanbul or Trabzon to Baku, take the ferry to Turkmenbashi and a 12-hour train ride across the desert to Ashgabat.

From the UK

The best summer fares to Almaty are about UK£450 return on KLM via Amsterdam. It's possible to buy an open-jaw return on this airline, eg into Almaty and out of Karachi.

To Tashkent the cheapest return fare is around UK£350 with Transaero, a reliable Russian airline. Other fares with Turkish Airlines or Lufthansa are UK£500 return. British Mediterranean fly to Tashkent (via Yerevan) and Bishkek (via Tblisi) but fares are generally higher.

Uzbekistan Airways' London–Tashkent (–Delhi) run (four weekly, UK£500 return) is comfortable, with good service and decent food (but the return is no match, with exhausted Delhi passengers sprawled everywhere and poor food from Tashkent). The routing means that for not much extra you can continue on from Tashkent to

Delhi or Bangkok, thus treating Tashkent as a stopover. Uzbekistan Airways also flies from Manchester. For details and prices contact **HY Travel** (☎ 020-7935 4775; 69 Wigmore St, London).

Kyrgyzstan Airlines (☎ 0121-523 5277) flies from Birmingham to Bishkek via İstanbul once a week for a bargain UK£195 one-way (UK£395 return). For details call the airline. Complaints about in-flight service are common.

The cheapest flights to Ashgabat are with Turkish Airlines from London via İstanbul (overnight), four times a week for UK£550 return. Turkmenistan Airways flies three times a week from London to Ashgabat (one-way US$405) and four times a week from Birmingham to Ashgabat.

To Afghanistan, the cheapest way is to fly to Dubai and pick up an Ariana flight to Kabul (US$210) from there. Other options include flying to Karachi and/or to Islamabad.

Discounted travel agencies include:
Bridge the World (☎ 0870-220 0012; www.bridge theworld.com)
STA Travel (☎ 020-361 6262; www.statravel.co.uk)
Trailfinders (☎ 020-7938 3366, 7938 3939; www.trail finders.co.uk)

From the USA & Canada

From North America you generally have the choice of routing your trip via İstanbul (Turkish Airlines), Moscow (Aeroflot) or a major European city (KLM, British Airways, Lufthansa etc). Stopovers can be lengthy. From the west coast it's possible to fly to Tashkent via Seoul on Asiana. It's always worth asking whether the airline will give you a free stopover.

From the USA, the best return fares to Central Asia at the time of writing were with Aeroflot from New York to Moscow and then Uzbekistan Airways to Tashkent, which was around US$1000 return. Return fares from the east coast were around US$1400 on Turkish Airlines to Tashkent, US$1700 to Almaty on KLM and US$1800 to Ashgabat with Lufthansa.

Uzbekistan Airways (☎ 212-489 3954) flies from New York JFK to Tashkent (via Belgrade) three or four times a week, an 18-hour flight for almost the same fare, but you may have difficulties finding a travel agent to book it.

Discounted agencies include:
STA Travel (☎ 800-777 0112; www.sta-travel.com)
Gateway Travel (☎ 800-441 1183)
Travel CUTS (☎ 416-979 2406; www.travelcuts.com)
Canadian travel discounter.

LAND
Border Crossings

Cross-border roads that are open to foreigners (by bus, taxi or hired car) are listed in the table on p466.

There are many crossings between Russia and Kazakhstan.

Car & Motorcycle

Although car or motorbike is an excellent way of getting around Central Asia, bringing your own vehicle is fraught with practical problems. Fuel supply is uneven, though modern petrol stations are springing up throughout the region. Prices per litre swing wildly depending on supply. Petrol comes in four grades – 76, 93, 95 and 98 octane. In the countryside you'll see petrol cowboys selling plastic bottles of fuel from the side of the road, often of very poor quality.

The biggest problem is the traffic police (Russian: GAI). Tajikistan's roads have almost as many checkpoints as potholes. In Uzbekistan there are police skulking at every corner, most looking for excuses to wave their orange baton and hit drivers (local or

---

SILK ROAD BY RAIL

Silk Road romantics, train buffs and nervous fliers can cross continents without once having to fasten their seatbelt or extinguish that cigarette. From Moscow (or even St Petersburg) you can take in the transition to Central Asia on the three-day train trip to Tashkent or Almaty. From here you can add on any number of side trips to Samarkand, Bukhara or even Urgench (Khiva), all of which are on the railway line. Then from Almaty it's possible to continue on the train to Ürümqi in China and even to Kashgar. From Ürümqi you can continue along the Silk Road by train east as far as Beijing, Hong Kong or Saigon, making for an epic transcontinental ride. It's not always comfortable and it will take some time so why do it? Because like Everest, it's there.

MAJOR BORDER CROSSINGS INTO CENTRAL ASIA

Border	Crossing	Means of Transport	Page	Comments
Iran–Turkmenistan	Gaudan/Bajgiran	car	p440	from Mashhad to Ashgabat; change at border
Iran–Turkmenistan	Saraghs	car/rail	p440	the best bet if you want to head straight for Mary
Iran–Afghanistan	Taybad/Islam Qala	bus	p403	change bus at border; alternatively, take the direct Mashhad–Herat bus
Azerbaijan–Turkmenistan	Turkmenbashi	Boat	p468	Upgrade when on board
China–Kazakhstan	Khorgos	bus	p157	buses run Yining–Almaty; to/from Ürümqi change buses at the border
China–Kazakhstan	Dustlyk	rail	p157	direct trains between Almaty and Ürümqi take 40 hours and cost US$60
China–Kyrgyzstan	Torugart Pass	car	p291	relatively expensive as you must hire your own transport
China–Kyrgyzstan	Irkeshtam Pass	car/bus	p157	check on the bus service from Osh to Kashgar (US$50) or take a taxi
China–Tajikistan	Qolma Pass	car	p352	due to open in 2004, connecting the Pamir region with the Karakoram Highway
Pakistan–Afghanistan	Khyber Pass	car	p403	arrange an armed escort through Pakistan's Tribal Areas
Pakistan–Afghanistan	Chaman	car	p403	not advisable at time of writing

otherwise) with a 'fine'. There are no motoring associations of any kind.

The state insurance offices, splinters of the old Soviet agency Ingosstrakh, have no overseas offices that we know of, and your own insurance is most unlikely to be valid in Central Asia. You would probably have to arrange insurance anew at each border. See Getting Around (p470) for more information on hiring a vehicle within Central Asia.

To read about a bicycle trip around Central Asia see www.tandemtoturkestan.com.

Train

There are three main rail routes into Central Asia from Russia. One comes from Moscow via Samara or Saratov, straight across Kazakhstan via Kyzylorda to Tashkent (3369km), with branch lines to Bishkek and Almaty (4057km). Another, the Turkestan-Siberian railway or 'Turksib' (see www.turksib.com for timetables) links the Trans-Siberian railway at Novosibirsk with Almaty. A third route goes around the other side of the Aral Sea via Urgench, Bukhara and Samarkand to Tashkent, with a branch line to Dushanbe, but services on this line are unreliable.

These routes don't have quite the romance or the laid-back feel of the Trans-Siberian railway, but they are usually cheaper and more frequent than flying, and allow Central Asia to unfold gradually, through plains, steppe and desert.

Another line crosses Kazakhstan via Karaghanda. From the Caspian Sea yet another line crosses Turkmenistan – the Trans-Caspian route. No international trains go to Turkmenistan. A line now links Mashhad in Iran with Ashgabat in Turkmenistan but at the time of writing no passenger trains were running between the two countries. An Almaty–Tehran train did run, once, in 2002, but Uzbekistan no longer allows other countries' transport to transit its territory.

Completed in 1992, after being delayed almost half a century by Russian-Chinese geopolitics, is a line from China via Ürümqi into Kazakhstan, joining the Turksib for connections to Almaty or to Siberia.

CLASSES

A deluxe sleeping carriage is called *spetsvagon* (SV, Russian for 'special carriage', abbreviated to CB in Cyrillic; some call this *spalnyy vagon* or 'sleeping carriage'), *myagkiy* (soft) or 1st class. Closed compartments have carpets and upholstered seats, and convert to comfortable sleeping compartments for two.

An ordinary sleeping carriage is called *ku peynyy* or *kupe* (which is the Russian for compartmentalised), *zhyoskiy* (hard) or 2nd class. Closed compartments are usually four-person couchettes and are comfortable.

A *platskartnyy* (reserved-place) or 3rd-class carriage has open-bunk accommodation. *Obshchiy* (general) or 4th class is unreserved bench-type seating.

With a reservation, your ticket normally shows the numbers of your carriage *(vagon)* and seat *(mesto)*. Class may be shown by what looks like a fraction: eg 1/2 is 1st class two berth, 2/4 is 2nd class four berth.

FROM CHINA
Apart from the long way around on the Turksib and Trans-Siberian trains, there's just one way to get in to or out of Central Asia by rail on the China side – the 1359km journey between Ürümqi and Almaty (48 hours, US$60). The trip duration includes around seven hours at the border for customs checks and to change bogies. Tickets are easily booked in either Ürümqi or Almaty (see p157).

FROM RUSSIA
Most trains bound for Central Asia depart from Moscow's Kazan(sky) station. Europe dissolves into Asia as you sleep, and morning may bring a vast panorama of the Kazakh steppe.

Train connections between Russia and Central Asia have thinned out in recent years. At the time of writing, fast trains left three times a week to/from Tashkent (No 5/6, 60 hours), every other day to/from Almaty (No 7/8, 50 hours) and once or twice a week to/from Bishkek (No 17/18, 75 hours). There are other, slower connections but you could grow old and die on them. Trains out of Moscow have even numbers; those returning have odd numbers.

Typical fares for a 2nd class *(kupeynyy)* berth are US$143 Moscow–Tashkent and US$117 Moscow–Almaty (via Astana).

Other offbeat connections include the Astrakan–Dushanbe (twice weekly), the St Petersburg–Astana (every other day) and Saratov–Nukus–Andijan (weekly) lines.

TRAVEL AGENCIES & ORGANISED TOURS

In this section we list reliable agencies who can help with the logistics of travel in Central Asia – whether it be visas, a few excursions or an entire trip. These include travel agencies, adventure tour operators and homestay agencies – many agencies combine these functions.

The following can arrange individual itineraries, accommodation, tickets and visa support.

Australia
Gateway Travel (☎ 02-9745 3333; www.russian-gateway.com.au; 48 The Boulevarde, Strathfield NSW 2135) Airfares to Central Asia, hotel bookings, homestays, visa invitations and airport transfers.

Passport Travel (☎ 03-9867 3888; www.travelcentre.com.au; www.russia-rail.com; Suite 11A, 401 St Kilda Rd, Melbourne, Victoria 3004) Accommodation and rail tickets.

Sundowners (☎ 03-9672 5300; www.sundowners.com.au; Suite 15, Lonsdale Court, 600 Lonsdale St, Melbourne, Victoria 3000) Small-group and independent tours into Central Asia.

The UK
Adventure Overland (☎ 020-8640 8105; www.adventureoverland.com; 9 Ridge Rd, Mitcham, Surrey CR42ET)

East-West Travel (☎ 020-7938 3211; travel@east-west.co.uk; 15 Kensington High St, W8 London) Independent itineraries and flights to the entire ex-Soviet Union; Consular service (☎ 020-7376 1555; consular@east-west.co.uk) This can arrange visas to all ex-Soviet republics.

Regent Holidays (☎ 117-921 1711; www.regent-holidays.co.uk; 15 John St, Bristol BS1 2HR) Short tours and can cobble together an individual itinerary, mini-treks, homestays in Bishkek and Torugart crossings (UK£185 per person from Bishkek to Kashgar).

Steppes East (☎ 01285-651 010; www.steppeseast.co.uk; 51 Castle St, Cirencester GL7 1QD) Arranges individual itineraries, and assists with border crossings and visas in conjunction with ground transport.

The USA
Mir Corporation (☎ 800-424 7289; www.mircorp.com; Suite 210, 85 South Washington St, Seattle, WA 98104) Independent tours, homestays and visa support with accommodation.

Red Star Travel (☎ 800-215 4378, 206-522 5995; www.travel2russia.com; Suite 102, 123 Queen Anne Ave N, Seattle, WA 98109) Organises tours, individual itineraries, accommodation, train tickets, visa support with booking.

SEA

The Baku (Azerbaijan) to Turkmenbashi ferry route (US$45 to US$100 foreigner price, 13 to 18 hours) across the Caspian is a fairly popular way to enter and leave Central Asia. Buy the cheapest seat: once on board you'll doubtless be offered a cabin by a crewmember, for which you should realistically pay US$10 to US$20. The best cabins have private bathrooms and are comfortable, although all are cockroach infested.

Boats usually leave several times a day in both directions, but there is no timetable. You'll simply have to arrive and wait until the ship is full of cargo. Stock up on food and water beforehand, as there is no food available on board.

Boats also sail occasionally from Turkmenbashi to Astrakan in Russia.

There are irregular boats every week or so between Baku and Aktau (24 hours, US$40 to US$60) in Kazakhstan. One of these ferries sunk in October 2002, killing all 51 people aboard.

GETTING AROUND

Flying is the least interesting and arguably the least safe mode of transport in Central Asia, but to some destinations and in some seasons it's the only sensible alternative. Trains are slow but crowded and generally not very convenient outside Kazakhstan. Buses are the most frequent and convenient way to get between towns cheaply, though trips can be cramped and vehicles are prone to breakdowns. The best option in many areas is a car: shared taxis or private drivers are often willing to take you between cities for little more than a bus fare (see p471).

The biggest headache for travellers crossing the region is that most inter-republic bus services have been cut. Travellers generally have to get a shared taxi or minibus to and from both sides of the border (see the boxed text p470). Crossings into Uzbekistan are the most tightly controlled, particularly coming from Tajikistan.

AIR

Flying saves time and takes the tedium out of Central Asia's long distances. It's also the only sensible way to reach some places, particularly in winter. But the Central Asian airlines have some way to go before meeting international safety standards on their domestic routes.

Apart from the national Central Asian airlines (see p461), there are several domestic airlines, including Kyrgyzstan's Itek Air and Altyn Air (www.altynair.kg in Russian only) and Kazakhstan's Air Astana, all of which are pretty good. Domestic and inter-republic services are no-frills; you might get a drink if lucky. For long flights consider packing lunch.

At the time of writing there were no Almaty–Bishkek or Dushanbe–Tashkent services. Major internal connections still run daily.

Flights between the biggest cities generally stick to their schedules, but those serving smaller towns are often delayed without explanation and cancellations are common, usually a result of fuel shortages (big-city flights get priority). Printed schedules are unreliable; routes and individual flights are constantly being cancelled or reintroduced. The only sure way to find out what's flying is to ask at an air booking office. In any case, confirm any flight 24 hours prior to departure.

Tickets for Central Asian airlines can be purchased from old Aeroflot municipal booking offices (most now renamed), from airline reservation desks in many major hotels (though they may attach fees of US$5 or more), at the airport right up to departure, or increasingly at private travel agents (aviakassa). You'll often need your passport and visa. Many booking offices have a special window for foreigners and/or for international flights. It is rarely possible to book a return flight. Check your ticket closely – mistakes are common.

The airfare diagram shows approximate one-way foreigners' fares in US dollar equivalents, for some major regional connections.

Check-in is 40 to 90 minutes before departure and airlines are entitled to bump you if you come later than that. Seating is a bit of a free-for-all (there are often no assigned seats), especially if the flight is overbooked. To minimise the risk of loss or theft, consider carrying everything on board.

Helicopter flights were once popular in the Tian Shan and Pamir Ranges but rising fuel costs have made most services prohibitively expensive (around US$1300 per hour).

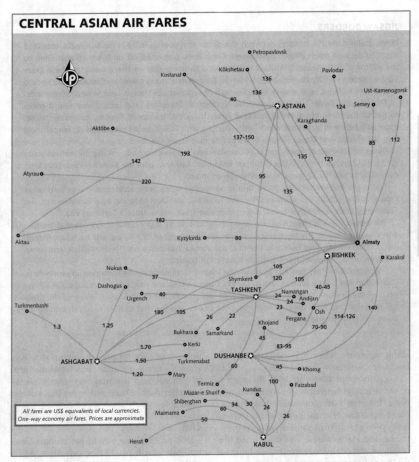

CENTRAL ASIAN AIR FARES

All fares are US$ equivalents of local currencies.
One-way economy air fares. Prices are approximate

Maintenance is also patchy; avoid them except in summer and go only if the weather is absolutely clear.

BUS

This is generally the best bet for getting between towns cheaply. The major transport corridors are served by big long-distance coaches (often reconditioned German or Turkish vehicles), which run on fixed routes and schedules, with fixed stops. They're relatively problem-free and moderately comfortable, with windows that open and sometimes with reclining seats. Luggage is locked safely away below. Journey times depend on road conditions but are somewhat longer than a fast train.

Regional buses are a lot less comfortable and a bit more...interesting. Breakdowns are common. They are also used extensively by small-time traders to shift their goods around the region, and you could gradually become surrounded by boxes, bags, urns and live animals.

Private minibuses, which often solicit passengers in front of bus stations, are a bit more expensive, sometimes faster, and usually more hair-raising. They may be called *marshrutnyy* (marsh-*root*-ni; Russian for 'fixed route') or *arenda* (Russian for 'for hire'). They generally have fixed fares and routes but no fixed timetable (or no departure at all if there aren't enough passengers to satisfy the driver), and will stop anywhere

JIGSAW BORDERS

When Stalin drew the borders between the different republics in 1924 no-one really expected them to become international boundaries. Areas were portioned off on the map according to the whims of Party leaders, without much regard to the reality on the ground. As these crazy jigsaw borders solidify throughout post-Soviet Central Asia, many towns and enclaves are finding themselves isolated, as the once complex web of regional ties shrinks behind new borderlines.

The Fergana Valley has been particularly affected. Travellers (and locals) may find it tricky to get to more remote areas or trekking bases by public transport. Borders sometimes close, especially between Uzbekistan and Tajikistan. Cars with Tajik number plates can no longer cross into Uzbekistan and Uzbek border guards often give locals the third degree.

Buses no longer run from central Uzbekistan into the Fergana Valley along the natural route via Khojand but rather take the mountain road from Tashkent over the Kamchik Pass. Only train connections exit the Fergana Valley through its mouth.

Trains are not immune to these border shenanigans, as lines occasionally veer into other republics. Trains from Astrakan and Khojand to Termiz and Dushanbe dip into Turkmenistan and Turkmen guards sometimes board the train to fine travellers without a Turkmen visa.

The bottom line is that there are now border checks at many hitherto disregarded borders and you need a visa any time you cross into another republic. If you are just transiting a third republic before heading back into the first you should invest in a double or multiple-entry visa. There are exceptions, eg the Tajikistan–Kyrgyzstan border.

These problems may be short-lived, as new transport connections are springing up everywhere. Uzbekistan has built a railway line to bypass Turkmenistan and roads have sprung up in Kyrgyz parts of the Fergana Valley to avoid Uzbek border guards. But these are just a few of the thousands of ties that bind the ex-Soviet republics to one another and to Russia, and disentangling them will take decades.

along the route. They may be clapped-out heaps or spiffy new Toyota vans.

Keep in mind that you're at the mercy of the driver as he picks up cargo here and there, loading it all around the passengers, picks up a few friends, gets petrol, fixes a leaky petrol tank, runs some errands, repairs the engine, loads more crates right up to the ceiling – and then stops every half-hour to fill the radiator with water.

Tickets

Most cities have a main intercity bus station (Russian: *avtovokzal*, Kyrgyz and Uzbek: *avtobekat*) and may also have regional bus stations (sometimes several) serving local towns.

Try to pick buses originating from where you are, enabling you to buy tickets as much as a day in advance. Tickets for through buses may not be sold until they arrive, amid anxious scrambles. In a pinch you could try paying the driver directly for a place.

Most large bus stations have police who sometimes create headaches for foreigners by demanding documents. Be wary of any policeman who approaches you at a bus station. Long-distance bus stations are, in general, low-life magnets, rarely pleasant after dark. Disregard most bus station timetables.

CAR

Car is an excellent way to get around Central Asia and it needn't be expensive. Main highways between capitals and big cities (eg Almaty–Bishkek–Tashkent–Samarkand–Bukhara) are fast and fairly well maintained. Mountain roads (ie most roads in Kyrgyzstan and Tajikistan) can be blocked with snow in winter and plagued by landslides in spring.

See Car & Motorcycle (p465) for advice about driving your own vehicle through Central Asia.

Hire

Almaty and Bishkek have a Hertz/Avis franchise and travel agencies can hire you out a Mercedes or jeep, but you are almost always better off hiring a taxi for the day. Some Central Asian travel agencies have a fixed per-kilometre rate eg US$0.25 per kilometre for a 4WD Niva.

Taxi

There are two main ways of travelling by car in Central Asia if you don't have your own vehicle: ordinary taxi or shared taxi.

ORDINARY TAXI

This form of travel is to hire an entire taxi for a special route. This is handy for reaching off-the-beaten-track places, where bus connections are hit-and-miss or nonexistent, such as Song-Köl in Kyrgyzstan. Select your driver with care, look over his car (we took one in Kyrgyzstan whose exhaust fumes were funnelled through the back windows) and assess his sobriety before you set off. See Taxi (p472) for more on Central Asian taxis.

You'll have to negotiate a price before you set off. Along routes where there are also shared taxis, this is four times the shared taxi per-person fare. Make sure everyone is clear which route you will be taking, how long you want the driver to wait at a site and if there are any toll or entry fees to be paid. You will need to haggle hard.

You can work out approximate costs by working out the return kilometre distance; assume the average consumption of cars is around 12 litres per 100km and times the number of litres needed by the per litre petrol cost (constantly in flux). Add to this a daily fee (anything from US$5 up to the cost of the petrol) and a waiting fee of around US$1 per hour and away you go.

SHARED TAXI

Shared taxi is the other main form of car travel around Central Asia, whereby a taxi or private car does a regular run between two cities and charges a set rate for each of the four seats in a car. These cars often wait for passengers outside bus or train stations and some have a sign in the window indicating where they are headed. Cars are quicker and just as comfortable as a bus or train, and can work out to be little more expensive than a bus. In Kyrgyzstan per-person fares are so cheap that two or three of you can buy all four seats and stretch out. Otherwise smaller cars can be a little cramped. The most common car is the Russian Zhiguli, fast being replaced by modern Daewoo models such as the Tico and Niva, both made in Central Asia.

These services are particularly useful in Kyrgyzstan along certain major routes such as Bishkek–Almaty, Bishkek–Osh, and Naryn–Bishkek. Other useful shared taxi routes are Urgench–Khiva and Ashgabat–Mary. There are a few shared taxis in Xinjiang (ie Yengisar–Kashgar) but they can be hard to find.

TRAIN

Lower-class train travel is the cheapest way to get around, but that also makes it attractive to everybody else, so it's the most crowded way. In general travelling in the summertime is best done at night. Kazakhstan is probably the only country where you'll find yourself using the train system much.

Connections

Trains are most useful to cover the vast distances in Kazakhstan. Certain corridors, such as the Turksib (Semey–Almaty) and Almaty–Tashkent, are well served by fast trains every other day. The daily overnight Tashkent–Bukhara run is particularly useful. The Samarkand–Bukhara train takes six hours and offers aeroplane-style seats. As an indication of journey times, Urgench–Tashkent and Tashkent–Almaty are each about 25 hours on a fast train.

Elsewhere, connections are drying up as fast as the Aral Sea; few trains run to Dushanbe any more (those that do take a very roundabout route and require a Turkmen transit visas) and there are no direct lines, for example, between Ashgabat and any other Central Asian capitals.

Many trains to and from Russia can be used for getting around Central Asia, and may be faster and in better condition. But any train originating far from where you are is likely to be filthy, crowded and late by the time you board it.

Tickets

Book at least two days ahead for CIS connections, if you can. You will probably need to show your passport and visa. A few stations have separate windows for advance bookings and for departures within 24 hours; the latter is generally the one with the heaving mob around it (beware of pickpockets). Many tourist hotels have rail-booking desks (including their own mark-up). Few travel agencies are interested in booking trains.

If you can't get a ticket for a particular train, it's worth turning up anyway. No matter how full ticket clerks insist a train is, there always seem to be spare *kupeynyy* (2nd class or sleeping carriage) berths. Ask an attendant. You'll have to pay at least the equivalent price of the ticket, often more, and usually in dollars. Shop around the attendants for the best offer (the money, of course, all goes into their pockets). You can sometimes upgrade this way.

A few sample *kupenyy* fares (one-way) from Tashkent are US$19 to Urgench, US$8 to Bukhara and US$3.50 to Samarkand. Fares from Almaty include Semey (US$16), Taraz (US$12) and Astana (US$20 or US$48 express).

HITCHING

In Central Asia there is generally little distinction between hitching and taking a taxi. Anyone with a car will stop if you flag them down (with a low up-and-down wave, not an upturned thumb) and most drivers will expect you to pay for the ride. If you can negotiate a reasonable fare (it helps to know the equivalent bus or shared taxi fare) this can be a much quicker mode of transport than the bus. There's also a good chance you'll be invited to someone's house for tea.

Hitching to parks and scenic spots is generally much easier on the weekends but you'll lose some of the solitude at these times.

LOCAL TRANSPORT

Most sizable towns have public buses, and sometimes electric trolleybuses. Bigger cities also have trams, and Tashkent has a metro system. Transport is still ridiculously cheap by western standards, but usually packed because there's never enough money to keep an adequate fleet on the road; at peak hours it can take several stops for those caught by surprise to even work their way to an exit.

Public transport in smaller towns tends to melt away soon after dark.

Bus, Trolleybus & Tram

Payment methods vary, but the most common method is to pay the driver cash on exit. Manoeuvre your way out by asking anyone in the way, *vykhodite?* (getting off?).

TAXI PRECAUTIONS

Avoid taxis lurking outside tourist hotels – drivers charge far too much and get uppity when you try to talk them down. Never get into a taxi with more than one person in it, especially after dark; check the back seat of the car for hidden friends too. Keep your fare money in a separate pocket to avoid flashing large wads of cash. Have a map to make it look like you know your route. If you're staying at a private residence, have the taxi stop at the corner nearest your destination, not the specific address.

Marshrutnoe Taxi

A *marshrutnoe taxi* (marsh-*root*-na-yuh tahk-*see*) or *marshrutka* is a minibus running along a fixed route. You can get on at fixed stops but can get off anywhere by saying *zdyes pazhalsta* (zd-*yes* pa-*zhal*-stuh; here please). Routes are hard to figure out and schedules erratic, and it's usually easier to stick to other transport. Fares are just a little higher than bus fares.

City Taxi

There are two kinds of taxis: officially licensed ones and anything else. Official taxis are more trustworthy, and sometimes cheaper – if you can find one. They may have meters but they're always 'broken' and you'll have to negotiate. Or let a local friend negotiate for you – they'll do better than you will.

Unofficial taxis are often private cars driven by people trying to cover their huge petrol costs. Anything with a chequerboard logo in the window is a taxi. Stand at the side of the road, extend your arm and wait – as scores of others around you will probably be doing. When someone stops, negotiate destination and fare through the passenger-side window or through a partially open door. The driver may say *sadytse* (sit down) or beckon you in, but sort the fare out first. It helps a lot if you can negotiate the price in Russian, even more so in the local language.

A typical fare across Tashkent at the time of writing was around US$2; about half that for Ashgabat or Bishkek. Fares go up at night and extra charges are incurred for bookings.

Health by Dr Trish Batchelor

CONTENTS

BEFORE YOU GO

Pack medications in their original, clearly labelled containers. A signed and dated letter from your physician describing your medical conditions and medications (using generic names) is also a good idea. If carrying syringes or needles, be sure to have a physician's letter documenting their medical necessity. If you have a heart condition, bring a copy of your ECG taken just prior to travelling.

If you take any regular medication, bring double your needs in case of loss or theft. In most Central Asian countries you can buy many medications over the counter without a doctor's prescription, but it can be difficult to find some of the newer drugs, particularly the latest antidepressant drugs, blood pressure medications and contraceptive methods.

Make sure you get your teeth checked before you travel – there are few good dentists in Central Asia. If you wear glasses take a spare pair and your prescription.

INSURANCE

Even if you are fit and healthy, don't travel without health insurance – accidents do happen. Declare any existing medical conditions you have – the insurance company *will* check if your problem is pre-existing and will not cover you if it is undeclared. You may require extra cover for adventure activities such as rock climbing. If you're uninsured, emergency evacuation is expensive – bills of over US$100,000 are not uncommon.

Make sure you keep all documentation related to any medical expenses you incur.

RECOMMENDED VACCINATIONS

Specialised travel-medicine clinics are your best source of information; they stock all available vaccines and will be able to give specific recommendations for you and your trip. Most vaccines don't produce immunity until at least two weeks after they're given, so visit a doctor four to eight weeks before departure. Ask your doctor for an International Certificate of Vaccination (otherwise known as the yellow booklet), which will list all the vaccinations you've received.

The only vaccine required by international regulations is yellow fever. Proof of vaccination will be required only if you have visited a country in the yellow-fever zone within the six days prior to entering Afghanistan and Kazakhstan.

Uzbekistan, Kazakhstan and Kyrgyzstan all require HIV testing if staying more than 15 to 30 days. Foreign tests are accepted under certain conditions, but make sure to check with the embassy of your destination before travelling.

The World Health Organization recommends the following vaccinations for travellers to Central Asia:

Adult Diphtheria & Tetanus Single booster recommended if none in the previous 10 years. Side effects include sore arm and fever.

Hepatitis A Provides almost 100% protection for up to a year; a booster after 12 months provides at least another 20 years' protection. Mild side effects such as headache and sore arm occur in 5% to 10% of people.

Hepatitis B Now considered routine for most travellers. Given as three shots over six months. A rapid schedule is also available, as is a combined vaccination with Hepatitis A. Side effects are mild and uncommon, usually headache and sore arm. In 95% of people lifetime protection results.

Measles, Mumps & Rubella Two doses required unless you have had the diseases. Occasionally a rash and flulike illness can develop a week after receiving the vaccine. Many young adults require a booster.

HEALTH

HEALTH

MEDICAL CHECKLIST

Recommended items for a personal medical kit:

- Antifungal cream (eg clotrimazole)
- Antibacterial cream (eg muciprocin)
- Antibiotics for skin infections (eg amoxicillin/clavulanate or cephalexin)
- Antibiotics for diarrhoea (eg norfloxacin, ciprofloxacin or azithromycin for bacterial diarrhoea; tinidazole for giardiasis or amoebic dysentery)
- Antihistamine – there are many options (eg cetrizine for day and promethazine for night)
- Antiseptic (eg Betadine)
- Antispasmodic for stomach cramps (eg Buscopan)
- Decongestant (eg pseudoephedrine)
- DEET-based insect repellent
- Diamox if going to high altitude
- Elastoplasts, bandages, gauze, thermometer (but not mercury), sterile needles and syringes, safety pins and tweezers
- Ibuprofen or another anti-inflammatory
- Indigestion tablets (eg Quick Eze or Mylanta)
- Iodine tablets (unless you are pregnant or have a thyroid problem) to purify water
- Laxative (eg Coloxyl)
- Oral rehydration solution for diarrhoea (eg Gastrolyte), diarrhoea 'stopper' (eg loperamide) and antinausea medication (eg prochlorperazine)
- Paracetamol
- Permethrin to impregnate clothing and mosquito nets
- Steroid cream for allergic/itchy rashes (eg 1% to 2% hydrocortisone)
- Sunscreen and hat
- Thrush (vaginal yeast infection) treatment (eg clotrimazole pessaries or Diflucan tablets)
- Ural or equivalent if prone to urine infections

Polio In 2002 only Afghanistan reported cases of polio. Only one booster is required as an adult for lifetime protection.

Typhoid Recommended unless your trip is for less than a week. The vaccine offers around 70% protection, lasts for two to three years and comes as a single shot. Tablets are also available; however, the injection is usually recommended as it has fewer side effects. Sore arm and fever may occur.

Varicella If you haven't had chickenpox discuss this vaccination with your doctor.

These immunisations are recommended for long-term travellers (more than one month) or those at special risk:

Tick-borne Encephalitis (Kyrgyzstan, Uzbekistan) Sore arm and headache are the most common side effects.

Meningitis Recommended for long-term backpackers aged under 25.

Rabies Side effects are rare – occasionally headache and sore arm.

Tuberculosis A Complex Issue Adult long-term travellers are usually recommended to have a TB skin test before and after travel, rather than vaccination.

FURTHER READING

Lonely Planet's *Healthy Travel – Asia & India* is a handy pocket size and packed with useful information, including pretrip planning, emergency first aid, immunisation and disease information, and what to do if you get sick on the road. Other recommended references include *Traveller's Health* by Dr Richard Dawood and *Travelling Well* by Dr Deborah Mills – check out the website (www.travellingwell.com.au).

IN TRANSIT

DEEP VEIN THROMBOSIS (DVT)

Deep vein thrombosis (DVT) occurs when blood clots form in the legs during plane flights, chiefly because of prolonged immobility. Though most blood clots are reabsorbed uneventfully, some may break off and travel through the blood vessels to the lungs, where they may cause life-threatening complications.

The chief symptom of DVT is swelling or pain of the foot, ankle or calf, usually but not always on just one side. When a blood clot travels to the lungs, it may cause chest pain and difficulty in breathing. Travellers with any of these symptoms should immediately seek medical attention.

To prevent the development of DVT on long flights, you should walk about the cabin, perform isometric compressions of the leg muscles (ie contract the leg muscles while sitting), drink plenty of fluids, and avoid alcohol and tobacco.

JET LAG & MOTION SICKNESS

Jet lag is common when crossing more than five time zones; it results in insomnia, fatigue, malaise or nausea. To avoid jet lag try drinking plenty of fluids (nonalcoholic) and eating light meals. Upon arrival, seek exposure to natural sunlight and readjust your schedule (for meals, sleep etc) as soon as possible.

Antihistamines such as dimenhydrinate (Dramamine), promethazine (Phenergan) and meclizine (Antivert, Bonine) are usually the first choice for treating motion sickness. Their main side effect is drowsiness. A herbal alternative is ginger, which works like a charm for some people.

IN CENTRAL ASIA

AVAILABILITY OF HEALTH CARE

Health care throughout Central Asia is basic at best. Any serious problems will require evacuation. The clinics listed below can provide basic care and may be able to organise evacuation if necessary.

Self-treatment may be appropriate if your problem is minor (eg traveller's diarrhoea), you are carrying the relevant medication and you cannot attend a recommended clinic. If you think you may have a serious disease, especially malaria, travel to the nearest quality facility immediately to receive attention. It is always better to be assessed by a doctor than to rely on self-treatment.

Buying medication over the counter is not recommended, as fake medications and poorly stored or out-of-date drugs are common.

To find the nearest reliable medical facility, contact your insurance company, your embassy or a top-end hotel.

INFECTIOUS DISEASES
Brucellosis

Risk: Kazakhstan, Kyrgyzstan, Tajikistan, Turkmenistan. It is rare in travellers but

---

INTERNET RESOURCES

There is a wealth of travel-health advice on the Internet. It's also a good idea to consult your government's travel-health website before departure, if one is available.

- Australia (www.dfat.gov.au/travel/)
- Canada (www.travelhealth.gc.ca)
- New Zealand (www.mfat.govt.nz/travel)
- South Africa (www.dfa.gov.za/consular/travel_advice.htm)
- UK (www.doh.gov.uk/traveladvice/)
- USA (www.cdc.gov/travel/)
- Lonely Planet (www.lonelyplanet.com) – good basic health information
- World Health Organization (WHO; www.who.int/country) – a superb book called *International Travel & Health* is revised annually and available online
- MD Travel Health (www.mdtravelhealth.com) – provides complete travel-health recommendations for every country and is updated daily
- The Centers for Disease Control and Prevention (CDC; www.cdc.gov) – good general information

---

common in the local population, it's transmitted via unpasteurised dairy products.

Hepatitis A

Risk: all countries. A problem throughout the region, this food- and waterborne virus infects the liver, causing jaundice (yellow skin and eyes), nausea and lethargy. There is no specific treatment for hepatitis A, you just need to allow time for the liver to heal. All travellers to Central Asia should be vaccinated.

Hepatitis B

Risk: all countries. The only sexually transmitted disease that can be prevented by vaccination, hepatitis B is spread by contact with infected body fluids, including via sexual contact. The long-term consequences can include liver cancer and cirrhosis.

HIV

Risk: all countries. HIV is transmitted via contaminated body fluids. Avoid unsafe sex, blood transfusions and injections (unless you can see a clean needle being used) in Central Asia.

Influenza

Risk: all countries. Present particularly in the winter months, symptoms of the flu include high fever, muscle aches, runny nose, cough and sore throat. Vaccination is recommended for those over the age of 65 or with underlying medical conditions such as heart disease or diabetes. There is no specific treatment, just rest and painkillers.

Leishmaniasis

Risk: Afghanistan, Kazakhstan, Turkmenistan, Uzbekistan. This sandfly-borne parasite is very rare in travellers but common in the local population. There are two forms of the disease – one which only affects the skin (causing a chronic ulcer) and one affecting the internal organs. Avoid sandfly bites by following insect avoidance guidelines.

Malaria

Risk: Afghanistan. Malaria is caused by a parasite transmitted by the bite of an infected mosquito. The most important symptom of malaria is fever, but general symptoms such as headache, diarrhoea, cough or chills may also occur. Diagnosis can be made only by taking a blood sample.

The risk for this serious and potentially deadly disease exists throughout Afghanistan below 2000m altitude from April until December. There is a slight risk of malaria in Tajikistan, Turkmenistan and Uzbekistan, but the disease is only present in the extreme south in the warmer summer months.

Two strategies should be combined to prevent malaria – general mosquito/insect avoidance and antimalaria medications. Before you travel, it is essential you seek medical advice on the right medication and dosage. To prevent mosquito bites, travellers are advised to take the following steps:

- Use a DEET-containing insect repellent on exposed skin. Natural repellents such as citronella can be effective, but must be applied more frequently than products containing DEET.
- Sleep under a mosquito net impregnated with permethrin.
- Choose accommodation with screens and fans (if not air-conditioned).
- Impregnate clothing with permethrin in high-risk areas.
- Wear long sleeves and trousers in light colours.
- Use mosquito coils.
- Spray your room with insect repellent before going out for your evening meal.

There are a variety of medications available:

Chloroquine & Paludrine The effectiveness of this combination is now limited in Afghanistan. Common side effects include nausea (40% of people) and mouth ulcers. Generally not recommended.

Lariam (Mefloquine) This weekly tablet suits many people. Serious side effects are rare but include depression, anxiety, psychosis and seizures. Anyone with a history of depression, anxiety, other psychological disorder or epilepsy should not take Lariam. It is considered safe in the second and third trimesters of pregnancy. Tablets must be taken for four weeks after leaving the risk area.

Doxycycline This daily tablet is a broad antibiotic that prevents a variety of tropical diseases. Potential side effects include photosensitivity (sunburn), thrush in women, indigestion, heartburn, nausea and interference with the contraceptive pill. Prevent potential ulceration of the oesophagus by taking the tablet with a meal and a large glass of water, and by waiting at least 30 minutes to lie down. It must be taken for four weeks after leaving the risk area.

Malarone This new drug is a combination of Atovaquone and Proguanil. Side effects are uncommon and mild, most commonly nausea and headache. It must be taken for one week after leaving the risk area.

Rabies

Risk: all countries. Still a common problem in most parts of Central Asia, this uniformly fatal disease is spread by the bite or lick of an infected animal – most commonly a dog. Having a pretravel vaccination means the postbite treatment is greatly simplified. If an animal bites you, gently wash the wound with soap and water, and apply iodine-based antiseptic. If you are not vaccinated you will need to receive rabies immunoglobulin as soon as possible and seek medical advice.

STDs

Risk: all countries. Sexually transmitted diseases most common in Central Asia include herpes, warts, syphilis, gonorrhoea and chlamydia. People carrying these diseases often have no signs of infection. Condoms will prevent gonorrhoea and chlamydia but not warts or herpes. If after a sexual encounter you develop any rash, lumps, discharge or pain when passing urine seek immediate medical attention. If you have been sexually active during your travels, have an STD check upon your return.

Tuberculosis

Risk: all countries. Medical and aid workers, and long-term travellers who have significant contact with the local population should take precautions against TB. Vaccination is usually given only to children under the age of five, but adults at risk are recommended pre- and post-travel TB testing. The main symptoms are fever, cough, weight loss, night sweats and tiredness.

Typhoid

Risk: all countries. This serious bacterial infection is spread via food and water. It gives a high and slowly progressive fever and headache, and may be accompanied by a dry cough and stomach pain. Be aware that vaccination is not 100% effective so you must still be careful what you eat and drink.

Traveller's Diarrhoea

Traveller's diarrhoea is defined as the passage of more than three watery bowel actions within 24 hours, plus at least one other symptom, such as fever, cramps, nausea, vomiting or feeling generally unwell. It is by far the most common problem affecting travellers – between 30% and 50% of people will suffer from it within two weeks of starting their trip.

Traveller's diarrhoea is caused by a bacterium and, in most cases, treatment consists of staying well hydrated; rehydration solutions such as Gastrolyte are the best for this. It responds promptly to treatment with antibiotics such as norfloxacin, ciprofloxacin or azithromycin. Loperamide is just a 'stopper' and doesn't get to the cause of the problem. It can be helpful, for example, if you have to go on a long bus ride. Don't take loperamide if you have a fever, or blood in your stools. Seek medical attention quickly if you do not respond to an appropriate antibiotic.

Amoebic Dysentery

Amoebic dysentery is actually rare in travellers but is often misdiagnosed. Symptoms are similar to bacterial diarrhoea, ie fever, bloody diarrhoea and generally feeling unwell. You should always seek reliable medical care if you have blood in your diarrhoea. Treatment involves two drugs: Tinidazole or Metroniadzole to kill the parasite in your gut, and a second drug to kill the cysts. If left untreated, complications such as liver or gut abscesses can occur.

Giardiasis

Giardia is a parasite that is relatively common in travellers. Symptoms include nausea, bloating, excess gas, fatigue and intermittent diarrhoea. 'Eggy' burps are often attributed solely to giardia, but work in Nepal has shown that they are not specific to giardia. The parasite will eventually go away if left untreated, but this can take months. The treatment of choice is tinidazole; metronidazole is a second option.

ENVIRONMENTAL HAZARDS
Altitude Sickness

This is a particular problem in high-altitude regions of Kazakhstan, Kyrgyzstan and Tajikistan. With motorable roads (such as the Pamir Highway) climbing passes of over 4000m, it's a problem not just restricted to trekkers.

Altitude sickness may develop in those who ascend rapidly to altitudes greater than 2500m. Being physically fit offers no protection. Risk increases with faster ascents, higher altitudes and greater exertion. Symptoms may include headaches, nausea, vomiting, dizziness, malaise, insomnia and loss of appetite. Severe cases may be complicated by fluid in the lungs or swelling of the brain.

To protect yourself against altitude sickness, take 125mg or 250mg of acetazolamide (Diamox) twice or three times daily, starting 24 hours before ascent and continuing for 48 hours after arrival at altitude. Possible side effects include increased urinary volume, numbness, tingling, drowsiness, nausea, myopia and temporary impotence. Acetazolamide should not be given to pregnant women or anyone with a history of sulfa allergy. For those who cannot tolerate

---

DRINKING WATER

■ Never drink tap water.

■ Bottled water is generally safe – check the seal is intact at purchase.

■ Avoid ice.

■ Avoid fresh juices – they may have been watered down.

■ Boiling water is the most efficient method of purifying it.

■ The best chemical purifier is iodine. It should not be used by pregnant women or those with thyroid problems.

■ Water filters should also filter out viruses. Ensure your filter has a chemical barrier such as iodine and a small pore size, eg less than four microns.

---

acetazolamide, the next best option is 4mg of dexamethasone taken four times daily. Unlike acetazolamide, dexamethasone must be tapered gradually upon arrival at altitude. Dexamethasone is a steroid, so it should not be given to diabetics or anyone for whom steroids are contraindicated. A natural alternative is gingko.

When travelling to high altitudes, avoid overexertion, eat light meals and abstain from alcohol. If your symptoms are more than mild or don't resolve promptly, see a doctor.

Food

Eating in restaurants is the biggest risk factor for contracting traveller's diarrhoea. Ways to avoid it include eating only freshly cooked food, avoiding food that has been sitting around in buffets, and eating in busy restaurants with a high turnover of customers. Peel all fruit, cook vegetables, and soak salads in iodine water for at least 20 minutes.

Insect Bites & Stings

Bedbugs don't carry disease but their bites are very itchy. They live in the cracks of furniture and walls and then migrate to the bed at night to feed on you. You can treat the itch with an antihistamine.

Lice inhabit various parts of your body but most commonly your head and pubic area.

Transmission is via close contact with an infected person. They can be difficult to treat and you may need numerous applications of an antilice shampoo such as permethrin. Pubic lice are usually contracted from sexual contact.

Ticks are contracted after walking in rural areas. They are commonly found behind the ears, on the belly and in the armpits. If you have had a tick bite and experience symptoms such as a rash at the site of the bite or elsewhere, fever or muscle aches, you should see a doctor. Doxycycline prevents tick-borne diseases.

Anyone with a serious bee or wasp allergy should carry an injection of adrenaline (eg an Epipen) for emergency treatment. For others, apply ice to the sting and take painkillers.

Skin Problems

Take meticulous care of any cuts and scratches to prevent complications such as abscesses. Immediately wash all wounds in clean water and apply antiseptic. If you develop signs of infection (increasing pain and redness) see a doctor.

Sunburn

Even on a cloudy day sunburn can occur rapidly, especially at high altitudes. Always use a strong sunscreen (at least factor 30), and always wear a wide-brimmed hat and sunglasses outdoors. If you become sunburnt stay out of the sun until you have recovered, apply cool compresses and take painkillers for the discomfort. One percent hydrocortisone cream applied twice daily is also helpful.

WOMEN'S HEALTH

Supplies of sanitary products may not be readily available in rural areas. Birth control options may be limited so bring adequate supplies of your own form of contraception.

Heat, humidity and antibiotics can all contribute to thrush. Treatment is with antifungal creams and pessaries such as clotrimazole. A practical alternative is a single tablet of fluconazole (Diflucan). Urinary tract infections can be precipitated by dehydration or long bus journeys without toilet stops; bring suitable antibiotics.

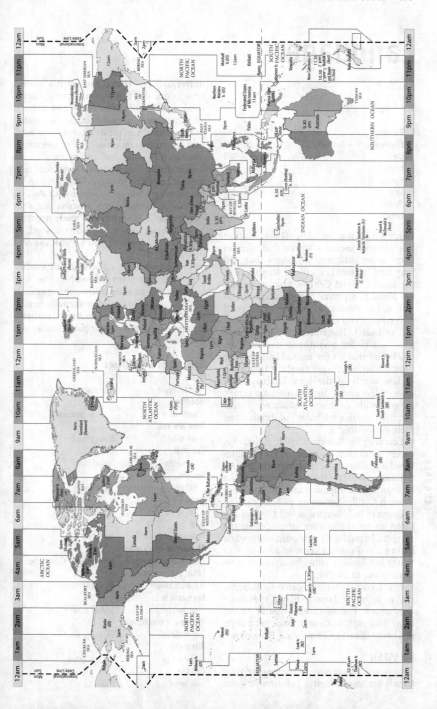

Language

CONTENTS

Central Asia is a multilingual area, and so this chapter includes words and phrases from seven different languages that you may find useful. The official languages of the former Soviet Central Asian countries are Kazakh, Kyrgyz, Tajik, Turkmen and Uzbek, but Russian is still the language of government and academia (rather like English in India). Therefore the one language most useful for a visitor is still Russian; you'll find that it's the second language for most adults, who were taught it in school. A few words of the local language will nonetheless give a disproportionate return in goodwill. At home, educated people normally speak a mishmash of Russian and their native tongue.

Learning the Russian Cyrillic alphabet is a very good idea, as most of the Cyrillic-based alphabets of Central Asia will then be familiar as well (see the two boxed texts The Russian Cyrillic Alphabet on p481 and Non-Russian Cyrillic Letters on p484). Learning to count in local languages will allow you to listen in on discussions of prices in the markets. In public it's now often worthwhile letting non-Russians know in advance that you're not Russian, either by saying so or by starting out in English.

For a comprehensive guide to Russian, get a copy of Lonely Planet's *Russian Phrasebook*. For an excellent guide to the other languages of Central Asia, get a copy of Lonely Planet's *Central Asia Phrasebook*.

RUSSIAN

Two words you're sure to use during your travels are здравствуйте *(zdrastvuyte)*, the universal 'hello' (but if you say it a second time in one day to the same person, they'll think you forgot you already saw them!), and пожалуйста *(pazhalsta)*, the multipurpose word for 'please' (commonly used with all polite requests), 'you're welcome', 'pardon me', 'after you' and more.

The easiest way to turn a statement into a question is just to use a rising tone and a questioning look, or follow it with *da?*, eg 'Is this Moscow?', Это Москва да? *(eta maskva da?)*. A sentence is made negative by putting не *(ni)* before its main word, eg 'This is not Moscow', Это не Москва *(eta ni maskva)*.

Two letters have no sound, but modify others. A consonant followed by the 'soft sign' ь is spoken with the tongue flat against the palate, as if followed by the faint beginnings of a 'y'. The rare 'hard sign' ъ after a consonant inserts a slight pause before the next vowel.

Greetings & Civilities

Hello.
zdrast·vuy·te — Здравствуйте.

Goodbye.
da svi·da·ni·ya — До свидания.

How are you?
kak di·la? — Как дела?

I'm well.
kha·ra·sho — Хорошо.

Yes/No.
da/net — Да/Нет.

good/OK
kha·ra·sho — хорошо

bad
plo·kha — плохо

Thank you (very much).
(bal'sho·ye) spa·si·ba — (Большое) Спасибо.

What's your name?
kak vas za·vut? — Как вас зовут?

My name is ...
mi·nya za·vut ... — Меня зовут ...

Where are you from?
at·ku·da vy? — Откуда вы?

Australia
af·stra·li·ya — Австралия

Canada
ka·na·da — Канада

France
fran·tsi·ya — Франция

Germany
ger·ma·ni·ya — Германия

Ireland
ir·lan·di·ya — Ирландия

New Zealand
no·va·ya ze·lan·di·ya — Новая Зеландия

the UK (Great Britain)
ve·li·ka·bri·ta·ni·ya — Великобритания

the USA
se she a/a·me·ri·ka — США/Америка

Language Difficulties

I don't speak Russian.
ya ni ga·va·ryu pa ru·ski — Я не говорю по-русски.

I don't understand.
ya ni pa·ni·ma·yu — Я не понимаю.

Do you speak English?
vy va·va·ri·te pa ang·liy·ski? — Вы говорите по-английски?

Could you write it down, please?
za·pi·shi·te pa·zhal·sta — Запишите пожалуйста.

Transport & Travel

To get off a *marshutnoe* minibus say *astanavitye pazhalsta.*

Where is ...?
gde ...? — Где ...?

When does it leave?
kag·da at·prav·lya·et·sya? — Когда отправляется?

What town is this?
ka·koy e·ta go·rat? — Какой этот город?

How much is a room?
skol'·ka sto·it no·mer? — Сколько стоит номер?

airport
ae·ra·port — аэропорт

bus
af·to·bus — автобус

hotel
gas·ti·ni·tsa — гостиница

railway station
zhi·lez·na da·rozh·nyy vag·zal — железно дорожный вокзал (abbr. ж. д.)

square/plaza
plo·shchat' — площадь (abbr. пл.)

street
u·li·tsa — улица (abbr. ул.)

toilet
tua·let — туалет

train
poy·ezt — поезд

THE RUSSIAN CYRILLIC ALPHABET

Cyrillic	Roman	Pronunciation
А, а	a	as the 'a' in 'father' (in stressed syllable); as the 'a' in 'ago' (in unstressed syllable)
Б, б	b	as the 'b' in 'but'
В, в	v	as the 'v' in 'van'
Г, г	g	as the 'g' in 'god'
Д, д	d	as the 'd' in 'dog'
Е, е *	e	as the 'ye' in 'yet' (in stressed syllable); as the 'yi' in 'yin' (in unstressed syllable)
Ё, ё **	yo	as the 'yo' in 'yore'
Ж, ж	zh	as the 's' in 'measure'
З, з	z	as the 'z' in 'zoo'
И, и	i	as the 'ee' in 'meet'
Й, й	y	as the 'y' in 'boy'
К, к	k	as the 'k' in 'kind'
Л, л	l	as the 'l' in 'lamp'
М, м	m	as the 'm' in 'mad'
Н, н	n	as the 'n' in 'not'
О, о	o	as the 'o' in 'more' (in stessed syllable); as the 'a' in 'hard' (in unstressed syllable)
П, п	p	as the 'p' in 'pig'
Р, р	r	as the 'r' in 'rub' (rolled)
С, с	s	as the 's' in 'sing'
Т, т	t	as the 't' in 'ten'
У, у	u	as the 'oo' in 'fool'
Ф, ф	f	as the 'f' in 'fan'
Х, х	kh	as the 'ch' in 'Bach'
Ц, ц	ts	as the 'ts' in 'bits'
Ч, ч	ch	as the 'ch' in 'chin'
Ш, ш	sh	as the 'sh' in 'shop'
Щ, щ	shch	as 'sh-ch' in 'fresh chips'
Ъ, ъ	-	'hard sign' (see p480)
Ы, ы	y	as the 'i' in 'ill'
Ь, ь	'	'soft sign'; (see p480)
Э, э	e	as the 'e' in 'end'
Ю, ю	yu	as the 'u' in 'use'
Я, я	ya	as the 'ya' in 'yard' (in stressed syllable); as the 'ye' in 'yearn' (in unstressed syllable)

* Е, е are transliterated ye when at the beginning of a word
** Ё, ё are often printed without dots

Money & Shopping

How much is it?
skol'ka sto·it? — Сколько стоит?

Do you have ...?
u vas est' ...? — У вас есть ...?

bookshop
knizh·nyy ma·ga·zin — книжный магазин

currency exchange
ab·men val·yu·ty — обмен валюты

LANGUAGE

EMERGENCIES – RUSSIAN

I need a doctor.
mne *nu*·zhin vrach — Мне нужен врач.

hospital
bal'*ni*·tsa — больница

police
mi·*li*·tsi·ya — милиция

Fire!
pa·*zhar*! — Пожар!

Help!
na *po*·mashch'!/ — На помощь!/
pa·ma·*gi*·ti! — Помогите!

Thief!
vor! — Вор!

---

market
ry·nak — рынок

money
den'gi — деньги

pharmacy
ap·*te*·ka — аптека

shop
ma·ga·*zin* — магазин

Time & Days

Dates are given as day-month-year, with the month usually in Roman numerals. Days of the week are often represented by numbers in timetables; Monday is 1.

When?	kag·*da*?	Когда?
today	si·*vod*·nya	сегодня
yesterday	vchi·*ra*	вчера
tomorrow	*zaf*·tra	завтра
Monday	pa·ni·*del*'nik	понедельник
Tuesday	*ftor*·nik	вторник
Wednesday	sri·*da*	среда
Thursday	chit·*verk*	четверг
Friday	*pyat*·ni·tsa	пятница
Saturday	su·*bo*·ta	суббота
Sunday	vas·kri·*sen*'e	воскресенье

Numbers

How many?	*skol*'ka?	Сколько?
0	nol'	ноль
1	a·*din*	один
2	dva	два
3	tri	три
4	chi·*ty*·ri	четыре
5	pyat'	пять

6	shest'	шесть
7	sem'	семь
8	*vo*·sim'	восемь
9	*de*·vit'	девять
10	*de*·sit'	десять
20	*dva*·tsat'	двадцать
30	*tri*·tsat'	тридцать
40	so·*rak*	сорок
50	pyat·di·*syat*	пятьдесят
60	shest·di·*syat*	шестьдесят
70	sem·di·*syat*	семьдесят
80	vo·sim·di·*syat*	восемьдесят
90	di·vya·*no*·sta	девяносто
100	sto	сто
1000	*ty*·sya·cha	тысяча

DARI

Dari is an Indo-European language belonging to the Persian subranch, which includes Farsi, Tajik and Pashto. Dari and Pashto are the official languages of Afghanistan, but Dari is the one most commonly used as a lingua franca (linking or market language). There's a fair degree of mutual intelligibility between the four Persian langauges, Dari, Farsi, Pashto and Tajik.

Like Farsi, Dari and Pashto are written using a modified alphabet of the cursive Arabic script. In the following list, **kh** is pronounced as the 'ch' in Scottish *loch*, **a** and **aa** are similar to the first and second 'a' in 'salami' respectively.

Dari Basics

Hello.	salaam aleykom
Do you speak English?	englisi yaad daari?
Yes/No.	bala/na
Goodbye.	bamaane khodaa
Please.	lotfan
Thank you.	tashakor
good/bad	khob/bad
OK	dorost
Excuse me /I'm sorry.	may bakhshi
How are you?	chetor asti?
I'm fine thanks, and you?	khob astam, shoma chetor astin?
My name is ...	naame ma ... ast.
Do you speak English?	englisi yaad daari?
I don't speak Dari.	ma dari yaad nadaarom
What is your name?	naamet chis?
I'm pleased to meet you.	Az didane shomaa khosh shodom.
Do you understand?	may faami?
I don't understand.	namayfaamam
Please repeat it.	az sar bego

Where is ...?	... da kojaas?
We need a doctor.	doktar kawr daarim
How much?	cheqadar?
How many?	chand taa?
airport	meydaane havaayi
bed	takht
boiled water	aawe jush
bread	naan
bus station	aystgaahe baas
expensive	geraan
friend	dost
hospital	shafaa khaana
hotel	hotal
meat	gosht
police	pulis
rice	birinj
room	otaaq
toilet	tashnaab
train station	aystgaahe tirayn
today	emroz
tomorrow	sabaa
yesterday	diroz
morning	sob
noon	chaasht
now	haale
later	pasaan tar
day	roz
night	shaw
Monday	do shanbay
Tuesday	say shanbay
Wednesday	chaar shanbay
Thursday	panj shanbay
Friday	joma
Saturday	shanbay
Sunday	yak shanbay
0	sefer
1	yak
2	du
3	se
4	chaar
5	panj
6	shash
7	haft
8	hasht
9	no
10	da
11	yaazda
12	duwaazda
13	sayzda
14	chaarda
15	paanzda
16	shaanzda

17	hafda
18	hažda
19	nozda
20	bist
30	si
40	chel
50	penjaa
60	shast
70	haftaad
80	hashtaad
90	navad
100	sad
1000	yak hazaar
first	aval
second	dowom
third	sewom

KAZAKH

Kazakh is a Turkic language. Since 1940 it has been written in a 42-letter version of the Cyrillic alphabet (see the two boxed texts The Russian Cyrillic Alphabet on p481 and Non-Russian Cyrillic Letters on p484). At least as many people in Kazakhstan speak Russian as Kazakh. Any political tension over language issues has been rather neatly sidestepped by making Kazakh the official state language, but permitting the predominant language in local regions to be used in written government business, and giving Russian national language status as 'language of interethnic communication'.

Russian is the first language for some urban Kazakhs as well as the large Russian minority who form about 35% of the population. Few people speak English or other western languages, but many of those who do tend to work in the tourist industry or with foreigners.

Street signs are sometimes in Kazakh, sometimes in Russian, sometimes in both. In this book we use the language you're most likely to come across in each town.

Kazakh Basics

Peace be with you.	asalam aleykum
Hello.	salamatsyz be
Goodbye.	qosh-sau bolyngdar
Thank you.	rakhmet
Yes/No.	ia/zhoq
How are you?	khal zhagh dayyngyz qalay?
I'm well.	zhaqsy
Do you speak English?	aghylshynsa bilesiz be?
I don't understand.	tusinbeymin

NON-RUSSIAN CYRILLIC LETTERS

Cyrillic	Roman	Pronunciation
Kazakh		
Ә, ә	a	as the 'a' in 'man'
Ғ, ғ	gh	as the 'gh' in 'ugh'
Қ, қ	q	a guttural 'k'
Ң, ң	n	as the 'ng' in 'sing'
Ө, ө	ö	as the 'u' in 'fur'
Ұ, ұ	u	as the 'u' in 'full'
Ү, ү	ü	as the 'oo' in 'fool'
Һ, һ	h	as the 'h' in 'hat'
I, i	i	as the 'i' in 'ill'
Tajik		
Ғ, ғ	gh	as the 'gh' in 'ugh'
Й, й	ee	as the 'ee' in 'fee'
Қ, қ	q	as the 'k' in 'keen'
Ӯ, ӯ	ö	as the 'u' in 'fur'
Х, х	kh	as the 'h' in 'hat'
Ч, ч	j	as 'j' in 'jig'
Uzbek		
Ғ, ғ	gh	as the 'gh' in 'ugh'
Қ, қ	q	a guttural 'k'
Ӯ, ӯ	u	as the 'oo' in 'book'
Х, х	kh	as the 'ch' in 'Bach'
Kyrgyz		
Ң, ң	ng	as the 'ng' in 'sing'
Ө, ө	ö	as the 'u' in 'fur'
Ү, ү	ü	as the 'ew' in 'few'

Where is...?	*... qayda?*
How much?	*qansha?*

airport	*aeroport*
bus station	*avtobus vokzal*
doctor	*dariger*
friend	*dos*
hospital	*aurukhana*
hotel	*qonaq uy/meymankhana*
police	*militsia*
restaurant	*restoran*
toilet	*azhetkhana*
train station	*temir zhol vokzal*

bad	*zhaman*
boiled water	*qaynaghan su*
bread	*nan*
expensive	*qymbat*
good	*zhaqsy*
meat	*yet*
rice	*kurish*
tea	*shay*

Monday	*duysenbi*
Tuesday	*seysenbi*
Wednesday	*sarsenbi*
Thursday	*beysenbi*
Friday	*zhuma*
Saturday	*senbi*
Sunday	*zheksenbi*

1	*bir*
2	*yeki*
3	*ush*
4	*tört*
5	*bes*
6	*alty*
7	*etti*
8	*sakkiz*
9	*toghyz*
10	*on*
100	*zhus*
1000	*myng*

KYRGYZ

Kyrgyz is a Turkic language that has been written using a Cyrillic script since the early 1940s (see the two boxed texts The Russian Cyrillic Alphabet on p481 and Non-Russian Cyrillic Letters opposite). Along with neighbouring countries Uzbekistan and Turkmenistan, Kyrgyzstan is in the process of changing over to a modified Roman alphabet. While international Roman letters have already been adopted for vehicle number plates, Kyrgyzstan is the slowest of these three countries in implementing the change from a Cyrillic to a Roman alphabet.

In 2000 the government gave Russian official-language status, but there is currently also a strong push to promote Kyrgyz as the predominant language of government, media and education. It's a move not without its detractors, who see it as a politically motivated means of discriminating against non-Kyrgyz–speaking minorities.

Kyrgyz Basics

Peace be with you.	*salam aleykum*
Hello.	*salam*
Goodbye.	*jakshy kalyngydzar*
Thank you.	*rakhmat*
Yes/No.	*ooba/jok*
How are you?	*jakshysüzbü?*
I'm well.	*jakshy*
Do you speak	*siz angliyscha süylöy süzbü?*
English?	
I don't understand.	*men tüshümböy jatamyn*

Where is ...?	*... kayda?*
How much?	*kancha?*
airport	*aeroport*
bus station	*avtobiket*
doctor	*doktur*
friend	*dos*
hospital	*oruukana*
hotel	*meymankana*
police	*militsia*
restaurant	*restoran*
toilet	*darakana*
train station	*temir jol vokzal*
bad	*jaman*
boiled water	*kaynatilgan suu*
bread	*nan*
expensive	*kymbat*
good	*jakshy*
meat	*et*
rice	*kürüch*
tea	*chay*
Monday	*düshömbü*
Tuesday	*seyshembi*
Wednesday	*sharshembi*
Thursday	*beishembi*
Friday	*juma*
Saturday	*ishembi*
Sunday	*jekshembi*
1	*bir*
2	*eki*
3	*üch*
4	*tört*
5	*besh*
6	*alty*
7	*jety*
8	*segiz*
9	*toguz*
10	*on*
100	*jüz*
1000	*ming*

TAJIK

Tajik, the state language of Tajikistan since 1989, belongs to the southwest Persian group of languages and is closely related to Dari, Pashto and Farsi. This sets it apart from all the other Central Asian languages which are Turkic in origin. Tajik was formerly written in a modified Arabic script and then in Roman, but since 1940 a modified Cyrillic script has been used (see the two boxed texts

The Russian Cyrillic Alphabet on p481 and Non-Russian Cyrillic Letters on p484).

In Dushanbe most people speak Tajik and Russian. Uzbek is also spoken by a significant percentage of the population.

Tajik Basics

Peace be with you.	*assalom u aleykum*
Hello.	*salom*
Goodbye.	*khayr naboshad*
Thank you.	*rakhmat/teshakkur*
Yes/No.	*kha/ne*
How are you?	*naghzmi shumo?*
I'm well.	*mannaghz*
Do you speak English?	*anglisi meydonet?*
I don't understand.	*man manefakhmam*
Where is ...?	*... khujo ast?*
How much?	*chand pul?*
airport	*furudgoh*
bus station	*istgoh*
doctor	*duhtur*
friend	*doost*
hospital	*bemorhona/kasalhona*
hotel	*mekhmon'hona*
police	*militsia*
restaurant	*restoran*
toilet	*khojat'hona*
train station	*istgoh rohi ohan*
bad	*ganda*
boiled water	*obi jush*
bread	*non*
expensive	*qimmat*
good	*khub/naghz*
meat	*gusht*
rice	*birinj*
tea	*choy*
Monday	*dushanbe*
Tuesday	*seshanbe*
Wednesday	*chorshanbe*
Thursday	*panjanbe*
Friday	*juma*
Saturday	*shanbe*
Sunday	*yakshanbe*
1	*yak*
2	*du*
3	*seh*
4	*chor*
5	*panj*
6	*shish*
7	*khaft*

8	khasht
9	nukh
10	dakh
100	sad
1000	khazor

TURKMEN

Turkmen, the state language of Turkmenistan since 1990, has been described as '800-year-old Turkish'. It belongs to the Turkic language family, forming part of the southwestern group together with the Turkish and Azeri (spoken in Azerbaijan). In Turkmenistan virtually everyone speaks Russian and Turkmen (except for Russians, who speak Russian only). English speakers are generally only found in the tourist industry and at some universities.

There's been a significant infiltration of Russian words and phrases into Turkmen, especially in this century (words to do with science and technology particularly). Turkmen conversation is punctuated with Russian, to the extent that sentences may begin in Turkmen, then slip into Russian midway through.

Three different scripts have been used to write Turkmen; Arabic, Roman and Cyrillic. Arabic was the first, though little Turkmen was ever written in it (there's a popular style of calligraphy, often used on monuments, in which Cyrillic script is rendered in such a way that it almost resembles Arabic script). A modified Turkish-Roman alphabet was used until 1940 when the Cyrillic alphabet took over. On 1 January 1996, Turkmen Cyrillic was officially replaced by another modified Roman alphabet called Elipbi, and the changeover to this has been quite rapid. As a result, you're much less likely to see Cyrillic in Turkmenistan than in any of the other former Soviet states that are making the change to a Roman alphabet.

Turkmen Basics

Peace be with you.	salam aleykum
Hello.	salam
Goodbye.	sagh bol
Thank you.	tangyr
Yes/No.	howa/yok
How are you?	siz nahili?
Fine, and you?	onat, a siz?
I don't understand.	men dushenamok
Do you speak English?	siz inglische gepleyarsinizmi?

Where is ...?	... niredeh?
How much?	nyacheh?

airport	aeroport
bus station	durolha
doctor	lukman
friend	dost
hospital	keselkhana
hotel	mikmankhana
police	militsia
restaurant	restoran
toilet	hajat'hana
train station	vokzal

bad	ervet
boiled water	gaina d'lan su
bread	churek
expensive	gummut
good	yakhsheh
meat	et
rice	tui
tea	chay

Monday	dushanbe
Tuesday	seshenbe
Wednesday	charshanbe
Thursday	penshenbe
Friday	anna
Saturday	shenbe
Sunday	yekshanbe

1	bir
2	ikeh
3	uch
4	durt
5	besh
6	alty
7	yed
8	sekiz
9	dokuz
10	on
100	yuz
1000	mun

UZBEK

Uzbekistan's three major languages are Uzbek, Russian and Tajik. Uzbek is the country's official language and, with 15 million speakers, it is the most widely spoken of the non-Slavic languages of all the former Soviet states. It belongs to the Turkic language family.

Uzbek was written in Roman letters from 1918 to 1941. Since then it has used a modified Cyrillic alphabet, but the country has been the most publicly anti-Russian of all the Central Asian countries, moving rapidly to a Roman script, and virtually eliminating Russian from public view in favour of written Uzbek. The shift away from both the Russian language and its alphabet is seen as a means of gaining better access to Western markets through closer alignment with Turkey.

While the majority of signs are now in Uzbek Latin, there is still sufficient evidence of Cyrillic to make familiarity with it a good idea (see the two boxed texts The Russian Cyrillic Alphabet on p481 and Non-Russian Cyrillic Letters on p484).

Uzbek Basics

Peace be with you.	asalom u alaykhum
Hello.	salom
Goodbye.	hayr
Thank you.	rakhmat
Yes/No.	kha/yuk
How are you?	qanday siz?
Do you speak English?	inglizcha bila sizmi?
Where is ...?	... qayerda?
How much?	qancha/nichpul?

airport	tayyorgokh
bus station	avtobeket
doctor	tabib
friend	urmoq/doost
hospital	kasalhona
hotel	mehmon'hona
police	militsia

restaurant	restoran
toilet	hojat'hona
train station	temir yul vokzali

bad	yomon
boiled water	qaynatilgan suv
bread	non
expensive	qimmat
good	yakhshi
meat	gusht
rice	guruch
tea	choy

Monday	dushanba
Tuesday	seyshanba
Wednesday	chorshanba
Thursday	payshanba
Friday	juma
Saturday	shanba
Sunday	yakshanba

1	bir
2	ikki
3	uch
4	turt
5	besh
6	olti
7	etti
8	sakkiz
9	tuqqiz
10	un
11	un bir
100	yuz
1000	ming

LANGUAGE

Glossary

Abbreviations

This glossary contains Afghan (Afg), Arabic (A), Kazakh (Kaz), Kyrgyz (Kyr), Russian (R), Tajik (Taj), general Turkic (T), Turkmen (Tur), Uzbek (U) and English terms you may come across in Central Asia.

A

-abad (T) – suffix meaning 'town of'
aerovokzal (R) – airport bus station
ak kalpak (Kyr) – felt hat worn by Kyrgyz men
akimat (T) – regional government office
aksakal (U) – revered elder
akyn (Kyr) – minstrel, bard
ala-kiyiz (Kyr) – felt rug with coloured panels pressed on
alangy (Kaz) – square
alpinistskiy lager (R) – see *alplager*
alplager (R) – mountaineers camp
apparatchik (R) – bureaucrat
apteka (R) – pharmacy
arashan (T) – springs
arenda (R) – literally 'lease' or 'rent', usually referring to buses that make a trip only if there are enough passengers
asalam aleykum (A) – traditional Muslim greeting, meaning 'peace be with you'
ASSR – Autonomous Soviet Socialist Republic
ATO – Afghan Tourist Organisation
aviakassa (T) – private travel agent
avtobus (R) – bus
avtostantsia (R) – bus stop or bus stand
ayollar hammomi (U) – women's bathhouse
azan (A) – Muslim call to prayer

B

babushka (R) – old woman; headscarf worn by Russian peasant women
balbal (T) – totemlike stone marker
banya (R) – public bath
basmachi (R) – literally 'bandits'; Muslim guerrilla fighters who resisted the Bolshevik takeover in Central Asia
batyr (Kyr & Kaz) – warrior hero in epics
beg (T) – landlord, gentleman; bay
beshbarmak (Kyr) – flat noodles with lamb, horse meat or vegetable broth
bishkek (Kaz & Kyrg) – see *pishpek*
bolnitza (R) – hospital
bolshoy rynok (R) – big farmers market
bosuy (Kyr) – see *yurt*
bufet (R) – snack bar selling cheap cold meats, boiled eggs, salads, breads, pastries etc
bulvar (R) – boulevard

bulvary (Kyr) – boulevard
burka (A) – enveloping veil worn by some Muslim women
buzkashi (T) – traditional pololike game played with a headless goat carcass

C

caravanserai – travellers inn
chabana (Kyr & Kaz)– cowboy
chaikhana (T) – teahouse
chay (T) – tea
chaykhana (T) – see *chaikhana*
chorsu (T) – market arcade
choy (U & Taj) – see *chay*
choyhona (T) – see *chaikhana*
chuchuk (Kaz) – see *kazy*
chuchvara (T) – dumplings
CIS – Commonwealth of Independent States; the loose political and economic alliance of most former member republics of the USSR (except the Baltic states); sometimes called *NIS*, for Newly Independent States
CPK – Communist Party of Kazakhstan

D

dacha (R) – a holiday bungalow
dangghyly (Kaz) – avenue
darikhana (Kaz) – pharmacy
darya (T) – river
dastarkhan (T) – literally 'tablecloth'; feast
dezhurnaya (R) – floor-lady; the woman attendant on duty on each floor of a Soviet-style state hotel
dom (R) – building
dom otdykha (R) – rest home
dopy (U) – black, four-sided skullcap embroidered in white and worn by men; also dopi, doppe or doppilar
drevniy gorod (R) – ancient city
duban (Kyr) – province

E

erkakli hammomi (U) – men's baths
eshon (A)– *Sufi* leader

G

GAI (R) – traffic police
gastronom (R) – state food shop
ghanch (T) – carved and painted plaster
gillam (T) – carpet
glasnost (R) – literally 'openness'; the free expression that was one aspect of the Gorbachov reforms
glavpochtamt (R) – main post office
gorod (R) – town
gosudarstvenny pvirodny park (R) – national park

Great Game – the geopolitical 'Cold War' of territorial expansion between the Russian and British empires in the 19th and early 20th centuries in Central Asia
GUM (R) – gosudarstvennyy universalnyy magazin; state department store

H
Hadith (A) – collected acts and sayings of the Prophet Mohammed
haj (A) – the pilgrimage to Mecca, one of the five pillars of Islam, to be made by devout Muslims at least once during their lifetime
hakimyat (Kyr) – municipal administration building
hammam (A) – bathhouse
hammomi (U) – baths
hanako (U) – see khanaka
hauz (T) – an artificial pool
hazrat (A) – honorific title meaning 'majesty' or 'holy'
Hejira (A) – flight of the Prophet Mohammed and his followers to Medina in AD 622

I
ikat (U) – tie-dyed silk
IMU – Islamic Movement of Uzbekistan
IRP – Islamic Renaissance Party; grouping of radical activists dedicated to the formation of Islamic rule in Central Asia
ISAF – International Security Assistance Force
Ismaili (A) – a branch of Shiite Islam

J
jailoo (Kyr) – summer pasture
jami masjid (A) – Friday mosque
jarma (Kyr) – fermented barley drink
jihad (A) – holy war

K
kala (T) – fortress
kalon (Taj) – great
karta (Kaz) – see kazy
kaskad (R) – dam
kassa (R) – cashier or ticket office
kazan (T) – cauldron
kazy (Kaz) – horse-meat sausage
-kent (T) – suffix meaning 'town of'
khanaka (A) – a Sufi contemplation hall and hostel for wandering ascetics; the room of an eshon in which he and other Sufis perform their zikr
khanatlas (U) – see ikat
kino (R) – cinema; also kinoteatr
köchösü (Kyr) – street
kökör (T) – kumys shaker
kökpar (Kaz) – see buzkashi
kolkhoz (R) – collective farm
komnaty otdykha (R) – rest rooms

kontrolno propusknoy punkt (R) – permit station
köshesi (Kaz & Karakalpak) – street
koshk (U & Tur) – fortress
koshma (Kaz) – multicoloured felt mats
kozlodranie (T) – see buzkashi
krytyy rynok (R) – covered market
kuchasi (U) – street
kumys (Kaz & Kyr) – fermented mare's milk
kupeynyy (R) – 2nd-class or sleeping carriage on trains; also kupe
kymys (Kyr) – see kumys
kyrort (R) – thermal-spring complex
kyz-kumay (Kyr) – traditional game in which a man chases a woman on horseback and tries to kiss her

L
laghman (T) – noodles
LOI – letter of invitation
loya jirga (Afg) – grand council
lux (R) – deluxe, though often a euphemism

M
mahalla (U) – urban neighbourhood
Manas (Kyr) – epic; legendary hero revered by the Kyrgyz
manaschi (Kyr) – type of akyn who recites from the Kyrgyz cycle of oral legends
manty (T) – small stuffed dumplings
marshrutka (R & T) – short term for marshrutnoe and marshrutnyy avtobus
marshrutnoe (R & T) – small bus or van that follows a fixed route but stops on demand to take on or let off passengers, with fares depending on distance travelled
marshrutnyy avtobus (R & T) – large bus that follows a fixed route but stops on demand to take on or let off passengers, with fares depending on distance travelled
maydoni (U) – public square
mazar (T) – tomb or mausoleum
medressa (A) – Islamic academy or seminary
mikrorayon (R) – micro region
militsia (R & T) – police
MSDSP – Mountain Societies Development Support Project
muezzin (A) – man who calls the Muslim faithful to prayer
mufti (A) – Islamic legal expert or spiritual leader
mujaheddin (A) – Muslim freedom fighter engaged in jihad
mullah (A) – Islamic cleric

N
nan (T) – flat bread
Naqshband – the most influential of many Sufi secret associations in Central Asia
Navrus (A) – literally 'New Days'; the main Islamic spring festival; has various regional transliterations (Nauroz, Nauryz, Nawruz, Norruz or Novruz)
NIS – Newly Independent States
non (U & Taj) – see nan

O
oblast (R) – province, region
oblys (Kaz) – province, region
OVIR (R) – Otdel Vis i Registratsii; Office of Visas and Registration

P
pakhta (T) – cotton
pakhtakor (T) – cotton worker
panjara (T) – trellis of wood, stone or *ghanch*
PCO – public call office
perestroika (R) – literally 'restructuring'; Gorbachov's efforts to revive the economy
piala (T) – bowl
pishpek (Kaz & Kyr) – churn for making *kumys*
pishtak – monumental Timurid-era entrance portals
platskartnyy (R) – hard sleeper train
ploshchad (R) – square
plov (T) – a rice dish with meat, carrots or other additions (traditionally prepared by men for special celebrations)
pochta bulimi (R) – post office
pol-lux (R) – semideluxe
polyclinic – health centre
propask (T) – military border permit
prospekt (R & T) – avenue
pulao (Afg) – see *plov*

Q
qala (U) – see *kala*
qymyz (Kaz) – see *kumys*
qyz-quu (Kaz) – see *kyz-kumay*

R
rayon (R) – district

S
samovar (R) – urn used for heating water for tea, often found on trains
samsa (T) – samosa
sharq (Taj & U) – east
shashlyk (A) – meat roasted on skewers over hot coals
shay (Kaz) – see *chay*
shaykhana (T) – see *chaikhana*
Shiite (A) – one of the two main branches of Islam
shosse (R) – highway
shubat (Kaz & Taj) – fermented camel's milk
shyrdak (Kyr) – felt rug with appliquéd coloured panels
skibaza (R) – ski base
SLLPCP – Sustainable Livelihoods for Livestock Producing Communities Project

SSR – Soviet Socialist Republic
stolovaya (R) – canteen, cafeteria
Sufi (A) – mystical tradition in Islam
suzani (U) – bright silk embroidery on cotton cloth

T
Taliban – plural of Talib, meaning student or seeker of knowledge; fundamentalist Islamic army that ruled Afghanistan
tebbetey (Kyr) – round fur-trimmed hat worn by men
telpek (Tur & U) – sheepskin hat worn by men
tim (T) – shopping arcade
toi (T) – celebration
Transoxiana – meaning 'the land beyond the Oxus'; historical term for the region between the Amu-Darya and Syr-Darya rivers
TsUM (R) – Tsentralnyy universalnyy magazin; central department store
turbaza (R) – holiday camp typically with Spartan cabins, plain food, sports, video hall and bar, usually open only in summer
Turkestan – literally 'the Land of the Turks'; covers Central Asia and Xinjiang (China)

U
ulak-tartysh (Kyr) – see *buzkashi*
ulama (A) – class of religious scholars or intellectuals
ulitsa (R) – street
umuvalnik (R) – portable washing basin
univermag (R) – universalnyy magazin; department store
uulu (Kyr) – meaning 'son of'
UXO – unexploded ordnance (land mine)

V
viloyat (U) – province
vodopad (R) – waterfall

Y
ylag oyyny (Karakalpak)– see *buzkashi*
yurt – traditional nomadic 'house', a collapsible cylindrical wood framework covered with felt

Z
zakazniki (R) – protected area
zapovednik (R) – nature reserve
zhyostkiy (R) – hard carriage on trains
zikr (A) – recitation or contemplation of the names of God; recitation of sacred writings; one part of traditional *Sufi* practice

Behind the Scenes

THIS BOOK

The 1st edition of this book was researched and written by John King, John Noble and Andrew Humphreys. Bradley Mayhew coordinated the 2nd edition. Richard Plunkett and Simon Richmond researched and wrote for that edition. This 3rd edition was again coordinated by Bradley Mayhew, who wrote all the front chapters, as well as Kyrgyzstan and Tajikistan. Also authoring were Michael Kohn (Kazakhstan and Uzbekistan), Paul Clammer (Afghanistan) and our anonymous Turkmenistan author. Dr Trish Batchelor wrote the Health chapter.

THANKS from the Authors

Special Thanks First and most important thanks go to Bruno De Cordier, the patron saint of independent travel in Central Asia, for sending endless updates and invaluable information on Tajikistan for this edition. Many thanks to both Bruno and Nurjamal for answering so many queries.

Bruno worked for different international development agencies and lived and travelled extensively in ex-Soviet Central Asia, Xinjiang and northern Pakistan for more than five years. He would like to thank Maxime Filandrov for all his friendship and help; Albert Longy and Nathalie Magnard for the good time in Badakhshan and the Eastern Pamir; Jamsho Dorobov and his family in Suchan for their hospitality; Alexandru Codreanu, Yusuf Mohammad, Abdelaziz and the rest of the OSCE staff in Kurgan-Tyube and Shartuz; Markus Häuser; and Daniël Züst from the Swiss development cooperation DEZA-DDC in Dushanbe. And

then last, but not least: Bugu for being a solid travel partner on life's path!

Bradley Mayhew In the Pamirs, thanks to Ubaidullah Mamadiev, Erik Engel and particularly to Robert Middleton for their generous help.

In Kyrgyzstan, Aigul and Anar Orozbaeva at CBT and Zamira at NoviNomad were generous with their time. Thanks to Kubat in Naryn for his hospitality. Genevieve Cahill and Almaz Kemelov in Karakol offered superb professional assistance, as did Ian Claytor of Celestial Mountains.

In Dushanbe thanks to Marielle Leseur at Acted (good luck in Murgab!) and to Paul Handley for trekking tips. Hi to Garth Willis and Ryan Schuchard.

Several travellers were generous with time and information, including James Down and Sally Reid. Thanks to John Oates for reports from the road; I don't think I will ever live down ordering you that bowl of congealed fat and hair in Osh! *Merci beaucoup* to Philippe Lamare for reports on his horse trip to Song-Köl and *chong rakhmat* to Miras Imanzhanov for a lift to Tash Rabat.

At Lonely Planet thanks to Janine, Mike, Paul and our mystery Turkmenistan author for their help throughout the book and to Judy Slatyer for joining me for five fun days in Kyrgyzstan.

My thanks and love as always to my wife Kelli for creating a home to come home to.

Paul Clammer Many people helped make my trip what it was, but the biggest thanks must go to the many Afghans who gave a smile, offered tea or corrected my bad Persian. To you all, *tashakor.*

THE LONELY PLANET STORY

The story begins with a classic travel adventure: Tony and Maureen Wheeler's 1972 journey across Europe and Asia to Australia. There was no useful information about the overland trail then, so Tony and Maureen published the first Lonely Planet guidebook to meet a growing need.

From a kitchen table, Lonely Planet has grown to become the largest independent travel publisher in the world, with offices in Melbourne (Australia), Oakland (USA), London (UK) and Paris (France).

Today Lonely Planet guidebooks cover the globe. There is an ever-growing list of books and information in a variety of media. Some things haven't changed. The main aim is still to make it possible for adventurous travellers to get out there – to explore and better understand the world.

At Lonely Planet we believe travellers can make a positive contribution to the countries they visit – if they respect their host communities and spend their money wisely.

Thanks to Abdullah Amiri and Mr Hussain in Kabul, Abdul Khalil (ATO) and Abdul Khalq Tawfiq in Bamiyan, and Sultan Hamidy, Faruk Tahiri and family for their hospitality in Herat.

Big thanks to Sally Cooper (Internews), Finne Lucey (GOAL), and Basir Noutash and Kristine Gutschow in Herat. Dr Shah Wali kindly gave permission to reprint OMAR's land-mine guidelines. Thanks also to Timor Shah and Robert Kluyver (FCCS), Ana Rodriguez (SPACH) and Linda Mogul.

Cheers to Dominic Medley. Lina Abirafeh contributed a great piece on Afghan women. Belinda Bowling, Anke Röhl, Guido Dingemans, Andrew Lange and Christine Dimmock all helped in their own ways. Tim Albone shared a hard road through the mountains when the Salang was closed.

Particular thanks to Vanni Cappelli (cat lover of Kabul) for the history lessons, to Jan Roos for looking after my stuff, and to both for being such fine company in Kabul.

Finally, the biggest thanks to Jo for her love and patience, and for knowing what that means to me.

Michael Kohn At Lonely Planet, many thanks are owed to the tireless assistance of Commissioning Editor Janine Eberle and Coordinating Author Bradley Mayhew.

In Kazakhstan, huge assistance came from VSOs Seamus Bennett, Mark Cripsey, Neil Warren, Ken Bealby, Serena and Clive Marriott, and Brian and Mary Crumblehulme. I am also indebted to former Almaty residents Rowan and Tristan Kennedy, and to adventurer extraordinaire Karlygash Makatova.

Elsewhere, great thanks to Jim Town and Sue Kennedy, and their respective students (KUBML and Pavlodar School #9), David Berghoff, Folke von Knobloch, Timur Chigirov, Elena Ponomareva, Leah McConaughey, Jeff Fearnside, Mike Roach, Helen Krylova, Linda Yoon, Chad Clay, Svetlana Voiskaliyeva and Askar Makhmudov.

In Uzbekistan, special thanks to Airat Yuldashev, Otabek Mirzakarimov, Murat Amanov, Alisher Khabibullaev and Tukhtamurad Karabaev in Tashkent; Laurel Scherffius in Kokand; and Eugene Rabinskiy and Helen Proud of Salom Travel in Bukhara.

I also received help along the way from Olga Daniels, Nodir Abdurahmonov, April Carman, Elyor Hatamov, Burt Herman, Bagila Bukharbayeva, Jahongir Khusainov, Rumil Gaifullin, Alisher Choriev, Pierre-Yves Tessier and Zarif Ziyaev. Thanks also to the many readers who wrote, and to fellow travellers Jeremy Meyer, Thomas Gay, Adam and Janet Goodvach, Emma Bush and Richard Entwistle.

Back home, thanks to Sue and Steve Kohn, J Norm and Baigalmaa.

Anonymous The author of the Turkmenistan chapter would like to extend his gratitude to people who took risks by speaking to him, the superbly helpful diplomatic community in Ashgabat and the wonderful Turkmen people. Special thanks to Alex, David, our superb guide Malcolm Tinning (BSI Travel), Emma Bush and Richard Entwistle.

CREDITS

Series Publishing Manager Robert Reid oversaw the redevelopment of this series with help from Virginia Maxwell and Maria Donohoe, and Regional Publishing Manager Kate Cody steered the development of this title. The series was designed by James Hardy, with mapping development by Paul Piaia. The series development team included Shahara Ahmed, Jenny Blake, Anna Bolger, Erin Corrigan, Nadine Fogale, Dave McClymont, Leonie Mugavin, Rachel Peart, Lynne Preston, Howard Ralley and Vivek Waglé.

This title was commissioned in Lonely Planet's Melbourne office by Janine Eberle. Cartography for this guide was developed by Shahara Ahmed. *Central Asia 3* was coordinated by Helen Christinis (editorial) and Daniel Fennessy (cartography). Kieran Grogan (with initial assistance from Andrew Weatherill) project managed this edition. Yvonne Bischofberger and Vicki Beale laid the book out. Annika Roojun designed the cover. Quentin Frayne coordinated the language content and Nick Stebbing solved some script issues. Thanks to Vivek Waglé for helping with the Health chapter. A talented team of editors, proofers, cartographers and designers assisted on this project: Katrina Webb, Emma Koch, Brooke Lyons, Margedd Heliosz, Nancy Ianni, Simon Williamson, Victoria Harrison, Barbara Delissen, Stephanie Pearson, Marion Byass, Julie Sheridan, Hunor Csutoros, Country Cartographics, Katherine Marsh, Tegan Murray, Karen Fry and Sonya Brooke.

THANKS from Lonely Planet

Many thanks to the hundreds of travellers who used the last edition and wrote to us with helpful hints, useful advice and interesting anecdotes:

A Husain Akbar, Paul Anderson, Mirhon Asadov, Rhea Ashmore **B** Krisztina Balazs, Shiriin Barakzai, Vio Barco, Daphna & Ranen Bardin, Yilmaz & Astrid Baris, Duncan Barker, Seamus Bennett, Mark Berkovich, Christopher Berresford, Fabio Bertino, Friedrich A Bielenstein, Aart Biewenga, Matthew Bisley, Gabriel Blanc, Amelia Blas, Alice Boyle, Paul Brand, David Bray, Henry Briscoe, Kenneth Brooker, Marl Allen Brown, Karin Bruce, Tom Bryson,

Sergey Bukharov, Bob Bunker, Rowland Burley, Sylvie Burnand, Alex Burnashev, John Burr, James Butterfield **C** Tom Chevanne, Summer Coish, Cheryl Collins, Brian Connellan, Susan Cook, Peter Cooper **D** Morgan Daniels, Armando de Berardinis, Bruno De Cordier, Philip-Carl De Cordier, Paul de Jong, Marianne de Swart, Corinna Deuscher, Andrew Dier, Marijke Dijkgraaf, Philippe Domogala, Catherine Douxchamps, Loeky Droesen, R Droux, Christine du Fresne **E** Ted Elder, Roy & Noga Eldor, Andy Evans **F** Jeff Fearnside, Ilja Fedoruk, Thomas Fertig, Dina Fesler, Alex Finck, Margaret & David Fitzgerald, Ruth Forbes, Steven Foundos, Dick Freed, Matteo Fumagalli **G** Jan Garvelink, Jacob Gautier, Thomas Gay, Bob Gibbons, Ashley Gilbertson, Efrat Gleitman, CJ Goble, Al & Susan Goff, David Goldblum, Owen Goldfrab, Simon Goss, Dagny Anne Greinus, Susan Griffiths, Stephan Gruenfelder, Micael Gustavsson, Kristina Gutschow, Matthias Gutzeit **H** Paul Haddock, Hugh Hadley, Grace Hafner, Ken Haley, Professor Daphne Hampson, Ron Hannah, Josie Hanneman, John Hardy, Kathleen Hardy, Marc & Claire Hasenohr, Esther Hecht, Jeff Hendrickson, Willaim Hendrik, Moritz Herrmann, Toby Hoeck, Dr Michael Hoffman, Kjetil Hope, Wendy Hoskins, Johanna Louise Houtekamer, Bram Hulzebos, Bob & Jo Hunter, Yvan Hutin **I** Hiroshi Ideka **J** Guy Jacobs, Rok Jarc, Marie Javins, Herbert Jehle, Brian Johns, Ross Johnson **K** Lucia Kadijk, Marty Karatsu, Ari Katz, Bryan Keith, Sue Kennedy, Mac Kenzie, Joann Kingsley, Denis Knowles, Geertje Koeman, Jolanda Koopmans, Jonathan Korowicz, David Kovar, Edyta Krakowiecka, Matthieu Kravos, Marlies Kriegenherdt, Kerstin Krolak, Hans-Peter Kuhn **L** Tomas Lackner, Fjoor Laridon, Amin Latipov, Richard Lax, Han Yo Le, John Leathers, Miki Lentin, Oded Levanoni, Elad Levi, Fanny Libin, Rolf Lienekogel, Maa Little, Catherine Loake, N Lobanov-Rostorsky, Stephen Lum **M** Damian MacCormack, Nicolas Maechler, Annette Magnusson, Antony Makepeace, Christine Martens, Jean Philippe Martinent, Rachel Mason, CN McCorquodale, BS McElney, Gregory McElwain, Michael McGrath, Natasha McKeown, Ann McMillan, Alex McPherson, Roberta Melchiorre, Jean-Marie Mell, Isabelle Merle, Natasha Milestone, Lesley Molyneux, Dr Herbert Müller Philipps Sohn, Helene Munson, Dale Myers **N** Ola Naess, Joanna Nathan, Caroline Naylor, Pamela Neil, Graham Nelson, Steve Newcomer **O** Darlene Oehlke, Lars Olberg **P** Daina Padgett, Olivier Pages, Larissa Pak, Rajan Parkash, Carlo & Emanuela Paschetto, David Patel, Tanya, Jason & Snortie Paterson, Dirk Pauwels, Farrell Payne, Matt Perrement, Piergiorgio Pescali, Tanya Peterson, Magnus & Sofie Petterson, Chris Phillips, Dave Pitney, Jürgen Pohle, Shawn Porter, Matthew Post, Lucy Potter, Guido Potters, Sian Pritchard-Jones, Helen Proud, Ryan Pyle **R** Nurmametov Radiy, Gary Rashba, Dominik Refardt, Tobias Reijngoud, Gene Richards, Sue & David Richardson, Adrian Rodwell, Roberto Rosiglioni, Dr Shimon Rumelt, Angry Russell, Martijn Rutte **S** Jane Salvage, Chris Scheupp, Mark Schiefelbein, Christian Schmidt, Meir Sela, Allegra M Sensenig, Jozef Serneels, Reda Sijiny, Tumer Sismanoglu, Ryan Skeie, Per-Olof Soderkvist, Per Sotvik, Clare Stableford, Robert John Hartley Stagg, Edwin Steele, Tobias Steinoe, Stephen Stewart, Stephan Stormer, John Sunblad, Judy & Ariana Svenson **T** Paul Taapken, Christine Tam, Gerham Tanew, Jane Taylor, Hilmi Temiz, Mark Temperley, Huw Thomas, Mark Thomas, Richard Thomas, V Thomspon, Mark Thornburg, Anna Timmins, Anneliese Tischler **U** Lars Uldall-Jensen, Emil Umetaliev **V** Kazbek Valiyev, Lars van der Bruggen, Misha van der Pijl, Sandra van Osch, Erik van Raaij, Andreas Voegelin, Folke von Knobloch **W** Kerry & John Wallace, Karen Watkins, Martha E Weeks, Jerry Phillips Winfield, Aleksandra & Georg Winterberger, Brian Wolfe, Ron Wurzer **Y** Pazu Yau, Jason Man-Kai Yeung **Z** Bla Zabukovec, Birgit Ziedoy, Bernd Ziermann, Trayah Zinger, Patrick Zoll

ACKNOWLEDGMENTS

Many thanks to the following for the use of their content:
Globe on back cover © Mountain High Maps 1993 Digital Wisdom, Inc.

index

Index

000 Map pages
000 Location of colour photographs

INDEX

INDEX

000 Map pages
000 Location of colour photographs

INDEX

512

MAP LEGEND
ROUTES

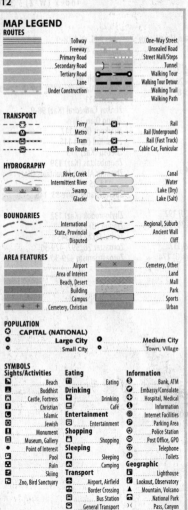

ROUTES
- Tollway
- Freeway
- Primary Road
- Secondary Road
- Tertiary Road
- Lane
- Under Construction
- One-Way Street
- Unsealed Road
- Street Mall/Steps
- Tunnel
- Walking Tour
- Walking Tour Detour
- Walking Trail
- Walking Path

TRANSPORT
- Ferry
- Metro
- Tram
- Bus Route
- Rail
- Rail (Underground)
- Rail (Fast Track)
- Cable Car, Funicular

HYDROGRAPHY
- River, Creek
- Intermittent River
- Swamp
- Glacier
- Canal
- Water
- Lake (Dry)
- Lake (Salt)

BOUNDARIES
- International
- State, Provincial
- Disputed
- Regional, Suburb
- Ancient Wall
- Cliff

AREA FEATURES
- Airport
- Area of Interest
- Beach, Desert
- Building
- Campus
- Cemetery, Christian
- Cemetery, Other
- Land
- Mall
- Park
- Sports
- Urban

POPULATION
- CAPITAL (NATIONAL)
- Large City
- Small City
- Medium City
- Town, Village

SYMBOLS

Sights/Activities	Eating	Information
Beach	Eating	Bank, ATM
Buddhist	**Drinking**	Embassy/Consulate
Castle, Fortress	Drinking	Hospital, Medical
Christian	Café	Information
Islamic	**Entertainment**	Internet Facilities
Jewish	Entertainment	Parking Area
Monument	**Shopping**	Police Station
Museum, Gallery	Shopping	Post Office, GPO
Point of Interest	**Sleeping**	Telephone
Pool	Sleeping	Toilets
Ruin	Camping	**Geographic**
Skiing	**Transport**	Lighthouse
Zoo, Bird Sanctuary	Airport, Airfield	Lookout, Observatory
	Border Crossing	Mountain, Volcano
	Bus Station	National Park
	General Transport	Pass, Canyon
	Taxi Rank	Spot Height
		Waterfall

LONELY PLANET OFFICES

Australia
Head Office
Locked Bag 1, Footscray, Victoria 3011
☎ 03 8379 8000, fax 03 8379 8111
talk2us@lonelyplanet.com.au

USA
150 Linden St, Oakland, CA 94607
☎ 510 893 8555, toll free 800 275 8555
fax 510 893 8572, info@lonelyplanet.com

UK
72–82 Rosebery Ave,
Clerkenwell, London EC1R 4RW
☎ 020 7841 9000, fax 020 7841 9001
go@lonelyplanet.co.uk

France
1 rue du Dahomey, 75011 Paris
☎ 01 55 25 33 00, fax 01 55 25 33 01
bip@lonelyplanet.fr, www.lonelyplanet.fr

Published by Lonely Planet Publications Pty Ltd
ABN 36 005 607 983

© Lonely Planet 2004

© photographers as indicated 2004

Cover photographs: Mir-i-Arab Medressa, Bukhara, Uzbekistan, Nevada Wier/Getty/The Image Bank (front); Tash Rabat caravanserai, Kyrgyzstan, Bradley Mayhew/Lonely Planet Images (back). Many of the images in this guide are available for licensing from Lonely Planet Images: www.lonelyplanetimages.com.

Printed through SNP SPrint Singapore Pte Ltd at
KHL Printing Co Sdn Bhd Malaysia